A DICTIONARY OF IRISH HISTORY
1800-1980

D. J. HICKEY
J. E. DOHERTY

GILL AND MACMILLAN

First published 1980 under the title
A Dictionary of Irish History Since 1800 by
Gill and Macmillan
Goldenbridge
Dublin 8
with associated companies throughout the world
This paperback reprint published 1987
© D. J. Hickey and J. E. Doherty, 1980
0 7171 1567 4
Print origination by Healyset, Dublin
Printed in Hong Kong

A catalogue record is
available for this book from
the British Library.

3 5 7 6 4

ABBREVIATIONS

ACC	Agricultural Credit Corporation
ADC	Aide-de-camp
ARA	Associate of the Royal Academy
b.	born
B.A.	Bachelor of Arts
BBC	British Broadcasting Corporation
c.	circa
CBS	Christian Brothers' School(s)
C.E.	Church of England
C.I.	Church of Ireland
CIE	Coras Iompar Eireann
C-in-C	Commander-in-Chief
d.	died
D.D.	Doctor of Divinity
D. Litt.	Doctor of Literature
DMP	Dublin Metropolitan Police
D.Sc.	Doctor of Science
DSO	Distinguished Service Order
E.	East
EAGGF	European Agricultural Guidance and Guarantee Fund
ed.	educated
EEC	European Economic Community
ESB	Electricity Supply Board
FF	Fianna Fail
FG	Fine Gael
GAA	Gaelic Athletic Association
GIS	Government Information Services
GOC	General Officer Commanding
GPO	General Post Office
ICTU	Irish Congress of Trade Unions
IDA	Industrial Development Authority
IRA	Irish Republican Army
IRB	Irish Republican Brotherhood
ITUC	Irish Trade Union Congress
JP	Justice of the Peace
KC	King's Counsel
LL.D.	Doctor of Laws
m.	married
M.A.	Master of Arts
Mass.	Massachusetts
M.D.	Doctor of Medicine
MP	Member of Parliament
MRIA	Member of the Royal Irish Academy
MRSAI	Member of the Royal Society of Antiquaries of Ireland
N.	North
NI	Northern Ireland
NICRA	Northern Ireland Civil Rights Association
NILP	Northern Ireland Labour Party
NUI	National University of Ireland
OBE	Order of the British Empire
O/C	Officer Commanding
Ph.D.	Doctor of Philosophy
P.P.	Parish Priest
QC	Queen's Counsel

QMG	Quartermaster-General
RA	Royal Academy
R.C.	Roman Catholic
RDS	Royal Dublin Society
Rev.	Reverend
RHA	Royal Hibernian Academy
RIA	Royal Irish Academy
RIC	Royal Irish Constabulary
RSAI	Royal Society of Antiquaries of Ireland
RTE	Radio Telefis Eireann
RUC	Royal Ulster Constabulary
S.	South
SDLP	Social Democratic and Labour Party
SJ	Society of Jesus
TCD	Trinity College Dublin
TD	Teachta Dala (member of the Dail)
UCC	University College Cork
UCD	University College Dublin
UCG	University College Galway
UDA	Ulster Defence Association
UK	United Kingdom
UPNI	Unionist Party of Northern Ireland
USA	United States of America
UUUC	United Ulster Unionist Council
UVF	Ulster Volunteer Force
VAT	Value Added Tax
VEC	Vocational Education Committee
W.	West

A NOTE ON CROSS-REFERENCES

Cross-references are indicated by an asterisk (*). Items have only been cross-referenced in cases where there is a direct connection between the subject of the entry and the item in question. Incidental connections are not cross-referenced. Thus, a statement that someone was born in Northern Ireland would not merit a cross-reference to the entry on Northern Ireland, whereas the entry on the Boundary Commission does have such a cross-reference.

Introduction

This is the first dictionary devoted solely to the events of Irish history. Although a small country, Ireland has had a history of great complexity: any work such as this which attempted to deal with events from earliest times to the present could only be contained within manageable limits at the cost of being severely restricted in scope. It has been necessary, therefore, to concentrate on a specified period. It seemed to us that the period since the Act of Union was the appropriate one to choose, for three main reasons. The availability of source materials is greater than for earlier centuries; proceeding from this, the modern period has been the subject of a great number of excellent and scholarly studies, on both general and specific subjects; finally, it would appear that the greatest public interest is focussed on the history of Ireland since the Union.

As it was, even the period since 1800 demanded that we be selective in the choice of our material. We have, however, attempted to define Irish history in the broadest terms possible within the limits of our brief. Happily, the day is gone when it was possible to suppose that 'history' meant political history and little else. We have sought, therefore, to include as many entries as possible on social affairs, literature and the arts, folk customs, religious developments, economics and population. Political and military concerns are, inevitably, central to this work, but it is our hope that they do not constitute a disproportionate element.

The decision to include a particular subject, while excluding another, has in every instance been our own. Herein lies an area of keen dispute and such judgments, no matter how carefully made, are an unfailing source of controversy. In making such decisions, we have tried to reconcile the demands of various catagories of readers: it is our hope that this volume will prove useful to the academic, the student and the general reader anxious to locate historical information in a readily accessible format.

Nomenclature, particularly in relation to titled persons, presented obvious problems of location. We have chosen to include such persons under the title or name by which they were popularly known.

D. J. Hickey
J. E. Doherty
December 1979

Acknowledgements

During the five years we have worked on this volume we have received generous assistance from a number of institutions and individuals. We wish to express our thanks to the Director (Alf MacLochlainn) and Staff of the National Library of Ireland; the staffs of the Cork City, Limerick City and Limerick County Libraries and of the Library of the National Institute of Higher Education, Limerick, John Killen (Reference Librarian) Linenhall Library, Belfast; L. Hamrock, Mayo County Library, Castlebar; Judith Bucke, Readers' Services, Library of the Queen's University of Belfast, Belfast Public Library, Kathleen O'Brien, Reference Librarian, Radio Telefis Eireann; P. O. Snodaigh, National Museum of Ireland; Coras Trachtala; the Departments of Education, Defence, Foreign Affairs and Posts and Telegraphs; Rose Mitchell, Government Information Services; S. E. Harper, Department of Finance, Northern Ireland, the Office of the Commissioner of Metropolitan Police, London; the Imperial War Museum, London; the Public Record Office of Northern Ireland; Adrian Munnelly, then Education Officer, Castlebar, Co. Mayo; Superintendent T. J. Kelly, P.R.O., Garda Siochana; Gerard Burns, Southern Education Library Board, Craigavon; Fr Paul Leonard, Editor, *Irish Messenger*; Austin Channing, *Ireland's Own*; Frank Hamilton, P.R.O., Shannon Free Airport Development Company; Mary Maher, P.R.O., Aer Lingus; Aer Rianta; Coras Iompar Eireann; Electricity Supply Board; John Higgins, P.R.O., Irish Shipping Ltd; Hugh Morris, Managing Director, Earagail Eisce Teo; Muintir na Tire; the Army Press Office; the Irish Air Corps; Terry Murphy and the Kilmainham Restoration Committee; John Trew, Editor, *The Belfast News-Letter*; *Cork Examiner*; *The Irish Independent*, *The Irish Press* and *The Irish Times*; John O'Shaughnessy, *The Limerick Chronicle*. Our thanks are also due to Senator Seamus Brennan, Sister Bridget, Fr John Browne, Anne and Robert Byrne, Mrs Dympna Cafferkey, Fr Michael Cribbin, Noel Doherty, Professor Samuel Fanning, Tom Ferris, Miss May Fitzmaurice, Fr John Fleming, David Lee, Liam and Margaret Leland, M. McCullough, Canon James D. McDyer, the late Michael McInerney, Declan Mc-Loughlin, F. M. McLoughlin, Mrs Florence Monteith Lynch, Thomas Molloy, Geraldine Neeson, Eamon O'Connor, Pearse O'Connor, Fr Christopher O'Dwyer, Cormac O'Malley, Maire T. Ní Riain, Joseph Scallan, Mainchin Seoighe, Fr Michael Smith, Michael V. Spillane, Fr Mark Tierney, Vincent Walsh, Derrick O. White and Tony White. We owe special thanks to William Lawlor, Richard Tobin and Captain William Treacy for their comments on sections of the manuscript and to our typist, Patricia Moran, for her work on the final draft. No words can fully express the debt we owe to our families for their encouragement and their willingness to live with this work for so long. Our inadequate thanks are due, therefore, to Anne, John, Michelle and Michael Hickey and to Caithlin, Patrick and Carmel Doherty.

A

ABBEY THEATRE. Founded in 1904 from a merger of the National Dramatic Company owned by the brothers Frank and William Fay, and the Irish Literary Theatre Society. At the suggestion of Willy Fay, a Manchester heiress, Miss Annie Fredericka Horniman bought the Mechanics Institute in Dublin (1904) as a home for the Irish National Theatre Company. With the aid of £1,500 provided by Miss Horniman, the Institute was adapted as the Abbey Theatre. The Abbey was opened on 27 December 1904 with performances of Yeats's *On Baile's Strand* and Lady Gregory's *Spreading the News*. The new theatre received an annual subsidy of £850 from Miss Horniman and a patent, made out to Lady Gregory, was granted by the government. The brothers Fay left the Abbey in 1908 and two years later the theatre was forced to become a self-supporting entity when Miss Horniman withdrew her financial assistance. In 1924 the Abbey was given an annual grant of £850 by the Free State government through its Minister for Finance, Ernest Blythe, which made it the first state-subsidised theatre in the English-speaking world. By 1949 the theatre had produced 449 plays of which 384 were classified as having been written for, or inspired by, the Abbey. Among the plays introduced by the Abbey in its earlier years were *The Well of the Saints* (Synge, 1905), *Deirdre* (Yeats, 1906), *The Playboy of the Western World* (Synge, 1907), which sparked off riots on its first production because of the use of the rather indelicate word 'shift', *The Country Dressmaker* (George Fitzmaurice, 1907), *The Workhouse Ward* (Lady Gregory, 1908), and the Sean O'Casey trilogy, *The Shadow of a Gunman* (1923), *Juno and the Paycock* (1924) and *The Plough and the Stars* (1926). Directors of the Abbey have included Augusta, Lady Gregory,* W. B. Yeats,* Edward Martyn,* J. M. Synge,* Ernest Blythe,* Brinsley MacNamara,* Frank O'Connor* and Walter Macken. Actors and actresses trained and employed by the Abbey have included F. J. McCormick,* Maire O'Neill, Sara Allgood,* William Shields (Barry Fitzgerald), Harry Brogan, Edward Golden, Cyril Cusack, J. M. Kerrigan, T. P. McKenna, Siobhán McKenna, Lennox Robinson, Arthur Sinclair and Ray McAnally. In 1925, the Peacock Theatre was constructed adjoining the Abbey. With a very small stage and seats for only 102 persons in the auditorium, it was designed for experimental productions and for performances by pupils of the Abbey School of Acting. The Abbey Theatre was gutted by fire in 1951 and the Company was housed at the Queen's Theatre until 1966, when it moved to the present site in Lower Abbey Street.

ABDICATION CRISIS (1936). The proposal of King Edward VIII to abdicate the throne of Great Britain in order to marry Mrs Wallis Simpson produced a constitutional crisis in 1936. Ireland was affected to the extent that the Free State* was a member of the British Commonwealth of Nations. The President of the Executive Council (Cabinet), Eamon de Valera,* took advantage of the crisis to introduce changes in the Constitution of 1922;* he was already working towards a new constitution and wished to have the crown removed from the Free State's affairs as far as possible. On 11 December, the day of the king's abdication, the Dail was summoned to debate two bills, under

1

guillotine so as to have them passed by the following night. The Constitution (Amendment No. 27) Act removed all references to the king and the Governor-General* from the constitution. The second, the External Relations Act,* recognised the king only 'for the purpose of the appointment of diplomatic and consular representatives, and the conclusion of international agreements . . . .' A new Constitution, *Bunreacht na hEireann*, was enacted in 1937 (*see* Constitution of 1937).

ABERCORN, 1st DUKE (1811–85). Hamilton, James; politician (Conservtive); landowner and Lord Lieutenant (1866–68, 1874–76); b. Edinburgh; ed. Harrow and Christ Church, Oxford. He succeeded to the title in 1818. He became an active and popular landlord on his estate which embraced parts of counties Londonderry and Donegal although his family seat was at Baronscourt, Co. Tyrone. During his first term as Lord Lieutenant he dealt firmly with the Irish Republican Brotherhood.* His second term was more peaceful and saw the rise of the Home Rule Party under Isaac Butt.* His efforts to place the advantages of secondary and university education within reach of Catholic children bore some fruit in the passage of the Intermediate Education Act, 1878 (*see* Secondary Education).

ABERCORN, 2nd DUKE (1830–1913). Hamilton, James; landlord and politician (Unionist); b. Brighton; ed. Harrow and Christ Church, Oxford. He was MP for Co. Donegal, where his family owned a 26,000 acre estate, from 1860 until 1880. He lost his seat at the height of the Land League agitation. After succeeding to the title in 1885 he became the chief spokesman for Ulster Unionists* and founded the Northwest Loyalist Registration and Electoral Association* in 1886 as part of the attempt to defeat the (first) Home Rule Bill.* In 1892 his 'We will not have Home Rule' became a Unionist catch-cry. When W. E. Gladstone* succeeded in getting the second

Home Rule Bill through the Commons in 1893 Abercorn presided over the Albert Hall Rally to oppose Home Rule.* He continued the fight in the Lords where the Bill was defeated. He became Chairman of the Tyrone County Council established by the Local Government Act, 1898. Abercorn opposed the Conservative policy of tenant-purchase but sold out large tracts of his own land under the Wyndham Act of 1903 (*see* Land Acts). He was a prominent member of the Ulster Unionist Council.*

ABERCORN, 3rd DUKE (1869–1953). Hamilton, James Gilbert Edward; politician (Unionist); son of the 2nd Duke; ed. Eton. He was MP, Derry City (1900–13), Lord Lieutenant, Co. Tyrone (1917–53), a member of the Senate of Northern Ireland (1921) and Governor of Northern Ireland (1922–45).

ABERDEEN, 1st MARQUESS (1847–1934). Gordon, John Campbell; politician (Liberal); Lord-Lieutenant (1886; 1905–15); b. Aberdeenshire; ed. Cheam School, St Andrew's University and University College, Oxford; M.A. (1877). His first term as Lord Lieutenant was from January to July 1886 when W. E. Gladstone* sought to carry Home Rule,* but failed. Aberdeen returned to the office when Henry Campbell-Bannerman* formed his government. He held the office for the longest term of any Lord Lieutenant. His wife, a domineering personality, once forced him to release James Connolly* from prison after a plea from Connolly's wife. The Aberdeens' period at the Viceregal Lodge was considered dull by Dublin society as the couple entertained as little and as cheaply as possible.

ACHILL MISSIONARY HERALD AND WESTERN WITNESS. Newspaper founded by Rev. Edward Nangle* as an organ for furthering his extreme evangelical views in Connaught; in the first issue (31 July 1837) the editor announced that his paper would 'bear a faithful and uncompromising testimony against the superstition and idolatry of the Church of Rome' and 'proclaim the glorious truths of the Gospel'. It was printed in Achill and was a constant source of irritation to the Catholic church in Connaught. It ceased to appear in the early 1850s. (*See* Second Reformation.)

ADAIR, GENERAL SIR WILLIAM (1850–1931). Soldier and Ulster Unionist; ed. Cheltenham; entered the Royal Marine Light Infantry (1867) and served in South Africa during the Boer War. He was Deputy Adjutant-General, Royal Marines (1907–11). Adair played a prominent role in the Ulster Unionist Party and was commander of the Antrim Ulster Volunteer Force.* He took charge of the landing and dispersal of the guns during the Larne Gun-running.*

AER LINGUS (AIR FLEET). Aer Lingus Teo. is an Irish government-owned public company, incorporated in 1936, which operates air services within Ireland and between Ireland and Britain and Europe. Aerlinte Eireann Teo. is an Irish government-owned public company incorporated in 1947 which operates services between Ireland and the United States and Canada.

On 27 May 1936, Irish Sea Airways (as Aer Lingus was first known) inaugurated its first route from Baldonnel military aerodrome to Bristol. The airline's solitary aircraft, a De Haviland Dragon, named *Iolar* (Eagle), was piloted by Captain O. E. Armstrong, and carried a full load of five passengers.

Later in 1936, the Bristol service was extended to London. This route as well as seasonal services to Liverpool and the Isle of Man, which were subsequently opened, comprised the company's network until the outbreak of World War II. In 1940 the airline's operational headquarters moved from Baldonnel to the newly completed Dublin Airport six miles north of the city centre. During World War II the company's operations were confined to a Dublin-Liverpool service, with Manchester as an alternative in adverse weather conditions. Shortly after the end of the war Aer Lingus embarked on an expansion programme. The airline's first three hostesses took up duty and by 1948 London, Liverpool, Glasgow, Manchester and the Isle of Man were added to the itinerary. Two continental routes, Dublin-Paris and Dublin-Amsterdam, were subsequently added.

With the continued rise of passenger and cargo traffic, the DC-3 was proving inadequate to meet demands. In 1954 Aer Lingus took delivery of four Viscounts from Vickers and they went into service on the continental routes. In that year also the airline became the first in the world to operate scheduled services to Lourdes – its fourteenth route. In recognition of the airline's part in promoting Lourdes Airport the company's then general manager, Dr J. F. Dempsey, was made a Freeman of Lourdes in 1963.

Jets were introduced on European services in 1965 and the company now operates Boeing 737s and BAC One-Elevens on these routes. In 1959 three Boeing 720 jet aircraft were ordered and the first of these went into service in December 1960. These were subsequently replaced by the larger 707-348C Boeing jets. Two new routes, to Chicago and Montreal, were opened in May 1966 and a fourth 707 was acquired. In 1971 Aer Lingus took delivery of two Boeing 747 (Jumbo) jets for transatlantic service.

Aer Lingus now provides scheduled services connecting Dublin, Shannon and Cork airports with the United States, Canada, Britain, Denmark, Netherlands, Belgium, France, Spain, Germany, Switzerland and Italy. Belfast is connected to Aer Lingus' North Atlantic routes by means of a local Belfast-Shannon service. The airline's charter service network, which also plays a significant role in Ireland's tourism efforts, is more extensive than the scheduled network.

An ancillary activities division was developed in the early 1970s to help

3

Key Results of 1978/79 (compared with previous year)

Operating Revenues	(IR£'000)	190,000 plus 16%
Operating Profit		7,316 minus 11%
Net Profit		4,019 minus 13%
Ancillary Activities Revenue		79,000 plus 18%
Operating Profit from Ancillary Activities		11,971 plus 28%
Passengers Carried		2,238,000 plus 11%
Cargo and Mail (Tons)		60,000 minus 6%
Passenger Load Factor		73% up four points
Staff (airline)		6,598 up 579
Staff (subsidary companies)		5,400 (900 added since 31 March)

Fleet at 31 March 1979

3 Boeing 747	Aircraft	397-seater
4 Boeing 707	Aircraft	176-seater
10 Boeing 737	Aircraft	110-seater
4 BAC One-Eleven	Aircraft	74-seater

Two further B737s have been added since 31 March and a further two are on order. No subsidies of any kind have been received by Aer Lingus since 1950.

augment returns from air transportation. Airline staff of all grades and qualifications have come from Australia, Bahamas, South Africa, Uganda, West Indies, Egypt, Singapore, Pakistan, and some thirty-five other countries for training with Ireland's national airline. Aer Lingus personnel have successfully travelled the airways of the world to sell Irish expertise and services, particularly in the fields of aircraft maintenance and component overhaul. The company has procured the former premises of Cement Ltd near Dublin for development of its component and overhaul services. In addition many world airlines are availing of such Aer Lingus services as aircraft leasing and brokerage, computer programming, computerised reservations, airport ground handling, on-site technical assistance and management. Of growing significance too is the air-line's diversification into the hotel industry. It now owns or leases seventeen hotels in the United States, Britain and France, and manages on contract a further six.

AER RIANTA. Aer Rianta, the Irish Airports Authority, was incorporated in 1937 in accordance with the terms of the Air Navigation & Transport Act of 1936. Initially a holding company for Aer Lingus,* Aer Rianta was additionally charged with responsibility for the promotion of aviation generally. Under the Air Companies Act, 1966, Aer Rianta's holding in the national airline was transferred to the Minister for Finance, while its own share capital was limited to a nominal £60,000. On 1 April 1969, responsibility for the management of Shannon and Cork Airports was vested in Aer Rianta.

The Authority derives its main income from landing fees. Other income sources are: airport retail and banking units, advertising, duty free shops (including a mail-order business with annual turnover in excess of £2.7m), restaurants and bars. Its College of Hotel Management at Shannon has won international acclaim and attracts students from many parts of the world. Castle Tours, a division of Aer Rianta, internationally promoted by Shannon Free Airport Development Company,* handles over 30,000 visitors in inclusive annual tours. It also organises the medieval banquets at Bunratty and Knappogue Castles (Co. Clare) and Dunguaire Castle, Co. Galway, which attract some 140,000 tourists each year.

Over three million passengers use the national airports annually and 66,000 metric tonnes of air freight pass through the air cargo facilities. General aviation makes frequent use of Aer Rianta facilities and some 140,000 landings are made each year by this category of aircraft. Some 2,000 employees are employed at the three national airports.

The National Airports

Dublin Airport: Formerly the military airport of Collinstown, it is situated some six miles north of the capital and covers 1,500 acres. The first flight from the new airport took place on 19 January 1940. Major overhaul of the airport and its facilities took place in the period before the introduction of the 'Jumbo' Jets in 1971. A new terminal, capable of accommodating six million passengers annually, was completed in 1972. The terminal was the largest structural contract of its type undertaken in Ireland at that time.

Shannon Airport: Located in the townland of Rineanna, Co Clare, the site is reputed to have been selected by Charles Lindbergh during his world air-route survey in the early thirties. Following the closure of nearby Foynes, which had catered for transatlantic flying boats during World War II, the airport at Rineanna

was completed in 1947. In that year also the Customs Free Airport Act established Shannon as the first Free Airport in the world, where transit passengers and goods were exempt from normal customs procedures. The first scheduled commercial transatlantic flight from Shannon – a Douglas DC4 (Skymaster) of American Overseas Airlines – operated from the airport on 24 October 1945.

Cork Airport: The smallest of the national airports, in the townland of Ballygarvan, some four miles from the city centre, serves the south-west of Ireland. It was opened in October 1961 at a cost of £1.9m. Serving largely a tourist market from the United Kingdom, the airport has also proved an important helicopter base for servicing the off-shore gas and oil exploration rigs operating off the south-west of Ireland.

AGAR-ROBERTES PROPOSAL. During the second reading of the (third) Home Rule Bill,* a Liberal MP, T. C. Agar-Robertes, proposed on 2 May 1912 that counties Londonderry, Down, Antrim and Armagh should be excluded from Home Rule; in June he introduced an amendment to give effect to this proposal for the partition of Ireland. It was opposed by the Liberal government supported by the Conservative leader, Andrew Bonar Law.* Partition came to be regarded as the only solution to the Home Rule question, with the counties of Fermanagh and Tyrone added to the four proposed by Agar-Robertes.

AGENTS, LANDLORDS'. *See* Middlemen.

AGISTMENT. *See* Tithes.

AGITATION. Title for the policy undertaken by Daniel O'Connell* in 1825 to further the fight for Catholic Emancipation;* again adopted in 1843 when he was fighting for Repeal. 'Agitation' consisted of mass-meetings, inflammatory speeches and a direct appeal to the passions and traditions of his audiences. It was highly unpopular with the government which brought the policy to an end in 1843 by proscribing his 'monster meeting' scheduled for Clontarf.

AGRARIAN CRIME. The law recognised four categories: crime against the Person, against Property, against Public Peace, and Intimidation by Threatening Letter. To combat these crimes numerous Peace Preservation Acts or Coercion Acts,* as they were known, were passed during the second half of the nineteenth century. The following are the figures for agrarian crimes between 1844 and 1919:

1844–50	7,958	1910	2,293
1851–60	4,153	1911	2,156
1861–70	3,889	1912	2,198
1871–80	5,434	1913	2,138
1881–90	14,100	1914	1,906
1891–95	1,794	1915	1,698
1896–1900	1,267	1916	1,792
1901	246	1917	1,858
1902	253	1918	2,563
1903	195	1919	3,600
1904	206		

(*See also* Secret Societies.)

AGRICULTURAL AND TECHNICAL INSTRUCTION ACT, 1899. The Act arose out of the recommendations of the Recess Committee* and was the brainchild of Sir Horace Plunkett* who became the first vice-president of the Department of Agriculture and Technical Instruction which was established under the Act in 1900; the first Secretary of the Department was a protege of Plunkett, Thomas Patrick Gill.* The new Department was financed from central and local funds and established a system of technical education* to provide opportunities for night classes in larger towns. The schools were non-denominational and their function was to provide education in practical subjects. An advisory Council of Agriculture of 104 members was established; there were two Boards, one each for Agriculture and Technical Instruction, on each of which the Council was represented; the Boards administered the Department's funds. The Department also provided a special agricultural scheme for the areas under the control of the Congested Districts Board;* by 1909, fifty-seven inspectors were employed for these areas. Agricultural instructors under the auspices of the Department worked throughout the country. The functions of the Department were taken over by the Department of Education of the Free State* in 1923; the schools administered by the Department continued as before until reorganised under the Vocational Education Act, 1930. In 1931 the Department of Agriculture and Technical Instruction was dissolved; the Technical Instruction branch was placed under the Department of Education and the Department of Agriculture took its present form.

AGRICULTURAL CREDIT CORPORATION. The ACC was established in 1927 under the Agricultural Credit Act as a limited company with a nominal share capital of £500,000. It was the first of the Irish state-sponsored bodies. Its aim was to advance working capital to farmers with their properties as security. By 1936 it had lent £1,250,000. The government's intention had been to revitalise Irish agriculture which suffered from a shortage of capital. However, most of the ACC's 16,500 transactions between 1927 and 1936 had been on too small a scale to achieve this aim. The average loan was just over £82, repayable over five to ten years; 239 transactions were for around £500 each. Bad debts amounting to £30,000 were written off during the same period. Irish agriculture did not undergo a radical transformation until the late 1960s after which Ireland entered the European Economic Community.* The ACC is now a public company with an authorised share capital of £10,000,000. Under the Agricultural Credit Act 1965, it is empowered to take deposits from any source. On 31 December 1976 it had just over £119,000,000 on deposit and was offering the widest possible range of credit facilities for agricultural purposes, with nearly £85,500,000 on loan.

AIKEN, FRANK (1898–   ). Politician (Fianna Fail); b. Co. Armagh; ed. CBS, Newry. He joined the Irish Volunteers* in 1913 and the Gaelic League* the following year. In 1917 he became a Sinn Fein organiser in South Armagh and was a commandant of the 4th Northern Division of the Irish Republican Army* during the War of Independence. He opposed the Treaty and, after attempting to remain neutral, fought against the Provisional Government; he became Chief-of-Staff of the Anti-Treaty republicans – the Irregulars – in 1923. Aiken was returned as abstentionist republican TD for Co. Louth in 1923 and three years later was a founder-member of Fianna Fail. When Eamon de Valera* formed his first government in 1932 Aiken became Minister for Defence (until 1939). During the Emergency,* he was Minister for Co-ordination of Defensive Measures (1939–45). He was Minister for Finance (1945–48); Minister for External Affairs (1951–54; 1957–68) and Minister for Agriculture (March to May 1957). He was Tanaiste from 1965 until his retirement to the back benches in 1969.

AIKENHEAD, MOTHER MARY (1787–1858). Religious; founder of the Sisters of Charity; b. Cork; at the age of sixteen she became a convert to Catholicism. With the assistance of Daniel Murray,* she spent three years in a novitiate at York after which she returned to Dublin to be professed. She opened her first convent of the Sisters of Charity in North William Street, Dublin, and was appointed Sister-General of the order which received papal recognition in 1816. By the time she died she had built eight other houses of the Order, an asylum for penitents and the hospital of St Vincent in Dublin (the first hospital in Ireland to be served by nuns).

AILTIRI NA hAISEIRI. 'Architects of the Revolution'; nationalist organisation active during the 1940s, founded by Gearóid Ó Cuinnegeáin from Craobh na hAiseiri of the Gaelic League.* Members of Ailtiri contested the general elections of 1943 and 1944 when they all lost their deposits. Membership in Limerick included Sean South.* Members of the organisation were later active in Clann na Poblachta.*

AIR CORPS. Section of the Defence Forces* established in 1922 upon the creation of the Free State. Having for its motto *Forfaire agus Tairiseacht* (Alert and Loyal), the Air Corps' functions are to train pilots and provide technical training, to maintain an air ambulance service (a helicopter squadron), air co-operation with the ground forces and military and survey photography for the Ordnance Survey; it also operates search and rescue aircraft, fishery protection from the air and VIP flights. Its headquarters are at Casement Aerodrome, Baldonnel, Co. Dublin.

The first military aircraft was a Martinsyde five-passenger plane which had been purchased by the Irish Republican Army* during the Treaty negotiations in case Michael Collins* should need to flee from London. It was christened 'The Big Fella' in his honour. Other planes held by the Air Corps in 1922 were eight Agro 504 Ks, eight Bristol fighters, four Martinsyde single-seater fighters and eight De Haviland 9A bombers, then the most modern available with a cruising speed of 90 mph and a range of 450 miles. The first Commanding Officer was Major-General Mac-Sweeney (1922–23). Cadets were recruited in 1926, the first to be recruited into the defence forces through competitive civil service examination.

During the Emergency* the Air Corps was responsible for the salvage of belligerent aircraft. Six Hawker Hinds and thirteen Hectors were purchased between 1940 and 1942. A squadron of Hurricane fighters was replaced by twelve Seafire aircraft in 1947.

The Air Corps has operated the Helicopter Rescue Service since 1962. The first actual sea rescue was on 8 August 1964 when a man and a boy were rescued from a drifting boat in Dublin Bay. By 1978 the HRS had engaged in 406 search and rescue operations in which a total of 103 lives were saved.

An officer of the Air Corps, James Fitzmaurice,* was a member of the crew of the *Bremen* which successfully completed the first east-west crossing of the Atlantic on 12—13 April 1928.

At the end of August 1979 the total strength of the Air Corps was 641: 84 officers, 193 NCOs and 364 men. There were also seven cadets.

ALIENS ACT, 1935. Act passed by the government of Eamon de Valera* along with the Irish Nationality and Citizenship Act.* The legislation defined as alien anyone who was not a citizen of the Irish Free State; it included British subjects in the category of aliens.

ALLAN, FRED (d. 1937). Fenian; he worked as a clerk on the Great Northern Railway. For his part in the Irish Republican Brotherhood,* he was unsuccessfully charged with treason-felony in 1884. He worked on the *Freeman's Journal* but broke his connection in 1891 when it lined up with the anti-Parnellites. Then he worked on the Parnellite *Irish Daily Independent* (see *Irish Independent*) of which he became business manager, turning the newspaper office into a virtual headquarters of the IRB. He was dismissed in 1899 when the newspaper got into financial difficulty. As secretary to the Supreme Council of the IRB he was co-ordinator for the 1898 centenary celebrations of the United Irishmen. He lost the support of many Fenians when he became private secretary to the Lord Mayor of Dublin and, in 1900, came in for strong criticism from his colleagues for organising a children's fete during

Queen Victoria's visit to Dublin (April); despite demands for his resignation, including one from John O'Leary,* he managed to retain his membership of the IRB. He was becoming increasingly alienated from the younger generation of republicans and in 1910 resigned. He opposed Bulmer Hobson,* Sean MacDiarmada* and *Irish Freedom.* He supported the Irish Volunteers* and after the Easter Rising of 1916,* became a Trustee of the Irish National Aid Association* and Irish Volunteers' Dependents' Fund.* He also supported Sinn Fein* and worked in republican courts during the War of Independence* and was imprisoned and interned until 1921. He supported the Treaty,* and served on the executive of Cumann na nGaedheal.*

ALLEN, WILLIAM. *See* Manchester Martyrs.

ALL - FOR - IRELAND LEAGUE. Founded by William O'Brien* in 1910 when he broke with the United Irish League* after that body rejected his call for a conference on the Irish question. The All-for-Irelanders had as their motto 'Conference, Conciliation, Consent'. They believed that only through a conference of all interested parties could a solution be found to the Irish question. This was not acceptable to John Redmond* and the majority of the Irish Parliamentary Party* from which O'Brien resigned. The League was strongest in Cork and the surrounding area. It opposed partition, saying, 'All for Ireland, Ireland for all'. The membership included prominent Unionists, Lord Dunraven,* Lord Barrymore (*see* Smith-Barry, A. H.), Lord Mayo* and Lord Castletown. The League was critical of Redmond's acceptance of the (third) Home Rule Bill.* O'Brien and T. M. Healy* represented the League at the Mansion House Conference* in 1918. The League ceased to have any influence after the general election of December 1918 which its parliamentary members did not contest.

ALLGOOD, SARA (1883–1950). Actress; b. Dublin; member of Inghinidhe na hÉireann.* Her talent was recognised by W. B. Yeats.* She studied elocution under Frank Fay* and later became a leading actress in the Abbey Theatre Company. She composed the music for Yeats's *Deirdre* (1906), and a year later made her appearance in what was to become one of her most celebrated roles — that of Pegeen Mike in *The Playboy of the Western World*. Her close personal friends included Augusta, Lady Gregory* and she was a frequent visitor to the Coole Park estate. She toured abroad with the Abbey Theatre Company to enthusiastic reviews and remained in the USA following the 1940 tour, taking out American citizenship in 1945. Miss Allgood moved to Hollywood but failed to achieve the success anticipated for her. She appeared in a succession of minor roles as an Irish domestic; her last appearance was in *Cheaper by the Dozen* in 1950.

ALLIANCE PARTY. Political party founded in Northern Ireland in April 1970; it attempted to provide a middle-ground between Catholics (regarded as republicans) and Protestants (regarded as unionists) as a result of the civil rights agitation organised by the Northern Ireland Civil Rights Association.* Alliance had three sitting members, led by Phelim O'Neill, when Stormont was prorogued and direct rule introduced in March 1972. The party subscribed to power-sharing and won eight seats to the Assembly (*see* Northern Ireland). It joined with the Social Democratic and Labour Party* and pro-Assembly Unionists led by Brian Faulkner* to form a power-sharing Executive. Alliance had one voting member, Oliver Napier, (Minister of Law Reform) and two non-voting members, Basil Glass (Deputy Chief Whip) and Robert Cooper (Minister of Manpower) on the Executive. The Assembly was destroyed by extremist Unionists. In the election to the Convention (*see* Northern Ireland) four-fifths of

the Alliance candidates saved their deposits and eight were returned.

ALLINGHAM, WILLIAM (1824–89). Writer and poet; b. Ballyshannon, Co. Donegal; ed. locally. He entered the Customs and Excise as a young man in London where he was a friend of the pre-Raphaelites (Millais and Rosetti illustrated his *Day and Night Songs* in 1854). He retired from the service (1870) to become sub-editor of *Fraser's Magazine* and was editor (1874–79). He married Helen Patterson, the distinguished water colour artist (22 August 1874). He contributed to leading periodicals of the day, including the *Athenaeum* and Dickens' *Household Words* and edited *The Ballad Book* (1872). His works include *Blackberries* (1850), *Poems* (1850), *Fifty Modern Poems* (1863), *Songs, Ballads and Stories* (1877), *Ashby Manor* (a play, 1882), *Evil May Day*, (1882, which contains his best known poem 'The Fairies'), *Irish Songs and Poems* (1887), *Flower Pieces and Other Poems* (1888). A selection from his diaries and autobiography was published in 1906.

ALL-IRELAND COMMITTEE. Founded in February 1897 to seek the implementation of the Report of a Royal Commission which had indicated that the country had been over-taxed during the Union. The Committee, which included Colonel E. J. Saunderson,* John Redmond,* Timothy Healy,* Sir Horace Plunkett* and John Dillon,* achieved little of value.

ALL-PARTY ANTI-PARTITION COMMITTEE (MANSION HOUSE COMMITTEE). Founded in January 1949, the Committee consisted of representatives of the major political parties in Eire. The members were the then Taoiseach, John A. Costello,* William Norton,* Sean MacBride,* Eamon de Valera,* and Frank Aiken;* the treasurer was Cearbhall O'Dalaigh. They organised a public collection, the Mansion House Fund, with a view to financing the peaceful reunification of Ireland. The Committee sponsored the publication of anti-partition propaganda, including *The Finances of Partition* and *Indivisible Ireland*. It also financed anti-partition candidates in Northern Ireland (*see* Anti-Partition League) and an Anti-Partition League in England.

AMBROSE, ROBERT (1855–1940). Surgeon and politician; b. Limerick; ed. Queen's University. He devoted much of his time to the promotion of an All-Red or All-British road from London to Australia, via British territory and on British ships. He was MP, W. Mayo, (1893–1910). In 1897 he introduced the first Bill for compulsory land purchase in Ireland. He also introduced a Bill to grant Co. Councils compulsory purchase powers to acquire land for reclamation and resale to the landless sons of small farmers, with mineral rights to remain with the Councils. He wrote on peasant proprietorship for England, Scotland and Wales, defending agricultural labourers. Ambrose was the author of *A Plea for the Industrial Regeneration of Ireland* (1909):

AMENDMENTS TO THE CONSTITUTION. *See* Constitution of 1937.

AMERICAN ASSOCIATION FOR THE RECOGNITION OF THE IRISH REPUBLIC. Founded by Eamon de Valera* on 16 November 1920 in an effort to bring Irish-American support into a single effective movement; this followed a split between himself and Clan na Gael,* which dominated the Friends of Irish Freedom.* The purpose of the AARIR, de Valera said, was to provide 'a co-ordinated and unified movement to supply the channels by which the popular sentiment in the country [USA] in favour of justice might express itself'. The AARIR was to raise money for the republican forces engaged in the War of Independence* with the British forces. The Association remained active during the War but was weakened by the split in the republican

movement after the Treaty.* By 1926 it had ceased to be of any importance.

AMERICAN COMMISSION OF INQUIRY. The inquiry was launched in the USA in August 1920 by Dr W. J. Moloney and Frank P. Walsh, to inquire into means of checking alleged excesses of British troops and police in Ireland.

The original committee of one hundred and fifty eminent Americans included Cardinal Gibbons, one Catholic archbishop, four Catholic bishops, seven Episcopal bishops, four Methodist leaders, the governors of five US states, eleven senators, the mayors of five large cities, college presidents, professors, editors and leaders of labour and industry representing, in all, thirty-six states. The commission called witnesses from Ireland and invited Lord French* and Hamar (later Sir Hamar) Greenwood* to attend. No British witness in fact testified. The Committee's Interim Report released early in 1921 focused world attention on prevailing conditions in Ireland and brought further pressure on the British government to bring about a cessation of hostilities.

AMERICAN LAND LEAGUE. Founded by Charles Stewart Parnell* and Michael Davitt;* the American branch of the Land League* was founded in New York as a result of a meeting called by Parnell in March 1880 during his American tour. A committee of seven was appointed, four of whom were members of Clan na Gael,* led by John Devoy.* The function of the American League was to rally support for the Land League in Ireland. *See* Land War.

'AMERICAN NOTE'. The American Note was delivered by the government of the USA to the Irish government in February 1944. The Americans had the support of the British government. The note demanded that the government of Eamon de Valera* should insist on the removal of German and Japanese diplomats from

Dublin. The Americans claimed that such diplomats had 'the opportunity for highly organised espionage'. In reply to the note, de Valera, who had a particularly poor relationship with David Gray, the US Ambassador to Ireland, pointed out that the Irish government had prevented attempts to use Ireland as a base for spying. He reiterated Ireland's position of neutrality in relation to the warring powers.

'AMERICAN WAKE'. A 'wake' was held for a prospective emigrant to the United States the night before his departure. Such gatherings, in marked contrast to those attendant upon the death of an aged person, were sad affairs. The reason for such an event was that the departing emigrant was unlikely to return to his home or townland. It was customary for all the guests at the 'wake' to accompany the emigrant on the first leg of his journey.

AMNESTY ASSOCIATION. The Amnesty Association was founded by John 'Amnesty' Nolan* in 1868 for the purpose of campaigning for the release of imprisoned members of the Irish Republican Brotherhood.* Fenians were held under notoriously harsh conditions in British prisons after the rising of 1867. The Association was supported by Isaac Butt* who became its President. When Butt founded the Home Government Association* in 1870 the Amnesty Association provided valuable support. The Association's agitation continued until 1872 by which time it had secured the release of important Fenians including John Devoy* and Jeremiah O'Donovan Rossa.* The Association resumed activities again in the 1890s to secure the release from imprisonment of convicted dynamiters.* A leading role in this campaign was played by Maud Gonne.* *See* Amnesty Association of Great Britain.

AMNESTY ASSOCIATION OF GREAT BRITAIN. The first branch of the Amnesty Association* in England was founded in London by Dr Mark Ryan* on 23 January 1892. The various branches amalgamated in August 1894 at a meeting held in Liverpool to form the Amnesty Association of Great Britain. The first president was Arthur Lynch* and other prominent members included John MacBride.* The AAGB remained in existence until it had fulfilled its task of securing the release of imprisoned Fenians, the last of whom, Thomas J. Clarke,* was released in 1898.

ANCIENT ORDER OF HIBERNIANS (AOH). Founded in 1641, the AOH took its modern form as a Catholic reaction to the Orange Order* in 1838. It had as its motto, 'Fidelity to Faith and Fatherland'. The Order was strongest in southern Ulster. During the nineteenth century it became one of the strongest Irish movements in the USA, where it played an important role in Irish political activity and where, during the 1880s, it was dominated by Clan in Gael.* In 1878 the AOH split over the admission of members of Irish descent instead of those of Irish birth. The split spread to Ireland (1884) and continued until 1902 when a conference established the Board of Erin.* The AOH gave its support to the Irish Parliamentary Party* under John Redmond, raising money for the cause of Home Rule. In 1904 Joseph Devlin became National President of the Board of Erin which represented the majority of the AOH membership. Those who did not recognise the Board amounted to some 1,500 members in twenty divisions. There was a further split in 1905 over the decision to register as a friendly society. In Ulster the AOH was an important part of Devlin's nationalist political machine and during the 1920s was the principal guardian of Catholic rights in the state of Northern Ireland. The AOH is no longer politically active. It is a friendly society, a benefit and social club.

AnCO: THE INDUSTRIAL TRAIN-ING AUTHORITY. AnCO was set up under the Industrial Training Act, 1967, to provide and promote training at all levels in commerce and industry. Five members of the AnCO Council are nominated by the employers' organisations, five are nominated by the Irish Congress of Trade Unions* and three are appointed by the Minister for Labour who also appoints the chairman. AnCO holds courses for men and women at its fourteen training centres. Most of the trainees are unemployed industrial or agricultural workers, or have been unable to find work on leaving school. Apprenticeship training is the responsibility of AnCO. It is carried out within firms and through day and block-release courses provided by the VECs. AnCO provides courses at its training centres for first-year apprentices.

ANDERSON, SIR JOHN, VISCOUNT WAVERLEY (1882–1958). Civil servant and politician (Conservative); Under-Secretary for Ireland (1920–21). While in Ireland he was responsible for putting out feelers for a Truce during the War of Independence.* His sympathies were with the state of Northern Ireland and he helped to persuade the British government to accept and finance the establishment of the Special Constabulary.* He was later Governor of Bengal (1933–37), Lord Privy Seal (1939) and Home Secretary (1939–40).

ANDERSON, SIR ROBERT (1841–1918). Civil servant and author; b. Dublin; ed. TCD; B.A. (1862), Bar (1863) and LL.D (1875). From 1868 he was adviser on political crime to the Home Office, in which capacity he investigated the Fenians* and the dynamiters* of the 1880s. Anderson supplied *The Times* with material for the Parnell Commission (*see* Parnellism and Crime) and was the author of the second series of articles, using material provided him by Henri Le Caron.* He was Head of the Criminal Investigation Department

(1888–1901). He was the author of a number of works on theological matters, including *The Silence of God* (1897), *The Bible and Modern Criticism* (1902), *Forgotten Truths* (1913) and *Misunderstood Texts of the New Testament* (1916). His *Criminal and Crime* was published in 1907.

ANDREWS, JOHN MILLER (1871–1956). Politician (Ulster Unionist); Prime Minister, Northern Ireland* (1940–43), b. Comber, Co. Down; ed. Belfast Academical Institute. A prominent member of the Ulster Unionist Council* and the Ulster Unionist Party he was also a member of the Orange Order* and served as Grand Master of the Council of World Orange Institutions (1949–56). Along with Sir Edward Carson* he sat as a non-labour member of the Ulster Unionist Labour Association,* 1918. Andrews was MP, Co. Down (1921–29) and Mid-Down and London-Derry (1929–53). He was Minister of Labour (1921–37) and Minister of Finance (1937–40) for Northern Ireland. In 1933 he stated that he had discovered that of the thirty-one porters employed at the parliament buildings 'there are thirty Protestants and only one Roman Catholic – there temporarily'. He succeeded Lord Craigavon* as Prime Minister in 1940 but he was unpopular with his younger colleagues who considered him too old-fashioned for the post. In 1943 he was overthrown and succeeded by Sir Basil Brooke (*see* Brookeborough, Lord).

ANDREWS, THOMAS (1843–1916). Politician (Ulster Unionist); b. Comber, Co. Down; ed. Belfast Academical Institute and Queen's College, Belfast. Andrews was MP for Co. Down. He was very active in the Ulster Unionist opposition to Home Rule.* President of the Ulster Liberal Unionist Committee (1892) and a member of the Ulster Defence Union (1893). He was a member of the Recess Committee.*

ANGLESEY, 1st MARQUIS (1768–1854). Paget, Henry William; Lord

Lieutenant (1828–29; 1830–33); b. London; ed. Westminster School and Christ Church, Oxford. After entering parliament for Carnarvon Boroughs (1790) he served in Flanders as a lieutenant-colonel of militia, but later, in the regular army, became one of the outstanding cavalry commanders of his time. He caused a celebrated scandal in 1809 by eloping with the sister-in-law of Arthur Wellesley, later Duke of Wellington.* As Lord Uxbridge, he served at Waterloo where he lost a leg. He succeeded Wellington as Commander-in-Chief in 1827. Anglesey was appointed to Ireland by the Duke of Wellington at the height of the agitation for Catholic Emancipation* organised by Daniel O'Connell* and the Catholic Association.* He became popular in Ireland when he indicated his support for Emancipation. He also favoured reforms in connection with tithes* and education. His plans were resolutely opposed by Wellington and King George IV.* He incurred the hostility of the (Protestant) Ascendancy* and the Orange Order* and earned the suspicion of the British government. Wellington informed him of his recall in December 1828; he was not in fact officially recalled until January 1829 and did not leave the Irish post until March of that year. By this time O'Connell's victory in the Clare by-election had made Emancipation inevitable. Anglesey returned to the Irish post when Wellington was succeeded by Earl Grey (1830). His second term in office was very different from his first. While he had supported Emancipation he totally opposed the new O'Connell campaign for Repeal of the Union, which led to bitter confrontation between himself and the Irish leader. His second term of office was also made more difficult by his poor relationship with the Chief Secretary, Lord Stanley (*see* Derby, 14th Earl) who was a member of the cabinet, from which Anglesey was excluded. Under pressure from the 1st Lord Monteagle who had prepared a report on education in 1828

Anglesey pressed for a system of non-denominational or 'mixed' education but was unable to make any headway despite the fact that Stanley favoured such a scheme (and did introduce a system of National Education in 1831 but without reference to Anglesey). Anglesey was thwarted also in his desire to break the monopoly of the Kildare Place Society* and to make grants available to Catholic bishops for educational purposes. A further reason for the unhappiness of his second term was the unrest in the country because of the anti-tithes campaign. Although he personally opposed the tithes, he was forced to support renewal of coercion* to deal with the rising crime rate, an issue which helped to bring down Grey's administration. He was succeeded by Richard Colley Wellesley.*

ANGLO-IRISH AGREEMENTS (1938). These were three agreements signed in London on 25 April 1938 between Eamon de Valera* and the British Prime Minister, Neville Chamberlain.* They were the results of talks which started in January of that year and brought the Economic War* to an end. The agreements were defensive, economic and commercial. The defensive agreement abrogated Articles 6 and 7 of the Treaty: the 'Treaty Ports' were returned to Ireland, a measure which was denounced by Winston Churchill* in the House of Commons. Under the economic agreement Eire agreed to pay £10,000,000 in full settlement of all British claims (which totaled £104,000,000); this amount covered the Land Annuities,* the withholding of which had precipitated the Economic War in 1932. The commercial agreement re-opened the British market to Irish cattle and food products; Ireland allowed duty-free access to British goods. The agreements were generally considered a triumph for de Valera and the defence agreement enabled Ireland to declare herself a neutral in World War II.

ANGLO-IRISH FREE TRADE AREA AGREEMENT (AIFTAA). The

13

AIFTAA came into effect on 1 July 1966. Under the terms of the agreement there was to be a gradual removal of protective tariffs on imports and exports between the Republic and the United Kingdom markets. The agreement was an important part of Irish economic policy during the 1960s (*see* Programmes for Economic Expansion). It was of particular importance for Irish agriculture as it gave unrestricted access to the UK for Irish store cattle and sheep. The butter quota to the UK was also increased. Irish agricultural and horticultural produce would not be regulated except by inter-governmental commodity agreement or some other arrangement. The British government also undertook to afford opportunities for the growth of imports from Ireland on terms no less favourable than those granted to British farmers. Under the agreement there was to be freedom of access to Irish fish and fishery products. Protective duties on textiles and clothing containing man-made fibres were to be eliminated. Agricultural exports showed an increase in 1967 as a result of the agreement; store cattle exports were 620,000 head as compared with an annual average from 1962 to 1966 of 510,000, and beef exports were 730,000 head compared with an annnual average of 340,000 head between 1963 and 1966.

ANGLO-IRISH TRADE AGREEMENT (1948). Under the terms of the AITA negotiated with the United Kingdom by the Minister for Agriculture, James Dillon,* the prices of Irish cattle and sheep were linked to British prices. *See also* Anglo-Irish Free Trade Area Agreement.

ANGLO-IRISH TREATY. *See* Treaty.

ANGLO-IRISH WAR. *See* War of Independence.

ANNAGHDOWN BOAT TRAGEDY (4 September 1828). Eleven men and eight women lost their lives when an old rowing boat foundered and sank at a point opposite Menlo Graveyard on Lough Corrib. Thirty-one people had boarded the boat at Annaghdown to travel the eight miles to the Fair of Fair Hill, Galway. Ten sheep and a quantity of lumber were also aboard. When one of the sheep became restless and drove his leg through a plank, a male passenger, in an effort to plug the leak, placed his overcoat over the hole and stamped it with his foot, thus driving the plank from the boat's bottom. The thirteen survivors received assistance from the 64th Regiment under the command of Major Dickson. A subsequent inquest under Coroner John Blakeney returned a verdict of 'accidental drowning'.

The tragedy was the subject of a poem by Anthony O'Raftery* 'Anach Cuain' subsequently translated by Dr Douglas Hyde* as 'The Drowning of Annach Doon'.

ANTI-COERCION ASSOCIATION. The Association was founded in England in 1880 by H. M. Hyndman and other British radicals. They sought to gather support for the Land League.* They used *The Radical* newspaper to attack the Liberal government on its Irish policies in which coercion played a major part.

ANTI-PARTITION COMMITTEE. *See* All-Party Anti-Partition Committee.

ANTI-PARTITION LEAGUE. The League was established in 1947 to protest against the continuing partition of Ireland into Northern Ireland and Eire. In the north it was supported by the Nationalist Party of Northern Ireland. *See also* All-Party Anti-Partition Committee.

ANTI-REPEAL UNION. *See* Ulster Loyalist Anti-Repeal Union.

ANTISELL, THOMAS (1818—93). Author and geologist; b. Dublin. He supported Young Ireland.* He was the author of *Agricultural Chemistry* (1845) and *Irish Geology* (1846). After the rising of 1848 he escaped to the USA where, as well as fighting with distinction in the Civil War (1861—65), he worked in the US Department of Agriculture where he became chief chemist.

AONTACHT EIREANN. Political party founded in 1971 by Kevin Boland* after he had quit Fianna Fail* in protest at the government's handling of affairs in relation to Northern Ireland. The party appealed for support for a united Ireland. It proposed that the Irish Republic should assist republicans in Northern Ireland in attempts to end the British presence and partition. Until 1973, the party had one member in Dail Eireann. In 1976 Mr Boland resigned from the leadership of the party, which had made little impact on Irish political life.

APPEAL TO THE IRISH RACE. *An Appeal to the Irish Race for the Sustainment of the Irish National Land Movement* was issued by the (Irish National) Land League* at its inaugural meeting on 21 October 1879 at the Imperial Hotel, Dublin. The *Appeal* was directed to the Irish in America as well as to 'all whom evil laws have scattered the world over, as well as to all other nationalities who sympathise with a wronged and impoverished people'. The Land League looked for support in its fight to destroy the landlord system as it operated in Ireland. This *Appeal* had the support of John Devoy,* and resulted in financial assistance which enabled the League to forward the cause of the Irish tenantry in its fight with the landlords and British authority in Ireland.

APPRENTICE BOYS. Ulster Unionist Protestant organisation founded in Derry to commemorate the actions of the apprentice boys who locked the gates of the city against James II in 1689. Closely associated with the Orange Order,* its annual march is held on 12 August. *See also* Royal Black Preceptory.

APPRENTICES, 'INDENTURED'. *See* 'Indentured' Apprentices.

ARBITRATION COURTS. During the agitation for Repeal, Daniel O'Connell* proposed that Arbitration Courts should be established to frustrate the operation of the Crown Courts. They operated briefly in 1843. The idea was revived during the War of Independence* when British administration in Ireland was wrecked by the Sinn Fein* takeover of local government. The republicans also established Land Arbitration Courts to settle disputes over land division. Decisions of the courts were executed by the Irish Republican Army.* Dail Eireann placed these courts under the jurisdiction of the Minister for Agriculture. *See also* Dail Courts.

ARBOUR HILL. Military Detention Centre built in 1842; the executed leaders of the Easter Rising of 1916* were buried in the grounds. It was closed down after the evacuation of the twenty-six counties by the British authorities and the establishment of the Free State in 1922. In 1975 it was reopened as a prison.

ARDAGH CHALICE, RECOVERY OF (1868). The Ardagh Chalice was unearthed by a Mr Quin of Ardagh, Co. Limerick, while digging potatoes in an old fort on his land. The find was examined by Bishop Butler of Limerick and Lord Dunraven who sent it to the Royal Irish Academy* for further examination. When the nature of the find had been ascertained Bishop Butler purchased it from Mr Quin (21 June 1871) and it was presented to the RIA in 1878. It is now in the National Museum, Dublin.

The chalice, which dates from the eighth century, is one of the most outstanding artefacts to survive from the golden age of Irish art.

ARMAGH RAILWAY DISASTER (12 June 1889). The worst disaster in Irish railway history, in which eighty people died, and nearly four hundred were injured, on the annual Armagh-Warrenpoint excursion of the Armagh Methodist Sunday School. The accident occurred when the engine stalled at a point near the end of its climb on the Dobbin's Bridge gradient. The engine was uncoupled and the train was divided to facilitate the climb. During the uncoupling, the front part of the train touched the rear portion which careered down the steep incline and smashed into the 10.35 Armagh-Newry train. A submission of *nolle prosequi* was entered before Justice O'Brien at Green Street Courthouse on 25 October and all concerned were discharged.

ARMOUR, REV. JAMES BROWN (1841–1928). Clergyman (Presbyterian); b. Lisboy, Ballymoney, Co. Antrim; ed. Queen's College, Belfast. He was a Presbyterian minister in Ballymoney from 1869 until his death. Founder of the Intermediate School, Ballymoney, and lecturer at Magee College, Derry. Rev. Armour was one of Ulster's best-known liberals of the nineteenth century. An impressive orator, he campaigned in support of Tenant Right* (or Ulster Custom), Home Rule* and for a Catholic University. He condemned the Ulster Unionism which developed in 1886 as a device to maintain the Ascendancy* in its old privileges. He opposed the Ulster Unionist Party* and the establishment of self-government in part of Ulster (*see* Northern Ireland). In October 1913 he was host to Sir Roger Casement* in Ballymoney.

ARMY. The National Army of the Free State* was established in January 1922 from among officers and men of the Irish Republican Army* who had supported the Treaty.* By June the Army was engaged in a Civil War,* fighting the section of the IRA which had rejected the Treaty. Following the Civil War the army was reduced from around 60,000 to 30,000, a measure which provoked the Army Mutiny* of

1924. The policy of reduction continued during the 1920s.

After coming to power in 1932 Eamon de Valera* recruited Volunteers from IRA men who had been active in the War of Independence* (1919–21). Distinctively uniformed, they were recruited during December 1933 and given the rank of captain. Another force, containing many former IRA men, was also established as the 'A' and 'B' Reserves. The strength of the combined army, volunteers and reserves in September 1939, just before the declaration of the Emergency* created by World War II, was 19,791:

	Officers	NCOs	Privates
Army	630	1,420	5,452
'A' and 'B' Reserves	194	544	4,328
Volunteers	237	557	6,429

Although Ireland was neutral the possibility of a German invasion following the fall of France in 1940 led to a massive recruitment drive which brought the strength up to 54,502 (April 1940). The regular strength was also augmented by the Local Security Force* (LSF) and the Local Defence Force* (LDF). However, desertion was not infrequent, as soldiers were attracted by the higher rates of pay in the British army and in factories engaged in war work. It was later estimated that during the course of the war some 7,000 deserted from the Irish armed forces. For this reason and through normal reduction the figure for the army in June 1944 was 36,211. The Army's strength was reduced to peace-time proportions during the late 1940s.

The Irish army served on a number of peace-keeping missions for the United Nations* since its first in the Congo (1961). Ten Irish soldiers were killed by Baluba tribesmen in an ambush at Niemba in 1961 while serving on the first peace-keeping mission. In all a total of twenty-six Irish soldiers died in the Congo. Subsequent peace-keeping missions were in Cyprus, Kashmir and the Lebanon.

At the end of 1979, while engaged

16

in a recruiting campaign to attract an extra 2,000 men and, for the first time, women, the army's strength was 11,933: 1,263 officers, 3,990 NCOs and 6,680 privates. There were also 59 cadets. *See also* Defence Forces.

ARMY COMRADES ASSOCIATION. The ACA was founded in February 1932 by Commandant Edmund (Ned) Cronin. At first it was confined to ex-officers and men of the Free State Army with the aim of upholding the Free State and commemorating those who had died during the War of Independence.* Its first President was Colonel Austin Brennan. During the general election of March 1932, which was won by Fianna Fail,* the ACA gave support to Cumann na nGaedheal.* In August it was opened to the general public and under a new president, Thomas F. O'Higgins, claimed a membership of 30,000. During the general election of January 1933 the ACA set itself to giving protection from the Irish Republican Army* to the Cumann na nGaedheal candidates during the violent campaign. The organisation was opposed to communism, which it identified with Fianna Fail and the IRA. The movement was now remodelled with view to greater discipline and in April 1933 its members took to wearing blue shirts. Members of the ACA became known as Blueshirts.* In July 1933 the presidency was assumed by General Eoin O'Duffy* who renamed it the National Guard.*

ARMY CONVENTIONS (26 March and 9 April 1922). The Army Convention of 26 March 1922 was demanded by officers of the Irish Republican Army* who were concerned that the establishment of the Provisional Government* and the acceptance of the Treaty* meant the abrogation of the Irish Republic as declared by the first Dail Eireann.* The Minister for Defence, Richard Mulcahy,* acceded to the demand but the cabinet proscribed the Convention and Mulcahy informed General Eoin O'Duffy* that anyone who attended the Convention would be taken to have severed his connection with the IRA. The Convention was attended only by the anti-Treaty IRA (soon to be known as the new IRA). The 211 delegates present appointed a sixteen-man executive as the supreme command of the IRA. The Convention resolved that the IRA should affirm its allegiance to the Irish Republic and that the IRA was the only legal army; it also called on the Provisional Government to cease recruiting for the National Army and the Civic Guards.* The Executive was granted authority 'if it considered fit' to suppress the general election scheduled for 16 June. It concluded by repudiating the authority of the Minister of Defence and his Chief of Staff (O'Duffy). The section of the IRA which supported the Free State became known as the old IRA. On 9 April a further Convention was held; 217 delegates attended. A new army constitution was drafted affirming the aims of the IRA and placing it under the control of the Executive. The Executive consisted of Liam Lynch, Chief of Staff; Rory O'Connor; Liam Mellows; Florence O'Donoghue; Joseph McKelvey; Liam Deasy; Ernie O'Malley; Sean Moylan, Sean O'Hegarty; Seamus Robinson; Peadar O'Donnell; Joe O'Connor; Frank Barrett; Thomas Maguire; P. J. Ruttledge and Thomas Hales. Before the end of the month republicans seized the Four Courts* and other buildings in Dublin and the Civil War* started in June. *See also* Army Mutiny (1924).

ARMY DOCUMENT. *See* Unity Proposals (May 1922).

ARMY MUTINY (1924). A major crisis for the government of the Free State arose in 1924, within a year of the Civil War, when W. T. Cosgrave* and his colleagues were presented with an ultimatum from the old IRA element within the national army. The ultimatum, signed by Liam Tobin and C. F. Dalton, was prompted by two factors. One was that the government had announced that the 60,000 strong army would have to be cut by nearly half now that there was peace in the country. The other factor was that the old IRA resented the influence within the army of the Irish Republican Brotherhood* to whom the Minister of Defence, General Richard Mulcahy* was thought to be sympathetic as a former member of the Supreme Council.* The ultimatum, presented on 6 March, demanded an end to demobilisation, the abolition of the Army Council established by Mulcahy and a declaration that the government was still committed to the ideal of an Irish Republic. In the absence of the President of the Executive Council, W. T. Cosgrave, who was ill, the crisis was handled by the Minister for Justice, Kevin O'Higgins.* The affair affected the government immediately as the Minister for Industry and Commerce, Joseph McGrath,* who was sympathetic to the old IRA, resigned his office in protest at the manner in which the Defence ministry had neglected the army's grievances. O'Higgins appointed General Eoin O'Duffy* to the command of the armed forces and had the two signatories arrested. Although now a private individual, McGrath assured the mutineers that their grievances would be investigated and the Army Council remodelled to their satisfaction. Shortly afterwards, when Free State troops attempted to arrest armed mutineers McGrath prevented bloodshed. The troops had acted without the authorisation of O'Duffy but on the orders of the Adjutant-General who had consulted with Mulcahy. The Adjutant-General and two other high-ranking officers were forced to resign as did Mulcahy. The mutiny came to an end when the legitimate grievances of the army had been conceded. Those who did not return to their posts were held to have 'retired'. By October the mutiny was over, largely due to O'Higgins's firm handling. It had been a costly affair in that two ministers had resigned and a number of army headquarters staff had been replaced. It had served to demonstrate how strong republican sentiment was among those who had supported the Free State. It had also clearly indicated the determination of the government to subordinate the national army to the civil authority. In the words of O'Higgins: 'Those who take the pay and wear the uniform of the state . . . must be non-political servants of the state'.

ARREARS ACT. An Act to enable tenants in arrears with their rents to benefit from the Land Act of 1881 (*see* Land Acts) was promised by W. E. Gladstone* to Charles Stewart Parnell,* under the terms of the so-called 'Kilmainham Treaty'.* There were some 130,000 tenants excluded from the working of the Act. Gladstone introduced an Arrears Act on 15 May 1882 and there was a fall in agrarian outrages. The Act provided £800,000 to pay off arrears, enabling the tenants to benefit from the fair rent clause in the 1881 Land Act.

ARTS COUNCIL. Founded in 1951 to promote and stimulate public interest and appreciation of the arts. The Council is financed by annual vote of funds from Dail Eireann.

ASCENDANCY (PROTESTANT). Term attributed by John Gifford* to the Protestant landowning class which dominated Irish social, political, cultural and economic life during the eighteenth and nineteenth centuries.

ASGARD, THE. A twenty-eight-ton white yacht owned by Robert Erskine Childers.* The *Asgard* sailed for the Roetigan lightship on 29 June 1914 to make a rendezvous with a tug containing arms for the Irish Volunteers.* The arms had been purchased by Darrell Figgis* in Hamburg. A second yacht, the *Kelpie*,* sailed a few days later to take part of the cargo. The *Asgard*, which had neither a radio nor an engine, included among its crew Childers' American wife, two

Donegal fishermen, and Gordon Shephard and Mary Spring Rice.* They made the rendezvous on 12 July and took on board 900 rifles and 29,000 rounds of ammunition which they landed at Howth on 26 July. *See also* Howth Gun-running.

ASHBOURNE ACT. *See* Land Acts.

ASHBOURNE, BATTLE OF (28 April 1916). During the Easter Rising of 1916,* Irish Volunteers led by Thomas Ashe* ambushed forty members of the Royal Irish Constabulary* at Ashbourne, Co. Meath. The fighting lasted several hours and ended with the surrender of the police when they ran out of ammunition. Eight policemen were killed and fifteen wounded.

ASHBOURNE, 1st BARON (1837–1913). Gibson, Edward; politician (Unionist); b. Dublin; ed. TCD; Bar (1860). He was returned as MP for Dublin University (TCD) in 1875 and became a prominent Conservative Party spokesman on Irish affairs, serving as Attorney-General from 1877 until 1880. Gibson was chief spokesman on the Irish land question and led the Conservative attack on W. E. Gladstone's Irish policy, 1880–85. He was raised to the peerage and appointed Lord Chancellor of Ireland in 1885, with a seat in the cabinet. In that year he drew up a Land Act which was introduced by the Salisbury caretaker government (*see* Land Acts). He was the author of *Pitt, Some Chapters in his Life and Times* (1898). His son, William, 2nd Baron Ashbourne (1868–1942), was a scholar and active member of the Gaelic League,* of which he was for a time president. He was born in Dublin, and educated at Harrow, TCD and Merton College, Oxford. Apart from contributions to a variety of learned journals he published *The Abbé Lemennais and the Liberal Catholic Movement* (1896).

ASHE, THOMAS (1885–1917). Republican; b. Kinard, near Dingle, Co. Kerry; ed. Ardmore School and De La Salle Training College, Waterford; National Teacher (1905). He was principal of Corduff National School, Lusk, Co. Dublin (March 1908–April 1916). Ashe was active in the Gaelic League* and the Irish Volunteers,* on whose behalf he went to the USA on a fund-raising mission in 1914. He supported James Larkin* during the Lock-Out in 1913 and was also a close friend of Sean O'Casey.* During the Easter Rising of 1916* he led local Volunteers at Ashbourne, Co. Meath. He was court-martialled for his role in the Rising (11 May 1916) and sentenced to life imprisonment. He was released on 17 June 1917. Ashe was an organiser in Sinn Fein* and the Volunteers and a leading republican propagandist. He campaigned for Eamon de Valera* in Clare during the 1917 by-election. He was arrested in August and charged with inciting the civil population, for which he was sentenced to two years imprisonment. After failing to secure recognition of the republicans' claim for political status in Mountjoy, he organised a hunger-strike among the Sinn Fein prisoners (20 September). On 25 September he died while being forcibly fed. An inquest, which opened on 27 September, closed on 1 November with a verdict which censured those responsible for the treatment inflicted on him.

ASKWITH INQUIRY. *See* Lock-Out.

ASQUITH, HERBERT HENRY, 1st EARL OF OXFORD AND ASQUITH (1852–1928). Politician (Liberal); Prime Minister (1908–16); b. Morley, Yorkshire; ed. City of London School and Balliol College, Oxford. He was returned as MP for E. Fife in 1886, gave his support to W. E. Gladstone on Home Rule* and served him as Home Secretary (1892–94). He became Chancellor of the Exchequer in the government formed by Henry Campbell-Bannerman* in 1905 and introduced Old Age Pensions* in 1908. Asquith succeeded Campbell-Bannerman as Prime Minister in 1908. He was immediately involved in a confrontation with the House of Lords when the Lords refused to accept the 'People's Budget' introduced by David Lloyd George* in 1909. He gained the support of the Irish Parliamentary Party, led by John Redmond,* for his struggle with the Lords when he made a public commitment to Home Rule at the Albert Hall on 10 December, prior to the general election (January 1910). Having removed the absolute veto of the House of Lords in 1911, Asquith introduced the (third) Home Rule Bill* in 1912. Between 1912 and 1914 the Ulster Unionists sought to prevent the passage of the Bill. The Ulster Volunteer Force* was established in January 1913 and a second force, the Irish Volunteers,* came into existence during the following November. In March 1914 Asquith's government sought an undertaking from the Army at the Curragh that it would be prepared to act in Ulster. This led to the Curragh Incident* which forced Asquith and his government to back down. He secured the resignation of Lord French and he himself replaced the Secretary of State for War. An attempt to solve the crisis over Home Rule by bringing the Unionists and the Nationalists together for the Buckingham Palace Conference* ended in failure (July 1914). He did succeed in getting them to agree to a suspension of the Home Rule Act for the duration of the war. Asquith added a proviso to the Act that the question of Ulster would be considered before the Act would be implemented. During the Easter Rising of 1916 he sent General Maxwell* to Ireland to restore order. Asquith came to Dublin for six days on 12 May and prevented any further executions. Upon his return to Westminster, he informed the cabinet that government in Ireland had broken down and he appointed Lloyd George to start negotiations with the Unionists and the Nationalists (*see* Irish Convention). In December 1916, following mounting criticism of his handling of the war, he was replaced as Prime Minister by Lloyd George.

ASSEMBLY OF NORTHERN IRELAND. *See* Northern Ireland.

ATHLONE MANIFESTO. *See* Republican Congress.

AUD, THE. Formerly the *Castro*, SMS *Libau* was disguised by the Germans to look like the Norwegian vessel *The Aud* in April 1916 to bring guns for the Irish Volunteers* in time for the Easter Rising of 1916.* The ship, commanded by Captain Karl Spindler with a crew of twenty-one officers and men, left Lubeck on 9 April with a cargo of 20,000 rifles, machine-guns and ammunition. Sailing under the Norwegian flag, the vessel carried a camouflage cargo of timber. It was intended that *The Aud* would rendezvous off Fenit, Co. Kerry, with a German U-boat, U-20, containing Sir Roger Casement* and Robert Monteith.* The ship carried no wireless and so was unaware that the date for its arrival off Fenit had been altered from Thursday 20 April to Sunday 23 April, the date of the proposed rising. As a result of the alteration there were no preparations by Austin Stack* and the Kerry Volunteers to meet the ship which hove-to for nearly twenty-four hours. The *Aud*'s presence attracted the attention of a British patrol boat, the *Bluebell*, which gave chase and forced Spindler to make for Queenstown (now Cobh). Rather than have his cargo fall into British possession, Spindler and his crew scuttled the ship and boarded a lifeboat, on 22 April. They were interned for the duration of the war.

AUXILIARIES. The Auxiliaries, mainly recruited from among demobilised officers of the British army, were organised at the end of July 1920 to augment the Royal Irish Constabulary* from which there had been nearly 600 resignations within three months. The Irish Republican Army* campaign during the War of Independence* had been directed mainly at the police force. In all about 1,500 'cadets', as they were offically known, were involved in supporting

20

the RIC. While they were nominally under RIC command, they were in fact separate both from the RIC and the other auxiliary force known as the Black and Tans.* The Auxiliaries were divided into companies of around 100 men and were stationed in particularly troublesome parts of the country. Their pay of £1 per day plus expenses made them the highest paid uniformed force of their time. They were granted three months leave. By mid-1921 there were fifteen companies operating between counties Dublin, Sligo, Longford, Roscommon, Meath, Cork, Kerry, Clare, Tipperary and Kilkenny. They were notorious for their indiscriminate heavy-handed justice and the ferocity of their reprisals.

B

BACHELOR'S WALK, DUBLIN (26 July 1914). A group of Irish Volunteers, returning from the Howth Gunrunning,* was halted at Clontarf by the Assistant Police Commissioner, Harrell. A regiment of the King's Own Scottish Borderers was present. Darrell Figgis* and Thomas Mc-Donagh* engaged Harrell in discussion, allowing the Volunteers to disperse with the arms. While awaiting the order to move, the soldiers were jeered at by a growing number of civilians. On the return journey to Dublin the regiment was subjected to personal abuse. At Bachelor's Walk, stones were thrown at the soldiers. An officer who had joined them along the way was unaware that their arms were ready to fire, and gave the order to face the crowd. While he was addressing the crowd of civilians, a shot was fired and this was followed by a volley. Three people were killed and at least thirty-eight injured. A subsequent Commission censured the use of the military. The incident caused widespread indignation throughout Ireland, particularly as the perpetrators of the Larne Gun-running,* which involved the seizure and imprisonment of Customs and police officers, remained unpunished.

BAILEY, WILLIAM FREDERICK (1857–1917). Lawyer and writer; b. Castletown Conyers, Co. Limerick; ed. TCD. He was called to the Irish Bar in 1881 and practised on the Munster Circuit. He was Barrington lecturer in Political Economy, TCD and Extern in English for the Intermediate Education Board. Bailey was one of the secretaries to the Royal Commission on Irish Published Works (1880), Legal Assistant to the Commissioners under the Irish Land Act of 1887 and Secretary to the Statistical and Social Inquiry of Ireland. He was President of the Statistical and Social Inquiry in 1902 and became a Privy Councillor in 1909. His works include *Local and Centralised Government in Ireland* (1888) and *Ireland Since the Famine* (1902). He also published editions of poetry, including works of Gray and Coleridge.

BAIRD, SIR ROBERT HUGH HANLEY (1855–1934). Newspaper proprietor; b. Belfast; ed. Belfast Academical Institute. He owned the *Belfast Weekly Telegraph* (1873), *Ballymena Weekly Telegraph* (1887), *Ireland's Saturday Night* (1894), *Belfast Telegraph* (1904), *Irish Daily Telegraph* (1904), *Larne Times* (1891). Baird was President of the Master Printers Federation (1910); Chairman, Ulster District Institute of Journalists (1910) and Irish Representative at the Admiralty, War Office and Press Committee between 1910 and 1934.

BALDWIN, STANLEY, 1st EARL BALDWIN OF BEWDLEY (1867–1947). English politician (Conservative) and Prime Minister (1923–24, 1924–29, 1935–37); ed. Harrow and Trinity College, Cambridge. In 1925 he engineered a tripartite agreement between the Irish Free State, Britain and Northern Ireland which shelved the Report of the Boundary Commission.* During the debate on the Statute of Westminster,* Baldwin argued strongly against a proposal by Sir Winston Churchill* that a restriction clause be inserted which would prevent the Free State from repudiating the Treaty; he said that such a clause would offend Irishmen all over the world as well as other dominions within the Commonwealth.

BALFE, MICHAEL WILLIAM (1808–70). Composer and singer; b. Dublin. He studied music in Dublin under O'Rourke and in Italy under Galli. Balfe was a child prodigy and had, at the age of seven, written a polacca for a military band. He spent a year in London before leaving for Italy in 1825. His first complete opera, *I Rivali di Se Stesso*, was produced at Palermo in 1830. Balfe returned to England in 1843 and on 27 November of that year *The Bohemian Girl* had its world premiere at Drury Lane. He wrote thirty operas, several cantatas and songs, and arranged many symphonies and accompaniments, including several for Moore's *Irish Melodies.*

BALFOUR, ARTHUR JAMES, 1st EARL BALFOUR (1848–1930). British politician; Chief Secretary (1887–91); Prime Minister (1902–5); b. Whittingehame, E. Lothian; ed. Eton and Trinity College, Cambridge; MP, E. Manchester (1885–1906). His period as Chief Secretary was distinguished by a mixture of coercion and conciliation. The Mitchelstown 'Massacre'* of September 1887 earned him the title of 'Bloody Balfour'. He described the Irish land system as 'essentially and radically rotten', formed a poor opinion of the greedier landlords and condemned absentee landlords. He made constructive efforts to deal with the land problems: by the Light Railways Act of 1889 he established a system of railways which linked the west of Ireland with the east; he established the Congested Districts Board* to deal with the particular problems of the west and although his Land Purchase Act of 1891 (*see* Land Acts) needed modification by his brother, Gerald Balfour,* it was nonetheless considered an enlightened approach to the problem. Balfour remained opposed to Home Rule* and used his influence to prevent any such measure from being considered. He succeeded his uncle, the Earl of Salisbury, as Prime Minister. Balfour was replaced as leader of the Conservative Party by Andrew Bonar Law* in 1911 but remained an important influence in the party.

BALFOUR, GERALD, 2nd EARL BALFOUR (1853–1945). Politician (Conservative); Chief Secretary (1895–1900); b. Whittingehame, E. Lothian, younger brother of Arthur James Balfour;* ed. Eton and Trinity College, Cambridge. While Chief Secretary his 1896 Land Act (*see* Land Acts) greatly simplified his brother's Act of 1891 and increased the amount of money available. He succeeded to the earldom in 1930 upon his brother's death.

BALL, FRANCIS ELRINGTON (1863–1928). Historian and antiquary; b. Portmarnock, Co. Dublin, third son of John Thomas Ball;* ed. privately. He was an authority on Swift whose *Correspondence* he edited (6 vols, 1910–14). His historical writings include *The Parish of Taney: a history of Dundrum* (with Everard Hamilton, 1895), *History of the County of Dublin* (6 parts, 1902–20), *The Vicinity of the International Exhibition of Dublin* (1907). His legal writings include *The Judges in Ireland 1221–1921*. This work assumed a great significance when records and documents were lost in the Four Courts* during the Civil War, and is

22

now cited as a primary authority in many instances.

BALL, JOHN (1818–89). Scientist, politician (Liberal) and Alpinist; ed. for the Bar but, although called in 1845, he never practised. He was appointed Poor Law Commissioner in 1846 but had to resign through ill-health. As a Liberal MP for Co. Carlow, Ball advocated the Disestablishment of the Church of Ireland,* a readjustment of land tenure, a system of equitable rents and a modern approach to valuation. He was Under-Secretary to the Colonies, 1855–57. Ball contested Limerick in 1858 where his support for the Italian liberators, Cavour and Sella, brought him into opposition with the local clergy. A keen mountaineer, he was first President of the Alpine Club in 1857. His works include *The Alpine Guide* (3 vols, 1866–68), and *What is to be done for Ireland* (1849). He also contributed many papers to geographical, scientific and botanical journals and periodicals.

BALL, JOHN THOMAS (1815–98). Jurist and writer; b. Portmarnock, Co. Dublin; father of Francis Elrington Ball;* ed. Trinity College, Dublin. He was called to the Bar (1840) and was a QC (1854). He was President of Trinity College Historical Society and a close associate of Isaac Butt* and many of the leading figures of the era. MP Dublin University (1865–75), Ball was Queen's Advocate from 1865, Lord Chancellor of Ireland 1875–80, Solicitor General (1868) and Attorney General (1868). He became Vice-Chancellor of Dublin University (1880–95). Ball opposed the Irish Church Act and helped to frame the constitution for the Disestablishment of the Church of Ireland.* He was a frequent contributor to the *Dublin University Magazine.* His other works include *Ballot considered in connection with extension of the franchise* (2nd ed., 1882), *The Reformed Church of Ireland, 1537–1886* (1886) and *Historical Review of the Legislative Systems* (1889).

BALL, NICHOLAS (1791–1865). Politician and judge; b. Dublin; ed. TCD. He was a close friend of Richard Lalor Sheil.* Ball was called to the Irish Bar in 1814. He visited Rome later in that year with Sir Thomas Wyse* and was suspected of plotting to gain support for the Veto.* Ball became Attorney General and Privy Councillor in 1835, and Judge of Common Pleas, 1839–65. In the latter capacity he was the second Catholic to hold the office following Catholic Emancipation.*

BALL, SIR ROBERT (1840 -1913). Astronomer; b. Dublin; ed. Chester and TCD. His interest in astronomy was stimulated while he was tutor to the sons of the 3rd Earl of Rosse* (1865–67) at Birr Castle in which grounds stood the Parsonstown Telescope.* Ball was appointed Professor of Applied Mathematics, Royal College of Science, Dublin (1867). He held the Chair of Astronomy at Dublin University from 1874 and was Royal Astronomer of Ireland (1874–92). His right eye became impaired in 1883 from continuous observations, necessitating its removal in 1897. From 1890 Ball was President of the Royal Zoological Society of Ireland and held the Chair of Astronomy at Cambridge from 1893 until 1913. He was president successively of the Royal Astronomical Society (1897–99) and of the Mathematical Association (1899–1900). His works include *Elements of Astronomy* (1880), *The Story of the Heavens* (1885) *StarLand* (1889), *Time and Tide* (1889), *The Cause of an Ice Age* (1891), *An Atlas of Astronomy* (1892), *In Starry Realms* (1892), *In the High Heavens* (1893), *Great Astronomers* (1895), *A Primer of Astronomy* (1900), *The Earth's Beginning* (1901), *The Story of the Sun* (1906) and *A treatise on spherical astronomy* (1908). He also edited several learned journals and contributed papers to leading domestic and international periodicals.

BALLINGARRY, CO. TIPPERARY. Scene of action during the Young

Ireland rising of 1848. Some former members of the movement who had formed the Irish Confederation* and who were now calling themselves the Irish League, held a conference at this Co. Tipperary village (July 1848) to determine future policy. The majority was in favour of avoiding an armed rising, but were opposed by William Smith O'Brien.* The police marched into the village and avoided a confrontation by taking refuge in the home of a widow, Mrs McCormack, whose five children were in the house when it was occupied by the constabulary under the command of Inspector Trent. During the next hour the 'rebels' attacked and shots were fired. A few attackers were killed while the police suffered no casualties. When police reinforcements arrived some hours later the 'rising' which O'Brien described as 'an escapade' was over. Michael Doheny,* James Stephens* and John Blake Dillon* escaped but William Smith O'Brien was arrested.

BALLINGLASS EVICTIONS (13 March 1846). Eviction by the landlord, Mrs Gerard, of the entire population of a Co. Galway village in order that the land might be more profitably turned to grazing. The tenants were not in arrears with rent and had, in fact, improved their holdings by reclaiming some four hundred acres of neighbouring bog-land. The incident received wide publicity and was 'personally investigated' by Lord Londonderry, who, in a statement to the House of Lords on 30 March 1846 said, 'I am deeply grieved, but there is no doubt concerning the truth of the evictions at Ballinglass. Seventy-six families, comprising 300 individuals had not only been turned out of their houses, but had even — the unfortunate wretches — been mercilessly driven from the ditches to which they had betaken themselves for shelter . . . these unfortunate people had their rents actually ready . . .' Despite widespread condemnation, the eviction order was not rescinded.

BAPTIST SOCIETY. The Baptist Society was founded in London in 1814 as a society for promoting the education of the poor. It established over sixty schools in Connaught where it used the Irish language as a medium of instruction. The Society was considered a proselytising agency for the established Church of Ireland.

BARBOUR, JOHN MILNE (1868–1951). Politician (Ulster Unionist); b. Lisburn, Co. Antrim; ed. Elstree, Harrow and Brasenose College, Oxford. He was MP for Co. Antrim (1921–29) and S. Antrim (1929–51). A member of successive Unionist governments of Northern Ireland, he was first Parliamentary and Financial Secretary to the Minister for Finance (1921–40), then Minister for Commerce (1925–41) and finally Minister for Finance (1941–43), serving under Lord Craigavon* and John Miller Andrews.*

BARING BROTHERS. A British mercantile house controlled by Thomas Baring (1799–1873) which was entrusted by Sir Robert Peel* with supplying Indian corn to Ireland between November 1845 and July 1846 following the failure of the potato crop (*see* Famine of 1845–49). The company declined to act beyond 1846 when the British government instructed them to restrict purchases to within the UK. Baring Brothers refused any commission for work performed in the cause of Famine relief. Their position as purchasers of Indian corn was assumed by Erichson, a corn-factor of Fenchurch St, London.

BARKER, FRANCIS (1773–1859). Physician; b. Waterford; ed. TCD and Edinburgh. Awarded his MD in 1810, he established the first fever hospital in Ireland at Waterford in 1802. Barker was Senior Physician to Cork St Hospital in 1804 and was Professor of Chemistry, TCD (1808–50). He was Secretary to the Irish Board of Health (1820–32). He edited *Dublin Pharmacopeia* (from 1826) and in collaboration with Dr Cheyne wrote *Epidemic Fevers in Ireland* (2 vols, 1821).

BARLOW, JANE (1857–1917). Author; b. Clontarf; a recluse, she sometimes wrote under the pseudonym 'Felix Ryark'. Her books and poems deal chiefly with pastoral themes. Her works include *Irish Idylls* (1892), *Bog-Land Studies* (poems, 1892), *Kerrigan's Quality* (1894), *Strangers at Lisconnel* (2nd series of *Irish Idylls*, 1895), *Maureen's Fairing* (1895), *Mrs Martin's Company* (1896), *A Creel of Irish Stories* (1897), *From the East unto the West* (1898), *From the Land of the Shamrock* (1901), *The Founding of Fortunes* (1902), *By Beach and Bog-land* (1905), *Irish Neighbours* (1907), *A Strange Land* (1908), *The Mockers and other verses* (1908), *Irish Ways* (1909), *Flaws* (1911), *Between Doubting and Daring* (verse, 1916).

BALLOT ACT (1872). Act which introduced the 'secret' ballot. It was of particular importance to Ireland as it enabled the tenant to vote against the wishes of his landlord in parliamentary elections. Within a few years, when the tenant saw that the ballot really *was* secret, he began to vote for non-landlord candidates. The principal result of the Act was seen in the general election of 1880 which marked the end of landlord interest in the Irish Parliamentary Party* and gave the new chairman of the party, Charles Stewart Parnell,* a greater measure of control over the members of the party, the majority of whom lacked independent means.

'BALTINGLASS, BATTLE OF'. Baltinglass, Co. Wicklow became the centre of political controversy in 1950 when James Everett,* TD for the county and Minister of Posts and Telegraphs in the (first) Inter-Party Government,* appointed Michael Farrell to the office of sub-postmaster. This office had been held by Miss

Helen Cooke, deputising for her invalid aunt, whose family had held the post since 1870. Members of the local community, supporting the Cooke family, objected. Allegations of political jobbery were denied but the minister's action became a national issue. Telegraph wires in Baltinglass were cut. Later in the year (December), Farrell resigned the office and Miss Cooke was officially appointed. It was believed that the Baltinglass affair contributed to the downfall of the Inter-Party Government (1951) which was involved in another controversy over the Mother and Child Scheme.*

BANGOR, 6th VISCOUNT (1868–1950). Ward, Maxwell Richard; politician (Unionist), ed. Harrow and the Royal Military Academy, Woolwich. He entered the army in 1887 and retired in 1912 with the rank of Major. He re-enlisted during World War I. Bangor was a prominent member of the Unionist Party* and of the Ulster Unionist Party.* He was Speaker of the Senate of Northern Ireland from 1930 until 1950.

BANIM, JOHN (1798–1842). Author; b. Kilkenny. He studied art in Dublin but turned to writing, modelling himself on Sir Walter Scott. Banim spent twelve years in London where he met Gerald Griffin.* His wife and children died in 1829 and Banim's health gave way. He was sent on a continental holiday through public subscription and granted a Civil List Pension of £190. He returned to Kilkenny in 1835 but his health had failed and he rarely ventured beyond his garden. With his brother, Michael, (1796–1874), a postmaster at Kilkenny for many years, he collaborated on several stories including *The Boyne Water* (3 vols, 1826), *The Anglo-Irish of the Nineteenth-Century* (3 vols, 1828), *The Renounced* (1830), *The Smuggler* (1833), *The Ghost-hunter and His Family* (1833), *The Town of the Cascades* (2 vols, 1864), *The Bit O'Writin'* (1865), *The Mayor of Wind-Gap and Canvassing* (1865),

The Peep O'Day; or John Doe and Crohoore of the Billhook (1865), *The Croppy* (1865), *Peter of the Castle* and *The Fetches* (1866), *The Conformists* (1881), *Father O'Connell* (3 vols, n.d.), *Clough Fionn* (n.d.). The brothers also produced a volume of songs, *Chaunt of the Cholera*, in 1831.

'BARNIES'. *See* Police.

BARRETT, MICHAEL (d. 1868). Fenian. He was closely associated with Captain John Murphy, who, with Jeremiah Sullivan, engineered the Clerkenwell Explosion.* Barrett was in Glasgow at the time of the explosion and was arrested for discharging firearms on Glasgow Green. False evidence was presented at his trial when he was charged with responsibility for the Clerkenwell explosion. He was found guilty and sentenced to be hanged. The sentence was carried out on 26 May before a crowd estimated at 2,000. Barrett's execution was the last public hanging to take place in England.

BARRINGTON, SIR JONAH (1760– 1834). Politician, judge and author; b. Abbeyleix, Co. Laois; ed. TCD where he read law. He was called to the Irish Bar in 1788 but had a brief military career before setting up practice. Elected MP for Tuam, Co. Galway (to the Irish House of Commons) he opposed the Union* and failed to win a seat in the post-Union general election. Barrington was appointed Judge in the Court of the Admiralty in 1803, a position he held until 1809 when he was dismissed on charges of embezzlement. He took up residence in France in 1809 and there wrote his *Historic anecdotes and secret memoirs of the legislative union* (2 vols, 1809–30) and *Personal Sketches of his own time* (2 vols, 1827). His *The Rise and Fall of the Irish Nation* (1833) is largely drawn from volume two of *Historic anecdotes*. This work contains the famous 'Red' and 'Black' list of members who voted on the Act of Union.

The Black list is a detailed analysis of the financial and positional advantages enjoyed by those who supported the legislative Union of Great Britain and Ireland.

BARRON, PHILIP FITZGERALD (1797–1860). Irish language enthusiast; b. Waterford. He was proprietor of the *Waterford Chronicle* (1825). A member of the RIA, he founded an Irish training college at Seafield, Bonmahon, Co. Waterford in 1835. Barron edited and wrote several tracts including *An Irish Primer* (three parts, 1835), *The Harp of Erin* (songs, 1835), *The Irish Catholic prayer book* (n.d.), and a magazine, *Ancient Ireland*, which he edited weekly from 1835. His publications did not meet with anticipated success and he suffered heavy financial losses. He retired to Paris where he died. Arthur Griffith* admired his work on behalf of the Irish language and referred to him as 'The first Gaelic Leaguer'.

BARRY, JOHN MILNER (1769– 1822). Physician; b. Bandon, Co. Cork; ed. Edinburgh, where he was awarded his M.D. in 1792. He introduced vaccination into Ireland in 1800 and two years later founded Cork Fever Hospital. Barry contributed to the leading medical and scientific journals of the era. His essays describe the physical dangers of alcoholism and he sought the imprisonment of habitual drunkards. He was also a strong advocate of female emancipation. His works include *An Account of the Nature of the Cow-pock* (1800) and *Report of the Fever Hospital of the City of Cork* (1818).

BARRY, KEVIN (1902–20). Republican soldier; b. Dublin. While a medical student at UCD, Barry took part in an attack on a British army bread van at Upper Church Street, Dublin (20 September 1920). He was discovered lying under the van with an automatic pistol (*see* Irish Republican Army *and* War of Independence).

Barry was court-martialled and sentenced to death. Despite pleas from all sections of the community to have the sentence commuted because of his youth, he was hanged at Mountjoy on 1 November. A fact generally lost in the political climate of the time was that a British soldier killed by the IRA during the raid was slightly younger than Kevin Barry. Barry's interrogation and hanging became the subject of a famous ballad.

BARRY, MICHAEL JOSEPH (1817–89). Young Ireland poet, and magistrate; b. Cork. He wrote verse for the *Nation* and *Spirit of the Nation* under the pseudonyms 'M.J.B.' and 'Brutus'. His best-known works are 'The Green Flag' and 'Step Together'. He was present at the first meeting of the Irish Confederation* and was later arrested for Young Ireland activities. Barry became bitterly disillusioned with the failure of the 1848 rising and underwent a complete *volte face*. He dissociated himself from Young Ireland and became a police magistrate in Dublin, earning a reputation as a dour wit. His writings include *A Treatise on the Practice of the High Court Chancery in Ireland* (with W. N. Keogh; 1840), *Ireland, as she was, as she is, and as she shall be* (1845), *Lays of the War* (1855), *The Pope and the Romagna* (1860), *Heinrich and Leonore* (1886). His *The Kishoge Papers* was a series of verse published anonymously in the *Dublin University Magazine* in 1842–43. Barry edited two editions of *The Songs of Ireland* (1845–46) and was for a period editor of the *Cork Southern Reporter*.

BARRY, TOM (1897–1980). Republican soldier; b. West Cork; ed. local National School. He enlisted in the British Army during World War I and served in Mesopotamia. He returned to Ireland in 1919 and became a prominent member of the Irish Republican Army* during the War of Independence.* Barry commanded an IRA unit in West Cork which he later developed into one of the leading Flying Columns of the war. The Column enjoyed remarkable success notably in ambushes at Kilmichael and Crossbarry. He opposed the Treaty and supported the republican side during the Civil War. Barry, in common with other leading republicans, was arrested by the de Valera administration in 1934. He called for a war against England in 1936 and demanded that the IRA should not answer the call by Frank Ryan* for republican volunteers to defend the Spanish republic (*see* Connolly Column). Barry resigned his position on the Army Council in 1937 and ceased to be an IRA activist in 1940. He was unsuccessful as an Independent candidate in Cork in 1946. He is the author of *Guerilla Days in Ireland* (1949) and *The Reality of the Anglo-Irish War 1919–21* (1974), a pamphlet refuting much of Liam Deasy's *Towards Ireland Free*.

BARRYMORE, 1st BARON. *See* Smith–Barry, Arthur Hugh.

BARTER, RICHARD (1802–70). Physician; b. Cooldaniel, Co. Cork; ed. London College of Physicians. He was Hon. Secretary to County of Cork Agricultural Society for many years. Barter introduced the Turkish Baths into these islands in 1842 when he opened the Hydropathic Institution at St Anne's, Blarney, Co. Cork.

BARTON, ROBERT CHILDERS (1881–1975). Republican politician; b. Glendalough, Co. Wicklow where he was reared with his cousin, Robert Erskine Childers;* ed. Rugby and Oxford. He was commissioned in the British army during World War I and sent to Dublin during the Easter Rising of 1916.* He became a convert to republicanism and was elected as Sinn Fein representative for Wicklow to the first Dail Eireann.* As first Minister for Agriculture (April 1919–August 1921), he was responsible for the Irish Land Bank. He was several times imprisoned for republican activities and was released from Portland during the Truce.* Barton was a member of the team which negotiated the Treaty.* Although he was a party to the signing of the Treaty and voted in favour of it in the Dail, he took the anti-Treaty side in the Civil War. He was captured and imprisoned in Portobello Barracks during the Civil War but managed to escape. He retired from politics at the end of the hostilities to manage his extensive estate in Co. Wicklow.

BATES, RICHARD DAWSON (1876— 1949). Lawyer and politician (Ulster Unionist); b. Belfast. After qualifying as a lawyer he became active in unionist movements: he was Secretary of the Ulster Unionist Council,* foundermember of the Ulster Volunteer Force* and a prominent voice in the Ulster Unionist Party. Bates was MP for E. Belfast and the Victoria Division (1921—43) and a member of the first cabinet of Northern Ireland, serving as Minister for Home Affairs (1921—23). In this office, he was responsible for the Civil Authorities (Special Powers) Act (Northern Ireland) 1922,* which was the principal weapon used by the Northern parliament to fight against the Irish Republican Army.*

BÉASLAÍ, PIARAS (1881—1965). Journalist and soldier; b. Liverpool. He arrived in Dublin in 1904 where he joined the Gaelic League* and the Irish Volunteers.* He edited the Gaelic League journal *An Fáinne* (1917—22) and the Volunteer journal, *An tÓglach.* Béaslaí worked closely with Michael Collins* at the headquarters of the Irish Republican Army during the War of Independence. He was captured and imprisoned in Mountjoy and escaped in March 1919 but was recaptured three months later. He was elected to the first Dail Eireann in which he represented East Kerry (December 1918). He supported the Treaty and was Major-General in the National Army during the Civil War. Beaslaí resigned from politics

in 1923 and from the service a year later, to devote his time to the language movement. His works include *Fear na Milliún Púnt* (1915), *Cluiche Cártaí* (1920), *Bealtaine 1916 agus Dánta Eile* (1920), *Political formulae instead of principles* (1922), *Michael Collins and the making of a new Ireland* (2 vols, 1926), *An Sgaothaire agus cúig drámaí eile* (1929), *An Danar* (drama, 1929), *An Bhean Chródha* (drama, 1931), *Eigse-na-Gaedhilge* (cuid 1—11, 1933—34), *Beirt na bodhaire bréige* (1936), *Cuigeachas* (1936), *An fear as Buenos Aires* (1936), *Michael Collins, Soldier and Statesman* (1937), *Blúire Páipéir* (drama, 1937), *Cormac na Coille* (n.d.), *Fear an sgéilín grinn* (drama, n.d.), *The Story of the Catholic Commercial Club, Dublin (1881— 1954)* (1957?). He edited Arthur Griffith's *Songs, Ballads and Recitations* (n.d.) and translated Goldsmith's *She Stoops to Conquer* into Irish in 1939.

BEAUFORT, SIR FRANCIS (1774— 1857). Mathematician and sailor; b. Navan, Co. Meath. He entered the British Navy at an early age and rose to rank of Admiral. While recovering from wounds received on an exploration, he assisted his brother-in-law Richard Edgeworth* with the construction of a telegraph line from Dublin to Galway (1803). He devised the Beaufort Scale (1805) to determine wind velocity. The scale was adopted by the Admiralty in 1838 and internationally in 1874. Beaufort conducted various nautical surveys for the British Navy, for which he was hydrographer from 1829—55.

BECKETT, SAMUEL (1906—   ). Bilingual novelist, poet and dramatist (French and English); b. Dublin; ed. Earlsfort House prep. school, Portora Royal School, Enniskillen and TCD, where he took B.A. in Modern Languages (French and Italian) in 1927. He taught for a short period in Belfast before emigrating to France to teach at the Ecole Normale Superieure, Paris. He met James Joyce* in Paris and occasionally worked as his secretary on the manuscript of *Finnegans Wake*. Beckett returned to Dublin to lecture in French at TCD but resigned after a two-year stay in 1932, and returned to Paris. He left Paris upon the fall of France (1940) and joined the French Resistance. He returned to Paris (1946). Beckett was awarded the Nobel Prize for Literature in 1969. His *En Attendant Godot (Waiting for Godot*; 1952*)* brought him world acclaim, and established him as a leading figure in the Theatre of the Absurd.

BEGGARS IN IRELAND. The number of beggars in Ireland during the nineteenth century was constantly increased by the evicted and famine-stricken. Several efforts were made to contain the number of beggars entering towns, including a licence system in which badges were issued to 'official' beggars who were then empowered to drive away all 'foreign' beggars. Dublin was virtually flooded with beggars in the wake of the Famine of 1817, and the charitable institutions of the capital were taxed beyond capacity. A group of public-spirited people made several efforts to alleviate the situation including the launching of an appeal to the citizens of Dublin. Their efforts met with little success and it was decided that more drastic action was needed. Accordingly, processions of beggars were led forth daily and taught to howl outside the doors of non-contributors. The scheme was attended with dramatic success and a figure of £9,000 was speedily collected. To distribute and organise the fund the Dublin Mendicity Institution was founded. Mr and Mrs S. C. Hall* recall an incident at Newmarket, Co. Cork when their tour was hampered by a crowd of beggars. They instructed them to return on the following day when each of them would receive one-halfpenny and were astonished when no less than ninety-two beggars awaited their bounty.

BEHAN, BRENDAN (1923–64) Dramatist, novelist and story teller; b. Dublin; ed. Sisters of Charity National School and Brunswick St CBS. A member of a family with a republican background and nephew of Peadar Kearney, author of the National Anthem,* Behan joined the Irish Republican Army* in 1937. Two years later the IRA declared 'war' on Britain and he was arrested in Liverpool in possession of explosives (December 1939). He was sentenced to three years Borstal detention. His experiences in Borstal until his release in December 1941 provided him with the material for his best-selling novel, *Borstal Boy* (1958). Four months after his return to Dublin he was sentenced to fourteen years imprisonment for the attempted murder of a policeman. His term of imprisonment in Mountjoy until his release under general amnesty (December 1946) provided the inspiration for his play, *The Quare Fellow*, which was first produced at the Pike Theatre on 9 November 1954. Following his release Behan travelled in the Kerry and Galway gaeltachtai perfecting his fluency in the Irish language. He also spent some time in London and Paris, working periodically as a house painter to support himself in lean times.

His play, *An Giall*, was first produced at An Damer in 1958. The longer version of it, in English, *The Hostage*, was produced in London by Joan Littlewood later that year. He contributed to Radio Eireann and the *Irish Press*. Other works include *Brendan Behan's Island* (1962), *The Big House* (play, 1963), *Hold Your Hour and Have Another* (1963, from his *Irish Press* articles, illustrated in book form by his wife, Beatrice), *With Breast Expanded* (1964), *Brendan Behan's New York* (1964), *Confessions of an Irish Rebel* (1965), *The Scarperer* (1966), *Moving Out* (play, 1967), and *A Garden Party* (play, 1967). His last work,

Richard's Cork Leg, was completed by Alan Simpson and received a posthumous production in Dublin in 1973.

BELFAST BOYCOTT (1920–22). The boycott of goods produced and distributed from Belfast was a reaction in the South of Ireland to the anti-Catholic rioting in Belfast during the summer of 1920. It was proposed by Sean MacEntee* but was opposed by Ernest Blythe* and Countess Markievicz.* It started in August on unofficial lines when shopkeepers in Galway city refused to stock goods originating in Belfast. The second Dail Eireann appointed Joseph Mc-Donagh* Director of the Belfast Boycott (August 1921–January 1922). From January 1922 until February the Boycott was directed by Michael Staines.* It ended as a result of the Craig-Collins Agreement.*

'BELFAST NEWS-LETTER, THE'. Founded by Francis Joy (1697–1790) – grandfather of Henry Joy McCracken – on 1 September 1737, the *News-Letter* is the oldest daily in Ireland and is second only to *Lloyd's List* (1719) as the oldest newspaper in these islands. Initially a bi-weekly with an early readership of approximately one thousand, it became a tri-weekly in 1851 and a daily newspaper in 1855. The earliest known copy of the paper is that of 9 January 1738 housed in the Linen-hall Library, Belfast. Its files date to 1738 (no copies of the thirty-two issues published in 1737 remain extant) and form a unique source for Irish history. The *News-Letter* of 27 August 1776 was almost certainly the first newspaper to publish on this side of the Atlantic to publish in full the text of the American Declaration of Independence under the headline 'Birth of the United States'. The paper has been published from its present address, 55 Donegall St, Belfast, since 1861. Its circulation as of 30 June 1979 was 72,580.

BELFAST PROTESTANT ASSOCIA-TION. Working-class anti-Catholic organisation founded in 1900 from Belfast lodges of the Orange Order.* The BPA was led by Arthur Trew and Thomas H. Sloan.* When Trew was imprisoned for twelve months in 1901 for inciting a riot during a Corpus Christi procession, the BPA was taken over by Sloan. Sloan was expelled from the Orange Order for making derogatory remarks about Colonel E. J. Saunderson* and used the BPA as the basis for the Independent Orange Order.

'BELL, THE'. Founded by Sean O'Faolain in 1940, it became the leading Irish literary journal of its time. Apart from fiction and poetry, it published articles on national and international affairs, pioneered new views and led the writers' struggle against censorship (*see* Censorship of Publications Act). *The Bell* appeared regularly throughout the Emergency* but ceased publication temporarily in April 1948. It appeared again in November 1950 and ran until 1955. Contributors included Peadar O'Don-nell* who edited it from 1946, Austin Clarke,* Oliver St John Gogarty,* Patrick Kavanagh* and Flann O'Brien (*see* O'Nolan, Brian).

BENNETT, EDWARD HALLORAN (1837–1907). Surgeon; b. Cork; ed. TCD; B.A. (1859); M.D. (1864). He was surgeon to Sir Patrick Dun's Hospital and Professor of Surgery at TCD (1873–1906). He was President of the Pathological Society (1880) and of the Royal College of Irish Surgeons (1884–86). Bennett was an authority on fractures and discovered 'Bennett's fracture' in 1880. He was one of the very earliest of Irish surgeons to employ Listerian methods during operations.

BENNETT, LOUIE (1870–1956). Trade unionist and suffragette. Closely associated with the cause of labour, she played a leading role in the Lock-Out.* As secretary of the Irish Women Workers' Union, she believed that a strong trade union movement was essential for a thriving Labour Party.* She opposed Labour's support for Fianna Fail* in 1927. Elected as the first female president of the Irish Trades Union Congress* in 1932, she was also elected to the Executive of the Labour Party in the same year.

BENSON, SIR JOHN (1812−74). Architect and engineer; b. Collooney, Co. Sligo. He was appointed surveyor to the East Riding of Cork in 1846 and superintended the Famine Relief works in the area. As Engineer to the Cork Habour Commissioners (1850) and architect to the Cork Corporation, he was responsible for many improvements to the city, including the erection of St Patrick's Bridge and the city's waterworks. Benson was also responsible for the great Industrial Exhibition which he presented in Dublin in May 1853 and for which he received a knighthood.

BERESFORD, LORD JOHN GEORGE (1773−1862). Archbishop of Armagh and Primate of All Ireland (C.I.), 1822−62; b. Waterford, a member of one of the wealthiest and most powerful families in Ireland; ed. Eton and Oxford. He was Dean of Clogher (1799), Bishop of Cork (1806), of Raphoe (1808) and of Clogher (1819). He founded a Protestant weekly paper, *The Patriot*. It has been estimated by one writer that Beresford's various church offices yielded him a total of £887,900 and that his family benefitted to the amount of £3m. Beresford spent £30,000 of his personal fortune in restoring Armagh Cathedral. He strongly opposed Catholic Emancipation* on the grounds that 'it would transfer from Protestants to Roman Catholics the ascendancy of Ireland'.

BERESFORD, MARCUS GERVAIS (1801−95). Archbishop of Armagh and Primate of All Ireland (C.I.), 1862−85; b. Dublin; son of George de la Poer Beresford, Bishop of Kilmore; ed. Richmond and Trinity College, Cambridge where he graduated B.A. (1824) and was ordained the same year. He held various curacies before 1854 when he became Bishop of Kilmore and Ardagh. An advocate of reform within his church as the movement for Disestablishment of the Church of Ireland* became stronger, he negotiated with W. E. Gladstone* terms under which disestablishment would be effected.

BERGIN, OSBORN (1872−1950). Scholar; b. Cork; ed. Queen's College, Cork and in Germany, specialising in Celtic Studies. He was Professor of Old Irish at UCD from 1908 to 1940. He was appointed first director of the School of Celtic Studies in the Dublin Institute for Advanced Studies in 1940 but he resigned within a year. His writings include *Maidean i mBéarra* (poems, 1918) and *Lebor na hUidre*, with R. I. Best,* 1929. He made several translations from Keating, translated Hans Christian Anderson into Irish (1912) and edited *Irish Grammatical Tracts* which appeared as a supplement to *Eriú* 1916−29.

BERNARD, JOHN HENRY (1860−1927). Scholar and Archbishop of Dublin (C.I.), 1915-19; b. India; ed. Privately and TCD; M.A. (1883). He was ordained in 1886 and became Chaplain to the Lord Lieutenant until 1902 when he was appointed Dean of St Patrick's, Dublin. He was Bishop of Ossory, Ferns and Leighlin until translated to Dublin. Archbishop Bernard was a Commissioner of both National (1897−1903) and Intermediate Education (1917). He was elected Provost of Trinity (1919−23). His writings include *Guide Book to Palestine (circ. A.D. 1350)* (1894), *The Irish Liber Hymnorum* (1898), *The Cathedral Church of St Patrick* (1903), *The relationship between Swift and Stella* (1908), *Easter Hope* (1916), *In war time* (1917), *Studia Sacra* (1917), *The Bernards of Kerry* (1922). He translated the works of

Kant and Eusebius and edited *The Works of Bishop Butler* (2 vols, 1900).

BERRY, JAMES (1842–1914). Folklorist and seanchai;* b. Bunowen, Louisburgh, Co. Mayo. He was educated at a local hedge-school* and by his uncle, Fr Edward O'Malley. Berry moved to Carna in Connemara in his youth and remained there for the rest of his life, working as a farm labourer. He collected folk-tales and invented stories in the traditional idiom, many of which were published in *The Mayo News*. He was a gifted seanchai; a large number of his stories deal with the period of the Famine of 1845–49*, and are a faithful depiction of the lives and folkways of the West of Ireland peasantry. There is a modern collected edition of his stories (edited by Gertrude Horgan).

BERWICK, REV. EDWARD (1750–1820). Pamphleteer; b. Co. Down. He was ordained (C.I.) in 1776 and held various livings before becoming chaplain to the Earl of Moira (later Marquis of Hastings). Berwick is best known as the author of the 'Pranceriana' squibs in which he resisted Provost Hely-Hutchinson's efforts to ban political debate at Trinity while nonetheless seeking student support for the parliamentary candidates of his (Hutchinson's) choice. Berwick lost his scholarship as a result but was reinstated on appeal to the Bishops of Armagh and Dublin who were on visit to the college. His works include *A Treatise on the Government of the Church* (1811), pamphlets and broadsides on *The Down County Election* published in 1790 and *Pranceriana* (an edition of the famous 'squibs') edited by Robert Dodsley (n.d.). He edited *The Rawdon Papers* (1819) and made various translations from the Greek.

BESSBOROUGH, 4th EARL (1781–1847). Ponsonby; John William; politician (Whig) and Lord Lieutenant (1846–47); the owner of extensive estates in Co. Kilkenny; ed. Christ Church, Oxford. Although he supported Catholic Emancipation* he was opposed by Daniel O'Connell* when he successfully contested the Kilkenny seat (1826). He won O'Connell's friendship shortly afterwards and introduced him to the House of Commons in February 1830. He retained Kilkenny in 1831 when the Bishop of Kildare and Leighlin, James Warren Doyle ('JKL'),* ordered his clergy not to oppose him. Appointed Home Secretary by his brother-in-law, Lord Melbourne,* in 1834 and raised to the peerage of the United Kingdom as Baron Duncannon of Bessborough. Lord Privy Seal from 1835 to 1839, he succeeded to his title in 1844. He became the first resident Irish landlord for a generation to become Lord Lieutenant in July 1846. His appointment was greeted with enthusiasm by O'Connell and the Irish people as the country was in the throes of the Famine of 1845–49.* Bessborough, however, proved unable to influence government policy. He died in office, 16 May 1847.

BESSBOROUGH, 6th EARL (1815–95). Ponsonby, Frederick George Brabazon; landlord; b. London; ed. Harrow and Trinity College, Cambridge where he was awarded M.A. (1837). He was called to the Bar at Lincoln's Inn (1840). Ponsonby succeeded to the title of Bessborough in 1880, but used the titles Baron Ponsonby and Baron Duncannon. A good landlord on his estates in Co. Kilkenny, he served as chairman of the Bessborough Commission* established by W. E. Gladstone* to examine land tenure in Ireland (1880) but his estate was involved in the Plan of Campaign* during the 1880s. He did not vote in the division on the second Home Rule Bill* (1893).

BESSBOROUGH COMMISSION. The Commission was appointed by Queen Victoria* on 29 July 1880 under the chairmanship of the 6th Earl of Bessborough. It was directed to investigate the workings of the Land Act of 1870 (*see* Land Acts) and to recommend further amendments for the purpose (1) of improving the relations between landlords and tenants in Ireland and (2) of facilitating the purchase of land by the tenantry. The other members of the Commission were Baron Richard Dowse, The O'Conor Don,* Arthur MacMurrogh Kavanagh* and William Shaw.* The Commissioners held sixty sittings throughout Ireland and interviewed 700 witnesses, including eighty landlords, seventy land agents, and 500 tenant-farmers. The Commission's sittings in Ireland were opposed by the Land League* because the tenants were not represented on the Commission. The Report of the Commission, including a minority report by The O'Conor Don, was signed on 4 January 1881. It found that the 1870 Land Act had not succeeded in its aims and that the Three Fs,* which was the basic demand of the Land League, should be granted. Arthur Kavanagh did not support the latter recommendation. In his minority report O'Conor Don stressed the need for absolute ownership of the land by the people who worked it. The Commission, whose findings were supported later in that month by the report of the Richmond Commission,* influenced the Land Bill which the Prime Minister, W. E. Gladstone,* introduced in the Commons in April 1881.

BEST, RICHARD IRVINE (1872–1959). Scholar; b. in Ulster. He studied Old Irish in Paris under H. d'Arbois de Jubainville whose *Le Cycle mythologique Irlandais* he translated into English. He was a friend of J. M. Synge,* Stephen McKenna,* Kuno Meyer* and James Joyce* who portrayed him unflatteringly in *Ulysses*. He became Assistant Director of the National Library of Ireland* in 1904 and was Director from 1924 to 1940. Best was Senior Professor of Celtic Studies at the Dublin Institute of Advanced Studies* (1940–47) and Chairman of the Irish Manuscript Commission* (1948–56). He was considered an authority on Irish Palaeography and

Philology, and made many translations from French into Irish and English. His works include *Bibliography of the Publications of Whitley Stokes* (1911), *Bibliography of Irish Philology and of printed Irish Literature in the National Library* (1913), *Bibliography of the Publications of Kuno Meyer* (1923), *Gein Branduib ocus Aedain* from the *Yellow Book of Lecan*, (1927), *Lebor na hUidre*, (edited with Osborn Bergin,* 1929), *The Ancient Laws of Ireland, Seanchas Már* (1931) and *Bibliography of Irish Philology and Manuscript Literature* (1942).

BETTER GOVERNMENT OF IRELAND BILL. *See* Government of Ireland Act (1920).

BETTY, LADY. A public hangwoman who held office at Roscommon Jail c. 1830. She murdered her only son for money without realising his identity, and when she gave herself up to the law she was sentenced to death. While she and a number of other prisoners were awaiting the sentence to be carried out, the hangman fell ill. Lady Betty volunteered to perform the office in return for her freedom. This was granted, and upon the death of the hangman she became the official executioner.

BIANCONI, CHARLES (1785–1875). Businessman; b. Tregelo, Italy. He was intended for the priesthood but left school at 15. He arrived in Dublin in 1802 where he worked for a print-seller. Bianconi became a print-seller on his own account and opened a shop in Carrick-on-Suir in 1807. He moved to Waterford in 1808 and there met Edmund Ignatius Rice* who taught him English. Bianconi never forgot his benefactor and had his daughter predeceased him, £50,000 would have gone to the Mount Sion School. Following Napoleon's defeat at Waterloo (18 June 1815), the demand for horses dropped and Bianconi seized the opportunity to purchase a horse and jaunting-car for a little under £10. The first Bianconi 'coach' ran from Clonmel (where 'Brian Cooney', as he was known in Clonmel, was now based), to Cahir on 6 July 1815, carrying six passengers at a return fare of 2d (slightly less than 1p). Bianconi set about extending his operations and his cars covered some 226 miles per day in 1816, 1,170 miles by 1825, 2,234 by 1836, rising to its peak of 4,244 miles by 1837. His fleet now consisted of 900 horses and 67 cars which were maintained at his vast stables and coach-house near Clonmel. He became a naturalised Irish citizen in 1831. With the introduction of the railway in 1838, Bianconi adapted his coaching business to provide 'feeder' services between stations, and purchased railway stock. He was Director of the Waterford and Limerick Railway Co. (1834) and a Director of the National Bank (1835). Bianconi was elected Mayor of Clonmel in 1844 and was Deputy Lieutenant of Co. Tipperary in 1863.

'BIBLICALS'. Evangelical clergymen active in Ireland among the Catholic population in the second decade of the nineteenth century, proselytising, preaching and distributing free Bibles (hence their name). They were more properly known as 'New Reformers'* and were part of the 'Second Reformation'.*

BIGGAR, JOSEPH GILLIS (1828–90). Politician (Nationalist); b. Belfast; ed. Belfast Royal Academy. He was reared as a Presbyterian but became a Catholic in 1877. He joined the Irish Republican Brotherhood* and became a member of the Supreme Council.* As an MP for Cavan in the Irish party led by Isaac Butt,* Biggar specialised in the technique of 'obstruction'. It was said of him that no member of parliament with such poor qualifications ever occupied so much of the House's time. This remark may be partly due to the fact that he had rather an ugly mumbling voice. Biggar once caused considerable consternation in the House by forcing the Prince of Wales to leave

the gallery by remarking 'I spy a stranger'. Biggar was active in the Land League* and a keen advocate of a strong Irish party acting on majority decisions.

BIGGER, FRANCIS JOSEPH (1863–1926). Historian and antiquarian; b. Belfast; ed. Liverpool and at the Royal Academical Institution, Belfast. He qualified as a solicitor in 1888 and became a member of the RIA and a Fellow of the Royal Society of Antiquaries of Ireland. Bigger was a frequent contributor to the archaeological journals of the era and was editor of the *Ulster Journal of Archaeology* (1894–1914). He was an enthusiast on all aspects of Irish culture and from his own resources restored ruined castles and churches and re-erected ancient grave stones and crosses. His works include *Vicinity of Belfast* (1894), *Northern Leaders of '98* (1900), *Labourers' Cottages for Ireland* (1907), *Irish Penal Crosses 1713–1781* (1909), *St Comgall of Bangor* (1909), *The Ulster Land War of 1770* (1910), *Four Shots from Down* (1918), *Relic of Penal Days* (1920), *Crossing the Bar* (1920).

BIRKENHEAD, 1st EARL OF (1872–1930). Smith, Frederick Edwin; lawyer and politician (Conservative); b. Birkenhead; ed. Birkenhead School and Wadham College, Oxford. A Fellow and Lecturer, Merton (1896) and Oriel (1897), he was Oxford Extension Lecturer in History (1898) and Extension Lecturer in Modern History, Victoria (1900). He entered the House of Commons in 1906 with a reputation for his wit and oratory. A leading spokesman with the Conservative Party on behalf of the Ulster Unionist Party,* he served in the Ulster Volunteer Force* as ADC to Edward Carson,* acting as Carson's 'Galloper' and becoming known to Irish nationalists, contemptuously, as 'Galloper Smith'. He became Solicitor-General in 1915 and then Attorney-General when he led the prosecution at the trial of Sir Roger Casement.*

Birkenhead was Lord Chancellor from 1919 until 1922. In this capacity he was a member of the British delegation which negotiated the Treaty of December 1921. He was Secretary for India from 1924 until 1928 when he resigned from politics and entered the city. He published many legal and historical works including *International Law* (1911), *Famous Trials of History* (1927) and *Turning Points in History* (1930).

BIRMINGHAM, GEORGE A. *See* Hannay, Canon James Owen.

BIRRELL, AUGUSTINE (1850– 1933). Politician (Liberal); Chief Secretary (1907–16); b. Liverpool; ed. Trinity Hall, Cambridge. He was called to the Bar in 1875. Birrell was elected MP in 1889 and earned a wide reputation as an orator. He failed to gain support for his Irish Council Bill* in 1907. During this tenure as Chief Secretary his main achievements were the passage of the Irish Universities (Ireland) Act* (1908) and the Land Purchase Act (1909) (*see* Land Acts). His casual approach to Irish affairs during his period as Chief Secretary failed to detect the rising tide of nationalism, and he left his government unprepared for the Easter Rising of 1916* (Birrell was on holiday in England when the rising broke out). He resigned his post immediately after the rebellion and left politics in 1918.

BLACK AND TANS. During the War of Independence,* the Royal Irish Constabulary* became the particular target of the Irish Republican Army* and recruitment into the regular police force suffered. The government recruited a new force in England from among demobilised soldiers which was intended to supplement the RIC. This body was placed under the new Commander in Chief of the forces in Ireland, General Sir Neville Macready.* There was a shortage of RIC uniforms for the new force and accordingly they were issued with khaki trousers (military) and dark green tunics (police). This combina-

tion reminded people in Munster of the famous Co. Limerick hunt, the Scarteen Black and Tans. The Black and Tans were located principally in trouble spots in the counties of Clare, Cork, Dublin, Galway, Kerry, Kilkenny, Limerick, Mayo, Meath and Tipperary. The notoriety which they have earned in Irish history stemmed from the ferocity of their reprisals to IRA successes. Some of the major incidents with which they were associated included the burnings of Bruff, Co. Limerick; Kilmallock, Co. Limerick; Balbriggan, Co. Dublin; Cork City; Miltown-Malbay, Co. Clare; Lahinch, Co. Clare; Ennistymon, Co. Clare; Tubbercurry, Co. Sligo; Midleton, Co. Cork and Trim, Co. Meath. They were also responsible for the murders of Tomás MacCurtain,* George Clancy* and Michael O'Callaghan, and the killings in Croke Park on Bloody Sunday, 21 November 1920.*

BLACK DIARIES. Alleged diaries of Sir Roger Casement* discovered while he was being held on charges of treason in 1916. The *Diaries* were shown to journalists in an attempt to stir up public opinion against Casement. Many entries in the diaries suggest that Casement was homosexual. They have been dismissed as forgeries by his defenders, notably by Dr Rex Mackay. Recent biographers, however, have supported their authenticity.

BLACKBURNE, FRANCIS (1782– 1867). Lawyer; b. Footstown, Co. Meath; ed. TCD. Called to the Bar in 1805, Blackburne administered the Insurrection Act in Limerick city and county (1822–24) and later played a leading role in suppressing anti-tithes agitation. He became Attorney-General for Ireland (1830– 35) and again in 1841. Blackburne was Master of the Rolls (1842) and Chief Justice of the Queen's Bench in 1846. He was commended for the zeal with which he prosecuted Daniel O'Connell,* William Smith O'Brien* and Thomas Francis Meagher.*

BLACKFEET. An agrarian secret society which operated during the 1820s and 1830s. *See* Secret Societies.

BLACKLEY, REV. WILLIAM LEWERY (1830–1902). Clergyman (C.I.); b. Dundalk; ed. Brussels and TCD where he was awarded M.A. (1854). He held various livings in England. He lectured and wrote on old age pensions and national insurance. His works include *National Insurance* (1878), *Collected Essays* (published 1880), *The British National Insurance Scheme* (1911).

BLANEY, NEIL T. (1922–   ). Politician (Fianna Fail and Independent Fianna Fail); b. Rossnakill, Co. Donegal; ed. National School and St Eunan's College, Letterkenny. He won his father's seat for Fianna Fail in 1948. He was Minister for Posts and Telegraphs (March–December 1957) and then Minister for Local Government until November 1966. In the first government formed by Jack Lynch,* he became Minister for Agriculture and Fisheries (from 1966). In May 1970 he was dismissed from the government by Mr Lynch and expelled from the party (November 1971). As the sole member of Independent Fianna Fail (until joined by Patrick Keaveney, June 1976–June 1977), Blaney maintained constant criticism of Fianna Fail and National Coalition governments on their policies for Northern Ireland and the republican movement (*see* Irish Republican Army *and* Sinn Fein). Mr Blaney's control of the Fianna Fail organisation in Donegal has been the subject of a study, *The Donegal Mafia* (1977). He headed the poll in the Connaught-Ulster constituency in the direct election to the European Parliament (June 1979).

BLASKET ISLANDS. Group of small islands off the south-west coast of Kerry, north of the entrance to Dingle Bay, the largest of which is Great Blasket. The islanders were frequently storm-bound for weeks at a time and a decision was made to evacuate the island. The last inhabitants were taken off the island in the steamer *Naomh Lorcan* in late November 1953. Prior to its evacuation the island was, with Iceland, the most westerly inhabited land in Europe. Many Irish language writers are associated with the area including Muiris O'Suilleabháin,* Peig Sayers, *Tomas O Criomthain* and `Robin Flower.*

BLENNERHASSETT, SIR ROWLAND (1839–1909). Politician; b. Blenerville, Co. Kerry, to a Catholic landowning family; ed. Downshire, Stonyhurst, Oxford, Louvain, Munich and Berlin (where he became acquainted with Bismarck). With the support of Lord Acton, Blennerhassett founded *The Chronicle*, a political and literary organ for liberal Catholics. He was elected Liberal MP for Galway City, (1865–75), for Kerry (1880–85), and supported Home Rule* during his political career. His *Peasant Proprietors in Ireland* was privately printed in 1884.

BLOODY SUNDAY (21 November 1920). The killing of eleven British intelligence agents, known as the Cairo Gang,* by members of Michael Collins' Special Intelligence Unit (*see* The Squad) provoked a reprisal later in the day by Black and Tans* in Croke Park. The soldiers fired into a crowd attending the Dublin-Tipperary match, killing twelve and wounding sixty (many more were injured in the resultant panic). One player, Michael Hogan of Tipperary, was killed. According to General Crozier* (who coined the phrase 'Bloody Sunday') the intention of the troops was to search for arms. The casualties would have been higher, had not officers of the Auxiliaries*ordered the Black and Tans to cease-fire. Later that day in Dublin Castle,* two Republican prisoners, Peadar Clancy and Dick McKee, both of whom had been captured the previous evening, were shot along with Conor Clune; the official explanation was that they were shot 'while attempting to escape'.

BLOODY SUNDAY (10 July 1921).
During the Belfast Boycott,* this
Sunday saw concerted attacks by
Orange factions and Special Constables upon Catholic persons and
properties in Belfast. Fifteen people
were killed, sixty-eight seriously
injured and 161 Catholic-owned
homes were razed. There was no
material damage to Protestant-owned
properties.

**BLOODY SUNDAY (30 January
1972).** The shooting by British Army
paratroopers of thirteen civilians
during a civil rights demonstration
in Derry. Massive anti-British demonstrations were provoked by the incident, notably in Dublin where the
British Embassy was burned down.
A subsequent Tribunal of Inquiry
headed by Lord Widgery exonerated
the army but found that none of the
victims had been armed.

BLUESHIRTS. 'Blueshirts' was the
popular name given to members of
the Army Comrades Association*
which, under the leadership of Commandant Edmund Cronin, adopted
blue shirts as a uniform in April 1933.
In July the leadership was given to
General Eoin O'Duffy* who had
been dismissed from his post as
Commissioner of the Garda Siochana*
by Eamon de Valera.* Duffy renamed
the movement the National Guard.
The basic philosophy of the Blueshirts came from the papal encyclical
Quadragesimo Anno and Mussolini's
theory of the corporate state. Leading
apologists for the movement were
Dr Michael Tierney and Dr J. J.
Hogan,* both of whom contributed
to *United Ireland* and the movement's
own newspaper, *The Blueshirt*, which
appeared between 1933 and 1935.
The effect of the Economic War* on
Irish agriculture gained support for
the Blueshirts. O'Duffy attacked the
de Valera administration and the Irish
Republican Army.* The government,
alarmed by the rhetoric of the movement and the public violence which
resulted, moved against the Blueshirts by banning unauthorised firearms, including those held by former
Cumann na nGaedheal ministers. In
August, O'Duffy announced that he
would hold a march to Leinster Lawn
where a commemorative rally would
be held in honour of Arthur Griffith,*
Michael Collins* and Kevin O'Higgins.* The government, alarmed at
the prospect of a clash between Blueshirt and IRA sympathisers, banned
the proposed march on 12 August.
The Military Tribunal established by
W. T. Cosgrave* in 1931 was revived
and the National Guard was outlawed.
Cumann na nGaedheal, disillusioned
with Cosgrave's leadership in the
wake of electoral failures, looked to
O'Duffy to head a new party which
was formed in September 1933 from
a merger of Cumann na nGaedheal,
the National Centre Party* and the
Blueshirts. The new party was known
as the United Ireland Party or Fine
Gael* with O'Duffy as president and
Cosgrave as one of his vice-presidents.
The National Guard became a youth
movement within Fine Gael under
the title of the Young Ireland Association. When the Blueshirts called for
the withholding of Land Annuities*
from the de Valera government,
O'Duffy's leadership became a source
of embarrassment. The government
introduced a bill to outlaw the wearing of unauthorised uniforms but it
was defeated in the Senate. Fine Gael
became even more disenchanted with
the movement generally when they
failed to make an impact during the
local government elections of 1934.
In August, J. J. Hogan resigned in
protest at O'Duffy's behaviour and
within a brief period O'Duffy resigned
under strong pressure. There was a
struggle between Ned Cronin and
O'Duffy for the leadership of the
Blueshirts. Cronin held onto the
Blueshirts and O'Duffy founded his
own league of Greenshirts. The Blueshirt movement was now in a decline
which continued throughout 1935.
There was a brief revival in 1936 when
O'Duffy led a brigade to Spain where
they supported General Franco until
their return in June 1937.

BLUNT, WILFRID SCAWEN (1840–1922). Diplomat and author; b. Sussex; ed. Stonyhurst. He entered the Diplomatic Service in 1858 and served in the major European capitals until 1872 when he inherited valuable properties. Travelled extensively in North Africa and Asia, his travels in India, in particular, made him a strong opponent of imperialism. He supported the Irish Parliamentary Party* and was imprisoned for two months in 1887 for advocating the Plan of Campaign.* Blunt was a prolific writer, many of his works reflecting his travels in the East. He was the author of three volumes of poetry, *In Vinculis* (1889), *A new pilgrimage* (1889) and *Poems* (1923). His *Diaries*, with a foreword by Augusta, Lady Gregory,* were published in two volumes (1919–20).

BLYTHE, ERNEST (EARNÁN DE BLAGHD) (1889–1975). Soldier, politician (Cumann na nGaedheal) and writer; b. Lisburn, Co. Antrim; ed. National School. He studied Irish through the Gaelic League* (1905–08) and worked as a farm labourer in Kerry to perfect his knowledge of the language. He joined the Irish Volunteers* and became their organiser in Munster and South Connaught; he was also Gaelic League organiser in Co. Cork. Blythe was arrested several times under Defence of the Realm Act.* He was elected to the Sinn Fein Executive (25 October 1917) and he represented Monaghan in the first Dail Eireann. Blythe was Minister for Trade and Commerce (April 1919–September 1922), Minister for Local Government in the Provisional Government (August–September 1922), Minister for Local Government and Public Health (September 1922–September 1923), Minister for Finance (September 1923–March 1932). He was Vice-President of the Executive Council of the Free State (July 1927–March 1932) and Director of the Abbey Theatre* (1939–67). His writings include *Fraoch agus Fothannain* (poetry, 1938), *The State and the* *Language* (1949), *Briseadh na Teorann* (a study of partition, 1955), *A New Departure in Northern Policy* (1959) and *The Abbey Theatre* (1963). His *Trasna na Bóinne* (1957) and *Slán le hUltaibh* (1969) are autobiographical.

BOARD OF ERIN (ANCIENT ORDER OF HIBERNIANS). Executive of the Irish branch of the Ancient Order of Hibernians,* created at the Conference of 1902 in an attempt to heal the breach between the Irish and American sections of the AOH. A minority in Ireland, around 6,500, refused to accept the reconciliation and abrogated the authority of the Board which represented 60,000 members in 700 branches. The National President was Joseph Devlin,* who used the AOH as his constituency machine in Belfast.

BOARD OF NATIONAL EDUCATION. *See* National Education.

BOARD OF WORKS. Also known as the Barrack Board, it was a branch of the government established in the eighteenth century and re-constituted in 1831. The Board had responsibility for administering public money for relief works to ease hardship through unemployment. During the first half of the nineteenth century it assumed responsibility for the upkeep of public buildings, drainage, waterways and canals. The Board played a prominent role as administrator of relief works during the Famine of 1845–49.* Its functions were further extended in the later part of the century to cover the loans of money for improvement to land, building labourers' cottages and working-class houses in towns. The Board also researched projects for the construction of railway and tram-lines.

BODENSTOWN SUNDAY. Annual commemoration for Theobald Wolfe Tone, founder of the United Irishmen* and generally regarded as the father of Irish republicanism, who is buried in Bodenstown, Co. Kildare. The ceremonies take place on the second last Sunday in June.

38

BODKIN, THOMAS PATRICK (1887–1961). Art expert; b. Dublin; nephew of Hugh Lane;* ed. Belvedere College, Clongowes Wood and the Royal University. He was called to the Bar in 1911 and practised until 1916. He was Secretary to the Committee of Charitable Donations and Bequests (1916–35). Bodkin was Director of the National Gallery of Ireland (1927–35). He was a member of the advisory Committee to the Minister for Education on National Museum Organisation (1927). Barber Professor of Fine Arts at Birmingham (1935–52) and life Governor of the University, he was the recipient of many honours including the Knighthood of St Gregory in 1952. He contributed articles to domestic and international journals, and was a frequent broadcaster on both British and Irish media. His writings include *Four Irish Landscape Painters* (1920), *Hugh Lane and his Pictures* (1932), *My Uncle Frank* (a biography of Hugh Lane, 1941), and *Reports of the Arts in Ireland* (1949).

BOLAND, FREDERICK H. (1904–). Civil servant and diplomat; b. Dublin; ed. Clongowes Wood College, TCD and King's Inns. He entered the Department of External Affairs in 1929. First Secretary, Paris (1932–34) and Head of Section (1934–36), he moved to the Department of Industry and Commerce where he was Principal Officer from 1945–50 and worked with the Minister for External Affairs, Sean MacBride,* on the *Long Term Recovery Programme.* He was Ambassador to the Court of St James (1950–56). Mr Boland was Permanent Representative of the Irish Republic at the United Nations (1956–64) and President of the General Assembly (1960–61). He became Chancellor of TCD in 1964.

BOLAND, GERALD (1885–1973). Politician (Fianna Fail); b. Manchester and raised in Dublin where he was educated at O'Brien Institute, Fairview after which he worked as a fitter with the Midland and Great Western Railway. A member of the Irish Volunteers,* he fought in the Easter Rising of 1916* and was later active in Sinn Fein* and the Irish Republican Army.* Having opposed the Treaty,* he fought against the Provisional Government* during the Civil War.* A supporter of Eamon de Valera,* Boland was a founder-member of Fianna Fail* in which he worked with Sean Lemass* to create the national constituency organisation which made it the best organised party in the state.

Boland was Minister for Posts and Telegraphs (February 1933– November 1936) and for Lands (November 1936–September 1939). As Minister for Justice (September 1939–February 1948) he was much criticised within republican circles for the measures used against the IRA during the Emergency.* He was again Minister for Justice from 1951 until his retirement to the back benches in 1954. He resigned his offices in the Fianna Fail organisation in sympathy with his son, Kevin Boland,* in 1970.

BOLAND, HARRY (1887–1922). Republican; b. Dublin; ed. Synge St CBS and de la Salle College, Castletown, Co. Laois. He joined the Irish Republican Brotherhood* in 1904, and was a prominent member of the Gaelic Athletic Association* and the Irish Volunteers.* He was imprisoned for a year for his part in the Easter Rising of 1916.* Upon his release in 1917 Boland became secretary of Sinn Fein* where he worked closely with his friend Michael Collins* in building up the Volunteers and the IRB. He represented Roscommon in the first Dail Eireann. Boland represented Dail Eireann in the United States in May 1919 and laid the groundwork for de Valera's fund-raising trip. During de Valera's American tour, Boland acted as his secretary and supported him in the rift with John Devoy* and Clan na Gael.* Boland rejected the Treaty claiming that it was a complete betrayal of the Republic established by the first Dail Eireann. He was re-elected for Roscommon in the general election of June 1922 and just over a month later was shot during the Civil War.

BOLAND, KEVIN (1917–   ). Politician (Fianna Fail and Aontacht Eireann); b. Dublin, son of Gerald Boland;* ed. St Joseph's CBS, Fairview. He was returned as Fianna Fail TD for Dublin South County (1957), and on his first day in the Dail became a member of the government formed by Eamon de Valera* in March, as Minister for Defence, a portfolio which he held until October 1961; Minister for Social Welfare (October 1961–April 1965) and Minister for Local Government in the government formed by Jack Lynch* in November 1966. Boland held the post until May 1970 when he resigned in protest at the dismissal of Neil Blaney* and Charles Haughey. He then broke with Fianna Fail, after resigning his seat, and founded Aontacht Eireann in 1971. The party failed to make an impact and he resigned from the leadership and from active politics in 1976.

BORD BAINNE. Established (1961) to promote export sales of butter, later (1964) assuming responsibility for the marketing of all Irish dairy produce in foreign markets.

BORD FAILTE EIREANN. 'Irish Welcoming Board', established under the Tourist Traffic Act, 1955 which changed the title of An Bord Failte to Bord Failte Eireann, which also assumed the publicity role of An Fogra Failte (dismantled under the Act). Working through an international network of offices the Bord's task is to promote Ireland as a holidaying and leisure centre. It gives assistance to those wishing to exploit their particular regions and areas as tourist resorts by providing grants and loans for festivals and entertainment and through the provision of finance to enhance and extend the tourist season. Since 1964 Bord Failte Eireann has operated through eight regional areas. They are Dublin:

Dublin city; Eastern Region: counties of Dublin, Kildare, Louth, Meath and Wicklow; South-Eastern Region: Waterford city and counties Carlow, Kilkenny, Tipperary (South Riding), Waterford and Wexford; Southern Region: Cork city and counties Cork and Kerry; Mid-Western Region: Limerick city and counties Clare, Limerick and Tipperary (North Riding); Western Region: counties Galway and Mayo;North-Western Region: counties Donegal, Leitrim and Sligo; Midland Region: counties Cavan, Laois, Longford, Monaghan, Offaly, Roscommon and Westmeath. The Bord is financed by annual state grant and derives additional revenue from registration fees, advertising and sales of photos and posters.

BORD IASCAIGH MHARA. The functions of the Board as defined in the Sea Fisheries Act (1952) are: to engage, facilitate or promote any arrangements or measures which are directly or indirectly conducive to the development of the Irish sea-fishing industry. The Board was reorganised in 1963 and assumed responsibility for Market Development, Fisheries Development and Investment Development.

BORD NA gCAPALL. Established in 1971 under the Horse Industry Act (1970). Its main functions are to assist the Minister for Agriculture and Fisheries in an advisory capacity on all aspects relating to horse breeding. The Board additionally administers a scheme providing for apprenticeships in farriery and in various ways promotes the non-thoroughbred horse industry.

BORD NA MÓNA. Established in 1946 to develop the country's resources. The industry diversified from providing peat for the turf-burning stations of the Electricity Supply Board* to manufacturing briquettes and producing horticultural peat-moss for a world-wide market.

BOTANIC GARDENS (DUBLIN).
Established by the Royal Dublin
Society* in 1795 with a grant of £300
from the Irish parliament. The Garden's first Director was Dr Walter
Wade. The forty-acre site, formerly
the demesne of the poet Thomas
Ticknell who was Secretary to the
Lords Justices of Ireland (1825–
40), had been a meeting place of
eighteenth-century *literati*, including
Joseph Addison, Richard Brinsley
Sheridan, Jonathan Swift and Sir
Richard Steele. Besides the unique
collection of plants, trees and shrubs,
many rare and exotic plants are
housed in the Garden's conservatories
which are the work of the architect,
Frederick Darley. The Botanic Gardens were taken over by the State in
1878.

BOUNDARY COMMISSION. The
Commission was established in 1924
in accordance with Article 12 of the
Treaty.* Its purpose was to 'determine in accordance with the wishes
of the inhabitants, so far as may be
compatible with economic and geographic conditions, the boundaries
between Northern Ireland and the
rest of Ireland'. Northern Ireland refused to nominate a commissioner
and an Ulster Unionist, J. R. Fisher*
was appointed by London. Eoin Mac-
Neill,* the Free State Minister for
Education, represented the south.
The jointly-appointed chairman was
Justice Feetham* of South Africa.
The Commission sat for most of 1925,
visiting border areas and taking sub-
missions. When the work was completed the commissioners agreed not
to disclose or publish their findings
until they could agree on a joint
report. However, on 7 November
1925, the British *Morning Post* revealed that the Commissioners would
leave the counties of Londonderry,
Tyrone, Fermanagh, Antrim and
Down as they were; part of east Donegal would go to Northern Ireland
and south Armagh would go to the
Free State. MacNeill resigned, saying
that he could not agree with such
findings and he accused the chairman

of having subordinated the wishes of
the border inhabitants to political
influence. Feetham had interpreted
the Commission's brief in accordance
with the letter of Article 12. On 3
December 1925 the three governments agreed that the border should
remain as fixed by the Government of
Ireland Act, 1920* and the Treaty.
The Free State and Northern Ireland
were relieved of their finâncial liabilities under the Treaty and Northern
Ireland was to hold such powers as it
had been given under the Government of Ireland Act. The Free State
assumed the total cost of the damages
incurred during the period 1919–22
and payment of Land Annuities* to
the United Kingdom Exchequer was
to be continued. The British Government transferred its powers under
the Council of Ireland* to Northern
Ireland. The *Report* of the Commission was published in 1969.

BOURKE, THOMAS FRANCIS (b.
1840). Fenian; b. Fethard, Co. Tipperary. Having emigrated to the USA
(1852), he trained as a house-painter
and joined the Fenians (1865). He
returned to Ireland in 1866 holding
the rank of General in the Fenian
Army and led a column in the rising
of 1867. Bourke was wounded and
captured while making his escape
at Ballyhurst, Co. Tipperary, following the rout of his inexperienced
soldiers. He was sentenced to be
hanged, drawn and quartered but
the sentence was commuted to penal
servitude for life. He was released
after serving some seven years of
his sentence and went to the United
States where he was elected to the
Council of the Fenians in New York
on 27 January 1876.

BOURKE, CANON ULICK (1829–
87). Clergyman (R.C.) and writer;
b. Co. Galway; ed. St Jarlath's, Tuam
and St Patrick's College, Maynooth.
He later taught Irish at St Jarlath's
where Dr Mark Ryan* was among his
pupils. Canon Bourke was a founder-
member of the Society for the Preservation of Irish and was one of the

most influential of the Irish language revivalists. He prepared books in the Irish language and had a special fount of type cast for his publications in the *Tuam News* and *Celtic Educator*. He was elected to the RIA in 1871 and appointed P.P. of Claremorris in 1878. His publications include *The College Irish Grammar* (1856), *Easy Lessons on Self-Instruction in Irish* (1874), *The Aryan Origin of the Gaelic Race and Language* (1875), *The Life and Times of Most Rev. John MacHale* (1882), *A plea for the evicted tenants of Mayo* (1883) and *Pre-Christian Ireland* (1887).

BOYCOTT, CAPTAIN CHARLES CUNNINGHAM (1832–97). Land-agent for Lord Erne's estate at Lough Mask, Co. Mayo; b. Norfolk; ed. Blackheath and Woolwich. He became land-agent at Lough Mask in 1873 and opposed the Land League* in their demands for rent reductions. He was one of the earliest victims of the 'moral Coventry' called for by Charles Stewart Parnell* in a speech at Ennis, Co. Clare on 19 September 1880, against those who transgressed Land League policy. The Dublin *Daily Express* and the *Daily Telegraph* established a fund which raised £2,000 to save Boycott's crops which were beginning to rot. The crops were saved by a work force of fifty Orangemen, mostly from Co. Cavan. Over 1,000 troops escorted the workers to and from their homes and remained at Lough Mask from 12–26 November while the crops were being harvested. The Boycott Relief Expedition, as it came to be known, cost the government an estimated £10,000, or as Parnell put it '. . . one shilling for every turnip dug from Boycott's land'. On 13 December 1880 the *Daily Mail* used the word 'Boycott' in capitals to describe the new weapon of the Land League. Boycott remained in Mayo until 1886 when he secured a post as a land-agent in Suffolk. He continued to holiday in Ireland and in December 1888 he appeared as a witness before the parliamentary commission on 'Parnellism and Crime'.*

BRAYTON, TERESA (1868–1943). Poetess; b. Kilbrook, Co. Kildare; ed. locally; assistant teacher at Newtown, Co. Kildare. Before emigrating to the USA in 1908 she had attracted wide attention with the publication of her verse in the national press. During her frequent visits to Ireland she became friendly with the future leaders of the Easter Rising of 1916,* and supported their cause in the USA by distributing pamphlets and organising fund-raising activities. Her works include *Songs of the dawn and Irish ditties* (1913), *The Flame of Ireland* (1926) and *Christmas Verses* (1934). Her best-known work is 'The Old Bog Road'.

BREATHNACH, MICHEÁL ('COIS FHAIRRGE') (1881–1908). Writer. A member of the Gaelic League,* he went to London where he became assistant Secretary of the London Gaelic League. He returned to Ireland in 1905 and taught in Tuam, Co. Galway. Because of chronic ill-health, he was forced to spend the winter months in Switzerland. He contributed many stories and essays to *An Claidheamh Soluis** and *Iris-leabhar na Gaeilge*. Breathnach's most important work is his *Stair na hÉireann* which was published by the Gaelic League in three parts between 1911–16.

BREEN, DAN (1894–1969). Republican soldier and politician; b. Grange, Donohill, Co. Tipperary. He became involved in nationalist activities at an early age and was sworn into the Irish Republican Brotherhood* by his close friend, Sean Treacy.* His exploits with the Third Tipperary Brigade of the Irish Republican Army* during the War of Independence* led to the government's offering a £1,000 reward for him. After the Truce* he went to the USA but returned at the request of Liam Lynch* to support the anti-

Treaty republicans during the Civil War.* He was elected TD for Tipperary while imprisoned at the end of the War. In April 1927 he became the first republican to take the Oath of Allegiance* (as a member of Clann Eireann). His Bill to have the Oath abolished was defeated 47−17. Breen's autobiography, *My Fight for Irish Freedom* (1924), is a highly colourful account of his life and times during the years 1913−23.

BRENAN, MICHAEL JOSEPH (1829−57). Young Ireland journalist and poet; b. Cork. He went to Dublin where he assisted John Mitchel* on the *United Irishman* and on that paper's suppression, he worked on the *Irish Felon*. He was arrested for Young Ireland activities in 1848 and imprisoned for a year. Brenan aided James Fintan Lalor* in the abortive insurrection in the south-east and upon its failure he emigrated to the USA. He settled in New Orleans where he became editor of the *New Orleans Times*. Brenan married Mary Savage, a sister of John Savage,* in 1851. The ceremony was attended by Richard Dalton Williams* and Thomas Devin Reilly.* Brenan was a very close friend of James Clarence Mangan* with whom he maintained a regular correspondence.

BRENNAN, LT GEN. MICHAEL (1896−   ). Soldier; Chief of Staff, Irish Army (1931−40); b. Meelick, Co. Clare; ed. locally. A member of the Irish Volunteers,* he was imprisoned for sedition shortly before the Easter Rising of 1916.* He commanded the East Clare Brigade of the Irish Republican Army* during the War of Independence.* A friend of Liam Lynch,* he held General Lucas prisoner after Lynch had captured him. Accepting the Treaty,* he enlisted in the Free State National Army as Commandant of the 1st Western Division, assuming control of barracks vacated by the Black and Tans. During the Civil War* he was O/C, Limerick Command until January 1923 and GOC, Limerick

from 24 January 1923. GOC, Southern Command from 29 February 1924 until he was appointed Adjutant General on 15 October 1925. He was Inspector General from October 1928 until his appointment as Chief of Staff on 15 October 1931.

BRENNAN, ROBERT (1881−1964). Journalist, diplomat and Director of Broadcasting, Radio Eireann (1947−48); b. Wexford; ed. locally. Active in the Gaelic League* and Sinn Fein,* he was recruited into the Irish Republican Brotherhood* by Sean T. O'Kelly and in 1913 became a member of the Wexford Irish Volunteers.* He was unable to get to Dublin when the Easter Rising of 1916 broke out but was imprisoned in the aftermath. Upon release he played a leading role in the re-organisation of the Volunteers and Sinn Fein, working as a propagandist for both organisations. He was National Director of Elections for Sinn Fein for the general election of December 1918 and was Under-Secretary of the Department of Foreign Affairs, Dail Eireann (February 1921−January 1922); and in this capacity organised the Irish Race Convention held in Paris in 1922. After rejecting the Treaty* he worked as propagandist for the republicans during the Civil War.* Later he worked as a reporter on *The Enniscorthy Echo*. Upon the establishment of *The Irish Press* by Eamon de Valera in 1931 Brennan became the first General Manager, a position he held until appointed Secretary of the Irish Legation in Washington by de Valera (February 1934−March 1938). He was Acting Chargé d'Affairs in Washington from March to September 1938 when he became Minister Plenipotentiary (Ambassador) a post he held from September 1938 to April 1947. Upon returning to Ireland he became Director of Broadcasting, Radio Eireann (May 1947−August 1948). His autobiography, *Allegiance*, was published in 1950.

BRENNAN, THOMAS (1842−1915). Land agitator; b. Mayo; ed. locally.

A member of the Irish Republican Brotherhood,* he worked in Dublin. With Isaac Butt* and John 'Amnesty' Nolan* he was prominent in the Amnesty Association.* Brennan was a member of the Land League* from the earliest days, having spoken at Irishtown, Co. Mayo,* and resigned his Dublin employment to become full-time secretary of the organisation. During a speech at Balla, Co. Mayo, on 22 November 1879, he called on the Royal Irish Constabulary* to assist the Land League and called for the implementation of a policy which later became known as 'boycotting': if a man took a farm from which another had been evicted, Brennan urged that he be treated 'as an unclean thing. Let none of you be found to buy with him or sell with him and watch how the modern Iscariot will prosper'. This line was taken during the following year by his companion on the Balla platform, Charles Stewart Parnell.* Brennan was prosecuted for his speech but the charge failed. Imprisoned with Parnell and other Land League figures in October 1881, he was a signatory to the 'No Rent Manifesto'.* He opposed the Ladies' Land League,* believing, like Parnell, that the ladies' activities would bring ridicule on the Land League movement. He emigrated to the USA after the Kilmainham 'Treaty'* and adopted a radical position within Irish-American politics.

BRENNAN, 'CAPTAIN' WILLIAM, 'BRENNAN ON THE MOOR', (d. 1840). Highwayman and folk-hero. He worked as a farm labourer at Kilmurray House for a Mr Grant, where he was caught while attempting to relieve a British officer guest of the burden of his watch. Brennan became an outlaw based in the Kilworth Mountains, Co. Cork and established a reputation throughout Munster as a Robin Hood figure. He was eventually arrested and hanged at Clonmel gaol. Brennan became the subject of a widely-known anonymous ballad, 'A Lament on the Execution of Captain Brennan'.

BRESLIN, JOHN J. (c. 1836–88). Fenian; b. Drogheda; ed. locally. A member of the Irish Republican Brotherhood,* he was employed as a hospital steward at Richmond Prison during the imprisonment of James Stephens* and secured an impression of the cell keys, enabling Stephens to escape (24 November 1865). He emigrated to the USA shortly afterwards and became a prominent member of Clan na Gael.* John Devoy* appointed him to supervise the rescue of Fenian prisoners from Fremantle, Australia, on the *Catalpa** (17 April 1876). Breslin was also involved with John P. Holland* on *The Fenian Ram* and worked for Devoy as Business Manager of *The Irish Nation.*

BRIGHT, JOHN (1811–89). British Liberal; b. Rochdale. He was a Quaker and a follower of the Manchester School of Economics. He visited Ireland in 1832 and 1849. His *Diaries* reveal his horror at the effects of the Famine of 1845–49.* Bright advocated sale of encumbered estates (*see* Encumbered Estates Acts) with provision for occupancy by tenants. He gave his name to the 'Bright Clause' which he persuaded W. E. Gladstone* to include in the Land Act of 1870 (*see* Land Acts); this stated that the government would put up some of the purchase money to enable a tenant to purchase his land. Bright opposed Home Rule* in the latter part of his life.

BRITISH RELIEF ASSOCIATION. Founded on 1 January 1847 at a meeting organised by Stephen Spring Rice at Messrs Rothschild's London offices, with the aim of 'alleviating distress caused by the potato failure in Ireland and Scotland'; five-sixths of funds was allocated to relieve distress in Ireland. Among those who contributed were Queen Victoria* (£2,000), Rothschild's (£1,000), the Duke of Devonshire (£1,000) and Charles Wood* (£400). The BRA appointed a Pole, Count Strzelecki* as agent for the distribution of relief and within a short time he was distributing £13,000 per week; £12,000 was also distributed for the clothing of children.

BROADCASTING ACT (1960). The Act set up an Authority to administer an Irish television service — Telefis Eireann (now RTE) which was to derive its revenue from commercial advertising and licence fees. *See* Radio Telefis Eireann.

BROIGHTER GOLD HOARD. While ploughing at Broighter, near Limavady, Co. Derry in February 1896, Tom Nicoll unearthed a treasure which has been described as '. . . the oldest, the rarest, the most beautiful ornaments ever discovered outside Ancient Egypt'. His employer, Joseph Gibson, sold the find to a Derry jeweller for a reputed 'few sovereigns'. The treasure was finally purchased by the British Museum for £600. The Royal Irish Academy subsequently claimed the find as 'treasure-trove' and following protracted litigation were awarded the treasure. The Broighter Gold Hoard contains the Broighter Collar — one of the classic examples of the La Tène period, dating from the First century A.D. The collection is now on display at the National Museum* and replicas are on view at the Ulster Museum, Belfast.

BRONTE (sometimes BRUNTY or PRUNTY) REV. PATRICK (1777–1861). Minor poet and father of the Bronte sisters; b. Emdale, Co. Down; ed. locally and at Cambridge. He was ordained in the Church of England in 1806 and held various livings in Essex and Shropshire before securing the perpetual curacy of Haworth, Yorkshire in 1820. He survived his wife and his seven children. His works are *The Rural Minstrel* (1813) and *The Maid of Killarney* (1818).

BROOKEBOROUGH, VISCOUNT (1888–1974). Brooke, Basil; politician (Ulster Unionist) and Prime Minister, Northern Ireland (1943–63); b. Fermanagh; ed. Winchester and Sandhurst. He served on the Western Front (1914–18). In 1921 he helped in the foundation of the 'B' Specials (*see* Special Constabulary) and was a member of the first Senate of Northern Ireland (1921). He was returned as the Ulster Unionist MP for Lisnaskea in 1929 and held the seat until 1968. Brooke was at first Assistant Whip of the Party from 1930 until 1933 when he became Minister for Agriculture (until 1941). Minister for Commerce (1941–43), he was a leading member of the younger generation of Unionists who were critical of the older members of the party, including the Prime Minister, John Miller Andrews.* Andrews resigned and in May 1943 Brooke replaced him as leader of the party and Prime Minister. He held the position for 20 years, the longest term of any Prime Minister of Northern Ireland. He replaced the older members of the government with younger men and set about planning the future growth of Northern Ireland, which was enjoying a new-found prosperity during World War II. The Labour government in Britain committed itself to aiding Northern Ireland to achieve parity with the rest of the UK in the spheres of education, medicine, social welfare, etc. These advances took place under Lord Brookeborough, as he became in 1952. A member of the Orange Order,* he had a history of anti-Catholic statements behind him and did nothing to resolve the sectarian tension which marked life in the Northern state. His government introduced internment to deal with the Irish Republican Army* and Saor Uladh* between 1956 and 1962. When he resigned office in 1963, he was replaced by a more liberal Unionist, Captain Terence O'Neill. He resigned his seat in 1968.

BROWNE, DR NOEL C. (1915–   ). Politician (Labour); b. Waterford; ed. Athlone, CBS, Ballinrobe, St Anthony's School, Eastbourne, Beaumont College, Windsor and

TCD where he qualified as a doctor. After contracting tuberculosis, he became a leading campaigner for the eradication of this disease, which had killed his parents. He became Clann na Poblachta TD for Dublin South East in 1948 and on his first day in Dail Eireann became Minister for Health in the first Inter-Party government.* His campaign against tuberculosis led to the virtual eradication of the disease. His attempt to implement the Mother and Child Scheme* led to a confrontation with the Catholic hierarchy and was a factor in the fall of the government (1951). He continued to hold his seat as an Independent (1951–53). He then became a member of Fianna Fail* but did not hold a seat (1953–57). Browne regained his seat as an Independent in 1957 and was a co-founder of the National Progressive Democratic Party* for which he sat from 1958 until 1963. In 1963 he joined the Labour Party,* holding a seat from 1969 until 1973, when he became a Senator. Although he was nominated by a Labour Party convention to contest Dublin Artane in 1977, he could not get ratification from the Administrative Council but won the seat as Independent Labour. He became the only sitting deputy of the Socialist Labour Party* later that year.

BROY, COLONEL EAMONN (1887–1972). Soldier and Commissioner of the Garda Siochana* (1933–38); b. Ballinure, Co. Kildare; ed. locally. He became a civil servant working in Dublin Castle and, as a Sinn Fein supporter, arranged for Michael Collins* to secure secret material during the War of Independence.* In April 1919 he brought Collins into the Castle to see the intelligence unit at work. Broy used his position to warn Collins of imminent raids. When his role was uncovered he was arrested but no action was taken against him, and Collins arranged for his release during the Truce.* He accompanied Collins to London during the Treaty negotiations. A

supporter of Eamon de Valera,* he rejected the Treaty. When de Valera dismissed General Eoin O'Duffy* in February 1933 Broy succeeded him as Commissioner of the Gardai. The opposition of the Blueshirts* to the Fianna Fail government produced unrest. Broy recruited ex-Irish Republican Army* soldiers into the Gardai; this auxiliary force was armed, unlike the regular Garda Siochana, and became popularly known as the 'Broy Harriers'. The force was disbanded when the Blueshirt movement disintegrated during 1935. Colonel Broy retired from the Commissionership in June 1938.

BRUCE, WILLIAM (1757–1841). Presbyterian minister; b. Dublin; ed. TCD and Warrington. He held various ministries, Glasgow (1776), Lisburn (1779), Dublin (1782) and Belfast (1789–1831). He was Principal of the Belfast Academy (1790–1822) and active in the Hibernian Bible Society. Bruce served in the Volunteers and was the last surviving member of the Rotunda Convention of 1783. He secured terms for the Presbyterian Church at the time of the Union.* He established The Belfast Literary Society (23 October 1801), wrote the address presented by the Presbyterians to George IV* (1821) and founded the Unitarian Society on 9 April 1831. His publications include *The State of Society in the age of Homer* (1827), *A Brief Commentary on the New Testament* (1836), and frequent contributions to the *Transactions* of the RIA and the *Dublin University Magazine.*

BRUGHA, CATHAL (1874–1922). Republican soldier and politician (Sinn Fein); b. Dublin; ed. Belvedere College. He was active in the Gaelic League,* the Gaelic Athletic Association* and the Irish Volunteers.* During the Easter Rising of 1916,* Brugha was second-in-command to Eamon Ceannt* at the South Dublin Union garrison and he was rendered lame as a result of wounds received in action. He was elected to the First Dail and was President of the Assembly from 21 January to April 1919 when he became Minister for National Defence, a position which he also held in the Second Dail, and throughout the War of Independence.* Brugha was one of the most impassioned opponents of the Treaty.* He fought on the Republican side in the Civil War.* When the Four Courts fell, Brugha took up a position in the Hamman Hotel and when this too came under heavy fire, he ordered his men to surrender. After they did so, he came out himself in a heroic last stand and was fatally wounded.

de BRÚN, MONSIGNOR PADRAIG (1889--1960). Clergyman (R.C.) and Gaelic scholar; b. Co. Tipperary; ed. Dublin, Paris and Gottingen. Ordained at Maynooth in 1913, he became Professor of Mathematics at the College the following year. He translated works from Greek, French and Italian into Irish, and was working on a translation of Dante's *Divine Comedy* when he died. Monsignor de Brún's works include translations into Irish of Shakespearean songs and sonnets, portions of *The Iliad*, three Sophoclean tragedies, *Antigone* (1926) and *Oedipus Rex* (1928). He was the co-author with Fr O Baoigheallain of *Beatha Iósa Críost* (*Life of Christ*, 1929). He was Chairman of the Dublin Institute of Advanced Studies,* Director of the Arts Council* and President of UCG.

BRUNSWICK CLUBS. Protestant clubs founded in 1828 by the Duke of Brunswick during the period of intense agitation for Catholic Emancipation.* The express purpose of such clubs was to oppose Emancipation. The members were known as 'Brunswickers' and were active during 1828–29, in opposition to the Order of Liberators.*

BRYANT, SOPHIE (1850–1922). Educationalist; b. Dublin; ed. privately and at Bedford College, London. Her father, Rev. W. A. Willock, played an important role in the Irish national educational movement. She became the first woman to take the D.Sc. in Moral Science in 1894. She was Consultant Commissioner to the Board of Education (1900–11). Her publications include *Educational Ends* (1887), *Celtic Ireland* (1889), *Short studies in character* (1894), *The Genius of the Gael* (1913) and *Liberty, Order and Law under Native Irish rule* (1923).

BRYCE, JAMES, 1st VISCOUNT BRYCE (1838–1922). Politician (Liberal); Chief Secretary (1905–07); b. Belfast; ed. Belfast High School, University of Glasgow, Trinity College, Oxford, and at Heidelberg. He was called to the Bar in 1867. He became Regius Professor, Civil Law, at Oxford (1870–93). Bryce was elected MP for Tower Hamlets in 1880 and became Under-Secretary for Foreign Affairs in 1886 and President of the Board of Trade (1894). During his career he was awarded some fifteen honorary degrees and was a prolific contributor to domestic and international journals in which he wrote extensively on Ireland and Irish affairs. His experiences in Ireland convinced him that some form of Home Rule* was inevitable and he urged Ulster politicians to safeguard the interests of Protestant Ulster. Bryce was a keen mountaineer and was President of the Alpine Club; Mount Bryce in the Rockies was named for him. His writings include *The American Commonwealth* (3 vols, 1888), *Impressions of South Africa* (1897), *South America, Observations and Impressions* (1912). He edited *Handbook of Home Rule* (2nd edition 1887) and wrote an introduction to *Two Centuries of Irish History*, (1888).

'B' SPECIALS. *See* Ulster Special Constabulary.

BUCKINGHAM PALACE CONFERENCE (21–24 July 1914). The

Conference was an attempt by King George V* to break the deadlock over the (third) Home Rule Bill.* Orange and Unionist movements in the northern counties were determined to prevent Home Rule, or, at the very least, not to become involved in it. An Amending Bill passed a month earlier provided for the exclusion of either four or six of the Ulster counties (the fate of Fermanagh and Tyrone had not yet been decided). Leaders of the Conference parties were: H. H. Asquith and David Lloyd George (Liberal), Lord Lansdowne and Andrew Bonar Law (Conservative), John Redmond and John Dillon (Nationalist), Sir James Craig and Sir Edward Carson (Unionist). The Conference, which lasted from 21–24 July, was presided over by the Speaker of the House of Commons. The king met each delegation separately to measure progress during the Conference. Due principally to lack of compromise, the Conference broke up inconclusively. The Government of Ireland Bill was passed and with it another Bill, postponing the implementation of Home Rule until the end of World War I. The Bills were given the Royal Assent on 18 September 1914.

BUCKLEY, TIM, 'THE TAILOR', (1863–1945). Storyteller; b. Kilgarvin, Co. Kerry; Tadgh O Buachalla in the Irish form of his name. He had little formal education. Buckley and his wife Anastasia or 'Ansty' (1872–1947) settled in Garrynapeaka, near Gougane Barra in West Cork where he plied his trade as a tailor. His stories, tales and observations earned him the friendship of many literary and artistic figures including Frank O'Connor,* Sean O'Faolain* and Seamus Murphy.* He was the subject of *The Tailor and Ansty* by Eric Cross.* It caused a furore upon its appearance in 1942 and led to discussions in the Senate.* Passages from the book were not read into the record of the House in case they might be peddled by 'pornographers'. The book also incurred clerical con-

demnation and was banned in Ireland until the 1960s. Local clergymen forced Buckley to burn copies of the book in his own fire-place. A collection of his lore in Irish, *Seanchas An Táilliúra*, collected in 1947 by Sean O Croinin, appeared in 1978.

BULFIN, WILLIAM (1864–1910). Newspaper owner, editor and writer; b. near Birr, Co. Offaly. He emigrated to Argentina in his teens where he worked as a gaucho until acquiring a successful newspaper in Buenos Aires. He returned to Ireland in 1902 and travelled all over the country by bicycle. His celebrated *Rambles in Erin* (1907) is a record of his tour of Ireland. His daughter, (d. 1976) married Sean MacBride.*

BUNREACHT NA hEIREANN. *See* Constitution of 1937.

BUNTING, EDWARD (1773–1843). Music-collector and organist; b. Armagh. He was trained as an organist by his brother in Drogheda. He travelled throughout Ireland collecting material for *The Ancient Music of Ireland* (1797). This work included sixty-six pieces of music previously unpublished. Many of the tunes were later used by Thomas Moore* for his *Melodies*. Bunting's second collection appeared in 1809 and contained, in addition to the history of the Irish harp, seventy-seven pieces arranged for the piano with words for twenty of the tunes. Bunting played an important role in the revival of the Irish language and culture and was instrumental in the staging of the Belfast Harp Festival in 1792. In 1813 he organised a Music Festival which featured organ and harp recitals and during this festival he conducted the first performance in Belfast of Handel's *Messiah*. Bunting toured the continent in 1815 and on his return to Ireland, he married and moved to Dublin. His *General Collection of the Ancient Music of Ireland*, dedicated to Queen Victoria,* appeared in 1840.

BURDETT, SIR FRANCIS (1770–1844). English radical politician. Burdett's Catholic Relief Bill (1825) which included state payment of the clergy and the disenfranchisement of the Forty-Shilling Freeholders* won the support of Daniel O'Connell.* The Bill passed the Commons but was rejected by the Lords.

BURKE, JOHN (1787–1848). Genealogist; b. Co. Tipperary. He left Ireland for England where he wrote a number of genealogical works. Those of Irish interest are *Genealogical and Heraldic Dictionary of the Peerage and Baronetage of the United Kingdom* (1826), *A General and Heraldic Dictionary of the Peerages of England, Ireland and Scotland* (1831), *A Genealogical and Heraldic History of the Commoners of Great Britain and Ireland* (5 vols, 1833–38), *The Knightage of Great Britain and Ireland* (with Sir John Bernard Burke, 1841).

BURKE, RICARD O'SULLIVAN (1838–1922). Fenian; b. Dunmanway, Co. Cork. He joined the Cork militia in 1853 and when his regiment was disbanded, he went to sea where he learned several languages as he voyaged around the world. Burke was in America at the time of the American Civil War (1861–65) and he joined the Federal Army. He organised Fenian Circles in the Army of the Potomac. Thomas J. Kelly* recommended him to James Stephens* as an arms-purchaser for the Fenians in Ireland. Using the pseudonym 'Edward C. Winslow', Burke built up contacts with Birmingham Small Arms manufacturers and imported Enfield rifles from the USA until he had some 2,000 stored in Liverpool. Burke organised the rescue of Colonel Kelly* and Captain Timothy Deasy* in Manchester (18 September 1867). He was betrayed by the Fenian spy John J. Corydon and arrested. He was held in the Clerkenwell House of Detention from which a Fenian rescue party attempted to free him (*see* Clerkenwell Explosion). Burke was sentenced to fifteen years' imprisonment and Michael Davitt* assumed his role as arms purchaser. Burke constantly feigned insanity while in prison and was eventually moved to Broadmoor Convict Lunatic Asylum from which he was released in 1872. He returned to the USA where he was employed in various engineering projects. He joined Clan na Gael* and continued his efforts in the Fenian cause.

BURKE, THOMAS HENRY (1829–82). Under-Secretary for Ireland (1869–82); b. Knocknagur, Co. Galway. He entered Dublin Castle* as a clerk in 1847 and worked in various departments attached to the Chief Secretary's Office. He was private Secretary to three Chief Secretaries: Edward Cardwell, Sir Robert Peel* and Chichester Fortescue-Parkinson.* Burke became Under-Secretary in 1869 and was closely associated with the coercion policy adopted during the Land War (1879–82). He was murdered by the Invincibles* on 6 May 1882 when he and the newly-arrived Chief Secretary, Lord Frederick Cavendish,* were walking in the Phoenix Park. *See* Phoenix Park Murders.

BURKE, FR THOMAS NICHOLAS ANTHONY (1830–83). Dominican preacher; b. Galway where his father owned a bakery. He received his early schooling locally at the hands of a Mr Magrath whose maxim was 'If I cannot drive it into your head, I'll drive it into you somewhere'. His conventional education began at the age of nine at the Galway Brothers of St Patrick. He continued locally at the school of Rev. Dr O'Toole and completed his studies at Michael Winter's Academy, Galway, where he was introduced to the classics. His interest in the latter prompted him to experiment with pebbles and shells in his mouth to test the articular range of his voice – emulating the great Athenian orator Demosthenes (385–322 B.C.). Burke was influenced by the writings of Thomas Davis* and by the oratorial powers of Daniel O'Connell.*

He entered the Dominican House in Denmark St, Dublin for a few days prior to his novitiate at Perugia, Italy. He received the habit on 29 December 1847, taking the name St Thomas Aquinas in religion, and was professed on 5 January 1849. Burke left Perugia on 3 January 1850 for Rome where he pursued his theological studies first at the Minerva and later at Santa Sabina. Appointed Novice Master at Woodchester, England in 1851, he arrived in London penniless and received financial assistance from Fr F. W. Faber (author of 'Faith of Our Fathers'). Burke was ordained on 26 March 1853 and ministered at Woodchester until 1855 when he was called upon to lead the Irish Novitiate at Tallaght. His fame as a preacher had preceded him and thousands flocked to hear him. Though frequently in ill-health with a stomach ailment, Fr Burke continued his preaching and mission work throughout Ireland and England. In one marathon sermon at Sheffield he preached for nearly three and a half hours on the Apostles' Creed. Rector of the Irish College, San Clemente, Rome from 1864, he returned to Ireland (August 1867) to the Friary of St Saviour, Dominic St, Dublin. When the remains of Daniel O'Connell were re-interred to the crypt beneath the tower at Glasnevin cemetry on 14 May 1869, Fr Burke preached the panegyric to an estimated 50,000 crowd. He was theological advisor to the Bishop of Dromore at the Vatican Council of December 1869 which decreed papal infallibility – which he himself opposed, fearing it would imperil Catholic unity. In 1871 Fr Burke preached one hundred and seventy-two sermons and conducted twenty-one retreats which necessitated an additional seven hundred and sixty addresses. In February 1872 he journeyed on a fund-raising tour to the United States but under the strain of preaching three times daily his lungs collapsed and he was forced to rest. His most popular lectures in America were his replies to J. A. Froude (1818–94) on the topic of Anglo-Irish relations. Fr Burke arrived home on 7 March 1873 having delivered some seven hundred sermons and lectures and having raised £80,000 for charity. During his last years he was in considerable pain and was sent by his superiors to Italy on a few occasions to improve his health. At his funeral in the presence of thirteen bishops, hundreds of priests and many thousands of the laity, a message of sympathy from Pope Leo XIII was read. It concluded '. . . The death of this great orator and excellent religious has placed in mourning not only his Order and all Ireland – but the Universal Church.'

BURTON, SIR FREDERICK WILLIAM (1816–1900). Portrait and water-colour artist; b. Corofin, Co. Clare. He sustained an accident in childhood which rendered his right arm useless. He was elected to the RHA in 1839. Burton was Director of the National Gallery, London (1874–94). He painted the leading celebrities of the day in Ireland, including Thomas Davis,* Samuel Ferguson* and Eugene O'Curry.* He executed the death mask of James Clarence Mangan.*

BUSHE, CHARLES KENDAL (1767–1843). Chief Justice (1822–41); b. Kilkenny; ed. TCD. He was called to the Bar in 1790 and elected MP for Callan, Co. Kilkenny in 1797. He opposed the Union.* A man of the highest integrity, Bushe was nicknamed 'Incorruptible'. He was equally renowned as an orator and wit. Henry Grattan* said of him, 'Bushe spoke with the lips of an angel'. Bushe was appointed Solicitor-General in 1805 and held the post until appointed Chief Justice. Apart from speeches reproduced in pamphlet form, his only published work is *Cease Your Funning* (1799).

BUTLER, MARY LAMBERT (MÁIRE DE BUITLÉIR) (c. 1872–1920). Writer; b. Co. Clare. She was a cousin of Sir Edward Carson.* She learned Irish in the Aran Islands and became active in the Gaelic League.*

Miss Butler edited the Eire Óg column of the *Weekly Independent*. A supporter of Arthur Griffith* in his Hungarian policy of 1904, she suggested to him the title of Sinn Fein.* She supported the Irish Volunteers* and wrote many articles to periodicals under the Irish form of her name. She is the author of *The Ring of Day* (1903).

BUTT, ISAAC (1813–79). Barrister and politician (Nationalist); b. Donegal; ed. TCD, where he had a brilliant academic career and was founder and editor of the *Dublin University Magazine* (1833). He took his B.A. in 1835 and in 1836 he became the first professor of Political Economy, TCD. He was called to the Bar in 1837. Butt was a convinced Unionist* at that time; he founded the *Protestant Guardian* and opposed Daniel O'Connell in the fight for Repeal.* His political opinions underwent a change as a result of the Famine of 1845–49;* in 1847 he published *The Famine on the Land* in which he pointed out that neglect of Irish grievances would lead to an anti-British coalition in Ireland. During the following year, he defended members of Young Ireland,* including William Smith O'Brien.* He now looked towards Federalism* as an answer to the Irish Question, and this remained his solution for the rest of his life. He was MP (Liberal-Conservative) for Harwich and later for Youghal (1852–65). Debts, accumulated through extravagant living and gambling, forced him to give up his political career and resume the Bar, and he returned to Ireland in 1865. His defence of the leaders of the Irish Republican Brotherhood,* between 1865 and 1867, gave him a national reputation which he consolidated by assuming the presidency of the Amnesty Association.* The desire to wrest the initiative from the revolutionary Fenians* led him to put forward his federal solution to the Irish demand for self-government; he envisaged a subordinate parliament in Ireland to deal with domestic affairs. He sought support principally from the propertied class, from both the Irish Liberals and Conservatives. In November 1869 Butt proposed in *The Nation* that a united nationalist party should be established. He called a meeting on 19 May 1870 and brought together differing shades of Irish political opinion. A few months later he founded the Home Government Association* which he replaced in 1873 with the Home Rule League.* Butt lacked the temperament and consistency needed to hold together a group with differing outlooks. As a constitutionalist he disapproved of the policy of 'obstruction' followed by the Fenian wing of the party which included Joseph Biggar* and John O'Connor Power.* He lost the support of those who disagreed with the concept of federalism and who were dissatisfied with their party's ineffective role at Westminster. The breach between Butt and the dissenting members became public in 1877. He lost the leadership of the Home Rule Confederation of Great Britain and Ireland* to Charles Stewart Parnell* in the same year. In 1878 he attempted to bring his party behind the Conservative government and was attacked at the Home Rule Conference in Dublin (January). This attack was renewed and strengthened at a meeting of the Home Rule League in February 1879; he died shortly afterwards. His writings include *The History of Italy from the Abdication of Napoleon* (2 vols, 1860), *Land Tenure in Ireland: A Plea for the Celtic Race* (1866), *The Power and the Land* (1867) and *Irish Federalism* (1870).

BYRNE, ALFRED (ALFIE) 1882–1956). Politician (Nationalist) and many times Lord Mayor of Dublin; b. Dublin; ed. locally. He was MP, Harbour Division of Dublin (1914–18) and Independent TD for various Dublin constituencies (1923–28, 1931–56). He was a member of the Senate from 1928 until his resignation in 1931. Three of his sons were at various times TDs. He was a candidate for the Presidency of Eire in

1938 but withdrew when Dr Douglas Hyde* became an agreed candidate. Alfie Byrne's record in local government was unique; he was Mayor of Dublin from 1930—39 and in 1954—55. He was popularly believed to have shaken the hand of every man, woman and child in the city and to have been on equal terms with everyone.

BYRNE, MYLES (1780—1862). United Irishman; b. Ballylusk, Co. Wexford. A farmer at Monaseed, he joined the United Irishmen* and commanded pikemen at the battle of Arklow (9 June 1798) where the rebels were forced to retreat; at Vinegar Hill (21 June) and, following the route of the United army by General Lake, he held out for a short time before joining Michael Dwyer* in Wicklow. He made his way to Dublin where he worked as a builder's clerk until he became involved in the rising of Robert Emmet* (23 July 1803). Emmet sent him to France to organise support and he entered the Irish Legion which he thought would be sent to Ireland but which fought on the continent. He was awarded a Legion of Honour by Louis Phillipe (1830). His three volumes of *Memoirs* were published in 1853. He is commemorated by a monument in Montmartre.

C

'**CAIRO GANG**'. Title for officers of British intelligence operating in Ireland during the War of Independence.* They worked independently of Dublin Castle.* On 21 November 1920 The Squad,* controlled by Michael Collins, assassinated eleven agents, provoking the events which led to the day's becoming known as 'Bloody Sunday'.*

'**CAKE, A**'. Irish custom, rather like a raffle, for the purpose of helping a distressed family. The family bought in drink and a large ornamental cake, some two or three stone in weight. The event normally took place on a Sunday or holiday and was attended by neighbours and friends from the surrounding townlands. The whole occasion became a social outing with music and dancing which attracted a crowd of several hundred. Revenue from the sale of drinks went to the hosts and helped to alleviate their distress.

CALLANAN, JAMES JOSEPH ('**JEREMIAH**') (1796—1829). Poet; b. Cork; ed. Maynooth and TCD. He was intended for the priesthood. On his leaving Trinity College he enlisted in the army. After a brief period in the service he purchased his release and thereafter made his living as a private tutor. He travelled around Ireland gathering legends and poetry which he included in his two published works, *The Recluse of Inchidony* (1829) and *Poems of James Joseph Callanan*, posthumously published in 1861.

CAMERON COMMISSION. The Commission was appointed by the government of Northern Ireland led by Captain Terence O'Neill* in January 1969 to investigate clashes between loyalist and civil rights marchers of the Northern Ireland Civil Rights Association* and the People's Democracy.* The Commission was chaired by Lord Cameron (a Scottish peer) and consisted of himself, Sir John Biggart and James Campbell. Their Report was issued as *Disturbances in Northern Ireland* (Cmd. 532, Belfast, HMSO 1969). The Commission, while criticising the civil rights movement, also found that loyalist groups had acted in a manner so as to deliberately provoke clashes with the marchers. It criticised loyalist agitators and found evidence that on 4–5 January 'a number of policemen were guilty of misconduct which involved assault and battery, malicious damage to property in streets in predominantly Catholic Bogside (Derry) . . . .' *See also* Hunt Committee.

CAMPAIGN FOR DEMOCRACY IN ULSTER. Founded in 1965 by left-wing British MPs, the CDU's aim was to oppose gerrymandering and discrimination in Northern Ireland against the Catholic population. It sought an official parliamentary inquiry into the Unionist government at Stormont.* CDU was supported by Gerry Fitt* and worked in close association with the Campaign for Social Justice in Northern Ireland.*

CAMPAIGN FOR SOCIAL JUSTICE IN NORTHERN IRELAND. Founded in 1964, it was a middle-class movement to highlight social injustice in Northern Ireland. It worked in close association with the Campaign for Democracy in Ulster* and the British Council for Civil Liberties; CSJNI helped to found the Northern Ireland Civil Rights Association* in 1967, into which it was absorbed.

CAMPBELL, GEORGE (1918–79). Artist; b. Arklow, Co. Wicklow; reared and ed. in Belfast where he worked in an aircraft factory during World War II. A co-founder of the Living Art Exhibition, he travelled frequently to Spain, a country which deeply influenced his work and which granted him the award of Knight Commander. Campbell, who was a member of the Royal Hibernian Academy,* exhibited in Dublin, London and in Spain. He received the Sacred Art Award (1961), the Open Award of the Arts Council of Northern Ireland (1962), the President Hyde Gold Medal (1966) and the Oireachtas Landscape Prize (1969). He worked also in stained glass (Galway cathedral and the Dominican church, Athy) and illustrated books.

An accomplished classical guitarist, he broadcast on BBC radio.

CAMPBELL-BANNERMAN, SIR HENRY (1836–1908). Prime Minister (Liberal), (1905–08); Chief Secretary (1884–85); b. Glasgow, surname Campbell (Bannerman was added in 1872); ed. Glasgow High School, Glasgow University and Trinity College Cambridge. He became MP for Stirling Burghs in 1868, which constituency he represented until his death. He supported W. E. Gladstone* on the Disestablishment of the Church of Ireland* and on granting Tenant Right* to Irish farmers (*see* Land Acts). In October 1884 he succeeded George Otto Trevelyan* as Chief Secretary of Ireland, in which post he won the admiration of Charles Stewart Parnell* who said of him '. . . he left things alone – a sensible thing for an Irish secretary'. Campbell-Bannerman supported Gladstone on the latter's conversion to Home Rule.* He became Secretary of State for War, 1893–95. In 1899 he succeeded Sir William Harcourt as leader of the Liberal Party. He attacked the government over the handling of the Boer War, and was supported in his attack by David Lloyd George* and by the members of the Irish Parliamentary Party.* When the Conservative government of Arthur J. Balfour* fell in 1905, Campbell-Bannerman formed a Liberal administration and declared his support for Home Rule. Opposition came from within his own party, now no longer dependent upon the support of the Irish MPs because of their absolute majority in the general election of 1906. As an alternative to Home Rule, Campbell-Bannerman sought to introduce a system of devolved government through the Irish Council Bill.* This measure fell in the face of Unionist and Nationalist opposition. He was succeeded as leader of the party and Prime Minister by H. H. Asquith.*

CAMPBELL, JOSEPH (1879–1944). Poet; b. Belfast; ed. locally. An early contributor to the Ulster Literary Theatre and to *Uladh* (1904), he spent much of his time collecting Ulster traditional songs and setting them to music, the best-known of which is 'My Lagan Love'. He spent some time in London where he became secretary of the Irish National Literary Society.* Prior to the outbreak of World War I he returned to Ireland and settled in Wicklow. Campbell opposed the Treaty* and was an outspoken critic of the Free State government. After being interned for two years on the outbreak of the Civil War,* he emigrated to the USA in 1924 and worked at Fordham University. He returned to Ireland in 1935 and settled near Glencree, Co. Wicklow. His works include *The Garden of the Rose* (1905), *The Rush Light* (1906), *The Manchild* (1907), *Judgement* (play, 1912), and *Earth of Cualann* (1916). *The Poems of Joseph Campbell* was published in 1963.

CANE, DR ROBERT (1807–58). Physician and historian; b. Kilkenny; ed. Dublin; M.D. (1836). He practised medicine in Kilkenny where he was prominent in local politics, becoming mayor in 1844. Cane sympathised with Young Ireland* but refused to aid the rising planned by William Smith O'Brien* which he believed was doomed to failure. He founded the *Celtic Union* (1853) and edited *The Celt* (1857). He published the *History of the Williamite and Jacobite Wars* (1859).

CANTING. A system whereby a lease held by an Irish tenant farmer was auctioned to the highest bidder when it fell in, giving the former occupier of the property no right to it unless he could meet the highest bid. It was common during the eighteenth century and persisted into the early decades of the nineteenth, a source of great insecurity and hardship among the peasantry.

CANTWELL, JOHN (1792–1866). Bishop of Meath (R.C.), 1830–66;

b. Rahan, Co. Offaly; ed. Navan and Maynooth. He was an ardent supporter of Repeal and frequently addressed the monster meetings organised by Daniel O'Connell.* He also lent his support to the efforts of Charles Lucas* and Charles Gavan Duffy* in their efforts on behalf of the Tenant League.*

'CAPUCHIN ANNUAL'. Published by the Capuchin Friary in Dublin from 1930 to 1977, the *Capuchin Annual*'s contributors included leading writers and politicians. It had only two editors, Fr Senan and Fr Henry, under whom many of its articles reflected a strong nationalist flavour. Apart from fiction and verse, it published articles on theology, history, literature and art. The distinctive cover, 'St Francis and the Wolf', designed by Sean O'Sullivan, RHA, did not change throughout the years. Many *Annuals* became collector's items for their superb photographs, many previously unpublished, and the commissioned illustrations.

CARBERY, ETHNA (1866–1902). Poetess, and language enthusiast; real name, Anna Johnston; b. Ballymena, Co. Antrim. She was a leading member of the Irish revival in Belfast where she edited *Shan Van Vocht** (1896–99). She was a frequent contributor to *The Nation** and *United Ireland.** Her works include *The Passionate Hearts* (1903) and *In the Celtic Past* (1904). She is best known for her ballad 'Roddy MacCorley' and her volume of poetry, *The Four Winds of Eirinn,* which was published posthumously in 1902. Shortly before her death she married the writer Seamus MacManus.*

CARDERS. An agrarian secret society active in Connaught in the early nineteenth century. The Carders took their name from the mutilation they inflicted on their victims by digging a steel comb used for carding wool through their victims' flesh. *See also* Secret Societies.

CAREY, JAMES (1845–83). Informer; b. Dublin where he worked as a bricklayer. He became a leading member of the Invincibles* and was involved in the Phoenix Park Murders.* Carey turned informer and his evidence led to the execution of five of his associates. He was murdered on board the *Melrose Castle*, off Capetown, by a member of the Invincibles, Patrick O'Donnell.

CARLETON, HUGH (1739–1836). Judge; b. Cork; ed. TCD; Bar (1764). He achieved notoriety as the Judge who condemned the brothers Sheares in 1798. Lord Kilwarden's death at the hands of a mob during Emmet's rebellion (1803), was due to the crowd having mistaken him for Carleton.

CARLETON, WILLIAM (1794–1869). Novelist; b. Clogher, Co. Tyrone, the youngest of fourteen children; ed. hedge school.* When his family was evicted in 1813 he joined the Ribbonmen* for a brief period. Carleton aspired to the priesthood but had a failing for women and drink. He became a Protestant on marriage and taught at the Erasmus schools in Dublin and Mullingar. On his return to Dublin (1826) he was employed by Caesar Otway* on the *Christian Examiner* and contributed to *Dublin University Magazine*,* *The Nation** and the *Irish Tribune*. He was awarded a Civil List pension of £200 in 1848. His works include *Father Butler* (1829), *Traits and Stories of the Irish Peasantry* (5 vols, 1830–33), *Tales of Ireland* (1834), *Fardorougha the Miser* (1837 ?) *The Misfortunes of Barny Branagan* (1841), *Jane Sinclair* (3 vols, 1843), *Art Maguire* (1845), *Denis O'Shaughnessy Goes to Maynooth* (1845), *Tales and Sketches* (1845), *Valentine M'Clutchy* (7 vols, 1845–48), *Roddy the Rover* (1847), *The Emigrants of Ahadarra* (1847), *The Tithe Proctor* (1849), *The Clarionet and other tales* (1850), *The Squanders of Castle Squanders* (2 vols, 1852), *Willy Reilly and his Dear Colleen Bawn* (3

vols, 1855), *Alley Sheridan and other stories* (1857), *The Double Prophecy* (2 vols, 1862), *Redmond Count O'Hanlon* (1862), *Barney Brady's Goose* (1869), *The Poor Scholar* *(1869)*, *Tubber Derg* (1869), *The Evil Eye* (1880), *The Red-haired Man's Wife* (1889) and *Phil Purcell the Pig Driver* (1895). Carleton's biography was written by D. J. O'Donoghue (2 vols, 1896) and revised by Patrick Kavanagh* in 1968.

CARLISLE, 7th EARL (1802–64). Howard, George William Frederick; politician (Whig), known as Viscount Morpeth (1825–48); Chief Secretary (1835–41) and Lord Lieutenant (1855–58); b. London; ed. Eton and Christ Church, Oxford. MP for Morpeth from 1826, he supported the efforts of Sir Francis Burdett* to secure Catholic Emancipation* in the House of Commons. As Irish Chief Secretary in the second administration formed by Lord Melbourne,* Morpeth worked with the Lord Lieutenant, Lord Mulgrave,* and the Under-Secretary, Thomas Drummond,* to form one of the most constructive Irish governments since the Union. He carried the Irish Tithes Act which brought an end to the widespread agrarian discontent over payment of tithes,* the Irish Municipal Relief Act (*see* Municipal Corporations Act) and the Irish Poor Law Act (*see* Poor Law). A member of the cabinet from February 1839 until the fall of Melbourne's government in July 1841, he was defeated in the Dublin by-election in 1842. He succeeded to the title in 1848. His published works included *Eleusis* (1821), *Paestum* (1821), *The Last of the Greeks* (1828), *Diary in Turkish and Greek Waters* (1854) and *The Second Vision of Daniel* (1858).

CARNARVON, 4th EARL (1831–90). Herbert, Henry Howard Molyneux; politician (Conservative); Lord Lieutenant (1885); ed. Eton and Christ Church, Oxford. He was Under-Secretary for the Colonies

(1858–59) and Colonial Secretary from 1866–68. Carnarvon gave his support to the Liberal measures for the Disestablishment of the Church of Ireland* and to the Lands Acts of 1870 and 1881 (*see* Land Acts). He accepted office in Lord Salisbury's caretaker government as Lord Lieutenant. Carnarvon was committed in principle to a limited measure of self-government for Ireland but *not,* as Charles Stewart Parnell appeared to believe, to Home Rule.* Within a short time of his assuming office the Conservatives introduced the Ashbourne Act (*see* Land Acts) and a Labourers' Act. Carnarvon held a private meeting with Parnell on 1 August 1885 to exchange opinions on the Irish question. He made it clear to Parnell that while he (Carnarvon) would support limited powers for an elective assembly, he would not accept any measure which would interfere with the legislative Union.* Parnell left the meeting apparently satisfied that he had achieved unanimity with Carnarvon. During the debate on Home Rule in June 1886 Parnell claimed that Carnarvon had stated that he was prepared to accept self-government for Ireland. Carnarvon refuted Parnell's version of their meeting. In 1887 when the *Times* published the series 'Parnellism and Crime',* Carnarvon proposed a special parliamentary commission to investigate the allegations and this was granted in 1888.

'CARRICK'S MORNING POST'. Daily newspaper founded by Richard Lonergan in 1812. Despite the fact that the paper derived the greater portion of its revenue from advertising, it managed to maintain an independent stance and gave a measure of support to Catholic Emancipation.* Lonergan ran into difficulties with his staff in 1825 the first labour problems to affect an Irish newspaper, when he took on apprentices against the wishes of his unionised staff. The latter physically attacked him and his non-union staff. Circulation of the *Post*

dwindled until the paper was bought by the *Dublin Times** in 1832.

CARROLL, PAUL VINCENT. (1900–68). Schoolmaster and playwright; b. Dundalk. He taught school in Glasgow (1921–37) where he was co-founder and director of Glasgow Citizens' Theatre. Carroll wrote for the Abbey Theatre* and was the recipient of many domestic and international theatrical awards, including the New York Drama Critics' Award (1937, 1939). His works include *Shadow and Substance* (1934), *Things that are Caeser's* (1934), *The White Steed* (1938), *The Old Foolishness* (1940), *Three Plays* (1944), *Two Plays* (1948), *The Devil came from Dublin* (1952) and *Irish Stories and Plays* (1958).

CARROLL, DR WILLIAM (1835–1926). Fenian; b. Rathmullan, Co. Donegal. He emigrated to the USA in 1838 where he qualified as a doctor, becoming Surgeon-General to the Federal Army during the American Civil War (1861–65). After the War, he settled in Philadelphia where he practised medicine and became a member of Clan na Gael.* Carroll became a leader in opposition to James Stephens* within the Fenian movement and was elected Chairman of Clan na Gael (1875–80). He was an advocate of the New Departure* with Charles Stewart Parnell,* but later had reservations regarding Parnell's motives and withdrew his support. He continued, however, to support John Devoy* and Clan policies.

CARSON, SIR EDWARD, BARON CARSON OF DUNCAIRN (1854–1935). Lawyer and politician (Unionist Party); b. Dublin; ed. Portarlington and TCD; called to the Irish Bar in 1889, he was Irish Solicitor-General, 1892. Carson established a reputation for his vigorous prosecution of the government's fight against the Plan of Campaign.* He represented Dublin University as a Unionist

(1892–1918). He was called to the English Bar in 1892 and to the Inner Bar two years later. Carson earned an outstanding reputation at the Bar and was a prominent advocate in many famous trials of the era including *Wilde v. the Marquis of Queensbury* in 1895 in which he successfully represented Queensbury. As English Solicitor-General (1900–06) he was a prominent advocate in many anti-government legal battles. Carson supported the demand for a Catholic University and lent his support to the Irish Universities Act of 1908.* He was elected leader of the Irish Unionist Party* in 1910. He was totally opposed to Home Rule,* and in 1911 he told a gathering of 100,000 Unionists at Craigavon, near Belfast, that should Home Rule become law, they would resist it and establish their own government of Ulster. He accepted the Agar-Robertes' Proposal* for the exclusion of four Ulster counties, Antrim, Armagh, Derry and Down, although in 1913 he had looked for the exclusion of the entire province. Carson played an influential role in the War Cabinet until his resignation in January 1918 because of the naval and military strategies of David Lloyd George.* In December 1918 he was elected MP for the Duncairn division of Belfast. Carson suggested the Council of Ireland* which he described as 'the biggest advance towards unity in Ireland'. He resigned the leadership of the Unionist Party to become Lord of Appeal in London (1921) and was succeeded as leader by Sir James Craig (*see* Craigavon, Lord). His *Ireland and Home Rule* was published in 1919.

CARTY, JAMES (1901–59). Historian; b. Wexford. He became assistant librarian at the National Library where he compiled two bibliographies, *Bibliography of Irish History, 1912–21* (1936) and *Bibliography of Irish History, 1870–1912* (1940). His other works include *A Class-book of Irish history* (book I–IV, 1930–33), *A junior history of Ireland* (2

parts, 1932–33), *Stair na h-Éireann le h-aghaidh na Soisear* (cuid I–II, 1935–36), *European History* (3 parts, 1937–40). He edited *Ireland from the Flight of the Earls to Grattan's Parliament* (1944), *Ireland from Grattan's Parliament to the Great Famine* (1949) and *Ireland from the Great Famine to the Treaty* (1951).

CASEMENT, SIR ROGER (1864–1916). Civil servant and Irish nationalist; b. Sandycove, Dublin; reared in Co. Antrim. He entered the British Foreign Service (1892) where he earned an international reputation as a humanitarian for his reports on atrocities committed by European employers in the Belgian Congo (now Zaire) and later in Putamayo, South America. His service in the tropics undermined his health and he was awarded a knighthood before retiring from the service in 1913. During visits to Ireland he became interested in Irish nationalist movements. He joined the Gaelic League* and became a close friend of Bulmer Hobson,* Alice Stopford Green,* and Francis Joseph Bigger.* He joined the Irish Volunteers* in 1913 and became a member of the Provisional Committee. Through his influential London friends he raised money for the purchase of arms. During a visit to the USA in 1914 he made contact with the German Embassy through John Devoy* and Clan na Gael.* Casement travelled to Berlin in October 1914 where he was unsuccessful in his efforts to raise an Irish Brigade from among Irish prisoners-of-war. He was later joined in Germany by Robert Monteith.* While in Germany Casement suffered from poor health, probably aggravated by his failure to achieve progress with the German authorities in his quest for an adequate supply of arms for the Volunteers. He felt that the German grant of 20,000 guns was inadequate and decided to return to Ireland to prevent the proposed Easter Rising of 1916.* He sailed for Ireland aboard a U-boat and arrived with Monteith and Bailey, one of the fifty or so who had answered his call to an Irish Brigade, at Banna Strand on Good Friday, 20 April. Casement was captured and taken to Dublin and later to London where he was being interrogated when the Easter Rising of 1916 broke out. He was charged with high treason. His defence was organised by George Gavan Duffy* whose cousin, Serjeant A. M. Sullivan, undertook the brief. The prosecution was led by F. E. Smith, later Lord Birkenhead.* Casement was convicted and sentenced to death. During July, while attempts were made to organise a reprieve, copies of his diaries were circulated (with government knowledge). These, the so-called Black Diaries,* indicated that he was homosexual and their release at that time was calculated to dissuade influential people from supporting the campaign for his reprieve now being waged by his friends in London, among them George Bernard Shaw.* The circulation of the diaries had the anticipated effect and Casement was hanged at Pentonville jail on 3 August. In 1965 the British Labour Government under Harold Wilson gave permission for the return of his remains to Ireland and he was re-interred in Glasnevin Cemetery, Dublin.

CASEY, JOHN KEEGAN (1846–70). Poet; b. Mount Dalton, Co. Westmeath; ed. locally and Ballymahon, Co. Longford. He wrote most of his poetry in his teens, contributing to *The Nation* under the pen-name 'Leo'. Principal teacher at Cleraun and Keenagh schools, he gave up teaching to work for the Irish Republican Brotherhood* and was among those arrested in 1867. He was sentenced to seven years' penal servitude but was released from Mountjoy within the year, because of ill-health. His best-known poems are the 'The Rising of the Moon', 'Máire My Girl' (written to his wife, Mary Briscoe) and 'Donal Kenny'. His works include *A Wreath of Shamrocks* (1866) and *The Rising of the Moon* (1869). *The London Review*, commenting on the

latter, stated, 'Mr Casey puts treason in a fascinating and intelligent manner'.

CASTLE DOCUMENT. Published on 19 April 1916, the document appeared to have been issued by Dublin Castle.* It gave instructions for the suppression of the Irish Volunteers,* ordered the occupation of key areas suspected of harbouring sedition, and called also for the arrest of certain individuals. The document was in fact a forgery, the work of Joseph Plunkett* and Sean MacDiarmada,* with the intention of provoking more Volunteers to support the Easter Rising of 1916.* It was partly successful in its objective in that it moved moderate Volunteers, including Eoin MacNeill,* towards a more belligerent position.

CASTLEREAGH, VISCOUNT, AND 2nd MARQUESS OF LONDONDERRY (1769–1822). Stewart, Robert; politician (Conservative); b. Co. Down; ed. Royal School, Armagh and St John's College, Cambridge; MP, Co. Down (1790). In his earlier years a liberal, Castlereagh supported the ideas of the United Irishmen* but, appalled by the excesses of the French Revolution, he became a noted Conservative. He supported the Catholic Relief Act of 1793. Following his appointment as Keeper of the Privy Seal by Lord Camden he became an important member of the Irish government; in March 1798 he became acting Chief Secretary and replaced Thomas Pelham in the post the following November. The rising of the United Irishmen in the summer of 1798 convinced him, as it did William Pitt,* of the need for a legislative union of the parliaments of Ireland and Great Britain (*see* Union). Castlereagh became a key figure in securing this union. Assisted by Lord Clare* he dispensed largesse, patronage, sinecures and titles on an unprecedented scale until he had turned the narrow majority against union (111–106 in January 1799) into a sizeable majority in favour (158–115 on 6 February 1800). After the Union he continued to sit for Co. Down and his worth in the imperial parliament was recognised by Pitt who continued him in the post of Chief Secretary for Ireland. He was President of the Board of Control (1802) and at the War Department (1804–06). After Pitt's death he spent a year out of office but then returned to the War Department (1807–09) where he was responsible for supplying the future Duke of Wellington during the Peninsular War. He resigned office after fighting a duel with his arch-rival, George Canning. In February 1812 he returned to office, this time as Secretary for Foreign Affairs. He was Minister Plenipotentiary to the allied sovereigns after Napoleon's defeat (1814–15) and played a leading role in the restoration of the old order in Europe at the Congress of Vienna. He had a nervous breakdown as a result of overwork. During 1820–22 he underwent bouts of acute depression and finally took his life with a razor.

'CAT AND MOUSE ACT'. Popular name for Prisoners (Temporary Discharge for Health) Act, introduced in 1913. The Act was originally used as a tactic against the Suffragette Movement. It was later invoked against hunger-striking republicans as an alternative to forcible feeding. Prisoners were released on parole but under the terms of the Act could be returned to prison at any time – usually when recovered from their hunger-striking ordeals.

CATALPA. Whaling vessel, built in 1844, bought for 5,250 dollars by Clan na Gael* for the rescue of six Fenians, Thomas Darragh, Martin Hogan, Michael Harrington, Thomas Hasset, Robert Cranston and James Wilson, from Fremantle on 17 April 1876. The rescue was planned by John Devoy* and John J. Breslin.* The Clan spent some 13,760 dollars equipping the vessel, which was 202 tons net, ninety foot long, twenty-five foot wide and twelve foot deep, for a whaling expedition. Only Captain George S. Anthony and one of his crew, Denis Duggan, a Fenian agent, knew the true purpose of the voyage. As it happened, they discovered that two members of the Irish Republican Brotherhood,* Denis Florence McCarthy and John Walsh* (later suspected of involvement in the assassination of Lord Frederick Cavendish)* were in Fremantle with an independent plan to rescue Fenians. On learning of the *Catalpa's* purpose, they agreed to co-operate with the Clan. On the morning of the rescue attempt, *Catalpa* hove-to in international waters off Fremantle. Captain Anthony took a whaling boat from the ship which was left to the command of the first mate, Samuel Smith (who had only recently become acquainted with the purpose of the voyage). The rescue went smoothly but while they were returning to the ship, a British naval cutter, *The Georgette*, attempted to put a boarding party on the *Catalpa*. This was resisted by Smith. Two days later, the *Catalpa* was again intercepted but although shots were fired across her bows *The Georgette's* captain decided against boarding the Fenian ship which was now flying the American colours. The rescued Fenians were landed at New York harbour at 2 a.m., on 19 August 1876. Captain Anthony received 3,166 dollars (which included a 1,000 dollars bonus) and Smith received 1,644 dollars which included a bonus of 200 dollars.

CATHOLIC ASSOCIATION. The Catholic Association of Ireland was the last in a line of movements which sought to secure Catholic Emancipation.* A Catholic Committee* had been revived in 1805 to press for full Emancipation; this committee included Daniel O'Connell. Government pressure forced the Committee to dissolve in 1812 and re-constitute as the Catholic Board* which in turn was harassed by the government. The Catholic Board was dissolved in 1814 and was re-established in 1823 by O'Connell and Richard Lalor Sheil* as the Catholic Association of Ireland. This Association broke with the aristocratic leadership of the past when in 1824 O'Connell allowed associate membership at the rate of one penny per month. This harnessed popular support and 'The Catholic Rent', as it became known, turned the Association into a mass movement: the rent, which earned for O'Connell the title of 'King of the Beggars', was collected at church doors all over the country every Sunday and within a year was bringing in £1,000 per month. The Association bridged class divisions, numbering among its supporters businessmen, professionals, tradesmen, small farmers, urban workers, priests, rural peasants and cottiers.* It became the first organised mass movement in Irish history to use constitutional methods. The method followed by O'Connell and Sheil was 'Agitation';* O'Connell's addresses to huge meetings were an integral part of the agitation. When the Association was suppressed by the government in 1825 O'Connell resorted to a favourite device and renamed it the New Catholic Association. The Association won its first victory in Waterford when Thomas Wyse* and a local Committee secured the election of Villiers Stuart* against the powerful Lord George Beresford (1826). This victory demonstrated the potential of the movement. Waterford also demonstrated a discipline and order among the electorate unique in an election of that period. Further successes followed: the Association returned a candidate in each of the by-elections in Louth, Monaghan and Westmeath. The culmination of the fight for Emancipation was the Clare by-election where O'Connell defeated the government candidate, William Vesey-Fitzgerald.* This latest victory made it clear that Emancipation could no longer be denied and, as the Duke of Wellington* and Sir Robert Peel* set about it, the Association dissolved itself (12 February 1829). *See also* Catholic Emancipation.

CATHOLIC ASSOCIATIONS (BELFAST AND DUBLIN).

Belfast
The Belfast Catholic Association was founded by the Bishop of Down and Connor (R.C.), Dr Henry Henry, as a local political machine in 1896. Dr Henry opposed the United Irish League* which became the official organisation of the Irish Parliamentary Party* under John Redmond* in 1900. Henry's attitude towards the UIL lost him support among his own clergy and, realising his failure, he consented to the disintegration of the BCA in 1905.

Dublin
The Dublin Catholic Association was founded in 1902 following the publication of an article in *The Irish Rosary*. The Association's first president was Edward Martyn.* The movement was supported by the *Irish Independent* and the *Irish Catholic,* both owned by William Martin Murphy.* Its purpose was to highlight anti-Catholic discrimination in employment. Although individual members of the Catholic hierarchy gave it support the Association lacked official approval. A Society for the Protection of Protestant Interests was founded in 1903, and in 1904 the Archbishop of Dublin (R.C.), William Walsh* warned that the existence of the DCA could be counter-productive in that it might lead to a Protestant boycott of Catholic businesses. The movement did not survive this warning.

CATHOLIC BOARD. The Board was a revival in 1812 of the Catholic Committee* which had been harassed by the Irish government under the Convention Act of 1793. The Board, which sought to continue the fight for Catholic Emancipation,* was immediately plunged into crisis by the revival of the Veto scheme. The struggle was between the aristocratic element led by Lord Fingall* who supported the Veto and the populist element led by Daniel O'Connell* who, with the support of the hierarchy, opposed it. This resulted in a victory for the anti-Vetoists but, coupled with government pressure, destroyed the Board which was dissolved in June 1814. The Catholic Committee-Board was resurrected as a popular movement by O'Connell and Richard Lalor Sheil* in 1823 as the Catholic Association.*

CATHOLIC BOY SCOUTS OF IRELAND (GASÓGA CATOLLICI NA hÉIREANN). The CBSI was founded in Dublin in 1927 by a Catholic priest, Fr Farrell. Its patrons are the members of the hierarchy and the organisation is divided on a diocesan, regional and parish basis. CBSI has 24,000 members and is a member of the Federation of Irish Scout Associations which is affiliated to the World Scout Conference. *See also* Scout Association of Ireland.

CATHOLIC COMMITTEE. The first Catholic Committee founded in 1760 was dissolved in 1793 following the passage of the Catholic Relief Act. The Committee was revived in 1805 and had a strong aristocratic flavour led by Lords Fingall and Kenmare, who lost much of their influence, however, when they supported the Veto.* The initiative now passed to the rising Catholic middle-class led by Daniel O'Connell.* By 1811 the government had become alarmed at the boldness of O'Connell's leadership and in February of that year the Convention Act of 1793 was invoked. This Act declared that 'the election or appointment of assemblies purporting to represent the people, or any description or number of the people of this realm, under pretence of preparing or presenting petitions ...' was illegal. An Emancipation Bill was introduced during 1812 and was defeated in committee. It had included the Veto which was opposed by O'Connell and the Catholic bishops. Prominent Committee members, including Fingall, were imprisoned during 1812 and the Com-

mittee dissolved to be reconstituted as the Catholic Board.*

CATHOLIC DEFENCE ASSOCIATION. Founded in Dublin in August 1851, by prominent members of the 'Irish Brigade',* George Henry Moore* and John Sadleir.* The CDA was intended to act as a permanent agency for the publication of Catholic grievances, but enjoyed rather limited success.

CATHOLIC EMANCIPATION (1829). Emancipation meant the right of Catholics to sit as MPs without having to subscribe to the Oath of Supremacy. Catholics were also virtually excluded from a wide range of public offices. Emancipationists sought equality between Catholic and Protestants in public life, the law and the army. Thomas Wyse* calculated that out of a total of 2,062 offices connected with the administration of justice in Ireland at that time (1828), 2,023 were filled by Protestants and thirty-nine by Catholics. The call for Emancipation towards the end of the eighteenth century had been ignored by George III* who believed that removal of the Oath of Supremacy would be in conflict with his coronation oath. The Catholic Committee* and the Catholic Board* failed to make any headway. After George's death in 1820, the new King, George IV,* in his earlier years pro-Emancipationist, proved as scrupulous as his father had been. An organised fight for Emancipation was undertaken by Daniel O'Connell* and Richard Lalor Sheil* for which purpose they founded the Catholic Association* in 1823. This Association attracted a support unparalleled in Irish history, and secured a series of election victories at Waterford, Louth, Monaghan, Westmeath and Clare. Following these successes, it became apparent to both the Duke of Wellington* and Sir Robert Peel* that Emancipation was inevitable and they applied pressure to George IV who eventually conceded. The Bill was prepared by Peel in March and steered through the Lords by Wellington, becoming law in April. In addition to Emancipation, which allowed O'Connell to take his seat, Peel curbed the power of the Catholic Association by disenfranchising the Forty-Shilling Freeholders* who had been the mainstay of the movement, by raising the qualification for franchise to a £10 valuation.

CATHOLIC EMANCIPATION CENTENARY (1929). To mark the centenary of Catholic Emancipation,* 1929 was assigned a year of National Celebration in Ireland. A one hundred and twenty-nine member committee was formed in Dublin to organise a week-long programme culminating in Pontifical High Mass and Solemn Eucharistic Procession at Phoenix Park on Sunday 23 June. The ceremonies were attended by international dignitaries of Church and State. His Holiness Pope Pius XI was specially represented by Monsignor Pisani, Archbishop of Constantia.

In its report on the final day's ceremonies the London *Times* commented '...Accommodation in the "Fifteen Acres" (Phoenix Park) had been arranged for 240,000 people, but it is estimated that more than 300,000 persons were present when Mass began at midday. The organisation was excellent. Every parish had its own section, and the presence of 10,000 stewards facilitated grouping to such an extent that there was no overcrowding and every member of the vast concourse was in his or her place when Mass began . . .'

The Centenary Celebrations afforded religious and civil authorities a unique experience in organisation and crowd control which was seen to good effect when the International Eucharistic Congress* was held in Dublin some three years later.

CATHOLIC RENT. *See* Catholic Association.

CATHOLIC UNION. Formed by Cardinal Paul Cullen* in 1872 in an effort to win support from the Home Government Association* led by Isaac Butt.* It was a total failure.

CATHOLIC UNIVERSITY OF IRELAND. Established under papal authority in 1854 to provide higher education for Catholics. John Henry Newman* accepted an invitation from the Archbishop of Dublin, Paul Cullen,* to become rector of the new university. Other academic posts were held by Gerard Manley Hopkins and Eugene O'Curry.* Cullen and Newman differed on the concept of the new university: Newman wished to provide a liberal education while Cullen sought a college which would provide the Catholic middle-class with an Irish Catholic education. The experiment was a failure because the Catholic University was not empowered to grant degrees. The University Act of 1879 attempted a solution by establishing an examining body, the Royal University,* which was empowered to grant degrees to any students who possessed the necessary standards. Fellowships of the Royal were distributed so as to provide an endowment in the region of £6,000 per annum to the Catholic University. While this was not wholly to the bishops' satisfaction it did enable Catholic students to graduate without attending Trinity College Dublin. As University College, the Catholic University was administered by the Society of Jesus from 1883 until it became a college of the National University of Ireland* in 1908.

CATTLE DRIVING. Term used for the empoundment of cattle owned by an Irish tenant in arrears with his rent. His cattle were driven to the nearest town and held there until the arrears were paid off.

CATTLE 'THATCHING'. Farmers occupying the poorer lands, such as those in Connaught barely existed at subsistence level. To overcome the lack of farm buildings or shelters for the cattle, farmers resorted to the covering or 'thatching' of individual cattle with straw to protect them in times of severe frost or snow.

CAVENDISH, LORD FREDERICK (1836–82). Politician (Liberal); b. Eastbourne, Sussex; ed. privately and at Trinity College, Cambridge. Cavendish was MP for the Northern Division of Yorkshire West Riding (1865–82) and was private secretary to W. E. Gladstone* (1872–73). He was appointed Chief Secretary for Ireland in May 1882 in succession to W. E. Forster* who had resigned in protest at the Kilmainham 'Treaty'.* Cavendish arrived in Ireland on 6 May 1882 and while walking that evening with T. H. Burke* in the Phoenix Park, Dublin, was murdered by the Invincibles.* *See* Phoenix Park Murders.

CEANN COMHAIRLE. Chairman of Dail Eireann.* The Ceann Comhairle of the first Dail Eireann was Sean T. O'Kelly* (1919–20), who was succeeded by Eoin MacNeill,* Ceann Comhairle during the Treaty debates. His successors in the office were Michael Hayes* (1922–32), Frank Fahy (1932–51), Patrick Hogan (1951–67), Cormac Breslin (1967–73), Sean Treacy (1973–77) and Joseph Brennan (1977–80). His deputy is known as the Leas Ceann Comhairle.

CEANNT, EAMONN (1881–1916). Republican; b. Ballymore, Co. Galway where his father had been a member of the RIC; ed. locally and North Richmond St CBS, Dublin, Ceannt worked as a clerk in the Treasury department of Dublin Corporation. He took a keen interest in the activities of the Gaelic League* which he joined in 1900. A skilled piper, he founded the Dublin Pipers Club and shortly afterwards (1911) played the uileann pipes in private audience to Pope Pius X. Having joined Sinn Fein* in 1908 Ceannt was inducted into the Irish Republican Brotherhood* by Sean Mac-Diarmada* (1913) and became a member of the Supreme Council* in

1915. A founder-member of the Irish Volunteers,* Ceannt, as Captain, 'A' Company, Fourth Battalion, assisted in the Howth Gun-running.* One of the seven signatories to the Easter Proclamation (*see* Easter Rising of 1916) he commanded the South Dublin Union area during the fighting. On the eve of his execution (7 May) from cell 88 in Kilmainham he wrote, '...I bear no ill will towards those against whom I have fought. I have found the common soldiers and the higher officers human and companionable, even the English who were actually in the fight against us. Thank God soldiering for Ireland has opened my heart and made me see poor humanity where I expected to see only scorn and reproach....'

CELTIC LITERARY SOCIETY. Founded by William Rooney* (first chairman) from the Leinster Literary Society in October 1893 with the objective of studying the Irish language, history, literature and music. The political policy of the CLS was 'independent action'. Membership included John O'Leary,* Frank Hugh O'Donnell and Arthur Griffith.* The exclusively male Society held weekly meetings at which debates and readings were held and maintained a manuscript journal, *An Seanachie.* Branches of the CLS were later absorbed by Cumann na nGaedheal* (1900).

CELTIC SOCIETY. Founded in 1845, the Society was devoted to the preservation of early Irish manuscripts and their publication. It was largely supported by academics and lacked popular support. The Society was the precursor of the Gaelic League* in its aims. It merged with the Irish Archaeological Society (founded in 1840) to become the Irish Archaeological and Celtic Society of which Prince Albert became Patron.

CENSORSHIP BOARD. The Board, consisting of five members appointed by the Minister for Justice, was appointed in 1930 under the Censorship of Publications Act (1926). It was empowered to recommend to the Minister works which it considered should be prohibited from sale in Ireland. In its zeal, the Board caused bans to be placed on some books of nearly every major Irish writer of the first half of this century, and on the works of most of the winners of the Nobel Prize for Literature. The terms of the Act were amended in 1946 to allow for appeals. The amendment also gave authority to Customs Officers to seize any literature which they considered infringed on the Act. A further amendment of 1967 allowed a reconsideration of all banned works, many of which were then allowed on sale and some of which were subjected to a further ban. Under this amendment a book is banned for a maximum of twelve years.

CENSORSHIP OF FILMS ACT. This Act of 1923 established a censorship board to examine films offered for commercial distribution in Ireland. The Act was in response to demands from religious and concerned lay bodies which pointed out to the government the necessity to guard against 'the dangers and actual evils arising out of the whole system of cinema shows in the picture houses of Dublin and of the country'. A Film Appeals Board was established in 1964.

CENTENARY CELEBRATIONS, 1898. 1898 marked the centenary of the rising of the United Irishmen.* A Committee was set up to co-ordinate the activities of the various bodies established throughout the country to celebrate the centenary. Among the clubs which were founded to this end were The Wolfe Tone Clubs, Fr Murphy Clubs, Oliver Bond Clubs, Lord Edward Fitzgerald Clubs, Napper Tandy Clubs, Sheares Brothers Clubs, etc. Nationalists, moderates and extreme republicans combined with literary and other figures in arranging the celebrations. Prominent among the activists were Maud Gonne,* John MacBride,* James Connolly* and William Butler Yeats.* The event was celebrated in USA, Australia and in South Africa.

CENTRAL BOARD. Sometimes called an Irish Board, the 'Central Board' scheme was put forward during 1884—85 by Joseph Chamberlain* who also called it a 'National Council'. It was part of his strategy to prevent Home Rule* for Ireland. Negotiations with Charles Stewart Parnell* on the scheme were conducted through Captain W. H. O'Shea* who led Chamberlain to believe that Parnell regarded the scheme as an acceptable solution to the Irish demand for self-government. This was not true, as the Board would have had very limited control and would have allowed only a small measure of local government, in such areas as land, communications and education, etc. Cardinal Manning assured Chamberlain that the Board would be acceptable to the Irish Catholic hierarchy. In May 1885 the Cabinet vetoed the Board idea. This rejection of his scheme increased Chamberlain's determination to destroy Home Rule.

CENTRAL COUNCIL OF THE REPUBLIC. *See* Comhairle na Poblachta.

CENTRE. Title for the head of a Circle of the Irish Republican Brotherhood.* The Centre held the rank of Colonel and theoretically he commanded 820 men. The first Head Centre or Chief Organiser of the IRB was James Stephens.*

CENTRE PARTY. *See* National Centre Party.

'CHALK SUNDAY'. In rural Ireland the last Sunday before the beginning of Lent was known as Chalk Sunday. It was customary on that day to make two chalk marks on the clothes of local bachelors to remind them that there were only two days left in which to get married.

CHAMBERLAIN, ARTHUR NEVILLE (1869–1940). Politician (Conservative); Prime Minister (1937–40); second son of Joseph Chamberlain;* ed. Rugby and Mason College, Birmingham; Mayor of Birmingham (1915–16); Director-General of National Service (1916–17); MP, Ladywood, Birmingham (1918–29), Edgbaston (1920–40); Postmaster-General (1922–28), Paymaster-General (1928); Minister of Health (1923, 1924–29, 1931); Chancellor of the Exchequer (1923–24; 1931–37). He succeeded Stanley Baldwin* as Prime Minister in 1937 and in 1938 reached an agreement with Eamon de Valera* which brought the Economic War* to an end. His policy of appeasement with Hitler and Mussolini subsequently damaged his political reputation. Chamberlain was forced out of office after the outbreak of World War II and succeeded by his severest critic, Sir Winston Churchill.* He was the author of *The Struggle for Peace* (1939).

CHAMBERLAIN, JOSEPH (1836–1914). Politician (Liberal and Liberal Unionist); b. Birmingham. He was a leading Birmingham industrialist and local politician, earning the popular title 'Radical Joe' for his work for local reform in sanitation and working-class housing. He was Mayor of Birmingham (1873–75) and MP, Birmingham (1876–85) and Birmingham West (1885–1914). In the negotiations leading to the Kilmainham 'Treaty',* he was an intermediary through Captain W. H. O'Shea* between W. E. Gladstone* and Charles Stewart Parnell* (April-May 1882). Chamberlain was a staunch imperialist and he opposed Home Rule* for Ireland, believing that it would herald the break-up of the Empire and Britain's world role. During 1884–85 he worked out a 'Central Board'* scheme for Ireland and was led by O'Shea to believe, wrongly, that Parnell would consider it as a settlement to Irish nationalist demands. He led the Liberal Unionists

against the Gladstonian Liberals and Home Rule. For the remainder of his career he continued to oppose Home Rule. He became a leading social-imperialist and tariff reformer.

'CHANGEDALE'. A feature of the Rundale* landholding system. The system allowed for a rotation of individual portions of land held by tenants to ensure that everyone shared both the good and bad holdings.

CHESTER BEATTY LIBRARY. The Chester Beatty Library at Shrewsbury Road, Dublin, was established in 1953 to house the priceless collection of Islamic and Oriental art and manuscripts bequeathed to Ireland by Sir Alfred Chester Beatty (1875–1968). Beatty, who became the first honorary citizen of Ireland, was born in New York where he attended the Westminister School, Dobb's Ferry. He completed his education at the Columbia Mining School and Princeton. By pioneering a new method of extracting copper from low-grade ore he made a fortune from international mining operations. He was sufficiently wealthy by 1913 to indulge his passion for oriental manuscripts of which he later had the largest private collection in the world. He specialised in miniatures and outstanding examples of calligraphy which are available in the Dublin Library.

CHICHESTER-CLARK, MAJOR JAMES DAWSON, LORD MOYOLA (1923–) Politician (Ulster Unionist) and Prime Minister, Northern Ireland, (1969–71); b. Castledawson, Co. Londonderry; ed. Eton; commissioned in the Irish Guards, he served in the Army Staff College. After retiring from the army in 1960 he was elected to the seat in South Derry vacated by his grandmother, Dame Dehra Parker.* He became Assistant Whip of the Ulster Unionist Party (1963), Chief Whip (1963–69), Leader of the House (1966–67) and Minister for Agriculture (1967–69). The attempted reforms of his cousin, Captain Terence O'Neill,* provoked his resignation from the government (23 April 1969) and helped to bring about O'Neill's own resignation (28 April). He then became leader of the party and the new Prime Minister. When violence erupted in Belfast in August 1969, he requested, and was granted, British troops. On 29 August the Home Secretary, James Callaghan, promised reforms in response to demands by the Northern Ireland Civil Rights Association.* Chichester-Clark proved unable to contain violence which erupted during 1970 between the Irish Republican Army* and Protestant paramilitaries. He was severely criticised by Rev. Ian Paisley* who demanded stronger action against the IRA. As the situation continued to deteriorate, Chichester-Clark requested more troops and when this was denied him in full, he resigned on 20 March. He was succeeded by Brian Faulkner.*

CHIEF SECRETARY. The Chief Secretary to the Lord Lieutenant* was the effective head of the Irish executive after the Union. With the Lord Lieutenant he was responsible for implementing United Kingdom Cabinet policy in relation to Ireland. He defended Irish policy in parliament and was responsible for the Irish Civil Service which was supervised by his Under-Secretary.* Although his office in Dublin Castle* was the centre of British administration in Ireland, the Chief Secretary spent the parliamentary year at Westminster and worked from the Irish Office* in London. Throughout the nineteenth century the Chief Secretary's office assumed an increasingly wide range of power and by the end of the century he controlled nearly all patronage in Ireland, the Royal Irish Constabulary,* the Dublin Metropolitan Police,* the General Registry Office, the General Prisons Board and the Crime Branch Special (the intelligence division of British administration in Ireland). He was *ex officio* president of the Local Government Board and the Department of Agriculture and Technical Instruction* and also sat on the Congested Districts Board* and on various charitable boards. The following is a list of Chief Secretaries from 1800 to 1922:

1800 Lord Castlereagh*
1801 Charles Abbot
1802 William Wickham
1804 Sir Evan Nepean
1805 Sir Nicholas Vansittart
1805 Charles Lang
1806 William Elliot
1807 Arthur Wellesley (*see* Wellington, Duke of)
1809 William Wellesley-Pole*
1812 Sir Robert Peel*
1818 Charles Grant*
1821 Henry Goulbourn*
1827 William Lamb (*see* Melbourne, Viscount)
1828 Francis Levenson Gower
1830 Sir Henry Hardinge
1830 Lord Stanley (*see* Derby, 14th Earl)
1833 Sir John Cam Hobhouse
1833 Edward John Littleton*
1834 Sir Henry Hardinge
1835 Viscount Morpeth (*see* Carlisle, 7th Earl)
1841 Lord Eliot (*see* St Germans, 3rd Earl)
1845 Baron Cottosloe*
1846 Earl of Lincoln
1846 Henry Labouchere*
1847 Sir William Somerville*
1852 Lord Naas (*see* Mayo, 6th Earl)
1853 Sir John Young
1855 Edward Horsman
1857 Henry A. Herbert
1858 Lord Naas
1859 Edward Cardwell
1861 Sir Robert Peel
1865 Chichester Fortescue-Parkinson*
1866 Lord Naas
1868 Lord Winmarleigh
1868 Lord Carlingford'
1870 Marquis of Hartington (*see* Devonshire, 8th Duke)
1874 Sir Michael E. Hicks-Beach*
1878 James Lowther*
1880 W. E. Forster*
1882 Lord Frederick Cavendish*
1882 Sir G. O. Trevelyan*
1884 Henry Campbell-Bannerman*

1885 Sir W. Hart Dyke
1886 W. H. Smith
1886 John Morley*
1886 Sir M. E. Hicks-Beach
1887 Arthur J. Balfour*
1891 William Lawless Jackson
1892 John Morley
1895 Gerald W. Balfour*
1900 George Wyndham*
1905 Walter Hume Long*
1905 James Bryce*
1907 Augustine Birrell*
1916 H. E. Duke
1918 Edward Shortt
1919 Ian Macpherson
1920 Sir Hamar Greenwood*

CHILDERS, ERSKINE HAMILTON (1905–75). Politician (Fianna Fail); President of Ireland (1973–75). He was the son of Robert Erskine Childers;* ed. Norfolk and Trinity College, Cambridge. After working as European manager of a Chicago-based travel agency (1928–31) he became advertising manager of *The Irish Press** (1931–36); he was then secretary of the Federation of Irish Manufacturers (1936–44). He was Parliamentary Secretary to the Minister for Local Government (1944–48), Minister for Posts and Telegraphs (1951–54), Minister for Lands, Forestry and Fisheries (1957–59), Minister for Transport and Power (1959–66), Minister for Transport and Power and Posts and Telegraphs (1966–69), and Tanaiste and Minister for Health (1969–73). He succeeded Eamon de Valera as President in 1973 and died in office two years later.

CHILDERS, HUGH CULLING EARLEY (1827–96). Politician (Liberal) and Chancellor of the Exchequer (1882–85); ed. Cambridge. He worked for some years as an education inspector in Australia. Upon his return to England he became a Liberal MP and was a close adviser to W. E. Gladstone.* As Chancellor of the Exchequer he supported Home Rule* for Ireland. The budget which he introduced in 1885 imposed tax and duties on beer and spirits and led to the defeat of the government. Upon Gladstone's return to office (January 1886) he became Home Secretary, again supporting Home Rule. He was chairman of the Royal Commission established in 1896 to investigate financial relations between England and Ireland; the Commission's Report suggested that Ireland had been consistently overtaxed during the Union, a finding which led to the foundation of the All-Ireland Committee.*

CHILDERS, ROBERT ERSKINE (1870–1922). Politician (Sinn Fein) and author; b. in England but reared at Glendalough, Co. Wicklow, at the home of his cousin, Robert Barton;* ed. Haileybury and Trinity College, Cambridge. He worked as Committee Clerk of the House of Commons (1894–1910). While serving during the Boer War he was wounded. In July 1914 he used his yacht, the *Asgard,** to ferry arms purchased by Darrell Figgis* from the North Sea to Howth (*see* Howth Gun-running). He served in the Royal Navy air force in 1916 and was awarded the D.S.O. During 1917–18, he was a member of the secretariat of the Irish Convention.* After settling in Ireland in 1919 he became totally committed to the republican cause and was elected to Dail Eireann* for Kildare-Wicklow. He succeeded Desmond FitzGerald* as Director of Publicity and editor of the republican propaganda paper, *The Irish Bulletin.** He was a member of the secretariat to the negotiating team which went to London in October 1921 for the Treaty* discussions. He strongly opposed the Treaty and supported the republicans during the Civil War* when he was Director of Publicity and editor of *The Republic of Ireland.* While visiting Barton's home he was arrested by Provisional Government* troops in November 1922. He was in possession of a revolver which had been presented to him by his former comrade, Michael Collins.* He was tried *in camera* under recent legislation which made possession of a revolver a capital offence and was sentenced to death (17 November). He was executed ten days later while an appeal was pending in the High Court. His was the first of a series of republican executions. Childers was the author of *The Riddle of the Sands* (1903), *War and the Arme Blanche* (1910), *The Framework of Home Rule* (1911), *Military Rule in Ireland* (1920), and *The Constructive Works of Dail Eireann* (1921).

CHILDREN'S LAND LEAGUE. In 1881 a Children's Land League was established by the Land League* and the Ladies' Land League.* The entire movement was outlawed in October 1881. Members of the Children's Land League were taught the following 'alphabet':

A is the army that covers the ground;
B is the buckshot we're getting all round;
C is the crowbar of cruellest fame;
D is our Davitt, a right glorious name;
E is the English who've robbed us of bread;
F is the famine they've left us instead;
G is for Gladstone, whose life is a lie;
H is the harvest we'll hold or we'll die;
I is the inspector, who when drunk is bold;
J is the jarvey, who'll not drive him for gold;
K is Kilmainham, where our true men abide;
L is the Land League, our hope and our pride;
M is the magistrate, who makes black of our white;
N is no rent, which will make our wrongs right;
O is Old Ireland, that yet shall be free'd;
P is the Peelers, who've sold her for greed;
Q is the Queen, whose use is not known;
R is the Rifles, who keep up her throne;
S is the sheriff, with woe in his train;
T is the toil that others may gain;
U is the Union that works bitter harm;
V is the villain that grabs up a farm;
W is the warrant for death or for chains;
X is the 'Express', all lies and no brains;
Y is 'Young Ireland', spreading the light;
Z is the zeal that will win the great fight.

CHOTAH, THE. Yacht, owned by Sir Thomas Myles,* which took part of the consignment of German arms purchased by Darrell Figgis* on behalf of the Irish Volunteers.* The *Chotah* received the guns from Conor O'Brien's yacht, the *Kelpie,* and had orders to land them at Kilcoole, Co. Wicklow on the same day (26 July) as the *Asgard,* owned by Robert Erskine Childers* landed the remaining part of the consignment at Howth (*see* Howth Gun-running). The *Chotah,* however, having taken aboard the arms from *Kelpie,* had a breakdown and did not deliver her cargo until 1 August.

CHRISTUS REX. Catholic clerical organisation founded in 1941 by Rev. Dr Cornelius Lucey, Professor of Ethics at Maynooth College* (later Bishop of Cork). Under the chairmanship of Dr Cathal B. Daly (Bishop of Ardagh and Clonmacnoise from 1967), the purpose of Christus Rex was to study social issues from a Catholic viewpoint.

CHURCH EDUCATION SOCIETY. A denominational society founded within the Church of Ireland in 1839 because of dissatisfaction with the system of National Education* established in 1831 by E. G. Stanley (*see* Derby, 14th Earl). The Society advocated free use of the bible in class and made no distinction between religious and literary training. In 1831 the Society had 825 schools with an enrolment of 43,627 students, 10,868 of whom were Catholics. Enrolment reached a peak in 1848 with 120,202 pupils. Sir Robert Peel* refused to allow separate grants for the Society in 1845 and the burden on the Society was considerable. The number of schools gradually fell from 1,885 in 1851 to 1,202 in 1870, in which year the Society was dissolved and its schools joined the National Education system.

CHURCHILL, LORD RANDOLPH HENRY SPENCER (1849–95). Politician (Conservative); b. Blenheim Palace, third son of the 7th Duke of Marlborough;* ed. privately and at Cheam, Eton and in Austria. He was Conservative MP for Woodstock from 1874. He made frequent visits to Ireland while his father was Lord Lieutenant (1876–80). While urging a policy of conciliation, Churchill opposed Home Rule,* the Kilmainham 'Treaty'* and the alliance between the Liberals and the Irish nationalists under Charles Stewart Parnell.* During one of his many speeches to the House on Irish affairs, he opposed the extension of the Crimes Act to Ireland. He was instrumental in arranging the Tory-Nationalist entente of 1885 which secured the Irish party's support against the Liberals in return for the dropping of Coercion.* With the announcement of Gladstone's conversion to Home Rule after the Hawarden Kite,* and Parnell's switch of support to the Liberals, Churchill made a positive move against Home Rule. On 23 February 1886 he spoke in Belfast using the slogan 'Ulster will fight; Ulster will be right', which became the watchword of Orangement and Unionists. He promised help, if required, from England, claiming that the fight against Home Rule was in reality a fight to defend the Empire. With the Liberals' failure to carry Home Rule, the Conservatives returned to power and Churchill was appointed Chancellor of the Exchequer and leader of the House of Commons (July 1886). He promised a general inquiry into affairs in Ireland as a result of which certain reforms were granted, including smallholdings for agricultural labourers, land transfers and land purchases. Churchill resigned his office on 23 December 1886 on the passing of the army and navy estimates, which he considered excessive.

CHURCHILL, SIR WINSTON LEONARD SPENCER (1874–1965). Politician (Liberal and Conservative); Prime Minister (1940–45; 1951–55); eldest son of Lord Randolph Churchill;* ed. Harrow and Sandhurst. Following an early career as a soldier in Cuba, India and the Sudan he was a war correspondent during the Boer War. He entered politics as a Conservative (1900–05) and then sat as a Liberal (1906–08), Conservative Liberal (1908–22) and Conservative (1924–65). He held various offices between 1905 and 1911 when he became First Lord of the Admiralty (until 1915). He supported Home Rule* for Ireland and arrived in Belfast in 1912 but had to speak in a field when he was denied the use of the Ulster Hall by hostile Unionists.* After Gallipoli (1915) he was replaced at the Admiralty and became Minister for Munitions (1917). As Secretary for the Colonies and Chairman of the cabinet commission on Irish affairs, Churchill played a leading role in the negotiations which led to the Treaty* (October–December 1921). He was adamant that Britain should hold ports in Ireland for defence purposes. Later (15 December) he defended the Treaty on the grounds that the reconquest of Ireland by force would have involved a costly campaign once the Truce* had been signed and that it would require the extension of martial law to the entire twenty-six counties. In 1922 he was responsible for the transfer of services to the Provisional Government* and the evacuation of Ireland by the British armed forces. He organised the meetings between Sir James Craig (*see* Craigavon, Lord) and Michael Collins* (January–March 1922) which led to the Craig-Collins Agreements.* While defending the Provisional Government in the Commons he put pressure on Collins to dislodge republicans from the Four Courts (*see* Civil War). He steered the

Irish Free State (Agreement) Bill, ratifying the Treaty, through the Commons in 1922. On 19 March 1926 he signed the Ultimate Financial Agreement* with the Free State's Minister for Finance, Ernest Blythe.* The question of the 'Treaty ports' for which he fought in 1921 came up again in 1938 and he unsuccessfully fought against their being returned to Eire. Churchill succeeded Neville Chamberlain* as Prime Minister (10 May 1940) and headed the coalition war cabinet until July 1945. He was unsuccessful in his attempts to secure from Eamon de Valera* the abandonment of Eire's neutrality, offering as an inducement an implied promise to recognise the principle of Irish unity when the war ended. His carping reference to the Irish neutrality policy in his victory speech provoked one of de Valera's most famous speeches (*see* de Valera). He was again Prime Minister from 1951 until 1955. His *The World Crisis: The Aftermath* (1929) contains his observations on Ireland's struggle for independence. He was awarded the Nobel Prize for Literature in 1953.

CINEMA IN IRELAND. The first films shown in Ireland were by the Lumieres at Dan Lowry's Music Hall (now the Olympia Theatre) on 20 April 1896. In 1909 the first Irish cinema, the Volta in Mary Street, Dublin, was opened in December under the management of James Joyce.* There were twenty cinemas in both Dublin and Belfast by 1915. Films with nationalist themes were made in Killarney by the Kalem Company (USA) in 1910. These works included *Rory O'More, Robert Emmet – Ireland's Martyr, Ireland the Oppressed* (starring Jack Clarke and Alice Hollister) and *You'll Remember Ellen* (starring Clarke and Gene Gauntier). Early Irish films made by the Film Company of Ireland included *Willy Reilly and His Colleen Bawn* (starring Brian McGowan and Frances Alexander) and *Paying the Rent* (1916). Following the introduction of talking films, Denis Johnston*

made a film version of *Guests of the Nation* (1934), featuring Barry Fitzgerald* and produced by the Gate Theatre.* Two years later Tom Cooper made *The Dawn* in Killarney. Rex Ingram (1893–1950), the Hollywood director whose works included the first versions of *The Four Horsemen of the Apocalypse* and *Scaramouche*, was born in Dublin. Another director, Herbert Brenon (1880–1958) who made the original versions of *Beau Geste* and *Peter Pan*, was born in Kingstown (Dun Laoghaire). The Russian director, Alexander Row, who made *King Frost* and *Cinderella*, was the son of a Wexfordman. Hollywood directors of Irish descent include John Ford who made *The Informer* (1935) from the novel by Liam O'Flaherty* and *The Plough and the Stars* (1936), featuring Barry Fitzgerald and F. J. McCormick.* Robert Flaherty (*Man of Aran*, 1934), Allan Dwan, Joseph Henabery and Raoul Walsh.

CITY AND COUNTY MANAGEMENT. *See* Local Government.

CIVIC GUARDS. *See* Garda Siochana.

CIVIL AUTHORITIES (SPECIAL POWERS) ACT (NORTHERN IRELAND), 1922. Generally known as the Special Powers Act and sometimes as the 'Flogging Bill', it was enacted by the parliament of Northern Ireland, granting the Minister for Home Affairs the powers to 'take all such steps and issue all such orders as may be necessary to preserve the peace'. The Minister had power to arrest without warrant and intern without trial, prohibit coroners' inquests, flog, execute, requisition land or property, ban any organisation and prohibit meetings, publications, etc. The Act received the Royal Assent on 7 April 1922 and was renewed every year until 1928 when it was renewed for five years. In 1933 it became permanent. Under the terms of the Act, internment was introduced for 1922–24, 1938–45, 1956–62 and 1971–

75. The power to flog was removed in 1968. The Act was reinforced by a Public Order Act, 1951.* The Special Powers Act was examined in 1969 by a commission under the Attorney-General for Northern Ireland, Basil Kelly. The Commission in their Report, issued in January 1970, recommended that an end should be put to the Act. The Commission further recommended that while internment should be retained, it should not be exercised at the will of the Minister for Home Affairs, but rather, by order of parliament. The armed forces in Northern Ireland from 1969 operated under the provisions of the Act. In February 1972, when two Northern Ireland politicians, John Hume and Ivan Cooper, appealed against a conviction for not having obeyed a dispersal order by soldiers, the Lord Chief Justice ruled that the military could not operate under the terms of the Act although they had been doing so for over eighteen months. A new Act, the Northern Ireland Act, 1972, was passed at Westminster, giving retrospective sanction to the army's activities.

CIVIL RIGHTS ASSOCIATION. *See* Northern Ireland Civil Rights Association (NICRA).

CIVIL WAR (1922—23). The Civil War was brought about by a breach in the nationalist movement over the Treaty* signed in London on 6 December 1921. On 7 January 1922 a vote in Dail Eireann showed a majority (64—57) in favour of acceptance. Those who rejected the Treaty were led by Eamon de Valera* and regarded themselves as the legitimate second Dail. Supporters of the Treaty were denigrated as 'Free Staters' by the republicans. Free Staters included most of the Irish Republican Brotherhood* and part of the Irish Republican Army.* The National Army was directed by the Minister for Defence, Richard Mulcahy.* General Eoin O'Duffy* was Chief of Staff of the

government forces. Pro-Treaty forces on the outbreak of the war were:

1st Northern Division
    Donegal — Four Brigades.
    Commandant Joseph Sweeney.
5th Northern Division
    Monaghan, East Cavan and South Fermanagh.
    Commandant Dan Hogan.
North Wexford Brigade
    North Wexford and South Wicklow.
    Commandant Joseph Cummin.
Carlow Brigade
    Carlow.
    Commandant Liam Stack.
Midland Division
    Longford, Leitrim and Fermanagh.
    Commandant Sean MacEoin.*
1st Western Division
    Clare and South Galway.
    Commandant Michael Brennan.
3rd Southern Division
    Leix, Offaly and part of Tipperary—
    Five Brigades.
    Commandant Michael McCormick.

Chief of Staff of the republicans or 'Irregulars' was Liam Lynch* and the Deputy Chief of Staff was Joseph McKelvey. Local Anti-Treaty commands were:

2nd Northern Division
    Tyrone and Derry — Four Brigades.
    Commandant Charles Daly.
3rd Northern Division
    Belfast, Antrim and North Down—
    Three Brigades.
    Commandant Joseph McKelvey.
Dublin No. 1 Brigade (independent)
    Dublin.
    Commandant Oscar Traynor.*
South Dublin Brigade (independent)
    South Dublin.
    Commandant Andrew MacDonnell.
2nd Western Division
    South Roscommon, South and East Mayo, North Galway.
    Commandant Thomas Maguire.
3rd Western Division
    North Roscommon, Sligo, part of Mayo.
    Commandant Liam Pilkington.

4th Western Division
   North and West Mayo, parts of
   Sligo and Galway.
   Commandant Michael Kilroy.
1st Southern Division
   Cork, Kerry and Waterford and
   West Limerick – Ten Brigades.
   Commandant Liam Lynch.
2nd Southern Division
   Kilkenny, Limerick and part of
   Tipperary – Five Brigades.
   Commandant Ernest O'Malley.*
4th Northern Division
(non-partisan at outbreak
of hostilities, later joined
Anti-Treaty faction)
   Armagh, West and South Down
   and North Louth – Three Brigades.
   Commandant Frank Aiken.*

Anti-Treatyites seized the Four
Courts* on 13 April 1922. This precipitated the Civil War proper on 28
June, when, in response to pressure
from Whitehall, government troops
commanded by Eoin O'Duffy moved
against the occupants. The bombardment of the Four Courts lasted until
30 June when Oscar Traynor ordered
a surrender. The republicans mined
the building before capitulation, resulting in the destruction of priceless
historical records. Among those captured by the government forces were
Rory O'Connor,* Liam Mellows,*
Ernie O'Malley, Joseph McKelvey
and Richard Barrett. During the
ensuing months the better-equipped
government forces recorded major
successes against the republicans who
were eventually forced to adopt the
guerilla tactics perfected in the War
of Independence.* The death of
Arthur Griffith* on 12 August and
of Michael Collins,* Commander-
in-Chief of the government forces,
on 22 August, saw the war enter a
new and terrible phase. On 27 September Mulcahy sought emergency
powers for the army. New legislation
was introduced by the Minister for
Home Affairs (later Justice), Kevin
O'Higgins,* establishing military
courts. Under the powers granted
to these courts unauthorised individuals could be executed for posses-

sion of arms. An early victim of the
new legislation was Robert Erskine
Childers* who was charged with
possession of a revolver (presented
to him by Michael Collins). Childers
was executed while an application
for habeas corpus was pending. The
republican deputies who had been
elected to the second Dail met in
Dublin on 25 October and called
on de Valera to resume the office
of President. They formed a government which met in secret session the
next day to issue a Proclamation.
This government was, however, unable to function in the prevailing
circumstances.

The Free State came formally into
existence on 6 December with W. T.
Cosgrave* as President of the Executive Council. On 8 December four imprisoned republicans, Rory O'Connor,
Liam Mellows, Richard Barrett and
Joseph McKelvey, were executed in
retaliation for the assassination of a
government deputy, Sean Hales. Between November 1922 and May 1923,
seventy-seven imprisoned republicans
were executed. Lynch announced on
1 February that his forces would
carry out reprisals if executions continued. On 9 February the government announced an amnesty. There
were unsuccessful attempts by a section of the IRA not involved in the
war (the Neutral IRA), and by the
Catholic bishops, to arrange a truce.
Eleven members of the IRA Executive met on 24 March in Co. Waterford. Among those present were
Aiken, de Valera, Austin Stack,*
Lynch and Tom Barry.* Lynch
opposed a motion for peace which had
been favoured by de Valera and Aiken.
This motion was defeated by six votes
to five and the meeting was adjourned
to 10 April. Later that same day
Lynch was killed in the Knockmealdown mountains. On 14 April Stack
was captured and more republican
commandants were taken in the ensuing weeks. At a further meeting
of the IRA Executive on 20 April,
Aiken again urged a suspension of
hostilities. De Valera, who was not
present, was authorised to announce

a temporary ceasefire. He signed the document on behalf of the republican government and Aiken for the army, to take effect from noon of 30 April. As the ceasefire contained no provision for the laying down of republican arms, it was ignored by the government. The government also made it clear that there could be no compromise on the Oath of Allegiance.* A further attempt by republicans to secure terms met with rejection on 8 May. On 13–14 May the Cabinet of the republican government met with the IRA Army Council and decided not to resume the war but neither, they stated, would they lay down their arms. This decision was rescinded by a Cease Fire and 'Dump Arms' order issued by Aiken on 24 May. At the same time de Valera issued a statement conceding defeat: 'Military victory must be allowed to rest for the moment with those who have destroyed the Republic'. Republicans were arrested throughout the country. In all 11,316 prisoners, including 250 women, were taken; the majority were released within a year.

The total damage of the Civil War is virtually incalculable. The death toll was not high (between six and seven hundred). It left a legacy of bitterness which was not fully assuaged decades later. The Civil War moulded the shape of the major political parties; Cumann na nGaedheal* was identified as the pro-Treaty party and bequeathed this image to its successor, Fine Gael.* Sinn Fein* split in 1925 and de Valera formed his own party, Fianna Fail,* a year later. The IRA, the military wing of Sinn Fein, continued its hostilities against the Cumann na nGaedheal government and apart from a brief period in the 1930s, against the ostensibly republican government of Fianna Fail. The Labour Party,* which had remained neutral during the Civil War, had to make its appeal to the electorate solely on economic issues which were sadly neglected in the State until the 1960s.

Principal engagements of the Civil War.
Dublin
    28 June–5 July 1922.
Blessington, Co. Wicklow
    2–7 July 1922.
Limerick
    2–20 July 1922.
Waterford
    28 June–21 July 1922.
Tipperary
    9–30 July 1922.
Carrick-on-Suir, Co. Tipperary
    28 July–2 August 1922.
Clonmel, Co. Tipperary
    8–10 August 1922.
Wexford and West Midlands
    June–July 1922.
Dublin
    6 July–5 August 1922.
Dundalk, Co. Louth
    28 June–15 August 1922.
Kilmallock, Co. Limerick
    21 July–5 August 1922.
Tralee, Co. Kerry
    2–6 August 1922.
Cork
    28 July–12 August 1922.
Béal na mBláth, Co. Cork (where General Michael Collins was killed)
    22 August 1922.

Skirmishing continued in Munster throughout the Summer of 1922 to April of 1923 when the death of the Chief-of-Staff, Liam Lynch,* effectively ended republican resistance. *See also* Pact Election *and* Unity Proposals.

'CLAIDEAMH SOLUIS, AN'. The official organ of the Gaelic League* first appeared on 17 March 1899 and weekly thereafter. It contained articles in both Irish and English. Its editors included Eoin MacNeill,* Patrick Pearse* and The O'Rahilly* who became Managing Editor in 1913 when the paper was re-organised. O'Rahilly commissioned an article from MacNeill who produced 'The North Began' (1 November 1913). As a result of this article the Irish Volunteers* was founded later that month. *An Claideamh Soluis* was at the centre of many controversies over the role of the language in Irish nationalism.

CLANCY, GEORGE (SEOIRSE) (1879–1921). Republican; b. Grange, Co. Limerick to a family of strong Fenian tradition; ed. locally and University College where he joined the Gaelic League* and was taught by Patrick Pearse.* Clancy formed a branch of the League in the College and persuaded many of his friends, including Thomas Kettle,* Francis Sheehy-Skeffington,* James Joyce,* Tomás MacCurtain* and Terence MacSwiney,* to take up the language. He taught Irish at Clongowes Wood before returning to Limerick in 1908 to continue teaching. He was a keen supporter of the Gaelic Athletic Association* and was friendly with its founder Michael Cusack.* Clancy was an influential member of the committee which helped to elect Eamon de Valera* to East Clare in 1917. He fell victim to the 'flu epidemic of 1918 and was forced to retire from his teaching duties. He became a superintendent of the Irish National Assurance Company and was elected Mayor of Limerick in January 1921. Shot dead at his home on the morning of 7 March by disguised members of the Black and Tans,* he was the model for Davin in Joyce's *Portrait of the Artist as a Young Man.*

CLANDILLON, SEAMUS (1878–1944). First Director of Broadcasting, 2RN and Radio Eireann; b. Lough Cutra, Gort, Co. Galway; ed. St Flannan's College, Ennis and the Royal University.* He was a teacher in Clonmel (1903–05) and at Clonakilty (1905–12). Clandillon entered the civil service as a Health Insurance Inspector in 1912. He became first Director of Broadcasting at Radio 2RN (now RTE) in 1925, training for the post at the BBC. Radio 2RN was shortly afterwards renamed Radio Eireann. On the opening day of the broadcasting service (1 January 1926) Clandillon and his wife, Mairéad Ní Annagain, a well-known singer, both sang traditional Irish airs. His wife was so frequently heard on the national service that she was referred to facetiously as 'Mairéad Ní On-Again'. In 1927 he refused to allow John Logie Baird give a talk on the Irish radio about television, claiming that the invention was unworkable. Clandillon retired from his post as Director in 1934 and returned to the Department of Health where he remained until 1943. He was succeeded as Director at Radio Eireann by Dr T. J. Kiernan. Clandillon was the author, in association with his wife, of *Londubh an Cairn* (1927), 'songs of the Irish Gaels, in Staff and Sol-Fa, with English Metrical Translations'. *See* Radio Telefis Eireann.

CLAN NA GAEL. Irish-American republican revolutionary organisation, sometimes known as the United Brotherhood, founded in New York on 20 June 1867 by Jerome J. Collins. It was a secret and oath-bound organisation recognising the Supreme Council of the Irish Republican Brotherhood* as the government of the Irish Republic 'virtually established'. The Clan attracted many of the leading IRB men who were forced to America, including Jeremiah O'Donovan Rossa* and John Devoy.* Devoy joined the Clan in 1871 and exerted a powerful influence on the organisation. Under his leadership the Clan became a party to the New Departure.* During the 1880s a section of the Clan was dominated by 'The Triangle' of Alexander Sullivan,* Michael Boland and Denis Feeley. They ordered a policy of terrorism which led to the emergence of a group which, under the direction of Dr Thomas Gallagher,* became known as the Dynamiters.* Devoy and Red Jim MacDermott* opposed this policy and wrested control of the movement from the Triangle by 1890. Influential members of the Clan during the 1890s were Joseph McGarrity* in Philadelphia, and Judge Daniel Cohalan* in New York. The Clan played an active part in the preparations for the Easter Rising of

1916.* In 1907 Thomas J. Clarke* came to Dublin from New York where he had been Devoy's assistant. He joined the IRB and became an inspiration to the younger generation of Fenians. The Military Council,* which planned the Rising, had been Clarke's idea. Members of the Clan led by Devoy met the German Ambassador to the USA, Count von Bernstorff, and his aide von Papen, in 1914, and were sympathetically received. The Clan later sent an emissary to Berlin to discuss how the German war effort and Irish nationalism might best be reconciled. Clan leaders were also hosts to Sir Roger Casement* in 1914 and arranged a meeting with the Ambassador who organised Casement's ill-fated mission to Germany. Shortly before the Rising, the Clan founded the Friends of Irish Freedom* 'to encourage and assist any movement that will help to bring about the National independence of Ireland'. The War of Independence* led to a split in the movement. In June 1920 Eamon de Valera,* as President of the Irish Republic declared by the first Dail Eireann,* became involved in a dispute with Devoy and Cohalan over lobbying presidential candidates on the question of American recognition for the Republic of Ireland. On 18 October Harry Boland* stated that the IRB in Ireland had been 'reluctantly compelled to sever connections between the Clan na Gael and the parent body in Ireland until such time as the will of the members of the Executive became operative and not the will of Judge Cohalan'. Devoy refused to accept this withdrawal of recognition. Cohalan and McGarrity, however, felt that without IRB acknowledgement, the Clan was meaningless, and broke with Devoy. Devoy regarded his faction as the true Clan and accepted the Treaty,* while McGarrity, leading a re-organised body, rejected it. McGarrity supported the anti-Treatyites in the Civil War* and continued to back the IRA after the movement was outlawed in June 1936. He provided aid during the

campaign against Northern Ireland and Britain in 1939 which provoked de Valera into passing the Offences Against The State Act.* The Clan ceased to be an active force after McGarrity's death in 1940.

CLANN EIREANN. Irish People's Party; founded by William Magennis* in 1925 as a breakaway from Cumann na nGaedheal* in protest at the settlement which shelved the Boundary Commission.* Clann Eireann was sympathetic to the aims of Fianna Fail* which was founded in 1926. It vanished from the political scene following the eclipse of its seven candidates in the 1927 general election; many of its members subsequently joined Fianna Fail.

CLANN NA POBLACHTA. 'Republican Family'; political party founded in July 1946 by Sean MacBride,* Noel Hartnett, Jack McQuillan and Michael Kelly, who became general secretary. The party, which was supported by some members of the Irish Republican Army,* saw itself as a modernising force and attracted support from many who wished to see a wide range of social reforms implemented. In 1947 the party won two out of three by-elections and MacBride entered Dail Eireann. The party's rapid growth prompted Eamon de Valera* to call a general election for 1948. Although most of its ninety candidates were inexperienced, the Clann won ten seats, and entered into coalition with Fine Gael,* Clann na Talmhan* and the Labour Party* to form the first Inter-Party Government.* Two ministries went to Clann deputies, MacBride (External Affairs) and Dr Noel Browne* (Health). The party supported the passage of the Republic of Ireland Act, 1948.* Dr Browne attempted to implement health reforms, including the eradication of tuberculosis* in which he was successful, and in maternity care, which brought him into conflict with the Catholic hierarchy and the Irish Medical Association (*see* Mother and

75

Child Scheme). He was not supported by his leader. The split between the two Clann ministers was echoed within the party and McQuillan resigned with Browne. Their resignations, and the controversy over Browne's health plans, helped to precipitate a general election. As the Clann was not prepared to remain in coalition, Fianna Fail* returned to power in 1951. Clann na Poblachta won only two seats. It won three seats in the 1954 general election but while MacBride supported the second Inter-Party Government his party did not participate in it and it fell in 1957 when he withdrew support over the government's measures against the IRA. He lost his seat in the 1957 general election. Only one Clann na Poblachta deputy, John Tully of Cavan, held his seat in 1961 and 1965. The party was dissolved and in 1969, Mr Tully was defeated when he ran as an independent.

CLANN NA TALMHAN. 'Family of the Land'; political party founded in 1938 at Athenry, Co. Galway by Michael Donnellan. It was loosely organised and had as its principal aim the defence of the small western farmer. The party's strongholds were in counties Galway, Mayo and Roscommon. It maintained constant criticism of the government's agricultural policies which it felt were inimical to the interests of the small farmer. The party secured fourteen seats in the general election of 1943. In 1944 Joseph Blowick became leader when Donnellan failed to hold his seat. Patrick Cogan, deputy leader of the party, left in 1947 to found a new party, the National Agricultural Party. The Clann secured seven seats in the 1948 election when it entered into the Inter-Party Government.* Its only minister in the coalition was Blowick who held Lands and Fisheries, while Donnellan, who had regained his seat, became a Parliamentary Secretary. Following the collapse of the Inter-Party Government in 1951 the party steadily lost support and having secured only two seats

in the 1961 general election, had disappeared from the political scene by 1965.

CLANRICARDE, 2nd MARQUESS AND 15th EARL (1832–1916). Burgh Canning, Hubert George de; landlord; ed. Harrow. He served in the diplomatic service from 1852 to 1863. He was MP (Conservative) for Co. Galway from 1867 until 1870 when he resigned his seat in protest at the first Land Act of W. E. Gladstone (*see* Land Acts). Clanricarde opposed the Land League* and was one of the most notorious of Irish absentee landlords. Evictions on his 57,000-acre estate at Woodford, Co. Galway led to a renewal of the land war through the Plan of Campaign* in 1885 when 186 of his 1,159 tenants were evicted. In a letter to *The Times* in 1889 T. W. Russell* wrote, 'Thank God there is but one Lord Clanricarde. If it were otherwise the country would be in a worse plight than it is'. Clanricarde refused to sell parts of his estates to those of his tenants who wished to buy out their holdings under the Land Acts. When the Congested Districts Board* was granted powers of compulsory purchase in 1909 it took four years before the Land Court was enabled to transfer his estates to the CDB for nearly £250,000.

CLARE, EARL OF (1749–1802). Fitzgibbon, John; lawyer and politician (Tory); b. Donnybrook, Dublin; ed. T.C.D.; Bar (1772). Although he was an indifferent lawyer he built up a considerable fortune at the bar (1772–73: £343.7s; 1783–89: £36,939 3s. 11d.). He became MP for Dublin University (1778). A staunch government supporter, he opposed the Patriot Parliament, the Volunteers, Henry Grattan,* parliamentary reform and Catholic Emancipation.* In 1789 he became the first native Lord Chancellor for nearly a century and was raised to the peerage as Baron Fitzgibbon; he was then created Viscount and Earl of Clare in 1795. He became the most powerful man in the country, sharing power only with John Beresford. He encouraged the savagery with which General Lake suppressed the United Irishmen* (1797–98) and threw his support behind Pitt's proposal for a legislative union of the Irish and British parliaments (*see* Union). However, Pitt intended union to be accompanied by Emancipation and Clare was one of the principals in having this dropped. During 1799 he assisted Lord Castlereagh in buying enough support for the government to ensure the passage of the Union (February–March 1800).

CLARENDON, 4th EARL (1800–70). Villiers, George William Frederick; Lord Lieutenant (1847–52); b. London; ed. privately. He entered the diplomatic service and saw service in St Petersburg (1820), before arriving in Ireland (1827) as adviser to the Lord Lieutenant, Lord Anglesey,* in connection with the union of the Irish and English excise boards. Clarendon was an advocate of free trade and was highly regarded by Daniel O'Connell.* In the first administration formed by Lord John Russell* Clarendon became President of the Board of Trade (July 1846) and in the following year was appointed Lord Lieutenant in succession to the 4th Earl of Bessborough.* Clarendon took office at the height of the Famine of 1845–49* and to deal with the general unrest he was granted formidable coercion powers in 1848. He opposed Young Ireland,* the Irish Confederation* and the Orange Order.* Following the affray at Dolly's Brae, he ordered that Lord Roden's name be struck from the commissioners of the peace. Clarendon was sympathetic to the plight of Irish landlords deprived of their rents through the famine, and lent his support to the Encumbered Estates Acts* of 1848 and 1849. He turned down an offer of the Foreign Office in 1851 and lost his Irish post the following year when Russell's ministry fell.

CLARKE, AUSTIN (1896–1974). Poet and scholar; b. Dublin; ed. Belvedere College, Mungret College and UCD. Clarke studied Old Irish literature and legends whose influences are evident in the style and metre of his poetry for which he received the National Award at the 1932 Tailtean Games. He became lecturer in English at UCD in 1916 in succession to Thomas MacDonagh.* His works include *The Fires of Baal* (1921), *The Sword of The West* (1921), *The Cattle-Drive in Connaught* (1925), *Pilgrimage* (1929), *The Flame* (1930), *The Bright Temptation* (romance, 1932), *The Singing Men of Cashel* (1936), *Night and Morning* (1938), *Sister Eucharia* (play, 1939), *Black Fast* (1940), *As the Crow Flies* (play, 1943), *The Viscount of Blarney and other plays* (1944), *First Visit to England* (1945), *The Second Kiss* (comedy, 1946), *The Plot Succeeds* (1950), *Poetry in Modern Ireland* (1951), *The Sun Dances at Easter* (1952), *The Moment Next to Nothing* (play, 1953), *Ancient Lights* (1955), *Too Great a Vine* (poetry, 1957), *The Horse-Eaters* (poetry, 1960), *Later Poems* (1961), *Twice Around the Black Church* (1962), *Forget-me-not* (1962), *Collected Plays* (1963), *Flight to Africa* (poetry, 1963), *Mnemosyne Lay in Dust* (1966), *Old Fashioned Pilgrimage* (poetry, 1967), *A Penny in the Clouds* (1968), *The Echo at Coole* (poetry, 1968), *Two interludes* (1968), *The Celtic Twilight and the Nineties* (1969).

CLARKE, JOSEPH (1758–1834). Obstetrician; b. Derry; ed. Edinburgh University where he was awarded M.D. in 1779. He returned to Dublin where he became Master of the Rotunda Hospital. Clarke instituted many reforms which greatly reduced the infant mortality rate at the hospital. His report on his seven years'

Mastership was described as 'one of the most valuable records in existence'.

CLARKE, MRS KATHLEEN (1879–1972).

Republican; b. Limerick, *née* Daly, the niece of John Daly* and sister of Edward Daly;* ed. locally. In 1901 she married Thomas J. Clarke.* They lived in the USA until their return to Ireland in 1907. She was closely involved in her husband's work within the Irish Republican Brotherhood* and played a leading role in Cumann na mBan.* After Clarke's execution for his role in the Easter Rising of 1916* she supported Sinn Fein* and the Irish Volunteers* in the struggle for an Irish Republic during the War of Independence.* She entered Ðail Eireann* as a TD for Dublin in 1921 and opposed the Treaty,* saying '. . . there is not power enough to force me, nor eloquence enough to influence me in the whole British Empire into taking that Oath [of Allegiance], though I am only a frail scrap of humanity'. She lost her seat in 1922, regained it in June 1927 but lost it the following September. She was defeated in a by-election in April 1928 and nominated to the Senate where she continued to sit after 1937 as a Taoiseach's nominee.

CLARKE, THOMAS J. (1858–1916).

Fenian; b. Isle of Wight where his father was serving in the British army. Clarke emigrated to the USA in 1880 where he joined Clan na Gael* and met Dr Thomas Gallagher,* with whom he embarked on a dynamiting mission to England. Clarke, using the alias 'Wilson', was arrested with Gallagher in 1883 and sentenced to life imprisonment as a treason-felon. While in prison both were subjected to the particularly harsh treatment reserved for felons; Clarke's health was undermined and Gallagher was driven insane. On his release in September 1898, Clarke returned to the USA where he resumed his Clan activities, working on the *Gaelic American** with John Devoy.* He married a niece of John Daly* in 1901 (*see* Clarke, Mrs Kathleen). He became a naturalised United States citizen in 1905, two years before he returned to Dublin where he set up a tobacconists shop which became a centre of nationalist activity. Elected to the Supreme Council of the Irish Republican Brotherhood,* Clarke urged the establishment of a Military Council* to examine the feasibility of an armed insurrection. The Dublin Central Branch of the Wolfe Tone Clubs Committee was established by him 'to propagate the principles of the United Irishmen and of the men of '98 . . .'. Under his influence and with Clan na Gael funds he, Bulmer Hobson* and Denis McCullough* gained control of *Irish Freedom** in 1910 and used it to propound a radical form of republicanism. As the senior member of the Provisional Government of the Irish Republic declared on Easter Monday 1916, Clarke was the first signatory to the Proclamation of Independence. Following the surrender he was court-martialled on 1 May and executed two days later. His *Glimpses of a Prison Felon's Life* appeared in 1922. *See also* Easter Rising of 1916.

CLERKENWELL EXPLOSION (13 December 1867).

Attempt by two Fenians, Captain John Murphy and Jeremiah Sullivan, to rescue Colonel Ricard O'Sullivan Burke* from the Clerkenwell House of Detention, London. Sullivan placed a barrel of explosives on a side-cart against the outer wall of the prison. He was chased by two policeman but escaped to make his eventual return to the USA. Two men and a woman, Ann Justice, were charged with the deaths of twelve people and injuries to over fifty others in the explosion, but were discharged for lack of evidence. A known Fenian, Michael Barrett,* who had been in Glasgow at the time of the explosion, was charged, found guilty and executed on 26 May 1868.

CLONCURRY, 2nd BARON (1773–1853). Lawless, Valentine Browne; b. Dublin; ed. Portarlington, Prospect School, King's School, Chester and TCD. He joined the United Irishmen* and was several times imprisoned. He travelled on the continent (1801–05) and then returned to Ireland to farm his estate. He supported Catholic Emancipation* and abolition of the tithes.* He did not actively support Repeal or Young Ireland.* Cloncurry was a friend of Fr Theobald Mathew* and was close to the Lord Lieutenant, Lord Anglesey.* He was active in attempts to provide relief during the Famine of 1845–49.* His *Personal Reminiscences* was published in 1849.

CLOSURE. Derived from the Irish word 'clabshur'. At the conclusion of the harvest it was customary to have feasting and dancing provided for the workers by the farm-owner. In certain parts of the country a custom prevailed whereby one of the workers placed an implement in the fire to signify that the work was at an end and a feast was demanded. The employer either pulled the implement out of the fire and gave the feast, or less frequently, let it burn to indicate refusal.

CLUSERET, GENERAL GUSTAVE PAUL (1823–1900). Soldier of fortune and briefly Fenian Commander-in-Chief; b. France. He was commissioned in the French army and served in several campaigns, being awarded the Legion of Honour in the Crimea (1855). Cluseret fought in Sicily under Garibaldi and in the Federal Army during the American Civil War (1861–65), where he attained the rank of Brigadier-General. He was introduced to James Stephens* by Colonel Thomas Kelly* in New York (1866). Cluseret accepted Stephens' invitation to become Commander-in-Chief of the Fenian Army on condition that the army would number 10,000. He travelled to England using documents (provided by the Fenians*) which allowed him inspect Woolwich Arsenal and Aldershot. His tour was interrupted by the premature Fenian rising in Kerry (March 1867). Cluseret had advised against a military rising because of lack of arms and returned to France when his advice was rejected.

CLUSKEY, FRANK (1930–   ). Politician (Labour); b. Dublin; ed. St Vincent's CBS, Glasnevin and Harvard; Branch Secretary, Workers Union of Ireland (1954–68). Labour member Dublin City Council (1960–73); Lord Mayor (1968–69); TD Dublin South Central (1965) and Dublin Central (1969). He was a member of the Committee on Public Accounts (1965–73), and Committee on Procedure and Privileges; Chief Whip, Labour Party (1969–73). In 1973 when the National Coalition Government* was formed Cluskey became Parliamentary Secretary to the Minister for Social Welfare and served in that post until the National Coalition lost office in June 1977. He succeeded Brendan Corish* as leader of the Labour Party shortly afterwards.

COAL-CATTLE PACT. An agreement which was concluded during the Economic War* in 1935 between the governments of Ireland and the United Kingdom. Under the terms of the Pact, England allowed an increase of one-third in the quota of Irish cattle allowed into the UK, in return for which Ireland agreed to import coal only from UK sources.

COERCION ACTS. Acts passed at Westminster giving the Irish administration special emergency powers during what were considered times of severe public unrest in the country. One hundred and five Coercion Acts were passed between 1800 and December 1921. *See also* Peace Preservation Act *and* Protection of Person and Property Act.

COFFIN SHIPS. During the Famine of 1845–49,* when emigration was at an unprecedented level, the enforcement of the Passenger Acts was impossible. Speculators, both native and foreign, were attracted to the lucrative Irish passenger trade. All types of ships, some little more than floating hulks, were employed on Atlantic crossings. Such vessels, because of their unsuitability for the rigours of the voyage and because of the insanitary and overcrowded conditions on board, became known as 'coffin ships'. Many of them were cargo vessels engaged principally in the timber trade and would have run empty on the outward voyage without the Irish emigrants. The majority of cargo ships made huge profits from the emigrant trade during the famine. British vessels were generally inferior to American. The fare was a quarter of that on vessels sailing from American ports. Passengers were crowded together without regard to sex, four to a berth (some six feet square). The Passenger Act of 1848 sought to end these conditions by legislating against the berthing together of single men and women. A further Act, in 1852, required all single men to be berthed together in a separate part of the steerage.

Stephen de Vere, a humanitarian Co. Limerick landlord, brother of the poet Aubrey de Vere,* described a voyage on an emigrant ship: '... Hundreds of poor people, men, women and children, of all ages, from the drivelling idiot of ninety to the babe just born, huddled together without light, without air, wallowing in filth and breathing a fetid atmosphere ... living without food or medicine, dying without the voice of spiritual consolation, and buried in the depths without the rites of the church' (quoted in *First Report from the Select Committee of the House of Lords on Colonisation from Ireland*, 1847). Herman Melville, author of *Moby Dick*, described a voyage from Liverpool to America: '... The bunks were rapidly knocked together and looked more like dog kennels than anything else. The emigrants talked soon of seeing America.

The agent had told them that twenty days would be an unusually long voyage. Suddenly there was a cry of 'Land' and emigrants crowded on deck expecting America, but it was only Ireland which they had left three or four weeks before in a steamboat for Liverpool.... The steerage was like a crowded jail. From the rows of bunks hundreds of thin, dirty faces looked out. Scores of unshaven men, seated on chests, smoked tea-leaves and created a suffocating vapour which was, still, better than the fetid air of the place'. (*Redburn: His First Voyage*, 1849).

The passengers were generally exploited by the crew. Vere Foster* recalled how, on a voyage on the *Washington*, he observed the surgeon hurl the chamber pots of women passengers overboard and heard him order them to use the privies on deck (which were filthy). The surgeon was overheard to say, 'There are a hundred cases of dysentery on the ship which will turn to cholera and I swear to God that I will not go amongst them; if they want medicines they must come to me'. On learning of this, one of the passengers collected money to placate the surgeon. The ship's doctor then claimed that the steerage passengers had 'plenty of money and if they would not look after him, he would not look after them'. Some passengers immediately offered a shilling provided that it was used to buy a rope to hang the doctor. (*Correspondence on the Treatment of the Passengers on Board the Emigrant Ship 'Washington'*, 1851). Since proper records were not kept, the exact number of lives lost as a direct result of coffin ships cannot be estimated. In 1847 alone 17,465 documented deaths occurred as a result of either typhus or cholera on board the ships. This figure represented one-sixth of all travellers on the ships concerned. It does not include the countless dead who were simply cast to the sharks without record, nor does it include the very many ships which foundered without trace on the voyage. *See also*

Emigration to the US, Grosse Isle *and* Point St Charles.

COHALAN, DANIEL (1859–1952). Bishop of Cork (R.C.), 1916–52; b. Kilmichael, Co. Cork; ed. St. Vincent's Seminary, Cork and Maynooth. After serving as curate at Kilbrittain, Co. Cork (1883) he was a professor at St Finbarr's Seminary and chaplain to the military prison. He was Professor of Theology at Maynooth (1886–1914) and was then appointed Bishop of Vaga and co-adjutor Bishop of Cork (1914–16). Dr Cohalan was an outspoken critic during the War of Independence,* condemning acts of violence on both sides. In particular, he denounced the policy of reprisals which was such a feature of the struggle between the Irish Republican Army* and the Black and Tans.* In July 1920, he pronounced an interdict on the killers of an RIC sergeant, shot dead in the church porch in Bandon. He declared that anyone killing from ambush would be excommunicated, and his life was threatened by the IRA. In August 1928 he condemned the British government which had allowed Terence MacSwiney* to die on hunger-strike in 1920. In addition to his contributions to the *Irish Ecclesiastical Review** and *The Catholic Bulletin*, he was the author of *Trinity College and the Trinity Commissions* (1908), *De Deo Uno et Trino, De Deo Creatore* (1909), *De Incarnatione* (1910), *Trinity College: Its Income and its Value to the Nation* (1911) and *De Sanctissima Eucharista* (1913).

COHALAN, JUDGE DANIEL (1865–1946). Irish-American leader; b. Middletown, New York, where he became an important figure in the Democratic Party, and was later prominent in the leadership of the Tammany Society (1908–11). In 1912 he was appointed a Judge of the Supreme Court of New York State. Cohalan was close to John Devoy* and played an influential role in a number of Irish-American societies, including Clan na Gael.* He played an important role in New York in preparations for the Easter Rising of 1916,* including the sending of Sir Roger Casement* to Germany (1914). He was chairman of the Irish Convention held in Philadelphia (22–23 February 1919) and was active in the Friends of Irish Freedom.* He broke with Eamon de Valera* late in 1919 and with Joseph McGarrity,* who had supported de Valera.

COLBERT, CON (1896–1916). Republican soldier; b. near Newcastle West, Co. Limerick; ed. Athea National School and CBS. He was employed as a clerk at Limerick railway station and later in the office of Kennedy's Bakery, Dublin. An early member of Fianna Eireann,* he was also drill instructor to St Enda's,* the school run by Patrick Pearse,* and later joined the Irish Volunteers* in a similar capacity. In the weeks preceding the Easter Rising of 1916,* he acted as bodyguard to Thomas J. Clarke.* Following the surrender of his detachment of Volunteers at Marrowbone Lane, Colbert assumed the command to save the life of his superior officer, and was executed at Kilmainham on 8 May.

'COLLEEN BAWN' MURDER, THE. The elopement and subsequent murder of a sixteen year old Limerick girl, Ellie Hanley (the 'Colleen Bawn'), resulted in one of the most sensational murder trials in Irish legal history. John Scanlan, a Co. Limerick squire, was convicted of the murder following a trial in which he was defended by Daniel O'Connell.* Scanlan was executed on 16 March 1820. His servant and agent in the murder, Stephen Sullivan, was tried separately and executed on 27 July 1820. The tragedy provided the plot for *The Collegians*, by Gerald Griffin,* a play, *The Colleen Bawn*, by Dion Boucicault and an opera, *The Lily of Killarney*, by Sir Julius Benedict. The

most factual account of events leading to the trial appeared in 1869
in *The True History of the Colleen
Bawn* by the Rev. Richard Fitzgerald
who was on vacation in the area from
Trinity College, Dublin, at the time
of the murder.

COLLINS, MICHAEL (1890–1922).
Soldier and politician (Sinn Fein); b.
Woodfield, Clonakilty, Co. Cork; ed.
Lissvaird and Clonakilty National
Schools. He went to London in 1906
where he worked as a clerk. On joining the Gaelic Athletic Association*
he came into contact with Dr Mark
Ryan,* Sam Maguire* and Peadar
Kearney.* Collins returned to Ireland for a period in 1915 and joined
the Irish Republican Brotherhood.*
When subsequently settling in Ireland
he was employed by Countess
Plunkett, mother of Joseph Mary
Plunkett,* and became acquainted
with Sean MacDiarmada* and Thomas
J. Clarke.* During the Easter Rising
of 1916* he fought in the GPO as
aide-de-camp to Plunkett and was
interned at Frongoch following the
surrender. Upon his release in December 1916, he became Secretary of the
Irish National Aid* and Irish Volunteer Dependents' Fund.* Collins was
a member of the Provisional Executive of the Irish Volunteers,* of
which he became Adjutant-General.

He resigned his position on the
Executive of Sinn Fein* to work
with Harry Boland* on the formation of an intelligence system which
became of vital importance during
the War of Independence.* Elected
to the first Dail Eireann,* he became
Minister for Home Affairs and subsequently (April 1919–August 1922)
Minister for Finance, in which capacity he organised the National Loan
which raised over £350,000. Collins,
as President of the Supreme Council,* held a unique position in the
IRA – rivalling that of Cathal Brugha*
who was Minister for Defence during
the War of Independence. Members
of Collins' personal staff known as
'The Squad'* made a series of attacks

on the British Intelligence system
operating from Dublin Castle, which
culminated in events leading to
Bloody Sunday (21 November
1920).* Through one of his contacts,
Eamonn Broy,* Collins had direct
access to Dublin Castle's operations:
he did, in fact, on one occasion visit
the Castle in broad daylight. Collins
reluctantly accepted nomination as a
delegate to London for the Treaty
negotiations and defended the signing of the Treaty during the Treaty
Debate (14 December 1921–10
January 1922). He was Chairman of
the Provisional Government.* The
Craig–Collins Agreements* were
brought about through his meetings
with Sir James Craig (*see* Craigavon,
Lord) in January and March 1922, in
an attempt to bring an end to the
continued unrest in Northern Ireland.
He met with Eamon de Valera*
(May, June 1922) and in an effort to
prevent a widening gap between pro
and anti-Treatyites he made a controversial Election Pact* which he
repudiated two days before the election.

Pressure from Westminster forced
the Irish government to move against
the republicans who had occupied
the Four Courts* and so precipitated
the Civil War.* Collins relinquished
his post as Minister for Finance to
become Commander-in-Chief of the
National Army during the struggle.
He began a tour of inspection of the
South on August 20 and was killed
in an ambush at Beal na mBlath, Co.
Cork, two days later. He was the
author of *The Path to Freedom*
(1922).

'**COLLOP**'. Amount of land deemed
capable of producing enough to
support one family or the number of
cattle that the family could rear by
pasture on it. It was the basis for the
division of common land in the
western parts of Ireland in the eighteenth and early part of the nineteenth century. As in the 'Rundale'*
system, the 'collop' was scattered
over several different fields so that

good and bad land was equally divided.

COLUM, PADRAIC (1881–1972). Poet and playwright; b. Longford; ed. locally. He moved to Dublin where he worked as a railway clerk and became one of the writers identified with the Irish Literary Revival. He remained a lifelong friend and correspondent of James Joyce.* Colum's play, *The Land*, was one of the Abbey Theatre's earliest successes in 1905. He founded the *Irish Review* which he edited with James Stephens* and Thomas MacDonagh.* Colum was charged with disorderly conduct in February 1907 when he was a leading activist in the anti-Synge riots directed against *The Playboy of the Western World*. He visited the USA twice before settling first in Connecticut and from 1939 in New York, working at his poetry, editing and lecturing. His works include *Studies* (1907), *Wild Earth* (verse, 1907), *The Bidder's House* (1909), *Thomas Muskerry* (play, 1910), *Eyes of Youth* (verse, 1911), *The Desert* (play, 1912), *My Irish Year* (1912), *A Boy in Eirinn* (1915), *The King of Ireland's Son* (1916), *The Adventures of Odysseus* (1920), *The Children of Odin* (1922), *Dramatic Legends and other poems* (1922), *Castle Conquer* (1923), *At the Gateways of the Day* (1924), *The Island of the Mighty* (1924), *The Bright Islands* (1925), *The Forge in the Forest* (1925), *The Voyagers* (1925), *The Road Round Ireland* (1926), *Creatures* (1927), *The Fountain of Youth* (1927), *Balloon* (comedy, 1929), *Orpheus, Myths of the World* (1930), *Old Pastures* (1930), *Three Men* (1930), *Poems* (1932), *The Big Tree of Bunlahy* (1933), *The Legend of St Columba* (1936), *Legends of Hawaii* (1937), *The Story of Lowry Maen* (1937), *Flower Pieces* (poems, 1938), *Where the Winds Never Blew* (1940), *The Frenzied Prince* (1943), *Collected Poems* (1953), *Flying Swans* (1957), *Ten Poems* (1957), *Arthur Griffith* (1959), *Our friend James Joyce* (with his wife, Mary, 1959), *Moytura* (play, 1963), and *Images of departure* (1969). He edited *An Anthology of Irish Verse* (1948), and *a Treasury of Irish Folklore* (1955).

COLWYN COMMITTEE. Committee set up under Lord Colwyn in 1923 to examine the question of Northern Ireland finances and contributions to be made to the Imperial Fund. The Committee suggested that the contribution to be made by Northern Ireland should be the residue after domestic expenditure had been met.

COMHAIRLE NA POBLACHTA. Central Council of the Republic; political party founded in 1929 from followers of the Irish Republican Army,* Sinn Fein,* Cumann na mBan* and socialist republicans. Prominent members included Sean MacBride,* Maud Gonne* and Frank Ryan.* It issued a weekly paper, *An Phoblacht.* Apart from their hostility to the Cumann na nGaedheal government the party's members had little in common and broke up within a brief period.

COMHALTAS CEOLTÓIRÍ ÉIREANN. An organisation founded in 1951 for the promotion of Irish traditional music, song and dance. There are over 250 branches throughout Ireland, England, the USA and Australia. It is financed through a state grant and voluntary subscriptions. The activities of the Comhaltas extend into many areas, including records, tapes, television and radio programmes. It also publishes a magazine, *Treoir*. The Comhaltas has done much to foster an appreciation of the heritage of Irish music, song and dance, both in Ireland and abroad. *See also* Gael Linn.

COMHDHÁIL NÁISIÚNTA NA GAEILGE. National Congress of the Irish Language; founded in 1943 as part of a movement to preserve and foster the language. It became a co-ordinating body for some eighteen associations and societies involved in the preservation and promotion of the native language and culture, including the Gaelic League.* In 1953 it became the patron of a new organisation, Gael Linn.*

COMMANDERS OF THE BRITISH FORCES IN IRELAND, 1801–1922.

1801	General Sir William Meadows.
1803	Lieut-General Henry Edward Fox.
1803	General William Lord Cathcart.
1806	General Charles, Earl of Harrington.
1812	General Sir J. Hope.
1813	General Sir George Hewett.
1816	General Sir George Beckwith.
1820	General Sir David Baird.
1822	Lieut-General Sir Samuel Auchmuty.
1822	Field-Marshall Viscount Combermere.
1825	Lieut-General Sir George Murray.
1828	Lieut-General Sir John Byng.
1831	Lieut-General Sir R. Hussey Vivian.
1836	Field Marshall Sir Edward Blakeney.
1855	Field Marshall Lord Seaton.
1860	General Sir George Brown.
1865	General Lord Strathnairn.
1870	General Lord Sandhurst.
1875	General Sir John Michel.
1880	General Sir Thomas M. Steele.
1885	General H.R.H. Prince Edward of Saxe Weimar.
1890	Field Marshall Viscount Wolseley.
1895	Field Marshall Earl Roberts.
1900	Field Marshall H.R.H. the Duke of Connaught.
1904	Field Marshall Lord Grenfall.
1908	General Sir Neville Lyttleton.
1912	Lieut-General Sir A. H. Paget.*
1914	Major-General L. B. Friend.*
1916	Lieut-General Sir J. G. Maxwell.*
1918	Lieut-General Sir F. C. Shaw.*
1920	General Sir C. F. N. Macready.*

COMMISSIONERS OF NATIONAL EDUCATION IN IRELAND. *See* National Education.

COMMISSION ON HIGHER EDUCATION. The Commission on Higher Education, appointed in 1960 to investigate higher education in Ireland, issued its Report in 1967. It recommended that UCC, UCD and UCG should be reconstituted as independent universities and that the constitution of TCD should be 'restated'. Other recommendations were that more finance should be made available for students in higher education and that instead of a new university, colleges should be established to concentrate on technological education. The Commission also urged the establishment of an authority for technological training and research and the appointment of a Commission for Higher Education.

Following on these recommendations the Higher Education Authority was established in September 1968 to examine and advise the Minister for Education on proposals for the co-ordination and development of the higher education system generally. It also advises the Minister on the allocation of funds for higher education. Another body, the National Science Council, which first met in January 1968, was established 'to advise the government on science and and technology, with particular reference to economic development, recognising the need to establish closer liaison between academic scientists and technologists, state research institutes and industrial firms'.

Five Regional Technical Colleges (RTCs), established between 1968 and 1970, soon joined by others in the early 1970s, were charged with training pupils for entry into trade and industry. They were to cover a wide variety of occupations, in engineering, science, commerce, catering, art and design.

Another development in line with

the recommendations of the Commission was the establishment in Limerick in 1972 of the National Institute for Higher Education (NIHE). A second one was opened in Dublin in 1980. The NIHE offers a wide variety of courses at both diploma and degree level, validated by the National Council for Educational Awards* (NCEA), working in close liaison with industry. The courses include computer programming, business studies, European studies, regional studies, public administration, electronic engineering, industrial electronics, material and production engineering, energy technology, chemical technology, industrial design (engineering) and industrial and management mathematical science.

A further result of the Commission's Report was the attempt by the then Minister for Education, Donogh O'Malley,* to merge common faculties within UCD and TCD. His attempt failed and remained a contentious issue in higher education during the 1970s. UCC, UCD and UCG became independent universities in 1980.

COMMONAGE. A large tract of land held in common by the Irish peasantry from the Middle Ages. It was a survival of the Gaelic system of land tenure in many respects; some land is still held 'in common' in parts of Kerry, Mayo and Donegal. Those holding rights to the commonage were entitled to graze their animals on it, free of rent-charge.

COMMONWEALTH LABOUR PARTY. Founded by Harry Midgely* in 1942 after he broke with the Northern Ireland Labour Party.* The CLP was pro-Unionist and it supported the involvement of Northern Ireland in the war effort. Of the party's six candidates who contested the general election in the North in 1945 only Midgely was returned, after which the CLP disintegrated.

COMMUNIST PARTY OF IRELAND (CPI). Founded in November 1921

after Roderic Connolly* took over the Socialist Party of Ireland.* Connolly was the first president and Walter Carpenter the first secretary of the CPI which was recognised by Moscow as the Irish section of the Comintern. The CPI opposed the Treaty* and put forward a republican-socialist programme: 'The basis of the war', [against the Free State] wrote Carpenter, 'must be broadened from a military to a military and social struggle with the Republicans attracting to their side the workers and small farmers'. The party, which never numbered more than 100, attracted support from socialist intellectuals such as Peadar O'Donnell* and Liam O'Flaherty.* O'Flaherty and Connolly co-edited the CPI's organ, *The Workers' Republic.* Three members of the party, Hedley, Dowling and McGrath, established the Munster Council of Action in December 1921 and organised twelve Soviets.* When the Comintern withdrew its recognition in 1923 and transferred it to the Irish Workers' League* led by James Larkin,* the CPI was dissolved. The Communist Party was re-established in 1933 by the Revolutionary Workers Group* and the Workers' Party of Ireland.* A leading member was Larkin's son, James Larkin, Jnr.* It was dissolved in 1941 and re-established as the Irish Workers' League in 1948. The IWL founded another communist party, the Irish Workers' Party, in 1962. This united with the Communist Party of Northern Ireland on 15 March 1970 to become the Communist Party of Ireland. The general secretary of the new CPI, which publishes the *Irish Workers' Voice*, was Michael O'Riordan.* A smaller communist party, the Communist Party, Marxist–Leninist, is also active.

COMPENSATION FOR DISTURBANCE BILL (1880). Introduced by the Chief Secretary, W. E. Forster,* on 18 June 1880, the Bill was designed as a temporary measure to deal with a deteriorating situation in Ireland brought about by famine and

Land League* agitation. It empowered the courts in certain cases to order a landlord to compensate a tenant upon eviction even if the eviction was for non-payment of rent, provided that the tenant could prove that inability to pay was a direct result of agricultural and economic depression. The Bill was to apply to designated areas in the west and south of the country and was for a period of eighteen months only. The Bill passed through the House of Commons but met with a devastating (282 votes to 5) defeat in the Lords. Contemporary reports estimated that the House had rarely been so crowded as during the debate on this Bill which so deeply affected the landlord class. Joseph Chamberlain* remarked, 'The Bill is rejected: the civil war has begun'. Rejection of the Bill was followed by an escalation of activities by the Land League.

COMYN, DAVID (DAITHI COIMIN) (1854–1907). Gaelic scholar; b. Co. Clare. He worked as a clerk in the National Bank and was a founder-member of the Society for the Preservation of the Irish Language (1876). He was the first editor of the Gaelic Union organ, the *Gaelic Journal* (1882). Comyn was instrumental in securing Irish as a subject in school curricula (1878). He was forced through ill-health to abandon his translation of Keating's *History of Ireland (Foras Feasa ar Éirinn)* in 1902, having completed one volume for the Irish Texts Society.* His library of books of Irish interest was presented to the National Library* in 1907 as the Comyn Bequest.

CONACRE. System of landholding by which a portion of land was rented for a season for the sowing of crops but without creating a relationship between landlord and tenant. A person holding a piece of land was often a poorer type of cottier* or landless agricultural labourer. Holding the land under conacre granted no legal rights to the land. Rent for conacre was paid in cash, labour, or a combination of both. This system was most commonly encountered in Munster and Connaught. According to the Devon Report of 1847, conacre in Leinster and Ulster was usually for a potato crop alone, but in Connaught and Munster, the crops included oats, hay and flax as well as potatoes. The owner manured the land before letting it out on conacre. The rent ranged from £6 to £14 per Irish acre in 1840. The principal defect in the practice was the nature of its speculative system; the labourer who took the land was frequently an indigent speculator who, dependent upon the weather, either made a profit or faced ruin. There were many cases of middlemen* renting the land and letting it out on conacre to desperate landless labourers or cottiers at a high profit. The system was particularly affected by the Famine of 1845–49.* *See also* Rundale *and* Spalpeen.

CONCANNON, HELENA (1878–1952). Writer and politician; b. Co. Derry. A prominent figure in the Gaelic League* before election to Dail Eireann in 1933, she became a Senator in 1938. She contributed to influential nationalist periodicals and journals and wrote religious articles for the *Irish Messenger*. Her works include *Makers of Irish History* (1920?), *Irish History for Junior Classes* (1921), *Daughters of Banba* (1922), *Defenders of the Ford* (1925), *A Garden of Girls* (1928), *The Poor Clares in Ireland* (1929), *White Horsemen* (1930), *Irish Nuns in Penal days* (1931), *St Patrick* (1931), *St Columban* (n.d.), *The Blessed Eucharist in Irish History* (1932), *Blessed Oliver Plunket* (1935), *The Queen of Ireland* (1938), *The Irish Sisters of Mercy in the Crimean War* (1950), and *Poems* (1953).

CONDON, EDWARD O'MEAGHER (1835–1915). Fenian; b. Cork. He emigrated to the USA where he became a member of the Fenians and fought in the American Civil War (1861–65). Condon returned to Ireland as a Fenian activist and was a party to the rescue of Colonel T. J.

Kelly* and Captain Timothy Deasy* in Manchester when Sergeant Brett was killed. Under the alias 'Shore' Condon was tried for murder with Allen, Larkin and O'Brien. His statement, 'I have nothing to regret, to retract, or to take home. I can only say "God Save Ireland"', to which the others chorused 'God Save Ireland', provided T. D. Sullivan* with the famous ballad of that name. Condon, because of his American citizenship, was reprieved, and upon his release returned to America where he supported the Allied cause during World War I. His *The Irish Race in America* appeared in 1889. *See* Manchester Martyrs.

CONGESTED DISTRICTS BOARD. Established by the Chief Secretary, Arthur J. Balfour* in 1891; it consisted of a body of commissioners whose duty it was to dispense assistance to the 'congested districts' – Donegal, Sligo, Leitrim, Roscommon, Galway, Clare, Limerick, Kerry and Cork. It was part of the Conservative policy of 'constructive unionism' or 'killing Home Rule with kindness'. The Board consisted of two Land Commissioners, five experts appointed by the Chief Secretary with the Chief Secretary himself sitting as an *ex officio* member. Regions under the Board's authority were areas in which the rateable valuation was less than thirty shillings. The entire territories added up to around three and a half million acres, with a population (1901) of about half a million. According to the Commissioners the population could be divided into two classes – 'the poor and the destitute'. Funds came from the disestablished Church of Ireland, amounting initially to £41,000. By 1912 it had attracted other funds and had assets of £530,000. The sums at its disposal were spent on building harbours, encouraging a fishing industry, curing fish, cottage industries and attempting to modernise farming methods. Under the Wyndham Act of 1903 (*see* Land Acts) the CDB was authorised to purchase extra land from large estates to enlarge the small holdings. In 1909 it was granted compulsory powers of purchase. It redistributed 1,000 estates totalling 2,000,000 acres. The Board was dissolved in 1923 by the government of the Free State and its functions handed over to the Land Commission.* One legacy of the CDB was the Co-Operative Movement* which was founded by Sir Horace Plunkett,* who had been shocked by his experiences while working as a member of the first Board.

CONGRESS OF IRISH UNIONS (CIU). Trades union congress founded in 1945 when the Irish Transport and General Workers' Union* led by William O'Brien* and followed by fourteen other unions, disaffiliated from the Irish Trades Union Congress* and the Labour Party.* The split was caused by the decision of the ITUC executive to send delegates to the World Trades Union Congress held in London in February 1945. O'Brien and his followers claimed that the WTUC was dominated by communists. The CIU gained from the growth of the Irish trade union movement during the 1950s and by 1958 had around 190,000 members in twenty-nine unions. It entered into negotiations with the ITUC in 1955 and four years later amalgamated with it to form the Irish Congress of Trades Unions.*

CONNAUGHT RANGERS' MUTINY (28–30 June 1920). The 'mutiny' was confined chiefly to members of 'B' and 'C' company, 1st Battalion, Connaught Rangers, quartered at Wellington Barracks, Jullundur, Punjab. The men at Jullundur, led by Private Joe Hawkes, refused to soldier because of atrocities being committed in Ireland by members of the Black and Tans* and Auxiliaries.* Their protest was joined two days later by a detachment of 'C' company at a hill-station in Solon, led by Private James Daly, a member of the Irish Republican Brotherhood.* In an attempt to rush the magazine at

Solon two men were killed (one, a Private Mears was not involved and was hit by a stray bullet; the other, Private Smith, was killed instantly). A third man, Private Egan, survived a bullet through his lung. While awaiting trial the men were subjected to very harsh treatment which caused the death of a Private Miranda. A subsequent general court-martial sentenced fourteen of the seventy-five protesters to death and the remainder to varying terms of imprisonment. Thirteen of the fourteen death sentences were commuted; the exception, James Daly, was executed by firing squad on 1 November 1920. The Connaught Rangers, like the Royal Irish Regiment, the Leinster Regiment, the Munster Regiment and the Dublin Fusiliers, was disbanded in 1922, upon the establishment of the Irish Free State.

CONNOLLY, JAMES (1868–1916). Socialist and trade union organiser; b. Edinburgh; self-educated. His early experience committed him to Marxist socialism and he was highly regarded as a socialist theorist. Connolly joined the British army to escape from poverty and served some time in Ireland. He deserted at the age of twenty-one and returned to Edinburgh where he married. He spent the next seven years in a variety of jobs and fell under the influence of the Scottish socialist, John Leslie. At Leslie's urging he came to Dublin in 1896 as an organiser for the Dublin Socialist Society.* After founding the Irish Socialist Republican Party* and *The Workers' Republic** (1898–99), he emigrated to the USA in 1903. During the next seven years he immersed himself in American socialism. He founded the Irish Socialist Federation and another newspaper, *The Harp*, which brought him to the notice of William O'Brien.* He returned to Dublin in 1910 having been assured of a position in the Socialist Party of Ireland* by O'Brien who eventually secured a position for him from James Larkin.* In June 1911 Connolly became Belfast or-

ganiser for the Irish Transport and General Workers' Union.* He was co-founder of the Labour Party* in 1912. He returned to Dublin to assist Larkin in the struggle against the Employers' Federation in the Lock-Out* and became actively engaged in the workers' defence force, the Irish Citizen Army.* Connolly returned to Dublin permanently in October 1914 and led the Labour movement following Larkin's departure to the USA. He revived *The Workers' Republic* after the *Irish Worker* was suppressed in December 1914. In *The Workers' Republic* he attacked the Irish Volunteers* for their inactivity. This paper too, was suppressed (February 1915).

On Easter Monday 1916 Connolly led his Citizen Army alongside the Volunteers under Patrick Pearse.* The Easter Proclamation of Independence bears evidence of Connolly's influence: 'We declare the right of the people of Ireland to the ownership of Ireland and to the unfettered control of Irish destinies . . . . The Republic guarantees . . . equal rights and opportunities to all its citizens . . . cherishing all the children of the nation equally, and oblivious of the differences carefully fostered by an alien government, which has divided a minority from a majority in the past . . .' He served as a Commandant in the General Post Office during the Easter fighting and was severely wounded. He was sentenced to death by the Military Tribunal for his role in the Rising and was shot propped in a chair on 9 May. His writings include *Erin's Hope* (1897), *The New Evangel* (1901), *Socialism Made Easy* (1909), *Labour in Irish History* (1910), *Labour, Nationality and Religion* (1910) and *The Re-Conquest of Ireland* (1915).

CONNOLLY, RODERIC (1901–). Trade unionist and politician (Labour Party); General Secretary, Labour Party; b. Dublin, son of James Connolly;* ed. locally. At the age of fifteen he fought alongside his father in the General Post Office during the Easter Rising of 1916,* after which he was interned (for eight days). Having organised the takeover of the Socialist Party of Ireland* in September 1921, he secured the expulsion of William O'Brien* and Cathal O'Shannon* (October), and renamed it the Communist Party of Ireland* for which he edited *The Workers' Republic.* * The CPI was short-lived and he later founded the equally short-lived Workers' Party of Ireland,* aided by Captain James Robert ('Jack') White.* TD for Louth (1943–45), Connolly was financial secretary of the Labour Party until 1977.

CONNOLLY COLUMN. The Connolly Column of the Abraham Lincoln Battalion of the International Brigade was formed from the republican volunteers, some eighty in number, who accompanied Frank Ryan* to Spain in December 1936 to support the republican government in the Spanish Civil War.* Members of the column, including the young poet Charlie Donnelly and Rev. R. M. Hilliard of Killarney, were killed while fighting in the battle of Jarama where Ryan was also wounded. In all, sixty-one of the 161 Irish republicans who served in the International Brigade were killed. Michael O'Riordan, who served in the column published its history, *Connolly Column* (1979).

CONOLLY, LADY LOUISE (1742–1821). Philanthropist and model landlord; *née* Lennox, daughter of the Duke of Richmond. On the death of her husband Thomas Conolly in 1803, she devoted herself to their magnificent estate at Castletown House. She anticipated the industrial school system by establishing schools which offered a practical education to children of her tenants and to the poorer children of the surrounding districts.

CONRADH NA GAEILGE. *See* Gaelic League.

CONSCRIPTION AND IRELAND. The question of introducing conscription in Ireland arose in 1916, following the heavy allied losses at Verdun (from February) and the Somme (from July). However, public unrest in Ireland after the Easter Rising of 1916* made it unlikely that conscription could be peacefully implemented. Realising this, the Prime Minister, David Lloyd George,* would say in the House of Commons in February 1917 that if a Conscription Act was passed it would produce only 160,000 men and '. . . You would get them at the point of the bayonet and a conscientious objection clause would exempt by far the greater number. As it is, these men are producing food which we badly need'. For the moment the question of conscription for Ireland was dropped. The situation changed in 1918 when between March and April the British Army lost more than 300,000 men on the Western Front. In March the Russians signed the Treaty of Brest-Litovsk with Germany. On 24 March the cabinet decided to raise the age limit for suitability from 42 to 50. Four days later the question of conscription for Ireland was once more discussed in the cabinet. It was agreed to wait for the report of the Irish Convention* which was to begin its final sitting on 4 April and would, it was hoped in England, provide a solution to the question of self-government for Ireland. On 7 April the war cabinet discussed both the extension of conscription and the introduction of Home Rule. The Chief Secretary, Henry Edward Duke, believed that conscription could successfully be introduced once the Convention provided a scheme for administration in Ireland. The Lord Lieutenant, Lord Wimborne,* did not feel that conscription would be acceptable before Home Rule was implemented. He urged the introduction of simultaneous home rule and conscription bills. On 9 April, Lloyd George introduced the Military Service (no. 2) Bill and was attacked by the Irish members led by Joseph Devlin* and John Dillon.* The Bill was passed (16 April 1918) and the

Irish members withdrew from the Commons and returned to Ireland where they joined forces with Sinn Fein.* Soon they were joined by the Catholic hierarchy, the trades unions, the Labour Party* and the Irish Volunteers.* The Bishops stated that 'conscription forced in this way on Ireland is an oppressive and inhuman law which the Irish have the right to resist by every means that are consonant with the law of God'. On 18 April the Lord Mayor of Dublin, Laurence O'Neill, brought the leaders together at the Mansion House. Among those present were Dillon, Eamon de Valera,* T. M. Healy,* William O'Brien* of the Labour Party and Arthur Griffith.* De Valera drafted a pledge to be taken all over Ireland on the following Sunday, 21 April: 'Denying the right of the British government to enforce compulsory service in this country, we pledge ourselves solemnly to one another to resist conscription by the most effective means at our disposal.' Anti-conscription demonstrations were held throughout the country and Committees of Defence were established. A National Defence Fund was launched. The Irish Trades Union Congress* called for a General Strike for 23 April and the call won a response everywhere except in Belfast. At the beginning of May the Irish executive was changed when Wimborne was replaced by Lord French* and Edward Shortt replaced Duke. They immediately set about a recruiting campaign instead of going ahead with conscription. On 11 November the war ended. A total of 49,000 Irishmen, out of the 150,000 who served in the British armed forces during the World War I, lost their lives.

CONSTABULARY. *See* Police *and* Royal Irish Constabulary.

CONSTITUTION AMENDMENT ACT, 1931. Introduced by the Cumann na nGaedheal* government led by William T. Cosgrave* during a period of intense republican activity, the Act established a Military Tribunal with power to deal with political crimes and to impose the death penalty. It empowered the government to outlaw associations and the police were given extensive powers of arrest and detention. The Act was used to outlaw a dozen societies and associations, including the Irish Republican Army* and Saor Eire.*

CONSTITUTION OF 1922 (FREE STATE). A Committee to draft a Constitution for the Free State was appointed in February 1922 under the chairmanship of Michael Collins.* Owing to the Civil War* much of the work fell to the deputy chairman, Darrell Figgis.* Other members were Hugh Kennedy,* James MacNeill,* Professor Alfred O'Rahilly,* James Douglas,* John O'Byrne, Kevin O'Sheil, James Murnaghan and an American lawyer, C. J. France. The secretariat consisted of R. J. P. Mortished,* E. M. Stephens and P. A. O'Toole. The Commission studied the constitutions of other countries and had many of them translated and collected into book form for the benefit of the legislature. Three drafts were submitted to the government. The Constitution consisted of seventy-nine articles and the Treaty.* It was subordinate to the Treaty insofar as it would become void and inoperative should any section of it be in conflict with the terms of the Treaty. The Constitution was accepted by the British government which recognised it by the Irish Free State (Constitution) Act 1922. The Constitution was published for the first time on 16 June, the day of the general election, so that a large proportion of the electorate had no opportunity of seeing it before they went to the polls. On 18 September a 'Bill to enact a Constitution for Saorstat Eireann for implementing the Treaty between Great Britain and Ireland' was introduced in the Dail by W. T. Cosgrave.* It was steered through the Dail by Kevin O'Higgins.* Article 1 declared that the Irish Free State was a co-equal member of the community of nations forming the British Commonwealth of Nations. The legislature was to be the Oireachtas,* consisting of the King, Dail Eireann* and the Senate.* Article 12 vested the 'Sole and exclusive' power of making laws in the Oireachtas. Executive authority was vested in the King. The state was to be governed by the Executive Council,* responsible to the Dail and consisting of Ministers appointed by the representative of the Crown, the Governor-General.* On 6 December the Free State or Saorstat came into existence. The Constitution was eventually replaced by the Constitution of 1937.

CONSTITUTION OF 1937 (ÉIRE). In May 1935 Eamon de Valera* instructed the law officer of the Department of External Affairs, John J. Hearn, to prepare the heads of a new constitution to replace the Constitution of 1922 (Free State). During 1936–37, de Valera worked on a Constitution which would make the Free State a Republic in all but name. In preparing drafts of the Constitution, he studied the *Code Sociale Esquisse d'Une Synthèse Social Catholique* published by the Union International d'Etude Sociale in Paris (1934). He also consulted recent papal encyclicals while drafting social sections of the new document to be known as *Bunreacht na hÉireann* (Constitution of Ireland). In addition he conferred with the leaders of the various religious denominations in the country while drawing up the clauses relating to the place of religious worship in the state. Under the Constitution, the new title of the state became Eire (Article 4). It affirmed the essential unity of the country, stating that 'the national territory consists of the whole island of Ireland, its islands and the territorial seas' (Article 2) but also stated that 'pending the reintegration of the national territory' the laws enacted by Dail Eireann under the Constitution would apply only to the twenty-six Counties (Article 3). Article 5 declared that

Ireland was a 'sovereign, independent, democratic state'. Irish was recognised as the first official language while English received recognition as the second language (Article 8). The legislature was to be the Oireachtas,* consisting of the President,* Dail Eireann* and the Senate.* The Dail was to be elected on universal franchise and the Senate would be partly nominated by the Taoiseach* and partly elected on a vocational basis. The Cabinet, to be selected by the Taoiseach and approved by the President and the Dail, could consist of no less than seven members and no more than fifteen. Articles 34 to 44 granted fundamental rights. These dealt with the rights of the individual and of the family, the right to education, private property and religion. So as to protect the basic social unit, the family, the State was prohibited from granting divorce. Article 44.1 recognised the special position of the Catholic Church as the church of the majority of the population in the state while also granting equal rights and recognition to all other religious denominations in the State. (The part of the Article granting special recognition to the Catholic Church was removed by referendum in 1972.) While the Constitution, which was published on 1 May 1937, met with a hostile reaction from the British press, it did not unduly disturb the British government. The Constitution was approved by the Dail on 14 June and submitted to the public in a referendum held on 1 July, the same day as the general election. During the election campaign de Valera appealed for a judgement based on the merits of the document and not along party lines. The result was a ratification by 685,105 votes to 526,945 (in the general election Fianna Fail received 599,040 first-preference votes). On 29 December, when the Constitution came into operation, the British government declared that the new Constitution did not affect Eire's membership of the Commonwealth of Nations. Eire became a Republic in name, as well as in fact, on Easter

Monday 1949 when the Republic of Ireland Act, 1948,* introduced by the first Inter-Party government,* became law.

CONVENTION OF NORTHERN IRELAND. See Northern Ireland.

CONWAY, FREDERICK WILLIAM (1782–1853). Journalist and publisher; b. Loughrea, Co. Galway. He founded the *Dublin Political Review* (1813) and *The Drama* (1821). Although Conway was a supporter of Catholic Emancipation,* he incurred the wrath of Daniel O'Connell* who nicknamed him 'Castle' Conway in reference to an alleged pension he received from Dublin Castle. Upon his death the sale of his extensive library took almost four weeks. Many of the books went to the library of TCD and other libraries in Dublin.

CONWAY, WILLIAM, CARDINAL (1913–77). Archbishop of Armagh and Primate of All Ireland (R.C.) 1963–77; b. Belfast; ed. Boundary St Primary School, CBS, Queen's University and Maynooth. He was ordained in 1937 and was awarded D.D. the following year. He taught at St Malachy's College, Belfast before becoming Professor of Moral Theology at Maynooth (1942–58). He was Dean of the Faculty of Common Law in 1947 and became Vice-President of Maynooth in 1957. Dr Conway was a member of the Income Tax Commissioners who recommended the introduction of Pay As You Earn (PAYE) in 1957. He served as Auxiliary to Cardinal D'Alton (1958–63), and succeeded him as Archbishop. He was present at the Second Vatican Council (1962–65) and was elevated to the College of Cardinals at the conclusion of the Council. He was one of the three chairmen of the first Synod of Bishops in Rome (1967) and a member of the Pontifical Commission for the Revision of Canon Law which led to the establishment of the International Theological Commission in 1969 and a papal direction on mixed marriages in 1970. Cardinal Conway was Papal Envoy to India in 1972. He initiated the establishment of Trocaire (the Catholic Development Agency for the Third World) in 1973. He was the author of *Problems of Canon Law* (1950) and contributed to *Irish Ecclesiastical Record,* * Christus Rex, The Furrow** and *The Irish Theological Quarterly*, which he at one time edited.

COOKE, REV. HENRY (1788–1868). Clergyman (Presbyterian) and leader of the Orange Order;* b. Grillagh, Co. Londonderry; ed. locally and at Glasgow College where he took Arts and Divinity, returning for the winter sessions of 1815–17 to study chemistry, geology, anatomy and medicine. He completed his education at Trinity College, Dublin and at the Royal College of Surgeons. Ordained (10 November 1808), he ministered at Randalstown, Co. Antrim until 1810 when he resigned to become a private tutor. From 1811 to 1818 he held the living at Donegore, Co. Antrim when he resigned to become minister at the Killelagh, Co. Down estate of Archibald Hamilton Rowan* (1751–1834). From 1821, when he publicly humiliated Smethurst, an English preacher conducting a mission at the invitation of Ulster Unitarians, Cooke became increasingly hostile to Arianism. His personal triumphs at the synods of Strabane, Co. Down (1827), Cookstown, Co. Tyrone (1828) and Lurgan, Co. Armagh (1829) forced the Arians to secede from the Synod of Ulster. In 1829 Cooke entered into spirited public debate with Rev. Henry Montgomery,* champion of Arianism. Cooke's extremist views were enunciated in *Orthodox Presbyterians* which he established in December 1829. At a Hillsborough, Co. Down meeting (30 October 1834) attended by more than 40,000 people, Cooke published the banns of a marriage between the established and Presbyterian churches of Ireland to guard against the onslaught of Roman Catholicism. His opposition to National Education* led to the Ulster Synod organising their own scheme which was recognised by the Board in 1840. A leading opponent of Daniel O'Connell,* Cooke challenged him to public debate on his visit to Belfast (January 1841) but O'Connell refused. At his urging the government endowed a theological college under the General Assembly, of which he became Professor of Rhetoric (1855) having been Dean of Residence, Queen's College, Belfast since 1849. He retired from active ministry in 1867, his May St, Belfast congregation having built a church for him in 1829. In his later years he was noted for his opposition to Disestablishment of the Church of Ireland.* Cooke published a *Family Bible* with notes and *Concordance of Scripture.*

CO-OPERATIVE MOVEMENT. A study group headed by Lord Monteagle sent R. A. Anderson* to the continent in 1890 to report on co-operative methods in Denmark and Sweden. The group was joined by Fr Thomas Finlay* and after making contact with the British Co-Operative Union formed an Irish section under the chairmanship of Sir Horace Plunkett.* The first co-operative creamery was established in Drumcolliher, Co. Limerick in 1890. By 1891 there were seventeen such creameries and this figure had reached sixty by 1894. Agricultural Societies were also established for the purchase of manure and seedlings. The Irish Agricultural Organisation Society* was formed in Dublin in 1894 under the presidency of Plunkett. In 1895 the first agricultural credit society was opened at Doneraile, Co. Cork. The movement established its own newspaper, the *Irish Homestead,** in March 1895 which became highly successful in the spread of co-operative ideals under its editor George Russell.*

An Irish Co-Operative Agricultural Agency Society was founded to purchase agricultural requisites for affiliated societies. This Society became the Irish Agricultural Wholesale Society in 1898 when it dropped agency-methods to undertake general trading.

Additional finance was provided in 1899 when the IAOS received a grant of £500 p.a. for five years from the Carnegie Trust and in 1900 the Department of Agriculture and Technical Instruction* began to operate. The Department made grants available to creameries for the purchases of pasteurising plants for which grants were also provided by County Councils. In 1900 there were 171 central creameries, 65 auxiliaries, 106 agricultural societies and 76 credit societies with a total membership of 46,206 and a turnover of £796,528. In 1910 United Irishwomen* was established and over the next few years it assumed control of home industries and poultry societies. World War I presented the co-operative movement with a major crisis when the state monies available from the Development Commission and the Congested Districts Board* were withdrawn. The Treaty of December 1921 led to the foundation of the Twenty-Six-County Free State and the societies in the Six-County state of Northen Ireland became a separate body as the Ulster Agricultural Organisation Society. The Free State made grants available to the IAOS. In 1923 the *Irish Homestead* was incorporated into Russell's *Irish Statesman*. In 1928, the Dairy Disposal Company was founded by the state, to rationalise the dairy industry. The Agricultural Credit Corporation* was established in 1927 and made cash available for expansion in agriculture. Between 1930 and 1939 the number of creamery societies fell from 279 to 219 while membership increased from 52,000 to 54,000 and turnover on dairy produce rose from £4,400,000 to £5,300,000. Non-creamery turnover rose by 11 per cent to 28 per cent. The 1940s, the period of the Emergency caused by World War II, was crucial for the movement. There was an increase in demand for dairy produce but a marked shortage of farm supplies. Societies were forced to diversify. Some undertook cereal milling and others entered poultry and egg mar-

keting fields, the sale and hire of agricultural machinery, bacon curing, flax
scutching and the operation of hatch-
eries. There was an expansion of co-
operative meat factories, notably
Clover Meats. Two creameries, Ballyclough and Mitchelstown, began the
manufacture of chocolate crumb and,
along with Golden Vale and Dungarvan, began to manufacture milk
powder while Mitchelstown and Golden Vale also went into cheese production. The Ballyclough creamery
pioneered artificial insemination in
cattle-breeding in 1946. A later development was the establishment of
co-operative livestock marts which
gradually took over from the traditional fairs. By 1961 the movement
had 108,000 members with a turnover of £65,000,000. In 1977 there
were 250 co-operatives affiliated to
the IAOS with 222,000 members and
an annual turnover of £173,000,000.
See also Gallagher, Patrick ('Paddy
the Cope') *and* McDyer, Canon James.

COPE, SIR ALFRED ('ANDY')
(1880–1954). Civil servant and
businessman. Following a career as
a detective in H.M. Customs and
Excise, Cope became Second Secretary at the Ministry of Pensions
(1919–20). He was appointed Assistant Under-Secretary in Ireland during
the War of Independence* in 1920.
He played an important role in the
attempt to secure a Truce.* In April
1921 he helped to bring about the
abortive meeting between Sir James
Craig* and Eamon de Valera* in
Dublin. Following the Treaty,* Cope
assisted General Sir Nevil Macready*
in supervising the withdrawal of
British forces from Ireland. He received a knighthood in 1922.

CÓRAS IOMPAIR ÉIREANN (CIE).
Córas Iompair Éireann, Ireland's
Transport Undertaking, came into
being on 1 January 1945 with the
amalgamation of the Great Southern
Railways Company (*see* Railways)
and the Dublin United Transport

Company under the terms of the
Transport Act 1944. A major scheme
of re-organisation was introduced in
February 1961 when management
was decentralised and the system
divided into five areas. A manager
was appointed to each area with headquarters in Dublin, Cork, Limerick,
Waterford and Galway. In 1964 a
new Transport Act provided CIE
with a subvention of £2m. per year
until 1969. By this Act a sum of £1m.
advanced to CIE from the Exchequer
was treated as a non-repayable grant.
The 1969 Act increased from £6m.
to £17m. the authority for capital
advances from the Exchequer to CIE.
CIE operates a network of inter-city
trains, using diesel-electric traction
and air-conditioned rolling stock.
Other rail passenger services, together
with suburban services in Dublin and
Cork, are also operated. The railway
freight system is in the process of
modernisation and new terminals are
being constructed at strategic locations throughout the country. The
worst rail disaster suffered by CIE
occurred on 31 December 1975. Five
people died and several were injured
when the 0805 train from Rosslare
Harbour to Dublin was derailed at
Tubberneering, near Gorey, Co. Wexford. CIE operates a network of provincial buses and provides express and
limited stop bus services between
certain cross-country routes. City bus
services in Dublin, Cork, Limerick,
Galway and Waterford together with
town services in Dundalk, Drogheda
and Sligo are also the responsibility
of CIE. A special feature of CIE's
role is the operation and administration of the countrywide free school
bus scheme comprising the employment of both CIE owned and private
contractor's vehicles. International
sea freight services are catered for by
Irish Ferryways, a subsidiary of CIE,
and Containerway and Road Ferry
Ltd. Air freight is catered for by
Aerlod Teo., a wholly owned CIE subsidiary. CIE also provides a nationwide
road freight network and operates
freight and sea-passenger services to
the Aran Islands.

CÓRAS NA POBLACHTA. Republican movement founded in 1940 by members of the Irish Republican Army* in an attempt to find a political role for the movement. It received little support and its place was taken by the more widely-based Clann na Poblachta* in 1946.

CÓRAS TRACHTÁLA (IRISH EXPORTS BOARD). Córas Trachtála in 1959 assumed the functions hitherto held by Coras Trachtal Teo. – to promote trade, particularly in its formative years, with Canada and the USA in an endeavour to reduce the dollar deficit. The Board now has offices in major cities including Brussels, Beirut, Dusseldorf, London, Los Angeles, Madrid, Manchester, Melbourne, Moscow, New York, Paris, Toronto, Warsaw and Zurich. Coras Trachtala provides a number of specialist services and facilities to assist exporters, including market information and research and market consultancy and advisory services. It administers grant schemes and incentives to exporters, assists engineering projects manufacturing materials for industrial or agricultural use, provides expertise on publicity and publications and fosters training courses for exporters. It works in close association with its associated bodies, the Kilkenny Design Centre and Shipping Services Ltd. In the year ending 31 March 1979 it received £6.09m. grant-in-aid from the Minister for Industry and Commerce.

CORISH, BRENDAN (1918–). Politician (Labour); leader of the Labour Party,* 1960–77; b. Wexford; ed. CBS. He became TD for Wexford in 1945 in a by-election caused by the death of his father, Richard Corish (TD 1921–45). He was Labour Party Whip (1947–49), vice-chairman of the Party (1946–49) and Chairman (1949–53). He served in the two Inter-Party Governments,* as Parliamentary Secretary to the Minister for Local Government and to the Minister for Defence (1948–51) and as Minister for Social Welfare (1954–

57). In 1960 he succeeded William Norton* as leader of the parliamentary Labour Party. Although Corish had publicly opposed the idea of coalition during the 1960s he supported it before the general election of 1973 when the National Coalition* defeated Fianna Fail.* He was Tanaiste and Minister for Health and Minister for Social Welfare until 1977. After the defeat of the National Coalition in June 1977, when Labour lost two seats, Corish resigned the leadership and was succeeded by Frank Cluskey.*

CORK DEFENCE UNION. A 'non-sectarian and non-political' organisation established in October 1885 'to unite together all friends of law and order of all classes in this country in a body for their mutual defence and protection'. The Union was opposed to Home Rule* and the National League.* Landowners, merchants, farmers, shopkeepers, artisans and labourers united under the presidency of the Earl of Bandon and his assistant, Viscount Doneraile, to assist those who had become victims of the National League's boycotting campaign. In March 1886 the Defence Union issued a pamphlet which listed cases of victimisation by the National League. *See also* Unionist Party.

'CORK EXAMINER'. Daily newspaper founded in 1841 by John Francis Maguire.* It was taken over by the Crosbie family, which still controls it, during the 1870s. The third most widely read morning paper in Ireland, it is mainly sold in Munster. The bulk of its readership is lower-middle class and skilled manual workers. The publishers also issue the *Cork Evening Echo* and the *Cork Weekly Examiner*. The *Examiner's* sales have increased from 57,329 in 1968 to 69,351 in 1979. The sales figure for the *Evening Echo* in that year was 42,705 while the *Holly Bough*, a special Christmas number of the *Cork Weekly Examiner*, sold 86,000 copies.

CORK GUNPOWDER EXPLOSION (3 November 1810).

Twenty-two people were killed and over forty injured, many seriously, when gunpowder stored in a labourer's house in Brandy Lane, Cork exploded. Three houses were reduced to rubble and several others, badly damaged by the explosion, were demolished. A subsequent inquiry revealed that several employees had been systematically stealing gunpowder from the Ballincollig gunpowder works which they then sold to quarrymen for blasting purposes. Figures compiled by factory authorities showed that almost half a ton was unaccounted for in the nine-month period preceding the disaster. During the course of the inquiry it was revealed that when the illicit gunpowder was brought home by the workers it had to be dried before resale. The method chosen for the drying was a lighted candle which was held over the gunpowder. On the night of the disaster at least one of the men involved in the operation was seen to be drinking heavily at a local tavern. This man lost a leg in the explosion and died on the way to hospital. A disaster fund was opened for the victims and their dependants to which over £12,000 was subscribed in two weeks.

CORKERY, DANIEL (1878–1968).

Writer and politician (Sinn Fein); b. Cork; ed. Presentation Brothers and St Patrick's College, Dublin, where he trained as a National Teacher. He was an influential figure in Cork in nationalist and literary movements, prominent in the Gaelic League* and Sinn Fein. With the assistance of other Gaelic Leaguers, including Terence MacSwiney,* he founded a theatre, An Dún, in 1908, for which he wrote plays in Irish. He gave early support to Seán O'Faoláin,* Frank O'Connor* and Seamus Murphy.* He was TD for Co. Cork in the second Dail Eireann and opposed the Treaty, giving support to the anti-Treaty forces during the Civil War. He was clerical assistant to the Co. Cork 'Inspector of Irish' from 1923 until 1928. Following the publication of *The Hidden Ireland* (1925) Corkery was awarded a doctorate by University College, Cork. Four years later he published his second major critical work, *Synge and Anglo-Irish Literature* and was appointed Professor of English in UCC in 1931 and held the post until he resigned in 1947. He was nominated to the Senate by the then Taoiseach, Eamon de Valera,* in 1951 and held the seat until 1954. He was co-opted to the Arts Council in 1952. Corkery's publications included *A Munster Twilight* (short stories, 1916), *The Threshold of Quiet* (novel, 1917), *The Lost Leader* (play; produced at the Abbey Theatre* in 1919 and published in 1920), *The Yellow Bittern and other plays* (1920), *The Hound of Banba* (short stories, 1920), *I Bhreasail* (poetry, 1921), *The Wager and other stories* (1950) and *The Fortunes of the Irish Language* (1954).

CORNWALLIS, CHARLES, 1st MARQUIS AND 2nd EARL (1738–1805).

Soldier; Commander-in-Chief and Lord Lieutenant (1798–1801); b. London; ed. Eton. An ensign in the 1st Grenadier Guards (1756), he attended military college in Turin. After succeeding to the title in 1762 he was joint vice-treasurer of Ireland (1769). Although he had opposed the taxation of America he accepted a command against the rebels in 1776, where, following initial successes, he was forced to surrender to General George Washington at Yorktown on 19 October 1781. He was Governor-General of India (1786–94), and upon his return became Master-General of the Ordnance with a seat in the cabinet (1795). He was sent to Ireland as C-in-C and Lord Lieutenant to suppress the rebellion of the United Irishmen* in 1798. He received the surrender of General Humbert in September. After the suppression of the United men, Cornwallis worked to secure the Union,* believing that it would be accompanied by Catholic Emancipation.* When he threatened to resign if the government did not honour its pledges to Union supporters, the government conceded. Shortly afterwards he joined with William Pitt* in resigning over the King's refusal to grant Emancipation (February 1801) but did not leave the Irish office until May. He later became C-in-C and Governor-General of India (1805) where he died at Ghazipur.

COSGRAVE, EPHRAIM MAC-DOWEL (1853–1925). Physician and antiquary; b. Dublin; ed. TCD, where he was awarded M.D. in 1875. He practised for some time in England before returning to Dublin, where he founded the Georgian Society (1909), and became President of the Royal College of Physicians of Ireland in 1914. He contributed antiquarian articles to *Proceedings* of the Royal Society of Antiquaries of Ireland. His best-known work (written in conjunction with L. R. Strangeways) is *Illustrated Dictionary of Dublin* which appeared in 1895.

COSGRAVE, LIAM (1920–   ). Politician (Fine Gael); b. Dublin; son of William T. Cosgrave;* ed. CBS, Synge Street, Dublin, Castleknock and King's Inns, Dublin. He became a Senior Counsel in 1958. He served in the army prior to his election to Dail Eireann in 1943. Cosgrave served in both the 1948 and 1954 Inter-Party Governments* as Parliamentary Secretary to the Taoiseach and to the Minister for Industry and Commerce (1948), and as Minister for External Affairs (1954–57). He was Chairman of the committee of the Ministers of the Council of Europe in 1955 and chairman of the first Irish delegation to the United Nations General Assembly (1956). In 1965 he succeeded James Dillon* as leader of Fine Gael. He was leader of the Irish parliamentary delegation to the Conference on Inter-Parliamentary Union, Rome, and was elected Vice-President of the IPU in 1972. Cosgrave became Taoiseach and leader of the National Coalition Government* (1973–77). On 20 June 1977, following a general election which saw his party lose eleven seats, he resigned from the leadership of Fine Gael and was succeeded by Dr Garret Fitzgerald.*

COSGRAVE, WILLIAM T. (1880–1965). Politician (Sinn Fein, Cumann na nGaedheal and Fine Gael); first President of the Executive Council of the Irish Free State (1922–32); b. Dublin; ed. CBS. As a member of the Irish Volunteers* he fought in the General Post Office during the Easter Rising of 1916.* He was sentenced to death for his part in the insurrection but this was commuted to life imprisonment and he was released in December 1916. He became treasurer of Sinn Fein and an alderman of Dublin Corporation. Cosgrave represented Carlow-Kilkenny in the first Dail Eireann and was Minister for Local Government (April 1919–September 1922) at which department his aide was Kevin O'Higgins.* He supported the Treaty.* He succeeded Arthur Griffith* as President of the second Dail (August 1922) and Michael Collins* as Chairman of the Provisional Government.* In December 1922 he became the first President of the Executive Council and was also Minister for Finance (September 1922–September 1923). In 1923 he founded the pro-Treaty party, Cumann na nGaedheal, of which he was leader until 1933. Criticism of his leadership grew following losses in the general elections of March 1932 and January 1933. He stood aside to allow General Eoin O'Duffy* assume the presidency of Cumann na nGaedheal's successor, the United Ireland or Fine Gael* party of which he became a joint vice-president. Within a short time he was called upon to assume the presidency which he did in 1935. He held the office and was leader of the opposition to Fianna Fail* governments until retirement in 1944. His son, Liam Cosgrave,* was later leader of Fine Gael.

COSTELLO, JOHN ALOYSIUS (1891–1976). Barrister, politician

(Fine Gael) and Taoiseach (1948–51; 1954–57); b. Dublin; ed. O'Connell's Schools, Dublin and UCD. He was called to the Bar in 1914 and held various offices before appointment as Attorney-General (1926–32). He was legal adviser to the Irish delegation during the Imperial Conferences of 1926, 1928 and 1932; he entered the Dail in 1933. When Fianna Fail* failed to secure a majority in 1948, Costello, although not leader of his party, was a compromise choice to lead a coalition government. As Taoiseach of the first Inter-Party Government* (1948–51), he supported the Republic of Ireland Act* which repealed the External Affairs Act* and formally established the Republic of Ireland on Easter Monday 1949. He was asked to lead the second Inter-Party Government in 1954. During his tenure of office as Taoiseach he was faced with a renewal of Irish Republican Army* activity against Northern Ireland. His efforts to deal with the campaign provoked a motion of No Confidence from the leader of Clann na Poblachta, Sean MacBride,* and when Fianna Fail supported the motion the government resigned (January 1957). Costello retired to the backbenches in 1963. He had been elected to the Royal Irish Academy in 1948 and was the recipient of many international honorary degrees.

COSTELLO, MAJOR-GENERAL MICHAEL JOSEPH (1904–). Soldier and businessman; b. Cloughjordan, Co. Tipperary; ed. CBS, Nenagh; his godfather was Thomas McDonagh.* Following his father's internment by the Black and Tans* during the War of Independence,* he joined the Irish Republican Army.* He supported the Treaty* and joined the National Army of the Free State, receiving the rank of Colonel during the Civil War.* Following a military course in the USA he organised the Irish Military College (1926). He was later Assistant Chief of Staff and commanded the 1st Division (Southern Command) during the Emergency,* 1939–45. After retiring from the army in 1945 he became Managing Director of the Irish Sugar Co., where he oversaw the introduction of worker-participation, and diversification into machinery and fertilisers, as well as experiments with food-growing on bogland. He was responsible for the establishment of Erin Foods Ltd. (1964).

COTTER, PATRICK (1760–1806). Giant; b. near Kinsale, Co. Cork. He was so tall he could, while following his trade as a stonemason, work on a ceiling without a ladder or any other support. He exhibited in England under the name 'O'Brien' claiming a height of eight feet seven and three-quarter inches at the age of twenty-six. His coffin plate gave his height as eight feet one inch but scientific calculation placed his height at seven feet, eleven inches, which makes him the tallest Irishman officially recorded. No hearse large enough to accommodate his nine feet four inch casket encased in lead, could be found, and his remains were borne to the grave by relays of fourteen men. In his will Cotter left £2,000 to his mother and a request that his remains be entombed within twelve feet of solid rock (to prevent exhumation for scientific research). His body was however exhumed and an arm is preserved in the Royal College of Surgeons, London.

COTTIER. One who rented a cabin and between one and one and a half acres of land upon which to grow potatoes, oats and possibly some flax. He held the ground on a year to year basis and his rent was often paid in labour. He could usually only get land which was considered too unprofitable for any other use. He kept a cow, a pig and some poultry. In addition, he usually had the right to graze his cattle on common land and to cut turf from a neighbouring bog by virtue of his holding (see Turbary-Right). While he was usually above the day-labourer who was frequently a very poor cottier, the cottier existed at subsistence level because of high rentals and the competition for land and labour among his class. The more prosperous type of cottier would work for his landlord and receive the balance in cash after his rent had been deducted. If work was not locally available he might have to become a migrant labourer. His income was usually supplemented by domestic industry. He had no incentive to improve his holding as any improvements would generally prompt an increase in his rent. The situation for cottiers worsened considerably during the early decades of the nineteenth century as the population continued to expand. After the Famine of 1845—49,* the cottier class almost completely disappeared. Contemporary accounts of the cottiers' lives are to be found in the works of William Carleton,* Arthur Young's *Tour in Ireland* (1777) and T. Campbell Foster's *Letters on the Condition of the people of Ireland* (1846). *See also* Conacre.

COTTOSLOE, 1st BARON (1808—1890). Fremantle, Thomas Francis; politician (Conservative); Chief Secretary (1845—46); b. London; ed. Oriel College, Oxford. MP from 1830, he was appointed Joint Secretary to the Treasury by Sir Robert Peel* (1834), and held the office in Peel's second administration (1841—44). He was Secretary for War in 1844. Cottosloe became Chief Secretary at the onset of the Famine of 1845—49* and spent some £50,000 on relief works, building piers and harbours in an attempt to stimulate a fishing industry. He was Deputy Chairman of the Board of Customs in 1846 and subsequently Chairman until 1873. He was created peer by Lord Beaconsfield (1874).

COUNCIL FOR THE STATUS OF WOMEN. Founded in 1968, the Council represents 250,000 women in thirty major organisations. The purpose of the Council is to provide liaison between the government and women's organisations. It concerns itself with discrimination against women and seeks implementation of the Report of the Commission on the Status of Women which was issued in 1973. The Council is the Irish section of the 'Women in Europe' secretariat and liaises with the Commission of the European Communities Directorate-General, Information.

COUNCIL OF AGRICULTURE. *See* Agriculture and Technical Instruction Act, 1899.

COUNCIL OF IRELAND. Incorporated into the Government of Ireland Act, 1920* the Council was intended as a meeting place for twenty representatives each from the Northern Ireland and Southern Ireland states. It was hoped that the Council would meet to discuss matters of mutual concern, trade, fisheries, transport, etc. It was viewed as a possible means whereby the two parts of the country might be brought together for cooperative purposes. However, following the Agreement which shelved the Boundary Commission* in December 1925 the powers of the Council in relation to Northern Ireland were transferred to the Northern Ireland government and plans for the Council were dropped. The idea was revived again in the Sunningdale Agreement* (December 1973). Unionist opposition in Northern Ireland and the subsequent collapse of the power-sharing Executive (*see* Assembly *in* Northern Ireland) put an end to the scheme.

COUNCIL OF STATE. As laid down in the Constitution of 1937* (Article 31) the Council of State is 'to aid and counsel the President on all matters on which the President may consult the said Council in relation to the exercise and performance by him of such of his powers and functions as are by this Constitution expressed to be exercisable and performable after consultation with the Council of State . . .' The *ex officio* members are the Taoiseach, the Tanaiste, the Chief Justice, the President of the High Court, the Chairman of Dail

Eireann, the Chairman of the Senate and the Attorney-General. In addition, it may also include any of those 'able and willing to act' who have held the offices of President, Taoiseach, or Chief Justice. The President may also appoint additional members up to the number of seven. Members of the Council of State hold office until the appointment of a new President. The President convenes meetings of the Council 'at such times and places as he shall determine' subject to Article 32.

COUNCIL OF THREE HUNDRED. First proposed by *The Nation*,* the proposal for a Council was taken up by Daniel O'Connell.* The proposal was for the sixty Irish nationalist MPs at Westminster to join with 240 others and form an independent Irish parliament under the Crown (300 had been the number of representatives in the Irish parliament before the Union*). An attempt to implement the proposal led to the trials of William Smith O'Brien,* John Mitchel* and Thomas Francis Meagher.* O'Connell sought to avoid the Convention Act of 1793 by proposing that those attending a meeting would not be delegates but simply bearers of the contributions of Repeal Rent from their areas (*see* Repeal Association). The Council never came into existence. A similar idea was later put forward by Arthur Griffith* but it was not received with enthusiasm.

'COUNSELLOR'. Popular name for Daniel O'Connell before 1829. It paid tribute to his success as a barrister. After 1829 he was known as the 'Liberator'.

COUNTY COUNCILS. *See* Local Government.

COURTS OF JUSTICE ACT, 1924. Act passed by the Free State government in an overhaul of the administration of justice. In ascending order, District, Circuit, High, Criminal Appeal, and Supreme Courts were created to replace the County Court system. Justices of the Peace and Resident Magistrates* were replaced by Judges, and the Petty Sessions abolished. Each Circuit Court area embraced around 400,000 people.

COVENTRY EXPLOSION (25 August 1939). The Irish Republican Army, led by Sean Russell,* declared war on Britain on 16 January 1939. This took the form of a series of explosions, some 120 in all, during the next months. The campaign culminated in the explosion at Broadgate, Coventry, when five people were killed and seventy injured. The Coventry Explosion caused outrage in Ireland and throughout the United Kingdom. The Fianna Fail government, which had already introduced the Treason Act* and the Offences Against the State Act,* introduced the Emergency Powers Act* in January 1940. Two republicans, Barnes and McCormick, were hanged in England in connection with the explosion in Coventry.

COWPER, 7th EARL (1834–1905). Grey, Francis Thomas de; politician (Liberal) and Lord Lieutenant (1880–82); b. London; ed. Bembridge, Harrow and Christ Church, Oxford. He was appointed to Ireland by W. E. Gladstone* at the height of the Land League agitation, when his Chief Secretary was W. E. Forster* with whom he had a poor relationship. Cowper considered resigning when he did not receive the full coercion measures which he felt the agitation required. He disapproved of Gladstone's handling of affairs with Charles Stewart Parnell* and was a reluctant party to the 'Kilmainham Treaty'* after which he resigned his office. He left Ireland on 4 May and the Phoenix Park Murders* two days later led to the introduction of a tough coercion bill which he had drafted shortly before his resignation. Cowper later opposed Home Rule* and was President of the Royal Commission on the Land Acts.*

COX, WALTER (WATTY) (1770–1837). Gunsmith and journalist. As printer and editor of the *Union Star*,* he launched savage attacks on the Orange Order* and exposed working-class grievances. He was a member of the United Irishmen* whose moderate leadership feared his vitriolic pen. Cox resigned the editorship of his paper, and made a deal with the Under-Secretary, Edward Cooke, in which Cox provided information to Dublin Castle on the United Irishmen.* He travelled to the USA and on his return founded the *Irish Magazine* and *Asylum of Neglected Biography* which, despite fines and imprisonment, he produced from 1808 to 1815. Cox was awarded a pension on condition he left Ireland, which he did in 1816. He returned in 1835, lost his annuity and spent his last two years in impoverished circumstances.

CRAIG, SIR JAMES. *See* Craigavon, 1st Viscount.

CRAIG-COLLINS AGREEMENTS (JANUARY AND MARCH 1922). Agreements reached between Sir James Craig,* Prime Minister of Northern Ireland and Michael Collins,* Chairman of the Provisional Government. There had been a breakdown of law and order on both sides of the border: Republican attacks continued across the border, while in the North there were Protestant pogroms against the minority population. The South was operating a- boycott against goods originating in Belfast (*see* Belfast Boycott). In an attempt to end the strife, Craig and Collins met in London through the good offices of Winston Churchill.* The first agreement was published on 21 January and sought an end to the Belfast Boycott, the reinstatement of Catholics in their jobs (some 10,000 had been dismissed in the pogrom), and the appointment of a sub-committee to examine proposals for a mutual agreement on the boundary between the two states. In the event however, the meeting proved fruitless. Catholics were not restored to

their jobs and Craig stated on 28 March that he would not accept the verdict of the forthcoming Boundary Commission* should it prove unfavourable to Northern Ireland. In the south, militant republicans continued the Belfast Boycott. A new meeting between the leaders was arranged for London as a result of which a more comprehensive agreement was reached and signed on 30 March, and counter-signed by the British government. The March Agreement began by stating, 'Peace is today declared'. It went on to say, 'From today, the two governments undertake to co-operate in every way in their power with a view to the restoration of peaceful conditions in the unsettled areas.'

The main terms of the Agreement were: special police in mixed districts would be composed half of Catholics and half of Protestants; an Advisory Committee composed of Catholics would be set up to assist in the selection of Catholic recruits for the special police; searches for arms would be carried out by police forces, consisting equally of Catholics and Protestants; a Committee was to be established in Belfast with an equal number of Catholic and Protestant members to hear and investigate complaints of intimidation, outrages, etc; IRA activity was to cease within the six northern counties (although Collins had little control over this). A further meeting between the two leaders would be arranged to see whether means could be devised to secure the unity of Ireland and if this failed, whether agreeement could be arrived at on the boundary question other than by recourse to the Boundary Commission. The Northern signatories undertook to use every method to secure the restoration of expelled workers and if this was impracticable to have them employed on relief works; both the Northern and Free State governments undertook to arrange the release of political prisoners imprisoned for acts committed before 31 March 1922. The Agreement concluded, 'The two governments unite in appealing to all concerned to refrain from inflammatory speeches and to exercise restraint in the interests of peace'. The Agreement, signed on behalf of the Provisional Government by Collins, Eamon Duggan,* Kevin O'Higgins* and Arthur Griffith* and by Craig, Lord Londonderry* and E. M. Archdale for the Northern Ireland government, was countersigned on behalf of the United Kingdom government by Churchill and L. Worthington Evans.* Both agreements remained inconclusive as none of the main terms were implemented. Catholics in the Northern state remained victims of institutional discrimination while IRA attacks on Northern Ireland, both from internal and cross-border bases, continued unabated.

CRAIG, WILLIAM (1924–   ). Politician (Ulster Unionist); ed. Dungannon Royal School, Larne Grammar School and Queen's University. He became Ulster Unionist MP for Larne (1960–73) and was Unionist Chief Whip, 1962–63. As Minister for Home Affairs, 1966–68, he opposed concessions to the Northern Ireland Civil Rights Association.* During the NICRA demonstration in Derry on 5 October 1968 he ordered the presence of the Royal Ulster Constabulary* and there was a severe riot in the city. He was dismissed by Captain Terence O'Neill* shortly afterwards and became a close associate of Rev. Ian Paisley.* On 2 October 1969 Craig warned that 'if Westminster were to take over and suspend our parliament . . . we would oppose such a takeover by any means within our power. This would not rule out the use of arms'. In February 1972 he founded Ulster Vanguard* and a year later its political wing, the Vanguard Unionist Party which he led in the Assembly and Convention (*see* Northern Ireland). He lost control of the party in 1975 when he appeared to suggest that power-sharing with the Catholic minority might be acceptable in certain circumstances.

CRAIGAVON, 1st VISCOUNT (1871–1940). Craig, James; politician (Ulster Unionist) and first Prime Minister of Northern Ireland (1921–40); b. Strandstown, Belfast, the son of a distillery millionaire; ed. prep school and at Merchiston Castle, Edinburgh. He left school at seventeen to work as a stockbroker in Belfast and London. Returning to Belfast in 1892, he founded his own firm and was a founder-member of the Belfast Stock Exchange. He served in the Royal Irish Rifles during the Boer War (1899–1902), rising to the rank of captain. After the war he resumed his business career and entered politics as Unionist MP for the East County Down Division (1906–18). Craig was second in influence only to Sir Edward Carson* in Unionist opposition to Home Rule.* He played a dominant role in the Ulster Unionist Council* and the Orange Order.* He supported the Ulster Volunteer Force* and was a party to the inconclusive Buckingham Palace Conference* (July 1914). During World War I he was QMG in the 36th (Ulster) Regiment and saw action on the Western Front, (1914–15). He was knighted in 1918. Following the war, he was returned for Mid-Down and represented the constituency at Westminster until 1921. He served as Parliamentary Secretary to the Minister for Pensions (1919–20) and as Parliamentary and Financial Secretary to the Admiralty (1920–21). He accepted the Government of Ireland Act, 1920* as the basis for the state of Northern Ireland, and, upon Carson's resignation, became leader of the Ulster Unionist Party and first Prime Minister of the new state. Prior to assuming office he met with the Sinn Fein leader, Eamon de Valera,* in Dublin in April 1921, but they discovered no common ground. During the Treaty negotiations, Craig informed David Lloyd George* that the position of Northern Ireland was not negotiable. During the War of Independence,* Northern Ireland was under attack from the Irish Republican Army.* Pogroms were directed against Catholics in the North, and the South responded with the Belfast Boycott.* Craig met with Michael Collins* in an effort to resolve the impasse. The meetings produced the Craig-Collins Agreements.* Craig refused to nominate a Northern Ireland representative to the Boundary Commission* and in December 1925 he attended a tripartite meeting which shelved the Commission's Report. He played a major role in ensuring that Northern Ireland would remain a Protestant State. In 1929 the abolition of proportional representation* in favour of the straight vote increased the chances of Unionist majorities in local government even in areas where there was a distinct Catholic majority. In 1932 Craig said, 'Ours is a Protestant government and I am an Orangeman' and 'I have always said that I am an Orangeman first and a politician and a member of this parliament afterwards'. He reacted to the Constitution of 1937* introduced by Eamon de Valera by calling a snap election in 1938 in which partition was the key issue, which resulted in an overwhelming victory for the Unionists. When de Valera suggested in October 1938 that the time had come to consider an All-Ireland parliament to be elected on P.R., he replied, 'I can only reiterate the old battle-cry — No Surrender'. Craigavon retired from office in 1940 and was succeeded by John Miller Andrews.*

CRAWFORD, LIEUT-COLONEL FREDERICK (1861–1952). Soldier and Unionist; b. Belfast where his father owned a chemical factory; ed. Methodist College, Belfast and University College, London. He worked in Harland and Wolff's shipyard as an apprentice electrical engineer. He founded Young Ulster* in 1892. Crawford held a commission in the Mid Ulster Artillery in 1894 and was a captain in the Donegal Artillery in 1898. He served in South Africa during the Boer War. Closely identified with Unionist resistance to Home Rule,* he was a founder-member of

the Ulster Volunteer Force* in 1913. In 1914 he was commissioned by the Ulster Unionist Council* to purchase guns in Hamburg for the UVF. The episode became popularly known as the Larne Gun-running.* When the state of Northern Ireland was established in 1921 Crawford sought legal status for the UVF but this was resisted by the government. He was appointed commandant of the new Special Constabulary* in South Belfast (1921).

CRAWFORD, ROBERT LINDSAY (1868–1945). Journalist; b. Lisburn, Co. Antrim; ed. privately. After a period in business he turned to journalism when he founded and edited the *Irish Protestant* (1901–06). As Grand Master of the Independent Orange Order,* he was the author of 'The Magheramore Manifesto'.* He became editor of the *Ulster Guardian* but lost the job when he was expelled from the Independent Orange Order for advocating Home Rule,* after which he emigrated to Canada (1910). Crawford was later trade representative in New York for the Free State.

CRAWFORD, WILLIAM SHARMAN (1781–1861). Politician (Liberal); b. Co. Down; MP Dundalk (1835). He supported Catholic Emancipation,* although he later quarrelled with Daniel O'Connell.* MP Rochdale (1841), he supported a federal solution to the Irish demand for a parliament. He fought throughout his career for the legalisation of the Ulster Custom* – the 'three Fs' – and supported the Tenant League.* Two of his bills attempting to secure Tenant Right* were defeated (1847, 1852). He was defeated when he stood for parliament in Down (1852), largely because of his identification with Tenant Right in the South of Ireland.

CREGAN, MARTIN (1788–1870). Painter; b. Co. Meath. He trained in the Dublin Society's School of Art, and in London under Sir Martin

Archer-Shee. Cregan first exhibited at the RA in 1812. He returned to Dublin (1822) and was an original member of the RHA the following year and President from 1832 to 1856, when he was succeeded by George Petrie.* Cregan is said to have painted over 300 portraits of the leading members of contemporary Irish society.

CRIME AND OUTRAGE (IRELAND) ACT, (29 NOVEMBER 1847). Legislation introduced in the British House of Commons by Sir George Grey in an attempt to stem the tide of violent agrarian discontent in Ireland, which had resulted in the murder of sixteen landlords within a twelve-month period. The Act gave the Lord Lieutenant power, at his discretion, to draft police into a district, such a district to be required immediately to repay the cost of the drafting. Arms were to be borne only by persons already licensed or holding official positions; JPs, naval and military officers etc; gamekeepers were allowed a gun, and householders might keep firearms within the house, for protection. When a murder had been committed, all male persons in the district between the ages of sixteen and sixty were liable to be called upon to assist in finding the criminal, and failure to assist was a misdemeanour, punishable by two years' imprisonment. The Bill received the royal assent on 20 December 1847, and to ensure its enforcement, three bodies of 5,000 troops were despatched to Arklow, Clonmel and Limerick City. *See also* Agrarian Crime.

CROKE, THOMAS WILLIAM (1824–1902). Archbishop of Cashel (R.C.) (1875–1902); b. Ballyclough, Co. Cork; ed. Charleville, Co. Cork and at the Irish Colleges, Paris, and Rome. He ministered in Cloyne, Co. Cork (1849–58) and taught at St Colman's College, Fermoy, Co. Cork, where he was President (1858–65). He was P.P., Doneraile, Co. Cork (1865–70). Dr Croke spent four

years as Bishop of Auckland, New Zealand before being translated to Cashel in 1875. He became a notable public figure, supporting land agitation and other forms of nationalism. He supported the Land League* but later condemned the No Rent Manifesto.* When the Plan of Campaign* was condemned by the Vatican as a result of the Persico* investigation, he devised an ingenious formula which allowed it to continue. He was the author of the *No Tax Manifesto*.* His opposition to the continued leadership of the Irish Parliamentary Party* by Charles Stewart Parnell* following the O'Shea divorce in 1890 was a major contribution to his being replaced as leader of the party by Justin McCarthy.* Dr Croke was a lifelong opponent of intemperance and established throughout his archdiocese branches of the temperance organisation, St Patrick's League of the Cross. He numbered among his close friends William O'Brien* and Sir Charles Gavan Duffy.* He was the first patron of the Gaelic Athletic Association,* and his name is perpetuated in Croke Park, Dublin, headquarters of the GAA.

CROKER, THOMAS CROFTON (1798–1854). Antiquary; b. Cork. He went to London in 1817 where he worked as a clerk at the Admiralty. He was first known as a painter and when he turned to literature he illustrated many of his own works. He was instrumental in the foundation of the Camden Society (1839), the Percy Society (1840) and was a founder-member of the British Archaeological Association in 1843. Croker returned frequently to the south-west of Ireland where he devoted himself largely to the collection of poetry and folklore. He was a frequent contributor to *Blackwood's Magazine* and to the *Morning Post*. His writings include *Researches in the South of Ireland* (1824), *Fairy Legends and traditions in the south-west of Ireland* (3 vols, 1825–28), *Harlequin and the eagle* (play, 1826), *Daniel O'Rourke* (1829), *The Christ-*

mas Box (1829), *Legends of the Lakes* (1829), *The Keen of the South of Ireland* (1844). Works which he edited include *The popular songs of Ireland* (1839), *The historical songs of Ireland illustrative of the struggle between James II and William II* (1841), *Popular Songs of the French invasions of Ireland* (4 vols, 1845–47).

CRONE, JOHN SMYTH (1858–1945). Physician and author; b. Belfast; ed. Belfast Academical Institution and Queen's College, where he qualified as a doctor. After working at the London Hospital he established a practice in Willesden where he worked for forty years. He was chairman of the Willesden District Council (1900–03), a member of the Middlesex Co. Council (1906) and Deputy Coroner (from 1917). Founder of the *Irish Book Lover* (1909) which he edited until 1924, he was president of the Irish Literary Society* (1918–25). Crone was co-editor with Francis Joseph Bigger* of the *Reliques of Barney Malone* (1894). He published *Francis Joseph Bigger 'In Remembrance'* (1927) and *A Concise Dictionary of Irish Biography* in 1928.

CROSS, ERIC (1905–   ). Chemist, writer and broadcaster; b. Newry, Co. Down. His major work, *The Tailor and Ansty*, created a sensation on its publication in 1942 and ran foul of the Censorship of Publications Board.* The book deals with the life of a West Cork tailor, Timothy Buckley,* preserving his personal philosophies, sayings and doings. Cross is a well-known short-story writer and a frequent broadcaster on Radio Eireann.

CROWLEY, PETER O'NEILL (1832–67). Fenian; b. Ballymacoda, Co. Cork. A farmer, he led a successful raid on Knockadoon coastguard station during the Fenian rising of 1867. He was wounded in Kilcloney Wood while evading capture in Co.

Tipperary. He was taken to Mitchelstown, Co. Cork where he died.

CROZIER, BRIGADIER-GENERAL FRANK PERCY (1879–1937). Soldier; Commandant, Auxiliaries* (August 1920–February 1921); ed. Wellington College. He served in the Boer War and retired in 1908. For a time he trained the Ulster Volunteer Force.* Serving again in the army during World War I, he held a commission of captain in the Irish Fusiliers, was a Lieutenant-Colonel in the Royal Irish Rifles (1916) and Brigadier-General in command of the 119th Infantry Brigade (November 1916). He was GOC of the 40th Division in France, (March–April 1919), fought in the Lithuanian Army and in the Polish Army against Russia (1919–20). As commandant of the Auxiliaries to the Royal Irish Constabulary* General Crozier became a centre of controversy when he resigned the post in February 1921. During the previous November he had been ordered by General Tudor* not to dismiss Auxiliaries for indiscipline. However, after a raid by Auxiliaries on a shop which they wrecked in Trim, Co. Meath on 9 February and the murder of two young men by Auxiliaries in Drumcondra, Dublin, Crozier dismissed Auxiliaries who were immediately reinstated by Tudor. His resignation drew attention to the indiscipline of the Auxiliaries and the Black and Tans.* He published *A Brass Hat in No Man's Land* (1930), *Impressions and Recollections* (1930), *Five Years Hard* (1932), *Angels on Horseback* (1932), *Ireland for Ever* (1932) and *The Men I Killed* (1937).

'CUBA FIVE'. Five Fenians who sailed to New York in January 1871 on the S.S. *Cuba* following their release from imprisonment in England for Fenian activities, became known as the 'Cuba Five'. The five were Jeremiah O'Donovan Rossa,* Charles Underwood O'Connell,* John Devoy,* John McClure and Henry Mulleda. The five received a tumultuous reception from New York's

Irish population on arrival and a resolution of welcome was passed by the US House of Representatives. All five continued to be active members of the Fenian movement in America.

CULLEN, PAUL, CARDINAL (1803–78). Archbishop of Dublin (1852–78) and first Irish Cardinal (1866); b. Ballitore, Co. Kildare; ed. Carlow; ordained in Rome (1829). He was appointed Archbishop of Armagh in 1849 and translated to Dublin in 1852. He embarked on an ambitious church-building programme throughout Ireland, and assisted and encouraged Catholic teaching orders. He convened the Synod of Thurles* in 1850 to bring the Irish church into line with Roman practices. Totally opposed to inter-denominational education, he attempted to provide for Catholic university education by establishing the Catholic University* and invited John Henry Newman* to be its first Rector. Although he had helped Frederick Lucas* to win Meath in 1852, Dr Cullen opposed the Independent Irish Party,* ordering his clergy to abstain from partisan politics except in cases where specific Catholic interests were involved. He promoted an Irish Brigade to defend the papacy against Garibaldi in 1859. He opposed the Fenians,* and in 1861 forbade the use of the pro-Cathedral, Dublin for the lying-in-state of Terence Bellew MacManus.* He attempted to channel nationalism to his own ends by founding the National Association* in 1864 to secure Disestablishment of the Church of Ireland.* At the Vatican Council of 1870, he was a staunch supporter of the definition of papal infallibility. He presided over the Synod of Maynooth in 1875. Throughout his life he remained unaffected by the criticism he provoked from both Irish and British politicians. He left an indelible mark on the organisational structures of the Catholic Church in Ireland.

CUMANN GAODHALACH NA hEAGLAISE. Founded by clergymen of the Church of Ireland in 1914 to give expression to 'all those aspirations for a more intense and real national character in the church'. Within four years the society had 140 members and was holding services in Irish and had published a hymnal in Irish and sponsored lectures on Irish religious literature. The movement was weakened by the new nationalism which arose in the wake of the Easter Rising of 1916.* In June 1916 it passed a resolution condemning the rising and affirming loyalty to the King. During the following year members of the executive sought to extract assurances from the committee that it would abide by the June 1916 resolution. When the resolution was rescinded by the committee in 1918, the executive founded another organisation, Comhluadar Gaodhalach na Fiadhnuise, which contained the majority of the CGE.

CUMANN LE BÉALOIDEAS ÉIREANN (THE IRISH FOLKLORE SOCIETY). *See* Irish Folklore Commission.

CUMANN NA mBAN. Women's organisation founded in Dublin in November 1913 at the same time as the Irish Volunteers* of which it became the women's division. It was led by Countess Markievicz* and Mrs Kathleen Clarke.* In November 1914, when the Cumann declared its support for the Volunteers, it lost some of its membership. By 1916 it had forty-three affiliated branches. The women supported the Easter Rising of 1916.* In its Constitution after the Rising, the Cumann declared itself 'an independent body of Irish women, pledged to work for the establishment of an Irish republic, by organising and training the women of Ireland to take their places by the side of those who are working for a free Ireland'. The Cumann continued to work for the republican movement during the War of Independence.* The majority of its members opposed the Treaty.* During the 1920s, led by

Maud Gonne,* they supported the Irish Republican Army* and were associated with some of the radical movements of the period.

CUMANN NA nGAEDHEAL (1900).

Founded on 30 September 1900 by Arthur Griffith* and William Rooney* to provide a co-ordinating body for smaller societies whose aim was to oppose English influences in Ireland. Its aims, propagated through Griffith's paper *The United Irishman,** were to diffuse a knowledge of Ireland's economic resources, support Irish industry, the study of Irish history, language, music and art and, in general, to combat the anglicisation of Ireland. Griffith was elected president and vice-presidents included Maud Gonne,* John MacBride,* John Daly,* Thomas J. Clarke* (then in the USA), John O'Leary* and Rooney. Griffith called upon the Cumann na nGaedheal Convention in 1902 to demand the withdrawal of the Irish Parliamentary Party* from Westminster. A year later the Executive constituted itself the National Council* to organise a protest against the visit of King Edward VII. Cumann na nGaedheal was later absorbed into Sinn Fein.* The name Cumann na nGaedheal was revived by W. T. Cosgrave* as the name for the political party formed by those who accepted the Treaty, in 1923 (see below).

CUMANN NA nGAEDHEAL. Political party founded by W. T. Cosgrave* in March 1923 for supporters of the Treaty.* As republicans did not enter the Dail until 1927 when Fianna Fail* broke with a policy of abstention, Cumann na nGaedheal formed governments until 1932. The party was identified with the commercial and propertied classes and the bigger farmers. It was strongest in the midlands and the east and weakest in the west. It was supported by the *Irish Independent,** the *Cork Examiner** and the *Irish Times.** Cosgrave led the party until it merged with others to form Fine Gael* in 1933. The party's strength from 1923 until 1932 was:

	Seats	Votes
1923	63	409,421
1927 (June)	47	315,277
1927 (Sept)	62	453,121
1932	57	449,506

	% Valid Poll	% of Electorate
1923	38.9	22.9
1927 (June)	27.5	18.2
1927 (Sept)	38.7	26.2
1932	35.3	26.6

For governments formed by the party *see* Governments. For details on the party in power *see*: Public Safety Acts; Irish Republican Army; Civil War; Army Mutiny; Boundary Commission; Land Acts; Agricultural Credit Corporation; Kevin O'Higgins; Electoral Amendment Act; Jinks Affair; Shannon Scheme *and* Electricity Supply Board; Land Annuities; Ultimate Financial Agreement; Army Comrades Association; Blueshirts.

CUMANN NA POBLACHTA. Republican League; political party founded by Eamon de Valera* in March 1922. It was supported principally by opponents of the Treaty.* Following the defeat of the republican cause in the Civil War the party became absorbed in Sinn Fein.* The majority of Cumann members rallied behind de Valera when he founded a new republican party, Fianna Fail,* in May 1926.

CUMANN POBLACHTA NA hÉIREANN. Irish republican party founded by Sean MacBride* in 1936, its aim was to provide a political platform for republicans opposed to the Republican Congress.* It received relatively little support from membership of the Irish Republican Army.* Soon after its first ard-fheis in November 1936, it disappeared. MacBride's next political party, Clann na Poblachta,* enjoyed a much greater measure of success.

107

CURRAGH INCIDENT. The incident sometimes known as the Curragh 'Mutiny' occurred in March 1914, shortly before the (third) Home Rule Bill,* which was strongly opposed by the Ulster Unionists,* was due to come into force. The War Office instructed General Sir Arthur Paget* to prepare plans for the protection of arms' depots in Ulster (14 March 1914). He was informed that while any officers who lived in Ulster would not be asked to act in the province, all others would be required to carry out their orders or be dismissed. Major-General Sir Hubert Gough* chaired a meeting of fifty-six officers at the Curragh Military Camp (20 March). They decided to offer their resignations rather than move against Ulster opponents of Home Rule.* Gough personally communicated the officers' decision to the War Office where it was sympathetically received by General Sir Henry Wilson.* The government, faced with a situation tantamount to mutiny, sidestepped the issue. Through the Army Council Gough was authorised on 23 March to inform the officers that the incident of the 'resignations' had been a misunderstanding. Gough stated in an interview with the *Daily Telegraph* that he had received a signed guarantee that in no circumstances would he or his officers be sent to enforce Home Rule upon Ulster. He declared that if the issue had to be resolved in open conflict, he would rather fight for Ulster than against it.

CURRAN, JOHN PHILPOT (1750–1817). Lawyer, orator and wit; b. Newmarket, Co. Cork; ed. TCD. He was called to the Bar in 1775, became a King's Counsel in 1782 and MP for Kilbeggan in 1783. During his career at the Bar he defended prominent United Irishmen including Hamilton Rowan, William Drennan, Oliver Bond, Napper Tandy, Theobald Wolfe Tone and the brothers Henry and John Sheares. Curran opposed the Act of Union.* His daughter, Sarah Curran,* became the fiancée of Robert Emmet* whose defence he subsequently refused. In 1807 he was appointed Master of the Rolls and held the post until 1814. Deserted by his wife, Curran's last years were spent alone and embittered in London, where he died. His remains were returned to Ireland for burial at Glasnevin in 1834.

CURRAN, SARAH (1782–1808). Daughter of John Philpot Curran* and sweetheart of Robert Emmet.* Virtually disowned by her father when her romance with Emmet became known, she left Dublin for Cork where, with her sister, she lived with the Penrose family. In Cork she met Captain R. H. Sturgeon of the Royal Staff Corps, a nephew of the Marquis of Rockingham. Following their marriage Sturgeon was posted to Sicily where they remained until 1808. Her health, impaired since the execution of Emmet, gave way shortly after they took up residence in Hythe, Kent, where she died on 5 May. Sturgeon, in deference to her wishes, had her body returned to the family seat in Newmarket, Co. Cork, for burial. A slab of Sicilian marble intended by him for her tombstone was delivered in error to Newberry, Mallow and never reached its true destination. Her grave is marked by a Celtic cross erected by the Newmarket citizens. Her tragic romance was featured in Washington Irving's *The Broken Heart* and in Thomas Moore's nostalgic air, 'She is far from the land'.

CUSACK, MICHAEL (1847–1907). Gaelic athletic enthusiast; b. Co. Clare. A teacher, he worked at Blackrock College and Clongowes Wood. He founded a school to assist young people entering the Civil Service or the University. He founded the Civil Service Academy Hurling Club and this experience germinated the idea of a Gaelic Athletic Association* of which he was co-founder in 1884. After his death the *Gaelic Journal* said of him that he 'was the living embodiment of the GAA'. Cusack was also the model for the Citizen in James Joyce's *Ulysses*.

CUSTOM HOUSE, DUBLIN (25 May 1921). The destruction of the Custom House was planned by Oscar Traynor,* O/C, Dublin Brigade of the Irish Republican Army.* It was on the suggestion of Eamon de Valera,* who sought to bring the civil service to a halt and at the same time attract international attention to the War of Independence.* Several hundred members of the IRA were involved in the action, with paraffin oil commandeered for the purpose and brought to the Custom House by lorry. The raiders entered by three doorways and ordered the evacuation of the building. A five-minute delay enabled Black and Tans* to arrive and a gunbattle took place, starting at 1.25 p.m. As a result of the fighting five IRA men were killed and about eighty wounded. The interior of the Custom House was destroyed by a fire which burned for eight days.

D

DAIL COURTS. Courts of law under the jurisdiction of Dail Eireann* were established during the War of Independence* to replace the British courts of law. In June 1920 they came under the authority of the Minister for Home Affairs, Austin Stack.* The courts' decrees were executed by police provided by the Dail on the basis of one officer for each brigade area. There were four types of court in operation: Parish Courts, District Courts, Circuit Courts (special sessions of the District Court held three times a year and presided over by a 'circuit judge') and a Supreme Court. The justice administered by the Dail Courts was based on the law as it stood on 2 January 1919. Attempts to suppress the courts failed but they were forced underground. During the period after the Truce* of July 1921 they were able to operate more openly. Upon the foundation of the Free State a new system of courts was established (*see* Courts of Justice Act, 1924).

DAIL EIREANN (21 January 1919– 5 December 1922). The Dail was the Constituent Assembly of Ireland. It first assembled on 21 January 1919, attended by Sinn Fein representatives who had been returned at the general election of December 1918. When the first Dail assembled at the Mansion House in Dublin there were twenty-seven Sinn Fein representatives present: thirty-four had been imprisoned since before the election while eight were unable to attend for other reasons. Cathal Brugha* was declared Acting President in the absence of Eamon de Valera,* President of Sinn Fein, who was imprisoned at Lincoln. Those present at the opening session approved the Constitution, the Declaration of Independence* and the Democratic Programme.* A *Message to the Free Nations of the World* was also approved. The Constitution approved by the Dail, as amended on 25 August 1921, was:

The Constitution of Dail Eireann
Article 1.
All legislative powers shall be vested in Dail Eireann, composed of Deputies, elected by the Irish people from the existing Irish parliamentary constituencies.

Article 2.
(*a*) All executive powers shall be vested in the members, for the time being, of the Ministry.
(*b*) The Ministry shall consist of a President of the Ministry, elected by Dail Eireann, and four Executive Officers, viz: A Secretary of Finance, A Secretary of Home Affairs; A Secretary of Foreign

Affairs; A Secretary of National Defence; each of whom the President shall nominate and have power to dismiss.

(c) Every member of the Ministry shall be a member of Dail Eireann, and shall at all times be responsible to the Dail.

(d) At the first meeting of Dail Eireann after their nomination by the President, the names of the Executive Officers shall be separately submitted to Dail Eireann for approval.

(e) The appointment of the President shall date from his election, and the appointment of each Executive Officer from the date of the approval by the Dail of his nomination.

(f) The Ministry or any members, therefore, may at any time, be removed by vote of the Dail upon motion for that specific purpose, provided that at least seven days notice in writing of that motion shall have been given.

Article 3.
A Chairman elected annually by the Dail, or in his absence a Deputy Chairman so elected, shall preside at the meetings of Dail Eireann. Only members of the Dail shall be eligible for these offices. In case of the absence of the Chairman and Deputy Chairman the Dail shall fill the vacancies or elect a temporary Chairman.

Article 4.
All monies required by the Ministry shall be obtained on vote of the Dail. The Ministry shall be responsible to the Dail for all monies so obtained, and shall present properly audited accounts for the expenditure of the same – twice yearly – in the months of May and November. The audit shall be conducted by an Auditor or Auditors appointed by the Dail. No member of the Dail shall be eligible for such appointment.

Article 5.
This Constitution is provisional and is liable to alteration upon seven days notice of motion for that specific purpose.

The first ministry appointed consisted of Cathal Brugha (President), Eoin MacNeill (Finance), Michael Collins (Home Affairs) and George Noble, Count Plunkett (National Defence). The second session of the first Dail was held on 1 April when de Valera was elected President (or Priomh Aire, First Minister). His first Ministry or Cabinet was: Michael Collins (Finance); Cathal Brugha (Defence); Arthur Griffith (Home Affairs); Count Plunkett (Foreign Affairs); William T. Cosgrave (Local Government); Constance Countess Markievicz (Labour); Eoin MacNeill (Industries); Ernest Blythe (Trades and Commerce); and Sean O'Kelly (Irish, from June 1920). Non-Cabinet Ministers were: Sean Etchingham (Fisheries); Robert Barton (Agriculture); and Lawrence Ginnell (Publicity).

On 20 August, Brugha proposed a motion that every deputy, officer, clerk of the Dail and each member of the Irish Volunteers* should swear allegiance to the Dail of the Irish Republic. The text of the Oath (which was approved) was: 'I, A.B., do solemnly swear (or affirm) that I do not and shall not yield a voluntary support to any pretended government, authority or power within Ireland hostile and inimical thereto, and I do further swear (or affirm) that to the best of my knowledge and ability I will support and defend the Irish Republic and the Government of the Irish Republic, which is Dail Eireann, against all enemies, foreign and domestic, and I will bear true faith and allegiance to the same, and that I take this obligation freely without any mental reservation or purpose of evasion, so help me God'. This Oath had the effect of turning the Volunteers into the Army of the Irish Republic, or, as they were known, The Irish Republican Army.*

On 10 September 1919, the Dail was declared a dangerous association and prohibited. Thereafter its meetings were in secret and ministers carried out their duties as best they could. The first Dail arranged for Arbitration Courts* to be established for the purpose of resolving agrarian disputes. These courts were fully operational by the summer of 1920. Arrangements were made for the establishment of a Consular Service and funds were allocated for afforestation and fisheries. A National Commission of Inquiry into the Industrial Resources of Ireland was appointed. In addition the Minister for Agriculture established Land Banks to advance funds to farmers. A Committee was appointed to draft the Constitution and Rules of Court, resulting in the creation of a Supreme, Parish and District Courts (*see* Dail Courts).

The Government of Ireland Act 1920* established two parliaments in Ireland, one for what the Act termed Northern Ireland and the other for 'Southern Ireland'. Elections to the new parliaments were held in May 1921. Sinn Fein won 128 out of 132 seats in the twenty-six counties, and sat in Dail Eireann, ignoring the existence of Northern Ireland and refuting the validity of the Southern parliament, the inaugural meeting of which on 28 June only the four Dublin University Unionist representatives attended. Its only other meeting was on 14 January 1922 for the purpose of transferring power to the Provisional Government. The Second Dail Eireann met at the Mansion House on 16 August 1921 to receive from de Valera the reports of his meetings with the British Prime Minister, embracing discussions by which a treaty might be found to end the War of Independence.* De Valera himself had rejected the proposals which offered Dominion status, and on 23 August the Dail, in secret session, rejected those terms. On 26 August, de Valera was elected President of the Irish Republic. The new Cabinet consisted of: Michael Collins (Finance); Austin Stack (Home Affairs); Arthur Griffith (Foreign Affairs); Cathal Brugha (National Defence);

W. T. Cosgrave (Local Government); and Robert Barton (Economic Affairs). Non-Cabinet members of the Ministry were: Countess Markievicz (Labour); Ernest Blythe (Trade and Commerce); Sean Etchingham (Fisheries); J. J. O'Kelly (Education); A. O'Connor (Agriculture); and Desmond Fitzgerald (Publicity). Plenipotentiaries to meet the British were appointed by the Dail on 14 September and negotiations began in London on 5 October. On 3 December, when the Cabinet met to consider the Articles of Agreement which had been worked out, there was a division. De Valera, who was holding to his own proposal of External Association.* would not accept the Articles as presented. The delegates returned to London under instruction not to sign any document until it had first been ratified by the Cabinet. On 6 December, under threat from Lloyd George that the alternative was 'immediate and terrible war', the delegates signed the document.

The second Dail debated the Treaty terms between 14 December 1921 and 10 January 1922. The debates were conducted in an atmosphere of bitterness as the gap between those who stood for the Republic of Easter 1916 and of January 1919 and those who found the Treaty terms acceptable, widened. The Dail voted on 7 January on the motion 'that Dail Eireann approves the Treaty'. The vote was 64 for approval, 57 against. De Valera resigned the Presidency on 9 January, and was replaced by Arthur Griffith. The second Cabinet of Dail Eireann from January–September 1922 consisted of: Arthur Griffith (President); Michael Collins (Finance); Eamon Duggan (Home Affairs); George Gavan Duffy (Foreign Affairs, July–August); Michael Hayes (Foreign Affairs, August–September); Richard Mulcahy (National Defence); W. T. Cosgrave (Local Government); Kevin O'Higgins (Economic Affairs). Non-Cabinet members were Joseph McGrath (Labour), Ernest Blythe (Trade and Commerce), Michael Hayes (Education), Patrick Hogan (Agriculture), Desmond Fitzgerald (Publicity), and Michael Staines (Director of the Belfast Boycott). On 8 June the second Dail adjourned; by the time it met again (30 June) the Civil War* had begun. This meeting of the Dail on 30 June was for the purpose of transferring power to the new Dail, elected on 16 June; having done this, the Dail again adjourned, having arranged a session for 1 July. This meeting however never occurred. Because of the war situation the Dail was not summoned and on 4 August it was prorogued.

The republican deputies refused to recognise the new Dail when it met on 9 September. They claimed that it was not the legitimate successor to the first and second Dails, stating that the oath was required before a deputy could take his seat and that it therefore derived its authority from the Treaty and not from the Irish people. The only republican who attended the opening was Lawrence Ginnell, who did so at de Valera's suggestion. Republicans called it the Provisional Dail but its supporters regarded it as the third Dail Eireann. The Free State came into existence on 6 December 1922 when it assumed the powers of the Provisional Government.

DALLAS, REV. ALEXANDER R.C. (1791–1869). English evangelical clergyman (C. of E.). His experiences on the continent during the Napoleonic wars left him obsessed with the evils of Catholicism, in particular the doctrine of papal authority. He served with the Church Mission Society prior to his ordination. During a visit to Ireland in 1840 he came into contact with Irish ultra-Protestantism and through Arthur Guinness was introduced to many influential people who persuaded him to remain in Ireland, where he won much support from Protestant landlords in the west of the country. He established his first mission at Castlekerke on Lough Corrib, where he also built a schoolhouse. During the Famine of 1845–49* he favoured spiritual rather than material assistance, and claimed that the misery of the people offered an ideal opportunity to win them away from Catholicism. In March 1849, he established the Irish Church Missions to Roman Catholics* with the support and assistance of the C.I. Bishop of Tuam, Thomas Plunket (*see* Second Reformation).

Assisted by Rev. Hyacinth D'Arcy,* Dallas founded missions at seven Co. Galway centres. In all he established twenty-five churches, eight parsonages and thirty schoolhouses in the process of which he attracted the hostility of the Catholic Church and alienated the more moderate Protestant clergy to whom his evangelical style was offensive. His chief opponents were Fr Patrick Lavelle* and the Archbishop of Tuam, John MacHale.* His publications include *Popery in Ireland : A Warning to Protestants* (1847), *Point of Hope in Ireland's Present Crisis* (1849), *Protestants in Ireland* (1851) and *Story of the Irish Church Missions* (1867).

DALTON, GENERAL EMMET (1898–1978). Soldier and filmproducer. He served in the Dublin Fusiliers during World War I where he attained the rank of major and was awarded the Military Cross. He became assistant Director of Training in the Irish Republican Army* and was a close friend and aide to Michael Collins.* During the War of Independence,* Dalton led a daring attempt to rescue Sean MacEoin* from Mountjoy Jail (14 May 1921). His party gained entrance but were discovered, and made a dramatic retreat. He travelled to England with Collins during the Treaty negotiations. Dalton supported the Treaty and was Director of Military Operations in the National Army of the Free State during the Civil War,* commanding the attack on the Four Courts.* He was placed in charge of operations to carry out his own suggestion that republican strongholds were vulnerable to attacks from the sea. He operated in Cork County during August 1922 and was with Collins at Béal na mBláth on the 22nd of that month when the latter was fatally wounded. Dalton subsequently moved to Hollywood and produced films for Paramount and MGM. He produced films in England and, later, with Louis Elliman, founded Ardmore Studios.

DALTON, JOHN (1792–1867). Historian; b. Bessville, Co. Westmeath; ed. locally and TCD. Called to the Irish Bar in 1813, he achieved his first major success a year later with the publication of *Dermid*. In 1827 he was awarded the Cunningham Medal of the RIA for his essay on *The Social and Political State of Ireland from the First to the Twelfth Century*. Dalton was appointed a commissioner of the Loan Fund Board, Dublin, in 1835. The new appointment afforded him a greater opportunity to pursue his study of Irish antiquities and archaeology. He was a frequent contributor to *Transactions* of the Royal Academy.* His works include *Lives of the Archbishops of Dublin* (1838), *History of the County of Dublin* (1838), *History of Drogheda* (2 vols, 1844), *The History of Ireland* (2 vols, 1844), *History of Dundalk* (with James Roderick O'Flanagan,* 1864), *King James the Second's Irish Army List* (1865).

DALY, EDWARD (1891–1916). Fenian; b. Limerick; ed. CBS. Both his father and his uncle, John Daly,* were prominent members of the Irish Republican Brotherhood.* His sister married Thomas J. Clarke* (*see* Clarke, Kathleen). A member of the Irish Volunteers,* he commanded at the Four Courts during the Easter Rising of 1916.* Following the surrender he was court-martialled, sentenced to death and executed on 4 May.

DALY, JAMES (1836–1910). Journalist and land agitator; b. Castlebar, Co. Mayo; ed. locally. As editor of *The Connaught Telegraph* he campaigned for land reform in his native county. He advised the tenants of Irishtown, Co. Mayo* and organised the meeting of 20 April 1879. President of the Castlebar Tenants' Defence Association, he played a leading role in the formation of the Land League of Mayo* and the (Irish National) Land League.* His evidence before the Bessborough Commission* influenced that body in its recommendations for land reform. Personality differences within the Land League led to a breach between Daly and other leaders and he became highly critical of the League's aims and organisation. He campaigned for the distribution of grazing land among smallholders and the landless, but opposed Michael Davitt* in the demand for nationalisation of the land. He supported Charles Stewart Parnell* in the demand for Home Rule,* defining it 'as unqualified control of Irish affairs by the Irish people'.

DALY, JOHN (1845–1916). Fenian; b. Limerick; ed. locally. He became an active member of the Irish Republican Brotherhood* in 1863 and led the Limerick City Company in the raid on Kilmallock Barracks during the rising of 1867. Following the rising he went to the USA where he was active in the Fenian movement. He returned during the Land War* and as a member of the Supreme Council* of the IRB became organiser for Connaught and Ulster. Later, while working as a mental hospital attendant in England he was again an organiser for the movement and assisted the Dynamiters.* Daly was arrested at Birkenhead in possession of explosives (1884) and was sentenced to life imprisonment. While in Portland prison he became acquainted with Thomas J. Clarke.* A Commission of Inquiry investigated Daly's allegation that he was being poisoned by prison staff and public agitation led to his release in 1896. While in prison Daly was elected MP for Limerick. Upon release he returned to Ireland and from there to the USA, where he embarked on an extensive lecture-tour. Daly opened a bakery in Limerick and was three times Mayor of the city (1899–1901). His nephew Edward Daly* and T. J. Clarke, who had married a niece, Kathleen (*see* Clarke, Kathleen) were executed for their roles in the Easter Rising of 1916.* The reminiscences of 'John Daly of Limerick' appeared in *Irish Freedom*,* 1912–13.

D'ARCY, REV. HYACINTH TALBOT (1806–74). Clergyman (C.I.) Evangelical; b. Glen Ierne, Clifden, Co. Galway, eldest son of John D'Arcy, a model landlord who developed Clifden; ed. TCD. He became an Evangelical while convalescing after the amputation of a leg, caused by a diseased knee-joint. Upon the death of his father in 1839, he became an active missioner around Clifden where he was highly popular, working in association with Rev. A. R. C. Dallas,* Rev. Edward Nangle,* and the Irish Church Missions to the Roman Catholics* (*see* Second Reformation). He helped to establish missions at Ballyconree, Errisconor, Claggan, Sellerna, Moyruss, Roundstone and Ballinahinch. When his estate was taken over by the Encumbered Estates' Court* in 1851 he was ordained by the Evangelical Bishop of Tuam, Thomas Plunket. Unlike many of his fellow-evangelicals, D'Arcy was highly popular with the peasantry whom he helped materially during the Famine of 1845–49.*

DARGAN, WILLIAM (1799–1867). Railway financier; b. Co. Carlow; ed. England where he was apprenticed in a surveyor's office. Having worked under Thomas Telford on the Holyhead Road project he returned to Ireland and became a contractor on several road schemes, including the Dublin-Howth Road. He built the first Irish railroad, the Dublin-Kingstown line, upon which the first train travelled from Westland Row on 17 December 1838. Later railroads which he built were the Ulster Railway Line (opened August 1839) and the Great Southern and Western (1843–50). He also built the Ulster Canal (1834–42). It was estimated that he paid around £4,000,000 in wages between 1845 and 1850. He financed the Dublin Industrial Exhibition of 1853 with a gift of £100,000 and also financed the building of the National Gallery (1864). Following a fall from a horse in 1866 his health declined and consequently his business interests and financial situation deteriorated. *See also* Railways in Ireland.

DAVIN, MAURICE (1864–1927). Athlete and co-founder of the Gaelic Athletic Association;* b. Deerpark, Carrick-on-Suir, Co. Tipperary; ed. locally. He was a member of a family celebrated for its athletic prowess. During the 1870s, he and his brothers, Tom and Pat, held more than half of the world's records for running, jumping, hurdling and weight-throwing. In 1884 he was a founder and first president of the GAA. The athletic grounds at his home at Deerpark fostered Irish athletics.

DAVIS, EUGENE (b. 1857). Fenian and poet; b. Clonakilty, Co. Cork; ed. locally, Louvain and Paris. Because of his involvement with Fenianism, he was forced to flee Ireland and travelled to Paris where he met James Stephens.* He was expelled from France with Stephens in 1885 and spent some time on the continent before returning to Dublin in 1887. Davis was a frequent contributor to *Irishman, United Ireland,* The Nation* and *Young Ireland* under various pseudonyms. He edited *The Reliques of John Keegan Casey* in 1878. A volume of his poetry, *A Vision of Ireland*, appeared in 1889, the same year in which *The Poetical Works of Eugene Davis* was published.

DAVIS, THOMAS OSBORNE (1818–45). Poet, journalist and Young Irelander; b. Mallow, Co. Cork; ed. TCD. Called to the Bar (1838), he never practised. He became joint-editor with John Blake Dillon* of the *Dublin Morning Regis-*

ter (1840) and was co-founder with Dillon and Charles Gavan Duffy* of *The Nation* (15 October 1842). His first poem, 'My Grave' appeared in the third issue over the signature 'A True Celt'. His nationalist verse gave the paper its distinctive character, introducing stirring and popular works with the purpose of awakening the spirit of Irish nationalism. This example was followed by other writers, many of whose contributions were collected into *The Spirit of the Nation* (1843). He was an influential member of Young Ireland* and a supporter of the Repeal Association.* His best-known poems included 'A Nation Once Again', 'The West's Asleep', 'Lament for the Death of Owen Roe O'Neill', 'Fontenoy', 'Clare's Dragoons', 'Tone's Grave' and 'My Land'. His prose works were edited by Thomas William Rolleston* in 1889. A *Life of Davis* was published by Duffy (1896) who also wrote a lengthy introduction to Davis's *The Patriot Parliament of 1689* (1893).

DAVITT, MICHAEL (1846–1906). Agrarian agitator, nationalist, trade unionist and journalist; b. Straide, Co. Mayo. The family were evicted from their small holding in 1850 and moved to Lancashire where he worked as a child labourer in a cotton-mill until his right arm was severed by machinery in 1856. Davitt joined the Irish Republican Brotherhood* and was involved in the raid on Chester Castle (11 February 1867). He was the chief arms purchaser for the Fenians until 1870 when he was sentenced to fifteen years imprisonment on a dubious charge of incitement to murder. During his imprisonment on Dartmoor he was subjected to very harsh treatment. He was released on ticket of leave in December 1877. He travelled to the USA where he met John Devoy* and returned in 1879 to his native Mayo where he at once involved himself in land agitation, being instrumental in the organisation of the mass meetings at Irishtown* in April and Westport in June. These meetings led to the foundation of the Land League of Mayo* in which Davitt played a vital role. Charles Stewart Parnell* was persuaded by Davitt to become involved in land agitation and they became partners in the New Departure.* Although he had ceased active membership of the Fenians by 1880, Davitt was imprisoned on a number of occasions through the Land League's vigorous prosecution of the Land War and under the Coercion Acts.* During his terms of imprisonment, he became familiar with the ideals of the English socialist movement, some of which influenced his subsequent agrarian demands. The Kilmainham 'Treaty'* led to a breach with Parnell. Davitt said of it, 'It was the vital turning point in Mr Parnell's career and he unfortunately turned the wrong way'. Davitt was elected MP for Meath in 1882 but was unseated by special writ of the House of Commons. He founded a short-lived newspaper in London, *The Irish World* (1890), but the paper collapsed on his resignation. His attempts to organise the Irish agricultural workers into the Irish Democratic Trade and Labour Union met with little success.

When Parnell's leadership of the Irish Parliamentary Party* was highlighted in the wake of the O'Shea divorce case, Davitt was one of his most vociferous critics. Elected MP for North Meath in 1892, Davitt was again unseated on petition but was returned unopposed for North-East Cork later in that year. He was, however, forced to resign the seat on being declared a bankrupt in 1893. Davitt supported Keir Hardie who accepted Home Rule,* but while Davitt favoured the foundation of a Labour Party, his commitment to the Liberal Party for the sake of Home Rule prevented his joining the new party – leading to a breach with the Labour leader which was not healed until 1905. Between 1895–99 Davitt represented East Kerry and South Mayo at Westminster, and was co-founder with William O'Brien* of the United Irish League.* He withdrew from parliament in protest against the Boer War and visited South Africa to lend support to the Boer cause. His experiences in South Africa inspired his *Boer Fight for Freedom* which was published in 1904. His support for undenominational education drew upon Davitt the wrath of Edward Thomas O'Dwyer,* Bishop of Limerick, and the Archbishop of Dublin, William Walsh.* Davitt's support for socialism in his latter years was based on the premise that Ireland could only achieve independence with the support of the British working class. This, along with his call for land nationalisation, made him a much misunderstood figure in Ireland. His writings include *The Prison Life of Michael Davitt* (1878), *Leaves from a Prison Diary* (2 vols, 1885), *Defence of the Land League* (1891), *Life and Progress in Australia* (1895), *Within the Pale* (1903) and *The Fall of Feudalism in Ireland* (1904).

DEASY, CAPTAIN TIMOTHY (1841–1880). Fenian; b. Clonakilty, Co. Cork. The family emigrated to the USA in 1847 and settled at Lawrence, Mass. In June 1861 Timothy Deasy, along with his brother Connie, enlisted in the 9th Massachusetts Regiment (comprised entirely of Irish emigrants). During the American Civil War (1861–65) Deasy fought in thirty-four engagements and was promoted to 1st Lieutenant. Upon his discharge, he joined the Fenians* and became a member of the Supreme Council of the Irish Republican Brotherhood.* He travelled to Ireland (26 August 1855) but was arrested in Skibbereen, Co. Cork, and ordered to leave the country. Deasy returned to Ireland and was in Ulster when recalled to Dublin by Colonel Thomas J. Kelly* to assist in the escape of James Stephens* from the Bridewell prison. Following Stephens' successful escape (24 November 1865), Deasy returned via France to the USA where he supported the proposed Fenian invasion of Canada led by Capt. John O'Neill.* Upon the failure of O'Neill's mission, Deasy returned to Ireland as second-in-command to Kelly and oversaw preparations for the Fenian rising in Cork. Deasy led the raid on Chester Castle and was fortunate to avoid arrest, as the authorities had been informed of the raid by the Fenian spy, J. J. Corydon. Capt. Deasy returned to Ireland where the Fenian rising had miscarried and from there travelled to England. He arrived in Manchester, where the authorities had been informed by Corydon of the presence of high-ranking Fenian officers, and was arrested with Kelly on 11 September. While he and Kelly were en route from the courthouse, the prison van was attacked by a number of Fenians and in the encounter, Sergeant Charles Brett was fatally injured (*see* Manchester Martyrs). Deasy and Kelly were rescued; the former narrowly avoided recapture when soldiers searched a farmyard but failed to check the barn in which, still manacled, he was hiding. Having eventually made his way to the USA in 1869, Deasy ceased his open connection with Fenianism. He became landlord of a saloon bar in Lawrence, Mass., where he was elected City Councillor and later served two terms in the Massachusetts House of Representatives. Apart from a secret visit to Ireland, Deasy remained in the US. His grave in Lawrence is marked as that of a Union officer of the American Civil War.

DECLARATION OF INDEPENDENCE. Drafted by a committee selected at a meeting of Sinn Fein representatives on 8 January 1919. The major part of it was framed by George Gavan Duffy.* The Declaration was read at the meeting of the first Dail Eireann* on 21 January. It was read in Irish, French, and English, and was approved by the Dail.

DECLARATION OF INDEPENDENCE
Whereas the Irish people is by right a free people;

And whereas for seven hundred years the Irish people has never ceased to repudiate and has repeatedly protested in arms against foreign usurpation;

And whereas English rule in this country is, and always has been, based upon force and fraud and maintained by military occupation against the declared will of the people;

And whereas the Irish Republic was proclaimed in Dublin on Easter Monday, 1916, by the Irish Republican Army, acting on behalf of the Irish people;

And whereas the Irish people is resolved to secure and maintain its complete independence in order to promote the common weal, to re-establish justice, to provide for future defence, to ensure peace at home and good will with all nations, and to constitute a national policy based upon the people's will, with equal right and equal opportunity for every citizen;

And whereas at the threshold of a new era in history the Irish electorate has in the General Election of December, 1918, seized the first occasion to declare by an overwhelming majority its firm allegiance to the Irish Republic;

Now, therefore, we, the elected Representatives of the ancient Irish people in National Parliament assembled do, in the name of the Irish Nation, ratify the establishment of the Irish Republic and pledge ourselves and our people to make this declaration effective by every means at our command;

We ordain that the elected Representatives of the Irish people alone have power to make laws binding on the people of Ireland, that the Irish Parliament is the only Parliament to which the people will give its allegiance;

We solemnly declare foreign government in Ireland to be an invasion of our national right which we will never tolerate, and we demand the evacuation of our country by the English Government;

We claim for our national independence the recognition and support of every free nation in the world, and we proclaim that independence to be a condition precedent to the international peace thereafter;

In the name of the Irish people we humbly commit our destiny to Almighty God who gave our fathers the courage and determination to persevere through long centuries of a ruthless tyranny, and strong in the justice of the cause which they have handed down to us, we ask His Divine blessing on this the last stage of the struggle we have pledged ourselves to carry through to freedom.

See also Easter Rising of 1916 *and* Democratic Programme.

DEFENCE FORCES. The Irish Defence Forces consist of the army*, the air corps,* the Forsai Cosanta Aitiuil* (FCA), the Naval Service* and Slua Muiri.* Figures for the individual forces in August 1979 were:

	Officers	NCOs	Men	Total
Army	1,263	3,990	6,680	11,933
Air Corps	84	193	364	641
Naval Service	65	213	394	672
FCA	692	3,096	15,675	19,463
Slua Muiri	24	91	277	392

DEFENCE OF THE REALM ACT (DORA).

First in a series of emergency legislation, passed on 27 November 1914, designed to prevent collaboration between Irish revolutionaries and Germany during World War I. It was extended to the supply and sale of liquor in May 1915. The Act gave sweeping powers of arrest to the Dublin Castle authorities and was used after the Easter Rising of 1916* to suppress suspect Irish revolutionary organisations. It was used against suspected persons, 1916–19, and during the War of Independence.* It ceased to function on 31 August 1921.

DEMOCRATIC PROGRAMME OF THE FIRST DAIL EIREANN.

Document drafted by Thomas Johnson* of the Labour Party and edited by Sean T. O'Kelly.* It was felt that the existence of such a programme would assist the Irish claim for self-government when Johnson attended the International Socialist Conference in Berne in 1919. The programme was proposed to Dail Eireann* when it met for the first time on 21 January 1919. The approved Dail version was:

We declare in the words of the Irish Republican Proclamation the right of the people of Ireland to the ownership of Ireland, and to the unfettered control of Irish destinies to be indefeasible, and in the language of the first President, Pádraig MacPhiarais, we declare that the Nation's sovereignty extends not only to all men and women of the Nation, but to all its material possessions; the Nation's soil and all its resources, all the wealth and all the wealth-producing processes within the Nation, and with him we re-affirm that all rights to private property must be subordinated to the public right and welfare.

We declare that we desire our country to be ruled in accordance with the principles of Liberty, Equality and Justice for all, which alone can secure permanence of Government in the willing adhesion of the people.

We affirm the duty of every man and woman to give allegiance and service to the Commonwealth, and declare it is the duty of the Nation to assure that every citizen shall have opportunity to spend his or her strength and faculties in the service of the people. In return for willing service, we, in the name of the Republic, declare the right of every citizen to an adequate share of the produce of the Nation's labour.

It shall be the first duty of the Government of the Republic to make provision for the physical, mental and spiritual well-being of the children, to secure that no child shall suffer hunger or cold from lack of food, clothing, or shelter, but that all shall be provided with the means and facilities requisite for their proper education and training as Citizens of a Free and Gaelic Ireland.

The Irish Republic fully realises the necessity of abolishing the present odious, degrading and foreign Poor Law System, substituting therefor a sympathetic native scheme for the care of the Nation's aged and infirm, who shall not be regarded as a burden but rather entitled to the Nation's gratitude and consideration. Likewise it shall be the duty of the Republic to make such measures as will safeguard the health of the people and ensure the physical as well as the moral well-being of the Nation.

It shall be our duty to promote the development of the Nation's resources, to increase the productivity of its soil, to exploit its mineral deposits, peat bogs and fisheries, its waterways and harbours, in the interests and for the benefit of the Irish people.

It shall be the duty of the Republic to adopt all measures necessary for the recreation and invigoration of our industries, and to ensure their being developed on the most beneficial and progressive co-operative and industrial lines. With the adoption of an extensive Irish Consular Service, trade with foreign Nations shall be revived on terms of mutual advantage and good will, and while undertaking the organisation of the Nation's trade, imports and exports, it shall be the duty of the Republic to prevent the shipment from Ireland of food and other necessaries until the wants of the Irish people are fully satisfied and the future provided for.

It shall devolve upon the present government to seek co-operation of the governments of other countries in determining the standard of social and industrial legislation with a view to a general and lasting improvement in the conditions under which the working classes live and labour.

DEMOCRATIC UNIONIST PARTY. Loyalist party founded by Rev. Ian Paisley* and Desmond Boal in 1971, as an opposition to the Ulster Unionist Party* then fragmenting as a result of divisions within the movement over concessions to the Catholic minority population. The DUP sought the maintenance of the Union with Great Britain, Unionist domination of the parliamentary institutions, and closer integration with Westminster. Dominated by Rev. Paisley, who stated, 'If the Crown in Parliament decreed to put Ulster into a United Ireland, we would be disloyal to Her Majesty if we did not resist such a surrender to our enemies', the party won eight seats in the June 1973 elections to the Assembly of Northern Ireland. It opposed the power-sharing Executive led by Brian Faulkner* who lost control of the Unionist Party in January 1974. The DUP was a party to the United Ulster Unionist Council* which helped to bring down the Executive and destroy the Assembly. *See also* Northern Ireland.

DENIEFFE, JOSEPH (1833–1910). Fenian; b. Kilkenny. A tailor by occupation, he became a member of Young Ireland* and of the Irish Confederation.* He emigrated to the USA in 1851 and later became a member of the Emmet Monument Association.* When returning to Ireland to see his ailing father in 1855, he was commissioned by John O'Mahony* and Michael Doheny* to

establish the Association in Ireland. He established contact with Irish nationalists, including Thomas Clarke Luby.* He had little success in Ireland and was about to return to the USA when he was contacted by James Stephens* in December 1857. On Stephens' behalf he raised £80 from members of the Emmet Monument Association and returned to Ireland where Stephens used the money to found the Irish Republican Brotherhood* on 17 March 1858. Following the failure of the Fenian rising in 1867 Denieffe returned to the USA and was closely associated with Clan na Gael.* He died in Chicago. His *Recollections of the Irish Revolutionary Brotherhood,* serialised in *The Gael* (New York) in 1904, appeared in an expanded edition as *A Personal Narrative of the Irish Revolutionary Brotherhood* (NY, 1906).

DENVIR, JOHN (1834–1916). Journalist and Fenian; b. Bushmills, Co. Antrim. He went to Liverpool as a youth and worked as a journalist. After joining the Irish Republican Brotherhood* he worked as an arms smuggler with Dr Mark Ryan,* Michael Davitt* and Ricard O'Sullivan Burke.* He left the IRB after the rising of 1867 and joined the Home Rule movement, becoming the first secretary of the Home Rule Confederation of Great Britain.* He published *The Nationalist* in Liverpool. In 1870 he began publication of the series *Denvir's Irish Library,* books on Irish history, archaeology and biography, each costing one penny. He was the author of *The Irish in Britain* (1892) and *The Life Story of an Old Rebel* (autobiography, 1910).

DEPARTMENT OF AGRICULTURE AND TECHNICAL INSTRUCTION. *See* Agriculture and Technical Instruction Act, 1899.

DERBY, 14th EARL (1799–1869). Stanley, Edward George Geoffrey; politician (Whig); Chief Secretary

(1830–33); Prime Minister (1852, 1858–59, 1866–68); b. Knowsley Park, Lancashire; ed. Eton and Christ Church, Oxford where he did not take a degree. First returned to parliament for Stockbridge (1822), he was close to George Canning under whom he served as Under-Secretary for the Colonies (1827). He turned down office under the Duke of Wellington.* Upon accepting office as Chief Secretary from Earl Grey he lost his seat but was elected for Windsor in 1831.

His outstanding achievement in Ireland was the creation of a system of National Education* which he outlined in a letter ('The Stanley Letter') to the 3rd Duke of Leinster.* He sought a system, he said, 'from which would be banished forever the suspicion of proselytism and which, admitting children of all religious persuasions, should not interfere with the peculiar tenets of any'. However, as the system developed it moved away from his non-denominational or 'mixed' ideal. Stanley held office in Ireland at a period of acute unrest over the tithes* which led to an increase in agrarian crime (*see* Secret Societies). After two years he succeeded in reducing the agitation by an act which made composition of the tithe for money payment compulsory. While dedicated to the preservation of the established Church of Ireland he helped to forward the Irish Church Temporalities Act* but without appropriation as had been proposed by his rival, Lord John Russell* (January 1832). Despite reservations about reform he introduced the reform bill for Ireland and proposed an increase in Irish representation at Westminster. He established the Irish Board of Works and secured improvements in the Shannon Navigation Scheme. In 1833 he secured coercion powers after a bitter struggle in cabinet. When his successor in the Irish office, E. J. Littleton,* tried to handle the unrest over tithes with further concessions the cabinet split over Russell's proposal for appropriation and

Stanley resigned. He followed other influential Whigs in joining Sir Robert Peel* in a new style of Conservative party, and held various posts in subsequent Tory governments. As Lord Derby he was Prime Minister three times.

DERRIG, THOMAS (1897–1956). Politician (Sinn Fein and Fianna Fail); b. Westport, Co. Mayo; ed. CBS and UCG. As a member of the Irish Volunteers* he was deported in May 1916 and upon his return became active in Sinn Fein. He was imprisoned in the German Plot series of arrests and again during the War of Independence.* Returned to Dail Eireann for South Mayo in 1921, he rejected the Treaty and although re-elected in 1922 did not take his seat. From 1923 he was TD for Carlow–Kilkenny. He was a founder-member of Fianna Fail* and was appointed Minister for Education in the first Fianna Fail government formed in 1932 by Eamon de Valera.* A keen supporter of the Gaelic League,* he advocated the policy of compulsory Irish in education. He continued in Education until 1948 apart from a short break (September 1939–June 1940), and was Minister for Post and Telegraphs (8–27 September 1939) and Minister for Lands (1951–54).

DERRYNAFLAN TREASURE HOARD. Found by Michael Webb and his sixteen-year-old son, Michael, Jnr, on 17 February 1980, while exploring the sixth-century monastic site of St Ruadhan of Lorrha. Located at Derrynaflan, in the parish of Killenaule, Co. Tipperary, the treasure, consisting of a chalice, strainer, large tray or paten, and a large bronze bowl, was unearthed with the aid of metal detectors. The chalice is decorated with panels of gold filigree and amber settings. The strainer is of gilt bronze, its bowl being divided by a central bronze plate. The large circular paten, considered the most significant find, is of complex construction and is decorated with stamped gold or gilded panels bearing interlaced and spiral motifs. Preliminary investigation suggested the chalice to be late eighth or early ninth century, while the strainer and paten appeared to be somewhat earlier. Widespread public interest was aroused when the treasure was displayed at the National Museum* prior to its removal to the British Museum to undergo a lengthy restoration process.

DESPARD, MRS CHARLOTTE (1844–1939). Radical; b. Kent, *neé* French, of a Co. Roscommon family, elder sister of the future Lord French;* ed. privately. A nonconformist from her early years, she espoused radical causes and was a noted suffragette. She was wounded during an altercation with the police outside the House of Commons and was seriously injured while in custody at Holloway prison. Following the death of her Irish husband, Maximilan Despard, in 1890 she moved from her Kent estate to live among the poor in the East End and became an active socialist.

Mrs Despard's career in Ireland, divided between Belfast and Dublin, was controversial. Her socialism made her suspect to both Protestants and Catholics: a Protestant mob drove her from her Belfast home while in Dublin a Catholic mob sacked her house in Eccles Street where she maintained a workers' college. She devoted her time and money to the welfare of hungry children during the Lock-Out of 1913.* She was known popularly among the Dublin working-class as Mrs 'Desperate'. A supporter of Sinn Fein,* she supported the Irish Republican Army* during the War of Independence* when her brother was Lord Lieutenant. He had disowned her because of her republican socialism, although she had expended some of her personal fortune paying off his debts. Later he refused to receive her when he was dying (1925).

Disillusioned by the Treaty* Mrs Despard left her Dublin home to her close friend Maud Gonne MacBride* and moved to Belfast where she supported Sean Murray and the Communist party in their efforts to unite Catholic and Protestant workers. Her friends in the republican movement included Peader O'Donnell.*

DE VALERA, EAMON (1882–1975). Politician (Sinn Fein, Cumann na Poblachta and Fianna Fail); President of Dail Eireann (1919–21), President of the Irish Republic (1921–22), President of the Executive Council of the Free State (1932–37), Taoiseach (1937–48, 1951–54 and 1957–59), and President of the Republic of Ireland (1959–73); b. New York; reared in Bruree, Co. Limerick and ed. locally, Charleville CBS, Co. Cork, Blackrock College and UCD. He taught mathematics at Rockwell, Belvedere and Carysfort Colleges and lectured for the Royal University* at Dominican, Loreto, Holy Cross and University Colleges. In 1908 he joined the Gaelic League* where he met his future wife, Sinéad Ni Fhlanagáin.

As commandant of the 3rd Brigade of the Irish Volunteers* at Boland's Mills during the Easter Rising of 1916,* he was the last commander to surrender. His sentence of death was commuted to life imprisonment and he was released on 16 June 1917. Shortly afterwards he was elected Sinn Fein MP for East Clare (5,010 votes to 2,035), which he represented until 1959. Arthur Griffith* stood aside in October to allow him to assume the presidency of Sinn Fein (1917–26); in November he was elected president of the Volunteers (1917–22). He was present at the Mansion House Conference* and drafted the anti-conscription pledge of 18 April 1918 (*see* Conscription and Ireland). After his arrest in the German Plot arrests on 17 May 1918, he was held at Lincoln Prison until his escape was engineered by Harry Boland* and Michael Collins* on 3 February 1919. While imprisoned he had been returned for four constituencies in the general election of

December 1918 and he was elected *Priomh Aire* or President of the first Dail Eireann (April 1919). Against the wishes of his cabinet colleagues he went to the USA in June 1919 to float the Dail Eireann External Loan, to secure recognition for the Irish Republic and to channel American influence into securing recognition of the Irish Republic by the League of Nations.* The success of his tour was marred when a rift developed between himself, Judge Daniel Cohalan* and John Devoy.* Despite Cohalan's powerful opposition de Valera succeeded in placing a resolution before the Republican Convention but it was rejected in favour of Cohalan's counter-proposal which sought 'recognition of the principle that the people of Ireland have the right to determine freely... their own government ...' The quarrel split the Friends of Irish Freedom* and de Valera founded a new organisation, the American Association for the Recognition of the Irish Republic* in June 1920. Before leaving America he entered into negotiations with the communist government in the Soviet Union for recognition of the Republic. Draft terms outlined plans for training the Irish Republican Army* in Russia and for the interests of the Catholic Church in Russia to be entrusted to representatives of the Irish Republic. De Valera loaned 25,000 dollars to the Soviet consul in New York and received as collateral a collection of the Russian Crown Jewels.*

De Valera returned to Ireland in January 1921. He was not an active participant in peace initiatives to end the War of Independence* but he had a fruitless meeting with Sir James Craig (*see* Craigavon, Lord) in Dublin on 5 May 1921 in an effort to secure cross-border detente. He was arrested on 22 June, the day upon which George V* opened the parliament of Northern Ireland. The government ordered his release and two days later he received an invitation to peace talks from David Lloyd George.* De Valera's invitation to

the Ulster Unionists* to attend preliminary discussions was rejected by Craig. After the Truce* (11 July) de Valera travelled to London and met three times with Lloyd George. On 20 July he received British proposals which he considered unacceptable because they offered only Dominion status, and did not recognise 'the indefeasible right of the Irish people to sovereignty and independence'. His own proposals, which offered a formula of External Association* with the British Commonwealth, were rejected by the British. The Irish cabinet supported de Valera's stand and the talks ended. In August 1921, accepting his new title of President of the Irish Republic, de Valera told members of the Dail, 'I am representing the nation and I shall represent the whole nation ... and I shall not be bound by any section of the nation whatever'. At a cabinet meeting on 9 September delegates for any future negotiations were selected. He gave as reasons for not being a delegate himself, that (a) while he remained in Ireland he could act as reserve should the talks break down; (b) that there was need for strong leadership at home to reconcile militant republicans to the concept of external association; (c) Arthur Griffith was a moderate while his own ideas on certain key issues were well known; (d) while remaining in Dublin he could mould and give free expression to national feeling. While his decision did not meet with unanimous approval, the Dail on 14 September ratified the choice of delegates. His correspondence with Lloyd George ended on 30 September with agreement to a conference between Irish and British delegations to discuss the Gairloch Formula.* He maintained a close interest from Dublin in the negotiations for a Treaty,* and informed Griffith on 2 December that the Articles of Agreement as drafted in London were unacceptable. Along with the rest of the cabinet, he understood that the plenipotentiaries would adhere to their written instructions by which they were to refer any settlement to Dublin before signing. Only the pleas of W. T. Cosgrave* dissuaded him from dismissing Griffith, Collins and Robert Barton* from the cabinet when they arrived back with the signed document. (Years later de Valera admitted that the only regret of his political life was that he had not ordered the arrest of the delegates upon their return from London.) In a private session of the Dail on 15 December he produced a new draft of the Treaty which became known as Document No. 2,* containing once more the idea of external association. He refused to allow it open for public discussion. After the Dail approved the Treaty by 64 votes to 57, he resigned the Presidency and was defeated by Arthur Griffith in a new election (60 votes to 58). Shortly afterwards he called a meeting of anti-Treaty TDs and formed Cumann na Poblachta. He reached an agreement with Griffith on 22 February 1922 that in the interests of avoiding a split in Sinn Fein a general election should be postponed for three months. Without recognising the authority of the Provisional Government* he continued to sit in the Dail, recognising only the ministry of the second Dail Eireann, presided over by Griffith.

In the opening phase of the Civil War* he was in the Hammam Hotel which he vacated on orders from Cathal Brugha* (3 July 1922). He was afterwards Adjutant to Sean Moylan,* Director of Operations in the Irregulars (anti-Treaty IRA). The IRA Executive authorised him on 24 March 1923 to negotiate peace terms with the Free State government. The government, however, refused to treat unless there was an unconditional surrender and this was rejected by the IRA. Following the death of Liam Lynch* and the collapse of the republican position de Valera and Frank Aiken* co-signed an order suspending IRA activity (24 May). Three days later he called for a Ceasefire and Dump Arms and the Civil War was over. He was arrested by

Free State troops in Ennis on 15 August and held at Arbour Hill and Kilmainham until 16 July 1924. Although prohibited from entering Northern Ireland he did so and was arrested and held in solitary confinement in Belfast Jail (1—29 November 1924). From 1924 until 1927 he led forty-four abstentionist TDs. They proclaimed their unalterable opposition to the partition of Ireland following the shelving of the Report of the Boundary Commission* in December 1925, when the Cosgrave administration agreed to accept the border as it was. De Valera, by now committed to constitutional opposition, refused to enter the Dail so long as the Oath of Allegiance* was required. In an attempt to strengthen the constitutional position he proposed at the Sinn Fein Ard-Fheis on 11 March 1926, 'That once the admission oath of the twenty-six county and six-county assemblies is removed, it becomes a question not of principle, but of policy, whether or not republican representatives should attend these assemblies'. His motion, opposed vociferously by Fr Michael O'Flanagan,* was defeated by 223 votes to 218. He resigned the presidency of Sinn Fein and set about establishing a constitutional republican party of his own, Fianna Fail. At the first Ard-Fheis of the new party, held on 24 November, he was elected President, a position which he held until 1959. He continued the struggle for the abolition of the Oath, seeking its removal under Article 48 of the constitution (under which 75,000 signatures could secure a referendum on an amendment to the Constitution). Forty-four Fianna Fail deputies were returned in the general election of June 1927 and on 23 June de Valera led the members of his party into the chamber. They were not allowed to take their seats without taking the Oath and so they withdrew. However, their position changed when the Electoral Amendment Act,* put through by Cosgrave after the assassination of Kevin O'Higgins* in July 1927, forced de

Valera and his followers either to take the Oath or remain permanently outside the Dail. When he led his followers into the Dail on 12 August he signed the book containing the Oath, saying, at the same time, 'I am not prepared to take an oath. I am not going to take an oath. I am prepared to put my name down in this book in order to get permission to go into the Dail, but it has no other significance'. The oath, he said, was 'an empty formula'.

The Dail was dissolved almost immediately and a new general election called for 15 September. Fianna Fail returned with fifty-seven seats. De Valera now presented his petition (with 96,000 signatures) but it was rejected by the government. For the next five years Fianna Fail and the Labour Party* provided the opposition to the government. De Valera attacked the payment of Land Annuities* and the economic policies of the Cosgrave administration. To further opposition he founded a party newspaper, the *Irish Press,* which first appeared on 5 September 1931. Leading up to the general election of 1932 he made a strong appeal to residual republican sentiment. The March election returned Fianna Fail with seventy-two seats to Cumann na nGaedheal's fifty-seven, and, supported by the Labour Party, de Valera formed his first administration. Making use of the Statute of Westminster,* he set about removing the Oath, but opposition from the Senate* led to a delay in actually deleting it from the Constitution. The withholding of the Land Annuities led to the Economic War* with Britain. In addition, the government had to deal with the rise of the right-wing movement known as the Blueshirts.* The threat from the right gained him the temporary support of Labour and the IRA. In an attempt to consolidate his position he called another election for January 1933 and gained five extra seats. His hand strengthened, he moved against General Eoin O'Duffy,* a prominent right-wing supporter, who was removed from the Commissionership of the Garda Siochana. He appointed a new Commissioner, Colonel Eamon Broy* who was permitted to recruit a new armed police auxiliary force from among the IRA. This firm approach saw the Blueshirts fade away during 1934—35 and with them went de Valera's need for the IRA which he outlawed in 1936. De Valera held the portfolio of External Affairs in all his administrations until 1948. He opened the 13th Assembly of the League of Nations on 26 September 1932, as President of the Council of the League. His message to the participating nations called on them to abide by the principles of the League, not to permit breaches of the smaller nations' rights by aggressive nations, and to work for disarmament. He supported Russia's admission in 1934 and favoured a policy of non-intervention in the Spanish Civil War (1936—39). For the session 1938—39 he was President of the Assembly and supported the appeasement policy adopted by Neville Chamberlain.* Throughout 1936—37 he worked on a new Constitution. He took advantage of the Abdication Crisis* of December 1936 to remove all references to the King and the Governor-General in the existing Constitution, retaining the King only for the purposes of external relations (*see* External Relations Act). The new Constitution of Eire* became operative on 29 December 1937. Despite radical changes in the position of the former Free State under de Valera's government, relations with Great Britain remained cordial. The Economic War had been blunted to some extent by the Coal-Cattle Pact* and he agreed in 1938 to meetings with Chamberlain with whom he signed a significant agreement in April 1938: the Anglo-Irish Agreement* ended the trade war between the two countries but also returned the so-called Treaty Ports* to Eire. This measure, which had been strongly opposed by Sir Winston Churchill,* afforded de Valera particular satisfaction.

When war broke out in September 1939, de Valera declared that 'the aim of government policy is to keep this country (Eire) out of war'. In this he had the support of members of all parties with the sole exception of James Dillon.* To deal with a new IRA campaign, directed against Northern Ireland and England, he introduced the Treason Act,* the Offences Against the State Act* and the Emergency Powers Act.* During the Emergency* as the period of World War II was known in Ireland, he enjoyed a good relationship with the British and German Ambassadors, but had a stormy one with the American Ambassador, David Gray. He resisted considerable pressure from the USA and Britain to enter the war effort (*see* American Note). His feeling was that Ireland could not aid Britain while the country was partitioned and he ignored Churchill's vague promise to examine the question of partition after the war. Britain heeded his protest against the extension of conscription to Northern Ireland, when he claimed that the nationalist minority would not tolerate it. On 2 May 1941, when a German air-raid left Belfast in flames, he ordered every unit save one of the Dublin Fire Brigade to assist the northern capital. He took the opportunity afforded by the hardships of the Emergency to describe his vision of Ireland. Speaking in a radio broadcast on St Patrick's Day 1943, he said:

The Ireland which we have dreamed of would be the home of a people who valued material wealth only as the basis of right living, of a people who were satisfied with frugal comfort and devoted their leisure to the things of the spirit; a land whose countryside would be bright with cosy homesteads, whose fields and villages would be joyous with the sounds of industry, with the romping of sturdy children, the contests of athletic youths, the laughter of comely maidens; whose firesides would be forums for the wisdom of old age. It would, in a word, be the home of a people living the life that God desires men should live.

His visit to the German Embassy on 30 April 1945 to offer his condolences on the death of Hitler earned him widespread unpopularity among the allies. However, he more than compensated for that at home when he made his celebrated reply to Churchill's attack on neutrality. The British leader, speaking in a victory broadcast on 13 May 1945, had said '. . . the approaches which the southern Irish ports and air-fields could so easily have guarded were closed by the hostile aircraft and U-boats. This indeed was a deadly moment in our life, and if it had not been for the loyalty and friendship of Northern Ireland, we should have been forced to come to close quarters with Mr de Valera, or perish for ever from the earth. However, with a restraint and poise to which, I venture to say, history will find few parallels, His Majesty's Government never laid a violent hand upon them, though at times it would have been quite easy and quite natural, and we left the de Valera Government to frolic with the German and later with the Japanese representatives to their heart's content . . .' During the course of his reply on Radio Eireann (17 May 1945) de Valera said:

. . . Allowances can be made for Mr Churchill's statement, however unworthy, in the first flush of victory. No such excuse could be found for me in this quieter atmosphere. There are, however, some things it is essential to say. I shall try to say them as dispassionately as I can.

Mr Churchill makes it clear that, in certain circumstances, he would have violated our neutrality and that he would justify his action by Britain's necessity. It seems strange to me that Mr Churchill does not see that this, if accepted, would mean that Britain's necessity would become a moral code and that when this necessity became sufficiently great, other people's rights were not to count. . . . That is precisely why we have the disastrous succession of wars – World War No. 1 and World War No. 2 – and shall it be World War No. 3?

. . . Mr Churchill is proud of Britain's stand alone, after France had fallen and before America entered the war. Could he not find in his heart the generosity to acknowledge that there is a small nation that stood alone not for one year or two, but for several hundred years against aggression; that endured spoliations, famine, massacres, in endless succession; that was clubbed many times into insensibility, but each time on returning consciousness took up the fight anew; a small nation that could never be got to accept defeat and has never surrendered her soul?

De Valera's speech did much to restore flagging morale in the wake of Churchill's speech which had been internationally reported.

The Emergency period, however, had left the country in poor shape economically. After sixteen years in power, his party was defeated by a coalition in the general election of 1948 and the first Inter-Party government* was formed. Three years later de Valera returned to power but his government, no more able to solve the mounting problems than its predecessor, was succeeded by another Inter-Party government in 1954. Fianna Fail won the election of 1957 and he returned to form his last government, at the head of the largest number of seats (78) held by any party until 1977. He retired from the office of Taoiseach in 1959 and was succeeded by his own choice, Sean Lemass.* De Valera won the Presidential election of 1959, defeating Sean MacEoin.* In 1966 he won again, defeating the Fine Gael candidate, Thomas F. O'Higgins. Prior to his retirement from office in 1973 he was the oldest serving head of state in the world.

DE VERE, AUBREY THOMAS (1814–1902). Poet; b. Curragh Chase,

Co. Limerick; ed. privately and TCD. Widely travelled, he was a friend of Wordsworth (by whom he was greatly influenced), Landor, Tennyson and Browning. He became a Roman Catholic in 1851, having had a close friendship with John Henry Newman.* Following his conversion to Catholicism his writings consisted mainly of devotional hymns, Irish bardic lore and ecclesiastical medievalism. His works include *The Waldenses* (1842), *The Search after Prosperine* (1843), *English Misrule and Irish Misdeeds* (1848), *Poems* (1855), *May Carols* (1857), *Innisfail* (1861), *The Infant Bridal* (1864), *Irish Odes* (1869), *The Legends of St Patrick* (1872), *Legends of the Saxon Saints* (1879), *The Foray of Queen Maeve* (1882), *Essays chiefly on Poetry* (1887) and *Medieval Records and Sonnets* (1893). His *Recollections* was published in 1897.

DEVLIN, JOSEPH (1872–1934). Politician (Nationalist); b. Belfast. He had little formal education. Devlin built up strong working-class support in Belfast and became a spokesman for the Catholic population by whom he was popularly known as 'Wee Joe'. He was a life-long opponent of the Orange Order* and a leading member of its Catholic counterpart, the Ancient Order of Hibernians.* Devlin was Home Rule MP for West Belfast, 1902–18, and sat with the Irish Parliamentary Party.* The United Irish League* in Ulster became his political machine as did the Board of Erin* which he controlled from 1905. In 1907 he supported the strike called by James Larkin* in Belfast. As leader of the Northern nationalists he accepted the Home Rule Bill of 1914 which temporarily excluded the six north-eastern counties from the jurisdiction of a Dublin government and was a major force in persuading a nationalist conference to accept it. During World War I, Devlin, in common with John Redmond,* encouraged Irishmen to join the British Forces (*see* Conscription and Ireland). After the general election of 1918, he became the leader of the Ulster nationalists but continued to sit at Westminster when the Government of Ireland Act of 1920 created the six-county state of Northern Ireland. For the general election of May 1921, held during the War of Independence,* Devlin signed an agreement with Eamon de Valera* not to contest seats where Sinn Fein* candidates were standing. He led the Nationalist Party of Northern Ireland* at Westminster and did not enter the parliament of Northern Ireland until 1925. Following his death, the Nationalist Party of Northern Ireland went into a period of decline which was not halted until after 1945.

DEVOLUTION. Proposal put forward by the Irish Reform Association* in August 1904 to secure devolved powers of self-government for Ireland through the extension of the local government system (*see* Local Government). The scheme had support from southern Unionist landlords led by the 4th Earl of Dunraven.* It was encouraged by the Under-Secretary, Sir Antony MacDonnell.* The devolution scheme was strongly opposed by the Ulster Unionists* who reacted by forming the Ulster Unionist Council.* The scheme had little support in the south among nationalists and led to the resignation of the Chief Secretary, George Wyndham.* The proposal met with no more enthusiasm when it was resurrected by Augustine Birrell* in the Irish Council Bill* of 1907.

DEVON COMMISSION. Appointed by Sir Robert Peel* under the chairmanship of Lord Devon, to investigate relations between landlords and tenants, mode of occupation of the land, cultivation of the land, need for improvement, and conditions and habits of the labouring class. The Commission first sat in 1843, and heard 1,000 witnesses. The widespread investigations of the Commission, contained in their Report issued

in 1847, were rendered academic by the onslaught of the Great Famine of 1845–49,* and the subsequent dislocation of the Irish economy.

DEVONSHIRE, 8th DUKE (1833–1908). Cavendish, Spencer Compton, Marquess of Hartington. Chief Secretary (1870–74); b. Lancashire, elder brother of Lord Frederick Cavendish;* ed. privately and Trinity College, Cambridge. He was Liberal MP from 1857 and became Marquess of Hartington in 1858. He supported his leader, W. E. Gladstone,* in the Disestablishment of the Church of Ireland.* Devonshire introduced the Bill for the Ballot Act which became law in 1872. Having refused the Viceroyalty of Ireland in 1869, he accepted the office of Chief Secretary in 1870 and was given wide powers of coercion to suppress the Ribbonmen.* His term of office saw the emergence of the Home Government Association* and the Home Rule League* led by Isaac Butt.*

DEVOY, JOHN (1842–1928). Fenian; b. Johnstown, Co. Kildare. He joined the Fenians in his teens and subsequently enlisted in the French Foreign Legion to gain military experience to assist in the fight for an Irish Republic. He returned to Ireland in 1862 and became an organiser for the Irish Republican Brotherhood* in the Naas area of Co. Kildare. Devoy, John Boyle O'Reilly* and Patrick 'Pagan' O'Leary* were appointed by James Stephens* to recruit members into the Fenian Brotherhood from among Irish soldiers serving with the British army (it was estimated that 15,000 soldiers were recruited). Following the arrest of prominent members of the Fenian leadership in 1865, Devoy became chief organiser, in which capacity he organised the escape of Stephens from Richmond prison. Devoy was arrested on 22 February 1866 and sentenced to fifteen years imprisonment, but was released in January 1871 on condition that he left these islands until the term of his sentence had expired. As one of the 'Cuba Five'* he went to the US where he worked as a journalist in Chicago and New York. He joined Clan na Gael* and built up its organisational and financial structures. Devoy masterminded the *Catalpa* expedition to rescue Fenian prisoners from Freemantle, Australia and had them brought to the US. He supported the New Departure* and through the Clan raised the finances which enabled Michael Davitt* and Charles Stewart Parnell* to continue the agitation, both in and out of parliament, for a satisfactory conclusion to the Land Question. Devoy supported the Plan of Campaign* but strongly opposed the terrorist wing of the Clan, known as the 'Triangle',* and finally won control from them in the late 1880s. Through his newspapers *The Irish Nation* and *The Gaelic American** he supported republicanism and continued to attack British imperialism. He maintained contact with nationalists in Ireland through his close friend, Thomas J. Clarke,* and supported Patrick Pearse* when he campaigned in the US seeking funds for the Irish Volunteers* and for his school, St Enda's,* in 1914. He arranged the contact between Roger Casement* and the German Ambassador in the same year, having himself unsuccessfully attempted to interest the German Ambassador in Washington in Ireland's potential as an ally in the German war effort. In 1920 Devoy broke with Eamon de Valera* and the IRB over the question of de Valera's American tactics. He supported the Treaty* and regarded the Free State as the first step in securing the ultimate aim of the republican movement. During his career Devoy was considered by the British authorities to be one of the Empire's most dangerous enemies. As late as 1916, he was described as the single most dangerous member of the republican movement. The Commission which sat to investigate the Easter Rising of 1916* found it incomprehensible that the same Devoy who helped organise the rising could have been involved with the Fenians of the 1860s.

DILLON, JAMES (1902–). Politician (Fine Gael); b. Dublin, son of John Dillon;* ed. Mount St Benedict, Co. Wexford and UCD. He studied business management in London and Chicago prior to his return as Independent TD for Donegal (1932–37). With Frank McDermot* founded the National Centre Party* and when it merged with Cumann na nGaedheal* to form Fine Gael* (September 1933) he became vice-president of the latter. He represented Co. Monaghan from 1937 until his retirement in 1968.

During the Emergency* he attacked the agreement on neutrality and was disowned by Fine Gael (18 July 1941). After his call for support for the Allies at the Fine Gael Ard Fheis was rejected (February 1942) he resigned from the party and sat as an Independent. He was returned as an Independent in the general elections of 1943, 1944 and 1948. Burying his differences with Fine Gael he accepted the Ministry of Agriculture in the first Inter-Party Government (1948–51). He rejoined Fine Gael before the general election of 1951. Dillon was again Minister for Agriculture in the second Inter-Party Government (1954–57). He was leader of Fine Gael from 1959 until his retirement to the back benches in 1965. He was succeeded as leader by Liam Cosgrave* and continued to be a member of the Council of State.*

DILLON, JOHN (1851–1927). Land agitator and politician (Nationalist). b. Blackrock, Co. Dublin, son of John Blake Dillon;* ed. Catholic University* and Royal College of Surgeons. While a medical student, he was present at the Home Rule conference when he proposed that the Home Rule Party should withdraw from the House of Commons before the division on the Balkan crisis. Later in that year (1879) he accused Isaac Butt,* leader of the party, of acting like a traitor. In

1879 Dillon became a leading agitator in the Land League,* and advocated the policy of boycott pursued by Charles Stewart Parnell.* Elected MP, Co. Tipperary (1880–83), Dillon continued his Land League activities. His views on agrarian reform and on Home Rule led to his being considered an extremist. He was prosecuted in November 1879, with other leading members of the Irish Parliamentary Party, for continued land agitation. Dillon travelled to the USA with Parnell on a fund-raising mission for the Land League, in which a sum of £30,000 was raised. Upon his return Dillon attacked the Land Bill of 1881 (*see* Land Acts). He was again arrested and imprisoned in May under the Coercion Acts* but was released in September. Dillon was a signatory to the No Rent Manifesto* which was in outline a policy he had himself advocated the previous year. His health caused him to retire briefly to the US in 1885 and upon his return he was nominated by Parnell as the party candidate in the Mayo East by-election, which constituency he represented until 1918. Despite Parnell's objections, Dillon became a leading figure in the Plan of Campaign* in which he was supported by William O'Brien* and Timothy Harrington.* He was again imprisoned in April 1887 under Coercion and upon his release resumed agrarian agitation, in particular his defence of the Munster farmers. With Archbishop Thomas William Croke* he devised a formula to circumvent the Papal decree of 1888 which condemned the Plan of Campaign and the boycott weapon. Upon his release from a further term of imprisonment, he travelled to the US with O'Brien to raise money for the Plan.

He was in the US when the crisis broke over Parnell's continuing leadership of the party in the wake of the O'Shea divorce. After some initial hesitancy, Dillon opposed Parnell and upon his return sought to save the party from fragmenting. He followed Justin McCarthy* in the rejection of Parnell and replaced McCarthy as leader of the anti-Parnellites in 1896. Dillon opposed Sir Horace Plunkett* in his efforts to help the small farmer. He supported O'Brien's United Irish League* which brought factions of the old Parnellite party together in 1900, and accepted John Redmond* as leader of the unified party. He opposed the financial terms of the Wyndham Land Act (*see* Land Acts), the Irish Council Bill,* and did not favour moves to have the Irish language made a compulsory subject for matriculation into the National University of Ireland.* Dillon supported the (third) Home Rule Bill* and was present at various meetings, including the Buckingham Palace Conference,* in an endeavour to settle the question of Ulster. Like other moderates he was worried by the rise of the Irish Volunteers* and the strong nationalist movement developing in Ireland under the aegis of the Irish Republican Brotherhood.*

He was trapped with his family in his Dublin residence during the Easter Rising of 1916* and was worried that the rebellion might prejudice the eventual granting of Home Rule. He made strong representations to the British authorities in an effort to prevent the executions and recriminations in the wake of the Rising and violently disagreed with Redmond's wholesale condemnation of those involved in the insurrection. Upon Redmond's death in March 1918, Dillon became leader of the parliamentary party and led the withdrawal from the House of Commons of the Irish members when the Military Service Bill passed on 16 April 1918 and he was a member of the Mansion House Committee* which organised the campaign against conscription. Towards the end of his political career he witnessed the emergence of Sinn Fein* as a political force and was himself defeated in East Mayo by an imprisoned Eamon de Valera* (December 1918), by a two-to-one majority. This hastened Dillon's withdrawal from the political scene and he retired from public life shortly afterwards. His son, James Dillon,* was later a prominent politician.

DILLON, JOHN BLAKE (1816–66). Lawyer and Young Irelander; b. Ballaghaderreen, Co. Roscommon; father of John Dillon;* ed. Maynooth and TCD; Bar (1842). He became a member of Young Ireland* and of the Irish Confederation.* With Thomas Davis* and Charles Gavan Duffy* he founded *The Nation* in 1842. Although opposed to the extremism of John Mitchel* at the conference of the Irish Confederation, Dillon took part in the Rising of 1848 and commanded the rebels at Killenaule. Following the collapse of the Rising he escaped to France and from there to the US, where he set up law practice with Richard O'Gorman.* In 1849 Dillon advocated a federal republic for Britain and Ireland. He returned to Ireland (1855) and was elected to the Dublin Corporation and to parliament as MP for Roscommon. John Mitchel said of him that he was all wrong on almost every question but that he was nevertheless better than most people who were all right.

DILLON, MYLES (1900–72). Scholar; b. Dublin, son of John Dillon;* ed. Dublin, Germany and France. He was Reader in Sanskrit, TCD (1928–30), UCD (1930–37), Professor of Irish, Wisconsin University (1937–46). Senior Professor at the School of Celtic Studies, Dublin Institute for Advanced Studies (1940), of which he was Director from 1960 to 1968. His works include *The Cycle of the Kings* (1946), *Early Irish Literature* (1948), *Irish Sagas* (1959), and *Lebor na gCert: The Book of Rights* (1962). He edited *Early Irish Society* (1954).

DINNEEN, REV. PATRICK (1860–1934). Clergyman (R.C.) and scholar; b. Co. Kerry; ed. National School and University College. He was ordained as a Jesuit and taught in colleges at Limerick and Dublin. He travelled to France (1899) and upon his return a year later he left the Jesuits. A prominent member of the Gaelic League,* he devoted the rest of his life to the study of Irish manuscripts in the National Library.* His most celebrated work was his *Foclóir Gaedhilge agus Béarla* (1904), an Irish-English Dictionary. The work appeared again in 1927, completely rewritten because the original plates had been destroyed during the Easter Rising of 1916.* The new edition was underwritten by the Irish Texts Society* and a grant of £1,000 from the government of the Free State. Fr Dinneen also wrote plays and published translations. His publications were *Litreacha Gaedhilge an Aosa Óig* and *Aistidhe Gaedhilge, le hAghaidh an Aosa Óig*, both published in 1908, and edited from Geoffrey Keating's *Foras Feasa ar Éirinn;* *Girle Guaire* (play, 1904), *Muinntear Chiarraidhe roimh an droc-saoghal* (1905), *Native History in National Schools* (1905), *Faoistin Naomh-Phadraigh* (1906: St Patrick's *Confession*, in Latin, Irish and English), *A Concise English-Irish Dictionary* (1910), *Mo Guidhir Fhearmanach* (1917), *Spioraid na Saoirse, Aisling ar an mBliadhain 1916* (1919), *Aisti ar Lithrídheacht Gréigre is Laidne* (1929), *Filidhe Móra Chiarraighe* (1929), *Earlamh Éireann* (1932), *Scéal na hÉireann do'n Aos Óg* (1932), and *Caiseal* (1935); he translated *A Christmas Carol* (1903) and Virgil's *Aeneid* (1931) into Irish.

DIRECT RULE. *See* Northern Ireland.

DISENDOWMENT. *See* Disestablishment of the Church of Ireland.

DISESTABLISHMENT OF THE CHURCH OF IRELAND (1869). The Disestablishment of the Church of Ireland was a major issue in the electoral policy put forward by W. E. Gladstone* in 1868. Despite opposition to the measure both in Ireland and England, he secured a mandate for Disestablishment with a majority of 112 and the Act passed the Lords at the end of July. The Act specified that the Church of Ireland would become a voluntary body as from 1 January 1871. The legislation also provided for the disendowment of the Church of its considerable landholdings, property and bequests (which had been valued at £600,000 p.a. in 1867). Apart from the churches and churchyards in use, the Church was to lose the rest of its holdings and property, to be vested in a body of Commissioners for Irish Church Temporalities. Compensation paid out under the Act amounted to £16m. which represented about one half the value of confiscated church property. The remainder was to be used for the relief of poverty, endowments for higher education, and for the encouragement of agriculture and fisheries (between 1871 and 1923, £13m. was paid out for these purposes). The land which the Church lost was offered to tenants and some 6,000 availed of the offer. Embodied in the Act was a general disestablishment of all religion in Ireland under which the Maynooth Grant and the Presbyterian *Regium Donum** were also abolished. Church of Ireland clergy were henceforth paid by the Representative Church Body.

DISRAELI, BENJAMIN, 1st EARL OF BEACONSFIELD (1804–81). Politician (Conservative); Prime Minister (1868; 1874–80); b. London, of a Jewish family. He was baptized in the Church of England in 1817 and continued his education in private schools until 1819. He joined the Conservative Party in 1834 and entered parliament in 1837. In 1844 he described the 'Irish Question' as 'a starving population, an absentee aristocracy, and an alien church, and ... the weakest executive in the world'. He broke with Sir Robert Peel* in 1845 following the Maynooth Grant and during the remainder of Peel's administration led the protectionist opposition to Peel's proposal for repeal of the Corn Laws at a period when Ireland had entered the

Famine of 1845–49.* As Chancellor of the Exchequer in Lord Derby's government (1858–59), Disraeli extended the process of bringing Irish taxation into line with British. He opposed Disestablishment of the Church of Ireland* but the measure was introduced by Gladstone's administration in 1869. During his next term of office (1874–80) the government had to contend with an emergent Irish Parliamentary Party,* in particular the radical fringe who engaged in the new policy of obstruction; this element of the party included Joseph Biggar,* Charles Stewart Parnell* and Frank Hugh O'Donnell.*

Disraeli's government passed two acts of consequence to Ireland. The first, in 1878, provided payment of government grants to secondary schools, based on results obtained in the Intermediate Board Examinations. The second, in 1879, was a further attempt to solve the question of university education in Ireland. It did not meet the demands of the Catholic hierarchy for a Catholic University* with degree-awarding powers but it established the Royal University of Ireland* whose examinations were open to all students. Both measures met with a tepid response in Ireland. A new agrarian crisis arose through the failure of the 1877 potato crop and a fall in agricultural prices and to meet the threat of eviction the Irish tenants organised the Land League* in 1879. It was left to Disraeli's successor, W. E. Gladstone,* to solve the new crisis.

DIXON, JOSEPH (1806–66). Archbishop of Armagh and Primate of All-Ireland (R.C.), 1852–66; b. Coalisland, Dungannon; ed. Maynooth; ordained 1829. He was Professor of Sacred Scripture and Hebrew at Maynooth from 1834 until 1852 when he succeeded Paul Cullen* to the primatial see of Armagh. Dr Dixon was highly regarded by John Henry Newman* and was a close friend of Cardinal Cullen. He convened and presided over the Synod of Ulster held in Drogheda (May 1854). He resumed the building of St Patrick's Cathedral which had been interrupted by the Famine of 1845–49,* and which was almost completed at the time of his death. He was the author of *A General Introduction to the Sacred Scripture* (1852).

DOCUMENT NO. 2. Alternative proposals for a Treaty between Ireland and Great Britain were first put forward by Eamon de Valera* at a private session of Dail Eireann on 14 December 1921 during the debate on the Treaty.* The proposals came up for discussion over the next few days in private session but when an attempt was made to discuss them in open session on 19 December de Valera sought to prevent it. He said that he had proposed 'the document for a distinct purpose to see whether we could get a unanimous proposition by this House. . . . It would cease to be of value unless it was a document that would command practically the unanimous approval of the assembly. It was given to the assembly to get objection to it . . . it was a paper put in, in order to elicit views'. In answer to a demand from Arthur Griffith* that he should let the Irish people see Document No. 2 de Valera said, 'I will produce it when this question, which is the only one before the House, the question of ratification or non-ratification [of the Treaty], is finished' (20 December). De Valera said on 4 January that he was formally giving notice that he would move the Document as an amendment to (the motion on) the Treaty. When it was circulated Griffith denied that it was the original document, claiming that six clauses had been omitted from the original draft. De Valera admitted that it had been amended 'as I would have done with any other document'. Collins referred to it as Document No. 3. Two days later, de Valera said that he was resigning (as President of Dail Eireann) and if he was re-elected he would place the Document before the new cabinet for submission to the House. Griffith stated on 7 Janu-

ary that the delegates in London had already had de Valera's proposals on External Association* rejected 'absolutely' by the British government. Document No. 2, he claimed, was putting up for a third time what had been turned down twice. The vote on the Treaty then took place and following the result (64 for, 57 against) de Valera resigned office. In Document No. 2, de Valera had proposed:

That inasmuch as the 'Articles of Agreement for a Treaty between Great Britain and Ireland' signed in London on December 6th, 1921, do not reconcile Irish National aspirations and the Association of Ireland with the Community of Nations known as the British Commonwealth, and can not be the basis of an enduring peace between the Irish and British peoples, DAIL EIREANN, in the name of the Sovereign Irish Nation, makes to the Government of Great Britain, to the Governments of the other States of the British Commonwealth, and to the peoples of Great Britain and of these several States, the following Proposal for a Treaty of Amity and Association which DAIL EIREANN is convinced could be entered into by the Irish people with the sincerity of goodwill.

This alternative differed on several important points from the Treaty. It declared in Article 1, 'That the legislative, executive, and judicial authority of Ireland shall be derived solely from the people of Ireland'. Article 2 was de Valera's old proposal of External Association: 'That, for purposes of common concern, Ireland shall be associated with the States of the British Commonwealth, viz: the Kingdom of Great Britain, the Dominion of Canada, the Commonwealth of Australia, the Dominion of New Zealand, and the Union of South Africa'. Whereas the Treaty included an Oath of Allegiance* which mentioned the King, de Valera's document proposed 'That, for purposes of the Association,

Ireland shall recognise His Brittanic Majesty as head of the Association' (Article 6).

Having dealt with Terms of Association (Articles 2 to 6), Document No. 2 stayed very close to the Treaty. Articles 7 to 10 dealt with Defence, giving guarantees to Britain of goodwill in the event of war: 'That for five years, pending the establishment of Irish coastal defence forces, or for such other period as the Governments of the two countries may later agree upon, facilities for the coastal defence of Ireland shall be given to the British Government . . .' (Article 8). An annex arising out of this article was identical to the one contained in the Treaty. Instead of Articles 12 to 15 of the Treaty, Document No. 2 contained an addendum dealing with Northern Ireland; headed North-East Ulster, it

RESOLVED:

That whilst refusing to admit the right of any part of Ireland to be excluded from the supreme authority of the Parliament of Ireland, or that the relations between the Parliament of Ireland and any subordinate legislature in Ireland can be a matter for treaty with a Government outside Ireland, nevertheless, in sincere regard for internal peace, and in order to make manifest our desire not to bring force or coercion to bear upon any substantial part of the Province of Ulster, whose inhabitants may not be unwilling to accept the national authority, we are prepared to grant to that portion of Ulster which is defined as Northern Ireland in the British Government of Ireland Act 1920, privileges and safeguards not less substantial than those provided for in the 'Articles of Agreement for a Treaty' between Great Britain and Ireland signed in London on December 6th 1921.

DOHENY, MICHAEL (1805–63). Young Irelander and poet; b. near Fethard, Co. Tipperary. Self-educated, he worked on his father's smallholding until he entered Gray's Inn in 1834. Doheny became a popular and highly respected member of the Bar on the Southern circuit. He joined the Repeal Association* and was a frequent contributor to *The Nation** over the signature 'Éiranach'. He was a member of the Irish Confederation* and though, like John Blake Dillon,* he was opposed to the extremism of John Mitchel, he nonetheless took part in the rising of 1848. Following the collapse of the rising he went to the US where he continued his legal career and was a founder-member of the Fenians* in 1858. His best-known poems are 'Acushla gal Machree' and 'The Outlaw's Wife'. His *In the Felon's Track* (1867) is an account of the 1848 Rising and its aftermath. His nephew, Edward L. Doheny (1856–1935), became a millionaire in the Californian and Mexican oil business, and was selected by Eamon de Valera* to lead the American Committee for Relief in Ireland in 1920.

DOHERTY, JOHN (1783–1850). Lawyer and politician (Conservative); b. Dublin; ed. TCD; B.A. (1806). He was called to the Irish Bar in 1808 and practised on the Leinster Circuit. He was MP for New Ross (1824–26) and Kilkenny (1826), Solicitor-General in 1827 and Lord Chief Justice of the Common Pleas in 1830. During his career at the Bar, he was involved in several famous trials including the Doneraile Conspiracy* in which Daniel O'Connell* represented the accused. In the House of Commons, Doherty was noted for his oratory and wit. He played a leading role in debates on the Irish question and favoured Catholic Emancipation* (one of the very few occasions on which he was at one with O'Connell). Doherty lost most of his fortune in railway speculation, and was a depressive in his later years.

DOLLY'S BRAE AFFRAY (12 July 1849). A battle between Catholic Ribbonmen* and Orangemen took place at Dolly's Brae near Magheramayo, Co. Down when the Catholics confronted an Orange Order* rally in Tullymore Park on the estate of the Earl of Roden.* The Orangemen had police and military protection and after a few hours' fighting some thirty Catholics were killed. The Orange victory at Dolly's Brae became part of Orange folklore. As a result of the fighting, legislation to prevent triumphalist processions was introduced but it failed to have any impact.

DONERAILE CONSPIRACY (1829). The area around Doneraile, Co. Cork, seat of the St Leger family, was the scene of intense Whiteboy activity. Following an attack on Dr Norcott (a local Protestant), landlords, led by George Bond Low, made a determined effort to end Whiteboy activity, not only in their area, but throughout North Cork. To this end a fund was launched and a sum of £732 collected for information leading to the arrest of Whiteboys. Perjured evidence presented by Owen 'Cloumper' Daly, his cousin Patrick Daly, William Nowlan, David Sheehan and Thomas Murphy, resulted in the appearance of twenty-one men in four stages before packed juries. Following a farcical trial (22 October) under Judges Torrens and Pennefather in which four of the prisoners were sentenced to death the following month, a brother of one of the accused yet to be tried, William Burke of Ballyhea, Co. Cork, decided to enlist the aid of Daniel O'Connell* in his defence. After a famous night ride to Derrynane, Co. Kerry, Burke succeeded in interesting O'Connell in the case. O'Connell set out almost immediately on an even longer journey to Cork, and arrived in court during the speech of the Solicitor-General, John Doherty.* Having secured Justice Pennefather's permission to breakfast in court, O'Connell sought to undermine the confidence of the Prosecutor, and by a series of timely interruptions, succeeded in switching the spotlight completely to the case for the defence. During the course of the perjured evidence

by Patrick Daly, Judge Pennefather beckoned O'Connell to approach the bench and drew his attention to the fact that the oral evidence now presented by the 'witness' was totally at variance with an earlier affidavit. O'Connell hopelessly confused the other 'witnesses' to such an extent that the jury, although confined for up to forty-eight hours, failed to agree and the trials were postponed. The remainder of the prisoners were acquitted and the sentence of death on the original four was commuted to transportation to New South Wales. The trial was the subject of the novel *Glenanaar* by Canon P. A. Sheehan.*

DONOVAN, ROBERT (1852–1934). Scholar; b. Leighlinbridge, Co. Carlow; ed. St. Kieran's College, Kilkenny and University College where he was Lecturer in English Literature (1886–87). He was a frequent contributor to *The Nation* * (1886–91), Commissioner of National Education in Ireland (1915), Chairman of the Proportional Representation Society of Ireland and of the Irish League of Nations Society. In 1927 he was Chairman of the Commission on Evil Literature and a member of the Censorship of Publications Board* in 1932.

DORA. *See* Defence of the Realm Act.

DOUGLAS, JAMES G. (1887–1954). Senator (1922–36; 1938–43; 1944–54); b. Dublin, to a prominent family in the Society of Friends in which he was a life-long activist; ed. Friends' School, Lisburn. During the War of Independence* he was treasurer and a trustee of the White Cross.* Upon the establishment of the Free State, he became a member of the Senate and was Vice-Chairman from 1922 to 1925 when he was also Chairman of the Joint Committee of the Dail and Senate on Standing Orders (Private Business). He was a member of the Committee which drafted the Constitution of 1922.*

DOYLE, JAMES WARREN ('J.K.L.') (1786–1834). Bishop of Kildare and Leighlin (R.C.), 1819–34; b. near New Ross, Co. Wexford where he witnessed the rising of the United Irishmen* in 1798; ed. locally, at the Augustinian College, New Ross (from 1799) and at the University of Coimbra in Portugal (1806–08). He served briefly with the Spanish Army during the Peninsular War and then worked as an interpreter with the British Mission in Lisbon (1808). After ordination (1809) he taught logic at New Ross Friary for four years, held the Chair of Rhetoric at Carlow College (1813) and was Professor of Theology there from 1814 until his appointment as Bishop.

As Bishop of Kildare and Leighlin he maintained a very close relationship with the Archbishop of Dublin, Daniel Murray.* He founded public libraries with a borrowing fee of one penny for the poor and revived the practice of parish retreats. In 1820 he organised a mammoth retreat in which the majority of the Catholic hierarchy and over 1,000 priests participated. A celebrated controversialist, in 1824 he advocated the union of the Catholic Church and the established Church of Ireland. He was a prolific letter-writer to the press, generally under the initials 'J.K.L.' (James, Kildare and Leighlin); his exchange of letters with Dr Magee, the Protestant Archbishop of Dublin, aroused widespread interest. Dr Doyle was the first member of the hierarchy to give public support to Daniel O'Connell* and the Catholic Association* in the fight for Catholic Emancipation.* When Emancipation was granted, he opposed the disenfranchisement of the Forty-Shilling Freeholders.* He was an influential witness along with O'Connell and others before a Select Committee inquiring into conditions in Ireland (March 1825). He was questioned on topics including the Sacraments, Miracles, Papal Authority, the Veto* and the payment of clergy. During a break in the proceedings the Duke of Wellington* was asked if they were still

examining Doyle, to which he replied, 'No, but Doyle is examining us'. He did not support O'Connell on Repeal, believing that reforming legislation would be sufficient for Ireland, and they were also opposed over the Poor Law.* Keenly interested in educational matters, he gave strong support to the National Education* system established in 1831 and when the landlords of the area did not make land available for the erection of schools he had schools built in graveyards. His best known pamphlets were *A Vindication of the Religious and Civil Principles of the Irish Catholics* (1822) and *On the origin, Nature and Destination of Church Property* (1831).

DRENNAN, WILLIAM (1754–1820). Poet and United Irishman; b. Belfast, son of a Presbyterian minister; ed. locally and at the University of Edinburgh where he received his M.D. (1778). After practising medicine in Belfast and Newry he moved to Dublin in 1789. He assisted Thomas Russell* and Theobald Wolfe Tone in the early organisation of the United Irishmen and wrote the manifesto of the new movement. Drennan, unable to reconcile himself to physical force, had little contact with the organisation after it went underground (1795). He was the originator of the phrase 'The Emerald Isle' in his poem, 'When Erin First Rose'. His 'Wake of William Orr', commemorating the execution of a United man on perjured evidence, was said to have caused the government more harm than the loss of a battle. Among his published works were *Glendalough and Other Poems* (1815), *Fugitive Pieces* (1815) and a translation of Sophocles' *Electra* (1817).

DREW, REV. THOMAS (1800–70). Religious preacher (C.I.); b. Limerick; ed. TCD where he graduated B.A. in 1826. Ordained in 1827, he later ministered in Belfast (from 1832) where he supervised the erection of twenty churches. As Grand Chaplain to the Orange Order,* he demanded the repeal of Catholic Emancipation* and the exclusion of Catholics from the British House of Commons. Unwilling to accept the findings of the official census of 1841 which indicated that Catholics formed the predominant religion in Ireland, he claimed it was a 'conspiracy' in that it did not show the true strength of the Protestant churches. The mission of the United Kingdom he said, was to 'Protestantise the world' (*see* Second Reformation). One of his daughters married the Orange leader, William Johnson.*

DRUMCOLLOGHER CINEMA TRAGEDY (5 September 1926). Forty-eight people lost their lives in the village of Drumcollogher, Co. Limerick, during a showing of *The Ten Commandments.* It occurred when a candle was upset near a reel of film, causing a flash fire among the remaining unprotected reels of celluloid. The audience panicked and stampeded to the one narrow exit which led to a wooden stairway (the only available means of exit). Two upstairs windows were barred on the exterior with rods of iron. The victims were buried in a communal grave in the local churchyard. A memorial library marks the location of the cinema. As a result of the tragedy stringent safety precautions were introduced internationally and a new type of film, which smouldered rather than flared, was developed.

DRUMMOND, THOMAS (1797–1840). Under Secretary (1835–40); b. Scotland; ed. Edinburgh University. He joined the Royal Engineers in 1815 and while in the army developed the 'Drummond' limelight and improved the heliostat. While serving with the Ordnance Survey of Ireland* he came into close contact with the peasantry, an experience which uniquely fitted him for understanding the principal grievances of the Irish. His term of office as Under-Secretary was conspicuous for its tolerance and contructiveness. The Irish Constabulary Act of 1836

encouraged Catholics to enter the police force which later became the Royal Irish Constabulary.* He was also involved in the establishment of the Poor Law* in Ireland. He had little sympathy for Irish landlords with whom he was very unpopular and to whom he pointed out, in replying to Tipperary magistrates, that 'property had its duties as well as its rights; to the neglect of these duties in times past is mainly to be attributed that diseased state of society in which such crimes can take their rise'. Stipendiary Magistrates,* independent of the landlords, were appointed, and his handling of the unrest over the tithes* resulted in a decrease in crime by 1840. The act of 1838 converted the hated tithe into a fixed rent and soldiers were no longer to be used for its collection. He died in office after a life of chronic ill-health.

'DRY LODGINGS'. Eighteenth-century term used to describe houses which offered accommodation to travellers in remote areas. Unlike post-houses which offered sustenance, neither food nor drink was available at a 'dry lodging' (hence the name). Accommodation was announced by the presence of a cloth or other sign attached to a makeshift pole. Frequently the traveller had to share a room with his landlord and family. *See also* 'Stradogue, sleeping in'.

DUBLIN CASTLE. The Castle was erected by order of King John (30 August 1204) in which is stated '. . . You have given us to understand you have no safe place for the custody of our treasures, and, because for this reason and for many others, we are in need of a strong fortress in Dublin, we command you to erect a castle there in such a place as you may consider to be suitable for the administration of justice and if need be, for the defence of the city . . .' A number of unsuccessful attempts were made to capture the Castle: in 1534 by Thomas Fitzgerald ('Silken

Thomas'), by Royalists in 1646 and by members of the Citizen Army* and the Irish Volunteers* during the Easter Rising of 1916.* Throughout its history the Castle was remote from, and at variance with, the rest of Ireland. During the Famine of 1845–49* the vice-regal court was maintained and receptions, balls and levees continued uninterrupted. Joseph Chamberlain* was prompted to comment in 1885 '... I say that the time has come to reform altogether the absurd and irritating anachronism which is known as Dublin Castle'.

Following the Treaty,* Dublin Castle was formally handed over to the Provisional Government* by the Lord Lieutenant, Lord FitzAlan* on 16 January 1922. A brief statement was subsequently released to the press: 'The members of Rialtas Sealadach na hÉireann (the Provisional Government of Ireland), received the surrender of Dublin Castle at 1.45 p.m. today. It is now in the hands of the Irish nation.' The Castle, which houses the State Record Office and State Apartments, is used during the inauguration of the President of Ireland, and is open to members of the public.

DUBLIN DRAMA LEAGUE. Founded in 1919 by William Butler Yeats,* James Stephens* and Lennox Robinson* to broaden the scope of drama offered by the Abbey Theatre,* which had confined itself to plays by Irish authors. The League proposed to organise a season of continental drama. Each play was to have a run of two days in the Abbey Theatre (on Sundays and Mondays). The first play produced by the new company was *The Liberators* by Srgjan Tucic (17 February 1919). Other authors whose works were presented included Strindberg, D'Annunzio, Eugene O'Neill, Euripides, George Bernard Shaw,* Lord Dunsany,* Cocteau, Chekhov, Pirandello and Chesterton. In 1928 the League was replaced by the Dublin Gate Theatre Company (*see* Gate Theatre) with the same policy except that it gave each play a run of at least one week.

DUBLIN INSTITUTE FOR ADVANCED STUDIES. Founded in 1940 by an Act of the Oireachtas. The functions of the Institute are to provide facilities for the furtherance of advanced study and the conduct and publication of research in specialised branches of knowledge. With the foundation of the Institute in 1940 two constituent schools were simultaneously established: the School of Celtic Studies and the School of Theoretical Physics. In 1947 a third School, the School of Cosmic Physics, was established, having three subsections: Astronomy, Cosmic Ray and Geophysics.

DUBLIN METROPOLITAN POLICE (DMP). Unarmed police force covering the area of Dublin city and county and Co. Wicklow, founded in 1786. The force evolved from the organisation of nightwatchmen and private security police. By 1839 they were fully organised, distinct from the Irish Constabulary (*see* Police *and* Royal Irish Constabulary), operating under their own code of regulations which was revised in 1889 and 1909. The 'G' Division of the DMP was responsible for gathering intelligence. The DMP were not involved in the War of Independence.* Under the Police Forces Amalgamation Act 1925, the DMP became part of the Garda Siochana* in April 1925.

'DUBLIN MORNING REGISTER.' Liberal newspaper founded in 1824 by Michael Staunton.* It supported Daniel O'Connell* in the struggle for Catholic Emancipation. The *Register* proved a new type of paper for Ireland in that it concentrated mainly on domestic events (most newspapers of the era carried more foreign, particularly British rather than Irish news) and it employed a permanent staff of trained reporters, which in the 1830s included Charles Gavan Duffy,* John Blake Dillon* and Thomas Davis.* Sales rose to a peak of 800 in 1835 but had declined to 300 by 1841, having been damaged by industrial disputes. It ceased publication in 1843.

'DUBLIN MORNING STAR.' Newspaper founded by Joseph Timothy Haydn* in February 1824. The paper was bitterly anti-Catholic and was also hostile to Dublin Castle.* It was noted for the libellous nature of its attacks, the first of which (in its maid⌐ ╕ issue), directed against the Castle, provoked a libel action in which Haydn was defended by Daniel O'Connell.* Because of the sensational nature of its content, the paper's circulation and advertising revenue rose rapidly, but a large number of costly libel actions had put it out of business by 1825.

'DUBLIN OPINION.' Leading satirical magazine from 1922 to 1972, appearing monthly. Its founding editor was Arthur Booth (d. 1926) and later editors were Charles E. Kelly and Tom Collins (1926—68), Gordon Clark (1968—70) and Lelia Doolan and Jack Dowling (1970—72). At its peak, it sold around 70,000 copies per issue and was noted for the bite of its political satire and cartoons. After 1972 it ceased to appear and was bought by Louis O'Sullivan who published it as a Christmas annual, edited by James D. O'Donnell.

'DUBLIN TIMES.' Newspaper founded in 1832 with the support of Dublin Castle.* It consisted almost entirely of advertising and was free, the first of its kind in Ireland; its non-advertising sections were particularly virulent in their denunciations of Daniel O'Connell,* the Repeal Movement* and the (Protestant) Ascendancy.* It enjoyed little success and ceased publication towards the end of 1833.

'DUBLIN UNIVERSITY MAGAZINE.' Monthly literary journal founded by Isaac Butt* in 1833. The editorial staff were all associated with Trinity College,* Dublin. (Protestant)

Ascendancy* and loyalist in tone, the magazine was, in Butt's words, to be a 'monthly advocate of the Protestantism, the intelligence, and the respectability of Dublin'. Butt was succeeded as editor by Charles Lever* in 1843. Lever lost some of the more distinguished contributors who included William Carleton,* George Petrie,* Eugene O'Curry,* John O'Donovan,* Sir Samuel Ferguson,* James Clarence Mangan,* William Bruce,* Sheridan Le Fanu* and Samuel Lover.* The magazine ceased publication in 1877.

DUBLIN WOMEN'S SUFFRAGE SOCIETY. See Irish Women's Suffrage Federation.

DUFFY, SIR CHARLES GAVAN (1816—1903). Young Ireland journalist; b. Monaghan; ed. Monaghan Public School and the Royal Belfast Academical Institute. He worked in Belfast on *The Belfast Vindicator* before moving to Dublin where he was co-founder with John Blake Dillon* and Thomas Osborne Davis* of *The Nation* in 1842. With the rest of the Young Irelanders he supported Daniel O'Connell* and the Repeal Association* until 1846 and was amongst those tried for sedition in 1843 with O'Connell, sentenced to imprisonment and then released by order of the House of Lords in 1844. In January 1847 he helped to found the Irish Confederation* of which he persuaded William Smith O'Brien* to accept the leadership. For his involvement in the July 1848 rising at Ballingarry, Co. Tipperary,* he was tried and acquitted four times. He became the leader of the Tenant League* with Frederick Lucas* in 1850 and was two years later a founder of the Independent Irish Party* and MP for New Ross, Co. Wexford. However, he became disillusioned with the failure of the party and emigrated to Australia in 1856. Entering public life in Australia, he rose to the position of Governor-General of Victoria and was knighted in 1873. He returned to Europe in 1881, and settled in the south of France. His principal works were *The Ballad Poetry of Young Ireland* (1845) which ran to fifty editions, *Guide to the Land Law of Victoria* (1862), *Young Ireland: A Fragment of Irish History* (1880), *The League of North and South* (1886), *Thomas Davis: The Memoirs of a Patriot* (1892), *A Short Life of Thomas Davis* (1896) and *My Life in Two Hemispheres* (1898).

DUFFY, GEORGE GAVAN (1882–1951). Lawyer and politician (Sinn Fein); son of Sir Charles Gavan Duffy;* ed. France and at Stonyhurst. He built up an extensive legal practice in London. In May 1916 he volunteered to arrange for the legal defence of Sir Roger Casement.* He returned to Ireland during the resurgence of Sinn Fein, was returned for South Dublin in the general election of December 1918, and helped to draft the Declaration of Independence.* In 1920 he represented the Irish Republic at the Peace Conference in Paris and was Ambassador to Rome one year later. Eamon de Valera* and Michael Collins* nominated him as a plenipotentiary at the Anglo-Irish negotiations which led to the Treaty* (he was the last delegate to sign). After succeeding Arthur Griffith* as Minister for Foreign Affairs in the government of the second Dail Eireann in July 1922 he resigned in the following month as a protest against the suppression of the Supreme Court. His suggestion that republican prisoners – Irregulars* – should be treated as prisoners-of-war was defeated (27 September 1922). He criticised the Constitution of 1922,* the government's policy of arrest and detention without trial, and attacked the execution of Robert Erskine Childers* while an appeal was pending in the High Court. Following a distinguished legal career, he became President of the High Court in 1946.

DUFFY, JAMES (1809–71). Publisher; b. Co. Monaghan. He moved to Dublin in early life as assistant to publisher John Daly. In 1831 Duffy entered the publishing business on his own account with *Napoleon's Book of Fate*, a twopenny version of *Boney's Oraculum*, then popular in Europe. It was a financial success and set him on a career which spanned forty years, during which he was reputed never to have taken a regular holiday. Duffy's publications, catering principally for the masses with cheap popular editions, were nevertheless well-produced. His green-covered books emblazoned with his trade mark of a golden harp encircled by a wreath of shamrocks were generally available in library and pocket editions. An excellent employer, he presented each of his employees with an annual Christmas Box varying from £3 to £20. Most of the works of the writers of Young Ireland* were published by Duffy. According to Charles Gavan Duffy* (no relation), 'The volumes projected by the Young Irelanders were nearly all published by James Duffy, whose enterprise and literality ultimately created a trade extending to India, America and Australia'. Among the writers whom Duffy published were Thomas Davis,* John Mitchel,* James Clarence Mangan,* Charles Gavan Duffy,* Thomas D'Arcy Magee,* Denis Florence McCarthy,* William Carleton,* Richard Dalton Williams,* John Banim,* Gerald Griffin* and Charles Kickham.*

DUGGAN, EAMON (EDMUND) JOHN (1874–1936). Politician (Sinn Fein, Cumann na nGaedheal and Fine Gael); b. Longwood, Co. Meath; ed. locally and Dublin where he qualified as a solicitor (1914). A member of the Irish Volunteers, he fought in the GPO during the Easter Rising of 1916* and was interned. Following his release he was again active in the Volunteers, becoming Director of Intelligence (1918). Representative for Louth–Meath in the first Dail Eireann, he was again imprisoned, from 1920 until the summer of 1921. He assisted in working out details of the Truce and was appointed to the team of plenipotentiaries to negotiate the Treaty* with Great Britain (October–December 1921). Duggan defended the Treaty in the Dail, stating 'I say under the terms of the Treaty that if the Irish people cannot achieve their freedom it is the fault of the Irish people and not of the Treaty'. TD for Co. Meath (1922–33), he was a Minister for Home Affairs in the Provisional Government* and Minister without Portfolio (September 1922–September 1923). He was Parliamentary Secretary to the Executive Council and Minister for Defence (1927–32). Duggan, who did not contest the general election of January 1933, was elected to the Senate and was the last member to take the Oath of Allegiance* (which was then abolished).

DUNGANNON CLUBS. Founded in 1905 by Bulmer Hobson* and Denis McCullough* in commemoration of the 1782 Volunteer Convention at Dungannon, Co. Tyrone. The clubs were non-sectarian, republican and separatist and flourished mainly in Ulster. They were described by Hobson as '. . . semi-literary, semi-political and patriotic . . .' Pamphlets urging the cultivation of the Irish language, non-co-operation with the British army, economic independence and self-sufficiency for Ireland, were produced by the Executive, which identified with the Irish Ireland movement of the time. The Dungannon Clubs were absorbed into Sinn Fein* between 1906 and 1908.

DUNGARVAN RIOT (29 September 1846). The riot in Dungarvan during the Famine of 1845–49 was the result of an attempt by starving, unemployed men to prevent the export of grain from the port. When the police had failed to restore order, a body of the 1st Royal Dragoons commanded by Captain Sibthorp was summoned. The Riot Act was read and when the crowd refused to disperse Sibthorp ordered his men to fire, killing two people and wounding several. This was the first riot at which loss of life occurred during the Famine.

DUNRAVEN AND MOUNT-EARL, 4th EARL (1841–1926). Quin, Windham Thomas Wyndham; landowner; b. Adare, Co. Limerick; ed. Rome and Christ Church, Oxford which he left without taking a degree in 1862 to become a cornet in the 1st Life Guards. He was war correspondent for the *Daily Telegraph* in Abyssinia (now Ethiopia) in 1867 and also covered the Franco-Prussian War and the siege of Paris (1870-71). On a visit to the USA in 1871 he hunted around the Platte River with 'Buffalo Bill' Cody and after another visit in 1874, when he explored the Yellowstone, he published *The Great Divide, the Upper Yellowstone* (1876). A noted yachtsman, he competed unsuccessfully in the Americas Cup in 1893 and 1895 with *Valkyrie II* (which sunk on the Clyde in 1894) and *Valkyrie III*. A strong Conservative, he was Under-Secretary of the Colonies (1885–86, 1886–87). During 1888–90 he was chairman of the Commission on Sweated Labour. He was a constructive Unionist and sought to bring about a peaceful solution to the land question and to the demand for Home Rule.* His *The Outlook in Ireland, the case for Devolution and Conciliation* was published in 1897 and reprinted in 1907. He was instrumental in the formation of the Land Conference* of 1902–03, of which he was chairman, and became president of the Irish Reform Association* a year later (*see* Devolution). Upon the foundation of the Free State in December 1922 he became a member of the first Senate.

Dunraven was a model landlord on his 39,000-acre estate at Adare, where he maintained a famous stud farm and experimented with growing tobacco until his factory burned down in 1916. He published *Cheap food for the people: an open letter to the people of Ireland* in 1925. Other published works included an 'historical notice of Adare' for

Memorials of Dunraven by his mother, Caroline, Countess of Dunraven (1865), *The Irish Question* (1880), *Self-Instruction in the Theory and Practice of Navigation* (1900), *The Legacy of Past Years* (1911), *Canadian Nights* (1914) and *Past Times and Pastimes* (1922).

DUNSANY, LORD (1878–1957). Plunkett, Edward John Moreton Drax; b. London, nephew of Sir Horace Plunkett;* ed. Eton and Oxford. Commissioned in the Coldstream Guards, he fought in the Boer War. On his estate in Co. Meath he befriended Francis Ledwidge* to whom he gave the use of his library. During World War I he fought in the Royal Iniskilling Fusiliers, the regiment which Ledwidge also joined. Dunsany was wounded in April 1916. A member of the British Academy of Letters, he was Professor of English Literature at Athens University (1940–41). His extensive output included novels, short stories, fantasies, plays, poetry and radio drama: *The Gods of Pagena* (1905), *Time and the Gods* (1906), *The Sword of Welleran* (1908), *The King of Elfland's Daughter* (1924), *The Charwoman's Shadow* (1926) and *The Curse of the Wise Woman* (1933); plays: *The Glittering Gates* (produced at the Abbey Theatre by W.B. Yeats in 1909), *The Gods of the Mountain* (1911), *A Night at an Inn* (1916), *The Laughter of the Gods* (1919), *The Tents of the Arabs* (1920), *If* (1921), *Alexander* (1925), *Lord Adrian* (1933) and *Plays for Earth and Air* (1937); radio dramas: *The Use of Man, The Bureau de Change, Atmospherics* and *The Aurora Borealis;* poetry: *Fifty Poems* (1930) and *Mirage Water* (1938). He edited and arranged for the publication of *The Complete Poems of Francis Ledwidge* (1919).

DUNSINK OBSERVATORY, DUBLIN. Founded in 1783 as the Observatory of Trinity College, Dublin. One of its early Directors was Sir William Rowan Hamilton.* The Observatory ceased to function on the birth of the Irish Free State in 1922 but was re-established by the Irish government in 1947 under the auspices of the Dublin Institute for Advanced Studies.* The Observatory now specialises in investigations of the sun, and its effects upon the earth, and precision-measurement of star brightness by electronic means.

DUTY-SERVICES. Services demanded by a landlord of a tenant under many of the leases issued to Catholic tenants in the eighteenth and early part of the nineteenth centuries. Such duties included furnishing the landlord or his agent with labourers or with one's own labour, or with horses for a set number of days per year, spinning flax for the landlord's use, carting his fuel or lime, or presenting gifts of poultry and eggs, etc., and of providing potatoes.

DWYER, MICHAEL (1771–1815). United Irishman; b. Co. Wicklow; uncle of Anne Devlin; ed. privately. Following the defeat of the 1798 insurgents he took to the hills for five years. A bounty of £1,000 was placed on his head, and £250 on each of his men, the most famous of whom were Hugh Byrne, Martin Bourke and Samuel McAllister (who was later to give his life for Dwyer). Due to join Robert Emmet* in the ill-fated rebellion of 1803 Dwyer never received the signal to rise. He surrendered voluntarily and was imprisoned at Kilmainham. Dwyer was sentenced to transportation to Botany Bay where the Governor was Captain William Bligh (of the *Bounty*). Bligh had him sent to Norfolk Island for six months and from there to Van Diemen's Land (Tasmania). On the removal of Bligh from the Governorship in 1808, Dwyer returned to Sydney where he became High Constable. His wife Mary died near Sydney in 1861 at the age of ninety-three.

DYNAMITERS. A dynamiting campaign in England during the 1880s was directed by the Fenians,* led by a triumvirate known as the Triangle.* Dynamiting activity was financed from the Skirmishing Fund* established by Jeremiah O'Donovan Rossa* and many of the dynamiters were trained by Dr Thomas Gallagher.* The campaign was not approved by the moderate leadership of Clan na Gael* and it served to alienate some British support for Irish reform.

An attempt was made to blow up Chester Castle in 1870 and James McKevitt and James McGrath were sentenced to penal servitude for attempting to blow up Liverpool Town Hall. Other attempts were made to destroy the Mansion House in London, the North-Western express near Wolverhampton, an infantry barracks at Salford, Lancashire, and the Victoria Docks in East London. A cache of weapons was found at Clerkenwell: it included 277 rifles, 276 bayonets, 7,925 cartridges for Schneider rifles, and 400 small pistols (the pistols and rifles were engraved with shamrocks). During 1883 Gallagher, Thomas J. Clarke,* William Ansburgh, Bernard Gallagher, John Kent and Alfred Whitehead were charged with the manufacture and possession of explosives. With the exception of Ansburgh and Bernard Gallagher, they were sentenced to penal servitude for life. Fenians were

usually charged under the Treason-Felony Act of 1848,* and were severely treated during imprisonment – on their release in 1896, Dr Gallagher and Whitehead were adjudged to be insane. In August 1884, John Daly* and James Francis Egan were tried for high treason and with possession of dynamite. Daly received a life sentence (he was released in 1896) and Egan was sentenced to twenty years penal servitude. On 13 December of that year William Francis Lomasney* *alias* Captain Mackey was killed along with two of his companions when an explosive charge they were placing against London Bridge exploded prematurely. Further dynamiting occurred in 1885 when attempts were made to destroy the London Metropolitan Railway Station near Tottenham Court Road, the Tower of London and the Houses of Parliament. For these attempts two men, Cunningham and Burton, were sentenced to fourteen years imprisonment. On 4 February two American citizens, Thomas Callan and Michael Harkin, were sentenced to fifteen years penal servitude for possessing dynamite. Harkin was released in 1891 and returned to the US where he died a year later, and Callan was released in 1893 on condition that he left England.

E

EARLY, BIDDY (c. 1799–1874). White witch; b. Faha Mountains, Co. Clare. She was a celebrated 'Wise Person',* specialising in eye diseases and able to cure illness in people and animals, rid people of curses and see into the future. Her home was near Feakle, Co. Clare, overlooking Kilbarron Lake. The source of her power was said to be a bottle, variously described as 'black', 'blue' or 'green'.

Her three husbands all died of excessive drinking of the presents of spirits brought to her by grateful and hopeful patients. She successfully resisted efforts by clergymen to prevent her from exercising her gift. Although crippled in her last years, she was said to have thrown her 'black bottle' into Kilbarron Lake just before her death. She was consulted by the Prince of Wales but the nature of his complaint was never revealed. She was buried in an unmarked grave in Feakle, Co. Clare.

EASTER RISING, 1916 (24 April—1 May).

The rising which started in Dublin on Easter Monday, 24 April 1916, had been planned by a secret Military Council* within the Irish Republican Brotherhood* in January. It was intended to be a national insurrection, starting on Easter Sunday. A series of mishaps destroyed the original plans. Eoin MacNeill,* Chief of Staff of the Irish Volunteers,* had not been informed and when he discovered on Thursday of the intended outbreak he confronted Patrick Pearse.* Pearse and Sean MacDiarmada,* believing that German arms would arrive, convinced him that the rising would be a success. The arms were expected on the *Aud** which had sailed from Germany to arrive off the Kerry coast on Friday, unaware that it was not expected until Sunday. Sir Roger Casement,* put ashore at Banna Strand in Co. Kerry from a German U-boat, was captured on Friday morning. Later that day the *Aud* was captured by a British patrol boat and the German captain scuttled the ship. When Mac-Neill discovered these facts on Saturday he countermanded Pearse's orders for a full mobilisation on Sunday morning. At a meeting held in Liberty Hall on Sunday morning the leaders decided to proceed with their plans on Easter Monday. As a result of the confusion the rising was almost exclusively confined to Dublin city.

Easter Monday, 24 April

The total rebel force was small: 1,558 volunteers led by Pearse and an estimated 219 of the Irish Citizen Army* led by James Connolly.* The General Post Office in Sackville Street (now O'Connell Street) was occupied at noon, and became rebel headquarters. A few minutes later Pearse appeared outside and proclaimed the Irish Republic:

POBLACHT NA hÉIREANN
THE PROVISIONAL GOVERNMENT
OF THE
IRISH REPUBLIC
TO THE PEOPLE OF IRELAND

IRISHMEN AND IRISHWOMEN: in the name of God and of the dead generations from which she receives her old tradition of nationhood, Ireland, through us, summons her children to her flag and strikes for her freedom.

Having organised her manhood through her secret revolutionary organisation, the Irish Republican Brotherhood, and through her open military organisations, the Irish Volunteers and the Irish Citizen Army, having patiently perfected her discipline, having resolutely waited for the right moment to reveal itself, she now seizes that moment, and supported by her exiled children in America and by gallant allies in Europe, but relying in the first on her own strength, she strikes in full confidence of victory.

We declare the right of the people of Ireland to the ownership of Ireland, and to the unfettered control of Irish destinies, to be sovereign and indefeasible. The long usurpation of that right by a foreign people and government has not extinguished the right, nor can it ever be extinguished except by the destruction of the Irish people. In every generation the Irish people have asserted their right to national freedom and sovereignty: six times during the past three hundred years they have asserted it in arms. Standing on that fundamental right and again asserting it in arms in the face of the world, we hereby proclaim the Irish Republic as a Sovereign Independent State, and we pledge our lives and the lives of our comrades-in-arms to the cause of its freedom, of its welfare, and of its exaltation among the nations.

The Irish Republic is entitled to, and hereby claims, the allegiance of every Irishman and Irishwoman. The Republic guarantees religious and civil liberty, equal rights and equal opportunities to all its citizens, and declares its resolve to pursue the happiness and prosperity of the whole nation and of all its parts, cherishing all the children of the nation equally, and oblivious of the differences carefully fostered by an alien Government, which have divided a minority from the majority in the past.

Until our arms have brought the opportune moment for the establishment of a permanent National Government, representative of the whole people of Ireland and elected by the suffrages of all her men and women, the Provisional Government, hereby constituted, will administer the civil and military affairs of the Republic in trust for the people.

We place the cause of the Irish Republic under the protection of the Most High God, Whose blessing we invoke under our arms, and we pray that no one who serves that cause will dishonour it by cowardice, inhumanity, or rapine. In this supreme hour the Irish nation must, by its valour and discipline, and by the readiness of its children to sacrifice themselves for the common good, prove itself worthy of the august destiny to which it is called.

Signed on Behalf of the Provisional Government.

Thomas J. Clarke
Sean MacDiarmada
Thomas MacDonagh
P. H. Pearse   Eamonn Ceannt
James Connolly   Joseph Plunkett

After it had been read, copies of the Proclamation were posted in the area around the GPO. The deployment of the rebels' forces was
1st Battalion, Commandant Edward Daly*: The Four Courts, the Mendicity Institute, Jameson's Distillery and North King Street;
2nd Battalion, Commandant Thomas MacDonagh*: Jacob's Factory;
The Irish Citizen Army, commanded by Michael Mallin,* took St Stephen's Green and the Royal College of Surgeons;
3rd Battalion, Commandant Eamon

de Valera*: Boland's Mills, the railway in Lansdowne Road, Westland Row Station, Mount Street Bridge and Northumberland Road;
4th Battalion, Commandant Eamon Ceannt* and Vice-Commandant Cathal Brugha*: the South Dublin Union, James's Street Hospital (now St Kevin's Hospital), Marrowbone Lane, Roe's Distillery, Ardee Street Bakery and Cork Street.
The Citizen Army under Captain Sean Connolly took City Hall. The rebels attacked Haddington Road and Beggars Bush Barracks. 2,500 British reinforcements from the Curragh arrived and engaged the rebels in the Dublin Castle area, and recovered City Hall. They attacked the Mendicity Institute which was held by Volunteers and members of na Fianna Eireann* under the command of Sean Heuston.* The South Dublin Union was also attacked.

Tuesday, 25 April
The attack on the Mendicity Institute continued. The British occupied the Shelbourne Hotel facing Stephen's Green. They attacked the Green and forced the Citizen Army to fall back on the Royal College of Surgeons. The army also recovered the *Daily Express* and *Evening Mail* building. General W. H. M. Lowe took command of the British forces in Dublin and established a cordon from Kingsbridge to College Green via Dame Street. British reinforcements arrived from Belfast and Templemore and artillery support from Athlone. The South Dublin Union was attacked and the army cordoned off the route from the North Wall to Kingsbridge (now Heuston) Station.

Wednesday, 26 April
The rebels burned the Linenhall Barracks where the garrison surrendered. The *Helga*,* a British gunboat, sailed up the Liffey and began shelling Liberty Hall. The British forces took up positions in Sackville Street. Two battalions of extra troops arrived from England, landing at Skerries, Co. Dublin. Reinforcements

from Kingstown (Dun Laoghaire) attacked the rebels at Lansdowne Road but were forced to retreat. Intense fighting took place at Mount Street Bridge, an outpost of de Valera's command. For nine hours twelve of his men held down two battalions; four rebels survived, while British casualties were four officers killed, fourteen wounded and 216 men killed and wounded (nearly half of the casualties for the whole week). The attack on the South Dublin Union continued. By the end of the day a cordon had been thrown around the city centre, north of the Liffey.

Thursday, 27 April
By now communications between rebel outposts had been cut. Having taken Sackville Street, the British commenced an artillery barrage on the GPO. Buildings on the street were soon on fire. Cathal Brugha was severely wounded in the fighting at the South Dublin Union where the British forces temporarily retreated. The shelling of the Four Courts commenced. Armoured cars entered the North King Street area while at the same time Boland's Mills was attacked.

Friday, 28 April
General Sir John Maxwell* arrived from England. The GPO, following the heavy bombardment, went on fire and Pearse decided to evacuate to the surrounding streets but came under heavy fire at the first attempt. The rebels managed to retreat to Henry Street at 8 p.m. The O'Rahilly* was killed leading his men into Moore Street. At Ashbourne, Co. Meath, Thomas Ashe,* having taken the police station, captured arms and ammunition but failed to take Ashbourne Barracks. His force lost two men in a battle with a relief force from Navan which lost eight soldiers.

Saturday, 29 April
The isolated rebels held out in Moore Street where they decided to negotiate terms of surrender for which preliminary arrangements were made by Nurse Elizabeth O'Farrell. General Lowe offered only unconditional surrender. At 3.30 p.m., Pearse agreed to surrender and handed his sword over to Lowe. Fifteen minutes later he signed orders to the other outposts:

'In order to prevent the further slaughter of Dublin citizens, and in the hope of saving the lives of our followers now surrounded and hopelessly outnumbered, the members of the Provisional Government present at Headquarters have agreed to an unconditional surrender, and the commandants of the various districts in the City and County will order their commands to lay down arms.'

The tricolour was hauled down from the roof of the GPO by British troops. On Monday, 1 May, the last incident of the rising took place at Bawnard House, near Fermoy, Co. Cork, the home of the Kent family, prominent republicans. After Thomas Kent* and his brothers returned home from being on the run during Easter Week their house was surrounded. Following a battle during which a constable of the RIC was killed and other policemen wounded, the family surrendered. Two of the brothers were wounded, one fatally. Thomas was sentenced to death and executed on 9 May.

Aftermath
Sixty-four republicans had been killed in action. Of the 20,000 British troops involved in the fighting during the week, 103 were killed and 357 wounded. Martial law was proclaimed and the leaders in the rising court-martialled. Between 3–12 May, fifteen men were executed, including Kent (in Cork):

3 May: Patrick Pearse, Thomas J. Clarke* and Thomas Mac-Donagh;

4 May: Joseph Plunkett,* Edward Daly, William Pearse* and Michael O'Hanrahan*;

5 May: John MacBride*;

8 May: Eamonn Ceannt, Michael Mallin, Con Colbert* and Sean Heuston;

9 May: Thomas Kent;
12 May: James Connolly and Sean MacDiarmada.

In August Sir Roger Casement was hanged for his part in events preceding the rising. Ninety-seven others were sentenced to death by court-martial but none of the sentences were carried out. There were 160 other courts-martial at which 122 people were sentenced to various terms of imprisonment. Some 2,000 men and women were imprisoned for rebel sympathies. All of those imprisoned were released between August 1916 and July 1917.

ECCLESIASTICAL TITLES ACT, 1851. The Act forbade Roman Catholic bishops in England to assume titles assigned to them by the Pope. The Pope's action had led to rioting directed against Catholics in some centres, most notoriously at Stockport, Cheshire. The passage of the Bill had been vigorously opposed by the Catholic Defence Association* led by George Henry Moore.*

ECONOMIC AND SOCIAL RESEARCH INSTITUTE (ESRI). Research organisation founded in 1960 with funds provided by the Ford Foundation. At first a purely economic research unit, its scope was widened to include social issues when financing was taken over by the Irish government in 1976. The ESRI had a staff of seventy in 1979 when its budget was £750,000, three-quarters of which was provided by the Department of Economic Planning and Development through a grant-in-aid. Twenty per cent of the ESRI's finance came from departments of the European Economic Community.*

ECONOMIC WAR. The War began after the Fianna Fail government withheld Land Annuities* from the British Exchequer in 1932. Britain held that this was in breach of the Financial Agreements of 1925 and 1926. Eamon de Valera* held that these agreements had never been ratified by Dail Eireann.* Britain imposed tariffs of 20 per cent on Irish cattle and agricultural produce entering the United Kingdom. De Valera then imposed tariffs on British goods entering the Free State: 5s (25p) per ton on coke and coal, 20 per cent on cement, machinery, electrical goods, steel and iron; 96 per cent of Irish goods went to Britain which was in a much better position than the Free State to engage in an economic war. As a result of the war, the value of Irish agricultural exports dropped from £35.8 million in 1929 to £13.5 million by 1935. The total value of exports to the UK fell from £43.5 million in 1929 to less than £18 million by 1935. The cattle trade was particularly affected as the numbers of cattle exported fell from 775,000 to just over 500,000. In 1934, a quota of 50 per cent of the 1933 figure was set and the export of store cattle was completely restricted. So was the entry to the UK of Irish beef and veal. The position improved in 1935 after the Coal-Cattle Pact.* Restrictions were further eased in 1936 and 1937. By the beginning of 1938 both governments were in a position to discuss ending the war. These talks between de Valera and Neville Chamberlain* took place between January and March 1938 and produced the Anglo-Irish Agreements.*

During the Economic War the government had sought to achieve a policy of self-sufficiency. It had appealed for an increase in wheat yields and by 1936 the acreage under wheat had risen from 21,000 in 1931 to 255,000. As Minister for Industry and Commerce Sean Lemass* endeavoured to float an industrialisation programme. He attempted to open up new export markets (US, Germany and France). To reduce the high unemployment figures, he embarked on an ambitious road-building programme costing £1 million. The government also began to resettle families from the Dublin tenement slums. The sugar-beet industry was extended, two cement factories were established in Limerick and Drogheda and tentative efforts at mineral exploitation were made. Between 1931 and 1938 there was a 44 per cent increase in industrial output and the numbers employed in industry rose from 110,000 to 166,000.

EDGAR, REV. JOHN (1798–1866). Clergyman (Presbyterian), philanthropist and temperance worker; b. near Ballynahinch, Co. Down; ed. Belfast and Glasgow; minister (1820); Professor of Theology, Belfast (1826). He started his temperance crusade in 1829 and won support from leading clergymen of all denominations. During the Famine of 1845–49* he worked on famine relief in Connaught, at the same time working for the propagation of his faith. He established industrial schools for training women in embroidery. He established a house in Brunswick St, Dublin (now Pearse St) to assist in the reform of prostitutes. During a tour of US in 1859 he raised £6,000 for educational purposes. His *Select Works* was published in Belfast in 1868.

EDGEWORTH, MARIA (1767–1849). Novelist; b. Black Bourton, Oxfordshire, daughter of Richard Lovell Edgeworth* who brought his family to Edgeworthstown, Co. Longford in 1782; ed. Derby and London. She was very small in stature and attempts to increase her height included suspending her for periods by the neck. She helped to rear her twenty-one brothers and sisters and was also the agent for her father's estate. She was very close to her father and collaborated with him on *Essays on Practical Education* (1797) and *Essays on Irish Bulls* (1803); in addition, she assisted him in the school which he established on the estate, and published educational books and moral tales such as *The Parent's Assistant, or, Stories for Children* (2 vols, 1796), *Harry and Lucy . . . being the first Part of Early Lessons* (1801), and *Moral Tales for Young People* (2 vols, 1801). Her

novels, starting with *Castle Rackrent* in 1800, made her internationally famous. Her work earned the admiration of Sir Walter Scott who acknowledged his debt to her in the General Preface to the Waverley Novels. She visited him at Abbotsford in 1823 and he returned the visit in 1825. During the Famine of 1845–49,* she used her own resources and successfully appealed for aid for the starving from her admirers around the world (from Boston came 150 barrels of flour addressed simply to 'Miss Edgeworth, for her poor'). Her other works included *Belinda* (3 vols, 1801), *Popular Tales* (1804), *Leonora* (1806), *Tales of Fashionable Life* (two series, 1809–12) – of which *Ennui* (1809) was volume III and *The Absentee* (1812) volume V – *Harrington* (1817), *Ormond* (1817) and *Helen*, her last novel, in 1834. She completed *Memoirs of Richard Lovell Edgeworth* (2 vols, 1820).

EDGEWORTH, RICHARD LOVELL (1744–1817). Landlord, politician, inventor and educationalist; b. Bath, Somerset; ed. privately and at Warwick, Drogheda, Longford, TCD and Oxford; four times married, he was the father of twenty-two children who were looked after by his eldest daughter, the novelist, Maria Edgeworth,* on whose work he insisted on collaborating and for which he often took undeserved credit. He settled in Ireland on his estate at Edgeworthstown, Co. Longford, in 1782 and proved an excellent landlord although his attempts to aid his tenantry were often misunderstood both by his Protestant neighbours and the Catholic tenants. He was MP for Johnstown, Co. Longford (1798–1800). In 1798, when the Ascendancy* prepared to meet the revolution led by the United Irishmen* and raised yeomen corps to fight their Catholic tenants, he raised the Edgeworthstown Infantry and to the concern of his Protestant neighbours, filled it with his Catholic peasantry; in the event, Dublin Castle* would not supply him with arms for his Infantry. In 1800 he opposed the Union,* objecting to the methods employed by the government to get a majority. He invented a plan for telegraphic communication between Dublin and Galway (1804) in order to get the racing results from Newmarket as soon as possible, and also invented a semaphore and velocipede. His several papers submitted to the Royal Irish Academy* included one on a method of bog reclamation (1810). He was deeply influenced by the writings of Rousseau and sought to rear his eldest son in accordance with the principles laid down in *Emile*, with very unhappy results. His works include *Essays on Practical Education* (2 vols, 1797), *Poetry explained for the use of young people* (1802), and *Essay on the Construction of Roads and Carriages* (1810). *The Memoirs of Richard Lovell Edgeworth, Begun by himself and completed by his Daughter, Maria Edgeworth*, (2 vols), appeared in 1820.

EDUCATION. During the nineteenth century separate education systems at elementary, secondary and third levels evolved in Ireland. These were not brought under central control until after 1920. In 1921 the Ministry of Education in Northern Ireland assumed control of its whole education system. In the Free State central control was assumed by the Department of Education in 1924. For primary education *see* National Education; for secondary education *see* Secondary Education, Technical Education *and* Vocational Education; for University Education *see* Trinity College, Dublin; Maynooth; Queen's Colleges; Catholic University; Royal University *and* National University of Ireland.

EDWARD VIII. *See* Abdication Crisis.

EDWARDS, HILTON (1903–   ). Actor, producer and director; b. London; ed. Grammar School, Finchley, and St Aloysius School, Highgate. After studying music and singing he spent two years with Doran's Shakespeare Company (1920–22) before joining the Old Vic. He was brought to Ireland to play Iago by Anew Mac-Master* who introduced him to Micheál MacLiammóir* in 1927. With MacLiammóir he founded the Gate Theatre* in 1928 and formed the most celebrated partnership in Irish theatrical history. He was principal producer-director at the Gate where he influenced, among others, Orson Welles, Geraldine Fitzgerald and James Mason, and produced over 350 plays. The director of three films, *Return to Glenascaul, From Time to Time* and *Hamlet at Elsinore*, he also appeared in Orson Welles' *Othello* and Bryan Forbes' *The Wrong Box*. He worked extensively in television, both for the BBC and for RTE, where he was Head of Drama from 1961 until 1963.

EGAN, PATRICK (1841–1919). Fenian; b. Ballymahon, Co. Longford; he worked in the North City Milling Co. in Dublin and rose to the position of Managing Director. He was a member of the Supreme Council* of the Irish Republican Brotherhood* and a founder-member of the Land League* of which he became Treasurer. When the League was outlawed in October 1881 he fled with the funds to Paris. He was implicated in the Phoenix Park Murders* along with Thomas Brennan.* Egan fled to the USA (1883) where he became a successful businessman and a citizen in 1888. He participated in American politics and Irish-American organisations and founded the National League of America of which he became president (1884–86). He was US Ambassador to Chile (1888). Later, Egan supported John Redmond* and the National Volunteers.*

EGLINTON, 13th EARL AND 1st EARL OF WINSTON (1812–61). Montgomerie, Archibald William; Lord Lieutenant (1852–53, 1858–59); b. Palermo, Sicily; ed. Eton. He succeeded to the title in 1819 and became a member of the House of Lords in 1834. His first term as Lord Lieutenant was noted for the extravagance of his entertainment, and his opposition to Catholic Emancipation* made him popular with the Irish administration. In 1854 he secured a commission of enquiry into National Education.* His second term at the Vice-Regal Lodge was from February 1858 until June of the following year.

EIGHTY-TWO CLUB. Founded in 1845 in memory of the Volunteers (1782) and the independent parliament of 1792. Its inaugural banquet was held in Dublin on 16 April 1845 and the guests included Daniel O'Connell,* Charles Gavan Duffy,* Michael J. Barry* and Thomas Davis,* who designed a uniform for the distinguished members. For a brief period, the Club raised hopes of an emulation of 1782 among its rather exclusive membership.

ÉIRE. The official name for Ireland in the Constitution of 1937.* Eamon de Valera* chose the name of a Queen of the ancient Tuatha de Danann tribe to break with the title of Free State* or Saorstat by which the twenty-six-county state had been known since 1922. In 1948 the name was changed by the Republic of Ireland Act* to the Republic of Ireland which became effective on Easter Monday 1949.

ELECTORAL AMENDMENT ACT, 1927. Introduced by W. T. Cosgrave* after the assassination of Kevin O'Higgins* (10 July 1927). The act provided that any candidate for a seat in Dail Eireann* would have to sign an affidavit to the effect that if he was elected he would take his seat and the Oath of Allegiance* within two months. The act ended the policy of abstention adopted by Eamon de Valera* and his followers. Mr de Valera, who had consistently refused to take the oath, announced that as it was 'an empty formula' he would go through the formality and enter the Dail, with his Fianna Fail party.

ELECTRICITY SUPPLY BOARD (ESB). The ESB was established by the Cumann na nGaedheal government under the Electricity (Supply) Act, 1927, which became law in August. The Board was granted a loan of £10,000,000 by the Executive Council* and was made responsible for control of and administration of a national network of generating stations, the first of which, at Ardnacrusha, Co. Clare, had been under way since September 1925 (*see* Shannon Scheme). The Act, which was to be the first of over thirty, provided for a Board of Control to consist of no less than three and no more than seven persons who were to be nominated by the Executive Council (later the Cabinet) for a period of no more than five years; members could be reappointed. The Act envisaged that the ESB would operate as a business enterprise and would not be subject to political interference. The ESB was to be a monopoly. By the mid 1930s, the Shannon hydro-electric scheme proved inadequate for the needs of the country and the Liffey was harnessed. By 1960 all Irish rivers of use had been surveyed and developed. Originally electricity supply had only been considered from the view of its usefulness to industry, then in its infancy; urban areas were the main beneficiaries. It was not until the act of 1945 that rural electrification was authorised. By 1977 there were very few single dwellings which had not yet been supplied with electricity. In 1945 an Electricity (Supply) Act raised state finance by 50 per cent. Legislation was also passed at the same time to authorise the establishment of turf-burning generating stations to be supplied by Bord na Móna.*

The price of electricity per unit in 1930 was 1.11p which compared very favourably with the rest of Europe; by 1940 this cost had been reduced to 0.61 per unit and by 1973 it had risen to 1.06. However, the oil crisis of 1973 was responsible for a dramatic increase in the cost thereafter: 1.19p (1974), 1.81p (1975), 2.18p (1976) and 2.56p in 1977. Unit consumption per head of population was 889 units in 1930, 1,846 (1939), 1,399 (1945), 2,016 (1950), 2,770 (1960), 5,609 (1970) and 7,070 in 1977. Unit production in 1930 was 60 million which had risen to eight billion in 1977, produced by twenty-nine stations. From nearly 50,000 customers in 1930 the ESB was supplying a million in 1977. In 1930 revenue stood at £500,000 and this had risen to £200 million in 1977. The ESB's fuel bill stood at £76 million in 1977. The ESB also controls the fishing rights for many Irish rivers used in hydro-electric schemes. As a result of the effects of the Shannon Scheme on salmon life in the river Shannon and its tributaries in the early years, the ESB became responsible for restoring fish stocks and fresh water fishing rights by Acts of 1935 and 1938.

ELIOT, LORD. *See* St Germans, 3rd Earl.

EMERGENCY. The period of World War II was known as the Emergency in the twenty-six-county state of Eire which remained neutral during the conflict.
Neutrality The Taoiseach and Minister for External Affairs, Eamon de Valera,* had stated the country's position in relation to a European war as early as April 1939 when he said, 'I have stated in this house and I have stated in the country, that the aim of government policy is to keep this country out of war, and nobody, either here or elsewhere, has any right to assume anything else'. A policy of neutrality was possible because the country had secured the return of the 'Treaty Ports' from Britain at the end of the Economic War* (March 1938).

Neutrality was supported by the major parties in Dail Eireann. The only dissent was from James Dillon* who resigned in protest from Fine Gael* (February 1942). De Valera had strong national support in his denial of Eire's ports to Britain and the USA. An all-party Consultative Defence Council was established to supervise government policy during the Emergency.

Relations with the British ambassador, Sir John Maffey, remained cordial during the war. On the whole neutrality in relation to Britain was benevolent. British flights over Eire were ignored and British intelligence agents were allowed to operate from the Foynes, Co.. Limerick, landing site for flying-boats. British airmen were repatriated and Irish citizens were free to join the British army or work in British factories.

Neutrality was strictly interpreted in relation to Germany with whose ambassador, Dr Edouard Hempel, de Valera had a very good relationship. Hempel was aware that Irish sympathies were generally with the Allies. The government protested strongly at German bombing of Irish targets which was stated by Germany to be accidental (*see* below). German agents found working in Ireland were interned (*see* Goertz, Hermann). Attempts by Germany to contact the Irish Republican Army* were circumvented by the severe measures taken to deal with the IRA (*see* below). De Valera's relationship with the American ambassador, David Gray, on the other hand, was extremely poor (*see* American Note).
Defence During the Emergency defence measures were supervised by the newly created Department for Co-ordination of Defensive Measures under Frank Aiken.* In September 1939 there was a total armed strength of 19,791 between the army,* the Volunteers and the 'A' and 'B' Reserves. A recruiting campaign undertaken at the start of 1940 brought the strength up to 54,502. However when it became clear that there was no immediate danger numbers began to fall until by 1944 the strength was 36,211. In addition to the regular forces, auxiliary forces were recruited as Emergency Durationists. The Local Security Force* (LSF) was established in May 1940 and the Local Defence Force* (LDF) in the following

September. The LDF numbered some 100,000 during the Emergency.

At the same time the Maritime Inscription was established as a part-time force to augment the Marine and Coastwatching Service in the defence of territorial waters, escort duties and port control (*see* Naval Service). A Minefield Section was established in 1941 to supervise minefields which were laid in Cork Harbour entrance, alongside the Deepwater Quay off Cobh, Co. Cork, at Belmont, Cobh, above Rushbrooke Dockyard and at Ballyhack in the approaches to Waterford. A 'Blockship' at Passage West, Co. Cork was kept ready for sinking in the channel to block the river to Cork. The Royal Navy also laid minefields outside Irish territorial waters along the south coast. After the war a minesweeping flotilla of the Royal Navy was based at Cobh; it swept or destroyed some 4,000 mines (1946—47).

Air-Raid Precautions (ARPs) were recruited for air raid duties. The Air Corps* was expanded. It purchased six Hawker Hinds in 1940 and thirteen Hectors during 1941—42. A squad of Hurricane fighters was built up. The Air Corps was responsible for dealing with crashed aircraft of which, during the Emergency, there were 160: 39 were American, 16 German and 105 British. Two hundred and twenty-three crewmen of the 830 involved in the crash-landings were killed.

The Irish Republican Army The IRA had started a 'war' against Northern Ireland and Britain in January 1939. The government dealt with this resurgence of IRA activity by introducing the Treason Act* (30 May 1939) and the Offences Against the State Act* (14 June). However, the IRA's successful raid on the army ammunition depot in the Phoenix Park at Christmas 1939 prompted extra measures. Additional powers were granted to the Minister for Justice, Gerald Boland,* in January 1940 under the Emergency Powers Act,* enabling him to intern members of the organisation. IRA activity continued during 1940. A bomb placed in Dublin Castle injured four members of the Special Branch (25 April 1940) and two policemen were killed in a gun-battle with the IRA on 7 May.

In an attempt to win German support the IRA produced 'Plan Kathleen'. German agents who made contact found the movement too disorganised and too harassed to be of any assistance to German operations. Two veterans of the IRA, Sean Russell* and Frank Ryan,* were in Germany in 1940 but none of their plans came to fruition.

The government's severe measures for dealing with the IRA during the Emergency took their toll. Some 600 were imprisoned and a further 500 were interned. Six members were executed, including the chief of staff, Charles Kerins, convicted of killing a Garda sergeant. Three members died on hunger-strikes between 1940 and 1946.

Rationing To ensure the distribution of foodstuffs and essential raw materials the Ministry of Supplies was established under Sean Lemass* on 16 September 1939. Rationing soon had to be introduced as the war interfered with normal shipping. As part of its campaign to influence Eire into supporting the Allies the British government also restricted shipping.

Petrol supplies were 20 per cent of normal, there was no domestic coal and only 16 per cent of usual gas supplies and 22 per cent of normal textiles were available. Tea was in short supply as only 25 per cent of normal supplies was on the market: between January and April 1941 the tea ration was cut from 2 oz. to 1 oz. and later this was further reduced to ½ oz. Despite the compulsory tillage policy (*see* below) which sought to increase the amount of land under wheat, bread was rationed in 1942. Coal was rationed to a half-ton per month and later there was none available. Bord na Mona* was established in 1944 to exploit native peat resources.

Irish Shipping Ltd* was incorporated in 1941 in an attempt to guarantee supplies of wheat but this failed to alleviate the situation. During the war twenty Irish ships were sunk with a loss of 138 lives.

Agriculture A compulsory tillage policy was introduced in 1940 and continued until 1948. Under this policy it was laid down that three-eighths of arable land in each holding had to be under tillage. As a result of this the net value of agricultural output increased by nearly 17 per cent. The overall tillage area rose from 1,500,000 acres (1938) to 2,600,000 (1945). Wheat, which had formerly been imported, now had to be home-grown and the wheat-growing area rose from 250,000 acres (1938) to 650,000 (1944).

These increases were obtained at the cost of over-utilising and under-fertilising the soil. The percentage of agricultural output exported showed a continuing decline during the Emergency. From a pre-war average of 34 per cent it had been reduced to 26 per cent by 1945 and to 20 per cent two years later. In addition, the cattle trade was severely affected by an outbreak of foot and mouth disease during 1941–42.

Bombing During the Emergency there were several incidents of German bombs falling in Ireland. A total of 828 people were killed, 740 of them in Belfast.

Three women were killed in a creamery in Campile, Co. Wexford when it was struck by a bomb on 26 August 1940. The German government apologised and paid £9,000 in compensation (March 1943). There were no fatalities among the casualties when bombs fell in Sandycove, Co. Dublin and Carrickmacross, Co. Monaghan, in December 1940. On the night of 1–2 January 1941 bombs fell near Drogheda, Co. Louth, in Wexford, Wicklow and Kildare. Three members of a family were killed that night when a bomb fell on their farmhouse at Knockroe, Co. Carlow.

The most serious bombing was in Belfast on Easter Tuesday 1941 when a total of 180 bombs left 740 people

dead and 1,511 injured. Fire brigades from the south went to Belfast to give aid.

The biggest number of casualties sustained in Eire was in Dublin on the night of 30–31 May 1941. Twenty-eight people were killed and 45 were injured, most of them when a 500-pound bomb landed on the North Strand. Two 25-pounders fell on the North Circular Road and Summerhill Parade. Arus an Uachtarain and the American Embassy were damaged when a 250-pound bomb landed in the Phoenix Park. The funerals of twelve of the victims were paid for by Dublin Corporation and attended by the Taoiseach and the government. The Irish government paid £344,000 in compensation to the bereaved and injured. The German government paid £327,000 to the Irish government in 1958.

EMERGENCY MEN. During the Land War* (1879–82) an Emergency Committee of the Orange Order* was established 'for the purpose of protecting loyal subjects in Ireland' against the activities of the Land League.* Financed by the Committee, emergency men, as they became known, took over the farms from which tenants had been evicted and worked them in the landlords' interests and provided labour for landlords who had been boycotted. They generally required police protection while engaged in 'emergency' work.

EMERGENCY POWERS ACT, 1940. Introduced by the government of Eamon de Valera* during the Emergency* in January 1940. The Act supplemented the Treason Act* and the Offences Against the State Act,* both designed to deal with the Irish Republican Army,* which, since January 1939, had been engaged in a campaign against Northern Ireland and Britain. The Emergency Powers Act granted the Minister for Justice, Gerald Boland,* powers to intern known or suspected members of the IRA or those who aided them, in a camp at the Curragh, Co. Kildare. *See also* Emergency Powers Act, 1976.

EMERGENCY POWERS ACT, 1976. Introduced by the National Coalition Government* following the assassination of Christopher Ewart-Biggs, British Ambassador to the Republic. The Act became the subject of great controversy as the Opposition, Fianna Fail,* claimed that the existing laws were sufficient to deal with the Irish Republican Army.* Section 2 of the Act empowered the Gardai to arrest without warrant and hold in custody for up to seven days persons suspected in connection with offences under the Offences Against the State Act 1939.* Section 2 was to remain in force for one year from the date of enactment (16 October 1976). Fianna Fail returned to power in July 1977 and in October Section 2 was allowed to lapse.

EMIGRATION TO THE UNITED STATES. Emigration from Ireland to the USA ran at a low level until the Famine of 1845–49* before which many Irish emigrants across the Atlantic were from Ulster. The pattern was changed by the Famine. Many who emigrated during the Famine had their passage paid by landlords anxious to get the indigent off the workhouse system since the government had made the maintenance of the destitute the responsibility of the Poor Law* in Ireland. The emigrant was not just the victim of the *laissez faire* economics of the time. He was also prey to the unscrupulous shipping agent who operated the emigrant lines. Many of the vessels employed on such runs were little better than floating hulks and were known as 'Coffin Ships'.* A low estimate places the number of those who died on the voyage across the Atlantic at 17,000. Many more died upon arrival or shortly afterwards.

Stringent regulations passed by Congress governing entry into the US prevented that country from witnessing the sort of misery which had become commonplace at Grosse Isle* in Canada. The number of Irish who entered the US in 1847 was nonetheless considerable: 52,946 landed in New York between May and December and 37,000 entered Boston. The following table gives the pattern of Irish emigration to the US in ten-year cycles from 1841 to 1960:

1841–50	780,719
1851–60	914,119
1861–70	435,778
1871–80	436,871
1881–90	655,482
1891–1900	388,416
1901–10	339,065
1911–20	146,181
1921–30	220,591
1931–40	13,167
1941–50	26,967
1951–60	57,332

Lord Dufferin in *Irish Emigration and Tenure of Land in Ireland* estimates the amount of money sent home from America by Irish emigrants between 1848 and 1864 to be in excess of £13,000,000 'and most of it was consumed in rents'.

EMMET, ROBERT (1778–1803). United Irishman; b. Dublin, younger brother of Thomas Addis Emmet* by whom he was influenced; ed. TCD where he was a friend of Thomas Moore.* On account of his connections with the United Irishmen* he was forced to leave college (February 1798). He went to Paris where he made contact with exiled United men and was joined by his brother in 1802. Napoleon led him to believe that there was to be a French invasion of England. After returning to Ireland he used a legacy to build up arms depots in Dublin. The outbreak of war between England and France (1803) seemed to offer an opportunity for a successful rising. An explosion at his ammunition factory on 16 July led to a premature rising on 23 July. Thomas Russell* in Ulster and Michael Dwyer* in Wicklow failed to co-ordinate with Emmet. Less than

100 rallied to him in Dublin and this was insufficient for an assault on Dublin Castle. They were joined by an unruly mob which was responsible for the murder of Lord Kilwarden and his nephew, Rev. Mr Wolfe, in Thomas Street. The rising collapsed inside an afternoon.

Emmet hid out under the name of Mr Ellis, protected by his housekeeper, Anne Devlin. He would not leave Dublin until he had met with his fiancee, Sarah Curran,* whose father, John Philpot Curran,* detested Emmet. He was captured at Harold's Cross on 25 August and tried before Lord Norbury.* Emmet's speech from the dock became one of the most celebrated patriotic speeches of the century, inspiring future generations of nationalists. He concluded his speech: 'Let no man write my epitaph; for as no man who knows my motives dare now vindicate them, let not prejudice or ignorance asperse them. Let them and me rest in obscurity and peace; and my tomb remain uninscribed and my memory in oblivion until other times and other men can do justice to my character. When my country takes her place among the nations of the earth, then and not till then, let my epitaph be written. I have done'. He was executed at noon on 20 September. His grave is unknown.

EMMET, THOMAS ADDIS (1764–1827).

United Irishman; doctor and barrister; b. Cork, elder brother of Robert Emmet;* ed. TCD; B.A. (1783), M.D. Edinburgh and Bar (1790). He became a barrister on the Leinster circuit and a member of the United Irishmen.* During the course of a trial in which he was defending United men in 1795, he took the oath publicly. He was essentially a constitutionalist, supporting electoral reforms and Catholic Emancipation,* and opposed the rising of 1798 which he believed was doomed to fail. Following his arrest (February 1798) he was a party to an 'honourable confession' with other leading United men. They were allowed to go into exile (1802) when he went to Paris where he met with Robert. Disapproving of revolutionary France, he went to the USA where he earned a distinguished reputation at the American Bar.

EMMET MONUMENT ASSOCIATION.

Precursor of the Irish Republican Brotherhood* founded in New York in 1855 by John O'Mahony* and Michael Doheny* with the object of gaining Irish independence by invading the country with an Irish-American army. One of its members, Joseph Denieffe,* returned to Ireland later in the year with instructions to establish a similar organisation in Ireland. He returned to New York late in 1857 with a commission from James Stephens* to raise enough money to finance the establishment of an underground movement in Ireland. Members of the Emmet Monument Association provided £80 which Stephens used to found the IRB in Dublin (17 March 1858). The Association was absorbed by the Fenians,* the American counterpart to the IRB.

ENCUMBERED ESTATES ACTS, 1848 and 1849.

The Acts allowed the sale of Irish estates which had been mortgaged and whose owners, because of the Famine of 1845–49,* were unable to meet their obligations. Under the act of 1849 an Encumbered Estates Court was established with authority to sell estates on the application of the owner or encumbrancer (one who had a claim on the estate). The first such court sat in Dublin on 24 October 1849. After the sale, the court distributed the money among the creditors and granted clear title to the new owners. The existing tenants on the estates were unprotected by legislation. Estates were generally bought by speculators. Between 1849 and 1857, 3,000 estates, totalling 5,000,000 acres, were disposed of under the Acts. Of the £21 million worth of land sold between 1848 and 1859 Irishmen purchased £18 million worth (7,180 out of 7,489 purchasers). The functions of the Court were assumed by the Landed Estates Court* in 1853.

ENSOR, GEORGE (1769–1843). Pamphleteer and political writer; b. Dublin; ed. TCD. He was called to the Bar in 1792. His works include *On National Government* (2 vols, 1810), *National Education* (1811), *Refutation of Malthus* (1818), *Addresses to the People of Ireland on the Degradation and Misery of their Country* (1823), *The Poor and their Relief* (1823), *A Defence of the Irish and the Means of their Redemption* (1825), *Irish Affairs at the close of 1825/1826* (1827), *Anti-Union: Ireland as She Ought to be* (1831), *Before and after the Reform Bill* (1842), etc. He produced pamphlets on the leading issues of the day and was generally sarcastic in his criticism of British rule in Ireland.

'ERIN'S HOPE'. Originally named *The Jacknell Packet*, the 200-ton brig sailed from New York for Ireland in April 1867 with thirty-eight Fenian officers aboard, commanded by Colonel Nagle. The vessel contained 5,000 breech-loading and repeating rifles, 1½ million rounds of ammunition and three unmounted cannons. The ship flew the English colours until Easter Sunday, 21 April, when it was rechristened *Erin's Hope*, and hoisted the green flag. It sailed into Sligo Bay in mid-May and was met by Ricard O'Sullivan Burke* who directed it southwards. At the beginning of June it reached Dungarvan, Co. Waterford. Off Cunnegar, a local fisherman unwillingly landed twenty-eight of the Fenians who were speedily captured. The ship then returned to the USA.

ERVINE, ST JOHN GREER (1883–1971). Novelist, playwright and drama critic; b. Belfast. He left school at the age of fourteen to work in an insurance office. While serving in the Dublin Fusiliers during World War I he lost a leg. Several of his plays were produced at the Abbey Theatre* of which he was manager (1915). He was Professor of Dramatic Literature to the Royal Society of Literature (1933–36) and drama critic for various newspapers, including *The Observer*. His works include the plays *Jane Clegg* (1911), *John Ferguson* (1914), *The First Mrs Fraser* (1931), and *Robert's Wife* (1937); novels, *The Wayward Man* (1927) and *Sophia* (1941); works on the theatre; a biography of General Booth and *Craigavon, Ulsterman* (1949).

ESMONDE, SIR OSMOND THOMAS (1896–1936). Diplomat and politician (Cumann na nGaedheal); son of Sir Thomas Esmonde;* ed. Downside and Balliol College, Oxford. He was Dail Eireann delegate to the USA, Canada and Australia (1920–21). In 1922 he represented the Provisional Government* in Spain. He was assistant secretary in the Department of External Affairs and delegate to the League of Nations* in 1923. He was returned as TD for Co. Wexford in 1923 and held the seat until 1936.

ESMONDE, SIR THOMAS HENRY (1862–1935). Politician (Nationalist); b. Pau, France; ed. Oscott; MP Co. Dublin (1885–91), West Kerry (1891–1900) and North Wexford (1900–18). During the Civil War* his country home at Ballynastragh, Co. Wexford was destroyed by the Irish Republican Army – the Irregulars – on 9 March 1923. He was returned to the Senate of the Irish Free State in 1922 as an independent. He lost his seat in 1934.

ETHER-DRINKING. Ether is a distillate of alcohol treated with sulphuric acid which needs to be adulterated in order to be taken with safety. In Ireland the adulterate was generally poteen.* Ether-drinking was confined to the Ulster counties of Tyrone, South Derry and North Fermanagh. According to *The Times* (March 1891) some 17,000 gallons were consumed annually; some of it was made locally, the rest either imported or smuggled. Drinking ether was sometimes equal in popularity to drinking whiskey. The technique was as follows: the drinker washed his mouth with cold water, drank a little water, held his nose, swallowed the ether and then followed it with more water (the water lessened the burning effects of the ether). In the course of a day up to half a pint might be drunk. According to Professor K. H. Connell in his essay on ether-drinking in *Irish Peasant Society* (Oxford 1968) a pintful would constitute an 'heroic debauch'. Vomiting was an occupational hazard. Chronic drinkers referred to the delightful music which they heard while tranquillised by the drink.

EUCHARISTIC CONGRESS. The thirty-first International Eucharistic Congress was held in Dublin, 22–26 June 1932. The Congress was sponsored by Most Rev. Dr Byrne, Archbishop of Dublin, Rev. D. T. Moloney was Congress Secretary and Mr Frank O'Reilly Director of Organisation. Many thousands of pilgrims arrived for the occasion. The first overseas visitors, who arrived on the *Duchess of Bedford*, were from Canada.

The Congress was formally opened at St Mary's Pro-Cathedral by His Eminence Cardinal Lorenzo Lauri, Cardinal Legate, in the presence of nine cardinals, over one hundred bishops and over one thousand priests and religious. An altar was erected on O'Connell Bridge where, following Solemn Procession of the Blessed Sacrament, Benediction was imparted by the Cardinal Legate. The Congress was organised as follows:

Wednesday 22 June: following Exposition, Midnight Mass was celebrated in every church throughout Dublin.

Thursday 23 June: Men's Day – over 250,000 men attended Mass at Phoenix Park.

Friday 24 June: Ladies' Day – some 200,000 women attended Mass at Phoenix Park.

Saturday 25 June: Children's Day – one hundred thousand children sang *Missa de Angelis* at their special Mass at Phoenix Park.

Sunday 26 June: An estimated one million people attended the Pontifical High Mass at Phoenix Park where Count John McCormack* sang 'Panis Angelicus'. Prior to the closing ceremonies, a special broadcast by His Holiness Pope Pius XI, during which he imparted his Apostolic Blessing, was relayed to the vast congregation.

EUROPEAN ECONOMIC COMMUNITY AND IRELAND. The Republic's entry to the EEC was approved by referendum on 10 May 1972 when 83 per cent of voters declared in favour. Membership became effective from 1 January 1973. Ireland's first Commissioner was Patrick J. Hillery* (later President of Ireland) who became Vice-President of the Commission with special responsibility for Social Affairs. He was replaced on 1 December 1976 by Richard Burke who was given responsibility for Taxation, Consumer Affairs, Transport and Relations with the European Parliament.

Between 1973 and 1978 the Republic was allocated a total of £1,123.4m. of which it had received £1,008.4m. (the disparity between the figures was due to the time lag between approval of payment and actual payment). For the period 1 January to 31 August 1979 the allocation was £319.1m. of which receipts totalled £290.4m.

Receipts from January 1973 to August 1979:

EAGGF	Guarantee Section	Common Agricultural	
EAGGF	Guidance Section	Policy	£1.188.7m.

European Social Fund	£61.3m.

European Regional Development Fund	£45.3m.

Miscellaneous	£3.5m.

Total	£1,298.8m.

The following loans were also received during the same period:

European Investment Bank	£325.5m.

European Coal and Steel Community	£1.4m.

Community Loan	£156.0m.

Total	£482.9m.

Between January 1973 and November 1979 Northern Ireland was allocated a total of £151.6m., of which it had received £80.4m. by end 1979:

EAGGF	£5.8m.
European Social Fund	£44.3m.
European Regional Development Fund	£30.3m.

During the same period Northern Ireland received loans totalling £73.3m. from the European Investment Bank:

1974 Short and Harland	£2.5m.
1977 Post Office	£18.5m.
1979 Department of Finance	£15.0m.
1979 Northern Ireland Electricity Service	£33.3m.
1979 Michelin (Belfast) Ltd.	£4.0m.

Money from EAGGF is also paid to beneficiaries in Northern Ireland through the Ministry of Agriculture, Fisheries and Food in Great Britain, but a separate record of payments to Northern Ireland is not maintained.

Direct elections to the European Parliament were held in Ireland on 7 June 1979. For the purpose of the elections to Europe the Republic of Ireland was divided into four constituencies (Dublin, Leinster, Connaught-Ulster and Munster). Northern Ireland was a constituency on its own.

Those elected were:

Dublin
Ritchie Ryan (Fine Gael)
John O'Connell (Labour)
Sile de Valera (Fianna Fail)
Michael O'Leary (Labour)

Leinster
Mark Clinton (Fine Gael)
Patrick Lalor (Fianna Fail)
Liam Kavanagh (Labour)

Connaught-Ulster
Neil Blaney (Independent)
Joe McCartin (Fine Gael)
Sean Flanagan (Fianna Fail)

Munster
T. J. Maher (Independent)
Eileen Desmond (Labour)
Tom O'Donnell (Fine Gael)
Jeremiah Cronin (Fianna Fail)
Noel Davern (Fianna Fail)

Northern Ireland
Rev. Ian Paisley
   (Democratic Unionist Party)
John Hume
   (Social Democratic and Labour Party)
John Taylor
   (Official Unionist Party)

EUROPEAN RECOVERY PROGRAMME. The ERP was instituted after World War II with finance provided by the USA under the Marshall Plan. Eire participated although it had been a neutral during the conflict (*see* Emergency). As a condition of participation the first Inter-Party Government* was required to draw up the Long-Term Recovery Programme.* Aid to the amount of 150 million dollars was made available and was employed on a variety of projects designed to boost the struggling economy.

'EVA OF THE NATION'. *See* Kelly, Mary Eva.

'EVENING HERALD'. A liberal newspaper founded in 1805 and owned by John Magee Jnr.* The paper supported the Catholic cause and earned the hostility of the Dublin Castle* administration. It changed its name to the *Sentinel* in 1814 and altered its policy, but a decline in readership and advertising forced it to close in 1815. Another paper of the same name is now published as the evening edition of the *Irish Independent.**

EVERETT, JAMES (1890–1967). Politician (Labour Party and National Labour Party); b. Wicklow; ed. locally. At first an organiser for the Co. Wicklow Agricultural Union which later amalgamated with the Irish Transport and General Workers' Union,* he was an ITGWU official in Wicklow in 1918. A member of Sinn Fein,* he was a judge in Kildare and Wicklow during the War of Independence. He represented Kildare/Wicklow in Dail Eireann from 1921 until his death. Everett was one of five ITGWU members of the parliamentary Labour Party who broke away in 1943 to form the National Labour Party.* He was a member of the (first) Inter-Party Government* in which he held the office of Minister of Posts and Telegraphs (1948–51). The two sections of Labour were reunited in 1950.

Everett became the centre of political controversy in 1950 over the so-called 'Battle of Baltinglass'* when he appointed Michael Farrell to the office of sub-postmaster over the wishes of the inhabitants of Baltinglass, Co. Wicklow. This led to allegations of political jobbery which affected the general election result of 1951 when Fianna Fail were returned strong enough to oust the Inter-Party Government. He was Minister for Justice in the second

Inter-Party Government (1954–57) and had become 'Father of the House' by the time of his death.

EVICTED TENANTS ACT, 1907. The Act greatly extended the Wyndham Act of 1903 (*see* Land Acts). It was introduced by the Chief Secretary, Augustine Birrell.* The Act enabled the Land Commissioners to acquire untenanted land compulsorily for the purpose of providing holdings for tenants, who, or whose predecessors, had been evicted from their holdings since the year 1878, and who had applied to the Commissioners before 1 May 1907. Up to 31 March 1911, as many as 12,398 applied for holdings as evicted tenants. Of these, 6,276 were rejected by the Commissioners following enquiry; 2,631 applied outside the prescribed time-limit; 2,830 were reinstated in holdings and the remaining 661 were still under consideration by the Commissioners.

EXECUTIVE AUTHORITY (EXTERNAL RELATIONS) ACT, 1936. *See* External Relations Act.

EXECUTIVE COUNCIL. Governing body of the Free State from 6 December 1922 until 29 December 1937. The Prime Minister was known as the President of the Executive Council. It was abolished by Eamon de Valera* through the Constitution of 1937,* after which the head of the government was known as the Taoiseach.* The Presidents of the Council were W. T. Cosgrave* (1922–32) and de Valera (1932–37).

EXTERNAL ASSOCIATION. Formula devised by Eamon de Valera* in 1921 in an attempt to bridge the gap between dominion status for Ireland and an 'isolated republic'. He described it as 'a certain treaty of free association with the British Commonwealth' and understood that it could be an inducement to Ulster Unionists* 'to meet whose sentiments alone this step could be contemplated'. External association would

not require an Oath of Allegiance.* The British government rejected the idea of external association when Lloyd George* met with de Valera in July 1921. The Draft for a treaty which the Irish plenipotentiaries brought to London involved the idea of external association but it was rejected during the negotiations. The essence of this, as de Valera said in a private session during the Treaty debates on 14 December, was that external association would recognise the king as head of the group (of Commonwealth countries) 'with no reference to Ireland'. During the debates he produced a document headed 'Proposed Treaty of Association between Ireland and the British Commonwealth', embodying the external association idea once again: 'That, for the purposes of common concern, Ireland shall be associated with the States of the British Commonwealth, viz: The Kingdom of Great Britain, the Dominion of Canada, the Commonwealth of Australia, the Dominion of New Zealand, and the Union of South Africa' (Article 2). This, Document No. 2,* as it became known, was unacceptable to advocates of the Treaty who felt that it differed very slightly from the Treaty under discussion. It went too far for opponents of the Treaty. De Valera continued to press for acceptance of the external association idea and achieved it in 1936 with the External Relations Act.*

EXTERNAL RELATIONS ACT, 1936. The Executive Authority (External Relations) Act was introduced in the Dail by Eamon de Valera* on 11 December 1936 at the same time as Edward VIII abdicated the throne (*see* Abdication Crisis). De Valera simultaneously introduced the Constitution (Amendment No. 27) Bill. Both Bills were under guillotine. The External Relations Act delimited the functions of the crown in the field of external relations of the Free State,* stating that so long as Ireland was associated with the Commonwealth of

Nations, 'with the following nations, that is to say, Australia, Canada, Great Britain, New Zealand and South Africa, and so long as the King recognised by those nations as the symbol of their co-operation continues to act on behalf of each of those nations (on the advice of the several governments thereof), for the purpose of the appointment of diplomatic and consular representatives and the conclusion of international agreements, the King so recognised may, and is hereby authorised to, act on behalf of Saorstat Eireann for the like purpose as and when advised by the Executive Council to do so'. External relations were now firmly in the control of the Executive Council or Cabinet and the link between Ireland and the Commonwealth at the same time maintained.

F

FACTION FIGHTING. Organised fights between followers of different factions or groups were common from the seventeenth century until the Famine of 1845—49.* In the nineteenth century factions consisted of families owing allegiance to a particular faction name: Caravats and Shanavests, later known as Three-Year-Olds and Four-Year-Olds; Coffeys and Reaskawallaghs, Cooleens and Black Mulvihills, Bogboys and Tobbers and hundreds of others. The fights usually took place at fairs* and markets, races, patterns* and other mutually arranged dates. The principal weapon was a stick, often well-seasoned; women were permitted to use stones but firearms were rarely used. These fights could involve several hundred people. Sylvester O'Halloran, a Limerick surgeon, became a celebrated specialist on head-injuries through treating victims of faction fights. Until 1837 the fights were listed as riots. After that date accurate reports were kept by the new Irish Constabulary* formed by Thomas Drummond* who sought to suppress the fighting. Daniel O'Connell* also opposed it as did the clergy. They had some success but it was the hardships occasioned by the Famine which led to a sharp decline in the practice. After the 1840s such fights were no longer common. However, they were slower to die out in Co. Tipperary, the home of faction fighting in the nineteenth century; the last recorded faction fight was at a fair in Cappawhite in 1887.

FAHY, FRANCIS ARTHUR (1854—1935). Song-writer and language revivalist; b. Kinvara, Co. Galway. He moved to London in 1873, joined the civil service and remained there for the rest of his life. He was a founder of the Southwark Irish Club* (1882) out of which grew the Irish Literary Society.* He contributed to a large number of Irish newspapers and journals, including *The Nation,** *United Ireland** and *The Freeman's Journal.** His work frequently appeared under the pen-name 'An Dreolin' ('The Wren'). *Irish Songs and Poems* appeared in 1887. His best-known piece was 'The Ould Plaid Shawl'. The London *Times* commented on his death, 'He had a part in the promotion of every Irish literary and social movement in London for the past fifty years'. P. S. O'Hegarty* edited *The Ould Plaid Shawl and Other Songs* (1949).

FAIRS. Markets held at traditional times of the year at established venues for the sale or interchange of goods. Labourers could also be hired at 'hiring-fairs'.* Pre-christian in origin, the oldest fair is traditionally held in Killorglin, Co. Kerry: Puck Fair, at which goats, horses and sheep are sold and 'King Puck' (a wild goat) is venerated. The second oldest fair was that of Cappawhite, Co. Tipperary, now lapsed. Other famous fairs are Ballinasloe, Co. Galway (horses), Spancil Hill, Co. Clare (donkeys and horses), Cahirmee, Co. Cork (horses, where Napoleon's white charger 'Marengo' was said to have been purchased), Ballycastle, Co. Antrim and Crossmaglen, Co. Armagh. Fairs attracted ballad-singers, stall-holders, confidence tricksters and general amusements. They could often be wild affairs owing to the large amount of drink consumed and in the last century commonly led to faction-fighting.* Donnybrook Fair in Dublin was celebrated for its fights which led to the use of the work 'donnybrook', meaning a fight involving large numbers.

FAMINE. Famine was a common feature of Irish life in the eighteenth and nineteenth centuries. During the nineteenth century, there were famines in 1800, 1807, 1817, 1821−22, 1830−34, 1836, 1839, 1845−49, 1878−81 and several times during the 1890s, in particular along the western seaboard which was always worst affected. These periods of famine took their toll of the population through death and emigration. Famine was often accompanied by 'famine fever' (dropsy, typhus and relapsing fever). In 1832 and 1849 there were outbreaks of cholera. Periods of famine produced agrarian unrest (*see* agrarian crime), often violent, and the harsh coercion measures introduced by the government to suppress the discontent of the starving generated a deep-seated hatred of the authorities. *See also* Famine of 1845−49.

FAMINE OF 1845−49. The Great Famine or 'Great Hunger' of 1845 to 1849, one of the worst catastrophes of modern Irish history, was caused by the failure of the potato through blight, the fungus *Phytophthora infestans*, which came to Europe from North America. The crisis was worse in Ireland than anywhere else because of the role of the potato in the Irish diet. For one-third of the population it was the sole article of diet. The poorest peasant rented some piece of land upon which to grow potatoes (*see* Conacre). Other crops were used to pay the rent. Even at the height of the famine, millions of pounds worth of food left Irish ports, often passing ships bringing in the hated Indian corn which, known colloquially as 'Peel's Brimstone', was distributed for relief.

The first signs of blight occurred in September 1845. It was hoped that the damage might be partial but when digging started in October, the full extent of the disaster was quickly realised. For the moment, however, there was no immediate distress as most people had something in reserve to use either as food or which could be pawned or sold to produce food. In an attempt to provide relief Sir Robert Peel* spent £100,000 on Indian corn which was distributed during November. He also appointed a scientific commission which issued *Advice concerning the potato crop to the Farmers and Peasants of Ireland* but this was of little practical use. Peel also set about the repeal of the Corn Laws but resigned on 5 December when this failed. When Lord John Russell* failed to form a government Peel returned to office until 29 June when he again resigned, having finally carried repeal of the Corn Laws. This time, Russell *did* form a government. Leading Irish public figures, including Daniel O'Connell,* tried in vain to impress upon the government the extent of the disaster. Between July 1845 and February 1846 over £1,000,000 worth of food left Ireland, for which armed escorts had to be provided at the ports (*see* Dungarvan riot). Relief schemes were introduced in March 1846, giving employment on road, pier and bridge-building to some 140,000. They were inefficiently (and in some cases corruptly) administered and did little for those most in need of relief.

Russell's administration was unsympathetic to Irish suffering. The men with most influence over the provision of finance, the Chancellor of the Exchequer, Sir Charles Wood,* and the Assistant Secretary of the Treasury, Charles Edward Trevelyan,* both firm believers in *laissez faire,* wanted Ireland to pay for its own relief. They called for an end to work-schemes and the distribution of relief. As distress mounted, the numbers employed on relief schemes increased from around 500,000 (December 1846) to 734,000 (March 1847). However, Trevelyan's Labour Rate Act* sought to force local landlords to pay for relief and called for an end to government schemes by 15 August 1847. Famine conditions throughout Europe led to speculation in corn. In Ireland, even where food was available to the peasants, they could not afford to buy it. As they failed to pay their rents, tenants were evicted. Starving people wandered the countryside seeking nourishment from berries, roots, nettles, even grass. The Poor Law system, which had never been intended to deal with a crisis of such magnitude, proved completely inadequate and deaths from malnutrition occurred in the workhouses. By the end of 1846 the Board of Works was collapsing under the strain. The government grain depots were opened in the West of Ireland in December, when grain was offered to the starving at the *market price plus 5 per cent.*

Private relief organisations were established during 1846. The Irish Relief Association raised £42,000 and the General Central Relief £63,000. The Ladies' Work Association provided clothes. Major attempts to deal with the crisis in the West of Ireland were made by the Society of Friends whose organisers included William Edward Forster* and James Hack Tuke.* Another organisation, the British Relief Association,* collected some £400,000, including £2,000 from Queen Victoria,* and appointed as agent in Ireland, Count Strzelecki.* The Temporary Relief of the Destitute Persons (Ireland) Act, generally known as the 'Soup Kitchen Act', became law in January 1847 and continued the policy of making Ireland pay for its own relief. Responsibility for looking after the starving rested with the Boards of Guardians of the Poor Law. The workhouses, already overburdened, were to be the principal units of relief. In protest, members of the Boards of Guardians resigned. Public works began to close down in anticipation of the Soup Kitchen Act's coming into force, throwing tens of thousands more onto the workhouse system. During 1847 soup became the chief item of diet for the starving, but there were too few soup-kitchens to meet the demand. Where they did exist, many soup-kitchens had the common failing that the soup was of such weak quality as to be virtually useless as nourishment. The soup-kitchens in the West of Ireland were distrusted by those most in need because of the involvement of Protestant clergymen, many of them evangelical New Reformers.* People who changed their religion in return for material aid were known as 'soupers'. 'Souperism',* as it was known, left an indelible mark on the Irish folk-memory.

Officials had for long been aware that it was only a question of time before fever would break out. When this occured in 1847 it produced a new crop of horrors as 'famine fever' swept the country. The Central Board of Health, which had been allowed to lapse in August 1846, was hastily reconvened. There were five categories of fevers: typhus ('Black Fever' or 'Spotted Fever'), relapsing fever ('Yellow Fever'), dysentery, hunger oedema ('Famine Dropsy') and scurvy ('Black Leg'). The two most prevelant causes of death were typhus and relapsing fever. Medical resources were grossly inadequate but the Board of Health prevented the death rate from being much higher. From February 1847 the Board oversaw 373 fever hospitals and 473 extra doctors until August 1850. 'Fever sheds' were set up. However, few local authorities were in a position, by this time, to provide finance and patients were moved onto the workhouse system as well. The Irish Fever Act placed responsibility for provision of facilities on Relief Committees which could call on central funds. They were slow to come into existence and when they did, many of them proved unwilling to assume full responsibility. Army tents were distributed by the government which cost some £120,000 in all, in an effort to combat the spread of disease. By September 1847 disease was on the decline. When American corn appeared in Europe during 1847, bringing down the price, there was little benefit to the starving Irish because the government cut back on relief works, leaving the workers without the small amounts of money needed to purchase meal. As a result, the numbers using soup-kitchens increased from slightly over 2,750,000 (May) to just over 3,000,000 (July). In July, the government announced that the money which had financed relief works and the soup kitchens would be forgiven but, at the same time, ordered rations to be finished and the soup-kitchens to cease by October. The potato did not fail in 1847 (although the yield was very low) but the government utterly failed to appreciate that the poor did not have any money at all and that the landlords were seizing corn in lieu of rent.

The new Lord Lieutenant, the 4th Earl of Clarendon,* appointed in May 1847 to succeed the 4th Earl of Bessborough,* stated in advance that he knew he would fail. He came to office in the middle of a financial crisis which forced the Bank of England to restrict credit. Consequently, Clarendon's appeal to the Treasury was rejected by Wood who pointed out that the Treasury was forgiving repayments on monies already advanced but would advance no more. In another move, Lord John Russell announced that there could be no more relief until the Irish Poor Law Rate of 5s (25p) in the £ was collected. Nearly £1,000,000 was col-

lected, frequently with the use of force. Property owners contemplated leaving the country. In response to the rising crime rate during the winter of 1847–48, much of it involving assaults on rates and rent collectors, the Crime and Outrage (Ireland) Act* was introduced. Fifteen thousand extra troops arrived and martial law was declared in troublesome districts. Clarendon was threatened with assassination and a number of landlords were murdered. Frightened property-owners now fled the country. Extremists in Young Ireland* who had formed the Irish Confederation* in January 1847 became more violent in tone. William Smith O'Brien,* Thomas Francis Meagher* and John Mitchel* were arrested in March 1848. The Treason-Felony Act* was introduced to deal with revolutionaries. O'Brien and Meagher, defended by Isaac Butt,* were acquitted in April, but Mitchel was sentenced to fourteen years transportation. Habeas corpus* was suspended in July and the Young Irelanders, alarmed, attempted an insurrection. O'Brien's call went unheeded in the midst of so much misery and after an affray at Ballingarry, Co. Tipperary,* the insurrectionists were either arrested or managed to escape.

When the potato crop failed again, the Treasury turned a deaf ear to appeals. Irish officials were ordered to collect the Poor Rates to finance the Poor Law Unions for which there was to be no more state money. Farms were abandoned as a new wave of emigration began from among the more prosperous tenant-farmers and small businessmen. High rates with no incoming rentals were beginning to have an adverse effect on landlords, many of them with mortgaged properties. The Encumbered Estates Act* established courts to effect the sales of bankrupt estates. At the end of December there was an outbreak of Asiatic cholera which continued until July 1849. Opthalmia was also widespread. As conditions showed no sign of relief, the government finally moved. A Rate-in-Aid was to be levied from the more prosperous Poor Law Unions to support those in distress. The Treasury would advance £100,000, £50,000 of it immediately, and an additional 6d (2½p) in the £ was to be paid by every Union. The landlords attacked this scheme and were supported by Twistelton, the Chief Constable for the Poor Law, who resigned in protest at what he called a policy of extermination. The numbers receiving outdoor relief had by now reached 768,902. A serious blow to those in distress occurred when the Society of Friends, having done all that was humanly possible, gave up their relief operations in Ireland. Cholera, disease, death and attempted revolution notwithstanding, it was announced that Queen Victoria would visit Ireland. She arrived on the royal yacht at Cobh, which was renamed Queenstown in her honour, on 1 August 1849.

The Census of 1851 told its own story when it recorded a population of 6,554,074 (compared to 8,177,744 in 1841). The Census Commissioners claimed that had the population continued to increase at its normal rate it would have been 9,018,799. The number of deaths due to the famine could not be calculated but it is fair to estimate that around 1,000,000 people died and that the remainder of the decline was due to emigration, a trend which continued until the 1960s.

FARMERS' PARTY. The Farmers' Party or Farmers' Union represented the more substantial farmer in Dail Eireann between 1922 and 1932. Its seven TDs returned in the general election of 1922 supported the Treaty. The party's greatest strength, fifteen seats, was achieved in the general election of 1923. It supported the Cumann na nGaedheal governments. In the first general election of 1927 the party returned with eleven seats but it suffered from the entry of Fianna Fail into politics and only held six seats in the second general election of that year. During the economic depression of 1929–32

one of its leaders, M. R. Heffernan, was Parliamentary Secretary to the Minister for Posts and Telegraphs (he joined Cumann na nGaedheal in 1932 as did some other leading members of the Farmers' Party). The party secured four seats in 1932 and those four members played a leading role in the foundation of the National Centre Party.* Over the next year the party disappeared and its supporters were absorbed by Cumann na nGaedheal and its successor, Fine Gael.*

FARMERS' UNION. *See* Farmers' Party.

FARNHAM, 11th BARON (1879–1957). Maxwell, Arthur Kenlist; Unionist; ed. Harrow and Sandhurst. As a lieutenant in the 10th Hessians, he served in the Boer War and later served in World War I. He was a representative Irish peer from 1908. Dedicated to opposing Home Rule* he was a member of the Irish Unionist Alliance.*

FAULKNER, ARTHUR BRIAN DEANE, LORD FAULKNER OF DOWNPATRICK (1921–77). Politician (Ulster Unionist); Prime Minister of Northern Ireland (March 1971–March 1972); b. Co. Down; ed. Elm Park Preparatory School, Armagh, St Columba's College, Rathfarnham and TCD. While working in the family textile business he was active in the Young Unionists.* Upon his election to Stormont as MP for East Down in 1949 he became the youngest member of the Northern Ireland parliament. He was Chief Whip (1956) and became Minister for Home Affairs in 1959 at the height of the Irish Republican Army* campaign which he suppressed with internment under the Special Powers Act.* As Minister for Commerce in 1963 he inaugurated a new era for the Northern economy, persuading companies such as ICI, Ford, Michelin, Goodyear and DuPont to set up plant.

He opposed concessions to the Northern Ireland Civil Rights Association.* On 23 January 1969, he resigned office in protest at the attempts by Captain Terence O'Neill* to introduce reforms at Westminster's request, and in protest at the appointment of the Cameron Commission.* When Major James Dawson Chichester-Clark* became Prime Minister (May 1969) Faulkner returned to serve as Minister for Development, declaring that he now favoured a policy of reform. Chichester-Clark proved unable to handle the deteriorating situation as more clashes occurred between the IRA and Protestant paramilitaries and Faulkner succeeded him as Prime Minister on 23 March 1971. He also held the Ministry of Home Affairs. His commitment to reform incurred Protestant-Unionist suspicions and his past association with internment, the Orange Order,* and previous opposition to reforms made him unattractive to Catholics. His announcement on 25 May that any soldier could shoot to kill on suspicion provoked a strong attack from the Social Democratic and Labour Party* whose support for his administration he tried to win in June when he announced the establishment of three committees for social, environmental and industrial affairs, two to be chaired by Opposition MPs. On 9 August he introduced internment, which, in the beginning, was directed at the Catholic population and led to increased support for the Provisional IRA. During the following month he engaged in tripartite talks with Edward Heath and Jack Lynch* but they proved unproductive. In October the British government published a Green Paper, *The Future of Northern Ireland: A Paper for Discussion* which implied the abolition of the Stormont system as it had existed for fifty years. While he resisted this, he did not reject the measure out of hand but his position was badly impaired by the events of Bloody Sunday (30 January 1972*). In February the right wing of his party founded Vanguard* of which William Craig became leader. On 22 March he met with Heath again in London where he refused to agree to a transfer of security to Whitehall

and also rejected Heath's suggestion of power-sharing. Two days later, Heath announced the abolition of Stormont and the introduction of Direct Rule from Whitehall.

During the next year Faulkner supported the Ulster Defence Association.* In December 1973 he was a party to the Sunningdale Conference,* having by now lost hard-line Unionist support. He became Chief Executive of the Assembly of Northern Ireland (*see* Northern Ireland) and following the collapse of the Executive, he formed his own party, the Unionist Party of Northern Ireland* which held five seats in the Convention (*see* Northern Ireland). Towards the end of 1975 he announced his retirement from politics and was raised to the peerage in January 1977. Two days after he was received into the House of Lords, (28 February) he was killed in a hunting accident.

FAY, FRANK (1870–1931). Actor, producer and elocution teacher; b. Dublin, elder brother of William Fay; ed. Belvedere College. He was a producer and founder of the Dublin Dramatic School and the Ormonde Dramatic Society (1898). Fay was also co-founder with his brother of the National Dramatic Society which was absorbed into the Irish National Theatre Society. He was a founder-member of the Abbey Theatre* in 1904. At the Abbey he was in charge of speech-training and is generally credited with creating the Abbey style. He played Shawn Keogh in the first production of *The Playboy of the Western World* (1907) and in the following year he accompanied his brother to the USA. Upon their return, they went to London (1914) and worked in both the Nottingham and Birmingham Reps. While Willy remained in England, Frank returned to the Abbey and became an elocution teacher in Dublin. He was the author of *A Short Glossary of Theatrical Terms* (1932), *Merely Players* and *The Joys of the Abbey Theatre* (1935).

FAY, WILLIAM G. (1873–1947). Actor-manager; b. Dublin, younger brother of Frank Fay; ed. Belvedere College. With his brother he worked in the Dublin Dramatic School and formed the Ormonde Dramatic Society where he taught elocution and stage-craft. His students included Sara Allgood.* He produced *Casadh an tSúgáin* (1901) by Douglas Hyde.* He became stage-manager of the Irish National Theatre Society,* founded from his own and his brother's National Dramatic Society. The foundation of the Abbey Theatre* in 1904 was mainly the result of his efforts to persuade Miss Annie Horniman to finance the new venture. He played Christy Mahon in the first production of *The Playboy of the Western World* in 1907. A year later he broke with the Abbey when he was refused full powers as Manager-Producer and, with Frank, went to the USA. Following a tour there, he returned to take up residence in England and remained there after Frank returned to Dublin.

FEDERALISM. The federal solution to the Irish demand for self-government proposed that an Irish parliament to legislate on purely domestic affairs should sit in Dublin while imperial affairs should be dealt with at Westminster. Daniel O'Connell* contemplated federalism during the struggle for Repeal* and incurred the suspicions of Young Ireland.* Sharman Crawford* accepted federalism as a solution, as did Isaac Butt and Charles Stewart Parnell* who nonetheless made it clear that he would still refuse to accept it as a final solution. Federalism was less acceptable to the more militant nationalists, many of whom were outright separatists, during the early years of the twentieth century (*see* Irish Republican Brotherhood).

FEETHAM, JUSTICE RICHARD (1874–1965). Judge; b. South Africa; ed. Marlborough and New College, Oxford; Bar (1899). Starting his career as Deputy Town Clerk of Johannesburg in 1902, he rose to become a Judge of the Supreme Court of South Africa, Transvaal Province (1923–30) and Judge-President, Natal Province Division (1931–39); Judge, Appellate Court Division, Supreme Court of South Africa (1939–44). In 1924 he accepted an invitation from the British government to serve as Chairman of the Boundary Commission.* His strict legalistic interpretation of Article 12 of the Treaty led to the shelving of the Report in December 1925. (*See* Boundary Commission.)

FENIANS. 'Fenians' was the name given by John O'Mahony* to the republican organisation which he founded in New York on 17 March 1858 at the same time as the Irish Republican Brotherhood* was founded in Dublin by James Stephens.* The name, chosen by O'Mahony in honour of the ancient Fianna, came to connote dedication to physical force to secure the independence of Ireland and the establishment of an Irish Republic. While the name also came to include the IRB they were separate organisations and until the Republic was achieved the Fenians were to recognise the Supreme Council of the IRB as the provisional government of the Republic. The function of the Fenians, whose offices were filled by election, was to serve as an auxiliary to the IRB, supplying it with officers, volunteers and arms. During the American Civil War (1861–65) Fenians fought in both armies. O'Mahony organised a Fenian regiment, the 99th, of the New York National Guard, of which he was Colonel. Fenian organisers also recruited among the regiments containing numbers of Irish-born or soldiers of Irish descent.

Discontent with O'Mahony's leadership and with Stephens' unwillingness to lead the IRB in a rising led to a reorganisation in 1865 when O'Mahony's powers as Head Centre were curbed by the creation of a Senate which could exercise a veto over him. When he proceeded with a scheme to finance a rising in Ireland by issuing bonds, he was deposed and replaced by W. R. Roberts. A further fragmentation occurred over proposals to launch raids on Canada. In 1866, as a result of these dissensions, there were three Fenian factions: the Fenian Brotherhood led by O'Mahony, the Senate wing led by Roberts and a group called 'United Irishmen' who supported the idea of attacking Britain through Canada. When Stephens did not call a rising during 1866 Fenian sympathy for him weakened and he arrived in New York accompanied by a prominent Fenian, Colonel Thomas J. Kelly*, to unite the movement. Stephens' arrival caused dismay, especially as he made it clear that he intended to support O'Mahony, after which he would return to Ireland and call the long-awaited rising. He threw himself into the tangled web of Irish-American politics with characteristic gusto which only made a bad situation worse. The Roberts wing went ahead with plans for a raid on Canada and O'Mahony, to forestall this plan, heedless of Stephens' advice, launched an expensive and unsuccessful raid on Compobello, off the coast of New Brunswick, in April 1866. In June, some 800 others led by General John O'Neill* went across the Canadian border and were easily defeated. As Stephens continued to procrastinate about returning to Ireland to organise the rising, feeling hardened against him and he was deposed in December 1866 and replaced by Colonel Kelly. In January 1867 Kelly, Captain John MacCafferty* and Ricard O'Sullivan Burke* sailed for Ireland. The Commander-in-Chief of the proposed rising was to be a French military adventurer, General Cluseret.*

The failure of the rising of 1867 convinced many that a new organisation was needed and Clan na Gael* was founded from among the O'Mahony Fenian Brotherhood and followers of the Senate wing. The Clan represented a long-lived form of Fenianism which helped to bring about Irish independence, assuming the same relationship to the IRB as

had formerly belonged to the Fenians proper. *See* Clan na Gael *and* Irish Republican Brotherhood.

FERGUSON, HARRY GEORGE (1884–1960). Sportsman and inventor; b. Growell, Hillsborough, Co. Down; ed. locally. He was employed in his brother Joe's Belfast engineering works. A keen motor-cyclist and car racer, Ferguson built an aeroplane with Joe Martin, a fellow employee, which, powered by an eight-cylinder air-cooled JAP engine, made a flight of some 130 yards about twelve feet off the ground on the Downshire estate at Hillsborough (31 December 1909). It was the first flight in Ireland by an aeroplane constructed entirely in Ireland. In the following year Ferguson won £100 when he flew some three miles at Newcastle, Co. Down (the prize money was awarded by the county council). Ferguson established his own engineering business, May Street Motors, in 1911. A supporter of the Ulster Volunteer Force,* he participated in the Larne Gun-Running* (April 1914). During the war he was an organiser in the scheme to increase food production through farm mechanisation. This led to the development of the Ferguson tractor which, with mounted ploughs, made his fortune. The only partner ever accepted by Henry Ford, he licensed Ford to produce the tractor in America in 1934. This unwritten agreement was repudiated by Ford's grandson in 1947. Ferguson took legal action and was awarded nine million dollars in settlement.

FERGUSON, SIR SAMUEL (1810–86). Antiquary and poet; b. Belfast; ed. Belfast Academical Institute and TCD; B.A. (1826); M.A. (1832). He was called to the Irish Bar in 1838 and was appointed QC in 1859. He retired from the Bar in 1867 to become Deputy Keeper of Irish Records, and was President of the Royal Irish Academy* in 1882. Politically a moderate, he sympathised with the aims of Young Ireland* (many of whom were his personal friends) but he opposed any form of violence. He founded the Protestant Repeal Association. His first poem 'The Forging of the Anchor' appeared in *Blackwood's Magazine.* He was a frequent contributor to the *Dublin University Magazine** but contributed only one poem to *The Nation** (24 November 1855). While chiefly recognised as a leading promoter of the Gaelic revival in Irish literature, Ferguson was also an antiquarian of note. His most valuable contribution in this field was *Ogham Inscriptions in Ireland, Scotland and Wales,* published posthumously in 1887, edited by his wife, Mary. His other works include *Lays of the Western Gael and other poems* (1865), *Congal, an Epic Poem* (1872) and *Remains of St Patrick* (a blank verse translation of the *Confession,* 1888). *Hibernian Nights Entertainment,* containing much of his prose writings, was posthumously published in 1887.

FIANNA EIREANN, NA. Republican youth movement founded in Dublin in August 1909 by Countess Markievicz* and Bulmer Hobson,* modelled on an earlier movement of the same name founded by Hobson in Belfast (1902). The Constitution declared:

Object: To re-establish the Independence of Ireland.
Means: The training of the youth of Ireland, mentally and physically, to achieve this object by teaching scouting and military exercises, Irish history and the Irish language.
Declaration: I promise to work for the independence of Ireland, never to join England's armed forces, and to obey my superior officers.

The chief instructor, Con Colbert,* and the Secretary, Eamon Martin, were members of the Irish Republican Brotherhood* for which Na Fianna was a recruiting ground. Hobson resigned the presidency after a few months and was succeeded by the Countess. Liam Mellows* joined Na Fianna in 1911 and became secretary of the Dublin District Council.

Branches of the organisation had by now been established in Belfast, Limerick, Cork, Waterford, Dundalk, Newry, Listowel and Clonmel. There were twenty-two *sluaghta* by 1912 (*slua:* crowd, pack or troop as for Boy Scouts). Na Fianna gained in importance from their patrons who included Patrick Pearse,* Dr Patrick McCartan* and Sir Roger Casement* and they actively supported the workers during the Lock-Out* of 1913. They were closely associated with the Irish Volunteers* and assisted at the Howth Gun-running* in July 1914. They continued their connection with the republican movement during and after the War of Independence,* as a junior branch of the Irish Republican Army.* Now known as Gluaiseacht Gasoglach agus Banochlach na hÉireann, Na Fianna are constituent members of Official Sinn Fein.* Their aims include the establishment in Ireland of a democratic socialist republic and the promotion of the Irish language and culture. They are non-sectarian and membership is open to boys and girls under fourteen years of age.

FIANNA FAIL. 'Soldiers of Destiny'; political party founded on 16 May 1926 by Eamon de Valera.* At the suggestion of Sean Lemass,* the party was sub-titled 'The Republican Party'. The aims of the party were the reunification of Ireland, the preservation of the Irish language, the distribution of large farms among the small farmers and a policy of protection and self-sufficiency for the Irish economy. The party broke with the Sinn Fein policy of abstention from Dail Eireann and entered the Dail on 11 August 1927. The party's newspaper, the *Irish Press,** was founded in 1931.

Fianna Fail came to power for the first time in March 1932 and formed the governments until February 1948. The party was out of power from 1948 until 1951 when it formed the government which lasted until 1954. It was out of power again until 1957 and formed governments from then

Year	Seats	Votes	% valid poll	% of electorate
1927 (June)	44	299,226	26.1	17.3
1927 (Sept.)	57	412,141	35.2	23.8
1932	72	566,498	44.5	33.8
1933	77	689,054	49.7	40.0
1937	69	599,040	45.2	33.7
1938	77	667,996	51.0	39.3
1943	67	557,525	41.9	30.7
1944	76	595,259	48.9	33.5
1948	68	553,914	41.9	30.8
1951	69	616,212	46.3	34.5
1954	65	578,960	43.4	32.8
1957	78	592,994	48.3	34.1
1961	70	512,073	43.8	30.6
1965	72	597,414	47.8	35.5
1969	75	602,234	45.7	34.7
1973	69	624,527	46.2	35.0
1977	84	811,615	50.6	38.4

until 1973. It returned to power in 1977. The party's strength since 1927 is shown in the table above.

The leaders of the party have been Eamon de Valera (1926–59); Sean Lemass (1959–66); John (Jack) Lynch (1966–79); Charles J. Haughey (1979–). For the members of the governments formed by Fianna Fail *see* Governments. For detail on the party in power *see* Land Annuities, Economic War, Irish Republican Army, Blueshirts, Abdication Crisis, External Relations Act (1936), Constitution of 1937, Anglo-Irish Agreement (1938), Offences Against the State Act, Emergency Powers Act, Emergency *and* Programmes For Economic Expansion.

FIANNA ULADH. 'Soldiers of Ulster'; the political wing of Saor Uladh* founded in 1953 by followers of Liam Kelly of Pomeroy, Co. Tyrone after he was imprisoned in Northern Ireland (he had been returned as abstentionist Sinn Fein MP shortly before his imprisonment). The party consisted of members of Kelly's own unit of the Irish Republican Army* and they contravened standard IRA practice by recognising the government of the Irish Republic in Dublin. Kelly was elected to the Senate with the help of Clann na Poblachta* in 1954. Fianna Uladh was short-lived although the military wing, Saor Uladh, continued its campaign until 1959. It was banned in 1956 as were Saor Uladh and Sinn Fein.*

FIGGIS, DARRELL (1892–1925). Author and politician (Sinn Fein); b. Rathmines, Dublin. He was taken to India as a child and worked on a tea plantation in Ceylon. Upon his return to Europe he worked in the tea-importation business in England and Ireland. He supported the Gaelic League,* Sinn Fein and the Irish Volunteers.* As a result of a meeting held at the home of Mrs Alice Stopford Green* on 8 May 1914 he went to Hamburg where he purchased arms for the Volunteers and had them transported to the North Sea where they were picked up by the *Asgard** and the *Kelpie** (*see* Howth Gunrunning). After the guns were landed he assisted Thomas MacDonagh in keeping the police and soldiers occupied while the Volunteers took the arms and ammunition to hiding places. He became Secretary of the re-organised Sinn Fein in 1917 and represented Co. Dublin in the first Dail Eireann. He supported the Treaty* and was acting chairman of the Committee which drafted the Constitution of 1922.* His wife killed herself in 1924 and following the death of his mistress he committed suicide. His writings include *A Vision of Life* (poems, 1909), *Broken Arcs* (1911), *A. E. George Russell, A Study of a Man and a Nation* (1915), *The Mount of Transfiguration* (1915), *The Gaelic State in the Past and the Future* (1917), *A Chronicle of Jails* (1917), *The Sinn Fein Catechism* (1918), *Children of Earth* (1918), *A Second Chronicle of Jails* (1919), *The Economic Case for Irish Independence* (1920), *The House of Success* (1921), *The Irish Constitution Explained* (1922), *The Return of the Hero* (1923) and *Recollections of the Irish War*.

FINE GAEL. 'Family (or Tribe) of the Gaels'; political party originally called the United Ireland Party founded in 1933 from a merger of Cumann na nGaedheal,* the National Guard* and the National Centre.* The first president of the party was General Eoin O'Duffy,* then leading the Blueshirts,* who was replaced by W. T. Cosgrave* in 1935. The principal supporters of the party were from industry, business, commerce, the professions and the more substantial farmers. Fine Gael was the principal opposition to Fianna Fail,* 1933–48, 1951–54 and 1957–73. It was the major party in the two Inter-Party Governments,* 1948–51 and 1954–57; it joined with the Labour Party* to form the National Coalition* government, 1973–77. The party's strength since 1933 is shown on the table opposite. The leaders of the party have been: General Eoin O'Duffy (who was not a member of the Dail), 1933–34; W. T. Cosgrave (1935–44); Richard Mulcahy (1944–59); James Dillon (1959–65); Liam Cosgrave (1965-77); Dr Garret Fitzgerald (1977–   ). For detail on the party in power, *see:* Inter-Party Governments, Republic of Ireland Act, Marshall Plan, European Recovery Programme, Long Term Recovery Programme, Industrial Development Authority, Land Rehabilitation Project, Mother and Child Scheme, United Nations and Ireland, National Coalition, Sunningdale Agreement *and* Emergency Powers Act 1976.

FINLAY, REV. THOMAS A., S. J. (1848–1940). Clergyman (R.C.) and political economist; ed. Maynooth; ordained 1876. He was Rector of Belvedere College (1882–87) and Classics Fellow of the Royal University* (1882). With his brother Peter he was Joint Professor of Mental and Moral Philosophy at University College. He was founder of the Lyceum Club (1884), founder-editor of *Lyceum,** (1887–94) and co-founder with Fr Matthew Russell of *The Irish*

Year	Seats	Votes	% valid poll	% of electorate
1933	59	(Fine Gael & the National Centre merged after the general election of January 1933)		
1937	48	461,171	34.8	26.0
1938	45	428,633	33.3	25.2
1943	32	307,490	23.1	16.9
1944	30	249,329	20.5	14.0
1948	31	262,393	19.8	14.5
1951	40	342,922	25.7	19.2
1954	50	427,037	32.0	24.3
1957	40	326,699	26.5	18.8
1961	47	374,099	32.0	22.4
1965	47	427,081	33.9	25.4
1969	50	449,747	34.1	25.9
1973	54	473,781	35.0	26.6
1977	43	488,767	30.5	23.1

*Monthly.** Fr Finlay was an ardent supporter of Sir Horace Plunkett* and the Co-Operative Movement.* He served as a member of the first committee of the Irish Agricultural Organisation Society* of which he was elected vice-president, and was editorial chairman of the *Irish Homestead.** He was Professor of Political Economy at the Royal University (1900) and at UCD (1909—30). He contributed to a wide range of journals, including *New Ireland Review, Studies** and *The Economic Journal.*

FISHER, JOSEPH R. (1855—1939). Journalist; b. Co. Down; ed. Royal Belfast Academical Institute, and Queen's University, Germany and France. During his career as a journalist he was Foreign Editor on the *Daily Chronicle* (1881), Assistant Editor, *The Standard* (1883—91) and Editor and Managing Editor of the *Northern Whig* (1891-1913). He was appointed by the British government to the Boundary Commission* when the government of Northern Ireland refused to nominate a member. He was the author of *Fisher's and Strahan's Law of the Press* (2nd ed., 1898), *Finland and the Tsars* (2nd ed., 1900) and *The End of the Irish Parliament* as well as contributions to *The Times' History of the War* and *Nineteenth Century.*

FITT, GERARD (1926—). Politician (Socialist Republican and Social Democratic and Labour Party); b. Belfast; ed. CBS. He worked as a merchant-seaman from 1941 until 1953 and thereafter at various jobs. He was a Councillor on Belfast Corporation for the Dock Ward which he also represented at Stormont as a member of the Republican Labour Party,* from 1962. In 1966 he was returned to Westminster as MP for West Belfast. He supported the civil rights movement during the 1960s (*see* Northern Ireland Civil Rights Association) and was injured in a demonstration in Derry (5 October 1968). After his return to Westminster with an increased majority in June 1970, he took part in talks which led to the foundation in August of the Social Democratic and Labour Party of which he became leader. This led to his expulsion from the Republican Labour Party. Although not consulted about the withdrawal of the SDLP from Stormont during 1971, he supported it. He was Deputy Chief Executive in the power-sharing Executive of the Assembly (*see* Northern Ireland) which lasted from July 1973 until May 1974. He also sat in the Convention (*see* Northern Ireland) from 8 May 1975 to 5 March 1976. He resigned from the SDLP in 1979.

FITZALAN OF DERWENT, 1st VISCOUNT (1855–1947). FitzAlan-Howard, Edmund Bernard, youngest son of the 14th Duke of Norfolk; politician (Conservative) and Lord Lieutenant (1921–22); ed. Oratory School, Edgbaston. He was MP for Chichester (1894–1921) and served as Lord of the Treasury (1905), Chief Whip (1913–21) and Joint Parliamentary Secretary at the Treasury (1915–21). Upon his appointment as Lord Lieutenant in 1921 during the closing stages of the War of Independence* he became the first Catholic to hold the office since the Union. He was in close consultation with the cabinet during the period preceding the Treaty. He was the last Lord Lieutenant and formally handed power over to Michael Collins* in January 1922.

FITZGERALD, AUGUSTUS FREDERICK. *See* 3rd Duke of Leinster.

FITZGERALD, BARRY (1888–1961). Stage-name of actor William Shields; b. Dublin; ed. Merchant Tay-

lor's School. After joining the Civil Service in 1911, he worked at the Abbey Theatre* but did not become a full-time actor until 1929. He was celebrated for his creation of Captain Boyle opposite F. J. McCormick* as 'Joxer' Daly in *Juno and the Paycock* and 'Fluther' Good in *The Plough and the Stars*, which he also played in the John Ford film version in 1936. Fitzgerald remained in Hollywood and appeared in a wide variety of films including *Ebb Tide* (1937), *Bringing Up Baby* (1938), *The Long Voyage Home* (1940), *How Green Was My Valley* (1942), *Ten Little Niggers* (1945), *Welcome Stranger* (1946), *Union Station* (1950), *The Quiet Man* (1952), *Rooney* (1957), and *Broth of a Boy* (1959). His most popular role was as Fr Fitzgibbon in *Going My Way* (1944).

FITZGERALD, DESMOND (1889–1947). Journalist and politician (Sinn Fein, Cumann na nGaedheal and Fine Gael); b. London of Kerry parentage. He was fluent in six languages and as part of his linguistic studies he studied the Irish language in Kerry. He became active in nationalist movements, including the Irish Volunteers* for whom he was an organiser in Kerry with Ernest Blythe.* During the Easter Rising of 1916,* he fought in the GPO, after which he was imprisoned. He was returned for Sinn Fein in Co. Dublin to the first Dail Eireann, and was substitute Director of Propaganda during the War of Independence.* Minister for Foreign Affairs in the Provisional Government, he held the same post (then known as External Affairs) in the Executive Councils* of the Free State (December 1922 – June 1927). He was Minister for Defence from June 1927 until March 1932, and was a member of the Senate from 1938 to 1947. A man of wide interests, he published poetry and drama and his interest in philosophy led to a visiting lectureship at Notre Dame University, USA. His son, Dr Garret Fitzgerald, was later leader of the Fine Gael party.

FITZGERALD, DR GARRET (1926–). Politician (Fine Gael); b. Dublin; ed. Bray, Ring College, Waterford, Belvedere College, UCD and King's Inns; B.A., Ph.D. and B.L. After working as Research and Schedules Manager of Aer Lingus* he became a Lecturer in the Department of Political Economy, UCD (1959–73), and was correspondent on economic affairs for the BBC, *The Financial Times* and *The Economist*. He was Managing Director of the Economist Intelligence Unit of Ireland (1961–67) and economic consultant to a variety of bodies. He became a Senator in 1965 and was returned as Fine Gael TD for Dublin South-East in 1969; he was opposition spokesman on education (1969–72) and on Finance (1972–73). When the National Coalition Government* was formed in March 1973 he became Minister for Foreign Affairs and presided over the Council of Ministers of the EEC from January to June 1975. Following the general election of June 1977 which returned Fianna Fail to office he succeeded Liam Cosgrave* as leader of the Fine Gael party.

FITZGERALD, GEORGE FRANCIS (1851–1901). Physicist; b. Dublin; ed. TCD, where he became Professor of Natural Philosophy in 1881. He developed the electro-magnetic theory of radiation. Following the Michaelson-Morley experiment he formulated the theory known as the Lorenz-Fitzgerald contraction. His hypothesis was an integral part of the Theory of Relativity published by Einstein in 1905.

FITZGERALD, JOHN DAVID, LORD (1816–89). Lawyer; b. Dublin; ed. privately. After a call to the Irish Bar in 1838 he practised on the Munster Circuit; QC (1847). MP for Ennis (1852) and Attorney-General (1855–56), he successfully defended himself in parliament in 1856 against accusations of complicity in the escape of John Sadleir* after bankruptcy. He was raised to the bench in 1860 and during the course of his career tried Fenians* (1865–67), and A. M. Sullivan,* Richard Pigott* and Charles Stewart Parnell* in 1880. He became a life peer in 1882 and three years later turned down the Lord Chancellorship.

FITZMAURICE, GEORGE (1887–1963). Dramatist; b. near Listowel, Co. Kerry; ed. locally. He worked in Dublin, first as a clerk and later in the Department of Agriculture. Most of his works were produced at the Abbey Theatre.* He contributed to the *Dublin Magazine* whose editor, Seamus O'Sullivan, was a close friend. He served in the British Army in France during World War I. His earliest success was with *The Country Dressmaker* (1907) and other works included *The Pie Dish* (1908), *The Magic Glasses* (1913) and *Twixt the Giltinans and the Carmodys* (1923). He was a recluse during his last years.

FITZMAURICE, COLONEL JAMES (1898–1965). Aviator; b. Dublin; after moving as a child to Portlaoise he was educated there by the Christian Brothers and at St Joseph's, Rockwell. Having worked for a short time in Waterford he joined the British army in 1912 but, as he was under age, his father had him released. Two years later he joined the 17th Lancers at the Curragh. He was sent to the Western Front where he was wounded and decorated in 1917. Before the end of the war he entered Cadet School in England and was commissioned in the Royal Flying Corps with which he flew a number of missions. After the war he was stationed at Folkestone, flying a mail service to Cologne until he resigned in 1921.

Upon joining the Air Corps* of the Free State he was stationed at Fermoy, Co. Cork. He was transferred to Baldonnel where he was Squadron Commander and Officer in Command of Training from 1 October 1924. Acting Commandant from 1 October 1925, he carried out the duties of the O/C, Army Air Corps from 11 October 1926 and was appointed commandant on 1 September 1927. He became a major on 13 April 1928.

Fitzmaurice first attempted to fly from Ireland to North America with Captain R. R. MacIntosh in September 1927 in a Fokker monoplane, 'Princess Xenia'. They abandoned the attempt after 500 miles and returned to land on the strand at Ballybunion, Co. Kerry. His second attempt was as a member of the crew of the 'Bremen' (D. 1167), a Junker, which left Baldonnel Aerodrome at dawn on 12 April 1928 to make the first east-west trans-Altantic crossing. He was accompanied by two Germans, Captain Kohl (co-pilot) and Baron von Heunfeld (observer). Following a difficult passage they made a forced landing on Greenly Island, Newfoundland, having flown 2,300 miles in 36½ hours.

He resigned from the Air Corps on 16 February 1929. After spending some years in the USA he returned and moved to England in 1939. He ran a servicemen's club in London and returned to live in Ireland in 1951. The 'Bremen' is on display at the Ford Museum, Deerborn.

FITZPATRICK, PATRICK VINCENT (1792–1865). Repealer; b. Dublin; ed. Maynooth. A close friend of Daniel O'Connell,* he assisted in the organisation of the Catholic Association.* He served as O'Connell's treasurer and was responsible for the collection of 'Rent' which after 1829 became the 'O'Connell Tribute' and performed the same service in the Repeal Association* after 1840. By occupation, he was Registrar of Deeds. He left his papers to W. J. Fitzpatrick* who edited them as *The Correspondence of O'Connell* (1888).

FITZPATRICK, WILLIAM JOHN (1830–95). Biographer; b. Dublin; ed. Clongowes Wood College; achieved notoriety in 1856 when he alleged, in *Who Wrote the Waverley Novels?*,

that Thomas Scott, brother of Sir Walter, was the real author. His best-known work, *The Sham Squire* (1865), sold over 10,000 copies; his other works included *Lord Cloncurry* (1855), *Lady Morgan* (1860), *Bishop Doyle* (2 vols, 1861), *Ireland Before the Union* (1863), *Archbishop Whately* (2 vols, 1864), *Irish Wits and Worthies* (1873), *Charles Lever* (1879), *The Life of the Very Rev. Thomas N. Burke O.P.* (2 vols, 1885), *The Secret Service under Pitt* (1892), and *Father Healy* (1895). His *History of the Dublin Catholic Cemeteries*, completed and edited by his son, appeared in 1900. He edited *The Correspondence of Daniel O'Connell* (1888) from papers left him by Patrick Vincent Fitzpatrick.*

FLAGS AND EMBLEMS ACT, 1954. Passed by the parliament of Northern Ireland, the Act gave the Minister for Justice the power to order the seizure of 'provocative emblems'. The main target of the act was the Irish Republican Army.*

FLANAGAN, JOHN WOULFE (1852–1929) Journalist; b. Roscommon; ed. Oscott College and Oxford; Bar (1877). He joined the staff of *The Times* in 1885 and produced the first series of articles on 'Parnellism and Crime'* (1887).

FLOOD, JOHN (1841–1909). Fenian; b. Dublin; ed. Clongowes Wood College. He became a journalist and a leading member of the Irish Republican Brotherhood.* After James Stephens'* escape from Richmond Prison, Flood sailed the vessel which took them to Scotland. He assisted Captain John MacCafferty* in the raid on Chester Castle (1867) and was arrested on his return to Dublin. After serving five years of a fifteen-year sentence in Australia, he settled in Queensland and worked as a journalist. He founded the first branch of the Land League* in Australia.

FLOOD, WILLIAM HENRY GRATTAN (1859–1928). Musicologist; b.

Lismore, Co. Waterford; ed. Mount Melleray and University College. Organist at Enniscorthy Cathedral from 1895, Flood edited Thomas Moore's *Irish Melodies* and the *Catholic Hymnal of Ireland.* He was Irish correspondent of *The Tablet* and the author of several works on the history of music, including *Story of the Harp* (1905), *History of Irish Music* (1905), *Story of the Bagpipes* (1911), *John Field of Dublin* (1920), *Introductory Sketch of Irish Musical History* (1922) and *Early Tudor Composers* (1925). He was also the author of *Diocese of Ferns* (1916) and *History of Enniscorthy* (1920).

FLOWER, ROBIN ERNEST WILLIAM (1881–1946). Scholar and poet; b. Meanwood, Yorkshire, of Anglo-Irish parentage; ed. Leeds Grammar School and Oxford after which he joined the staff of the British Museum (1906) where he became Deputy Keeper of Manuscripts (1929–44). He came to Ireland in 1910 to perfect his studies in Old and Middle Irish and was directed to the Blasket Islands* where he mastered the language and was known affectionately as 'Bláithín' (Little Flower). He held lecturing appointments in Celtic Studies at University College, London, the British Academy, the Royal Society of Literature, and Boston, Yale and Chicago universities. His works include *Eire and Other Poems* (1910), *Hymenea and Other Poems* (1918), *Ireland and Medieval Europe* (1928) and *An Irish Journal: the Story of the Blaskets* (1933); translations from the Irish: *Love's bitter-sweet: translations from the Irish poets of the 16th and 17th centuries* (1925), *Poems and Translations* (1931) and *The Islandman* (1934) from *An tOileánach* by Tomás Ó Criomhthain.* He edited *Dánta Grádha* (1916) by T. F. O'Rahilly and completed with Standish Hayes O'Grady* the *Catalogue of the Irish Manuscripts in the British Museum* (1926). His *Seanchas ón oileán thiar* was written from the speech of Ó Criomhthain and appeared in 1956.

FLYING COLUMN. The principal unit used by the Irish Republican Army* during the War of Independence.* The column consisted of a small group with an intimate knowledge of their operational terrain. It was highly manoeuvrable and operated on an independent basis. Members of the column were often 'on the run' for days at a time and used their knowledge of the countryside and the inhabitants to the best advantage. Prominent leaders of flying columns were Tom Barry* (West Cork), Dan Breen* and Dinny Lacey* (Tipperary), Frank Aiken* (Louth) Ernie O'Malley,* (Limerick-Tipperary), and Sean MacEoin* (Longford).

FOGARTY, MICHAEL (1859–1955) Bishop of Killaloe (R.C.), 1904–53; b. Kilcoleman, Nenagh, Co. Tipperary; ed. locally and Maynooth. Professor of Philosophy and Canon Law, Carlow (1886–89). Professor of Dogmatic and Moral Theology, Maynooth (1889–1904), he was widely recognised for his nationalist sympathies. During the Clare by-election of 1917 he came out publicly in favour of Sinn Fein* and supported Eamon de Valera.* His support for Dail Eireann* and the Irish Republic led to attempts by Auxiliaries* to murder him (December 1920). In 1954 he received the title of Archbishop upon appointment as Assistant to the Pontifical Throne.

FOLEY, JOHN HENRY (1818–74). Sculptor; b. Dublin; ed. at the schools of the Royal Dublin Society and the Royal Academy where he first exhibited in 1849. His Irish works included the statues of Oliver Goldsmith and Edmund Burke and the O'Connell Memorial in O'Connell Street, Dublin. He was one of the four Irish sculptors who worked on the Albert Memorial in London (the others were Patrick McDowell, John Lawlor and Samuel Ferris Lynn); Foley was responsible for the group representing 'Asia'. Other works were Lord Canning (Calcutta), Lord Clyde (Glasgow), John Stuart Mill and Sir Charles Barry (London) and Stonewall Jackson (Richmond, Virginia).

FOLKLORE OF IRELAND SOCIETY. *See* Irish Folklore Commission.

FORAS FORBARTHA TEO., AN. The National Institute for Physical Planning and Construction Research. Founded in 1964 with aid from the United Nations, An Foras Forbartha provides research training and specialist studies relating to all aspects of the environment. It is financed by a grant from the Department of the Environment (formerly Local Government).

FORD, PATRICK (1837–1913). Journalist; b. Galway; ed. locally. He emigrated to the USA in 1841 and settled in Boston where he completed his education and was apprenticed to a printer. His journalistic career began in 1855 as editor and publisher of *The Boston Sunday Times* which failed in 1860. He fought in the Union army during the American Civil War (1861–65). From 1864 to 1866 he edited *The Charleston Gazette*. He founded *The Irish World* in 1870 and printed and published it from New York until his death. It became one of the most influential of Irish-American newspapers, with large sales in Ireland, where it was several times banned by the authorities. In it he advocated self-government, and supported the Fenians* and the Land League* for which he raised money and helped to organise 2,500 branches in the USA. Following the split in the Irish Parliamentary Party* (1890–91) he supported John Redmond* and accepted the Home Rule Bill of 1912 as the answer to Ireland's demand for self-government. *The Irish World* was edited by his nephew, Robert, from 1913 to 1920. Ford was the author of *The Criminal History of the British Empire* (1881) and *The Irish Question and American Statesmen* (1885).

FORSAÍ COSANTA ÁITIUIL (FCA). Auxiliary branch of the Defence Forces* established after the Emergency* to replace the Local Defence Force* (LDF). The FCA was administered by the regular army which operated annual training camps. It became a separate organisation on 3 September 1979 when it had a total of 19,463 personnel: 692 officers, 3,096 NCOs and 15,675 men.

FORSTER, WILLIAM EDWARD (1818–86). Politician (Liberal) and Chief Secretary (1880–82); b. Bradpole, Dorset, to a Quaker family; ed. Bristol and Tottenham, London. He worked in the wool business, eventually settling in Bradford where he entered a partnership in a wool concern (1842–86). He visited Connemara during the Famine of 1845–49* on a relief mission. MP for Bradford (1861–86), he supported reform and was Under-Secretary of the Colonies (1865). In 1870 his Elementary Education Act failed to secure assent to clauses on compulsory education. He oversaw the passage of the Secret Ballot Act, 1872.*

W. E. Gladstone* appointed him Chief Secretary at the height of the Land War* inaugurated by the Land League* against which he fought, while defending himself from the 'advanced' wing of his own party. Although he pressed for coercion* he had to wait until January 1881 to get strong measures. His position was not helped by his poor relationship with the Lord Lieutenant, the 7th Earl of Cowper.* He was criticised in England for his failure to secure convictions in the trials of Charles Stewart Parnell,* John Dillon* and other Land League leaders (December 1880 – January 1881). On 7 January 1881 he was granted power to hold persons in prison upon 'reasonable suspicion' of crime, outrage or conspiracy and soon had 900 imprisoned under this authority. His health weakened under the strain of office. By October he had Dillon, Michael Davitt,* Parnell and William O'Brien* imprisoned and when they issued the No Rent Manifesto* he suppressed the League. With Parnell imprisoned the crime rate soared and in spite of several attempts upon his life, Forster travelled throughout the country seeking to win acceptance for Gladstone's Land Law (Ireland) Act of 1881 (*see* Land Acts). He was by now a hated figure, popularly known as 'Buckshot' Forster as a result of his humane substitution of buckshot for bullets for the Royal Irish Constabulary* (the substitution, in fact, made the police more apt to open fire). He broke with Gladstone over the Kilmainham 'Treaty',* announcing his resignation on 4 May 1882. Following the assassination of his successor, Lord Frederick Cavendish,* on 6 May he offered to resume the post temporarily but Gladstone rejected the offer. Forster played no further part in Irish affairs apart from his accusation in 1883 that Parnell and others were conniving in criminal activities. He devoted himself to colonial interests and became chairman of the Imperial Federation League which he launched in 1884.

FORTESCUE-PARKINSON, CHI-CHESTER, LORD CARLINGFORD (1823–98). Politician (Liberal); Chief Secretary (1865–66, 1868–70); ed. privately and Oxford where he was awarded M.A. (1847). He was MP for his native Co. Louth (1847–74). In 1851 he opposed the Ecclesiastical Titles Bill.* He assumed the additional surname of Parkinson in 1852 to comply with the terms of the will of Parkinson Ruxton of Ardee who bequeathed him an estate. After serving as Junior Lord of the Treasury (1854–55) he was Under Secretary of State for the Colonies (1857–58, 1859–65) and became Chief Secretary for Ireland in November 1865. He introduced a bill to secure compensation for improvements made to tenants' holdings but as it was overshadowed by the issue of parliamentary reform he withdrew it in 1866. In the first administration formed by W. E. Gladstone* he became Chief Secretary for the second time (De-

cember 1868) and assisted the Prime Minister with the drafting of proposals for the Disestablishment of the Church of Ireland.* He also helped to draft Gladstone's Land Act of 1870 (*see* Land Acts). To deal with the agitation which occurred in 1870, he was granted a Peace Preservation Act but the feeling within the cabinet was that he was not strong enough for the Irish post and he was replaced (*see* Devonshire, 8th Duke). After losing his seat in 1874 he was raised to the peerage as Lord Carlingford. He wrote a minority report as a member of the Richmond Commission.*

FORTY-SHILLING FREEHOLDERS. Those who held a lease for life of a house or land, in which the lessee had an interest worth forty shillings a year, known as a 'forty-shilling freehold', were granted the vote in 1793. This placed Protestants and Catholics on equal terms but the Catholic was still unable to become a member of either house of parliament because of the Oath of Supremacy (*see* Catholic Emancipation). The more forty-shilling freeholders a landlord had on his land, the greater his influence in elections and it was noted by contemporaries that landlords were now encouraged to divide their estates into even smaller holdings for that reason. However, with the passage of the Emancipation Act of 1829, the qualification for the franchise was raised from forty shillings to £10. One consequence was to reduce the electorate from 230,000 to around 14,000.

FOSTER, VERE HENRY LEWIS (1819–1900). Educationalist and philanthropist; b. Copenhagen; ed. Eton and Oxford. After joining the diplomatic service he was posted to Rio de Janeiro (1842–43) and Montevideo (1845–47). While visiting Ireland with his brother during the Famine of 1845–49* he devoted himself to social welfare, in particular to the welfare of emigrants. He travelled on coffin ships* in order to experience the conditions of travel and revealed gross exploitation of emigrants by captains and crews which led to legislation to ensure stricter control. It was estimated that he used his personal fortune to pay the fares of some 25,000 emigrants. His experiences with emigrants convinced him of their need for a good standard of education and he interested himself in teaching methods, building parish schools.

He designed and published his famous 'Vere Foster Copy Books' in 1868, selling over one million. He also designed children's copy-books with script 'headlines' of mottoes such as 'More Haste, Less Speed', etc. He claimed that good copper-plate handwriting was the most essential lesson a child could learn. In 1868 he founded and became the first president of the Irish National Teachers' Association (later Organisation, the INTO). He moved to Belfast in 1870 and spent the remainder of his life assisting the poor. He died in poverty, his funeral attended by a handful of people and his passing noted by only two newspapers. Among the educational aids which he inspired were *Elementary Drawing Copybook* (1868), *Copybooks* (1870), *Drawing Copybooks* (1872), *Public School Copybooks* (1881), *Simple Lessons in Watercolour* (1883), *Drawing Book . . . in Pencil and Water-Colour* (1884), *Painting for Beginners* (1884) and *Upright Writing Charts* (1897).

FOUR COURTS. The Four Courts, the centre of the Irish judiciary, was seized by the 3rd Battalion of the Dublin Brigade, Irish Republican Army,* on 14 April 1922. Other buildings occupied at the same time included the Kildare Street Club and the Ballast Office. These seizures had not been authorised by the IRA Executive but over the next two months many prominent republicans joined the original garrison of 180. No attempt was made for the moment by the Provisional government* to dislodge the republicans although their presence was a severe embarrass-

ment to Arthur Griffith,* the President of Dail Eireann,* and Michael Collins,* the Chairman of the Provisional government. Both of them were under pressure from their colleagues and from the British government to take some action against the occupying force. No action was taken until events in June forced the government to act. The general election of 16 June resulted in a victory for the Treaty supporters and placed the Provisional government in a strong position. On 22 June, General Sir Henry Wilson* was assassinated in London and the British government, attributing the murder to the IRA, demanded immediate action against the Four Courts. The British issued an ultimatum on 25 June to the effect that they would consider the Treaty breached if the Provisional government did not act. While the government was deliberating the republicans forced it to act by kidnapping the Deputy Chief of the National Army, General J. J. O'Connell, on 26 June. Griffith presided over a specially convened meeting and the decision was taken to move against the Four Courts.

At 3.40 a.m. on 28 June the garrison was called upon to surrender. When this demand was ignored the government commenced shelling the building at seven minutes past four. The Civil War* had begun. The Four Courts garrison issued the following proclamation:

Oglaigh na hÉireann
PROCLAMATION
Fellow citizens of the Irish Republic:
The fateful hour has come. At the dictation of our hereditary enemy our rightful cause is being treacherously assailed by recreant Irishmen. The crash of arms and the boom of artillery reverberate in this supreme test of the Nation's destiny.

Gallant soldiers of the Irish Republic stand rigorously firm in its defence and worthily uphold their noblest traditions. The sacred spirits of the Illustrious Dead are with us in this great struggle. 'Death before Dishonour' being an unchanging principle of our national faith as it was of theirs, still inspires us to emulate their glorious effort.

We therefore appeal to all citizens who have withstood unflinchingly the oppression of the enemy during the past six years to rally to the support of the Republic and recognise that the resistance now being offered is but the continuance of the struggle that was suspended by the truce with the British. We especially appeal to our former comrades of the Irish Republic to return to that allegiance and thus guard the Nation's honour from the infamous stigma that her sons aided her foes in retaining a hateful domination over her.

Confident of victory and of maintaining Ireland's Independence this appeal is issued by the Army Executive on behalf of the Irish Republican Army.

(*Signed*)
Commdt.-Gen. Liam Mellows,
Commdt.-Gen. Rory O'Connor,
Commdt.-Gen. Jos. McKelvey,
Commdt.-Gen. Earnán Ó Máille,
Commdt.-Gen. Seamus Robinson,
Commdt.-Gen. Sean Moylan,
Commdt.-Gen. Michael Kilroy,
Commdt.-Gen. Frank Barrett,
Commdt.-Gen. Thomas Deerig
   [*sic*, Derrig],
Commdt. T. Barry,
Commdt. F. Ó Faolain,
Brig. Gen. J. O'Connor,
Commdt. P. Ó Ruitléis.

After the building was shelled for two days, for the most part with amateur gunners, a government force of 2,000 attacked the Four Courts and the republican garrison proved unable to withstand the attack. Before surrendering, the republicans mined the records office, resulting in the destruction of documents dating back to the twelfth century. The garrison surrendered at 3.30 p.m. on 30 June. Among those captured were Liam Mellows,* Rory O'Connor* and Ernie O'Malley* (who signed the surrender). Among those who escaped was Cathal Brugha* who continued the fight for a few more days from the Hammam Hotel. General Liam Lynch,* Chief of Staff of the IRA, made his escape from Dublin to continue the republican struggle in the south for a further year. The attack on the Four Courts resulted in sixty-five killed, 270 wounded and twenty-five buildings destroyed. *See also* Civil War.

FOX, CHARLOTTE MILLLIGAN (1864–1916). Folk-song collector; b. Omagh, Co. Tyrone; founded Irish Folk Song Society (1904). She travelled throughout Ireland collecting folk songs and airs on gramophone and published *Annals of the Irish Harpists* (1911), from the papers of Edward Bunting.*

FOYNES, CO. LIMERICK. Landing site for transatlantic flying boats known as 'Yankee Clippers' which landed between the mainland and Foynes Island from 1937 to 1945, when Foynes was eclipsed by the opening of Shannon Airport at Rineanna, Co. Clare to transatlantic aircraft. During its years of operation, Foynes was used as a landing-place by Pan-American, Imperial Airways (afterwards British Airways) and American Overseas Airlines (afterwards TWA).

FREE STATE. Established on 6 December 1922 under the Treaty,* the Irish Free State consisted of twenty-six counties. It had a two-tier legislature made up of Dail Eireann* and the Senate.* The state was governed by an Executive Council,* the first President of which was W. T. Cosgrave.* The State's Constitution came into force in 1922 and lasted until the Constitution of Eire* came into operation on 29 December 1937 when the title 'Eire' was substituted for 'Free State'. Since 1949 the state has been known as the Republic of Ireland.

'FREEMAN'S JOURNAL'. Newspaper founded in Dublin in 1763. In 1802 it was controlled by Philip Whitfield

Harvey who, in receipt of a government pension of £200 p.a., supported Dublin Castle.* During the period 1809–12 it fell into dispute with the Chief Secretary, William Wellesley-Pole, and became more independent. Prominent editors and owners of the paper included Michael Staunton,* Sir John Gray* and Edward Dwyer Gray,* senior and junior. The paper supported Catholic Emancipation,* Repeal,* the Land League* and Home Rule.* In the early years of the twentieth century it supported moderate nationalism and the Irish Parliamentary Party* under John Redmond.*

Its support for the Treaty* and the government of the Free State led to its destruction: on 29–30 March 1922 the plant was raided by the Irish Republican Army* which destroyed the presses, and burned down the building. The cause of the IRA's anger was an official report from the Free State Army headquarters on the (IRA) Army Convention of 26 March, which appeared in the paper. The Dail voted £2,600 compensation to the paper, which appeared for a while as a typed sheet. It appeared once more late in April as a twenty-four-page newspaper but it ceased publication during the following year and was incorporated into the *Irish Independent.* *

FRENCH OF YPRES, LORD (1852–1925) Soldier and Lord Lieutenant (1918–21); b. John Denton French, of a Roscommon family living in Kent. His career in the army started in 1874 and he rose to become C-in-C of the British Expeditionary Force to France (1914) and C-in-C of the Home Guard (1915-18). He received £50,000 in 1915 and was created viscount for services to the crown. During the crisis over Conscription and Ireland* in 1918 he claimed to the cabinet that with 'a slight augmentation' of troops he could enforce conscription (25 March 1918). On 11 May he replaced Lord Wimborne* as Lord Lieutenant with the widest powers of any viceroy, under the Defence of the Realm Act.* He assured David Lloyd George* that he would prevent 'any German intrigues' and within a week he had arrested supporters of Sinn Fein,* the Irish Volunteers* and other nationalist organisations on charges of involvement in a German Plot.* Following the Sinn Fein victory in the general election of December 1918 and the establishment of Dail Eireann* on 21 January 1919 he asked the cabinet to release imprisoned nationalists (this commenced on 4 March 1919). Within a short time the country was in the midst of the War of Independence.* He persuaded his former subordinate, General Sir Nevil Macready,* to take office as C-in-C of the armed forces. The arrival of the Auxiliaries* and Black and Tans* during the summer of 1920 led to an intensification of the war. In December, martial law was declared and French became a virtual dictator. In all, a dozen attempts were made on his life by republicans; following a particularly narrow escape on 19 December 1920 at Ashtown he confined himself to the Viceregal Lodge. Throughout the spring of 1921 attempts were made to negotiate with the Irish Republican Army.* As a conciliatory measure French was removed and replaced by the first Catholic Lord Lieutenant, Lord Fitz-Alan of Derwent.* Upon his return to England he was created Earl.

FRENCH, WILLIAM PERCY (1854–1920). Engineer, artist and songwriter; b. Cloonyquin, Co. Roscommon; ed. Kirk Langley, Derbyshire, Windermere College, Foyle College and TCD; B.A. (1876) and B.E. (1880). While a student he sold the rights to 'Abdulla Bulbul Ameer' for £5. In 1891 he met Houston Collinson (1865–1920) with whom he later collaborated. French was the author of some of the best-loved Irish songs, including 'Phil the Fluther's, Ball' (1889), 'The Mountains of Mourne' (1896), 'Are ye right there Michael' (1902) – which led to a celebrated libel case brought against him by the West Clare Railway – 'Eileen Oge' (1903). 'The Darlin' Girl from Clare' (1906) and 'Come back Paddy Reilly to Ballyjamesduff' (1912). During World War I he gave charity performances on the continent and in England (with Collinson). He was a talented artist and painted several Irish scenes for King George V. He died of heart failure at Formby, Lancashire, pre-deceasing his friend, (now Canon) Collinson, by one week.

FRIEND, MAJOR-GENERAL SIR LOVICH BRANSBY (1856–1944). Soldier; GOC, Ireland (1914–16); b. Wollet Hall, North Crag, Kent; ed. Cheltenham College, and Royal Military Academy, Woolwich. Following commission as a lieutenant in the Royal Engineers (1873), he served in South Africa and Egypt. With the rank of major-general he was in charge of Administration in Ireland (1912–14) before appointment as GOC. In 1915 he recommended to the Chief Secretary, Augustine Birrell,* that the Irish Volunteers* should be proscribed but Birrell rejected this advice. Following the outbreak of the Easter Rising of 1916* he was succeeded by General Maxwell.*

FRIENDS OF IRELAND GROUP. The Friends were left-wing Labour MPs who came together in 1945 to express their opposition to the rule of the Ulster Unionist Party* in Northern Ireland. They hoped to influence the Labour government led by Clement Attlee but failed. A leading member was Geoffrey Bing, himself an Ulsterman. The group was no longer active after the fall of the first Inter-Party Government* in 1951. *See also* Northern Ireland.

FRIENDS OF IRISH FREEDOM. A republican organisation founded at the first Irish Race Convention* in New York (4–5 March 1916). It was supported by the United Irish League,* the Ancient Order of Hibernians* and other leading Irish-American organisations but it was dominated by Clan na Gael* whose members held fifteen out of seventeen executive seats. The aim of the organisation was 'to encourage and assist any movement that will tend to bring about the National Independence of Ireland'. The first president was Victor Herbert, the treasurer was Thomas Hughes Kelly and the secretary, John D. Moore. The FOIF supported the Easter Rising of 1916* and in the aftermath of the rising, raised 350,000 dollars through the Irish Relief Fund to assist dependants. Diarmuid Lynch* was appointed Secretary in 1918 and held the post until 1932. By 1920 there was a 'regular' membership of over 100,000 and 484 'associate' branches with a membership of 175,000. During the War of Independence,* the FOIF helped to raise over five million dollars for the newly-declared Irish Republic through the promotion of Bond Certificates. This followed an appeal from the President of Dail Eireann, Eamon de Valera,* then in the US. In October 1920, a rift developed between de Valera and the American Fenian leaders, John Devoy* and Judge Daniel Cohalan* which resulted in a split between the FOIF and the Irish Republican Brotherhood* in Ireland. Before leaving the US, de Valera founded a new organisation, the American Association for the Recognition of the Irish Republic* to continue the work of the FOIF. The FOIF was wound up in 1932 following litigation concerning the monies it had collected for the Irish Republic, most of which were returned to the original donors.

FRIENDS OF RELIGIOUS FREEDOM AND EQUALITY. Founded in October 1862, the FRFE was a short-lived organisation led by George Henry Moore* for the purpose of calling a conference to discuss the religious issues of the day. It was attended by twenty-six Irish Liberal MPs. They demanded the repeal of the Ecclesiastical Titles Act* and the Disestablishment of the Church of Ireland.* The Friends had the support of Archbishop Paul Cullen* of Dublin. They called on Irish Liberals to oppose any United Kingdom governments not prepared to meet their demands.

FUNERAL PROCESSIONS. When the deceased had been waked (*see* Wake) the priest sprinkled earth from the grave into the coffin or, alternatively, blessed earth for throwing on to the coffin at interment. The latter was a relic of the Penal Laws of the eighteenth century when a Catholic priest was not allowed to officiate in Catholic graveyards. When the coffin was taken from the house it was placed on four chairs before being raised onto the shoulders of the bearers. When it was placed on their shoulders the four chairs were knocked over. Four men bore the coffin in relays, in accordance with their closeness of kinship and friendship to the deceased. Whenever possible they had the same surname as the deceased. The funeral procession was by the longest possible route to the graveyard. The cortege consisted of relatives following immediately behind the bearers; men preceded women who were followed by pony-traps and cars etc. The cortege halted at cross-roads for short prayers. Anyone coming from the opposite direction to a funeral was expected to join the procession and take at least three steps with it. Traditionally, in no circumstances did a funeral procession ever cross another person's land. Mr and Mrs S. C. Hall* noted the rivalry which they observed when two funeral processions approached a cemetery. It was a matter of honour, as to who entered first. To the Hall's astonishment the funeral processions, at one moment reverently approaching the gate of the cemetery, were the next moment running at full speed in competition. 'Such encounters', the Halls noted, 'become a contest of speed if not of blood'. With the advent of the motor-car many of the traditions associated with funeral processions were no longer observed. They are still extant in some rural areas.

'FURROW, THE'. Theological journal founded in February 1950 by Canon James Gerard McGarry (d. 1977). Published in Maynooth, it became the most important organ of its type published in Ireland, dealing with theological, liturgical, ecumenical and pastoral affairs. Its advanced views, sometimes irritating to the conservative Catholic hierarchy, were vindicated by the Second Vatican Council (1962–65). The *Furrow* introduced continental theological thinking into Ireland and had a profound influence on a younger generation of Irish theologians.

G

GAEL LINN. A non-profit making cultural organisation, Gael Linn was founded in May 1953 under the patronage of Comhdháil Náisiúnta na Gaeilge.* Its activities were directed by Donal Ó Moráin and financed initially by a donation of £100 from Ernest Blythe.* Regular finance for its activities came from a football pool. In addition to its principal aim of fostering the Irish language and culture, Gael Linn sought to provide a means of livelihood for people in the Gaeltachtai.* This led to a scheme to exploit the fishing potential of the west coast. In 1958 Gael Linn bought and refitted old lifeboats which were then sold to Galway fishermen on hire-purchase for £400 each. It later invested some £150,000 in three private oyster beds at Ros Muc, Co. Galway. The Industrial Development

Authority* assisted in the establishment of a freezing and lobster-holding plant at Carna, Co. Galway, a form of enterprise further developed by Gaeltarra Eireann.

Gael Linn's work in Irish culture has been varied. One of its first ventures was to make fortnightly and then weekly newsreels in Irish which were shown throughout the country by the Rank Organisation until 1961. With the assistance of film-makers George Morrison, Colm O'Laoghaire and Louis Marcus it also produced two documentaries on Irish history, *Mise Eire* (1959) and *Saoirse* (1961) for which the music was composed by Sean O'Riada.* It also made *Peil* and *Christy Ring* under the sponsorship of Player-Wills. Gael Linn produces recordings of traditional Irish music and since 1954 has sponsored scholarships to enable young people to live in the Gaeltachtai during their holidays.

'GAEL, THE'. Newspaper published by the Gaelic Athletic Association* in 1887. Among contributors to the literary section, which was edited by John O'Leary,* were T. W. Rolleston,* Ellen O'Leary,* Douglas Hyde* and W. B. Yeats.* The paper had a successful two-year run as a weekly.

'GAELIC AMERICAN'. Fenian newspaper published by John Devoy* in New York; the first edition appeared on 13 September 1903 and it ran until 1927. Devoy's assistant on it until 1907 was Thomas J. Clarke.*

GAELIC ATHLETIC ASSOCIATION (CUMANN LUTHCLEAS GAEL). Amateur sporting association. The GAA owes its origin to a circular issued (27 October 1884) by Michael Cusack* and Maurice Davin* requesting attendance at 'a meeting which will be held at Thurles on 1 November to take steps for the formation of a Gaelic Association for the preservation and cultivation of our National Pastimes, and for providing amusements for the Irish

people during their leisure hours'. The meeting, which took place in the billiard room of Hayes' Hotel, was also attended by John Wyse Power, John McKay, J. K. Bracken, P. J. Ryan and St George McCarthy. Davin was elected first president and Cusack, Wyse Power and McKay were elected secretaries. Dr T. W. Croke,* Archbishop of Cashel, became the 'Association's first patron (18 December 1884). Michael Davitt* and Charles Stewart Parnell,* also patrons, were among prominent nationalists who quickly identified themselves with the emergent Association. The GAA was anti-British in outlook and imposed a ban (now rescinded) upon its members, which prevented them from participating in or observing certain specified non-Gaelic games. Its rules also excluded those serving in the crown forces from membership. Largely a rural movement, the Association originated and fostered 'county' loyalties (still a distinctive feature) among its supporters. Its rapid spread attracted the attention of the Irish Republican Brotherhood* which supported many of its ideals. The majority of the Association's members subsequently supported the Gaelic League,* na Fianna Eireann* and the Irish Volunteers.*

Football (peil), hurling (iománaídheacht) and handball (liathróid láimhe) are the principal games fostered under the umbrella of the GAA. The All-Ireland Finals, hurling and football, are played annually in September at Croke Park Dublin (headquarters of the association), and are relayed by sound and vision to many corners of the globe. Today the GAA through its sponsorship of Scór, Féile na nGael and Scór na nÓg, plays an important social and cultural role in Irish life. *See also* Maguire, Sam.

GAELIC LEAGUE (CONRADH NA GAEILGE). Founded on 1 July 1893 by Dr Douglas Hyde,* Eoin MacNeill* and Fr Eugene O'Growney,* the League was dedicated to the 'de-Anglicisation of Ireland' through the revival and preservation of Irish as a spoken language. Hyde hoped that a non-political and non-sectarian league would offer common ground upon which all sections of Irish political and religious opinion could meet for a cultural purpose. Through its newspaper, *An Claideamh Soluis*,* and through the publication of stories, poetry and plays in Irish, the League expanded quite rapidly although it was to remain largely an urban organisation. An annual festival of native culture, an tOireachtas, was established in 1897 and the League successfully campaigned to have St Patrick's Day accepted as a national holiday. Timirí* or travelling teachers journeyed to the remoter parts of the country where Irish was no longer spoken and encouraged the formation of classes. In 1905 the first college for training teachers of the language was established at Ballingeary, Co. Cork and soon Irish was being taught as part of the primary and secondary schools' curricula. The League had some 600 branches by 1908 and one year later Irish was accepted as a compulsory subject for matriculation to the new National University of Ireland.*

Against Hyde's wishes the League had by 1915 taken a political stance under Patrick Pearse.* At the Árd Fheis of that year in Dundalk it was resolved that the political independence of Ireland was a primary aim. This led to Hyde's resignation and his lead was followed by many of the moderate members. In 1920 the League issued its educational policy which was to have Irish recognised and implemented as the principal language of Ireland and for the language to become the medium of instruction in all schools within five years. *See also* Gaeltachtai *and* Gael Linn.

GAELIC SOCIETY. Short-lived scholarly society founded in 1807, it was devoted to the discovery, translation and publication of early Irish manuscripts. Some of its members

independently published a grammar of Irish but the society itself published little. Among its members was Edward O'Reilly.*

GAELTACHT AREAS ORDER, 1956. *See* Gaeltachtai.

GAELTACHTAI. Areas of Ireland in which Irish is the vernacular of the majority of the people. Two types of Gaeltacht are distinguished; the Fíor-Gaeltacht in which 80 per cent or more of the population speak Irish, and the Breac-Gaeltacht in which 25 to 79 per cent speak the language. By the Gaeltacht Areas Order (1956) Gaeltacht districts were declared in Counties Clare, Cork, Donegal, Galway, Kerry, Mayo and Waterford.

In 1835 it was estimated that 50 per cent of Irish people spoke the language. By 1851 the Census put the figure at 1½ million people (30 per cent) and by 1871 13 per cent spoke only Irish. There was a possibility that the language might disappear completely, and in the second part of the century determined efforts were made to preserve it. In the main such revival groups tended to be too localised and were patronised almost exclusively by scholars and academics. One of these groups, the Gaelic League,* did enjoy a large measure of success. Irish became compulsory at primary school level in 1922, and in 1923 it became essential as a qualification for entry into the civil service of the Free State. The Constitution of 1922* declared that Ireland had two official languages, Irish and English; the Constitution of 1937* made Irish the first official language. The following figures show the numbers returned as Irish-speaking between 1891 and 1946. Irish-speaking in this context means those who speak both Irish and English. The figures in parentheses give the percentage of the whole population of the twenty-six-county area of what is now the Irish Republic.

1891	664,387	(19.2)
1901	619,710	(19.2)
1911	533,717	(17.6)
1926	543,511	(18.3)

aged 3 and over

1926	540,802	(19.3)
1936	666,601	(23.7)

(Gaeltacht area: population 426,685 of which 238,338 were Irish-speaking.)

1946	588,725	(21.2)

(Gaeltacht area: population 398,202 of whom 192,963 were Irish-speaking.)

The following figures give the population of the Gaeltacht as defined in the Gaeltacht Areas Order (1956): *1956* 85,703; *1961* 78,524; *1966* 73,630; *1971* 70,568.

GAELTARRA ÉIREANN. *See* Gaeltachtai.

GAFFNEY, REV. HENRY (1896–1974). Clergyman (R.C.), dramatist and novelist; b. Cuffe's Grange, Co. Kilkenny; ed. CBS, Kilkenny, Dominican College, Newbridge, Lisbon and Rome. Following his ordination in Rome (1923) he ministered in a variety of Dominican Houses in Ireland. The family of Patrick Pearse* commissioned him to dramatise the Pearse stories which were published as *The Stories of Patrick Pearse.* He was commissioned by the literary executors of Canon Patrick A. Sheehan* to complete the Canon's last novel, *Tristram Lloyd* (1928). His popular novel, *The Boys of Ben Edair*, was based on his altar boys at St Saviour's Church, Dublin. Fr Gaffney was the author of a number of religious plays for Radio Eireann and published lives of noted Dominicans. He was editor of *The Irish Rosary*.

GAIETY THEATRE. Opened in South King Street, Dublin, 27 November 1871 by the Gunn brothers, John and Michael. The architect was C. J. Phipps. The theatre was completed in the short period of twenty-six weeks from the laying of the first stone. Goldsmith's *She Stoops to Conquer* shared opening billing with the burlesque *La Bella Sauvage* performed by Mrs John Wood's company.

'GAIRLOCH FORMULA'. During the talks between Eamon de Valera,* President of Dail Eireann and David Lloyd George,* the British Prime Minister, (14–21 July 1921), a state of deadlock had been reached. De Valera wanted an independent Irish Republic whereas Lloyd George would offer no more than Dominion Home Rule. The 'formula' was a response to a letter dated 12 September 1921, from de Valera, which was delivered to Lloyd George while on a fishing holiday at Gairloch, in Scotland. The letter, which was released for publication, stated that Ireland had 'formally declared its independence and recognises itself as a sovereign state'. The formula which Lloyd George then proposed was delivered 29–30 September. It stated that the British government could not afford to recognise the independence and sovereignty of Ireland. It went on to say: 'The proposals which we have already made have been taken by the whole world as proof that our endeavours for reconciliation and settlement are no empty form, and we feel that conference not correspondence is the most practical and hopeful way to an understanding such as we ardently desire to achieve. We, therefore, send you herewith a fresh invitation to a conference in London on October 11th, where we can meet your delegates as spokesmen of the people whom you represent with a view to ascertaining how the association of Ireland with the community of nations known as the British Empire may best be reconciled with Irish national aspirations'. This last sentence became the basis for the talks which commenced between an Irish delegation led by Arthur Griffith* and Michael Collins* and the British delegation led by Lloyd George in October 1921. As a result of these discussions, the Treaty* was signed on 6 December 1921.

GALE. A 'gale', derived from the word *gavelkind*, was the twice-yearly payment of rent. During the eighteenth century and for most of the following century, rents were high and the *gale-day*, the day upon which the rent fell due, assumed great importance for the Irish peasant. Non-payment led to an increase in his debts and could lead eventually to eviction. A *hanging-gale* was an arrears of rent, of which Edward Wakefield observed in 1812, 'The hanging-gale is one of the greatest levers of oppression by which the lower classes are kept in a kind of perpetual bondage . . . this debt hangs over their heads like a load, and keeps them in a continuous state of anxiety and terror'.

GALLAGHER, FRANK (1893–1962). Journalist and author (under the pen-name 'David Hogan'); b. Cork; ed. locally. A member of the Irish Volunteers,* he worked under Robert Erskine Childers* on the publicity staff of the first Dail Eireann.* During the War of Independence,* he was several times imprisoned and went on hunger-strikes (the longest for forty-one days and the shortest for three). He edited the *Irish Bulletin* (1920–22). When Eamon de Valera* founded the *Irish Press* in 1931 Gallagher became editor and later that year was imprisoned under emergency legislation introduced by W. T. Cosgrave. Until he became Director of the Government Information Bureau (*see* Government Information Services) in 1940, he worked as Deputy Director of Radio Eireann. From 1954 he was on the staff of the National Library.* His works include a journal of his hunger-strikes, *Days of Fear* (1928), *Four Glorious Years* (1953), an account of the War of Independence, and *Indivisible Island* (1957), a history of partition in Ireland.

GALLAGHER, PATRICK ('PADDY THE COPE') (1873–1966). Co-operative pioneer; b. in the Rosses, Co. Donegal. He had to leave school at the age of nine to augment the family budget. His first employer was a Strabane farmer who paid him £3 for six months work. As a youth he went to Scotland for the potato-picking season and there had his first experience of the co-operative system. He returned to Donegal with the intention of establishing a co-operative in his native parish. While he had the support of the Co-Operative Movement* he had to overcome intensive resistance from 'middlemen' in his own area. He was supported in his efforts by George Russell* ('AE'). He started the Templecrone Co-Op Society with capital of £1.75p in 1906 and had a turnover in the first year of £490; by 1975 this had reached £1,170,000. His nickname was a mispronunciation of 'Co-Op'. His autobiography, *My Story* (1939), is an eminently readable account of his early life and the seemingly insurmountable obstacles which he encountered in attaining his objective.

GALLAGHER, DR THOMAS (1851–1925). Fenian dynamiter; b. Glasgow. He went to the USA where he became a prominent member of the Fenians and directed training for the Dynamiters.* His students included Thomas J. Clarke* who accompanied him to England in March 1883. Gallagher was unaware that they were under surveillance by the British Secret Service. He was arrested with Clarke and others on 4 April and sentenced to life imprisonment as a 'Treason-Felon'* and treated so harshly under the 'special' conditions for those sentenced under this category that he became deranged. Agitation over his treatment led to his release in 1896. He returned to New York where he died in a sanatorium without ever having recovered his sanity.

GALLICANISM. Gallicanism, the idea which upholds the partial autonomy of the national Catholic Church, was commonly found in the Irish hierarchy in the first half of the nineteenth century. It was propagated in the writings of Dr Lewis Delahogue, Professor of Moral Theology at St Patrick's College, Maynooth, from 1798. When he resigned the Chair in 1820 he was succeeded by Dr John MacHale* who, as Archbishop of Tuam (1834—81), was the outstanding example of an Irish Gallican. Another leading Gallican was Fr Patrick Lavelle* who was several times protected by Dr MacHale from Dr Paul Cullen,* the leading Ultramontanist.

From the time of his arrival in Ireland as Archbishop of Armagh (1849—52), Cullen made strenuous efforts to combat Gallicanism in the hierarchy. Before Cullen's time the majority of Irish bishops had been products of Maynooth, an institution which he viewed with apprehension. Under his influence, as Archbishop of Dublin (1852—78) the complexion of the hierarchy changed until only half of the bishops had a Maynooth background. Ultramontanism* became a feature of the Irish hierarchy in the second part of the nineteenth century.

A residue of Gallicanism remained, as was evident during the Land War* when priests were found supporting the Land League* and the Plan of Campaign,* particularly in the south where they took their lead from the Archbishop of Cashel, Dr Thomas William Croke.*

GANLY, PATRICK (1809—99). Geologist; b. Dublin; ed. TCD. He was employed on the Boundary Survey and General Valuation of Ireland. His correspondence with Sir Richard John Griffith* formed the basis for the latter's revision of the *Geological Map of Ireland*. Three manuscript volumes of Ganly's letters are in the Valuation Office, Dublin. In a paper read before the Geological Society of Dublin in 1856 he first put forward the method of current-bedding to determine the orientation of strata.

GARDA SIOCHANA. 'Guardians of the Peace'; unarmed police force established in the Autumn of 1922

under the title 'Civic Guards'; on 31 July, on a motion by Cathal O'Shannon,* the name was changed to Garda Siochana. The first Commissioner was Michael Staines* who was succeeded in September 1922 by General Eoin O'Duffy.* The force had an initial strength of 4,000 which, by the Garda Siochana Act (1924), was raised to 6,300. This consisted of one Commissioner, five Supervising Officers, twenty-seven Chief Superintendents, 150 Inspectors and Superintendents, 1,200 Sergeants and 4,918 Gardai. The Garda Siochana Act of 1958 provided for the entry of women into the force and by 1974 there were twenty Ban Gardai stationed in the larger towns. The Garda Training Depot is in Templemore, Co. Tipperary. In 1977 the force consisted of one Commissioner, two Deputy Commissioners, four Assistant Commissioners, one Surgeon, thirty-eight Chief Superintendents, forty Superintendents, 188 Inspectors, 300 Station Sergeants, 1,500 Sergeants and 6,742 Gardai. There is a Technical Bureau in Dublin Castle which oversees criminal records, fingerprinting, mapping, photographic department, ballistics and investigation.

GARRETT, JAMES R. (1818—55). Ornithologist; b. Belfast. Under the will of Lord Kelvin* he and Robert Patterson were entrusted with the completion of Thompson's *Natural History of Ireland* (1849—50).

GATE THEATRE. Founded in 1928 by Hilton Edwards* and Micheál MacLiammóir.* Its policy, to provide Ireland with the best of international drama as well as non-peasant drama by Irish writers in both English and Irish, was similar to that of the Dublin Drama League* which it replaced. Each play was to have a one-week run. The first production was of Ibsen's *Peer Gynt* on 14 October 1928. Until 1930 the company played at the Peacock Theatre attached to the Abbey Theatre.* The Concert Rooms of the Rotunda were leased in 1930 with funds provided by public subscription and a limited company was formed with Edwards as Managing Director. The first production at the new premises was Goethe's *Faust*. Lord Longford* became a director in 1931 and his company, after the foundation of Longford Productions in 1936, leased the premises for six months annually. Edwards and MacLiammóir performed at the Gate as well as producing, directing and, in MacLiammóir's case, writing and designing. Among the actors who worked with the company were Coralie Carmichael, Geraldine Fitzgerald, James Mason, Gearoid Ó Lochlainn and Orson Welles. Early productions mounted at the Gate included works by Shakespeare, W. B. Yeats,* George Bernard Shaw,* Aeschylus, Ibsen, Sheridan, Cocteau, Strindberg, Chekhov, Elmer Rice, Gertrude Stein and MacLiammóir.

GAYNOR, REV. EDWARD (1850–1936). Clergyman (R.C.) and musician; b. Moate, Co. Westmeath. ed. Athlone, Castleknock and Ballina. He spent his early ministry in Sheffield where he founded the very successful Sheffield Choral Union. He returned to Ireland and ministered in Cork where he re-organised the Vincentian Choir to include female voices. Though not noted for his preaching, his Sunday's Well church in Cork was packed to capacity every Sunday to hear the seventy-strong choir which he energetically conducted from the pulpit. He composed several motets of which *Pauperes Sion, Anima Christi* and *Panis Angelicus* were the most popular. He also edited a hymnal consisting of 201 hymns, which included twenty-nine compositions and seventy-six of his own arrangements.

GENERAL ASSOCIATION. *See* O'Connell, Daniel.

GENERAL STRIKE. *See* Lock-Out of 1913.

GEOGHEGAN, ARTHUR GERALD (1810–89). Poet and antiquarian;

b. Dublin. He entered the excise service in 1830 and was later Surveying General Examiner (1854) and collector of Inland Revenue (1857). His poetry was signed with three asterisks although *The Nation** (21 August 1852) noted that he also signed his work with the figure of a hand. An early member of the Kilkenny Archaeological Society, he was a frequent contributor to its journal as well as to *The Nation* and to *The Irish Monthly*.* His long narrative poem 'The Monks of Kilcrea' appeared anonymously in *Scraps of Irish History* (1858). He settled in London in 1869 and exhibited his vast collection of antiquities.

GEORGE III (1738–1820). King of Great Britain and Ireland (1760–1820); b. London; ed. privately. At the outset of his reign he ordered that the Lord Lieutenant* should reside continuously in Ireland. There was widespead discontent among the Irish peasantry who suffered from the remnants of the Penal Laws, from high rents, taxes and tithes;* this discontent manifested itself in the rise of secret agrarian societies such as the Whiteboys'.* Towards the end of the eighteenth century the demand for Catholic Emancipation* caused him great uneasiness as he brooded over the consistency of Emancipation with his coronation oath. The advice generally given him was that Emancipation would not be inconsistent with the oath but he continued to oppose it and any measure of Catholic relief. The insurrection of the United Irishmen* in 1798 convinced him, as well as his Prime Minister William Pitt* of the necessity for a legislative Union between Ireland and England but he refused to assent to Pitt's proposition that Union be accompanied by Catholic Emancipation. His refusal on this led to Pitt's resignation (5 February 1801). The King became insane (February–March) and Pitt gave an undertaking that he would not raise the question of Catholic relief. The King again became deranged in 1810 and was permanently incapacitated from 1811 onwards. The Prince of Wales, later George IV,* was Regent until 1820.

GEORGE IV (1762–1830). King of Great Britain and Ireland (1820–30); b. London, son of George III;* ed. privately. In 1811 his father was declared permanently insane and he became Regent. Although he had earlier supported Catholic Emancipation,* he now urged the suppression of the Catholic Committee* and was as opposed to Catholic relief as his father had been. He influenced the defeat of the Catholic Relief Bill introduced by Henry Grattan* in 1819. After ascending the throne he made an official visit to Ireland (May–September 1821) when Daniel O'Connell* was among those who attended on him to demonstrate their loyalty. The King resolutely refused the proposal for Emancipation put forward by the Duke of Wellington* and Sir Robert Peel* after O'Connell's victory in the Clare by-election in 1828. There were fears that he might become insane under the pressure which the prospect of Emancipation appeared to place upon him. However, he announced in January 1829 that a measure of Catholic relief would be introduced, and then declared on 1 March that he would rather abdicate than concede it. Three days later he informed Wellington and Peel that he had never understood that Emancipation would mean the repeal of the Oath of Supremacy and so he could not agree to it. When Wellington and Peel tendered their resignations, he gave in. It was in deference to his wishes that O'Connell had to contest Clare a second time before he could take his seat.

GEORGE V (1865–1936). King of Great Britain and Ireland and Emperor of India (1910–36); b. London; ed. privately. He became King at the height of the battle between H. H. Asquith* and the House of Lords but avoided involvement in it (*see* Parliament Act of 1911). The deadlock between the Ulster Unionists and the Irish nationalists over Home Rule* was a source of concern to him and in 1914, in an attempt to overcome the crisis, he persuaded Asquith to hold the Buckingham Palace Conference.* In September 1914 he signed the Government of Ireland Act* which was then suspended for the duration of World War I. On 22 June 1921 he formally opened the parliament of Northern Ireland. In the course of his speech he appealed for an end to the War of Independence,* saying, 'I speak from a full heart when I pray that my coming to Ireland today may prove to be the first step towards an end of strife amongst her peoples, whatever their race or creed. In that hope I appeal to all Irishmen to pause, to stretch out the hand of forbearance and conciliation, to forgive and forget and to join in making for the land which they love a new era of peace, contentment and goodwill'. The King's appeal was followed immediately by an invitation from the Prime Minister, David Lloyd George* to Eamon de Valera* to attend a conference. This was followed by the Truce.*

GERMAN-IRISH SOCIETY. Short-lived society founded in Berlin in January 1916 which contributed 50,000 marks for Sir Roger Casement,* then in Germany to purchase arms for the Irish Volunteers.*

'GERMAN PLOT'. Dublin Castle* announced in May 1918 that evidence had been found that 'certain subjects . . . domiciled in Ireland' had entered into 'treasonable communication with the German enemy'. This came at the height of the Irish campaign to resist conscription (*see* Conscription and Ireland). On 15 May almost the entire leadership of Sinn Fein* was arrested, with the exception of Cathal Brugha* and Michael Collins.* No evidence of such a plot was ever found and its apparent purpose was to discredit the leaders of the anti-conscription campaign and discredit the Sinn Fein movement in the eyes of the American authorities. One result of the arrests was increased support in Ireland for Sinn Fein.

GILBERT, SIR JOHN THOMAS (1829–98). Historian; b. Dublin; ed. Bective College, Dublin, and Prior Park College, Bath. He was a member of the Royal Irish Academy* of which he was Librarian for thirty-four years. Editor of *Contemporary History* (1841–52), he was co-founder with John Henthorn Todd* of the Irish Celtic and Archaeological Society. His attack on the competence of the editors of the *Calendars of Patent and Close Rolls of Chancery in Ireland* in 1863 was subsequently proven justified. He helped to establish the Public Record Office* of which he was secretary from 1867 to 1875. His unique collection of historical and archaeological works passed to the Dublin Corporation after his death. His works include *Calendar of Ancient Records of Dublin up to 1730, Historical Literature of Dublin* (1851) and *The Streets of Dublin* (1852–55), both of which became *History of the City of Dublin* (1861) and *History of the Viceroys of Ireland (down to 1500)* (1865).

GILL, MICHAEL HENRY (1794–1879). Printer and publisher; b. Co. Offaly. Apprenticed to the University Press of TCD, he became its sole lessee in 1842. He purchased in 1856 the stock, copyrights and premises of the Dublin printer, James McGlashan, and founded the publishing house of McGlashan and Gill which produced the monumental *Annals of the Four Masters* in seven volumes between 1849 and 1851 (2nd, edition, 1856). The imprint became M. H: Gill and Son in 1876 and through association with Macmillan of London became Gill and Macmillan in 1968. The company specialises in educational and historical works.

GILL, THOMAS PATRICK (1858–1931). Politician (Nationalist) and civil servant; b. Ballygraigue, Nenagh, Co. Tipperary; ed. CBS, Nenagh and TCD. After editing the *Catholic World* in New York and working as associate editor of the *North American Review* (1883–85) he became MP for South Louth as a member of the Irish Parliamentary Party* (1885–92). He was fund-raising with John Dillon,* William O'Brien* and Timothy Harrington* in America when the crisis over Parnell's leadership occurred in the party. Upon his return he tried to heal the division, failed and resigned. Through his close friendship with Sir Horace Plunkett* he was appointed secretary of the Recess Committee* and later occupied a similar post in the department of Agriculture and Technical Instruction* (1900–23). He was a member of the War Committee for Supply and Distribution of food and materials for agriculture and industry (1914–19), and a member of the General Assembly of the Institute of Agriculture, Rome, President of the Grand Committee on Economic and Social Policy (1920), Chairman of the Free State Central Savings Committee and President of the Irish Technical Education Association (1925–29).

GILMORE, GEORGE (1898–   ). Socialist republican; b. Belfast; ed. locally and Dublin where he lived for most of his life. A member of the Irish Republican Army,* he opposed the Treaty after the War of Independence and was secretary to Sean Lemass* during the Civil War. A member of the Army Council of the IRA, he supported Peader O'Donnell* and Frank Ryan* in their efforts to fuse republicanism and socialism in movements such as Saor Eire* and Republican Congress.* He attempted to secure an agreement with Soviet Russia for the training of IRA officers who were unable to train in the hostile political climate in the Free State. He was frequently imprisoned for republican activities. Gilmore, who led a raid on Mountjoy in March 1926 and rescued nineteen republican prisoners, was sentenced to five years imprisonment after the IRA was outlawed (7 December 1931). While imprisoned, along with his brother Charlie, he led a campaign for political status. They were released on the accession of Fianna Fail* to power in March 1932. Later in the year, he was wounded by police near Kilrush, Co. Clare (14 August). With Frank Ryan and others, he organised a short-lived Citizens' Army in opposition to the orthodox IRA. He described the Republican Congress about which he wrote a pamphlet (1934) as 'an organising centre for anti-imperialist activities on the part of people irrespective of their party or organisational affiliations'.

GINNELL, LAWRENCE (1854–1923). Politician (Nationalist) and writer; b. Co. Westmeath; largely self-educated; called to Irish and English Bars. Popularly known as 'The Member for Ireland' Ginnell was MP for Co. Westmeath from 1906 until 1918. He was an impassioned orator and was several times ejected from the House of Commons for his refusal to follow procedure. He changed his allegiance from the Irish Parliamentary Party* after the Easter Rising of 1916* and joined Sinn Fein* of which he became treasurer. After election for Westmeath to the first Dail Eireann* he became Director of Publicity (April 1919–August 1921). He was imprisoned in May 1919. In August 1922 he acceded to a request from Eamon de Valera* and became the only anti-Treatyite to enter the Dail in August 1922; after demanding the credentials of the Dail he was forcibly removed and became a member of the republican 'Council of State' formed by the 'government' led by de Valera from a remnant of the second Dail (October 1922). He died while in the USA. His writings include *The Brehon Laws* (1894), *The Doubtful Grant of Ireland* (1899) and *Land and Liberty* (1908).

'GIRLCOTTING'. Derived from the word 'boycotting', girlcotting referred to the practice during the Land War* of girls being warned by the Land League* against marrying boycotted farmers.

GLADSTONE, WILLIAM EWART (1809–98). Politician (Liberal-Conservative, Tory and Liberal); b. Liverpool; ed. Eton and Christ Church, Oxford. After entering politics in 1832 as MP for Newart he was aided during the early years by Sir Robert Peel* who appointed him vice-president of the Board of Trade in 1841 (although Gladstone had sought the Chief Secretaryship of Ireland). He became a member of the cabinet two years later but resigned in 1845 over Peel's introduction of the Maynooth Grant which, however, he supported from the backbenches. Returning to office within a short time, as Colonial Secretary, he supported Peel's repeal of the Corn Laws. Before the Famine of 1845–49* Gladstone had said of Ireland, 'Ireland, Ireland! that cloud in the West, that coming storm, that minister of God's retribution upon cruel and inveterate and but half-atoned injustice! Ireland forces upon us these great social and great religious questions – God grant that we may have courage to look them in the face and to work through them'. He was in opposition throughout the period of the Famine. He was Chancellor of the Exchequer from 1852 to 1855 and from 1859 to 1865. As Leader of the Commons in 1865 he opposed the Whigs' attempt to introduce a Reform Bill, which split the party and the government fell. He now took up the cause of Irish grievances. His proposal for the Disestablishment of the Church of Ireland* was opposed by Benjamin Disraeli* and the Conservative government which fell when Gladstone won his resolution that the House go into committee on the issue. After the general election, fought on the sole issue of Disestablishment, Gladstone formed his first administration (1868–74), saying 'My mission is to pacify Ireland'.

Having secured Disestablishment in 1869 he introduced the Land Act of 1870 (*see* Land Acts). Although the Act was considered a failure in its attempt to legalise the Ulster Custom* (or Tenant Right), it initiated a policy which continued in his second administration (1880–85). In 1873 he tackled a further problem, that of suitable university education for Catholics whose needs were not catered for either in the Queen's Colleges* or in the Catholic University.* His Irish University Bill sought to abolish the Queen's College in Galway and amalgamate the other two (Cork and Belfast) along with Trinity College, Dublin, Magee College and the Catholic University into one national, non-sectarian university. It was opposed by all shades of Irish religious and political opinion and led to the fall of his government. During his period in opposition (1874–80) he suggested that the Lord Lieutenancy should be abolished and that the Prince of Wales might become the permanent Viceroy. This proposal did not meet with the approval of Queen Victoria.* During a three-week visit to Ireland in 1877 he met with the Catholic Archbishop of Dublin, Dr Paul Cullen.*

When Gladstone formed his second government in April 1880 Ireland was in the throes of a land agitation led by the Land League.* The Irish executive, led by Lord Cowper* and William Edward Forster,* was determined to resist the League but in 1881 Gladstone conceded the demand for the Ulster Custom and peasant proprietorship (*see* Land Acts). Charles Stewart Parnell* was imprisoned in October and unrest mounted until he and Gladstone came to an understanding in the Kilmainham 'Treaty'* which led to Parnell's release (2 May 1882). The Representation of the People Act of 1884 established universal male household franchise and, with the Redistribution Act, worked in Ireland to the distinct advantage of the Irish Parliamentary Party.* When his government was defeated over the budget in June 1885 Gladstone resigned. He refused to bargain with Parnell

over Home Rule* and the Liberals lost the support of the Irish party which went to the Conservatives. However, Gladstone recovered Irish support when the 'Hawarden Kite'* announced in December that he now favoured Home Rule. The Liberals were not united on Home Rule and Gladstone lost the support of the Whigs and later of Joseph Chamberlain* and the Radicals. Following the defeat of the (first) Home Rule Bill* he went to the country and lost. He was again in opposition, 1886–1892. Upon returning to office in 1892 he introduced his (second) Home Rule Bill* which passed the Commons but was lost in the House of Lords (1893). In 1894 he resigned office and the leadership of the party and retired to his Bible studies.

GLENAVY, 1st BARON (1851–1933). Campbell, James Henry Mussen; lawyer and politician (Unionist) b. Terenure, Co. Dublin; ed. Kingstown School and TCD where he had an outstanding academic career (Senior Moderator and gold medallist in Classics, History, Law and Political Economy). He was called to the Bar in 1878, became QC in 1890 and was Unionist MP for the St Stephen's Green Division of Dublin (1898–1900), and for Dublin University (1903–16). He was Solicitor-General (1901–05), Attorney-General (1905, 1916), Lord Chief Justice (1916–18) and Lord Chancellor of Ireland (1918–21). Created Baron Glenavy in 1921, he was Vice-Chancellor of TCD (1919–31) and first Chairman of the Senate of the Free State (December 1922–28).

GLENTORAN, 1st BARON (1880–1950). Dixon, Herbert; politician (Ulster Unionist); ed. Rugby and Royal Military College, Sandhurst. He served in the Boer War and World War I. First returned to parliament as MP for the Pottinger Division of Belfast at Westminster (1918–21). He was MP for East Belfast (1921–29) upon the creation of the state of

Northern Ireland, and for the Bloomfield Division of Belfast (1929–50). He was Chief Whip (1921–42) and Minister for Agriculture (1941–43), serving under two Prime Ministers, Lord Craigavon* and John Miller Andrews.*

GODKIN, JAMES (1806–79). Writer; b. Gorey, Co. Wexford. Ordained a dissenting minister, he was sent as a missionary among Catholics in Connaught in 1834 by the Irish Evangelical Society. He became a journalist in 1845 and contributed articles on religion and agrarian reform to various periodicals. He founded *The Christian Patriot* in Belfast (1849) and was editor of *The Derry Standard* and Dublin correspondent for the London *Times*. Godkin was active on behalf of the Tenant League* in 1850 and his writings on agrarian reform were widely read and highly influential, as was his writing on Church reform. As a Special Commissioner for *The Times* he travelled Ulster and the south of Ireland making observations on the system of land-holding in different parts of the country. His reflections were published as *The Land War in Ireland* (1870). His other major works included *Ireland and her Churches* (1867) and *Religious History of Ireland; Primitive, Papal and Protestant* (1873). He was awarded a pension by Queen Victoria* for his *Illustrated History of England from 1820 to the death of the Prince Consort.*

GOERTZ, HERMAN (1890–1947). German spy; b. Lubeck. He read law at Heidelberg and was called to the Bar, and won the Iron Cross while serving in Belgium and Russia during World War I. In 1935 he joined the Luftwaffe and was imprisoned in England for espionage (1935–39). Goertz returned to Germany upon release and was transferred to the Abwehr in January 1940. He was sent to Ireland on 5 May 1940 and was contacted by the Irish Republican Army* shortly afterwards. His Dublin contact was raided and sentenced to five years imprisonment under the Emergency Powers Act, 1940.* While hiding out in Dublin, Goertz came to the conclusion that the IRA would be of little practical use to Germany. He was arrested on 27 November and interned in Athlone Prison until September 1946. He moved to Dublin where he became secretary of the 'Save the German Children Fund' until his re-arrest on 12 April 1947, along with former German prisoners for deportation in accordance with an Allied request to Ireland. On 23 May he committed suicide in a Dublin police-station.

GOGARTY, OLIVER ST JOHN (1878–1957). Surgeon, poet, wit, author and Senator; b. Dublin; ed. Stonyhurst and TCD; M.D. (1907). During his student days he was a close associate of James Joyce* with whom he shared a Martello tower in Sandycove (September 1904). Joyce later used him as a model for Buck Mulligan in *Ulysses*. He established a successful practice as a throat surgeon and was also a celebrated sportsman, motor-cyclist, archer and aviator. During the Civil War he was kidnapped by republicans and escaped by plunging into the Liffey (December 1922). He was a member of the Senate (1922–36). Disillusioned with Ireland, he spent his later years in the USA. His wide range of literary friends included W. B. Yeats,* George Moore* and George Russell.* His works include *Poems and Plays* (1920), *An Offering of Swans* (1924), *As I Was Going Down Sackville Street* (1937), *Others to Adorn* (1938), *I Follow St Patrick* (1938), *Elbow Room* (1939), and *It isn't This Time of Year at All* (1954, autobiography).

GOMBEEN MEN. Sometimes called 'meal-mongers', the 'gombeen men' were generally people with average-sized farms who accumulated a small amount of capital which they loaned out at high interest-rates. The name 'gombeen' meant usurer and he sold meat or potatoes at the top price during times of scarcity. More frequently they loaned money to people in desperate circumstances, who would be unlikely to be in a position to repay the full amount for a lengthy period. In his *Letters on the Condition of the People of Ireland* (1846) Thomas Campbell Foster recalled that he had been given an instance of a gombeen man who made a loan of £1 at an interest rate of 50 per cent per month or 600 per cent per annum. As many of the peasants were chronically short of cash gombeen men were found in nearly every rural community. If the loan was not repaid he could bring ruin upon his creditor by seizing his property. Many gombeen men also acted as landlords' agents or middlemen.*

GONNE MacBRIDE, MAUD (1866– 1953). Nationalist and suffragette; b. near Aldershot where her father, a British Army officer, was stationed; ed. privately. Her early life was divided between Dublin, London and Paris where her lover, Millevoye, edited *La Patrie*. John O'Leary* introduced her to Fenianism (1886) and to W. B. Yeats* (1889). For a time she supported the Irish Republican Brotherhood* but later became dissatisfied with its lack of an aggressive policy. She was influenced by Arthur Griffith* and James Connolly.* During the famine of the 1890s in Donegal and Mayo she led peasant agitation over the land system. A prominent member of the Amnesty Association* which agitated for the release of treason-felons* held in Portland prison, she organised counter-attractions to loyalist celebrations for the jubilee of Queen Victoria.* She visited the USA in 1897 on behalf of the 1898 Centenary Celebrations.* A member of Cumann na nGaedheal,* the Irish Transvaal Committee which organised support for the Boers, and of the National Council,* Maud Gonne founded the republican-suffragette organisation, Inghinidhe na hÉireann,* at Easter 1900. With James

Connolly she organised protests against the visit of Queen Victoria and again visited the USA to gather support for the Boers (1900 and 1901). In 1902 she took the lead in Yeats' *Cathleen ni Houlihan.*

Griffith introduced her to Major John MacBride* (1900) to whom she was married in Paris (1903). When the marriage broke up within a few years she became unpopular in Ireland and took up residence in Paris while MacBride returned to Dublin. She edited a news sheet for Irish causes, *L'Irlande Libre*, and contributed to *Bean na hÉireann* (The Irishwoman). Her writings advocated physical force as a method of achieving Irish independence. Following MacBride's execution for his part in the Easter Rising of 1916,* she returned in 1917 and a year later was imprisoned during the German Plot* series of arrests. She contrived to escape from Holloway prison. During the War of Independence* she worked for the White Cross* and, having opposed the Treaty,* founded the Women's Defence League. For the rest of her life she supported the republican movement. Imprisoned during the Civil War,* she went on hunger-strike and was released after twenty days (January 1923). She supported her son, Sean MacBride,* in his attempts to establish constitutional-republican parties, Cumann Poblachta na hÉireann,* Comhairle na Poblachta* and Clann na Poblachta.*

Her autobiography, *A Servant of the Queen*, was published in 1938.

GOODMAN, CANON JAMES (1829– 96). Musician; b. Dingle, Co. Kerry; ed. TCD. Ordained in 1851, he became Professor of Irish in TCD in 1879. Between 1884 and 1896 he collaborated with James Harnett Murphy translating St Luke into Irish. He translated *St Patrick's Breastplate* from ancient to modern Irish – it was set to music by Sir Robert Stewart in 1888 and later by Sir Charles Stanford.* While a curate at Ardgroom, Castletownbere, Co. Cork (1858–66) he was visited by the most famous of the Kerry musicians, including the blind Dingle fiddler, Thomas Kennedy. He collected over 1,000 tunes which he sent in four volumes to Patrick Weston Joyce.* Dr Douglas Hyde,* after hearing him perform on the uileann pipes, described him as 'the best piper I have ever heard'.

GOOLD, THOMAS (c. 1766–1846). Lawyer; b. Cork; ed. TCD. After a career of dissipation which cost him £10,000 he settled down to the study of law and was called to the Bar in 1791. He opposed the Union and his *Address to the People of Ireland on the subject of the Proposed Union* (1799) was widely read. After the Union he was a very prominent member of the legal profession and was appointed Master in Chancery in 1832.

GORDON, LT COL. SIR ALEXANDER ROBERT GISBORNE (1882–1967). Soldier and politician (Ulster Unionist); b. Co. Down; ed. Rugby and Sandhurst Military College; he was commissioned in the Royal Irish Regiment (1901) and served in World War I. After retiring in 1921 he was recommissioned as a Major (1940–42). He was MP for East Down (1929–49), Minister in the Senate (1951–61) and Speaker of the Northern Ireland parliament (1961–64).

GORDON, REV. JAMES BENTLEY (c. 1749–1819). Clergyman (C.I.) and historian; b. Neeve Hall, Derry; ed. TCD and ordained in 1773. He held the living of Canaway, Co. Cork (1796) and was Rector at Killegney, Co. Wexford (1799). His works included *Terraques or a New System of Geography and Modern History* (4 vols, 1790–98), *A History of the Rebellion of 1798* (1801) to which he was an eye-witness, *A History of Ireland* (1805), and *An Historical and Geographical Memoir of the North American Continent* (1820).

GORE-BOOTH, CONSTANCE. *See* Markievicz, Countess.

GORE-BOOTH, EVA SELENA (1870–1926). Suffragette and poet; b. Lisadell House, Sligo, sister of Constance (*see* Markievicz, Countess). She emigrated to Manchester in 1897 and became involved in trade unionism and the fight for women's franchise. She was soon recognised as a writer on political and economic subjects. Her first book, *Poems* (1898), was greeted by William Butler Yeats* as a work of 'poetic feeling . . . and great promise'. Her work appeared in *The Irish Homestead,* and *New Ireland Review.** One of her best known works was 'The Little Waves of Breffni' which appeared in *The One and The Many* (1904). Other works were *The Three Resurrections and the Triumph of Maeve* (1905), *The Agate Lamp* (1912), *The Perilous Light* (1915), *Broken Glory* (1918) and *The House of Three Windows* (1926). A complete edition of her works was published in 1929, edited by her friend and fellow suffragist, Esther Roper.

GOSSOON. From the French word 'garcon', he was a small boy who was at the beck and call of the butler and cook in an Irish household. When serving as messenger boys, some of them are recorded to have covered over fifty miles on foot in a surprisingly quick time.

GOUGH, GENERAL SIR HUBERT DE LA POER (1870–1963). Soldier; b. London, he was reared in India until he was seven; ed. privately in India; Laleham, Eton and Versailles. After entering the Royal Military College, Sandhurst (1887) he was gazetted as a 2nd Lieutenant in the 16th Lancers (1889) and served in India and South Africa when he saw action at the relief of Ladysmith (28 February 1900). Known popularly as 'Goughie' since his Sandhurst days, he was the youngest Brigadier-General in the army while serving in Ireland. Gough was an accomplished horseman, riding thirty-one races and being placed in twenty-eight of them during an eighteen months' spell.

When the War Office ordered General Sir Arthur Paget* to prepare to protect arms' depots in Ulster, Gough led the 'mutiny' of the officers at the Curragh (March 1914), travelling to London where, after a meeting with General Sir Henry Wilson,* he succeeded in having the original order revoked (*see* Curragh Incident). He later served on the Western Front.

GOULBURN, HENRY (1784–1856). Politician (Conservative) and Chief Secretary (1821–27); b. London; ed. Trinity College, Cambridge; B.A. (1805) and M.A. (1808). He entered parliament in 1808 and became Under-Secretary at the Home Office two years later. His appointment under Richard Colley Wellesley* was unpopular in Ireland because of his earlier opposition to the Catholic Disability Removal Bill. Within two years he was confronted by the national agitation for Catholic Emancipation organised by the Catholic Association* under Daniel O'Connell. In 1823 he introduced the Irish Tithe Composition Act (*see* Tithes). His Act of February 1825 (Goulburn's Act*) to suppress unlawful societies failed in its purpose as O'Connell simply changed the name of the Catholic Association to the New Catholic Association and continued the agitation. He supported the Duke of Wellington* and Sir Robert Peel* in their opposition to the grant of Emancipation. He was later Home Secretary under Peel (1834–35) and Chancellor of the Exchequer (1841–46).

GOULBURN'S ACT (1825). The Act was introduced by the Chief Secretary, Henry Goulburn,* in an attempt to suppress the Catholic Association.* Under the Act, political associations of more than fourteen days' duration were outlawed. Daniel O'Connell* circumvented the Act by changing the name of the Association to the New Catholic Association. When it expired in 1827 the Act had failed in its purpose.

GOVERNMENT INFORMATION SERVICES. Founded in 1934 as the Government Information Bureau attached to the Department of the President of the Executive Council. The GIS, as it was known after 1973, is attached now to the Department of the Taoiseach. The first Director was Shan O'Cuiv* (1934–40) who was succeeded by Frank Gallagher.* The title of Director was later changed to that of Head of the GIS. The function of the GIS is to facilitate communication between the government, departments of state and the general public. It provides official documents to the media as well as news, arranges press conferences for Ministers and officials, briefs correspondents on the background to official statements and interprets public feeling to government departments. It co-operates with the Department of Foreign Affairs in disseminating information abroad.

GOVERNMENT OF IRELAND ACT, 1920. Known as the 'Better Government of Ireland Act', it repealed the 1914 Home Rule Act in an attempt to satisfy the nationalist demand for Home Rule.* At the time of its passage the War of Independence* had started. The Act attempted to find a compromise solution to the Irish question by granting a large measure of Home Rule to the 'south' while making the six north-eastern counties of Ulster (Londonderry, Tyrone, Fermanagh, Antrim, Down and Armagh) a separate state of Northern Ireland within the United Kingdom. The powers granted under the Act were similar to those granted under the (third) Home Rule Bill* but with the addition that partition was conceded. A Northern Ireland parliament would sit in Belfast and a parliament of Southern Ireland would meet and legislate for the south. In addition, a Council of Ireland* was to be established to consider questions of common concern. Forty-two Irish members would sit at Westminster where imperial matters would be dealt with. Elections under the Act were held in May 1921. In the north forty out of fifty-two seats were won by the Ulster Unionists* and on 22 June King George V* formally opened the parliament of Northern Ireland. In the south, however, the Act was virtually ignored. Elections were held in May but were boycotted by Sinn Fein* which used the occasion to return members to Dail Eireann; no Sinn Fein candidate was opposed. Four Unionists representing the University of Dublin, Trinity College, were elected for that constituency but as they were the only members present, the parliament of Southern Ireland was adjourned. It met once more to dissolve itself and hand its powers over to the Provisional Government.* *See also* Treaty.

GOVERNMENTS OF IRELAND 1919–1977.

This entry lists the governments of the twenty-six county area known successively as the Irish Free State, Eire and the Republic of Ireland. For governments of Northern Ireland, see separate entry on Northern Ireland.

First Dail Eireann
1. 21 January– 1 April 1919
Sinn Fein
C. Brugha (President)
E. MacNeill (Finance)
M. Collins (Home Affairs)
Count Plunkett (Foreign Affairs)
R. Mulcahy (National Defence)

2. 1 April 1919–26 August 1921
E. de Valera (President)
A. Griffith (Home Affairs)
M. Collins (Finance)
C. Brugha (Defence)
W. T. Cosgrave (Local Government)
Count Plunkett (Foreign Affairs)
E. MacNeill (Industries)
Countess Markievicz (Labour)
Ernest Blythe (Trade and Commerce)
S. O'Kelly (Irish)
Non-Cabinet Members
S. Etchingham (Fisheries, from 29 June 1920)
R. C. Barton (Agriculture)
L. Ginnell (Publicity)

Second Dail Eireann
1. 26 August 1921–9 January 1922
Sinn Fein
E. de Valera (President)
A. Griffith (Foreign Affairs)
M. Collins (Finance)
C. Brugha (Defence)
W. T. Cosgrave (Local Government)
A. Stack (Home Affairs)
R. C. Barton (Economic Affairs)
Non-Cabinet Members
K. O'Higgins (Assistant, Local Government)
Countess Markievicz (Labour)
E. Blythe (Trade and Commerce)
S. Etchingham (Fisheries)
J. J. O'Kelly (Education)
D. Fitzgerald (Publicity)
Count Plunkett (Fine Arts)
A. O'Connor (Agriculture; Deputy, Economic Affairs from 14 October 1921)

2. 10 January–9 September 1922
Sinn Fein
A. Griffith (President; Foreign Affairs from 25 July; died on 12 August)
M. Collins (Finance; killed on 22 August)
W. T. Cosgrave (Local Government)
K. O'Higgins (Economic Affairs)
R. Mulcahy (Defence)
G. Gavan Duffy (Foreign Affairs until 25 July)
M. Hayes (Foreign Affairs from 12 August; non-Cabinet member as Minister for Education)
E. Duggan (Home Affairs)
Non-Cabinet Members
E. Blythe (Trade)
J. McGrath (Labour)
D. Fitzgerald (Publicity)
P. Hogan (Agriculture)
M. Staines (Director of Belfast Boycott, January–February)

Provisional Government
1. January–August 1922
Sinn Fein
M. Collins (Chairman and Minister for Finance)
E. Duggan (Home Affairs)
W. T. Cosgrave (Local Government)
J. McGrath (Labour)
K. O'Higgins (Economic Affairs)

F. Lynch (Education)
P. Hogan (Agriculture)
J. J. Walsh (Postmaster-General, from 22 April)
E. MacNeill (without portfolio)
Non-Cabinet Member
H. Kennedy (Law Officer)

2. August–6 December 1922
Sinn Fein
Following the death of Michael Collins (22 August 1922) W. T. Cosgrave became Chairman and Minister for Finance. The other members of the government were:
D. Fitzgerald (External Affairs)
K. O'Higgins (Home Affairs)
R. Mulcahy (National Defence)
E. Blythe (Local Government)
J. McGrath (Labour, Industry and Commerce and Economic Affairs)
E. MacNeill (Education)
P. Hogan (Agriculture)
J. J. Walsh (Postmaster-General)
Non-Cabinet Member
H. Kennedy (Law Officer)

From 6 December 1922 until 29 December 1937, the governments of the Irish Free State were known as the Executive Councils.

1. 6 December 1922–21 September 1923
Sinn Fein
W. T. Cosgrave (President and Minister for Finance)
K. O'Higgins (Home Affairs)
E. MacNeill (Education)
R. Mulcahy (Defence)
J. McGrath (Industry and Commerce)
D. Fitzgerald (External Affairs)
E. Blythe (Local Government)
E. Duggan (without portfolio, to 14 December)
Non-Cabinet Members
J. J. Walsh (Postmaster-General)
P. Hogan (Agriculture)
F. Lynch (Fisheries, from 14 December)
H. Kennedy (Attorney-General).

2. 21 September 1923–23 June 1927
Cumann na nGaedheal
During the period in office of this Executive Council the nomenclature

of some departments changed. In 1924 the office of Postmaster-General was changed to the Minister of Posts and Telegraphs; Home Affairs became Justice; Local Government became Local Government and Public Health and Agriculture became Lands and Agriculture (until 1928).
W. T. Cosgrave (President; Minister for Defence from 19 March until 20 November 1924)
K. O'Higgins (Vice-President and Minister for Justice)
E. Blythe (Finance)
R. Mulcahy (Defence, until 19 March 1924)
P. Hughes (Defence, from 24 November 1924)
D. Fitzgerald (External Affairs)
J. McGrath (Industry and Commerce, until 7 March 1924)
E. MacNeill (Education, until 24 November 1925)
J. M. O'Sullivan (Education, from 24 November 1925)
P. McGilligan (Industry and Commerce, from 7 March 1924)

Not members of the Executive Council
J. J. Walsh (Posts and Telegraphs)
P. Hogan (Lands and Agriculture)
F. Lynch (Fisheries)
J. A. Burke (Local Government and Public Health)
H. Kennedy (Attorney-General, until 5 June 1924)
J. O'Byrne (Attorney-General, 5 June 1924–9 January 1926)
J. A. Costello (Attorney-General, from 9 January 1926)

3. 23 June–12 October 1927
Cumann na nGaedheal
W. T. Cosgrave (President and Minister for Justice from 10 July)
K. O'Higgins (Vice-President; Minister for Justice and for External Affairs until his death on 10 July)
E. Blythe (Finance; Vice-President from 10 July)
D. Fitzgerald (Defence)
P. McGilligan (Industry and Commerce)
P. Hogan (Lands and Agriculture)

J. J. Walsh (Posts and Telegraphs)
F. Lynch (Fisheries)
J. M. O'Sullivan (Education)
R. Mulcahy (Local Government and
Public Health)
*Not a member of the Executive
Council*
J. A. Costello (Attorney-General)

4. 12 October 1927–9 March 1932
Cumann na nGaedheal
In 1928 Lands and Agriculture re-
verted to its former title of Agri-
culture, and Fisheries became Lands
and Fisheries.
W. T. Cosgrave (President)
E. Blythe (Vice-President; Minister
for Finance and Posts and
Telegraphs)
J. Fitzgerald Kenny (Justice)
D. Fitzgerald (Defence)
P. McGilligan (External Affairs and
Industry and Commerce)
P. Hogan (Agriculture)
F. Lynch (Lands and Fisheries)
J. M. O'Sullivan (Education)
R. Mulcahy (Local Government and
Public Health)
*Not a member of the Executive
Council*
J. A. Costello (Attorney-General)

5. 9 March 1932–8 February 1933
Fianna Fail
E. de Valera (President and
External Affairs)
S. T. O'Kelly (Vice-President and
Local Government and Public
Health)
S. MacEntee (Finance)
S. Lemass (Industry and Commerce)
J. Geoghegan (Justice)
F. Aiken (Defence)
J. Ryan (Agriculture)
P. J. Ruttledge (Lands and Fisheries)
J. Connolly (Posts and Telegraphs)
T. Derrig (Education)
*Not a member of the Executive
Council*
C. A. Maguire (Attorney-General)

6. 8 February 1933 to 21 July 1937
Fianna Fail
In 1934 Lands and Fisheries reverted
to its former title of Lands.

E. de Valera (President and External
Affairs)
S. T. O'Kelly (Vice-President and
Local Government and Public
Health)
S. MacEntee (Finance)
S. Lemass (Industry and Commerce)
P. J. Ruttledge (Justice)
F. Aiken (Defence; Lands from
29 June to 11 November 1936)
J. Ryan (Agriculture)
J. Connolly (Lands until 29 May
1936)
T. Derrig (Education)
G. Boland (Posts and Telegraphs to
11 November 1936; then Lands)
O. Traynor (Posts and Telegraphs
from 11 November 1936)
*Not members of the Executive
Council*
C. A. Maguire (Attorney-General to
2 November 1936)
J. Geoghegan (Attorney-General,
2 November–22 December 1936)
P. Lynch (Attorney-General from
22 December 1936)

7. and 1. 21 July 1937–30 June
1938
Fianna Fail
On 29 December 1937 the Constitu-
tion of Eire* came into operation.
The last Executive Council of the
Free State then became the first
government of Eire (Ireland). The
President of the Executive Council
was replaced by the Taoiseach,* and
his deputy was known as the
Tanaiste.*
E. de Valera (President; after 29
December 1937 known as the
Taoiseach; External Affairs)
S. T. O'Kelly (Vice-President; after
29 December 1937 known as the
Tanaiste; Local Government)
S. MacEntee (Finance)
P. J. Ruttledge (Justice)
F. Aiken (Defence)
S. Lemass (Industry and Commerce)
J. Ryan (Agriculture)
T. Derrig (Education)
G. Boland (Lands)
O. Traynor (Posts and Telegraphs)
*Not a member of the Executive
Council or Cabinet*
P. Lynch (Attorney-General)

199

2. 30 June 1938–2 July 1943
Fianna Fail
During the Emergency* created by World War II two new Cabinet posts were created: Minister for Supplies and Minister for Co-ordination of Defensive Measures.

E. de Valera (Taoiseach and External Affairs; Education, 27 September 1939–18 June 1940; Local Government and Public Health, 15–18 August 1941)
S. T. O'Kelly (Tanaiste; Local Government until 8 September 1939; Education, 8–27 September 1939; Finance from 16 September 1939)
S. MacEntee (Finance until 16 September 1939; Industry and Commerce, 16 September 1939–18 August 1941; Local Government and Public Health from 18 August 1941)
P. J. Ruttledge (Justice until 8 September 1939; Local Government and Public Health, 8 September 1939–14 August 1941)
F. Aiken (Defence until 8 September 1939; Minister for Co-ordination of Defensive Measures from 8 September 1939)
S. Lemass (Industry and Commerce until 16 September 1939; Minister for Supplies from 16 September 1939 and also Industry and Commerce again from 18 August 1941)
J. Ryan (Agriculture)
T. Derrig (Education until 8 September 1939; Lands from 8 September 1939; Posts and Telegraphs 8–27 September 1939; Education from 18 June 1940)
G. Boland (Lands until 8 September 1939 and then Justice)
O. Traynor (Posts and Telegraphs until 8 September 1939 and then Defence)
P. J. Little (Posts and Telegraphs from 27 September 1939)
Not members of the Cabinet
P. Lynch (Attorney-General until 1 March 1940)
K. Haugh (Attorney-General from

1 March 1940 to 10 October 1942)
K. Dixon (Attorney-General from 10 October 1942)

3. 2 July 1943–9 June 1944
Fianna Fail
E. de Valera (Taoiseach and External Affairs)
S. T. O'Kelly (Tanaiste and Finance)
G. Boland (Justice)
S. MacEntee (Local Government and Public Health)
S. Lemass (Industry and Commerce and Supplies)
F. Aiken (Co-ordination of Defensive Measures)
O. Traynor (Defence)
J. Ryan (Agriculture)
T. Derrig (Education)
P. J. Little (Posts and Telegraphs)
S. Moylan (Lands)
Not a member of the Cabinet
K. Dixon (Attorney-General)

4. 9 June 1944–18 February 1948
Fianna Fail
The Departments of Supplies and Co-ordination of Defensive Measures were dissolved in 1945 when the war ended. The Emergency, however, continued. In 1947 Local Government and Public Health was divided into two new departments. Local Government and Health. The Department of Social Welfare was created in 1947.
E. de Valera (Taoiseach and External Affairs)
S. T. O'Kelly (Tanaiste and Finance to 16 June 1945 when he became President of the State)
S. Lemass (Industry and Commerce; Supplies to 21 July 1945; Tanaiste from 14 June 1945)
G. Boland (Justice)
F. Aiken (Co-ordination of Defensive Measures to 19 June 1945; Finance from 16 June 1945)
O. Traynor (Defence)
J. Ryan (Agriculture to 21 January 1947 and then Health and Social Welfare)
T. Derrig (Education)
S. MacEntee (Local Government and Public Health to 21 January 1947 and then Local Government)

P. J. Little (Posts and Telegraphs)
S. Moylan (Lands)
P. Smith (Agriculture from 21 January 1947)
Not members of the Cabinet
K. Dixon (Attorney-General to 30 April 1946)
C. O'Dalaigh (Attorney-General from 30 April 1946)

5. 18 February 1948–14 June 1951
First Inter-Party Government
J. A. Costello (Taoiseach; Health from 11 April 1951)
W. Norton (Tanaiste and Social Welfare)
S. MacEoin (Justice to 7 March 1951; Defence from 7 March 1951)
P. J. McGilligan (Finance)
S. MacBride (External Affairs)
D. Morrissey (Industry and Commerce to 7 March 1951; Justice from 7 March 1951)
T. F. O'Higgins (Defence to 7 March 1951; Industry and Commerce from 7 March 1951)
N. Browne (Health to 11 April 1951)
J. Dillon (Agriculture)
R. Mulcahy (Education)
J. Blowick (Lands)
J. Everett (Posts and Telegraphs)
T. J. Murphy (Local Government to 29 April 1949)
M. C. Keyes (Local Government from 29 April 1949)
Not members of the Cabinet
C. Lavery (Attorney-General to 21 April 1951)
C. F. Casey (Attorney-General from 21 April 1951)

6. 13 June 1951–2 June 1954
Fianna Fail
E. de Valera (Taoiseach)
S. Lemass (Tanaiste and Industry and Commerce)
S. MacEntee (Finance)
G. Boland (Justice)
O. Traynor (Defence)
F. Aiken (External Affairs)
J. Ryan (Health and Social Welfare)
T. Derrig (Lands)
P. Smith (Local Government)
S. Moylan (Education)
T. Walsh (Agriculture)
E. Childers (Posts and Telegraphs)

Not members of the Cabinet
C. O'Dalaigh (Attorney-General to 11 July 1953)
T. Teevan (Attorney-General from 11 July 1953)

7. 2 June 1954–12 February 1957
Second Inter-Party Government
The Department of the Gaeltacht was created in July 1956.
J. A. Costello (Taoiseach)
W. Norton (Tanaiste and Industry and Commerce)
S. MacEoin (Defence)
G. Sweetman (Finance)
J. Everett (Justice)
T. F. O'Higgins (Health)
J. Dillon (Agriculture)
R. Mulcahy (Education; Gaeltacht, 2 July–24 October 1956)
J. Blowick (Lands)
M. Keyes (Posts and Telegraphs)
L. Cosgrave (External Affairs)
B. Corish (Social Welfare)
P. O'Donnell (Local Government)
P. J. Lindsay (Gaeltacht from 24 October 1956)
Not a member of the Cabinet
P. McGilligan (Attorney-General)

8. 20 March 1957–23 June 1959
Fianna Fail
Mr de Valera resigned the office of Taoiseach on 17 June 1959 but continued to carry out the duties of the office in accordance with Article 28 (10) and (11) of the Constitution until his successor, Sean Lemass, was appointed on 23 June 1959. De Valera then became President of the State.
E. de Valera (Taoiseach)
S. Lemass (Tanaiste and Industry and Commerce)
J. Ryan (Finance)
O. Traynor (Justice)
K. Boland (Defence)
F. Aiken (External Affairs; Agriculture to 16 May 1957)
P. Smith (Local Government and Social Welfare to 27 November 1957; Agriculture from 27 November 1957)
S. MacEntee (Health; Social Welfare from 27 November 1957)

S. Moylan (Agriculture, 16 May—
16 November 1957)

E. Childers (Lands)

J. Lynch (Education; Gaeltacht to
26 June 1957)

N. Blaney (Posts and Telegraphs to
4 December 1957; Local
Government from 27 November
1957)

M. O'Morain (Gaeltacht from 26
June 1957)

J. Ormonde (Posts and Telegraphs
from 4 December 1957)

Not a member of the Cabinet

A. O'Caoimh (Attorney-General)

9. 23 June 1959—12 October 1961

Fianna Fail

The Department of Transport and
Power was created in July 1959.

S. Lemass (Taoiseach)

S. MacEntee (Tanaiste, Health and
Social Welfare)

J. Ryan (Finance)

O. Traynor (Justice)

K. Boland (Defence)

F. Aiken (External Affairs)

P. Smith (Agriculture)

E. Childers (Lands to 23 July 1959
and Transport and Power from
27 July 1959)

J. Lynch (Industry and Commerce)

N. Blaney (Local Government)

M. O'Morain (Gaeltacht to 23 July
1959; Lands from 23 July 1959)

P. J. Hillery (Education)

G. Bartley (Gaeltacht from 23 July
1959)

M. Hilliard (Posts and Telegraphs)

Not a member of the Cabinet

A. O'Caoimh (Attorney-General)

10. 12 October 1961—21 April 1965

Fianna Fail

S. Lemass (Taoiseach; Justice, 8
October—3 November 1964)

S. MacEntee (Tanaiste and Health)

J. Ryan (Finance)

F. Aiken (External Affairs)

P. Smith (Agriculture to 8 October
1964)

E. Childers (Transport and Power)

J. Lynch (Industry and Commerce)

N. Blaney (Local Government)

M. O'Morain (Lands and the
Gaeltacht)

P. J. Hillery (Education)

M. Hilliard (Posts and Telegraphs)

G. Bartley (Defence)

K. Boland (Social Welfare)

C. Haughey (Justice to 8 October
1964; Agriculture from 8 October
1964)

B. Lenihan (Justice from 3 November
1964)

Not members of the Cabinet

A. O'Caoimh (Attorney-General to
16 March 1965)

C. Condon (Attorney-General from
16 March 1965)

11. 21 April 1965—10 November
1966

Fianna Fail

In July 1965 Agriculture became Agriculture and Fisheries. The Department of Labour was established in
July 1966.

S. Lemass (Taoiseach)

F. Aiken (Tanaiste and External
Affairs)

J. Lynch (Finance)

B. Lenihan (Justice)

M. Hilliard (Defence)

E. Childers (Transport and Power)

C. Haughey (Agriculture and
Fisheries)

P. J. Hillery (Industry and Commerce
to 13 July 1966; Labour from
13 July 1966)

N. Blaney (Local Government)

K. Boland (Social Welfare)

M. O'Morain (Lands and the
Gaeltacht)

J. Brennan (Posts and Telegraphs)

G. Colley (Education to 13 July
1966; Industry and Commerce
from 13 July 1966)

S. Flanagan (Health from 13 July
1966)

D. B. O'Malley (Health to 13 July
1966; Education from 13 July
1966)

Not a member of the Cabinet

C. Condon (Attorney-General)

12. 10 November 1966—2 July 1969

Fianna Fail

Mr Lemass resigned as Taoiseach and
leader of Fianna Fail in November

1966, to be succeeded by Mr Jack Lynch.

J. Lynch (Taoiseach; Education, 10–26 March 1968)
F. Aiken (Tanaiste and External Affairs)
C. Haughey (Finance)
B. Lenihan (Justice to 26 March 1968 and then Education)
K. Boland (Local Government)
N. Blaney (Agriculture and Fisheries)
G. Colley (Industry and Commerce)
E. Childers (Transport and Power, Posts and Telegraphs)
M. O'Morain (Lands and the Gaeltacht to 26 March 1968, then Justice)
D. B. O'Malley (Education to 10 March 1968)
M. Hilliard (Defence)
S. Flanagan (Health)
J. Brennan (Social Welfare)
P. J. Hillery (Labour)
P. Faulkner (Lands and the Gaeltacht from 26 March 1968)
Not a member of the Cabinet
C. Condon (Attorney-General)

13. 2 July 1969–14 March 1973
Fianna Fail
During the course of this government there was a major crisis over Northern Ireland; two ministers, C. Haughey and N. Blaney, were dismissed and two, K. Boland and M. O'Morain, resigned.
In January 1973 Ireland entered the European Economic Community. The Department of External Affairs was renamed Foreign Affairs.
J. Lynch (Taoiseach)
E. Childers (Tanaiste and Health)
C. Haughey (Finance to 6 May 1970)
M. O'Morain (Justice to 4 May 1970)
N. Blaney (Agriculture and Fisheries to 6 May 1970)
K. Boland (Local Government and Social Welfare to 6 May 1970)
P. J. Hillery (External Affairs to 3 January 1973, when he became a Vice-President of the Commission of the European Communities with special responsibility for Social Affairs)
G. Colley (Gaeltacht; Industry and Commerce to 8 May 1970 and then Finance)
B. Lenihan (Transport and Power to 3 January 1973 and then Foreign Affairs)
J. Brennan (Labour to 8 May 1970 and then Labour and Social Welfare)
S. Flanagan (Lands)
P. Faulkner (Education)
J. Gibbons (Defence to 8 May 1970 and then Agriculture and Fisheries)
P. J. Lalor (Posts and Telegraphs to 8 May 1970 and then Industry and Commerce)
R. Molloy (Local Government from 9 May 1970)
D. O'Malley (Justice from 7 May 1970)
G. Cronin (Defence from 9 May 1970)
G. Collins (Posts and Telegraphs from 9 May 1970)
M. O'Kennedy (Without Portfolio, 18 December 1972–3 January 1973, and then Transport and Power)
Not a member of the Cabinet
C. Condon (Attorney-General)

14. 14 March 1973–5 July 1977
Inter-Party National Coalition
On 1 November 1973 a Department of the Public Service was established, under the Minister for Finance. The Gaeltacht became a separate department at the beginning of the government's term. On 8 February 1977 Fisheries was detached from Agriculture to become a separate department also.
L. Cosgrave (Taoiseach; Defence, 2–15 December 1976)
B. Corish (Tanaiste, Health and Social Welfare)
R. Ryan (Finance; and the Public Service from November 1973)
P. Cooney (Justice)
P. S. Donegan (Defence to 1 December 1976; Lands, 2 December 1976–7 February 1977; Fisheries from 8 February 1977).
G. Fitzgerald (Foreign Affairs)
J. Tully (Local Government)

203

M. Clinton (Agriculture and Fisheries to 7 February 1976 and then Agriculture)
M. O'Leary (Labour)
J. Keating (Industry and Commerce)
T. Fitzpatrick (Lands to 1 December 1976 and then Transport and Power)
C. C. O'Brien (Posts and Telegraphs)
R. Burke (Education until 2 December 1976 when he became a Commissioner of the European Communities with responsibility for Taxation, Consumer Affairs, Transport and Relations with the European Parliament)
P. Barry (Transport and Power to 1 December 1976 and then Education)
T. O'Donnell (Gaeltacht)
O. J. Flanagan (Defence from 16 December 1976)
D. Costello (Attorney-General)

15. 5 July 1977–11 December 1979
Fianna Fail
The new government created a Department for Economic Planning and Development. In addition, the titles of three departments were changed: Transport and Power to Tourism and Transport, Local Government to Environment, and Industry and Commerce to Industry, Commerce and Energy. The office of Minister of State, to replace that of Parliamentary Secretary, was created in November 1977. Ministers of State were not to be members of the Cabinet.
J. Lynch (Taoiseach)
G. Colley (Tanaiste, Finance and the Public Service)
G. Collins (Justice)
M. O'Kennedy (Foreign Affairs)
J. Gibbons (Agriculture)
D. O'Malley (Industry, Commerce and Energy)
B. Lenihan (Fisheries)
C. Haughey (Health and Social Welfare)
P. Faulkner (Tourism and Transport, and Posts and Telegraphs)
R. Molloy (Defence)
J. Wilson (Education)

G. Fitzgerald (Labour)
D. Gallagher (Gaeltacht)
M. O'Donoghue (Economic Planning and Development)
S. Barrett (Environment)
Not a member of the Cabinet
A. J. Hederman (Attorney-General)

16. 11 December 1979–
Fianna Fail
Mr Lynch resigned on 11 December 1979 and was succeeded by Charles J. Haughey. The Department of Economic Planning and Development was abolished. Tourism and Transport became a separate department. It was announced that a Department of Energy would be established at a later date.

C. J. Haughey (Taoiseach)
G. Colley (Tanaiste; Tourism and Transport)
M. O'Kennedy (Finance)
B. Lenihan (Foreign Affairs)
G. Collins (Justice)
R. MacSharry (Agriculture)
D. O'Malley (Industry, Commerce and Energy)
P. Power (Fisheries and Forestry)
M. Woods (Health and Social Welfare)
A. Reynolds (Posts and Telegraphs)
P. Faulkner (Defence)
J. Wilson (Education)
G. Fitzgerald (Labour)
M. Geoghegan-Quinn (Gaeltacht)
S. Barrett (Environment)

Not a member of the Cabinet
A. J. Hederman (Attorney-General)

GOVERNORS-GENERAL. In accordance with Article 3 of the Treaty* the post of Governor-General of the Irish Free State was created in December 1922. He represented the crown in Ireland and occupied the Viceregal Lodge (now Arus an Uachtarain) in the Phoenix Park. The office was abolished by Eamon de Valera* upon the passage of the External Relations Act* (December 1936). Under the Constitution of 1937* the head of the Irish state was the President. The three Governors-General were Timothy Michael Healy* (1922–28), James MacNeill* (1928–

32) and Domhnall Ó Buachalla* (1932—37).

GRAHAM, REV. JOHN (1774— 1844). Clergyman (C.I.) and poet; b. Co. Longford; ordained (1799). He became Rector of Tamlaght-Ard, Co. Londonderry. A leading member of the Orange Order,* much of his poetry appeared over the pen-name 'Apprentice Boy'. He was said to have written witty parodies of Moore's *Melodies*.

GRAINGER, REV. JOHN (1830— 91). Clergyman (C.I.) and antiquary; b. Belfast. He filled his house at Broughshane, Co. Armagh with zoological and archaeological specimens from all over the world, many of them unlabelled and unlocalised. Before his death he directed that the material should go to the City of Belfast and much of it was catalogued by Robert Lloyd Praeger.*

GRANARD, 8th EARL (1874— 1948). Forbes, Bernard Arthur; politician (Liberal); ed. Oratory School. He was commissioned as a lieutenant in the 3rd Battalion of the Gordon Highlanders and was ADC to the Lord Lieutenant, Lord Cadogan. He served in the Boer War and resigned from the army after reaching the rank of captain (1905). He was assistant to the Postmaster-General in Henry Campbell-Bannerman's government (1906). During World War I, he commanded the 5th Battalion of the Royal Irish Fusiliers. He sat in the Irish Convention* of 1917—18. During the Civil War his home at Castle Forbes, Newtown Forbes, Co. Longford, was extensively damaged by the Irish Republican Army* — the Irregulars — on 26 January 1923.

GRAND JURY. From the time of Charles I (1625—49) the Grand Jury was the body responsible for the administration of the county unit. Described as 'the gentlemen of most consequence in the county', the members were generally the lead-ing landowners but peers could not serve. In Ireland in the nineteenth century they were generally C. of I. (*see* Ascendancy). The upper limit of members was twenty-three and the position was honorary. They met at the assizes to assist the judges on circuit and their chief function was to strike the rate or 'cess' for the county. They had the right to demand forced labour for road maintenance. The Grand Jury *Presentments*, the printed abstracts of the presentments as passed by the Grand Jury of each county, form a record of local taxation from 1663 until the dissolution of the Grand Jury system in 1898. Under the Local Government Act, 1898 a new system of elected County and District Councils came into operation and took over the Jury's functions. *See also* Local Government.

GRAND ORANGE LODGES. *See* Orange Order.

GRANT, CHARLES, BARON GLENRIG (1778—1866). Politician (Whig) and Chief Secretary (1818—21); b. Bengal; reared in England and ed. Magdalene College, Cambridge. Although called to the Bar (1807) he did not practise and became an MP in 1811. During his period at the Irish Office he adopted measures to conciliate the Catholic population. He unsuccessfully attempted to suppress Orange Order demonstrations, establish a system of National Education (which did not come until 1831) and effect changes in the police and magistracy. He was later Colonial Secretary (1835) when he achieved the total abolition of slavery in Cape Colony. When Lord John Russell* and other influential Whigs sought his dismissal he resigned in 1839.

GRATTAN, HENRY (1746—1820). Politician and orator; b. Dublin; ed. TCD. Having read law at the Middle Temple he was called to the Bar in 1772. MP (1775), he was a prominent member of the opposition, a noted champion of free trade and the demand for the legislative independence of the Irish parliament. When the parliament did achieve independence in 1782 it became popularly known as 'Grattan's Parliament' although he consistently refused office. During the life of the parliament he sought Catholic Emancipation, introducing a bill which was defeated in 1794. He was in England during the United Irishmen's* rising of 1798 and was accused of sympathising with the objectives of the rebels. He strongly opposed the Union* and was allowed the singular privilege of addressing the House of Commons on the motion while sitting down because of his illness. Following the Union he resided in England, and was MP for Malton (1805–06), and for Dublin (1806–20). For the rest of his life he continued to press for Emancipation. His bill in 1808 proposed Emancipation with the Veto* and was defeated by 281 votes to 128. His next bill was defeated by two votes in 1819. His integrity and oratorical powers won the support of even his enemies. He had a peculiar style of gesticulation while speaking, flapping his hands and arms around and producing a very eccentric impression until the audience became enraptured by the power of his eloquence.

GRAVE-DIGGING. Among the Irish there were many customs and ceremonies associated with burial. A grave was usually dug on the morning of a funeral, or the evening before when the shovels and forks used were placed across the open grave in the form of a cross. By tradition, graves were not dug on a Monday. It was considered a privilege to dig the grave and those who were asked were selected carefully in accordance with their closeness of friendship with the deceased. It was also customary for the chief mourner to provide whiskey to be drunk at the graveyard by the grave diggers and important mourners.

GRAVES, ALFRED PERCEVAL (1846 – 1931). Poet and writer; b. Dublin, son of Bishop Charles Graves;* ed. Windermere College and TCD. His early writings appeared in *Dark Blue* at Oxford and *Kattabos* at TCD. Later contributions appeared in the leading periodicals of the day including *Fraser's Magazine*, the *Spectator* and *Punch*. He graduated B.A. in 1870 and entered the Home Office as private secretary to the under-secretary Winterbotham. He became editor of Everyman's Irish Library and secretary of the Irish Literary Society.* Graves' first volume of verse, *Songs of Killarney*, appeared in 1872; other works include *Irish Songs and Ballads* (1880), *Songs of Old Ireland* (set to music by Sir Charles Stanford,* 1883) and the work by which he is best known, *Father O'Flynn and Other Lyrics* (1889). A leader of the Irish Literary Revival, he edited several works of Irish interest including *Songs of Wit and Humour* (1884), *The Irish Songbook with Original Irish Airs* (1894), *The Irish Fairy Book* (1909), *The Book of Irish Poetry* (1915), *A Treasury of Irish Prose and Verse* (1915), *A Celtic Psaltery* (1917), *Irish Doric in Song and Story* (1926), and *The Celtic Song Book* (1928). His first wife died in 1886 and he remarried in 1892. By his second marriage he became father of Robert and Charles Graves. Graves spent many years as a school inspector and was co-author of a work on school management. His last years were spent at Harlech, North Wales, where he wrote his autobiography *To Return to All That* (1930), a reply to his son Robert's *Good-bye to All That* (1929).

GRAVES, CHARLES (1812–99). Bishop of Limerick (C.I.), 1866–99; father of Alfred Perceval Graves;* ed. Bristol and TCD; B.A. (1835) and Fellow of TCD in 1836. He was elected to the RIA in 1837 and was awarded M.A. the following year. He was Professor of Mathematics, TCD (1843) and took his D.D. in

1851. He became Dean of Castle Chapel, Dublin, in 1860 and the following year was elected President of the RIA. He became Dean of Clonfert in 1864 and was translated to the see of Limerick in 1866. Bishop Graves was awarded a Fellowship of the Royal Society (1880) and an Honorary D.C.L. by Oxford University (1881). His major published mathematical work was his translation of Charles' *On the General Properties of Cones of the Second Degree and of Spherical Cones* (1841), in which his notes aroused considerable excitement among contemporary mathematicians. Much of his work was published in the RIA *Proceedings*, and several of his poems appeared in *Kattabos*, while many others were printed for private circulation. His sonnet to Wordsworth, which pleased the poet, appears on page 35 of Grosart's edition of Wordsworth's prose writings. He had an interest in archaeology and in Irish history and worked on the interpretation of ogham stones and successfully urged the translation of the Brehon Laws into English (1851).

GRAVES, ROBERT JAMES (1796–1853). Physician; b. Dublin; ed. TCD; M.B. (1818). After a stay on the continent, when he travelled with the artist Turner in the Alps and Italy, he became physician to the Meath Hospital and founded the Park Street School of Medicine. Clinical Lecturer to the Irish College of Physicians (of which he was President, 1843–44), he discovered 'Graves' Disease' (exopthalmic goitre), and made advances in the treatment and feeding of fever patients. His lectures were collected and published as *Clinical Lectures on the Practice of Medicine* (1843).

GRAY, EDMUND DWYER (1845–88). Journalist and politician (Nationalist); b. Dublin, son of Sir John Gray,* whose newspaper, the *Freeman's Journal,** he inherited. Politically he was a moderate within the Irish Parliamentary Party.* In 1879, during the course of a debate over a

speech which Charles Stewart Parnell* had made in Limerick, Parnell accused him of cowardice; they were eventually reconciled through the intervention of Archbishop Thomas William Croke* of Cashel and Gray placed the *Journal* behind Parnell and the Land League.* He presided over the meeting of 17 May 1880 at which Parnell was elected chairman of the party. In 1886 he and his paper supported Parnell in the controversy over the nomination of Captain W. H. O'Shea* to contest the Galway by-election.

GRAY, SIR JOHN (1816–75). Journalist and politician (Repeal); b. Claremorris, Co. Mayo; father of Edmund Dwyer Gray.* He was editor and part proprietor of the *Freeman's Journal* of which he became sole owner in 1850. He was tried along with Daniel O'Connell* and others during the state trials of 1843–44. Gray was instrumental in securing for Dublin its first efficient water supply.

GREAT NORTHERN RAILWAY. *See* Railways in Ireland.

GREAT SOUTHERN RAILWAYS. *See* Railways in Ireland.

GREAT SOUTHERN AND WESTERN RAILWAY. *See* Railways in Ireland.

GREAT STRAND STREET, SIEGE OF. In March 1933 a part of the congregation at the Pro-Cathedral, Dublin, which had been listening to a sermon from a Redemptorist priest, marched from the church to the headquarters of the Revolutionary Workers' Group* at 64 Great Strand Street. On their way they smashed windows at Unity Hall and were joined by members of the Store Street Mission congregation. They surrounded 64 Great Strand Street, harangued and intimidated those inside and broke windows, etc. The incident was symptomatic of the prevailing anti-Communist hysteria for much of which over-zealous members of the Catholic Church were responsible.

GREEN, ALICE STOPFORD (1847–1929). Historian; b. Kells, Co. Meath; ed. privately. She married the historian J. R. Green in 1877 and assisted him on his work when his health failed. After his death (1883) she completed his *The Conquest of England* (1883) and *Town Life in the Fifteenth Century* (2 vols, 1894). Her London home was a salon for a wide range of writers, scholars and politicians. She was sympathetic to the Irish demand for Home Rule* and at the suggestion of her close friend, Sir Roger Casement,* organised the 'London Committee' to collect money for arms for the Irish Volunteers.* The sum of £1,500 was used by Darrell Figgis* to purchase the arms which were brought to Ireland on the *Asgard** and the *Kelpie** (*see* Howth gunrunning). Although she disapproved of the Easter Rising of 1916* she moved house from London to Dublin and supported the Treaty.* W. T. Cosgrave* nominated her to the first Senate to which she presented a casket containing a scroll upon which was to be inscribed the names of all senators; after the abolition of the Senate in 1936 the casket and scroll went to the RIA. Her major works were *The Making of Ireland and Its Undoing* (1908), *Ourselves Alone and Ulster* (a pamphlet, 1918), and *A History of the Irish State to 1014* (1925).

GREEN, REV. WILLIAM SPOTSWOOD (1847–1919). Clergyman (C.I.) and naturalist; b. Youghal, Co. Cork; ed. TCD. He was rector at Carrigaline, Co. Cork for many years. A keen adventurer, he was the first to reach the summit of Mount Cook (12,349 ft) in New Zealand (1881). He surveyed the peaks and glaciers of the Selkirks for the Canadian government (1888) and dredged and trawled with A. C. Haddon* to a depth of 1,200 fathoms off the southwest coast of Ireland to explore marine fauna for the RIA. In 1890 he left the church to become an Inspector of Fisheries, a post he retained until retirement in 1914. He was for many years a member of the Congested Districts Board.*

'GREEN KNIGHTS'. Title used by members of the Brunswick Clubs* when referring to the Order of Liberators* led by Daniel O'Connell.

GREENSHIRTS. *See* Blueshirts.

GREENWOOD, SIR HAMAR, 1st VISCOUNT (1870–1948). Politician (Conservative) and Chief Secretary (1920–22); b. Canada; ed. Public School, Whitby and Toronto University where he qualified as a lawyer. He became an MP in 1906. Supporting David Lloyd George* in the rigorous prosecution of the War of Independence,* he accepted the appointment of Chief Secretary at the peak of the fighting. At a time when Coroners' Inquests had returned over twenty charges against crown forces, he admitted to knowledge of only one such charge. He was a member of the British team which negotiated the Treaty.*

GREER, SAMUEL McCURDY (1810–80). Politician; b. Springvale, Co. Londonderry; ed. Belfast Academy and Glasgow University; Irish Bar (1833). He began public life in 1844 when he supported the call for land reform and the secret ballot. A founder-member of the Tenant League,* he failed many times to be returned to parliament before finally winning Derry City (1857–70). He was Recorder of Derry (1870–78) and a county court judge (1878–80).

GREGG, REV. JOHN (1798–1878). Bishop of Cork, Cloyne and Ross (C.I.), 1862–78 and evangelical; b. Cappa, near Ennis, Co. Clare; ed. TCD; ordained in 1826, he became curate at the French Church, Portarlington. He was given the living of Killsallaghan, Co. Dublin, was incumbent of Bathesda Chapel (1836), which was built for him, and was Archdeacon of Kildare (1857) while retaining his incumbency at Trinity Church. During his term as Bishop the Cathedral of St Fin Barre in Cork was erected, designed by William Burges. One of the most celebrated evangelicals of his time, he was the author of *A Missionary Visit to Achill and Erris* (1850). His son, Robert Samuel Gregg,* was Archbishop of Armagh. *See also* Second Reformation.

GREGG, ROBERT SAMUEL (1834–96). Archbishop of Armagh and Primate of All Ireland (C.I.), 1893–96; b. Killsallaghan, Co. Dublin; ed. TCD; B.A. (1857) and M.A. (1860). After ministering at Rathcooney, Co. Cork (1860) he was incumbent of Christ Church, Belfast (1863) until his appointment as Rector of Carrigrohane (1865) and precentor of St Fin Barre's Cathedral, Cork, where his father, John Gregg,* was bishop. His talent for financial affairs was given full rein and his administration of the diocesan finances became a model for the Church of Ireland after disestablishment (1871). He became Dean of Cork in 1874 and a year later Bishop of Ossory, Ferns and Leighlin. He succeeded his father as Bishop of Cork, Cloyne and Ross (1878) where he completed his father's work on St Fin Barre's.

GREGORY, AUGUSTA, LADY (1852–1932). Dramatist and folklorist; b. Roxborough, Co. Galway, *née* Persse; her mother was related to Standish O'Grady;* ed. privately. She married Sir William Gregory in 1880 and after his death took up residence at the estate of Coole Park, Co. Galway (1892). Apart from editing her father-in-law's papers and her husband's *Autobiography* (1894), her literary career did not start until she was nearly fifty. She first met William Butler Yeats* in 1896 at Tulira, Co. Galway, home of their mutual friend, Edward Martyn.* From 1897 Yeats spent holidays at her home, collecting folklore with her in the area around Kiltartan. They collaborated on *The Pot of Broth* (1902).

Lady Gregory was fascinated and stimulated by the wealth of Irish story, myth, legend and fairy-lore of a peasantry which spoke English while thinking in Irish, so producing a unique idiom. To express this language, she wrote in the Kiltartan dialect or 'Kiltartanese' as it came to be known. The fruit of her interest appeared in *Cuchulainn of Muirthemne* (1902), *Poets and Dreamers* (1903) and *Gods and Fighting Men* (1904).

Her gifts as a dramatist blossomed after she became involved in the Irish Literary Theatre* of which she was a co-founder with Yeats and Martyn in 1898. From this venture was formed the Abbey Theatre* of which she was an active director until 1928 when ill-health forced her to retire to Coole Park. Between 1901 and 1928 she wrote more than forty plays, most of which were produced at the Abbey. Apart from her many adaptations and translations, her plays dealt with the lives, sufferings, superstitions and humours of the peasantry. They are written in a heightened language and exaggerated poetry based on the idiom with which she was familiar from her tenants' cottages.

Her home at Coole Park was open to the major figures of the Irish literary revival and to visiting *literati*. The famous 'Autograph Tree' bears the initials of Yeats, John Millington Synge,* George Russell * (AE), George Moore,* Sean O'Casey* and George Bernard Shaw.*

Lady Gregory's published works include *Spreading the News* (1904), *The Rising of the Moon* (1904), *The Gaol Gate* (1906), *The Workhouse Ward* (1908), *The Kiltartan Handbook* (1909), *The Kiltartan Wonder Book* (1910), *The Kiltartan Moliere* (1910), *Our Irish Theatre* (1913), *Shanwalla* (1915), *The Kiltartan Poetry Book* (1918), *The Golden Apple* (1920), *Visions and Beliefs in the West of Ireland* (1920), *Hugh Lane's Life and Achievement* (1921) and *Sancho's Master* (1927). Her

Journals 1916–30 were edited by Lennox Robinson* in 1946.

GREGORY, WILLIAM (1766–1840). Civil Servant; Under-Secretary (1821–31); b. Coole Park, Co. Galway; ed. TCD and Cambridge; B.A. (1783) and M.A. (1787); MP Portarlington in the last Irish House of Commons (1789–1800), he became Civil Under Secretary to the Lord Lieutenant in 1812 and when this office was united with that of the Military Under Secretary in 1821 he became the first holder of the joint post. Because Gregory was adviser to so many Viceroys and Chief Secretaries Daniel O'Connell* once called him the real ruler of Ireland. He was particularly close to Sir Robert Peel* and was an adviser during the period leading up to Catholic Emancipation.* He lost much of his influence following the retirement of Sir William Saurin* and upon the accession of Lord Anglesey* to the office of Lord Lieutenant in 1831 he was forced to retire. A selection of his papers was edited by his daughter-in-law, Augusta, Lady Gregory,* in 1898.

de GRAY, THOMAS PHILIP, 1st EARL de GRAY (1781–1859). Lord Lieutenant (1841–44); b. Whitehall, London; ed. St John's College, Cambridge; M.A. (1801); First Lord of the Admiralty (1834–35). During his term as Lord Lieutenant de Grey opposed any form of Repeal; to Sir Robert Peel* he wrote, '. . . Let no morbid sensibility, or mawkish apprehension of invading the constitution which might influence some hearts, or perhaps secure some trifling support, be allowed to weigh'. He resigned office in 1844.

GRIFFIN, GERALD (1803–40). Dramatist, novelist and poet; b. Limerick, ninth son of a brewer; ed. chiefly at hedge school.* He became editor of *The Limerick Advertiser* in his teens, and moved to London (1823) where he received help from John Banim* and William Maginn.* Griffin wrote for *The Literary Gaz-*ette (over the signature 'Oscar') and contributed light dramatic pieces to Covent Garden (over the pseudonym 'G. Joseph'). His first popular success was achieved in 1826 with the publication of *Holland Tides and Other Tales*. He returned to Ireland where he published three volumes of *Tales of the Munster Festivals* (1827). He entered the Irish Christian Brothers* in Dublin (September 1838) and was shortly afterwards transferred to the North Monastry, Cork as a teacher. His works include *Tales Illustrative of the Five Senses* (1830), a further series of *Tales of the Munster Festivals* (1832), *Tales of my Neighbourhood* (1835), and *Duke of Monmouth* (1836). His most enduring work, *The Collegians*, which appeared anonymously in 1829, subsequently provided the plot for *The Colleen Bawn* by Dion Boucicault (1860) and Sir Julius Benedict's opera *The Lily of Killarney* (1861). A memoir of Griffin's life, by his brother William, appeared in 2 volumes (1842–3) and his *Poetical and Dramatic Works* appeared between 1857 and 1859.

GRIFFITH, ARTHUR (1871–1922). Journalist and politician (Sinn Fein); b. Dublin; ed. CBS, Strand Street. After leaving school to become an apprentice printer, he worked on the *Irish Independent* * and *The Nation*.* He was an admirer of Charles Stewart Parnell.* Through the Eblana Debating Society and the Leinster Debating Society he came into contact with William Rooney* by whom he was deeply influenced. A founder-member of the Celtic Literary Society,* he was active in the Gaelic League* and the Irish Republican Brotherhood of which he was a member until 1910. Griffith's favourite authors included Thomas Davis* and John Mitchel* whose *Jail Journal* he edited in 1914.

During a slump in the printing trade he accepted an invitation to join John MacBride* in South Africa. During the two years from January 1897 he worked in Johannesburg, helped to organise a 'Ninety-Eight Celebration' and gave support to the Boers. Then, in answer to a call from Rooney, he returned to Ireland to edit a new nationalist paper, the *United Irishman*. He also founded the Irish Transvaal Society to organise Irish support for the Boers. He joined Rooney in founding Cumann na nGaedheal* on 30 September 1900. While in Paris to attend the International Exhibition in 1900 he introduced Maud Gonne* to MacBride.

His *The Resurrection of Hungary: A Parallel for Ireland* sold over 30,000 copies in 1904. Basing his concept on the *ausgleich* between Austria and Hungary in 1867, he advocated a dual monarchy for Ireland and the rest of the United Kingdom. In 1905 he outlined his ideas on the economic future of Ireland to the National Council,* reflecting the influence of the German economist, Friedrich List (protective tariffs which would allow light industries to develop). He put forward a proposal for the re-afforestation of Ireland and for the creation of a mercantile marine, etc. His central idea was economic self-sufficiency for a self-governing Ireland. It became part of the programme adopted by Sinn Fein. His new paper, *Sinn Fein*,* replaced the *United Irishman* in 1906 and continued to appear despite adverse circumstances until it was suppressed by the government in 1914.

Griffith's Sinn Fein policy incurred the hostility of John Redmond* and the Irish Parliamentary Party.* Neither did his constitutionalism appeal to a younger generation of activists who were under the influence of the militant republicanism of Thomas J. Clarke.* Others, however, like Bulmer Hobson,* saw the potential value of Sinn Fein to the IRB. Griffith opposed the Home Rule Bill of 1912, commenting, 'If this is liberty the lexicographers have deceived us'. He called on Redmond and the Irish party to withdraw from Westminster and, borrowing an idea from Daniel O'Connell,* called for the establishment of a Council of Three Hundred* to govern Ireland. Although he joined the Irish Volunteers* in 1913 he was not invited onto the Provisional Committee lest the new organisation should be too closely identified with Sinn Fein. He took part in the Howth Gun-running* (July 1914).

After the suppression of another of his papers, *Eire* (1914–15), he published a short-lived compilation called *Scissors and Paste* in which he reproduced headlines from continental, British and American newspapers, giving an unofficial slant to the news. He did not take part in the Easter Rising of 1916,* having been persuaded by Sean MacDiarmada* that his services would be more valuable after the insurrection. Under martial law regulations he was arrested and imprisoned on 3 May (the authorities had erroneously believed the rebellion to be the work of Sinn Fein); he was held at Reading Gaol until February 1917.

Sinn Fein, moribund before the rising, was now revived, this time as the republican political movement. Griffith stood aside to allow Eamon de Valera* to assume the presidency and became a vice-president himself. He was a member of the Mansion House Committee* which organised resistance to conscription, (*see* Conscription and Ireland) and was arrested under the 'German Plot'* series of arrests. While imprisoned he was returned to represent East Cavan for Sinn Fein.

Acting President of Dail Eireann* during de Valera's American tour, he was again arrested in December 1920 and held until July 1921 when he was released under the terms of the Truce.* Shortly afterwards he was appointed to head the Irish delegation to the negotiations with the British government (October–December 1921). Outmanouevred by David Lloyd George,* Griffith promised that he would not break off the negotiations over Ulster if all other questions were satisfactorily concluded. Lloyd George held him to this promise and gave him to understand that partition would be temporary and that a Boundary Commission* would effectively abolish it. Afterwards,

Griffith defended the Treaty,* saying, 'I signed the Treaty not as an ideal thing, but fully believing, as I believe now, it is a Treaty honourable to Ireland, and safeguards the vital interests of Ireland. . . . We have done the best we could for Ireland'.

He defeated de Valera in the election for the Presidency of the Dail and appointed his close colleague, Michael Collins,* to the post of Chairman of the Provisional Government.* As the country moved towards Civil War* he led a delegation to London to assure the British government that the Treaty would be honoured (May 1922). Following the general election of 16 June 1922, which resulted in a victory for the pro-Treaty candidates, he agreed to the bombardment of the garrison at the Four Courts* which precipitated the Civil War. Along with Collins, he prosecuted the war until his death from a cerebral haemorrhage on 12 August 1922.

Griffith was the first Irish leader to be buried as a Head of State.

GRIFFITH, SIR RICHARD JOHN
(1784–1878). Geologist and civil engineer; b. Dublin; ed. Dublin, London and Edinburgh. He surveyed the coal-fields of Leinster (1808) and was engineer to the Commission on Irish Bogs (1809–12). His major work was the *Geological Map of Ireland*, compiled during his survey of every parish and townland of Ireland, which became a standard reference upon its adoption by the Ordnance Board in 1855. He supervised the *Valuation of Ireland*, the Primary Valuation* (*see also* Griffith's Valuation). He was Deputy-Chairman of the Board of Works (1846), Chairman (1850–64), and was retained in an unpaid advisory capacity on his resignation. His name was connected with almost every major undertaking of the era in Ireland.

'GRIFFITH'S VALUATION'.
The Primary Valuation* drawn up by Sir Richard Griffith* under the Valuation Act (1852). The Valuation became highly controversial as it was 'only a relative valuation of property to regulate the taxation of Ireland, and not for the purpose of fixing a letting value'. Griffith stated that the land had been valued 'from twenty-five to thirty per cent under its letting value . . . according to a scale of agricultural prices, not according to rents'. His successor as Commissioner, John Ball Greene, claimed it was unjust to use Griffith's Valuation as an estimate for fair rents. During the Land War,* however, the Land League insisted that tenants offer payment of rent based on Griffith's Valuation and no other, and if that was not acceptable to the landlords then to withhold rent entirely.

GROSSE ISLE.
Islet, measuring three miles long by one mile broad, situated on the St Lawrence and sited thirty miles downriver from the city of Quebec. The area was first chosen as a quarantine station in 1832 to isolate cholera victims arriving from Ireland and England. In 1847, however, the flight from the Irish famine brought thousands flocking to Canada and completely overwhelmed the meagre facilities available to Dr George Douglas, medical superintendent of the quarantine station. The island's hospital had sufficient room for 200 cases, but by 28 May 1847, 850 cases of typhus and dysentery were already on the island, a figure which had reached 1,800 by 10 June and 2,500 a month later. To deal with this overwhelming influx, the superintendent had, at his disposal, a staff of only fourteen, who were expected to minister to the needs of the sick on the island, and also to examine and treat passengers on off-shore ships. Today, two monuments preserve the memory of the thousands who died on the island. The first, in a wooded hollow, once the site of the emigrant cemetery, was erected by Dr Douglas and his assistants. It commemorates on two sides the four doctors who died in their efforts to ease the sufferings of an unfortunate people. On the west face of the monument an

inscription reads: 'In this secluded spot lie the mortal remains of 5,424 persons who flying from Pestilence and Famine in Ireland in the year 1847 found in America, but a Grave'. The second memorial, a Celtic Cross carved in granite, bearing inscriptions in English, French and Irish, was erected by the Ancient Order of Hibernians* in 1909.

GRUBB, THOMAS (1800–78). Optical manufacturer; b. Kilkenny. He made reflectors and refractors for the observatories at Armagh, Dunsink, Glasgow and Melbourne and assisted the 3rd Earl of Rosse* in the construction of the Parsonstown Telescope* (1845). Grubb was the author of many learned papers on comparative and defining powers of different telescopes and on optical instruments.

GUERNSEY, WELLINGTON (1817–85). Composer and poet; b. Mullingar, Co. Westmeath. He wrote and composed a large number of songs, and set several poems by Thomas Davis,* Gerald Griffin* and others to music. He arranged the music and composed symphonies for *The Songs of Old Ireland* (edited by Rev. Joseph Fitzgerald, 1843) and also arranged *The Songs of Ireland* (1860) for publication. His best known melodies are 'I'll hang my harp on a Willow Tree' and 'Poor Old Ned'.

GUINNESS, SIR ARTHUR EDWARD, 1st BARON ARDILAUN (1840–1915). Businessman and politician (Unionist); b. Clontarf, Dublin, eldest son of Sir Benjamin Lee Guinness;* ed. Eton and TCD. He was head of the brewery at St James' Gate from 1868 to 1877. A committed Unionist, he was MP for Dublin (1868–69, 1874–80), and was created Baron Ardilaun of Ashford, Co. Galway in 1880. With his brother Edward Cecil Guinness,* he financed the Dublin Exhibition of Arts and Science (1872). He restored Marsh's Library, built the Coombe Lying-In Hospital, financed the laying out of St Stephen's Green

for the benefit of Dublin citizens and bore half the expense of the choir of St Patrick's Cathedral. In 1899 he bought Muckross estate in Co. Kerry to prevent it from falling into the hands of commercial interests. He was President of the Royal Dublin Society* (1897–1913). Guinness used the Dublin *Daily Express* and the *Evening Mail* to forward the Unionist case against Home Rule.

GUINNESS, SIR BENJAMIN LEE (1798–1868). Brewer and philanthropist; b. Dublin. He assumed control of Arthur Guinness Son & Co. in 1855. Under his guidance the company developed an immense export trade, and he became the richest man in Ireland. He was Lord Mayor of Dublin in 1851. At a personal cost of £150,000 he restored St Patrick's Cathedral, Dublin (1860–65), saving the historic building from almost certain ruin. In recognition of this and many other philanthropic acts, the citizens of Dublin and the Dean and chapter of the Cathedral presented him with addresses of gratitude for his donations to the city.

GUINNESS, EDWARD CECIL, 1st EARL OF IVEAGH (1847–1927). Businessman and philanthropist; b. Clontarf, Dublin, youngest son of Sir Benjamin Lee Guinness;* ed. privately and TCD. He inherited a share of the family firm upon his father's death in 1868 and became a manager in the business. When it went public in 1886 he became chairman, a post he retained after his retirement (1889). His philanthropy was as diverse as that of his brother, Sir Arthur Edward Guinness.* He provided £250,000 to clear some seven acres of Dublin slums, donated £250,000 to build housing for the London and Dublin poor (£200,000 for London and £50,000 for Dublin), and donated £250,000 to the Lister Institute of Tropical Medicine. In 1891 he was created Baron Iveagh. During the Boer War (1899–1902) he equipped and maintained field hospitals for the British Army. While his politics were strongly Unionist, he was respected by Irish nationalists and he continued to provide donations for Irish charities after the establishment of the Free State in 1922. In his later years he moved to his estate at Elveden in England where he entertained Kings Edward VII and George V during their shooting holidays. He became the first Earl of Iveagh and Viscount Elveden in 1919.

GWYNN, DENIS ROLLESTON (1893–1971). Historian; son of Stephen Lucius Gwynn.* He worked at the British Ministry of Information during World War I. He claimed later in his *The Life and Death of Roger Casement* (1930), that while employed there, he learned that a senior Ministry official, G. H. Mair, had photographed the Casement 'Black Diaries'* for distribution to foreign embassies and journalists in 1916. Gwynn was Research Professor of Modern History at University College Cork (1946–63) and was a frequent contributor to leading journals of the era, including *Studies** and *Irish Ecclesiastical Record.** A prolific writer, his works include *The Catholic Reaction in France* (1924), *The Irish Free State, 1922–27* (1928), *A Hundred Years of Catholic Emancipation* (1929), *Charles Butler* (1929), *Daniel O'Connell* (1929), *Daniel O'Connell and Ellen Courteney* (1930), *Pius XI* (1932), *The Life of John Redmond* (1932), *De Valera* (1933), *The O'Gorman Mahon* (1934), *John Keogh* (1935), *The Vatican and the War in Europe* (1940), *Young Ireland and 1848* (1949), *Cardinal Wiseman* (1950). He edited *Reminiscences of a Maynooth Professor* (1925) by Dr Walter MacDonald.*

GWYNN, EDWARD (1868–1941). Scholar; ed. St Columba's College, Rathfarnham and TCD, of which he became Fellow (1893) and Provost in 1927. He became a member of the RIA (1896) and Todd Lecturer, during which period he worked on the translation of the verse parts of the *Dinnshenchas*, the prose of which had been translated by Whitley Stokes.* His work on this occupied him for thirty-seven years. He also catalogued MSS. in the Trinity College Library and in the Library of the RIA.

GWYNN, STEPHEN LUCIUS (1864–1950). Journalist, novelist, critic, poet and politician (Nationalist); b. Co. Dublin, a grandson of William Smith O'Brien;* ed. St Columba's College, Dublin and Brasenose College, Oxford. After teaching classics for ten years he worked as a freelance journalist in London (1896–1904). He was MP for Galway City from 1906 to 1918 and served with the Connaught Rangers in World War I. He attended the Irish Convention* in 1917–18. His literary works include *Tennyson* (1899), *The Decay of Sensibility* (1900), *The Old Knowledge* (1901), *The Fair Hills of Ireland* (1906), *Robert Emmet* (1909), *Henry Grattan and his Times*, *The Masters of English Literature*, *Thomas Moore* (both 1904), *John Redmond's Last Years* (1919), *Sir Walter Scott* (1930), *Horace Walpole* (1932), *Mary Kingsley* (1932), *Dean Swift* (1933), *Goldsmith* (1935), and *Robert Louis Stevenson* (1939). His *Collected Poems* appeared in 1923 and his autobiography, *Experiences of a Literary Man*, in 1926.

H

HABEAS CORPUS. An Irish *Habeas Corpus* Act was passed in 1782. It was suspended by the government in times of open rebellion or violent agrarian unrest: 1798, 1848, 1881 and 1920. A notorious occasion on which the Act was suspended was on 22 July 1848, when a Bill to suspend the Act until March 1849 passed through all its stages in one day, and was rushed through the Lords in similar fashion on the following Monday. The Provisional Government* suspended *habeas corpus* in 1922. Erskine Childers* was executed on 24 November while an application was pending in the High Court.

HALL, ANNA MARIA (1800–71). Author; b. Dublin *née* Fielding. She spent most of her childhood at Bannow, Co. Wexford. She went to London in 1815, where in 1824, she married author Samuel Carter Hall with whom she collaborated on several works including *Ireland: its Scenery and Character* (3 vols, 1841–43). Her studies of Irish peasant life, including *Tales of the Irish Peasantry* (1840), are considered an invaluable contribution to the knowledge of pre-Famine conditions in Ireland. Her early writings appeared in her husband's *Amulet* and were published as *Sketches of Irish Character* in 1829.

In London she campaigned on behalf of temperance movements and supported the drive against consumption. She inaugurated a fund in honour of Florence Nightingale which amounted to over £40,000. A bibliography of the writings of Mrs Hall and her husband shows that individually and in collaboration they produced in excess of 500 works. Her writings include *The Chronicles of a Schoolroom* (1829), *The Buccaneer* (1829), *The Outlaw* (1832), *The French Refugee* (1837), *Lights and Shadows of Irish Life* (1838), *Marian* (1840), *The White*

Boy (1845), *A Woman's Story* (1857), *The Flight of Faith* (1862).

HAMILTON, REV. JAMES ARCHIBALD (1747–1815). Astronomer; b. Athlone; ed. Athlone and TCD. He built an observatory at Cookstown, from which he made a particular study of Mercury and was appointed first astronomer, Armagh Observatory (1791); Dean of Cloyne (1804). Many of his papers on astronomy are in the library of the Royal Irish Academy.*

HAMILTON, SIR WILLIAM ROWAN (1805–65). Mathematician and linguist; b. Dublin. He had little formal education until he entered TCD in 1823. A child prodigy, he had shown particular aptitude in languages and was capable of conversing in nine by the time he was seven years of age. At fourteen years of age he was fluent in fourteen languages, including Hebrew, Greek, Latin, Syriac, Sanskrit and Hindustani.

He became Professor of Astronomy at TCD in 1825 and was President of the RIA in 1837. He discovered the formula of quaternion multiplication while walking with his wife on Broom Bridge, Dublin (16 October 1843). Hamilton scratched the theory on the masonry as he had no other means of recording the formula.

His writings include *Lectures on Quaternions* (1835) and *The Elements of Quaternions* (1835). He also contributed widely to learned journals and was elected a Corresponding member of the Academy of St Petersburg.

HANGING-GALE *See* Gale.

HANNA, REV. HUGH 'ROARING' (1824–92). Clergyman (Presbyterian) and pamphleteer; b. Dromara, Co. Down; ed. Belfast. He was ordained in 1852 and shortly afterwards commenced the building of St Enoch's, the largest of Belfast's Presbyterian churches. An impassioned preacher, his 'sermons' frequently incited violence against the Catholic population. In 1857 he defied Belfast magistrates who proscribed preaching in the city centre because they wished to keep it non-sectarian, and sparked off days of rioting. Rev. Hanna founded many elementary schools in Belfast and was appointed a Commissioner of National Education in 1880.

HANNAY, REV. JAMES OWEN (1865–1950). Clergyman (C.I.) and author; b. Belfast; ed. variously in England, he completed his studies at TCD. He was ordained in 1889 and was curate at Delgany, Co. Wicklow and later Rector at Westport, Co. Mayo. He was Donnellan Lecturer, TCD (1901–02) and a member of the General Synod of the Church of Ireland (1905–15), and Chaplain to the British Legation in Budapest (1922–24). He became Rector of Mells in 1924 and remained there until 1934, during which period he lectured at Durham and Oxford Universities.

Canon Hannay was an extremely active worker in the Gaelic League* during his Westport ministry. In this capacity he incurred the suspicion of the Catholic parish priest of Tuam, and to avoid a possible split in the Branch, Canon Hannay withdrew from the executive in 1906. He believed that it was vital that the Church of Ireland should accept the realities of Irish nationalism, and in 1912 he protested at a special meeting of the General Synod which expressed attachment to the Union. He was a prolific author, both under his own name and under the *nom-de-plume* George A. Birmingham; his works include *The Spirit and Origin of Christian Monasticism, The Wisdom of the Desert* and *A Wayfarer in Hungary* (1925), *Isaiah* (1937) and *God's Iron: A Life of the Prophet Jeremiah* (1939); his twenty-nine novels published under the name George A. Birmingham included *Spanish Gold* (1913), *The Lost Tribes* (1914),

Minnie's Bishop and other stories, The Island of Mystery (1918), *Up the Rebels* (1919), *A Public Scandal* (1922), *The Grand Duchess* (1924), *Goodly Pearls* (1926), *The Mayor's Candlesticks* (1929), *Fed Up* (1931), *Two Fools* (1934), *Mrs Miller's Aunt* (1936), *Appeasement* (1939), *Laura's Bishop* (1949); he edited *Irish Short Stories* in 1932; his plays included *Eleanor's Enterprise* (1911), and *Send for Dr O'Grady* (1923).

HARDEBECK, CARL GILBERT (1869–1945). Musician and collector of Irish traditional music; b. Clerkenwell, London, of German parentage; blind from birth, he was educated at Normal School for the Blind, London and trained as an organist, pianist and music teacher. He moved to Belfast in 1893 where he was co-partner in an unsuccessful musical warehouse business, losing his entire capital in less than three years. He became a music teacher, and, in 1904, organist at St Peter's Cathedral, Falls Road, Belfast. His first entry at a Feis Ceoil won First Prize in 1897, a feat which he repeated until 1908. He studied native music in Donegal and invented a type of Gaelic Braille which was later adopted by the National Institute for the Blind. He continued his work in the Gaeltacht districts of Galway, Kerry and Mayo. Hardebeck became an Irish nationalist under the influence of the writings of Patrick Pearse.* Master of the School of Music in Cork (1919), he held the Chair of Irish Music in UCC but was forced to supplement his income by working as a pianist at a local cinema. He returned to Belfast in 1923 to resume his career as a composer. He moved to Dublin in 1932 and was employed by the state to continue his work as a collector. His text book on Irish music, begun in 1926, was never published. Many works which he collected were published at his own expense and involved considerable financial losses. Despite his acknowledged contribution to Irish music and the consequent debt owed him by researchers, scholars and students,

Hardebeck was never honoured by an Irish university. He died in comparative poverty and his widow was given some financial security by a Hardebeck Testimonial Fund which was established by the editor of the *Capuchin Annual.*

HARDIMAN, JAMES (1782–1855). Antiquarian; b. Galway where he was reared and educated as a native speaker of Irish. After studying law in Dublin he was appointed sub-commissioner of Public Records where John O'Donovan* worked under him for a time. He was later Librarian, Queen's College, Galway. A member of the Royal Irish Academy* for which he translated *Ancient Irish deeds and writings,* his works included *History of the Town and County of Galway* (1820), *Irish Ministrelsy* with translations (2 vols, 1831), *The Statutes of Kilkenny* (1843) and an edition of O'Flaherty's *Iar-Connacht* (1846) for the Irish Archaeological Society.

HARDY, REV. EDWARD JOHN (1849–1920). Clergyman (C.I.) and author; b. Co. Armagh; ed. Royal School, Portora, and TCD. Ordained in 1874, he was army chaplain to the British forces (1878–1908) and was Donnellan Lecturer, TCD (1898–99). His most famous book, *How to be Happy Though Married* created a sensation upon its publication (1884) and was translated into several languages.

HARDY, PHILIP DIXON (1793–1875). Printer, publisher and poet; b. Dublin; ed. TCD; B.A. (1847). He introduced steam printing into Ireland (1833). Hardy edited and printed the *Dublin Penny Journal* from its second edition. He also edited *The National Magazine* and *The Friend of Ireland, containing an exposure of the errors and superstitions of the Church of Rome* (Vols 1–10, 1838–39). He was the author of *Wellington* (poem, 1814), *Bertha: a tale of Erin* (poetry, 1817), *A Wreath from the Emerald Isle* (1826), *The Northern*

Tourist (1830), *The New Picture of Dublin* (guide book, 1831), *The Holy Wells of Ireland* (1836), *Legends, tales and stories of Ireland* (1837), *The Northern Cottage, or The Effects of Bible Reading* (1842), *The Inquisition* (1849), *The Maynooth Grant considered religiously, morally and politically* (1853), *Hardy's tourists' guides through Ireland: in four tours* (1858) and *The Pleasure of Religion and Other Poems* (1869).

HARLAND, SIR EDWARD JAMES (1831–95). Shipbuilder and politician (Conservative); b. Scarborough. He became an engineer after serving an apprenticeship in a Newcastle-on-Tyne shipbuilding firm. After coming to work in Robert Hickson's shipyard in 1854, he bought the firm for £5,000 four years later. He entered into partnership with G. W. Wolff in 1862 and together they laid the basis for what became the biggest shipbuilding firm in the world, Harland and Wolff. Occupied with his estate at Ormiston, Co. Down, Harland brought his head draughtsman, William James Pirrie,* into partnership in 1874 and left the direction of the business to him. Mayor of Belfast in 1885 and created baronet, he was MP for North Belfast (1889–95). Under Pirrie's management the Harland and Wolff firm became Belfast's biggest single employer, with 12,000 employees by 1914.

'HARP, THE'. *See* Connolly, James.

HARP SOCIETY, THE. Founded in Belfast (1808) by Dr James Mac-Donnel and Edward Bunting*. The principal aim of the Society was to enable blind children earn a living by teaching them the harp. A secondary aim was the promotion of the study of the Irish language, history and antiquities. Its president was the Earl O'Neill and membership included Rev. James Bryson and Rev. John McCracken (brother of Henry Joy McCracken). The Society ran into financial difficulties in 1819 but was rescued through the patronage of the

Marquis of Hastings, the Marquis of Downshire, Sir Francis McNaughton and Major Charles Kennedy; and with in excess of £1,000 collected by a supporting committee in Calcutta (prominent among whom was Lt Col Casement, ancestor of Sir Roger Casement*). The Society remained active until 1830 when many of its functions and membership were absorbed by the newly-formed Ulster Gaelic Society.

HARRINGTON, TIMOTHY CHARLES (1851–1910). Politician (Nationalist) and land agitator; b. Castletownbere, Co. Cork; ed. TCD. He founded *The Kerry Sentinel* in 1877 and used it to further Land League agitation in Co. Kerry. He was MP for Kerry (1880), for Co. Westmeath (1883) and for the Harbour Division, Dublin (from 1885). As Hon. Secretary to the Irish Parliamentary Party* he devised the Plan of Campaign* which he published in *United Ireland* on 23 October 1886 and thereafter, with John Dillon* and William O'Brien* played a leading role in the agitation. Harrington was called to the Bar in 1887 and acted as counsel for Charles Stewart Parnell* during the sittings of the Commission on 'Parnellism and Crime'* (1888–89). He was on a fund-raising tour of the USA with Dillon on behalf of the Plan when the split occurred in the Parnellite party. He supported his leader from the USA and continued his allegiance on his return. He was Lord Mayor of Dublin (1901–02) and continued to sit as a member of the Redmondite Irish Party until his death.

HARRIS, MATTHEW (1825–90). Fenian and politician (Nationalist); b. Ballinasloe, Co. Galway; ed. at a hedge school. He became a successful building contractor, a political activist and a supporter of Daniel O'Connell,* Young Ireland* and the Tenant League.* As a Fenian he was the chief gun-runner for the Connaught circles. He enlisted Michael Davitt's support for land reform in Mayo

which led to the foundation of the Land League.* Harris was campaign manager for John O'Connor Power* in the 1874 election in Mayo and sat as MP for East Galway from 1885 until his death. He was extremely active in agrarian agitation in Co. Galway where he founded the Ballinasloe Tenants' Defence Association and supported the Plan of Campaign*. Harris was suspicious of clerical interference in Irish politics and was an early critic of the Papal Rescript of 1888.

HARRISON, HENRY (1867–1954). Writer; b. Hollywood, Co. Down; ed. Westminster School and Balliol College, Oxford where he was secretary to the Oxford Union Home Rule Group. He supported Charles Stewart Parnell* and was a member of the Irish Parliamentary Party* (1890–92). He supported Parnell after the split in the party. Harrison was commissioned in the Royal Irish Regiment (1915). He was Secretary to the Irish Dominion League; Irish correspondent of *The Economist* (1922–27) and editor of *Irish Truth* (1924–27). His works include *Parnell Vindicated* (1931), *Ireland and the British Empire* (1937), *Conflict and Collaboration* (1937), *Parnell, Joseph Chamberlain and Mr Garvin* (1938), *Ulster and the British Empire* (1939), *Help or Hindrance* (1939) and *The Nationality of Ireland* (1942). He challenged *The Times* in 1947 when its *History of The Times* distorted the facts in connection with the forgeries in 'Parnellism and Crime'*; the fourth volume of the *History* acknowledged the misrepresentation and included a corrigendum. His last work was *Parnell, Joseph Chamberlain and the Times* (1953).

HAUGHEY, CHARLES (1925–). Politician (Fianna Fail); Taoiseach (1979–); b. Castlebar, Co. Mayo; reared in Dublin where he was educated at Scoil Mhuire, Marino, St Joseph's CBS, Fairview, UCD and King's Inns. Although called to the Bar he never practised law, concentrating instead on a career in accountancy. He was a founder of the firm of Haughey and Boland (1950) and a year later married Maureen, daughter of Sean Lemass.* Haughey, who joined the Fianna Fail party in 1948, became a member of the Dublin City Council (1953–55) but failed to gain a Dail seat in either the 1954 general election or a by-election in 1956. He was first returned as a TD for Dublin North East in 1957.

After serving as Parliamentary Secretary to the Minister for Justice (1960–61) he became Minister for Justice in 1961. He was Minister for Agriculture and Fisheries (1964–66). In 1966 he was a contender with George Colley for the leadership of the party in succession to Lemass, who wished to retire. When Jack Lynch* was nominated to contest the election Haughey withdrew and Lynch defeated Colley by fifty-two votes to nineteen. As Minister for Finance (1966–70) he was responsible for the introduction of tax exemption on the literary earnings of creative writers.

His career as a minister was abruptly interrupted when, following allegations that arms had been smuggled into the republic, his resignation was demanded by Jack Lynch who also demanded the resignation of Neil T. Blaney.* This was followed by their trial on charges of conspiring to import arms. They were found not guilty and Haughey called on Lynch to resign. While Blaney continued outside the party, Haughey remained a member. His rehabilitation began in 1972 when he was re-elected to the National Executive of Fianna Fail. He was opposition spokesman on Health (1975–77) and upon Fianna Fail's return to office in June 1977 was appointed Minister for Health and Social Welfare. His Family Planning Bill during 1978 and 1979 was a major source of public controversy: having guided it through the Dail he succeeded Lynch as leader of the party and Taoiseach on 11 December 1979, having defeated Colley by forty-four votes to thirty-eight.

'HAWARDEN KITE'. The 'Kite' was the unauthorised disclosure (16 December 1885) by Herbert Gladstone, son of W. E. Gladstone,* that his father now favoured Home Rule* as a solution to the Irish question. The publication of the announcement in the press embarrassed the Liberal Party, and had the effect of alienating Conservative support for any measure of Home Rule. Charles Stewart Parnell* then entered into an alliance with Gladstone and the Liberals. When the Liberals returned to power in January 1886, their commitment to Home Rule was a major factor in the division which followed within the party.

HAYDEN, MARY TERESA (1862–1942). Scholar; b. Dublin; ed. Alexandra College and Royal University of Ireland* where she took B.A. (1885) and M.A. (1887) in Modern Languages and was appointed Junior Fellow in English (1895). When the National University of Ireland* was founded, she became the only woman on the Senate (1909–24). She was closely associated with the Gaelic League* and sat on the executive. With George A. Moonan she was the author of *A Short History of the Irish People* (1921).

HAYDN, JOSEPH TIMOTHY (1786–1856). Journalist; b. Limerick where he founded and edited both the *Limerick Star* and the *Limerick Times.* He went to London in 1839 and continued his journalistic career. He worked for some time in the Admiralty records department for which he received a pension of £25 per annum. Haydn's most famous work, *Dictionary of Dates,* appeared in 1841, and ran to twenty-five editions before 1900. He also edited Lewis' *Topographical Dictionary* (4 vols, 1849).

HAYES-McCOY, GERARD A. (1911–75). Military historian; b. Galway; ed. Patrician Brothers and UCG, Edinburgh and London. He was Assistant Keeper at the National Museum*

(1939–58) and Professor of History, UCG (1959–75). A member of the Royal Irish Academy* and of the Irish Manuscripts Commission,* he was a committee member of the Military History Society of Ireland* and a frequent contributor to its journal, *The Irish Sword*. Professor Hayes-McCoy was the author of *Scots Mercenary Forces in Ireland* (1939), *Irish Battles: A Military History of Ireland* (1969), three chapters in the *New History of Ireland*, Volume III (1976) and *A History of Irish Flags from earliest times* (1979). He edited *The Irish At War* (1964).

HAYES, MICHAEL (1889–1976). Scholar and politician (Sinn Fein and Cumann na nGaedheal); b. Dublin; ed. CBS, Synge Street, and UCD; M.A. (1920) and called to the Bar in 1929. He was a member of the Gaelic League* and of the Irish Volunteers,* and fought under Thomas MacDonagh in Jacob's Factory during the Easter Rising of 1916,* after which he was imprisoned. Active in Sinn Fein, he was imprisoned in Mountjoy, Arbour Hill and Ballykinlar, Co. Down, during the War of Independence;* at Ballykinlar he was Director of Education for the prisoners, and organised classes in Irish, History, English, French and Spanish. While imprisoned he was elected to the second Dail Eireann and took his seat upon his release in August 1921 after the Truce. He supported the Treaty* and was Minister for Education from January to September 1922, and Minister for External Affairs from August to September. He was Ceann Comhairle (Speaker) of Dail Eireann from 1922 to 1932, and lost his seat in the general election of January 1933.

He sat in the Senate from 1933 until 1965. A lecturer in Modern Irish at UCD (1933–51) and Professor (1951–60), he was a member of the Royal Irish Academy, the Governing Body of UCD, the Senate of NUI, the Royal Society of Antiquaries and of the Military History Society. He was for many years chairman of the Standing Committee and National Council of Fine Gael. His publications included an essay on 'Thomas MacDonagh and the Rising' in *1916 and UCD* (1966), 'Impressions of Dail Eireann' (in *Capuchin Annual*, 1969) and 'Michael Collins' (*Capuchin Annual*, 1972).

HAYES, MICHAEL ANGELO (1820–77). Painter; b. Waterford. Noted for his sporting and military pictures, his best-known works were 'Punchestown', 'Sackville Street' and the Bianconi 'Travelling-Car' prints which in many cases form the only contemporary records of those conveyances. He was one of the first painters to realistically represent horses in movement.

HAYES, RICHARD (1878–1958). Scholar and politician (Sinn Fein); b. Bruree, Co. Limerick; ed. locally. He was influenced by Rev. Eugene Sheehy* and a boyhood friend was Eamon de Valera*. A member of the Irish Volunteers, he fought at Ashbourne under Thomas Ashe* during the Easter Rising of 1916 for which he was sentenced to twenty years' imprisonment. Returned as TD for East Limerick to the first Dail Eireann, he supported the Treaty* which he described as 'a compromise without dishonour'. An authority on Irish military emigrants ('The Wild Geese'), he was appointed Film Censor (1940–54). He was awarded an honorary doctorate by the National University of Ireland. His works include *Ireland and Irishmen in the French Revolution* (1932), *Irish Swordsmen of France* (1934), *The German Colony in Co. Limerick* (1937), *The Last Invasion of Ireland* (1937), *Old Irish Links with France* (1940) and *Biographical Dictionary of Irishmen in France* (1949).

HEALY, TIMOTHY MICHAEL (1855–1931). Politician (Nationalist) and author; first Governor-General of the Irish Free State (1922–28); b.

Bantry, Co. Cork; ed. CBS Fermoy, Co. Cork. He emigrated in his teens and worked as a railway clerk at Newcastle-upon-Tyne. He was parliamentary correspondent for *The Nation* and he reported the role played by the party at Westminster and highlighted the emergence of Charles Stewart Parnell.* Healy was MP for Wexford (1880–83) and acted as Parnell's secretary during the American tour of 1880. Following Parnell's triumphant reception in Montreal he referred to his leader as 'the uncrowned king of Ireland'. At Westminster, Healy was an obstructionist, noted for the severity of his language and the biting sarcasm of his wit. He was called to the Bar in 1884 and was an expert in agrarian law. This proved of immense value during the debate on the Land Act of 1881 (*see* Land Acts) and enabled him secure an amendment (the 'Healy Clause') which protected tenants from rent increases arising from their own improvements to property. He was returned as MP for Co. Monaghan in 1883 after his release from imprisonment on charges of treason. Healy broke with Parnell over the Galway by-election in 1886, and during the campaign he publicly referred to Katharine O'Shea* as Parnell's mistress. He was MP for South Londonderry (1885–86) and for North Longford (1887–92). With Timothy Harrington,* John Dillon* and William O'Brien,* he played a prominent role in the Plan of Campaign* (1886–91). When the split occurred in the Irish Parliamentary Party (1890–91), he played a leading part in the attack on Parnell, and on the Parnellite wing led by John Redmond* after Parnell's death. With Justin McCarthy* and Dillon he led the anti-Parnellite Irish National Federation* from which he was expelled in 1895. He was unsuccessful in his attempt to found a clericalist party, the People's Rights Association.* From 1892 until 1910 he was MP for North Louth. Healy represented the employers during the Inquiry into the Lock-Out* of 1913. His final parliamentary seat was North-East Cork (from 1910) and this he lost when Sinn Fein* annihilated the Irish Parliamentary Party in December 1918.

When the Free State was established in December 1922 he was a popular choice as the King's representative, the Governor-General. His writings include *Why There is an Irish Land Question and an Irish Land League* (1881), *A Record of Coercion* (1881), *Loyalty Plus Murder* (1884), *A Word for Ireland* (1886), *Key to the Land Law (Ireland) Act,* 1887 (with his brother Maurice Healy, MP), *Under Which Flag? or Is Parnell to be Leader of the Irish People?* by a Gutter Sparrow (1890), *Why Ireland is Not Free* (History of the Irish Nationalist Party 1875–98; 1898), *Stolen Waters* (1913), a shorter version of the same book under the title *The Great Fraud of Ulster* (1917), and *Letters and Leaders of My Day* (2 vols, 1928).

HEDGE-SCHOOLS. System of schools which became widespread during the eighteenth century to provide education for Catholics who were prevented by the Penal Laws* from attending schools either in Ireland or abroad. William Edward Hartpole Lecky, the historian, wrote, 'The legislation on the subject of Catholic education may be briefly described, for it amounted to universal, unqualified, and unlimited proscription'. Hedge-schools have been traced back to the seventeenth century but it was not until a century later that they became widespread and, to a certain extent, institutionalised. The hedge-school curriculum then included Latin, Greek, Arithmetic, Irish, English, History and Geography.

The hedge-schoolmasters were often itinerant educators, establishing their schools at will. They faced a major problem in finding suitable texts and students were often taught from works such as *Irish Rogues and Rapparees*, Ovid's *Art of Love, His-*

tory of Witches and Apparitions, Moll Flanders and the biography of Freney the highwayman. Payment to the schoolmaster varied throughout the country and depended on the size of the school, the standing of the teacher and the need for education. It could be as little as £20 per annum, or as much as £50 per annum. One teacher lamented that he had taught school for sixpence per quarter. Generally the teacher would, in addition, receive payments in kind, of turf, fowl, butter, vegetables, etc. He was a respected figure in the community and was frequently called to assist when letters had to be written; he was also consulted about drawing up wills, leases, measuring land or arbitrating in disputes. Thomas Crofton Croker,* writing of the celebrated Munster hedge schoolmasters, pointed out that '. . . next to the lord of the manor, the parson, and the priest, he is the most important personage in the parish'.

Among the most famous poets of the eighteenth century there were several hedge schoolmasters, including Donncadh Rua MacConmara, Eoghan Ruadh O'Suilleabhain and Bryan Merriman.* Some of the best-known teachers were Eugene Cavanagh, Peter Daly, John Fitzgerald (Cork), Richard Fitzgerald, Philip Fitzgibbon, James Fortune (Wexford), Pat Frayne (Monaghan), Peter Gallagher, Francis Grace, Maurice Gorman, Sean Kennedy, Dr Lanigan (later Bishop of Ossory), Pat Lynch, Denis McCarthy, Richard McElligott (who taught Gerald Griffin), Charles McGoldrick, John Nash, Peter O'Doirnin, Michael O'Lanagan and Tomás Rua O'Sullivan (who forgot to include the letter 'S' in his Irish *Dictionary*). Matt Tuohy, who was one of the last hedge schoolmasters, had a school in Killaloe where he charged 2s. 6d. (12½p) per week for instruction in Latin, Greek, Irish, Sums and Dancing.

Hedge schools continued into the first part of the nineteenth century but they were gradually supplanted by the schools established by Lord Stanley (*see* Derby, 14th Earl) in the system of National Education (1831).

HEENEY, PATRICK (1881–1911). Musician; b. Dublin; ed. St Patrick's National School. Although he could not write music he collaborated with Peadar Kearney* and worked out the music (on his melodeon) for Kearney's 'The Soldier's Song' which became the National Anthem. Other songs for which he provided the music included 'Michael Dwyer Keeps His Word' and 'The Flag of Green'.

'HELGA'. Built in Liffey Dockyard as a fishery protection vessel in 1908, *Helga II* was operated by the Department of Agriculture and Technical Instruction as a police patrol boat. One hundred and fifty-six feet long, 323 tons, it was taken over by the Admiralty on 27 March 1915 as an 'armed steam yacht'.

On the morning of 29 April, during the Easter Rising of 1916,* the *Helga* sailed up the Liffey and bombarded Liberty Hall, headquarters of the Irish Citizen Army.* It was also used in the attack on the insurgents' stronghold at Ringsend.

Renamed the *Muirchu* it was the first fishery protection vessel of the Free State's Coastal and Marine Service (*see* Naval Service). It was then returned to the Department of Agriculture and Fisheries (1924). It was armed for its duties until 1927. The *Muirchu* re-entered the Naval Service on 12 December 1939, shortly after the establishment of the Marine and Coastwatching Service during the Emergency.*

The ship was sold to the Hammond Lane Foundry in January 1947 but sank during passage to Dublin, off the Saltee Islands (8 May 1947). There were no injuries to crewmen.

HELY-HUTCHINSON, RICHARD, 1st EARL OF DONOUGHMORE (1758–1825). Politician; b. Dublin, son of John Hely-Hutchinson, Provost of TCD. He inherited the title in succession to his mother, Baroness of Donoughmore. As MP for Sligo and later for Taghmon, he supported efforts to secure Catholic Emancipation.* He was created Viscount Suirdale in 1797 and a year later commanded the Cork Legion during the rising of the United Irishmen.* For his support of the Union* he was created Earl in 1800 and became an Irish representative peer in the House of Lords. He continued his support of Catholic Emancipation and approved of the government's efforts to rule Ireland through coercive measures. He held the post of Postmaster General from 1805 to 1808.

HENEBRY, REV. RICHARD (1863–1916). Gaelic scholar; b. Co. Waterford; ed. Waterford and Maynooth College* where he was ordained in June 1892. A brilliant linguist, he excelled at Irish, English and Hebrew. He held a curacy at Manchester, 1892–96, after which he studied Celtic Philology at the German Universities of Frieburg and Griefswald (1896–97). He was appointed to the Ancient Order of Hibernians-endowed Chair of Irish at the University of Washington (1900–03). During his stay in the USA, he became a close friend of Captain Francis O'Neill,* Chief of Chicago Police, and a well-known collector of Irish traditional music. On his return to Ireland, Dr Henebry's contributions to *The Leader* on 'Revival of Irish' attracted attention from leading Gaelic scholars of the era. In 1908 he was appointed Professor of Celtic, UCC, a position he retained until his death. He inaugurated a class for 'Ancient Irish' and he attracted one of the largest classes at the College. An accomplished violinist, Seamus Clandillon,* when Director of Radio Eireann,* said of him '. . . I have heard Dr Henebry's rendering on his violin of "Táim-se in Chodladh" – and it seemed to me that I heard the age-old plaint of the Gaelic race, and sensed the undying hope which under God has brought our people through seven centuries of blood and tears . . .' Dr Henebry's works include *The Sounds of Munster Irish* (1898) *Eachtra an Ghobáin*

Saoir so (1910), *A Handbook of Irish Music* (1928). His collected works appeared as *Schríbhne Risteárd De Hindebergh* in 1929.

HENNESSY, WILLIAM MAUNSELL (1829–89). Scholar; b. Castlegregory, Co. Kerry. He spent some time in the USA and upon his return worked on the staff of *The Nation*, and was an active member of Young Ireland.* From 1868 he worked in the Public Record Office,* where he became Assistant Deputy Keeper. He won a high reputation for his scholarship in Irish history and literature, in particular for his Essays on MacPherson's *Ossian and Ossianic Literature* (1871). His other works include *Pedigree of the White Knight* (which he revised, 1856), *Chronicum Scotorum* (with glossary of the rarer words, 1866). He edited the *Annals of Logh Cé* (1871) and translated *Tripartite Life of St Patrick* (1871). He also edited translations of the *Book of Fenagh* (1875), *Poets and Poetry of Munster* (1883) and *Mesca Ulad* (1889). Following the deaths of his wife and daughter, he became a depressive in his later years.

HENRY, AUGUSTINE (1857–1930). Botanist; b. Cookstown, Co. Tyrone. He joined the Chinese Imperial Maritime Customs in 1882 and, for the next eighteen years, travelled extensively throughout the world collecting and studying tree specimens. While Reader in Forestry at Cambridge (1907) and Professor of Forestry at the Royal College of Science, Dublin (1913), he published many papers and acted as adviser on diseases of Irish cultivated trees. He collaborated with Elwes on *Trees of Great Britain and Ireland* (7 vols, 1906–13).

His unique collection of tree and plant specimens was donated to the Botanic Gardens* where it was separately catalogued in 1957.

HENRY, PAUL (1876–1958). Artist; b. Belfast. His father, Robert, was nephew of John Mitchel;* ed. Belfast Academical Institution, by private tutor and in Paris. He visited Achill in 1912 and set up home there until 1919. He moved to Dublin (1920) and to Bray, Co. Wicklow in 1950. Henry is known particularly for his Achill scenes and for his poster design. His 'Connemara Landscape' which he designed for the London, Midland and Scottish Railway in 1925 had the largest sale of any British poster to that period. Throughout his life he was red-green colour blind and was totally blind for the last thirteen years of his life. His paintings have had almost fifty international exhibitions. His autobiography, *An Irish Portrait*, was published in 1951 and *Further Reminiscences* in 1977.

HEUSTON, SEAN (1891–1916). Republican; b. Dublin; ed. CBS. He worked in Limerick as a railway clerk in 1908, and organised and trained Na Fianna Eireann.* After returning to Dublin in 1913, he became a founder-member of the Irish Volunteers.* At the request of Patrick Pearse* he assisted Con Colbert* in training the boys of St Enda's* in drill and musketry. A captain in the Volunteers, Heuston commanded the Mendicity Institute during the Easter Rising of 1916.* For three days his small force prevented several hundred reinforcements arriving at Kingsbridge (now Heuston) Station from linking up with British troops in Dublin. Following a court-martial he was executed on 8 May.

HEYTESBURY, 2nd BARON (1779–1860). A'Court, William; Lord Lieutenant (1844–46); ed. Eton. He entered the diplomatic service (1801) and served in Naples, Vienna, Malta and the Barbary States. He was Envoy Extraordinary to Spain (1822), Ambassador to Portugal (1824) and to Russia (1828). Heytesbury became Lord Lieutenant on 26 July 1844. In 1845 the potato crop failed at the beginning of what was to become the worst famine in Irish history (*see* Famine of 1845–49). Like most British politicians he failed to realise the crucial role of the potato in the

Irish economy. He proved unsympathetic to pleas for aid from prominent Irish leaders led by Daniel O'Connell.* Upon the fall of Peel's administration in July 1846 Heytesbury was replaced by the 4th Earl of Bessborough.*

'HIBERNIA'. Review covering current, literary and economic affairs since 1937. For 394 editions it appeared as a monthly (until October 1968). It was published fortnightly until September 1977 when it became a weekly. Founded by the Knights of Columbanus* as a vehicle for the expression of their right-wing views, it subsequently passed out of their control and gradually became one of the principal organs for liberal debate in Ireland.

'HIBERNIAN JOURNAL'. Anti-administration newspaper purchased by Thomas McDonnell in 1788. The paper initially supported the United Irishmen* but lost influence when McDonnell resigned from the movement. Following McDonnell's death in 1809 it continued an independent line for a brief period, until its new owners, J. B. and Edward Fitzsimons made it a vehicle for Dublin Castle propaganda. The anti-Catholic line of the paper continued until 1821 when it lost Castle support following an editorial in which it stated that if Catholic Emancipation* was granted, Protestants could not be held responsible for their actions. The lack of Castle support through advertising and the publication of proclamations was a severe financial blow and the paper ceased publication in 1822 when its readership had fallen to less than a hundred.

HICKEY, REV. WILLIAM (1788–1875). Clergyman (C.I.), agriculturist and author; b. Murragh, Co. Cork; ed. TCD and Cambridge; he was awarded a B.A. in 1809 and M.A. in 1832. He held various curacies from 1820 until settling in Mulrankin (1834). With Thomas Boyce he was founder of the South Wexford Agricultural Society (the first of its kind in Ireland). Rev. Hickey set out to educate the peasantry in agriculture and husbandry with a series of Handbooks (under the pseudonym 'Martin Doyle'), starting with *Hints to Small Farmers* (1830). He contributed prose and verse to the *Dublin Penny Journal* and was a frequent letter-writer to provincial and national newspapers on all aspects of agricultural life. The Royal Literary Fund awarded him an annual pension for his services to Irish agriculture. His works include *The Flower Garden* (1834), *A Cyclopaedia of Practical Husbandry* (1839), *Farm and Garden Produce* (1857) and *Cottage Farming* (1870). He also attempted to improve the relationship between landlord and tenant and wrote several booklets on the theme, including *An Address to the Landlords of Ireland* (1831) and *The Labouring Classes in Ireland* (1846). Rev. Hickey edited the *Irish Farmers' and Gardeners' Magazine* (1834—42) and *The Illustrated Book of Domestic Poultry* (1854).

HICKS-BEACH, SIR MICHAEL, 9th BARONET AND 1st EARL ALDWYN (1837—1916). Politician (Conservative); Chief Secretary (1874—78; 1886); ed. Eton and Christ Church, Oxford; MP from 1864. He was Parliamentary Secretary to the Poor Law Board (1868). During his first term as Irish Chief Secretary he was the unwitting cause of singling out Charles Stewart Parnell* for the attention of the Irish Republican Brotherhood;* on 30 June 1876 Hicks-Beach referred to 'the Manchester Murderers' and Parnell, claiming that the Chief Secretary was looking at him, stated '... I do not believe and never shall believe, that any murder was committed at Manchester'. Although hostile to Home Rule* on which he claimed that the Irish party itself was not united, he was sympathetic to Irish reforms. He strongly opposed the (first) Home Rule Bill* introduced by W. E. Gladstone* in 1886 and when Gladstone's administration fell, became Chancellor for the second time in a Conservative government. When he became Chief Secretary later in 1886 he found Ireland in the throes of a new land agitation, the Plan of Campaign.* In 1887 he was succeeded at the Irish office by Arthur J. Balfour.* He was President of the Board of Trade (1888—92) and Chancellor of the Exchequer (1895—1902).

HICKSON, MARY AGNES (1826—99). Historian; b. Co. Kerry; as a local historian she contributed an immense amount of family and local history to the *Kerry Evening Post;* author of *Selections from Old Kerry Records* (first series, 1872; second series, 1874) and *Ireland in the Seventeenth Century* (2 vols, 1884).

HIGGINS, FREDERICK ROBERT (1896—1941). Poet; b. near Foxford, Co. Mayo. He worked as an office boy in Dublin and later became an official in the Irish labour movement. His poetry was first published by Arthur Griffith* in *Sinn Fein.* Higgins edited economic and literary journals and in 1935 became joint-editor, with W. B. Yeats,* of *Broadsides.* He was managing director of the Abbey Theatre* from 1935 and a founder-member of the Irish Academy of Letters.* He was a close friend of Padraic O Conaire* on whose death he wrote a lament, 'Padraic O Conaire Gaelic Storyteller'. His works include *Salt Air* (1924), *Island Blood* (1925), *Arable Pastures* (1933), *The Gap of Brightness* (1940). His poetry dealt principally with the natural beauty of the West and Midlands of Ireland.

HIGHER EDUCATION AUTHORITY. *See* Commission on Higher Education.

HILLERY, PATRICK (1923—   ). Politician (Fianna Fail); President of Ireland (1976—   ); b. Miltown Malbay, Co. Clare; ed. National School, Rockwell College and UCD; M.D. (1947). He was elected TD, West Clare in 1951 and represented the constituency until 1973, serving as a member of several Fianna Fail governments as Minister for Education (1959—65), Industry and Commerce (1965—66), Labour (1966—69) and External Affairs (1969—72). While Minister for External Affairs, Dr Hillery was responsible for the conduct of the negotiations which led to the Republic's accession to the European Economic Community in 1973. He left Irish politics to become the Irish Commissioner and a Vice-President of the Commission of the EEC in which he had responsibility for Social Affairs (1973—76). Following the resignation of Cearbhall O Dálaigh* Dr Hillery became an agreed candidate for the Presidency and was elected in November 1976.

HIRING-FAIR. A fair at which men and boys offered themselves for employment to substantial farmers for the agricultural season. While it was the prerogative of the hirer to strike a bargain over wages, it was possible for the one hiring himself to bargain for additional benefits in kind (bacon, potatoes, clothing, footwear, etc.). Those who hired themselves out were often known as 'spalpeens'.

HOBSON, BULMER (1883—1969). Republican; b. Belfast; ed. Quaker's School. He founded Na Fianna Eireann* in Belfast in 1903 and the movement was re-organised at his suggestion in 1909 by Countess Markievicz.* Denis McCullough* recruited him into the IRB in 1904 and together they founded the Dungannon Clubs in 1905. He was a pioneer of the Sinn Fein idea and became vice-president of the movement in 1907. He founded a journal, *The Republic* (1906—07), and also worked on *The Peasant* (1908) in Dublin. At his suggestion *Irish Freedom* was founded in 1910. He became chairman of the Dublin Centre of the IRB, was a member of the Leinster executive and then a member of the Supreme Council.* He played a major role in the establishment of the Irish Volunteers* in 1913

but lost the confidence of Thomas J. Clarke,* Sean MacDiarmada* and other influential Fenians when he supported a demand by John Redmond* for half of the seats on the controlling body of the Volunteers (June 1914). John Devoy* dismissed him from *The Gaelic American* and he was also forced to resign from *Irish Freedom* and from the Supreme Council. After he accidentally discovered the plans for the Easter Rising of 1916* he informed Eoin MacNeill* and helped him in the attempt to prevent the rising, but was held prisoner by the leaders until it had started. After 1916 he withdrew from public life and secured a minor civil service post in the Free State, which he held until his retirement to Connemara in 1946. His autobiography, *Yesterday, Today and Tomorrow,* was published in 1969.

HOGAN, JAMES J. (1898—1963). Historian; b. Kilfrickle, Co. Galway; ed. Clongowes Wood College and UCD. He was a member of the Dublin 3rd Battalion of the Irish Volunteers. In Galway during the Easter Rising of 1916,* he was organiser for the Volunteers in the Loughrea district. He served in the East Clare Flying Column during the War of Independence.* In 1920 he was appointed Professor of History at UCC after publishing *Ireland in the European System,* but did not take up the appointment until 1923 (he held it for forty years). Before taking up his Cork post, he entered the Free State national army for a short time, having supported the Treaty. In 1928 he was a founder-member of the Irish Manuscripts Commission* and joint-editor with Eoin MacNeill of *Analecta Hibernica.* During the rise of the Blueshirts,* 1932—33, he supported its anti-communism and contributed to Cumann na nGaedheal and Fine Gael newspapers. His pamphlet, *Could Ireland become Communist?* (1935), was widely-read. He was a regular contributor to *Studies* and *Proceedings* of the Royal Irish Academy; he

226

was the author of *Election and Representation* (1943).

HOGAN, JOHN (1800–58). Sculptor; b. Tallow, Co. Waterford; ed. locally. His family moved to Cork where in 1814 Hogan was employed as a solicitor's clerk, and then as a draughtsman and wood-carver. He was employed by Dr Murphy, Bishop of Cork, to carve twenty-seven statues in wood and bas-relief panel for the North Chapel. Under the patronage of Lord de Tabley, Hogan went to Rome where he remained until 1849, apart from two visits to Ireland (1829, 1840). Having earlier refused membership of the Royal Hibernian Academy,* he was elected a member of the prestigious Vir Tuosi del Pantheon (the first person from these islands to be so honoured: 1837).

Hogan's first work in Rome was the 'Italian Shepherd Boy' (1826). Other works include 'The Dead Christ' (Carmelite Church, Dublin, 1828), Rev. Theobald Mathew (1840, 1844), James Warren Doyle ('J.K.L.') (Carlow Cathedral, 1840), Daniel O'Connel (City Hall, Dublin, 1846; the Crescent, Limerick, 1857), Thomas Steele (RHA, 1851), Thomas Davis (Mortuary Chapel, Mount St Jerome Cemetery, Dublin, 1853), Robert Graves (Royal College of Physicians, Dublin, 1853) and Bishop Brinkley of Cloyne (Cloyne, Co. Cork, and statue at TCD).

HOGAN, PATRICK J. (1891–1936). Politician (Sinn Fein and Cumann na nGaedheal); b. Co. Clare; ed. locally. A member of the Irish Volunteers, he was returned as Sinn Fein TD for Co. Galway in the general election of 1921. As Minister for Agriculture from 1922 to 1932 in the Provisional Government* and succeeding Cumann na nGaedheal governments, he was considered one of the outstanding ministers. He introduced the 1923 Land Act (*see* Land Acts) and attempted to reform agriculture through his Dairy and Livestock-Breeding Acts. After losing his Dail seat in 1932 he was a member of the Senate until his death in a car accident.

HOLLAND, JOHN P. (1841–1914). Submarine inventor; b. Liscannor, Co. Clare. He joined the Irish Christian Brothers* and became a teacher, working in Dundalk (1869–73) where he demonstrated a model submarine. Forced through ill-health to abandon teaching, he left the Brothers and emigrated to the USA where his plans for a submarine were rejected by the US Navy (1875). Holland offered his services to John Devoy,* the Fenian leader of Clan na Gael.* The Clan provided him with 6,000 dollars with which he built an experimental boat, the *Holland No. 2,* over the next two years. Between 1879 and 1881 he built the *Holland No. 3,* known as the *Fenian Ram.* The vessel, which was armed with underwater cannon, was intended to be used against British ships in the Atlantic and for an invasion of Ireland by Fenians.* There is no evidence to suggest that the submarine was ever used in combat. The experiments cost the Clan around 60,000 dollars and it became disillusioned with the inventor's projects. In 1898 *Holland No. 9* was completed and this proved the prototype for future American and British submarines. Shortly after his death, World War I vindicated Holland's faith in the submarine as an effective weapon.

HOLLOWAY, JOSEPH (1861–1944). Diarist; b. Dublin. He attended every play and many of the rehearsals at the Abbey Theatre* and kept a diary of his observations. The complete record spans fifty years and 221 volumes, and was published in edited form as *Joseph Holloway's Abbey Theatre* in 1967. The diary also records Holloway's impressions of the Easter Rising of 1916.*

HOLMES, ROBERT (1765–1859). Lawyer; b. Dublin; ed. TCD and called to the Bar in 1785. He resigned from the lawyer's corps of the Yeomen during the rising of the United Irishmen in 1798 in protest at atrocities committed by the government forces under General Edward Lake. A strong opponent of the Union,* he published an appeal to the Irish legislature to reject it. He was imprisoned in 1803 on suspicion of having supported the uprising of his brother-in-law, Robert Emmet.* Holmes became father of the northeast circuit and rejected any offers of government advancement, earning the nickname 'Bitter Bob'. He supported the Repeal Association* in whose cause he published *Case of Ireland Stated* (1847). He continued at the Bar until his eighties, and represented *The Nation** in 1846, and John Mitchel* in 1847.

HOME GOVERNMENT ASSOCIATION. Founded in May 1870 by Isaac Butt.* Its sole aim was the establishment of a federal system for the United Kingdom, which would grant Ireland a domestic parliament responsible for internal affairs. The Association, which never became a national movement, contained Catholics and Protestants, Orangemen and Repealers, liberals and conservatives, veterans of Young Ireland* and a few Fenians.* It gathered little electoral support and election results indicated that on its own, federalism or Home Rule was not a popular issue. It was succeeded in 1873 by the Home Rule League.*

HOME RULE. The term 'Home Rule', first used in the 1860s, meant an Irish legislature with responsibility· for domestic affairs. It was variously interpreted. Isaac Butt,* founder of the Home Government Association* and the Home Rule League* from which developed the Irish Parliamentary Party,* saw it as part of a federal system for the United Kingdom: a domestic parliament for Ireland while the imperial parliament at Westminster would continue to have responsibility for imperial affairs. Republicans, represented by the Fenians* and the Irish Republican Brotherhood,* wanted total separa-

tion from Britain and complete autonomy for Ireland but for the moment they were prepared to co-operate with Home Rulers. Charles Stewart Parnell* sought, as an interim measure, a Dublin parliament with a limited amount of legislative power. Arthur Griffith* envisaged a dual monarchy upon the Austro-Hungarian model. To Unionists,* and in particular to Ulster Unionists and the Orange Order,* Home Rule meant a parliament in Dublin dominated by the Catholic Church and interfering with Ireland's economic progress. The Liberal Party, under W. E. Gladstone,* committed itself to Home Rule while the Conservatives sought to divert attention from the demand by implementing a policy of moral force or constructive Unionism ('Killing Home Rule by kindness').

The first Home Rule Bill, introduced by Gladstone on 8 April 1886, was defeated on 8 June by 343 votes to 311 in the House of Commons. His second Bill, in 1892, passed the Commons but was rejected by the House of Lords. The Liberal government formed by Henry Campbell-Bannerman in 1905 was not dependent upon the support of the Irish party, then led by John Redmond.* However Campbell-Bannerman's successor, H. H. Asquith,* needed Redmond's support to secure the passage of the Parliament Act* in 1911 and promised Home Rule in return. The third Home Rule Bill was introduced by Asquith on 11 April 1912. Opposition to the Bill was led by Sir Edward Carson* for the Unionists. The House of Lords used its veto to delay the passage of the Bill. Asquith's government vacillated and attempted to reach a compromise with Redmond and Carson, considering the exclusion of some part of Ulster. Partition was acceptable to neither side but by the summer of 1914 nothing had been settled. The Buckingham Palace Conference* in July failed to reach a settlement and after the outbreak of war in August, Asquith secured from the Irish parties an agreement to the suspension of the Act for the duration of the war. It was signed into law by King George V* on 18 September. The Unionists were given to understand that the Act would not become operative until some provision had been made for part of Ulster.

By 1919 events in Ireland, particularly in the aftermath of the Easter Rising of 1916,* had made Home Rule an irrelevance. This was clearly demonstrated when Redmond's party was routed by Sinn Fein* in the general election of December 1918. The republican tradition had won when, in January 1919, the Sinn Fein representatives opened Dail Eireann* and declared the establishment of an Irish Republic. The British government attempted to settle the problem during the War of Independence* by the passage of the Government of Ireland Act 1920.* Home Rule became a reality under the Treaty* in 1922 when the Free State* was established for the twenty-six southern counties and the state of Northern Ireland,* established under the Government of Ireland Act 1920, continued in existence.

HOME RULE BILL, FIRST (1886). The first Home Rule Bill was introduced in the House of Commons by W. E. Gladstone* on 8 April 1886; it was defeated in the Commons by 343 votes to 311 on 8 June. The Bill proposed an Irish legislature of two Orders, one containing 103 members of whom 75 were to be elected (for a ten-year term) on a restricted franchise and 28 were to be peers; the second Order was to consist of 204 members elected on the existing franchise for a five-year term.

The legislative functions of the Irish assembly would be restricted: it would not have the power to make laws dealing with the Crown, war or peace, defence, treaties, titles of honour, treason, alienage and naturalisation, navigation, trade, beacons, quarantine, lighthouses, coinage, weights, copyrights, the undenominational nature of education or the establishment or endowment of reli-

gion. Ireland would not be represented in the imperial parliament. The Irish executive would be the Crown represented through the Lord Lieutenant* who would have power of veto and who would have the aid and advice of the Executive committee of the Irish Privy Council.

Ireland would control its own taxes with the exception of customs and excise. The revenue at the disposal of the Irish government would be the gross revenue collected in Ireland from Irish and imperial taxes, and Crown lands. Ireland would bear the cost of collecting the revenue. The Irish contribution to the imperial exchequer was to be calculated at a fixed maximum which could be diminished but could not be exceeded, and which was to be revised in thirty years. The cost for 1886 would have been £3,242,000. Judges were to be appointed by the Irish government. The Dublin Metropolitan Police* were to remain under imperial control for two years and the Royal Irish Constabulary* were to be permanently under imperial control. However, it was envisaged that Ireland would ultimately create a new police force under the control of local authorities. This measure of self-government was accepted by Charles Stewart Parnell* as a temporary measure. He felt that having achieved such progress, it would be possible to make advances as the occasion arose.

HOME RULE BILL, SECOND (1893). W. E. Gladstone* introduced his second Home Rule Bill in January 1893. It was strongly resisted in the Commons and was only forced through with repeated use of closure. In September it was rejected by the House of Lords.

Under the 1893 Bill, it was proposed that Ireland should again have a two-tier legislature; there would be a Council of forty-eight members elected for an eight-year term on a restricted franchise, and an Assembly of 103 members elected for five years on the existing franchise. As in the

1886 Bill, disagreements were to be settled by joint majority vote. The same restrictions applied as in the 1886 Bill. Ireland would have eighty representatives in the imperial parliament. Certain powers relating to landlord/tenant relations and the purchase and letting of land were to be reserved to the imperial parliament. The executive was to be the same as in the 1886 Bill, but a limit of six years was placed on the Lord Lieutenant's term of office. The system of taxation was to be the same as in the 1886 Bill. Revenue was to be the true Irish revenue derived from imperial taxes, revenue from Irish taxes and Crown lands and an imperial grant of one-third of the annual cost of the police forces (DMP and RIC). Ireland's contribution to the imperial exchequer for six years would be one-third of the true revenue raised in Ireland, which in 1893 amounted to approximately one twenty-seventh of the total imperial expenditure. This scheme would be revised after six years. Judges would be appointed by the Irish government but for six years judges of the Supreme Court would be appointed by the imperial parliament. The Dublin Metropolitan Police* and the Royal Irish Constabulary* were to be under imperial control permanently but again it was envisaged that locally controlled police forces would gradually replace them.

HOME RULE BILL, THIRD (1912). H. H. Asquith* introduced the third Home Rule Bill to the House of Commons on 11 April 1912. It met with strong opposition in the Commons from Ulster Unionists* and Conservatives and the third reading was not carried until January 1913. It was then defeated in the House of Lords who, since the Parliament Act of 1911,* could delay it for two years. The Bill was signed into law by King George V* on 18 September 1914. By agreement with the Ulster Unionists and the Irish Parliamentary Party,* it was suspended for the duration of World War I, leaving the question of

exclusion unresolved. However, by the time the war ended the Easter Rising of 1916* had changed public opinion in Ireland and the Act was not acceptable to nationalists. It was superseded by the Government of Ireland Act, 1920.

The third Bill provided for two Houses, a Senate of forty members to be nominated by the Lord Lieutenant* in the first instance and thereafter elected for five-year terms under the existing franchise, and a House of Commons of 164 members elected for five-year terms under the same franchise. Disagreements were to be resolved by joint majority. Restrictions on the legislature were the same as those in the 1893 and 1886 Bills, and in addition, it was prevented from making laws on religious belief or ceremony as a condition of marriage. Ireland was to have forty-two representatives in the imperial parliament. The imperial parliament retained control of Old Age Pensions (1908–11), National Insurance, the Labour Exchanges, the Post Office, Savings Banks and Friendly Societies for a minimum of ten years until a Resolution of Transfer had been passed by the Irish parliament. In addition, it reserved in perpetuity control of tax collection and land purchase. The executive, as in 1886 and 1893, was to be the Lord Lieutenant acting on behalf of the Crown and aided and advised by the Privy Council. The Irish parliament was to have the power to vary imperial taxes and to impose new taxes but it could not vary the rate of income tax on incomes below £5,000 per annum. It also would have power to impose customs duties on articles subject to imperial Customs Duty (including alcohol, tea, coffee, sugar, tobacco and cocoa). Irish revenue was to be raised from sums transferred from the imperial treasury, consisting of the revenue derived from Irish taxes and a fixed annual grant from the imperial parliament (£500,000 for three years, to be reduced by £50,000 per annum, until it reached £200,000). The cost of reserved services was to be borne by the imperial parliament. Ireland's contribution to the imperial parliament was to be fixed by a Joint Exchequer Board after total revenues equalled total charges for three consecutive years. It would be fixed on the basis of an equitable contribution by Ireland to the common expenses of the United Kingdom. Judges were to be appointed as laid down in the 1886 Bill and the police would be controlled by the Irish parliament except for the Royal Irish Constabulary* which would be controlled by the imperial parliament for six years.

HOME RULE CONFEDERATION OF GREAT BRITAIN. Founded in 1873 by Isaac Butt* to harness the support of the Irish people in Britain for Home Rule*. It gained the support of Irish exiles in Wales and Scotland as well as in England. Butt was replaced as president by Charles Stewart Parnell* in 1877. The Confederation was gradually infiltrated by members of the Irish Republican Brotherhood* who recognised the potential of the movement to spread their influence among the large Irish population in the British industrial centres.

HOME RULE LEAGUE. Founded in 1873 to replace the Home Government Association.* Its leader was Isaac Butt* and its principal aim was to obtain self-government for Ireland through a federal system for the United Kingdom. Under Butt's guidance the League became identified with the popular issues of the day, such as denominational education, land reform and Home Rule.* In spite of being unprepared for the 1874 general election – the first held under the Secret Ballot Act of 1872 – the League secured fifty-nine seats, two of which were in Ulster (Cavan). The League marked the first positive step by Irish members towards a separate and distinct party at Westminster which was realised by the Irish Parliamentary Party.*

HOME RULE PARTY. *See* Irish Parliamentary Party.

HOME RULE UNION. Organised by the British Liberal Party in 1886. Two years later it had sixty affiliated Liberal Associations. It disseminated propagandist literature, much of it supplied by the Irish Press Agency,* in an attempt to foster support for Home Rule.* The Union provided lecturers (most of them Parnellite members of the Irish Parliamentary Party*) throughout Britain. It collapsed following the split in the Parnellite party (1890–91).

HONE, EVIE (1894–1955). Artist; b. Dublin. She studied art under Sickert, Meninsky and Byam Shaw before moving to Paris where she worked under Lhote and Gleizes. Her development took her away from painting and into stained glass. A friend and fellow-student of Mainie Jellet,* she joined Sarah Purser* in 1932 and workly closely with her and Michael Healy in the development of the Irish stained glass industry. Her works in stained glass include 'Deposition' (Municipal Gallery of Modern Art, Dublin), the great window of Eton College, and windows in the Jesuit seminary at Rahan, Co. Offaly, St Mary's, Kingscourt, Co. Cavan, Farm Street Jesuit Church, London, and in the new Cathedral of Washington D.C.

HOPE, JEMMY (1764–1847). Poet and United Irishman; b. Templepatrick, Co. Antrim, the son of a weaver. Largely self-educated, he was apprenticed to a linen-weaver and, after serving his term, became a journeyman. A member of the Roughfort Volunteers, Hope came into contact with leading United Irishmen* of the day, including Samuel Neilson, Thomas Russell* and Henry Joy McCracken. He became a recruiting agent for the United Irishmen in Dublin in 1796. Following the collapse of the 1798 rising he remained on the run in Ulster for five months before making his way to Dublin where he

231

worked in the Coombe. He supported his friend Robert Emmet* in planning the insurrection of 1803 and was in effect quartermaster and chief organiser of the rising. He was on an organisational tour in Ulster when the rising occurred and his deputy failed to alert Michael Dwyer* in Wicklow. Hope escaped arrest and returned to Belfast in 1806 where he worked for some time for the McCracken family. His last employment was as clerk to Joseph Smyth, publisher of the *Belfast Almanac*.

Hope was socialist in outlook. George Gilmore* has compared his influence in his own time to that of James Fintan Lalor* and James Connolly* at later periods. His poetry, much of it written in the closing years of his life, was included by R. R. Madden* in *Literary Remains of the United Irishmen*.

HOUSES, CLASSES OF. The Census Commissioners classified Irish houses in the nineteenth century in four main categories: in the fourth class were all mud cabins having only one room; third class were also of mud but with two to four rooms, having windows; the second class was a good farmhouse with from five to nine rooms, with windows; in the first class were all houses of a better description. The figures from 1841 to 1861 are as follows:

	1841	1851	1861
Class 1	40,080	50,164	55,416
Class 2	264,184	318,758	360,698
Class 3	533,297	541,712	489,668
Class 4	491,278	135,589	89,374

HOWTH GUN-RUNNING. The running in of guns to Howth, Co. Dublin for the Irish Volunteers* was planned by Eoin MacNeill,* Bulmer Hobson,* The O'Rahilly,* Robert Erskine Childers,* Mary Spring Rice, *Sir Roger Casement* and Darrell Figgis.* The guns, having been purchased in Germany by Figgis, were taken to Howth by Childers in his yacht, the *Asgard*,* and arrived on 26 July 1914. The 900 rifles and 29,000 rounds of ammunition were collected by Volunteers and members of Na Fianna Eireann.* The successful landing was in emulation of the Larne Gunrunning of April 1914. Later that evening, there was a confrontation between soldiers and sympathisers of the Volunteers at Bachelor's Walk.* See also *Chotah* and *Kelpie*.

HULL, ELEANOR HENRIETTA (1860–1935). Scholar and poet; b. England; ed. Alexandra College, Dublin. She pursued her studies in Old Irish under Kuno Meyer* and Standish Hayes O'Grady.* On completion of her education, she moved to London where her early writings appeared in *The Cornhill Magazine*. A member of the London Branch of the Gaelic League,* she was instrumental in the founding of the Irish Texts Society* of which she was long-time secretary. She was also president of the London Irish Literary Society.* Her works include *Cuchulain Saga* (1898), *Pagan Ireland* (1904), *Early Christian Ireland* (1904), *A text book of Irish Literature* (2 vols, 1906–08), *Cuchulainn the Hound of Ulster* (1909), *Poem Book of the Gael* (1912), *Northmen in Britain* (1913), *History of Ireland* (2 vols, 1926, 1931), and *Folklore of the British Isles* (1928).

HUME, JOHN (1937–   ). Politician (Social Democratic and Labour Party); b. Derry city; ed. St Columb's

College, Maynooth and Queen's University, Belfast. In turn a teacher and a businessman (in the salmon business), his administrative abilities were utilised in founding a housing association and a credit union which he pioneered among the Derry Catholic population. He was President of the Credit Union League of Ireland (1964–68). A pacifist, he was a member of the Northern Ireland Civil Rights Association* (NICRA) and was present at the riot which ensued when NICRA members were attacked by police in Derry on 5 October 1968. Four days later he was co-founder and vice-chairman of the Derry Citizens' Action Committee.

Hume, who won the Foyle seat to the Northern Ireland parliament from Eddie McAteer* in 1969, played a leading role in the prevention of rioting in Derry on 16 November 1969. A founder-member and deputy chairman of the SDLP, he was returned as MP for Londonderry to the Assembly of Northern Ireland (1973–74) and was Minister for Commerce in the power-sharing Executive (January – May 1974). He held his seat in the election to the Convention to draft a constitution (1975–76). Following the failure of the Convention he took up a position in the commission of the European Economic Community. In June 1979, he was one of those members elected to represent Northern Ireland in the first directly-elected European Parliament. He was elected to the position of leader of the SDLP in succession to Gerry Fitt* who resigned in November 1979.

HUMPHRIES, FR DAVID (1834–1930). Clergyman (R.C.) and land agitator; b. Boher, Co. Tipperary; ed. Maynooth for the archdiocese of Cashel where his bishop was Thomas William Croke.* A radical on the land question, he supported the Land League* and played a leading role in the organisation of the rent-strike in Tipperary town where he was a curate (1889–95). He formulated the plan for New Tipperary* in the fight

against A. J. Smith-Barry (*see* Barrymore, Lord) during the Plan of Campaign.*

HUNT, JOHN (1900–76). Antiquarian; b. near Newmarket-on-Fergus, Co. Clare. He received his final education at UCC and graduated M.A. in medieval sculpture. He worked on many of the major excavations in Limerick and Clare including Lough Gur, and supervised the restoration of Bunratty Castle, Co. Clare. In 1965 he bought Craggaunowen Castle, Co. Clare, and restored it. A frequent contributor to specialist publications throughout the world, his major work was *Irish Medieval Figure Sculpture 1200–1500* (1974). He bequeathed his collection of antiquities to the National Institute of Higher Education, Limerick.

HUNT COMMISSION. The British government appointed a Commission of Inquiry in August 1969 under the chairmanship of Lord John Hunt to examine the recruitment, organisation, structure and composition of the Royal Ulster Constabulary,* and the Special Constabulary* in Northern Ireland. The other members of the Commission were Sir James Robertston and Robert Mark. The Report of the Commission, on the *Re-organisation of the Police in Northern Ireland* issued in October, recommended that the RUC should be relieved of all duties of a military nature and that its function should be restricted to intelligence-gathering, the protection of important persons and the enforcement of specified laws. The Commission also proposed that there should be a Police Authority for Northern Ireland, whose membership should reflect the proportions of the different religions in the community. It was recommended that the Special Constabulary should be disbanded and replaced by a locally-recruited part-time force to operate under the authority of the GOC, Northern Ireland.

In spite of objections from Ulster Unionists* the report was implemented. The Special Constabulary, particularly unpopular with the Catholic population in Northern Ireland, was disbanded on 1 April 1970 and the RUC lost its military powers. A new force, the Ulster Defence Regiment,* was established for security duties. However, the government of Northern Ireland, headed by Major James Dawson Chichester-Clark,* did grant the new body many of the old powers of the 'B' Specials and many of the former Special Constabulary became members of the UDR. *See also* Cameron Commission.

HYDE, DR DOUGLAS (1863–1947). Gaelic scholar; first President of Ireland (1938–45); b. Sligo, he was reared in Frenchpark, Co. Roscommon; ed. TCD where he took a B.A. (1884) and LL.D. (1887). Throughout his life he played a leading role in efforts to preserve the Irish language. He was a member of the Society for the Preservation of the Language at TCD, and later of the Gaelic Union. With W. B. Yeats* he founded the Irish Literary Society* in London (1891) and the National Literary Society in Dublin (May 1892). In November 1892 he delivered a manifesto to the NLS under the title 'The Necessity for de-Anglicising Ireland' in which he urged the Irish people to assert their separate cultural identity. In July 1893 he became co-founder of the Gaelic League* and remained its President until 1915. During the 1890s he organised a successful campaign to force the Post Office to accept letters and parcels addressed in Irish. As 'An Craoibhin Aoibhinn' (The Sweet Little Branch) he published poetry and drama in Irish. His *Casadh an tSúgáin* (1901) was one of the earliest plays in the language.

In 1897 Hyde became an assistant editor of the New Irish Library.* He was the editor of *Ciolla an Fhuiga* (1901) published by the Irish Texts Society* of which he was president and for which he edited volume 36 (folktales) in 1939. As a member of the Commission on Secondary Education he successfully fought Professor J. P. Mahaffy* for the inclusion of the Irish language on the curriculum (1901). In 1906 he was a member of the Royal Commission on University Education and he was successful in his efforts to have Irish included as a compulsory subject for matriculation. He was Professor of Modern Irish at the National University (1908–32) and was Dean of the Faculty of Celtic Studies. Dr Hyde was a member of the Senate of the NUI (1909–19). He was Chairman of the Irish Folklore Institute (1930–34) and was awarded the Gregory Medal in 1937. In 1938 he was the unopposed candidate for the presidency of Ireland (Eire). While in office, he published three volumes for private circulation: *The Children of Lir* (1941), *Songs of Columcille* (1942) and *Dánta Éagsamhla.* His publications included *Leabhar Sgéaglaigheachta* (1889), *Cois na Teinneadh* (Beside the Fire, 1890), *Amhráin Grádh Chúige Connacht* (Love Songs of Connaught, 1893), *The Three Sorrows of Storytelling* (1895), *The Story of Gaelic Literature* (1895), *The Story of Early Irish Literature* (1897), *An Sgéalaidhe Gaodhalach* (Cuid 1, 1898; Cuid II, 1899; Cuid III, 1901), in a French translation (1899) and republished in Irish type (1933); *A Literary History of Ireland* (1899), *Medieval Tales from the Irish* (Vol. 1 for the Irish Texts Society, 1899); *Ubhla den Chroibh* (poetry, 1900), *Casadh an tSúgáin* (play, 1901), *Trí Sgéalta* (1902), *Filidheacht Gaedhalach* (1903), *Abhráin an Reachtabhraigh* (1903; enlarged edition, *Abhráin agus Dánta an Reachtabhraigh,* in 1933); *The Bursting of the Bubble, An Pósadh, An Cleamhnas, King James and The Tinker and the Fairy* (plays, 1905), *The Religious Songs of Connaught* (1906), *Sgéaluidhe Fíor na Seachtmhaine* (1909), *Maistín an Bhéarla* (play, 1913), *Legends, Saints and Sinners from the Irish* (1915), *The History of Charlemagne* (edited and translated from *The Book of Lismore* and other vellum

MSS.; volume XIX for the Irish Texts Society, 1919); *An Leath-ranna* (1922), *Oct Sgéalta Ó Choillte Mágnach* (1936), *Imeasg na nGaedheal*

ins Oileán Úr (1937), and *Sgéalta Thomáis Uí Chatasaigh* (1939); his autobiography, *Mise agus an Conradh*, appeared in 1931.

I

IBERNO-CELTIC SOCIETY. Scholarly society founded in Dublin in 1818 with the object of preserving the 'venerable remains of Irish literature, by collecting, transcribing, illustrating and publishing the numerous fragments of the Law, History, Topography, Poetry, and Music of Ancient Ireland . . .' Its members included Edward O'Reilly* whose *Chronological Account of nearly Four Hundred Writers* (1820) was the Society's only publication; other members were Sir George Petrie* and James Hardiman.*

IMPERIAL CONFERENCES (1926–31). As a member of the British Commonwealth of Nations the Irish Free State was represented at the Imperial Conferences at which the status of the member nations was defined. At the early Conferences the Free State delegation was led by Kevin O'Higgins.* O'Higgins worked in close association with the Canadian and South African delegations but as Ireland was the most recent addition to the Commonwealth it was felt politic to allow the other two delegations to lead on the issues concerning which there was agreement.

The most thorny issue at the Imperial Conferences of the 1920s was the exact status of the member nations of the Commonwealth in relation to the imperial parliament. A breakthrough came in 1926 when Arthur James Balfour* defined that relationship as being between

autonomous communities within the British Empire, equal in status, in no way subordinate one to another in any aspect of their domestic or external affairs, though

united by common allegiance to the Crown and freely associated as members of the British Commonwealth of Nations.

This, the 'Balfour Definition' as it became known, led forward to the Statute of Westminster* in 1931. By then O'Higgins' place had been taken by Patrick McGilligan* who played a leading role in writing the final draft of the Statute under which the parliaments of the Commonwealth nations were free to repeal or reject the legislation of the imperial parliament.

INCUMBERED ESTATES ACTS. *See* Encumbered Estates Acts.

'INDENTURED' APPRENTICES. Malpractice promoted chiefly by American merchantmen when touching at Irish ports. Young boys were invited on board ship where they were forced to sign 'agreements' as apprentices for a number of years. However, the practice was to use them for the return voyage and then turn them adrift. J. K. Trimmer in his *Further Observations on the Present State of Ireland* (London 1812) observed, 'This traffic in Irishmen has been of long continuance, and to a very great extent; as lately as last year I witnessed an American vessel freighted with nearly three hundred of these poor deluded self-sold men'.

INDEPENDENT IRISH PARTY. Founded in September 1852 from an alliance of the Irish Brigade* and the Tenant League,* the Independent Irish Party consisted of some forty Irish MPs led by Charles Gavan Duffy,* George Henry Moore* and Frederick

Lucas.* Members were pledged to be 'independent of and in opposition to' all British governments which did not (1) concede the demands of the Tenant League for land reform and (2) repeal the Ecclesiastical Titles Act.* The party also sought the Disestablishment of the Church of Ireland.* It was viewed with hostility by the Catholic Archbishop of Dublin, Dr Paul Cullen,* who distrusted Duffy and forbade priests to take an active part in political matters. He also was alarmed lest the party might provoke the government into an anti-Catholic reaction.

The election of 1852 resulted in a Tory administration led by Lord Derby who refused to consider the League's land reform bill. The party helped to unseat the government which was succeeded by a Liberal administration under Lord Aberdeen (December). Two members of the party, John Sadleir* and William Keogh,* accepted office from the government, breaking their pledges and dealing the party a severe blow when their example was followed by other members. Within a year the number of Irish independents had been reduced to twenty-six.

Lucas complained to Rome about Archbishop Cullen's ordinance on clerical involvement in politics and when he took his case to Rome (December 1854 – May 1855) both clerical and lay opinion was outraged. Six members of the party forwarded a memorial to Rome, further alienating public opinion in their constituencies. The party lost its three leaders within a short time when Lucas died (1855), Duffy emigrated (1856) and Moore was unseated (1857). The idea of an independent Irish party did not arise again until 1873 with the emergence of the Home Rule League* under Isaac Butt.*

INDEPENDENT ORANGE ORDER. Breakaway from the Orange Order* founded by T. H. Sloan* in 1902. Based on the militant Belfast Protestant Association,* the Institution was predominantly working-class. It co-operated with the Ancient Order of Hibernians* and others in the general strike organised in 1907 by James Larkin.* A leading intellectual was Robert Lindsay Crawford,* author of the 'Magheramore Manifesto'.* Independents fared badly in the 1912 local elections. The Independent Orangemen maintained their working-class character. Supporters of the Rev. Ian Paisley,* they co-operated in 1974 with the Ulster Workers' Council* in the May strike which brought down the Assembly of Northern Ireland. The Independent Orange Institution represents a very small part of the Orange movement.

INDUSTRIAL DEVELOPMENT AUTHORITY (IDA). State-sponsored body founded in 1949 as an agency of the Department of Industry and Commerce. While it was financed by a grant-in-aid and its board was appointed by the Minister for Industry and Commerce, the IDA was relatively free of the restrictions governing the Civil Service. Its function was to investigate areas of possible industrial development. For this purpose it brought together financial and industrial experts, with a brief to plan industrial growth and to examine the protectionist structure of Irish industry. In 1970 the IDA merged with An Foras Tionscail (The Industrial Institute) to become an autonomous state-sponsored body with responsibility for attracting foreign investment and aiding foreign and national industrial expansion. The Authority achieved its best-ever performance during 1979 when it exceeded its job target by 5,000. It negotiated some 1,500 new industrial projects with an employment potential of 35,000 over the next five years.

INGHINIDHE NA hÉIREANN (DAUGHTERS OF IRELAND). Nationalist movement founded by Maud Gonne* at Easter 1900 with the assistance of Countess Markievicz* and Francis Sheehy-Skeffington.* It supported Irish separatism, the Irish-Ireland* movement and was opposed to the Irish Parliamentary Party*. The organisation was instrumental in preventing the Corporation of Dublin from presenting a Loyal Address to Queen Victoria* in 1900 on the occasion of her visit to Ireland. Inghinidhe na hEireann produced a magazine, *Bean na hÉireann*, from 1908. The movement was absorbed into Cumann na mBan* in 1913.

INGRAM, JOHN KELLS (1823– 1907). Scholar; b. Newry, Co. Down; ed. locally and at TCD where he had a distinguished academic career. He was Professor of Oratory at Trinity (1852–66) and Professor of Greek (1866–77) before becoming Librarian in 1879. Ingram was a member of the Commission for Publication of the Ancient Laws and Institutes of Ireland and was President of the RIA and of the Statistical Society of Ireland. His work for *Encyclopaedia Britannica* on Political Economy (1888) was translated into ten languages, including Japanese.

His works include *A History of Slavery and Serfdom* (1895), *Outlines of the History of Religion* (1900), *Human Nature and Morals according to A. Comte* (1901), *Practical Morals* (1904) and *The Final Transition* (1905). He contributed verse to *Kattabos, The Dublin University Magazine* and *The Nation*. His best known poem 'The Memory of the Dead' ('Who fears to speak of '98'?) was published anonymously in *The Nation* in April 1843.

INSTITUTE FOR INDUSTRIAL RESEARCH AND STANDARDS (IIRS). Founded in 1946 and reconstituted in 1961 under the Institute for Industrial Research and Standards Act. Its purpose is to promote the application of science and technology in industry. The IIRS offers Technical Advisory Services and Research Development Programmes. The Institute's Board is appointed by the Minister for Industry and Commerce. IIRS is also the Irish national standards organisation, responsible for drawing up standard specifications, some of which can be made compulsory by ministerial order. The Institute represents Ireland on international standards bodies.

INSTITUTE OF PUBLIC ADMINISTRATION (IPA). Founded in 1957 by a group of civil servants working in local government and semi-state bodies. The aim of the Institute was to examine public administration in Ireland and seek guidelines for improvement. It runs in-service and degree courses, and encourages research on the public service and its history; publishes periodicals and books concerned with the whole area of public administration. The first director (1960–76) was Dr Thomas J. Barrington.

INTERMEDIATE EDUCATION. *See* Secondary Education.

INTERMEDIATE EDUCATION ACT, 1878. *See* Secondary Education.

INTER-PARTY GOVERNMENTS. Since the foundation of the state in 1922 there have been three inter-party or coalition governments. The first inter-party government was in office from 18 February 1948 until 13 June 1951; the second was in office from 2 June 1954 until 12 February 1957, and the third, known as the National Coalition Government,* was in office from 14 March 1973 until 5 July 1977. The constant members of all three coalitions were Fine Gael and the Labour Party.

18 February 1948 – 13 June 1951
The first inter-party government was a coalition of Fine Gael (31 seats), the Labour Party (14), Clann na Poblachta (10), Clann na Talmhan (7) and National Labour (5). They entered into coalition in order to break the monopoly on government held by Fianna Fail since 1932. This apart, the parties had little in common. By agreement the office of Taoiseach went to John A. Costello* because the leader of the Fine Gael Party,

Richard Mulcahy,* was not acceptable to Clann na Poblachta.

The Fine Gael ministers were Patrick McGilligan* (Finance), Sean MacEoin* (Justice, until 7 March 1951 when he was succeeded by Daniel Morrissey); Thomas F. O'Higgins (Defence, until 7 March 1951, when he was succeeded by MacEoin); Daniel Morrissey (Industry and Commerce, until 7 March 1951 when he was succeeded by T. F. O'Higgins); Richard Mulcahy (Education); James Dillon,* who had left Fine Gael in 1942, became Minister for Agriculture.

Labour was represented by the party's leader, William Norton* (Tanaiste and Minister for Social Welfare), and by T. J. Murphy (Local Government until 29 April 1949 when he was succeeded by Michael Keyes). James Everett of National Labour was Minister for Posts and Telegraphs.

Clann na Poblachta's Sean MacBride* and Dr Noel Browne* were Ministers for External Affairs and Health respectively. Joseph Blowick of Clann na Talmhan was Minister for Lands and Fisheries.

For details of the government's period in office *see* Battle of Baltinglass, Republic of Ireland Act 1948, Long Term Recovery Programme, Industrial Development Authority, Land Rehabilitation Project *and* Mother and Child Scheme.

2 June 1954 – 12 February 1957
The parties to the second inter-party government were Fine Gael (50), Labour (19) and Clann na Talmhan (5). Clann na Poblachta (3), shattered since the Mother and Child Scheme,* agreed not to oppose the government. The Fine Gael members of the government were John A. Costello (Taoiseach), Gerard Sweetman (Finance), Sean MacEoin (Defence), Liam Cosgrave* (External Affairs), Richard Mulcahy (Education and Gaeltacht from 2 July – 24 October 1956), T. F. O'Higgins (Health), James Dillon (Agriculture), P. J. Lindsay (Gaeltacht from 24 October 1956).

Labour ministers were William Nor-

ton (Tanaiste and Industry and Commerce), Brendan Corish* (Social Welfare), James Everett (Justice), Patrick O'Donnell (Local Government), and Michael Keyes (Posts and Telegraphs). Joseph Blowick of Clann na Talmhan was Minister for Lands.

The Irish Republican Army* started a new campaign against Northern Ireland in 1956 and Sean MacBride proposed a vote of 'No Confidence' in the government's handling of the situation which, with Fianna Fail support, led to the government's defeat. For further details *see* United Nations and Ireland *and* Gaeltachtai. *See also* National Coalition.

INVINCIBLES. The group known as the Irish National Invincibles was founded in 1881 during the Land League agitation as a breakaway from the Irish Republican Brotherhood.* Most of the leaders, including John McCafferty,* P. J. Tynan and James Carey,* had close connections with both the Land League and the Fenians.* A terrorist organisation, it plotted the deaths of Superintendent John Mallon* of the G Division of the Dublin Metropolitan Police and William Edward Forster,* the Chief Secretary whose successor, Lord Frederick Cavendish,* they assassinated on 6 May 1882, along with his Under-Secretary, Thomas Henry Burke* (*see* Phoenix Park Murders). The Invincibles were abhorred by the orthodox Fenians and were utterly condemned by Charles Stewart Parnell.* They had the support of a handful of extremists in Ireland and in the USA where they were generally out of touch with Irish opinion. Five of them were hanged for the Phoenix Park murders and the organisation disappeared.

IRELAND ACT, 1949. Act introduced by the British government as a reaction to the Republic of Ireland Act* which came into effect on Easter Monday, 1949. The Ireland Act declared, '. . . that part of Ireland heretofore known as Eire ceased, as from the eighteenth day of April, nineteen hundred and forty-nine, to be part of His Majesty's Dominions' and then went on to state '. . . that Northern Ireland remains part of His Majesty's Dominions and of the United Kingdom and it is hereby affirmed that in no event will Northern Ireland or any part thereof cease to be part of His Majesty's Dominions and of the United Kingdom without the consent of the Parliament of Northern Ireland'. *See also* Northern Ireland.

'IRELAND'S OWN'. Weekly magazine founded in 1902 by Edward O'Cullen, editor of the Wexford-based newspaper, *The People.* From its inception it had good sales and was particularly popular with Irish people abroad. Regular features include a four page ballad-supplement, 'Songs of Your Country', 'Land of Saints', 'What's In Your Name?', ghost stories, a children's section and readers' services. Some of the most popular writers for the magazine have included Annie M. P. Smithson, Mrs N. T. Pender, Victor O'D. Power (whose 'Kitty the Hare' stories are still reprinted although the author died in the late 1920s) and Paul Vincent Carroll.* The most requested poem has proven to be John Locke's 'Morning on the Irish Coast'. Circulation had risen from 20,000 in 1939 to 68,000 in 1979.

IRISH ACADEMY OF LETTERS. Founded in 1932 by William Butler Yeats* and George Bernard Shaw,* its aims were to promote a bi-lingual creative literature in Ireland by supporting work of intellectual and poetic quality by writers of Irish birth or descent; to counter any obstacle that would hamper literary activity; and to develop a public appreciation for all work which should, in the Academy's opinion, contribute to the creation of a distinctive Irish literature. Membership of the Academy is limited to thirty-five.

IRISH AGRICULTURAL LABOURERS' UNION. One of several attempts to unionise the widely-exploited agricultural workers. It was founded in 1873 by W. C. Upton, Isaac Butt* and Joseph Arch (leader of the British agricultural workers). Its inaugural meeting, held at Kanturk, Co. Cork, was attended by some 3,000 people but within a few months it had collapsed. *See also* Irish Federated Trade and Labour Union.

IRISH AGRICULTURAL ORGANISATION SOCIETY (IAOS). Founded in 1894 by Sir Horace Plunkett,* Fr Thomas Finlay* and their associates in the Co-Operative Movement,* to co-ordinate the activities of the various Irish co-operative units. The IAOS published a co-operative journal, *The Irish Homestead,* * edited by George W. Russell.* The IAOS is governed by a Committee of twenty-four, eighteen of whom are nominated by affiliated co-operatives and the remaining six are co-opted. In 1977 there were 250 affiliated co-operatives with a total membership of 222,000 and a combined turnover of £173,000,000. *See also* Co-operative Movement.

IRISH BATTALION OF ST PATRICK. Eight companies of soldiers were raised in Ireland in 1860 to serve Pope Pius IX in his resistance to Italian nationalists who desired to unify the country. They were recruited by papal ambassadors with the help of the editor of *The Nation,* A.M. Sullivan,* who promised 10,000 but raised 1,400, consisting of two units of 700 men each. The volunteers, of different backgrounds and education, were paid 1½d. per day but were enjoined to take consolation at the opportunities afforded them for martyrdom in the service of the pope. Numbers involved might have been greater had the British government not issued prohibitions against recruitment for the Pope's cause. In Italy the Battalion was led by an ex-militia officer from Louth, Major Myles O'Reilly, who organised what was originally an undisciplined mob into a fine fighting force. Living conditions experienced by the volunteers were appalling, par-

'ticularly at Ancona and Spoleto. Under O'Reilly the Spoleto garrison defended the town with notable bravery before it was forced to surrender after a twelve-hour bombardment (17 September 1860). By the end of the year many of the Irish had returned home, some with the papal medal inscribed 'Pro Petri sede' ('For the Seat of Peter').

'IRISH BRIGADE'. A group of Liberal MPs numbering about twenty-four who banded together in order to oppose the Ecclestiastical Titles Bill* during the 1851 parliamentary session became known as the 'Irish Brigade'. They had the approval of the Archbishop of Dublin, Paul Cullen,* when they founded an extra-parliamentary movement called the Catholic Defence Association.* The Brigade, later to be known facetiously as 'The Pope's Brass Band',* included George Henry Moore,* William Keogh* and John Sadleir*. The Tenant League* entered into an alliance with the Brigade in August 1852 and formed the Independent Irish Party.* The new alliance had immediate success at the polls when, in the 1852 general election, forty out of forty-eight of its candidates were returned. Within a short time however, the Brigade had disappeared.

'IRISH BULLETIN'. Periodical published by Dail Eireann during the War of Independence.* It was first issued on 11 November 1919 and ran until 1921. Translated into French and Spanish, it was circulated on the continent and also in the USA. The British government was embarrassed by its accounts of events in Ireland and frequent efforts were made by Dublin Castle authorities to suppress it, including the capture of most of the printing equipment and the circulation of forged 'Bulletins'. Amongst those associated with the production of the Bulletin were Desmond Fitzgerald,* Robert Erskine Childers* and Frank Gallagher.*

IRISH CHRISTIAN BROTHERS. Catholic teaching order founded by Edmund Ignatius Rice* in Waterford where he founded his first school, Mount Sion, in 1802 (officially opened on 7 June 1803). The community of four lived at first in accordance with the rules of the Presentation Order. On 15 August 1808, with three communities, the Brothers (or 'Monks' as they were more popularly known) were given vows of poverty, chastity and obedience for one year, and a religious habit, by the Bishop of Waterford, Dr Power, who had been authorised by Propaganda Fidei (Rome). Seven members took perpetual vows in 1809. Encouraged by public subscriptions and on the invitation of the Bishop of Cork the Brothers moved to Cork. By 1812 they had moved to Dublin and were running three schools within five years, with funds raised from church door collections. In Dublin they were given support by Daniel O'Connell* and Richard Lalor Sheil.* In order to keep the scattered communities unified the Brothers requested a Papal Brief which was granted in 1820 and two years later Edmund Rice was elected Superior General of the new Order. The Brothers concentrated on the provision of elementary education for those who could not otherwise afford any. Their schools remained outside the system of National Education* established in 1831.

The Christian Brothers now provide education at both primary and post-primary levels. They have also established communities in England, in Africa, North and South America, Australia and New Zealand.

IRISH CHRISTIAN FRONT. Rightwing movement founded in 1935 by Patrick Belton, ex-member of the Fianna Fail and National Centre parties. The Front was a non-party organisation, closely associated with the Blueshirts,* dedicated to resisting the alleged threat to Ireland of international communism. It had the tacit support of the Catholic Hierarchy in its efforts to put pressure on the Fianna Fail government to sever diplomatic relations with the Republican government in Spain and, shortly afterwards, to support General Franco in his armed opposition to that government. The Front was opposed by the left-wing of the Irish Republican Army* which was led by Peadar O'Donnell,* and Frank Ryan.* During the Spanish Civil War the Front collected funds for medical supplies for Nationalists. It had little support and soon faded away.

IRISH CHURCH ACT. *See* Disestablishment of the Church of Ireland.

IRISH CHURCH MISSIONS TO ROMAN CATHOLICS, SOCIETY FOR. Evangelical proselytising organisation founded by Rev. Alexander R. C. Dallas* on 28 March 1849. Part of an intensive Evangelical campaign in Ireland which won influential support during the controversy leading up to the Ecclesiastical Titles Act* of 1851, its purpose was, in the words of its founder, 'The great work of the enlightenment of large bodies of Roman Catholics in Ireland, by the affectionate preaching of an outspoken Gospel in antagonism to Roman dogma . . .' It concentrated much of its activities on the West of Ireland which was most affected by the Famine of 1845–49.* This brought the Missions, the first of which was founded at Castlekerke on Lough Corrib, into conflict with the Catholic Archbishop of Tuam, John MacHale, but gained the support of the Protestant Bishop, Thomas Plunket. In 1853, Dallas finally persuaded the less extreme Irish Society* to aid the ICM but within three years the partnership was dissolved as the Irish Society became alarmed at the Missions' aggressiveness' (*see* Second Reformation).

The ICM had some success in its early years but two factors eventually militated against it: the contempt in which the Catholics held one who changed his religion (*see* 'jumper', 'souperism' and 'perverts') and the

waning of Evangelical fervour in England during the late 1850s, depriving the Missions of extensive funds. The ICM wound up upon the death of the founder (1869). The Missions had little support from the Church of Ireland whose moderate members disapproved strongly of evangelicalism, but it soured relations between the Catholic Church and the Church of Ireland in many areas for a considerable time. It also prompted the appointment to Ireland of Ultramontanist Dr Paul Cullen,* as Archbishop of Armagh.

IRISH CHURCH TEMPORALITIES ACT, 1833. Act which suppressed ten sees of the Church of Ireland and reduced the revenues of the remaining twelve. Opposed by Daniel O'Connell,* it was a minor concession to those who sought the Disestablishment of the Church of Ireland.*

'IRISH CITIZEN, THE'. The official organ of the Irish Women's Suffrage Movement; first appeared in 1912, edited by James Cousins and his wife, Margaret. Contributors included Hanna and Francis Sheehy-Skeffington.* It ran until 1920.

IRISH CITIZEN ARMY. Founded as a workers' defence corps during the Lock-Out* by James Larkin* and James Connolly* on 23 November 1913. The purpose of the army, at the suggestion of its first drill-master, Captain J. R. White,* was to keep the unemployed trades unionists occupied, but its immediate purpose was to protect the workers from attacks by the Dublin Metropolitan Police* and the employers' hired bullies. The Army's headquarters was at Liberty Hall, and it was confined to Dublin. While it was close to the Irish Volunteers,* founded at the same time, the Citizen Army maintained a separate identity. It published a weekly newspaper, *The Irish Worker.* After the Lock-Out ended in the spring of 1914 the membership dwindled and the remaining 200 or so were taken over by Connolly, who re-organised them. The general secretary of the Army was Sean O'Casey.*

The ICA now had two aims, both of them identified with Connolly: the ownership of the land of Ireland by the people of Ireland and the establishment of a 'Workers' Republic'. The Army continued to have close contact with the Volunteers and in September 1914 it assisted in the recovery of the Volunteer headquarters from the National Volunteers* led by John Redmond.* Connolly, impatient at Volunteer inactivity, considered using his Army to start an insurrection in Dublin in the hope that it would spark off a national uprising. On 6 October 1915 he and Countess Markievicz led a feint attack on Dublin Castle. He was unaware that the Military Council* within the Irish Republican Brotherhood* had decided to stage an insurrection during the coming year. After he was taken into the Council's confidence (January 1916) he committed the Irish Citizen Army to the Easter Rising of 1916.* He led his small band of some 200 on to the streets of Dublin on Easter Monday. He held the command in the General Post Office, headquarters of the Provisional Government of which he was a member, and his army was deployed mainly in St Stephen's Green and the Royal College of Surgeons under the command of Michael Mallin.* A detachment of the Army attacked Dublin Castle and registered the first casualty of the rising when they shot Constable O'Brien of the DMP at the entrance. Five prisoners were taken and then the Citizen Army evacuated the Castle, unaware that they had in fact taken it (there was no other guard on duty that day). They then took up a position just opposite the Castle where they were attacked that afternoon by the Dublin Fusiliers and the Royal Irish Rifles. The Citizen Army force in St Stephen's Green held out for a time. Mallin was executed in May, as was Connolly.

The Irish Citizen Army remained in existence after the rising, although numerically weak, and fought alongside the Irish Republican Army* during the War of Independence.* Countess Markievicz influenced many members of the Army in refusing to accept the Treaty* and they supported the republicans – the Irregulars – during the Civil War.* In June 1922 members of the Citizen Army were involved at the Four Courts and took over Findlaters' in O'Connell Street from where they were dislodged. They took over the Hammam Hotel when the Four Courts fell. The end of the Civil War in May 1923 and the mass arrests of republicans and sympathisers, coupled with the victory of constitutionalism, left the Citizen Army without a further role to play.

IRISH CONFEDERATION. Founded 13 January 1847 by members of Young Ireland* who had seceded from the Repeal Association* led by Daniel O'Connell. The Confederation, led by William Smith O'Brien,* promoted the establishment of Confederate Clubs throughout the country whose membership included Charles Gavan Duffy,* John Blake Dillon,* Thomas Francis Meagher,* John Mitchel* and Michael Doheny.* The Confederation proclaimed the right of Ireland to self-government and the need for self-reliance. It disavowed the use of physical force or separation from England. However, the radical views of James Fintan Lalor* began to attract the support of a minority within the Confederation led by Mitchel, Doheny and Thomas Devin Reilly.* Lalor insisted that there could be no support for the demand for self-government unless it was linked with land agitation. This view was too radical for most of the moderates and Mitchel, Doheny and Reilly broke with them and founded *The United Irishman.*

The outbreak of revolution in France in February 1848 gave a new impetus to the Repeal movement and to the Confederate Clubs, with the demand for Repeal of the Union and, the establishment of a national parliament being taken up throughout Ireland. John Mitchel and Thomas Francis Meagher went beyond the call for Repeal to demand the establishment of an Irish Republic and published a series of articles outlining military tactics for the proposed uprising. Smith O'Brien suggested that a National Guard be recruited. Confederates marched in England alongside the Chartists who were led by Feargus O'Connor.* A deputation to Paris met Lamartine but received little encouragement from him. In March the Confederate leader, O'Brien, was arrested along with Mitchel and Meagher and charged with sedition. The charges against the first two failed, but in May, Mitchel was tried under the Treason Felony Act* and sentenced to fourteen years transportation. Aided by Fr John Kenyon,* leaders of the movement, Duffy, Dillon and Reilly, began to plot insurrection. On 22 July parliament suspended Habeas Corpus: Duffy, Meagher, Doheny and Thomas D'Arcy McGee* were arrested and membership of the Confederate Clubs was declared an offence. The suspension of Habeas Corpus provoked the Confederate leaders still at liberty into calling for an armed rebellion. Their attempts were unsuccessful. Smith O'Brien's tour of the south-east produced little support, and the 'Young Ireland Rising' ended with a brief skirmish under O'Brien's leadership at Ballingarry, Co. Tipperary.*

The Irish Confederation collapsed as did the parent movement, Young Ireland. Its legacy was considerable, however: two members of the movement, James Stephens* and John O'Mahony,* later founded the Irish Republican Brotherhood or Fenians.* The ideas of many Young Irelanders, including those of Thomas Davis,* reflected in *The Nation,** inspired future generations of nationalists.

IRISH CONGRESS OF TRADE UNIONS (ICTU). Formed in 1959 from an amalgamation of the Irish Trades Union Congress* (ITUC) and the Congress of Irish Unions* (CIU). The purpose of Congress was to co-ordinate, advise and generally assist affiliated unions of which, in 1959,

there were ninety-three with a membership· of 438,000. Congress offers training and educational services for shop stewards, officials and members. It has several sub-committees which deal with a wide range of headings, disputes, demarcation, trades union organisation, industrial relations, etc. Congress representatives are involved in the negotiation of national wage agreements with employers. In 1977 there were ninety-two trades unions with a total membership of 564,000 affiliated to Congress; 45 per cent of these were in three unions, the Irish Transport and General Workers Union,* the Workers' Union of Ireland* and the Amalgamated Transport and General Workers' Union.

IRISH CONSTABULARY. *See* Police *and* Royal Irish Constabulary.

IRISH CONVENTION (JULY 1917 – APRIL 1918). An attempt by David Lloyd George* to secure a final settlement of the demand for Home Rule.* The ninety-five members, who met in July 1917 under the chairmanship of Sir Horace Plunkett,* included representatives of the Ulster Unionist Party. the southern Unionists and the Irish Parliamentary Party. There were also a number of independents, including Edward MacLysaght* and George Russell.* However, it was boycotted by Sinn Fein* and the Labour Party.* The Convention made no headway in reconciling the nationalist demand for self-government with the Unionist demand that Ireland remain within the United Kingdom. John Redmond,* in an attempt to form an alliance with the southern Unionists and isolate the Ulster Unionists, suggested that a native parliament should waive the right to collect customs duties, and alienated members of his own party. The Convention ended in failure in April 1918 with a Report, signed by less than half of the members, which recommended self-government. A minority report to the government stated that it would be dangerous to extend conscription to Ireland (*see* Conscription and Ireland). In the general election which followed the Convention, in December 1918, the Irish Parliamentary Party* retained only six seats while the abstentionist Sinn Feiners won seventy-three.

IRISH CO-OPERATIVE MOVEMENT. *See* Co-Operative Movement.

IRISH COUNCIL (1847). Formed in 1847, prompted by the experiences of the Famine of 1845–49.* The Council was representative of all classes, religions and political opinions and included John O'Connell* and John Mitchel* among its members. It attempted to devise a system to alleviate famine distress, but, as conditions deteriorated, chaos ensued and the professional and landlord elements within the Council sought coercion* and the Council disintegrated. Its sole achievement had been an investigation which it had conducted into the prevailing social conditions.

IRISH COUNCIL. *See* Council of Ireland.

IRISH COUNCIL BILL (1907). Also known as the Devolution Bill, it was an attempt by the Chief Secretary, Augustine Birrell,* to grant Ireland devolved powers of home government. The bill was largely drafted by the Under-Secretary, Sir Antony MacDonnell.* The proposed Council was a compromise between the Home Rule and Unionist positions; it proposed to grant Ireland domestic control of eight out of forty-five government departments, including Education, Local Government, Public Works, Agriculture and the Congested Districts Board.* There was to be a chamber of 106 members, eighty-two of whom were to be nominated by the government. Although some nationalists, including Patrick Pearse,* were prepared to accept it, the proposal was rejected by Sinn Fein,* the United Irish League,* John Redmond* and the Irish Parliamentary Party.*

IRISH COUNTRYWOMEN'S ASSOCIATION (BANTRACHT NA TUAITHE). Founded in April 1935 from the Society of United Irishwomen,* the ICA is dedicated to the general improvement of rural life and concentrates on home and farm management instruction, handicrafts and general cultural activities. It is governed by the General Council to which each of the 900 guilds is entitled to send a delegate. The ICA has a residential college at Termonfeckin, Co. Louth (An Grianan) where a Horticultural College was opened in 1966 with aid from the Kellogg Foundation (USA). The ICA is affiliated to the Associated Country Women of the World and publishes a monthly magazine, *The Irish Countrywoman.* Its 28,000 members make it the largest women's organisation in Ireland.

IRISH CREAMERY MILK SUPPLIERS' ASSOCIATION (ICMSA). Non-political organisation founded in 1950 by John Feely to 'promote the interests of all engaged in agriculture and to advise, protect and regulate the agricultural industry in Ireland'. A member of the General Committee of the International Catholic Rural Association (Rome), the ICMSA is one of the leading pressure-groups within the agricultural sector. Members are active in commercial and co-operative agencies and have founded an Investment Society. It finances and promotes educational opportunities for young people in agriculture. Policies are decided by a National Council of sixty members who are elected annually. During 1979 the ICMSA held talks to consider a merger with the other large farming organisation, the Irish Farmers' Association* (IFA).

'IRISH DAILY INDEPENDENT'. See *Irish Independent.*

'IRISH DEMOCRAT'. Short-lived socialist newspaper produced by Peadar O'Donnell* and published in Dublin, 1937–38, to replace *The Republican Congress.* Another newspaper of the same name appeared in London from 1944 until 1968.

IRISH DOMINION LEAGUE. Founded on 27 June 1919 by Sir Horace Plunkett* with Henry Harrison* as secretary. The League sought self-government for Ireland within the British Empire. It looked for an end to representation at Westminster and the regulation of fiscal relations by Treaty. The time was not auspicious for such a proposal as the first Dail Eireann* had met on 21 January and declared an Irish Republic; the War of Independence* had already started. The proposal had no appeal to the Ulster Unionists* and the League disappeared.

'IRISH ECCLESIASTICAL RECORD.' Monthly journal founded in March 1864 by the Catholic Archbishop of Dublin, Dr Paul Cullen.* The *Record's* purpose was to communicate Roman encyclicals, decisions and instructions to the clergy, and was part of the Archbishop's effort at bringing the Catholic Church in Ireland more into line with Roman practice. The first editors were Rev. George Conroy and Rev. (later Archbishop) Patrick Moran,* Dr Cullen's nephew.

IRISH EDUCATION ACT (1892). The Act was designed to make National Education* compulsory but it had limited effectiveness. It abolished the payment of fees for all children between the ages of three and fifteen who were attending state-aided primary-level schools. A School Attendance Act followed in 1894 but the local authorities generally proved indifferent about implementing it.

IRISH FARMERS' ASSOCIATION (IFA). Founded on 1 January 1970 from an amalgamation of the National Farmers' Association,* the Irish Sugar Beet and Vegetable Growers' Association, the Leinster Milk Producers, the Cork and District Milk Producers and the Irish Commercial Horticultural Association. It is a member of the EEC-based farmers' union, COPA, in which it represents the interests of over 150,000 Irish farmers.

IRISH FEDERATED TRADE AND LABOUR UNION: Founded by Michael Davitt* in Cork in 1890, it was a further effort to establish a trade union for the estimated 300,000 agricultural labourers in rural Ireland. A previous attempt had been made with the Irish Agricultural Labourers' Union.* The IFTLU sought universal suffrage, free education, land settlement, houses for workers and reduced working hours. It broke up as a result of the split in the Irish Parliamentary Party* in the years 1890—91, although a remnant of it persisted into the 1920s. Another attempt to organise the agricultural workers was made with the Irish Land and Labour National Association.*

IRISH FEVER ACT (27 April 1847). Legislation introduced to contain the widespread fever which accompanied the Famine of 1845—49.* The Act gave local bodies wide preventative powers including the erection of temporary fever hospitals and proper burials for the famine dead. The legislation was responsible for the provision of additional accommodation for some 23,000 patients in extra hospitals and dispensaries. Total cost of the operation, including staffing, was £119,055 which was made a free grant to the Unions by the government. The Act remained in force until August 1850.

IRISH FOLK MUSEUM. *See* Knock, Co. Mayo.

IRISH FOLKLORE COMMISSION (COIMISIÚN BÉALOIDEAS ÉIREANN). Founded in 1927 as An Cumann le Béaloidas Éireann (The Folklore of Ireland Society), its purpose was to collect and preserve oral tradition. Aided by a government grant, the Royal Irish Academy* and An Cumann Le Béaloidas Éireann established the Irish Folklore Institute for the systematic and scientific collection and examination of Irish folklore and the publication of the preserved material. Later known as the Irish Folklore Commission, it has published valuable collections as well as the folklore periodical, *Béaloideas*, which has appeared since 1927, and maintains a library of MSS., built up by collectors throughout the country.

IRISH FOLKLORE INSTITUTE. *See* Irish Folklore Commission.

IRISH FREE STATE (CONSTITUTION) ACT. Statute of 1922 which incorporated the Free State Constitution of 1922* giving it constitutional recognition in English law.

'IRISH FREEDOM'. Republican newspaper published by members of the Irish Republican Brotherhood* from 1910 until 1914. The paper was managed by Sean MacDiarmada* and the principal contributors included Bulmer Hobson,* who edited it for a time, and Patrick S. O'Hegarty.* It was financed by a subscription of 1s (5p) per month from each member of the IRB. Under the control of the younger IRB element the paper became a vehicle for a more radical expression of republicanism, encouraged by John Devoy* and Clan na Gael.* It attracted contributions from Patrick Pearse* and Thomas MacDonagh.* As a result of its increasingly extremist and radical tone, calling on Irishmen to resist British imperialism and not support Britain in World War I, it was suppressed by the authorities in December 1914. Another paper of the same name was published by the republican movement in Dublin from 1939 to 1944 and in Belfast in 1951.

IRISH GEORGIAN SOCIETY. Society for the preservation and protection of buildings of architectural merit. Founded in 1958 by Desmond and Marie-Gabriella Guinness, Percy Le Clerk and William Dillon, the Society was registered as a company in 1970.

'IRISH HISTORICAL STUDIES'. Historical journal founded in 1938 as the joint journal of the Irish Historical Society and the Ulster Society for Irish Historical Studies; the original joint editors were R. Dudley Edwards and T. W. Moody.

'IRISH HOMESTEAD'. Journal edited by George W. Russell* from its foundation in 1895 as the organ of the Co-Operative Movement.* The *Homestead* had the financial backing of Sir Horace Plunkett.* Under Russell it became an influential publication, attracting contributions from his many friends in the literary revival, including W. B. Yeats.* In 1923 it merged with the *Irish Statesman,* also edited by Russell with Plunkett's support.

IRISH HOSPITALS SWEEPSTAKE. The first 'Sweep' was held on the Manchester November Handicap of 1930. Total prize money amounted to £409,233 and first prize of some £208,792 was shared by three Belfast men. The Hospitals Trust (1940) was founded to administer the Irish Hospitals Sweepstake under the provisions of the Public Hospitals Acts (1933–40). Over four hundred institutions which afford free medical or surgical treatment are beneficiaries under the terms of the Act. Up to and including the Irish Sweeps Cambridgeshire Draw of 1972, a total of 129 Sweepstakes, for which the Hospitals and Prize Fund figures are as follows, had been held:
Hospitals Fund £97,382,923
Prize Fund £226,168,430
Joseph McGrath* played a leading role in the introduction of the scheme and the McGrath family still maintain a controlling interest in the Trust.

IRISH INDEPENDENCE PARTY. Nationalist political party founded in Northern Ireland in October 1977 by Frank McManus and Fergus McAteer. The party called for a British withdrawal from Northern Ireland.

'IRISH INDEPENDENT'. National daily newspaper founded as the *Irish Daily Independent* by Charles Stewart Parnell* following the split in the Irish Parliamentary Party (December 1890 — January 1891). The first issue appeared on 18 December 1891, two months after Parnell's death. A companion paper, *The Evening Herald*, was also published. From the beginning the paper employed many members of the Irish Republican Brotherhood,* including the president of the Supreme Council, Fred Allan,* so that the *Independent's* offices became a regular rendezvous for foreign and native republicans. John Redmond* controlled the paper during the 1890s when it soon ran into financial difficulties, losing readers to both *The Daily Nation* and *The Freeman's Journal.* In 1900 the *Independent* merged with *The Daily Nation* controlled by William Martin Murphy,* an anti-Parnellite. The paper became *The Irish Independent* in 1905 and in 1906 another companion paper, *The Sunday Independent*, began publication.

The Irish Independent was identified during the 1920s with support for the Treaty and for the pro-Commonwealth position of Cumann na Gaedheal;* it gave support to Fine Gael* during the 1930s. The largest-selling morning newspaper, around 55 per cent of its readership comes from the AB socio-economic grouping (upper middle and middle-class managerial, administrative and professional). Its offices in Middle Abbey Street, Dublin, were the former site of *The Nation* offices. Circulation figures for the three newspapers in June 1979 were: *Irish Independent*, 181,600; *Evening Herald*, 120,150; *Sunday Independent*, 280,800.

IRISH-IRELAND. Generic title for the forms of cultural nationalism which took shape during the 1890s and in the first decade of the twentieth century. The most potent expressions of Irish-Ireland were found in the Gaelic Athletic Association,* the Gaelic League,* Cumann na nGaed-heal led by Arthur Griffith* and his early Sinn Fein movement. The idea was also promoted by the Irish literary movement and the Abbey Theatre.* The Irish-Irelanders sought cultural and economic independence and they aimed to achieve a genuine independence which would not be possible without self-sufficiency. There was not always agreement among the different groups or personalities as to how these aims could be achieved. In 1905 David P. Moran* of *The Leader* published a collection of essays under the title 'A Philosophy of Irish Ireland' based on a series of articles he published between 1893 and 1900; stating his concept of Irish nationalism, he pointed to what he saw as flaws in the Irish idea of Irish culture, identity and independence. In their enthusiasm Irish-Irelanders often developed a complete intolerance for Britain and all things British, regarding their near neighbour as the seat of all the influences which were, in their opinion, corrupting Irish national values.

IRISH LABOUR DEFENCE LEAGUE. Originally the Workers' Defence Corps,* it was renamed the ILDL after the first convention of the WDC on 7 July 1931. It consisted of the left-wing members of the Irish Republican Army* and Dublin trades unionists. The League was outlawed by the government on 17 October 1931 along with eleven other radical organisations, and disappeared within a short time.

IRISH LABOUR LEAGUE. Founded in 1891 by the Dublin branch of the National Union of Gasworkers and General Labourers. The League sought the nationalisation of transport. It failed within a short time through lack of support.

IRISH LABOUR PARTY. *See* Labour Party.

IRISH LAND AND LABOUR ASSOCIATION. Founded in Cork by D. D. Sheehan at the end of the nineteenth century, it sought to organise agricultural labourers and small tenant farmers, as a successor to the Irish Democratic Labour Federation. Its platform included a demand for 'houses for the people, land for the people, work and wages for the people, education for the people, state pensions for old people and that all local rates should be paid by the ground landlords'. It did not have widespread support and attracted the attention of William O'Brien* of the United Irish League* but he failed to make it more than a local organisation. After the foundation of the Labour Party* (1912) the ILLA broke up and its members were mainly absorbed into the new labour movement.

IRISH LITERARY SOCIETY. Formed in London in 1891 from the Southwark Literary Club,* the aim of the ILS was to encourage and stimulate a new school of literature which would be thoroughly and distinctively Irish although in the English language. Founder-members of the Society included W. B. Yeats,* T. W. Rolleston,* Charles Gavan Duffy,* Douglas Hyde,* and R. Barry O'Brien.* The Irish National Literary Society* was founded in Dublin a year later, with the identical aims and involving many of the same people.

IRISH LITERARY THEATRE. Founded at the end of 1898 by William Butler Yeats* after he broke with the Irish National Literary Society.* He was aided by Augusta, Lady Gregory* and Edward Martyn.* The first productions by the ILT were Yeats' *The Countess Cathleen* and Martyn's *The Heather Field* (1899). One of the first plays written in Irish, *Casadh an tSúgáin* ('The Twisting of the Rope') by Douglas Hyde,* was produced by the Literary Theatre in 1901. The aims of the Theatre met with disapproval from some sections of Irish-Ireland,* led by Arthur Griffith and D. P. Moran who denounced it as false and offensive. The quarrel between Yeats and his critics was essentially one of differing philoso-

phies: to Griffith and his followers literature was a powerful instrument for propaganda in a war with Britain, while to Yeats art was an end in itself. The ILT joined with the National Dramatic Company of Frank Fay* and Willy Fay* in 1902 to form the Irish National Theatre Society. One of the new company's first productions was *The Shadow of the Glen* by John M. Synge* in 1903, which was savagely attacked by Griffith. From the Literary Theatre the Abbey Theatre* developed from 1904 onwards a school of dramatists, actors and actresses through whose work Ireland made a distinctive contribution to modern drama.

IRISH LOYAL AND PATRIOTIC UNION (ILPU). Political association of Unionists* founded in May 1885. The aim of those involved, mostly businessmen, landowners and academics, was to organise resistance to Home Rule,* the demand for which was being pressed strongly at Westminster by the Irish Parliamentary Party.* ILPU candidates contested the general election of November 1885 hoping to win seats in the south of Ireland where Unionist representation was particularly weak but only one of the five candidates was returned (for the University of Dublin, Trinity College). This defeat appeared to end the Union's hopes of becoming a strong political force and thereafter it concentrated on disseminating anti-Home Rule propaganda. In 1891 the Union became the Irish Unionist Alliance.*

'IRISHMAN'. See *Voice of Labour.*

IRISH MANUSCRIPTS COMMISSION (COIMISIÚN LÁIMHSINBHISI ÉIREANN). Established in 1928 with Eoin MacNeill* as first chairman, the Commission's brief was to investigate and report on existing manuscripts of literary, historical and general Irish interest and importance, and to edit and publish such manuscripts. Additionally, it hoped to revise and republish significant works no longer generally available. In March 1930 the Commission began publication of *Analecta Hibernica* which reports on important manuscript collections and on varying aspects of the work being undertaken. At the end of 1979 the IMC had published 134 volumes and had thirty-eight others in preparation.

'IRISH MONTHLY'. Founded 1873 and edited until 1912 by Rev. Matthew Russell,* a magazine of a religious and literary character. Many of the leaders of the literary revival at the end of the nineteenth century, including W. B. Yeats,* contributed to it. Other contributors were Aubrey de Vere,* T. D. Sullivan* and Denis Florence McCarthy.*

IRISH NATION LEAGUE. Founded by nationalists in Ulster after the Easter Rising of 1916,* the League's purpose was to oppose any proposal for the partition of Ireland. Numerically weak, it made little impact in Ulster and none outside the province. *See also* Northern Ireland.

IRISH NATIONAL AID ASSOCIATION. Founded after the Easter Rising of 1916,* its purpose was to raise funds for the dependants of the deceased and imprisoned Irish Volunteers.* Within a short time the Association amalgamated with the Irish Volunteers Dependants' Fund* which became a national organisation.

IRISH NATIONAL ALLIANCE. Republican organisation founded in 1894 by members of Clan na Gael* led by a militant, William Lyman. Dr Mark Ryan* organised it in Ireland and England.* While the INA followed the rules and constitution of the Irish Republican Brotherhood,* except that it substituted a pledge for the oath, it was completely opposed to the IRB which it attacked for its conservatism. The dispute between the two republican organisations was fought out in the columns of various republican newspapers, including the INA's *Irish Republic*. It had a military wing, the Irish National Brotherhood.

The INA won away some of the more radical members of the IRB. Through the activities of travelling organisers such as James F. Egan it became a force in the west of Ireland where the tradition of radical secret societies persisted. However, it did not become a national movement. Its decline was steady, mainly due to lack of funds, and by 1900 there were only two circles left out of the original fourteen in Dublin. It had support from Maud Gonne* and W. B. Yeats.*

IRISH NATIONAL ANTHEM. *See* National Anthem.

IRISH NATIONAL BROTHERHOOD. *See* Irish National Alliance.

IRISH NATIONAL CLUB. Founded in London in January 1899 largely from among those who organised the '98 Centenary Celebrations,* including Dr Mark Ryan.* Its object was 'To promote a healthy spirit of nationality among London Irishmen and the study and encouragement of Irish history and literature'. The Club supported the Gaelic Athletic Association* and Gaelic League.*

IRISH NATIONAL FEDERATION. Constituency organisation formed in March 1891 by the anti-Parnellite majority which seceded from the (Irish) National League* as a result of the split in the Irish Parliamentary Party* over the leadership of Charles Stewart Parnell.* The leaders of the INF were Justin McCarthy,* John Dillon,* William O'Brien* and Timothy M. Healy.* The latter was expelled in 1895. The INF was stronger than the National League which entered a period of rapid decline during the 1890s; in December 1891 the NL had 13,000 members compared with the INF's 83,000; two years later the figures were 6,500 (NL) and 47,000 (INF). When McCarthy resigned in 1896 Dillon became the leader. By 1898 the INF had 221 branches compared to NL's six. Disputes between different branches of the formerly united parliamentary party led to increasing disillusionment among the rising generation of Irish nationalists. The rise of the United Irish League* (founded by O'Brien in 1898) led to a reassessment of the situation and in 1900 the NL and the INF united under John Redmond,* accepting the UIL as a new constituency organisation.

IRISH NATIONAL FORESTERS. Founded in Dublin in 1877 as a benefit society to provide relief for members and their families. The leaders included members of the Irish Republican Brotherhood* while other members were prominent in nationalist organisations. To qualify for membership one had to be Irish by birth or descent. The chief officials were known as the High Chief Ranger and the High Sub-Chief Ranger and each branch was led by a Chief Ranger and Sub-Chief Ranger. The Foresters' purpose was to assist members in search of employment and the organisation was regarded with great suspicion by Dublin Castle. The INF is still in existence, wholly as a benefit society.

IRISH NATIONAL INVINCIBLES. *See* Invincibles.

IRISH NATIONAL LAND LEAGUE. *See* Land League.

IRISH NATIONAL LEAGUE. *See* National League.

IRISH NATIONAL LIBERATION ARMY (INLA). Left-wing splinter of the Official Irish Republican Army* formed in 1975, before which it had been known as the People's Liberation Army (1974). It was involved in the feud between the Official IRA and the Irish Republican Socialist Party.* The INLA claimed credit for the assassination of the British Conservative Shadow Secretary of State for Northern Ireland, Airey Neave, on 30 March 1979.

IRISH NATIONAL LITERARY SOCIETY. Literary movement founded in Dublin in 1892 by W. B. Yeats* and Douglas Hyde.* The Society was modelled on their Irish Literary Society* founded in London the previous year. The INLS was dedicated to the revival and preservation of old Irish customs and culture and to combating foreign influences in the culture of Ireland, through the development of Anglo-Irish literature. Hyde and Yeats held different viewpoints as to how best the aims of the Society could be achieved and Yeats ultimately withdrew from its ranks to found the Irish Literary Theatre.*

IRISH NATIONAL SOCIETY. Founded in London in 1844 during the agitation for Repeal.* It was designed to bring Irishmen together, regardless of their political or religious beliefs. The membership included Maurice O'Connell,* the Earl of Clanricarde and Lord Castlereagh. It did not survive the break up of the Repeal Association.*

IRISH NATIONAL TEACHERS' ORGANISATION. The oldest teachers' trade union in Ireland, founded in 1868, for those employed in schools within the National Education system. In 1977–78 it had 19,244 members. Originally known as the Irish National Teachers' Association, its first president was Vere Foster.*

IRISH NATIONAL UNEMPLOYED MOVEMENT. *See* Workers' Party of Ireland.

IRISH NATIONALITY AND CITIZENSHIP ACT (1935). Act introduced by the Fianna Fail government, by which Irish nationals ceased to be British subjects.

IRISH NEUTRALITY LEAGUE. A short-lived nationalist body founded in 1914 with the aim of keeping Ireland from involvement on the side of Britain in World War I. During its short life the League organised an intense anti-recruiting campaign. *See* Conscription and Ireland.

IRISH NEWS AGENCY. Established by Sean MacBride* in 1949 during the term of the Inter-Party Government of 1948—51 to publicise Ireland abroad. It published *Eire-Ireland,* edited by Conor Cruise O'Brien, and was abolished by Frank Aiken* in 1957.

IRISH OFFICE. Established in 1801 at the time of the Union,* the Irish Office was where the Chief Secretary* transacted business while in London for the parliamentary session. According to a report on 'The Organisation of the Permanent Civil Service' drawn up by Stafford Northcote and Charles Edward Trevelyn* in 1853, it was not clear exactly what the Irish Office staff did. It was abolished after the Treaty.*

IRISH PARLIAMENTARY PARTY (HOME RULE PARTY). The Irish Parliamentary Party, or Home Rule Party, also known as the Nationalist Party, grew out of the Home Rule League* founded by Isaac Butt in 1873. In the beginning it was a loose association of interests bound by a rather vague agreement that they were 'deeply impressed with the importance of unity of action upon all matters that can affect the parliamentary position of the Home Rule Party, or the interests of the Home Rule cause'. The aim of the fifty-six Home Rulers returned in the general election of 1874 was to sustain and support each other in the manner 'best calculated to promote the grand object of national self-government which the Irish nation has committed to our cause'. The members also resolved that they would 'individually and collectively hold ourselves aloof from and independent of all party combinations'. Butt's leadership of the party was weak and he proved ineffectual in his attempts to focus parliamentary attention upon Irish affairs during the Conservatives' period in office (1874—80). A thorough consti-

tutionalist, he disapproved of the Fenian element in his party which, led by Joseph Biggar,* John O'Connor Power* and Frank Hugh O'Donnell,* adopted a policy of 'obstructing' parliamentary business. In 1875 they were joined by Charles Stewart Parnell.*

William Shaw* succeeded Butt as leader in 1879. He and his moderate followers remained aloof from the Land War prosecuted by the Land League* under the leadership of Parnell. The war, financed by Clan na Gael* in America, was the outcome of a partnership between constitutionalists and revolutionaries, known as the New Departure.* At the height of the Land War the general election of April 1880 returned sixty-one Irish members styling themselves Home Rulers. On 17 May, Parnell was elected chairman of the party by twenty-three votes to Shaw's eighteen. His ascendancy over the party was confirmed when, in January 1881, a group of twelve, led by Shaw, later known as 'nominal Home Rulers or 'Whigs', seceded. Parnell's followers fought the case of the tenant-farmers and the Land League at Westminster where his closest aides were John Dillon,* Timothy Harrington* and Timothy Healy.* He also established a party organ, *United Ireland,* edited by William O'Brien* who became an MP in 1883. The result of the combined agitation by the party in London and the Land League in Ireland was the Land Act, introduced by W. E. Gladstone* in 1881 (*see* Land Acts).

During the three years from 1882 to 1885 Parnell built up a constituency organisation, the (Irish) National League,* financed by local collections, by money from Irish business interests (in particular the drink trade) and by money from America where a branch of the National League was also established. Parnell's party became the first modern political party in Europe, in that its members could draw salaries from National League finances, it operated under a Whip (Tim Healy) and after 1884 members were bound by a pledge. The party pledge was imposed at the Dungarvan Convention in August 1884. Drawn up by Harrington, the text was: 'I . . . pledge myself that in the event of my election to parliament, I will sit, act and vote with the Irish parliamentary party and if at a meeting of the party convened upon due notice especially to consider the question, it be decided by a resolution supported by a majority of the entire parliamentary party that I have not fulfilled the above pledge I hereby undertake to resign my seat'.

Home Rule dominated Ireland during 1885. Gladstone's government fell in June 1885 over the drink provisions in the budget introduced by H. C. E. Childers.* Parnell had received little encouragement from the Liberals on Home Rule, and, believing that the Conservatives would introduce some measure of Home Rule, he placed the support of the party behind them, for the general election. The Irish party benefitted from the Representation of the People (1884) and Redistribution Acts. In addition, the party had clerical support. In the words of Thomas William Croke,* the nationalist Archbishop of Cashel, speaking in June 1885, 'Three years ago, the Irish Parliamentary Party was disliked, and distrusted by many of the best men in the land. Today the bishops, as a body, and the priests universally, thoroughly believe in their honour and honesty and have confided to them, accordingly, their most sacred interests' (he had in mind the party's support for the case for grants for Catholic schools). The Home Rulers won 86 seats, exactly the difference between the Liberals (335) and the Conservatives (249). Parnell held the balance of power. The Conservatives contented themselves with the Ashbourne Land Purchase Act (*see* Land Acts) and made no move on Home Rule. Then in December the 'Hawarden Kite'* announced Gladstone's conversion to Home Rule. When the Conservatives introduced coercion* in January

1886 Parnell switched Irish support to the Liberals. Gladstone formed his third administration committed to Home Rule and introduced the (first) Home Rule Bill* on 8 April. Two months later it was defeated in the House of Commons as Unionists,* Conservatives and the Liberal Unionists, led by Joseph Chamberlain,* combined against it. Gladstone lost the general election of July 1886 and the Home Rulers returned with eighty-five seats. Parnell and his party were committed to supporting Gladstone and the Liberals in opposition.

Between 1887 and 1890 the party and its leader were constantly in the public eye as a result of a libel action taken against *The Times* over a series of articles entitled 'Parnellism and Crime'.* At the same time a special parliamentary commission investigated Parnell's role in the Land War. The articles were proved to be forgeries and the commission cleared him after an exhaustive enquiry. But the party was soon plunged into its greatest crisis over Parnell's involvement in the *O'Shea v O'Shea and Parnell* divorce case. The trial was a victory for Captain W. H. O'Shea* whose wife, Katharine O'Shea,* had been Parnell's mistress since 1880.

The revelations in the divorce court forced Gladstone to announce that the Liberals could not support Home Rule while Parnell led the Irish party. The party was now forced to choose between the leader and the cause. In addition, he was condemned by the Catholic hierarchy. The party, which had re-elected him Chairman for the forthcoming session, was forced to re-consider and a long drawn out struggle took place in Committee Room 15 of the House of Commons (1–6 December 1890) when Parnell refused to relinquish the leadership. Justin McCarthy, followed by a total of 45 members, withdrew, leaving Parnell with 28 followers, including one of the chief lieutenants, John Redmond.* The split within the party divided the country long after Parnell's death (October 1891). As a result of the split during the 1890s, there were several different factions at Westminster fighting for Home Rule. McCarthy, Dillon, O'Brien and Healy formed a new constituency organisation, the Irish National Federation,* while Redmond retained control of the National League. In 1895 Healy left the INF and founded the clericalist People's Rights Association.* When McCarthy resigned from leadership of the anti-Parnellites in 1896 he was succeeded by Dillon. The factions were forced to re-unite by the swift success of a new organisation, the United Irish League,* founded by William O'Brien in 1898. Two years later the factions came together and recognised the UIL as the new constituency organisation. Redmond was accepted as leader of the re-united Home Rule Party, numbering eighty-two. In addition, the party benefited from the Local Government Act, 1898 which transferred power from the (Protestant) Ascendancy class to Nationalists (*see* Local Government).

The Redmondite party did not, however, have the solidarity of the old Parnellite party. The highly individualistic Tim Healy was a maverick and his bitter opponent, William O'Brien, leading a personal following of around 8 MPs ('O'Brien's Young Men'), was at loggerheads with the party over the Land Conference* and the Irish Reform Association.* However, the size of the party and the accession to power of the Liberals under the Gladstonian Home Ruler, Henry Campbell-Bannerman,* forced the Unionists* and in particular the Ulster Unionists* to re-organise against the possibility of another attempt at Home Rule. Redmond's position was weak as the Liberals did not need Irish support from 1905 until 1910. H. H. Asquith,* who succeeded Campbell-Bannerman in 1908, was not a strong supporter of Home Rule and Redmond had to resist suggestions that he break the Liberal connection. The party took consolation from the fact that its opponents at home, the Fenians and Sinn Fein,* were numerically small. In the North

Leitrim by-election of 1908 a former member of the party, C. J. Dolan, standing for Sinn Fein, was defeated by a Redmondite. By that time, the Home Rule party could take credit for constructive legislation: rural and local housing improvements, reinstatement of evicted tenants, protection for tenants in towns, and the Irish Universities Act (1908) which established the National University of Ireland.*

The situation changed before the general election of 1910. Asquith, seeking Irish support for his attempt to break the power of the House of Lords (a traditional enemy of Home Rule), promised in a speech on 10 December 1909 at the Albert Hall, that Liberal policy '. . . while explicitly safeguarding the supremacy and indefectible authority of the imperial parliament, will set upon Ireland a system of full self-government in regard to purely Irish affairs'. The state of the parties after the general election (January 1910) was: 275 Liberals, 273 Conservatives and Unionists, 40 Labour and 81 Home Rulers (although 11 of them were Independent Nationalists, not subject to Redmond's whip). A second general election (December 1910) left Asquith in a strong enough position to secure the passage of the Parliament Act of 1911* which left the Lords with power to delay legislation for two years. The removal of their power of veto, however, ensured the eventual passage of the (third) Home Rule Bill.* The Ulster Unionists and the Conservatives fought hard to prevent the passage of the Bill which was introduced on 11 April 1912. The Irish party was prepared to concede all reasonable accommodation to the Unionists except partition of the country, but the rise of the Ulster Volunteer Force* in January 1913 and the Irish Volunteers* in November 1913 led to a government fear of civil war. In an attempt to resolve the deadlock between the Unionists and Nationalists the Buckingham Palace Conference* was held in July 1914. Redmond and Dillon represented the

Irish party and Sir James Craig* and Sir Edward Carson* the Unionists. The Conference ended in failure after only three days. In view of the European situation the Unionists and the Nationalists agreed to the suspension of Home Rule after it became law, for the duration of World War I, leaving the position of Ulster unresolved.

The party had accomplished the aim of Butt and Parnell. Congratulatory messages poured in from Ireland and wherever Irish people were gathered, and the heroes of the past were called upon by *The Freeman's Journal** to bear witness to Redmond's triumph.

The Easter Rising of 1916* took the party as much by surprise as it did the government and the Irish people. Redmond denounced the organisers as traitors and pawns of Germany. It appeared to the party to be a deliberate attempt to undo the work which had been accomplished. Redmond and the party now set their hopes upon the Irish Convention* of 1917–18, which was boycotted by Sinn Fein and broke up inconclusively in the summer of 1918. By then, Redmond was dead (March 1918) and John Dillon became the last leader of the party. During 1918 the party held its own when it won three by-elections. Its demise was aided by a serious miscalculation of the British government when it attempted to introduce conscription (*see* Conscription and Ireland). This attempt united the country outside of Ulster as it had not been united for years. Although Dillon attended the Mansion House Conference* which co-ordinated the anti-conscription campaign, the party suffered for its past identification with British policy on Ireland. Another series of arrests, triggered by the so-called German Plot,* further alienated nationalist public opinion. The final stage in the struggle between the Home Rule party and Sinn Fein, the old and the new nationalism, took place during the general election of December 1918. It was a bitterly fought contest which resulted in the virtual annihilation of the party, which retained only six seats, four of them in Ulster constituencies. Symbolically, Dillon lost his Mayo seat to the imprisoned leader of Irish republicanism, Eamon de Valera.* The party was vanquished except for the Northern nationalist remnant led by Joseph Devlin,* who sat at Westminster until 1925. On 21 January 1919 Sinn Fein representatives formed Dail Eireann and declared an Irish Republic.

'IRISH PEASANT'. Newspaper founded in 1905 by James McCann, a Dublin stockbroker and nationalist MP. Initially the paper was of almost exclusive Co. Meath interest but under the dynamic editorship of William Ryan* (Liam O'Riain) it became of national importance. Under him the paper played a leading role in Irish-Ireland* and highlighted the philosophy of the Gaelic League* and of the Catholic hierarchy towards the Irish language, and Irish nationalism. The paper fell foul of the Catholic hierarchy and was condemned by Cardinal Logue* as 'a most pernicious anti-Catholic print'. The McCann family closed the paper in December 1906. Ryan's *The Plough and the Cross* (1910) is an account of the paper. He was unsuccessful in his attempt to continue the *Irish Peasant* as *The Peasant* which folded within a year.

'IRISH PEOPLE'. Newspaper founded by James Stephens* as the official organ of the Irish Republican Brotherhood* in November 1863. The Fenians* published another paper of the same name in New York. *The Irish People* was edited by John O'Leary* with Charles J. Kickham* and Thomas Clarke Luby* as the chief contributors. Jeremiah O'Donovan Rossa* was business manager. The paper was outspoken in its republicanism and was suppressed in September 1865 and many of the personnel arrested (although Stephens remained free for a month). Another newspaper, *The Flag of Ireland*, was published by the IRB from 1868 to 1874.

'IRISH PEOPLE'. Weekly newspaper founded by William O'Brien* as the organ of the United Irish League.* Very critical of the Irish Parliamentary Party* from which O'Brien had broken away, the first issue appeared on 16 September 1899. Under O'Brien's editorship the paper supported the idea of securing self-government for Ireland through conciliation and conference. He was succeeded as editor in 1907 by John Herlihy. The paper never had a large circulation and was constantly in financial difficulties. It ceased publication in 1908.

'IRISH PRESS'. Daily newspaper founded in September 1931 by Eamon de Valera* to provide a forum for Fianna Fail.* Its first editor was Frank Gallagher.* The editorial policy was controlled by de Valera and later by his son, Major Vivion de Valera. Over half of its readership is from skilled manual and lower-middle class workers. It had a circulation of 98,790 (1979). The company also publishes *The Sunday Press* which was founded in September 1949 and had a circulation of 386,083 (1979), and *The Evening Press,* founded in September 1954, with a circulation of 171,780 (1979).

IRISH PRESS AGENCY. Founded in October 1886 under the management of J. J. Clancy, MP, the Agency's purpose was to distribute information in England on Irish affairs. It issued pamphlets dealing with the land question, Ulster and Home Rule. The Agency was partly financed by the Irish Parliamentary Party* which contributed £13,000 between 1886 and 1890. It also worked through the Home Rule Union.* It collapsed after the split in the Irish party (1891).

IRISH RACE CONVENTIONS. The first Irish Race Convention was held in New York on 3–4 March 1916 under the auspices of Clan na Gael;* it founded the Friends of Irish Freedom.* At another Convention held in Philadelphia in February 1919 John Devoy* and Judge Daniel Cohalan* organised a mass demonstration in favour of the Irish Republic which had been declared on 21 January 1919 by the first Dail Eireann.* The IRC wished to gain the support of President Wilson of America for recognition of the Republic at the Paris peace talks but their efforts ended in failure when the convention's delegates to the peace talks failed to gain a hearing.

IRISH REFORM ASSOCIATION. Established in 1904 as a reconstitution of the Land Conference.* The leading organiser was the 4th Earl of Dunraven* who was supported by some thirty landlords. Their programme of August 1904 showed their aim to be a devolution* of some power to an Irish body. The Association won the support of Sir Antony MacDonnell* who, with Dunraven, issued a further proposal (September 1904) calling for a council for Ireland which would have considerable powers to legislate and control over its own finances. The proposal was strongly attacked by the Unionists* and those opposed to Home Rule* and led to the resignation of the Chief Secretary, George Wyndham.* *See also* Irish Council Bill.

IRISH REPUBLICAN ARMY (IRA). The Army of the Irish Republic was, in the first instance, the army which gave its allegiance to the Irish Republican Brotherhood.* The IRB regarded itself as the government of the Irish Republic 'virtually established'. The insurrection of 1867 failed and it was not until the IRB took over the Irish Volunteers* for the Easter Rising of 1916* that the IRA was re-established. Following the establishment of the first Dail Eireann* in January 1919 the Volunteers were recognised as the Army of the Irish Republic and in this capacity they prosecuted the War of Independence.* Although Cathal Brugha* was Minister for Defence in the government of Dail Eireann, Michael Collins,* who re-organised the Volunteers during 1917—18, with Harry Boland,* had much more influence through membership of the Supreme Council* of the IRB. The IRA could not hope to win a war against Britain by the gun alone and its object, in association with the political movement, Sinn Fein,* was to make British administration in Ireland impossible. Their campaign was so successful that during the spring of 1921 David Lloyd George* put out peace feelers which resulted in the Truce* of July 1921 and later in the Treaty* of December 1921.

The Treaty split the IRA as it divided the country. Many members of the IRA followed Collins into the Free State* to become members of the National Army, while those who rejected the Treaty took arms against the Provisional Government* which established the Free State. Those who accepted the Treaty were known as the 'Old IRA' while those who rejected it were known during the Civil War* as the 'New IRA', or the Irregulars. Under the Chief of Staff, Liam Lynch,* the Irregulars continued to hold out against the Free State until May 1923 when Eamon de Valera* and Frank Aiken* agreed to surrender. The republican movement was now faced with a dilemma: whether to enter the Dail and seek a republic constitutionally, or to remain outside the Dail opposing the Free State. This division within Sinn Fein was paralleled by a division in the IRA. The IRA withdrew from Sinn Fein in 1925 when de Valera proposed a constitutional role for Sinn Fein and then formed his own party, Fianna Fail* (1926).

There was a rapprochment between Fianna Fail and the IRA leading up to the general election of 1933. Imprisoned members of the IRA (which had been outlawed by W. T. Cosgrave*) were released by Frank Aiken. The alliance lasted during the crisis posed by the Blueshirts when former members of the IRA were inducted into the army and the Garda Sioch-ana.* Fianna Fail lost IRA support when de Valera outlawed the movement in 1936. An attempt to carry the IRA in a leftward direction during the 1920s and 1930s was unsuccessful. The prime movers behind this shift in emphasis were Peadar O'Donnell,* George Gilmore* and Frank Ryan.* This led to short-lived movements such as Saor Eire* and the Republican Congress.* The socialist wing of the IRA was never more than a small minority until the 1960s. In 1936 left-wing supporters did answer Frank Ryan's call to aid the Spanish republican government in the Civil War (1936—39). At the same time, prominent IRA leaders like Sean Mac-Bride* had realised the futility of trying to win the republic by force. They lost, however, to the more militant wing, led by Sean Russell,* which declared war on Northern Ireland and Britain in January 1939. The militants, hoping unsuccessfully for support from Joseph McGarrity* and Clan na Gael in the USA, demanded that England 'withdraw from every part of Ireland as an essential preliminary to arrangements for peace and friendship between the two countries'. In 1939 a series of bombings throughout Britain startled public opinion in England and Ireland. In all seven people were killed and 137 injured. The most notorious incident was at Coventry. The de Valera government and the government of Northern Ireland both moved against the IRA. The Special Powers Act was invoked in Northern Ireland and the Dublin government passed a Treason Act* and an Offences Against the State Act.* After the outbreak of World War II de Valera introduced the Emergency Powers Act* which allowed for the internment of the IRA, hundreds of whom were interned and some of whom were executed. Committees of republican sympathisers were formed to help republicans, under the guidance of the former chief of staff, Sean MacBride, now a highly respected barrister with a long record of defending republicans. These committees and the released internees combined under Mac-Bride to form a new republican party, Clann na Poblachta,* in 1946. The new party ran on a reformist, republican platform and joined the first Inter-Party Government* of 1948–51 which passed the Republic of Ireland Act.*

Clann na Poblachta was not a member of the second Inter-Party Government (1954–57) but MacBride agreed not to oppose it. However, when the government moved against the IRA, which started another campaign against Northern Ireland in 1956, he joined Fianna Fail in a motion of No Confidence and brought it down. The campaign of 1956–62, directed by Cathal Goulding and Ruari O'Bradaigh, received little support among the Catholic population in Northern Ireland and had failed by 1960. A splinter republican movement in Co. Tyrone called Fianna Uladh,* led by Liam Kelly of Pomeroy, also failed. Both Northern Ireland and the Republic introduced internment. In 1962 the campaign was over. The only effect of the campaign, which had, unlike others, concentrated on military and police targets, had been to harden Ulster Unionists* in their determination to resist a united Ireland. Far-reaching economic changes took place in Ireland during the 1960s as a result of the Programmes for Economic Expansion drawn up by T. K. Whitaker and implemented by Sean Lemass. The IRA was influenced by the shift in emphasis. These changes were signalled in 1965 when Lemass became the first head of a southern government to recognise the northern state, when meeting with the Prime Minister, Captain Terence O'Neill. At the same time, the Nationalist Party, led by Eddie McAteer, accepted the position of official opposition at Stormont. The most significant change in the IRA was that, at least for the moment, it turned its back on the physical-force tradition, and, under the influence of Dr Roy Johnson, founder of the Wolfe Tone Society,* moved leftwards to apply a

Marxist analysis to Irish economic and social questions. A leader in the movement to the left was Tomas Mac Giolla. A new generation of Catholics in Northern Ireland had less interest in republicanism and a united Ireland than in social justice. This led to the formation of the Northern Ireland Civil Rights' Association* in 1967. Initially the IRA acted solely as stewards on the NICRA marches and had no other involvement. Loyalist paramilitary attacks on the marchers, as at Burntollet when a People's Democracy* march was attacked in January 1969, forced the IRA to go on the offensive. When the British Army, brought to Northern Ireland in August 1969, appeared to Catholics to be acting in a partisan manner, the IRA reverted to its traditional role and declared war on the Army. Before this happened, however, the Sinn Fein-IRA movement once again split.

The split resulted from a difference of outlook. The war, as it became, between the loyalist and nationalist populations in Northern Ireland, led to a breach between the northern IRA and southern command. The socialist face of the movement was now, the northern IRA felt, irrelevant to the new situation. They had been restrained throughout 1968 and into 1969, so much so that they did not defend their traditional territories from attacks by loyalist paramilitaries (13 August 1969). August 1969 was crucial. The rioting by loyalists in Catholic areas where the people were unarmed caused alarm both in the south and in Britain. The southern government, led by Jack Lynch,* appealed unsuccessfully for United Nations intervention. Mr Lynch announced that his government would not stand by while innocent people were attacked because of their religion. His declaration, however, was not followed by any positive initiative and, at the same time, the northern IRA was growing restless at its own inactivity. The inactivity was due, to a large extent, to lack of money and arms. However, late in 1969, guns and money came from southern sympathisers, thus enabling the northern command to break away from the purely socialist part of the movement (January 1970). The northerners and their sympathisers became known as the 'Provisional' IRA. It had its headquarters in Kevin Street, Dublin; the army was led by Sean MacStiophan (John Stevenson) and the political wing, 'Provisional' Sinn Fein, was led by Ruari O'Bradaigh (Rory Brady). It published a newspaper, *An Phoblacht*, in which it sought support for the traditional republican aim of an end to British involvement on Irish soil, and the establishment of a united 32-county Republic. The other Sinn Fein-IRA became known as 'Official'. Led by Tomas Mac Giolla, it propounded the doctrine of a socialist republic, and offered a social and economic policy. It contested local elections. The Officials' headquarters was in Gardiner Place, Dublin, whence it issued *The United Irishman*. In the beginning the differences between the two IRAs were not manifestly large but they grew to such an extent that they treated each other with as much hostility as they did the British.

The first task facing Captain O'Neill's successors, Major James Chichester-Clark* and Brian Faulkner,* was, they claimed, to destroy the IRA, Neither succeeded in doing it. In February 1971 the first British soldier was killed and in the following August, Faulkner introduced internment. Internment did not break the IRA but it alienated the Catholic population and gained more support for the Provisionals. Stormont was suspended in March 1972 and direct rule from Whitehall was substituted for self-government. The leader of the British Labour Party, Harold Wilson, then in opposition, had talks with the Provisionals in Dublin in the same month. Four months later, in July, the Secretary of State for Northern Ireland, William Whitelaw, held discussions with them but as he could not guarantee British disengagement from the north the talks were fruitless. The war between the IRA and

the loyalist paramilitaries and the British Army continued, marked by great ferocity, bombings and sectarian assassinations. In December 1974 top Provisionals, including MacStiophan's successor, Daithi O'Conaill (David O'Connell) and Ruari O'Bradaigh, met for secret talks with a group of Protestant clergymen in an hotel in Feakle, Co. Clare. While there were no significant long-term benefits from the discussions, on 20 December the Provos announced a truce for Christmas. The conflict was, however, resumed in 1975.

Since that date, the Provisionals' campaign has passed through three main phases. In 1976, the level and nature of violence was similar to the years 1973–75, although there was a notable increase in the numbers killed. In the following two years, the influence of the Peace Movement* and an increasingly tough security policy resulted in a dramatic fall in the statistics of violence. This had the effect, however, of forcing the IRA to regroup and rethink and it tightened the internal security around its active service units. In August 1979, it was responsible for the assassination of Lord Mountbatten in Co. Sligo and for the killing of eighteen soldiers in an ambush in Co. Down. It subsequently rejected an appeal by Pope John Paul II to end the campaign. By the end of 1979 there was a general belief that while the IRA could not win, neither could it be beaten completely.

IRISH REPUBLICAN BROTHERHOOD (IRB). The movement which was to become known as the IRB was founded in Dublin on 17 March 1858 by James Stephens,* using funds provided by John O'Mahony* who at the same time, founded the Fenians* in New York. Although the American and Irish organisations were separate, the entire republican movement was popularly known as the Fenians. The Fenians were in fact an auxiliary of the IRB. In the beginning, the Irish organisation was called the Irish Revolutionary Brotherhood, but this was eventually changed to the Irish Republican Brotherhood. Among themselves the members referred to it as 'The Society', 'The Organisation' or 'The Brotherhood'. Their watchword was 'Soon or Never' and their aim was to overthrow British rule in Ireland and to create an Irish Republic.

Stephens, as Head Centre, organised the IRB along lines which he believed were best designed to ensure secrecy. He divided the organisation into Centres; under each Centre who was known as 'A' there were nine captains (Bs); each captain had nine sergeants (Cs) and under each sergeant nine privates or Ds. Each member of the IRB had to swear an oath, of which there were several versions, one of which went: 'I, A.B., in the presence of Almighty God, do solemnly swear allegiance to the Irish Republic now virtually established; and that I will do my utmost, at every risk, while life lasts, to defend its independence and integrity; and finally, that I will yield implicit obedience in all things, not contrary to the laws of God, to the commands of my superior officer. So help me God. Amen'. Leading recruiters for the IRB were Stephens, John Devoy,* Patrick 'Pagan' O'Leary,* and William Roantree.*

The IRB quickly incurred the hostility of the Catholic Church and was denounced by the hierarchy in 1863. Two years later it was condemned by the Archbishop of Dublin, Dr Paul Cullen,* and, after the rising of 1867, it was denounced by Pope Pius IX (1869). Nonetheless, it gathered support among the lower orders of clergy. Its newspaper, *The Irish People,* appeared from 1863 until it was suppressed in 1865. Three years later it was replaced by *The Flag of Ireland* which was suppressed in 1874. Stephens resisted pressure from America for a rising until, in December 1866, he lost the confidence of the Fenians who replaced him with Colonel Thomas J. Kelly.* Kelly and his followers arrived in London in January 1867 where General Clus-

seret* was in charge of the military venture. The rising was ruined by a combination of bad planning and betrayal. The police and military speedily defeated Fenian forces at Stepaside, Glencullen and Tallaght, all near Dublin; Drogheda, Kilmallock and Ardagh, Co. Limerick, Drumcliffe, Co. Sligo, Ballyknockane and Knockadoon coastguard station, Co. Cork, and Ballyhurst, Co. Tipperary. For their role in suppressing the rising, the police force became the Royal Irish Constabulary.* An attempt to rescue Colonel Kelly, who had been arrested in England, resulted in the death of a police sergeant in Manchester for which three men, Allen, Larkin and O'Brien, who became known as the Manchester Martyrs, were hanged. In December of that year an attempt to rescue Ricard O'Sullivan Burke resulted in the Clerkenwell Explosion.* The rising and its aftermath caused widespread concern in England and drew attention to Irish affairs. Irish agitation was led by Isaac Butt,* who defended many leading Fenians. When W. E. Gladstone* formed his first government in 1868 he said, 'My mission is to pacify Ireland'.

In 1873 the IRB was re-organised. The most important point made in the new constitution was that the Irish people should decide the fit hour for inaugurating war against England. The IRB would support every movement designed to further the cause of Irish nationalism and independence. As an experiment, some members, Joseph Biggar* and John O'Connor Power* most notably, joined the Home Rule League and sat at Westminster where they adopted a policy of 'obstruction'. The new constitution also laid down that all members had to swear an oath undertaking to do their utmost to establish an independent Ireland, to be faithful to the Supreme Council* and the government of the Irish Republic and to obey their superior officers and the constitution of the IRB. Members in towns and parishes elected an officer to be known as a Centre who would be governed by a County Centre. All recognised the President of the Supreme Council as President of the Irish Republic. Soldiers of the IRB were termed the Irish Republican Army.* Clan na Gael,* founded in New York in 1867 in an attempt to heal the divisions within the Fenian movement there, was recognised as the American auxiliary of the IRB.

The experiment with constitutionalism ended in 1877 when Fenians who remained members of the Irish Parliamentary Party* were expelled from the Supreme Council. Two years later, however, the rise of the Land League* brought prominent IRB men back into the alliance which was then known as the New Departure.* Republicans were much less prominent in the National League,* the constitutional body which replaced the Land League in 1882. Parnell briefly recovered extremist support during the winter of 1890–91 when, following the split in his party, the 'hillside men' rallied to him, encouraged by the violence of his language. Numbers in the IRB were falling during the 1890s, however; official sources estimated that they had fallen from 11,000 to around 8,000. The IRB still had considerable influence as it adopted a policy of infiltrating nationalist organisations from the foundation of the Gaelic Athletic Association* in 1884 onwards. During the 1890s it engaged in a bitter struggle with the Irish National Alliance,* a splinter of Clan na Gael, which had a military wing, the Irish National Brotherhood. The battle between these two republican movements was fought out, for the most part, in the columns of various republican newspapers from1895 until the turn of the century when it ended in victory for the IRB, then led by Fred Allan.*

The IRB recovered support in 1898 when it took a leading role in the '98 Celebrations to commemorate the rising of the United Irishmen.* The nationalist political leader, John Redmond,* shared a common platform with Allan, Arthur Griffith,* Maud Gonne* and James Connolly,* often posing Dublin Castle a major headache in deciding who was and who was not a member of the IRB (Griffith was, while Maud Gonne and Yeats both had close associaitions with the INA). Despite an apparent resurgence in 1898, however, the IRB was losing to open organisations such as Griffith's Cumann na nGaedheal* and the Dungannon Clubs* founded by Bulmer Hobson; these two organisations formed the basis for Sinn Fein.* The revival of the IRB which occurred after 1904 was due to young men such as Hobson, Denis McCullough* and Sean MacDiarmada,* all three of them working in Belfast. They were inspired by Thomas J. Clarke* who arrived from New York in 1907 as an emissary from John Devoy. Most of them were involved in the early stages with the formation of Sinn Fein. By 1912 the RIC had assured Dublin Castle that there was a revival of the IRB but the castle authorities did not take the warning too seriously. In fact, the numerical strength of the IRB at this stage was low – 1,660 members in Ireland and 367 in Great Britain.

In November 1913 Hobson and MacDiarmada played a leading role in the formation of the Irish Volunteers,* destined to become the Irish Republican Army during the Easter Rising of 1916.* The Rising was planned by a small group in the Military Council,* formed in 1915 under Clarke's guidance. Following the collapse of the Rising, the IRB was reorganised under Michael Collins* and Harry Boland.* The Supreme Council was expanded to fifteen members (four co-opted by the original eleven) and a subordinate Military Council was established. The President of the Supreme Council was Thomas Ashe,* who, following his arrest in August 1917, embarked upon a hunger-strike during which he died while being forcibly fed. In accordance with a long-standing IRB tradition his funeral was used as a republican demonstration. Sean MacGarry replaced Ashe as president with Michael Collins as secretary. By the summer of 1918 there were 350 IRB circles with a total membership of 3,000. As each Volunteers' unit was dominated by members of the local circle, the power of the IRB, working in secret, was enormous. This strength compensated for the defection of IRB members who believed that the time for secrecy had vanished with the Easter Rising. When Sinn Fein contested the general election of December 1918 on an abstentionist platform many of the candidates were chosen by the Supreme Council. When Sinn Fein representatives met in the Mansion House on 21 January 1919 and declared Dail Eireann* the parliamentary assembly of the Irish Republic it seemed that the IRB had achieved its central objective. The IRB's influence declined during the War of Independence* as the authority of the IRA increased. Even where membership of the two organisations overlapped the officers' loyalty to the Dail took precedence over their oath to the IRB. The Supreme Council favoured the Treaty,* about which Collins had kept members informed during the negotiations which preceded it. The vote within the Council was eleven in favour, four against. Outside of the IRB there was a strong feeling among critics of the Treaty, in particular Eamon de Valera,* that the Council was using its influence to win support for the Treaty. While supporting the Free State,* the Council looked forward to severing the link with England and financed a newspaper, *The Separatist,* which expounded this theme (it ran from February to September 1922).

During the Civil War* the IRB split. Towards the end of 1922 Free State army officers re-organised and established circles within the army itself, under the leadership of Liam Tobin. They established the Irish Republican Army Organisation with the support of members of the Dail, including the Minister for Industry and Commerce, Joseph McGrath.* The rejection by the government of the officers' demand for a guarantee that the Free State government was still working towards an Irish republic led to the Army Mutiny* in 1924. This presented the government with its first major crisis since the end of the Civil War. However, the government broke the mutiny. The IRB dissolved itself later that year. Funds belonging to the IRB lay in a bank until 1964 when the surviving trustees handed the amount (£2,835) over to Mrs Kathleen Clarke,* widow of Tom Clarke. She had revived the Wolfe Tone Memorial Committee of 1898 to erect a statue to Wolfe Tone and the United Irishmen. This Committee added to the IRB funds and a statue at Stephen's Green was unveiled by Eamon de Valera, then President of the Irish Republic, in November 1967.

IRISH REPUBLICAN DEFENCE ASSOCIATION. Founded in London in 1937 to organise Irish support in Britain for the Irish Republican Army* and its aim of securing a thirty-two county republic. It supported the IRA campaign against Britain which started in January 1939.

IRISH REPUBLICAN SOCIALIST PARTY. Founded in December 1974 as a breakaway from Official Sinn Fein* by Seamus Costello and Ms Bernadette McAliskey (*née* Devlin). With a membership of around 1,000 throughout Ireland, it was registered as a political party in May 1975. It sought a united Ireland organised on socialist lines. In its early days the movement engaged in a feud with the Official IRA, mainly in Northern Ireland. Having survived one assassination attempt, Costello was killed by a gunman in Dublin on 5 October 1977. The party publishes a newspaper, *The Starry Plough.*

IRISH SELF-DETERMINATION LEAGUE OF GREAT BRITAIN. Founded in March 1919 to support Sinn Fein* and the first Dail Eireann* in the fight for Irish independence; the President was P. J. Kelly and the Vice-President Art O'Brien;* Sean McGrath was General Secretary. The

League held classes in the Irish language and on Irish music, etc., and distributed Sinn Fein literature.

IRISH SHIPPING LTD. Established in March 1941, the company was charged with the provision and operation of ships to maintain the vital foodstuffs and raw materials link from overseas – a minimum of 155,000 tonnes deadweight being laid down for this purpose by the Irish government.

The first ship acquired was the Greek vessel *Vassilios Destounis* which was renamed *Irish Poplar.* Nine other vessels, including *Irish Pine* and *Irish Oak,* which were chartered from the US government, were acquired in 1941. Both these ships were lost during World War II; *Irish Pine* disappeared with all hands on a voyage to the US (November 1942) and *Irish Oak* was sunk in the North Atlantic (May 1943) but her entire crew were rescued by a sister ship, the *Irish Plane.* During World War II the Irish Merchant Fleet suffered the loss of one-hundred and fifty-two seamen from nineteen ships.

In 1948 *Irish Rose,* a vessel of 2,210 tonnes deadweight, became the first new ship to be built for Irish Shipping Ltd. During the late 1960s the company switched from its established North America/Canada cargo runs to international tramp shipping. Its tramp fleet now comprises a total of 159,467 tonnes deadweight: *Irish Rowan* (27,532), *Irish Cedar* (27,572), *Irish Pine* (26,091), *Irish Maple* (26,091), *Irish Oak* (26,061) and *Irish Larch* (26,120).

In April 1978, the *Saint Killian* (7,128 tonnes) joined the *Saint Patrick* (5,285) on the Rosslare/Le Havre-Cherbourg service. To 31 March 1979, 162,000 passengers and 36,100 cars were carried on the ferry. This represented an increase of 38 per cent and 44 per cent respectively over the previous year's levels. Freight carryings by the service were some 200 per cent up on the previous year's level, boosting the Group's profit (to 31 March 1979) to £4,823,000.

Irish Shipping has a 99.96 per cent holding in Irish Continental Line Ltd, and in its subsidiary companies Southern Development Ltd, Donwell Ltd, Herat Ltd, and Pennyroyal Ltd. Irish Continental Line Ltd, which also has a 50 per cent shareholding in Ferrytours Ltd, operates the Rosslare to Le Havre and Cherbourg car/passenger and roll-on/roll-off freight service. The company also has a substantial interest in Associated Port Terminals Ltd, a stevedoring firm which is based at Dublin. Other company interests include holdings in the Insurance Corporation of Ireland Ltd, the Property Corporation of Ireland, Irish Mainport Holidays Ltd, and Celtic Bulk Carriers.

Employment in the Irish Shipping Group increased by almost 15 per cent to 947 in 1979. In addition employment in associated companies increased by almost 9 per cent to 970 within the same period.

IRISH SOCIALIST REPUBLICAN PARTY. Founded in Dublin on 29 May 1896 by James Connolly* as a successor to the Dublin Socialist Party. The party had little popular support. Connolly used its newspaper, *The Workers Republic,* * to further his social and nationalist ideals. Following Connolly's departure to the USA in 1903 the party was reorganised by William O'Brien* as the Socialist Party of Ireland.*

IRISH SOCIETY. The Irish Society 'for promoting the Scriptural Education and Religious Instruction of Roman Catholics chiefly through the Medium of Their Own Language' was founded in 1818. Its leaders were all members of the Established Churches of Ireland and England who wished to avoid proselytising and concentrate on producing the Bible and The Book of Common Prayer in the Irish language. Between 1836 and 1850 the society spent around £4,000 a year on the provision of Bibles and instructors. The members also supported the campaign for a Chair of Irish in Trinity College Dublin (the Chair was established in 1838). The Society's efforts were directed in the main at the poorer parts of Ireland where they sought to win converts through encouragement rather than open proselytisation. The Irish Society attempted to avoid association with the militantly proselytising Irish Church Missions* established in 1849 by Rev. Alexander R. C. Dallas.* However, the Society came under such strong pressure from influential figures in the Established Church, both in England and in Ireland, that in 1853 it entered into an alliance with the ICM. Within three years, alarmed at the 'aggressiveness' of Dallas and his movement, the Irish Society broke away. Its membership and influence were by now considerably reduced and only the Dublin branch remained active for a short time.

'IRISH STATESMAN'. Weekly review established with the aid of Sir Horace Plunkett* in 1919, under the editorship of Warre Bradley Wells. It ceased publication temporarily in April 1920 due to the War of Independence* but was revived by Plunkett in September 1923. The *Statesman* took over the *Irish Homestead** and was edited by George Russell* until it ceased publication in 1930.

IRISH SUGAR COMPANY (COMHLUCHT SIÚICRE ÉIREANN TEO). Founded in 1933, the company has four factories at Carlow, Mallow, Thurles and Tuam, which produce sugar from beet. The company also distributes fertiliser and ground limestone to farmers and manufactures specialised agricultural machinery under the brand name 'Armer'. A decision to diversify into food processing was made in 1959, largely through the urgings of the then Managing Director, Major General Michael Joseph Costello.* In 1964 Erin Foods Ltd was formed; in 1967 it joined H. J. Heinz Ltd, to gain international distribution for its produce.

IRISH TEXTS SOCIETY, THE. Founded in 1899 by Eleanor Hull* in association with Dr Douglas Hyde,* Robin Flower,* P. W. Joyce,* Frank A. Fahy* Miss N. Borthwick, T.D. Fitzgerald, David Comyn* and others, for the purpose of publishing texts in the Irish language. Many of the Society's early publications were, in fact, bilingual. Among its most notable achievements was the promotion of Rev. P. S. Dinneen's revised *Irish-English Dictionary (Foclóir Gaedhilge agus Béarla)* in 1927. Other translations were undertaken by the Society under the editorships of Standish Hayes O'Grady,* Tomas Ó Máile,* Douglas Hyde, Eoin MacNeill and David Comyn.

'IRISH TIMES'. Daily newspaper founded by Major Laurence E. Knox in 1859, Ireland's first penny newspaper. The unofficial organ of the (Protestant) Ascendancy* for many years, it was bought by Sir John Arnott upon Knox's death in 1873. Its most famous editor (1934–54) was R. M. Smyllie.* Its Unionist attitudes have gradually changed until in more recent years it has become the principal forum for liberal views. With sales of 70,000 (January 1979), *The Irish Times* is in the third place of the four morning dailies. It devotes more space and gives greater depth of coverage to international news than any of the other national dailies.

IRISHTOWN, CO. MAYO. Village where a meeting on 20 April 1879 initiated the land agitation which led to the establishment of the Land League.* The meeting, organised by James Daly* and Michael Davitt,* was in protest at the evictions ordered by a local landlord, Canon Bourke. Between 8,000 and 10,000 tenant-farmers attended, focusing attention on the desperate conditions under which land was held during a time of famine. After Irishtown the Fenians* and the Irish Parliamentary Party* became involved in what was soon a land war. As a result of the Irishtown meeting, and a similar one held in Westport, the Land League of Mayo* was founded on 16 August in Castlebar. The (Irish National) Land League was established two months later.

IRISH TRADE AND LABOUR UNION. An attempt in 1890 to form a trade union, which had the support of Michael Davitt.* The movement failed within a short time through lack of worker support.

IRISH TRADES UNION CONGRESS (ITUC). Formed in Dublin 1894 to further the interests of the trades union movement. The ITUC was largely apolitical in its early years but after 1910 it took on a political complexion with the entry of James Larkin and James Connolly. In 1912 Congress passed a motion by Connolly calling for the formation of an Irish Labour Party as a result of which the Irish Labour Party and Trades Union Congress was formed (*see* Labour Party). The ITUC was an all-Ireland body and also contained a large number of trades unions with their headquarters in Britain. This last factor was a major cause of tension within Congress with the growth of militant nationalism leading to the War of Independence.*

During the 1920s and '30s Congress was dominated by William O'Brien* of the ITGWU whose quarrel with his former leader, Larkin, split the trade union movement. In 1945 O'Brien split Congress and the Labour Party when he withdrew the ITGWU from Congress and was followed by fourteen other unions. They formed a rival Congress of Irish Unions.* The ITUC remained representative of the whole island and still contained a large proportion of British-based unions within the 145,000 affiliated members. It gave autonomy to its members in Northern Ireland who elected their own Northern Committee. During the 1950s there was a growth in Irish trade union membership. In 1958 the ITUC had 250,000 members in some

sixty-four unions while CIU had around 190,000 in thirty unions. In 1955 negotiations began between the Congresses as a result of which they amalgamated to form the Irish Congress of Trade Unions* in 1959.

IRISH TRANSPORT AND GENERAL WORKERS' UNION (ITGWU). Founded by James Larkin* on 4 January 1909 after he had broken with the National Union of Dock Labourers. The ITGWU was formed from among the Dublin members of the NUDL and sought to attract carters and general labourers. In 1910 it was affiliated to the Irish Trades Unions Congress* and by 1911 had a membership of 5,000. Larkin was general secretary and other prominent members were Thomas Foran, P.T. Daly and William O'Brien.* James Connolly* became Belfast organiser in June 1911. Under Larkin's leadership the union's campaign for members brought it into conflict with William Martin Murphy* and the Dublin employers who sought to prevent their workers from joining it. This led to the Lock-Out* (September 1913-February 1914). By the time the Lock-Out ended, the ITGWU was in financial straits and Larkin went to the USA at the end of 1914 to raise money for both it and the Labour Party.* During his absence the leader was James Connolly. Following the Easter Rising of 1916,* after which Connolly was executed, the leadership devolved on O'Brien, Daly and Foran who built it up over the next few years until there were forty branches with 14,000 members. By the end of 1918 this had risen to 210 branches with 68,000 members and a year later there were 350 branches with 100,000 members, making it the biggest union in the country.

O'Brien's rise to power within the Union caused discontent among a section led by Daly who sought to enlist the aid of Larkin, still in America. When Larkin returned in 1923 he attempted to resume control but was defeated by O'Brien and Thomas

Johnson.* Larkin then assumed control of the Workers' Union of Ireland* in 1924 and the split reduced the ITGWU to 60,000 members. The quarrel between the ITGWU and Larkin's syndicalist WUI was a constant source of tension within the Irish labour movement throughout the 1930s and into the 1940s. Eventually, after Larkin was reunited with the Labour Party and the WUI affiliated to the ITUC, O'Brien and the ITGWU diaffiliated from the party and Congress in 1945. Five ITGWU parliamentary members formed the rival National Labour Party,* and O'Brien and the ITGWU formed the rival Congress of Irish Unions.* This breach was not healed until twelve years after Larkin's death when the two congresses united to form the Irish Congress of Trades Unions* in 1959. The ITGWU is the largest union in Ireland with 155,000 members in 172 branches.

IRISH UNIONIST ALLIANCE. Founded in 1891 from the Irish Loyal and Patriotic Union,* the Alliance's purpose was to resist Home Rule.* It represented a small but influential number of Unionists,* mainly from the south where they had extensive business and landowning interests which, they believed, would be jeopardised by self-government. Although the Alliance was never numerically strong it had considerable influence among Conservatives in England where its chief spokesmen were Lord Midleton* and Lord Lansdowne. As it included peers and their close associates, the Alliance held considerable weight in the House of Lords, then overwhelmingly Conservative and anti-Home Rule. It was, however, more propagandist than political, as there was little chance of southern Unionists winning seats in the south. During the debates on the (second) Home Rule Bill* (1892-93) and subsequently, the Alliance used its resources to disseminate anti-Home Rule propaganda in Ireland and throughout the United Kingdom. The IUA played a leading role in the

Joint Committee of Unionist Associations* and during the debate on the (third) Home Rule Bill* (1912–14) it brought Conservative MPs to Ireland and sent Unionist spokesmen to England and Scotland. Upon the passage of the Bill and its signing into law in September 1914 southern Unionists were forced to come to terms with the immediate prospect of self-government and following a split within the Alliance they formed the Unionist Anti-Partition League.

See also Unionist Party *and* Ulster Unionist Party.

IRISH UNIVERSITIES ACT, 1908. Introduced by the Chief Secretary, Augustine Birrell,* it attempted to solve the vexed question of acceptable higher education for Catholics. Under the Act, the Royal University* was abolished and two new universities were constituted: Queen's University of Belfast (*see* Queen's Colleges), and the National University of Ireland,* made up from the old Queen's Colleges of Galway and Cork, with University College, Dublin. The Catholic Hierarchy was prominently represented on the Governing Body of NUI which was declared to be a non-denominational university.

IRISH VOLUNTEERS. Founded on 25 November 1913 as the result of an article by Eoin MacNeill* in *An Claideamh Soluis** of 1 November. In the article, entitled 'The North Began', MacNeill suggested that southern nationalists should form a volunteer movement on the lines of the Ulster Volunteer Force.* He was then approached by Bulmer Hobson* of the Irish Republican Brotherhood* who organised a public meeting at the Rotunda where the new force was established. It attracted followers of Sinn Fein,* the Gaelic Athletic Association* and the Gaelic League* as well as members of the IRB who envisaged a future role for the new force. By May 1914 membership was around 80,000 and funds were collected through John Devoy* and Clan na Gael* in the USA and by Sir Roger Casement* and Alice Stopford Green* in England. In July 1914 Darrell Figgis* and Robert Erskine Childers arranged for the purchase of guns in Germany (*see* Howth gunrunning).

There were now two armed volunteer armies in the country. The Ulster Volunteer Force had made clear its commitment to resist Home Rule* at all costs, and had been given the support of Andrew Bonar Law* and the Conservatives. John Redmond* was fighting for Home Rule without partition at Westminster but he was concerned lest the Volunteers should prevent the passage of the (third) Home Rule Bill.* To ensure control of the Volunteers he demanded half of the seats on the Provisional Committee. As the alternative was to split the movement, his demands were conceded in June, much to the anger of extremists in the IRB. By September, when the Home Rule Act was suspended for the duration of World War I, membership numbered 180,000. The British government rejected an offer of the Volunteers as a defence force for Ireland. On 20 September, in the course of a speech at Woodenbridge, Co. Wicklow, Redmond urged Volunteers to support Britain in the war against Germany 'for the freedom of small nations'. His call was answered by a majority of the Volunteers which became known as the National Volunteers,* leaving some 11,000 Irish Volunteers, who opposed involvement in the War. This minority reorganised in October 1914. MacNeill became Chief of Staff, Hobson (no longer acceptable to the IRB) Quartermaster and The O'Rahilly* Director of Arms. Three key posts were in the hands of the IRB: Patrick Pearse* was Director of Military Organisation, Joseph Plunkett* Director of Military Operations and Thomas Mac Donagh* Director of Training. All three later became members of the secret IRB Military Council* which organised, under the influence of Thomas J. Clarke,* the

Easter Rising of 1916* for which the Volunteers provided a ready-made army.

Despite the failure of the military insurrection, the executions and mass arrests which followed it led to a revitalisation of the Volunteer movement. On 21 January 1919 the first Dail Eireann* met and proclaimed the Irish Republic. In 1920 the Volunteers took an oath to the Republic and became the Irish Republican Army.*

The Manifesto of the Irish Volunteers, read by MacNeill at the Rotunda on 25 November 1913, said, in part:

'At a time when legislative proposals, universally confessed to be of vital concern for the future of Ireland, have been put forward, and are awaiting decision, a plan has been deliberately adopted by one of the great English political parties, advocated by the leaders of that party and by its numerous organs in the Press, brought systematically to bear on English public opinion, to make a display of military force and the menace of armed violence, the determining factor in the future relations between this country and Great Britain.

The party which has thus substituted open force for the semblance of civil government is seeking by this means not merely to decide an immediately political issue of grave concern to this nation, but also to obtain for itself the future control of all our national affairs. It is plain to every man that the people of Ireland, if they acquiesce in this new policy by their inaction, will consent to the surrender not only of their rights as a nation, but of their civic rights as men. . . .

Are we to rest inactive in the hope that the course of politics in Great Britain may save us from the degradation openly threatened against us? British politics are controlled by British interests, and are complicated by problems of great importance to the people of Great Britain. In a crisis of this kind the duty of safeguarding our rights is our duty first and foremost. If we remain quiescent by what title can be expect the people of Great Britain to turn aside from their own pressing concerns to defend us? Will not such an attitude of itself mark us out as a people unworthy of defence?

Such is the occasion, not altogether unfortunate, which has brought the inception of the Irish Volunteer movement. But the Volunteers, once they have been enrolled, will form a prominent element in the national life under a national government. The nation will maintain its Volunteer organisation as a guarantee of the liberties which the Irish people shall have secured . . .

The object proposed for the Irish Volunteers is to secure and maintain the rights and liberties common to all the people of Ireland. Their duties will be defensive and protective, and they will not contemplate either aggression or domination. Their ranks are open to all able-bodied Irishmen without distinction of creed, politics, or social grade. Means will be found whereby Irishmen unable to serve as ordinary Volunteers will be enabled to aid the Volunteer forces in various capacities. There will also be work for women to do, and there are signs that the women of Ireland, true to their records, are especially enthusiastic for the success of the Irish Volunteers.

We propose for the Volunteers' organisation the widest possible basis. Without any other association or classification the Volunteers will be enrolled according to the district in which they live. As soon as it is found feasible, the district sections will be called upon to join in making provision for the general administration and for united co-operation. . . .

In the name of national unity, of national dignity, of national and individual liberty, of manly citizenship, we appeal to our countrymen to recognise and accept without hesitation the opportunity that has been granted them to join the ranks of the Irish Volunteers, and to make the movement now begun, not unworthy of the historic title which it has adopted.'

IRISH VOLUNTEERS' DEPENDANTS' FUND. Established in 1916 through the efforts of Mrs Kathleen Clarke* to aid the dependants of those involved in the Easter Rising of 1916.* Initial funds were provided by £3,000 in gold remaining from money sent by Clan na Gael* to finance the insurrection. An early appeal on behalf of the IVDF in *The Irish Independent* on 15 July 1916 listed the executive as follows: Mrs Clarke, president; Mrs Ceannt, vice-president; Sorcha Nic Mathgamhna, treasurer; E. Mac Raghnaill, secretary; Mrs Pearse, Mrs MacDonagh, Miss E. O'Hanrahan, Miss M. Daly, and Miss L. Colbert. The principal aim of the IVDF was 'to provide adequately for the dependants of the men executed, killed in fighting, imprisoned or deported for their participation in the Insurrection of Easter Week'. The IVDF merged with the Irish National Aid Association* in August 1916. Michael Collins,* released from Frongoch at Christmas 1916, became Chief Organiser and Secretary of the Fund at a salary of £2.50 per week and remained in the post until 1918. Dail Eireann* later assumed responsibility through the Ministry for Home Affairs. The distribution of the funds gathered support and sympathy from all sections of the public and was used to further the reorganisation of Sinn Fein.*

IRISH WOMEN'S SUFFRAGE FEDERATION. The first Irish women's suffrage association was the Dublin Women's Suffrage Society founded in 1875. As the scope of the society broadened, it became the Irishwomen's Suffrage and Local Government Association. Women were granted the vote for local government elections under the Local Government Act of 1898. The IS & LGA and scattered local suffrage societies were absorbed by Louie Bennett* and Helen Chenevix in 1911 into the Irish Women's Suffrage

Federation. Presidents of the Federation included Mary Hayden,* while George Russell* was one of its vice-presidents. Under the Representation of the People Act, 1918, women over the age of thirty received the vote. Among the first Irish women to exercise the franchise was Anna Haslam, a veteran suffragette, then aged eighty-nine, who had sown the seed of female emancipation over forty years earlier.

'IRISH WORKER'. Weekly newspaper founded by James Larkin* in May 1911 to represent the trade union and labour movement (*see* Irish Transport and General Workers' Union *and* Labour Party). The paper, in which Larkin, William O'Brien* of Labour and James Connolly* attacked capitalism, imperialism, employers, the bourgeoisie and the Irish Parliamentary Party,* sold an average of 20,000 copies per issue. During its first years it was sued for libel seven times as a result of Larkin's policy of denouncing individuals by name. Its nationalism attracted the attention of Dublin Castle* which suppressed it for its anti-war sentiments (December 1914 – January 1915). After Larkin's departure for the USA in October 1914, Connolly edited the paper until it was suppressed. *The Irish Worker* was revived by Larkin and edited by his son, James Larkin Jnr,* from October 1930 until March 1932.

IRISH WORKERS' AND FARMERS' REPUBLICAN PARTY. Radical movement founded in 1930, its objectives were 'to break the connection with England' and 'to bring about the closest co-operation between workers in . . . rural districts . . . in cities . . . all victims of the same exploiting agencies' (Irish capitalism and British imperialism). Like other groups such as the Workers' Revolutionary Party* and Peadar O'Donnell's Irish Working Farmers' Committee,* the IWFRP lacked popular support. It was outlawed on 17 October 1931.

IRISH WORKERS' LEAGUE. Marxist organisation founded by James Larkin* in 1923. It replaced the Communist Party of Ireland* as the Irish section of the Comintern. The IWL's Marxism won very little support and it was absorbed by Larkin's Workers' Union of Ireland.* Larkin represented the IWL at the Comintern congresses in Moscow in 1924 and 1928. It failed in its attempt to establish a revolutionary workers' party. Larkin was the League's candidate in the general election of June 1927 when he won his seat but was disqualified.

IRISH WORKERS' PARTY. *See* Communist Party of Ireland.

IRISH WORKING FARMERS' COMMITTEE. Radical movement founded in the West of Ireland in the late 1920s by Peadar O'Donnell* and Sean Hayes. It attracted the support of the left-wing of the Irish Republican Army.* Largely rural based, it had little success because of the difficulty of organising the smaller farmer and the exploited hired agricultural labourers. The older farmer, even if poor, was too conservative and too attached to his holding to support the idea of co-operative farming on the lines envisaged by O'Donnell. It was banned by the government along with eleven other organisations, including Saor Eire,* the Friends of Soviet Russia, the Workers' Revolutionary Party* and the IRA in October 1931.

'IRISH WORLD'. Radical newspaper founded by Patrick Ford* in 1870, its sub-title was 'American Industrial Liberator'. It supported extremist Fenian policy in America, in Ireland, and in Britain. It played a large role in securing help for the Land League* both in America and in Ireland, and for the Irish Parliamentary Party* in the struggle for Home Rule.* The paper often took an unpredictable line, mirroring the changes of policies and friendships of its editor. After Ford's death the paper was edited by his nephew, Robert, and it supported the Redmondite cause until the latter's death.

J

JACOB, ARTHUR (1790–1874). Oculist; b. Maryborough (Portlaoise). He studied surgery under his father at Dr Steevens's Hospital, Dublin, and in Edinburgh where he received his M.D. (1814). After completing studies in Paris and London he returned to Dublin in 1819. He was co-founder of the Park St School of Medicine; Professor of Anatomy at the Royal College of Surgeons of Ireland (1826–69) and three times President of the RCSI. The City of Dublin Hospital was founded by him in 1832 and he edited the first forty-two volumes of his *Dublin Medical Press* from 1839 to 1859. He discovered 'Jacob's Ulcer'. Apart from articles on the eye which he published in the *Cyclopaedia of Anatomy* and in the *Cyclopaedia of Practical Medicine*, he was the author of *A Treatise on Inflammation of the Eyeball* (1849) and *Cataract and the Operation for its Removal by Absorption* (1851).

JACOB, JOSHUA (c. 1805–77). Founder of White Quakers; b. Clonmel, Co. Tipperary; ed. Quaker Schools. He followed a business career in Limerick and Dublin. He established the White Quakers – a sect which wished to revive the early spirit of the Quaker movement. The new sect re-adopted the practice of wearing undyed garments, abstained from eating meat and condemned all manifestations of the modern world, including clocks, watches, and even bells. The movement established centres in Clonmel, Dublin, Waterford and Mountmellick. Upon the death of his wife Abigail, Jacob married a Catholic. He then abrogated the movement, resumed his business career, and allowed his children to be educated in the Catholic faith.

JAMES CONNOLLY WORKERS' EDUCATION CLUB. *See* Workers' Party of Ireland.

JEBB, JOHN (1775–1833). Author and Bishop of Limerick (C.I.), 1822–27; b. Drogheda, Co. Louth; ed. Celbridge, Derry City and TCD where he graduated M.A. in 1801. Following his ordination in 1799 he was appointed curate at Mogarvane, Co. Tipperary. He accompanied Alexander Knox to England in 1809 and became acquainted with William Wilberforce and other leading reformers. Upon his return he received the rectorship of Abington, Co. Limerick. During one of his frequent visits to London he arranged publication there of his most celebrated work: *Essay on Sacred Literature* (1820). As Archdeacon of Emly (from 1820), he devoted himself to the welfare of his district, and his was one of the relatively few areas to be trouble-free during the disturbances which accompanied the famine of 1822. His career as bishop was interrupted when he became paralysed in 1827, after which he went to live in England. Like his friend Knox, he anticipated the Oxford Movement. His most widely-read works include *Sermons* (1815), *Practical Theology* (1833), *Piety without Asceticism* (1831), and *Thirty Years of Correspondence between . . . Bishop Jebb . . . and Alexander Knox* (2 vols, 1836).

JELLETT, MAINIE (1896–1943). Artist; studied in Dublin, London and Paris. She was a close friend of Evie Hone* with whom she held an exhibition at the St Stephen's Green studio of Jack Butler Yeats* in 1921. This exhibition was condemned by traditionalists, including George Russell.* She was selected by the Irish government to design the murals for the Irish Pavilion at the Glasgow Exhibition (1938). Her 'Deposition', oil on canvas (Municipal Gallery of Modern Art, Dublin), is considered an excellent example of religious art.

269

JINKS AFFAIR. Alderman John Jinks of Sligo was a member of the National League Party,* led by Captain Redmond. The National League and the Labour Party had entered into an alliance with Fianna Fail in August 1927 for the purpose of ousting the Cumann na nGaedheal government. On 16 August a vote of No Confidence was called by Thomas Johnson,* leader of the Labour Party. Because Jinks was not present the result was a tie of seventy-one votes and the government was saved by the casting vote of the Speaker, Michael Hayes.* Jinks' absence became a celebrated source of Irish political lore. His non-appearance has been generally attributed to the intervention of two Cosgrave supporters, Major Bryan Cooper and R. M. Smyllie,* editor of *The Irish Times.* They were suspected of having furnished Jinks with liberal entertainment, making it impossible for him to attend the division. Cosgrave dissolved the Dail on 25 August and called a new election in which he secured a comfortable majority. During the following year when a discussion arose as to the name of a horse newly purchased by the National Stud, Cosgrave suggested 'Mr Jinks'. The horse subsequently won the 1929 English Two Thousand Guineas at odds of 5 to 2.

JOHNSON, THOMAS (1872–1963). Trade unionist and politician (Labour), Senator (1928–38) and member of the Labour Court (1946–55); b. Liverpool. He left school at twelve to work in an office and came to Ireland in 1892. He moved from Kinsale to Belfast in 1901 to work as a commercial traveller and served on the strike committee organised by James Larkin* during the Belfast general strike of 1907. A founder-member of the Labour Party in 1912, he was vice-chairman of the executive which, along with William O'Brien,* he dominated until 1923. He was a member of the Mansion House Conference* called in 1918 to oppose conscription (*see* Conscription and

Ireland). When he called a strike on behalf of the anti-conscription movement and published *A hand book for rebels; a guide to successful defiance of the British Government,* he lost his job in Belfast and moved to Dublin where he became treasurer of the Irish Transport and General Workers' Union.*

Johnson agreed to the abstention of the Labour Party from the general election of December 1918 so as not to split the Sinn Fein vote. He was co-author of the Democratic Programme* adopted by the first Dail Eireann. He accompanied Cathal O'Shannon* to the Socialist International held in Berne in 1919. His enemies accused him of supporting the Treaty* and he never denied the charge which damaged his standing among republicans. Returned as Labour TD for Co. Dublin in the election of June 1922, he voted against W. T. Cosgrave* in the election for President of the Executive Council. He was leader of the seventeen-man Labour parliamentary party and of the official opposition until 1927.

Johnson was critical of the government's handling of the Civil War,* denouncing in particular the policy of executing imprisoned republicans. His economic policy called for the reduction of indirect taxation, for tariffs on imports and for less reliance on private industry. He opposed the payment of the Land Annuities* to Britain. Between 1924 and 1926 he spearheaded a Labour demand for a radical overhaul of the educational system.

The return of James Larkin from the USA in 1923 led to a division in the Labour movement when Johnson and William O'Brien resisted Larkin's attempt to regain control of the ITGWU. He retained his seat in Dail Eireann in the general election of that year which reduced Labour representation from seventeen to fourteen seats. The first general election of 1927 gave Labour twenty-two seats and he led opposition to the Public Safety Act which followed the assassination of Kevin O'Higgins.* He agreed to support Fianna Fail* on condition that Labour would participate in a coalition with Fianna Fail and the National League.* Fianna Fail's entry into constitutional politics provided a serious opposition to the Cosgrave government and on 16 August, Johnson called for a vote of No Confidence. The government was saved only by the absence of Alderman John Jinks of Sligo (*see* Jinks Affair). In September he lost his seat to James Larkin Jnr,* and resigned as secretary of the party in 1928. He represented Labour in the Senate until 1936 when the upper house was abolished by Eamon de Valera.* On the establishment of the Labour Court* in 1946 he became a founder-member.

JOHNSTON, FRANCIS (1761–1829). Architect, known as 'The Wren of Ireland'; b. Co. Armagh. He was responsible for some of Dublin's finest buildings including St George's Church, Temple Street (1802); Chapel Royal, Dublin Castle (1807–16); the General Post Office (1815–17). Johnston adapted the Parliament House for the Bank of Ireland (c. 1803) and worked on major alterations at the Vice-Regal Lodge (now Aras an Uachtarain) in 1816. He acted as adviser and restorer on several projects including Nelson Pillar (1808–09) and was instrumental in the founding of the Royal Hibernian Academy* in 1823. Johnston was a keen campanologist and had a bell-tower erected in his garden but following objections from his neighbours he presented the peal to St George's, Drumcondra, Dublin.

JOHNSTON, WILLIAM (1829–1902). Politician (Unionist) and prominent member of the Orange Order; b. Ballykilbeg, Co. Down; ed. TCD; B.A. (1852); Bar (1872). He joined the Orange Order in 1848 and was closely associated with it for the rest of his life. He was imprisoned under the Party Processions Act (1867). His violent speeches in opposition to the Land League* led to his dismissal from a post as inspector of fisheries. Returned as MP for South Belfast in 1885, he became the first Irishman to be elected because of imprisonment. During his career in parliament until his death he remained a strong opponent of Home Rule.* He supported security of tenure for the tenant farmers and was also a strong supporter of the temperance movement and of female emancipation. His seat was won by T. H. Sloan.*

JOHNSTON, WILLIAM DENIS (1901–). Dramatist; b. Dublin; ed. St Andrew's, Dublin, Marchiston Castle, Edinburgh, Christ Church, Cambridge and Harvard Law School. After a call to the Irish and Northern Bars he briefly practised law. Under the stage-name E. W. Tocher he appeared in Abbey Theatre productions. He married the Abbey actress Shelagh Richards in 1928. He was a director of the Gate Theatre* from 1931 to 1936 where his first play, *The Old Lady Says 'No'*, was produced after it was rejected by the Abbey, and where he produced the first wholly Irish film, an adaptation of Frank O'Connor's *Guests of the Nation* (1934). Johnston worked as a script writer and director for BBC Radio (1936), script writer for BBC Television (1938) and Censor for the American networks from 1939. He was a BBC war correspondent from 1942 and was awarded the OBE in 1946. After becoming drama critic at Radio Eireann in 1947 he held visiting professorships at American universities before settling in the Channel Islands (1967). His works include *The Old Lady Says 'No'* (1929; the title comes from the note which W. B. Yeats sent to the author telling him that Augusta, Lady Gregory had rejected it), *The Indiscreet Goat* (1931, ballet), *The Moon in the Yellow River* (1931), *A Bride for the Unicorn* (1933), *Storm Song* (1934), *The Golden Cuckoo* (1939), *The Dreaming Dust* (1940), *A Fourth for

Bridge (1947), *Strange Occurrence on Ireland's Eye* (1956), *The Scythe and the Sunset* (1958), *In Search of Swift* (1959) and *J. M. Synge* (1955). His autobiography, *Nine Rivers from Jordan* (1953) is based on his experiences as a war correspondent.

JOINT COMMITTEE OF UNIONIST ASSOCIATIONS. Founded in 1907 as the co-ordinating body of northern and southern Unionist organisations in the fight against Home Rule.* The Joint Committee brought together the Ulster Unionist Council* and the Irish Unionist Alliance.* Following the passage of the (third) Home Rule Bill* in 1914, the Committee had little relevance for Northern Unionists and was abandoned by tacit agreement.

JOLY, REV. JASPER ROBERT (1819–92). Clergyman (C.I.) and bibliophile; b. Clonbullogue, Co. Offaly; ed. TCD (which he entered at the age of thirteen). He received his B.A. in 1837, M.A. in 1840 and LL.B. and LL.D. in 1857. Called to the Bar, he did not practise but took Orders and was appointed Vicar-General of the Diocese of Tuam, Co. Galway. A council member of the Royal Dublin Society,* Dr Joly executed a Deed of Gift and Trust (8 April 1863) conveying to the Society his vast collection of books and manuscripts. A proviso in the Deed stipulated that whenever a public library should be established in Dublin by Act of Parliament, the RDS would transfer the collection to it. The National Library* was formally opened on 29 August 1890 with the Joly collection as a nucleus. The collection contains 23,000 printed volumes and includes a large quantity of unbound papers and prints. It includes also an extensive collection of Irish and Scottish song music and a French section dealing with the Napoleonic and Revolutionary eras.

JOYCE, JAMES AUGUSTINE ALOYSIUS (1882–1941). Novelist, poet and dramatist; b. Dublin; ed.

Clongowes Wood and Belvedere Jesuit Colleges. After reading English, French and Italian at UCD he was awarded B.A. by the Royal University (1902). His close associates at University College included George Clancy, Thomas Kettle* and Francis Skeffington (*see* Sheehy-Skeffington, Francis). Under Clancy's influence he attended Gaelic League* classes but became so annoyed at the hostile attitude towards English of the teacher, Patrick Pearse,* that he gave up studying Irish.

In 1904 Joyce left Dublin with his common-law wife, Nora Barnacle, and settled in Trieste where he taught languages while working on *Dubliners* (1914) and *A Portrait of the Artist as a Young Man* (1916). He returned to Dublin in October 1911, as a member of a Triestine partnership, to open a cinema, the Volta. It opened on 20 December but within a short time, he lost interest and returned to Trieste in January 1912. He settled in Zurich (1915–19) and worked on *Ulysses* (1922). After taking up residence in Paris (1920) he began work on *Finnegans Wake* (1939), known before publication as *Work in Progress.* His eyesight deteriorated rapidly and any Irish visitor to Paris was likely to be pressed into service as a secretary. This select group included Samuel Beckett.* For most of his life he was supported by his brother, Stanislaus, his publisher Sylvia Beach and an American benefactor, Harriet Weaver. On the outbreak of World War II in 1939 he sought refuge in Zurich where he remained until his death. His poems *Chamber Music,* appeared in 1907, *Exiles* (a play) in 1918 and *Pomes Penyeach* in 1927.

JOYCE, PATRICK WESTON (1827–1914). Scholar, historian and collector of folk-music; b. Ballyorgan, Co. Limerick; brother of Robert Dwyer Joyce;* ed. at hedge-school and at Kilfinane, Kilmallock, Galbally (Co. Limerick) and Mitchelstown, Co. Cork. He completed his education at TCD where he took his B.A. in 1861 and M.A. three years later. Joyce was an active member of the Society for the Preservation of the Irish Language. He was elected to the RIA in 1863 and was President of the Royal Society of Antiquaries (1906–08). A prolific writer, the majority of his works were written following his retirement as Principal of Marlborough Street Training College, Dublin in 1893 (a post which he had held since 1874).

His works include *Ancient Irish Music* (1872), *A Handbook of School Management* (1876), *How to Prepare for Civil Service Examinations* (1878), *Old Celtic Romances* (1878), *The Geography of the Counties of Ireland* (1883), *Irish Music and Song* (1888), *A Child's History of Ireland* (1898), *A Reading Book of Irish History* (1900), *A Social History of Ancient Ireland* (1903), *A Concise History of Ireland* (1903), *A Smaller Social History of Ancient Ireland* (1906), *The Story of Ancient Irish Civilisation* (1907), *The Wonders of Ireland* (1911), *Outlines of the History of Ireland* (1921).

His first collection of music in 1872 contained the air 'Mor Chluana' which was adapted as 'An tAmhrán Dochais' ('The Song of Hope') and became the official salute to An Taoiseach. Joyce's last collection, *Old Irish Folk Music and Songs* (1909) contained 824 previously unpublished airs. The work by which he is best known, *The Origin and History of Irish Names and Places*, appeared in three volumes (1869, 1875 and 1913).

JOYCE, ROBERT DWYER (1830–83). Physician, poet and Fenian sympathiser; b. Glenosheen, Co. Limerick, brother of Patrick Weston Joyce;* ed. hedge school* and at Queen's College, Cork, where he graduated M.D. in 1857. He was employed by the Commissioners of National Education and became principal of the Clonmel Model School and later (1866) became Professor of English at the Catholic University.* Joyce contributed verse to the leading periodicals of the era including *The Nation,** *Harp*, *The Celt*, *Irishman* and the

*Irish People.** He left Ireland in 1866 disillusioned with Fenianism when the anticipated rising failed to materialise in 1865. He practised medicine in Boston and lectured at Harvard medical school.

In the USA Joyce became closely associated with the Fenian movement and with its leaders John Devoy,* Jeremiah O'Donovan Rossa,* James J. O'Kelly* and the Fenian poet John Boyle O'Reilly.* He supported the New Departure* though convinced that Irish freedom could be won only by the gun. He experimented with new methods of gun-casting and researched into ways of improving Fenian gunpowder factories. He returned to Ireland in September 1883 and died at his brother's home a few weeks later. His works include *Ballads, Romances and Songs* (1861), *Legends of the Wars in Ireland* (1868), *Irish Fireside Tales* (1871), *Ballads of Irish Chivalry* (1872), *Deirdre* (1876) and *Blanaid* (1879). His best known poems are 'The Leprachaun' ('In a shady nook one moonlit night . . .'), 'The Boys of Wexford', 'The Wind that shakes the barley' and a lament on the death of the Fenian leader, Peter O'Neill Crowley.*

JOYCE, WILLIAM ('LORD HAW-HAW') (1906–46). Nazi sympathiser and propagandist; b. New York and brought to Galway with his family in 1909; ed. at Jesuit School in Galway. He went to England in 1922 and eleven years later joined Oswald Mosley's British Union of Fascists from which he was expelled in 1937. Joyce then founded his own movement, the National Socialist League, which recognised Adolf Hitler as a figurehead. He left England in 1939 and placed himself at Hitler's service. His first broadcast was on 18 September 1939. Because of his mock British accent he became known as 'Lord Haw-Haw'. His broadcasts, introduced by 'Germany calling, Germany calling', had a wide audience throughout Europe, including Britain. He became a naturalised German in 1940. Joyce was captured near the Danish border in May 1945, tried for treason at the Old Bailey, London, found guilty and hanged. His remains were returned to Galway for burial in 1976.

'JUMPER'. Among the peasant Catholics the name was used to designate those who changed their religion. It was an expression of contempt and those who 'jumped' from the Catholic to another religion were often obliged to leave their homes for another part of the country. *See also* 'Perverts' *and* Souperism.

'JUNO'. Norwegian vessel from which some forty cases of arms (960 weap-ons) were spirited away as she lay at anchor in Cork harbour (11 August 1880). Some of the boxes were subsequently found by the authorities but the great majority of the haul was never recovered.

JURIES PROTECTION ACT, 1929. Introduced by the Cumann na nGaedheal government in response to unsettled conditions in the Free State. There was widespread agitation by republican and left-wing groups and a growth in cases of intimidation of jurymen in political trials. The Bill was opposed by Fianna Fail and was only passed with the use of the guillotine.

K

KANE, SIR ROBERT (1809–1890). Scientist; b. Dublin; ed. TCD and Paris. Kane first attracted notice in 1831 with the publication of *Elements of Practical Pharmacy.* He became a Licentiate of the King's and Queen's College of Physicians in 1832 and in the same year founded *The Dublin Journal of Medical Science.* He was Secretary to the Council of the Royal Irish Academy* in 1842 and was Professor of Natural Philosophy to the Royal Dublin Society* from 1841 to 1847. Kane was a member of Peel's Commission to investigate Potato Blight in Ireland (1845). At his suggestion the government established the Museum of Irish Industries of which he became first Director in 1846. The first President of the Queen's College Cork, now UCC (1849–73), and held a number of other influential appointments, including Commissioner of National Education (1873), President of the RIA (1877), and Vice-Chancellor of the Royal University (1880). He contributed articles to leading scientific journals of the era and edited *The Philosophical Magazine* in 1840. His major works were *Industrial Resources of Ireland* (1844, a collection of his lectures which became the economic blueprint of Young Ireland), and *The Large and Small Farm Question Considered* (1844).

KANE, REV. ROBERT ROUT-LEDGE (1841–98). Clergyman (C.I.); b. Mountstewart, Co. Armagh. After being brought up as a strict fundamentalist Presbyterian, he joined the Church of Ireland for which he was ordained in 1869. He was Rector of Tullylist (1872–82) and incumbent, Christ's Church, Belfast (1882). A prominent member of the Orange Order,* he strongly opposed the Catholic religion and the Irish nationalist demand for Home Rule.*

KAVANAGH, ARTHUR MacMUR-ROUGH (1831–89). Politician (Conservative) and landlord; b. Borris, Co. Carlow. Born without proper limbs, he learned to ride, shoot, draw and write. He travelled extensively throughout Europe and the East with his brothers, all of whom predeceased him. Father of a large family, Kavanagh was renowned for his justice both as a magistrate and landlord. He represented Co. Wexford (1866–68) and Co. Carlow (1868–80) until he lost his seat in the general election to Edmund D. Gray. Kavanagh opposed Disestablishment of the Church of Ireland* but supported the Land Act of 1870 (*see* Land Acts). His outstanding career which so totally overcame his handicaps made him the subject of a number of stories and books.

KAVANAGH, PATRICK (1904–67). Poet; b. Iniskeen, Co. Monaghan; ed. locally. Having worked as a small farmer and cobbler and published his first collection, *The Ploughman and Other Poems* (1936), he moved to Dublin in 1939. His newspaper, *Kavanagh's Weekly*, enlivened Dublin's intellectual life during the 1950s with biting attacks on a variety of topics. He published *A Soul for Sale* (1947) which included 'The Great Hunger' written in 1942, and *Come Dance With Kitty Stobling* (1960). He also published two semi-autobiographical novels, *The Green Fool* and *Tarry Flynn* (1948). His *Collected Poems* appeared in 1964.

KEARNEY, PEADAR (1883–1942). Ballad-writer and author of the Irish National Anthem;* b. Dublin, an uncle of Brendan Behan;* ed. Model School, Dublin. He worked as a messenger boy before turning to house-painting. Kearney was a member of the Irish Republican Brotherhood* and the Gaelic League* and in the latter association taught Irish in Dublin where his students included Sean O'Casey.* Keenly interested in the theatre, Kearney worked for some time in an unpaid capacity at the early Abbey Theatre* before being employed as a props man in 1910. He met Patrick Heeney* in 1903 and four years later they collaborated on the 'The Soldier's Song'. Having joined the Irish Volunteers* on their formation, Kearney was touring with the Abbey in England when he was alerted for the Easter Rising of 1916.* He returned immediately and fought under Thomas MacDonagh* in the Jacob's Factory command. He avoided capture in the aftermath of the rising and retained close links with Sinn Fein.* A close friend of Michael Collins,* Kearney was interned at Ballykinlar (1920–21) during the War of Independence.* After the Treaty he was official censor at Portlaoise jail during the Civil War.* He took little further interest in politics and returned to his trade as a house-painter. Apart from 'The Soldier's Song' his best-known ballads are 'The Tri-Coloured Ribbon', 'Down by the Glenside', and 'Whack Fol the Diddle'.

KEATING, SEAN (1889–1977). Artist; b. Limerick; ed. St Munchin's College and the Royal College of Art, Dublin. He was a protegé of William Orpen* under whom he worked in London. After returning to Ireland in 1916 he visited the Aran Islands which were a source of artistic inspiration for the rest of his life. He taught at the National College of Art and Design. His works included a canvas of 72 feet by 24 feet for the New York World's Fair of 1939 and a mural (24 feet by 12 feet) for the main hall of the headquarters of the International Labour Organisation in Geneva. He was a member of the Royal Hibernian Academy* of which he was president for twelve years.

KEEN (CAOINE). From the Irish word 'caoineadh' to cry. As an integral part of the Irish ceremony of death, there was a ritual crying over the body of the deceased by near relatives and other mourners. Four people noted for their keening (usually older women), were hired for their talent of crying in a dramatic and anguished manner over the body of a deceased. A traveller in Co. Kildare in 1683 commented, 'as soon as the bearers have taken up the body, they begin their shrill cries and hideous hootings ... this now may be heard two miles away . . .' The traditional form of the keen had the refrain 'Ochon!, ochon!, Ullaghon

O' with lines addressed to the corpse asking why he or she had gone away leaving grieving relatives, and listing the virtues of the departed. Keening was condemned by the Catholic Church Synod and in various Pastorals. In 1800 Dr Thomas Bray, Archbishop of Cashel, issued a pastoral letter which roundly condemned the practice: '. . . .We also condemn and reprobate, in the strongest terms, all unnatural screams and shrieks and fictitious tuneful cries and elegies, at wakes, together with the savage custom of howling and bawling at funerals . . .' The custom was still extant in Ireland up to the earlier part of the twentieth century.

KELLY, LIAM. *See* Fianna Uladh *and* Saor Uladh.

KELLY, MARY EVA (1826–1910). Poet; b. Headford, Co. Galway. A keen supporter of Young Ireland,* she contributed verse to *The Nation** under the pen-name 'Eva' and became widely known as 'Eva of the Nation'. When her fiancé Kevin Izod O'Doherty* was transported in 1848 for his political activities, she promised she would await his return. They were married in 1855 shortly after his return to Ireland. Her husband established a medical practice in Brisbane where he died in 1905. Following his death she experienced some financial distress and a fund was opened on her behalf by sympathisers in Australia, Ireland and England. Her best-known poems included 'The People's Chief', 'Tipperary' and 'Murmers of Love'.

KELLY, COLONEL THOMAS J. (1833–1908). Fenian; b. Galway. A printer by trade, he emigrated to the USA where he fought with the 10th Ohio Regiment during the American Civil War (1861–65) and became a Fenian. In March 1865 he was sent to Ireland to urge the Head Centre of the Irish Republican Brotherhood, James Stephens,* to call an insurrection. Kelly then became Chief of Staff within the IRB and took part in the

rescue of Stephens from Richmond Jail (24 November 1865). He escaped to England with Stephens following the arrest of John Devoy* in February 1866. When Stephens was deposed from his offices within the movement (December 1866), Kelly replaced him as Head Organiser for Ireland and England with the office of Acting Chief Executive of the Irish Republic. In January 1867 he returned to England from America accompanied by Fenian officers. He established his headquarters in London and aided by General Cluseret,* Ricard O'Sullivan Burke* and Godfrey Massey,* he planned the rising for 11 February. It was intended that this should be preceded by a raid on Chester Castle but the plan misfired and the rising was postponed. With the capture of Massey, the plans for the rising were totally disrupted and it was a failure. Kelly was arrested along with Timothy Deasy* in Manchester on 11 September. They were rescued a week later by Fenians from a police-van: this led to the death of a policeman for which three were hanged (*see* Manchester Martyrs). Kelly and several others prominent in the Fenian movement escaped to the USA and faded into relative obscurity.

'KELPIE'. Yacht owned by Conor O'Brien used by the Irish Volunteers* for gun-running in July 1914 as a companion vessel to the *Asgard.** The *Kelpie* sailed from Dublin on 2 July to rendezvous in the North Sea with Darrell Figgis* who had purchased arms in Hamburg. Because the owner and his yacht were so well known to the authorities, the *Kelpie's* cargo of arms was transferred to the *Chotah** for landing at Kilcoole, Co. Wexford.

KENNEDY, HUGH BOYLE (1879–1936). Lawyer and judge; b. Dublin; ed. University College where he was a contemporary of James Joyce* with whose views on literature and religion he quarrelled (as editor of the college magazine, *St Stephen's*, he rejected a critical essay by Joyce which was hostile towards the works of George A. Moore* and W. B. Yeats*). He was Law Officer to the Provisional Government* from January to December 1922 and first Attorney-General of the Free State* from 1922 to 1924. He was first Chief Justice of the Free State (1924–36).

KENNEDY, JOHN PITT (1796–1879). Soldier and engineer; b. Carndonagh, Co. Donegal; ed. Foyle College, Derry and the Military Academy, Woolwich. After working abroad he returned to Ireland (1831) and interested himself in progressive farming. As manager of estates at Lough Ash and Clogher he operated model farms and built schools where emphasis was placed on land reclamation. He became Inspector-General to the Board of National Education in 1837, but, finding his plans frustrated, resigned after two years. Following a period in Australia and India he returned and was secretary to the Devon Commission.* During the Famine of 1845–49* he was secretary to the Famine Relief Committee and Superintendent of Relief Works in West Limerick (1846) where he was also agent for Lord Devon's estates. He was placed in command of the defence of Dublin during the 1848 rising of Young Ireland* when he distributed £600 worth of arms to Orange volunteers. After returning to India (1849) with Sir Charles Napier he built the military road which still bears his name, in Tibet. He lived in England after 1852 and promoted a construction company in 1872.

KENNEDY, PATRICK (1801–73). Author and bookseller; b. Wexford. After moving to Dublin in 1823 he set up as a bookseller in Anglesea Street and was a regular contributor to the *Dublin University Magazine*.* His writings include *Legendary Fictions of the Irish Celts* (1866), *The Banks of the Boro* (1867), *Evenings in the Duffrey* (1869), and *Bardic Stories of Ireland* (1871). Works which he edited include *The Fireside Stories of Ireland, The Irish Book of Anecdotes, Humour, Wit and Wisdom* (1872) and *Household Stories* (1891).

KENT, THOMAS (1865–1916). Land agitator and republican; b. Bawnard House, Fermoy, Co. Cork to a family of strong nationalist tradition; ed. locally. He joined the Irish Volunteers* and organised the disruption of British Army recruitment in Ireland. A leading member of the Volunteer Executive in Cork, in which his brothers Richard, David and William figured prominently, he was on the run during the Easter Rising of 1916.* On his return home, the house was surrounded on 1 May by a party of soldiers and policemen who wished to arrest the entire family. In an engagement which resulted in the death of a constable and in several casualties to the military, and during which David Kent was wounded, the family was forced to surrender through lack of ammunition. Richard Kent attempted to escape and was shot dead. The remainder of the family, including their eighty-year old mother, was arrested. Thomas and William were tried by court martial and the latter was acquitted. Thomas Kent was executed on 9 May, becoming one of the 'sixteen dead men' of the Easter Rising.

KENYON, REV. JOHN (1812–69). Clergyman (R.C.) and Young Irelander; b. Limerick; ed. Maynooth. After ordination he ministered in Templederry, Co. Tipperary where he was later parish priest. A supporter of Young Ireland,* he contributed to *The Nation*.* Disapproving of the moral force argument put forward by Daniel O'Connell,* he supported John Mitchel* and John Martin,* a life-long friend, in the demand for a militant policy. He supported the Young Irelanders when they seceded from the Repeal Association* in July 1846 and established the Irish Confederation* in January 1848. Fr Kenyon faced a Limerick mob in 1847 when he opposed John O'Connell,* MP for Limerick. However, he did not support William Smith

O'Brien* and the insurrection of 1848 (*see* Ballingarry, Co. Tipperary), as he believed that the Famine of 1845—49* had sapped the energies of the people. He accompanied John Martin to Paris in 1866 to meet Mitchel for the last time. During the visit he persuaded Mitchel to visit the Irish College where they received a standing ovation from the clerical students.

KEOGH, WILLIAM NICHOLAS (1817—78). Politician (Independent Irish Party) and judge; b. Galway; ed. TCD where he was a noted public speaker. After his call to the Bar in 1840, he practised on the Connaught circuit where he built up a considerable reputation as an advocate although his knowledge of law was not profound. Upon his return as Conservative MP for Athlone (1847) he became the only Irish Catholic Conservative at Westminster. A cofounder of the Catholic Defence Association* with John Sadleir* and George Henry Moore,* he became a member of the Independent Irish Party in 1852 and seconded the Tenant Right Bill introduced by William Sharman Crawford* in that year. He supported his party in bringing down Lord Derby's government in 1852 but then helped to destroy it when he accepted office as Solicitor-General from Lord Aberdeen. Three years later he became Attorney-General and a Judge of the Court of Common Pleas in 1857. He was special commissioner at the trials of the Fenians* in 1865 when he was noted for the ferocity of his remarks when sentencing. As judge during the Galway county election petition of 1872 when the nationalist, John P. Nolan,* was unseated in favour of Captain Le Poer Trench (a Conservative), Keogh's remarks led to questions in the House of Commons; a petition by Isaac Butt* to have him removed from the bench was defeated. From 1856, when he had been embarrassed by the revelations of fraud and embezzlement surrounding his close associate, John Sadleir, he showed symptoms of mental instability. While visiting Germany he committed suicide. His works include *A Treatise on the Practice of the High Court Chancery in Ireland* (with M. J. Barry, 1840), *Ireland Under Lord Grey* (1844), *Ireland Imperialised* (1863) and *An Essay on Milton's Prose Writings* (1863).

KETTLE, ANDREW (1833—1916). Land agitator and close associate of Charles Stewart Parnell;* b. Swords, Co. Dublin; ed. locally. A tenant-farmer with properties in Co. Dublin, he was involved in the fight for security of tenure in the Tenant League* of the 1850s. He later supported Michael Davitt* and was instrumental in persuading Parnell to support the land agitation of the late 1870s. He presided at the first meeting of the national Land League* at which Parnell became President (October 1879). Parnell pressed him into standing for the Irish Parliamentary Party* in April 1880 but clerical opposition led to his defeat by 154 votes.

Kettle proposed in February 1881 that the answer to the government's coercion policy was that 'the whole Irish party should rise and leave the House, and cross to Ireland and carry out a no-rent campaign'. This policy of concentration, as it was known, was opposed by Parnell and a modified version of it was adopted. He was appointed to organise resistance to coercion for which he was imprisoned at Naas and later in Kilmainham. He was a signatory to the No Rent Manifesto.* Ill-health led to his release at Christmas 1881. Following the Kilmainham Treaty* he retired from active politics to work his farms, then in poor condition, but he continued to give passive support to Parnell's policies. He continued to support Parnell after the split (*see* Irish Parliamentary Party). His son, Thomas Kettle,* was a member of the IPP under John Redmond.* Kettle's memoirs, *Material for Victory: The Memoirs of Andrew J. Kettle*, were published in 1958.

KETTLE, THOMAS M. (1880–1916). Politician (Nationalist); b. Dublin, son of Andrew Kettle;* ed. CBS, Clongowes Wood College and University College, Dublin. A close friend of James Joyce* and a noted orator, he was called to the Bar but never practised. President of the Young Ireland branch of the United Irish League,* he edited the short-lived, controversial *Nationalist* with Francis Sheehy-Skeffington,* who was, like himself, married to one of the Sheehy sisters. As MP for East Tyrone (1906–10) he supported Home Rule* and became an authority on the economic implications of Irish self-government. Critical of what he regarded as narrow-minded nationalism, he taught that Ireland, in order to achieve a true identity, should absorb European influences. He became the first Professor of Economics in the Dublin college of the National University of Ireland* in 1908.

Kettle supported the Irish Volunteers* for whom he purchased weapons in Belgium in 1914. Following the outbreak of World War I he acted as war correspondent of *The Daily News*. In November 1914 he joined the Dublin Fusiliers and toured Ireland as a recruiting officer. Following the murder of Sheehy-Skeffington during the Easter Rising of 1916,* he volunteered for active service and was sent to the western front where he was killed at Givenchy during the Battle of the Somme.

A gifted speaker with an incisive mind and devastating wit, his death was regarded as a great loss to Ireland's political and intellectual life. His writings included *The Open Secret of Ireland* (1912), *Poems and Parodies* (1916), and two posthumous publications, *The Ways of War* (1917) and *The Day's Burden* (1918).

KICKHAM, CHARLES JOSEPH (1828–82). Author and Fenian; b. near Cashel, Co. Tipperary, a cousin of John O'Mahony.* His formal education ended at the age of thirteen when gunpowder exploded in his face, virtually destroying his hearing and sight. A supporter of the Repeal Association* and Young Ireland,* he contributed verse to *The Nation*,* *The Celt* and *The Irishman*. Having founded a branch of the Irish Confederation* in Mullinahone in 1848, he was forced into hiding after the unsuccessful rising at Ballingarry, Co. Tipperary* in July 1848.

He joined the Irish Republican Brotherhood* in 1860, visiting the USA on its behalf three years later. At the invitation of James Stephens* he joined the editorial staff of *The Irish People*.* Following his arrest in 1865, he was tried before Judge William Keogh* and sentenced to fourteen years imprisonment. After serving periods in Pentonville, Portland and Woking prisons he was released in 1869 with his health severely impaired and returned to Mullinahone. Following the annulment of the return of Jeremiah O'Donovan Rossa* as MP for Tipperary, Kickham stood and polled even better (1,664 votes) but was defeated by four votes. In spite of his ill-health he moved to Dublin and resumed his career in the IRB. He became a member of the Supreme Council* (1872) of which he was chairman until his death. His death was hastened by an accident in Blackrock, Co. Dublin when he was knocked down by a jaunting car. The church of his native parish was closed to his remains and he was buried without the presence of local clergymen. The funeral oration was delivered by John Daly* of Limerick.

Kickham's first novel, *Sally Cavanagh*, appeared in 1869. Despite the national reputation which he gained from his ballads and stories, a national collection had to be taken up for him in 1878. In 1873 he published his most famous work, *Knocknagow, or, The Homes of Tipperary*. *For the Old Land* appeared in 1886. His ballads include 'Patrick Sheehan' which forced the government to award a pension to a veteran of the Crimean War, 'Rory of the Hill' and 'The Irish Peasant Girl'.

KILDARE PLACE SOCIETY. Popular name for the Society for the Education of the Poor in Ireland. Founded in 1811, it was a Protestant organisation which aimed to provide a system of undenominational education, in which the Bible could be read by all Christian denominations without comment or notes. The Society was awarded a state grant of £7,000 in 1817 which, by 1831, had become £30,000. By the early 1830s, the Society was instructing some 137,639 pupils in 1,621 schools. A suspicion of proselytisation for the Church of Ireland made it unpalatable to the clergy and laity of the Catholic Church in Ireland.

KILDARE STREET CLUB. Founded in 1782 by Burton Conyngham it soon became a familiar meeting-place for members of Grattan's Parliament (1782–1800). It remained a venue for politicians for many years. In 1975 the Kildare Street Club merged with the University Club.

KILLEN, JAMES BRYCE (1845–1916). Fenian and land agitator; b. Kells, Co. Antrim; ed. Queen's College, Belfast. He was called to the Bar in 1869. A member of the Irish Republican Brotherhood,* he supported Michael Davitt* in the foundation of the Land League of Mayo.* Killen was arrested near Sligo with Davitt and James Daly* (19 November 1879) and charged with seditious speeches, but the government dropped the charges and released the trio. Killen later edited *The Northern Star* in Belfast and also worked as a journalist in Dublin.

KILMAINHAM 'TREATY'. Title for the agreement negotiated between Charles Stewart Parnell* and William Ewart Gladstone* in April 1882. Parnell and leading members of his party had been imprisoned under the Coercion Act in October 1881 for opposing Gladstone's 1881 Land Act (*see* Land Acts). Following Parnell's imprisonment, agrarian outrages increased, the imprisoned leaders issued a 'No Rent Manifesto'* and the Land League* was suppressed by the government. There was considerable pressure on Gladstone to resolve the deteriorating situation in Ireland, while Parnell was anxious to leave prison for political and private reasons. In April 1882 Parnell passed a letter to Gladstone through Captain W. H. O'Shea* in which he (Parnell) stated that if tenants in arrears and leaseholders were brought within the scope of the 1881 Land Act the Irish party would 'co-operate cordially for the future with the Liberal Party in forwarding Liberal principles and measures of general reform'.

By the terms of the 'Treaty', it was agreed that the 130,000 tenants in arrears and some 150,000 leaseholders would be allowed the benefits of the Act and coercion* would be dropped. Parnell agreed to use his influence to counter the violence and to end the land agitation by accepting the amended Act as a settlement of the land question, while collaborating with the Liberals on Gladstone's Irish policy. Parnell and his lieutenants were released on 2 May. The murder four days later in the Phoenix Park of Lord Frederick Cavendish* and T. H. Burke,* provoked Gladstone into introducing further coercive measures and seriously endangered the Irish party-Liberal alliance. The 'Treaty' was received without enthusiasm by Michael Davitt* and other radicals on the land question.

KING'S COUNTY (OFFALY). Title for the territory of modern Co. Offaly, named by English planters in honour of King Philip II of Spain, husband of Queen Mary (1553–58), during the Plantation of Laois and Offaly. The official title of King's County was replaced by Offaly upon the establishment of the Free State in 1922. The administrative centre, Philipstown, was then re-named Daingean.

KING'S INNS LIBRARY, DUBLIN. Founded in 1787 and maintained by Benchers of the King's Inns. The present building was designed by Frederick Darley in 1827 and houses a unique collection of Irish county histories and almost 10,000 pamphlets.

'KING'S SHILLING' (*or* **'QUEEN'S SHILLING**). Bounty payable to a recruit by the recruiting sergeant upon enlistment in the British Army. One who had enlisted was sometimes contemptuously referred to as having 'taken the shilling'.

KINNEAR, REV. JOHN (1824– 1909). Clergyman (Presbyterian) and politician (Liberal); b. Clonaneese, Co. Tyrone; ed. Belfast and ordained in Letterkenny, Co. Donegal, where he ministered for the remainder of his life. Sympathetic to the tenant cause, he supported Tenant Right* and was returned as MP for Co. Donegal in the general election of April 1880 during the Land War.* The first clergyman with a congregation to sit in the House of Commons, he held the seat for five years. He bequeathed his extensive library to Presbyterian College, Belfast.

KIRK, THOMAS (1781–1845). Sculptor; b. Cork. He studied in the Dublin Society's schools. He was an original member of the RHA and a regular exhibitor at the Royal Academy. His most famous work was the figure of Nelson for Nelson Pillar in Dublin.

KNIGHTS OF COLUMBANUS, ORDER OF. Founded in Belfast by Canon James O'Neill in 1915. Structured on Masonic lines, the Order's aim was to cherish 'fraternal charity and to develop practical Christianity among its members'. An earlier group, the Columban Knights, merged with it in 1922. Dedicated to opposing 'British socialism' and 'Orange Ascendancy', branches of the Order were founded in Dublin in 1917 and in Cork two years later. By 1935 it had 6,000 members drawn, for the most part, from the professional and business classes. Its activities were cloaked in secrecy which earned the suspicion of outsiders. The Order received formal recognition from the Catholic Church in 1934.

KNOCK, CO. MAYO. Scene of a reported apparition by the Virgin Mary on Thursday, 21 August 1879. According to the witnesses, Dominic Beirne (aged 28), Dominic Beirne (20), Margaret Beirne (70), Margaret Beirne (10), Mary Beirne (26), Patrick Beirne (16), Judith Campbell (40), John Curry (6), John Durkan (11), Mrs Hugh Flatley (68), Patrick Hill (13), Mary McLoughlin (26), Catherine Murray (8½), Bridget Trench (75) and Patrick Walsh (65), the Virgin Mary appeared on the southern gable of Knock Church. She was accompanied by St Joseph and St John the Evangelist. The witnesses described an altar to the right of the gable, on which a cross and a lamb with angels were visible. Although it was raining heavily at the time, the witnesses, who got very wet, stated that there was no rain in the area of the apparition. An ecclesiastical commission examined the witnesses in 1879 and another commission examined the survivors in 1936. As a result of the report of the apparition, Knock became a major centre of pilgrimage. The Knock Shrine Society was founded in 1935 by Justice Liam D. Coyne. An Irish Folk Museum was opened at Knock on 1 August 1973, with the aim of showing the social and economic background to Ireland at the time of the apparition (*see* Land War). *The Light of Other Days* (1974) by Thomas Neary with photographs by Seamus Malee shows the contents of the museum.

KNOX, REV. ROBERT (1815– 83). Clergyman (Presbyterian); b. Clady, Urney, Co. Tyrone; ed. locally and Glasgow University. M.A. (1837) and Belfast College. He played an important role in promoting the union between the Synod of Ulster and the secessionists, a unity which

281

led to the General Assembly of the Presbyterian Church in Ireland (1840). Ordained in April 1840, he became a Presbyterian missionary in the south of Ireland until his appointment as Minister of the Linenhall Church in Belfast (1842). Knox was a prolific builder of churches and schools. He founded and edited the monthly *Irish Protestant* and was also co-founder of the Sabbath School Society. He became widely known for his newspaper controversy on the subject of baptismal regeneration with Rev. Theophilus Campbell. For many years he had promoted the creation of a world-wide Presbyterian Alliance and he was making preparations for it to be held in Belfast in 1884 when he died.

KNOX, ROBERT BENT (1808–93). Archbishop of Armagh and Primate of All Ireland (C.I.), (1885–93); b. Dungannon Park Mansion, Co. Tyrone; ed. TCD. B.A. (1829) and M.A. (1834). Ordained in 1832, he became Chancellor of Ardfert (1834), prebendary of St Munchin's, Limerick (1841) and Bishop of Down, Connor and Dromore (1848) in succession to Bishop Richard Mant. Convinced that Disestablishment of the Church of Ireland* was inevitable, Bishop Knox set about the re-organisation of his diocese: he founded the Belfast Church Extension Society in 1862 and also founded the Diocesan Board of Missions. During 1867–68 he proposed the reduction of the Church hierarchy to one archbishopric and five bishoprics. He succeeded Marcus Gervais Beresford* as Archbishop of Armagh in 1885. His *Ecclesiastical Index* was published in 1830.

L

LABOUCHERE, HENRY, BARON TAUNTON (1798–1869). Politician (Whig); Chief Secretary (1846–47); b. Essex; ed. Winchester, Christ Church, Oxford where he was awarded B.A. (1821) and M.A. (1828), and Lincoln's Inn. He was not called to the Bar. He entered politics as MP for Michael Borough (1826) and had a varied career (Vice-President of the Board of Trade, Under-Secretary for War and the Colonies, President of the Board of Trade) until he accepted office as Chief Secretary from Lord John Russell,* serving under a new Lord Lieutenant, the 4th Earl of Bessborough.* He took office at a time of crisis as the potato crop had failed in 1845 (*see* Famine of 1845–49). While some measures of relief had been laid down by Sir Robert Peel* and the head of the Treasury, Charles Edward Trevelyn,* the steps were inadequate as neither the Irish executive nor the British government realised the full extent of the crisis. None of the measures to be taken, as laid down in the Labour Rate Act,* anticipated that the 1846 crop might also fail. Bessborough, on 5 October, endeavoured to cope with the worsening situation and Labouchere issued a statement, known as the 'Labouchere Letter', virtually repealing the Labour Rate Act. His purpose was to have the money for relief work spent usefully rather than 'in the execution of works comparatively unproductive'. He envisaged that the monies would be spent upon drainage works and subsoiling. However, the terms of the letter were vague, and his scheme ran into difficulty in that the landowners were unwilling to make themselves liable for repaying the expense in each district. Another difficulty was the opposition of Trevelyn who told him, 'The scheme laid down in your letter is practically inefficient, both as a measure of relief and as a measure of improvement'. Labouchere proved remarkably casual in the face of an epidemic of fever during the winter of 1846–47. He informed the House of Commons that it was not necessary to introduce extra powers for the health authorities, in spite of the fact that the Central Board of Health had not yet been re-established and the Poor Law* workhouses were patently unable to cope with the strain thrown upon them by the outbreak. Although he had reports from doctors, ministers and magistrates calling attention to the extent of the outbreak, he told the Commons that 'accounts given . . . were, to a great extent, undoubtedly inaccurate' (25 January 1847). He was succeeded in the Irish office by Sir William Somerville* and became President of the Board of Trade once more. He retired from office in 1852 when Russell's government fell but returned to office three years later as Secretary for the Colonies (until 1858). He was created Baron Taunton in 1859 and entered the House of Lords in 1860.

LABOUR COURT. Created by the Industrial Relations Act 1946 and granted revised powers under the Industrial Relations Acts of 1969 and 1975, the purpose of the Court is to provide Industrial Relations Officers to prevent or settle disputes. The first Chairman of the Court was R. J. P. Mortished* and its members included Thomas Johnson.* The Court originally consisted of an employers' representative nominated by the Federated Union of Employers, a workers' representative nominated by the Irish Congress of Trade Unions,* a neutral chairman and two deputy chairmen appointed by the Minister for Labour. The Court now consists of a chairman, two deputy chairmen and six members, three each for the employers and the workers. In carrying out its functions, the Court is not subject to the control of the government or of any Minister, and its ancillary services are available to management and unions free of charge. The Court investigates trade disputes and then issues recommendations. Subject to the provisions of the Industrial Relations Acts, the Court also registers agreements on wages and working conditions. It provides chairmen and/or secretaries for the Joint Industrial Council and it establishes Joint Labour Committees whose proposals on wages and conditions the Court may ratify. The Court has Equality Officers who investigate and make recommendations on claims arising from alleged discrimination on pay and employment.

LABOUR PARTY. The Irish Labour Party was founded in Clonmel in 1912 by James Connolly* and James Larkin.* From 1918 it was known as the Irish Labour Party and Trade Union Congress until 1930 when the Irish Trade Union Congress* became an autonomous body. The party sought to provide a non-sectarian platform for workers to achieve Connolly's ideal of a workers' republic. It supported the nationalist cause between 1916 and 1921 but under pressure from Sinn Fein,* abstained from the general election of December 1918 to avoid a split in the nationalist vote. The party played no direct role in the establishment of Dail Eireann* although its leader, Thomas Johnson,* drew up the original draft of the Democratic Programme.* Labour took no official position on the Treaty but party members returned in the general election of June 1922 were obliged to take their seats in the Dail. Labour was the main opposition party to Cumann na nGaedheal* governments from 1922 until 1927 when Fianna Fail* entered the Dail. In 1932 it helped Fianna Fail to power. It moved away from Fianna Fail during the later 1930s. In 1930 it dropped the aim of a workers' republic and nationalisation of the means of production, readopted the policy in 1936, but under pressure from the Catholic Hierarchy, dropped

	Seats	Votes	% Valid Poll	% Electorate
1922	17	132,428	21.1	12.9
1923	14	130,509	12.4	7.3
1927(June)	22	158,211	13.8	9.1
1927 (Sept)	13	111,231	9.5	6.4
1932	7	98,286	7.7	5.8
1933	8	79,221	5.7	4.6
1937	13	135,758	10.3	7.6
1938	9	128,945	10.0	7.6
1943	17	208,812	15.7	11.5
1944	8	139,499	11.5	7.9
1948	14	149,088	11.3	8.3
1951	16	151,828	11.4	8.5
1954	19	161,034	12.0	9.1
1957	12	111,747	9.1	6.4
1961	16	136,111	11.6	8.1
1965	22	192,740	15.4	11.5
1969	18	224,500	17.0	12.9
1973	19	184,656	13.7	10.3
1977	17	186,410	11.6	8.8

it again in 1939. The party again adopted the aim of nationalisation in 1969. It has been a minority party in three governments: the two Inter-Party Governments* (1948–51; 1954–57) and the National Coalition Government* (1973–77). The table shows its strength since 1922. The leaders of the Labour Party have been:

James Larkin (1912–14)
James Connolly (1914–16)
Thomas Johnson (1916–27)
T. J. O'Connell (1927–32)
William Norton (1932–60)
Brendan Corish (1960–77)
Frank Cluskey (1977–   )

For Labour Party members of governments *see* Governments.

LABOUR RATE ACT, 1846. Legislation introduced by Lord John Russell* during the Famine of 1845–49.* The Act stated that (*a*) The district in which Public Works were being carried out would in future have to bear the total expense of such works; (*b*) Works were to be approved and executed by the Board of Works, the cost to be met by a Treasury advance repayable within 10 years at 3½ per cent, and the money for repayment was to be raised by a rate levied on all poor-ratepayers locally. The whole burden and expense of supplying food to the famine-stricken during the remainder of 1846 and for 1847 was thus made a local charge, the British government no longer bearing half the cost of Public Works. The Act occasioned great public indignation and it was repealed almost in its entirety by order of the Lord Lieutenant some six weeks later. *See* Labouchere, Henry, Baron Taunton.

'LABOUR WORLD'. Founded in London in September 1890 by Michael Davitt,* it was a weekly newspaper intended as a 'journal of progress for the masses'. It was circulated in Ireland. Beginning with a print of 60,000 copies the paper was at first successful but then ran into difficulties because it was under-capitalised. It collapsed after eight months.

LACEY, DENIS ('Dinny'; 1890–1923). Republican soldier; b. Attybrack, Co. Tipperary; ed. National School. Active in the Gaelic League,* Lacey aided Sean Treacy* and Dan Breen* in the re-organisation of the Irish Volunteers* and Sinn Fein* in Tipperary after the Easter Rising of 1916, and was a member of the 3rd Tipperary Brigade of the Irish Republican Army.* In October 1920, following Treacy's death, he became O/C of the Flying Column planned by Treacy to operate throughout South Munster. He led raids at Thomastown (28 October) and against the Black and Tans* and Royal Irish Constabulary* at Lisnagaul in the Glen of Aherlow (13 November). Rejecting the Treaty,* he persuaded large numbers of his men to join him and continue the fight against the Provisional Government* in the Civil War.* He led a raid on Clonmel Barracks in February 1922 and took 300 rifles, 200,000 rounds of ammunition, seven machine-guns, a few

hundred boxes of bombs, twelve armoured cars, ten Lancia cars and Crossley tenders and two armoured Lancias. After holding the region around Carrick-on-Suir for a short time in December he was forced back into the hills and was killed in the Glen of Aherlow in February 1923.

LADIES' LAND LEAGUE. Founded in 1881 as the Central Land League of the Ladies of Ireland by Anna Parnell* at the urging of Michael Davitt;* its members included Katharine Tynan* and Mrs A. M. Sullivan. The ladies aided the Land League* by collecting data on estates throughout the country. They compiled a book jocosely called 'The Book of Kells', providing information on the landlord system. When Davitt, Charles Stewart Parnell* and other leaders in the land movement were imprisoned during the year the ladies took over the organisation of the movement and oversaw the underground publication of *United Ireland.* The league was the first radical movement in Ireland organised by women and was denounced by John MacHale,* the Archbishop of Tuam, and Edward McCabe,* the Archbishop of Dublin. The Chief Secretary, W. E. Forster,* attempted to suppress it under statutes designed to curb prostitution and succeeded in enhancing the ladies' status as nationalists. Parnell was concerned by the ladies' activities, as were the more conservative members of the Land League and the Irish Parliamentary Party.* Upon his release from prison in May 1882 Parnell set about dismantling the organisation and suppressed it in August of that year.

LADY CLARES. Agrarian secret society which operated in Connaught and West Munster during the early decades of the nineteenth century. *See* Secret Societies.

LALOR, JAMES FINTAN (1807–49). Land agitator; b. Tenakill, Queen's County (Laois); ed. Carlow Lay College. As a result of a con-

285

genital spinal disease he suffered from chronic ill-health. While working as a farmer he was deeply influenced by local land reformers led by William Conners and broke with his father, who supported Daniel O'Connell* in the view that land reform would follow Repeal.* He wrote to Sir Robert Peel* in 1843, outlining his view of the land question. Peel afterwards established a Commission of Inquiry into the land issue but to Lalor's disappointment there were no concrete results. He divided his time between Belfast and Dublin until 1846, when his ill-health brought about a reconciliation with his father and he returned home to begin a detailed analysis of the land problem. He supported Young Ireland* when it broke with O'Connell in 1846, still holding to his belief that there could be little progress in the fight for Repeal until the issue was linked to land reform. 'A secure and independent agricultural peasantry is the only base on which a people rises or ever can be raised; or on which a nation can safely rest', he said. His view that only those who work on the land could own it, expressed in *The Nation,* during 1847, attracted the attention of more militant Young Irelanders who were now in the Irish Confederation.* These included John Mitchel,* Thomas Devin Reilly* and Michael Doheny.* This extremism was not supported by William Smith O'Brien* and the editor of *The Nation*, Charles Gavan Duffy,* who, however, continued to allow him the use of the paper in which Lalor suggested that tenants, affected by the Famine of 1845–49,* should start withholding rents. His attempts, with Doheny, to establish tenant-right societies in counties Kilkenny and Tipperary were a failure as was the effort to organise a rent strike. He co-edited Mitchel's paper, *The Irish Felon,* with John Martin.*

Following the attempted insurrection led by Smith O'Brien at Ballingarry, Co. Tipperary* in 1848, Lalor was arrested in Templederry where the parish priest, Fr John Kenyon,* was his close friend. He was released from prison when the authorities became concerned about his health. By now he was close to Thomas Clarke Luby* with whom he became involved in a Waterford-Tipperary secret organisation whose members included John O'Leary* and Charles J. Kickham.* He became discouraged when his fellow-members of the executive showed no interest in financing a new newspaper. During the summer of 1849 he travelled around south Tipperary, and stayed with Fr Kenyon. In September the organisation wished to attempt another insurrection which he prepared to lead at Cashel (16 September) but the force which arrived to support him was so small that he sent them home. He returned to Dublin where he died two days later.

His influence in his lifetime was confined to a small, if select, circle but he was destined to be a major influence on future agitators. His doctrine that '. . . the entire ownership of Ireland, moral and material . . . is vested of right in the people of Ireland' made a deep appeal to Michael Davitt* and the Land League* and to James Connolly,* Patrick Pearse* and Arthur Griffith.* His younger brother, Peter Lalor (1823–89), led insurgent miners in Australia at Eureka stockade (3 December 1854) and rose to the rank of Postmaster-General and later Speaker of the Australian parliament.

LAND ACTS 1860–1933. Between 1860 and 1923 a series of Land Acts transformed the landholding system in Ireland. In 1870 there were some 13,000 landlords, one-third of whom lived outside the country; 300 of them had estates of more than 10,000 acres. There were over 500,000 tenants, 135,000 of whom had leases while over 400,000 held land by verbal agreement and could be evicted at six months' notice. Within a generation the position of the landlords was altered as the land passed into the hands of the former tenants so that, after the Wyndham Act of 1903, more than half of the holdings were held by a new class of peasant proprietors. The political as well as the social and economic consequences of this shift in power was enormous; the peasant of the 1870s and 1880s, a radical in the days of the Land League* and the Plan of Campaign,* became the conservative of the 1890s and thereafter. The 1870 Act introduced by W. E. Gladstone* was in response to a widespread call for redress to the obvious injustices of the system. His next Act, in 1881, was a response to the Land War,* prosecuted by the Land League against the landlords. The rest of the major Acts were introduced by Conservative governments, responding, to a large extent, to a trend which had gathered its own momentum. The Act of 1923 was the first introduced by a native government.

1860 Landlord and Tenant Law Amendment (Ireland) Act

Known as Deasy's Act after its sponsor, Richard Deasy, Irish attorney-general, it strengthened the position of the landlord. The Act declared that the relationship between landlord and tenant was 'deemed to be founded on the express or implied contract of the parties and not upon tenure or service'. It allowed the landlord to recover the landholding at the termination of a lease or yearly letting. As the tenant was often in no position to bargain, the Act enabled the landlord to set what terms he wished. In essence, it was overturned by the Act of 1870.

1870 Landlord and Tenant (Ireland) Act.

In this Act Gladstone attempted to give legal status to the Ulster Custom* (the 'Three Fs' or Tenant Right). It proved, however, difficult to define. The Act also sought to compensate tenants for disturbance in occupancy and for their improvements, but it proved a failure in practice. The so-called 'Bright Clause' made provision for purchase of his holding by the tenant who could borrow up to two-thirds of the price, repayable at 5 per cent over 35 years. The average price was 23½ years' rental. In all, 877 tenants took advantage of the Act to purchase their holdings.

1881 Land Law (Ireland) Act.

In drawing up his second Act, at the height of the Land War, Gladstone was able to draw upon the Richmond and Bessborough Commissions,* both of which had recommended the legislation of the Ulster Custom. The Act established the principle of dual ownership by landlord and tenant, gave legal status to the Ulster Custom throughout the country, provided for compensation for improvements and disturbance and established a Land Commission* and a Land Court.* The intention was not to destroy landlordism, in Gladstone's words, but to make it impossible. It was, however, a complicated piece of legislation (there were over 14,000 speeches made during the debates, 2,000 points of order and some 800 amendments proposed and rejected). It also provided for land purchase; three-quarters of the money to be advanced by the Land Commission, to be repaid over 35 years at 5 per cent: 731 tenants bought under this Act. More important from the tenants' point of view was their right to take their rents to the Land Court for reduction under the Fair Rent clause; in most cases, reductions of between 15 per cent and 20 per cent were awarded. The Act had little other immediate benefit, as the situation on the land had deteriorated rapidly during the Land War, with evictions and starvation commonplace. It had excluded nearly 280,000 tenants who were either leaseholders or in arrears with their rent.

1882 Amending Act (to deal with arrears)

The Arrears Act was a result of the Kilmainham 'Treaty',* made between Gladstone and Parnell. The

Land Commission was empowered to cancel arrears of rent due by tenants of less than £30. The conditions were that the tenants should pay the 1881 rent, and that the tenant and the state should pay equal amounts but not more than a total of two years. The money came from the Church Surplus Fund. In all, £2,000,000 was written off, according to one estimate.

1885 Purchase of Land (Ireland) Act (Ashbourne)

Known as the 'Ashbourne Act' after the 1st Baron Ashbourne* who introduced it, the Act allowed a tenant to borrow the full amount of the purchase price, to be repaid over 49 years at 4 per cent. Five million pounds was made immediately available, and this was supplemented in 1888. Between 1885 and 1888 some 25,400 tenants purchased their holding, many of them in Ulster. In all, 942,600 acres were purchased; this made an average holding of thirty-seven acres at a purchase price of 17½ years' rental.

1887 Land Act

The first Land Act introduced by Arthur J. Balfour* was an amendment to the 1881 Act, extending the terms of the Act to leaseholders.

1888 Land Purchase Act

Also introduced by Balfour, it provided a further £5,000,000 to the amount granted for purchase by the Ashbourne Act.

1891 Land Act

Balfour's major Land Act came at the end of the land agitation known as the Plan of Campaign.* It provided £33,000,000 for purchase but contained so many daunting clauses that it was not successful until amended five years later. Only £13,500,000 of the purchase money was taken up at the time. It substituted peasant proprietorship for dual ownership as the principle of land tenure. At the same time Balfour created the Congested Districts Board* to deal with distress in the economically backward areas of the West of Ireland.

1896 Land Act

Introduced by Gerald Balfour,* it amended the 1891 Act, increasing the amount available for purchase and removing the clauses which made the earlier Act so unattractive. It empowered the Land Court to sell 1,500 bankrupt estates to tenants. Between 1891 and 1896, 47,000 holdings were bought out.

1903 Land Act (Wyndham Act).

Introduced by George Wyndham,* it was based to a large extent on the recommendations of the Land Conference of 1902.* It approached the situation from the landlords' point of view, offering them an incentive to sell out their entire estates, by offering a bonus. The Act stipulated that individual purchase would not be permissible and that the landlord should sell large areas, including non-tenanted land as well as tenanted. The incentive offered was a 12 per cent bonus in addition to the agreed price; the landlord could sell his demesne lands to the Estate Commissioners and buy them back on the same annuity terms as the tenants. Money was raised by the issue of 2¾ per cent Guaranteed Land Stock. Prices for the holdings ranged from 18½–24½ years' purchase on rents fixed by the Land Courts under the 1881 Act, or 21½–27 years on rents fixed in or after 1896. The whole sum would be advanced at 3¼% repayable over 68½ years. The Act contained a provision which forbade subdivision or mortgaging. Because the terms of the Act were considered to favour the landlord at the expense of the tenant, it was opposed by Michael Davitt,* John Dillon,* Thomas. Sexton* and *The Freeman's Journal.* This Act, however, did more than any of the previous ones to bring about the major change in the Irish landholding system, by transferring holdings to the tenantry. By 1908 £28,000,000 had been advanced and arrears of sales equalled some £56,000,000. This £84,000,000 accounted for around seven million acres (an average price of £12 per acre). By 1909 around one million acres remained to be disposed.

1907 Evicted Tenants Act.
Introduced by Augustine Birrell,* the Act enabled 735 tenants to be reinstated at a cost of £390,000.

1909 Land Act.
This also was introduced by Birrell. Land Stock worth £33,000,000 had been issued and the stock had fallen to 87; financing the remaining £56,000,000 was a problem and led to the passage of an Act. In future, landlords were to be paid 3½ per cent Stock as a 'bonus'; this varied from 3 per cent to 18 per cent according to the purchase price. If the price was less than 16 years' purchase it was to be 3 per cent. This Act also introduced an element of compulsory purchase; the landlord had to sell if the majority of his tenants sought purchase. Between the Wyndham Act of 1903 and the Birrell Act of 1909, 256,000 holdings were purchased for £82,000,000.

Land Acts by Native Irish Governments.
When the Free State was established on 6 December 1922, 316,000 holdings, amounting to 11 million acres, had been purchased. Three-quarters of a million acres had been given to 35,000 allottees, mostly in the districts under the supervision of the Congested Districts Board. About 100,000 holdings remained to be dealt with, amounting to three million acres.

1923 Land Law Act.
Under this Act the Congested Districts Board and the Estates Commission were abolished; the Land Commission was reconstituted.

1923 Land Act (Hogan Act).
Introduced in Dail Eireann by the Free State Minister for Agriculture, Patrick Hogan,* the Act made compulsory the sale and purchase of all the land not yet dealt with. Rents fixed before 1911 were reduced by 35 per cent and rents fixed later by 30 per cent. Annuities were calculated on 4¾ per cent over 66½ years. The vendor was to receive approximately fourteen years purchase of the rent originally paid. In addition, the State paid 10 per cent to the vendor and paid his legal and other expenses. The Act also dealt with the question of arrears. All arrears due up to 1920 (between 1919 and 1922 very few rents were paid) were forgiven; arrears subsequent to 1920 were reduced by 25 per cent. Sub-tenants illegally on the land were recognised as tenants, and sub-letting or sub-division of land was again prohibited.

1927 Land Law Act.
Introduced by Hogan also, it was made necessary by the accumulation of arrears. Due to the post-war economic depression, there had been a general laxity in the payment of annuities, rents and rates. Under the Act arrears were funded and added to the annuities. Sub-tenants illegally in possession were confirmed and sub-letting was again prohibited.

1933 Land Act.
By 1930 default on annuities amounted to 10 per cent, so that by 1933 the amount involved was £4,611,381. In 1932, Fianna Fail came to power, having promised that Land Annuities* would no longer be paid to the British Exchequer. They would, however, continue to be collected, but many of the new owners were withholding. The 1933 Act, introduced by the new Minister for Agriculture, James Ryan,* wiped out all arrears prior to 1930, and funded subsequent arrears. Annuity repayments were reduced by ½ per cent because of the Economic War,* which had resulted from the withholding of annuities by the Free State government. The Land Com-

mission could compulsorily acquire land for those who had no land or for those who needed more. The Commissioners were also empowered to take back land which they themselves had vested in the tenants. The Act also abolished fixity of tenure. Between 1870 and 1933 tenants in the area of the twenty-six counties bought out 450,000 holdings, a total of 15 million acres out of 17 million. The total cost of £130,000,000 gave an average price of £8.67 per acre.

LAND AND LABOUR ASSOCIA-TION. *See* Irish Land and Labour Association.

LAND ANNUITIES. Sums of money payable to the United Kingdom Exchequer by Irish tenants who purchased their holdings under a series of Land Acts* from 1870 onwards. After the creation of the Free State in 1922 the amounts were collected by the Irish Exchequer which forwarded them to London. The payment of the annuities was unpopular and the Minister for Agriculture, Patrick Hogan,* introduced a series of bills which were passed by the Dail to collect arrears which accumulated during the period of unrest from 1916 until 1923. During the 1920s, Peadar O'Donnell* and Colonel Maurice Moore* called for the annuities to be retained in Ireland. This became an issue during 1931–32 when Fianna Fail* promised that if returned it would withhold the annuities from the British Exchequer. On coming to office in March 1932 Eamon de Valera* withheld payment. This led to the Economic War* when Britain imposed duties on Free State agricultural produce to compensate for the loss of the annuities. De Valera called a new election in January 1933, and during the campaign announced that the annuities would continue to be collected but that the amounts would be reduced by half. Within a short time his political opponents, Eoin O'Duffy* and the Blueshirts,* had organised a campaign of non-payment and the

government reacted by seizing cattle and goods in lieu of payment. Payment to the Free State Exchequer was resumed within a short time. As part of the agreement which ended the Economic War in 1938 Eire (formerly the Free State) paid the United Kingdom £10,000,000 in final settlement of all claims arising from the dispute.

LAND ARBITRATION COURTS. *See* Arbitration Courts.

LAND COMMISSION. Established under the Land Act of 1881 (*see* Land Acts), its main purpose was to work out 'fair rents' under the Act. It was also given responsibility for overseeing the land purchase schemes introduced under later acts. Under the Free State Act of 1923 (*see* Land Acts) it took over the estates where landlord and tenant had a dual interest and arranged for the land to be passed to the tenant under the stipulated Land Annuities.* In 1923 it absorbed the functions of the Congested Districts Board.* It now redistributes land.

LAND COMMITTEE. *See* Land Conference.

LAND CONFERENCE. The suggestion for a land conference to find a final settlement to the land question came from Captain John Shawe-Taylor in a letter to the press on 2 September 1902. He suggested that a group of representatives of the Unionists and landlords should meet with tenants' representatives in Dublin. His proposal was addressed to the 2nd Duke of Abercorn;* A. H. Smith-Barry, Lord Barrymore,* The O'Conor Don* and Col E. J. Saunderson,* for the landlord side. As tenants' representatives he suggested the leader of the Irish Parliamentary Party, John Redmond,* William O'Brien,* Timothy Harrington* and Thomas William Russell.* The Shawe-Taylor proposal had the support of the Chief Secretary, George Wyndham,* and his Under-Secretary, Sir Antony Mac-Donnell.* The invitation was turned down by the nominated Unionists who were replaced by the 4th Earl of Dunraven,* the Earl of Mayo, Col W. H. Hutcheson-Poe and Col Nugent-Everard. The tenants' representatives were as proposed. Dunraven chaired the Conference when it met in December. After a two-week session the members produced a report which made four important recommendations. First, the government should undertake a massive scheme of land purchase which would be fair both to landlord and tenant; second, that such a scheme should not be compulsory; third, that the landlords should receive a fair price for the sale of their estates; fourth, the repayments, (so as not to be a burden on the tenant purchasers) should be Land Annuities spread over 68½ years. These proposals were almost totally incorporated into the Wyndham Act of 1903 (*see* Land Acts). The Conference also suggested that the Congested Districts Board* should be reformed, a settlement made for evicted tenants and better housing should be provided for labourers. The members of the Conference, in particular William O'Brien, felt that their efforts had been so successful that the conference method might be employed to solve the question of Home Rule* to mutual satisfaction. The members remained as the Land Committee throughout 1903 and during 1904 they reconstituted themselves as the Irish Reform Association* to examine the question of self-government.

LAND COURT. Established under the Land Act of 1881 (*see* Land Acts) to arbitrate between the landlord and tenants in rent disputes, improvements and compensation. The Court, additionally, had the power to annul any existing unfair clause or condition.

LAND LEAGUE. The (Irish National) Land League was founded in Dublin on 21 October 1879 at a meeting presided over by Andrew Kettle* and attended by Michael Davitt* and Charles Stewart Parnell,* who was elected president. The League, a reaction to the worsening conditions experienced by tenant-farmers during the agricultural depression of the late 1870s, was modelled on the Land League of Mayo.* From the beginning the League was supported by individual members of the Irish Republican Brotherhood,* the Irish Parliamentary Party* and the Fenians* in America. This linking of the revolutionary, constitutional and agrarian factions came to be known as the New Departure.* Funds for the League came from John Devoy* and Clan na Gael* in the USA. While the League, according to its constitution, was a moral force movement, in the eyes of the government it was synonymous with physical force, containing as it did the legacy of the old secret societies, the Whiteboys* and the Ribbonmen.* The radical nature of the Land League was demonstrated in its constitution. Its Declaration of Principles stated: 'The land of Ireland belongs to the people of Ireland, to be held and cultivated for the sustenance of those whom God decreed to be the inhabitants thereof. Land being created to supply mankind with the necessaries of existence, those who cultivate it to that end have a higher claim to its absolute possession than those who make it an article of barter to be used or disposed of for purposes of profit or pleasure. The end for which the land of a country is created requires an equitable distribution of the same among the people who are to live upon the fruits of their labour in its cultivation'.

In this declaration the Land League was much influenced by the teachings of James Fintan Lalor.* Its aims, protection of the tenant and the abolition of landlordism, were to be achieved, the League stated, by 'every means compatible with justice, morality, and right reason'. It also intended to 'expose the injustice, wrong or injury which may be inflicted upon any farmer . . . either by rackrenting, eviction, or other arbitrary exercise of power which the existing laws enable the landlords to exercise over their tenantry . . .' The economic depression of the 1870s had caused widespread hardship among the tenant-farmers as starvation and eviction became daily reminders of the precarious nature of the system under which they held their land. So far as the small tenant-farmers were concerned the primary aim of the League was to secure tenant-right or the Ulster Custom* known as the Three Fs, (Fair Rent, Free Sale and Fixity of Tenure). Others sought to completely destroy landlordism and establish peasant proprietorship. The League united the country outside of the north-eastern part of Ulster. The first truly democratic organisation in modern Irish history, it brought together those of different classes, religious and political persuasions. The agricultural labourers joined forces with their natural enemies, the farmers who exploited them, and the townsmen, suffering also from landlordism, were at one with the farmer. Clergy, many of them from the tenant-farmer class, were ceaseless organisers at local level. The League was also supported by Archbishop Thomas William Croke,* and by Bishop Thomas Nulty* of Meath, the first member of the hierarchy to give support. Most of the hierarchy, however, remained aloof from the agitation. The slogans of the League became the catch-cries of the people: 'Down with Landlordism', 'The land for the people', 'Keep a firm grip upon your lands' and 'Pay no rent'. The conservative press denounced the new movement as communistic, but the fight won the support of *The Nation, The Irishman* and the *Flag of Ireland,* both owned by Richard Pigott,* the *Freeman's Journal* (after 1880), and the *Irish World.* Parnell bought two of Pigott's papers and founded *United Ireland* which, under the editorship of William O'Brien,* was

the most outspoken League organ. The most powerful weapon of the League was the 'boycott' outlined by Parnell in a speech at Ennis on 19 September 1880. He asked his audience, 'What are you to do to a tenant who bids for land from which a neighbour has been evicted?' There were answering cries of 'Shoot him' and 'Kill him' to which he replied 'No' and went on . . . 'you must show him on the roadside when you meet him, you must show him in the streets of the town, you must show him at the shop-counter . . . and even in the house of worship, by leaving him severely alone, by putting him into moral Coventry . . .' This policy of 'moral Coventry', which had been advocated by John Dillon* in October 1879, was soon put into effect on an estate managed in Mayo by Captain Charles Conningham Boycott* and became the most effective weapon. It became difficult even to secure burial in some parts of the country for those who had been 'boycotted'. American support for the League remained strong throughout the Land War. Dillon, Davitt and Parnell toured the US in January 1880, and on 2 February, Parnell addressed the House of Representatives. Upon his return he was elected Chairman of the Irish Parliamentary Party (17 May).

The task of fighting the League fell to the Chief Secretary William E. Forster.* His attempt to defuse the situation failed on 3 August, when his Compensation for Disturbance Bill* was defeated in the House of Lords. The Land League policy of boycotting, from September onwards, increased pressure on him to adopt a tough line with the League and he had the leaders arrested. The 'state trials' of Parnell, Davitt, Dillon, Matt Harris* and others began on 23 December 1880 and collapsed one month later when the jury disagreed. Meanwhile, the Bessborough Commission* issued its report, recommending the reformation of land law and the implementation of the Three Fs. This call was reinforced when the Richmond Commission* issued a report later in the month (January 1881). The League's activities, however, had forced the Prime Minister, W. E. Gladstone,* into contemplating his second Land Act. On 7 January, the Queen's speech gave notice that a Land bill would be introduced for Ireland but, at the same time, a coercion bill would also be introduced to deal with the lawlessness throughout the country (*see* Agrarian Crime). On 24 January, Forster introduced the Protection of Person and Property (Ireland) Bill.* The Irish members obstructed it, forcing the House into the longest sitting on record (41 hours: 31 January – 2 February). Obstruction had been used for the last time, however, when the debate was brought to an end by the Speaker's motion of closure (2 February). On the following day Davitt was arrested and thirty-six protesting Irish members were expelled from the House. The Coercion Act became law on 2 March and *habeas corpus* was suspended.

The Prime Minister introduced his bill (*see* Land Acts) on 7 April. He proposed to grant the Three Fs, but the Act would exclude leaseholders and those in arrears from taking advantage of it. Parnell opposed it although on 19 May twenty-six members of his party gave the bill their support. It became law on 22 August. Returning home, Parnell urged the Land League Convention of 15 September to 'test the Act' in the new Land Court.* In fact, the Act was acceptable to those League members who were in a position to take advantage of it. Parnell, in the meantime, continued his attack on Gladstone and the Act until he was imprisoned on 13 October. Six days later, he signed the No Rent Manifesto* which, as he had anticipated, was condemned by moderate opinion throughout the country, including Dr Croke of Cashel. The government responded to the Manifesto by suppressing the League on the next day. The League's place was now taken by the extremist Ladies Land League.* The situation in Ireland, with Parnell

imprisoned and a rising crime rate, deteriorated during the winter of 1881–82. During the spring of 1882 Parnell was in touch with members of the government through Captain William H. O'Shea* and in April he came to an agreement with Gladstone known as the Kilmainham 'Treaty'.* He was released from prison on 2 May and the land war appeared to be over. However, on 6 May, the new Chief Secretary, Lord Frederick Cavendish* (replacing Forster who had resigned in protest at the 'Treaty'), and the Under-Secretary, Thomas H. Burke,* were murdered by the Invincibles* (*see* Phoenix Park Murders). The Invincibles were known to have close contacts with prominent figures in the suppressed Land League. The agitation, however, was over.

The Land Act of 1881 began to operate. Most of those who applied for rent reductions under the Fair Rent clause secured reductions of up to 25 per cent. It was a complicated piece of legislation and few purchased under it, but it answered the League's demands. Gladstone later admitted that without the League there would not have been a Land Act in 1881. The League had shown the Irish tenant the value of solidarity. Through it the tenant-farmers and agricultural labourers had enhanced their self-respect. The League had started the process which eventually broke the power of the landed gentry in Irish social and economic life. Parnell's leadership had made him a national figure, and when he founded the National League* in 1882 he built it upon the framework of the Land League, using many of the same local personalities.

LAND LEAGUE OF MAYO. Founded 16 August 1879 by James Daly* and Michael Davitt* following meetings at Irishtown* and Westport, Co. Mayo. The first president was a Westport barrister, J. J. Louden, who also farmed 7,000 acres. Supported by Charles Stewart Parnell,* the League soon spread into a national organisation, the (Irish National) Land

League* which modelled itself on the constitution of the Land League of Mayo. The LLM sought the legalisation of the Ulster Custom.*

LAND WAR. Fought between 1879 and 1903, the Land War can be divided into three phases: 1879–82, when there was a violent struggle between landlords and the tenants led by the Land League;* 1886–91, a more subdued struggle called the Plan of Campaign,* mainly confined to Munster; 1891–1903, a more conciliatory phase when the transfer of the land-holdings to the tenants was effected through a series of Land Acts* introduced by Arthur J. Balfour,* Gerald Balfour* and George Wyndham.* In the strictest sense the term 'Land War' refers to the first phase. Tenants' leaders at different stages were Michael Davitt,* Charles Stewart Parnell,* John Dillon* and William O'Brien* MP.

LAND REHABILITATION PROJECT (1949). Introduced by the Minister for Agriculture in the first Inter-Party Government,* James Dillon.* The scheme was intended to put unused land into production over a ten-year period, recovering some four million acres at a total cost of £40m. The project was considered one of the major achievements of the Inter-Party Government.

LANDED ESTATES COURT. Formerly the Encumbered Estates Court, it was established in 1852, to guarantee the titles of estates being sold as a result of the bankruptcy of their owners, either before or during the Famine of 1845–49.* Its functions were taken over in 1877 by the Land Judges, Chancery. *See* Encumbered Estates Acts.

LANDED IMPROVEMENT ACT, 1847. Act designed to empower the State to advance money for agricultural use in Ireland. It was administered by the Commissioners of Public Works. Many of the loans were used for drainage. In 1848 £350,000 was borrowed and the same amount in 1849; it fell to £250,000 in 1850.

LANE, DENNY (1818–95). Poet and businessman; b. Cork; ed. TCD where he was a close friend of Thomas Davis.* He was a prominent member of Young Ireland* and contributed to *The Nation.* His political activities led to his being detained for four months in 1848. Lane became president of the Cork Literary and Scientific Society, and was a director of the Cork Gas Co., and involved in other businesses, including railways. He was the author of 'Carrig Dhoun' and 'Kate of Araglen'.

LANE, SIR HUGH (1875–1915). Art-dealer and collector; b. Ballybrack House, Co. Cork, nephew of Augusta, Lady Gregory;* ed. privately. He moved to London where he worked for Colnaghi's from 1893 until 1898 when he established his own art-dealing business. An acknowledged art expert, he befriended Sarah Purser* and commissioned a series of portraits from John B. Yeats.* During a trip to Paris in 1905 he began his modern collection which, owing to his discernment, grew into one of the most valuable in the world. When the Dublin Corporation opened a Municipal Gallery in Harcourt Street in 1908 he organised a Franco-Irish exhibition and one year later was knighted for his services to art. He housed his collection, including works by Renoir, Pisarro, Monet, Manet, Degas and Corot in his Chelsea home which he bought in 1909. He had a vision of a gallery for modern art linked with the National Gallery* and spanning the Liffey (to replace the 'Ha'penny Bridge'). In 1912 he commissioned Sir Edward Lutyens to design such a gallery but his offer of his collection of Impressionists was rejected by the Dublin Corporation which was not prepared to justify the cost. The controversy over the gallery prompted W. B. Yeats* to write *To a Wealthy Man Who Promised a Second Subscription to the Dublin Municipal*

Gallery if it were Proved the People Wanted Pictures. Lane took his collection to London in 1914 and presented it to the National Gallery, London. During the controversy he was appointed Director of the National Gallery of Ireland. He travelled to the USA in 1915 to repair his finances which had been injured by World War I and was drowned returning in the *Lusitania* (7 May 1915). His will contained an unsigned codicil making a gift of thirty-nine pictures from his modern collection to the National Gallery of Ireland. This marked the beginning of bitter litigation concerning the future of the Lane collection. Sarah Purser, supported by Lady Gregory and Yeats, formed the Friends of the National Gallery of Ireland in 1924 to campaign for the return of the paintings from London. The Municipal Gallery was established in 1930 with a room for the collection. An interim settlement between the Municipal Gallery and the National Gallery, London worked out in 1959 provided an arrangement under which the paintings would rotate between London and Dublin every five years for a twenty-year period.

LANE, TIMOTHY O'NEILL (1822– 1915). Lexicographer; b. Co. Limerick. Trained as a teacher, he worked in Templeglantine, Co. Limerick from 1852 until he moved to London (1877) where he worked as a clerk. He spent some time in Paris as a newspaper correspondent. The work of producing and publishing his *English-Irish Dictionary* (1904) was said to have cost him some £3,000.

'LANE COLLECTION'. *See* Lane, Sir Hugh.

LANIGAN, JOHN (1758–1828). Historian and clergyman (R.C.); b. Co. Tipperary; ed. Rome where he was ordained. He was for some years Professor of Hebrew at Pavia University. After returning to Ireland in 1794 he became assistant librarian to the Royal Dublin Society* and was appointed Librarian in 1799. His major work was *An Ecclesiastical History of Ireland from the first introduction of Christianity to the beginning of the 13th Century* (4 vols, 1799–1829). He had an obsession about stones which eventually led to his being confined to a mental asylum in Finglas, Co. Dublin, where he died.

LANSDOWNE, 3rd MARQUESS (1780–1863). Petty-Fitzmaurice, Henry; politician (Whig) and landowner in Kerry and Limerick; b. London; ed. Westminster School, Edinburgh University and Trinity College, Cambridge. As MP for Clane (1803–07) he attracted attention in the House of Commons for his wide knowledge of economic questions. After losing his seat in 1807 due to his supporting Catholic Emancipation* he then opposed it. In 1809 he succeeded his half-brother and entered the House of Lords where he advocated liberal causes. He was President of the Council under Lord Grey (November 1830) and under Lord Melbourne,* (from 1835 to 1841). While he opposed Daniel O'Connell* and the demand for Repeal* he sought justice for Ireland, supporting Sir Robert Peel* on repeal of the Corn Laws. He spoke on distress in Ireland in the Lords during the Famine of 1845–49* (on 15 February 1847) but expressed himself as filled with 'horror and dread' at the attempt by Lord John Russell* to place the burden of financing relief on landowners. He was generally regarded as a good landlord on his Irish estates. Lansdowne was a patron of Thomas Moore* to whom he gave frequent financial assistance.

LARCOM, SIR THOMAS (1801–79). Soldier and civil servant; Under-Secretary (1853–68); ed. Royal Military Academy, Woolwich. After working on the Ordnance Survey in England (1824–26) he became director of the Irish Ordnance Survey (1828–45) and employed, among others, John O'Donovan,* George Petrie* and

Eugene O'Curry.* As Census Commissioner in 1841 he introduced large-scale changes, including a systematic classification of occupation and the collection of statistics on the general conditions of the population. He was a commissioner on Colleges (1845), of Public Works (1846–49) and assisted on the commission established to investigate the reform of Dublin Corporation (1849). After a period as deputy chairman of the Board of Works (1850–53) he became Under-Secretary where he was faced by the Fenians* whose activities he attempted to curb by a firm but fair approach. He sought to have the law dispensed in Ireland on the same principles as obtained throughout the rest of the United Kingdom.

LARKIN, DENIS (1908–). Trade unionist and politician (Labour); b. Rostrevor, Co. Down, second son of James Larkin* and brother of James Larkin, Jnr;* ed. St Enda's College* by Patrick Pearse. After working with London Arco Trading he returned to Dublin to assist his brother and father in the Workers Union of Ireland,* (1923–77). A member of the executive of the Irish Trade Union Congress* from 1949, he was vice-president of Congress (1973–74) and president (1974–75). He presided over the Employer-Labour Conference which negotiated the National Pay Agreement of 1974. A member of Dublin Corporation for thirty years, he was chairman of the Housing Committee and Lord Mayor (1955, 1959). He served on the Administrative Council of the Labour Party and was TD for Dublin North-East (1954–57, 1965–69). He was a member of the European Trade Union Conference Executive and of the European Social Fund Committee and the only trade unionist on the European Special Commission to Combat Poverty.

LARKIN, JAMES (1876–1947). Socialist, trade unionist and politician (Labour); b. Liverpool of Irish parentage. He was sent at the age of five to his grandparents in Newry, Co. Down. After returning to Liverpool in 1885 he became a labourer and later worked as a seaman. He became a dock foreman in Liverpool in 1894, but lost the position when he struck in sympathy with the men he was supervising. Working for the National Union of Dock Labourers, he was sent to Belfast in 1907 and within a short time had organised a wave of strikes (including one by the Royal Irish Constabulary* which had been sent in to quell the strikers). For a short time he succeeded in getting the workers to bridge the sectarian, political and cultural divides. They won small increases in wages but the consciousness of solidarity did not last. His activities in Belfast alienated the NUDL and he was transferred to Dublin in 1908, where he re-formed the Irish branch of the Independent Labour Party and began to organise the Dublin casual and unskilled workers. Within a year he had called three strikes and was suspended by the NUDL which refused to finance his industrial action. This led to the foundation of his own union, the Irish Transport and General Workers' Union* (December 1908–January 1909).

He called strikes on the Irish dockland and in Dublin organised a temperance campaign and succeeded in ending the system whereby casual labourers were paid in public houses. His strike tactics alienated employers and the leaders of the Irish Trades Union Congress,* leading to his expulsion in 1909. His union was not re-affiliated until 1911, shortly after which he became president of Congress. In June 1910 he was sentenced to one year's imprisonment on a charge of misappropriating Cork dockers' money while working for the NUDL (at most he was guilty of sloppy accountancy and not of wilful embezzlement). He was released on 1 October 1910 following a petition from the Dublin Trades' Council to Lord Aberdeen.* From 1911 onwards he attacked the Dublin employers in his newspaper, *The*

Irish Worker. As he led a series of strikes involving carters, dockers, railwaymen and tram workers, he aroused misgivings among the employers who were led by William Martin Murphy.* Murphy unified the employers to resist Larkin's demand for employer-labour discussions on wages, hours and general conditions. During 1912 the situation further deteriorated by which time, as a prominent member of Congress, he backed a call from James Connolly* for a Labour Party. By 1913 his own union had 10,000 members and he had secured wage increases for dock labourers and brought the agricultural labourers around Co. Dublin within the ITGWU. The employers' attempt to prevent workers from joining the ITGWU led to the Lock-Out* in 1913. He organised assistance from England and the USA to feed the workers in a campaign known as the 'Fiery Cross'. By the end of January 1914, however, when the Lock-Out was ending as workers returned to work, Larkin's union was depleted both numerically and financially. The tone of *The Irish Worker* became increasingly bitter and in August it was suppressed by Dublin Castle.* In October he went on a lecture-tour of the US to raise funds, leaving the union in the hands of Connolly and William O'Brien.*

Larkin's 'visit' to the US became a nine-year stay as he involved himself in the American labour movement, particularly with the syndicalist International Workers of the World for which Connolly had previously worked. He lacked the money to return home and eventually was arrested and imprisoned for his trade union activity. During his imprisonment (in Sing Sing) he was annually re-elected general secretary of the ITGWU. From his prison cell he denounced the Treaty.* In January 1923 he was released on the orders of Governor Al Smith and returned home to Ireland to a triumphant reception.

The Easter Rising of 1916,* the execution of Connolly, the rise to prominence of O'Brien in the ITGWU

and of Thomas Johnson* in the Labour Party, the establishment of the Free State in the middle of the Civil War,* all had served to change Ireland as he had known it. He made no allowance for the changes and attempted to regain control of the union. This was resisted by O'Brien and Johnson who engineered his expulsion. He lost a court case for control and was declared a bankrupt. With his brother, Peter, and son, James Larkin Jr,* he formed a new union, the Workers' Union of Ireland,* which won support from Dublin workers. He secured recognition from the Communist International in 1924 and visited Russia as representative of the Irish Section of the Comintern. The split in the labour movement continued during the 1930s during which period he built up the WUI. He returned to the Labour Party again after playing a prominent part in securing amendments to the Trade Union Act* of 1941, and in opposing the Wages Standstill Order* of the same year. He won back his Dail seat for Labour after O'Brien failed to prevent his getting the party's nomination. His return to Labour precipitated another bitter fight which ended in 1945 with the ITGWU disaffiliating from Congress and five members of the Labour parliamentary party forming National Labour.* During his last two years he led a fight against rising prices.

LARKIN, JAMES, JNR (1904–69). Trade unionist and politician (Labour); b. Liverpool, eldest son of James Larkin;* ed. Liverpool and St Enda's College* where he was taught by Patrick Pearse. He spent three years at the Lenin School, Moscow, after visiting there with his father (1924) and later worked with him in the Workers' Union of Ireland.* Standing as a Communist, he won the Dublin seat held by Thomas Johnson* in September 1927. A founder-member of the Workers' Revolutionary Groups* for which he was returned to Dublin Corporation (1930), he failed to retain his Dail seat in the

1932 general election. He became chairman of the Communist Party of Ireland* (1933). Along with his father he was accepted into the Labour Party in December 1941 and became a member of the executive. He succeeded his father as general secretary of the WUI in 1947 and was the first trade unionist to present a case in the Labour Court* in the same year. During the 1950s he played a leading role in efforts to unify the trade union movement which had been split in 1945, and which was finally united in 1959 with the foundation of the Irish Congress of Trade Unions* of which he was twice president. He was succeeded as general secretary of the WUI by his brother, Denis Larkin.*

LARMINIE, WILLIAM (1850–1900). Writer and prominent member of the Irish literary revival; b. Castlebar, Co. Mayo; ed. locally and TCD. He worked as a civil servant in the India Office in London for some years. He returned to Ireland in 1887. His poetry was deeply influenced by old Irish verse. His works include *Fand and Moytura* (1892), *West Irish Folk-Tales* (1894) and *Glanluas and other Poems* (1889).

LARNE GUN-RUNNING. The mission to buy German guns and land them in Larne for the Ulster Volunteers was carried out by Frederick Crawford* with the support of Sir James Craig (*see* Craigavon, Lord), Sir Edward Carson* and the Ulster Unionist Council.* Thirty-five thousand rifles and 5,000,000 rounds of ammunition were landed at Larne from the *Clyde Valley* on the night of 24–25 April 1914. The guns were taken over by General Sir William Adair,* assisted by Captain Sir Wilfrid Spender. Guns were also landed at Donaghadee. The Larne Gun-running stimulated the rival volunteer army in the south, the Irish Volunteers,* into organising the Howth Gun-running* in July.

LARTIGUE RAILWAY. Monorail invented by Francis Marie-Theresa Lartigue to link the Co. Kerry towns of Listowel and Ballybunion (a distance of eight miles). Built for £33,000, the Lartigue monorail was the only one operated in these islands and opened on 29 February 1888. Its first run was on 5 March when the standard time of one hour was set. The engine was a steam locomotive. Care had to be taken, when loading, to ensure that there was an even distribution of passengers on each side. This militated against an effective timetable. The single fare was 10d (slightly more than 4p) and the return fare was 1/3 (about 6½p). The highest recorded number of passengers carried was on 11 August 1911 when 1,500 were conveyed between 10.30 a.m. and 2 p.m. from Listowel for a pattern* in Ballybunion. Machinery and rolling stock were damaged during the Civil War* and the line was closed on 14 October 1924.

LATIMER, REV. WILLIAM THOMAS (1842–1919). Presbyterian historian; b. Ballynahetty, Co. Tyrone; ed. Queen's College, Belfast, where he graduated B.A. in 1870. He was ordained in 1872. Rev. Latimer contributed historical articles to leading journals of the era. His works include *A History of the Congregation of Eglish* (1890), *History of Irish Presbyterians* (1893), *Life of Dr Cooke* (1897), *The Ulster Scot* (1899), *The Battles of the Yellow Ford and Benburb* (1919).

LAVELLE, REV. PATRICK (1825–86). Clergyman (R.C.) and nationalist; b. Murrisk Mullagh, Louisburgh, Co. Mayo; ed. Maynooth and the Irish College, Paris, where he was an outstanding student. He was forced to resign his professorship in Paris following a bitter dispute with the Rector, Rev. Thomas Miley.* Upon his return to Ireland he was appointed to Mt Partry (Tourmakeady), first as Administrator and later as Parish

Priest (1858–69). With the encouragement of his friend, John Mac-Hale,* Archbishop of Tuam, he played a leading role in combating the evangelical New Reformers* whose operations within his parish were supported by the Church of Ireland Bishop of Tuam, Thomas Plunket.* Fr Lavelle's attack on Bishop Plunket over the treatment of tenants at Tourmakeady led to an editorial in the London *Times* and questions in the House of Commons (1860). The affair was known as 'The War in Partry'.

Vice-President of the National Brotherhood of St Patrick, Fr Lavelle supported the Irish Republican Brotherhood* and came into conflict with Paul Cullen,* Archbishop of Dublin. After delivering the funeral oration over the grave of the Fenian, Terence Bellew McManus,* Fr Lavelle was supported by Archbishop MacHale when Dr Cullen attempted to have him suspended. Appointed Parish Priest of Cong, Co. Mayo (1869). Following the Galway election of 1872 which led to a celebrated court case (for clerical intimidation), he was denounced by Judge William Keogh,* after which he dropped from national prominence. Fr Lavelle's main publication was *The Irish Landlords Since the Revolution* (1870).

LAVERY, LADY HAZEL (1881–1935). Noted beauty; her portrait, by her husband, Sir John Lavery,* decorated Irish paper currency from 1928 until 1977; b. Chicago (*née* Martyn) she accompanied her mother to Europe and remained there to study art. She married Sir John, her second husband, in London (1910). Among her close friends in London were George Bernard Shaw,* Lord Birkenhead* and Sir Winston Churchill.* During the War of Independence,* she became interested in Irish affairs and formed a close friendship with Michael Collins* while the Treaty negotiations in London (October–December 1921) were in session. Her best-known paintings are of her husband and of Shaw. In 1927

Kevin O'Higgins* suggested that Sir John be appointed Governor-General so as to give Lady Lavery an opportunity to display her talent as a hostess but the idea was dropped after O'Higgins' death in July 1927.

LAVERY, SIR JOHN (1856–1941). Artist; b. Belfast. He studied art in Glasgow where he was a member of the 'Glasgow School'. After further studies in London and Paris under Bouguereau and Robert-Fleury, he built up a considerable reputation as a portraitist, in particular for his portraits of women. He married the noted beauty Hazel Martyn in 1910 (*see* Lavery, Lady Hazel). Knighted for his work as official war artist in 1918, his best-known works were 'Hazel Lavery' (Municipal Gallery of Modern Art, Dublin), 'Polymnia' (National Gallery, Rome), 'A Lady in Black' (National Gallery, Berlin), 'Spring' (the Luxembourg, Paris), 'Game of Tennis' (New Pinelothek, Munich) and 'Cardinal Logue' (Belfast Gallery). His portrait of his wife decorated Irish paper currency from 1928 to 1977.

LAW, ANDREW BONAR (1858–1923). Politician (Conservative); Prime Minister (1922–23); b. Kingstown, New Brunswick, Canada, of Ulster descent; ed. Gilbertfield School, Hamilton and Glasgow High School. He was elected MP for Blackfriars and Hutcheson division of Glasgow in 1900. A prominent supporter of Joseph Chamberlain,* he was opposed to Home Rule* for Ireland. He denounced the 'People's Budget' introduced by David Lloyd George* in 1909, calling it 'pure and unadulterated socialism', a view shared by the leader of the Unionists, Walter Hume Long.* His rise to power was swift and on 13 November 1911 he became leader of the Conservatives as a compromise between Long and Austen Chamberlain. His denunciation of Home Rule was severe as H. H. Asquith* sought to carry the Government of Ireland Act 1914. Law assured the Ulster Unionists* at Blenheim Palace

(July 1912), 'I can imagine no length of resistance to which Ulster will go which I shall not be ready to support'. Addressing agitated Unionists in Ulster and in England, he supported the 'No Surrender' stand taken by Sir Edward Carson* and James Craig (*see* Craigavon, Lord). He supported the formation of the Ulster Volunteer Force* in January 1913. In July 1914 he was present at the Buckingham Palace Conference* which unsuccessfully attempted to break the deadlock. When Home Rule was passed and suspended in September he claimed that it was a breach of faith with Ulster Unionists.

After bringing about the coalition war cabinet of May 1915 he became Chancellor of the Exchequer and was responsible for the raising of War Loans. He urged the extension of conscription to Ireland (*see* Conscription and Ireland) and during his period as a member of the cabinet he reached an understanding with the new Prime Minister, Lloyd George, on Ulster's position in relation to Home Rule. After the failure of the Irish Convention* he issued a joint letter with the Prime Minister on the eve of the general election of December 1918, pointing out that Ireland could not leave the Empire nor would the six north-eastern counties be forced against their will into Home Rule. He supported the Government of Ireland Act, 1920.* He attended the Peace Conference in Paris occasionally and was a signatory to the Treaty of Versailles, 28 June 1919. After resigning his post as Leader of the House of Commons (March 1921) he severed his relationship with the Ulster Unionists who soon became the ruling party in the new state of Northern Ireland. His term as Prime Minister was cut short through ill-health (October 1922–May 1923), and he died five months after his resignation.

LAW, HUGH (1818–83). Lawyer and politician (Liberal); Lord Chancellor (1881–83); b. Co. Down; ed. Dungannon and TCD. Called to the Bar in 1840 and a QC from 1860, he drafted the bill for the Disestablishment of the Church of Ireland* and also assisted W. E. Gladstone* in drafting the Land Act of 1870 (*see* Land Acts). MP for Co. Londonderry (1874–83), he was Attorney-General in 1880 when he unsuccessfully prosecuted Charles Stewart Parnell* and leaders of the Land League* for alleged conspiracy.

LAW ADVISER. Official of the Irish government at Dublin Castle* whose duty was to advise the government and the Irish magistracy on points of law. Magistrates based their judgements upon his advice. Such a close connection between the Executive and the judiciary was considered injurious in practice as the course of 'law and order' was variously interpreted according to the prevailing political climate. The last such offical was John Nash.

LAWLESS, EMILY (1845–1913). Poet and novelist; b. Kildare, daughter of the 3rd Lord Cloncurry; ed. privately. She travelled widely in Europe. Her works include *Hurrish* (1886) *Ireland: Story of the Nation* (1888), *Major Lawrence F.L.S.* (1888), *Plain Francis Mowbray and other tales* (1889), *With Essex in Ireland* (1890), *Grainne: The story of an Island* (1892), *Maelcho* (1894), *Traits and Confidences* (1898), *With the Wild Geese* (poetry, 1902), *Maria Edgeworth* (1904), *The Book of Gilly* (1906), *The Races of Castlebar* (with Shan F. Bullock, 1913), *The Inalienable Heritage* (poetry, 1902). *The Poems of Emily Lawless*, edited by Padraic Fallon, was published in 1965.

LAWLOR, JOHN (1820–1901). Sculptor; b. Dublin; ed. Royal Dublin Society school. He enjoyed considerable success after moving to London (1845) where he sculpted many of the statues in the House of Commons. He was responsible for the 'Engineering' group on the Albert Memorial. His best-known works in Ireland are the statues of Bishop Delany (Cork) and Patrick Sarsfield in Limerick.

LAWRENCE, WILLIAM (1841–1932). Photographer; b. Dublin; ed. locally. Lawrence was a toymaker in Upper Sackville Street (now O'Connell Street), Dublin, where he had a shop. During the 1870s he opened a photographic department in his toyshop and was so successful that he closed down the toymaking end of the business to concentrate on photography. His chief photographer, Robert French, travelled throughout the country, amassing a vast collection of photographic plates of people and places. The Lawrence Collection of 40,000 plates was bought by the National Library* for £300 in 1942. It is a major source of photographic material for Ireland between 1880 and 1910 and has been used in many books and documentary films.

LEADBEATER, MARY (1758–1826). Author; b. Ballintore, Co. Kildare, *née* Shackleton, into a prominent Quaker family. She visited London in 1784 and was introduced to many influential people, including Edmund Burke and Sir Joshua Reynolds. She was horrified by the atrocities which accompanied the rising of the United Irishmen* in 1798, an account of which may be found in *The Leadbeater Papers* (2 vols, 1863). Her works also included *Cottage Dialogue* (1814), *Cottage Biography* (1822) and *Biographical Notices of Members of the Society of Friends* (1823).

LEAGUE OF NATIONS. The Irish Free State became a member of the League of Nations on 10 September 1923, having registered the Treaty with the League. The registration of the Treaty and Ireland's admission to membership were opposed by the British government which claimed the right to represent the countries making up the British Commonwealth of Nations. In 1926 the Free State was unsuccessful when it stood for

election to the Council of the League but was elected to the Council in 1930 with the support of other Commonwealth countries. The Irish permanent delegate to the League was Sean Lester* (1929–34). When Eamon de Valera* formed his first administration in 1932 he held the Ministry of External Affairs and was elected President of the Council (September 1932). He urged that the smaller nations form a bloc of their own: 'All the small states can do if the statesmen of the greater states fail in their duty, is resolutely to determine that they will resist with whatever strength they may possess every attempt to force them into war against their will' (1936). He supported the League's policy of non-intervention during the Spanish Civil War* (1936–39) and was President of the Assembly (1938–39). He also supported attempts by Neville Chamberlain* to appease Hitler. Ireland's representative, Sean Lester, was the last Secretary-General of the League (1940–45). *See also* United Nations.

'LEAGUE OF NORTH AND SOUTH'. *See* Tenant League.

LEAGUE OF YOUTH. Name adopted in 1934 by the Young Ireland Association,* more popularly known as the Blueshirts.*

LEAHY, DR PATRICK (1807–75). Theologian and Archbishop of Cashel (R.C.), 1857–75, b. near Thurles, Co. Tipperary; ed. Maynooth. Following ordination he became Professor of Theology at St Patrick's seminary, Thurles, where he was also president until 1855. Highly regarded by the then Archbishop of Armagh, Paul Cullen,* he was appointed one of the honorary secretaries at the Synod of Thurles* and was later vice-rector of the Catholic University* (May 1854–September 1855). He became parish priest and dean of Cashel in September 1855 and Archbishop two years later. One of his first acts was to enforce an ordinance on the closure of public houses on Sundays. He made determined efforts to abolish faction fighting* in Munster. He started the Cathedral at Thurles which was completed by his successor, Thomas William Croke.*

LEAMY, EDMUND (1848–1904). Lawyer and politician (Nationalist); b. Waterford; ed. locally and at Tullybeg. He qualified as a solicitor (1878) and was called to the Bar (1885). Leamy was returned as MP for Waterford in 1880 and later for Cork (1885), South Sligo (1887) and Kildare (1900) as a member of the Irish Parliamentary Party.* He remained faithful to Charles Stewart Parnell* after the split (December 1890). Parnell appointed him editor of *United Ireland* after it had been taken forcibly from the anti-Parnellites.

LE CARON, HENRI (1841–94). Fenian informer; b. Colchester, real name Thomas Billis Beach. An apprentice draper, he went to the USA in 1861 and enlisted in the 8th Pennsylvanian Reserves using the title Major and the name Le Caron. He was Assistant Adjutant-General in 1865. During the Civil War (1861–65) he joined the Fenians.* He settled in Nashville, Tennessee, where he studied medicine. His career as an informer began in 1866 when he notified the authorities of a Fenian raid to be undertaken on Canada by Captain John O'Neill* whose confidence he had won. The raid was defeated by the Canadian authorities on 1 June 1866. When he visited England during the following year he made contact with Robert Anderson* of the Home Office to whom he relayed extensive information on Fenianism in Ireland, England and America. Between 1868 and 1870 he earned £2,000 from the Home Office for information, and frustrated a second raid on Canada. A founder-member of Clan na Gael,* he was privy to information on the New Departure* and formed a close friendship with Alexander Sullivan* of the terrorist Triangle* and was also

friendly with John Devoy.* Devoy commissioned him to visit Europe with packets for John O'Leary* and Patrick Egan* in Paris in 1881; while passing through London he gave Anderson an opportunity to study the packets. Egan accompanied him to London on the return journey from Paris and introduced him to Charles Stewart Parnell* who commissioned him to bring about an understanding between the constitutionalists and the Fenians in America. After he returned to the US he was denounced for his Fenianism when he stood for election to the House of Representatives (1885). After returning to England permanently in December 1888 he was cross-examined in February 1889 during the hearings of the Special Commission on 'Parnellism and Crime'.* His testimony did not damage Parnell but revealed his own extraordinary career as a double agent. He spent the next five years in England, quietly, apart from a nervous breakdown shortly before his death. In his autobiography, *Twenty-Five Years in the Secret Service* (1892), he claimed that his spying had been motivated by patriotism and not by money. He had been paid £10,000 for his attempt to smear Parnell.

LECKY, WILLIAM EDWARD HARTPOLE (1838–1903). Historian and politician (Liberal-Unionist); b. near Dublin; ed. Cheltenham and TCD. As MP for the University of Dublin from 1895 he opposed Home Rule.* He supported Sir Horace Plunkett* and the Co-Operative Movement.* His works include *Leaders of Public Opinion in Ireland* (essays on Swift, Flood, Henry Grattan and Daniel O'Connell; 1862), *The History of England in the Eighteenth Century* (written to counteract Froude's *History of Ireland;* 1878–90), *Democracy and Liberty* (1896), *The Map of Life* (1899), and *A History of Ireland in the Eighteenth Century* (1892), culled from a twelve-volume *History of England*.

LEDWIDGE, FRANCIS (1891–1917). Poet; b. Slane, Co. Meath; ed. locally to the age of fourteen when he was employed by a farmer. His first poems, written in his early teens, appeared in the *Drogheda Independent*. While working as a labourer and ganger on road works he was secretary of the Slane branch of the Meath Labour Union (1912). Lord Dunsany* gave him access to the Library at Dunsany Castle where Ledwidge met Katharine Tynan* with whom he corresponded regularly. He enlisted in Dunsany's regiment, the 10th (Irish) Division, Iniskilling Fusiliers. While home on leave in May 1916, saddened by the executions of the leaders of the Easter Rising of 1916,* he wrote an elegy to his friend Thomas MacDonagh* ('He shall not hear the bittern cry . . .'). He was killed by shell-fire while road-laying in preparation for an assault on Ypres and was buried in the second plot of Artillery Wood cemetery near the village of Boesinghe, Belgium. His works, *Songs of the Fields*, *Songs of Peace* and *Last Songs*, were collected by Dunsany and published as *The Complete Poems of Francis Ledwidge* (1919). This volume was extended by his biographer, Alice Curtayne, and published as *Complete Poems* (1974).

LE FANU, JOSEPH SHERIDAN (1814–73). Novelist; b. Dublin, grand-nephew of Richard Brinsley Sheridan; ed. TCD. He was called to the Bar in 1839 but did not practise. His journalistic career began in 1839 when he issued the *Dublin Evening Mail*. He also edited the *Dublin University Magazine* (1869–72) of which he was later proprietor and in which he serialised many of his novels. He was the author of twelve gothic novels, the most widely-read of which were *The Cook and the Anchor* (1845), *Torlough O'Brien* (1847), *Uncle Silas* (1864), *The Tenants of Malo* (1867) and *In a Glass Darkly* (1872).

LEFROY, THOMAS LANGLOIS (1776–1869). Judge and politician (Conservative); b. Co. Limerick; ed. TCD. He was called to the Irish Bar in 1797. He was MP for the University of Dublin (1830–41), Baron of the Irish Court of Exchequer (1841–52) and Lord Chief Justice of the Queen's Bench (1852–66). During his period on the bench (where he remained until his ninetieth year) he delivered sentence on many of the leading Irish nationalists.

LEGION OF MARY. Roman Catholic organisation founded in Dublin on 7 September 1921 by Frank Duff, Fr Michael Toher and Mrs Elizabeth Kirwan. The Legion, which is guided by Duff's *Legion of Mary Handbook*, engages in charitable activities.

LEINSTER, 3rd DUKE (1791–1874). FitzGerald, Augustus Frederick; landowner; succeeded to the title while a boy; ed. Eton and Oxford. A Whig, he supported Catholic Emancipation* and parliamentary reform. He was Grand Master of the Freemasons in Ireland where he lived on his large estate at Carton, Co. Kildare. In 1831 he received a letter from Lord Stanley (*see* Derby, 14th Earl), outlining a proposal for a system of National Education* in Ireland. This 'Stanley Letter', as it became known, was the basis for the non-denominational system which originated in 1831. Leinster was the first chairman of the Board of Commissioners, a post which he held until his resignation in 1850.

LEINSTER HOUSE. The Home of Dail Eireann* and the Senate* since 1921. Kildare House, as it was originally known, was begun in 1745 as the town house of Lord Kildare, heir to the Duke of Leinster. The house was sold in 1815 to the Dublin Society (*see* Royal Dublin Society) under whose aegis it was the home of the nucleus of the National Gallery,*

National Library* and National Museum.* Dail Eireann occupies the former RDS lecture theatre and the Senate is in the saloon in the north wing.

LEITRIM, EARL OF (1806–78). Clements, William Sydney; politician (Conservative) and landowner; b. Dublin. After a career in the army where he reached the rank of lieutenant-colonel and was MP for Leitrim (1839–47), he succeeded to title and estates in Leitrim and Donegal in 1854. Notoriously litigious, he prosecuted some 180 tenants and spent so much on courts costs (even as far as the House of Lords) that he seriously reduced the income of his estates. On his 57,000 acre estate near Milford in Co. Donegal, he refused to allow the Ulster Custom* to his tenants after the passage of the 1870 Land Act (*see* Land Acts). His tenants claimed that he used his position as landlord to seduce girls on his estates. Leitrim was murdered at Woodquarter near Mulroy Bay, outside Milford, while journeying to Manorhamilton, Co. Leitrim. His three murderers were never apprehended, although several people were arrested and later released. His assassination was a prelude to the Land War* which broke out one year later. A cross was erected in 1960 at the spot where he was killed; it commemorates Michael Hegarty, Michael McElwee and Niel Sheilds 'who, by their heroism at Cratlagh Wood on 2nd April 1878, ended the tyranny of landlordism in Ireland'.

LEMASS, SEAN (1900–71). Politician (Fianna Fail); Taoiseach (1959–66); b. Dublin; ed. CBS. A member of the Irish Volunteers,* he fought in the GPO during the Easter Rising of 1916* and later in the Irish Republican Army* during the War of Independence.* He opposed the Treaty* and was a member of the Four Courts garrison. Elected to Dail Eireann in June 1922, he abstained and was a member of the alternative republican government

formed by Eamon de Valera* during the Civil War. He was a founder-member of Fianna Fail* in 1926 and was, with Gerald Boland,* responsible for building up the constituency organisation which made the party the strongest in the country. After Fianna Fail entered the Dail in 1927 he played an important part in the opposition to the Cumann na nGaedheal government. He described Fianna Fail in March 1928 as 'a slightly constitutional party'. Lemass had a deep interest in economics and industry and propounded a doctrine of self-sufficiency, advocating protection for industry. When he became Minister for Industry and Commerce in de Valera's first government he was the youngest member of the cabinet. He held the ministry until 1948 apart from a short break (16 September 1939–18 August 1941).

His initial approach to the Irish economy was based on the old Sinn Fein protectionist theories of Arthur Griffith.* Lemass gave priority to employment and the protection of native industry, playing a crucial role in the Cabinet Economic Committee. His pragmatic approach to all problems made Industry and Commerce a key ministry in the attempt to foster economic recovery during the depression of the 1930s. Despite the fall in the value of agricultural exports during the Economic War* and a lack of capital for investment along with the increased cost of vital imports of raw material, his achievements were considerable. Foreign investment was only encouraged where it filled a need that could not be met by native industry. A Housing Act made £3,400,000 available for house-building (between 1932 and 1942 a total of 132,000 houses were built), and £1,000,000 was provided for road-building. He investigated the possibility of establishing two cement factories but this did not come to fruition until 1936 when two were built at Limerick and Drogheda. Twenty-six thousand pounds was provided for mineral exploration. He introduced a number of Control of Manufactures Acts between 1932 and 1934 and a series of Conditions of Employment Acts oversaw a gradual improvement in working conditions. Two million pounds was provided for industry and business firms with a view to finding new markets for Irish manufactured products. The Industrial Credit Company was established in 1933 with an advance of £6,000,000 and he urged the Department of Education to undertake the establishment of factory courses for industrial apprentices in an attempt to overcome the acute shortage of skilled labour. Lemass established bodies to investigate the expansion of the turf industry and the possibility of increasing electricity output. The sugar-beet industry was expanded and he extended the role of the state further into industry by widening the range of semi-state bodies, creating a managerial class within the protected industries. On the whole, this energetic approach was successful: net industrial output rose from £25,600,000 (1931) to £36,000,000 (1938). Employment in manufacturing industry rose from 110,000 to 166,000 during the same period, although this had to be offset against losses in agricultural employment.

During the Emergency* he was appointed Minister of Supplies, with responsibility for rationing. In this capacity he controlled the distribution of raw materials and fuel resources to industry. His value to de Valera and the government received public recognition when he succeeded Sean T. O'Kelly* as Tanaiste in June 1945. His work of the 1930s could not be continued during the post-war period as a lack of capital coupled with rising prices and inflation deepened the economic depression. There was also widespread industrial unrest. Fianna Fail was out of office from 1948 until 1951 and when Lemass returned to Industry and Commerce the economy was still in trouble: inflation, unemployment and high emigration proved the main problems. The government was unable to solve the economic crisis and it was defeated in the 1954 general election by the second Inter-Party Government.* Lemass again held Industry and Commerce in de Valera's last administration (March 1957–June 1959). It was his final term in the Department and saw the beginning of a new age in which foundations were laid for the economic prosperity of the 1960s. In this work he depended upon the Secretary of the Department of Finance, T. K. Whitaker,* who outlined the first Programme for Economic Expansion in May 1958 (*see* Programmes for Economic Expansion). Implementing the programme became Lemass's first priority when he succeeded de Valera as Taoiseach in June 1959.

Under Lemass, foreign companies were offered tax-free 'holidays' and new bodies were established while existing bodies were streamlined and strong efforts were made to boost export industries. The planned economy began to show results: output increased by almost one-quarter between 1958 and 1963. Unemployment fell by one-third and there was a sharp decrease in emigration (a reduction of 40 per cent during 1961–66 over the figures for 1956–61). His economic plans laid, Lemass announced in 1961 that Ireland would apply for membership of the European Economic Community (but due to French resistance to Britain, Ireland did not become a member until 1973). His public statements in 1962 indicated also that Ireland would ally herself with the Western political system as he denounced communism, and praised the USA for acting as guardians of liberty. Changes in Irish thinking under Lemass were signalled very forcibly by one of his last public acts when he travelled to Belfast in 1965 to have tea with Captain Terence O'Neill.* This seemed to offer a more liberal policy in relation to Northern Ireland. From 1961 to 1965 he led a minority government with Fianna Fail holding 70 seats to a combined opposition of 74. In the general election of 1965 his party gained two seats, to hold 72 against a combined opposition of 72. When he retired in November 1966, his departure was the signal for a struggle between contenders for the leadership, in particular between his son-in-law, Charles J. Haughey,* and George Colley, both of whom, in the event, were defeated by Jack Lynch.*

LENIHAN, MAURICE (1811–95). Historian and journalist; b. Waterford. He was a close friend of Daniel O'Connell,* Richard Lalor Sheil,* George Petrie,* Fr Theobald Mathew* and Thomas Francis Meagher.* He organised many of O'Connell's meetings for the Repeal Association.* The founder of *The Tipperary Vindicator* (1844), he took over *The Limerick Reporter* (1849) and was later Mayor of Limerick city and High Sheriff of the county. He was the author of *Limerick, Its History and Antiquities* (1866).

LESTER, SEAN (1888–1959). Journalist and diplomat; b. Co. Antrim; ed. locally, he worked as a journalist on nationalist and republican newspapers. He was news editor of *The Freeman's Journal* in 1923 when he entered the Department of External Affairs where he remained until 1929. From 1929 to 1934 he was permanent delegate to the League of Nations.* He served on the Council of the League and presided over arbitration on the Peru-Colombia and Bolivia-Paraguay disputes. Lester was High Commissioner in Danzig (1934–37), Deputy Secretary-General of the League (1937–40) and last Secretary-General (1940–46). He received the Woodrow Wilson Foundation Award in 1945. *See also* League of Nations and Ireland.

LEVER, CHARLES JAMES (1806–72). Physician, author and diplomat; b. Dublin; ed. TCD, Gottingen and Louvain. He practised medicine at various centres in Ireland and was very active during the cholera epidemic of 1832. During W. M. Thackeray's Irish tour of 1842 they met and Thackeray acknowledged Lever's assistance by dedicating the *Irish Sketch Book* to him. He edited the *Dublin University Magazine** (1842–45) and then went to the continent with his family, settling in Florence (1847). His postings as British Consul included Spezia (1857) and Trieste (1867–72). When conferring the consulship at Trieste upon him, Lord Derby remarked, 'Here is £600 a year for doing nothing, and you Lever, are just the man to do it'. Lever's prolific literary output was stimulated by his need to meet his gambling debts. He has been accused of fostering the image of the stage Irishman, an accusation also levelled at Samuel Lover* with whom he is frequently confused. In Lever's case it was the accompanying illustrations by Hablot K. Browne which led to charges of stage Irishry. His writings include *Harry Lorrequer* (1837), *Charles O'Malley* (1841), *Tom Burke of Ours* (1844), *Arthur O'Leary* (1844), *The O'Donoghue* (1845), *The Knight of Gwynne* (1847), *Con Cregam* (1849), *Barrington* (1862), *Cornelius O'Dowd on Men, Women and Things in General* (in *Blackwood's Magazine*, 1864), and *Luttrell of Arran* (1865). A thirty-three-volume collected edition of his work appeared between 1876 and 1878.

'LEVIATHAN'. Title of the seventy-two-inch Parsonstown Telescope* built by the 3rd Earl of Rosse* at Birr Castle, Co. Offaly, in 1845.

LIA FÁIL. 'Stone of Destiny' (ancient inauguration stone of the Kings of Tara); Lia Fail was the title of a movement founded in 1957 by Fr John Fahy to agitate against land purchases by foreigners. It failed to achieve popular support.

LIBERTY LEAGUE. Founded in the spring of 1917 by Count Plunkett* who hoped that it would replace both Sinn Fein* and the Irish Nation League.* It acquired some support but the enterprise was clouded with confusion; Sinn Fein continued to gather support and by mid-1917 the League had disintegrated.

LICHFIELD HOUSE COMPACT. An informal agreement reached at the home of the Earl of Lichfield between Daniel O'Connell* and Lord Melbourne* in March 1835. The agreement was that O'Connell's Repealers and the radicals would assist the Whigs in opposing the government led by Sir Robert Peel.* In return for this help, the Whigs agreed that upon returning to office they would provide a settlement to the tithes* question. Melbourne also promised a measure of municipal reform to help Catholics in local government. Peel's administration fell on 11 April and Melbourne formed a new government. The tithes question was satisfactorily settled and in 1840 a Municipal Corporations Act* was introduced. The unwritten agreement reached at Lichfield House lasted until the end of the Melbourne administration in 1841.

LIGHTHOUSE SERVICE OF IRELAND, THE. The Commissioners of Irish Lights are the statutory lighthouse authority for Ireland. Originally lighthouses were operated by private individuals and in 1660 King Charles II granted letters patent to Sir Richard Reading to erect six lighthouses on the coast of Ireland, two of which were to be placed at Howth, Co. Dublin, one at the 'Olde Head of Kingsale', Co. Cork, one at Barry Oges Castle, near Kinsale, one at Hook Tower, Co. Wexford and the last at the 'Isle of Magee', near Carrickfergus, Co. Antrim.

In 1704 control of the lighthouses was vested in certain Commissioners and in 1786 an act was passed setting up the Corporation for Preserving and Improving the Port of Dublin. This body subsequently divided to bring about the Port of Dublin Corporation in 1854. In 1867 this latter body became the Commissioners of Irish Lights while the former became

the Dublin Port and Docks Board — titles which they retain to this day. Some of the best-known Irish lighthouses are: Fastnet Rock, Co. Cork, Hook Tower, Co. Wexford, Kish, Co. Dublin, Tory Island, Co. Donegal and Tuskar Rock, Co. Wexford.

Two Light Vessel Stations, Coninbeg, off Co. Wexford and South Rock, off Co. Down, are also maintained by the Commissioners who tour the Irish coast annually on board the lighthouse tender *Granuaile* for an inspection of the entire lighthouse network. The lighthouse service is financed from the General Lighthouse Fund.

'LIMERICK CHRONICLE'. The oldest newspaper in the Republic of Ireland. Founded by John Ferar in 1766, the paper appeared twice weekly up to 1862 when it appeared thrice weekly. It is now published by Limerick Leader Ltd every Tuesday and has a circulation of 12,000. During its long history it has carried reports ranging from the American War of Independence (1776–81), the French Revolution (1789), the 1798 Rebellion, the trial of Robert Emmet (1803), the Fenian Rising (1867) to the marriage of eighty-year old Biddy Early* to young Patrick O'Brien (23 July 1869). Its files are much sought after by researchers and scholars and form an invaluable historical record. From January 1980 the paper has appeared in tabloid format when, printed in web offset, colour was introduced for the first time.

LIMERICK DECLARATION. A declaration made in 1868 by some 1,600 priests in Limerick to the effect that Repeal was the only possible final solution to the Irish question. The Declaration had been organised by the Catholic Dean of Limerick, Dr O'Brien. *See also* Repeal Association.

LITTLE CHRISTMAS (Nollaig na mBan). Also known as Women's Christmas to distinguish it from the feast of Christmas proper (known as 'Men's Christmas'), Little Christmas fell on 6 January. It was the day when the holly was taken down and burned and twelve candles were lighted in honour of the Twelve Apostles.

LITTLETON, EDWARD JOHN, 1st BARON HATHERTON (1791–1863). Politician (Whig); Chief Secretary (1833–34); b. Wolverhampton, surname Walhouse; ed. Rugby, Brasenose College, Oxford and Lincoln's Inn (1810–12). He changed his name to Littleton to benefit from a grand-uncle's will and entered politics in 1812. Littleton supported Catholic Emancipation* and introduced the Electoral Franchise in Ireland Bill which became one of the 'wings' of the Catholic Relief Bill of Sir Francis Burdett* in 1825. Daniel O'Connell* unsuccessfully supported him for the speakership of the House of Commons. He became Chief Secretary in 1833 under Richard Colley Wellesley.* Concerned over the question of tithes,* he introduced an Irish Tithes Arrears Act which advanced £1,000,000 to the Irish tithes-owners and on 20 February introduced his bill for the commutation of the tithes into a land tax payable to the state. At the same time his opposition to Repeal* led to a breach with O'Connell who opposed the commutation bill. In the interim, the cabinet was debating the renewal of coercion.* Littleton was prepared to accept a minimum of coercion if O'Connell would support the tithes bill, a trade which was acceptable to O'Connell. However, Littleton was not a member of the cabinet, which over-ruled his recommendation and introduced a severe measure of coercion, leading to charges of duplicity from O'Connell. The revelation of Littleton's dealings with O'Connell damaged the government but Lord Grey refused to accept his offer of resignation. His tithes bill was rejected by the House of Lords and in November he and the rest of the government resigned. A new government was formed by Lord Melbourne.* Littleton became Baron Hatherton in 1835.

LLOYD GEORGE, DAVID, 1st EARL (1863–1945). Politician (Liberal); Prime Minister (1916–22); b. Manchester of Welsh parents and raised by an uncle in Caernarvonshire. Largely self-educated, he qualified as a solicitor. After entering politics in 1890, he became a public figure through opposing the Boer War. While Chancellor of the Exchequer in the first government formed by Herbert H. Asquith* his 'People's Budget' provoked such opposition from the House of Lords as to force Asquith to seek the support of John Redmond* and the Irish Parliamentary Party to break the Lords with the Parliament Act* (1911). In return the Irish received the (third) Home Rule Bill.* As Minister for Supply in Asquith's government, Lloyd George's criticism of the Prime Minister's handling of the war led to the fall of Asquith whom he succeeded in December 1916. Following the Easter Rising of 1916* he was anxious to find a peaceful solution to the Irish question and released the last of the internees from Frongoch, including Michael Collins.* In May 1917 he offered Redmond immediate Home Rule with six counties of Ulster excluded for a period of five years. Redmond, rejecting partition, suggested an Irish Convention* which Lloyd George established. He was anxious to solve the Irish question, as he intended to introduce conscription which he did not believe could be achieved without Home Rule. The Convention failed but he conceded the demands of the army and tried to introduce conscription for Ireland, triggering off massive resistance and furthering the rise of Sinn Fein* (*see* Conscription and Ireland).

Sinn Fein swamped the Irish Parliamentary Party in the general election of December 1918 but Lloyd George's government did not recognise Dail Eireann* and during the War of Independence* he continued to seek a solution which would keep Ireland within the Empire. He believed that he had found it in the

Government of Ireland Act 1920* which established the state of Northern Ireland,* but was ignored in the south. In response to the complete breakdown of law and order, as the Irish Republican Army* played havoc with the Royal Irish Constabulary,* he sent the Black and Tans* and the Auxiliaries* in, to aid the police. Their failure to subdue the IRA forced him to try and make contact with Sinn Fein leaders but Eamon de Valera* was not prepared to treat with him through intermediaries and Lloyd George was not prepared to treat with Collins whom he regarded as the leader of a band of assassins.

He helped to draft the conciliatory speech made by King George V* at the opening of the Northern Ireland parliament on 22 June 1921 and two days later, he invited de Valera to attend a conference in London, reluctantly agreeing to a Truce* which began on 11 July. He met with de Valera and his party four times, on 14, 15, 18 and 21 July. On the 20th, he presented de Valera with a proposal for Dominion Home Rule within the Empire. De Valera rejected this, but Lloyd George persuaded him to present it to the cabinet in Dublin which also rejected it. Lloyd George continued to correspond with de Valera during August and September without making any advance. Then, on 29 September, he telegraphed the 'Gairloch Formula' which de Valera accepted as the basis for discussions. The Irish plenipotentiaries, led by Arthur Griffith* and Collins, began discussions with Lloyd George and his team on 11 October.

During the negotiations which led to the Treaty* he played a crucial role, using a combination of charm, cunning and bullying which made him a devastating force at the conference table. On 24 October he met with Griffith and Collins only, in a move to reduce the numbers involved in discussion. He raised the question of the Crown and the Irish presented de Valera's formula of External Association* which Lloyd George had rejected in July. Griffith now re-jected Lloyd George's proposals on the acceptance of the Crown and it was decided to continue negotiations, leaving the question of the Crown as the last item of discussion. Lloyd George now broached the question of Ulster. From the beginning he had been placed in an invidious position in that Sir James Craig (*see* Craigavon, Lord) had made it clear that there could be no bargaining with Northern Ireland. Griffith received the impression on 3 November that if Ulster proved intractable the British ministers involved would resign their posts rather than use force. Lloyd George offered a Boundary Commission* as an inducement and then met Craig on 5 and 7 November; Craig rejected any suggestion which would change the status of Northern Ireland. Griffith, however, was so taken with the idea of a Boundary Commission that he said he would not 'queer his (Lloyd George's) pitch' on Ulster. On 12 November Lloyd George translated this assurance from Griffith into a commitment that if Ulster was presented with the alternatives of an all-Ireland parliament (already rejected by Craig) or a Boundary Commission, Griffith would not break off negotiations over Ulster. He then triumphed at the Liverpool Unionist Conference where the die-hards intended to condemn his government for negotiating with Sinn Fein. He was not satisfied with the Irish reply to his draft proposals for a Treaty in that they would not accept the Crown and Empire. No advance was made when he met with Craig again on 24 November. Four days later, he made it clear to Griffith that any British government which accepted abrogation of the Treaty would be ruined. Later that evening, his team offered the Irish an opportunity to insert into the Treaty 'any phrase they liked' which would ensure that the position of the Crown in Ireland would be no more than it was in relation to Canada or any other Dominion. He met with Griffith, Collins and Eamon Duggan* on 29 November and offered them a form of Oath of Allegiance* different from the one subscribed to by other Dominion parliaments, which the Irish rejected. Two days later he sent for them and presented them with a draft for a Treaty which Griffith took to Dublin on 2 December while Lloyd George met with Collins and Robert Erskine Childers* to discuss financial arrangements on Ulster.

After rejecting counter-proposals from the Irish cabinet, Lloyd George met with Collins on 5 December. He then met with the King, attended a cabinet meeting and afterwards met the Irish delegation. He offered full financial autonomy and stated that there would be no further concessions. To their astonishment, the Irish were now presented with an ultimatum. Holding up two letters, one containing the Articles of Agreement for a Treaty, the other containing the news that Sinn Fein had refused to come into the Empire, he demanded to know which one he should send to Craig. Was it to be war or peace? Without allowing the delegates any opportunity to get in touch with Dublin, he demanded that they sign the Treaty immediately or both sides would be free to resume warfare within three days. This ultimatum was considered a major factor in persuading the delegates to sign. Lloyd George's role in the negotiations earned him a legendary reputation in Irish popular myth for unparalleled deceit. His government fell in 1922 and thereafter he remained on the backbenches. He refused an invitation to join the National Government in 1940. Shortly before his death he was created Earl Lloyd of Dwyfor.

LOCAL APPOINTMENTS COMMISSION. Body established in 1926 for recruitment to the senior administrative and professional posts in local government authorities. Such posts have to be advertised and filled by competition to be conducted under the auspices of the Commissioners, in Dublin.

LOCAL DEFENCE FORCE (LDF). Volunteer force formed during the Emergency* in September 1940 under the Defence Forces (Temporary Provisions) Act which created a new type of soldier, the Emergency Durationist. It was recruited from the 'A' group of the Local Security Force* (LSF). Fully armed and uniformed, the 100,000 members served as an auxiliary to the regular army and were under the direct control of the Chief of Staff and a special Local Defence Directorate. In the event of an invasion the LDF was to be the first line of defence which would locate and harass the enemy and provide the army with vital information. *See also* Defence Forces *and* Forsai Cosanta Aitiuil.

LOCAL GOVERNMENT. Local government in Ireland during the nineteenth century was based on the county, each of which was governed by a Grand Jury* which solely represented the (Protestant) Ascendancy* class. The county, rather than a smaller unit as in England, was chosen for administrative convenience and because the native population was considered unfit to govern itself. The Grand Jury financed local expenditure by raising a cess or levy upon the occupiers of the land within its jurisdiction (each barony, of which there are now 273, was made to pay for its own roads, etc.). Borough corporations, most of which were created by royal charters in earlier centuries, were reformed and reconstituted under the Municipal Corporations (Ireland) Act 1840.* Some town commissioners were established under an act of 1828 and under private acts, but most came into existence under the Town Improvements (Ireland) Act 1854. Commissioners were made responsible for the provision of lighting, cleaning services and water supply in all towns with a population, of more than 1,500. The Local Government Board was established in 1872 to take central control but it allowed a large measure of autonomy to local authorities. The administration of health facilities during the nineteenth century was mainly the responsibility of the Poor Law Boards of Guardians for each Union district. Under the Poor Relief (Ireland) Act, 1851, (the Medical Charities Act), the Boards were to divide their Unions into dispensary districts, each with a salaried Medical Officer. The Public Health Acts of 1874 and 1878 granted the borough corporations and the town commissioners considerable power in regard to the provision of health facilities and housing services. In addition, there were boards to administer lunatic asylums, boards for the county infirmaries and boards for the fever hospitals. The Boards of Guardians received extra responsibility when in 1883 they were authorised to provide rural housing.

The Local Government Act 1898, which rationalised the existing web of authorities and boards, was one of the most sweeping measures introduced during the century. Established on democratic principles which included female suffrage, it abolished the Grand Jury, destroying the power of the Ascendancy, and effectively handing control to nationalists. Four new authorities, all elected, replaced the old system: County Councils, Borough Corporations, Urban District Councils and Rural District Councils. Larger towns within each county continued to be governed by town commissioners. The duties of the Boards of Guardians (not abolished until 1923) were confined to poor relief while their other functions were taken over by the county councils (responsibility for mental hospitals, fever hospitals and county infirmaries). The Local Government (Ireland) Act, 1919 extended the system of Proportional Representation* to twenty-six town councils and Urban District Councils and to 200 other local authorities. Further changes in administration occurred after the creation of the Free State* (December 1922). The old Boards of Guardians were replaced by Boards

of Health (later Boards of Health and Public Assistance). A new system of Home Assistance replaced the old workhouse relief, to be granted to 'any poor person who is unable by his own industry or other lawful means to provide for himself or his dependants the necessaries of life or necessary medical or surgical treatment'. Two years later under the Local Government Act, 1925, the Rural District Councils were abolished and their functions assumed by the Boards of Health. Outside of urban areas the Boards were authorised to provide for sanitation, housing, drainage, water supplies and general public health services. Members were appointed from the County Councils. Between 1922 and 1942 a series of reforms to secure maximum efficiency in local government were introduced; as part of these reforms a Local Appointments Commission* was established in 1926, to select qualified personnel for a wide range of administrative and professional posts in local government.

The chief executive in local government is the County or City Manager, a salaried official who may only be removed from office by the Minister of the Environment. The management system was first introduced in Cork under the Cork City Management Act, 1929; it was extended to Dublin in 1930, Limerick (1934), Waterford (1939) and to the counties in 1942. The functions of local authorities are divided into two classes under the Management Acts: 'reserved functions' which are the prerogative of the elected members and 'executive functions' which devolve on the manager. Elected members are responsible for policy decisions and the manager must act in conformity with general policy as laid down by the members. In recent times the general functions of the local authorities have been in relation to (*a*) the provision, maintenance and improvement of public roads; (*b*) the assessment of housing needs, the enforcement of minimum standards, provision of housing for those unable to provide it for themselves and the provision of grants and loans for other persons providing or reconstructing their own houses; (c) the provision of public water supplies and sewerage systems, refuse collection and burial grounds; (d) the preparation and implementation of development plans, the control of development and the preservation and improvement of amenities; (e) environmental services, amenity services, protective and regulatory services. Health services are now the responsibility of the Regional Health Boards (since 1 April 1971).

Rates on private dwelling houses were abolished as from 1 January 1978 and local authorities now receive finance from central funds to replace this source of revenue. There are twenty-seven County Councils, four County Borough Corporations, fifty-six Borough Corporations and Urban District Councils and twenty-eight Town Commissioners.

LOCAL GOVERNMENT BOARD. Established in 1872, it took over responsibility for the Poor Law* from the Poor Law Commissioners. It supervised the dispensary system, adjudicated between local authorities, controlled hospitals, administered the Housing Acts and Public Health Acts, and took responsibility for public hygiene and distressed areas. Additionally, after 1908, it paid out Old Age Pensions.*

LOCAL GOVERNMENT (IRELAND) ACT, 1919. Act which extended the system of Proportional Representation* to twenty-six town and urban district councils and to 200 other local authorities.

LOCAL OPTION PARTY. Prohibition party founded in Northern Ireland in 1929 to contest the general election of that year. The party was led by Presbyterian clergymen, including Rev. A. Wylie Blue. Its platform was that people in a particular local authority area should be enabled to vote in favour of preventing the sale of drink. There was a strong prohibitionist following in Northern Ireland, which had not been satisfied by the Licensing Act (NI) 1923, an attempt to provide a compromise between publicans and temperance bodies. The party contested three seats in the election against Unionist candidates and lost all three.

LOCAL SECURITY FORCE (LSF). Organisation formed in May 1940 during the Emergency* as an nonmilitary auxiliary to the regular army (*see* Defence Forces). At first it was divided into 'A' and 'B' groups, both of which were trained by the Garda Siochana.* 'A' group were men suitable for military service willing to assist the regular forces in the field while the 'B' group performed auxiliary police duties. Under the Defence Forces (Temporary Provisions) Act, 'A' group was reorganised as the Local Defence Force (LDF) in September 1940 under the direct control of the army Chief of Staff. 'B' group continued to be known as the Local Security Force under the control of the Gardai.

LOCK-OUT (1913). The Lock-Out was the culmination of a battle between organised labour in Dublin led by James Larkin* and the Dublin employers led by William Martin Murphy,* a struggle which had first started when Larkin founded the Irish Transport and General Workers' Union* in January 1909. The period between 1909 and 1913 was one of acute economic crisis for labourers who, together with their families, numbered 100,000 or around one-third of the population of Dublin. When Larkin called on the employers to take part in discussions in 1911, Murphy, who had organised nearly 400 employers, rejected the demand. He was determined to destroy Larkin, the union and 'Larkinism' in general. In August 1913 the united employers demanded from their workers a written undertaking that they would not join Larkin's or any other union. Those who refused were dismissed.

Larkin called out the workers of the Dublin Tram Company (of which Murphy was a director) on 26 August and the call was answered by 700 of the 1,700 employees. The Dublin Metropolitan Police* helped to restore the tram service and Larkin and others were arrested the next day and released on bail. Murphy called a meeting of the Employers' Federation for 29 August. Two days later the police made a brutal attack on people in the Dublin streets after Larkin succeeded in addressing a small crowd from the Imperial Hotel (owned by Murphy). The action of the police set the tone for the next few weeks as Larkin and the employers became locked in combat. The coal merchants locked out their workers on 2 September, the same day as two four-storey tenement houses collapsed, killing seven and injuring many others. On the next day the Employers' Federation decided to lock out their workers and by 22 September some 25,000 workers were unable to work. A government inquiry into events in Dublin started on 29 September under the direction of Sir George Askwith. The employers were represented by Timothy M. Healy* and Larkin spoke for the workers. British as well as Irish trade unionists gave evidence. The Askwith Report condemned the tactic of the sympathetic strike (Larkin's favourite weapon) but also stated that the employers had no right to impose anti-union restrictions on their workers. The employers alienated public opinion by rejecting the Report. The employers' behaviour provoked a scathing denunciation from George Russell* who issued an *Open Letter for the Dublin Employers* ('Masters of Dublin') under his pen-name 'AE' (7 October). On the same day they were condemned by *The Times*. None of this, however, benefitted the unemployed workers and their families who were led by James Connolly,* newly arrived from Belfast after Larkin was imprisoned for seven months on 27 October (he was released within a short time).

The situation of the workers' children caused grave concern and with Larkin's approval in late October Mrs Dora Montefiore and Lucille Rand arrived in Dublin to arrange for the children to be taken to England where they would be guaranteed shelter, food and clothing. This proposal was attacked by the Archbishop of Dublin, William Walsh,* who accused the ladies of proselytising. They were arrested on charges of kidnapping, and the concentrated efforts of the Dublin clergy ensured that when Delia Larkin took over the project she was defeated. However, the clergy were now enjoined by Walsh to see to the distribution of relief in the tenements. The plight of the workers and the children also attracted the attention of nationalists like Patrick Pearse,* Thomas MacDonagh* and of humanitarians like Francis Sheehy-Skeffington.* In November the workers' situation appeared desperate as there was no end to the lock-out in sight. George Bernard Shaw* arrived in Dublin to take part in a demonstration. Connolly, now leading the trade unionists' Irish Citizen Army,* attacked the Liberal government, and David Lloyd George* attributed Liberal by-election reverses to Larkin. Connolly closed Dublin port and Larkin, released from jail, embarked on the 'Fiery Cross' campaign to gain help in England, gathering food and clothing for the workers and their families and sailing shiploads of aid up the Liffey. His campaign in England ran into difficulties when he called upon the British unions to help the Irish dockers by closing the docks. This was not acceptable to the British Trade Union Congress which was sensitive to the notion of Larkin's dictating to British unions. He then attacked the British union leaders, J. H. Thomas and J. H. Wilson, and soon the only major British labour figure to remain friendly was Keir Hardie. The British unions helped to open negotiations with the Dublin employers during December but on 20 December the talks broke down. Aid from England which, along with American and continental aid, had been considerable, began to dry up and by the end of the month the workers were seeking a return to work. The Dublin clergy urged workers to go back and during the second half of January 1914 many applied to return provided they did not have to sign an undertaking not to join the ITGWU. In February the workers' cause received a severe blow when the British Trade Union Congress announced that the Dublin Relief Fund would be wound up on 11 February. By the end of that month the lock-out was over.

LOGUE, MICHAEL, CARDINAL (1839–1924). Archbishop of Armagh and Primate of All-Ireland (R.C.), 1887–1924; b. Carrigart, Co. Donegal; ed. hedge school* and Maynooth (1857–65); ordained (1866). He was Professor of Dogmatic Theology at the Irish College, Paris from 1866 until 1874 when he was appointed curate of Glenswilly (1874–76). He became Dean of Maynooth, Professor of Irish (1876–78) and Professor of Theology (1878). During his eight years as Bishop of Raphoe (1879–87) he distributed large amounts to the famine-stricken tenant-farmers (collecting £30,000 on one visit to the USA). He undertook an ambitious afforestation scheme, planting some 25,000 trees around Glenswilly. A strong supporter of the total abstinence movement, he preached widely on the abuses of poteen-making. Having been co-adjutor bishop to the Archbishop of Armagh, Dr McGettigan, for nine months, he succeeded him in December 1887.

A conservative, he regarded the Plan of Campaign* as a tactical mistake and opposed Charles Stewart Parnell* as leader of the Irish Parliamentary Party* after the divorce. He was a patron of the Gaelic League* and criticised the Board of Intermediate Education for its failure to promote the Irish language. During the crisis in 1918 over the proposal to extend conscription to Ireland he supported the anti-conscription coalition (*see* Conscription and Ireland). He opposed Sinn Fein* when it became a physical force movement and denounced the British forces and the government for the policy of official reprisals during the War of Independence.* He was involved in peace 'feelers' with the Assistant Under-Secretary, A. W. Cope.* He appealed for an end to the Civil War* and issued a letter on 18 November 1923 exhorting the Free State government to release all republican prisoners not guilty of crime, and calling upon the imprisoned members of the Irish Republican Army* to abandon the hunger-strike weapon.

LOMASNEY, WILLIAM FRANCIS MACKEY (1841–84). Fenian; b. Cincinnati, Ohio, of Cork parents; his father was a Fenian. Lomasney was better known under his alias of Captain Mackey. He came to Ireland in 1865 to establish contact with James Stephens* and the Irish Republican Brotherhood,* but after a short time was arrested and allowed to leave the country. He returned to Ireland in January 1867 to take part in the rising planned by Thomas J. Kelly.* Although the rising was a failure Lomasney held out until February 1868, having captured Ballyknockane police barracks (April 1867) and made sorties against barracks and gunsmiths. He was sentenced to twelve years' imprisonment. As a result of agitation by Isaac Butt* and the Amnesty Association* he was released in 1871 and returned to the US where he established a bookselling business in Detroit. He supported the Land League* and later joined the dynamiting campaign organised by Dr Thomas Gallagher.* Lomasney was killed with his companions on 12 December 1884 while attempting to destroy London Bridge.

LONDONDERRY, 6th MARQUESS OF (1852–1915). Stewart, Charles Stewart Vane-Tempest; politician

(Unionist) and landowner; Lord Lieutenant (1886–89); b. London; ed. Eton and Christ Church, Oxford; MP for the family seat, Co. Down (1878–84). During his term as Lord Lieutenant the Irish executive had to contend with the renewal of the land war in the form of the Plan of Campaign.* He gave his complete support to his Chief Secretary, Arthur J. Balfour.* He was Postmaster-General (1900–02), President of the Board of Education (1902–05) and Lord President of the Council (1903–05). Londonderry opposed Home Rule* and was active in Ulster Unionist efforts to combat it. He helped to organise the Solemn League and Covenant* and the Larne Gunrunning.*

LONDONDERRY, 7th MARQUESS OF (1878–1949). Stewart, Charles Stewart Henry Vane-Tempest; politician (Ulster Unionist) and landowner; b. London; ed. Eton and Sandhurst. He was Conservative MP for Maidstone (1906–15) and second-in-command of the Home Guard during World War I. Londonderry was a well-known air enthusiast and served as Under-Secretary for Air (1920–21). He owned an estate of some 50,000 acres in Co. Down and was an active member of the Ulster Unionist Party.* Upon the establishment of the state of Northern Ireland in 1921 he became Minister for Education. He was unsuccessful in his attempt to establish a system of education which would not be segregated on religious lines. He was leader of the Northern Ireland Senate (1921–26), Secretary of State for Air (1931–35) and Lord Privy Seal and leader of the House of Lords (1935). He was the author of *Ourselves and Germany* (1938) and *Wings of Destiny* (1943).

LONDONDERRY HOUSE AGREEMENT. Agreement reached on 6 April 1911 between the Union Defence League* and the Joint Committee of the Unionist Association of Ireland,* at the home of Lord Londonderry.

Under the agreement the UDL was to collect funds for the Unionist cause and act as a propaganda bureau in England, Scotland and Wales, for the case against Home Rule.*

LONG, WALTER HUME, 1st VISCOUNT LONG OF WRAXALL (1854–1924). Politician (Conservative); Chief Secretary (1905); b. Bath; ed. privately, and at Harrow and Christ Church, Oxford, where he did not take a degree. He became an MP in 1880. After a career as Parliamentary Secretary to the Local Government Board (1886–95) and President of the Board of Agriculture (1895–1900), he succeeded George Wyndham* as Chief Secretary in March 1905. Although Long spent a very short time in office (until December 1905) he was praised by his successor, Augustine Birrell,* for leaving the country in a harmonious state. He lost his seat in South Bristol in the general election of 1906 and was returned as MP for South Co. Dublin, succeeding Colonel E. J. Saunderson* as leader of the Unionist Party.*

He was unwilling to take the post, but the Unionists persuaded him on the grounds that they needed his parliamentary experience. When he won another seat, the Strand Division of Westminster, in January 1910 he was succeeded as leader of the Unionists by Sir Edward Carson.* A founder of the Union Defence League* in 1907, he became president of the Budget Protection League established to oppose the 'People's Budget' introduced by David Lloyd George* in 1909. In 1910 he was a contender with Austen Chamberlain for the leadership of the Conservative Party. Both of them withdrew to allow the leadership to go to Andrew Bonar Law.* Long introduced the Franchise Bill of 1917 which became law in time for the general election of December 1918 and allowed women over thirty the right to vote. He published *My Memories* in 1923.

LONG TERM RECOVERY PROGRAMME. White paper drawn up in

1949 by the first Inter-Party Government* as part of Ireland's application for Marshall Aid.* The Programme was drawn up by the Minister for External Affairs, Sean MacBride,* and the Secretary of the Department, Frederick H. Boland.* The programme emphasised the value of livestock production for the export market. Its major achievement was the Land Rehabilitation Project* undertaken by the Minister for Agriculture, James Dillon.* However, owing to the prevailing economic situation, the programme was not a success. It marked the beginning of economic planning which bore fruit a decade later in the Programmes for Economic Expansion.* Later benefits of the LTRP included the establishment of the Central Statistics Office, Coras Trachtala and the Industrial Development Authority.*

LONGFORD, CHRISTINE, LADY (1900–80). *Née* Trew; author; b. Oxford and ed. Somerville College, Oxford where she met the future 6th Lord Longford* whom she married in 1925. She collaborated with him at the Gate Theatre* of which she was Managing Director (1961–64) and in Longford Productions. A member of the Irish Academy of Letters,* her works include the novels, *Making Conversation* (1931), *Country Places, Mr Jiggins of Jigginstown* (1933), *Printed Cotton* (1935), *Anything But the Truth* (1937), and *Sea Change* (1940); dramatisations of *Pride and Prejudice, The Absentee, The Watcher* and *The Avenger;* and the plays, *Lord Edward* (1942), *The United Brothers* (1942), *Patrick Sarsfield* (1943), *Earl of Straw* (1944), *Tankardstown* (1950), *Mr Supple* (1950) and *The Hill of Quirke* (1958).

LONGFORD, 6th EARL (1902–61). Pakenham, Edward Arthur Henry; actor and producer; ed. Oxford where he met his future wife (*see* Longford, Christine, Lady). In 1931 he became a director of the Gate Theatre* founded by Hilton Edwards* and Micheál MacLiammóir.*

Five years later, Longford founded his own company, Longford Productions, which leased the Gate for six months annually to stage a wide range of international drama. He was the author of *Yahoo* (1933) in which Hilton Edwards played Jonathan Swift. Longford's company toured the Irish provinces. He translated the *Oresteia* of Aeschylus, *Oedipus* (Sophocles), *The Bacchae* (Euripides) and *Tartuffe* and *Le Bourgeois Gentilhomme.* His company disbanded after his death.

LORD LIEUTENANT. The Lord Lieutenant or Viceroy, senior member of the Irish executive, who, with the Chief Secretary* and the Under-Secretary,* was responsible for the implementation of Irish policy. His office was in Dublin Castle* while his home was at the Vice-Regal Lodge (now Arus an Uachtarain) in the Phoenix Park. Although the Lord Lieutenant was responsible for the civilian government of Ireland and also controlled the military forces of the Crown, actual power in Ireland was vested in the Chief Secretary who was an MP, and sometimes a member of the cabinet.

The function of the Viceroy was largely ceremonial. De Tocqueville noted in 1835: 'The political tendency ... is to leave the Lord Lieutenant only the appearance of authority and to concentrate the real power in the hands of the Minister in London'. R. Barry O'Brien* said later that the Lord Lieutenant wore the insignia of command and signed the log but the Chief Secretary was the captain of the ship. A Lord Lieutenant's popularity was often determined by the generosity of his entertainment. As political power had shifted from Dublin after the Union* much of the glitter of a capital city disappeared and the vice-regal ceremonials offered rare glimpses of pomp and circumstance. Only one Lord Lieutenant, Lord FitzAlan of Derwent,* the last man to hold the office, was a Roman Catholic.

The following is a list of Lords

Lieutenant from 1800 to 1922 (those with a dagger(†) indicate persons either born, or owning land, in Ireland):

1800 Lord Cornwallis
1801 3rd Earl of Hardwicke
1806 6th Earl of Bedford
1807 4th Duke of Richmond
1813 Viscount Whitworth
1817 1st Earl Talbot of Hensol
1821 Richard Colley Wellesley, Marquess†
1828 1st Marquess of Anglesey
1829 3rd Duke of Northumberland
1830 1st Marquess of Anglesey
1833 Richard Colley Wellesley
1834 9th Earl of Haddington
1835 2nd Earl of Mulgrave
1839 Chichester Fortescue-Parkinson, Baron Carlingford†
1841 Thomas Philip de Grey, 1st Earl
1844 2nd Baron Heytesbury
1846 4th Earl of Bessborough†
1847 4th Earl of Clarendon
1852 13th Earl of Eglinton
1853 3rd Earl of St. Germans
1855 7th Earl of Carlisle
1858 13th Earl of Eglinton
1859 7th Earl of Carlisle
1864 John Wodehouse, 1st Earl of Kimberley
1866 1st Duke of Abercorn†
1868 John Poyntz Spencer, 5th Earl
1874 1st Duke of Abercorn
1876 7th Duke of Marlborough
1880 7th Earl of Cowper
1882 John Poyntz Spencer, 5th Earl
1885 4th Earl of Carnarvon
1886 1st Marquess of Aberdeen
1886 6th Marquess of Londonderry†
1889 3rd Earl of Zetland
1892 1st Marquess of Crewe
1895 5th Earl of Cadogan
1902 2nd Earl of Dudley
1905 1st Marquess of Aberdeen
1915 2nd Baron Wimborne
1918 1st Earl French of Ypres
1921 1st Viscount FitzAlan of Derwent

LOVER, SAMUEL (1797–1868). Novelist, portraitist and song-writer; b. Dublin; ed. privately. He worked briefly in his father's stockbroking business which he entered as a youth.

A member of Royal Hibernian Academy,* he helped to found the *Dublin University Magazine.** Failing eyesight forced him to abandon painting, a field in which his best-known work was a study of Paganini. After moving to London in 1835 he became a member of a literary circle including Charles Dickens with whom he was co-founder of *Bentley's Miscellany*. He developed an 'Irish Evening' which included monologues, recitals and stories; this became a major source of income when he toured Ireland, Britain, Canada and the USA. His works include *Legends and Stories of Ireland* (two series, 1831–34), *Rory O'More* (1836), *Songs and Ballads* (1839) and *Handy Andy* (1842). He composed over 300 songs set to old Irish airs, the most popular of which were 'Molly Bawn', 'The Angel's Whisper', 'The Low-Backed Car' and 'What Will you Do Love?'

LOWTHER, JAMES (1840–1904). Politician (Conservative); Chief Secretary (1878–80); ed. Westminster. MP from 1865, he was Parliamentary Secretary to the Poor Law Board (1868) and Under-Secretary for the Colonies (1874–78). During his term as Chief Secretary there was widespread unrest as a result of an agricultural depression and he had to deal with a rising crime rate and the Land League.* Upon the change of government in May 1880 he was replaced by William Edward Forster.*

LOYAL NATIONAL REPEAL ASSOCIATION. *See* Repeal Association.

LOYALIST ASSOCIATION OF WORKERS. Founded by Billy Hull in Belfast in 1971 from among former supporters of his Workers' Committee for the Defence of the Constitution. LAW had strong support from workers at Harland and Wolff's shipyard, Mackie's foundry and Gallaher's tobacco factory. It developed close links with the Ulster Defence Association* and with Rev. Ian Paisley.* LAW organised a series of lightning one-day strikes to highlight loyalist demands and played a leading part in the general strike of 1974 which destroyed the power-sharing Executive of the Assembly of Northern Ireland.

LOYALIST COALITION. *See* United Ulster Unionist Council.

LUBY, THOMAS CLARKE (1822– 1901). Nationalist; b. Dublin; ed. TCD. He supported the Repeal Association,* joined Young Ireland* and was a contributor to *The Nation*. After the breach with Daniel O'Connell* and the Repeal Association he joined the Irish Confederation* and befriended James Fintan Lalor* by whom he was deeply influenced. Following the collapse of the 1848 rising (*see* Ballingarry, Co. Tipperary) organised by William Smith O'Brien,* he attempted to revive the fighting by working with a secret society in Dublin to which Lalor also belonged. Their attempt was unsuccessful and he was imprisoned after his arrest at Cashel, Co. Tipperary. He became a founder member of the Irish Republican Brotherhood* in 1858 and accompanied James Stephens* on an organising tour, and worked on *The Irish People* (1863–65). He was among those arrested in 1865 when he was sentenced to twenty years imprisonment of which he served six before his release in 1871 as a result of agitation by the Amnesty Association.* Following his release he went to Belgium, and from there to the US where he joined Clan na Gael.* A supporter of Jeremiah O'Donovan Rossa,* he was a trustee of the Skirmishing Fund,* some of which was used to finance dynamiting.* He was suspicious of the Irish Parliamentary Party* and opposed the New Departure and the Land League.*

LUCAS, FREDERICK (1812–55). Journalist and politician (Tenant League); b. England; ed. at Quaker School. After converting to Catholicism (1839), he founded *The Tablet* (1840) which became an influential weekly organ of English Catholicism.

A keen student of Irish affairs, he was impressed by the manner in which Irish Catholics showed their opposition to the government and came to Ireland with his newspaper in 1849. In the aftermath of the Famine of 1845–49,* he became involved with Charles Gavan Duffy* in the Tenant League (1850). He quickly established an ascendancy over his colleagues, although he lacked certain qualities of leadership: he was an impatient man, given to outbursts of violent language and lacking tact, although he was given credit by all who knew him for his sincerity. His friends included John Henry Newman* who continued the friendship despite the warnings of Archbishop Paul Cullen.*

When the 'Irish Brigade' was established in 1851 to fight the Ecclesiastical Titles Act, Lucas successfully advocated that the Tenant League join with it to form the Independent Irish Party.* He was returned as MP for Meath in 1852, with the help of Archbishop Cullen. Over the new few years relations between Dr Cullen and the party deteriorated and the Tenant League attributed the loss of the Louth by-election to the Archbishop's intervention (February 1854). Lucas appealed to Rome, arriving there in December 1854. He had an interview with the Pope on 9 January 1855 and then met Dr Cullen on 24 January. When Cullen explained his views to him, Lucas became, if anything, even more vehement. Supported in Rome by Cullen's old opponent, Dr John MacHale,* Archbishop of Tuam, Lucas had a second interview with the Pope (26 February) but it achieved nothing. The League and the Independent party suffered badly from clerical and lay reaction to Lucas's visit to Rome. Still waiting for a result of his appeal to Rome, he died from a heart-attack probably precipitated by worry.

LUNACY. Until the first decade of the nineteenth century there was no organised provision of relief for the mentally afflicted, with the exception of Jonathan Swift's hospital and certain cells in the infirmaries. The Richmond in Dublin (1810) and a hospital in Cork were the only other places which offered containment. The mentally afflicted were otherwise guarded at home or became wanderers. Asylums were built after 1821 until there were twenty-three of them, containing 6,200 patients, operating under the Inspectors of the Lunatic Asylums in Ireland. Before the establishments were provided for, the household had to support its own afflicted. A witness before the Committee on Poor Law gave the following statement in 1817: 'When a strong man gets the complaint [mental illness] the only way they [his family] have to manage is by making a hole in the floor of the cabin, not high enough for a person to stand up in, with a crib over it to prevent his getting up. The hole is about four feet deep, and they give this wretched being his food there, and there he generally dies. Of all human calamities I know of, none are equal to this in the country parts of Ireland I am acquainted with.'

'LYCEUM'. Literary review founded by Fr Thomas A. Finlay* S.J., in 1887, attached to University College. The review published matters of literary, topical, political and cultural interest and attracted a wide range of distinguished contributors. In 1893 it was replaced by *New Ireland Review.**

LYNCH, ARTHUR (1864–1934). Soldier and politician (Nationalist); b. Ballarat, Victoria, Australia to an Irish father and a Scottish mother. After working as a civil and electrical engineer, doctor, surgeon, and journalist he settled in London during the 1890s and gave support to Irish nationalist movements such as the Gaelic League* and the Amnesty Association.* Under commission from *Collier's Magazine* he covered the Boer War (1899–1902) and while in South Africa befriended Major John MacBride* with whom

he formed a pro-Boer 'Irish Brigade'. The Brigade, which included Afrikaaners, French and Germans, saw no action but he was given the rank of Colonel. He was returned as MP for Galway in 1900 and upon his return to London to take his seat was arrested (January 1903), put on trial for high treason and sentenced to death. He was pardoned in 1907 and later was MP for Clare. During World War I he served in the British Army for which he recruited in Ireland. He lost his seat in 1918 when the Irish Parliamentary Party* was routed by Sinn Fein* and practised medicine in London until his death.

LYNCH, JEREMIAH ('DIARMUID') (1878–1950). Republican; b. Tracton, Co. Cork; ed. locally. After working as a post office clerk in Cork and as a clerk in the British civil service, he went to the USA (1896) where he became involved in the Gaelic League* and the New York Philo-Celtic Society. His contacts in America included John O'Leary,* Jeremiah O'Donovan Rossa* and John Devoy.* He returned to Ireland in 1907 and was initiated into the Irish Republican Brotherhood* one year later by Sean T. O'Kelly,* later becoming Divisional Centre for Munster on the Supreme Council* from 1911 to 1916. He accompanied Thomas Ashe* to the US on a fundraising tour for the Gaelic League and the Irish Volunteers,* collecting £2,000. In September 1915, he was detailed by Patrick Pearse* to find a suitable landing place for an arms ship before the proposed Easter Rising of 1916* and selected Fenit, Co. Kerry as the landing place for the *Aud** for April 1916. Pearse also appointed him in January 1916 to alert Cork, Kerry, Limerick and Galway for the rising. After fighting in the GPO during Easter Week he was imprisoned at Pentonville until June 1917 after which he went once more to the US where he was appointed national secretary of the Friends of Irish Freedom.* In his absence he was elected to the first

Dail Eireann* but resigned his seat in 1920. He supported Eamon de Valera* on the fund-raising drive of 1920 and opposed the Treaty,* remaining secretary of the FOIF until 1932 when he returned to Ireland. Between 1936 and 1940 he collected material from survivors of the 1916 rising in an attempt to produce a factual account of the operations in the GPO during Easter Week. This appeared in *The IRB and the 1916 Insurrection* edited by Major Florence O'Donoghue* in 1957. He returned to his native Tracton in 1939 and remained there for the rest of his life.

LYNCH, JOHN ('JACK') (1917–). Politician (Fianna Fail); Taoiseach (1966–73; 1977–79); b. Cork; ed. North Monastery, Cork, UCC and King's Inns; qualified as a lawyer. After working in the Department of Justice from 1936 he was called to the Bar in 1945 and resigned to practise on the Munster Circuit. He won a national reputation as a sportsman with the Gaelic Athletic Association* and by the time he retired from sport in 1952 he had the unique distinction of winning six consecutive All-Ireland medals, for hurling (1941, 1942, 1943, 1944 and 1946) and for football (1945). Returned as TD for Cork city in 1948, he was Parliamentary Secretary to the Government and the Minister for Lands (1951– 54); Minister for the Gaeltacht (19 March–June 1957), Vice-President of the Consultative Assembly of the Council of Europe (1958), Minister for Education (1957–59), Minister for Industry and Commerce (1959– 65), President of the International Labour Conference (1962) and Minister for Finance (1965–66).

He succeeded Sean Lemass* as leader of the Fianna Fail party and Taoiseach in 1966 after a determined bid for the leadership by three other candidates, Charles J. Haughey, George Colley and Neil T. Blaney.* Under his leadership the party gained three extra seats in the general election of 1969 (from 72 in 1965 to 75).

Almost immediately he had to face a major crisis as the civil rights movement in Northern Ireland provoked loyalist reactions (*see* Northern Ireland Civil Rights Association). In August he promised that the southern government would not 'stand by' (or 'stand idly by' as many commentators would have it) while the Catholic minority in the North was subjected to harassment by Protestant paramilitaries. In January 1970 the Irish Republican Army* split into Provisionals and Officials. The leader of the opposition, Liam Cosgrave,* alleged in April that members of Lynch's government were providing arms for the Provisional IRA. On 6 May he dismissed Haughey and Blaney; two other members of the government, Kevin Boland* and Michael O'Morain, resigned. Then and subsequently he enunciated the line that a united Ireland could only come about through consent and not through violence.

His government moved against the IRA by introducing the Offences Against the State (Amendment) Act. The events of Bloody Sunday (30 January 1972)* shocked public opinion but he continued to state that only consensus from within the North could solve the problem. He met Edward Heath and Brian Faulkner* for an unproductive meeting at Chequers. But in March, Heath introduced direct rule for Northern Ireland from Whitehall.

Mr Lynch's government fell in March 1973 after a general election campaign during which he claimed success for his government's policy on the North and on security. Just before the date of the election, the Labour Party* and Fine Gael* announced a fourteen-point programme for a National Coalition* and won. He led Fianna Fail in opposition from 1973 until 1977, when, after an intensive personal canvass of the country during June, he led the party back into government with an unprecedented 84 seats, having secured 20,079 first-preference votes in his Cork city constituency.

By mid-1979, however, there was widespread criticism within the party of his style of leadership and during his tenure as President of the EEC he unexpectedly announced his resignation which took effect on 11 December 1979 when he was succeeded as leader of the party and Taoiseach by Charles J. Haughey.*

LYNCH, LIAM (1890–1923). Republican soldier; b. Anglesborough, Ballylanders, Co. Limerick; ed. locally. Trained for the hardware business, he worked in Mitchelstown and Fermoy, Co. Cork. He was active in the re-organisation of the Irish Volunteers* in Co. Cork (1917) and played a prominent part in the opposition to conscription (*see* Conscription and Ireland). During the War of Independence* he commanded the Cork No. 2 Brigade of the Irish Republican Army* and was among the leaders of the Irish Republican Brotherhood.* He captured the RIC Barracks at Araglin, Co. Cork (April 1919) and led an attack on British troops in Fermoy (September) for which there were executions in reprisal. After capturing General Lucas and two colonels on 26 June 1920 (Lucas escaped five weeks later, for which his captors were relieved as he was costing them a small fortune in food and drink), he was himself captured on 12 August but the British soldiers did not recognise him. He and his party were released, except for Terence MacSwiney.*

As a member of the Supreme Council* of the IRB Lynch was an influential figure in the War of Independence although he was not a member of Dail Eireann.* He opposed the Treaty.* Throughout the early months of 1922, as the nationalist movement split over the Treaty, he hoped for some way of avoiding an open confrontation in order to preserve the Republic. This was not possible and the country moved towards civil war. When a convention of the IRA resolved on 26 March 1922 to re-affirm allegiance to the Republic he was appointed Chief-of-

Staff. They established an Army Executive and abrogated the authority of the Minister for Defence. Within a short time the Executive split over tactics and he resigned. He disapproved of the seizure of the Four Courts* in April but on 27 June joined the garrison just before the Provisional Government* attacked. He subsequently made his escape to the south where he assumed command of the 1st Southern Division of the IRA or Irregulars,* the largest command, being one-quarter of the total force.

He arrived in Mallow on 29 June and on the following day announced that he was Chief-of-Staff of the IRA with military command of the south and west. His assistant was Ernie O'Malley.* Lynch now appeared to hope that the hostilities might be confined to Dublin and that if Republicans could control the rest of the country the Provisional Government would recognise its hopeless position and allow the Republic to function. He moved to Limerick at the beginning of July and attempted to avoid clashes between pro and anti-Treaty forces to hold what became known as the 'Munster Republic' (south of a line from Limerick to Waterford). Fighting broke out in Limerick on 7 July and a week later he abandoned the city to the pro-Treaty forces and moved to Clonmel to establish a new headquarters. He took up a position in Fermoy shortly afterwards but was forced to abandon it on 11 August, leaving the barracks in flames. He directed that the IRA should break up into small 'active service units' (or flying columns as they had been known during the War of Independence) in order to operate more effectively against the Provisional Government's troops. From now until May 1923 the republicans were increasingly hemmed in by the National Army. He was a member of the Army Council which hoped to negotiate terms of peace that would 'not bring this country within the Empire'. This was unrealistic as the Provisional Government controlled

most of the twenty-six counties and was on the verge of establishing the Free State (which came into existence on 6 December 1922). In addition, the Catholic Hierarchy had by now roundly condemned the republicans in arms against the Provisional Government.

Lynch revealed some of his desperation when, on 27 November, he sent a letter to the Speaker of the Dail, stating that as 'the illegal body over which you preside has declared war on the soldiers of the Republic and suppressed the legitimate parliament of the Irish People' (the Second Dail Eireann), 'we therefore give you and each member of your body due notice that unless your army recognises the rules of warfare in future we shall adopt very drastic measures to protect our forces'. Three days later he issued the 'Orders of Frightfulness',* as they became known, outlining for all battalion commanders fourteen categories of persons who were to be shot on sight. The killing on 7 December of a TD, Sean Hales, and the wounding of the Deputy Speaker, Padraic O'Máille, provoked the government into executing imprisoned republicans. Thereafter property rather than persons became republican targets. On 9 February Lynch rejected a plea from the captured republican, Liam Deasy, that the republicans should unconditionally surrender within nine days. Lynch called on republicans in arms

not to surrender, but over the next two months, more of his battalion commanders were captured by the government. Despite the hopelessness of his position he attempted to carry on the fight. A meeting of the Executive was called to consider the new situation, as by now both Eamon de Valera* and Frank Aiken* favoured coming to terms with the Free State government. Accompanied by Aiken, he journeyed to Cork to attend the meeting, stopping at a hideout in Co. Tipperary en route. On 10 April, the day of the meeting, he was shot by a party of government troops in the Knockmealdown mountains and died in Mitchelstown.

LYNCH, PATRICIA (1897–1972). Writer; b. Cork; she worked as journalist in Dublin where she covered the Easter Rising of 1916.* Her wide output of children's fiction made her an international reputation. *The Turf Cutter's Donkey* (1935) was her most popular work.

LYONS, JOHN CHARLES (1792–1874). Antiquary; b. Co. Westmeath; ed. locally and at Oxford. A self-taught mechanic, he built his own printing press upon which he printed *Grand Juries of Westmeath 1727–1853* and *Book of Surveys,* now regarded as valuable genealogical and antiquarian material. He was one of the earliest Irish authorities on orchids.

M

MAAMTRASNA 'MASSACRE' (18 August 1882). The murder of five members of the Joyce family who were occupying boycotted land in a remote Co. Galway area became known as the Maamtrasna Massacre. Only the youngest son, Patrick, survived the attack. Michael Joyce, prior to his death, gave evidence which led to the arrest of ten men who were subsequently charged with the murders. Two of the arrested, Anthony Philbin and Thomas Casey, became witnesses for the Crown. Five of the accused, Michael Casey, Patrick Joyce, Thomas Joyce, John Casey and Martin Joyce, had their death sentences commuted to penal servitude for life. Patrick Joyce, Patrick Casey and Myles Joyce were executed at Galway by William Marwood* on 15 December 1882.

McADAM, JAMES (1801–81). Geologist and librarian; b. Belfast, brother of Robert Shipboy McAdam;* ed. TCD. A Fellow of the Royal Geological Society, he made preliminary investigations into Irish geology during the construction of the Irish railroad system (his work was aided by the blastings made necessary by mountainous terrain). He was the first librarian of Queen's College, Belfast (1845) and founder of the city's Botanic Gardens. He contributed to the *Journal* of the Geological Society of Dublin and possessed an extensive geological museum.

McADAM, ROBERT SHIPBOY (1808–95). Linguist; b. Belfast, brother of James McAdam.* He was fluent in thirteen languages and encouraged the study of Irish, advocating the preservation of Gaelic manuscripts as part of a preservation programme. He published a Gaelic *Grammar* and was principal founder of the *Ulster Journal of Archaeology* which he edited from 1853 to 1862.

MACALISTER, ROBERT ALEXANDER STEWART (1870–1950). Archaeologist; b. Dublin; ed. TCD, Germany and Cambridge. He was Director of Excavations for the Palestine Exploration Fund (1900–09) and Professor of Celtic Archaeology at UCD (1909–43). Dr Macalister was also a musician of note and composed a suite in D minor for the piano and organ. He was organist and choirmaster at the Adelaide Road Church, Dublin. His works include *Studies in Irish Epigraphy* (3 vols, 1897–1907), *The Archaeology of Ireland* (1927), *Tara, Ancient Pagan Sanctuary of Ireland* (1931), *Ancient Ireland* (1935) and *The Secret Language of Ireland* (1937).

MACARDLE, DOROTHY (1889–1958). Historian and dramatist; b. Dublin; ed. Alexandra College and University College, Dublin. She taught English at Alexandra College. Active in the Gaelic League* and Sinn Fein,* she supported the Easter Rising of 1916 and became a follower of Eamon de Valera.* She rejected the Treaty* and supported the republicans during the Civil War.* Her *The Irish Republic* (1937) became a standard history of events leading up to the establishment of the Free State* in 1922. She covered the period of de Valera's involvement with the League of Nations from Geneva (*see* League of Nations and Ireland). During World War II she worked for refugee children about which she wrote *Children of Europe* (1949). Her other works include the plays, *Atonement* (1918), *Ann Kavanagh* (1922), *The Old Man* (1925); a volume of short stories, *Earthbound* (1924), and *Uneasy Freehold* (1944), *Fantastic Summer* (1946), *Tragedies of Kerry* (1946), *Dark Enchantment* (1953), and *Shakespeare, Man and Boy* (1961).

McATEER, EDDIE (1914–   ). Politician (Nationalist); b. Coatbridge,

Scotland. His family moved to Derry in 1916 where he was educated at St Columb's College. He worked first as a civil servant and later as an accountant. Through his brother, Hugh, he had close connections with the Irish Republican Army.* Returned to Stormont as MP for Mid-Derry in 1945, he took the initiative in setting up a convention which led to the foundation of the Anti-Partition League (*see* Nationalist Party of Northern Ireland). This had close connections with the Fianna Fail government. He was MP for Foyle (1953–69). He became leader of the reorganised Nationalist Party in 1964 and led it as official opposition at Stormont from 1965 until 1969 when he lost his seat to John Hume. McAteer was an unsuccessful candidate in the elections for the Assembly of Northern Ireland in 1973 (*see* Northern Ireland).

McAULEY, MOTHER CATHERINE (1778–1841). Religious; foundress of the Order of Mercy; b. Dublin. Following the death of her mother in 1798, she lived at her uncle's home until 1803 when he became companion to a Mrs Callaghan at Coolock, Dublin, on the death of whose husband, William, in 1822 she inherited some £27,000. Catherine developed a keen interest in the education of poorer children and visited France where she studied Catholic methods of education. She also studied the methods used by the Kildare Place Society.* Encouraged by Archbishop Daniel Murray* of Dublin, she opened a school on 24 September 1827 and a small orphanage shortly afterwards. With two companions, Mary Ann Doyle and Elizabeth Hanley, Miss McAuley was professed on 12 December 1831 and returned to Baggot Street, Dublin. The new Order of Mercy, which received formal papal approval in 1835, operated under rules modified from those of the Presentation order with an additional vow to the service of the under-privileged. The spread of the Order was rapid and by 1887, 175 houses had been established in

Ireland alone. The congregation now has houses throughout the five continents.

MacBRIDE, MAJOR JOHN (1865–1916). Republican; b. Westport, Co. Mayo. He joined the Irish Republican Brotherhood in the 1880s but quickly became disillusioned, describing it as '. . . older men . . . sitting on their backsides and criticising and abusing one another'. A member of the Celtic Literary Society in Dublin, he was influenced by Arthur Griffith.* After emigrating to South Africa he became assayer for the Rand Mining Corporation. He persuaded Griffith to join him (1897) and they organised the 1898 Centenary Celebrations.* Their sympathies were with the Boers for whom, after Griffith returned home, MacBride and Arthur Lynch* organised an Irish Brigade.

After returning to Ireland he was defeated when he stood for election in South Mayo (1900). Griffith introduced him to Maud Gonne* whom he married in 1903 and by whom he had one son, Sean MacBride.* He returned to Ireland while his wife and son remained in Paris (until 1917). Still supporting Griffith, he became vice-president of Cumann na nGaedheal,* and a member of the National Council* and of Sinn Fein.* He also became a member of the revitalised IRB and served on the Supreme Council. In *Irish Freedom** he stated that of '. . . the lessons learned on the battle field of South Africa . . .' one was '. . . that the English army is of very little account as a fighting force'. Although he had nothing to do with the planning of the Easter Rising of 1916* he participated in it, at Jacob's Factory under Thomas MacDonagh,* for which he was executed on 5 May.

MacBRIDE, SEAN (1904–   ). Republican and politician (Clann na Poblachta); b. Paris, son of Maud Gonne* and Major John MacBride;* ed. St Louis de Gonzaga, Paris, Mount St Benedict and UCD. He opposed the Treaty,* fought in the Irish Republican Army* during the Civil War* and was imprisoned for a short time (1923—24). A leading member of Comhairle na Poblachta* (1929), he organised the first convention of Saor Eire* in 1931. His call for the creation of a republican political party was opposed by the Army Council when he was Chief-of-Staff of the IRA (1936—38). He was ousted from the Council by Sean Russell* but with the passage into law of the Constitution of 1937* he felt that there was no further need for the IRA, and severed his connection in protest at the bombing campaign or 'war' launched by Russell against Britain in 1939.

Called to the Bar in 1937 and to the Inner Bar in 1943, MacBride won a national reputation during the 1940s for his defence of republicans charged under the Treason Act,* Offences Against the State Act* and the Emergency Powers Act.* In 1946 he founded Clann na Poblachta* which attracted republicans and others who were discontented with Fianna Fail government. MacBride led his party into coalition with Fine Gael and others to form the first Inter-Party Government* in which he was Minister for External Affairs (1948—51). He drew up the White Paper which formed the basis for the Long-Term Recovery Programme* (1949). When the Mother and Child Scheme* introduced by the Minister for Health, Dr Noel Browne,* (also a member of Clann na Poblachta) proved unacceptable to the bishops, the government and the Irish Medical Association, MacBride demanded his resignation. The government fell shortly afterwards. MacBride did not participate in the second Inter-Party Government but agreed not to oppose it. However, when a new IRA campaign started in 1956, and prompted harsh government measures, he proposed a motion of 'No Confidence' which, with Fianna Fail support, brought down the government (January 1957).

He was deeply involved with human rights organisations and was secretary-general of the International Commission of Jurists (1963—70). A founder-member of Amnesty International of which he was chairman, he was also a member of the Council of Minorities' Rights Group, Irish Representative to the Council of Europe Assembly, and United Nations Commissioner to Namibia. He was awarded the Nobel Peace Prize in 1976 and won the Lenin Peace Prize one year later. His works include *Civil Liberty* (1948) and *Our People—Our Money* (1951).

MacCABE, ALEXANDER (ALASDAIR MacCABA) (1886—1972). Politician (Sinn Fein), teacher and businessman; b. Sligo; ed. Summerhill College and St Patrick's Training College. He worked as a national teacher and became principal of Drumnagranchy National School (1907). After joining the Irish Republican Brotherhood* in 1913 he represented Connaught in the Supreme Council* in 1915—16. His republicanism led to his dismissal from his teaching post in 1915. He was responsible during the Easter Rising of 1916* for creating diversions in Counties Longford, Cavan and Sligo. Following the collapse of the rising he went on the run, and assisted George Noble, Count Plunkett,* during the Roscommon by-election (1917), after which he was imprisoned. He was returned as Sinn Fein TD for Sligo-Mayo in December 1918. MacCabe was close to Michael Collins* during the War of Independence,* and was imprisoned at the Curragh from July 1920 to July 1921. He supported the Treaty* and became a member of Cumann na nGaedheal.* He resigned during the Army Mutiny* (1924), retired from politics shortly afterwards and resumed his teaching career. Later he was co-founder of the Educational Building Society (1935) of which he became Secretary and Managing Director.

McCABE, EDWARD, CARDINAL (1816—85). Archbishop of Dublin and Primate of Ireland (R.C.), 1878—85; b. Dublin; ed. Maynooth where he was ordained in 1838. Early in his career he was patronised by Archbishops Daniel Murray* and Paul Cullen.* As parish priest of St Nicholas' Without (1853), he built several churches and schools and was Vicar-General of the Dublin archdiocese. His health broke in 1865 and he was transferred to Kingstown (Dun Laoghaire) where he built a new church and hospital. He became Archbishop Cullen's assistant in 1877 and succeeded him a year later. He became a cardinal in 1882. He issued a circular on the question of university education for Catholics in 1879. Opposed to the Land League,* he denounced agrarian unrest (see Agrarian Crime) and condemned the 'No Rent Manifesto'.* His life was threatened by extremists. He was a member of the Mansion House Committee for the Relief of Poverty. He was succeeded by William Walsh.*

McCAFFERTY, CAPTAIN JOHN (b. 1838). Fenian; b. Sandusky, Ohio of Irish parentage. He joined the Confederate Army during the American Civil War (1861–65) and became a skilled guerrilla tactician. As an officer of 'Morgan's Guerrillas' he was involved in many daring exploits including the capture of an ammunition dump behind enemy lines and its successful transportation down the Mississippi, raked by fire from Federal batteries. While serving in the army, McCafferty became converted to Fenianism and at the conclusion of hostilities he travelled to Ireland to assist with preparations for the proposed rising. He was introduced by John Devoy* to leading Dublin Fenians on 17 January 1866 as their probable leader in the forthcoming rising. When the anticipated rising failed to materialise, McCafferty with John Flood, organised the raid on Chester Castle (11 March 1867), which was betrayed by John J. Corydon. McCafferty was arrested in Dublin Bay and was sentenced to death on 1 May but the sentence was later commuted to life imprisonment. Released and deported in 1871, he

returned to Ireland where he was involved in the Mayo by-election of 1874 when he challenged the Fenian candidate John O'Connor Power* to a duel. McCafferty was a prominent member of the Invincibles* during the period of the Phoenix Park Murders,* following which he fled the country and lived the remainder of his life in relative obscurity.

MacCAFFREY, REV. JAMES (1875–1935). Clergyman (R.C.) and historian; b. Fivemiletown, Co. Tyrone; ed. Maynooth where he was ordained in 1899 and spent two years at the Dunboyne Establishment. After studies in Paris and Freiburg he was awarded a doctorate in 1906 and became Professor of Ecclesiastical History at Maynooth. His publications included *A History of the Catholic Church in the Nineteenth Century* (1909), *School History of the Catholic Church* (1912), and *History of the Catholic Church from the Renaissance to the French Revolution* (1915). He edited *The Black Book of Limerick* (1907), *Archivum Hibernicum* and the *Irish Theological Quarterly*.

McCALL, JOHN (1822–1902). Author; b. Clonmore, Co. Carlow; ed. locally. He moved to Dublin in 1839 and worked in grocery and spirit shops before establishing his own business in 1856. He lived for the remainder of his life in Patrick Street in the Dublin Liberties. A prolific contributor of stories and humorous pieces to leading periodicals, including *Science and Literature*, *Argosy*, *The Irish National Guard*, *The Catholic Advocate* and *The People's Journal*, he published *Antiquities and History of Cluain Norp Medhoe in the County of Carlow* (1862) and the lives of poets in *The Irish Emerald* (1892–93). He also published a number of almanacs: *Lady's and Farmer's Almanack* (1861–76), *Old Moore's Almanack* (1875–1902), *Nugent's Moor's Almanack* (1886–98) and a *History of Almanacks* (1897). His son, P. J. McCall (1861–1919) was the author

of the ballad 'Boolavogue', a founder-
member of the Irish National Literary
Society* and a popular lecturer on
old Dublin.

MacCANN, MICHAEL JOSEPH
(1824–1883). Journalist and scholar;
b. Galway; ed. locally. He was appointed to a professorship at St
Jarlath's College, Tuam, on the recommendation of Archbishop John
MacHale.* His best known work,
'O'Donnell Abu', appeared in *The
Nation* on 23 January 1843 under
the title 'The Clanconnell War Song',
and was subsequently translated into
several languages. He edited two short-
lived periodicals, *The Harp* (1857)
and *The Irish Harp* (1863).

McCARTAN, DR PATRICK (1878–
1966). Republican; b. Carrickmore,
Co. Tyrone; ed. Monaghan, St
Patrick's College, Armagh and St
Malachy's, Belfast. After moving to
the USA (1905) he worked as a barman in Philadelphia, joined Clan na
Gael* and became a close associate
of Joseph McGarrity.* He returned
home in 1905, qualified as a doctor
and practised in Co. Tyrone. He maintained a close association with the
Irish Republican Brotherhood,* in
particular with the younger men
such as Sean MacDiarmada,* Bulmer
Hobson* and Denis McCullough,*
and with Thomas J. Clarke* who
returned to Ireland in 1907. Mc-
Cartan kept McGarrity closely informed on Irish developments. He
edited *Irish Freedom* for a short
time in 1910. He was elected MP
for the Tullamore Division of King's
County (Offaly) in 1918 and represented Laois-Offaly in the first Dail
Eireann.* As representative of the
Irish Republic he travelled to the
USA but was refused an audience
with President Wilson. He failed
to resolve the differences between
Eamon de Valera,* Judge Daniel
Cohalan* and John Devoy.* On a
visit to Russia in December 1920
he secured a Treaty of Recognition
between the Irish Republic and the
USSR, but it was never signed. He

brought part of the Russian Crown
Jewels* to America as collateral for
a 25,000 dollar loan advanced by
de Valera to communist representatives in Washington.
During the Treaty* debate he said,
'I am a republican and will not en-
dorse, but I will not vote for chaos.
Then I will not vote against it'. In
fact, he voted for approval and then
returned to his medical practice. He
ran as an Independent Republican in
the Presidential election of 1945 and
came third to Sean MacEoin* and
the victor, Sean T. O'Kelly.* He was
a member of the Senate (1948–51).
His *With de Valera in America* was
published in 1935.

McCARTHY, DENIS FLORENCE
(1817–82). Poet and scholar; b. Dublin; ed. locally and Maynooth but he
turned from clerical studies to the
law. He did not practise after his call
to the Bar, and was appointed to the
Chair of English Literature at the
Catholic University.* Apart from contributions to *The Nation* and the
Dublin University Magazine, his publications included translations from
the Spanish of fifteen Calderon plays
(for which he was awarded a medal
by the Royal Academy of Spain),
Ballads, Poems and Lyrics (1850),
*Ode on the Death of the Earl of
Belfast* (1856), *Under Glimpses and
Other Poems* (1857), *Bell-Founder
and Other Poems* (1857), *Shelley's
Early Life* (1872) and *The Centenary
of Moore, an Ode* (privately printed,
1880). He edited *The Book of Irish
Ballads* (1846) and *The Poets and
Dramatists of Ireland* (1846). His
Collected Poems appeared in 1882,
although with many notable omis-
sions.

McCARTHY, JUSTIN (1830–1912).
Politician (Irish Parliamentary Party)
and author; b. Cork; ed. locally. While
working for *The Cork Examiner*
(1848–52) he covered the trials
of Young Ireland leaders, William
Smith O'Brien* and Thomas Francis
Meagher,* whose cause he espoused.
After moving to England he worked

on *The Northern Daily News* in Liverpool (1854–60) and *The Morning Star* (1860–64) in London, of which he was editor (1864–68). He was leader writer of *The Daily News* from 1870. McCarthy taught himself to read German, Italian, French and Spanish. At the invitation of Charles Stewart Parnell* he successfully contested the Longford seat in 1880, after which he became vice-chairman of the party and one of Parnell's chief lieutenants. He was MP for Derry City (1886–92) and North Longford (1892–1900).

After the revelations in the divorce court of Parnell's relationship with Mrs Katharine O'Shea,* McCarthy was informed by W. E. Gladstone* that Parnell was no longer acceptable to the Liberal Party as leader of the Irish party. He proved unable to convince Parnell of this and when Gladstone's publication of his position precipitated a split in the Irish Parliamentary Party, McCarthy became a leader of the anti-Parnellites (1–6 November 1890). Those who followed his withdrawal from Committee Room 15 included his son, Justin Huntly McCarthy.*

McCarthy was chairman of the anti-Parnellite constituency organisation, the Irish National Federation.* His followers won 72 seats in the general election of 1892 when he lost Derry but regained Longford. Ill-health and failing eyesight led to his resignation from the chairmanship of the party in 1896 and he was succeeded by John Dillon.* McCarthy went blind shortly afterwards and the remainder of his works were dictated. He was granted a civil list pension of £300 per annum. Apart from fictional works (*Dear Lady Disdain*, 1875, *Miss Misanthrope*, 1879, and *Mononia*, 1901), and lives of the four Georges and William IV, Sir Robert Peel, and Pope Leo XIII, he published *A History of Our Own Times* (1877–1905), *The Story of Mr Gladstone* (1898), *Modern England* (1898), *Reminiscences* (1899), *The Reign of Queen Anne* (1902), *The Story of an Irishman* (1904),

Irish Recollections (1911), and *Our Book of Memories* (with Mrs Campbell Praed, 1912).

McCARTHY, JUSTIN HUNTLY (1861–1936). Politician (Irish Parliamentary Party) and author; b. London, son of Justin McCarthy; ed. University College School and University College, London. Widely travelled, he visited Europe, Egypt, the Holy Land and the USA. As a member of the Irish party (1884–92) he supported Charles Stewart Parnell* until December 1890 when he followed his father in breaking with Parnell's leadership over the O'Shea divorce case. A prolific author, his works included verse: *Serapion* (1883); fiction: *The Flower of France* (1906), *The Fair Irish Maid* (1911), *The Golden Shoe* (1921), and *Truth and the Other Thing* (1929); translations of the *Rubaiyat* of Omar Khayyam and *The Thousand and One Days*; plays: *The Candidate, The Wife of Socrates, If I were King, The O'Flynn, Stand and Deliver;* history: *Outline of Irish History* (1883), *England Under Gladstone* (1884), *Ireland Under the Union* (1887), *The Case for Home Rule* (1887), and *A Short History of the United States* (1898).

McCLEERY, SIR WILLIAM VICTOR (1887–1957). Orangeman and politician (Ulster Unionist); ed. privately. A leading businessman in Northern Ireland, he was president of the North Antrim Unionist Association (1922–45). Prominent in the Orange Order,* he was a member of the Grand Orange Lodge of Ireland, Grand Master of Antrim Orange Lodges, member of the Imperial Black Chapter of the British Commonwealth, Grand Master of the Grand Orange Lodge of Northern Ireland (1954) and Grand Master of the Imperial Grand Orange Council of the World (1955). Returned as MP for North Antrim in 1945, he was Minister for Labour and National Insurance (1949) and Minister for Commerce (1949–53).

McCORMACK, JOHN, COUNT (1884–1945). Tenor; b. Athlone; ed. locally by the Marist brothers and at Summerhill College, Sligo (to 1902). As a member of the Dublin Palestrina choir, he studied under its director, Vincent O'Brien, and continued his tuition under Vincenzo Sabatini in Milan. Entered by friends as a competitor in the Feis Ceol of 1903 he chose 'Tell Fair Irene', from Handel's *Atalanta*, and 'The Snowy Breasted Pearl'. When he had finished, the audience burst into spontaneous applause (contravening a Feis Rule). In awarding him the Gold Medal, Maestro Luigi Denza commented, 'I don't have to tell you who the winner is – as you yourselves have chosen him'. McCormack represented Ireland at the St Louis Fair (1904) and received £50 for recording ten cylinders for the Edison Bell Company in the same year. His operatic debut was in Mascagni's *L'Amico Fritz* at the Teatro Chiabrera, Savona (December 1905), appearing under the name 'Giovanni Foli'. In July 1906, he married singer Lily Foley. He made his Covent Garden debut on 15 October 1907 in *Cavalleria Rusticana* when he was the youngest tenor to appear there up to that time. McCormack's American debut at Manhattan Opera House (10 November 1909) was against the wishes of its then manager, Oscar Hammerstein, who commented, 'An Irish tenor in opera? I don't think so!' However, as the singer left the stage, having played the role of Alfredo in *La Traviata*, Hammerstein clapped him on the back and said 'You'll do, Mike'. McCormack retired from the operatic scene in 1923, his last appearance being at Monte Carlo where he played Gritzko in Mussorgsky's *La Foire de Sororchintzi* on 17 March.

Although he supported Irish nationalist causes, he became an American citizen in 1917. Pope Benedict XV created him a Papal Chamberlain (Count) and a Commander of the Order of St Gregory in 1928. His films included *Song O' My Heart* (1930) for which he was paid 500,000 dollars and *Wings of the Morning* (1937). He came out of retirement in 1938 to tour on behalf of the Red Cross and other charitable organisations. However, in early 1945, it was discovered he was suffering from the emphysema which led to his death on 16 September 1945. A *Discography* was published by L.F.X. McDermott Roe in 1956.

McCORMICK, F. J. (1891–1947). Stage-name of actor Peter C. Judge; b. Skerries, Co. Dublin; ed. locally. After working for a time as a GPO clerk in London, he entered the Irish Civil Service and adopted his stage-name. His first film role was in *Fun at Finglas Fair* (1915). He entered the Acting School of the Abbey Theatre* in 1921 at the same time as Eileen Crowe (1891–1978) to whom he was married in 1925. They toured America and Canada with the Abbey and were widely acclaimed for their performances in *Juno and the Paycock* as 'Joxer' Daly and Bessie Burgess. He had an unusually wide range, playing in Yeats' version of Sophocles' *Oedipus the King, Don Quixote* (to the Sancho Panza of his close friend, Barry Fitzgerald), *King Lear, Caesar and Cleopatra, The Plough and the Stars* (Jack Clitheroe) and *The Well of the Saints* (the Saint). McCormick rejected Hollywood offers but appeared in the John Ford film version of *The Plough and the Stars* (1936) and won acclaim for his appearances in *Hungry Hill* (1946) and *Odd Man Out* (1947) in which he created the part of 'Shell'.

McCULLOUGH, DENIS (1883–1968). Republican; b. Belfast, the son of a Fenian; ed. CBS. A piano-tuner by trade, he established his own business in Belfast in 1909. He later moved it to Dublin (1919) where he traded under the name McCulloughs Limited, which became McCullough Pigott Limited in 1968. After joining the Irish Republican Brotherhood* in 1901, he became disillusioned

329

with its lack of discipline and its deep-seated traditionalism. He began recruiting younger men, including Bulmer Hobson* with whom he founded the Dungannon Clubs.* Co-opted to the Supreme Council* (1906), he became Ulster representative and director of the IRB in Ulster. He played a leading role, along with Hobson, Sean MacDiarmada* and Thomas J. Clarke,* in moving the IRB along more militant lines after the foundation of the Irish Volunteers,* and was imprisoned from August to November 1915. As President of the Supreme Council he supported the Easter Rising of 1916* but was not informed of the final details. He was delegated to bring 132 Volunteers from Belfast to Coalisland, Co. Tyrone, where he was to link up with Dr Patrick McCartan* and travel south to Fermanagh to join Liam Mellows* in Connaught. Due to the general confusion surrounding the rising he returned with his men to Belfast on Sunday evening, and so had no direct involvement with it. He was arrested on the following Friday. His account of events appeared in *The Capuchin Annual* (1966) under the title '1916: The events in Belfast'.

MacCURTAIN, TOMÁS (1884–1920). Politician (Sinn Fein); first republican Lord Mayor of Cork (30 January 1920); b. Ballyknockane, Co. Cork, the youngest of a family of twelve; ed. Burnfoot National School. He moved to Cork in 1897 and there completed his education at the North Monastry CBS. A member of the Gaelic League,* he became secretary of the Blackpool Branch in 1902. He left his employment as a clerk to the City of Cork Steam Packet Co. to become a Gaelic League teacher in Limerick, Tipperary and East Cork, but returned to Cork in 1907 to work at a local mill. MacCurtain joined Sinn Fein in 1907 and was on the Cork Executive Committee (1909–11). He was inducted into the Irish Republican Brotherhood* in 1907. When Na Fianna Eireann* was established in Cork, he acted as treasurer and Irish teacher (1911–14). With Terence MacSwiney* he joined the Irish Volunteers* on their formation in Cork (14 December 1913) and was secretary and later Brigade Commandant of the City Battalion. When John Redmond* called for Volunteer support for the British war effort, MacCurtain was one of his strongest critics and presided at a public meeting in Cork on 22 January 1916, at which Fr Michael O'Flanagan* was principal speaker, to protest against the application of economic conscription by local employers (*see* Conscription and Ireland).

The entire Volunteer movement in Cork had been mobilised in preparation for the Easter Rising of 1916* and orders issued to meet at Crookstown. On learning of Mac-Neill's countermanding order, MacCurtain decided to avoid further confusion and allowed units to proceed as arranged to Crookstown where exercises took place. Remaining in the area until the following night, he was astonished to learn that a rising had in fact taken place on Easter Monday. Awaiting a confirmatory despatch from General Headquarters in Dublin, he made the decision that Cork Volunteers would act only in a defensive capacity. During the week of fighting in Dublin, Bishop Daniel Cohalan* and the Lord Mayor of Cork, T. C. Butterfield, arranged a compromise with Capt Dickie on the British side. The agreement stipulated that no Volunteer arrests would be made in Cork provided the local volunteers surrendered their arms. Guarantees made on the British side were not honoured and MacCurtain and ten other volunteers were arrested on 2 May. This was the first of his many arrests and he served varying terms at Richmond Barracks, Dublin, Frongoch, Reading and Ledbury.

During the War of Independence,* MacCurtain was active in the organisation of an efficient despatch system between county and city brigades, drilling, discipline and the capture of arms. He made several prolonged tours of inspection throughout the county. He was murdered at his home at 1.12 a.m. on the morning of Saturday, 20 March, by members of the Royal Irish Constabulary* in semi-disguise. On Saturday 17 April 1920, a coroner's court recorded that '. . . the murder was organised and carried out by the Royal Irish Constabulary . . .' District-Inspector Swanzy, one of the police officers charged with the murder by the coroner's court, was shot dead in Lisburn, Co. Antrim, on 22 August 1920.

MacDERMOT, FRANK (1886– 1975). Politician (National Centre and Fine Gael) and author; b. Coolavin; ed. Downside and Oxford; qualified as a barrister. After serving in the British Army during World War I, he worked in a merchant bank in New York. He returned to Ireland in the late 1920s and was returned as Independent TD for Co. Roscommon in 1932. Later in that year, with James Dillon,* he founded the National Centre Party,* which secured 11 seats in the general election of January 1933. Its opposition to the Fianna Fail government brought the party close to Cumann na nGaedheal* and the Blueshirts* and he was instrumental in bringing about a merger of the parties into Fine Gael* (September 1933), of which he became vice-president. When the new party supported Mussolini's invasion of Abyssinia, he resigned in 1936. He became a member of the Senate upon nomination by Eamon de Valera* in 1937 and resigned in 1942 when he became US correspondent for *The Sunday Times*. He was later Paris correspondent for the same paper. His historical study, *Theobald Wolfe Tone*, appeared in 1939.

MacDERMOTT, JAMES ('RED JIM'). Fenian informer; b. Dublin, illegitimate child of a Dublin lawyer whom he subsequently blackmailed. After fighting in the Irish Papal Brigade and receiving a medal from Pope Pius IX (1860), he returned to Ireland and joined the Irish Republican Brotherhood;* at the same time entering the pay of the British secret service. He moved to New York where he became secretary to John O'Mahony* who ignored warnings about him from James Stephens.* He aided the split within the American Fenians, 1865– 66. During the 1880s he was a close associate of many of the Dynamiters,* some of whom he betrayed. After his arrest (while drunk) in Dublin in 1884 documents in his possession were seen by Michael Davitt* who denounced him. MacDermott was released on the orders of the Under-Secretary with instructions to associate Parnell with the dynamiting campaign. Publication in the House of Commons of his activities forced MacDermott's rapid return to America, where he faded into obscurity.

McDERMOTT, MARTIN (1823– 1905). Author; b. Co. Leitrim; trained as an architect. A member of Young Ireland,* he contributed to *The Nation* and *The Irish Felon*. A founder-member of the Southwark Literary Club* and of the Irish Literary Society,* he published *Songs and Ballads of Young Ireland* (1896). His work included 'The Cúilin', and an edition of *The New Spirit of the Nation* and of Thomas Moore's *Life of Lord Edward Fitzgerald*, both in the *New Irish Library* series published by Sir Charles Gavan Duffy.*

MacDIARMADA, SEÁN (1884– 1916). Republican; b. Co. Leitrim. He had little formal education and emigrated to Scotland as a youth, working in Glasgow at a variety of jobs. Upon his return to Ireland he worked as a barman in Belfast where he was for a time involved in the Ancient Order of Hibernians.* He met Bulmer Hobson* and Denis McCullough* who employed him as an organiser for the Dungannon Clubs* and inducted him into the Irish Republican Brotherhood* in 1906. He organised the Sinn Fein campaign for C. J. Dolan in the North

Leitrim by-election (1908) and moved to Dublin when the Dungannon Clubs were absorbed into Sinn Fein around the same time. At McCullough's insistance, he was appointed full-time organiser for the IRB (1908) and during the next few years, he travelled around the country building up the organisation. MacDiarmada was co-founder of *Irish Freedom* which he edited for a short time. An attack of polio in 1912 left him crippled but he continued to work for the IRB. When the Irish Volunteers* were founded in November 1913, he saw its potential as an army for the IRB. In July 1914 he was estranged from Hobson as a result of Hobson's agreement to the take-over of the Volunteers by John Redmond.* MacDiarmada was imprisoned during 1915 under the Defence of the Realm Act* and after his release he was co-opted onto the secret Military Council* at Clarke's suggestion. He was co-author with Joseph Plunkett* of the 'Castle Document'* which was intended to produce a favourable climate for the rising within the Volunteer movement. When the plans were discovered by Hobson and Eoin MacNeill* on Holy Thursday, MacDiarmada persuaded MacNeill that the arrival of the *Aud** would mean the success of the rising. However, when the news of the scuttling of the *Aud* and of the capture of Sir Roger Casement* reached MacNeill, he called off the rising and MacDiarmada and his colleagues changed the date to Easter Monday. He was a member of the Provisional Government of the Irish Republic which was declared on Easter Monday and remained with his colleagues within the GPO until the building was burned. He was executed on 12 May 1916.

MacDONAGH, DONAGH (1912– 68). Author; b. Dublin, son of Thomas MacDonagh;* ed. Belvedere College and UCD. After a call to the Bar in 1935, he practised on the Western Circuit until his appointment as a district justice. He was co-editor with Lennox Robinson* of *The Oxford Book of Irish Verse* (1956). A student of folklore, and a radio broadcaster, his hobby was collecting Dublin slang. His works included numerous short stories, a volume of poetry, *Veterans* (1941) and the play, *Happy as Larry* (1946).

MacDONAGH, JOSEPH (1883– 1922). Republican; b. Cloughjordan, Co. Tipperary, younger brother of Thomas MacDonagh;* ed. National School and Rockwell College. He entered the revenue department of the civil service. After the Easter Rising of 1916* and his brother's execution, he became active in the re-organised Sinn Fein* and was for a short time headmaster of St Enda's College.* He represented North Tipperary in Dail Eireann (1918–22) and was an alderman of Dublin Corporation (1920–22). MacDonagh was imprisoned three times during 1919–20. With W. T. Cosgrave* he established an insurance brokerage, Cosgrave and MacDonagh, which, after he resigned, became Cosgrave and Boland. He was Director of the Belfast Boycott* in 1921. Opposed to the Treaty,* he was arrested at the commencement of the Civil War* and died shortly after his release in November 1922.

MacDONAGH, THOMAS (1878– 1916). Republican; b. Cloughjordan, Co. Tipperary; ed. Rockwell College. He taught in St Kieran's College, Kilkenny (1901–03) when he joined the Gaelic League.* After moving to St Colman's College, Fermoy, Co. Cork, where he taught from 1903 to 1908, he became a founder-member of the Association of Secondary Teachers, Ireland (ASTI). He moved to Dublin in 1908 where he formed a close friendship with Patrick Pearse* and taught at St Enda's College* while reading for his B.A. (1910) and M.A. (1911) after which he became a lecturer in the English Department, UCD. He was co-editor with Joseph Mary Plunkett* of *The Irish Review* and co-founder with Plunkett and Edward Martyn* of the Irish Theatre, which produced his play *Pagans* in 1915.

MacDonagh was a founder-member of the Irish Volunteers* (November 1913) for whom he was Director of Training and organiser of the march to Howth in July 1914 for the collection of guns off the *Asgard (see* Howth Gun-running). A year later he organised the parade for the funeral of Jeremiah O'Donovan Rossa.* He joined the Irish Republican Brotherhood* in September 1915 and was co-opted in April 1916 to the secret Military Council* which planned the Easter Rising of 1916.* For his role as O/C, 2nd Battalion, at Jacob's Factory during the rising, he was executed on 3 May.

His works included *Through the Ivory Gate* (poems, 1902), *April and May* (poems, 1903), *The Golden Joy* (poems, 1906), *When Dawn is Come* (a play produced at the Abbey Theatre, 1908), *Songs of Myself* (poems, 1910), *Metempsychosis: or a Mad World* (play, 1912), and *Lyrical Poems* (1913). His dissertation for a Ph.D., *Literature in Ireland*, appeared after his death in 1916.

MacDONALD, DR WALTER (1854–1920). Clergyman (R.C.) and author; b. Emil, Mooncoin, Co. Kilkenny; ed. St Kieran's College, Kilkenny and Maynooth where he was ordained in 1876. After teaching in St Kieran's he returned to Maynooth in 1881 as Professor of Dogmatic Theology and, for a time, Professor of Canon Law. He was head of the Dunboyne Establishment. His first major publication, *Motion, Its Origin and Conservation*, in which he examined the relationship between theology and science, was condemned for being in conflict with the doctrine of free will and placed on the *Index Librorum*; subsequent theological works were refused an imprimatur. During his career at Maynooth he was involved in a number of controversies. He pressed for the appointment of professors by open competition and for security of tenure. Dr MacDonald also supported Charles Stewart Parnell* after the split in the Irish Parliamentary Party and Parnell's condemnation by the hierarchy. He championed the cause of Fr Michael O'Hickey* who had been dismissed by the bishops and supported James Larkin* and the Irish Transport and General Workers' Union.* His circle of friends included Sean O'Casey.* He again came into conflict with the bishops when he pressed for reforms in the managerial system in National Education,* and for supporting the right of Catholics to enter Trinity College, Dublin.

His works included *Ethical Questions of Peace and War* which caused controversy upon publication in 1919, *Some Ethical Aspects of the Social Question* (1920) and *A History of the Parish of Mooncoin* (1960). His *Reminiscences of a Maynooth Professor* was published in 1925, edited by Denis Rolleston Gwynn.*

MacDONNELL, SIR ANTONY PATRICK (1844–1925). Civil Servant; Under Secretary (1902–08); b. Shragh, Co. Mayo; ed. Summerhill College, Sligo, Athlone and Queen's College, Galway where he read French and German and won the Peel Gold Medal in 1864. After entering the Indian Civil Service in 1864 he became an expert on the organisation of famine relief about which he wrote *Food-Grain Supply and Famine Relief in Bihar and Bengal* (1876). He was known popularly within the service as 'The Bengal Tiger'. After retiring, due to ill health, in 1881, he returned to the service eight years later and became Lieutenant-Governor of the United Province of Agra and Cudh in 1893, where he was again responsible for famine relief operations in 1896. He accepted the Irish post under persuasion from George Wyndham,* the Chief Secretary. MacDonnell insisted that law and order would be maintained in Ireland, that he would be given more power than the Under-Secretary normally had, and that any solution to the land question should include voluntary sale. He also demanded educational and economic reforms. He was sympathetic to the Liberal Party and his brother was a member of the Irish Parliamentary Party.* Thus to the Unionists he appeared to be a home ruler and to the home rulers he appeared a renegade. In his efforts to expedite a solution to the land question he supported the Land Conference* which influenced Wyndham's Land Act (see Land Acts). He was criticised by the Unionists for his support of the new Act. Following Wyndham's departure, hastened by the controversy over Devolution,* MacDonnell served under Walter Long,* James Bryce* and Augustine Birrell.* He played a prominent role in drafting the ill-fated Irish Council Bill* which proposed devolution and was denounced from all sides. When he failed to secure support for suppressing disorder he resigned in 1908. He later served as chairman of the Royal Commission on the Civil Service (1912—14) and attended the Irish Convention (1917— 18). He urged Lord French* in October 1918 to drop the idea of introducing Conscription (see Conscription and Ireland). MacDonnell refused to accept a seat in the Senate of the Free State (December 1922).

MacDONNELL, ENEAS (1783—1858). Journalist; b. Westport, Co. Mayo; ed. Tuam and Maynooth. He was called to the Bar but chose a journalistic career, becoming editor of the *Dublin Chronicle* in 1815. One year later he was prosecuted for libel for which he was sentenced to six months' imprisonment. His newspaper strongly opposed the government and supported the Catholic Association* for which he later made London agent. He was a prolific pamphleteer for the Association until he quarrelled with Daniel O'Connell* and became a government supporter.

McDYER, CANON JAMES DANIEL (1911—). Clergyman (R.C.) and founder of Glencolumbkille Co-Operative Society (1962); b.

Kilraine, Glenties, Co. Donegal; ed. local National School, St Eunan's College, Letterkenny and St Patrick's Maynooth. Ordained (1937) Fr McDyer was curate at Wandsworth, London, when he was appointed by Bishop Amigo of Southwark as chief fund-raiser to help rebuild the bombed-out church of St Mary Cray, Kent, for which he raised several thousand pounds. Fr McDyer ministered at Brighton before being appointed curate at Tory Island off the Donegal coast where he remained for four and a half years. Appointed P.P., Glencolumbkille (6 March 1961) he was appalled at the high emigration level and the inexorable decline of the community. Amid local scepticism and apathy he founded Glencolumbkille Co-Op which fostered and encouraged local hand knitters. His Errigal Co-Op (1962), a vegetable growing and processing project, grew from an initial work force of thirty to one hundred and fifty-three. Vegetable processing was abandoned in favour of fish-processing in 1973. Aided by Comhluct Siuicre Eireann* and Gaeltarra Eireann and under Fr McDyer's chairmanship, the new co-op achieved early profitability and in 1975 became Earagail Éisc Teo. with a permanent staff of twenty-five peaking to a seasonal ninety. Profit in 1978/79 was some £750,000 from a 95 per cent export market.

Other successful ventures launched by Fr McDyer are: a machine knit co-op (1967), holiday village of some thirty cottages (1970) and a sportswear factory (1979). The Co-Op also owns the Glenbay Hotel and the Glencolumbkille craft shop in Anne St, Dublin.

Fr McDyer's pet project is the Glencolumbkille Folk Village which spans three centuries of Donegal life and includes among its novel features a century-old schoolhouse and a shebeen complete with still (nonproductive!). Appointed Canon at neighbouring Carrick in 1974 he takes a close interest in local youth and sponsors a Gaelic cabaret during summer months when children perform

Irish songs and dances for visitors to Glencolumbkille.

McELLIGOTT, THOMAS J. ('PRO PATRIA') (1888–1961). Policeman and republican; b. Duagh, Co. Kerry; ed. National School. He joined the Royal Irish Constabulary* in 1907 and rose to the rank of sergeant. Realising, as did Jeremiah Mee,* the pressures which nationalistically-minded policemen would undergo during the coming years, he supported republican causes. He established the Irish Branch of the British National Union of Police and Prison Officers of which he became chairman in April 1918. His public support for Sinn Fein,* the anti-conscription campaign (*see* Conscription and Ireland), and labour, using the pen-name 'Pro Patria', forced his resignation from the RIC in May 1919. He was by now a close friend of Thomas Johnson.*

His experience of the RIC made him valuable to the republicans and he provided Michael Collins* with information for the Irish Republican Army.* He became an inspector with the White Cross* and established the 'Resigned and Dismissed Members of the RIC and DMP (1916–21)'. Although he opposed the Treaty* he was nominated by Collins and Arthur Griffith* to advise on the new police force for the Free State, the Civic Guards (*see* Garda Siochana). He recommended that the new force should be unarmed. He was imprisoned during the Civil War* and went on hunger-strike for thirty-five days.

He supported Fianna Fail* and negotiated with Eamon de Valera* on behalf of the 'Resigned and Dismissed Members of the RIC and DMP'. He was critical of the financial agreement made between de Valera and the British government in 1938, ending the Economic War.* During the 1940s he became interested in socialist economic theory and published pamphlets, including *National Monetary Policy* and *National Agricultural Policy* (1943). Disillusioned with Fianna Fail, he supported Clann na Poblachta* and worked for the welfare of republican prisoners during the 1950s.

MacENTEE, SEÁN (1889–). Politician (Sinn Fein and Fianna Fail); b. Belfast; ed. St Malachy's College and the Belfast Municipal Institute of Technology where he qualified as an engineer. A member of the Irish Volunteers,* he fought in the Easter Rising of 1916* for which he was sentenced to death. When his sentence was commuted to life imprisonment, he served terms in Dartmoor, Lewes and Portland prisons until released under general amnesty (17 June 1917). He was returned as Sinn Fein MP for South Monaghan in December 1918 while again imprisoned. Upon release, he took his seat in Dail Eireann* where he opposed the Treaty.* After supporting the republicans in the Civil War,* he became National Treasurer of Sinn Fein in 1924. He followed Eamon de Valera* in the break with Sinn Fein and was a founder-member of Fianna Fail, of which he was joint-treasurer until 1932, national executive member from 1926 and national vice-president from 1955 until 1965.

He was a member of all Fianna Fail governments until he retired to the backbenches in 1965: Minister for Finance (March 1932–September 1939), Industry and Commerce (September 1939–August 1941), Local Government and Health (August 1941–February 1948), Finance (June 1951–54), and Health (March 1957–April 1965). He was a member of the Council of State* from 1948 and Tanaiste* from June 1959 to April 1965. After retiring from active politics in 1969 he resumed his profession of consulting engineer. He published *Poems* in 1918 and *Episode at Easter* in 1966.

MacEOIN, GENERAL SEÁN (1894–1973). Soldier and politician (Cumann na nGaedheal and Fine Gael); b. Bunlahy, Co. Longford where, following his education at Kilshrule, he became a blacksmith. After joining the Irish Volunteers* he became a company commander in 1914 and later battalion commander of the 1st Battalion, Longford Volunteers. As a commandant in the Irish Republican Army* he played a leading role in the War of Independence* and reached the rank of general. He led the IRA in one of the most celebrated ambushes of the war, when, on 3 November 1920, anticipating an attack by the Black and Tans* on Ballinalee, he prepared for them and routed them after an all-night battle, earning the nickname 'The Blacksmith of Ballinalee'. In March 1921, after he had defeated Auxiliaries* on 2 February, he was captured and sentenced to death. A rescue attempt, planned by Michael Collins* and executed by Emmet Dalton,* failed. Eamon de Valera* then made his release one of the conditions for a truce. Acting under instructions from Collins, MacEoin nominated Eamon de Valera for the position of 'President of the Irish Republic' (August 1921). He followed Collins in accepting the Treaty,* saying, 'As long as the armed forces of Britain are gone and the armed forces of Ireland remain we can develop our own nation in our own way'. He took possession of Longford Barracks from the British garrison (January 1922) and during the Civil War* was GOC, Western Command of the Free State National Army, of which he was Chief of Staff (1923). General MacEoin was TD for Sligo and Longford (1929–65). He served in the two Inter-Party Governments,* as Minister for Justice (February 1948–March 1951) and Defence (March–June 1951; 1954–57). He was an unsuccessful candidate in two presidential elections, losing to Sean T. O'Kelly* in 1945 and to Eamon de Valera in 1959. He retired from politics in 1965.

MacFADDEN, REV. CANON JAMES (1842–1917). Clergyman (R.C.) and land agitator; b. Carrigart, Co. Donegal; ed. locally and Maynooth College. As parish priest in Gweedore (from 1875) he was prominent in the Land

League,* for which he wrote several pamphlets on the land question. During the Plan of Campaign* he was imprisoned (1888) for inciting parishioners to withhold their rents. While he was being arrested at Derrybeg chapel for a repetition of the offence, a fracas developed between the tenants and the Royal Irish Constabulary* in which Inspector Martin was killed (3 February 1889). The canon and twelve others were charged with manslaughter. He was bound to the peace for two years while the others received sentences of up to thirty years imprisonment. He played little part in the national agitation after that and finished his clerical career as parish priest of Inishkeel, Glenties (1901–17). The canon who was locally known as 'An Sagart Mor' ('The Big Priest') for the uncompromising manner in which he managed his parish and parishioners, visited the USA twice (1898–99; 1900–02) to collect money to build Letterkenny cathedral.

McGARRITY, JOSEPH (1874–1940). Republican; b. Carrickmore, Co. Tyrone; ed. National School. After emigrating to the USA in January 1892 he settled in Philadelphia where he worked at a variety of jobs until he bought a tavern and liquor business (which he lost in 1919). After joining Clan na Gael* in 1893 he became district officer for Philadelphia (17 January 1904) and was elected to the executive (25 September 1912). He was to wield a great influence over Irish affairs through financial support which, over the course of his life, was said to have cost him 100,000 dollars. McGarrity was kept informed on Irish affairs through his close friends Dr Patrick MacCartan* and Thomas J. Clarke* and through the visits to America of leading Irish republicans and nationalists. He encouraged the Dungannon Clubs,* the Gaelic League,* the Gaelic Athletic Association,* Sinn Fein* and the Irish Volunteers* and was President of the American Volunteers' Aid Association. He was responsible in September 1911 for the prosecution in Philadelphia of the players of the Abbey Theatre* for performing 'an immoral play', *The Playboy of the Western World.*

After the Easter Rising of 1916* he supported the reorganisation of the Volunteers as the Irish Republican Army* and the restructuring of Sinn Fein as the republican political movement. Throughout the War of Independence* he supported Dail Eireann* through the Friends of Irish Freedom.* His *Irish Press*, founded to support the republican cause, ran from 23 March 1918 to 6 May 1922 and cost him 60,000 dollars. McGarrity managed the tour in the USA undertaken by Eamon de Valera* (1919–20). He supported de Valera in the dispute with John Devoy* and Judge Daniel Cohalan* which split the Friends of Irish Freedom in 1920. As de Valera's substitute in America he then ran the American Association for the Recognition of the Irish Republic.*

McGarrity opposed the Treaty* and visited Ireland in February 1922, after which he supported the anti-Treaty IRA during the Civil War.* Following the defeat of the republicans he continued to give support to the militant IRA. As leader of the extremists in Clan na Gael he described de Valera's entry into Dail Eireann in 1927 as an 'act of treason'. He was later temporarily reconciled with de Valera but broke completely with him when the de Valera government moved against the IRA in 1936. One of his last acts was to support Sean Russell* in the demand for an IRA 'war' against Britain but he could only drum up token financial support in America for the venture. His holiday in Ireland in 1939 was terminated when he was served with an expulsion order. He returned to the US via Hamburg where he discussed aid for the IRA with Hermann Goering (this came to nothing).

McGarrity's invaluable library of 10,000 volumes, many of them quite rare, passed to Villanova University when Clan na Gael proved unable to house them in accordance with his will. His poetry, *Celtic Moods and Memories*, with a foreword by Padraic Colum,* was published in New York in 1942. IRA communiques are still sometimes signed with his name.

McGEE, THOMAS D'ARCY (1825–68). Journalist and Young Irelander; b. Carlingford, Co. Louth; ed. Wexford. He emigrated to the USA in 1842 and worked as a clerk on *The Boston Pilot* which he later edited. Through the influence of Daniel O'Connell* he returned to Europe to become parliamentary correspondent of *The Freeman's Journal** and subsequently of *The Nation** in which he published patriotic verse under a variety of pen-names ('Amergin', 'Montanus', 'Sarsfield', 'Gilla-Patrick', etc.). He was active in Young Ireland* and was secretary of the Irish Confederation.* Upon his return from Scotland, where he had been sent on an abortive mission to secure help for the rising of 1848, he was sheltered by Dr Edward Maginn,* Bishop of Derry, whose life he later published (1857). Dr Maginn aided his escape to America.

He founded *The New York Nation* but was forced out of business when he denounced the clergy for having contributed to the failure of the rising of 1848. After moving to Boston he founded *The American Celt* (1850) which, initially republican, became moderate and constitutional. Following accusations of treachery from Irish-Americans, he moved to Buffalo and from there back to New York where he was attacked by Thomas Devin Reilly* and other influential figures. He moved to Canada and settled in Montreal (1857) where he founded *The New Era* and entered politics. McGee played a prominent role in guiding Canada towards Dominion Home Rule, was President of the Council of the Legislative Assembly (1862, 1864) and Minister for Agriculture and Emigration (1867). Following his denunciation of Fenian raids on Canada he was assassinated in Ottawa on 7 April 1868. His works include *The Life of Art MacMurrough* (1847), *Irish Writers of the Seventeenth Century* (1847), *History of the Irish Settlers in North America* (1852) and *A Popular History of Ireland* (3 vols, 1862–69). A collected edition of his poems, edited by Mrs J. Sadleir, appeared in New York in 1869.

McGILLIGAN, PATRICK (1889–1979). Politician (Cumann na nGaedheal and Fine Gael); b. Coleraine, Co. Londonderry; ed. St Columb's College, Derry city, Clongowes Wood College, Dublin and UCD where he was awarded B.A. (1910) and M.A. (1915). He was called to the Bar in 1921 and to the Inner Bar in 1946. From 1934 he was Professor of Constitutional Law, International Law, Criminal Law and Procedure at UCD. He was a member of the Senate of the National University of Ireland.*

Having joined Sinn Fein* upon graduation, McGilligan became a civil servant as secretary to Kevin O'Higgins* in the first Dail Eireann* after unsuccessfully contesting the Derry seat in the general election of 1918. He was later TD for the National University (1923–37), Dublin North West (1937–48) and Dublin Central (1948–51). He succeeded Joseph McGrath* as Minister for Industry and Commerce (1924–32) when he launched the first National Loan. He was a member of the Free State delegation which negotiated the tripartite agreement of December 1925 which shelved the Report of the Boundary Commission.* As Minister he persuaded sceptical cabinet colleagues to back the Shannon Scheme* and the Electricity Supply Board.* Following the assassination of O'Higgins (July 1927) he also held the Ministry of External Affairs (1927–32) and, as leader of the Irish delegation to the Imperial Conferences he drafted the final version of the Statute of Westminster.*

During his term as Minister for Finance in the first Inter-Party Government* (1948–51) he introduced the first Keynesian budgets. He increased the Social Welfare budget and established the Industrial Development Authority* (IDA). McGilligan was also active in the negotiations which led to the repeal of the External Relations Act of 1936 and the declaration of the twenty-six-county Republic of Ireland. He was responsible for the return to Russia of the Russian Crown Jewels.* Owing to ill-health he turned down the offer of a Ministry in the second Inter-Party Government (1954–57), accepting instead the office of Attorney-General. He was the last survivor of the first Free State government.

McGRATH, JOSEPH (1888–1966). Politician (Sinn Fein and Cumann na nGaedheal); b. Dublin; ed. CBS, James Street. After leaving school at the age of fourteen, he worked at various jobs. He joined the Irish Volunteers* in 1913 and fought in the Easter Rising of 1916.* A member of the reorganised Sinn Fein and Irish Volunteers, he was imprisoned several times between 1916 and 1918. Returned for Dublin in the general election of December 1918, he replaced Countess Markievicz as Minister for Labour in Dail Eireann following her arrest in September 1920. On 26 November he was imprisoned along with Arthur Griffith* and others. He supported the Treaty* and was Minister for Labour in the second Dail and in the Provisional Government.* In addition, he was Minister for Industry and Commerce and Economic Affairs (until September 1922). A founder-member of Cumann na nGaedheal, he was Minister for Industry and Commerce until 7 March 1924 when he resigned over the government's handling of the Army Mutiny.* His sympathies were with the Irish Republican Army* element within the National Army. As a private citizen he attempted to act as an intermediary between the army officers and the government.

McGrath then left politics and pursued a very successful business career. He helped to push the Shannon Scheme* for which he acted as Director of Labour. He founded Waterford Glass and Donegal Carpets. An authority on bloodstock and horse-racing, he had international successes in the racing world. He was the founder of the Irish Hospitals Sweepstake.*

McGRATH, SEAN (1882–1954). Republican; b. Ballymahon, Co. Longford; ed. locally. After emigrating to England he became a clerk in British Rail Company, London, in 1908, and quickly established himself in the Gaelic League* and the Irish Republican Brotherhood.* A close friend of Michael Collins* in London, he joined the Irish Volunteers* and was responsible for buying guns for shipment to Volunteers in Ireland. He served with the London Corps in the GPO during the Easter Rising of 1916,* after which he was interned in Frongoch with Collins until the end of 1916. Arrested again in March 1918, he was imprisoned for a year. McGrath was a founder member of the Irish Self-Determination League of Great Britain of which he was general secretary until 1924. He disapproved of the Treaty* and remained in England during the Civil War.* He was among the League activists who were deported in March 1923 but returned to London when a ruling of the House of Lords declared that the deportations were illegal. He was then charged with conspiracy for which he served one year of a two-year jail sentence.

McGREEVY, THOMAS (1893–1967). Scholar, poet and critic; b. Kerry; ed. privately and UCD. He served as an artillery officer with the British forces in Flanders during World War I and was later Lecturer d'Anglais at the University of Paris (1926–33). A close friend of Samuel Beckett* and James Joyce,* he was at Joyce's death-bed in Zurich (1941). As Director of the National Gallery of Ireland (1950–64) he formed a close friendship with Jack B. Yeats* and was executor of his will. His works

included *Poems* (1934) and *Pictures in the Irish National Gallery* (1945) as well as contributions to journals and articles in *The Capuchin Annual* and *The Father Mathew Record.*

MacHALE, JOHN (1791–1881). Archbishop of Tuam (R.C.), 1834–81; b. Tobbernavine, Co. Mayo; ed. at a local hedge-school, Castlebar and Maynooth College* which he entered in 1807. Following his ordination in 1814 he was appointed lecturer in Theology (1814–20) at the College, and was Professor of Theology (1820–25). His first writings, attacking the system of religious education in schools, appeared in the press in 1820 under the pen name 'Hierophilus'. When appointed coadjutor Bishop of Killala, Co. Mayo, in 1825, Dr MacHale became the first Irish prelate since the Elizabethan era to complete his education entirely in Ireland. In 1826 he joined with J. W. Doyle ('JKL')* in his condemnation of the proselytising activities of the Kildare Place Society.* He supported Daniel O'Connell* in the struggle for Catholic Emancipation.* O'Connell referred to him as 'The Lion of the Tribe of Judah' or 'The Lion of St Jarlath's', which the archbishop's critics unkindly turned to the 'The Lion of the Tribe of Dan'. A partial failure of the harvest in Connaught during 1830 resulted in Dr MacHale travelling to London where he unsuccessfully attempted to obtain government aid for the impoverished. Because of ill-health he was recommended a complete change of climate by his doctors and spent some sixteen months in Rome. Shortly after his return to Ireland he was appointed Archbishop of Tuam, despite representations to the Vatican by the British government to prevent his appointment. The new system of National Education* was strongly opposed by MacHale and he refused to allow schools within his archdiocese to be governed by the Act. He supported the Repeal Association* and was at one with O'Connell in his denunciation of the Charitable

Donations and Bequests Act (1844) and the establishment of the Queen's Colleges* which he referred to as the 'godless colleges'.

The proselytising activities of the Rev. Edward Nangle* were a continuing source of worry to MacHale. Nangle had established a colony on Achill Island in 1834 and with the 'New Reformers'* during the 'Second Reformation'* posed a constant threat to Catholic influence. MacHale visited the island in 1835 and to combat the proselytising activities he increased the number of priests and established the Franciscan Monks of the Third Order on the island. During the Famine of 1845–49,* the Archbishop worked tirelessly to aid the starving peasantry. He bombarded the British press, the British and Irish governments and in particular Lord John Russell,* in his efforts to alleviate distress. Additionally, he personally acknowledged every donation sent from all over the world to aid the starving people. The death of his friend O'Connell in 1847 deeply affected him. He was strongly opposed to Young Ireland,* particularly in its acceptance of a system of mixed religious education. Although he had proposed Paul Cullen* for the Archdiocese of Armagh, they were frequently opposed on major issues, including the concept of a Catholic University* as established by Cullen's nominee, John Henry Newman.* MacHale, who had supported Tenant Right* in 1850, was opposed to the Land League* in Connaught. His denunciation of the proposed Westport meeting, following upon the success of that at Irishtown, Co. Mayo,* intimidated many political figures with the notable exception of Charles Stewart Parnell.* Dr MacHale attended the Vatican Council of 1870 where he spoke and voted against the dogma of Papal Infallibility (which the Council defined). His last major public appearance was in Dublin in August 1879 where he unveiled a statue to his friend, Sir John Gray,* editor of the *Freeman's Journal.*

A native Irish speaker, he was the author of an *Irish Catechism* in 1840 which remained in use in Connaught for nearly a century. His translation of *Moore's Melodies* into Irish in 1841 was said to have 'greatly pleased the poet'. He translated Book I of *The Iliad* into Irish verse (1844), Book II (1846), Book III (1851), Book IV (1857), Books V and VI (1860), Book VII (1869) and Book VIII (1871). He translated the Pentateuch into Irish as part of an Irish translation of the Bible (1861). *Toras na Chroice* (1854) was a rendering into Irish of *The Way of the Cross* of St Alfonso Ligouri.

MACKAY, J. J. (1775–1862). Botanist; b. Kirkcaldy, Scotland; ed. locally where he worked for some years as a gardener. He came to Ireland in 1803 and travelled extensively, particularly to the west of the country studying the flora of the region. His *A Catalogue of the Rare Plants of Ireland* was published in *Transactions* of the RDS in 1806. He was assistant Botanist TCD (1804–05), first curator of TCD's Botanic Gardens (from 1806) and associate of the Linnean Society (1806). He discovered several species of plants new to these islands, all of which he enumerated in his papers to the RDS; his major work, *Flora Hibernica,* was published in 1836.

McKENNA, STEPHEN (1872–1934). Scholar and journalist; b. Liverpool. He worked for a time in Dublin as a bank clerk and then as a journalist in London and Paris until 1897 when he went to support the Greeks during the Graeco-Turkish war. In his capacity as a journalist he covered the Russian revolution of 1905. Upon resigning his post with the *New York World* he returned to Dublin to work on the *Freeman's Journal* and for the Irish language revival. A close friend of Arthur Griffith,* Thomas MacDonagh* and leaders of the Irish Volunteers,* he supported the Easter Rising of 1916* which broke out while he was ill. His offer of aid to the rebels in the GPO was rejected as they believed that he was too sick to be of help and they sent him home. His poem 'Memories of the Dead', published under the pen-name 'Martin Daly' in 1916, was a tribute to the insurgents. He moved to London following the death of his wife in 1923. McKenna's translation of Plotinus in five volumes appeared between 1917 and 1930 and his *Journals and Letters*, edited by E. R. Dodds with a preface by Padraic Colum,* in 1936.

MACKEY, CAPTAIN. Alias used by the Fenian, William Francis Lomasney.*

MacLIAMMÓIR, MICHEÁL (1899– 1978). Actor, designer, artist and writer; b. Cork, real name Willmore which he later gaelicised to Mac-Liammóir. He was reared in London, mainly self-educated and appeared at the age of ten in H. Beerbohm Tree productions of *Macbeth*, *Peter Pan* and *Oliver Twist*. He spent some time in Spain and then returned to London where he became the youngest student at the Slade (1915) and studied art. During this period he also joined the Gaelic League* and fell under the literary influence of W. B. Yeats.* Returning to Ireland in 1916, he joined Sinn Fein* before again travelling abroad. Apart from Irish and English, he spoke German, French, Italian and Spanish. As an adolescent he wrote children's fairy tales in Irish and English.

MacLiammóir returned to Ireland to work with his brother-in-law, Anew MacMaster,* who introduced him to Hilton Edwards* in 1927. He founded Taibhdhearc na Gaillimhe* whose first production was his *Diarmuid agus Gráinne* for which he also designed the sets. Returning to Dublin, he founded the Dublin Gate Theatre Studio (*see* Gate Theatre) with Hilton Edwards. Their first production was Ibsen's *Peer Gynt* (12 October 1928). It marked the start of the most productive partnership in Irish theatrical history, during which MacLiammóir designed nearly 300 productions for their theatre.

He played a wide range of roles, in his own works, plays by native dramatists and in international classics. His parts included Robert Emmet in *The Old Lady Says 'No'* (1929), Larry Doyle in *John Bull's Other Island*, Brack in *Hedda Gabler*, Romeo, Richard II, and Gypo Nolan in *The Informer*. Edwards directed him in a notable production of *Hamlet* at the Gate in 1931; he re-created the role in a celebrated production at Elsinore in 1952. His performance as Oscar Wilde in the one-man show *The Importance of Being Oscar* (1960) won international acclaim, was filmed by RTE and BBC and recorded by CBS.

In the early years of the Gate Theatre he befriended the young Orson Welles with whom he worked on the latter's film of *Othello* (1951), playing Iago to Welles' lead. Their experiences appear in MacLiammóir's *Put Money in Thy Purse* (1952) and he also made *An Introduction to the Making of Othello* (1952) for television. In 1953 he played Edgar to Welles' Lear in a New York television production directed by Peter Brook. Other film appearances were in Edwards' *Return to Glenascaul* (made during a break in filming Othello), *The Kremlin Letter* (1970) and *What's the matter with Helen?* (1971). Apart from adaptations for the stage of *Jane Eyre, The Picture of Dorian Gray* and *A Tale of Two Cities*, his plays included *Ford of the Hurdles* (1928), *Where Stars Walk* (1940), *Dreary Shadows* (1941), *Ill Met by Moonlight* (1946), *Portrait of Marian* (1947), *The Mountains Look Different* (1948), *Home for Christmas* (1950), *A Slipper for the Moon* (1954), the one-man show *I Must be Talking to My Friends* (1965), and *Prelude in Kazbec Street* (1973). His prose works included *All for Hecuba* (1946), *Aistreori Faoin Dhá Solas* (1956) which he translated as *Each Actor on his Ass* (1961), *Ceo Meala Lá Seaca* (1952), *Theatre in Ireland* (1954), *Bláth agus Taibhse* (1966), *An Oscar of No Importance* (1968), and *W. B. Yeats and His World* (1970).

MacLysaght

His autobiography, *Enter a Goldfish: Memoirs of an Irish Actor, Young and Old*, appeared in 1977.

MacLYSAGHT, EDGEWORTH ANTHONY (EDWARD) (1887–   ). Genealogist; b. at sea *en route* to Australia, his surname was Lysaght until 1920. He was reared in Raheen, Co. Clare; ed. Oxford which he left without taking a degree but later took M.A. in history at UCC. He worked on the family farm which became an horticultural nursery in 1913. After joining Maunsels, the publishers, in 1916, he came into contact with the leading literary figures of the period. He sat in the Irish Convention,* 1917–18, identified with the nationalist cause, and was imprisoned in 1921 during the War of Independence.* Having worked as a journalist in South Africa from 1932, he returned to Ireland in 1938 and became an inspector with the Irish Manuscripts Commission.* On the staff of the National Library* (1943–55), he worked in the manuscripts division and oversaw the Genealogical Office. He retired from the chairmanship of the IMC in 1973. His writings include *An Afraic Theas* (1947), *Irish Life in the Seventeenth Century* (2nd ed, 1950), *Irish Families: Their Names and Origins* (4 vols, 1957–65), *More Irish Families* (1960), *Supplement to Irish Families* (1964) and *Guide to Irish Surnames* (1964). His autobiography, *Changing Times: Ireland since 1898*, appeared in 1978.

MacMAHON, JAMES (1865–1954). Civil Servant; Under Secretary (1918–22); b. Belfast; ed. CBS, Armagh, St Patrick's College, Armagh and Blackrock College, Dublin. He was Assistant Secretary to the Post Office in Ireland, 1913–16 and Secretary, 1916–18. As Under Secretary he served three Chief Secretaries, including Sir Hamar Greenwood.* MacMahon was the last man to hold the position of Under Secretary and in 1922 helped to oversee the withdrawal of the British Administration from southern Ireland.

MacMANUS, FRANCIS (1909–65). Writer and broadcaster; b. Kilkenny; ed. CBS, St Patrick's College, Dublin and UCD. After working as a journalist he joined Radio Eireann where he became Director of Features in 1947. He inaugurated the Thomas Davis Lectures in 1953. A member of the Irish Academy of Letters,* his works included the trilogy based on the life of the eighteenth-century poet, Donncadh Rua MacConmara: *Stand and Give Challenge* (1934), *Candle for the Proud* (1936) and *Men Withering* (1939); *This House was Mine* (1937), *The Wild Garden* (1940), *The Fire in the Dust* (1950) and a biography of *St Columbanus* (1962). His play, *The Judgement of James O'Neill*, was produced at the Abbey Theatre in 1947. He edited *The Yeats We Knew* (1965) and *The Years of the Great Test: Ireland 1926–39* (1967).

MacMANUS, SEAMUS (1861–1960). Author; b. Mountcharles, Co. Donegal; ed. locally and at a teacher-training college in Enniskillen, Co. Fermanagh. He worked as a school-teacher for some years before emigrating to the USA (1899); he married Ethna Carbery* in 1901. He was the author of the plays *The Townland of Tawney* (1904) and *The Hard Hearted Man* (1905). His other works included *Ireland's Case* (1915), *The Story of the Irish Race* (1921), *We Sang for Ireland* (1950); collections of short stories: *A Lad of the O'Friels* (1906), *Top O' The Morning* (1920) and *The Bold Blades of Donegal* (1937); verse: *Ballads of a Country Boy* (1905); *The Rocky Road to Dublin* (autobiographical) appeared in 1938.

MacMANUS, TERENCE BELLEW (1823–60). Young Irelander and Fenian; b. Temo, Co. Fermanagh. He emigrated to Liverpool where he established a successful shipping agency and joined the Repeal Association* and Young Ireland.* He retired from business in 1848 and returned to Ireland, joining William Smith O'Brien* in the attempted insurrection at Bal-

342

lingarry, Co. Tipperary.* He was sentenced to death but the sentence was commuted to transportation. After escaping from Tasmania with Thomas Francis Meagher* in 1852 he made his way to the USA where he died impoverished following the collapse of his business interests. His body was returned to Ireland by the Fenians but the Catholic Archbishop of Dublin, Dr Paul Cullen,* refused permission for a lying-in-state at the Pro-Cathedral, Dublin. Dr Cullen's ban on Catholic clergy participating in the ceremonies was broken by Fr Patrick Lavelle.* The funeral gained national attention for the Irish Republican Brotherhood.*

MacMASTER, ANEW (1894–1962). Actor-Producer. He made his stage debut with Fred Terry in London (1911) and remained with Terry's company until 1914. He toured Australia (1921) and came to Ireland in 1925, touring rural areas offering seasons of Shakespearean productions which were immensely popular. He was noted for his Shylock, Richard III and Coriolanus. A close friend of Micheál MacLiammóir* and Hilton Edwards,* he brought them together (1927). He toured abroad and returned to Ireland after World War II. 'Mac', as he was known, was noted for the encouragement which he gave to young talent. His autobiography, *Mac*, appeared in 1968.

MacNAMARA, BRINSLEY (1891–1963). Author; b. Delvin, Co. Westmeath, real name John Weldon; ed. locally. He became a director at the Abbey Theatre* until 1928 when he resigned during the controversy surrounding *The Silver Tassie* (*see* O'Casey, Sean). He was drama critic of *The Irish Times*. His first novel, *The Valley of the Squinting Windows* (1919), caused widespread protest in his native area and led to his father being forced to retire from the schoolteaching position which he held. MacNamara wrote several plays for the Abbey, including *The Rebellion at Ballyscullion* (1917), *The Land for*

the People (1920), *The Glorious Uncertainty* (1923), *Look at the Heffernans* (1926), *The Master* (1928), and *Margaret Gillian* (1935).

MacNEILL, EOIN (1867–1945). Historian and politician (Sinn Fein and Cumann na nGaedheal); b. Glenarm, Co. Antrim; ed. privately and at St Malachy's College, Belfast. While reading law he worked as a junior clerk in the civil service and through research in the library of the Royal Irish Academy* became an authority on Old Irish. His suggestion for a new organisation to promote the preservation and use of the Irish language led to the foundation of the Gaelic League* in 1893 of which he was vice-president. He edited *Irisleabhar na Gaedhilge* (1894) and was a co-founder of the Feis Ceoil in the same year. As editor of *An Claideamh Soluis** in 1899 he began to use the Gaelic form of his name, Eoin, instead of John.

A man of wide interests, he studied entomology, botany and science as well as the literature and laws of ancient Irish civilisation. He was appointed first Professor of Early and Medieval Irish History at UCD in 1908. His wide circle of friends included Sir Roger Casement, Robert Erskine Childers, Alice Stopford Green, Thomas Kettle, Mary Spring Rice, Michael Cusack and Augusta, Lady Gregory. The publication of his article 'The North Began' in *An Claideamh Soluis* (1 November 1913) in response to an invitation from The O'Rahilly,* led to the foundation of the Irish Volunteers,* of which he became Chief-of-Staff. He supported John Redmond* and the Irish Parliamentary Party* in their belief that the (third) Home Rule Bill* would answer Ireland's demand for Home Rule. However, when Redmond demanded control of half of the seats on the Provisional Committee, Mac Neill rejected the demand. He helped to plan the Howth Gun-running* and opposed Redmond in his call for Volunteers to join the British Army.

MacNeill was unaware that Patrick

Pearse and other influential Volunteer leaders were members of a secret Military Council* within the Irish Republican Brotherhood which was planning a rising at Easter 1916. Informed of the proposed rising by Bulmer Hobson,* MacNeill confronted Pearse but was persuaded by Sean MacDiarmada* and Thomas MacDonagh* not to interfere with the plans. However, when MacNeill learned that the *Aud** had been scuttled and Casement arrested, he again confronted the leaders, whereupon Pearse informed him, 'We have used your name and influence for what they were worth, but we have done with you now'. As Chief-of-Staff, MacNeill countermanded the orders issued by Pearse, creating total confusion among the Volunteers. The militants went ahead with their plans, rising on Easter Monday.

MacNeill was generally blamed for having virtually destroyed the rising but shortly before their executions, Pearse and MacDonagh exonerated him from all blame. He was interned in England with thousands of other Volunteers and members of Sinn Fein. Eamon de Valera,* the senior surviving commandant from the rising, ordered a general salute when MacNeill entered prison and he was rehabilitated within the nationalist movement. He was a signatory to the 'Message to the President and Congress of the United States' (June 1917). In the general election of December 1918 he was returned for Derry and became Minister for Finance in Dail Eireann (January–April 1919). When Michael Collins* replaced him at Finance, MacNeill became Minister for Industries (April 1919–August 1921). A supporter of the Treaty,* he was Ceann Comhairle during the Treaty debate.

MacNeill was Minister without Portfolio in the Provisional Government* (January–August 1922) and Minister for Education (August–December 1922). He also held Education in the first Executive Council of the Free State (December 1922–November 1925). His son, Brian, who opposed the Treaty, joined the republicans (Irregulars) in the Civil War and was killed in action in Co. Sligo in 1922. He was the Free State representative on the Boundary Commission* which began its deliberations in November 1924. At the conclusion of their sittings the three Commissioners agreed that their Report should not be published until its findings were unanimously acceptable. MacNeill believed that the findings would favour the Free State but on 7 November 1925 an obvious 'leak' to the *Morning Post* revealed that there would be no significant change to the border. He resigned from the Commission on 20 November, informing the Dail that he obviously had a different interpretation of article 12 of the Treaty than had Mr Justice Feetham,* Chairman of the Commission. MacNeill refused to accept the Report and he resigned from the government which signed an agreement with Britain and Northern Ireland – effectively shelving the findings of the Commission. His brother, James MacNeill,* was the second Governor-General of the Free State (1928–32).

MacNEILL, JAMES (1869–1938). Governor-General of the Free State (1928–32); b. Glenarm, Co. Antrim, brother of Eoin MacNeill;* ed. Belvedere School, Blackrock College, Dublin, and Emmanuel College, Cambridge. He joined the Indian Civil Service in 1890 and later served in the West Indies and Fiji as an immigration investigator. He was Chairman of Dublin County Council (1922) and a member of the committee which drafted the Constitution of 1922. High Commissioner of the Free State (1922–28), he succeeded T. M. Healy* in the office of Governor-General. MacNeill and the office were slighted when Eamon de Valera* formed the first Fianna Fail government in 1932. This led to an exchange of letters and when MacNeill published the acrimonious correspondence concerning his office, he was dismissed.

MacNEILL, JOHN GORDON SWIFT
(1849–1926). Lawyer and politician
(Nationalist); b. Dublin; ed. TCD
and Oxford. Called to the Bar (1876)
and KC (1903), he was Professor of
Criminal Law, King's Inns, Dublin
(1882–88) and Professor of Constitutional Law, UCD from 1909. Elected
MP for South Donegal (1887–1918),
he showed a strong interest in reform.
His motion for disallowing votes of
the directors of the Mombassa Railway led to the defeat of the Salisbury
government in 1892 and its replacement by a Liberal administration,
pledged to Home Rule and led by
W. E. Gladstone.* He established
the principle that Ministers of the
Crown could not hold directorships
in public companies, and also secured
the abolition of flogging in the Navy
(1906). His published works include
The Irish Parliament (1885), *English
Interference with Irish Industry*
(1886), *How the Union was Carried*
(1887), *Titled Corruption* (1894),
*Constitutional and Parliamentary
History of Ireland* (1917), *Studies
in the Constitution of the Irish Free
State* (1922) and *What I have Seen
and Heard* (1925).

McQUAID, JOHN CHARLES (1895–
1973). Archbishop of Dublin and
Primate of Ireland (R.C.), (1940–
72); b. Cootehill, Co. Cavan; ed. UCD
where he took an M.A. in Classics
and was ordained a priest in the Holy
Ghost Fathers. After post-graduate
studies in Rome he was appointed
Dean of Studies, Blackrock College
(1928–31), where he was President
(1931–39). He was among those consulted by Eamon de Valera* when
the draft of the Constitution of 1937
was being prepared.

As Archbishop he was noted for
his interest in educational and social
matters. He established the Advisory
Commission on Secondary Schools
and encouraged the Society of Jesus
to open the Catholic Workers' College
(1948). His concern for poverty-
stricken emigrants led to the foundation of the Catholic Social Service
Conference and the Catholic Social

Welfare Bureau. During the economic
depression of the 1940s he acted as a
mediator in industrial disputes, often
alongside James Larkin* whose death-
bed he attended.

He opposed the Mother and Child
Scheme* which was a part of the
1947 Health Act. After consultations
with de Valera the controversial aspects of the Act were shelved. When
the scheme was revived by Dr Noel
Browne* in 1950 Dr McQuaid led
the episcopal opposition. He met with
the Taoiseach, John A. Costello,*
who agreed that a serious question
of 'faith and morals' was involved.
Dr McQuaid was adamant that the
hierarchy could not accept either the
concept of freedom of choice for
patients in selecting a doctor, the
lack of a means test or sex education.
Dr Browne was forced to resign. The
scheme, suitably modified, was introduced by Fianna Fail in 1953. A conservative man, he was able to assure
his flock after his return from a session of the Second Vatican Council
that 'No changes will worry the tran-
quility of your Christian lives'. A
deeply private man with an enduring
suspicion of the media, he did little
to explain the reasoning behind certain of his decisions. The creation of
a diocesan office for maintaining contact with the media effected little
change in this situation. He resigned
his See in 1972 and went into retirement and was succeeded by Dr
Dermot Ryan.

MACRA NA FEIRME. 'Sons of
the Farms'; voluntary organisation
founded in 1944 to assist the personal development of its members
and to provide opportunities for
learning the skills and theory of farming. Other aims of Macra include the
encouragement of leadership ability,
the improvement of relationships between farming and non-farming sections of the community, and the
provision of a medium of social contact between young people of both
sexes. Macra has links with similar
organisations abroad with whom it
arranges exchange visits.

MACREADY, GENERAL SIR CECIL FREDERICK NEVIL (1862–1945). Soldier; GOC British forces in Ireland (1920–23); b. Aberdeen; ed. Marlborough and Cheltenham; commissioned in the Gordon Highlanders in 1881. Promoted Lieutenant-Colonel in 1900, while serving in the Boer War, he became a General in 1918. He was Commissioner of the Metropolitan Police (1918–20), and under pressure from his former commanding officer, Lord French,* accepted the post of GOC of the British forces in Ireland in 1920 during the War of Independence.* The arrival of the Auxiliaries* and Black and Tans* during 1920 to supplement the Royal Irish Constabulary* resulted in an escalation of the war between the police and the Irish Republican Army.* Disapproving of the tactics for which the Black and Tans and Auxiliaries became notorious, he threatened in December 1920 that he would 'break any officer who was mixed up in reprisals'. At the same time he admitted that the police had a difficult job and that they had no clear code under which to operate. When General Sean MacEoin* was captured in March 1921, he met with him in attempt to negotiate with the IRA but the meeting proved fruitless. Macready believed that the IRA would not agree to negotiate if laying down arms was a preliminary – an opinion not welcomed by the Prime Minister, David Lloyd George.*

He met with the IRA leaders on 8 July 1921 in the Mansion House where it was agreed that a Truce should commence three days later. Under pressure from Eamon de Valera,* Macready agreed as a preliminary to release MacEoin who was under sentence of death. He was an adviser to the British government during the negotiations which led to the Treaty and attended some of the cabinet meetings. His last act was to oversee the withdrawal of British forces from Ireland during January 1922, from his headquarters at the Royal Hospital. He was present at the start of the Civil War. He retired from active service in 1923 and published *Annals of an Active Life* in 1942.

MacRORY, JOSEPH, CARDINAL (1861–1945). Archbishop of Armagh and Primate of All Ireland (R.C.), (1927–45); b. Ballygawley, Co. Tyrone; ed. locally, Armagh Diocesan Seminary and Maynooth where he was ordained in 1885. Before becoming Bishop of Down and Connor (1915–27) he was head of the Catholic Academy, Dungannon, Professor of Moral Theology and Scripture in the Diocesan Seminary, Birmingham and Professor of Sacred Scripture at Maynooth. He succeeded Patrick Cardinal O'Donnell* to the Archdiocese of Armagh in 1927 and became a Cardinal in 1929. He was an outspoken critic of the anti-Catholic discrimination practised in Northern Ireland.

MacSWINEY, MARY (MÁIRE NIC SUIBHNE; c. 1872–1942). Republican; b. London and reared in Cork, sister of Terence MacSwiney;* ed. Queen's College, Cork and trained as a teacher, after which she taught for a time in London before returning to teach in Dublin. A member of nationalist organisations, including the Gaelic League,* she was arrested after the Easter Rising of 1916, and, having been dismissed from her teaching post, established her own school after her release later in the year. Called St Ita's, it was modelled on St Enda's founded by Patrick Pearse. The school was located in her home where she was assisted by her sister, Eithne, (d. 1954) and Terence. Active in Sinn Fein,* she visited the USA in 1920 and gave evidence before the American Commission on conditions in Ireland (*see* American Commission of Inquiry). Following her brother's death on hunger-strike, she represented Cork in Dail Eireann.* Her speeches were among the most impassioned in opposition to the Treaty* which she described as 'the grossest act of betrayal that Ireland ever endured'. If it was accepted, she said, she would use her influence as a teacher to teach rebellion against the proposed Free State.* She was imprisoned for a brief period after the fall of the Four Courts (July 1922). Returning to Cork she ran the republican headquarters there during the Civil War* for which she was again imprisoned (1922–23). She supported Eamon de Valera* until he broke from Sinn Fein and established Fianna Fail.* For the rest of her life she refused to recognise the legitimacy of the Free State and Eire, foregoing grants for her school rather than do so.

MAcSWINEY, TERENCE (1879– 1920). Republican; politician (Sinn Fein); b. Cork, brother of Mary Mac-Swiney;* ed. locally and the Royal University. He became a technical instructor in Cork where he was a member of the Gaelic League* and of the Irish Volunteers.* With his assistant Tomás MacCurtain,* he mobilised local volunteers in anticipation of the Easter Rising of 1916.* MacSwiney was arrested and interned for a period in 1916. Upon release he became an active member of the re-organised Volunteers and of Sinn Fein for which party he represented Mid-Cork in the first Dail Eireann. He succeeded the murdered Tomás MacCurtain as Lord Mayor of Cork (30 March 1920). When arrested under the Defence of the Realm Act,* on 19 August 1920, MacSwiney embarked on a hunger-strike in Brixton prison which captured international attention. Representations to have him released were unsuccessful and after fasting for seventy-four days, he died. A guard of honour of Volunteers in prohibited uniform accompanied his funeral through the streets of London watched by thousands of Irish exiles. He was the author of several works including *Battle Cries* (poems, 1918), and *The Revolutionist* (1914). His best-known work, the essay *Principles of Freedom*, was published in New York in 1921.

MacWHITE, MICHAEL (1883–1958). Diplomat; b. Clondora, Co. Cork. After serving in the British Army during World War I, he went to the USA with the French Military Mission (1918). He was Secretary to the Dail Eireann Delegation to the Paris Peace Conference (1920–21). Upon the establishment of the Free State (December 1922) MacWhite was appointed Permanent Delegate to the League of Nations from 1923 to 1929 (*see* League of Nations and Ireland). He was vice-president of the International Labour Conference at Geneva (1928). He held diplomatic postings as Irish Envoy Extraordinary and Minister Plenipotentiary to the USA, (1929– 38), and to Italy (1938–50).

MADDEN, RICHARD ROBERT (1798–1886). Historian; b. Dublin. He qualified as a doctor in London and became a member of the Royal College of Surgeons (1829). He was a magistrate in Jamaica and Colonial Secretary in West Australia. After returning to Dublin he became secretary to the Dublin Fund Board (1858–60). Upon discovering Anne Devlin living in extreme poverty in Dublin in 1843 Madden arranged for her support for the rest of her life. She died during one of his absences abroad, and was buried in a pauper's grave; upon his return he arranged for her reinterment in a plot beside the grave of Daniel O'Connell* in Glasnevin Cemetery. His publications included *Breathings of Prayer in Many Lands* (1838), *Egypt and Mohamed Ali* (1841), *The United Irishmen: Their Lives and Times* (4 vols, 1842–46), *The Connexion between the Kingdom of Ireland and the Crown of England* (1845), *The Life and Times of Robert Emmet* (1847), *The Literary Life and Correspondence of the Countess of Blessington* (3 vols, 1855), *Galileo and the Inquisition* (1863), *Ancient Literary Frauds* (1863), *Historical Notice of the Penal Laws Against Roman Catholics* (1865), *Exposure of Literary Frauds Concocted in*

Ireland (1866) and *History of Irish Periodical Literature* (2 vols, 1867).

MAGEE, JOHN, JNR (1780–1814). Journalist; b. Dublin. Succeeding his father as owner and editor of *The Evening Post*, he ran it upon the same liberal, anti-government lines. He was found guilty of a libel on the Dublin police in 1812 and a year later was again tried for a libel, this time on the Duke of Richmond. The offending article, in fact, was most likely written by Denis Scully.* Magee's defence was conducted by Daniel O'Connell who made a four-hour speech which was generally regarded as his best and was reprinted as *The Trial of John Magee* (1813). Despite the brilliant defence Magee was found guilty, fined £500 and sentenced to two years' imprisonment. Upon his release he was again prosecuted for libel; he was fined £1,000 and imprisoned for six months.

MAGENNIS, PROF. WILLIAM (1869–1946). Academic and politician (Cumann na nGaedheal and Clann Eireann); b. Belfast; ed. CBS, Belvedere and University College; M.A. in Philosophy from Royal University, of which he became a Fellow. He was editor of *Lyceum*,* 1890–92, and of its successor, *New Ireland Review*,* 1893. He was Professor of Philosophy at Carysfort Training College and of Metaphysics at UCD. Professor Magennis was TD for the National University (1922–36). In 1925 he founded Clann Eireann after breaking with Cumann na nGaedheal in protest at the agreement on the Report of the Boundary Commission.* He was a member of the Senate from 1937.

'MAGHERAMORE MANIFESTO'. Document prepared by Robert Lindsay Crawford* for the Independent Orange Order,* it was ratified at a meeting of the members held at Magheramore, near Larne, Co. Antrim, in 1905. Crawford called on all Orangemen, whether in the Grand Lodges or in the Independent Institutions to '. . . hold out the hand of friendship to those who, while worshipping at other shrines, are yet our countrymen . . .' The Manifesto also called for compulsory land purchase, a national university for Ireland and it attacked the Ulster Unionist Council.* Crawford's views led to his expulsion from the Independent Orange Order in 1908.

MAGINESS, WILLIAM BRIAN (1901–67). Politician (Ulster Unionist); b. Lisburn, Co. Antrim; ed. locally and TCD. He was called to the Bar at King's Inns (1922). Maginess was MP for the Iveagh Division of Co. Down (1938–64). He served as Under-Secretary to the Minister for Agriculture (1941–43), Parliamentary Secretary to the Minister for Commerce (1943–45), Minister for Labour and National Insurance (1945–49), Commerce (1949), Home Affairs (1949–53), and Finance (1953–56). He was Attorney-General (1956–64).

MAGINN, DR EDWARD (1802–49). Bishop of Derry (R.C.), 1845–49; b. Fintona, Co. Tyrone; ed. Irish College, Paris where he was ordained in 1825. Following his return to Ireland he supported Daniel O'Connell* and the Repeal Association* during the 1840s but supported Young Ireland* in its break with O'Connell in 1846. He was co-founder of the Ulster Tenant Right Association* in 1847. He gave shelter to Thomas D'Arcy McGee* after the collapse of the 1848 rising. McGee published a biography of the bishop in 1857.

MAGUIRE, JOHN FRANCIS (1815–72). Newspaper proprietor, author and politician (Repealer); b. Cork; ed. locally. He read law in Cork. While a student he was a keen supporter of Daniel O'Connell* and a frequent contributor to newspapers and periodicals on a wide variety of national topics. He founded *The Cork Examiner** in 1841. Called to the Bar in 1843, he rarely practised owing to his literary and political commitments. Maguire was MP for Dungarvan, Co. Waterford, 1852–65, and for Cork, 1865–72. A witty and persuasive speaker, many stories are told of his repartee. On one occasion, he faced a particularly vigorous and volatile opposition at a Mallow, Co. Cork election meeting. To the consternation of his supporters, Maguire remained placid in the face of some highly personal abuse. At the end of the meeting, a large body of opponents followed him to the station and continued to insult him. Finally, in exasperation and in an attitude of prayer he proclaimed *'Sed libera nos a malo'*.

At Westminster he succeeded in promoting a Private Member's Bill effecting a change in the law relating to Irish paupers in England. As the law stood, no Irish pauper could claim relief unless he had resided five years in an English parish. The new law provided relief after a residence of six months. Maguire lent his support also to Tenant Right* and to Disestablishment of the Church of Ireland.* He was Lord Mayor of Cork in 1853, 1862, 1863 and 1864. During his mayoralty he was a strong advocate of the temperance campaign of Fr Theobald Mathew* whose crusade received wide publicity in *The Cork Examiner*. As Lord Mayor he was extremely active in the promotion of local industries and he was instrumental in breaking the monopoly enjoyed by British merchant shipping in the port of Cork. Maguire was closely connected with demands for National Education* and was an early advocate of a system of technical instruction. He visited Rome in 1856 and was received in audience by Pius IX, whose *Pontificate* he wrote on his return. A strong supporter of female emancipation, his novel, *The Next Generation* (1871) reflects a society in which women's rights universally obtain. His other writings include *The Industrial Movement in Ireland* (1852), *Life of Father Mathew* (1862) and *The Irish in America* (1868).

MAGUIRE, SAM (1879–1927). Republican; b. Dunmanway, Co. Cork; ed. locally. After leaving school he entered the civil service as a clerk in the London General Post Office. A supporter of the Irish Republican Brotherhood,* he was involved in the Gaelic League,* the Gaelic Athletic Association* and the Irish Volunteers.* As Chief Intelligence Officer of the Volunteers in England, he became a close associate of Michael Collins.* For his role in supplying arms to the Volunteers during the War of Independence* he was imprisoned and dismissed from his civil service post. Upon the creation of the Free State, he returned to Ireland and worked for a short time in the civil service before ill-health forced his retirement to Dunmanway in 1924. A keen sportsman, Maguire captained the London teams which contested the All-Ireland Football Finals of 1903, '05 and '06. The present All-Ireland football trophy, 'The Sam Maguire Cup', wrought to the design of the Ardagh Chalice, was presented to the GAA as a memorial to his work for the cause of Irish nationalism. The cup was first won by Kildare, who defeated Cavan in 1928.

MAHAFFY, SIR JOHN PENTLAND (1839–1919). Scholar and clergyman (C.I.); Provost of Trinity College, Dublin (1914–19); b. Vevey, Switzerland; ed. TCD (from 1856) where he had a brilliant scholastic career, was ordained and became a Fellow (1864) and senior Fellow (1899). He was passed over for the Provostship in 1904 when it went to Dr Anthony Traill.* Internationally renowned for his learning and wit, his most famous pupil was, perhaps, Oscar Wilde.

Generally hostile towards developing Irish nationalism during 1900–01, he opposed the efforts of Douglas Hyde* and the Gaelic League* to have the Irish language placed on the curriculum for secondary schools; he said of Irish that it was impossible to find in it a text that was not 'either religious, silly or indecent'. Later, in November 1914, he denied the use of the College to a meeting which was to be addressed by Patrick Pearse.* W. B. Yeats was also one of the speakers. He remained in the College during the Easter Rising of 1916* and later gave the use of Regent's House for the sittings of the Irish Convention* (1917–18).

He published works on Kant's philosophy, Irish history, poetry, Egyptian papyri and Trinity plate as well as on the art of speaking. First Professor of Ancient History at Trinity (1869–1901), his scholastic field was Greek society and literature. Among his published works were a translation of Kuno Fischer's *Commentary on Kant* (1866), *Prolegomena to Ancient History* (1871), *Greek Social Life from Homer to Menander* (1874), *Rambles and Studies in Greece* (1876), *History of Classical Greece* (1880), *Sketch of the Life and Teachings of Descartes* (1880), *The Decay of Modern Preaching* (1882), *The Story of Alexander's Empire* (1887), *Greek Life and Literature from Alexander to the Roman Conquest* (1887), *The Art of Conversation* (1889), *The Greek World under Roman Sway* (1890), *Problems in Greek History* (1892), *Plindera Petrie Papyri* (3 vols, 1891–93; vol. 3 with J. G. Smyly), *An Epoch in Irish History, 1591–1660* (1904) and *The Particular Book of Trinity College* (1918).

MAHON, CHARLES JAMES PATRICK, THE O'GORMAN MAHON (1800–91). Adventurer and politician; b. Ennis, Co. Clare; ed. privately and at TCD where he graduated M.A. in 1825. He joined the Catholic Association* and supported Daniel O'Connell* who, at his urging, successfully contested Clare in 1828. Mahon was elected for Clare in 1830 but was unseated on charges of bribery and was succeeded by Maurice O'Connell.* He again contested the seat in 1831 but was unsuccessful when O'Connell chose not to support him. Called to the Bar in 1834, Mahon did not practise but chose instead to travel ex-

tensively. He travelled to Paris where he met Talleyrand and became acquainted with King Louis Phillipe. From France he travelled to Africa, the East and South America, returning to Ireland in 1846. Mahon represented Ennis at Westminster (1847–52) before losing the seat to J. D. Fitzgerald. Following his election defeat he set out for France in 1853 and from there travelled to Russia where he became a lieutenant in the Tsar's international bodyguard, and then toured China and India before serving respectively in the Turkish and Austrian armies. He became a general in the army of Uruguay and later commanded the Chilean fleet against Spain. He continued as a soldier-of-fortune in Brazil where he was a colonel in the national army. In the American Civil War (1861–65) he fought on the Northern side and on the Confederate surrender he took ship to Paris where he became a colonel in the regiment of chasseurs serving Napoleon III. Mahon took up residence in Berlin in 1867 and became a close friend of Bismarck. He returned to Ireland in 1871 and supported the campaign for Home Rule.* He was a delegate to the Home Rule Convention of 1873. He supported Charles Stewart Parnell* and in 1879 won the Clare seat, holding it in the general election of 1880. He was out of politics, 1885–87, until elected for Carlow which he represented until 1891. During the controversy surrounding Parnell's involvement in the O'Shea divorce and the subsequent split in the Irish Parliamentary Party,* Mahon was an anti-Parnellite. A note duellist, he is said to have been involved in at least thirteen encounters.

MAHONY, REV. FRANCIS SYLVESTER; 'FR PROUT' (1804–66). Poet, wit and eccentric; b. Cork; ed. Amiens, Paris and Rome where he wrote 'The Bells of Shandon'. He joined the Society of Jesus and taught briefly at Clongowes Wood College (1830). He ministered in Cork for a while (1832) but left the order, although he remained a priest under special dispensation from the Holy See. He went to London where his writings first appeared as 'The Prout Papers' in *Fraser's Magazine*. His work also appeared in *Bentley's Miscellany* and *The Cornhill Magazine*. He travelled widely throughout Europe and Asia, becoming fluent in several languages. His friend Charles Dickens persuaded him in 1846 to become the Rome correspondent of *The Daily News* and his articles appeared under the pseudoynm 'Don Jeremy Savonarola, Benedictine Monk'. An eccentric in dress and habit, he was described by Blanchard Jerrold as 'trudging along the boulevards with his arms clasped behind him; his nose in the air . . . his deep-seeking eye wandering sharply to right and left and sarcasm . . . playing like jack-o'-lantern in the corners of his mouth'. Politically a conservative, he opposed the Repeal Association and Daniel O'Connell. Apart from his translations of Thomas Moore* and Richard Millikin, his works were published in *Reliques of Fr Prout* (illustrated by Daniel Maclise, 2 vols, 1836) and *The Last Reliques of Fr Prout*, edited by Blanchard Jerrold (1876). Following his death in Paris, his body was returned to Cork and placed in the family vault in Shandon.

MALLET, ROBERT (1810–81). Engineer; b. Dublin; ed. TCD where he was awarded B.A. in 1830. As a partner in the Victoria Foundry he supervised the operation of raising the 133-ton roof of St George's Church, Dublin. His firm built equipment for Guinness's Brewery, a number of swivel bridges over the Shannon (1836) and the Nore viaduct. From 1845 to 1848 Mallet surveyed the River Dodder in an attempt to improve the Dublin water supply system. He was involved in the erection of Fastnet Lighthouse (1848–49) and many terminal railway stations. His invention of the buckled plate was patented in 1852. He manufactured mortars for use in the Crimea (1854). After moving to London in 1861

he surveyed and wrote works on mechanics. A member of the Institute of Civil Engineers (1842) and a Fellow of the Royal Society (1854), he was awarded the Cunningham Medal by the Royal Irish Academy (1862).

MALLIN, MICHAEL (1880–1916). Republican; b. Dublin; ed. locally. Having spent some years with the British Army in India, he became a republican and on returning to Ireland joined the Irish Citizen Army* of which he became Chief-of-Staff. During the Easter Rising of 1916* he was commandant of the Citizen Army detail in the St Stephen's Green area where Countess Markievicz* was his second-in-command. He was executed on 9 May. Countess Markievicz later stated that Mallin's bearing, courage and example were instrumental in her decision to become a Catholic.

MALLON, JOHN (b. 1839). Policeman; b. Meigh, Co. Armagh, ed. Newry Model School. After working for a period as an apprentice to a draper in Newry, he joined the Dublin Metropolitan Police* in 1858. He won rapid promotion, becoming director of the detective branch, 'G' Division. For the most part, his career was devoted to investigating underground movements, including the Fenians, the Irish Republican Brotherhood, Clan na Gael, the Invincibles and the Irish National Alliance. He was active against the Land League and his most famous arrest was when he took Charles Stewart Parnell into custody at Morrison's Hotel on 12 October 1881 (Parnell refused to leave until he had received 10 per cent off his bill). Mallon investigated the Phoenix Park Murders* and the activities of the Dynamiters.* Exchange Court Clerk to Dublin Castle (1892–94), he had reached the rank of Assistant Commissioner when he retired in 1901. He was still alive when *Irish Conspiracies: Recollections of John Mallon* by F. M. Bussy appeared in 1910.

MALONE, REV. SYLVESTER (1822–1906). Clergyman (R.C.) and historian; b. Kilmally, Co. Clare; ed. Maynooth. He was a curate in Kilkee and later parish priest in Sixmilebridge, Co. Clare, and vicar-general while parish priest in Kilrush (1872–1906). A keen supporter of the Gaelic League,* he bequeathed £100 to encourage the study of the language. His *Church History of Ireland* (1867) became a standard reference work.

MANCHESTER MARTYRS. Three Fenians, William Philip Allen, Michael Larkin and Michael O'Brien, who were executed for the murder of Sergeant Charles Brett, during the rescue of the Fenian leaders, Thomas J. Kelly* and Timothy Deasy,* in Manchester on 18 September 1867. Following the escape of Kelly and Deasy some sixty Irishmen were rounded up by the police over the next twenty-four hours. Five of them, Allen, Larkin, O'Brien, Edward O'Meagher Condon* and Thomas Maguire, were charged with complicity in the murder of Sergeant Brett.

The rescue and the killing of Brett sparked off widespread anti-Irish feeling: newspapers carried anti-Irish articles and the verdict at the inquest on Brett was 'wilful murder against Allen and others unknown', *before* the trial had commenced.

The five, who were held in chains during the trial, were found guilty and sentenced to death. There was disquiet at the nature of some of the evidence which led to their conviction. One leading witness, Frances Armstrong, had no less than forty-three convictions for drunkenness and another, Emma Halliday, was awaiting trial on a charge of theft which, because of previous convictions, carried a penalty of penal servitude. Two days before the date of execution Maguire was given a 'free pardon' following representations from journalists who had covered the trial. Condon's sentence was commuted.

The public execution of Allen, Larkin and O'Brien on 23 November aroused widespread indignation in Ireland. The 'Manchester Martyrs', as they became known, were accorded a public funeral in Dublin where an estimated 60,000 people marched in the procession over a route stretching for four miles. Their executions alienated Irish nationalist opinion from any belief in British justice and helped to increase recruitment into the Irish Republican Brotherhood.*

Edward O'Meagher Condon had finished his speech from the dock: 'I have nothing to regret, or to retract, or take back. I can only say, "God Save Ireland".' His words were taken up by the others who repeated 'God Save Ireland'. This phrase became the title of a ballad by T. D. Sullivan.* The ballad became the marching song of the IRB and the unofficial anthem of nationalist Ireland.

MANDEVILLE, JOHN (1849–88). Agrarian agitator and politician (Irish Parliamentary Party); b. Mitchelstown, Co. Cork. Mandeville was active in the Plan of Campaign* and was closely associated with William O'Brien* in the organisation of tenants' resistance on the Kingston estate, near Mitchelstown. This led to a summons to trial which was the occasion of the Mitchelstown Massacre.* He was imprisoned in Tullamore Jail with O'Brien, and, like many others in the Plan, refused to wear prison uniform. Under the orders of Arthur J. Balfour* the prisoners were not allowed to wear their own clothing and Mandeville was kept naked in a cell (November 1887). He died in July 1888, a few months after his release. His death aroused great indignation in England and Ireland, as it was attributed to ill-treatment in prison.

MANGAN, JAMES CLARENCE (1803–49). Poet; b. Dublin; ed. Saul's schools which he left prematurely to aid his impoverished family. While working in a scrivener's office (1818–21) Mangan began his studies of European languages including French, German, Italian and Spanish as well as Latin. He began drinking heavily early in life and also became addicted to opium. His early literary contributions were reserved chiefly for almanacs to which he subscribed under a variety of pseudonyms including Peter Puff *Secundus*, P. V. M'Guffin, 'An Idler' and M.E., Dublin. His later poetry appeared in *The Comet, The Dublin Penny Journal, The Satirist* and in the first and subsequent editions of *The Nation*, and in the *United Irishman*. To the editor of the latter, John Mitchel,* Mangan wrote in 1849 '. . . Insignificant an individual as I am, and unimportant to society as my political opinions may be, I, nevertheless, owe it, not merely to the kindness you have shown me, but to the cause of my country, to assure you that I thoroughly sympathise with your sentiments, that I identify my view of public affairs with yours, and that I am prepared to go to all lengths with you and your intrepid friend, Devin Reilly, for the achievement of our national independence . . .' Mangan was employed by George Petrie* copying topographical matter for the Ordnance Survey.

An eccentric in dress and habits, Mangan was frequently seen in the Dublin streets dressed in a large pointed hat and a cloak, while a pair of dark green spectacles emphasised the paleness of his features. He was said to have carried two umbrellas, even in the warmest weather. He fell victim to the cholera epidemic during the Famine of 1845–49* and died in the Meath Hospital, Dublin, where his last writings, which he was carrying inside his hat, were inadvertently destroyed by a ward orderly. W. B. Yeats* admitted that Mangan had been an important influence. James Joyce* was also influenced by him and read a paper on Mangan to the Literary and Historical Society of UCD (1 February 1902) and five years later delivered a lecture on the

poet to students at the Universita del Popolo, Trieste. Mangan's poetry, including his 'Dark Rosaleen' and 'Woman of Three Cows', was edited for a New York edition by John Mitchel in 1859.

MANNIX, DANIEL, CARDINAL (1864–1963). Archbishop of Melbourne (R.C.), 1917–63; b. Charleville, Co. Cork; ed. locally, St Colman's, Fermoy and Maynooth. Following his ordination (1890) he was appointed Professor of Philosophy at Maynooth (1891), and Professor of Theology in 1894. Vice-President of the College (1903), he was President, 1903–12. Dr Mannix was co-adjutor Bishop of Melbourne from 1912 until 1917, when he was appointed Archbishop. An outspoken nationalist, he strongly condemned the extension of conscription to Ireland (*see* Conscription and Ireland). He was particularly virulent in his denunciation of the excesses committed by the Black and Tans* and the Auxiliaries.* Before he left on a trip to Ireland in July 1920 he received the Freedom of the City of New York. *En route* to Ireland he was arrested (8 August 1920) and taken to Penzance, Cornwall, to prevent his addressing meetings in Ireland on nationalist issues. Prevented also from speaking at meetings in Liverpool, Manchester and Glasgow, he nevertheless succeeded in addressing huge torchlight gatherings throughout England and Scotland. An outspoken opponent of war, he said of Hiroshima in 1945 that such a question was not new: '. . . all such bombings, no matter by whom, are indefensible and immoral'.

MANSION HOUSE COMMITTEE. Established in 1918 as a central board to co-ordinate the activities of the various nationalist movements involved in Sinn Fein.* The members included Arthur Griffith,* George Noble, Count Plunkett* and, later in the year, W. T. Cosgrave* and Eamon de Valera.*

MANSION HOUSE CONFERENCE. Called by the Lord Mayor of Dublin, Laurence O'Neill, on 18 April 1918 to discuss the British government's proposal to introduce conscription in Ireland. Conference delegates, who represented all shades of nationalist opinion, included Arthur Griffith,* John Dillon,* T. M. Healy,* Eamon de Valera,* Joseph Devlin,* William O'Brien, MP,* and William O'Brien* of the Labour Party. De Valera drafted an anti-conscription pledge to be taken at church doors throughout Ireland on Sunday, 21 April. The delegates co-ordinated an anti-conscription campaign. *See also* Conscription and Ireland.

MANSION HOUSE FUND. *See* All-Party Anti-Partition Committee.

MARIA DUCE. Right-wing Catholic movement founded by Rev. Dr Denis Fahy, a Holy Ghost priest, active during the 1940s. A minority movement, it campaigned against Article 44 of the Constitution of 1937, claiming that the article was not strong enough in defence of the Catholic Church. Maria Duce published *Fiat.*

MARIAN YEAR (1954). The Marian Year was celebrated to commemorate the centenary of the proclamation of the Dogma of the Immaculate Conception by Pope Pius IX in 1854. Because of the special devotion traditionally reserved for the Virgin Mary, the year held a special significance for Ireland. Knock, Co. Mayo* was the centre for a large number of pilgrimages, many hundreds of wayside shrines and grottos were erected throughout the country, while many girls born in that year were given the name of 'Marian'. The Marian Year officially ended on 8 December – the Feast of the Immaculate Conception.

MARKIEVICZ, CONSTANCE, COUNTESS (1868–1927). Republican; b. Lissadell House, Co. Sligo, sister of Eva Gore-Booth;* ed. privately. She studied art at the Slade and in Paris and married Casimir Markievicz, a Polish artist, in 1900, by whom she had one daughter, Maeve, who was reared by Constance's mother, Lady Gore-Booth. The marriage was not a success and Markievicz left Ireland to live in London. She became a follower of Sinn Fein* although she disagreed with the pacifism of its leader, Arthur Griffith.* At the suggestion of Bulmer Hobson* (with whom she lived for some time at a Raheny, Dublin, Commune), she founded a youth organisation, Fianna Eireann,* in 1909. She joined Inghinidhe na hEireann* for which she wrote a pamphlet, *A Call to the Women of Ireland* (1909) and contributed also to the suffragette newspaper, *Bean na hEireann*, and to Griffith's *United Irishman*. During the Lock-Out of 1913,* she organised soup kitchens in the Dublin slums and became an officer in the Irish Citizen Army,* commanded by her friend, James Connolly.* Her involvement in the Citizen Army led to some bitterness in the movement and prompted the resignation of its general secretary, Sean O'Casey.* During the Easter Rising of 1916* she served as second-in-command to Michael Mallin* at the St Stephen's Green command. She was sentenced to death for her role in the rebellion but the sentence was commuted. She became a Catholic shortly afterwards.

In the general election of 1918 she was returned for the St Patrick's division of Dublin – the first woman to be elected to the House of Commons. As a member of Sinn Fein, however, she did not sit at Westminster but became a member of the first Dail Eireann with a cabinet post as Minister for Labour (April 1919–August 1921), although she spent much of this period in prison. She again held the Ministry of Labour in the second Dail but was not a member of the cabinet. She was vehement in her denunciation of the Treaty: 'It is the capitalist interests in England and Ireland that are pushing this Treaty to block the march of the working people in England and Ire-

Marriage

land .... Now I say that Ireland's freedom is worth blood, and worth my blood, and I will willingly give it for it, and I appeal to the men of the Dail to stand true.' From its inception she was an irreconcilable opponent of the Free State and supported the republicans (Irregulars) during the Civil War, for which she was imprisoned (1923–24). She was returned as Sinn Fein abstentionist TD for Dublin City South in the general election of 1923. Four years later, during the general election of June 1927, she conducted her own highly individual campaign but died one month later in a public ward of Sir Patrick Dun's Hospital.

MARLBOROUGH, 8th DUKE (1822–83). Churchill, John Winston Spencer; Lord Lieutenant (1876–80); b. Norfolk; ed. Eton, Oriel College, Oxford; MP (Conservative), Woodstock (1844) as Marquis of Blandford until he succeeded to the dukedom in 1857; Privy Councillor (1866); Lord President of the Council (1867–68). He first rejected an offer of the Irish Lord Lieutenancy from Benjamin Disraeli* in 1874 but accepted office two years later. Marlborough was popular during his term of office when nationalist aims were channelled by Isaac Butt in to the path of the Home Rule Party (*see* Irish Parliamentary Party). The late 1870s was also a period of severe agricultural depression and by 1879 there was famine, particularly along the western seaboard. Marlborough and his wife, Frances Anne, daughter of the 3rd Marquess of Londonderry, set themselves to administering famine relief, setting up a fund which collected £12,484. With the fall of the Disraeli administration in 1880, he left office and was succeeded by the 7th Earl of Cowper.* *See also* his son, Churchill, Lord Randolph.

MARRIAGE. The pattern of marriage changed considerably in Ireland during the nineteenth century particularly in the wake of the Famine of 1845–49.* Prior to the Famine,

the custom was one of early marriage. K. H. Connell accepted this as a major factor in the population increase which was a marked feature in Ireland between 1780 and the Famine. Contemporary observers noted the incidence of early marriage. Campbell Foster commented, 'If there is any evil more prominent than another in the social condition of Ireland, it is the improvident and early marriages which are contracted . . . a lad is no sooner sixteen or seventeen years of age, than he marries some girl of fifteen or sixteen . . . he has a family growing up about him before he is a man'. The principal cause of early marriages, according to the contemporary accounts, was the reckless subdivision of land which made it possible for a newly-wedded couple to earn their subsistence.

Late marriages became a feature of Irish rural life after the Famine. In 1945–46, the average marrying-age of Southern farmers was 39 while that of the bride was 30. One in four males were between 65 and 74 years of age. Census returns indicated a pattern of late marriages and a declining birth-rate. There were 4.5 marriages per one thousand of population for the period 1871–81; for 1951–56 the figure was 5.4 per one thousand, and for 1958, 5.3 per one thousand.

Contemporaries paid regular tributes to the chastity of Irish women and noted the low rate of pre-marital and extra-marital sexual activity. Lord Radnor told de Tocqueville in 1833 that he (Radnor) had heard it said that morals in Ireland and Scotland were better than in England. Monsignor Nolan of Carlow told de Tocqueville (20 July 1835), 'Their morals, in the narrow sense of the word, are very chaste'. The Bishop of Kilkenny, Monsignor Kinsley, told him (24 July 1835), 'Their morals are pure' and 'twenty years of confession have taught me for a girl to fall is very rare, and for a married woman practically unknown. .... A woman suspected is lost for her whole life. I am sure that there are not twenty illegitimate children a year among the Catholic population of Kilkenny which numbers 26,000'. Factors which pevented promiscuous activity were fear of the clergy and of contempt within the community for those who transgressed the strict moral codes of rural Ireland.

Prominent among the influential folk in the rural community was the match-maker.* His function was to arrange marriages between boys and girls of different families. An important consideration in arranging a marriage, whether through the matchmaker or not, was the wealth of the individuals being 'matched'. It was important that the girl have a dowry, either of cattle, money or land. It was important that she should not be matched with one who was deemed a social inferior. Landless sons were thrown on their wits, and strove to find a mate within the landowning community. Marriage in rural Ireland after the Famine and into the twentieth century was decided along predominantly mercenary lines.

Until the 1850s marriages were performed in the home where the couple intended to live, in rural Ireland generally in the home of the bridegroom's parents. Those attending the wedding ceremony marched in procession from the home of the bride's parents to that of the groom's, on foot, in traps or on horseback. Drink, usually whiskey and wine, was provided at both houses. Feasting began as soon as the procession arrived at the house where the ceremony was to be performed. If those responsible for the wedding entertainment were poor, neighbours would provide what was necessary for the merrymaking. The officiating priest was expected to remain for the duration of the festivities and to this end, it was presumed that he would perform his parochial duties before arriving. The wedding service was usually performed in the kitchen and as many people as wished could be registered as witnesses. Neither the bride nor groom were allowed to sing at their own wedding. At mid-night strawboys — young men dressed in straw and wearing masks — arrived and requested admittance. These were singers and musicians and the party received a fresh impetus from their arrival. The entertainment normally continued into the early hours of the morning.

There were many superstitions attached to marriage ceremonies. It was considered lucky to get married on a sunny day, and unlucky to be married on a wet day; it was good luck to hear a cuckoo on the morning of the wedding or to see three magpies as the bridal party proceeded to the ceremony. It was unlucky to be married on a Saturday, or to meet a funeral on the way (in which case the party either turned back or went to the place of marriage by an alternative route).

MARSHALL AID FOR IRELAND. The first Inter-Party Government* signed an agreement with the USA in June 1948 whereby Eire was to receive aid to the amount of £47,000,000. It was conditional upon the government's drawing up a programme outlining the country's import requirements for the next three years. This Long-Term Recovery Programme* was drawn up by the Minister for External Affairs, Sean MacBride.* Eire also had to join the Organisation for European Economic Development. By the end of 1950 some 150,000,000 dollars had been received. While it did not solve the major problems — emigration, rising prices, low wages and unemployment — it was used to benefit agriculture (*see* Land Rehabilitation Project), a housing programme and a restructuring of the social welfare system.

MARTIN, HARRIET MARY LETITIA (1815–50). Philanthropist and author; b. Co. Galway, granddaughter of Richard Martin;* her benevolence during the Famine of 1845–49* brought the estates of her family to bankruptcy. She was known to her tenants as the 'Princess of

Connemara' because of her charity. On the loss of her 200,000 acre farm when the mortgage was foreclosed, she went to Belgium where she married Arthur Bell and wrote several novels under the name Letitia Bell Martin. She died on the voyage to America following a difficult birth. Her best-known novel *Julia Howard* (1850) is a moving account of the ravages of the famine in the West of Ireland.

MARTIN, JOHN (1812–75). Young Irelander, journalist and politician (Nationalist); b. Loughorne, Co. Down; ed. Newry where he was a school-fellow of John Mitchel* whose sister, Henrietta, he later married. A member of the Repeal Association,* he was also active in Young Ireland.* He supported James Fintan Lalor* on the land question and assisted Mitchel on *The United Irishman*.* He co-edited *The Irish Felon* with Lalor and was arrested for membership of the Irish Confederation.* Found guilty of treason-felony, he was transported to Tasmania where he remained from 1849 until 1854 and two years later he returned to Ireland. A supporter of tenant-right during the 1850s and 1860s he opposed the extremism of the Irish Republican Brotherhood* although he did deliver the oration for the Manchester Martyrs* in 1867. His lecture-tour of the USA enjoyed popular success (1869–70). Martin was a founder-member of the Home Government Association* and became MP for Meath in 1871. He became ill immediately after Mitchel's death and died nine days after his brother-in-law's funeral. His seat was won by Charles Stewart Parnell.*

MARTIN, RICHARD (1754–1834). Politician and landowner; b. Dublin. The first member of his family to conform to the established Church of Ireland, he was educated at Harrow and Trinity College, Cambridge. After a call to the Bar in 1781, he practised on the Connaught Circuit. His estate of around 200,000 acres in Connemara, extending for thirty miles from his house at Ballinahinch, was the largest in Ireland. He represented Jamestown, Co. Leitrim (1776–83) and Lanesborough (1798–1800) in the Irish House of Commons and supported the Union. He continued to hold a seat at Westminster until after the general election of 1826. The contest for his seat was fought amid great unrest and Martin's retention of it was petitioned by James Staunton Lambert who held it when the House of Commons removed Martin's name by a majority of 84 votes in 1827.

Martin's love of duelling earned him the nick-name 'Hairtrigger Dick' from his close friend the Prince of Wales (*see* George IV). His love of animals earned him the popular name of 'Humanity Dick'. He tabled a private member's bill in 1822 'to prevent the cruel and improper treatment of cattle' and was a founder-member of the Royal Society for the Prevention of Cruelty to Animals in 1824. A popular landlord in the west, he was widely respected for his defence of the oppressed and during his period in parliament gave his support to Catholic Emancipation.* After losing his seat in 1827 he retired to Boulogne where he died.

MARTIN, VIOLET FLORENCE (1862–1915). Novelist (under the pen-name 'Martin Ross'); b. Ross House, Co. Galway, grand-daughter of Charles Kendal Bushe;* ed. Alexandra College, Dublin. Violet Martin was the co-author of a number of popular books, written in collaboration with her cousin, Edith Anna Oenone Somerville.* Having suffered a serious accident in 1898, her last years were spent in confinement. Her collaborator continued to publish books which she stated were written in conjunction with the deceased, claiming that they communicated through spiritual means. Trinity College, Dublin, awarded her a posthumous honorary D. Litt. in 1932. The works of which she was co-author include *An Irish Cousin* (2 vols, 1899; with 'Geilles Herring' [Somerville]), *Naboth's Vineyard* (1891); *The Real Charlotte*

(1894), *Beggars on Horseback* (1895), *The Silver Fox* (1898), *Some Experiences of an Irish R.M.* (1899), *All on the Irish Shore* (1903), *Further Experiences of an Irish R.M.* (1908), *Some Irish Yesterdays* (1908), *Dan Russell, the Fox* (1911), and *In Mr Knox's Country* (1915). Somerville claimed that Violet Martin was co-author of a biography of their grandfather, Bushe, *Incorruptible Irishman* (1937).

MARTYN, EDWARD (1859–1923). Dramatist; b. Masonbrook, Co. Galway; ed. Belvedere College, Dublin, Beaumont, Windsor and Christ Church, Oxford. He supported the Gaelic League* and was an influential figure in the Irish literary revival of the 1890s. In 1894 when he discussed with George Augustus Moore* the idea of writing native drama in the English language he was instrumental in bringing about Moore's decision to return to Ireland. Martyn's neighbour was Augusta Lady Gregory* to whom he introduced W. B. Yeats* in 1896. From this meeting there developed the Irish Literary Theatre.* He had a passion for music and established the Palestrina Choir in the Pro-Cathedral Dublin in 1899, in which the youthful John McCormack* was shortly destined to sing. The choir became the *Schola Cantorum* of the Archdiocese in 1903. Martyn also played a leading role in the reform of Irish church architecture and in the stained-glass revival. He wrote *The Heather Field* for the Irish Literary Theatre in 1899.

A fervent Catholic, Martyn was distressed when Yeats' *The Countess Cathleen* was criticised on moral grounds and he threatened to break with the Theatre. With Lady Gregory and Yeats, he was a member of the first Board of Directors of the Abbey Theatre,* but later severed his connection with it, dissatisfied with its policy of peasant drama. In the nationalist developments of the time, he gave support to the National Council* and Sinn Fein* of which he was President (1905–08). Following

his break with the Abbey he became co-founder with Thomas MacDonagh* and Joseph Mary Plunkett* of the Irish Theatre – a short-lived experiment at Hardwicke St, Dublin in 1914. His health deteriorated and he lived his remaining years as a recluse on his Ardrahan estate. His will directed that he be buried in a pauper's grave and that his body should be donated to a Dublin hospital for dissection. His works included the satiric novel, *Margante the Lesser* (1890) and the plays *Maeve* (1899), *The Bending of the Bough* (with George A. Moore, 1900), *The Placehunters* (1902), *The Enchanted Sea* (1902), *Romulus and Remus* (1907), *Grangecolman* (1912), *The Dream Physician* (1914) and *The Privilege of Place* (1915).

MARWOOD, WILLIAM (1820–83). Hangman at Kilmainham; b. Horncastle, Lincolnshire; a cobbler by trade. Having watched several executions he was appalled by the victim's suffering and suggested a more humane method: the descent of a body into a pit beneath the scaffold which would cause death instantly due to dislocation of the vertebrae. Marwood was invited to become public executioner and his first engagement was at Lincoln in 1871. He performed some executions at Kilmainham. His most famous victims, however, were criminal rather than political: Charles Peace, Dr Lamson and Kate Webster. Following an execution it was his custom to hand to the assembled pressmen his card inscribed, 'William Marwood, Executioner, Horncastle'.

MASSEY, GODFREY. Illegitimate son of William Massey of Castleconnell, Co. Limerick. His mother, Mary Condon, reared him in the USA under the name Patrick Condon. He worked in New Orleans for a time and served in the British Army during the Crimean War (1854–56). Inspired by a speech of James Stephens,* he joined the Fenians* in New York, c. 1860. He fought in the American Civil War (1861–65), serving in the

Confederate Army and reaching the rank of colonel. In January 1867 he was sent to Ireland by the Fenians with money to pay the officers of the Irish Republican Brotherhood,* in preparation for the rising in March being planned by General Cluseret* and Colonel Thomas Kelly.* On the date of the rising, he was arrested at Limerick Junction and provided the authorities with information which effectively destroyed any hope of a rising for that year.

MATCH-MAKER. Person who undertook to arrange a marriage between parties. He was a highly-regarded member of the community, whose function was to pair people according to social background, an important consideration in a rural community where a person's wealth was judged according to the size of his farm and the amount of livestock he possessed. The match-maker was paid for his services, generally by both parties.

MATHEW, REV. THEOBALD (1790–1856). Temperance preacher and Capuchin priest; b. Thomastown, Co. Tipperary; ed. Maynooth, where he was ordained in 1814. He ministered briefly at Kilkenny but left the diocese after he was wrongly accused by the bishop of having administered Paschal Communion (a privilege reserved for certain dioceses). He ministered in Cork for over twenty years, founding schools and working among the poor. Fr Mathew was celebrated for his work during the cholera epidemic of 1832. As a pastor, he was particularly disturbed by the incidence of drunkenness among the poor. In 1838, encouraged by Protestant philanthropists in Cork, he began a temperance crusade which grew into one of the oustanding movements of the 1840s.

The extent of the problem facing a temperance reformer may be judged from the following figures: while the consumption of spirits in England was seven and one-ninth pints per annum per head of population, in Ireland the figure was nearly thirteen pints per annum. Contemporary accounts show that excessive drinking was a serious social problem; de Tocqueville was told, 'But when the chance of a drunken orgy offers, they [the Irish poor] do not know how to resist it. They become turbulent and often violent and disorderly. . . . Acts of violence are rather frequent, but they all arise from drunkeness or political passions'. In August 1835 de Tocqueville was also told by a judge of the Assizes Court in Galway that drinking was the chief cause of faction-fighting.*

Fr Mathew's temperance campaign in Cork met with such a favourable response that he extended it into a national campaign. Thousands of people travelled to attend and to take the 'pledge' of abstinence. In Limerick city, 10,000 people, about half of whom had travelled a considerable distance to hear him preach, were said to have taken the pledge. Between 1839 and 1844 he was reputed to have administered five million pledges. Revenue from consumption of drink dropped from £1,435,000 in 1839 to £352,000 in 1844. Publicans went bankrupt – one figure suggests around 20,000. The police, it was said, were in danger of becoming redundant for want of crime to keep them occupied. The campaign earned the praise of Daniel O'Connell* who said that he could not have held his mass meetings for Repeal if the population had not first been converted to sobriety. Fr Mathew urged his converts to replace drinking as a pastime by taking up dancing and music.

When he took his campaign to the US in 1849, his fame had preceded him and he was met by a deputation of the New York City Council, greeted by the Mayor, and dined with President Taylor. Hundreds of thousands of Irish-Americans took the pledge. By the time he returned home he was in ill-health as a result of his exertions. He spent almost a year in Madeira but on his return to Cork again undermined his health by the intensity of his labours. He supported the temperance work of the United Kingdom Alliance (1853).

MATURIN, REV. CHARLES ROBERT (1782–1824). Clergyman (C.I.) and author; ed. TCD; B.A. (1800). He was curate at Loughrea and Dublin and author of extremely popular Gothic novels, the most famous of which was *Melmoth the Wanderer* (1820). His play, *Bartram* (1816), was performed at Drury Lane with Kean and earned him £1,000. Another, *Manuel* (1817) was less successful. He corresponded with Lord Byron and Sir Walter Scott.

MAXWELL, CONSTANTIA ELIZABETH (1886–1962). Historian; first woman professor in Trinity College, Dublin. b. Dublin; ed. St Leonard's School, St Andrews and TCD. She was Lecturer in History (1909–39), Professor of Economic History (1939–45) and Professor of Modern History (1945–51). Her writings include *Short History of Ireland* (1914), *Irish History from Contemporary Sources* (1923), *Dublin Under the Georges* (1936), *Country and Town in Ireland under the Georges* (1940), *A History of Trinity College* (1946), *The Stranger in Ireland from the reign of Elizabeth to the Great Famine* (1954). She edited Arthur Young's *Tour of Ireland* (1925).

MAXWELL, GENERAL SIR JOHN GRENFELL (1859–1929). Soldier; b. Liverpool; ed. Cheltenham College and Royal Military Academy, Sandhurst (1878). He was commissioned in the 42nd Foot in 1879. His military career took him to the Sudan (1885–89) and he fought in the Boer War. Maxwell was Chief Staff Officer to the Duke of Connaught in Ireland (1902–04), and commander of the Force in Egypt (1909–12). He retired on half-pay but was recalled to duty on the outbreak of World War I. Attached to French headquarters as head of the British Military Mission until after the Marne, he again commanded in Egypt until 1916. Al-though he did not want the post, he accepted command in Ireland during the Easter Rising of 1916,* arriving on 28 April, with complete control over the country under martial law. He isolated 'infected patches' of rebels in Dublin and within two days, the rising was over. Maxwell executed fifteen rebels and arrested and held thousands of others who were suspected of being sympathisers. His handling of the Irish situation was widely criticised but he was defended by the Prime Minister, Herbert Asquith,* and was awarded the GCB. He was appointed C-in-C of the Northern Command in England (November 1916). He spent a further period in Egypt with Lord Milner before retiring in 1922.

MAXWELL, REV. WILLIAM HAMILTON (1792–1850). Clergyman (C.I.) and historian; b. Newry, Co. Down; ed. TCD; B.A. (1812); ordained (1813). He ministered in Balla, Co. Mayo. A contributor to the leading periodicals of the time, he edited *The Naval and Military Almanac* (1840–41). He published *O'Hara* (1825), *Stories of Waterloo* (3 vols, 1829), *The Field Book* (1833), *Wild Sports of the West* (1838), *The Victories of the British Armies* (2 vols, 1839), *Life of Wellington* (3 vols, 1838–41), *History of the Irish Rebellion of 1798* (1845) and *The Irish Movements* (1848).

MAYNE, RUTHERFORD (1878–1967). Dramatist; b. Japan; ed. Belfast, real name Samuel Waddell; brother of Helen Mayne (1899–1965). He was a distinguished Latin scholar and a founder-member of the Ulster Theatre in which he acted for a time and for which he later wrote. His works were also produced at the Abbey Theatre. They include *The Turn of the Road* (1906), *The Drone* (1908), *The Gomeril* (1909), *Red Turf* (1911), *Neil Gallivan* (1912), *If* (1913), *Industry* (1915), *Phantoms* (1928), *Peter* (1930) and *Bridgehead* (1934).

MAYNOOTH, ST PATRICK'S COLLEGE. St Patrick's College, Maynooth, Co. Kildare was founded in 1795 by the Irish parliament, at the prompting of William Pitt.* The College was intended both as a seminary for clerical students and as a place of higher education for lay students. The lay college was discontinued in 1817. Maynooth students were generally intended for ministering in their own dioceses. During the nineteenth century, diocesan seminaries were established throughout the country, and their students went on to further study at Maynooth. The original grant of £9,000 for Maynooth was increased by Sir Robert Peel* in 1845 to an annual grant of £26,000. This, the Maynooth Grant, caused resentment among nonconformist groups. The Maynooth Grant was discontinued in 1871 as part of the general disendowment of religion in Ireland (*see* Disestablishment of the Church of Ireland) and was replaced by a capital sum of £369,000. In 1910 Maynooth became a 'recognised' college of the National University of Ireland.* It is now a constituent college of the NUI. Maynooth consists of a seminary, a pontifical university (since 1899) and a lay college (since 1966). The college is the responsibility of the trustees, who are the Catholic bishops.

MAYO, 6th EARL, LORD NAAS (1822–72). Bourke, Richard Southwell; politician (Conservative); Chief Secretary (1852, 1858 and 1866); b. Dublin; ed. privately and TCD where he did not take a degree. During the Famine of 1845–49,* he helped in the distribution of famine relief. He was MP, Co. Kildare (1847–52), Coleraine (1852–57) and Cockermouth (1857–58). He spent three short periods in office as Chief Secretary and opposed Disestablishment of the Church of Ireland.* In office, he was conciliatory but determined to suppress agitation. He sought finance for schools of all denominations and also supported tenant demands for compensation for improvements.

He was Governor-General of India in 1869, an appointment made by Benjamin Disraeli* and allowed to stand by W. E. Gladstone.* He was assassinated while visiting a penal colony at Fort Blair.

MAYO, 7th EARL (1851–1927). Bourke, Dermot Robert Wyndham; Unionist; ed. Eton; he served in the army as a cornet in the 10th Hussars (1870) and as a lieutenant in the Grenadier Guards (retired in 1876). He was a representative peer for Ireland (1890) and supported the All For Ireland League* (1910). He was a prominent opponent of Home Rule. Mayo attended the Irish Convention (1917–18). Following the Treaty he accepted the Free State and became a member of the Senate (1921).

MEAGHER, THOMAS FRANCIS (1822–67). Young Irelander; b. Waterford; ed. Clongowes Wood College. After working as a journalist he studied law for a time. He supported Young Ireland* and became a close friend of William Smith O'Brien* and John Mitchel.* Meagher was the immediate cause of the break between Young Ireland and the Repeal Association:* in the course of a speech at Conciliation Hall he angered Daniel O'Connell* when, refusing to 'stigmatise the sword', he made a speech in which he used the word 'sword' eight times and earned from W. M. Thackeray the title 'Meagher of the Sword'. He was a founder-member of the Irish Confederation.*

Meagher was sent to France after the revolution of February 1848 as an emissary from Young Ireland and returned with a gift from the French for the citizens of Dublin – the tricolour,* which was later adopted as the national flag of Ireland. For his role in the rising at Ballingarry, Co. Tipperary,* he was transported to Tasmania where he joined Mitchel. After informing the authorities that he was retracting his parole not to escape, he escaped and made his way to the USA where he became a popular lecturer on Irish affairs and entered American politics. He also explored Central America and the Rocky Mountains.

Upon the outbreak of the Civil War (1861–65) he became Brigadier-General of the New York Irish Brigade (the 69th, 88th and 63rd New York Volunteers), later known as 'Meagher's Brigade'. The Brigade's banners displayed the Irish harp and a wreath of shamrocks embroidered in gold on a field of emerald silk. It was distinguished for its bravery in action, and fought at Bull Run (August–September 1862), Antietum (September 1862), Fredericksburg (December 1862) and Chancellorsville (May 1863). It was virtually annihilated during the last two battles but was in action at Gettysburg (July 1863) and Bristole's Station (October 1863). Meagher retired with the rank of full lieutenant-general and then entered politics to become Territorial Secretary (1865) and Acting-Governor of Montana (1865–66). While returning to explore the Northern Territory for the second time, he fell overboard his ship in mysterious circumstances and was drowned. He is commemorated by a statue in Helena, the capital of Montana. His speeches, with some personal reminiscences and two of his poems, were published in Dublin in 1916, in a volume edited by Arthur Griffith.

MEANY, STEPHEN JOSEPH (1825–88). Journalist and Fenian; b. Ennis, Co. Clare; ed. locally. After working on *The Freeman's Journal* he founded *The Irish National Magazine*. Following imprisonment for membership of Young Ireland (1848), he emigrated to the USA where he worked as a journalist and joined the Fenians (1864). After his arrival in England as a Fenian emissary in 1866, he was arrested and imprisoned. During his period in prison he composed verse, including 'Three Cheers for the Red White and Blue'. Upon release (1868), he returned to America where he was admitted to the Bar and edited *The Evening Democrat* in Connecticut.

He assisted in the defence of the Dynamiters.* His remains were returned from the US for burial in Ennis in March 1888.

MEE, JEREMIAH (1889–1953). Policeman; b. Knickanes, Glenamaddy, Co. Galway; ed. National School. Having joined the Royal Irish Constabulary* in 1910 he was stationed at a variety of posts until July 1919 when he was transferred to Listowel, Co. Kerry. He supported the policemen's union (*see* McElligott, Thomas J.). On 16 June 1920, Mee and his colleagues refused orders to hand over Listowel barracks to military control and accept the more dangerous assignments to outlying barracks. He became spokesman for the barracks.

Addressing the 'mutineers', the RIC Divisional Commander for Munster, Lieutenant-Colonel G. B. Smyth,* pointed out that the RIC were to go on the offensive against the Irish Republican Army:* 'You may make mistakes occasionally and innocent persons may be shot, but that cannot be helped, and you are bound to get the right parties some time. The more you shoot, the better I will like you . . .' Rather than co-operate with the Black and Tans,* Mee and some of his colleagues at Listowel resigned (6 July).

He was unemployed for a time until he secured a job with the White Cross* (February 1922). After internment during the Civil War* from 12 August to 13 September 1922, he was employed by the BP Oil Company but was dismissed when he organised a strike against the company's policy of discriminating against Catholics for promotions. He was then employed by Russian Oil Products (ROP) Ltd, from 1926 until 1932, when he joined the Department of Local Government and Public Health in Longford, Mullingar and Dublin.

His *Memoirs* offer a unique insight into the RIC. They were written during 1951–52 and appeared in *Reynold's News* (25 November 1951–6 January 1952) and in *The Leitrim Leader* (15 March–26 April

1952). Extensively rewritten, they appeared in book form, edited by J. Anthony Gaughan, in 1975.

MEITHEAL. Irish custom of providing a few days of free labour for a neighbouring farmer by turf-cutting, harvesting, etc. This voluntary assistance was repaid in turn, so that a large circle of co-operation operated among farmers in a given locality. The labour was also repaid by the provision of food and drink at the end of the work period, with dancing, singing and story-telling.

MELBOURNE, 2nd VISCOUNT (1779–1848). Lamb, William; politician (Whig); Chief Secretary (1827–28) and Prime Minister (1834; 1835–41); b. Brocket Hall; ed. Eton, Trinity College, Cambridge and Glasgow University; he read law at Lincoln's Inn and was called to the Bar (1804) but did not practise. He entered politics as MP for Westminster (1805) and represented different constituencies for the rest of his political career. In April 1827 he accepted the post of Chief Secretary. While he was known to favour Catholic Emancipation,* he disapproved of the agitation led by Daniel O'Connell.* Although he disagreed with the methods used by the Catholic Association,* he was aware that Ireland could not be peacefully governed without reaching an accommodation with O'Connell and so he cultivated the Irish leader's friendship. Melbourne's wish to open public offices to Catholics was opposed by the (Protestant) Ascendancy.* While this was a new approach and earned him popularity among Catholics, it increased the suspicions of the Orange Order.* At the request of the Duke of Wellington,* he agreed to remain Chief Secretary until 1828 but spent much of his time in London. When Wellington's administration fell in the wake of Emancipation, he became Home Secretary in Lord Grey's government (1830–34). As Home Secretary he was very involved in Irish affairs. He intended his government of Ireland to be 'firm but fair'.

He encouraged Lord Stanley in the implementation of the National Education system in the hope that constructive measures might win the Irish away from O'Connell's new cause, Repeal. However, 1830–31 was a period of cholera outbreak and there was widespread discontent. Melbourne agreed with the need for Poor Law,* but did not feel that it could yet be established. In 1832 the government attempted to put an end to the long-standing grievance of the tithes,* when the system was adjusted and there was a redistribution of the Church of Ireland's income. An attempt to reform the Church of Ireland was made in 1833. Melbourne's main energies as Home Secretary were devoted to combating trade union agitation brought about by a severe economic depression.

He became Prime Minister for the first time in July 1834 but by the end of the year he was replaced by Sir Robert Peel* whose administration fell 100 days later. Melbourne's second government lasted until 1841. This was a period of continuing reform in Ireland, brought about by Lord Mulgrave,* Lord Morpeth* and Thomas Drummond.* The Lichfield House Compact* gained the support of O'Connell and English radicals for Melbourne's ministry. O'Connell had campaigned during the 1835 election on a cry of 'Repeal, sink or swim', but, while Melbourne was not prepared to consider Repeal, O'Connell had no option but to support a reforming policy on Ireland. The Compact gained O'Connell Tithe Commutation (1838) and the extension of the Poor Law to Ireland. Melbourne's offer of the Mastership of the Rolls was rejected by O'Connell. In 1840 the Melbourne ministry introduced local government reforms in the Municipal Corporations Act.* His government fell in 1841 and Sir Robert Peel returned to office.

MELLOWS, LIAM (1892–1922). Republican; b. Ashton-under-Lyne near Manchester; reared by his grandparents near Inch, Co. Wexford; ed.

Cork, Portobello and the Royal Hibernian Military School. He started work as a clerk in Dublin in 1905. Through Na Fianna Eireann,* he became closely associated with Bulmer Hobson,* Sean MacDiarmada* and Thomas J. Clarke* and was sworn into the Irish Republican Brotherhood* by Con Colbert* in 1912. Appointed Fianna organiser in 1913, he worked closely with Countess Markievicz* in building up the movement and travelled throughout Ireland as a republican propagandist. As a socialist, he was influenced by James Connolly.* Upon the foundation of the Irish Volunteers* in 1913 he became a member of the Provisional Committee.* He was sent to Galway as Volunteer organiser for South Connaught where he was twice arrested, and deported to England on the second occasion. Connolly arranged for his return to Ireland (disguised as a priest) for the Easter Rising of 1916* after which he went on the run in Co. Clare until arrangements were made for his escape. He was smuggled to England and from there to the USA.

He was arrested late in November 1917 in New York for using false papers and released on bail (for two years). Although he was out of touch with developments in Ireland he maintained contact with the re-organised Volunteers and Sinn Fein.* During de Valera's tour of America in 1920 Mellows acted as advance agent. He supported de Valera in the dispute with Judge Daniel Cohalan* and John Devoy.* Mellows was regarded with suspicion by Irish-Americans whose loyalty to America clashed with their loyalty to Ireland. After his return to Ireland in 1920 he became involved in the Irish Republican Army* and was appointed Director of Purchases during the War of Independence.* He represented Galway in the first Dail Eireann and played a leading role in opposition to the Treaty,* which he called 'the betrayal of the Republic' and '. . . a new Coercion Act in the biggest sense in which any Coercion Act was ever

made in Ireland'. He seconded the motion for the re-election of de Valera as President of Dail Eireann (9 January 1922, when de Valera lost to Arthur Griffith).

Mellows was for a time editor of the republican organ *Poblacht na hEireann* and was a member of the Four Courts garrison when the Civil War* broke out. Following the collapse of the Four Courts he was arrested and imprisoned at Mountjoy by the Provisional Government. From prison he issued the *Notes from Mountjoy* which appeared in the *Irish Independent* on 21 September 1922. He called for the defence of the Republic and urged the establishment of a civilian republican government to counter the Provisional Government. When de Valera became 'President of the Irish Republic' (only existing in name) Mellows was named Minister for Defence, although still imprisoned. He was executed by the Provisional Government (along with three others) on 8 December 1922 in reprisal for the assassination of Sean Hales TD, on 7 December.

MEYER, KUNO (1858–1919). Scholar; b. Hamburg; ed. Gelehrtanschule of the Johanneum, Hamburg and at the University of Leipzig where he read German and Celtic Philosophy. He was Lecturer in Teutonic Languages at the University of Liverpool (1884–95) and Professor (1895–1915), and founded the School of Irish Learning in Dublin in 1903. Apart from contributions to scholarly journals, his publications of Irish interest included *The Irish Odyssey* (1885), *Bryth and Gael* (1896), *Liadan and Cuirithir* (1902), and *The Lay of Adamnan* (1904); his translations included *The Vision of MacConglinne* (1892), *The Voyage of Bran* (1895), *Fianaigheacht* (1910) and *Ancient Irish Poetry* (1913).

MIDDLEMAN. Leaseholders, holding land from a landlord who was often an 'absentee', and sub-letting the land at an inflated rent were known as 'middlemen'. The system was often observed by outsiders to be one of the more blatant evils of a land-holding system noted for its uneconomic and inefficient nature. In many cases there were layers of middlemen involved, as the sub-tenant, instead of working the land, might in turn sub-let it and thus became a middleman to one tenant, while being a sub-tenant to another middleman. T. Campbell Foster noted, 'Sometimes these middlemen underlet the whole at an increased rent to one man, who again underlets to farmers and cottiers at a further increased rent; and this second middleman, as he usually extracts a most extortionate rent, employs himself in watching his tenants and pouncing on every shilling they make; and sometimes, the farmers, in such a case, to enable them to pay these high rents, let out fragments of land manured to cottiers, in what is termed as "con-acre" for which the general rent is £8 to £10 per acre'. It was not unusual for the 'head middleman' to be an absentee, like the head landlord. Foster stated, 'The prejudices of the middlemen, and their habit of realizing a profit without trouble, must therefore be overcome, or rather the middleman must be got rid of, where possible, as an useless incubus, and a practical intelligent farmer be obtained in his place'.

While contemporary accounts generally portray the middlemen as a rapacious class, there were middlemen who attempted to assist the tenantry. However, so long as there was an expanding population putting continual pressure on land and food resources there were few who could envisage an end to the system. The worst abuses of the system were eliminated by the Famine of 1845–49.* *See also* Conacre, Cottier *and* Gombeen Men.

MIDGLEY, HARRY (1893–1957). Politician (Labour and Ulster Unionist). He became a carpenter and was later a trade union official and a member of the Independent Labour Party. He served in World War I. Midgley was defeated when he contested the first general election in Northern Ireland as an anti-partitionist (1921). As a member of the Labour Party, he was MP for Belfast Dock (1933–38), and Willowfield (1941–47). He broke with the Northern Ireland Labour Party* in 1942 and founded the Commonwealth Labour Party.* During World War II he was Minister for Public Security (1943–45) and then a back-bencher. He joined the Ulster Unionist Party in 1947 and was Minister for Labour (1949–52) and Education (1952–57). He was a prominent member of the Orange Order.*

MIDLAND GREAT WESTERN RAILWAY. *See* Railways in Ireland.

MIDLETON, 1st EARL (1856–1942). Brodrick, St John; b. Co. Fermanagh landowner and prominent Unionist; ed. Eton and Balliol College, Oxford; Conservative MP for Surrey (1885) and Guildford Downs (1885–1906). He was Financial Secretary to the War Office (1886–92), Under-Secretary of State for War (1895–98), and for Foreign Affairs (1898–1900), Secretary of State for War (1900–03), and for India (1903–05). Midleton was closely associated with Unionist movements resisting Home Rule* for Ireland and he was a member of the Irish Convention,* 1917–18. He was the author of *Ireland, Dupe or Heroine* (1932), and *Records and Reactions, 1856–1939* (1939).

MILESMEN. Part-time constabulary who patrolled the Irish roads at night in the early years of the nineteenth century.

MILEY, REV. JOHN (1805–61). Clergyman (R.C.); b. Co. Kildare; ed. Maynooth and Rome. After returning to Ireland in 1835 he became a supporter of Daniel O'Connell,* to whom he became private chaplain. Especially interested in educational reform, he published several pamphlets on the subject. He accompanied O'Connell to Europe in 1847 and attended him in his last moments. In deference to O'Connell's last wishes, he conveyed the body to Ireland from Genoa and preached the panegyric in the Pro-Cathedral, Dublin. He was Rector of the Irish College, Paris (1849–59) and parish priest of Bray, Co. Wicklow from 1859. His several religious works included *History of the Papal States* (1852).

MILITARY COUNCIL (IRB). The Military Council or 'Military Committee' as it was also known was formed in 1915 at the suggestion of Thomas J. Clarke,* a member of the Supreme Council of the Irish Republican Brotherhood.* The Council consisted of a small group of revolutionaries who intended to use the Irish Volunteers as the army for a rising which they planned towards the end of 1915. Original members of the Council were Patrick Pearse,* Joseph Mary Plunkett* and Eamonn Ceannt.* In September 1915 they were joined by Clarke and Sean MacDiarmada.* In January 1916 they revealed their plans to James Connolly* who then became a member. The final member, Thomas MacDonagh,* was recruited in April. The Council was a secret group within a secret group and its existence was unknown to the leaders of the Volunteers.* The resulting confusion produced a situation very different to what the Council originally intended. *See also* Irish Republican Brotherhood *and* Easter Rising of 1916.

MILITARY HISTORY SOCIETY OF IRELAND. Founded in January 1949 to pursue research into the history of warfare in Ireland and of Irishmen at war; it produces a magazine, *The Irish Sword.*

MILITARY PENSIONS ACT, 1934. Act introduced by Eamon de Valera* to provide pensions for the members of the Irish Republican Army* who had supported the republican cause during the Civil War* (1922–23). The pensions drew support away from the IRA with which he was now on distant terms. Figures provided by the Minister for Finance on 10 November 1937 indicated that £457 was paid out in 1934–35, £54,305 in 1935–36 and £164,845 in 1936–37.

MILITARY SERVICE (No. 2) ACT, 1918. Act introduced in August 1918 by the government of David Lloyd George.* It proposed to extend conscription to Ireland, but it met with such widespread resistance that it had to be abandoned (*see* Conscription and Ireland).

MILLIGAN, ALICE (1866–1953). Author; b. Omagh, Co. Tyrone; ed. Methodist College, Belfast and King's College, London. She contributed to *United Ireland* and *Sinn Fein*, sometimes using the pen-name 'Irish Olkyrn'. She was the founder-editor of *Shan Van Vocht** with Ethna Carbery.* Apart from collaborating with her father on *Glimpses of Erin* and with her brother on *Sons of the Sea Kings*, she was the author of a *Life of Wolfe Tone* (1898), *The Last of the Fianna* (play, 1900), *Hero Lays* (poetry, 1908) and *The Daughter of Donagh* (play, 1920).

MILROY, SEAN (1877–1946). Journalist and politician (Sinn Fein, Cumann na nGaedheal); b. Maryport, Cumberland. He came to Ireland to work in the nationalist cause and became a close friend of Arthur Griffith* and a supporter of Sinn Fein.* Milroy joined the Irish Volunteers* and was imprisoned in Mountjoy (June–August 1915). He fought in the Easter Rising of 1916* and on the surrender he was imprisoned in Reading Jail. On 19 April 1917 he was elected to the National Council, a body representative of the nationalist organisations. Elected to the Executive of the Volunteers (19 November 1917), he was an unsuccessful Sinn Fein candidate at East Tyrone in April 1918. Shortly after his election to Dublin Corporation he became a director of elections for Sinn Fein in the general election of 1918. Arrested prior to the election, he was imprisoned at Lincoln Jail from which he escaped with Eamon de Valera.* Milroy assisted the establishment of the Irish Self-Determination League of Great Britain.* He was elected MP for Fermanagh-Tyrone to the first parliament of Northern Ireland (24 May 1921) but did not take his seat. After election as Sinn Fein TD for Cavan on 16 August 1921 he sat in Dail Eireann* where he was secretary to the Dail Sub-Committee on Ulster and spokesman on Northern affairs. Milroy supported the Treaty: 'I believe that this Treaty is one which gives Ireland real power, real authority and real freedom'. He was re-elected to Dail Eireann in 1923 but resigned his seat in 1924 following the Army Mutiny,* and broke with Cumann na nGaedheal* following the shelving of the Boundary Commission.* He ran as an Independent Republican but failed to regain his seat. Elected to the Senate* in 1928 where he supported Cumann na nGaedheal, he remained there until the House was abolished in 1936 by Eamon de Valera. Milroy was the author of a pamphlet, *The Case of Ulster*, in 1922.

MINISTERS AND SECRETARIES ACT, 1924.

Introduced by the Free State government of W. T. Cosgrave* for the purpose of streamlining the administrative system by uniting the various bodies under eleven ministerial departments. The eleven departments were: President of the Executive Council (now the Department of the Taoiseach), Finance, Justice, Local Government and Public Health, Lands and Agriculture, Industry and Commerce, Fisheries, Posts and Telegraphs, Education, Defence and External (now Foreign) Affairs. Lands was attached to Fisheries from 1928 to 1934 and thereafter it was a separate ministry. An amendment Act of 1946 removed Public Health from Local Government and created a new department of Health from 1947. In 1947 also, a new department of Social Welfare was created.

MITCHEL, JOHN (1815–75). Young Irelander and journalist; b. Dungiven, Co. Londonderry; son of a Presbyterian minister; ed. Derry City until his family moved to Newry (1822) where he met John Martin,* later his associate and brother-in-law. After taking a law degree at Trinity (1834) Mitchel worked at a law office in Banbridge, Co. Down, where he came into conflict with the local Orange Order. Visits to Dublin brought him into contact with Charles Gavan Duffy* and Thomas Davis* and he joined Young Ireland* and contributed to *The Nation*.* Following Davis' death in 1845 he accepted Duffy's invitation to become principal contributor to *The Nation* and moved with his family to Dublin. Following the break between Young Ireland and Daniel O'Connell,* he became a leading member of the Irish Confederation* (1847). He fell under the influence of James Fintan Lalor* and advocated an extreme policy to defend the tenantry suffering during the Famine of 1845–49.* A member of the Irish Council,* he became disillusioned with its failure and, breaking with the Confederation in January 1848, established his own paper, *The United Irishman*.*

Between February and March 1848 he advocated that the starving peasantry should withhold the harvest, not pay rent or rates, resist distraint and eviction, ostracise all who would not co-operate, and arm themselves. His paper provided advice on the organisation of barricades and noted that railway tracks could be used as pikes. He also pointed out that vitriol could be used against soldiers. The tone of his paper led to his arrest in May. The paper was suppressed and he became the first man tried under the new Treason-Felony Act,* before a packed jury which found him guilty. He was sentenced to fourteen years' transportation.

He was joined in Tasmania by his friend, Thomas Francis Meagher,* with whom he gave parole to the governor not to escape. After withdrawing his parole, he escaped on

8 June 1853 and made his way to the USA. He worked as a journalist in New York and then moved to Tennessee where he farmed. During the Civil War (1861–65) he supported the Confederacy for which he was imprisoned by the victorious North. He consistently denounced the Fenians* during his time in America. After his return to Ireland in 1874, he was returned as MP for North Tipperary (1875), but was unseated by the government on the grounds that he was a convicted felon who had not served his sentence. A second election again returned him but he died while his victory was being celebrated. His most famous work was *Jail Journal*, which first appeared in 1854 in his New York newspaper, *The Citizen*. It details his prison experiences and philosophy and influenced generations of Irish nationalists. Other writings included *The life and Times of Aodh O'Neill, Prince of Ulster* (1845), *History of Ireland from the Treaty of Limerick* (1858), and *The Last Conquest of Ireland (Perhaps)*. He also edited the works of James Clarence Mangan* (1859) and Thomas Davis (1868).

MITCHELSTOWN 'MASSACRE'. The Mitchelstown 'Massacre', as it became popularly known, occurred on 9 September 1887 at Mitchelstown, Co. Cork, during the Plan of Campaign.* On that day William O'Brien* MP and John Mandeville,* MP, were ordered to appear before magistrates. Although they refused to comply with the order, a large crowd of tenant-farmers gathered in the town. The police, under orders from the Chief Secretary, Arthur J. Balfour,* to suppress all disorder connected with the Plan, fired into the crowd, killing three people and wounding others. The attack was defended by the Lord Lieutenant, the 6th Marquess of Londonderry.* As a result of an official investigation two officers, Captain H. Segrave and the County Inspector of the Royal Irish Constabulary,* Inspector Brownrigg, were held responsible and the latter forced to resign.

MODEL SCHOOLS. Established in 1846 as part of the training system for teachers, the Model Schools were administered directly by the Commissioners for National Education. Selected trainees were supervised in their teaching of 100 pupils for six months in each District Model School. Each was intended to produce six male and two female teachers annually, who would then take a two-year training course. Following an examination the trainees completed their training in the Central Model School in Dublin. The Schools were denounced by the Catholic hierarchy because, unlike the National Schools which were under their management where the Catholic population warranted it, Model Schools were directly controlled by the Commissioners. As a result of hierarchical condemnation in 1861 no further Model Schools were built. The bishops objected to their religiously-mixed boarding character. Two years later, the hierarchy ordered that no priest was to send any person from the schools under his control to be trained in a District Model School, nor was any priest to employ as teachers persons who had been trained in one. They also ordered that Catholic children were to be withdrawn from the Models, and repeated this in 1866.

Chichester Fortescue-Parkinson* strongly criticised the Schools for their failure to turn out sufficient trainees (only 400 were available to meet the annual demand for 900). He proposed that future Models should be under local management. However, shortly afterwards the Commissioners recommended that in schools run by religious, pupils of sufficient calibre should be recognised as 'first-class monitors'; as those regarded as 'class monitors' were in fact becoming trained teachers, this undermined the whole basis of the Model Schools. The Powis Commission* recommended that they be abolished. A number of Model

Schools, as they are called, still exist, directly administered by the Department of Education.

Since 1833, there had been a system of Agricultural Model Schools. In theory they were national schools with facilities for teaching the children the rudiments of agricultural theory and practice. In fact, they were quite often simply national schools with gardens of variable size attached. Those who emerged with the suitable qualifications could be sent on to a Central Agricultural School or College for further study. The system was extremely inefficient because facilities were lacking to carry out teaching on the level hoped for by the planners. The Powis Commission recommended that the 'agricultural' model schools be reduced and that there should be centralisation based on the farms and gardens of the Model School at Glasnevin. This was eventually done.

MOLLY MAGUIRES. An anti-landlord agrarian secret society which flourished in Ireland from 1835 to 1855, it spread to the USA where, as an off-shoot of the Ancient Order of Hibernians,* it was active in the Pennsylvanian coalfields. The members, who were all Catholics, dressed in women's clothing when committing their outrages, hence their name. The Molly Maguires was organised primarily for the execution of a concerted campaign of violence, arson and sabotage against those whom the coal miners considered their oppressors. Membership of the society in America expanded rapidly after the American Civil War (1861–65). In 1875 the Molly Maguires brought about a strike in the coalfields of Pennsylvania. It was broken through the efforts of James McParlan, a Pinkertons' agent who infiltrated the society and won the confidence of its leaders. McParlan's evidence resulted in the conviction and execution of leading figures of the movement and the imprisonment of many others. The society was disbanded in the US in 1877.

In January 1979 Governor Shapp of Pennsylvania signed a posthumous pardon for one John Kehoe who had been hanged for membership of the Molly Maguires more than a century earlier. In the course of his speech Governor Shapp commented '. . . We can be proud of the men known as the Molly Maguires, because they defiantly faced allegations to make trade unionism a criminal conspiracy. These men gave their lives on behalf of the labour struggle'. *See also* Secret Societies.

MONAHAN, JAMES HENRY (1804–78). Judge; b. Portumna, Co. Galway; ed. TCD; B.A. (1823) and Bar (1828). After having been counsel for Daniel O'Connell* during the state trials of 1843–44, he became Solicitor-General in 1845. He was elected Conservative MP for Galway in 1847. He prosecuted the leaders of the Young Ireland* insurrection of 1848 and Fenians* (1865–67). A Catholic, he opposed the system of jury-packing which he attempted to prevent in courts at which he presided.

MONETARY REFORM. Maverick one-man political party founded by Oliver J. Flanagan prior to the general election of 1943. The party's conception of monetary reform was to print more money. Flanagan secured his seat for Laois-Offaly, the party faded away and he became a prominent member of Fine Gael.*

MONTEAGLE, 1st LORD (1790–1866). Spring Rice, Thomas; politician and landowner; b. Limerick, ed. Cambridge. He was Tory MP for Limerick from 1820 until 1832 when he lost to an O'Connellite and then became MP for Cambridge. He was chairman of a commission appointed to report on the education of the poor in 1828. The Report issued by the commission recommended the creation of a system of united ('mixed') education under a governing body which would protect children from interference with their religious beliefs. Other recommendations were that the governing board should superintend the model schools* and print books for literary and religious teaching. Spring Rice was bitterly disappointed at the government's lack of response to the Report, but the recommendations were noted by E. G. Stanley (*see* Derby, 14th Earl) when establishing the National Education system in 1831.

Spring Rice presided over a select committee which issued a report opposing any system of compulsory relief for the poor in 1830. He also opposed the extension of the Poor Law* to Ireland. A good landlord upon his estate, Mount Trenchard, Foynes, Co. Limerick, he saw emigration as a possible solution to overpopulation and in 1847 secured the establishment of a select committee to examine 'colonisation' (i.e., emigration). Monteagle had, during the Famine of 1845–49,* paid the passage of tenants who emigrated.

MONTEITH, ROBERT (1880–1956). Nationalist; b. Newtownmountkennedy, Co. Wicklow; ed. Kilquade National School. He enlisted in the British Army in 1896 (giving his age as 18). He served in the Royal Horse Artillery in India for a time and then fought in the Boer War where he was at the relief of Ladysmith. Disillusioned by his army experiences, and following further service in India, he returned to Ireland and worked in the Ordnance Survey* in Dublin. In spite of his loyalist background, Monteith joined the Irish Volunteers* and lost his job. His military experience made him a valuable asset and he was appointed instructor. Thomas J. Clarke* delegated him to go to Germany to assist Sir Roger Casement* there in recruiting an Irish Brigade from among Irish prisoners-of-war. Monteith went to New York where his passage to Norway was arranged by Clan na Gael.* Upon his arrival in Germany in 1915, he found Casement in poor health. He was informed by the German general staff in 1916 that 20,000

guns were to be sent to Ireland on the *Aud** for the Easter Rising of 1916,* but that there would be no men. Monteith considered this inadequate and decided to accompany Casement to Ireland to prevent the rising. Along with Sergeant Bailey of the abortive Irish Brigade, they travelled to Ireland on a U-boat which landed them off Fenit, Co. Kerry. Upon landing at Banna Strand, Casement was found to be too ill to travel and Monteith and Bailey journeyed to Tralee where Bailey was captured. By now suffering from a bout of malaria, Monteith made his way to Cork where he was nursed by Capuchin monks. He eventually worked his passage to New York where he lived for the next few years. Eamon de Valera* appointed him organiser of the American Association for the Recognition of the Irish Republic* (1920–22). Monteith later settled in Detroit where he worked in Ford's factory.

MONTGOMERY, REV. HENRY (1788–1865). Clergyman (Presbyterian); b. Killead, Co. Antrim; ed. privately and Glasgow College which he entered in 1804 and graduated M.A. in 1807. Ordained in 1809, he held the living at Dunmurry, Co. Antrim until his death. As headmaster of the English school in the Belfast Academical Institution (from 1817) he vehemently refuted the assertions of Rev. Henry Cooke* who had denounced it to the Royal Commission on Education in January 1824 as 'a seminary of Arianism'. Montgomery led the Arian secessionists in their withdrawal from the Synod of Ulster and was engaged in spirited public debate with Cooke thereafter. The new Remonstrant Synod consisting of three presbyteries and seventeen congregations, held their first meeting on 25 May 1830. A supporter of religious liberty Montgomery advocated Catholic Emancipation and supported National Education* but opposed Repeal.* He defeated his old adversary Cooke in April 1841 in the latter's efforts to exclude Arians from professorships at the Belfast Academical Institute. A prolific pamphleteer Montgomery edited *Bible Christians* for many years.

MONTGOMERY, HUGH DE FELLENBURG (1844–1924). Landowner and Ulster Unionist; ed. Christ Church, Oxford. He succeeded to an estate of approximately 12,500 acres in counties Fermanagh and Tyrone in 1863, living at Blessingbourne, Co. Tyrone. An excellent landlord, he granted rent reductions during the crisis of 1879 to 1882 but was highly critical of the succession of Land Acts* (1881–1903), and condemned the idea of compulsory purchase as destructive of the Union. Although he was critical of the Orange Order,* the threat of Home Rule* reconciled him to it. He was suspicious of Sir Edward Carson* whose commitment to Unionism, Montgomery believed, could lead to the neglect of Ulster Unionists. A member of the executive of the Irish Loyal and Patriotic Union,* he published anti-Home Rule pamphlets and was a member of the advisory committee of the Ulster Unionist Council.* In this capacity he helped to draft the Solemn League and Covenant* (1912). He reluctantly accepted the idea of six-county exclusion from Home Rule and was 'Father of the Senate' of Northern Ireland (1921–24).

MOORE, GEORGE AUGUSTUS (1852–1933). Novelist and dramatist; b. Moore Hall, Co. Mayo, son of George Henry Moore* and brother of Colonel Maurice Moore;* ed. Oscott, Birmingham. He spent most of his life in London. In 1894 Edward Martyn* acquainted him with the ideals of the Irish Literary revival and when he returned to Dublin, Moore became a member of a group including Augusta Lady Gregory,* John Millington Synge* and W. B. Yeats,* which created a native drama in the English language. During this period Moore collaborated with Martyn on *The Bending of the Bough* (1900), with Yeats on *Diarmuid and Grania* (1901) and produced a volume of short stories, *The Untilled Field* (1903). His literary evenings became celebrated occasions for bringing native and visiting literati together. James Joyce* took exception to his exclusion from these gatherings – Moore considered him socially inferior, and was later to say that his own *Confessions of a Young Man* (1888) was superior to Joyce's *Portrait of the Artist as a Young Man*. Moore's conversion to Protestantism earned him notoriety in Ireland. His works include a three-volume autobiography – *Ave* (1911), *Salve* (1912) and *Vale* (1913) – collectively titled *Hail and Farewell*. He published thirty-five books in all, including *Parnell and his Island* (1887), *Esther Waters* (1894), *Memoirs of My Dead Life* (1906), *The Making of an Immortal* (1927), *The Passing of Essenes* (1930) and *A Communication to My Friends* (1933).

MOORE, GEORGE HENRY (1811–70). Politician; b. Moore Hall, Co. Mayo; father of George Augustus Moore* and Colonel Maurice Moore;* ed. Oscott College, Birmingham and Christ College, Cambridge. He was elected MP for Co. Mayo in 1847 and won a reputation in the House of Commons as a distinguished speaker. An excellent landlord on his Co. Mayo estate, he supported Tenant Right.* He was a founder of the Catholic Defence Association* and was leader of the 'Irish Brigade'.* He was prominent in the formation of the Independent Irish Party* which resulted from the merger of the Brigade and the Tenant League Association.* Moore lost his parliamentary seat in 1857 following charges of clerical interference in his election campaign. He was re-elected in 1868 and held the seat until his death.

MOORE, COLONEL MAURICE GEORGE (1854–1939). Soldier; b. Moore Hall, Co. Mayo, son of George Henry Moore* and younger brother of George Augustus Moore;* ed. St Mary's College, Oscott, Birmingham, and at Sandhurst Military College. Commissioned in the Connaught Rangers in 1875, he fought in the Kaffir and Zulu Wars (1877–79) and in Natal. He commanded the 1st Battalion of the Connaught Rangers (1900–06), forming a cavalry corps which distinguished itself during the Boer War. After settling in Ireland he supported John Redmond* and the Irish Parliamentary Party* in the fight for Home Rule.* He became instructor of the Irish Volunteers.* Following the establishment of the Free State,* he campaigned for the withholding of Land Annuities,* and supported Captain William Redmond* and the National League Party.* A founder-member of Fianna Fail* in 1926, he was later a member of the Senate.* He was the author of *An Irish Gentleman, George Henry Moore* (1913), and *The Rise of the Volunteers, 1913–17* (1938).

MOORE, ROBERT ROSS ROWAN (1811–64). Political economist; b. Dublin; ed. TCD. He was a close friend of Thomas Davis.* Moore campaigned for Free Trade and was a member of the Irish Anti-Slavery Society which fought against the practice of shipping indentured apprentices* to the Caribbean.

MOORE, THOMAS (1779–1852). Poet and composer; b. Dublin; ed. Samuel White Academy and TCD, from which he graduated B.A. in 1798. While at TCD he formed a close friendship with Robert Emmet* on whose execution in 1803 he wrote 'Oh! Breathe Not His Name'. Moore arrived in London in April 1799 and under the patronage of Lord Moira published *Odes of Anacreon* (1800). An accomplished harpsichordist, Moore was a popular figure on the London social scene; Shelley mentions him in *Adonais*: '. . . from her wilds Ierne sent, The sweetest lyrist of her saddest wrong . . .' Moore's literary reputation was further enhanced with the publication of *The Political Works of the late Thomas*

Little Esq. in 1801. His opera *The Gipsy Prince* was, however, taken off the London Haymarket after a few performances (July 1802). In 1803 Moore declined the post of Chief Laureate of Ireland and in the same year secured a position as Registrar of the Admiralty in Bermuda. In March 1811 he married sixteen-year old Elizabeth ('Betsy') Dykes (she died in 1867 having survived her husband and five children). Moore's deputy in Bermuda absconded with the proceeds of a vessel and cargo, leaving him liable for some £6,000. Through the good offices of his publisher Longman, and Lord Lansdowne, the debt was discharged on payment of £1,000.

Lord Byron, a close friend, died in 1824, having entrusted his *Memoirs* to Moore. Byron's relatives were opposed to publication and Moore burned the manuscript for which he had accepted an advance of two thousand guineas. A strong advocate of Catholic Emancipation* and supporter of Daniel O'Connell,* Moore twice refused to stand as a Repeal candidate for Limerick. The most popular of his works, his *Melodies*, appeared in their tenth and last edition in 1834. A clause in the contract stipulated that he '. . . should visit town (London) at regular intervals and make a vogue for the latest songs by singing them publicly . . .' His other writings include *The Fudge Family in Paris* (1817), *Lalla Rookh* (1817), *Rhymes for the Road* (1823), *Fables for the Holy Alliance* (1823), *Loves of the Angels* (1823), *Memoirs of Captain Rock* (1824), *Memoirs of Right Hon. R. B. Sheridan* (1825), *Evenings in Greece* (1825), *The Epicurean* (1827), *Odes (Political)* (1828), *Letters and Journals of Lord Byron* (1829), *Life of Fitzgerald* (1831), *Travels of an Irish gentleman in search of a religion* (1833), *History of Ireland* (1835) and *The Fudges in England* (1835). His collected poems were published by Longman in ten volumes (1843). Moore's executor, Lord John Russell,* arranged for the publication of *Memoirs, Journals and Correspond-*

ence of *Thomas Moore* which appeared in eight volumes, 1853–56.

MORAN, DENIS PATRICK (1872–1936). Journalist; b. Waterford; ed. privately and Castleknock College. Having moved to London in 1888, he was active in the Gaelic League* and the Irish Literary Society.* Returning to Ireland in 1898, he edited the *New Ireland Review** in which he expressed his disillusionment with Irish nationalism. Two years later he founded *The Leader* (1 September 1900) which quickly established itself as an influential force in the Irish – Ireland movement. Moran called for a thoroughly political, cultural and economic nationalism, expressed in *Philosophy of Irish Ireland,* where Ireland would be a self-governing land 'living, moving and having its being in its own language, self-reliant . . . developing its own manners and customs, creating its own literature out of its own distinctive consciousness . . .' He organised a 'Buy-Irish' campaign. Moran criticised virtually every part of the nationalist movement, including the Gaelic League, W. B. Yeats* and the literary revival ('. . . one of the most glaring frauds that the credulous Irish people ever swallowed . . .'), Sinn Fein* (the 'Green Hungarian Band'), the Irish Republican Brotherhood* and the Irish Parliamentary Party* ('West Britons' and 'shoneens'). One of Moran's most vitriolic reviews was of *The Playboy of the Western World* by J. M. Synge* in 1907; he condemned in particular its attitude towards Irish women. He played no public role after the Easter Rising of 1916* and his paper, not geared for the changes taking place after the establishment of the Free State,* lost its influence.

MORAN, PATRICK FRANCIS, CARDINAL (1830–1911). Bishop of Ossory (R.C.), 1872–84, and Archbishop of Sydney (1884–1911); b. Leighlinbridge, Co. Carlow, the nephew of Dr Paul Cullen,* under whose patronage he was edu-cated at the Irish College, Rome from the age of twelve. Following ordination in 1853 he became vice-rector of the college (1856) and Professor of Hebrew at the College of Propaganda. He was co-founder and co-editor of *The Irish Ecclesiastical Review** in 1864 and returned to Ireland as private secretary to Cardinal Cullen in 1866. Four years later he became co-adjutor bishop of Ossory, and within two years, its bishop. Following his translation to Sydney he built up the archdiocese, raising the number of churches from 75 to 189 for a Catholic population which grew from 96,000 to 195,000. He published *Memoir of Oliver Plunkett* in 1861.

MORE O'FERRALL, RICHARD (1797–1880). Politician (Liberal); b. Balyna, Co. Kildare. He refused to enter TCD because of religious scruples. A close friend of Bishop James Warren Doyle ('JKL')* and Daniel O'Connell,* he was MP for Kildare (1831–47), Longford (1851–52) and Kildare (1859–65). In 1832 he was a member of a commission which investigated the state of Ireland. He accepted office from Lord Melbourne,* as Lord of the Treasury (1835). Appointed Governor of Malta (1847), he resigned after four years in protest at the Ecclesiastical Titles Act.* Magistrate, Grand Juror and Deputy Lieutenant of Kildare, upon his death he was the oldest serving Privy Councillor in Ireland.

MORGAN, SYDNEY, LADY (1777–1859). Poet and novelist; b. probably at sea, daughter of an actor whose original name was MacOwen; ed. by tutor and at Huguenot School, Clontarf, Dublin. She was employed as a governess from the age of eighteen by which time she had written several poems. The first volume of her *Poems* appeared in 1801 and her first novel, *St Clair,* was published two years later. She married the physician T.C. Morgan in 1812, shortly before he received a knighthood. With her husband she made frequent continental journeys, beginning with a visit to

France in 1816. Her subsequent book *France* (1817) was the centre of controversy: Lady Morgan was severely attacked by critics, notably by Gifford in *The Quarterly Review*. Her next travel work, *Italy*, also provoked the hostility of critics although Lord Byron writing to Thomas Moore* described it as '. . . fearless and excellent on the subject'. Although not an admirer of Daniel O'Connell,* Lady Morgan strongly advocated Catholic Emancipation* and her novels reflected her liberal outlook on Irish affairs. Her husband, (who had assisted her in several of her works) died in 1843 and Lady Morgan was awarded a civil list pension of £300 per annum. Author of over seventy works from which she grossed in excess of £25,000, her writings include *The Novice of St Dominic* (1805), *The Wild Irish Girl* (1806), *The Lay of an Irish Harp* (1807), *The First Attempt* (a comic opera, 1807), *Patriotic Sketches* (1807), *O'Donnell* (1814), *Florence McCarthy* (1819), *Absenteeism* (1825), *The O'Briens and the O'Flahertys* (1827), *Passages from my Autobiography* (1859). *Lady Morgan's Memoirs: Autobiography, Diaries and Correspondence* was edited by W. H. Dixon and published shortly after her death.

MORIARTY, DAVID (1814–77). Bishop of Kerry (R.C.), 1856–77; b. Kilcarragh, Co. Kerry; ed. locally, Boulogne and Maynooth where he was ordained in 1839. He was Vice-President of the Irish College, Paris and President of All-Hallows, Drumcondra (1847–54), before becoming co-adjutor bishop of Kerry (1854–56). During the 1850s he was suspected by his friend, Paul Cullen,* Archbishop of Dublin, of being a Young Ireland sympathiser. Following the rising of the Irish Republican Brotherhood* in Kerry in 1867 he became notorious for the vehemence of his alleged condemnation, when he called down upon the Fenians 'God's heaviest curse, His withering, blasting, blighting curse' and then informed his

public that 'hell was not hot enough and eternity not long enough to punish these miscreants'. His reported sermon was not approved by his fellow members of the hierarchy and Cullen privately indicated his disapproval of it. A Unionist at heart, Moriarty opposed Home Rule* and unsuccessfully put forward his own anti-Home Rule candidate in Kerry in the general election of 1874. He attended the Vatican Council in 1870 and disapproved of the definition of papal infallibility, claiming that this was not the right time to promulgate it, although he accepted it once it had been approved by his fellow-bishops.

MORLEY, JOHN, 1st VISCOUNT (1838–1923). Journalist and politician (Liberal); Chief Secretary (February–July 1886; 1892–95); ed. Cheltenham College and Lincoln College, Oxford; Bar (1873). As editor of *The Fortnightly Review* he was one of the most influential political and intellectual forces in England. After first meeting Charles Stewart Parnell* in 1879, he acted as confidante and go-between for the Irish party and W. E. Gladstone.* He defended the Land League.* After his return as MP for Newcastle-on-Tyne (1883) he supported Joseph Chamberlain* until they broke over Home Rule* in 1886 when he made the celebrated accusation that Chamberlain had played Casca to Gladstone's Caesar. He accepted office in February 1886 when the 1st Marquess of Aberdeen* became Lord Lieutenant. Until July he was consulted by Gladstone on the (first) Home Rule Bill* which was defeated that month. Morley supported Parnell when *The Times* published 'Parnellism and Crime'* and discouraged him from taking any action against the paper. He was closely involved with Parnell and Gladstone after the *O'Shea v O'Shea and Parnell* divorce decision (November 1890). Gladstone wrote him a letter on 24 November, to be shown to Justin McCarthy* who was to make known its contents to Parnell: if Parnell remained at the head of the Irish party it would render Gladstone's leadership of the Liberals 'a nullity'. When Parnell was re-elected chairman of the party (25 November) Gladstone published the letter.

Morley was noted for his over-caution during his second term as Chief Secretary. He helped Gladstone to carry the second Home Rule Bill* through the Commons (1893) and attacked the privileges of the (Protestant) Ascendancy* in Ireland, removing some of the more intransigent from magistracies. He was Lord President of the Council (1910–14). His works include *The Struggle for National Education* (1873), *On Compromises* (1874), *Burke* (1879), *The Life of Richard Cobden* (1881), *Life of Gladstone* (3 vols, 1903) and *Recollections* (1917).

MORPETH, VISCOUNT. *See* Carlisle, 7th Earl.

MORRISON, SIR RICHARD (1767–1849). Architect; b. Midleton, Co. Cork. Intended for the church, he showed little enthusiasm for orders and was placed as a student under James Gandon. Knighted in 1841, Morrison built up an extensive practice which included work on the court-houses at Carlow, Clonmel (where he lived for a time), Dundalk, Galway, Naas and Wexford. He made extensive alterations to the cathedrals of Cashel and Roscommon and the Pro-Cathedral, Dublin. He published a volume of *Designs* in 1793.

MORTISHED, RONALD JAMES PATRICK (1891–1957). Labour leader; b. London of a Limerick father; ed. London Council schools, Strand School, Morley College and the London School of Economics. He entered the British Civil Service in 1908 and later became a member of the (Irish) White Cross* and of the Reconstruction Committee (1921). Mortished served as Secretary to the Committee which drafted the 1922 Constitution of the Irish Free State. He was assistant secretary of the

Labour Party* and of the Irish Trade Union Congress* (1922–30). He served in the International Labour Organisation (1930–46) and was chairman of the Labour Court (1946–52). He published *The World Parliament of Labour* in 1946.

MOSSOP, WILLIAM STEPHEN (1788–1827). Medallist; b. Dublin; ed. Samuel White Academy, Dublin. He struck his first medal in 1805. Mossop produced a series of medals on most of the leading celebrities of the era, including the first engraving of Daniel O'Connell* (1816). He produced a variety of commemorative medals and designed the seals for most public bodies in Ireland. A selection of his original steel discs may be observed in the Royal Irish Academy.*

'MOTHER AND CHILD SCHEME'. The Mother and Child Scheme, as it was popularly known, was part of the 1947 Health Act drafted by the Fianna Fail* government. The terms of the scheme were unacceptable to the Catholic hierarchy and when this was brought to the attention of Eamon de Valera* by the Archbishop of Dublin, John Charles McQuaid,* the scheme was shelved. The Fianna Fail government was replaced by the first Inter-Party Government* in February 1948 and two years later, the scheme was revived by the socialist Minister for Health, Dr Noel Browne.* After consultations with the Consultative Child Health Scheme (consisting of medical specialists, and representatives of the local authorities and of the Departments of Health, Education and Social Welfare) a draft of the scheme was prepared in June 1950.

The Scheme, which was not to be compulsory, proposed a system of education 'in respect of motherhood' for *all* mothers and children up to sixteen years of age. There was to be no means test. The Irish Medical Association (IMA), with which Dr Browne had a poor relationship, objected to the concept of 'socialised medicine'. In July, Dr Browne told the Dail that he would not agree to a means test, and received the backing of the cabinet. During October the bishops considered the Scheme and expressed disquiet at clauses which had already been rejected in 1947 (the lack of a means test and freedom of choice of doctor). An episcopal commission, consisting of Dr McQuaid, Dr Michael Browne of Galway and Dr Staunton of Ferns, was established. At a meeting with Dr Browne on 11 October 1950, the bishops indicated their objections and heard Dr Browne's reply. Dr Browne left the meeting under the impression that he had satisfactorily met their objections. Dr Browne again rejected the idea of a means test on 24 October 1950, when the IMA indicated the lack of resources at the disposal of the State. The bishops made it clear to the government that they considered there was an important issue of 'faith and morals'. The family, they stated, was the final arbiter in regard to sex education. They also objected to non-Catholics treating Catholic mothers-to-be or offering them sex education which might be at variance with accepted Catholic social teaching. The debate continued until March 1951. During this time the relationship between Dr Browne and the leader of his party, Sean MacBride,* deteriorated. At the same time he was at odds with the leader of the government, John A. Costello,* and with his cabinet colleagues. The government, by now, wished to concede to the episcopal and medical demand for a means test.

On 6 March, Dr Browne said that there would be no more delays and published the Scheme, having refused his colleagues' request for the inclusion of a means test. Details of the Scheme were circulated to the hierarchy and two days later the bishops rejected it on the grounds that none of their objections had been met. They provided Mr Costello with a copy of their correspondence with the Minister for Health. Dr Browne pointed out that he had met the bishops' objections. A major misunderstanding had apparently taken place, and he met with Dr McQuaid on 24 March and agreed that the bishops had the right to decide issues of 'faith and morals'. In April the bishops' convention rejected the Scheme 'as opposed to Catholic social teaching'. The government refused to support the Minister and abandoned the Scheme, conceding to all the bishops' objections. Dr Browne had by now also been rejected by his own party: MacBride had demanded his resignation. He resigned and published his correspondence with the hierarchy. The government fell in June 1951. The new Fianna Fail government introduced a public health act scheme with a means test.

'MOUNTAIN DEW'. *See* Poteen.

MOYLAN, SEAN (1888–1957). Politician (Fianna Fail); b. Cork; ed. National School which he left at twelve. Active in Irish Volunteers* in Cork and in the Irish Republican Army* during the War of Independence* in Cork. He was returned as republican TD in 1922 but did not take his seat as he opposed the Treaty.* He was Director of Operations in the new IRA (or Irregulars) during the Civil War* when his assistant was Eamon de Valera.* He continued to support Sinn Fein* until de Valera founded the Fianna Fail* party (1926). Moylan was Minister for Education in de Valera's government (June 1951–June 1954). After losing his seat in the 1957 general election, he was nominated to the Senate* by de Valera who wished to have him in the government as Minister for Agriculture (March–November 1957). Moylan was one of only two Senators who have held ministerial posts (the other was Joseph Connolly, Minister for Posts and Telegraphs, 1932–36).

MUINTIR NA TIRE (IRISH COUNTRY DEVELOPMENT MOVEMENT). 'The People of the Countryside'; community development association founded by Canon John Hayes, P.P., Bansha, Co. Tipperary (17 May 1931). It is registered as a friendly society. Fr Hayes adopted the Belgian organisation Boerenbond Belge (fl. 1890) as a model for the Irish movement which stated as its aim:

'. . . to unite the rural communities of Ireland on the Leo XIII principle that there must exist friendly relations between master and man; that it is a mistake to assume that class is hostile to class, that well-to-do and working men are intended by nature to live in mutual conflict. This new rural organisation . . . intends to unite in one body the rural workers of the country, not for the purpose of attacking any one section of the community, but to give the agricultural workers in Ireland their due and proper position in the life of the nation.'

The organisation sought to achieve its aims by the introduction of informal 'Fireside Chats' and later by rural week-ends culminating in its first full rural week at St Declan's Irish College, Ardmore, in 1937, which was opened by Eamon de Valera* and attended by church dignitaries, farmers, agricultural workers and members of the professions. The rural week was later replaced by a National Conference. Through its publications *The Landmark* and *Rural Ireland* (sold at church doors on Sundays), the association kept members informed of the efforts and achievements of guilds all over the country. These publications have now been replaced by a monthly bulletin.

To Muintir must go much of the credit for the rapid extension of the rural electrification scheme, the establishment of local industries, the erection and extension of leisure facilities (mostly accomplished by voluntary labour), the establishment of group water-schemes and the provision of free school meals (or hot drinks) to children in many rural schools. The association also pioneered community information services. Latterly

Muintir has been working in close harmony with the EEC Social Fund on Community Development and in July 1977 received a grant of £50,000 for community development in areas undergoing structural change in Ireland.

MULCAHY, GENERAL RICHARD JAMES (1886–1971). Soldier and politician (Cumann na nGaedheal and Fine Gael); b. Waterford; ed. locally and at CBS, Thurles, Co. Tipperary. A member of the Gaelic League,* he joined the Irish Volunteers* in 1913 and was second-in-command to Thomas Ashe* at Ashbourne during the Easter Rising of 1916.* Imprisoned for his role in the Rising, he became, upon release, deputy Chief-of-Staff of the Volunteers in which capacity he worked closely with Michael Collins.* As Chief-of-Staff of the Irish Republican Army* he was elected to the First Dail Eireann* where he acted as Minister for Defence until Cathal Brugha* assumed the Ministry in April 1919. Mulcahy supported the Treaty* and became Minister for National Defence in the Second Dail and in the Provisional Government,* while acting as Chief-of-Staff of the National Army. In these capacities he retained contact with that section of the IRA which had rejected the Treaty and he was a signatory to the Army Document* which attempted, in the interests of national unity, to secure a compromise between supporters and opponents of the Treaty. Mulcahy was responsible for the prosecution of the fight against the Republicans during the Civil War,* during which he met Eamon de Valera* on 6 September 1922 in an unsuccessful attempt to end hostilities. On 10 October 1922 Mulcahy's request for Special Emergency Powers to prosecute the war against the Republicans was granted, and he received a virtual *carte blanche* to expedite their defeat. He remained Minister for Defence in the Free State government until March 1924, when he resigned during the Army Mutiny.*

In June 1927, he became Minister for Local Government (until March 1932). Prominent in the Blueshirt movement, Mulcahy was a founder-member of Fine Gael* which party he represented until losing his Dail seat in May 1943. Having regained his seat in 1944, and now leader of Fine Gael in succession to W. T. Cosgrave,* he was not an acceptable head of government to the parties of the first Inter-Party Government:* he served instead as Minister for Education (February 1948–June 1951) to the compromise Taoiseach, John A. Costello.* He was Minister for Education in the second Inter-Party Government (June 1954–March 1957) and Minister for the Gaeltacht (July–October 1956). He was succeeded as leader of Fine Gael by James M. Dillon* in October 1959. In 1961 he retired from the Dail where in later years he had represented the constituency of South Tipperary.

MULGRAVE, 2nd EARL (1797–1863). Phipps, Constantine Henry; Politician (Whig); Lord Lieutenant; b. England; ed. Harrow and Trinity College, Cambridge, where he graduated M.A. in 1818. He supported Catholic Emancipation* and movements towards parliamentary reform. His liberalism brought him into conflict with his family and he left England for Italy. Upon his return in 1822 he was elected MP for Higham Ferrars. He succeeded to the title in 1831. Having held the governorship of Jamaica and been Lord Privy Seal under Melbourne's administration, Mulgrave was appointed Lord Lieutenant in 1835. Daniel O'Connell* and the Irish party received his appointment with enthusiasm. Mulgrave headed one of the most constructive Irish governments of the century. His Chief Secretary was Viscount Morpeth* and the Under-Secretary was Thomas Drummond.* Mulgrave's attempts to win Ireland to the Union through concessions earned him wide criticism. He supported Drummond in the removal from office of magistrates noted for their anti-Catholic prejudices, and denounced the influence of Orangemen in public life. Mulgrave incurred further hostility on the occasions when he openly consulted the Catholic hierarchy on key issues. He several times exercised viceregal prerogative to commute death sentences. Created Marquis of Normanby in 1839, Mulgrave retired from Ireland to become Secretary of War and the Colonies in 1839.

MULHOLLAND, ANDREW (1791–1866). Cotton and linen industrialist; b. Belfast. He rebuilt his mill after a fire in 1828 and within two years was producing some of the earliest flax-yarn to be machine-spun in Ireland (previously flax had to be sent to Manchester to be spun and later re-imported as yarn). Mulholland was Lord Mayor of Belfast in 1845 and donated the great organ to the Ulster Hall. Other offices which he held included J.P., Deputy Lieutenant and High Sheriff for the counties of Antrim and Down. He retired from public life in 1860.

MULLINS, THOMAS (1903–78). Politician (Fianna Fail); b. New Rochelle, New York; ed. New York until he came to Ireland in 1914. He continued his education at St Enda's.* A member of Na Fianna Eireann* and the Irish Volunteers,* he supported Sinn Fein after the Easter Rising, of 1916 and was a member of the Irish Republican Army during the War of Independence.* Imprisoned on Spike Island, Wormwood Scrubs (where he went on hunger-strike) and Ballykinlar Camp (1920–21), he rejected the Treaty and supported the Irregulars (anti-Treaty IRA) during the Civil War* when he was captured and sentenced to death. During his imprisonment in Mountjoy he went on a 41-day hunger-strike. Mullins was a founder-member of Fianna Fail, building up an organisation in West Cork for which he was returned to Dail Eireann (1927). Close to leading radicals of the IRA, he supported Saor Eire* and was prominent in the fight against the Blueshirts.* He organised public relations for the Fianna Fail government which entered office in 1932. Having lost his seat he contested Co. Dublin in the by-election of 1947 when he lost to Sean MacBride.* Mullins organised the Fianna Fail victory of 1957 and became a member of the Senate and general secretary of Fianna Fail until 1973.

MUNICIPAL CORPORATIONS ACT, 1840. Introduced by the Whig administration during its period of alliance with Daniel O'Connell.* Under the terms of the Act, fifty-eight Corporations were dissolved and ten remaining corporations were reconstituted with selective town councils (Belfast, Clonmel, Cork, Drogheda, Dublin, Kilkenny, Limerick, Londonderry, Sligo and Waterford). Towns which had less than £100 valuation were administered by the Poor Law Guardians. The franchise for the incorporated towns was a £10 valuation. The Act marked a further step in the reform of Irish municipal government. *See also* Local Government.

MUNSTER COUNCIL OF ACTION. *See* Communist Party of Ireland *and* Soviets.

MURPHY, GERARD (1901–59). Scholar; b. Clones, Co. Monaghan; ed. Mount St Benedict, Gorey and at UCD where he read Celtic Studies. He worked in the National Library under Richard Best.* He spent four years in Switzerland before returning in 1930 to become Lecturer in Bardic Poetry and Early Irish Literature at UCD, and was appointed Professor of the History of Celtic Literature in 1948. Over a twenty-year period (1933–53) he translated parts II and III of the *Dunaire Finn* (*The Book of the Lays of Finn*) for the Irish Texts Society.* His other works include *Glimpses of Gaelic Ireland* (1948), *Ossianic Lore* and *Romantic Tales of Medieval Ireland* (1955), *Saga and Myth in Ancient Ireland* (1955). He contributed to *Studies* and *Eriu*

and edited *Journal of Modern Irish Studies* (1939), *Early Irish Lyrics* (1956) and *Early Irish Metrics* (with vocabulary) in 1961.

MURPHY, JOHN (1771–1847). Bishop of Cork (R.C.), 1814–47 and bibliophile. Following his ordination in Lisbon he returned to Cork where he became an early patron of the sculptor John Hogan.* He developed a keen interest in the Irish language and amassed a library of manuscripts and books which grew into the largest private library in Ireland and which, after his death, entailed division into three separate lots for disposal. He bequeathed over 100 Irish volumes to Maynooth.* His brother, Francis Stack Murphy, was a noted scholar and lawyer.

MURPHY, PATRICK (1834–62). Giant; b. Co. Down. He was exhibited in every European country with the exception of Ireland as the tallest known living man — at eight foot one inch. Following his death at Marseilles, his remains were embalmed for re-interment at Kilbroney, Co. Down.

MURPHY, SEAMUS (1907–75). Sculptor; b. Mallow, Co. Cork; ed. St Patrick's National School, Cork. He left school at fourteen and was apprenticed to a headstone designer. He attended evening classes at the Cork Art School, and won a scholarship to Paris in 1932. Murphy set up his own studio in 1933 and supported himself by designing headstones. He won international fame as a sculptor and conversationalist. Much of his work is found in Cork city and county. His autobiography, *Stone Mad*, was a bestseller in 1966.

MURPHY, WILLIAM MARTIN (1844–1919). Businessman and politician (Nationalist); b. Bantry, Co. Cork; ed. Belvedere College, Dublin. Having constructed railways in the UK and financed similar undertakings in the Gold Coast (now Ghana) and in South America, he returned to

Ireland where he constructed Irish rail and tramways and purchased newspaper and other interests. He was proprietor of the *Irish Catholic* and *Irish Independent*.* Murphy was elected MP for St Patrick's Division of Dublin (1885–92). He was the chief promoter and Chairman of the Committee of the Irish International Exhibition of 1907. Alarmed at the militancy of the James Larkin-dominated Irish Transport and General Workers' Union,* Murphy formed a 400-strong Employers' Federation of which he was President. He was also President of the Dublin Chamber of Commerce. Although he held he was not 'in principle' opposed to his employees being members of organised 'worker combinations', Murphy demanded in August 1913 that they submit a written undertaking not to join Larkin's union. He told his employees in the Dublin United Tramway Co. that the directors had no objection to the men forming a 'legitimate union'. He felt that there was sufficient talent among his staff to undertake such a project without allying themselves to a 'disreputable organisation' which would place them under the 'strike monger' and the 'unscrupulous man, who used men as tools to make him the labour dictator of Dublin'. Larkin retaliated by calling out the tramway workers and in September Murphy and his fellow-employers locked out the workers in a vicious confrontation known as the Lock-Out of 1913.* This ended in victory for the employers in the short term, although its long-term effects greatly assisted the development of trade unionism in Ireland.

During World War I, Murphy recruited for the British Army in Ireland. On 25 November 1915 he convened a meeting of Irish employers at which a scheme was put forward to dismiss able-bodied men so as to force them to enlist. He was Chairman of the Finance and General Purposes Committee, Dublin Castle, for the Red Cross Hospitals (1915–19). In his will, Murphy left a personal estate of £264,005 which allowed for bequests to charities and to individual employees. He was the author of *The Home Rule Act 1914 Exposed*, in which he advocated colonial status for Ireland.

MURRAY, DANIEL (1768–1852). Archbishop of Dublin and Primate of Ireland (R.C.), 1823–52; b. Arklow; ed. locally and at the Irish College, Salamanca, where he was ordained in 1790. As a curate in Arklow he witnessed the Battle of Arklow during the rising of the United Irishmen* in 1798. Dr Murray was strongly opposed to the Veto* in 1808 and in the following year was appointed co-adjutor Bishop of Dublin at the request of the ailing Archbishop, Dr John Troy. He was sixth President of Maynooth College from June 1812 to November 1813, when he was succeeded by Dr Crotty.* As Archbishop he determined upon a policy of detente with the government, a policy which was frequently criticised by nationalists whom he further alienated in 1844 when he attended a viceregal levee. Dr Murray's acceptance of the system of National Education* led to a prolonged quarrel with the Archbishop of Tuam, John MacHale.* He accepted a position on the Board of Education as one of the two serving Catholic members (the other was A. R. Blake), and in so doing had the support of Rome and the majority of Irish bishops. When the controversy arose over the Queen's Colleges as an answer to the Catholic demand for a university, he supported Archbishop MacHale and Daniel O'Connell* in their denunciation of the 'godless colleges'. During the later years of his episcopate, discipline within his See relaxed and it was left to his successor, Paul Cullen, to initiate reforms.

MURRAY, THOMAS CORNELIUS (1873–1959). Dramatist, b. Macroom, Co. Cork; ed. National School and St Patrick's Training College, Dublin, where he qualified as a teacher in

1893. He worked in a number of schools in Co. Cork before he became headmaster of the Model School in Inchicore, Dublin, where he remained until his retirement in 1932. An outstanding member of the group of dramatists known as the 'Cork Realists' whose works were performed at the Abbey Theatre (*see* Robinson, Lennox), he was director of the Authors' Guild of Ireland and a member of the Irish Academy of Letters* of which he became vice-president. His best-known works were *Maurice Harte* (1910), and *Autumn Fire* (1924); other plays included *Birthright* (1910), *The Briery Gap* (1917), *Spring* (1918), *Aftermath* (1920), *The Pipe in the Fields* (1927), *The Blind Wolf* (1928), *A Flutter of Wings* (1929), *Michaelmas Eve* (1932), *A Stag at Bay* (1934), *Spring Horizon* (1937), *A Spot in the Sun* (1938) and *Illumination* (1939).

MYLES, SIR THOMAS (1857–1937). Surgeon; b. Limerick; ed. TCD. He entered Dr Steevens's Hospital in 1881. Myles was Secretary to the Dublin Hospitals' Committee (1885), Professor of Pathology at the Royal College of Surgeons (1889) and President of the Royal College of Surgeons (1900–02). He was Honorary Surgeon to the King in Ireland. His yacht, the *Chotah*, was used to transmit German guns for the Irish Volunteers (*see* Howth Gun-running). Upon the outbreak of World War I he became Consulting Surgeon to HM's Forces with the rank of Lieutenant-Colonel in the RAMC. Sir Thomas contributed specialist articles to a variety of medical and international journals.

N

NALLY, PATRICK W. (1857–91). Athlete and republican; b. Balla, Co. Mayo; ed. locally. A celebrated all-round athlete, in June 1876 he finished either first or second in sixteen out of seventeen competitions. He was sworn into the Irish Republican Brotherhood* by Dr Mark Ryan* and became chief organiser in Connaught. He was delegate to the Supreme Council* in 1879 and a founder-member of the Land League* of which he became secretary. While walking with Michael Cusack* in the Phoenix Park, he discussed the lack of an organisation for native athletics and from this conversation the Gaelic Athletic Association* developed. He fled from Mayo because of his republican activities, in particular his involvement in the so-called 'Crossmolina Conspiracy' but was captured and sentenced to ten years' imprisonment (1881–91). Harsh treatment in Mountjoy Jail led to his death shortly after release. A monument to his memory was unveiled in Balla by Mark Ryan in 1900.

NANGLE, REV. EDWARD (1799–1883). Evangelical clergyman (C.I.); b. Kildalkey, Athboy, Co. Meath; ed. TCD. He ministered at Athboy and Arva, Cavan, until his health broke. Nangle was secretary to the Sunday School Society of Ireland and worked also for a firm of publishers of religious tracts in Dublin. In 1831 he rented Achill Island and founded a Protestant missionary colony. His settlement, encouraged by the noted Protestant militant, Robert Daly, later Bishop of Cashel, flourished. Nangle founded a school, a church, a hospital and a printing press from which flowed tracts, pamphlets and articles for his propagandist newspaper, the *Achill Missionary Herald and Western Witness*, in which he attacked the 'superstition and idolatory of the Church of Rome'. He was a noted controversialist and incurred the hostility of both the Catholic and Protestant clergy. Although accused during the Famine of 1845—49* of using monies to further missionary work rather than give relief, and of operating a policy of 'souperism',* contemporaries were impressed by the amount of temporal aid which he gave. By 1853, he had gained a notable number of converts from the Catholic church and his activities became a source of some concern to the Catholic authorities in the west, and in particular to the Archbishop of Tuam, John MacHale.* Nangle purchased the estate of his former landlord, Sir Richard O'Donnell, for £17,500 from the Encumbered Estate Court.* While rector of Skreen (1852—73) he paid less attention to his colony. A fluent Irish speaker, he published a popular *Introduction to the Irish Language* (1854) which he hoped to use for the purpose of winning the natives from the Catholic Church. By 1879 however, his colony was almost defunct and he spent his remaining years in violent opposition to the Land League.*

NAPIER, SIR JOSEPH (1804—82). Lawyer and politician (Conservative); b. Belfast; ed. Belfast and TCD. Called to the Bar in 1831, he became QC in 1844 and was MP for Dublin University (1848—58). As Attorney-General (1852) he introduced the Ecclesiastical Code which bears his name. A strong supporter of the Established Church, he opposed the Disestablishment of the Church of Ireland* during his tenure as Lord Chancellor of Ireland (1858—59). Napier published specialist works on law and education and was a member of the judicial committee of the Privy Council (1868—81).

NATHAN, SIR MATHEW (1852—1937). Under-Secretary (1914—16); b. England; ed. privately and in the Royal Military Academy, Woolwich. He was commissioned in the Royal Engineers in 1890 and served at the War Office, to which he returned after seeing service in Africa and the Colonies. He held various offices before his appointment in 1914 as Under-Secretary for Ireland to the Chief Secretary, Augustine Birrell.* Nathan's *sang froid* in the face of nationalist hostility and crisis, once considered a virtue, became a distinct liability. Birrell was to dub him 'Nathan the Unwise' as, despite the overwhelming evidence of Volunteer activity during the Easter period in 1916, he took no precautionary action. As late as Easter Sunday, by which time the *Aud** with the arms intended for the Irish Volunteers,* had been scuttled and Sir Roger Casement* arrested, Nathan believed that a rising could be averted by arresting Volunteer leaders. On 10 April, he had stated that he did not believe that nationalist leaders meant an insurrection or that there were sufficient arms even if they did; in any case, he went on, 'revolutions never happen after noon'. He was trapped in Dublin Castle during the Easter Rising of 1916* and resigned on 3 May. A Royal Commission into the Easter insurrection blamed him for not having sufficiently impressed upon Birrell the necessity for action against the Volunteers at the end of the previous year. Nathan was succeeded as Under-Secretary by H. E. Duke and was subsequently Governor of Queensland (1921). A scholarly man by temperament, Nathan was a Fellow of the Royal Society of Antiquaries, a member of the Royal Historical Society and Vice-President of the Royal Geographical Society (1929—32). He was the author of *Annals of West Coker* (1937).

'NATION, THE'. Journal founded by Charles Gavan Duffy* in 1842. The motto of the paper, the first edition of which appeared on 15 October, was 'To create and foster public opinion, and make it racy of the soil'. The principal contributors were Thomas Davis* and John Blake Dillon* who, along with Duffy, had been trained in journalism by Michael Staunton* on *The Morning Register. The Nation* was quickly established as the organ of Young Ireland.* Through the publication of articles, stories, poems, ballads and historical pieces it strove to create in its readers a consciousness of Ireland's separate identity, its right to independence and the need for self-reliance. Edited at first by Davis who published many of his poems in it, the paper became widely read by the peasantry who clubbed together to pay the 6d (2½p) to purchase it and then, in many cases, had to find someone who could read it to them. By 1843 it was selling 10,000 copies at a time when 1,000 copies was a highly respectable sales figure, and was estimated to have a readership in the region of 250,000. Davis said of it that it would work to realise a 'nationality of the spirit as well as the letter . . . which would embrace Protestant, Catholic, and Dissenter – Milesian and Cromwellian – the Irishman of a hundred generations and the stranger who is within our gates . . .' (22 July 1843). Asked about the tone of the paper a reader replied, 'Wolfe Tone'.

The Nation supported Daniel O'Connell* and the Repeal Association* and advocated withdrawal from Westminster and the establishment of an Irish parliament in Dublin. It ceased to support him in 1846 when he declared that physical force could never be a solution to Ireland's problem and Young Ireland broke with the Repeal Association.

The paper mirrored Young Ireland in support of the Queen's Colleges* which brought it into conflict with the nationalist Archbishop of Tuam, John MacHale.* After Davis' death (September 1845) the new chief writer was John Mitchel,* until he broke with the paper over Duffy's policy of moderation (1847). Following the collapse of the 1848 rising at Ballingarry, Co. Tipperary,* Duffy became a constitutionalist and the paper supported the Tenant League* and, for a short time, the Independent Irish Party.* Follow-

ing Duffy's departure for Australia (1855), *The Nation* was owned by A. M. Sullivan.* It published a letter in 1858 from the former leader of Young Ireland, William Smith O'Brien,* warning the people against joining secret societies – by implication the Irish Republican Brotherhood.* Although the paper's influence was now beginning to wane, it formed an important platform of support for the Disestablishment of the Church of Ireland* and for the proposal by Isaac Butt* for a united nationalist party. Throughout the 1880s the paper supported Charles Stewart Parnell,* the Irish Parliamentary Party,* the Land League* and the New Departure.* During the split in the party following on Parnell's involvement in the O'Shea divorce case (*see* Irish Parliamentary Party) the paper was anti-Parnellite. *The Nation* ceased publication in 1891. *The Irish Independent** complex now occupies the site of its former office in Dublin.

NATIONAL AGRICULTURAL LABOURERS' UNION. The NALU was a British union which extended its activities to Ireland in 1873 in an attempt to prevent Irish migrant labourers strike-breaking in England. The Irish leader was P. F. Johnson of Kanturk, Co. Cork, in which area some Labourers' Clubs were formed. The union took on a pro-Home Rule complexion when Isaac Butt* and P. J. Smyth* became president and vice-president respectively. It was not a success, however, and faded after 1877.

NATIONAL ANTHEM. 'Amhrán na bhFiann' or 'The Soldier's Song', the Irish national anthem, was written by Peadar Kearney* with music by Patrick Heeney* in 1907. First sung by Sean Kavanagh in Dublin, the words were published in *Irish Freedom** by Bulmer Hobson in 1912 and during the following year the tune was adopted by the Irish Volunteers.* After the Easter Rising of 1916, the song became popular among the interned Volunteers and supplemented the unofficial anthem, 'God Save Ireland'. 'The Soldier's Song' was informally adopted as the national anthem of the Free State* in 1924 and two years later, on the motion of W. T. Cosgrave, it was ruled that it should be recognised as the national anthem.

NATIONAL ASSOCIATION. Inaugurated 29 December 1864 with the encouragement of the Catholic Archbishop of Dublin, Paul Cullen,* who hoped to weaken the influence of the Irish Republican Brotherhood.* The National Association adopted a programme of Tenant Right,* Disestablishment of the Church of Ireland* and freedom of education. Prominent supporters included W. J. O'Neill Daunt* and Sir John Gray.* It received strong support from the Catholic hierarchy but was publicly opposed by John MacHale,* Archbishop of Tuam and Thomas Nulty,* Bishop of Meath. The NAI was short-lived due to its poor organisation, insufficient finances and internal wranglings. Many of its supporters were absorbed into the Home Government Association* established by Isaac Butt* in 1870.

NATIONAL CENTRE PARTY. Founded by James Dillon* and Frank MacDermot* from the National Farmers' and Ratepayers' League* in 1932—33. Its principal aims were to secure monetary reform, tariff protection, de-rating of agricultural land, reduction of legal fees and wages stability. The party secured eleven seats in the 1933 general election. Ideologically, the party was close to Cumann na nGaedheal,* and when the Fianna Fail administration of Eamon de Valera* banned the Blueshirts* in August 1933, the NCP merged with Cumann na nGaedheal's successor, Fine Gael.

NATIONAL COALITION GOVERNMENT. Government formed in 1973 from a coalition of Fine Gael* and the Labour Party.* The partners to the Coalition published a fourteen-point programme before the general election of February 1973 in which they secured an overall majority over Fianna Fail;* Fine Gael returned with 54 seats and Labour with 19, while Fianna Fail secured 69.

Liam Cosgrave* became Taoiseach and selected the following cabinet: Brendan Corish,* leader of the Labour Party, (Tanaiste and Minister for Health and Social Welfare); Dr Garret Fitzgerald,* Fine Gael (Minister for Foreign Affairs); Patrick Cooney, Fine Gael (Justice); Richard Ryan, Fine Gael (Finance); Patrick S. Donegan, Fine Gael (Defence to December 1976, succeeded by Oliver J. Flanagan, Fine Gael, in January 1977); Michael O'Leary, Labour (Labour); Justin Keating, Labour (Industry and Commerce); Dr Conor Cruise O'Brien, Labour (Posts and Telegraphs); Tom O'Donnell, Fine Gael (Gaeltacht); Richard Burke, Fine Gael (Education, until January 1977 when he was succeeded by Peter Barry, Fine Gael); Thomas Fitzpatrick, Fine Gael (Lands); Mark Clinton, Fine Gael (Agriculture); James Tully, Labour (Local Government). The Attorney-General (with a cabinet seat) was Declan Costello, until 1977 when he resigned and was replaced by John Kelly, a former Parliamentary Secretary to the Taoiseach and Chief Whip.

Despite its pre-election hopes, the Coalition proved unable to stabilise prices; inflation continued to mount until 1978. Overall there had been price increases of 100 per cent in many areas. The government removed VAT from food (1973), electricity, heating, oils, clothing and footwear (1976) and subsidised staple food items. It also increased Social Welfare payments and reduced the Old Age Pension qualifying age to sixty-six. Supplementary and pay-related schemes were introduced to ease the burden of heavy unemployment (around 160,000 by mid-1977). By 1974 the government was in a position to negotiate with the employers and trade unions to produce a national pay agreement with pre-determined increases over a twelve-month period.

Agriculture boomed from 1974 to 1977, due principally to EEC demand for Irish beef and agricultural produce. The government concentrated on tax inequities but their scheme to tax the larger farms, on a system based on rateable valuation and notional income, evoked mounting criticism from farming organisations.

The Minister for Local Government, James Tully, made more finance available for local authority housing. His target of 25,000 new houses per annum stretched available resources to the limit and while figures issued by his Department indicated that this target was being met the depression within the building industry continued. Mr Tully was also accused of a gerrymander (or 'Tullymander' as political pundits put it) in his re-drawing of the constituency boundaries for national elections. Political commentators felt that Fianna Fail faced an uphill struggle in the next general election as a result of Mr Tully's re-shaping of the constituencies. A further act of Mr Tully (which was to have a significant effect on the general election result) was the lowering of the voting age from 21 to 18 years, making the young vote one quarter of the entire electorate.

The Coalition initiated new approaches on the question of Northern Ireland and Mr Cosgrave was party to a meeting with Brian Faulkner* and Edward Heath, the British Prime Minister, at Sunningdale* in December 1973. Security was a major concern of the Coalition Government which was dedicated to the destruction of the Irish Republican Army* and kindred subversive organisations. The Criminal Law (Jurisdiction) Act 1976 extended the criminal law of the Republic and created new offence categories. The Bill was referred by the President, Cearbhal O'Dalaigh,* to the Supreme Court and held to be constitutional. The Act was rein-forced by the Emergency Powers Act 1976 which increased the maximum penalties for offences under the Offences Against the State Act.* This Act was also referred by the President to the Supreme Court but it too was held to be constitutional. During 1976–77 there was widespread criticism of the conditions alleged to obtain in Portlaoise jail which had become a maximum security prison for convicted IRA members. The government consistently refused to allow independent investigations of the prison system and evoked widespread comment by their refusal. There was no noticeable diminution in the level of IRA activity by the time the government went out of office (June 1977) but there was a sustained demand for more gardai to deal with the high level of organised and petty crime.

At the end of 1976 came a disquieting incident destined to have far-flung implications for the Coalition. The Minister for Defence, Patrick Donegan, speaking at a function for Army personnel, referred to the President as a (reportedly) 'thundering disgrace' for his action in referring the Emergency Powers Act 1976 to the Supreme Court. This attack on the President's use of his powers caused a political furore. The opposition called for the Minister's resignation, or at the very least, his dismissal from the cabinet. The Taoiseach (Liam Cosgrave) declined to act and although Mr Donegan apologised, the President resigned, maintaining that as the office had been denigrated, he had no alternative. In December 1976, Mr Donegan, in a cabinet re-shuffle, left Defence to become Minister for Lands and later Minister for Fisheries. Further damage was done to the Coalition's prestige at the Fine Gael Ard-Fheis in May 1977. In an unscripted aside, Mr Cosgrave referred to the Coalition's critics in the media. He referred to these critics as 'blow-ins' and requested them to 'blow-out'. This apparent intolerance of criticism, while greeted with obvious enthusiasm by the delegates, was received with sobriety by the media and neutral observers.

In the ensuing general election in June, Fianna Fail swept back to power with a record 84 seats. The implications of the defeat for the Coalition partners ran deep. Almost immediately, Liam Cosgrave resigned the leadership of Fine Gael and was succeeded by Dr Garret Fitzgerald.* Frank Cluskey* replaced Brendan Corish as leader of the Labour Party. The Coalition had presided over the 20th Dail which sat for a record total of 404 days, or 3,250 hours – 979 of them during 1975.

NATIONAL CORPORATIVE PAR- TY. Founded by General Eoin O'Duffy* in 1935 after he had been ousted from the League of Youth.* The NCP, which was inspired by the ideals of Benito Mussolini and his Fascist party, was actively supported by a number of former Blueshirts.* It failed within a brief period through lack of popular support.

NATIONAL COUNCIL. Formed by members of Cumann na nGaedheal* Executive to protest against the pro- posed visit to Ireland of King Edward VII in 1903. The Council, whose chairman was Edward Martyn,* in- cluded Arthur Griffith,* Maud Gonne,* Major John MacBride* and John O'Leary* among its members. It also attracted the support of the Irish Republican Brotherhood* through Dr Mark Ryan* and John Daly.* The Council remained in existence long after its original aim had been accomplished and finally merged with Sinn Fein.*

NATIONAL COUNCIL FOR EDU- CATIONAL AWARDS (NCEA). Es- tablished in 1972 as part of the re- organisation of third-level education, the NCEA was empowered to vali- date awards issued by non-university institutions. Its purpose was to plan and co-ordinate facilities, '. . . to pro- mote maximum interaction between the autonomous university sector

and the non-university sector . . . to avoid random development as be- tween either sector which might lead it to unnecessary duplication of scarce resources'. Its degree-awarding powers were removed in 1973 by the Minister for Education in the National Coalition Government* and restored in 1977 by the Minister in the new Fianna Fail government.

NATIONAL DEMOCRATIC PARTY. *See* National Unity and the National Democratic Party.

NATIONAL EDUCATION. The Irish system of national education was founded in 1831 under the direction of the Chief Secretary, E. G. Stanley.* (*see* Derby, 14th Earl). His concept of a non-denominational system was outlined in a letter to the 3rd Duke of Leinster* who was invited to become president of the commis- sioners of national education. In the system as established no material peculiar to any denomination was used in schools, and ministers and priests were precluded from teaching posts. From its inception the system was attacked by the major Irish religious denominations (Catholic, Church of Ireland and Presbyterian) and by the powerful Orange Order.* Opposition from the Presbyterian Church, headed by Dr Henry Cooke,* led to a protracted series of negotia- tions until a formula was devised in 1840 which allowed for Presbyterian participation in the system without religious scruple. The Church of Ireland established its own Church Education Society* in 1839. The Society's schools (which had Catho- lics on the rolls) were denied a grant by Sir Robert Peel* and ran into financial difficulties as the National Education system developed. In 1870 it entered the national system and came under the jurisdiction of the board of commissioners, making use of the non-vested system.

The Catholic Church largely ac- cepted the system from its introduc- tion and the Archbishop of Dublin, Daniel Murray,* became a member of the Board. Support was also forthcoming from Bishop James Doyle* ('JKL') of Kildare and Leighlin and William Crolly, Archbishop of Armagh. In 1835, 941 individual Catholic clergy applied for grants. In 1836 the Christian Brothers withdrew from the system, their founder Edmund Ignatius Rice* holding that a system for Catholics should be thoroughly Catholic. One of the most significant opponents of the National Education system was the influential nationalist Archbishop of Tuam, John MacHale,* who would not allow national schools in his archdiocese. His opposition was based on the premise that the schools were anti-nationalist (Irish was not taught) and anti-Catholic. The death of Dr Murray and the succession of Paul Cullen* to the archdiocese of Dublin led to a change in the Church's attitude particularly after the Synod of Thurles* in 1850. Henceforth the Church concerned itself with demands for radical changes in the rules governing the system and in opposing the Model Schools.*

The national schools were built with the aid of the commissioners of national education and local trustees. The parent community was responsible for providing the site which was then vested in the trustees who were frequently landlords or local clergymen. Patronage was usually vested in the local bishop of the diocese. The patron appointed a manager (a minister or parish priest). Managers had virtually unlimited powers of hiring and firing and normally employed only teachers of their own denominations. Provided that the school complied with its regulations the Board itself exercised no authority in relation to the powers of the managers. Managers of many national schools during this period acquired deserved reputations as petty tyrants.

Although it had not been originally intended, a second category of national school, the Non-Vested school, emerged during the 1830s. Such establishments operated a uni-que set of rules approved by the Board. Some of these rules were in fact quite restrictive: Clergymen whose faith differed from that of the manager were forbidden to give religious instruction on school premises while religious instruction became a managerial prerogative. The proportion of non-vested schools, 68 per cent in 1850, rose to 75 per cent in 1880 but dropped to 66 per cent in 1900. The number of 'mixed' schools fell steadily in the second half of the century. The figure of 'mixed', or inter-denominational, schools in 1862 was just over 53 per cent, which had dropped to 35 per cent by the turn of the century.

The commissioners were incorporated in 1844 and their efforts to control all future schools built with their aid was strenuously and successfully opposed by the Catholic bishops. Included among the duties of the commissioners was the responsibility for producing textbooks. The range of textbooks produced was accepted as of a high standard by neutral observers. The system, however, alienated nationalist feeling: little Irish history was taught; neither Irish singing nor the Irish language were included in school curricula. Much controversy was excited in 1879 when the 'payments by results' system, already operating in England, was introduced. This system, however, was abolished in 1897 when a new scale came into operation.

The system of training teachers for the national schools had been considered generally unsatisfactory since its introduction in the mid 1840s. The Model Schools had been greeted with suspicion by the Catholic hierarchy and had failed to produce the required number of teachers: this led to many untrained teachers working in the national schools. In 1874 there were 2,640 trained to 5,000 untrained teachers operating in Catholic schools, compared with 426 trained and 380 untrained in Church of Ireland schools. Training schools were established in 1883 when St Patrick's Drumcondra (Dublin) opened to Catholic males and Our Lady of Mercy, Carysfort, Co. Dublin to Catholic female teachers. Church of Ireland trainees attended the Kildare Place Training College.

In the last quarter of the century a number of schools with residences attached were constructed under the National Teachers Residences (Ireland) Act of 1875. There were 1,970 applications for loans and eighty-three applications for grants, all of which were approved. By the end of 1919, 2,200 schools had residences attached. Illiteracy was no longer a major problem in Ireland by the end of the century and the National Education system had played a vital part in its virtual elimination. Ireland had had free primary education before the majority of its industrialised Western European neighbours. The following table gives a breakdown on the number of children attending primary schools in Ireland:

1833	107,042
1843	355,320
1850	804,000
1880	1,083,298
1900	745,861

The parliamentary grant for the national schools rose from £125,000 in 1850 to £1,145,721 in 1900.

The Board of Commissioners was dissolved when the Free State was established, and the national schools, along with the secondary and tertiary colleges, came under the jurisdiction of the newly-created Department of Education in 1924. In 1958, in the twenty-six counties, there were 4,869 national schools employing 13,554 teachers and catering for 504,401 pupils. The budget for the national system was in excess of £9m. For the school year 1977–78 there were 3,489 national schools with a total of 536,476 pupils.

NATIONAL FARMERS' AND RATE-PAYERS' PARTY. Founded in October 1932 by Patrick Belton and Frank MacDermot* who became its leader. Its principal aims were the promotion of agriculture, stronger representation of farmers in Dail

Eireann, an end to the Economic War* and the removal of partition by mutual consent between Northern Ireland and the Free State. A short time after James Dillon* joined it the NFRP became the National Centre Party.*

NATIONAL FARMERS' ASSOCIATION (NFA). Representative organisation for Irish farmers, founded in 1955. Under the leadership of Rickard Deasy, the NFA engaged in a bitter struggle to secure price increases for agricultural producers. It was affiliated to the International Federation of Agricultural Producers. The NFA merged with other organisations in 1969 to form the Irish Farmers' Association,* launched on 1 January 1970.

NATIONAL FOLK THEATRE OF IRELAND. *See* Siamsa.

NATIONAL GALLERY OF IRELAND. Established by Act of Parliament under a Board of Governors and Guardians, the Gallery was officially opened in 1866 by the Lord Lieutenant, the Earl of Carlisle.* Its architect was Charles Lanyon and the Gallery's first Director was George Mulvany ([Mulvaney] 1806–69). Early financial assistance was provided from a testimonial of £5,000 to William Dargan* in acknowledgement of his services to the Dublin Exhibition in 1853. The thirty-eight galleries display some 1,300 paintings and sculptures and approximately 600 watercolours and drawings. Painters represented include Fra Angelico, Breughel, Canaletto, Cezanne, Chardin, Constable, Corot, Cozens, David, Degas, Delacroix, El Greco, Gainsborough, Goya, Hals, Hogarth, Millet, Monet, Murillo, William Orpen,* Rembrandt, Rubens, Tintoretto, Turner, Van Dyck, Whistler, John Butler Yeats* and Jack Butler Yeats.* Principal gifts and bequests to the Gallery have been bestowed by the Countess of Miltown, Sir Hugh Lane,* George Bernard Shaw,* Sir Alfred Chester Beatty and the Friends of the National Collections. The Gallery's three main sources of income are government grant, the Lane Fund and the Shaw Bequest (one-third of the residual estate of G. B. Shaw).

NATIONAL GUARD. Title assumed by the Army Comrades Association* when General Eoin O'Duffy* became leader in July 1933. The members were popularly known as the Blueshirts.* In September the National Guard merged with Cumann na nGaedheal* and the National Centre Party* to form the United Ireland Party which became known as Fine Gael.*

NATIONAL INDUSTRIAL AND ECONOMIC COUNCIL. Established in 1963 during the first Programme for Economic Expansion (*see* Programmes for Economic Expansion). Its function is to create an awareness, in the industrial and commercial sectors, among trades unions, government departments and agencies and the general public of the needs and problems of the Irish economy through the publication of a regular series of reports.

NATIONAL INSTITUTE FOR HIGHER EDUCATION. *See* Commission on Higher Education.

NATIONAL INSURANCE ACT, 1911. Major scheme of insurance introduced by the Liberal government in 1911 to insure manual workers against ill-health and unemployment. The Act applied to manual workers earning less than £160 per annum, and was administered through 'approved societies'. It offered benefits for sickness, maternity and medical needs. Contributions were made by the insured person, the employer and the government. Payment was 10 shillings (50p) for male and 7s 6d (37½p) for female workers.

NATIONAL LABOUR PARTY. Political party founded in 1943 by five members of the Labour Party* after the Irish Transport and General Workers' Union* disaffiliated from the party. National Labour members secured four seats in the general election of 1944 and one more in 1948. The party joined the (first) Inter-Party Government* (1948–51) in which one member, James Everett,* held office as Minister for Posts and Telegraphs. Talks between National Labour and the parent party started in 1949 and they were reunited in June 1950.

NATIONAL LAND LEAGUE. Organisation for small farmers, founded by the Ballinagall Land Club (near Mullingar, Co. Westmeath) under the chairmanship of Dan McCarthy in 1965, with the support of Peadar O'Donnell.* The 7,500 strong organisation (1979), which opposed Ireland's entry into the European Economic Community,* opposes the purchase of Irish land by foreigners and seeks the redistribution of large holdings among the smaller farmers.

NATIONAL LEAGUE. The Irish National League, inaugurated by Charles Stewart Parnell* on 17 October 1882, replaced the Land League.* It was the constituency organisation of the Irish Parliamentary Party,* with the aims of securing '(1) national self-government; (2) land law reform; (3) local self-government; (4) extension of the parliamentary and municipal franchise; (5) development and encouragement of the labour and industrial resources of Ireland'. The League, built up by Tim Harrington,* the Secretary, William O'Brien* and T. M. Healy* had 1,261 branches by December 1885. Meetings throughout the country were addressed by Nationalist MPs at the rate of around thirty per month.

Parnell controlled the organisation through his manipulation of the League's Council, the governing body. Of the Council's forty-eight members, sixteen were MPs and the remainder representatives of local branches. He dominated the sixteen parliamentary members and so, for a majority, only needed nine of the thirty-two local representatives. In 1884 he made Catholic priests *ex-officio* delegates to the League's Conventions, by which time he had the support of the Catholic hierarchy.

In the USA the Irish National League of America was established but soon fell under the control of Clan na Gael* and was of limited use to Parnell and the Irish League.

In Ireland, the League's principal functions were to organise county conventions at which candidates for the general elections were chosen, and to provide financial support for the parliamentary party, which, from 1884, gave financial assistance to its MPs who lacked independent means. The new organisation within the constituencies produced results when the Parnellite party returned with eighty-five seats in Ireland after the general election of November 1885. In the following year, leading members of the League, Harrington, O'Brien, Healy and John Dillon* organised the Plan of Campaign,* leaving the prosecution of the Plan in each area to the local branch of the League. The amount of money raised increased from £11,616 (1884–85) to £47,275 (1885–86). The League split during 1890–91 as a result of the division within the party over Parnell's involvement with Mrs Katharine O'Shea.* The Parnellites, led by John Redmond,* held control of the League, while the anti-Parnellites established the Irish National Federation.* Membership of the League steadily decreased, from 13,108 in December 1891 to 6,500 in December 1893. By 1899 there were only six active branches. The rise of the United Irish League* brought about the reunification of the Irish party in 1900 and the UIL replaced the National League as the constituency organisation.

NATIONAL LEAGUE OF THE NORTH. Political party founded in 1928 by Joseph Devlin* who became its first president. The League was supported by former adherents of the (Irish) National League.* It sought the unification of Ireland while recognising the state of Northern Ireland. Devlin led his handful of followers as an opposition at Stormont* to the governing Ulster Unionist Party.* As the Unionists traditionally secured around forty of the fifty-two seats at Stormont the National League had to fight for the remaining dozen or so and so was of little use as a lobby. It lost support in the years 1932–34 and disappeared after the death of Devlin in 1934. *See also* Nationalist Party of Northern Ireland.

NATIONAL LEAGUE PARTY. Political party founded in September 1926 by Captain William Redmond.* The party incorporated the ideals of the Irish Parliamentary Party* and the National League* which had been controlled by the Captain's father, John Redmond.* The National League Party offered a programme of co-operation with Britain and Northern Ireland and sought to break the established political pattern in the Free State. League candidates won eight seats in the general election of June 1927; Redmond entered a pact with Fianna Fail and the Labour Party in an attempt to oust the Cumann na nGaedheal government. Prior to a vital division one League member, Rice, joined the government party and another, John Jinks of Sligo, failed to appear (*see* Jinks Affair). This ensured the government survival for a further period of office, after which W. T. Cosgrave* called another election which reduced the League's parliamentary presence to two. The party merged with Cumann na nGaedheal between 1931 and 1932.

NATIONAL LIBRARY OF IRELAND. Founded under the Dublin Science and Art Museum Act 1877, the National Library of Ireland (NLI) was officially opened on 29 August 1890. It was designed by Thomas

Deane. The nucleus of the new library's collection was 30,000 books from the Royal Dublin Society* and 23,000 volumes which had been held by the RDS in trust under a bequest from Rev. Jasper Joly.* The Joly Gift included a large collection of Irish and Scottish song music and a section of Napoleonic literature. Under its first Director, William Archer (1877–95), the NLI was one of the five libraries in the United Kingdom to use the Dewey system of classification. The library also receives all Irish publications under the Irish Copyright Act. Other Directors have included Thomas W. Lyster (1895–1920), Robert Lloyd Praeger* (1920–22), Richard Irvine Best* (1924–40) and Richard J. Hayes* (1940–67). The library is administered by the Department of Education through a Board of Trustees, four of whom are nominated by the Minister for Education and eight by the RDS. The library, which administers the Genealogical Office in Dublin Castle, contains 500,000 printed books, 40,000 manuscript items and 1,000,000 feet of microfilm.

NATIONAL MUSEUM OF IRELAND. Established in 1877 following investigations by a Select Committee (1862, 1864) into scientific institutions in Dublin. As a result of the Committee's Report the government agreed to support the library, Botanic Gardens* and the museum of the Royal Dublin Society.* The Dublin Museum Act of 1877 formally established the museum which was opened on 29 August 1890. Its collection is spread over four divisions: Natural Science, Art and Industrial (endowed by the RDS), Irish Antiquities (formed from a gift of the Royal Irish Academy in 1890) and Irish Folk Life (formed in 1974). Famous treasures housed in the Museum, which is administered by the Department of Education, include the Broighter Collar (1st century), St Patrick's Bell (5th century), the Tara Brooch (c. 700 A.D.), the

Ardagh Chalice (8th century), the Lismore Crozier (c. 1110) and the Cross of Cong (1123).

NATIONAL PARTY. Political party founded in 1924 as a result of the crisis over the Army Mutiny.* Led by Joseph MacGrath,* its membership was drawn almost exclusively from Cumann na nGaedheal.* The party demanded the reinstatement of the leaders of the Mutiny, but failed to secure it. In July the group, supported by the Labour Party,* challenged the government on the Appropriations of the Executive Council but their combined opposition, totalling eighteen votes, posed no serious threat to the government. With the exception of Sean Milroy* who unsuccessfully sought re-election, the National Party members resigned their seats in the autumn of 1924. The party disappeared from the political scene during 1925.

NATIONAL PETITION MOVEMENT. Founded at the offices of *The Nation** in 1859 at the urging of an Irish academic in France, J. P. Leonard who, in a letter to the newspaper, urged that Ireland should 'take England at her word'. He was referring to the support given by Lord John Russell* and *The Times* to the right of self-determination (they were actually referring to Italy). The National Petition, directed by T. D. Sullivan,* collected 500,000 signatures at church doors throughout the country. They were presented to parliament by The O'Donoghue. John Devoy,* who claimed in his *Recollections* that the National Petition 'gave Fenianism its first real start in Dublin' stated that the local branches of the NPM were sworn into the Irish Republican Brotherhood.*

NATIONAL POLITICAL UNION. Organisation founded and controlled by Daniel O'Connell* as the political machine of the Repeal Party (*see* Repeal Association) in 1832. Although it originally contained Whigs it became completely nationalist within a short period.

NATIONAL PROGRESSIVE DEMO-CRATIC PARTY. Socialist political party founded in 1957 by Dr Noel Browne.* The party won two seats in the general election of 1961 but was dissolved in 1963 when Dr Browne joined the Labour Party.*

NATIONAL REPEAL ASSOCIA-TION. *See* Repeal Association.

NATIONAL UNITY AND THE NATIONAL DEMOCRATIC PARTY. Movement founded in Northern Ireland in 1959 by a group of Catholic graduates who supported the idea of a United Ireland while recognising the constitution of Northern Ireland. It opposed violence (this was during a new campaign by the Irish Republican Army*). National Unity members put their expertise at the disposal of the Nationalist Party* but became disillusioned with the party's lack of policy and leadership. In 1964 it attacked the Nationalist Party which then produced a thirty-nine-point programme and under a new leader, Eddie McAteer,* prepared to adopt a more constructive role as the voice of the Catholic population. The movement then founded its own party, the National Democratic Party,* which committed itself to a pronouncement that the unification of Ireland could only come about when it was desired by the majority in Northern Ireland. In 1970 the NDP joined the Social Democratic and Labour Party.*

NATIONAL UNIVERSITY OF IRE-LAND. Established under the Irish Universities Act of 1908, introduced by the Chief Secretary, Augustine Birrell.* With the founding of the NUI the government hoped to placate the demand of the Catholic hierarchy for a Catholic system of university education. The move however incurred the hostility of Ulster Unionists.* The NUI was to consist of the old Queen's Colleges* of Cork and Galway, excluding the Queen's College of Belfast which became a full university. The third constituent college of the NUI was University College, Dublin. The Catholic hierarchy was given a major role in the governing body of each of the three constituent colleges. St Patrick's College, Maynooth was a 'recognised' college of the NUI until 1967 when it became a full constituent college. The NUI was theoretically non-denominational, and was forbidden by charter from having Chairs of Theology or Sacred Scripture. During the term of office of the National Coalition government (1973–77) the Minister for Education, Richard Burke, announced plans for a reshaping of NUI; UCD was to become a full university and both UCC and UCG would continue as constituent colleges. However, no legislation had been introduced by the time his government went out of office.

NATIONAL VOLUNTEERS. The Irish Volunteers* had been founded in November 1913. In September 1914 John Redmond* called on the Volunteers to help the British war effort and the Volunteer movement split when the separatists seceded from it, retaining the title Irish Volunteers. Redmond's followers became known as the National Volunteers. The National Volunteers numbered around 170,000, the vast majority of the original Volunteers. Contingents served in the British Army on the Western Front, but, unlike the Ulster Volunteer Force,* they were not permitted to maintain their Volunteer identity. The minority of the Irish Volunteers, some 12,000, formed the basis of the force which fought in the Easter Rising of 1916.*

NATIONALIST PARTY OF NORTH-ERN IRELAND. The Nationalist Party in Northern Ireland led by Joseph Devlin* was the northern section of the Irish Parliamentary Party.* Its six MPs abstained from the parliament of Northern Ireland when it was opened in June 1921. The Nationalists did not enter until three years later when two members, Devlin and T. G. McAllister, took their seats (there were ten members by then). The domination of the Northern Ireland parliament by the Ulster Unionist Party* rendered the small Nationalist Party so ineffective that members saw little reason to sit and they refused to accept the title of official opposition. Under a new constituency organisation, the National League of the North,* the party won eleven seats in the general election of 1929, the first held after the abolition of proportional representation. Three years later, Devlin led the members out of the chamber in protest at the Unionist government and did not return until October 1933. After his death in 1934 the National League was almost completely without direction and the party began to disintegrate through abstentionism and internal wranglings. The party was reorganised in preparation for the general election of 1945 and adopted a new title, the Anti-Partition League, reflecting its principal aim of ending the partition of Ireland. It gained ten seats, but, its anti-partition stance apart, was largely ignored by the government. Four years later, it had nine seats but its ineffectual leadership of the Catholic population was losing it ground to the Irish Republican Army* which was then reorganising. Throughout the 1950s, new organisations like Saor Uladh* and Fianna Uladh supported the IRA in an unsuccessful attack on the Unionist system. By the mid-1950s, the party was coming under pressure from a rising generation of educated, middle-class Catholics who founded a new constitutional movement, National Unity,* in 1959.

National Unity attacked the Nationalist Party for its lack of leadership, policy and relevance to the Catholic population. The Nationalists reacted by again reorganising, this time under Eddie McAteer.* The party produced a thirty-nine-point programme in 1964, seeking an end to unemployment, the public ownership of key industries and the establishment of training schemes. A year later, following the meeting between Sean Lemass* and Captain Terence O'Neill,* the party agreed to become the official opposition. But within a short time, traditional loyalism clashed with the Northern Ireland Civil Rights Association* and once again, the Nationalists lost ground to a new movement. In 1969 McAteer's own Derry seat was taken by John Hume. The party disappeared within a short time and was replaced by the Social Democratic and Labour Party* (1970).

The party's strength from 1921 to 1969 was: 1921 (6 seats), 1925 (10), 1929 (11), 1933 (9), 1938 (8), 1949 (9), 1953 (7), 1958 (8), 1962 (9), 1965 (9) and 1969 (6).

NATIONALIST POLITICAL FRONT. *See* National Unity.

'NATIONALITY'. Nationalist journal (1915–19) published by Arthur Griffith* and edited by Griffith and Seamus O'Kelly.* It advocated that nationalists should have the right of Irish independence discussed at any post-war peace conference and should refuse to accept partition as a solution to the Irish question. Strongly supported by separatists, it did not survive long in the turmoil of the period.

NAVAL SERVICE. The first Irish navy, known as the Coastal and Marine Service, was established in May 1923 to prevent gun-running and to provide fishery protection. Commanded by General Joseph Vize, with headquarters at Portobello Barracks, Dublin, its vessels included the *Muirchu,* formerly the *Helga,** six Mersey Class trawlers, six Canadian Castle Class trawlers, two Drifters, five River Patrol boats (on the Shannon and the Lee and in Waterford), three motor launches and two steam launches. At the time the Service had 139 officers (fifteen of them army officers), thirteen cadets and 213 ratings. It was disbanded in March 1924 and the personnel either demobilised or transferred to the Army.*

Coastal defence until 1938 was the responsibility of the 'South Irish Flotilla' of the Royal Navy. The SIF consisted of two ships, H.M.S. *Tenedos* and H.M.S. *Thracian*. Under the terms of the Treaty* Britain retained mooring rights in three Irish ports, Lough Swilly, Berehaven and Cork, known as the 'Treaty Ports'. The Royal Navy withdrew from the Treaty Ports on 11 July 1938 following the agreement which ended the Economic War.*

The outbreak of World War II created a problem of Irish coastal defence (see Emergency) and led to the creation of a new Naval Service. It was established on 5 September 1939 as the Marine and Coastwatching Service with three craft borrowed from the Air Corps.* Commanded by Colonel T. A. Lawlor, the service was augmented by the Maritime Inscription in September 1940, the size of the fleet was increased and a Minesweeping Section was established (1941). The Maritime Inscription, separate from the Naval Reserve, was a localised organisation, each section of which was responsible for a designated coastal area or port. It was reorganised as Slua Muiri on 10 June 1947.

The Service was divided into the 'Marine Service' and the 'Marine and Coastwatching Service' on 17 July 1942. By then there were two patrol vessels, six MTBs, a mine planter and a training ship. After the war the Coastwatching Service was disbanded (19 November 1945).

In accordance with a government decision of 15 March 1946 a new Marine Service was established as a permanent arm of the Defence Forces.* Commanded by H. J. A. Jerome, formerly of the Royal Navy, it continued to have its base and dockyard at Haulbowline, Cork and became known officially as the Naval Service in 1947 when it had 400 ratings. The first cadets, enlisted in December 1946, were trained at the Royal Naval College, Dartmouth. Three corvettes, *Macha* (1946–68), *Maev* (1946–69) and *Cliona* (1947–71), performed fishery protection duties. They were replaced during 1970–71 by three former minesweepers: *Grainne, Banba* and *Fola*. The Service's first custom built ship, *Deirdre*, built at Verolme, Cork Dockyard, was commissioned on 19 June 1972.

The Naval Service undertook to carry out a Hydrographic Survey in 1963. Training courses for boy fishermen were carried out under naval direction from 1964 to 1968 and courses for Irish Merchant Navy Officers started in October 1966. At the end of August 1979, while engaged in a recruiting drive to expand the strength to 1,250, the strength of the Service was 672: 65 officers, 213 NCOs and 394 ratings. There were also 24 cadets.

NEW CATHOLIC ASSOCIATION. New title of the Catholic Association* adopted by Daniel O'Connell* in 1825 when the government declared the Catholic Association an illegal body. The government's failure to suppress O'Connell's organisation left the NCA free to organise his election victory in Clare (1828) which was followed by the grant of Catholic Emancipation.*

'NEW DEPARTURE'. A policy of co-operation between Fenians,* land agitators and members of the Irish Parliamentary Party,* called the 'New Departure' by John Devoy,* was brought about as a result of the economic depression of the late 1870s which destroyed the standard of living of Irish tenant-farmers. The idea was first mooted in talks held between Devoy and Michael Davitt* and then developed by Charles Stewart Parnell.* The initiative was taken by Devoy after he had been assured by Dr William Carroll,* his colleague in Clan na Gael,* who had met Parnell in Paris early in 1878, that Parnell was 'safe' on the national question and favoured 'the absolute independence of Ireland'. On 26 October 1878, Devoy published in the *New York Herald* the text of a cablegram which he had sent to Parnell; in the cablegram he had outlined a policy of co-operation which could be undertaken on the basis of a 'general declaration in favour of self-government instead of simple federal Home Rule' and 'a vigorous agitation of the land question on the basis of a peasant proprietary, while accepting concessions tending to abolish arbitrary eviction'. In January 1879 Devoy, accompanied by Davitt, went to Paris to meet leaders of the IRB; the President of the Supreme Council, Charles J. Kickham,* would not consider any policy of co-operation with constitutionalists but it was understood that individual Fenians might participate. Later that year, in June, Parnell accepted Davitt's invitation to attend a meeting of tenant-farmers at Westport, Co. Mayo. Fenians and some ex-Fenians joined land agitators and members of the Nationalist Party on the platform. With the foundation of the Land League of Mayo,* and later the (Irish National) Land League,* the New Departure had produced its first fruits. In operation, it was pragmatic: the Fenians in America provided the money for the Land League and Parnell; the Land League mounted a national campaign to secure land reform and Parnell (leader of the Irish Parliamentary Party from May 1880) represented these ideas at Westminster. This combination was viewed with some fear by the government and the Chief Secretary, W. E. Forster,* sought in vain to crush the land agitation. While the Land League was a moral force movement and rejected violence, there were so many Fenians in it that violence could hardly be avoided. In addition, the condition of the tenant-farmers, particularly in the West of Ireland, was so desperate that violence was an inevitable reaction. The outcome of the New

Departure was the Land Act of 1881 (*see* Land Acts). In October 1881 the Land League was suppressed by Forster and this marked the end of one phase of the new policy of co-operation. American aid continued for the (Irish) National League* which Parnell established in 1882 and later aided another phase of the land agitation, the Plan of Campaign.* The policy of co-operation between American Fenians and Irish nationalists did not end until the establishment of the Free State (1922).

'NEW IRELAND REVIEW'. Journal published by the staff of University College Dublin from 1893. The *Review* developed from *Lyceum.* It appeared for the last time in February 1911 and was eventually replaced by *Studies* in March 1912.

NEW IRISH LIBRARY. The NIL was a series of nationalist books issued by Sir Charles Gavan Duffy* after he settled in London in 1880. In 1897 Douglas Hyde* became Assistant Editor. Titles in the series included Duffy's *Four Years of Irish History* (1883), *A Short Life of Thomas Davis* (1896) and *My Life in Two Hemispheres* (1898); other titles included *The Patriot Parliament* (1893) by Thomas Davis, *The Bog of Stars* (1893) by Standish James O'Grady; *The New Spirit of the Nation* (1894) and *The Irish Song Book* (1894), both edited by Alfred Percival Graves, *The Story of Gaelic Literature* (1895) by Dr Douglas Hyde, *The Life of Sarsfield* (1895) by John Todhunter and *Bishop Doyle ('J.K.L.') A Biography and Historical Study* (1896) by Michael MacDonagh.

NEWMAN, JOHN HENRY, CARDINAL (1801–90). Clergyman (C.E. and R.C.); b. London; ed. Trinity College, Oxford, where he became a Fellow of Oriel College and was ordained in 1824. Appointed tutor at Oriel in 1826, he became Vicar of St Mary's Oxford in 1827. Newman, who moved from Low to High Church, became a leader of the Oxford Movement and one of the best-known of the Tractarians. He was the author of *Tract 90* in which he demonstrated that the Thirty-nine Articles were consistent with Catholicism. He resigned his living in the Church of England in 1843 and two years later, joined the Roman Catholic church. Following ordination in Rome (1847) he was awarded D.D. On his return to England he founded the Oratorian Congregation at Edgbaston, Birmingham. He was created a cardinal in 1879.

Newman was consulted during 1850-51 by Paul Cullen,* Archbishop of Armagh, for advice on the establishment of the Catholic University.* He accepted an offer of the rectorship on 18 July 1851 and was formally appointed on 12 November, three years before the foundation of the new university. The *Discourses* which Newman delivered in the presence of Dr Cullen and other members of the hierarchy at the Rotunda in Dublin between 10 May and 7 June 1852 were the basis for *The Idea of A University Defined* (1873). His rectorship was a source of conflict although he had a good working relationship with Cullen, by now Archbishop of Dublin. However, his insistence that English professors should be among those appointed, while supported by Cullen, was opposed by John MacHale* and some of the more nationalistic bishops. Newman officially took up office on 18 May 1854. He did not enjoy the degree of autonomy which he had expected, the university was in chronic financial difficulties and had no power to award degrees. In addition, his desire to return to his order in Birmingham made the Irish position unsatisfactory, and he resigned on 12 November 1858. His autobiography, *Apologia Pro Vita Sua,* was published in 1864.

NEW REFORMATION. *See* 'Second Reformation'.

'NEW REFORMERS'. Evangelical clergymen, sometimes known as 'Biblicals', who were active between 1822 and 1860. They were actively encouraged by the Church of Ireland Archbishop of Dublin, William Magee, who said, in 1825, '... in Ireland the reformation may ... be truly said only now to have begun'. The 'New Reformation' was also called the 'Second Reformation'.*

NEW THEATRE GROUP. Socialist theatre founded in Dublin in 1937. The group, which concentrated on works by dramatists such as Maxim Gorky, Ernst Toller and Eugene O'Neill, had its headquarters in Charlemont Road, Dublin. It ran until 1945.

'NEW TIPPERARY'. Established by Rev. David Humphries* and William O'Brien* when A. H. Smith-Barry,* landlord of Tipperary town, evicted 146 tenants during the Plan of Campaign.* O'Brien opened 'New Tipperary' under the auspices of the Tenants' Defence Association* on 12 April 1890. The attendance included Michael Davitt* and 'thirty distinguished English gentlemen' including six English MPs. Three of the streets were named after O'Brien, Davitt and Charles Stewart Parnell.* Some forty local shopkeepers established businesses in the town which became a tourist attraction for a short time. Magistrates refused to grant liquor licences. Smith-Barry failed in his efforts to have Thomas William Croke,* Archbishop of Cashel, condemn the project but the venture collapsed within a few years, having cost the organisers of the Plan £50,000. The land reverted to Smith-Barry who had the town levelled.

NEW ULSTER POLITICAL RESEARCH GROUP. Founded in 1978 by the Ulster Defence Association* to consider the future of Northern Ireland. It was led by Tommy Lyttle,

Harry Chicken and Glen Barr. The Group proposed an independent state of Northern Ireland.

NIGHT OF THE BIG WIND (6–7 January 1839). The storm on the night of 6–7 January 1839 probably caused more widespread damage in Ireland than any storm in recent centuries. This night has become legendary as 'The Night of the Big Wind'. Pressure had fallen rapidly over the West of Ireland on the morning of 6 January. Heavy rain commenced before noon, whipped by strong winds which soon spread all over the country and built up to hurricane force. The gale continued till the evening of the 7th. The register of observations taken at the Phoenix Park recorded gale-force winds from 2100 on 6 January to 1800 on 7 January inclusive. The reading on 7 January at 0900 records: 'Pressure 28.721 inches (972.6 mbs), Temperature 40°F (4.4°C). Rainfall for past 24 hours .115 inches; clear, and blowing a gale. A hurricane from about two to four in the morning. Upwards of 100 trees along the pathway in the Park from Dublin Gate to Mountjoy torn up.'

Damage was widespread; it was estimated that over 2,500 valuable trees were blown down in the Dublin area and some 5,000 houses had damage ranging from complete destruction to broken windows. A County Mayo landlord who had over 70,000 trees felled on his vast estate complained, 'My estate is now as bald as the palm of my hand'. P. W. Joyce,* a boy at the time, slept soundly through the storm and on awakening the following morning was astounded at the scene of desolation which greeted him: 'The entire countryside had been swept clean as if by some gigantic broom.' John O'Donovan* had been conducting research in Glendalough, Co. Wickow and was staying at a local hotel. At midnight the window of his bedroom was blown in, and fearing that the wind would lift the roof, O'Donovan leapt out of bed and closed the shutters. To keep them closed however, he was obliged to lie prone on the window sill where he remained, naked, until the storm showed some signs of abating, several hours later.

NINETEEN-THIRTEEN CLUB. Socialist society founded by David Thornley in 1957, in commemoration of James Connolly,* James Larkin* and the Lock-Out of 1913. Numerically small, it was absorbed by the National Progressive Democratic Party* later in the year, from which Thornley shortly withdrew. It had little support, but served as a short-lived ginger-group within Irish socialism.

NO RENT MANIFESTO. The Manifesto was drawn up by William O'Brien* and issued from Kilmainham Jail by the leaders of the Irish Parliamentary Party, Charles Stewart Parnell* and John Dillon* on 18 October 1881. They added the names of Michael Davitt* and Patrick Egan* to the document which called on the supporters of the Land League* to withhold payment of rent. The leaders of the League objected to the exclusion from the Land Act of 1881 (*see* Land Acts) of leaseholders and tenants in arrears with rent – a total of some 280,000 – and hoped to bring pressure on the government by organising a rent strike. Parnell signed the document reluctantly as a token gesture to the extremist element within his movement. Michael Davitt, who was imprisoned in England, denounced it, feeling that it would lead to a revival of agrarian violence (there *was* a dramatic increase in agrarian crime* but this was principally attributed to the fact that the League was for a lengthy period without the moderating influence of its imprisoned leaders).

The Manifesto alienated influential members of the Catholic hierarchy, in particular Archbishop Thomas W.

Croke* of Cashel. It was also received with hostility by many members of the League who stood to benefit under the terms of the new Land Act. On 20 October the government reacted to the Manifesto by declaring the Land League an illegal organisation. The text of the Manifesto was:

Mr Gladstone has by a series of furious and wanton acts of despotism driven the Irish tenant farmers to choose between their own organisation and the mercy of his lawyers . . .

You have to choose between all-powerful unity and unpopular disorganisation; between the lands for the landlord and the land for the people. We cannot doubt your choice. Every tenant farmer in Ireland is today the standard-bearer of the flag unfurled at Irishtown and can bear it to glorious victory. Stand together in the face of the brutal and cowardly enemies of your race. PAY NO RENT UNDER ANY PRETEXT. STAND PASSIVELY, FIRMLY, FEARLESSLY BY while the armies of England may be engaged in their hopeless struggle against a spirit which their weapons cannot touch. . . .

If you are evicted you shall not suffer. The landlord who evicts will be a ruined pauper, and the government who supports him with its bayonets will learn in a single winter how powerless its armed force is against the will of a united and determined and self-reliant nation.

Charles Stewart Parnell, Kilmainham Jail

Andrew Kettle

Michael Davitt, Hon. Sec., Portland Jail

Thomas Sexton, Head Organiser, Kilmainham Jail

Patrick Egan, Treasurer, Paris.

NO TAX MANIFESTO. The so-called No Tax Manifesto arose from a letter by the Archbishop of Cashel, Thomas W. Croke,* published in the *Freeman's Journal* on 17 February 1887. The Archbishop, a supporter of nationalist causes, had contributed to a defence fund for nationalist MPs on trial in connection with the Plan of Campaign.* The constant need for subscriptions to defend nationalist activists from legal harrassment prompted the letter from the Archbishop. Among other things, he said, 'We pay taxes to a government that uses them not for the public good and in accordance with the declared wishes of the tax-payers, but in direct and deliberate opposition to them. . . . Our money goes to purchase bludgeons for policemen to be used in smashing the skulls of our people. The policeman is pampered and paid; the patriot is persecuted. Our enforced taxes go to sustain the one – we must further freely tax ourselves to defend the other. How long, I ask, is this to be tolerated?'

The letter received wide approval and aroused such interest that the government contemplated prosecuting Croke for inciting people to withhold their taxes. The idea of prosecution, however, was dropped on the advice of Cardinal Manning who believed that such an action would make Croke even more popular. The government complained to Rome and the Vatican expressed its displeasure at the letter. To clarify his position, Dr Croke wrote a further letter to the *Freeman's Journal* in which he stated, 'It never entered into my head to recommend a general uprising against the payment of taxes. . . . I trust to constitutional agitation alone for the restoration of our national rights'.

NOLAN, JOHN 'AMNESTY' (d. 1887). Republican; a member of the Irish Republican Brotherhood,* Nolan worked in a Dublin drapery shop. He earned his nickname 'Amnesty' for his energy and devotion as secretary of the Amnesty Association* which was established, under the Presidency of Isaac Butt, to secure the release of Fenians imprisoned during the 1860s. Many Fenians, imprisoned as 'treason-felons', were treated very harshly in English jails. He emigrated to the USA in 1877 and settled in New York where he died impoverished. He is sometimes confused with John 'Jackie' Nolan, another Fenian, who died in 1920 after spending fifteen years in prison in Canada. A fund was raised by Patrick Ford* to aid Nolan in his last months and it was employed to raise a memorial to him in Calvary Cemetery, New York. Michael Davitt* later paid for a monument to be erected to him in Glasnevin Cemetery, Dublin.

NOLAN, COLONEL JOHN PHILLIP (1838–1912). Soldier and politician (Irish Parliamentary Party); b. Ballinderry, Co. Galway; ed. Clongowes Wood College, TCD and Woolwich Military College. He served in the Abyssinian campaign and reached the rank of Colonel. After his return as MP for Co. Galway in 1871 he was unseated on grounds of clerical intimidation. This led to a court action during which Judge William Keogh* made a savage attack on the Catholic clergy for their role in the election. Once more elected in 1874, Nolan held his seat as a member of the Irish Parliamentary Party until 1896. He introduced Charles Stewart Parnell* to the House of Commons in 1875 and supported him thereafter. After seconding Parnell's nomination as chairman of the party in November 1890 after W. E. Gladstone* had withdrawn support, he continued to urge Parnell to remain as chairman. On 1 December he put forward an amendment to a proposal by John Barry in an attempt to win time for Parnell: the amendment, which was defeated, proposed that the meeting be postponed until the party members could meet with their constituents and then hold a meeting in Dublin. He lost his seat in 1896 but regained it in 1900 and supported John Redmond.*

NORBURY, 1st EARL (1745–1831). Toler, John; lawyer, judge and politician (Conservative); b. Co. Tipperary; ed. TCD where he graduated M.A. in 1766. Called to the Bar in 1770, he is reputed to have begun his legal career with £50 and a brace of duelling pistols. Norbury, according to his contemporaries had a poor knowledge of law – an ignorance which was eventually to become notorious. He began his political career in 1776 as MP for Tralee, Co. Kerry. As a politician, he placed his services at the disposal of the government, trimming his beliefs to the prevailing political wind. A leading opponent of Catholic Emancipation* and political reform, he became Solicitor-General in 1789 and Attorney-General in 1798, in which capacity he ruthlessly prosecuted the leading United Irishmen.* He voted for the Union* in 1800 and received a Chief Justiceship and a Baronetcy as reward. His appointment to the bench was opposed by his political supporters and opponents. Lord Clare* protested that Norbury was unfitted to sit on the bench. Their fears were confirmed: Norbury ran his court like a circus, attracting a large segment of Dublin's loungers to the free 'entertainment'. He displayed a complete indifference to the feelings of those in the dock: having acquitted a manifestly guilty defendant, he informed an astonished prosecution that he was attempting to compensate for having sentenced six innocent men to death at an earlier court-sitting. He had a voluminous knowledge of Milton and Shakespeare and frequently entertained the court by impromptu recitals. Despite the attempts of Daniel O'Connell* and other leading advocates to have him removed, he remained on the bench until 1827 when his senility and outrageous behaviour forced his removal. He was raised to the peerage as Earl Norbury in 1827. His most famous case was in 1803 when he presided at the trial of Robert Emmet.* Norbury was an excellent social companion and enjoyed a good reputation as a landlord.

NORTHERN IRELAND. Northern Ireland, established under the Government of Ireland Act 1920,* consists of the six Ulster counties of Antrim, Armagh, Down, Fermanagh, Londonderry and Tyrone. Its 5,238 square miles are approximately one-sixth of the land area of Ireland, and the population of 1,256,561 (1926) was about one-third of the population of the whole island. The principal religious denominations were Catholic (33.5 per cent), Presbyterian (31.3 per cent) and Church of Ireland (27 per cent).

The parliament of Northern Ireland, consisting of the King, Senate and House of Commons, was opened by George V* on 22 June 1921. Parliament had sovereign powers apart from certain excepted areas: the crown, peace and war, treaties, the armed forces, dignities and titles, treason, naturalisation, domicile, trade outside of Northern Ireland, cables and wireless, air and navigation; lighthouses, ` coinage, weights and measures, trade marks, copyright, patents and the Supreme Court. Certain other matters were also reserved to the imperial parliament: the postal service, savings banks, design of stamps, imposition and collections of customs duties, income tax, surtax, purchase tax and profits tax. The parliament was prohibited from passing laws which discriminated against or endowed any religion. It could not repeal any act passed at Westminster nor pass any act repugnant to the statutes of the United Kingdom.

The legislature consisted of two houses, a House of Commons of 52 members, and a Senate of 26 members, 24 of whom were elected by the Commons. The first general election, held on 24 May 1921, was the first in the history of the British Isles to use Proportional Representation.* The election returned 40 members of the Ulster Unionist Party;* the remaining 12 seats were divided between the Nationalist Party of Northern Ireland,* led by Joseph Devlin,* and Sinn Fein,*

neither of whom initially recognised the new state. (The Nationalists entered parliament in 1924.)

The Ulster Unionist Party formed all the governments of Northern Ireland until 1972. The first Prime Minister was Sir James Craig (*see* Craigavon, Viscount). The other ministries were Finance, Home Affairs, Labour, Education, Commerce and Agriculture. A Ministry of Health and Local Government was created in 1944. There was a Ministry of Public Security during World War II and a Ministry of Community Relations was established in 1971. Under the terms of the Treaty* (Articles 11–16), Northern Ireland could opt out of the Irish Free State, in which case a Boundary Commission would be established. By the end of 1925 the Commission and its Report were a dead letter and the arbitrary boundary, chosen on the basis of the area which would provide a Unionist majority, remained permanently fixed.

From the beginning, the Irish Republican Army* was a threat to Northern Ireland which was established during the War of Independence.* A second problem for the government was widespread unemployment which created severe social discontent. To protect itself from the IRA the state had at its disposal the Civil Authorities (Special Powers) Act (Northern Ireland) 1922* under which the Minister for Home Affairs had unlimited powers of arrest and detention. The Act, which was renewable, was made permanent in 1933. Action was also taken to lessen the influence of the Catholic population which was assumed to be sympathetic to the IRA and the unification of Ireland. Although Proportional Representation was supposed to be the method of election, it was abolished for local government elections in 1922. It was abolished for central government elections in 1929 and replaced by the direct vote. Local government elections were held on a rate-paying franchise and business firms had a multiple vote (the company vote). Gerrymandering of the constituencies for local government elections also helped to ensure permanent Unionist majorities. The system worked so successfully that Derry City, Armagh District Council and Fermanagh County Council had Unionist majorities whereas they were all areas with Catholic majorities. Protestant employers were encouraged not to employ Catholics and local authorities adopted the same policy. Allocation of public authority housing favoured Protestant applicants. While there were Catholics in the Royal Ulster Constabulary,* an auxiliary, the Special Constabulary,* was wholly Protestant. Many Unionist politicians, most members of the government and all the Prime Ministers of Northern Ireland maintained very close contact with the Orange Order* and the majority were, in fact, members.

Until World War II the economy was depressed. The unemployment rate was 23 per cent in 1923 and 25 per cent during the 1930s. The high rate of unemployment placed a heavy burden on the Northern exchequer and the depressed state of the economy was reflected in the lack of social services. Hospitals were inadequate and the workhouse system was still being used in the 1940s. Between 1919 and 1936 around 50,000 houses were built in the six-county area and it was believed that a further 100,000 were needed. Around 85 per cent of rural dwellings had no running water as late as 1939. Tuberculosis* was responsible for almost 50 per cent of deaths in the 15−25 age-group. World War II was a watershed in the history of Northern Ireland. As Eire was neutral the ports of Northern Ireland were vital to the Allied war effort, giving access to the sea lanes. The state also produced war materials. Tanks (550), ships (150, totalling 500,000 tons) and bombers (1,000) were built in Northern Ireland. Within a short time unemployment fell from 25 per cent

to 5 per cent. The Harland and Wolff shipyard underwent a transformation. Employment at the shipyards rose from 7,300 (1938) to 20,600 (1945). In the engineering works employment rose from 14,000 to 26,000 and in the aircraft industry it rose from 5,800 to 23,000. Total employment in industry rose from 27,000 to 70,000. In addition, some 60,000 people migrated to England. The agricultural sector reaped the benefits of increased demand, which led to an increase in the tillage area from 400,000 acres to 800,000. Between 1939 and 1948 wages nearly doubled (although much of the increase was accounted for by the rise in agricultural wages, traditionally very low). Belfast, Derry and Larne became important naval bases. Derry was chosen as a depot for American destroyers as early as March 1941 and was a base for escort groups for convoy protection later. From January 1942, Northern Ireland provided training bases for US and Canadian military personnel. It was designated a strategic base for American aircraft-carriers in 1943. Belfast became the assembly point for the bombarding ships of the US Western Forces which sailed for Normandy on 3 June 1944. German planes made four raids on Belfast during April and May 1941 (on two occasions units of the Dublin Fire Brigade were dispatched to aid Belfast).

Changes continued after the war. In accordance with the 'step by step' policy which sought to ensure that the citizens of Northern Ireland enjoyed parity of services with the remainder of the United Kingdom, the Welfare Services were established. This was achieved at the expense of financial autonomy as the Treasury in London gained more control over the North's finances. The New Industries (Development) Act, 1945, assisted businesses to adjust to post-war conditions. The government could buy or develop land and build or lease factories. Grants were offered towards industrial services. By the end of 1955, 143 firms had taken advantage of the act and were employing 21,000 people. The New Industries branch of the Ministry of Commerce also helped fifty firms to add a total of 4,900 employees to their payrolls. Advances made by Northern Ireland after the war threw into further relief the less prosperous condition of the Southern state and was used by Unionists to justify the existence of partition. Anti-Partition propaganda antagonised the Unionists as did the Republic of Ireland Act, 1948,* which led to the Ireland Act,* reiterating the position of Northern Ireland within the United Kingdom.

After 1956 there was a renewal of militant republican activity when the IRA attacked the North. Both the Northern and Southern governments reacted by introducing internment, but in fact the IRA received no support among the Catholic population in the North, and called off the campaign in 1962. One year later the traditionalist Prime Minister, Lord Brookeborough,* resigned and was succeeded by Captain Terence O'Neill.* O'Neill broke with the Unionist policy of ignoring the Republic. He invited Sean Lemass,* Taoiseach of the Republic, to visit him at Stormont in February 1965 and repaid the visit later in the year. His actions were severely criticised by extreme loyalists, led by Rev. Ian Paisley,* who viewed with concern a policy of *rapprochement* with the South, coming so soon after the ecumenism enunciated by the Second Vatican Council. As 1966, the year of the fiftieth anniversary of the Easter Rising of 1916 approached, traditional Unionists were outraged when O'Neill allowed commemorations in Northern Ireland. One reaction was an anti-republican campaign by the newly-revived Ulster Volunteer Force.*

Within a year this was followed by demands for civil rights by a new generation of Catholics. The Northern Ireland Civil Rights Association,* founded in February 1967, attracted all shades of political and religious opinion but inevitably it had a Catholic majority. They demanded reforms in local government: 'one man, one vote'; a new system for allocation of local authority housing and equal civil rights for all. They organised protest marches, the first of which was held in Dungannon in protest at the housing policy (24 August 1968). Shortly afterwards, a more radical organisation, the People's Democracy,* was established by students at Queen's University, Belfast. Unionists and militant Protestants were alarmed at the manner in which protest was spreading.

Following an attack upon the People's Democracy marchers at Burntollet in January 1969, and the misbehaviour of policemen in Derry afterwards, the RUC became a discredited force among Catholics. The Cameron Commission* later found that some police had been involved in the rioting. The Minister for Commerce, Brian Faulkner,* resigned at the idea of the police being investigated, and O'Neill, attacked from within his government and outside, called a general election for 24 February 1969. He received only 47 per cent of the vote in his own Bannside constituency where his opponent, Ian Paisley, polled 6,331 votes. The Unionists were now split into 24 pro-O'Neill and 12 anti-O'Neill members. The election had another significance: it spelled the ruin of the old Nationalist Party of Northern Ireland whose leader, Eddie McAteer,* lost his seat to John Hume, a supporter of the civil rights campaign. Under pressure from Westminster O'Neill announced the introduction of 'one man, one vote' for local elections. He was immediately attacked by his own party and resigned on 28 April 1969. He was succeeded by Major James Dawson Chichester-Clark,* who proved unable to prevent clashes between the two communities. After serious rioting in July 1969 the Labour Home Secretary, James Callaghan, issued what became known as the Downing Street Declaration on

19 August. The Declaration promised reforms, including reforms in the RUC. Local Government reforms were to continue, an independent Housing Authority would be established, discrimination against Catholics in public employment would be abolished and an ombudsman would be appointed. The Hunt Commission* recommended that the RUC should be disarmed and the Special Constabulary abolished (it was replaced by the Ulster Defence Regiment*). British troops were by now keeping the peace in Northern Ireland.

However, the British Army soon lost the support of the minority population as searches for arms and military actions became identified with hostility towards and harassment of the Catholic areas of Belfast and Derry. In January 1970 the IRA split into Provisional and Official and clashes between the IRA and loyalist paramilitary organisations continued.

Two new political parties, both aimed at the centre, appeared during 1970: the Social Democratic and Labour Party* and the Alliance Party.* The breach in the Unionist Party grew during 1970 and 1971. When Chichester-Clark resigned in March 1971 he was succeeded by Brian Faulkner. As a gesture of goodwill he made David Bleakley, of the Northern Ireland Labour Party,* Minister of Community Relations and brought a Catholic, Dr Gerard B. Newe, into the cabinet in October as a temporary junior minister. It was soon evident that reforms would have to wait until the IRA had been destroyed. SDLP members walked out of parliament in July 1971 and remained abstentionists for the rest of the session.

Faulkner introduced internment in August 1971. Internment camps were established at Long Kesh, Magilligan and on the vessel *Maidstone*. Initially internment was used exclusively against the Catholic population. The operation was mishandled: many IRA leaders escaped while some of the persons arrested were

the victims of mistaken identity. The operation led to an upsurge of support for the IRA. The level of violence increased considerably: there were twice as many explosions for the period from August to December 1971 as there had been from January to July.

Following Bloody Sunday* (30 January 1972), Faulkner was summoned to London for talks with Edward Heath and members of the Conservative cabinet. He was told by Heath that security would now become the responsibility of Whitehall and that if violence did not cease, Stormont would be suspended and replaced by direct rule from London. Violence continued, some of it in England when the officers' mess at the headquarters of the 16th Parachute Regiment at Aldershot was bombed, killing civilians and a Catholic priest on 22 February. The Official IRA claimed that it was revenge for Bloody Sunday. An explosion at the Abercorn restaurant on 4 March killed three and mutilated over 130 people. The IRA claimed that it was the work of Protestant paramilitaries but later that month claimed responsibility for an explosion in Donegall Street in which six people were killed and 150 injured.

Unionist backbenchers issued a statement on 15 March warning Faulkner that direct rule was unacceptable. Faulker was summoned to London on 21 March where he was told that internment would have to be phased out. Whitehall was to assume complete responsibility for law and order. Faulker rejected this and returned to Belfast where his cabinet supported his stand. Heath announced the suspension of Stormont on 24 March and the introduction of direct rule under the Northern Ireland (Temporary Suspension) Act. William Whitelaw became the first Secretary of State for Northern Ireland. There were over 21,000 British troops in Northern Ireland by July 1972.

In a White Paper published on

20 March 1973 the British government proposed the abolition of Stormont and its replacement by an Assembly which would govern Northern Ireland through a power-sharing Executive. Elections to the Assembly were held on 28 June and the Assembly met on 31 July. The 78 members were made up of two main groupings: 52 Pro-Assembly and 26 Anti-Assembly. The Pro-Assembly members broke down into Faulknerite Unionists (24), SDLP (19), Alliance (8) and the Northern Ireland Labour Party (1). Anti-Assembly members were made up of Anti-White Paper Unionists (8), Democratic Unionist Party members led by Rev. Ian Paisley (8), the Vanguard members (7) and Other Loyalists (3). Talks were held between those who accepted power-sharing, the Faulknerite Unionists, the SDLP and Alliance, on 5 October. The Executive was announced on 22 November. There were eleven members: six Unionists, four members of the SDLP and one member of Alliance. Brian Faulkner became the Chief Executive and Gerry Fitt, of the SDLP, the Deputy Chief Executive. In December the anti-White Paper Unionists formed the United Ulster Unionist Council,* also known as the Loyalist Coalition. (For the full Executive see below.)

Representatives of the Executive were present for tripartite talks with the British and Irish governments at Sunningdale on 6–9 December. The Sunningdale Agreement* was a breakthrough so far as relations between the Irish Republic and Northern Ireland were concerned, but on 5 January 1974 when the Executive formally took office, the Unionist Party rejected Sunningdale and power-sharing. Later that month, on 23 January, the 'Official' (anti-Faulkner) Unionists, the DUP and Vanguard withdrew from the Assembly. In February, eleven of the twelve Northern Ireland members returned in the general election to Westminster gave their support to the Loyalist Coalition. The Coalition supported the general strike called by the Ulster Workers' Council on 14 May in an attempt to destroy power-sharing. On 28 May the strike brought Northern Ireland to a standstill. The Executive collapsed and direct rule was resumed. Faulkner established the Unionist Party of Northern Ireland* on 24 June 1974. The Ulster Unionist Party was now hopelessly fragmented.

The Labour government published a new White Paper on the North on 4 July, announcing another attempt to restore order. This was to be a Constitutional Convention, to be elected on 1 May 1975. The result of the elections was a victory for the Loyalist Coalition which secured 47 out of the 78 seats: the 47 seats were divided between the Official Unionists (19), the DUP (12), Vanguard (14) and Other Loyalists (2). Those supporting power-sharing had 31 seats between them: SDLP (17), Alliance (8), UPNI (5) and NILP (1). The Convention, which was to produce a report by 7 November 1975, met on 8 May under the chairmanship of the Lord Chief Justice of Northern Ireland, Sir Robert Lowry, 'to consider what provision for the Government of Northern Ireland is likely to command the most widespread acceptance throughout the whole community'.

The parties within the Convention submitted five different reports for consideration. In the nature of the Convention, the two with the greatest support were those of the UUUC and the SDLP. The UUUC rejected power-sharing and accused the SDLP of wishing to make Northern Ireland part of a united Ireland. It sought full parliamentary powers for Stormont, and no interference from Westminster. In short, it sought what the British government had already implicitly rejected – a return to the old Unionist-dominated Stormont. The SDLP report blamed the UUUC for the failure to produce a unanimous report and continued to seek power-sharing with offices for the minority population. These were the views of the two strongest parties and the smaller parties advocated positions somewhere between the two poles. The Convention was unable to produce an acceptable unanimous draft for the British government. When a vote was taken it was a victory for the report submitted by the UUUC Loyalists (42 votes to 31). In hope of breaking the deadlock the British government extended the life of the Convention by another six months, bringing it up to 7 May 1976, and referred the report back for consideration (14 January 1976). Negotiations between the parties began again but produced only the same responses and demands. In March, admitting that the Constitutional Convention had been a failure, the government dissolved it.

Population of Northern Ireland, 1926–71

1926	1,256,561
1937	1,279,745
1951	1,370,921
1961	1,425,042
1971	1,536,065

Governors

3rd Duke of Abercorn (December 1922 – September 1945)
Lord Granville (September 1945 – November 1952)
Lord Wakehurst (December 1952 – November 1964)
Lord Erskine (December 1964 – November 1968)
Lord Grey (December 1968 – July 1973)

Distribution of Seats in General Elections 1921–74

Dates of Elections	Union-ists	Indep. Un.	Libs.	Lab.	Nats.	Abst. Sinn Fein	Repubs. Rep. Lab. Soc. Rep. Ind. Lab.	Indeps. & Others
24. 5.1921	40	–	–	–	6	6	–	–
28. 4.1925	32	4	–	3	10	2	–	1
22. 5.1929	37	3	–	1	11	–	–	–
30.11.1933	36	2	–	2	9	2	–	1
9. 2.1938	39	3	–	1	8	–	1	–
14. 6.1945	33	2	–	2	9	–	3	3
10. 2.1949	37	2	–	–	9	–	2	2
22.10.1953	38	1	–	–	7	2	3	1
20. 3.1958	37	–	–	4	8	–	2	1
31. 5.1962	34	–	1	4	9	–	3	1
25.11.1965	36	–	1	2	9	–	2	2
24. 2.1969	36	3	–	2	6	–	2	3

Assembly					
28. 6.1973	Anti-White Paper Unionists	DUP	Vanguard	Faulk-nerite Unionists	Alliance	SDLP
	8	8	7	24	8	19

	NILP	Other Loyalists
	1	3

Convention					
1. 5.1975	Official Unionists	DUP	Vanguard	UPNI	Alliance	SDLP
	19	12	14	5	8	17

	NILP	Other Loyalists
	1	2

A. Governments of Northern Ireland (1921–72)

Prime Ministers
Sir James Craig, Lord Craigavon (June 1921–November 1940)
John Miller Andrews (November 1940–May 1943)
Sir Basil Brooke, Lord Brookeborough (May 1943–March 1963)
Captain Terence O'Neill (March 1963–April 1969)
Major James Dawson Chichester-Clark (May 1969–March 1971)
Arthur Brian Deane Faulkner (March 1971–March 1972)

Finance
H. M. Pollock (1921–37)
J. M. Andrews (1937–41)
J. M. Barbour (1941–43)
J. M. Sinclair (1943–53)
W. B. Maginess (1953–56)
G. B. Hanna (1956)
T. O'Neill (1956–63)
J. L. O. Andrews (1963–65)
H. V. Kirk (1965–72)

Home Affairs
R. D. Bates (1921–43)

W. Lowry (1943–44)
J. E. Warnock (1944–45)
W. B. Maginess (1945–53)
G. B. Hanna (1953–56)
T. O'Neill (1956)
W. W. B. Topping (1956–59)
A. B. D. Faulkner (1959–63)
W. Craig (1963–64)
R. W. McConnell (1964–66)
W. Craig (1966–68)
W. J. Long (1968–69)
R. W. Porter (1969–72)

Labour
J. M. Andrews (1921–37)
D. G. Shillington (1937–39)
J. F. Gordon (1939–43)
W. Grant (1943–45)
W. B. Maginess (1945–49)
H. Midgley (1949–51)
I. Neill (1951–62)
H. V. Kirk (1962–64)
W. J. Morgan (1964–72)

Agriculture (known as Agriculture and Commerce until 1925)
E. M. Archdale (1921–33)
Sir B. Brooke (1933–41)
Lord Glentoran (1941–43)
R. Moore (1943–60)

H. W. West (1960–67)
Major J. D. Chichester-Clark (1967–69)
P. R. H. O'Neill (1969–72)

Commerce
J. M. Barbour (1925–41)
Sir B. Brooke (1941–43)
Sir R. T. Nugent (1943–49)
W. V. McCleery (1949–53)
Lord Glentoran (1953–61)
J. L. O. Andrews (1961–63)
A. B. D. Faulkner (1963–69)
P. R. H. O'Neill (1969)
R. H. Bradford (1969–71)
R. J. Bailie (1971–72)

Education
Lord Londonderry (1921–27)
Viscount Charlemont (1927–33)
J. H. Robb (1933–43)
Rev. R. Corkey (1943–44)
Lt Col S. H. Hall-Thompson (1944–52)
H. Midgley (1952–57)
W. M. May (1957–62)
I. Neill (1962–64)
H. V. Kirk (1964–66)
W. J. Long (1966–68)
W. K. Fitzsimmons (1968–69)
P. R. H. O'Neill (1969)
W. J. Long (1969–72)

Health
W. Grant (1944–49)
Dame Dehra Parker (1949–57)
J. L. O. Andrews (1957–61)
W. J. Morgan (1961–64)
W. Craig (1964–65)
W. J. Morgan (1965–69)
R. W. Porter (1969)
W. K. Fitzsimmons (1969–72)

Public Security
W. Grant (1941–42)
H. Midgley (1942–45)

Development
W. Craig (1965–66)
W. K. Fitzsimmons (1966–68)
I. Neill (1968–69)
W. J. Long (1969)
A. B. D. Faulkner (1969–71)
R. H. Bradford (1971–72)

Community Relations
D. Bleakley (1971)
W. B. McIvor (1971)

B. Executive of Northern Ireland (5 January–28 May 1974).
Chief Executive: A. B. D. Faulkner
Deputy Chief Executive: G. Fitt
Finance: H. V. Kirk
Agriculture: L. Morrell
Commerce: J. Hume
Education: W. B. McIvor
Health & Social Services: P. Devlin
Manpower Services: R. Cooper*
Environment: R. Bradford
Community Relations: I. Cooper*
Local Government, Housing & Planning: A. Currie
Planning & Coordination: E. McGrady*
Law Reform: O. Napier
Information: J. Baxter.
*Holders of Ministerial offices outside the Executive.

C. Secretaries of State for Northern Ireland (1972–)
1972–73 William Whitelaw
1973–74 Francis Pym
1974–77 Merlyn Rees
1977–79 Roy Mason
1979– Humphrey Atkins

NORTHERN IRELAND CIVIL RIGHTS ASSOCIATION (NICRA). Founded in Belfast in February 1967, NICRA was a broadly-based movement embracing a wide spectrum of political opinion. Its members were concerned with the lack of civil rights in the Northern Ireland state, and particularly with discrimination in the allocation of public authority housing. It was based on the Campaign for Social Justice founded in Dungannon by Patricia and Con McCluskey and was modelled on the National Council for Civil Liberties in Britain, to which it was affiliated. NICRA included among its aims 'one man, one vote' in local elections, the removal of gerrymandered electoral boundaries and of discriminatory practices within local government authorities, the establishment of machinery to investigate complaints against local authorities, the allocation of public housing on a points system, the repeal of the Civil Authorities (Special Powers) Act* and the disbandment of the 'B' Specials (*see* Special Constabulary).

NICRA's first major public involvement was on 24 August 1968 when the movement organised a march from Coalisland to Dungannon, protesting at anti-Catholic discrimination by the Dungannon authorities. The march attracted over 3,000 and received wide media coverage. Another march was called for 5 October in Derry city – one of the most depressed regions within Northern Ireland. The march, banned by the Minister for Home Affairs, William Craig,* was the scene of a violent clash between the marchers and the RUC. Civil rights agitation spread throughout the North, provoking counter-demonstrations from Unionist traditionalists, led by Rev. Ian Paisley.* Both Paisley and the Minister for Home Affairs regarded NICRA as a front for the IRA, the Communist Party and subversives in general.

Police action in Derry triggered off three days of rioting in which eleven policemen and seventy-seven civilians were injured. Students protesting in support of NICRA and against events in Derry founded the People's Democracy* in Belfast on 9 October. The Prime Minister of Northern Ireland, Captain Terence O'Neill,* found his reform efforts strongly opposed within his own party and by the powerful Orange Order. As NICRA gained only minor concessions, the situation in Northern Ireland continued to deteriorate. The British Army was called in to maintain order when the Royal Ulster Constabulary and the 'B' Specials were no longer able to contain the situation (August 1969). Caught in a maelstrom of terrorism and reprisal, NICRA's role became less effective. It continued in existence, however, and in June 1977 issued a statement declaring the RUC an unacceptable police force.

NORTHERN IRELAND LABOUR PARTY (NILP). Social democratic party founded in 1923. Based on the trade union movement, the NILP contained Catholics and Protestants but because of the primacy of constitutional issues in Northern Ireland politics it was unable to muster sufficient support to make an impact. Its attempt to remain neutral on the question of partition was unsuccessful and during the debate on the issue during 1948–49 the party gave its support to the Unionist government. Its opponents formed the Republican Labour Party.* After the declaration of the Ireland Act 1949* the NILP stated that it '. . . accepts the constitutional position of Northern Ireland, the close association with Britain and the Commonwealth . . . we are not seeking a mandate to change'. During the civil unrest of the 1960s the party supported the agitation for civil rights, but lost ground to the new parties, the Social Democratic and Labour Party* and the Alliance Party.* Although it does not have MPs at Westminster, the NILP maintains close contact with the British Labour Party. The party's strength in the Northern Ireland parliament has been: 1925 (3 seats), 1929 (1), 1933 (2), 1938 (1), 1945 (2), 1949 (0), 1953 (0), 1958 (4), 1962 (4), 1965 (2) and 1969 (2). *See also* Northern Ireland.

NORTHERN RESISTANCE MOVEMENT. Founded in Northern Ireland in 1971 after the introduction of internment, the NRM brought republicans and radicals together in opposition to the government's policies. The Movement included members of the People's Democracy* and the Provisional Irish Republican Army.* During 1971–72 the NRM organised protests but it was considerably weakened in July 1972 when the Provisionals made a truce with the British government. *See also* Northern Ireland.

NORTHWEST LOYALIST REGIS-TRATION AND ELECTORAL ASSOCIATION. Formed to fight against Home Rule* by the 2nd Duke of Abercorn* in 1886. Its purpose was to organise the Unionist vote in north-west Ulster, the counties of Donegal, Tyrone and London-derry in order to prevent a clash of interests at the polls between loyalist groups. Such an occurrence in Lon-donderry South in 1885 had allowed the return for the constituency of a nationalist, Timothy Healy.* The Association only had limited success, as the Liberal Unionists, concerned with a possible loss of identity to the Ulster Unionists, formed their own Liberal Unionist Association.

NORTON, WILLIAM (1900–63). Politician; leader of the Labour Party (1932–60); b. Kildare; ed. locally. After becoming a post office clerk in 1918 he was elected in 1920 to the national executive of the Post Office Workers' Union, for which he was honorary organising secretary (1922–23), honorary general secre-tary (1923–24) and full-time secre-tary (1924–57). He was President of the Executive Council of the Postal, Telegraph and Telephone International (1926–60).

Norton was returned as Labour TD for Co. Dublin in 1926 but lost his seat the following year. Upon his return for Kildare in 1932 he became leader of the party. This coincided with the election victory of Fianna Fail,* led by Eamon de Valera.* Labour supported the Fianna Fail opposition to the Blueshirts* whom Norton denounced as 'Hitlerite'. He criticised the government's handling of the Land Annuities* and during the Economic War* said that tariffs were not the answer to Ireland's economic problems. However, he supported the government's position during the war.

At the Labour Party's annual con-ference of 1936 he succeeded in having a resolution on public owner-ship incorporated into the constitu-tion. At the same time he urged the removal from the constitu-tion of the aim of the 'Workers' Republic' which had been criticised by the Catholic hierarchy. Calling for its removal, he said 'The Labour party is a political party and objec-tions have been taken by the hierarchy to the term "Workers' Republic". If the Conference wants to avoid the deliberate misrepresentation which opponents would apply against us, it is necessary to delete the term from the constitution'.

The general election of 1943 was a critical test of his leadership. He supported the return of James Larkin* to the parliamentary party and was attacked by Larkin's old opponents, the Irish Transport and General Wor-kers' Union.* Labour increased its representation from nine (1938) to seventeen seats. However, the ITGWU disaffiliated from the party and the union's members of the par-liamentary party established National Labour.* Following the general elec-tion of 1944 he was leading only eight deputies. Four years later the party secured fourteen seats and joined the first Inter-Party Govern-ment* in which Norton held the posts of Tanaiste and Minister for Social Welfare. The breach between the Labour Party and National Labour was healed in 1950, a year before the end of the Inter-Party Government. He was again Tanaiste in the second Inter-Party Govern-ment in 1954 when Labour returned with nineteen seats. This time he held the Ministry of Industry and Commerce. The party lost seven seats in the general election of 1957. He resigned the leadership three years later and was succeeded by Brendan Corish.*

'NOTES FROM IRELAND'. A Con-servative-Unionist bulletin on Irish affairs which first appeared on 25 September 1886, following the fail-ure of the (first) Home Rule Bill* to pass the Commons. The *Notes* repor-ted the efforts of the Irish Parliam-entary Party* to secure support for Home Rule and provided facts on

Ireland for the imperial parliament, the media and the general public. It appeared until 1914 when the (third) Home Rule Bill* became law.

NUGENT, SIR ROLAND THOMAS (1886–1962). Politician (Ulster Unionist); b. Portaferry, Co. Down; ed. Eton, Trinity College, Cambridge and the University of Bonn. After entering the diplomatic service in 1910, he served in the Foreign Office (1913–18). He was Director of the Federation of British Industry (1916–17 and 1919–32). Minister without Portfolio in the government of Northern Ireland (1944–45), he was Minister for Commerce (1945–49), Minister in the Senate (1949) and Speaker of the Senate (1950–51).

NULTY, THOMAS (1818–98). Bishop of Meath (R.C.), 1867–98; b. Oldcastle, Co. Meath; ed. Gilson Endowed School, Diocesan College, Navan and Maynooth where he was ordained in 1846. One of the earliest members of the Catholic hierarchy to take an active interest in the land question, he supported the New Departure* and the Land League.* He issued a pastoral letter on the land question in 1881. Dr Nulty supported the Irish Parliamentary Party,* initiating a 'church door' collection to defray the election expenses of Charles Stewart Parnell,* MP for Meath, in 1880. Following the No Rent Manifesto* he expressed surprise at the condemnation issued by Thomas William Croke,* Archbishop of Cashel. After the split in the Irish party over Parnell's involvement in the O'Shea divorce case, Dr Nulty's denunciation of Parnellism was as forthright as his earlier support had been: 'Parnellites are anti-Catholic', he stated in January 1892, and in July he described it as '... Paganism ... it impedes, obstructs and cripples the efficiency and blights the fruitfulness and the preaching of the Gospel . . .' Following a pastoral letter during the Meath by-election of 1892 the election result was annuled on the grounds of clerical intimidation.

O

OATH OF ALLEGIANCE (1919). The following is the text of the Oath of Allegiance administered to the members and officers of the first Dail Eireann in August 1919: 'I ... do solemnly swear (or affirm) that I do not and shall not yield a voluntary support to any pretended government, authority or power within Ireland hostile and inimical thereto, and I do further swear (or affirm) that, to the best of my knowledge and ability, I will support and defend the Irish Republic and the Government of the Irish Republic, which is Dail Eireann, against all enemies, foreign and domestic, and I will bear true faith and allegiance to the same, and that I take this obligation freely, without any mental reservation or purpose of evasion, so help me God.'

OATH OF ALLEGIANCE (1922). The Oath of Allegiance was laid down in Article 4 of the Treaty and Article 17 of the Constitution of 1922. The text was: 'I ... do solemnly swear true faith and allegiance to the Constitution of the Irish Free State as by law established and that I will be faithful to H. M. King George V, his heirs and successors by law, in virtue of the common citizenship of Ireland with Great Britain and her adherence to and membership of the group of nations forming the British Commonwealth of Nations.' This Oath was abhorrent to the anti-

Treatyite republicans. Under the leadership of Eamon de Valera* they refused to take their seats in Dail Eireann.* Their abstentionist policy was brought to an end by the Electoral Amendment Act.* On 11 August 1927, de Valera and the members of his Fianna Fail party signed their names in the book containing the Oath while affirming that they were not taking the Oath, which they called an 'empty formula'. During the general election of March 1932 de Valera stated that they would abolish the Oath if he was returned to power. After Fianna Fail's victory, the Oath was removed on 3 May 1933 by the Removal of Oath Act.*

O'BRENNAN, ELIZABETH ('LILY'; 1878–1948). Republican; b. Dublin; ed. Dominican Convent, Eccles Street. She joined Cumann na mBan* of which she was later vice-president and secretary. A sister-in-law of Eamonn Ceannt,* she fought in the Easter Rising of 1916* and was afterwards a leader of the Irish National Aid Association* and a member of Sinn Fein.* As a staff-member of the Ministry of Labour in the first Dail Eireann, she assisted with the organisation of the Belfast Boycott.* She became typist to Arthur Griffith* following his election as President of the Dail (January 1922), and remained in the civil service.

Ó BRIAIN, ART (1872–1949). Republican; b. London; ed. St Charles College, London, and qualified as a civil engineer. He joined the Gaelic League* in 1899 and was President of the London organisation (1914– 35). After joining the Irish Volunteers* and becoming President of the Sinn Fein Council of Great Britain (1916–23), O'Briain was co-founder of the Irish Self-Determination League of Great Britain, and its Vice-President (1919–22) and President (1922–24). He was appointed official spokesman for Sinn Fein* by the first Dail Eireann during the War of Independence. After opposing the Treaty* he was dismissed by the Provisional

Government in June 1922. O'Briain and others were deported from England in March 1923 but returned after a declaration by the House of Lords that their deportations were illegal. He was among those subsequently charged with conspiracy and served two years' imprisonment until released by the Labour government in July 1924. The republican movement in England split over accusations that O'Briain had revealed important information at his trial and that an excessive amount of money had been spent on his defence. He worked as Managing Editor of *The Music Trades Review* (1924–35). In 1935 he became Irish Minister Plenipotentiary to France and Belgium. He retired in October 1939 and settled in Ireland where he became deputy chairman of Mineorai Teo.

Ó BRIAIN, LIAM (1889–1974). Scholar and republican; b. Dublin; ed. O'Connell Schools and UCD where he became an assistant in the French Department (1910–11). After receiving a travelling scholarship in Celtic Studies he worked in Berlin under Kuno Meyer* and at Bonn University under Rudolf Thurneysen. Upon returning to Ireland in 1914 he resumed his work in the French Department at UCD (1914–15). A member of the Irish Volunteers,* he fought in the Easter Rising of 1916,* after which he was interned. He was later imprisoned during the War of Independence.* A member of the executive of the Gaelic League* (1915–27), he was Professor of Romance Languages at UCG (1917–58). He was a founder-member of Taibhdhearc na Gaillimhe* in which he acted and for which he was secretary from 1928 until 1938. Dean of the Arts Faculty, UCG for twenty years, he was a member of the Governing Body and a member of the Senate of the National University of Ireland.* He also served on the Censorship Appeals Board, the Board of the Abbey Theatre* and was a member of the Military History Society of Ireland.

O'BRIEN, CHARLOTTE GRACE (1845–1909). Philanthropist and poet; daughter of William Smith O'Brien;* ed. St Columba's College and by private tutor. A prolific pamphleteer, her observations on emigrant conditions, when reprinted in the *Pall Mall Gazette* (6 May 1881), resulted in a Board of Trade investigation into the White Star Line and in stricter government control of emigrant ships. She was active in opposition to the Coercion Act of 1881 and was a keen supporter of the Land League.* She contributed to *The Nation* and *United Ireland* and had a wide circle of influential friends including Douglas Hyde, Aubrey de Vere and John Boyle O'Reilly. Troubled by increasing deafness in her later years she nevertheless travelled extensively. Her works include *Light and Shade* (1878), *Drama and Lyrics* (1880), *Lyrics* (1886), and *Cahirmoyle* (1888).

O'BRIEN, FLANN. *See* O'Nolan, Brian.

O'BRIEN, JAMES FRANCIS XAVIER (1828–1905). Republican; politician (Nationalist). He studied medicine in Paris and subsequently travelled to South America where he fought in the war in Nicaragua in 1856. Later in the US he met James Stephens,* joined the Fenians* and became a member of the Supreme Council.* Having served as an assistant surgeon in the American Civil War (1861–65), he returned to Ireland to take part in the Rising of 1867. He led an attack on Ballyknockane Barracks, Co. Cork, where he was captured and sentenced to death. He was released in 1869 and took little further part in the movement, devoting himself instead to his merchant business in Dublin. He supported Charles Stewart Parnell* and was treasurer of the National League.* He was MP for Mayo (1885–95) and for Cork (1895–1905). He became an anti-Parnellite following the split in the Irish Parliamentary Party.*

O'BRIEN PETER, LORD ('PETER THE PACKER'; 1842–1914). Lawyer; b. Ballynalacken, Co. Clare; ed. TCD where he graduated M.A. He was called to the Bar in 1864 and became a QC in 1880. As Crown Counsel at Green Street, Dublin, during the trials of prominent Land League* members (1881–82), he was noted for his hostility towards the defendants. His activities during these trials led to the accusation of his 'packing' juries – hence his nickname, 'Peter the Packer'. He was Solicitor-General, 1887–89, when he was created Lord Chief Justice. Awarded a baronetcy in 1891, he was raised to the peerage in 1900. His *Reminiscences* appeared in 1916.

O'BRIEN, REV. RICHARD BAPTIST (1809–85). Clergyman (R.C.) and author; b. Carrick-on-Suir, Co. Tipperary; ed. locally and Maynooth. He was parish priest in Newcastle West, Co. Limerick until 1865 when he was appointed Dean of Limerick. A contributor to *The Nation* and *The Irish Catholic Magazine,* he founded the Catholic Young Men's Society. His novels were *Ailey Moore* (1856), *Jack Hazlitt* (1875) and *The Daltons of Crag* (1882).

O'BRIEN, RICHARD BARRY (1847–1918). Historian; b. Kilrush, Co. Clare; ed. privately and at the Catholic University.* He was called to the Bar in 1874. As a journalist in London he edited *The Speaker.* His membership of the Home Rule Confederation of Great Britain* brought him into contact with Charles Stewart Parnell* and leading members of the Irish Parliamentary Party. A member of the London Gaelic League,* O'Brien promoted the study of Irish literature, language and history. He was Chairman of the League (1892–1906) and President (1906–11). Following the split in the Irish Party (1890), O'Brien remained loyal to Parnell and for a period acted as his unofficial private secretary. His two-volume biography of Parnell (*The Life of Charles Stewart Parnell*) was published in 1898. His other works include *The Irish Land Question and English Public Opinion* (1879), *The Parliamentary History of the Irish Land Question* (1880), *Fifty Years of Concessions to Ireland* (1883), *Fifty Years of Irish History* (2 vols, 1883–85), *Lord Russell of Killowen* (1901), *England's Title in Ireland* (1905), *Studies in Irish History* (second series, 1906) and *Dublin Castle and the Irish People* (1909); he also edited *Two Centuries of Irish History* (1888), *The Autobiography of Wolfe Tone* (1893) and *Speeches of John Redmond* (1910).

O'BRIEN WILLIAM (1852–1928). Politician (Nationalist), journalist and land agitator; b. Mallow, Co. Cork; ed. Cloyne Diocesan School. He matriculated to Queen's College, Cork where he won a law scholarship but was unable to continue his studies through ill-health. He worked on the Cork *Daily Herald* (1868–76) and *The Freeman's Journal* (1876–81). While reporting a Home Rule Meeting in Tralee in 1878, he met Charles Stewart Parnell* for the first time. A strong supporter of the Land League,* O'Brien accepted Parnell's invitation to edit the Parnellite newspaper, *United Ireland,* which he did from 1881 to 1890. As editor of *United Ireland,* which he once described as 'an insurrection in print', O'Brien was one of the most influential journalists in the country. This led to his imprisonment with Parnell in October 1881. He was author of the 'No Rent Manifesto'.* After his release in April 1882 he became a leading organiser of the new Parnellite constituency organisation, the National League,* and was returned as MP for Mallow (1883). He became one of Parnell's principal lieutenants in the Irish Parliamentary Party.*

O'Brien, with Tim Harrington, T. M. Healy and John Dillon was a leader of the Plan of Campaign* (1886–91). In August 1886 he accompanied John Redmond* and Michael Davitt* to the Fenian Convention in Chicago where they secured Clan na Gael* support for Parnell and the party. For his Plan of Campaign activities he was arrested with Dillon in Loughrea, Co. Galway (December 1886); they were tried in February 1887 and acquitted when the jury disagreed. Returned as MP for North-East Cork in 1887, his organisation of a rent-strike on the Kingston estate near Mitchelstown led to a magistrate's order for a court appearance in the town on 9 September, along with John Mandeville, MP. Although they did not appear a large crowd gathered and in the resulting disorder three people were killed in what became known as the Mitchelstown 'Massacre'.* They were imprisoned on 2 November 1887 and, refusing to wear prison garb, suffered hardship which resulted in Mandeville's death shortly after his release early in 1888. O'Brien was re-arrested on 8 April 1888 but succeeded in an appeal against his three months' sentence of hard labour. Arrested again on 24 January 1889, he escaped from the courtroom and went to England, having been sentenced to four months *in absentia*. He was arrested in Manchester shortly afterwards and served his sentence in Clonmel and Galway. During this period he still led the Plan of Campaign but failed to secure support from Parnell who, fearing his Liberal alliance would suffer, remained aloof from the agitation. By 1889 when the plan was in difficulties it required all of O'Brien's efforts to secure a measure of support from Parnell for the Tenants' Defence Association* which was launched in November 1889 (while he was again imprisoned, September – December). Upon his release, he threw himself wholeheartedly into the New Tipperary* project which ultimately ruined the Plan by eating into the available finance.

He skipped bail with Dillon in October 1890 and went to the USA via France. While fund-raising in America, they were absent when the crisis in the party broke over the revelations in the divorce court concerning Parnell's *affaire* with Mrs Katharine O'Shea.* The American group sent a telegram expressing their confidence in Parnell's leadership but repudiated him after the publication of the 'Manifesto to the Irish People', on 29 November. After the split in the party on 6 December, O'Brien was an anti-Parnellite. At the request of the American delegates he travelled to France and met with Parnell in Boulogne on 30 December. He declined Parnell's proposal that he (O'Brien) should be chairman of the party instead of Justin McCarthy.* They were joined by Dillon in January 1891 but the fruitless talks were terminated by Parnell on 10 February. O'Brien and Dillon were imprisoned upon arrival in England, and transferred to Galway jail from which they were released on 30 July.

Although returned for Cork City in 1892, O'Brien took up residence in Mayo and played only a peripheral role in politics during the early 1890s. He was horrified by the famine conditions he encountered in Mayo, and, in an attempt to win concessions, he founded a new movement, the United Irish League* on 28 January 1898. With its call of 'The Land for the People' O'Brien's new movement became a national one. Within two years his success had prompted the re-unification of the Irish Parliamentary Party under John Redmond.* Although a member of the party, O'Brien expressed his own views in his new paper, *The Irish People* (1899–1908). By 1900 he had become convinced that no solution to the Irish demand for self-government or to the land question could come about without bringing together all major Irish groupings, in particular Unionists and Nationalists, landowners and tenants. His emphasis was on 'conference' and 'conciliation', and he was one of the most enthusiastic members of the Land Conference (1902–03), whose recommendations influenced the Wyndham Land Act of 1903 (*see* Land Acts). Although he had reservations about the Act he believed that the confer-

ence had been successful. He broke with the party in November 1903 when it refused to accept that the conference could be successfully applied to the question of self-government, and he was a member of the Land Conference's successor, the Irish Reform Association.* After he was returned unopposed for Cork City (1904) he refused to take the party pledge in May 1905. His attempts to negotiate with Sinn Fein* were a failure and, realising the futility of his isolated position, he formally re-joined the Irish party in January 1908, followed by T. M. Healy. Almost immediately he clashed with the party when he opposed the government's attempts to dilute the Land Act of 1903. Suffering from ill-health and fatigue, he resigned his seat in April 1909.

Within two years he was back in politics, with a new paper, *The Cork Accent,* and his seat for Cork regained, (January 1910). Still seeking 'conference' and 'conciliation', he founded a new party, the All-For-Ireland League.* His support however, was principally confined to the south and financing his newspapers, after *The Cork Accent* gave way in 1911 to the anti-socialist *Cork Free Press,* depleted his wife's fortune. Completely opposed to any form of partition, he voted against the (third) Home Rule Bill* (25 May 1914). He lost much nationalist support in Cork, however, when he spoke on recruiting platforms during 1914–15. Following the Easter Rising of 1916* he recognised that the country was moving towards Sinn Fein and did not contest the general election of December 1918 in which the Irish Parliamentary Party was annihilated. Earlier that year he had been a member of the Mansion House Conference* to oppose conscription (*see* Conscription and Ireland). Now he retired to his home in Mallow. On the foundation of the Free State he declined to be nominated to the Senate.* Shortly before he died he also declined to be nominated in the Fianna Fail interest.

O'Brien had a wide circle of friends

which included Thomas William Croke,* Archbishop of Cashel (who travelled to London to officiate at his wedding, 11 June 1890, the last occasion on which the leading members of the Irish party met in peace). His works included 'Christmas on the Galtees', an account of tenants' conditions, which appeared in *The Freeman's Journal* during the winter of 1877—78 and attracted the attention of Dr Croke and Canon Sheehan; *When We Were Boys* (1890), *Irish Ideas* (1893), *A Queen of Men* (1898), *Recollections* (1905), *An Olive Branch in Ireland* (1910), *The Downfall of Parliamentarianism* (1918), *Evening Memories* (1920), *The Responsibility for Partition* (1921), *The Irish Revolution* (1921), *Edmund Burke as an Irishman* (1924), *The Parnell of Real Life* (1926) and *Irish Fireside Hours* (1927).

O'BRIEN, WILLIAM (1881—1968). Trade unionist; b. Ballygurteen, Clonakilty, Co. Cork; ed. CBS, Dungarvan and in Carrick-on-Suir. After his family moved to Dublin in 1896 he fell under the influence of James Connolly* and joined the Irish Socialist Republican Party* of which he became financial secretary and treasurer. A master-tailor by trade, he was chairman of the Amalgamated Society of Tailors (1904). He was a founder-member of the United Socialist Party. A delegate to the Dublin Trades Council, he was a member of the executive of which he became vice-president (1913) and president (1914).

O'Brien was a founder-member of the Irish Transport and General Workers' Union,* to which he devoted the the rest of his life. He persuaded Connolly to return from the USA in 1910 and within a short time had him appointed Belfast organiser of the ITGWU. As a member of the executive of the Irish Trades Union Congress,* he masterminded a takeover by the Larkinites and was secretary of the committee which organised the Lock-Out of 1913,* for which he

was imprisoned. He was also a member of the Irish Neutrality League* during World War I and sat on the Anti-Conscription Committee (1915).

Through his involvement with Connolly and the Irish Citizen Army* he was interned after the Easter Rising of 1916 in which he had played no direct part. After his release in August 1916 he worked for the National Aid and Volunteers' Dependents Fund* (1916—18). During this period also he played a leading role in the re-organisation of the ITGWU which by 1920 had 100,000 members (from 10,000 in 1913). As general secretary and a member of the executive of the Labour Party* he assisted Thomas Johnson* in drafting the Democratic Programme.* During the War of Independence, he gave 'unofficial' assistance to the Irish Republican Army and to the first Dail Eireann. He was imprisoned in Wormwood Scrubs in 1920.

O'Brien had a brief parliamentary career. He was returned for Labour during the session 1922—23 and then lost his seat. Re-elected in the first general election of 1927 (June) he lost his seat in the second (August). After this, he concentrated on union activities as general secretary of the ITWGU. He was financial secretary of the Labour Party (1931—39) and chairman of its administrative council (1939—41). He resisted Larkin's attempts to regain control of the union in 1923. When Larkin forcibly took over the union's headquarters O'Brien successfully took the case to court. Larkin then founded a rival union, the Workers' Union of Ireland,* which, taking Dublin support from the ITGWU, reduced O'Brien's union membership to around 60,000. The battle was resumed in 1943 when Larkin and his son, James Larkin Jnr,* were admitted to the Labour Party. Having failed to exclude them, O'Brien led the ITGWU to disaffiliate from Labour and formed a rival Congress of Irish Unions* for his supporters. Having reached the statutory age limit he retired from the ITGWU in 1946 but remained as an adviser to the union. His autobiography, *Forth the Banners Go,* appeared in 1969.

O'BRIEN, WILLIAM SMITH (1803–64). Politician (Repeal); b. Dromoland Castle, Co. Clare; ed. Harrow and Trinity College, Cambridge. He entered politics as a Tory Emancipationist MP for Ennis (1828–41), supporting the Catholic Association* with whose leader, Daniel O'Connell,* he had an uneasy relationship. In 1831 he unsuccessfully drafted a Bill to relieve the aged, infirm and helpless poor in Ireland. He also supported the fight against the Tithes,* and, in 1838, proposed that peasants should be granted ownership of reclaimed land.

Although he joined O'Connell's Anti-Tory Association in 1835, O'Connell and the Catholic Vicar-General of the Limerick diocese opposed him when he successfully contested the Limerick seat. O'Brien disclaimed any connection with O'Connell so as not to ' . . . compromise the independence which as a Member of Parliament I shall never cease to claim for myself'. He did not publicly support O'Connell until 1843, and then only for a few years. In opposition to anti-Repeal tactics by the Irish administration he resigned his position as a Commissioner of the Peace after the dismissal in 1843 of pro-Repeal magistrates. He then joined the Repeal Association* of which he was a critical supporter. He protested against O'Connell's state trial and imprisonment (1843–44). At a meeting of the Association in November 1844 he proposed the Repeal Pledge. During this period he was highly respected by *The Nation* group of Young Ireland,* and, bridging the gap between 'Young' Ireland and what O'Connell called 'Old' Ireland, jocularly called himself 'Middle-Aged' Ireland. Young Ireland, provoked by John O'Connell,* moved further away from the Association. One issue which caused tension was Young Ireland's support for the Queen's Colleges,* the solution proferred by O'Connell's old enemy, Sir

Robert Peel,* to end the demand for a Catholic university. O'Brien supported the 'godless colleges' as they were described by O'Connell and the Archbishop of Tuam, John MacHale.* The breach between O'Brien and O'Connell was widened in December 1845 when O'Connell supported the repeal of the Corn Laws to assist Ireland, already in the throes of the Famine of 1845–49.* O'Brien also objected to O'Connell's alliance with the Whigs against Peel. Any alliance with an English party ran counter to O'Brien's concept of an Irish party: 'I believe it to be for the interests of Ireland that administration after administration should be shipwrecked until England shall have learnt that it would be wise as well as just on their part to conform to our demand for a national legislature'. In July 1846 Young Ireland withdrew from the Repeal Association.

Although he did not agree with the Young Ireland extremists, led by James Fintan Lalor, John Mitchel and Thomas Francis Meagher, he accepted the position of official spokesman in the House of Commons. In January 1847 he was persuaded by Charles Gavan Duffy to become leader of the Irish Confederation.* By this time the Famine was widespread throughout the country. The government reacted to unrest by introducing severe laws, the Treason Felony Act* (April 1848) and the suspension of habeas corpus.* In March 1848 when he, Mitchel and Meagher were placed on trial the charges failed, but Mitchel was re-tried in May under the new law and sentenced to fourteen years' transportation. O'Brien had earlier rejected Mitchel's call for an insurrection but by summer he had been converted to the belief that there was no alternative, when the Confederation was outlawed on 26 July. He attempted to raise support in the south-east, along the Tipperary-Kilkenny border, but was greeted without enthusiasm. The rising, for the most part centred on Ballingarry, Co. Tipperary,* was a failure and within days the leaders had either been captured or had surrendered. Of the small number who made their escape one was his *aide-de-camp,* James Stephens,* who later founded the Irish Republican Brotherhood.* O'Brien was captured and condemned to death, a sentence which was commuted to transportation to Tasmania where he remained until released in 1854.

After his release he visited Poland and the USA where he received a warm reception from his former colleagues and admirers. He returned to Ireland in 1856. His actions in 1848 had not been characteristic and he reverted now to his innate conservatism, using the columns of *The Nation* to attack militant secret movements, including the IRB. He played little further part in the public affairs and died in Wales. His daughter, Charlotte Grace O'Brien,* was a noted philanthropist in the cause of emigrants' travel conditions.

Ó BUACHALLA, DOMHNALL (1866—1963). Politician (Sinn Fein and Fianna Fail); Governor-General (1932—37); b. Maynooth, Co. Kildare where he later owned a shop and was active in nationalist causes. A member of the Irish Volunteers* he led a detachment from his home to Dublin to fight in the GPO after the outbreak of the Easter Rising of 1916.* Following a period of internment he was active in the anti-conscription campaign (*see* Conscription and Ireland) and was returned as MP for Kildare in the general election of December 1918. Rejecting the Treaty, he supported the Irregulars (anti-Treaty IRA) during the Civil War* when he was for a time imprisoned. A founder-member of Fianna Fail, he was a member of Dail Eireann from 1927 until he lost his seat in 1932 when his close friend, Eamon de Valera,* formed the first Fianna Fail government. At de Valera's request, O'Buachalla agreed to accept the office of Governor-General, with the Irish title of *An Seanascal* (Chief Steward). As it was de Valera's in-

tention to phase out the office, O'Buachalla did not reside at the Vice-Regal Lodge but in a small house in Monkstown, commuting by bicycle instead of official automobile. Neither did he appear at official functions. Following the abolition of the office in 1937, he retired.

Ó CADHAIN, MÁIRTÍN (1907—70). Writer and republican; b. Cois Fharraige, Connemara, Co. Galway; ed. National School and St Patrick's Training College, Dublin. Active in the Gaelic League* he became a schoolteacher but lost his post because of his membership of the Irish Republican Army.* During the Emergency,* he was imprisoned at the Curragh where he taught Irish and other subjects to his fellow-prisoners. He became a translator on the Oireachtas staff in 1949. Fluent in eight languages and a lecturer in Modern Irish at TCD from 1956, he became Professor in 1969 and a Fellow in 1970. His novel, *Cré na Cille* (1949), was chosen by UNESCO for translation into several European languages. *An tSráith ar Lár* (1967) was awarded the £2,000 Butler Family Prize. His other works included *Idir Shúgradh agus Dáiríre* (short stories, 1953), *An Aisling* (1961), *Mr Hill, Mr Tara* (1964) and *An tSráith Dá Togáil* (1970).

O'CALLAGHAN, JOHN CORNELIUS (1805—83). Historian; b. Dublin; ed. Clongowes Wood and Blanchardstown. Called to the Bar in 1829, he did not practise. He contributed to the *The Nation* and was a member of the Repeal Association*, for which he designed membership cards in 1843. A supporter of Daniel O'Connell,* he, with John Hogan,* the sculptor, placed a crown upon O'Connell's head at a monster meeting held at Tara. O'Callaghan also contributed to *The Comet* and to *The Irish Monthly.* He edited Charles O'Kelly's *Macariae Excidium* (an account of the Williamite campaign in Ireland, in 1846). His monumental *History of the Irish Brigades in the Service of*

France took twenty-five years to complete and he was unable to find a publisher in Ireland. The work was published in Glasgow in eight volumes in 1890.

O'CASEY, SEAN (1880–1964). Dramatist; b. Dublin. He was largely self-educated. While working as a labourer he became involved in the Gaelic League,* the labour movement and the Irish Citizen Army,* of which he became general secretary. Deeply influenced by the ideologies of James Connolly* and James Larkin,* he was inducted into the Irish Republican Brotherhood by Ernest Blythe, but never became an active member of the organisation. His trilogy, *The Shadow of a Gunman, Juno and the Paycock* and *The Plough and the Stars,* all dealing with aspects of the struggle for Irish independence between 1913 and 1922 were produced at the Abbey Theatre.* He moved to England in 1926, where he remained for the rest of his life. His next play, *The Silver Tassie* (1928) was rejected by the Abbey directors, a decision which wounded him deeply. Many now consider it a modern classic. His later works failed to excite the critical enthusiasm that greeted his first three, nor did they achieve the same commercial success.

His other works were *Within the Gates* (1933), *Windfalls* (1934), *The Star Turns Red* (1940), *Purple Dust* (1940), *Red Roses for Me* (1942), *Oakleaves and Lavender* (1946), *Cock-a-Doodle-Dandy* (1949) and *The Bishop's Bonfire* (1955). His *Collected Plays* appeared between 1949 and 1951. His six-volume *Autobiographies* appeared between 1939 and 1954. He also published volumes of essays, *The Flying Wasp* (1936), *The Green Crow* (1956), *Under a Colored Cap* (1963) and *Blasts and Benedictions* (1967).

Ó COILEÁIN, SEÁN (1754–1816). Poet and schoolmaster, known as 'The Silver Tongue of Munster'; b. West Cork to a dispossessed family; ed. Timoleague and Cork. He was in-tended for the priesthood but became a schoolmaster at Myross in Carbery. His works include *Machtnamh an Duine Dhoilghíosaigh (Meditation of the Sorrowful One), An Buachaill Bán (The Fair-Haired Boy)* and a translation of Campbell's *The Exile of Erin.* He was compiling a *History of Ireland* at the time of his death.

Ó CONAIRE, PÁDRAIC (1883–1928). Irish writer and storyteller; b. Galway; ed. Rosmuc and Blackrock College. Following a brief career as a merchant seaman, he worked for several years in the British civil service. While in London, he began to write in Irish and returned to Ireland in 1914. He was winner of two Oireachtas prizes for short stories (1904, 1909) and wrote many stories for children. His works include *Bairbre Ruadh* (a play, 1908) *Deoraidheacht* (1910), *An Sgoláire Bocht* (1913), *Tír na nIogantas* (1913), *An Chéad Chloch* (1914), *Brian Og* (a novel, 1926) *Beagnach Fíor* (1927), *Fearfeasa Mac Feasa* (1930). His most successful work, *M'Asal Beag Dubh* (1944), has been reprinted several times.

O'CONNELL, CHARLES UNDERWOOD (d. 1902). Fenian; b. Co. Offaly. He emigrated to the US where he fought in the American Civil War (1861–65) and became a Fenian. Sent to Ireland on a mission in 1865, he was arrested with documents in his possession intended for James Stephens* relating to the Fenian movement in the US. O'Connell served part of his ten-year sentence in Portland and Mill Bank prisons, until released as a result of agitation by the Amnesty Association.* He was a member of the Cuba Five* which included John Devoy* and Jeremiah O'Donovan Rossa* who landed in New York in January 1871 and were greeted with an address from the House of Representatives. His latter years were spent in relative obscurity in the United States.

O'CONNELL, DANIEL (1775–1847). Lawyer and politician (Repeal); b. Carhen, near Cahirciveen, Co. Kerry; fostered at the age of three at a herdsman's hut at Teirmoile, he was educated at a local hedge-school* and at Redington, near Cobh, Co. Cork. Taken under the patronage of his uncle, Maurice 'Hunting-Cap' O'Connell (1727–1825), his later education and that of his brother, Morgan, was at St Omer (January 1791 – August 1792) and at Douai (August 1792 – January 1793). He read law at Lincoln's Inn (1794–96) and continued his studies in Dublin where he was called to the Bar in 1798. O'Connell approved of the liberal principles of the United Irishmen,* their call for reform and for Catholic Emancipation,* but he disagreed with their rising in open rebellion (1798). He had been a member of the Lawyer's Corps of Artillery in 1797 and returned to Kerry during the rising, which was suppressed with great savagery.

His first public speech, in opposition to the Union,* was made to the Catholic citizens of Dublin at the Royal Exchange on 13 January 1800. Within ten years of starting his career at the Bar, he became one of the best-known advocates in the country. Popularly known as 'The Counsellor', he established himself as the champion of the ordinary Catholic. O'Connell opposed the Veto* and protested against papal interference in Irish affairs. In February 1816 the Vatican conceded defeat on the Veto controversy. He issued an *Address to the Catholics of Ireland* on 1 January 1821, calling for united action by all religious denominations to secure Repeal of the Act of Union. But it was the struggle for Emancipation which occupied O'Connell during the 1820s. He was a co-founder of the Catholic Association* in 1823. It only became a movement of consequence when he created an associate membership which enabled ordinary people to become involved in its affairs for one penny per month ('The Catholic Rent'). He utilised the Catholic Rent

as a central fighting fund of tens of thousands of pounds. An outstanding mob orator, he toured the country, controlling millions of followers. When the government reacted by suppressing the Catholic Association under Goulburn's Act,* he renamed it the New Catholic Association and continued the campaign. The first major test of his organisation came in 1826 when it defeated the Beresfords to return William Villiers Stuart* as MP for Waterford. This was followed by other victories until, in 1828, he was himself returned for Clare. His bitterest critic, Sir Robert Peel,* with whom he had nearly fought a duel in a notoriously complicated affair, and the Prime Minister, the Duke of Wellington,* conceded defeat. At the King's insistence, O'Connell was not allowed to take his seat until he had been re-elected for Clare. On 4 Feburary 1830 O'Connell became the first Catholic in modern history to sit in the House of Commons.

During his parliamentary career from 1830 to 1847, he was associated with a wide variety of issues. He opposed slavery in the West Indies and in America (where his stand aroused considerable ill-feeling), the monopoly enjoyed by the East India Company, Jewish disabilities, the blasphemy laws and flogging in the army. Free trade, a reduction in the national debt, manhood suffrage, parliamentary reform and the liberal movements in Belgium, Poland and Spain were among causes he espoused.

After the Doneraile Conspiracy* trial in October 1829, he retired from the Bar to become a full-time politician. For the remainder of his life, he was supported by 'The O'Connell Tribute', a public collection managed by Patrick Vincent Fitzpatrick,* out of which O'Connell paid all his expenses. He was the leader of a party, or 'O'Connell's Tail' as it was sometimes known, which included a number of his kinsfolk, all committed to the cause of Repeal. Believing that Repeal would not be granted for some time, O'Connell soùght reform. He resisted pressure to fight for it too soon, saying, 'I would make ... (revolution) with public opinion and I would put a little Irish spirit into it (the House of Commons)'. During the 1830s, he confounded those who expected him to be out of place at Westminster. He astonished members by the force of his oratory, his passion and, not infrequently, his invective. He supported the Reform Act of 1832 which increased the electorate. In the first election held under the act, he was returned for Dublin City. His 'household brigade' of three sons, two sons-in-law and one brother-in-law were also returned. Now he was leading around forty members (the Tail). During this period Ireland was in turmoil as peasant grievances focused on tithes.* In 1834 he introduced a motion to reduce tithes by two-thirds.

O'Connell rejected the offers of the Attorney-Generalship and Mastership of the Rolls for Ireland in the new ministry formed by Lord Melbourne, on the grounds that acceptance of office would damage his credibility in Ireland. Melbourne was shortly succeeded by Sir Robert Peel and O'Connell became party to the Lichfield House Compact* which pledged his support to the Whigs on their return to office. Shortly afterwards, Peel was displaced by Melbourne. O'Connell's influence was soon apparent when his enemies were removed from office and replaced by those with whom he had a good relationship. The new Irish executive, the 2nd Earl of Mulgrave,* Viscount Morpeth (see Carlisle, 7th Earl) and Thomas Drummond* was one of the most constructive of the century. The alliance was denounced by the Tories and regarded with suspicion by radicals and with caution by the parties themselves. The years of Whig alliance were not personally happy; his wife, whom he had married against his family's wishes, died; the 'O'Connell Tribute' was in decline and in addition, he became involved in a series of unfortunate business ven-

tures. On the political front he had some successes. In September 1836 he founded the General Association. The aims of the Association were household suffrage, triennial parliamentary elections, one-member electoral districts, free trade and the abolition of the property qualification for MPs. O'Connell described it as the Catholic Association on a 'broader basis' and it was a prototype for the Repeal Association.* The General Association was dissolved after the election of 1837 which returned forty-six Repeal candidates, and in the following year, O'Connell founded the Pre-Cursor Society* which had Repeal as its aim.

He pressed for a solution to the question of the tithes, a major cause of Irish rural unrest. He sought a reduction in the amount, abolition of arrears and the appropriation of the surplus to popular education (a suggestion denounced by the Catholic clergy). The first of his aims was achieved in 1838. He was also involved in the debates on the provision of relief for the indigent and sick in Ireland, but he unsuccessfully opposed the introduction of the Poor Law.* O'Connell met with further success when his demand for reforms in municipal government became law through the Municipal Corporations Act* in 1840. One of its first consequences was that he became Lord Mayor of Dublin (1841–42). The Repeal Association* or the 'National Association of Ireland for full and prompt Justice and Repeal', was launched on 15 April 1840. The cumbersome title was changed to the Loyal National Repeal Association in January 1841. His chief lieutenant was his favourite son, John O'Connell.* During these early years O'Connell attracted the support of a new generation, Young Ireland,* which, under Thomas Davis* and his colleagues at The Nation,* gave Repeal a new platform while other press support came from the Pilot. O'Connell announced that 1843 would be the Year of Repeal. The agitation entered a new phase as he organised what The

Times called 'Monster Meetings' upon historic sites where hundreds of thousands came to listen to his impassioned oratory and then dispersed peacefully. The ageing Liberator addressed crowds at Mullingar (150,000), Mallow (400,000), Lismore (400,000) and Tara where the crowd was estimated at between 800,000 and one million. He called his last meeting at Clontarf for 8 October 1843, confident that the government, overwhelmed by the weight of public opinion, would have to concede Repeal. But the Prime Minister, Sir Robert Peel, was determined to oppose the agitation. The Clontarf monster meeting was proscribed and to the dismay of his followers O'Connell obeyed the law and called it off as hundreds of thousands made their way to the historic meeting-place. He now adopted a new tactic, calling for the establishment of Arbitration Courts* which would take over from the government's courts of justice. A Council of Three Hundred* would come together to form a national representative assembly. This forced the government's hand and along with his son, John, and other leaders of the Repeal agitation, he was put on trial for conspiracy.

The state trial of O'Connell for 'intimidation and demonstration of great physical force' was held before a carefully 'packed' jury and resulted in a verdict for the Crown. O'Connell was sentenced to a year's imprisonment, fined £2,000 and ordered to give securities of £5,000 for seven years' good behaviour. Before entering prison in May 1844 he went to the House of Commons, from which he had been a conspicuous absentee during the Year of Repeal. He was cheered by the opposition, made a brief speech and returned to Dublin where he was lodged in the Richmond Bridewell Prison. In September, the House of Lords condemned his trial for its injustices and ordered his release. O'Connell emerged from prison physically and mentally weakened, already suffering from the softening

of the brain which eventually killed him. He no longer believed that Repeal could be won and in October 1844 divided the Repeal Party when he stated his opinion that a federal system, in which Ireland would continue to be represented, was preferable to simple Repeal of the Union. He was denounced by *The Nation* and Young Ireland, and withdrew his support for Federalism, but his wavering was a cause of concern to his supporters. He resumed his seat in parliament where he opposed the Charitable Bequests and Donations Act which had been denounced by his close friend, John MacHale,* Archbishop of Tuam. He reluctantly supported Peel's endowment of Maynooth College.* However, his opposition to the Queen's Colleges* led to friction with Young Ireland in 1845 and within a year he and they were split irreconcilably.

O'Connell's control over the Repeal Association had by now passed to his son, John. Young Ireland militants led by Thomas Francis Meagher* forced O'Connell's hand. The old man denounced talk of militant action: 'It is, no doubt, a very fine thing to die for one's country, but believe me, one living patriot is worth a whole churchyard full of dead ones.' The O'Connells feared that talk of rebellion such as appeared under Mitchel's name in *The Nation* would lead to the suppression of the Repeal Association and they demanded that all members subscribe to peace resolutions. Young Ireland seceded from the Association and O'Connell and his son were left with a movement which was a pale shadow of former years.

Ireland was by now in the throes of the Famine of 1845—49.* O'Connell supported Lord John Russell* whose Whig administration (after June 1846) was responsible for Ireland. O'Connell, helplessly watching the situation deteriorate, provided what assistance he could on his own estate. By the end of 1846 his physical condition gave cause for concern and he spent most of his time in prayer. He spoke in the House of Commons for the last time on 8 February 1847. He was barely audible and aroused sympathy even among his enemies who listened in respectful silence as he pleaded for aid for his starving country. In March, acting on the advice of his personal physician, he set out for Italy. His journey to Rome was attended by receptions, addresses and adulation. Following his death in Genoa on 15 May, his heart was buried in Rome. His body was returned to Ireland, accompanied by his private chaplain, Rev. John Miley,* on board *The Duchess of Kent.* He was buried in Glasnevin Cemetery.

O'CONNELL, REV. FREDERICK (1876–1925). Clergyman (C.I.) and grammarian; b. Co. Galway; ed. TCD. Ordained in 1902, he was Rector of Achonry (1907) and became Assistant Director of Radio Eireann (1925). A native Irish speaker, he was an authority on Old Irish and worked on the *Dictionary* prepared by the Royal Irish Academy.* He was Lecturer in Queen's University, Belfast, and he edited the works of An tAthair Peadar O Laoghaire.* His other works included a translation of *Cúirt a' Mhean Oíche* ('The Midnight Court', 1909), *A Grammar of Old Irish* (1912), *An Irish Corpus Astronomiae* (1915), *The Writings on the Walls* (1915), *The Age of Whitewash* (essays, 1921), a translation of O Laoghaire's *Don Ciochte* (1921, under the pen-name 'Conall Cearnach'), *Irish for Self-Tuition* (1922), *Old Wine and New* (essays, 1922), *The Fatal Move and other stories* (1923) and a translation into Irish of *Dr Jekyll and Mr Hyde.*

O'CONNELL, LT-GEN. J. J. ('GINGER') (1887 – 1944) Soldier; b. Co. Mayo; ed. locally and University College, Dublin. Following service in the US army (1912–14), he returned to Ireland and joined the Irish Volunteers.* Eoin MacNeill,* attempting to prevent the Easter Rising of 1916,* despatched him to Cork to take command of the Volunteers. After the collapse of the rising O'Connell was interned. He was attached to the headquarters staff of the Irish Republican Army during the War of Independence,* as Assistant to the Chief of Staff, General Richard Mulcahy.* O'Connell, who supported the Treaty*, became Deputy Chief of Staff of the Free State Army. He was kidnapped by Ernie O'Malley* on 26 June 1922 and lodged with the Four Courts* garrison. His kidnapping precipitated the formal outbreak of the Civil War* when the Provisional Government attacked the Four Courts two days later. O'Connell was assistant to General Eoin O'Duffy* and Mulcahy during the Civil War.

After the Civil War he was Chief Lecturer at the Army School of Instruction (1924–29), Director of No. 2 Bureau (Intelligence Branch) from 1929 to 1932, Quartermaster-General (1932–34) and Director of Military Archives (1934–44).

O'CONNELL, JOHN (1810–58) Politician (Repeal); b. Dublin, third son of Daniel O'Connell; ed. Clongowes Wood College and TCD. After reading law at King's Inns, he was called to the Bar but never practised, becoming instead his father's chief lieutenant. As MP for Youghal (1832–37) Athlone (1837–41) and Kilkenny (1841–47) he was the leading member of his father's so-called 'Household Brigade' of related political hacks. In 1843 he was tried along with his father and imprisoned at Richmond Prison until their release was ordered by the House of Lords (1844). As his father's health declined he became dominant in the Repeal Association.* Lacking both charm and tact, he alienated Young Ireland,* forcing its leaders, William Smith O'Brien, Charles Gavan Duffy, Thomas Francis Meagher and John Mitchel, to leave in 1846. One year later, the Association was dissolved, his father was dead and he closed down the headquarters at Conciliation Hall.

During the rising of July 1848 organised by the Irish Confederation* (Young Ireland) he visited France and upon his return, moved closer to the government. As MP for Limerick, he helped to topple Lord John Russell* and the Whigs in 1851. Having been censured by his constituency, he took the Chiltern Hundreds. He opposed the Tenant League.* Known to his followers as the 'Young Liberator', he was returned in 1853 for Clonmel, and spent four undistinguished years in the House of Commons until he accepted a sinecure as clerk in the Hanaper Office in Dublin. His writings include *An Argument for Ireland* (1844), *The Repeal Dictionary* (1845), and *Recollections* (1846). He published an edition of his father's *Life and Speeches* in 1846.

O'CONNELL, MAURICE (1803–53). Politician (Repeal); b. Dublin, eldest son of Daniel O'Connell;* ed. Clongowes Wood College, TCD, and Gray's Inn, London, where he was called to the Bar. With his father's assistance he was returned as MP for Clare (1831), defeating The O'Gorman Mahon.* He represented Tralee from 1832 until 1835. O'Connell eloped in dramatic fashion with a Clare girl, Frances Scott, escaping by yacht across the Shannon estuary, and later marrying her in a Catholic marriage ceremony in Tralee and a Protestant one in Kenmare. The marriage broke up after they had four children. He was renowned for his numerous *affaires* and had at least four illegitimate children. A fluent speaker of Irish, he contributed prose and verse to a number of periodicals.

O'CONNELL, MORGAN (1804–85). Soldier and politician; second son of Daniel O'Connell.* At his father's urging, he joined Devereux's Irish Legion which supported Simon Bolivar, for whom the elder O'Connell had a great admiration, in the struggle against Spain. He won little distinction as a soldier, and was shipwrecked when returning home. He became MP for Meath (1832–40), and was Assistant Registrar and later Registrar of Deeds of Ireland.

O'CONNELL, PETER (1775–1826). Lexicographer; b. Co. Clare. He spent practically his entire life preparing a comprehensive dictionary of the Irish language. His researches took him to the Hebrides, the Scottish Highlands, South Wales and all over Ireland. He had difficulty in finding a publisher for the completed work. When Daniel O'Connell* was asked to assist he is reputed to have said, 'the man was a fool to waste his life on such a useless labour'. The manuscript was later sold for a crown (25p) and is preserved in the British Museum. There is a copy in the library of Trinity College, Dublin.

O'CONNELL, THOMAS J. (1882–1969). Trade unionist and leader of the Labour Party (1927–32); b. Bekan, Co. Mayo; ed. National School and St Patrick's College, Drumcondra, where he qualified as a teacher (1902–16). General Secretary of the Irish National Teachers' Organisation* (1916–48), he was Labour TD for Co. Galway (1922–27) and for South Mayo (1927–32). When Thomas Johnson* lost his seat in 1927 O'Connell succeeded him as leader of the parliamentary party. During his tenure as leader O'Connell followed a policy of co-operation with Fianna Fail as an opposition to the Cumann na nGaedheal government. This policy was more beneficial to Fianna Fail than to Labour, which lost six seats in the general election of 1932. O'Connell lost his seat and was succeeded as leader by William Norton.* O'Connell was a member of the Senate (1941–44; 1948–51; 1954–57), served on the Youth Unemployment Commission (1943–51), on the Central Council of the Irish Red Cross (1927–40) and was Director of the World Federation of Educational Associations (1927–40). He was the author of the centennial *Story of the Irish National Teachers' Organisation 1868–1968* (1968).

O'CONNELL TRIBUTE. *See* O'Connell, Daniel.

423

O'CONNOR, FEARGUS (1794–1855) Politician (Radical) and Chartist leader; b. Connorville, Co. Cork, son of Roger O'Connor. He read law at TCD and Gray's Inns, London. Active in the tithes* agitation during the 1830s, he supported the fight for Repeal* and was returned as MP for Co. Cork in 1832, but he soon quarrelled with Daniel O'Connell.* He was unseated three years later, on the grounds that he lacked the necessary property qualifications. O'Connor remained in England where he became a leading radical and became, for many, the embodiment of Chartism. In *A Series of Letters from Feargus O'Connor to Daniel O'Connell* (1836) he proposed an alliance between the Irish peasantry and the British working-class; he also accused O'Connell of dictatorship (O'Connell always referred to him as 'Balderdash'). His newspaper, *The Northern Star,* was very widely read. His activities led to his imprisonment (1840–41) after which he was returned as MP for Nottingham (1847–52) and continued to agitate long after the collapse of Chartism. Increasingly violent behaviour led to his incarceration in a mental asylum where he died.

O'CONNOR, FRANK (1903–66). Writer; b. Cork, real name Michael O'Donovan; ed. CBS. Along with his friend Sean O'Faolain* he was deeply influenced by Daniel Corkery,* supported the republicans during the War of Independence and was interned during the Civil War. He was a librarian in Cork (1925–28) and in Ballsbridge, Dublin (1928–38). Widely read in Old Irish literature and culture, he lectured at Harvard (1952, 1954) and at Chicago University (1953). W. B. Yeats* compared O'Connor as a short story writer to Chekhov. His works were *Guests of the Nation* (1931), *The Saint and Mary Kate* (1932), *The Wild Bird's Nest* (1932), *Bones of Contention* (1936), *Three Big Brothers* (1937), *The Big Fellow* (1937; a study of Michael Collins), *Lords and Commons* (1938), *Fountains of Magic* (1939), *Dutch Interior* (1940), *Three Tales* (1940), *A Picturebook* (1942), *Crab Apple Jelly* (1944), *The Midnight Court* (1945; a translation of Brian Merriman's *Cúirt a' Mheán Oíche), Towards an Appreciation of Literature* (1945), *Selected Stories* (1946), *Irish Miles* (1947), *Art and the Theatre* (1947), *The Common Chord* (1947), *The Road to Stratford* (1948), *Leinster, Munster and Connaught* (1950), *Traveller's Samples* (1950), *The Stories of Frank O'Connor* (1953), *More Stories of Frank O'Connor* (1954), *Short Stories of Frank O'Connor* (1956), *The Mirror in the Roadway* (1956), *Domestic Relations* (1957), *The Book of Ireland* (1958), *Kings, Lords and Commons* (1960; translations from Irish poetry); *An Only Child* (1961; autobiography), *The Little Mountains* (1962), *The Lonely Voice* (1963, a study of the short story), *Collection Two* (1964) and *The Backward Look* (1966), a study of Irish literature. He had a long association with the Abbey Theatre,* and was the author of three plays in collaboration, *In the Train* (1937) *The Invincibles* (1937), and *Moses' Rock* (1938), and two on his own, *Time's Pocket* (1939) and *The Statue's Daughter* (1940). *My Father's Son,* the second volume of his autobiography, appeared posthumously in 1968.

O'CONNOR, JOHN (1850–1928). Republican and politician (Nationalist); b. Mallow; ed. locally. He worked as a commercial traveller and a van-driver. After joining the Irish Republican Brotherhood,* he became secretary of the Supreme Council and was imprisoned five times under coercion acts. He met with Charles Stewart Parnell* and others in March 1878 for discussions which led to the New Departure.* Although Parnell and the Archbishop of Cashel, Thomas William Croke, supported him for the Tipperary seat in 1885 the county convention of the National League* refused his nomination; he received it only when Parnell called a second convention and personally piloted it through. He lost the seat in 1890 through remaining loyal to Parnell after the split in the Irish Parliamentary Party.* He was called to the Bar in 1893.

O'CONNOR, ROGER (1761–1834). United Irishman and eccentric; b. Connorville, Co. Cork, father of Feargus O'Connor;* ed. TCD. He was called to the Bar in 1783. His membership of the United Irishmen* led to his imprisonment at Fort George in Scotland until 1803. O'Connor was noted for his eccentricity: tracing his descent from the last man to hold the title of High King in the twelfth century, Rory O'Connor, he considered himself the lawful King of Ireland, using the acronym 'ROCK' (Roger O'Connor, King). His home at Dangan Castle burned to the ground shortly after he had taken out a large insurance on it. In order to capture love letters incriminating his friend, Sir Francis Burdett,* he robbed the Galway Mail Coach for which he was tried and acquitted. His *Chronicles of Eri* (2 vols, 1822) are imaginary annals.

O'CONNOR, RORY (1883–1922). Republican; b. Dublin; ed. St Mary's College, Clongowes Wood and University College, Dublin, where he graduated in Arts and Engineering; he also held diplomas from the College of Science. He spent four years (1911–15) working in Canada as a railway engineer before returning at the request of the Irish Republican Brotherhood* and was wounded in the Easter Rising of 1916. After a period of internment, he left the IRB, believing with Eamon de Valera and Cathal Brugha, that its secrecy had damaged the rising and that such a movement could not achieve popular support.

O'Connor was close to Michael Collins and became Director of Engineering of the Irish Republican Army during the War of Independence. He rejected the Treaty* and became chairman of the Military Council of the IRA, repudiating the authority of Dail Eireann in March 1922. He played a leading part in the establishment of a republican garrison in the Four Courts* in April 1922 and rejected the Election Pact between Collins and de Valera. While he disapproved of attempts to find a compromise formula to prevent outright civil war between the republicans and the supporters of the Provisional Government,* he accepted the truce of May which did not require the IRA to evacuate the Four Courts. Following the government's attack on the garrison (28 June) he was captured and became one of the four republicans executed on 8 December in reprisal for the assassination of Sean Hales, TD. The executions were the responsibility of the Minister for Home Affairs, Kevin O'Higgins,* at whose wedding O'Connor had been best man.

O'CONNOR, TIMOTHY POWER ('TAY PAY') (1848–1929). Journalist and politician (Irish Parliamentary Party); b. Athlone; ed. Queen's College, Galway. He moved to England in 1870, became a popular journalist and built up close contacts with the Liberal Party. A strong supporter of the Home Rule Confederation of Great Britain,* he became MP for the Scotland Division of Liverpool (1880–1929), and the only member of the Irish party to sit for an English constituency. O'Connor supported the Land League and Charles Stewart Parnell. Describing himself as 'an advanced radical', he advocated the extension of the Irish land legislation to the British working-class. He toured the US in 1881 and again in 1909 on fund-raising missions.

He helped to draw up the *Manifesto to the Irish in England*, published in November 1885 before the general election when Parnell called on the Irish voters to oppose Liberals. O'Connor was returned for two constituencies (Liverpool and Galway). When he decided to sit for Liverpool Parnell's nomination of Captain W. H. O'Shea* for the Galway seat led to a crisis in the party. O'Connor supported Parnell after some initial opposition. Later, he opposed Parnell during the leadership crisis provoked by the divorce case. He was 'Father of the House of Commons' in his later years and was Official Film Censor from 1917.

He founded and edited *The Star* (1887) when his reviewers included George Bernard Shaw.* O'Connor established *The Sun* (1893) and his most popular paper, *T. P.'s Weekly* in 1902. As editor of the latter he once turned down an application for a job from James Joyce.* His works include *Life of Lord Beaconsfield* (1876), *Gladstone's House of Commons* (1885), *The Parnell Movement* (1886), *Life of Charles Stewart Parnell* (1891), and *Memoirs of an Old Parliamentarian* (1929).

O'CONNOR, REV. WILLIAM ANDERSON (1820–87). Clergyman (C.I.) and historian; b. Cork; ed. locally and TCD which he entered when almost thirty. He held various curacies in Liverpool, Manchester and Chester and wrote several theological works. He is best remembered in Ireland for his *History of the Irish People* (2 vols, 1882)—a strong indictment of English rule, and *The Irish Massacre of 1641* (1885). *Essays in Literature and Ethics,* edited by W. E. A. Axon, were published in 1889.

O'CONOR, CHARLES OWEN, THE O'CONOR DON (1838–1906). Politician (Conservative) and author; b. Dublin to a prominent Catholic family; ed. Downside. As MP for Co. Roscommon (1860–80) he supported agrarian, taxation and educational reforms about which he published pamphlets including *Irish Land Tenure, Taxation of Ireland* and *Freedom of Education.* O'Conor was appointed High Sheriff of Sligo in 1863. He sat on several royal commissions including those on Penal Servitude (1863), Factories and Workshops (1875), Registration Deeds (1878) and on the Reformatories and Industrial Schools Commission (1896). He is best known for his association with the Bessborough Commission* of 1880 when he issued a minority report. He played a major role in the passage of the Irish Sunday Closing Bill. O'Conor was President of the RIA and of the Society for the Preservation of the Irish language. His best-known work, *The O'Conors of Connaught,* was published in 1891.

O'CONOR, MATTHEW (1773–1844). Historian and lawyer; b. Co. Sligo; ed. for the priesthood but turned instead to law; his brother, Rev. Charles O'Conor, was a noted scholar and antiquary. He published *Irish Catholics from the Settlement in 1691* (1813) and a *Military History of the Irish Nation comprising a Memoir of the Irish Brigade in the Service of France with . . . Official Papers (A.D. 1550–1738)* in 1845. It was later superseded by John Cornelius O'Callaghan with his *Irish Brigades in the Service of France.*

Ó CRIOMHTHÁIN, TOMÁS (1856–1937). Fisherman. He lived all his life on the Blasket Islands* rearing ten children on a rocky smallholding. He was a friend and tutor to many visiting writers, notably Robin Flower.* His autobiography *An tOileánach (The Islandman)* appeared in 1929 and is regarded as a classic. In his last year he dictated stories to Robin Flower which were published as *Seanchas ón Thiar* in 1965.

Ó CUIV, SHAN (1875–1955) Journalist and educationalist; b. Macroom, Co. Cork. He worked on several papers, including *The Freeman's Journal* and *The Evening Telegraph.* He was first director of the Government Information Bureau. Author of many text-books in the Irish language, his works include *Domhnall Donn agus Sgéiline Eile* (1929).

O'CURRY, EUGENE (1796–1862). Scholar; b. Dunaha, Co. Clare. A self-taught authority on Irish manuscript material, he worked for a time as Keeper of the Limerick Lunatic Asylum until he was employed by George Petrie* as a researcher for the Historical Department of the Ordnance Survey* (1834). In this capacity, along with John O'Donovan,* he pioneered a scholarly assessment of Irish manuscripts throughout Irish and English institutions. He translated rare manuscripts and drew up a catalogue of those in the British Museum (1849, 1855), work which was completed by Robin Flower* in this century. O'Curry was appointed Professor of Archaeology and Irish History by John Henry Newman at the Catholic University. His lectures, delivered during 1854–56, were published in 1860 (the twenty-one lectures made a volume of some 700 pages) as *Lectures on the Manuscript Materials of Ancient Irish History.* He made facsimiles of rare beauty of *The Genealogical Manuscript of Duald Mac Fhirbhis* (1836), *The Book of Lismore* (1839), *The Book of Lecan* and other MSS. He was a member of the Celtic Society* (1853) for which he also made translations.

Ó DÁLAIGH, CEARBHALL (1911–1977) President of Ireland (1974–76); ed. CBS Dublin, and UCD. He was Irish editor of *The Irish Press,* 1931–40, called to the Bar in 1934 and to the Inner Bar in 1945. He was Attorney-General (1946–48, 1951–53), under Fianna Fail governments. He was appointed Judge of the Supreme Court in 1953 and was Chief Justice and President, 1961–73. When Ireland entered the European Economic Community (1973) he became Irish representative at the European Court of Justice, and President of the First Chamber in 1974. He was an agreed candidate for the presidency in 1974 and was thus returned unopposed to succeed Erskine Hamilton Childers* as President of Ireland. In 1976 he referred two Bills of the National Coalition government to the Supreme Court under Article 26 of the Constitution; these were the Criminal Law (Jurisdiction)

Bill and the Emergency Powers Bill. While speaking to the army in Mullingar, the Minister for Defence, Patrick S. Donegan, reportedly referred to the President as 'a thundering disgrace' because of his actions. When it appeared that no disciplinary action was to be taken against the Minister by the Taoiseach, Liam Cosgrave,* the President resigned in November 1976, and was succeeded by Patrick Hillery.*

O'DALY, JOHN (1800–73). Author and bookseller; b. Fernane, Co. Waterford; ed. at local hedge-school.* After moving to Dublin he established a bookshop in Anglesea Street and issued many works concerning the Irish language, with Edward Walsh* as his chief collaborator. He provided translations from which James Clarence Mangan* created a new style of poetry in the English language using Irish rhythms and technical devices. His works included *Reliques of Jacobite Poetry* (1844), *Fein-Teagasg Gaoidheilge* (1846), *Fenian Poems* (1861), *The Irish Language Miscellany* (1876) and *Key to the Study of Gaelic* (1899).

O'DOHERTY, KEVIN IZOD (1823–1905). Young Irelander; b. Dublin; studied medicine. A member of the Repeal Association,* he was active in Young Ireland* and contributed to *The Nation.* He supported the Irish Confederation* and was co-founder with Richard Dalton Williams of *The Irish Tribune* which replaced *The United Irishman* after the transportation of his friend, John Mitchel. Along with Thomas Francis Meagher* he was transported for his role in the 1848 rising. He worked as a doctor in St Mary's Hospital, Hobart, during his period of transportation, meeting periodically with Mitchel, whose escape he organised (in *Jail Journal* Mitchel calls him 'St Kevin'). On his release in 1855 he returned to Europe and married the patriotic poet, Mary Eva Kelly* ('Eva' of *The Nation*), who had waited for his return.

A Fellow of the Royal College of

Surgeons of Ireland (1857), he studied medicine for a time in Paris before returning to Australia where he settled in Brisbane and built up a considerable medical practice. He entered politics, becoming a member of both houses of the Australian legislature. On his return to Ireland he was returned as MP for North Meath in 1885. He failed to establish a practice in London and returned to Australia in 1888. After failing to re-establish his practice there he died in poor circumstances. A collection was taken up for his widow in her last years.

O'DONNELL, FRANK HUGH (1848–1916). Politician (Nationalist) and author; b. Co. Donegal; ed. Queen's College, Galway, where he was awarded M.A. in 1869 and specialised in languages. After initiation into the Irish Republican Brotherhood* by Dr Mark Ryan,* he had a brief association with the movement. He worked as a journalist in London, on *The Morning Post,* specialising in foreign affairs. Following his return as Home Rule MP for Galway in 1874 he was unseated on the grounds of clerical intimidation and for libelling his opponent, but three years later won the Dungarvan, Co. Waterford, seat which he held until 1885. A distinguished speaker, he became a noted obstructionist, along with The O'Gorman Mahon,* Joseph Biggar* and Charles Stewart Parnell.*

A vain man, O'Donnell made no secret of his feelings of intellectual superiority over most of his colleagues to whom he became known as 'Crank Hugh' after Timothy Healy* gave him the nickname. He hoped for the chairmanship of the Irish Parliamentary Party in succession to Isaac Butt* but was eventually defeated by Parnell (May 1880) whose leadership he refused to accept (referring to Parnell once as 'my runaway errant boy'). He also refused to support the Land League,* and broke with the Parnellite wing of the party in 1881. He resigned his seat four years later and concentrated on journalism.

He sued *The Times* for publication of the series on 'Parnellism and Crime'* (1887–88) but lost the case because his counsel would not call Parnell as a witness. During the trial, Parnell secured evidence which indicated that Richard Pigott* was the author of forged letters upon which *The Times* rested much of its case. His principal works were *The Lost Hat* (1886), *How Home Rule was Wrecked* (1895), *The Message of the Masters* (1901), *The Ruin of Education in Ireland* (1902), *The Stage Irishman of the Pseudo-Celtic Drama* (1904), *Paraguay on Shannon* (1908) and *History of the Parliamentary Party* (2 vols, 1910).

O'DONNELL, JOHN FRANCIS (1837–74). Poet and journalist; b. Limerick; ed. locally. He commenced writing verse for *The Kilkenny Journal* when fourteen years of age. He worked for some time on Munster papers and was sub-editor of *The Tipperary Examiner.* After moving to London, where in 1860 he became editor of *Universal News,* he was encouraged in his work by Charles Dickens. O'Donnell returned to Ireland for a brief period in 1861 to fill a vacancy on the staff of *The Nation* but returned to London the following year. He contributed prose and verse under various pseudonyms to the leading periodicals of the day, including *The Irish People,* *The Lamp, The Boston Pilot, Duffy's Fireside Magazine, Dublin Review* and *Chamber's Journal.* He was for a period editor of *The Tablet,* before accepting a post as agent-general in the New Zealand office. Although a prolific writer, only three volumes of his work have been published: *The Emerald Wreath* (1865), *Memories of the Irish Franciscans* (1871), and *Poems* (1891).

O'DONNELL, PATRICK, CARDINAL (1856–1927). Archbishop of Armagh and Primate of All Ireland (R.C.), 1924–27; b. near Glenties, Co. Donegal; ed. locally and Maynooth where he was ordained in

1880, after which he became Professor of Theology and Prefect of the Dunboyne Establishment. As Bishop of Raphoe (1888—1922) he was the youngest member of the Irish hierarchy. He was Rector of the Catholic University.* A keen agrarian reformer, he supported the Irish Parliamentary Party.* He was co-adjutor to Cardinal Logue* from 1922 until he succeeded him two years later. When created Cardinal in 1925 he was the youngest member of the College of Cardinals. Cardinal O'Donnell issued all his pastoral letters in Irish and English.

O'DONNELL, PEADAR (1893—). Socialist republican and writer; b. Meenmore, Dungloe, Co. Donegal; ed. National School and St Patrick's Training College, Dublin, where he trained as a teacher. He taught on Arranmore Island before leaving for Scotland to aid migrant workers from Donegal in their strike for better pay and conditions. A member of the Irish Republican Army,* he fought during the War of Independence and opposed the Treaty. He supported the occupation of the Rotunda by Liam O'Flaherty* in January 1922 and also was a member of the IRA garrison which took the Four Courts* in the following April. After the collapse of the garrison he was imprisoned along with his close friend, Liam Mellows.* After escaping in 1924 he resumed his career in the IRA and was returned as a republican member of Dail Eireann (not recognised by the IRA).

He had little faith in violence which he felt could not bring about his ideal of a workers' republic in the tradition of James Connolly.* In an effort to achieve this aim, he attempted to steer the IRA towards socialist republicanism, but apart from Frank Ryan* and George Gilmore* he received little support. He was a member of the Executive and Army Council of the IRA from 1924 until his expulsion with Frank Ryan in 1934. O'Donnell started an agitation against the payment to the British

Exchequer of Land Annuities* and persuaded Colonel Maurice Moore to gain Fianna Fail support. He proposed the re-organisation of Sinn Fein* in 1927 so as to avoid the proliferation of republican sects and groups but received little support. His attempt to form a League of Republican Workers also ended in failure. During the years 1928—30 he founded a number of short-lived revolutionary groups, including the Irish Working Farmers' Committee* and the Workers' Revolutionary Party* for which he edited *The Workers' Voice*. A founder-member of Saor Eire* for which he edited *An Phoblacht,** he was imprisoned in 1931.

During the 1930s he played a leading role in the fight against the Blueshirts.* He helped to establish the Republican Congress* in 1934, whose paper, *Republican Congress,* he edited, and was again imprisoned in March 1934. In Spain when the Spanish Civil War (1936—39) broke out, he supported the republican government and upon his return to Ireland, helped to organise the Connolly Column* which Frank Ryan led to Spain in December 1936. He later led the campaign to save Ryan who was captured and imprisoned by the Franco government (1939). O'Donnell contributed articles and short stories to a wide variety of Irish and international magazines and journals, including *An tÓglach, Ireland Today, The Dublin Magazine* and *The Irish Booklover*. He assisted Sean O'Faolain on *The Bell* as Managing Editor and Editor.

His books include *Storm* (1925), *Islanders* (1928), *Adrigool* (1929), *The Knife* (1930), *For or Against the Ranchers* (1932), *Wrack* (a play, 1933), *On the Edge of the Stream* (1934), *Muintir an Oileáin* (1935), *The Big Window* (1955), and *Proud Island* (1975). He published two autobiographical volumes, *The Gates Flew Open* (1932) and *There Will be Another Day* (1963).

O'DONOGHUE, DANIEL, THE O'DONOGHUE (1833—89). Politician

429

(Whig); b. Kerry; ed. Stonyhurst. He supported the Catholic University* and the Tenant League.* After succeeding John Sadleir* as MP for Tipperary he was expelled from the House of Commons. He was MP for Tralee (1865—85). In 1862 he challenged Sir Robert Peel, 3rd Baronet, to a duel for referring to him as 'a mannikin traitor'. He was declared a bankrupt in 1870. A supporter of Charles Stewart Parnell,* he appealed to the electorate in the general election of 1880 to return him as 'at the end of so many years in parliament I should be sorry to lose my seat'. He retired in 1885.

O'DONOGHUE, FLORENCE 'FLORRIE' (1894—1967). Republican and author; b. Rathmore, Co. Kerry. He spent most of his life in Cork where he joined the Irish Volunteers in 1917, becoming brigade adjutant and later intelligence officer in the 1st Cork Brigade of the Irish Republican Army.* During the Emergency* he was assistant intelligence officer in the Southern Command (April 1940 — April 1943), and in the 1st Southern Division (April 1943 — November 1945). During this period he edited the Irish army's journal, *An Cosantóir*. He retired from the army at the end of the Emergency, with the rank of Major. He spent some years building up the reference library of the Bureau of Military History. Apart from contributions to a wide range of journals and newspapers, his writings included an edition of the papers of Diarmuid Lynch,* a biography of Liam Lynch* *(No Other Law*, 1954), *The IRB and the Rising* (from Diarmuid Lynch's papers, 1956), *Tomas MacCurtain* (1958) and *The Mystery of the Casement Ship* (1965).

O'DONOVAN ROSSA, JEREMIAH (1831—1915). Republican; b. Rosscarbery, Co. Cork; ed. locally in an Irish-speaking environment. He worked distributing relief during the Famine of 1845—49.* After establishing a grocery business in Skibbereen he founded the Phoenix National and Literary Societies* in 1856, which, at the invitation of James Stephens,* became part of the Irish Republican Brotherhood* (1858). Rossa, as he was known after his birthplace, became a leading organiser in the new movement, to the detriment of his business. Financial difficulties forced him to emigrate to the USA where he remained until 1863, when he returned to become business manager of *The Irish People.* * He was arrested along with other IRB leaders in 1865 and tried before Judge William Keogh who sentenced him to life imprisonment after Rossa had attacked him in a speech lasting eight hours. As a treason-felon* he was treated with great harshness. While imprisoned he was returned as MP for Tipperary (1869). Agitation by the Amnesty Association* led to questions being asked in the House of Commons by George Henry Moore,* as a result of which a commission was established to examine his conditions of confinement and he was released in 1871.

He accompanied John Devoy* to New York with other released Fenians, to receive an address of welcome from the House of Representatives (*see* Cuba Five). O'Donovan Rossa worked as an hotel manager in New York while contributing to *The Irishman* whose owner, Richard Pigott,* financed the education of his sons at St Jarlath's College, Tuam. Active in the Fenians,* Rossa became Head Centre in 1877, by which time the movement was in disarray. He organised a Skirmishing Fund* for a dynamiting campaign in Ireland (*see* Dynamiters). His plan for a band of 'skirmishers' to prosecute a war against Britain was opposed by Devoy and Dr William Carroll* and he broke with Clan na Gael* in 1880.

Through his newspaper, *United Ireland*, he attacked British imperialism, lecturing throughout America on the theme. He returned to Ireland for a short visit in 1894 and for two years in 1904. Heavy drinking and attacks upon former colleagues alienated him from the republican movement. He died in New York and his remains were returned to Ireland where, for a rising generation of republicans, he remained a symbol of the spirit of Fenianism. His burial at Glasnevin Cemetery was the occasion for an oration by Patrick Pearse* who, extolling O'Donovan Rossa's undying spirit, proclaimed: 'Life springs from death; and from the graves of patriot men and women spring living nations. The Defenders of this Realm... think that they have pacified Ireland ... but the fools, the fools, the fools! – they have left us our Fenian dead, and while Ireland holds these graves, Ireland unfree shall never be at peace'.

O'Donovan Rossa's *Prison Life*, published in New York in 1874, was reprinted as *Irish Rebels in English Prisons* (1882, 1899) and was later abridged as *My Years in English Jails* (1967). His autobiography, *Rossa's Recollections, 1838–1898*, was published in 1898.

O'DONOVAN, JOHN (1809–61). Antiquary and scholar; b. Slieverue, Attateemore, Co. Kilkenny. Upon the death of his father in 1817 he moved to Dublin where he completed his education and was imbued by his uncle Patrick with a love of Irish culture. O'Donovan, who was in the main a self-taught scholar, worked under James Hardiman* in the Irish Record Office (1826). From 1829 he was employed under George Petrie* in the Historical Department of the Ordnance Survey along with Eugene O'Curry.* While working for the Ordnance Survey he listed 62,000 Irish place-names. He was co-founder, with O'Curry and James Henthorn Todd,* of the Irish Archaeological Society (1841). From 1836 he worked at the cataloguing of Irish MSS in the library of TCD. Called to the Irish Bar in 1847, he became Professor of Celtic Studies in the Queen's College, Belfast, in 1852 and was employed by the Commission for the Publication of the Ancient Laws of Ireland to translate the *Senchus Mór*.

Apart from contributions to *The Dublin Penny Journal* and *The Irish Penny Journal*, he published a translation of the *Irish Dictionary* by Peter O'Connell (1828), *The Banquet of Dun na nGedh* and *The Battle of Magh Rath* (1842), *Tracts Relating to Ireland* (1843), *The Tribes and Customs of Hy-Many, commonly called O'Kelly's Country* (1844), *Tribes and Customs of Hy-Fiachrach, commonly called O'Dowda's Country* (1844), *Grammar of the Irish Language* (1845), *Primer of the Irish Language* (1845), *Leabhar na gCeart* ('The Book of Rights', edited from *The Book of Lecan* and *The Book of Ballymote*, 1847), *Annals of the Four Masters* (7 vols, 1848–57) and *Three Fragments of Irish Annals* (1860). His *Letters*, dealing with his work on the Ordnance Survey and other matters of antiquarian interest, were edited in fifty volumes by Fr Michael O'Flanagan* (1924–32).

O'DUFFY, GENERAL EOIN (1892–1944). Soldier and Chief of Police (1922–33). b. Castleblayney, Co. Monaghan; ed. locally. After a period of apprenticeship in Wexford he returned to Monaghan and worked as an engineer and architect until he became an auctioneer and valuer. During the War of Independence* he was attached to headquarters staff of the Irish Republican Army.* Returned as TD for Monaghan in August 1921, he supported the Treaty.* When the Provisional Government* was established in January 1922 he became Assistant Chief of Staff of the new National Army and during the Civil War* was GOC, South-Western Command. In September 1922 he was appointed to command the newly-formed police force, the Garda Siochana.*

Although there had been a breakdown of law and order during the War of Independence and the Civil War which followed (still in progress when he took up office), O'Duffy agreed that the new police force should be unarmed. He showed tremendous energy as Commissioner but was so closely identified with Cumann na nGaedheal* that he incurred the suspicion of Eamon de Valera and Fianna Fail* when they assumed office in March 1932. O'Duffy had also been closely associated with the Army Comrades Association* which had campaigned against Fianna Fail. Declaring that he lacked 'full confidence' in him, de Valera dismissed him in February 1933. O'Duffy rejected an offer of the office of Controller of Prices but accepted a pension of £520 per annum.

Following his dismissal he accepted an invitation to take command of the ACA, soon popularly known as the Blueshirts.* Changing the title to the National Guard,* O'Duffy organised fascist-style marches, flags, salutes ('Hail, O'Duffy') etc. Staunchly anti-communist, he made no secret of his admiration for Mussolini's concept of the corporate state. By August 1933 the activities of the Blueshirts led to its being declared illegal by the government.

When the Blueshirts merged with Cumann na nGaedheal to form the United Ireland or Fine Gael* party in September 1933, he became the first president of the new party. He soon became an embarassment. He attacked the government and the IRA which he called communist. He urged that farmers, suffering from the effects of the Economic War,* should withhold payment of their Land Annuities* and rates to the de Valera government. The party leadership, conscious that he was not a member of Dail Eireann, became disillusioned with him, increasingly so when Blueshirt candidates did poorly in the local government elections of 1934. His wild and unpredictable speeches alarmed moderates in Fine Gael. In an attempt to attract more members to the Blueshirts he issued a new programme, republican and anti-British in tone, calling for an end to partition. Opposition within Fine Gael led to his resignation from the Presidency (August 1934). However, he attempted to retain the leadership of the Blueshirts but was ousted when he was opposed by the former

leader of the ACA, Commandant Ned Cronin.

By 1936 his small following was in decline but had a temporary revival when he called for support for Franco in the struggle against the Spanish republican government (*see* Spanish Civil War). Supported by the Catholic Church in Ireland and by right-wing national newspapers, he led around 600 followers to Spain. They returned in the summer of 1937, having seen little action. *Crusade in Spain,* his account of the Blueshirts in Spain, was published in London in 1938.

O'Duffy continued to sympathise with fascist-style discipline and during World War II he was contacted by Germany which hoped that he could be used to induce the IRA to undertake a policy of sabotage against Britain. This idea, based on an ingenious misreading of his relationship with the IRA, came to nothing. He was given a state funeral.

O'DWYER, EDWARD THOMAS (1842–1917). Bishop of Limerick (R.C.), 1886–1917; b. Tipperary; ed. Maynooth where he was ordained in 1867. He was curate at St Michael's Limerick. During his period as bishop he was hostile to the land agitation and the Plan of Campaign; he accepted the Papal Rescript of 1887 as binding upon priests and laity, withdrawing from priests in his diocese the power of absolving anyone supporting the Plan. Although he was occasionally a severe critic of the Irish Parliamentary Party* he refused to sign the episcopal condemnation of Charles Stewart Parnell* issued by the Archbishop of Dublin, William Walsh* (4 December 1890). Generally noted for his individualism, he was rarely at one with his fellow-members of the hierarchy.

During World War I he advocated that Ireland remain neutral and criticised the pro-British policy of John Redmond.* When a party of Irish emigrant workers was attacked in Liverpool in November 1915 he wrote to the press, saying, in part, '. . . Their crime is that they are not ready to die for England. Why should they? What have they or their forebears ever got from England that they should die for her? . . . Win or lose, Ireland will go on, in our old round of misgovernment intensified by a grinding poverty which will make life intolerable'. His letter was issued as a pamphlet by nationalists and also published as a postcard.

He again became nationally prominent when he became the first member of the hierarchy to defend the rebels who had organised the Easter Rising of 1916.* In reply to a request from General Maxwell* that he discipline two of his priests, both noted nationalists, O'Dwyer said, 'You remember the Jameson raid, when a number of buccaneers invaded a friendly state, and fought the forces of the lawful government? If ever men deserved the supreme punishment it was they, but officially and unofficially, the influence of the British Government was used to save them and it succeeded. You took care that no plea of mercy should interpose on behalf of the poor young fellows who surrendered to you in Dublin. The first information which we got of their fate was the announcement that they had been shot in cold blood. Personally, I regard your action with horror, and I believe it has outraged the conscience of the country. Then the deporting of hundreds and even thousands of poor fellows without a trial of any kind seems to me an abuse of power as fatuous as it is arbitrary, and altogether your regime has been one of the worst and blackest chapters in the history of the misgovernment of the country'. This stand was in marked contrast to that of his fellow-bishops and earned him the admiration and respect of nationalists throughout the country. Local bodies all over the country sent him resolutions and he was presented with the Freedom of the City of Limerick on 14 September 1916.

O'FAOLAIN, SEAN (1900–   ). Writer; b. Cork, under the English form of his name, John Whelan; ed.

National School, Presentation Brothers College and UCC where he was awarded M.A. (1924). Deeply influenced by Daniel Corkery,* he adopted the Irish form of his name, and later joined the Irish Republican Army while at university during the War of Independence. After rejecting the Treaty he became a bomb-maker in the IRA during the Civil War, working also as Acting Director of Publicity in Cork and Dublin (1922–23). After teaching in CBS, Ennis, he returned to UCC and later went to Harvard where he was a Commonwealth Fellow (1926–29). He taught at Strawberry Hill (1929–33) when he was befriended by Edward Garnett. Upon returning to Ireland in 1933 he became a founder member of the Irish Academy of Letters.* His magazine *The Bell,* * founded in 1940, was the leading Irish literary magazine of its time.

His wide literary output includes criticism, translations, one play and a study of the Irish: *Lyrics and Satires of Tom Moore* (1929), *Midsummer Night's Madness and Other Stories* (1932), *A Nest of Simple Folk* (1933), *The Life of Eamon de Valera* (1933), *Constance Markievicz* (1934), *There's a Birdie in a Cage* (1935), *Bird Alone* (1936), *A Born Genius* (1936), *A Purse of Coppers* (1937), *She had to do something* (play, 1937), *Autobiography of Wolfe Tone* (edited 1937), *King of the Beggars* (life of Daniel O'Connell, 1939), *The Silver Branch*, (translations from the Irish, 1938), *Come Back to Erin* (1940), *The Great O'Neill* (1942), *The Story of Ireland* (1943), *Teresa and Other Stories* (1947), *The Irish* (1947), *The Short Story* (1948), *Summer in Italy* (1949), *Newman's Way* (1952), *South to Sicily* (1953), *The Vanishing Hero* (1956), *The Finest Stories of Sean O'Faolain* (1957), *I Remember, I Remember* (1961), *Vive Moi!* (autobiography, 1964), *The Heat of the Day* (1966) and *Talking Trees* (1970). He edited *The Short Story: A Study in Pleasure* (1961).

OFFENCES AGAINST THE STATE ACT, 1939. Introduced by the Fianna

Fail government in June 1939 in response to the campaign by the Irish Republican Army.* The Act provided for the establishment of Military Tribunals and under Part II suspects could be arrested and interned without trial. Part II of the Act was brought into force again in 1957 to deal with a renewed IRA campaign and 100 republicans were interned.

OFFICIAL IRISH REPUBLICAN ARMY. *See* Irish Republican Army.

OFFICIAL SINN FEIN. *See* Sinn Fein.

O'FLAHERTY, LIAM (1896–). Writer and socialist; b. Inishmore on the Aran Islands; ed. National School, Clongowes Wood and Blackrock Colleges after which he spent a brief period at UCD. After joining the Irish Volunteers* he enlisted in the Irish Guards under the name 'Ganley' and saw action on the Western Front where he was wounded. After the war, in London, he joined a number of socialist organisations. He supported the Irish Republican Army during the War of Independence. O'Flaherty worked as a sailor, travelling to Rio de Janeiro where he taught Greek at the Colegio Anglo Brazileiro, and to America where he lectured, and worked as a labourer and as an oyster fisherman. He opposed the Treaty.

A founder-member of the Communist Party of Ireland,* he advocated the seizure of buildings in Dublin but was opposed by Roddy Connolly* and members of the party. He was sales manager of *The Workers' Republic.** While the party leaders were on a visit to Russia, he led the seizure of the Rotunda in Dublin on 18 January 1922, flew the red flag and became commander-in-chief of the garrison where he was joined by Peadar O'Donnell.* They sought to draw attention to the social problems brought about by heavy unemployment and demanded the creation of a workers' republic on the lines of James Connolly (*see* Soviets). After four days they were attacked by the

Provisional Government* and surrendered, having proclaimed an Irish Soviet Workers' Republic. He supported Rory O'Connor in the occupation of the Four Courts. During the 1930s he supported the socialist wing of the Irish Republican Army* which, led by Frank Ryan,* went to Spain to help the republican government in the struggle with General Franco (1936–39).

His first novel, *Thy Neighbour's Wife,* was published in 1923; other works were *Spring Sowing* (1923) *The Black Soul* (1924), *The Informer* (1925, which won the James Tait Black Memorial Prize and was turned into a successful motion picture by John Ford), *Civil War* (1925), *The Terrorist* (1926), *Mr Gilhooly* (1926), *The Child of God* (1926), *The Tent and Other Stories* (1927), *The Life of Tim Healy* (1927), *The Assassin* (1928), *Red Barbara and Other Stories* (1928), *The House of Gold* (1929), *The Return of the Brute* (1929), *The Mountain Tower and Other Stories* (1929), *A Tourist's Guide to Ireland* (satire, 1929), *Two Years* (1930), *Joseph Conrad: An Appreciation* (1930), *I Went to Russia* (1931), *A Cure for Unemployment* (1931), *The Puritan* (1931), *The Ecstasy of Angus* (1931), *Skerrett* (1932), *The Wild Swan and Other Stories* (1932), *The Martyr* (1933), *Shame the Devil* (1934), *Holywood Cemetery* (1935), *Famine* (1937), *The Short Stories of Liam O'Flaherty* (1937), *Land* (1946), *Two Lovely Beasts and Other Stories* (1948), *Insurrection* (1950), *Duil* (1953), *The Stories of Liam O'Flaherty* (1956) and *The Wounded Cormorant and Other Stories* (1973).

O'FLANAGAN, JAMES RODERICK (1814–1900). Lawyer and author; b. Fermoy, Co. Cork; ed. locally. He travelled widely on the continent before returning to Ireland in 1838 when he was called to the Bar and practised on the Munster Circuit. A prolific writer, his works include *Impressions at Home and Abroad* (1837), *The Blackwater in Munster*

(1844), *History of Dundalk* (with John Dalton, 1861), *The Bar Life of O'Connell* (1875), *The Irish Bar* (1878–79), *The Munster Circuit* (1880), *Annals, anecdotes, traits and traditions of the Irish Parliaments, 1172–1800* (1895) and his autobiographical *An Octogenerian Literary Life* (1896). He edited several magazines, including the *Irish National Magazine* and *Fermoy Illustrated Journal of Instruction and Amusement* (1885–86).

O'FLANAGAN, REV. MICHAEL (1876–1942). Clergyman (R.C.), republican and land agitator; b. near Castlerea, Co. Roscommon; ed. National School, Summerhill College and Maynooth, where he was ordained in 1900 for the Elphin diocese. When he was sent to the USA on a fund-raising mission for his bishop he brought with him thirty-two sods of turf, one for each Irish county, and charged Irish-Americans one dollar to 'tread once more their native sod'. He returned in 1907 to teach at Summerhill College (until 1912). As a curate in Co. Roscommon (1912–14) he was deeply involved in land agitation, demanding 'land for the people' and leading a campaign against the Congested Districts Board over turbary-right.* He then ministered in Clifoney, Co. Sligo.

During the North Roscommon by-election he campaigned for Sinn Fein* and Count Plunkett. He became vice-president of Sinn Fein (25 October 1917) and was prominent in the anti-conscription campaign (*see* Conscription and Ireland). His republicanism and his attempt to recruit other priests into Sinn Fein led to his suspension by his bishop in June 1918. During the War of Independence, Fr O'Flanagan, known as 'the Sinn Fein priest' supported Dail Eireann and the Irish Republican Army, and served as a judge in the Dail courts. He visited America (1921–26) as a Sinn Fein propagandist, having rejected the Treaty. On his return he attended the Sinn Fein Ard-Fheis of 1926 and

opposed the proposal by Eamon de Valera* that if the Oath of Allegiance* was removed, it would be a matter of policy rather than principle for republicans to enter the Dail. With Fr O'Flanagan's influence the motion was defeated by 223 votes to 218. After de Valera left Sinn Fein to form Fianna Fail,* O'Flanagan blamed him for splitting the republican movement. Disillusioned, he resigned from Sinn Fein in 1927 although he continued to support it. Fr O'Flanagan was silenced by his bishop in 1932. Still a republican, he supported the IRA which, led by Frank Ryan,* went to Spain to aid the republican government against General Franco (1936–39). He visited Canada and the USA in 1937 on behalf of the Friends of the Irish Republic and the North American Commission to aid Spanish Democracy. Upon his return he settled in Dublin and devoted himself to the study of Irish literature. He edited fifty volumes of the *Letters* of John O'Donovan* (1924–32).

Ó FOGHLUDHA, RISTEÁRD (1873–1957). Scholar; b. Youghal, Co. Cork. He taught in England where he also worked as a journalist. Upon his return to Ireland he became editor with An Gúm and was first director of the Place Names Commission (1946). In addition to editions of Irish poets and translations from French and Russian, he published *Log-Ainmneachta* (1935), a dictionary containing some 7,000 entries on Irish place-names.

'AN tÓGLACH'. Newspaper, successor to *The Irish Volunteer*. Published by the Irish Volunteers,* the first issue appeared on 15 August 1918. It was declared an illegal publication and appeared irregularly. People found in possession of a copy could be charged under the Defence of the Realm Act.* Sixteen numbers appeared between 15 August 1918 and 15 December 1918, and a further seventeen between 15 January 1920 and the following October. It appeared intermittently during 1921 and 1922 and ceased publication after the Civil War. Its editors included Ernest Blythe.

O'GORMAN, NICHOLAS PURCELL (1778–1857). Politician; b. Co. Clare; father of Purcell O'Gorman;* ed. TCD. He was imprisoned during the rising of the United Irishmen in 1798. Called to the Bar in 1803, he was a close friend of Daniel O'Connell,* from whom he was later estranged, and supported him in the opposition to the Veto. He was later prominent in the Catholic Association* and accompanied O'Connell during the Clare by-election (1828) after which he went to London with O'Connell for his entry to the House of Commons.

O'GORMAN, PURCELL (1820–88). Soldier and politician (Nationalist); b. Dublin, son of Nicholas Purcell O'Gorman;* ed. TCD where he was awarded B.A. in 1840, after which he joined the Army. He served in Ceylon, Mauritius and in the Crimea (1854–55). His adverse comments on Judge William Keogh* led to his being relieved of his office as Justice of the Peace. He was returned as MP for Waterford for the Home Rule League* in 1874, and held the dubious distinction of being the heaviest member of the House of Commons. His association with the Irish obstructionists did not save him from defeat in the general election of 1880.

O'GORMAN, RICHARD (1826–95). Young Irelander; b. Dublin; ed. TCD. He was a member of the Repeal Association* and of Young Ireland.* A close associate of John Mitchel with whom he seceded from the Irish Confederation,* he was one of the principal organisers of the rising of 1848 and was attempting to get support in Limerick when the rising in Tipperary collapsed. He escaped to France and from there to Constantinople (Istanbul), making his way to the USA where he practised law in New York in association with John

Blake Dillon.* Close to Irish-American politics at Tammany Hall in which fellow countrymen Richard 'Boss' Croker and John Kelly were influential, he ended his career as a judge of the New York Supreme Court.

O'GRADY, STANDISH, 1st VISCOUNT GUILLAMORE (1766–1840). Lawyer; b. Mount Prospect, Co. Limerick; ed. TCD where he read law and later practised on the Munster Circuit. As Attorney-General he prosecuted Robert Emmet* in 1803. He was Chief Baron of the Exchequer for Ireland and was created Viscount Guillamore of Cahir (1831) and Baron O'Grady of Rockbarton. His nephew was Standish Hayes O'Grady.*

O'GRADY, STANDISH HAYES (1832–1915). Antiquarian; b. Castleconnell, Co. Limerick; ed. Rugby and TCD. Although qualified as a civil engineer, he worked under the guidance of Eugene O'Curry* and John O'Donovan* copying Old Irish manuscripts. After working for some years in the USA as an engineer, he returned to Ireland and began work on *A Catalogue of Irish MSS. in the British Museum* upon which O'Curry had worked and which was completed by Robin Flower and published in 1926. His major work was *Silva Gadelica* (2 vols, 1892), tales from ancient Irish manuscripts.

O'GRADY, STANDISH JAMES (1846–1928). Writer; b. Castletown Berehaven, Co. Cork; ed. Tipperary Grammar School and TCD, where he had an outstanding academic career and excelled also as a debater and as a sportsman. He was called to the Bar in 1872 but practised little, turning instead, under the influence of the works of John O'Donovan,* to a study of the Old Irish myths and legends, although he knew little Irish. His works, which influenced the Irish literary revival of the 1890s, popularised the Irish sagas, and included *History of Ireland – Heroic Period* (2 vols, 1878–81), *Early Bardic Literature of Ireland* (1879), *Finn and His Com-*

panions (1892), *The Bog of Stars and other stories* (1893), *The Coming of Cuchulain* (1894), *The Chain of Gold* (1895), *The Flight of the Eagle* (1897), *The Departure of Dermot* (1913), and *The Triumph and Passing of Cuchulain* (1919).

O'GROWNEY, REV. EUGENE (EOIN) (1863—99). Clergyman (R.C.) and scholar; b. Co. Meath; ed. St Finian's College, Navan, and Maynooth where he was ordained in 1888. A close friend of Dr Douglas Hyde,* he assisted in the foundation of the Gaelic League* in 1893 and was editor of *The Gaelic Journal.* He was Professor of Celtic Literature and Language at Maynooth from 1891 until ill-health forced his resignation in 1894 when he was succeeded by Fr Michael O'Hickey.* Fr O'Growney went to the USA on medical advice, continuing to write his column of Irish lessons for *The Weekly Freeman* and working for the language revival movement in the Irish-American press. He died in Los Angeles where a subscription was raised to have his remains returned to Maynooth (1901). His *Simple Lessons in Irish* were collected and published in four parts (1897—1900) and *Leabhar an tAthair Eoghain,* his complete works, edited by Agnes O'Farrelly, was published in 1904.

O'HAGAN, THOMAS, LORD (1812—85). Lawyer and politician (Liberal); b. Belfast; ed. Royal Belfast Academical Institution; called to the Bar in 1836. He edited *The Newry Examiner* (1836—40) before practising law. Among his clients was Charles Gavan Duffy* whom he defended in a libel suit (1842) and in the state trials of 1843—44. Respected by Daniel O'Connell,* he supported a federal solution to the Irish demand for self-government. MP for Tralee (1863), he was Solicitor-General and Attorney-General (1861—62), before becoming a judge in 1865. On his appointment as Lord Chancellor in 1868 he became the first Catholic in modern times to hold the office. He was created a peer in 1870 and reappointed Chancellor ten years later, but resigned within a year. He took part in the O'Connell centenary celebrations of 1875. His *Speeches and Papers* appeared 1885—86.

O'HANLON, REV. CANON JOHN (1821—1905). Clergyman (R.C.) and writer; b. Stradbally, Queen's County (Laois); ed. locally, at Ballyronan and Carlow. He went to Quebec in 1842 and from there to the US where he was ordained in 1847. After returning to Ireland in 1853 he held various appointments in the archdiocese of Dublin. His works include *The Irish Emigrant's Guide for the United States* (1851), *Life of St Laurence O'Toole* (1853), *Life of St Malachy* (1859), *Life of St David* (1869), *Irish Folklore* (1870), *The Buried Lady, a Legend of Kilronan* (under the penname 'Lageniensis', 1883), *Lives of the Irish Saints* (10 vols, 1875—1903) and *Irish-American History of the United States* (1903).

O'HANRAHAN, MICHAEL (1877—1916). Republican; b. New Ross, Co. Wexford to a family of strong Fenian tradition; ed. CBS and Carlow College. An Irish language enthusiast, he was a member of the Gaelic League* and of Sinn Fein.* A founder-member of the Irish Volunteers,* he became Quartermaster-General of the force. O'Hanrahan was second-in-command to Thomas MacDonagh* at Jacob's Factory during the Easter Rising of 1916.* He was executed at Kilmainham on 4 May. His brother, Henry, was also sentenced to death but the sentence was commuted to life imprisonment. O'Hanrahan was the author of *A Swordsman of the Brigade* (1915), *When the Normans Came* (1919) and *Irish Heroines* (1919).

O'HART, JOHN (1824—1902). Genealogist; b. Co. Mayo. He had little formal education and joined the Royal Irish Constabulary from which he resigned to become a schoolteacher.

Associate in Arts of Queen's University, Belfast, a Fellow of the Royal Historical and Archaeological Association of Ireland and a member of the Harlean Society, he was the author of *Irish Pedigrees* (2 vols, 1876) and its supplement, *The Irish and Anglo-Irish Gentry when Cromwell Came to Ireland* (1884).

O'HEGARTY, PATRICK SARSFIELD (1879—1955). Republican and author; b. Cork; ed. CBS. He worked variously as a law clerk (1895), post office clerk (1897) and a bookseller (1918). A member of the Irish Republican Brotherhood, he edited a number of nationalist publications including *Irish Freedom* (1911—14), *An tÉireannach* (1913), *The Irish World* (1918—19) and *The Separatist* (1922). While on the Supreme Council* he accepted the Treaty. His works included *John Mitchel* (1917), *The Indestructible Nation* (1918), *Sinn Fein, an Illumination* (1919), *Ulster; A Brief Statement of Fact* (1919), *A Short Memoir of Terence MacSwiney* (1922), *The Victory of Sinn Fein* (1924), and *A History of Ireland Under the Union 1801—1922* (1952). He published bibliographies of Standish O'Grady (1930), Patrick H. Pearse (1931), Joseph Mary Plunkett (1931), Thomas MacDonagh and Seamus O'Kelly (1934), The O'Rahilly, Thomas J. Clarke, Michael O'Hanrahan and Countess Markievicz (1936), Terence MacSwiney and Francis Sheehy-Skeffington (1936), Arthur Griffith, Michael Collins and Kevin O'Higgins (1937), Darrell Figgis (1937), Dr Douglas Hyde (1939), Joseph Campbell (1940), James Clarence Mangan (1941), William Allingham (1945), James Joyce (1946), Robert Erskine Childers (1948), and Sir Roger Casement (1949).

O'HICKEY, REV. MICHAEL (1861—1916). Clergyman (R.C.) and language revivalist; b. Carrick-on-Suir, Co. Waterford; ed. locally and Maynooth where he was ordained in 1884. After ministering in Scotland until 1893 he returned to Ireland and succeeded Fr Eugene O'Growney* as Professor of Celtic Literature and Languages at Maynooth. A vice-president of the Gaelic League,* Professor O'Hickey sought the inclusion of Irish in the national education curriculum and in the universities. This brought him into conflict with the bishops who were unsympathetic to the language and who objected to his pamphleteering in its cause. He published *The Irish Language Movement* in 1902 and travelled throughout the country, lecturing on the Irish language and calling for cultural and national self-reliance. The Maynooth Trustees (the bishops) forced his resignation from the Gaelic League in 1903. His campaign for compulsory Irish for matriculation to the National University of Ireland* brought him into conflict with Dr Daniel Mannix,* the President of Maynooth, and Cardinal Logue,* in 1908 and after publishing *An Irish University, or else* — (1909) and *The Irish Bishops and an Irish University* (1909) he was dismissed from his professorship. Aided by Dr Walter MacDonald,* he appealed to Rome where he presented his case in June 1910, but, outmanoeuvred by the hierarchy, he received no recompense. He retired to his brother's home in Carrick-on-Suir where he remained until his death.

O'HIGGINS, KEVIN CHRISTOPHER (1892—1927). Politician (Sinn Fein and Cumann na nGaedheal); b. Stradbally, Queen's County (Laois); ed. Clongowes Wood College, Maynooth from which he was expelled (for drinking) and UCD where he took B.A. and LL.B. degrees and qualified as a solicitor. As a student he contributed articles to several newspapers. He was called to the Bar in 1923. A member of the Irish Volunteers,* he was returned for Laois-Offaly to the first Dail Eireann where he was noted for his sharpness of intellect and intolerance of indecisiveness. He was assistant to the Minister for Local Government, William T. Cosgrave* from January 1919 to January

1922. O'Higgins defended the Treaty saying, on 19 December 1921, '. . . I say it represents such a broad measure of liberty for the Irish people and it acknowledges such a large proportion of its rights, you are not entitled to reject it without being able to show that you have a reasonable prospect of achieving more'. He rejected Document No. 2* put forward by Eamon de Valera.* O'Higgins argued that allegiance to the Constitution of the Free State was stronger than faith to the King of England as called for in the Oath of Allegiance.*

After working as assistant to Michael Collins,* Minister for Finance, he became Minister for Economic Affairs in the cabinet formed by Arthur Griffith* in January 1922 and held a similar position in the Provisional Government.* He recommended road and house-building programmes as well as drainage schemes to deal with the high unemployment figures, (130,000 – 150,000 in March 1922). Condemning republicans who took arms against the Provisional Government, he said in May 1922, '. . . if civil war occurs in Ireland it will not be for the Treaty. It will be for a Free State versus anything else. It will be for a vital fundamental principle – for the right of the people of Ireland to decide any issue, great or small, that arises in the politics of this country'. During 1922 he was a regular traveller between Dublin and London, supervising the withdrawal of British forces from Ireland, while playing a leading role in drafting the Constitution of 1922.*

He was Minister for Home Affairs in the Cumann na nGaedheal governments from 1922 to 1927, working closely with Cosgrave, on whose behalf he handled the Army Mutiny* of 1924. As Minister for Home Affairs (and Minster for Justice after 1924) he was responsible for suppressing civilian disorder and for supervising the prison system. He was party to the decision that four republican prisoners, including Rory O'Connor,* who had been best man at his wedding, should be executed in reprisal

for the assassination of Sean Hales TD on 7 December. His father was murdered by republicans in front of his family (February 1923). O'Higgins was associated with the implementation of the unpopular Public Safety Acts* designed to destroy the Irish Republican Army* and reduce the crime rate which characterised the unrest in the wake of the Civil War.*

He represented the Free State at the League of Nations,* and attended the annual Imperial Conferences which shaped the evolution of the British Commonwealth of Nations into sovereign autonomous bodies, a concept which he had outlined at one stage during the Treaty debates.

O'Higgins was assassinated on 10 July 1927 near his home at Booterstown while on his way to Mass, by a group of republicans acting independently of the IRA (which disapproved of the killing). Alarmed by the boldness of the killing, Cosgrave introduced a severe Public Saftety Act and an Electoral Amendment Act.*

OIREACHTAS. Legislature of the Republic of Ireland, consisting of two Houses, Dail Eireann* (the Lower House) and Seanad Eireann or the Senate* (the Upper House). The office of President is also part of the Oireachtas but the President may be a member of either House.

'OIREACHTAS COMPANION'. Series of five volumes published between 1928 and 1945 by a member of the Oireachtas staff, William J. Flynn. The purpose of the *Companion* was to 'set out, in short compass and in attractive form, a budget of valuable information for ready reference'. It dealt with the political system, the functions of the Dail, Seanad, etc., and gave background information on electoral results.

O'KELLY, JAMES J. (1845–1916). Republican and politician (Irish Parliamentary Party); b. Dublin; ed. locally. After joining the Irish Republican Brotherhood* in 1860, he joined the French Foreign Legion (1863), leaving it within a short time to return at the request of John Devoy.* He fought in the Mexican War (1864) and upon his return became a member of the Supreme Council* in 1867. Opposed to the rising of 1867, he afterwards played a leading role building up the IRB in England, working with Michael Davitt as an arms purchaser. Under commission from the *New York Herald* (for which Devoy worked) he was a war correspondent in Cuba where he was arrested and court-martialled by the Spanish authorities. He served as a war correspondent for the *Daily News* in Egypt where his contact with followers of the Mahdi convinced him that Clan na Gael* should provide 20,000 soldiers for the war in the Sudan against Britain but the scheme was rejected by Devoy and the Clan.

While visiting France to meet John O'Leary* he was introduced to Charles Stewart Parnell* in August 1877. Through contact with Devoy he played a role in bringing about the New Departure.* His fund-raising drive in the USA in 1879 was reported to have netted £800,000 (a claim which was generally regarded with scepticism). His proposals for the reorganisation of the IRB were rejected by the Supreme Council. He was active in the Land League* and was returned as MP for North Roscommon in 1880 as a Parnellite supporter. In May 1881 he introduced Parnell to Henri Le Caron.* Later that year (October), he was imprisoned for his League activities. He continued to support Parnell after the split in the party (1890–91) and supported John Redmond* after Parnell's death.

O'KELLY, JOHN J. 'SCEILG' (1872–1957). Republican and writer; b. Valentia Island, Co. Kerry; ed. locally. After moving to Dublin, he joined the Gaelic League* of which he was president (1919–23). He was returned as Sinn Fein member for Louth-Meath to the first Dail Eireann in which he was Leas Ceann-Comhairle (Deputy Speaker) from 21 January 1919 to August 1921 and Minister for Irish;

he was Minister for Education (26 August 1921 – January 1922). Resolutely opposed to the Treaty, he followed a policy of abstention after 1922 and succeeded to the Presidency of Sinn Fein when Eamon de Valera* left in 1926 to form Fianna Fail.*

He was editor of *Banba*, *The Catholic Bulletin* and *An Camán*, publishing his Irish works under the pen-name 'Sceilg'. His publications included *Saothar ar Sean i gCéin* (1904), *Beatha Lorcáin Naomhtha Uí Tuathail* (Life of St Laurence O'Toole; 1905), *Brian Boróimhe* (1906), *Beatha an Athair Tíobóil Maitiu* (Life of Fr Mathew; 1907), *Leabhar na Laoitheadh* (1912), *Eachtra an Amadáin Mhóir* (1912), *Ireland: elements of her early story from the coming of Caesar to the Anglo-Norman invasion* (1921), *The Oath of Allegiance and all that it implies* (1925), *Trí Trugha na Scéaluidheachta* (1927), *Eachtraidheacht* (1928), *Taistealiudheacht nó cúrsa na truinne* (1931), *Partition* (1940), *Cathal Brugha* (1942), *Éigse Eireann* (1942), *Amhráin an áird-teastaig* (1943), *Spelling made easy* (1946), *O'Connell Calling, or the Liberator's Place in the World* and *Ireland's Spiritual Empire: St Patrick as a World Figure* (1952).

O'KELLY, SEAMUS (1880–1918). Writer; b. Loughrea, Co. Galway; ed. locally. The youngest newspaper editor of his time, he edited *The Southern Star* at the age of twenty-four (1904–05). He edited *The Leinster Leader*, *The Dublin Saturday Evening Post* and *The Sunday Freeman*. His wide circle of nationalist and literary friends included Arthur Griffith,* W. B. Yeats,* Seamus O'Sullivan,* George W. Russell* and James Stephens.* He aided Griffith in editing *Nationality* and on 14 November 1918, following a raid on the Harcourt Street offices by Crown forces, was found dead at his desk. The cause of death was established as a heart attack probably precipitated by the raid. P. S. O'Hegarty* said, regarding the circumstances of his death, 'He died for Ireland as surely and as finely as if he had been shot by a Black and Tan'.

His works included plays for the Abbey Theatre,* *The Shuiler's Child* (1909), *The Parnellite* (1911), *Meadowsweet* (1912) and *The Bribe* (1914); short stories: *By the Stream of Kilmeen* (1910), *Waysiders* (1917), *Hillsiders* (1917), *The Golden Barque* (1920) and *The Weaver's Grave* (1920); novels: *The Lady of Deer Park* (1917) and *Wet Clay* (1919). *Poems – Ranns and Ballads* was published in 1918.

O'KELLY, SEÁN THOMAS (SEÁN T. Ó CEALLAIGH) (1883–1966). President of Eire (1945–49) and first President of the Irish Republic (1949–59); politician (Sinn Fein and Fianna Fail); b. Dublin; ed. North Richmond CBS. Employed as a junior assistant in the National Library,* he was a keen student of Irish and joined the Gaelic League* in 1898, becoming a member of the governing body, the Ciste Cnótha, in 1910, and general secretary in 1915. He was manager of *An Claideamh Soluis.* O'Kelly was a founder-member of Sinn Fein* and of the Irish Volunteers.* He was a Staff-Captain in the GPO during the Easter Rising of 1916,* and was interned after the collapse of the insurrection.

He was returned for Dublin to the first Dail Eireann where he became Ceann Comhairle on 21 January 1919 and was a member of the Irish delegation which unsuccessfully sought a hearing at the Paris Peace Conference. After rejecting the Treaty he supported the republicans (the Irregulars) during the Civil War, after which he was Sinn Fein envoy to the USA (1924–26). A founder-member of Fianna Fail, he became vice-president of the Executive Council* when Eamon de Valera* took office in 1932. He was Minister for Local Government and Public Health (1932–39), Tanaiste (1937–45) and Minister for Finance (1939–45). He succeeded Dr Douglas Hyde* to the Presidency of Eire in 1945 and was succeeded by de Valera in 1959 as President of the Republic of Ireland.

Ó LAOGHAIRE, AN tATHAIR PEADAR (1839–1920). Writer and scholar; b. Clondrohid, Co. Cork; ed. Carriganima National School, Macroom, Kanturk, St Colman's College, Fermoy and Maynooth where he was ordained in 1867. He ministered in Glountane (1867–68), Kilworth (1869–72; 1882–84), Rathcormac (1872–78), Macroom (1878–80), Charleville (1880–82), Doneraile (1884–91) and Castlelyons where he was a parish priest from 1891. A supporter of the Land League,* he was dedicated to the language revival and was a founder-member of the Gaelic League,* of which he said, 'It was not till the start of the Gaelic League that I really began to live in a worthy sense' (*The Irish Peasant,* July 1906). However, he later quarrelled with League leaders, including Eoin MacNeill,* who objected to his archaic form of spelling and his adherence to 'caint na ndaoine' (speech of the people). Later, he attempted to devise a new form of orthography.

He did not begin to write seriously until his mid-fifties and his famous autobiography, *Mo Sgéal Féin,* was written when he was sixty-six. His output, however, was prolific; a bibliography published in *Celtica* in 1954 lists 487 items. He made many translations into Irish, including the works of Cervantes and Thomas à Kempis. His style in adaptations of ancient sagas was chosen as a model by many Irish scholars, including Osborn Bergin.* He was the first writer to have a collection of short stories published in Irish, *Ar nDóithín Araon* (1894), and the first to have a play produced in the Irish language, *Tadgh Saor,* in Macroom, Co. Cork, in 1900. His most famous work, *Séadna,* a Faustian tale, was serialised in *The Gaelic Journal* (1894), and published in book form ten years later. Other works included *An Craos Demhain, Niamh* (1907), *Sliabh na mBan Bhfionn* (1914), *Ag Seideadh* *agus ag Ithe* (1918), and *Criost mac Dé* (1925).

OLD AGE PENSIONS. The old age pension was provided by the Old Age Pensions Act of 1908 introduced by H. H. Asquith.* The non-contributory old-age pension of 5s. (25p) per week was granted to those over seventy whose incomes did not exceed 10s. (50p). Ireland, with a large population of indigent elderly, benefited greatly from the pension which was administered by the Local Government Board. In 1910 £2,400,000 was spent on old-age pensions in Ireland.

'OLD ROBIN'S REMARKS'. Almanac printed in Belfast in the 1830s which predicted all manner of calamities for the year ahead. Its credibility suffered a mortal blow, however, when a boy apprentice was overheard by a prospective buyer asking his Master, 'Sir, what will I put in for March?'.

OLDHAM, CHARLES HUBERT (1860–1926). Lawyer and economist; ed. TCD where he had a distinguished career. Called to the Irish Bar, he worked on the northern circuit and founded the Protestant Home Rule Association* in 1886. He was later principal of the Rathmines School of Commerce and was appointed first Professor of Commerce in the National University of Ireland in 1909. He was the author of *Economic Development in Ireland* (1900), *Technical Education for Commerce* (1902), *The Economic and Industrial Condition of Ireland* (1908), *The Woollen Industry of Ireland* (1909), *The History of Belfast Shipbuilding* (1910), *The Public Finances of Ireland* (1911), *The Keystone of Irish Finance* (1912), and *Some Perplexities in regard to the Agricultural Statistics of Ireland* (1924).

O'LEARY, ELLEN (1831–89). Republican and writer; b. Tipperary, sister of John O'Leary.* She contributed verse to the Fenian organ, *The Irish People** (1863–65), and to *The Nation*,* *The Irish Fireside, The Irishman* and *The Boston Pilot*. She mortgaged her property to provide £200 for the escape of James Stephens* from Richmond Prison (November 1865). A volume of her verse, *Lays of Country, Homes and Fireside*, edited by T. W. Rolleston,* was published in 1891.

O'LEARY, JOHN (1830–1907). Republican; President of the Supreme Council of the Irish Republican Brotherhood* (1885–1907); b. Tipperary; ed. Carlow, the Queen's Colleges of Cork and Galway and TCD, where he studied medicine but did not graduate. Influenced by *The Nation** and Young Ireland,* he took part in the rising of 1848 (*see* Ballingarry, Co. Tipperary) for which he was arrested and imprisoned. Upon his release he supported James Fintan Lalor* in 1849.

His connection with the Fenians* began when he accepted a commission from James Stephens* to go to the USA to inform John O'Mahony* of developments. Later, he worked on *The Irish People** whose staff also included his sister, Ellen O'Leary.* When the paper was suppressed in 1865 he was arrested and sentenced to twenty years' imprisonment. After serving nine years in English prisons, he was released on condition that he went into exile until the period of his sentence was expired. He spent most of this time in Paris, visiting the US in 1872 and 1880. Charles Stewart Parnell* and Joseph Biggar* visited him in Paris in August 1877 and in March of 1879, he met with Parnell and John Devoy* to discuss the proposed New Departure.* While refusing any compromise with constitutionalism, he also denounced terrorism and agrarian agitation.

O'Leary returned to Dublin in 1885. His hostility towards the Irish Parliamentary Party* and its constituency organisation, the National League,* made him unpopular. When the party split in 1890 over Parnell's involvement in the O'Shea divorce case, he came out in support of Parnell whose extremism now made him attractive to the Fenians. Within a short period of settling in Ireland, he had attracted certain of the young generation of Irish nationalists and writers to whom he was a symbol of Young Ireland and the early Fenian movement. These included W. B. Yeats,* Douglas Hyde,* Katharine Tynan* and Maud Gonne.* Yeats, in particular, was influenced by him and sought his advice while editing *Folk Tales of the Irish Peasantry* (1888), *Stories from Carleton* (1889) and *Representative Irish Tales* (1890). O'Leary published works by Yeats and others of his generation in the literary section of *The Gael.* He also helped to finance *Poems and Ballads of Young Ireland* (1888) which its editors dedicated to him. He was president of the IRB committee established to organise the centenary celebrations of the United Irishmen* in 1898 and of the Young Ireland Society. In 1900 he became the first president of Cumann na nGaedheal.*

His works include *Young Ireland, the Old and the New* (1885), *What Irishmen should Know, How Irishmen Should Feel* (1886), *Introduction* to the writings of James Fintan Lalor (1895) and *Recollections* (2 vols, 1896).

O'LEARY, PATRICK, 'PAGAN' (b. c.1825). Republican; b. Macroom, Co. Cork. After running away from home as a youth he went to the USA where he studied for the priesthood. He abandoned his clerical studies to fight in the Mexican War (1846–48), during which he was wounded in the head, afterwards demonstrating symptoms of mental instability. His title 'Pagan' came from his disapproval of Christian values, in particular that of charity. O'Leary held that the worst thing that had happened to the Irish was their conversion to Christianity which had taught them to love their enemies. He held St Patrick in low esteem. Apart from St Patrick, the principal targets of his abuse were England, Rome, Queen Victoria* (whom he called 'Mrs Brown') and the Pope to

whom he referred familiarly as 'the boss'. After returning to Ireland, he played an important role alongside John Devoy* and William Roantree* as a recruiting officer for the Irish Republican Brotherhood.* He was particularly active among Irish soldiers in the British Army and was said to have recruited several thousand into the organisation. After his arrest in Athlone while he was administering the Fenian oath to a soldier in 1867, he was sentenced to several years' imprisonment. Following his release he again went to America where he faded into obscurity. He is occasionally confused with John O'Leary.*

O'MAHONY, EOIN (1904–70). Genealogist and broadcaster popularly known as 'The Pope'; b. Cork; ed. Presentation College, Cork, Clongowes Wood College, UCC, TCD and King's Inns. He was a noted public speaker during his university career. For a time a barrister on the Munster circuit, he became active in Fianna Fail* in the early 1930s but later failed to secure either a Dail or Senate seat. His attempt to secure a nomination to contest the 1966 presidential election was also a failure. His expertise as a genealogist led to seven years broadcasting on Radio Eireann as host of the 'Meet the Clans' programme which made him a household name. While visiting Professor at the University of South Illinois (1966–68) he annotated the university's collection of Irish writings. A contributor to a wide variety of journals, he was the author of *Catholic Organisation in Holland* and *The Pathology of Democracy.*

O'MAHONY, JOHN (1815–77). Republican; b. Kilbeheny, Co. Limerick; ed. Cork and TCD where he took a classics degree. A supporter of the Repeal Association, he later joined Young Ireland* and supported William Smith O'Brien* during the rising of 1848. After the collapse of the rising he unsuccessfully attempted to organise another one. He escaped to France where he made a precarious living teaching English and was in contact with James Stephens.* He went to New York in 1853, and, along with his friend Michael Doheny,* joined the Emmet Monument Association. He supported himself by making a distinguished translation of Geoffrey Keating's *History of Ireland* (1857).

After resuming contact with Stephens he raised 400 dollars which enabled the latter to establish the Irish Republican Brotherhood* in 1858. Simultaneously, O'Mahony founded an American counterpart, known as the Fenians.* He visited Ireland in 1860 and returned a year later to attend the controversial funeral of Terence Bellew MacManus.* During the American Civil War (1861–65) he organised a Fenian* regiment, the 99th of the New York National Guard, in which he held the rank of colonel.

As Head Centre of the Fenians in America, his secretary was 'Red Jim' MacDermott,* a spy for the British government. Despite warnings from Stephens and others, O'Mahony continued to trust MacDermott and defended him even after his treachery had been unmasked. When the Fenians were reorganised in 1865, his position as Head Centre was assumed by Colonel W. E. Roberts who became leader of the anti-O'Mahony ' Senate' wing. The 'Senate' advocated an attack on Britain through Canada. O'Mahony disapproved and urged Stephens to call the long-awaited Irish rising. Instead, Stephens arrived in New York, attempting unsuccessfully to heal the breach between O'Mahony and Roberts. Stephens himself was deposed and replaced by Colonel Thomas J. Kelly.* O'Mahony, attempting to recover his own position, tried to capture the island of Compo Bello, off New Brunswick, but was betrayed by MacDermott. After the collapse of Kelly's Irish venture in 1867, O'Mahony lost his small wing of the American movement, much of which was absorbed into Clan na Gael* in 1867. O'Mahony's last years were spent in poverty. His remains were brought back to Ireland in a reenactment of the MacManus funeral.

Ó MÁILLE, TOMÁS (1883–1938). Scholar; b. Connemara; ed. locally, University College, Manchester, Freiburg, Baden and Berlin. Professor of Irish at UCG, he was a close friend of Micheál Breathnach* with whom he wrote Irish texts for the Linguaphone language system (1927). His works include *The Language of the Annals of Ulster* (1910), *History of the Verbs of Existence in Irish* (1911), *An Gaoth Aniar* (1920), *MacDatho* (1927), *Medb Chriachna* (1934), *Diarmad Dann* (1936), *An Béal Beo* (1936). He edited *An Stoc* and *Amhráin Cearbhalláin* (1916) and co-edited *Amhrann Chlainne Gaedheal* (1905).

O'MALLEY, DONOUGH (1921–68). Politician (Fianna Fail); b. Limerick; ed. Crescent College and UCG where he qualified as an engineer. A prominent member of the Fianna Fail organisation in Limerick, he was returned as TD for Limerick East (1961–68). He was Minister for Health (April 1965–August 1966). As Minister for Education (August 1966 until his death), he tackled several aspects of Irish education: he established free education for all in primary and secondary education, closed small rural schools, bussed children to larger schools in urban areas and introduced Intermediate and Leaving Certificate courses in the vocational system. His proposal for a merger of TCD and UCD to avoid duplication of courses excited national controversy, and is still periodically discussed.

O'MALLEY, ERNEST 'ERNIE' (1898–1957). Republican and writer; b. Castlebar, Co. Mayo. His family moved to Dublin (1906) where he was educated at O'Connell's Schools and UCD where he studied medicine. A member of the Irish Volunteers,* he joined the rebels on the Thursday of the Easter Rising of 1916* after which he was interned. As a staff captain in the Irish Republican Army* during the War of Independence* he held a roving commission as an organiser for Michael Collins.* At the request of Sean Treacy* he was attached to the Third Tippeary Brigade with which he took part in the attack on Hollyford Barracks (10–11 May 1920) and was wounded during the attack on Rear Cross Barracks (11 July). While serving in Co. Kilkenny later in the year he was captured and imprisoned for three months under the name 'Bernard Stewart'. He did not reveal his identity even under severe torture. After escaping in February 1921 he took command of the Second Southern Division (March).

O'Malley was the first divisional commander to reject the Treaty* and repudiate the authority of the Provisional Government.* He raided Clonmel Barracks (26 February 1922), provoking a protest from the British government to the Provisional Government. He was O/C, headquarters section of the garrison at the Four Courts,* and he remained in the building after the Provisional Government commenced bombardment on 28 June. One of the last to leave, he triggered off an explosion which destroyed the Public Record Office. He was captured but almost immediately escaped and, as the Civil War* spread, went to Wexford where he took part in the raid on Enniscorthy Castle.

As a member of the IRA Executive and O/C of the Northern and Eastern areas, he was appointed to the Army Council (16 October 1922) and became Assistant Chief of Staff of the Irregulars (anti-Treaty IRA). In November 1922, during a raid on a house in which he was sheltering in Ailesbury Road in Dublin, he was severely wounded, captured and imprisoned at Mountjoy where he remained under sentence of death until July 1924. He undertook a forty-one-day hunger-strike in 1923 and was returned as Sinn Fein TD for North Dublin in the general election of 1923. Under medical advice that he would not walk again he was released in 1924. He refused to take his Dail

seat while the Oath of Allegiance* was mandatory.

O'Malley recovered his health and left Ireland for Spain where he spent two years in the mountains and was in contact with the Basque Separatist Movement. Upon his return to Ireland in 1927 he decided against resuming his medical studies and travelled to the USA. While there he helped to raise money for a Fianna Fail newspaper, *The Irish Press.** He travelled in California, New Mexico and Mexico, working at a variety of jobs. Having settled for a time in Taos, New Mexico, where he lived with an American family, he wrote poetry and drafted early versions of *On Another Man's Wound* and *The Singing Flame.* He was Irish representative at the Chicago World's Fair (1933). He moved to New York where he married.

He returned to Ireland in 1935 and divided his time between his homes in Mayo and Dublin. O'Malley was elected to the Irish Academy of Letters* in 1947. *On Another Man's Wound,* his account of the period from 1916 to the end of the War of Independence, was serialised in *The Irish Press* and published in London in 1936. The sequel, *The Singing Flame,* dealing with the period of the Civil War, was published in 1978, edited by Frances-Mary Blake from the manuscript in the library of UCD.

O'MARA, JAMES (1873–1948). Politician (Nationalist and Sinn Fein); b. Limerick, elder brother of Stephen O'Mara; ed. locally, he entered the extensive family business. Briefly a member of the Irish Parliamentary Party* (resigned 1907), he supported the Irish Volunteers* and Sinn Fein,* in which he was active after the Easter Rising of 1916.* He was returned as Sinn Fein member for Limerick to the first Dail Eireann* but spent most of his time in the USA where he was sent by Eamon de Valera* to raise funds in 1919. When de Valera toured America, O'Mara frequently accompanied him, acting as a trustee for the Dail Eireann funds. Following policy disagreements with de Valera in May 1921, he resigned from the Dail and resumed his business interests.

O'MARA, STEPHEN M. (1885–1926). Republican; b. Limerick, younger brother of James O'Mara; ed. locally, he entered the family business. Like his older brother, he was a strong nationalist, supporting the Irish Volunteers* and Sinn Fein* in which interest he was a member of the Limerick Corporation. He became Mayor of Limerick after the assassination of George Clancy* in March 1921. He succeeded his brother as trustee of the Dail Eireann funds in May 1921 and worked for a time in the USA.

O'NEILL, FRANCIS (1849–1936). Collector of Irish dance and folk music; b. Tralibane, Bantry, Co. Cork; ed. local National School. Intended for the Irish Christian Brothers,* O'Neill ran away to sea (1865). Having completed several voyages he was shipwrecked for some weeks on Baker's Island in the Pacific. Later (1869–70), he taught school at Edina, Knox Co., Missouri and worked in a freight yard before joining the Chicago Police Force in July 1873. During an encounter with a gunman the following month, he was shot in the back (the bullet was never extracted) and he was promoted for his bravery. His awakening interest in Irish music was shared by a fellow officer, Sergeant James O'Neill, who transcribed the tunes that Francis had collected. O'Neill was appointed Chief of Police (1901) and held the post until his retirement in 1905. His critics have suggested that during his tenure of office, the Chicago Police Force contained an unusually high proportion of Irish musicians. His published works include *The Music of Ireland* (1903), *The Dance Music of Ireland* (1907), *O'Neill's Irish Music* (1908), *Irish Folk Music* (1910), *Irish Minstrels and Musicians* (1913) and *Waifs and Strays of Gaelic Melody* (1916).

O'NEILL, GENERAL JOHN (1834–73). Fenian; b. Monaghan. He emigrated to the USA where he served in the Union Army during the Civil War (1861–65) and joined the Fenian Brotherhood in which he was appointed a general. He befriended Henri Le Caron* who became his confidant and betrayed many of his plans. Leading 800 men he crossed the Canadian border on 31 May 1866 and seized the village of Fort Erie. He defeated Canadian Volunteers at Fort Ridgeway but on 3 June retreated back to the US, suffering total casualties of eight killed and twenty wounded (the Canadians had twelve killed and forty wounded). A second raid across the Vermont border was a failure as Le Caron betrayed the plans. He was arrested and imprisoned by the American authorities and became a civilian upon his release, working for a firm of land speculators. He is commemorated in the capital of Holt County.

O'NEILL, CAPTAIN TERENCE, LORD O'NEILL OF THE MAINE (1914–   ). Politician (Ulster Unionist); Prime Minister of Northern Ireland (1963–69); b. London, grandson of Dame Dehra Parker;* ed. privately and Eton. A captain in the Irish Guards (1939–45), he was returned as MP for Bannside, Co. Antrim, in 1946. He was Parliamentary Secretary to the Minister for Health (1948–52), Deputy Speaker of the House (1953–56) and Minister for Home Affairs (1956). As Minister for Finance (1956–63) his efforts to attract industries and foreign investment were quite successful.

He succeeded Lord Brookeborough* as leader of the Unionist Party and Prime Minister in 1963. Loyalists were opposed to his gesture of inviting Sean Lemass* to take tea at Stormont on 14 January 1965. He returned the visit, to Dublin, later in the year. This policy of *rapprochement* was condemned by hardliners, led by Rev. Ian Paisley,* who were further alienated when the Prime

Minister allowed peaceful commemorations of the Easter Rising of 1916 during 1966.

There was an increasing demand from the Catholic minority population for an end to the discrimination which characterised the Northern Ireland state at local government level (*see* Northern Ireland). O'Neill agreed to the abolition of the business vote but he rejected other demands put forward by the Northern Ireland Labour Party and the Irish Congress of Trade Unions. There was a revival of the Ulster Volunteer Force* to 'protect the loyalist heritage' and Rev. Paisley founded the Ulster Constitution Defence Committee* with its militant wing, the Ulster Protestant Volunteers,* for the same purpose. On 28 June, having returned from a commemoration of the Battle of the Somme, he proscribed the UVF for its role in killings at Watson's Bar in Malvern Street. He survived a revolt of his own followers who were led by Brian Faulkner* and William Craig.*

Following demands by the Northern Ireland Civil Rights Association* and the People's Democracy,* he announced a five-point programme of civil rights, in November 1968. The division within the cabinet over his concessions became public when he dismissed the Minister for Home Affairs, William Craig, in December.

The disturbances which accompanied the People's Democracy march in January 1969 received widespread media coverage and led to harsh criticism of Paisleyites and the police. There was a public demand for an investigation of the attack at Burntollet on the marchers, and, under pressure from Westminster, O'Neill announced the establishment of the Cameron Commission.* This led to the resignation of Brian Faulkner, deputy leader of the Unionist Party and Minister for Commerce (23 January).

Challenged for leadership of the party and attempting to unify it, O'Neill called a general election for 24 February. In his own constituency he was opposed by Rev. Paisley who polled 6,331 votes to his 7,741. He secured twenty-three votes in the leadership contest, with Faulkner opposing him, Craig abstaining and ten walking out. As unrest continued he commented on 5 March: 'We are all sick of marchers and countermarchers. Unless these warring minorities rapidly return to their senses, we will have to consider a further reinforcement of the regular police duties. . . . Enough is enough. We have heard sufficient for now about civil rights; let us hear a little about civic responsibilities.' His position continued to be eroded and when his cousin, Major James Chichester-Clark,* Minister for Agriculture, resigned on 23 April, O'Neill's moral authority within the party was shattered. He resigned on 28 April. In the election for a new leader, when Chichester-Clark defeated Faulkner by one vote (17 to 16), the decisive vote was O'Neill's. He resigned from politics in January 1970; his seat went to Rev. Paisley. Shortly afterwards O'Neill was raised to the peerage as Lord O'Neill of the Maine. His *Autobiography* appeared in 1972.

O'NEILL DAUNT, WILLIAM JOSEPH (1807—94). Novelist and politician (Home Rule); b. Tullamore, Co. Offaly; MP (Repealer) for Mallow (1832). He was a convert to Catholicism and supported the policies of Daniel O'Connell* and the Repeal Association.* He was a close friend of Charles Gavan Duffy.* Daunt favoured Disestablishment of the Church of Ireland.* He acted as intermediary between the Catholic Archbishop of Dublin, Paul Cullen,* and the Home Government Association* and became secretary of the latter at a salary of £400 p.a. In 1874 he retired to his residence at Kilcasan, Co. Cork. His novels include *Saints and Sinners, The Wife Hunter* and *Kilgarvan;* other works were *Inishfoyle Abbey* (under pseudonym 'Ignatius Moriarty'; 3 vols, 1840), *Ireland Under the Legislative Union* (1843), *Hugh Talbot: A Tale of the Irish Con-*

fiscations of the Seventeenth Century (1846), *Ireland and her Agitators* (1857), *How the Union Robs Ireland* (1873), *Eighty-Five Years of Irish History* (1886) and *A Life Spent for Ireland* (1896).

O'NOLAN, BRIAN ('MYLES NA GOPALEEN') (1911–66). Writer; b. Strabane, Co. Tyrone; ed. locally and UCD where he was awarded M.A. He worked as a civil servant. His first novel, *At-Swim-Two-Birds,* written under his fiction pseudonym of Flann O'Brien, became a cult work upon its appearance in 1939 but received little recognition owing to the war; it won critical acclaim on its re-appearance in 1960. A recognised Irish language scholar, he satirised political and revivalist approaches to the preservation of the language in *An Béal Bocht (The Poor Mouth)* in 1941. His play, *Faustus Kelly,* a satire on Irish politics, was produced at the Abbey Theatre* in 1943 and revived in 1978. Under the pen-name 'Myles na Gopaleen' he contributed a regular column, 'Cruiskeen Lawn', to *The Irish Times,* from 1939 until his death; a collection of pieces from the column was published as *The Best of Myles* in 1968. His other works included *The Third Policeman* (written in 1940, published 1967), *The Hard Life* (1961) and *The Dalkey Archive* (1965) dramatised by Hugh Leonard as *The Saints Go Cycling In.*

O'RAHILLY, REV. ALFRED (1884–1969). Academic and clergyman (R.C.); President of University College, Cork (1944–54); b. Listowel, Co. Kerry; ed. Blackrock College where he knew Eamon de Valera.* He studied for the priesthood in the Society of Jesus but left the Order. Having taken M.A. and Ph.D. degrees he became assistant lecturer in Mathematics at UCC in 1914, becoming Professor shortly afterwards. Active in Sinn Fein* after the Easter Rising of 1916, he was a member of Cork Corporation where he proposed Tomás MacCurtain* and later Terence MacSwiney* for the Lord Mayoralty.

He was imprisoned on Spike Island (January–June 1921). Having been an adviser to the Irish plenipotentiaries on constitutional matters, he accepted the Treaty and was TD for Cork from 1922 to 1924 when he resigned the seat. He represented the Free State at an International Conference in Geneva and was President of one of the Commissions.

After resuming his academic career in Cork, he went to Harvard and upon his return established the Chair of Sociology which he held without salary. As President of UCC he oversaw the expansion of the college's facilities, particularly the library where he raised the number of books from 50,000 to 500,000 and established the Cork University Press. He also instituted courses for the diploma in Social Sciences. Apart from his work on electrodynamics, he contributed to *The Dublin Review* and *Studies,* which he co-edited for a time. After retiring from the Presidency of UCC he resumed his clerical studies and was ordained in 1955. When he died he had been raised to the rank of Monsignor.

O'RAHILLY, MICHAEL JOSEPH 'THE O'RAHILLY' (1875–1916). Nationalist and journalist; b. Kerry; ed. Clongowes Wood College and UCD. Due to ill-health he spent some time in the USA where he married. Upon his return to Ireland he settled in Dublin, and, falling under the influence of Arthur Griffith,* became active in Sinn Fein.* He was also a member of the Gaelic League* and became Managing Director of its journal, *An Claideamh Soluis,* in 1913. His request for a contribution from Eoin MacNeill* led to the publication of 'The North Began' which attracted the attention of the Irish Republican Brotherhood.* At the request of Bulmer Hobson,* O'Rahilly asked MacNeill to help form a Volunteer organisation in the south and when it was founded in November 1913 he became chairman of the arms sub-committee, helping to plan the Howth Gun-running.*

He became Director of Arms on the central executive of the secessionist Irish Volunteers, after the split in September 1914 over the call by John Redmond* for Volunteers' support for the British war effort. He supported MacNeill's bid to retain the Irish Volunteers as a pressure group until after World War I – unless the government first attempted to suppress them. Like MacNeill, he was unaware that the Military Council* within the IRB had planned to use the Volunteers during the Easter Rising of 1916.* When he was informed of the rebels' plans he supported MacNeill in the attempt to call off the rising. Having failed to avert it, he joined the rebels and became a member of the GPO garrison. He was killed while leading a charge against a British barricade in Moore Street on the Friday of Easter Week.

ORANGE ORDER. Protestant organisation founded after a battle on 21 September 1795 between the Catholic Defenders and the Protestant Peep-O'-Day Boys at the Diamond, Co. Armagh. Originally known as the Orange Society, members inaugurated a campaign of violence against Catholic peasants, driving thousands of them to seek refuge outside Ulster. The first Loyal Orange Lodge was in Dyan, Co. Tyrone, and the first Grand Master was James Sloan of Loughgall. Another Protestant organisation, the Royal Black Preceptory,* founded shortly afterwards (1796), maintained strong links with the Orange movement.

The foundation of the Orange Order, modelled on the Freemasons, mirrored Protestant reaction to the Catholic Relief Act of 1793 which precipitated fears that increasing reforms, leading to Catholic Emancipation, would give Catholics control over Irish economic and political life. Orangemen, whose oath went, 'I . . . do solemnly swear that I will, to the utmost of my power, support and defend the King and his heirs as long as he or they support the Protestant ascendancy', had three principal aims:

protection of Protestants from Catholics, support for the Protestant religion and the maintenance of the monarchy and the constitution. They looked to the victory of King William of Orange over James II at the Boyne (1 July 1690 or 12 July in the new style). Orangeism was also strong but less vehement in Great Britain.

While the Orange movement was united in opposition to the United Irishmen* it was not united in its attitude towards the Act of Union. The aristocracy, the gentry and professionals generally supported the government in bringing it about but the rank and file members suspected that it might be followed by Emancipation (*see* Veto; Pitt, William; *and* Union). When the Union was carried and became law on 1 January 1801, the Orange Order saw itself firmly cast in the role of guarantor of the Protestant supremacy in Ireland.

Lord Cornwallis* and Lord Castlereagh* unsuccessfully attempted to suppress the Order of which the government was clearly suspicious. However, membership, always strongest in the north-east, declined during the early decades of the nineteenth century, and the Grand Orange Lodge of Ireland, the ruling body, was dissolved in 1825. At the same time, the Order, under the direction of the Duke of Cumberland, the King's brother, reorganised to fight Daniel O'Connell* and the Catholic Association.* The Grand Orange Lodge was reconstituted in 1828, as O'Connell's drive proved inexorable and prominent members formed Brunswick Clubs* to lobby against Emancipation which was granted in 1829.

Having lost this fight, the Orange Order strengthened itself to oppose 'Repeal of the Union', O'Connell's battle-cry during the 1830s. At Hillsborough in Co. Down, the Orange Presbyterian preacher, Dr Henry Cooke,* called for a united front by Protestants to combat the effects of Emancipation (30 October 1834). This was followed by sectarian rioting. The Irish government became alarmed, as did Liberals in England,

and the Duke of Cumberland, to forestall government action, dissolved the Grand Orange Lodge again in 1836.

The defeat of the Repeal demand and the onset of the Famine of 1845—49 prevented the Order from clashing with the government. The Grand Orange Lodge was reconstituted once more, in 1845. The Order opposed the Tenant League of the 1850s, supported the Ecclesiastical Titles Act and indicated the dangers of the Irish Republican Brotherhood during the 1860s. It suffered a major defeat in 1869 when W. E. Gladstone carried the Disestablishment of the Church of Ireland. It had more success in combating the effects of the Land League in Ulster and organised a force of harvesters for Captain Charles Boycott* when he was ostracised by the League in Mayo during the winter of 1880.

The imminent threat of Home Rule* in 1886 led to a popular revival of the Order. British Conservative politicians, led by Lord Randolph Churchill,* wooed the Orange Lodges by playing 'the Orange card'. Membership, for some time largely working and lower-middle class, was increased by the middle classes and the Protestant aristocracy to whom Home Rule was an economic threat.

The influx of the middle-class employers, businessmen and professionals led to tension within the movement once the immediate threat of Home Rule had vanished (1893). A strong working-class element, led by T. H. Sloan,* broke away in 1902 to form the Independent Orange Institution* and in 1907 co-operated with the Ancient Order of Hibernians* (traditional enemy of the Order) and the Dungannon Clubs* to take part in the general strike organised by James Larkin.*

When the public discussions of Devolution* in 1903—04 and the fall of the Conservative government in 1905 led to fears of Irish self-government the Order played a leading role in the formation of the Ulster Unionist Council.* It received 122 out of 760 seats on the Council as well as eighteen seats on the 300-strong Standing Committee. The Parliament Act of 1911 made Home Rule inevitable within a few years and Orange leaders organised the Solemn League and Convenant* and the Ulster Volunteer Force.*

The Orange Order played a prominent role in the new state when Northern Ireland came into existence in 1921. Most Ulster Unionists* were members of Orange Lodges as were all of the state's Prime Ministers. The first Prime Minister, Sir James Craig, later Lord Craigavon,* publicly stated in 1932 that he was an Orangeman first and Prime Minister and a member of the Northern Ireland parliament second. Legislation and discrimination against the Catholic population were not seriously questioned by the British government until the agitation by the Northern Ireland Civil Rights Association* in the 1960s.

The Orange Lodges hold processions annually on 12 July to commemorate King William's victory at the Boyne in 1690. *See also* Apprentice Boys.

ORDER OF LIBERATORS. Founded by Daniel O'Connell* in 1824 to promote the fight for Catholic Emancipation.* Its aim was to protect the Forty-Shilling Freeholders* who voted against their landlords. Members of the Order wore a green ribbon and a medal. O'Connell was popularly known as the Liberator for his work to secure Emancipation, which was granted in 1829.

'ORDERS OF FRIGHTFULNESS'. Title for instructions issued by Liam Lynch* to the anti-Treaty Irish Republican Army* (the Irregulars) during the Civil War,* on 30 November 1922. The 'Orders' listed fourteen categories of persons who were to be regarded as legitimate targets for republicans to shoot on sight and have their properties destroyed. Those listed included members of Dail Eireann who had voted for the Special Emergency Powers granted to the Minister for Defence of the

Provisional Government,* and Senators, Unionists, hostile journalists, High Court judges, businessmen and those described as 'aggressive Free State supporters'. On 7 December, on the day after the Free State* officially came into existence, republicans killed a TD, Sean Hales. The government executed four imprisoned republicans in reprisal and over the next few months, seventy-seven republicans in all were executed. The policy outlined in the 'Orders' was later abandoned.

ORDNANCE SURVEY OF IRELAND. Begun in 1830 by Colonel Thomas Colby of the Royal Engineers, assisted by Lieutenant Thomas Larcom,* whose idea it was that the survey should embrace every item of local information relating to the country. John O'Donovan,* from whom Larcom had learned Irish, was employed on the survey along with Edward O'Reilly* and George Petrie.* The surveyors were given various headings under which to list their material. Each heading was broken down into further sub-titles as follows:

Natural Topography: Hills, Bogs, Woods, Climate. Further information was added by the surveyor to include types of crop, sowing and harvest times.

Ancient Topography: Ecclesiastical, Pagan, Military and Miscellaneous. Information under this heading included lists of ruined churches, graveyards, holy wells, prehistoric monuments, standing stones and giants' graves. A sketch of local folk-life and tradition appeared under the 'Miscellaneous' section.

Modern Topography: Towns, Machinery, Communications, General Appearance and Scenery and Social Economy. Information compiled under this heading included a list of the number of houses in a town, frequently with an entry on the occupation of the inhabitants, a note of the machinery of the district, road-widths and notes on construction, destinations and fares of mail-coaches. The 'General Appearance & Scenery' section depended to a great extent on the scenic taste of the compiler.

Social Economy: This section related to the habits of the people, their food, drink, dress, amusement, dialects and customs. One researcher noted that the men 'were prone to whiskey while the women squander all their money on tea'. For amusement, dancing and tea parties were listed as being most popular. The violin and the highland pipe were the musical instruments most common. A subsidiary heading, 'Obstructions to Improvements', listed sheeben* houses as a social ill.

The first report of the Survey appeared in 1839 but the government decided to discontinue the Survey on the grounds of expense. A Commission of 1843 examined Petrie and other witnesses and recommended that the Survey be continued, but the government rejected its findings.

O'REILLY, EDWARD (1770–1829). Lexicographer and antiquarian; b. Co. Cavan. After moving to Dublin in 1791 he began the study of Irish. He was assistant secretary to the Iberno-Celtic Society* and worked in the library of TCD preparing catalogues of manuscripts in the Irish language. At the time of his death he was working on Irish nomenclature for the Ordnance Survey* under George Petrie.* He published *Irish-English Dictionary* (1817) and his *Chronological Account of nearly 400 Irish Writers,* financed by the Iberno-Celtic Society, appeared in 1820.

O'REILLY, JOHN BOYLE (1844–90). Fenian and writer; b. Dowth Castle, Co. Louth; ed. privately. Apprenticed to a newspaper compositor in 1855, he went to England in 1858 and settled in Preston until returning to Ireland in 1863. He joined the Irish Republican Brotherhood* and, at the suggestion of John Devoy,* enlisted in the 10th Hussars in Drogheda in 1864 to recruit soldiers for the IRB. He was detected and sentenced to death (9 July 1866) but the sentence was commuted to twenty years' penal servitude. After transportation to Western Australia in 1868 he escaped to the US (1869) where he worked on the staff of the *Boston Pilot* (1870–76) of which he was later owner-editor (1876–90). He gave support to Clan na Gael.* His works include *Songs from the Southern Seas* (1873), *Songs, Legends and Ballads* (1878), *Moondyne* (a novel of Australian convict life which ran through twelve impressions from 1880), *The Statues in the Block* (1881) and *In Bohemia* (1886). He edited the first edition of *The Poetry and Songs of Ireland* (1889). A keen sportsman and athlete, he also edited *Ethics of Boxing and Many Sports* (1888).

Ó RIADA, SEÁN (1931–71). Composer and musician; b. Adare, Co. Limerick. During his early years he used the English form of his name, John Reidy. He was Assistant Music Director, Radio Eireann, Music Director at the Abbey Theatre and Lecturer in Irish Music at UCC. In 1961 he formed Ceoltoiri Chualann from among a group of musicians with whom he became acquainted at the Abbey Theatre and some of whom, after his death, formed the Chieftains. His compositions included works for string orchestra, *Hercules Dux Ferrariae* and *Nomos No. 2*. His scores for the films *Mise Eire* (1959) and *Saoirse* (1961) enjoyed immense popularity. He wrote two *Masses* in Irish, one of which was first heard at his funeral service.

O'RIORDAN, MICHAEL (1917–   ). Politician (Communist); b. West Cork; ed. CBS until he left at fourteen and became involved in the youth movement of the Irish Republican Army, Na Fianna Eireann.* He was influenced by the writings of James Connolly. O'Riordan fought in the Spanish Civil War on the republican side in 1938. He returned to Ireland where he was interned at the Curragh during the Emergency,* (1940–43).

During his internment he studied Irish under Máirtín Ó Cadhain* and became converted to communism. Upon release in 1943 he returned to Cork where he joined the Labour Party* from which he was expelled in 1945. He founded the Cork Socialist Party before moving to Dublin in 1947 where he became involved in the Irish Workers' League.* He was a member of the Irish Workers' Party* for which he contested the general election of 1951 when he ran foul of the Catholic hierarchy. In 1967 O'Riordan became general secretary of the IWP and when it merged with other organisations to become the Communist Party of Ireland* (1970) he continued to hold the office, advocating a pro-Moscow line for the CPI.

Ó RIORDÁIN, SEÁN (1905–57). Archaeologist; b. Cork; ed. locally and trained as a primary teacher. After teaching for a time he went abroad to continue archaeological studies. He was Professor of Archaeology at UCC and later in UCD. His publications include *Excavation of a Cairn in Townland of Curraghbinny* (1933), *Recent Acquisitions from Co. Donegal in the National Museum* (1935), *Excavations at Lissard, Co. Limerick and other sites in the locality* (1936), *Fulacht Fiadha Discovery at Kilnagleary, Co. Cork* (1937), *Excavations at Cush, Co. Limerick* (1940), *Antiquities of the Irish Countryside* (1942), and his account of the 1939 excavations at Lough Gur, Co. Limerick published in *Proceedings* of the Royal Irish Academy (1951). His *New Grange and the Bend of the Boyne,* with Dr Glyn Daniel, appeared in 1964.

O'RIORDÁIN, SEÁN (1917–77). Poet; b. Ballyvourney, Co. Cork; ed. National School and North Monastery CBS, Cork. He worked in Cork and contributed a regular column to *The Irish Times.* His volumes included *Eireaball Spideóige* (1952), *Brosna* (1964), *Rí na n-Uile* (1967) and *Línte Liombó* (1971), which earned for him a reputation as a leading poet in the Irish language.

O'SHANNON, CATHAL (1889–1969). Socialist and journalist; b. Randalstown, Co. Antrim; reared in Derry City where he was educated at St Columb's College. A member of the Gaelic League and the Irish Republican Brotherhood, he was a founder-member of the Irish Volunteers.* He worked with James Connolly as an organiser for the Irish Transport and General Workers' Union* in Belfast and also assisted on *The Workers' Republic** in Dublin. Although he had not been in action during the Easter Rising of 1916 he was interned. A prominent member of the Labour Party* and Irish Trades Union Congress,* he was active in the anti-conscription campaign during 1918. He unsuccessfully urged that Labour should contest the general election of December 1918 but remained close to leaders of Sinn Fein and worked with Thomas Johnson* on the early drafts of the Democratic Programme* adopted by the first Dail Eireann.

He was an Irish Labour delegate to the Socialist International Conference held in Berne in 1919 when he and Johnson presented the Irish case for self-determination, published as *Ireland at Berne*. Editor of *The Voice of Labour** (1918–19) and *The Watchword of Labour** (1919–20), he was arrested in March 1920 during a swoop on union officials. O'Shannon was also a founder-member of the Socialist Party of Ireland* from which he was expelled along with William O'Brien after it had been taken over by Roderic Connolly late in 1921. An advocate of Labour Party neutrality towards the Treaty, he was acting chairman of the party's delegation to Dail Eireann on relief for the unemployed (10 January 1922). He headed the poll in Louth-Meath in the general election of 16 June 1922 and was deputy chairman of the Labour parliamentary party until he lost his seat a year later. He edited the Labour newspapers, *The*

Voice of Labour and *The Watchword* (1930–32). O'Shannon worked for the ICTU and the Congress of Irish Unions.* Upon the establishment of the Labour Court* in 1946 he became the first workers' representative and held the position until his retirement in 1969. He edited *Fifty Years of Liberty Hall* (1969).

O'SHEA, MRS KATHARINE (1845–1921). Mistress and later wife of Charles Stewart Parnell;* b. Rivenhall, Essex. She married Captain William H. O'Shea* in 1867. Financial circumstances forced her to live with her aunt, Mrs Benjamin Wood, at Eltham. Mrs O'Shea supported her husband's political career after he was returned as a nominal Home Ruler for Clare in 1880 and acted as hostess at his dinners. She engineered a meeting in July 1880 with Parnell, leader of the Irish Parliamentary Party,* and within a short time, was having an *affaire* with him, which her husband appears to have acquiesced in and used to further his career. (For events between 1880 and 1891 *see* O'Shea, Captain William H., Parnell, Charles Stewart *and* Irish Parliamentary Party.)

Following a divorce trial initiated by her husband (December 1889–November 1890), she married Parnell (June 1891) and settled in Brighton where he died in her arms on 6 October in that year. She spent the rest of her life mourning for him. She published *Charles Stewart Parnell: His Love Story and Political Life* (1914) but much of her recollections were rebutted by Henry Harrison* in his *Parnell Vindicated* (1931).

O'SHEA, CAPTAIN WILLIAM HENRY (1840–1905). Politician (Home Ruler); b. Dublin; ed. St Mary's College, Oscott and TCD; cornet in the 18th Hussars (1858). A spendthrift, he lived off his wits and his father, a Dublin solicitor. He received little income from his small Irish property, from which he was an absentee landlord. Unsuccessful business transactions in Spain where he had small mining interests rendered his financial position precarious.

His marriage to Katharine (*née* Wood) was not successful, as shortage of money and general neglect led to his wife's moving with their children to live at Wonersh Lodge, Eltham, where her aunt, Mrs Benjamin Wood, possessed an estate. With the assistance of The O'Gorman Mahon he was returned as nominal Home Ruler for Clare in 1880, having promised to meet Mahon's election expenses which, in the event, were borne by Mrs Wood. O'Shea supported Charles Stewart Parnell* for the leadership of the Irish Parliamentary Party.* Katharine O'Shea's love affair with Parnell began shortly afterwards and while O'Shea apparently ignored it, he occasionally used it to his own advantage. However, he challenged Parnell to a duel in July 1881 but it did not take place. When a daughter was born to his wife in 1882 he acknowledged the child as his own although it was certainly Parnell's.

During the spring of 1882 he acted as intermediary between Parnell and Joseph Chamberlain* in the negotiations which led up to the Kilmainham Treaty.* Katharine was in communication with W. E. Gladstone.* O'Shea glorified his role within the Irish party, on one occasion telling Chamberlain, 'eighteen months ago he [Parnell] used every effort to induce me to take over the leadership of the party'. In May 1882 O'Shea delivered Parnell's offer of resignation to Gladstone after the Phoenix Park Murders.*

His relations with Parnell worsened considerably between 1882 and 1885. Two girls, recognised within the family as Parnell's, were born in 1883 and 1884. O'Shea became more sensitive to the possibility of a scandal and urged discretion on his wife. In fact, most members of the Liberal government and of the Irish party were aware of the triangular relationship. In 1884 he founded the Irish Land Purchase and Settlement Company with Parnell; it failed shortly afterwards. In addition, his political

career suffered because he neglected his constituents and showed little interest in the Home Rule cause, concentrating instead on cultivating influential politicians who might be of use to his financial schemes. The Clare branch of the National League* passed a motion of no confidence in him in June 1884 and in the following October, when he rejected the party pledge, it became obvious that he would not hold the Clare seat.

During 1885 he increasingly put pressure on his wife and Parnell to secure a seat for him in the general election. Parnell backed him for the Exchange Division of Liverpool after failing to have him nominated for Mid-Armagh. After losing the election O'Shea insisted in 1886 that he should be put forward for the Galway seat in the February election. The Galway by-election placed Parnell in a dangerous position as influential members of the party believed that he was being blackmailed by O'Shea. There was an open revolt which was only suppressed when Parnell made the Galway election a test of his leadership of the party. O'Shea won but then resigned the seat in the following June, to the astonishment of his colleagues. No adequate explanation was offered, but it may have been due to a change within the relations of the *ménage à trois* when Parnell moved into Mrs O'Shea's residence at Eltham.

As O'Shea's hatred of Parnell intensified, he was suspected of having forged the letters to the *The Times* which formed the basis for the series 'Parnellism and Crime' (they were, in fact, the work of Richard Pigott). O'Shea appeared as a witness before the Special Commission on 31 October 1888 'to refute the slanders which had been circulated about me by Mr Parnell and his friends . . .' He had, by that time, published an unflattering portrait of the Irish leader in *The Times* (2 August 1888). He informed the Commission that he believed that Parnell's signatures on the letters were genuine. Immediately afterwards he went to Spain on a business trip and was in Madrid when Richard Pigott committed suicide (28 February 1889).

Mrs Wood's death in May 1889 led to a crisis. The only reason he had refrained from suing for divorce was that a scandal would have deprived his wife of her aunt's fortune (estimated at £200,000). Mrs O'Shea was left around £145,000 worth of stocks and land, but the Captain could not benefit under the will. He sued for divorce on 24 December, citing Parnell as co-respondent. (Mrs O'Shea afterwards alleged that O'Shea had had an *affaire* with her sister, Anna Steele.) The courtroom revelations destroyed Parnell's reputation in England and led to a split in the Irish party when Gladstone repudiated Parnell's continuing leadership.

Captain O'Shea was granted a decree *nisi* on 18 November 1890, receiving custody of the children under sixteen (including Parnell's two daughters). For the remainder of his life, he lived off the money which he received in a court settlement of Mrs Wood's will. He took up residence in Brighton where his former wife and Parnell had spent their brief married life.

Ó SÚILLEABHÁIN, MUIRIS (1904–50). Writer; b. Great Blasket Island; raised in Dingle, Co. Kerry, he returned to the island at the age of four; ed. on the island. He intended to emigrate but joined the recently formed Garda Siochana in 1926. His account of life on the island in *Fiche Blian ag Fás* (1933) was translated by Moya Llewelyn Davies and George Thomson as *Twenty Years a-Growing*. It was an immediate success and has been translated into many languages. He resigned from the Gardai in 1934 but never completed his projected second book, to be called *Fiche Blian fé Bláth, (Twenty Years in Flower)*. He drowned while swimming in Galway Bay.

O'SULLIVAN, JOHN MARCUS (1891–1948). Scholar and politician

(Cumann na nGaedheal); b. Killarney, Co. Kerry; ed. St Brendan's College, Killarney, Clongowes Wood and UCD. He was awarded a Ph.D. at Heidelberg (1906) and became Professor of Modern History at UCD. TD for North Kerry (1924–32), he served as Parliamentary Secretary to the Minister for Finance (1924–26) and was Minister for Education (1926–32). He was an Irish delegate to the League of Nations* in 1924, and from 1928 to 1930. He published several works of criticism in German.

O'SULLIVAN, REV. MORTIMER (1791–1859). Clergyman (C.I.) and evangelical; b. Clonmel, Co. Tipperary where, as a youth, he changed from Catholicism to the Church of Ireland in which, after taking a degree at TCD (1816), he was ordained. He ministered in Tipperary, Dungannon, Co. Tyrone, Waterford and Dublin before moving in 1827 to Killyman, Co. Armagh, where he was rector. In his early years a liberal, he became a controversial evangelical and a member of the Orange Order* as he became convinced that Protestants must unite or be destroyed by Catholicism.

He was the author of impassioned attacks on the Irish landlord system and gave evidence before the Select Committee on the State of Ireland in 1825; he published his evidence, along with that of Dr William Phelan, as *Evidence on the State of Ireland* (1826). He engaged in a celebrated controversy with the Catholic Archbishop of Dublin, Dr Daniel Murray,* in 1835. Later Donnellan Lecturer at TCD (1851), he was chaplain to the Earl of Carlisle. His brother, Rev. Samuel O'Sullivan, was a more extreme evangelical.

His works include *Captain Rock Detected* by 'A Munster Farmer' (1824), *A Guide to an Irish Gentleman in search for a Religion* (2 vols, 1833), *The Case of the Protestants of Ireland Stated, with notes* (1836), and *Romanism as it rules in Ireland,* with Rev. Robert James McGhee (1840), an attack on Ultramontanism.* *See also* Second Reformation.

O'SULLIVAN, SEAMUS (1879–1958). Poet; b. Dublin, real name James Sullivan Starkey; ed. University College. The founder of *The Dublin Magazine* to which all the leading writers of the period contributed, he was a founder-member of the Irish Academy of Letters* and winner of the Gregory Medal (1957). His volumes of verse include *The Twilight People* (1905), *The Earth Lover: Selected Lyrics* (1910), *Collected Poems* (1912), *Requiem* (1917), *The Lamplighter and Other Poems* (1919), *Personal Tales* (1936), *Poems* (1938), *Collected Poems* (1940), and *Dublin Poems* (1946); prose works include *Mud and Purple* (1917), *Essays and Recollections* (1944) and *The Rose and Bottle* (1946).

OTWAY, REV. CAESAR (1780–1842). Evangelical clergyman (C.I.) and writer; b. Tipperary; ed. locally and TCD where he took his B.A. in 1810. Having taken Orders he held rural curacies until his appointment as assistant chaplain to Magdalen Asylum, Dublin, and to a minor post in St Patrick's Cathedral, Dublin. He was a noted preacher and his sermons attracted wide attention. In 1825, in conjunction with Dr Singer, Otway was co-founder of *The Christian Examiner* – the first religious magazine published in Ireland associated with the Established Church. An eccentric, he was obsessed with the imaginary sexual practices of nuns and priests, writing prolifically about them. He toured Ireland during 1826, collecting stories of 'beastly rites', generally involving priests, and visited Lough Derg and other places of Catholic pilgrimage. His tour provided him with material for his *Sketches in Ireland* (published in 1827 under the initials 'O.C.'). In 1832 he co-edited the *Dublin Penny Journal* with Dr George Petrie,* on which the *Dublin University Magazine* commented, 'Without containing one line that would mark the religious or political partialities of the writers, it contains more matter illustrative of the history and antiquities of Ireland than any previous publications'.

William Carleton* became a frequent contributor to the *Christian Examiner*, many of his articles later appearing as *Traits and Stories of the Irish Peasantry*. Otway published *A Tour of Connaught* (1839) and *Sketches in Erris and Tyrawley* (1841).

P

PACT ELECTION. The 'Pact Election' was the general election of 16 June 1922 which was in effect being held on the issue of the Treaty.* The Pact was an attempt by Michael Collins,* representing the pro-Treaty position, and Eamon de Valera,* for the anti-Treatyites, to allow the forthcoming election to be held in fair conditions and not on the basis of pro- and anti-Treaty. The Programme was agreed on 20 May and it was criticised by supporters on both sides. The British government took a very unfavourable view of it. Two days before the Election, Collins repudiated the Pact. The short text was:

We are agreed:
(1) That a National Coalition panel for this Third Dail, representing both parties in the Dail and in the Sinn Fein organisation, be sent forward, on the ground that the national position requires the entrusting of the government of the country into the joint hands of those who have been the strength of the national situation

during the last few years, without prejudice to their present respective positions.

(2) That this coalition panel be sent forward as from the Sinn Fein organisation, the number from each party being their present strength in the Dail.

(3) That the candidates be nominated through each of the existing party Executives.

(4) That every and any interest is free to go up and contest the election equally with the National-Sinn Fein panel.

(5) That constituencies where an election is not held shall continue to be represented by their present deputies.

(6) That after the election the Executive shall consist of the President, elected as formerly; the Minister for Defence, representing the Army; and nine other ministers – five from the majority party and four from the minority, each party to choose its own nominees. The allocation will be in the hands of the President.

(7) That in the event of the coalition government finding it necessary to dissolve, a general election will be held as soon as possible on adult suffrage.

See also Dail Eireann, *and* Treaty.

PADLOCKS. According to the poet-historian, A. M. Sullivan,* padlocks were first used in Ireland after the Famine of 1845–49 when traditions of hospitality had been greatly weakened.

PAGET, SIR ARTHUR (1851–1928). Soldier, C-in-C of the British Army in Ireland (1911–17). After entering the Scots Guards in 1869 he served in the Ashanti War (1873), became a Colonel in 1895, and served in the Sudan (1885, 1888–89), Burma (1887) and South Africa (1899–1902). He became a Major-General in 1900. Shortly after his posting to Ireland, he was ordered by the War Office to prepare plans for the protection of arms' depots in Ulster (14

March 1914). As a result, he went to London on 18 March to query the position should any officer be unwilling to serve in action in Ulster. He was informed that officers who lived in Ulster would be exempt but that the remainder would have to carry out their orders or be dismissed from the service. Upon his return to Ireland two days later, he informed his senior officers of the position. Major-General Sir Hubert Gough* and fifty-seven officers stated that they would accept dismissal rather than serve in action against Ulster, thus initiating the so-called Curragh Incident* or 'Mutiny'. After the Easter Rising of 1916* Paget was superseded by General Maxwell* and retired from the Irish command in the following year.

PAISLEY, REV. IAN RICHARD KYLE (1926–   ). Clergyman (Free Presbyterian) and politician (Democratic Unionist); b. Armagh; ed. Primary School, Sixmilesbridge and Model School, Ballymena. He was awarded a diploma of the Theological Hall of the Reformed Presbyterian Church, Belfast, and, after a short seminar at the Barie School of Evangelism, South Wales, was ordained to the ministry by his father (1946). He was a co-founder and Moderator of the Free Presbyterian Church of Ulster (1951).

During the 1950s, Rev. Paisley became a noted opponent of Catholicism and any form of liberalism in the Protestant churches. In August 1959 he led a verbal attack on the Methodist, Dr Donald Soper, in Ballymena, Co. Antrim. He opposed ecumenism and, to this end, visited Rome to protest against the Second Vatican Council (10–16 October 1962). On 4 June 1963 he held a mass-meeting to protest at the lowering of the flag on the City Hall, Belfast, as a mark of respect on the death of Pope John XXIII. The improvement in relations between Northern Ireland and the Republic of Ireland, due to meetings between Captain Terence O'Neill* and Sean Lemass,* led to Paisley's denunciation of O'Neill as a traitor (25 February 1965). He founded the Ulster Constitution Defence Committee* and the Ulster Protestant Volunteers* in April 1966 to oppose any commemorations in the North of the Easter Rising of 1916. He also led protests at 'Romeward' trends within the Presbyterian Church. His behaviour was denounced by O'Neill (15 June 1966) and he was imprisoned from 20 July to 19 October 1966 for refusing to be bound to the peace. By now recognised as the champion of fundamental Protestantism, he was awarded a Doctorate of Divinity by the Bob Jones University, Greenville, South Carolina.

Rev. Paisley was alarmed at the growth of the Northern Ireland Civil Rights Association* which he claimed was a front for the IRA. Aided by Major Ronald Bunting he halted a civil rights march in Armagh (30 November 1968). Another target was the People's Democracy* and militant Protestants, led by Bunting, harassed the PD march which left Belfast on 1 January 1969 for Derry. On 4 January, the loyalist faction made a concerted attack on the unarmed PD marchers at Burntollet Bridge. Later that month Paisley and Bunting were imprisoned. In the general election of 24 February he stood against O'Neill in the Bannside division, polling 6,331 votes to the Prime Minister's 7,745. In April, O'Neill resigned and was succeeded on 1 May by Major James Chichester-Clark. Rev. Paisley strongly criticised Chichester-Clark's attempts to balance the Catholic demand for concessions and the Unionist right-wing demand for maintenance of the Protestant-Unionist supremacy. He was released from prison under general amnesty (6 May). He and his supporters were outraged by the disbandment of the Special Constabulary* on 1 April 1970.

He was returned to Stormont* for the Bannside division on 16 April 1970 as a Protestant Unionist and in June returned for the North Antrim Westminster seat. Chichester-Clark was replaced by Brian Faulkner* as Prime Minister (March 1971) and six months later Paisley and Desmond Boal founded the Democratic Unionist Party.* Unionism continued to fragment as the pace of the war between the IRA and the British Army accelerated and when Faulkner proved unable to restore peaceful government, direct rule was introduced on 30 March 1972. Over the next few years, Paisley was a leader in the demand for the restoration of Stormont but British governments were now committed to some form of 'power-sharing' between the two communities in Northern Ireland; Rev. Paisley denounced this as undemocratic. He was elected to the Assembly (*see* Northern Ireland), where he was a member of the opposition to the power-sharing Executive. He was a strong supporter of the strike by the Ulster Workers' Council* which brought about the collapse of the Executive in May 1974. As a member of the United Ulster Unionist Council,* he sat in the Constitutional Convention (1975) which succeeded the Assembly. He subscribed to the majority Convention report, which effectively called for the restoration of the old Stormont. The British government rejected these proposals and the Convention dissolved. In 1977 he attempted to secure a change in British security policy on Northern Ireland by calling another general strike. The strike was a failure, however, as it did not involve the power workers. He topped the poll in the Northern Ireland constituency in the European Parliament election of 1979, with 170,688 first-preference votes.

Rev. Paisley has controlled the *Protestant Telegraph* since its foundation in 1966. His other publications include a *History of the 1859 Revival* (1959), *Christian Foundation* (1960), *Ravenhill Pulpit* (Vols I & II, 1966–67), *Exposition of the Epistle to the Romans* (1968, written while in prison) and *Billy Graham and the Church of Rome* (1970).

PAN-CELTIC SOCIETY. Literary society of the 1880s later absorbed by the Irish National Literary Society.* Its members, who included W. B. Yeats, T. W. Rolleston and Douglas Hyde, published *Poems and Ballads of Young Ireland* (1888), dedicated to John O'Leary and *Lays and Lyrics of the Pan-Celtic Society* (1889). Membership was restricted to those who had published a story, essay, poem or sketch in a recognised Irish magazine or newspaper.

PARKER, DAME DEHRA (1882–1963). Politician (Ulster Unionist); b. Kilrea, Co. Londonderry, *née* Dawson; ed. privately. She was twice married: in 1901 to Lt Col Robert P. D. Spencer Chichester (d. 1921) and in 1928 to Admiral H. W. Parker (d. 1940). MP for Londonderry City and County (1921–29) and South Londonderry (1933–60), she was an important force in the Unionist Party. Parliamentary Secretary to the Minister for Health, Northern Ireland (1937–44), in 1949 she became the first female member of the NI Cabinet as Minister for Health (until 1957 when she resigned). When she resigned her seat in 1960, it was won by her grandson, Major James Dawson Chichester-Clark.* She was alleged to have directed that her other grandson, Captain Terence O'Neill,* should succeed Lord Brookeborough* as Prime Minister and that he, in turn, should be succeeded by Chichester-Clark (which was precisely what happened).

PARLIAMENT ACT, 1911. Introduced by the Liberal government of H. H. Asquith,* it removed from the House of Lords the power to defeat a Bill outright, and replaced it with the power to veto a Bill for two years. It was prompted by the Lords rejection of the so-called 'People's Budget' introduced in 1909 by David Lloyd George. Asquith's dependence on John Redmond and the Irish Parliamentary Party resulted in the (third) Home Rule Bill of 1912 which was thus assured of passage, as the Lords had been the principal Unionist guarantee of blocking it.

PARLIAMENT OF SOUTHERN IRELAND. *See* Southern Ireland.

PARNELL, ANNA CATHERINE (1852–1911). Land agitator; b. Avondale, sister of Charles Stewart Parnell;* ed. Metropolitan School of Art. She organised a Famine Relief Fund during the depression in the late 1870s and visited the USA (1879–80) for fund-raising purposes. While she supported the Land League,* she found its policy timid and was critical of the Land Act of 1881 (*see* Land Acts). Prompted by her sister, Frances ('Fanny') Parnell,* she established the Ladies' Land League* and spoke at its first public meeting at Claremorris, Co. Mayo (31 January 1881). Her extremism was denounced by the Archbishop of Tuam, John MacHale, and the Archbishop of Dublin, Edward McCabe, both of whom objected to women in public life. She was the first outstanding female agitator in modern Irish history.

Her brother disapproved of her leadership of the Ladies' Land League during his term in Kilmainham (October 1881–May 1882) and cut off its funds when he was released, as a result of which she became estranged from him. Anna moved to England where she lived in retirement until she drowned at Ilfracombe. She was the author of an unpublished book, *The Tale of a Great Sham,* which was extremely critical of the Land League. It is preserved in the National Library of Ireland.*

PARNELL, CHARLES STEWART (1846–91). Politician (Irish Parliamentary Party, of which he was leader, 1880–90); b. Avondale, Co. Wicklow. His schooling included a period at a girls' school in Yeovil, Somerset, where he contracted typhoid and had to be sent home; private tuition and a school in Kirk Langley, Derbyshire, from which he was expelled; and Great Ealing

School. His father died in 1859 and he inherited the Avondale Estate, after which the family lived at a succession of homes in the Dublin district during the 1860s. After attending a cramming academy in Chipping Norton he entered Magdalene College, Cambridge, from which he was sent down in 1869. He travelled on the continent (1871) and visited the USA where his brother, John Howard Parnell,* was farming in Alabama.

Parnell unsuccessfully contested a Dublin seat for the Home Rule League* in 1874. He won the Meath seat vacated upon the death of John Martin* in April 1875 and began his parliamentary career by joining the obstructionists, Joseph Biggar* and John O'Connor Power.* He came to the attention of extreme nationalists when, during an exchange with Michael Hicks-Beach* on 30 June 1876, Parnell stated, 'I wish to say as publicly and directly as I can that I do not believe, and never shall believe, that any murder was committed at Manchester' (*see* Manchester Martyrs). This attracted the interest of the Irish Republican Brotherhood* and in the same year he accompanied O'Connor Power to the US where they tried unsuccessfully to present President Grant with a congratulatory message on the occasion of the centenary of the Declaration of Independence. Upon his return, Parnell became a vice-president of the Home Rule Confederation of Great Britain,* against the wishes of the party leader, Isaac Butt. Having played a leading role in several marathon obstructive filibusters, Parnell was elected President of the HRCGB (28 August 1877). At the same time he visited Paris where he met John O'Leary* and J. J. O'Kelly,* both of whom were impressed by him. In December at a reception for Michael Davitt* he met Dr William Carroll of Clan na Gael* who assured Parnell that the movement could be relied on as an ally in the struggle for Irish self-government. This led to a meeting between influential constitutionalists, Parnell and Frank Hugh O'Donnell,*

and leading Fenians, O'Kelly, O'Leary and Carroll, in March 1878. It was followed, on 25 October, by a telegram from John Devoy who proposed a policy of co-operation between the constitutionalists and the separatists to pursue Home Rule and the land agitation.

Within a year Parnell had become the leader of the New Departure,* as it became known, holding the position of President of the Land League.* On platform after platform throughout the autumn of 1879 he repeated his message that the tenants should keep a 'firm grip on their homesteads'. Accompanied by John Dillon,* he left for America on 21 December, to secure support for Home Rule* and money for famine relief. His tour was so successful that Timothy M. Healy* was brought to America to deal with the press and correspondence. Parnell addressed the House of Representatives on 2 February 1880 and in March moved to Canada where he was so well received in Toronto that Healy dubbed him 'the uncrowned king of Ireland'. He and his companions collected £70,000 for famine relief and the Land League before returning to Ireland in time to fight the general election in April. Sixty-one committed Home Rulers were returned in the election. Among those returned was Captain William Henry O'Shea* with whose wife, Katharine O'Shea,* Parnell began an *affaire* later in the year. At a meeting of the new party, attended by forty-one members, Parnell was elected chairman in succession to William Shaw* by twenty-three votes to eighteen. The new Chief Secretary, W. E. Forster,* introduced a Compensation for Disturbance Bill* (18 June) which was rejected by the Lords (3 August). Violence in Ireland increased. When parliament was prorogued (7 September) Parnell returned to Ireland and continued the land agitation. He made his celebrated 'moral Coventry speech' in Ennis, Co. Clare on 19 September:

'When a man takes a farm from which another has been evicted, you must show him on the roadside when you meet him, you must show him in the streets of the town, you must show him at the shop-counter, you must show him at the fair and at the market-place and even in the house of worship, by leaving him severely alone, by putting him into a sort of moral Coventry, by isolating him from the rest of his kind, as if he were a leper of old, you must show him your detestation of the crime he has committed, and you may depend upon it if the population of a county in Ireland carry out this doctrine, that there will be no man so full of avarice, so lost to shame, as to dare the public opinion of all right-thinking men within the county and to transgress your un-written code of laws.'

The first victim of this policy was Captain Charles Cunningham Boycott.* In an attempt to break the Land League, Forster prosecuted the leaders. The trial of Parnell, Biggar, Dillon and others began on 28 December and collapsed on 23 January 1881. The government promised coercion (Protection of Person and Property Bill) and land reform. Parnell's policy was to fight coercion and secure suitable amendments in the land legislation (*see* Land Acts). He was suspended from the House of Commons on 1 August and returned to Ireland where he was joined by Dillon.

Parnell's attack on the Land Bill was aided by his own newspaper, *United Ireland,** and its editor William O'Brien.* Parnell rejected a demand for a 'No Rent Campaign' at this time. His tactic was to wait and test the Act in the Land Court which was to be established in October. However, on 13 October he was arrested following his description of W. E. Gladstone* as 'this masquerading knight-errant, the pretending champion of the rights of every other nation except those of the Irish nation . . . the man who, by his own utterances, is prepared to carry fire and sword into your homesteads, unless you humbly abase yourselves

before him and before the landlords of the country . . . I say it is not in Mr Gladstone's power to trample on the aspirations and rights of the Irish nation with no moral force behind him.' He was joined at Kilmainham by many of his colleagues.

Parnell now agreed to the No Rent Manifesto* on 18 October. The Land League was suppressed immediately but the agitation, to his dismay, was carried on by the Ladies' Land League,* led by his sister, Anna Catherine Parnell.* The negotiations which led to the so-called Kilmainham 'Treaty'* were conducted through the O'Sheas. He was released on 2 May 1882 and returned immediately to London. He was there when he learned of the Phoenix Park Murders* and was so shocked that he offered to resign if Gladstone felt that it would serve any purpose. Gladstone now came under attack for his Kilmainham deal with Parnell. Parnell, who was also attacked, led the obstruction of the new coercion measure which, however, became law in July. He also suppressed the Ladies' Land League. The land agitation was halted, at least temporarily, when the Arrears Bill became law on 18 August.

Parnell now sought to turn his experience and mass support to Home Rule* and to this end, he founded the National League* in Dublin on 17 October 1882. During the next few years his hold over the party and the country strengthened. A measure of his popularity was the Parnell Tribute which, despite condemnation by the Catholic hierarchy, raised £37,011 17s in 1883 when it was known that his Avondale estate was in financial difficulties. One year later, it became clear that he had also won over the bishops, led by the influential Thomas William Croke,* Archbishop of Cashel, and Thomas Nulty,* Bishop of Meath. When the bishops made the party the guardian of Catholic educational interests in 1884, he said, 'I need scarcely say how highly my colleagues and I value the mark of confidence in us which the resolutions of the hierarchy convey'.

By 1885 Parnell was leading a party well-poised for a general election, in which he hoped to secure between 70 and 80 seats. His statements on Home Rule were designed to secure the widest possible support, as when he stated in Cork on 21 January 1885: 'We cannot ask the British constitution for more than the restitution of Grattan's parliament, but no man has the right to fix the boundary to the march of a nation. No man has the right to say to his country, "Thus far shalt thou go and no further", and we have never attempted to fix the *ne plus ultra* to the progress of Ireland's nationhood, and we never shall'.

Gladstone's government fell in June 1885 over the budget introduced by H. C. E. Childers* and a Conservative caretaker administration took office under Lord Salisbury. Parnell was now in a bargaining position. He had contacts with two prominent Conservatives, Lord Randolph Churchill* and the 4th Earl of Carnarvon,* the new Lord Lieutenant. While Churchill appeared to believe that Parnell had committed the Irish party to the Conservatives for the forthcoming general election, Carnarvon believed that Parnell had stated that he would not seek to break the Union in the search for Home Rule, that Parnell would be prepared to accept something on the lines of the Central Board* outlined by Joseph Chamberlain.* Through Mrs O'Shea, Parnell was also in touch with Gladstone but the outcome of their messages was that Gladstone was not prepared to bargain against Tory offers.

Parnell issued a manifesto to the Irish in Great Britain on 21 November, calling on them to vote Conservative where they were faced with Liberal or Radical candidates. The result of the election gave the Liberals 335 seats, Conservatives 249 and the Irish party 86. Parnell thus held the balance between the two British parties and placed his seats behind the Conservatives to keep Salisbury in power. Then, in December, Herbert Gladstone revealed in the Hawarden Kite* that his father was about to come out in favour of Home Rule (17 December). The Conservatives now moved away from any consideration of Home Rule.

At the same time a new land crisis had developed which led to the Plan of Campaign* during 1886. Parnell did not associate with the Campaign although it was supported by his chief lieutenants. The government moved to curb the agitation and in January Salisbury announced a new measure of coercion. Parnell switched support to the Liberals, the Conservatives fell, and Gladstone took office committed to Home Rule.

Parnell's leadership was immediately put to the test, when, under pressure from Mrs O'Shea, he forced Captain O'Shea's candidature for the Galway seat in the by-election of February 1886. Against the opposition of some of the most powerful members of the party, Parnell succeeded in having O'Shea returned but only by placing his leadership of the party at stake.

Gladstone introduced the (first) Home Rule Bill* on 8 April 1886. During the debate on the second reading Parnell was reminded that he had said that Ireland would not rest until the final link was broken. Now, to a point-blank question as to whether he accepted the bill 'as a final settlement of the [Irish] question' he answered 'Yes'. Unionist* opposition in Ireland was increasing, particularly among the Ulster Unionists who were in alliance with Churchill. At the same time, Joseph Chamberlain was leading Liberal-Unionists in opposition. On the second reading on 7 June it was defeated (341 seats to 311). Parliament was dissolved on 25 June and Home Rule became the central issue of the general election. The Irish party campaigned throughout Britain, seeking support for the Liberals. The result was a defeat: a total of 394 anti-Home Rulers to 191 Liberals. The Conservatives had a majority of 118 over the combined Irish and Liberal members. The Conservatives returned to office and Parnell and his party were committed to the Liberals.

When Parnell moved to Eltham to take up residence with Mrs O'Shea in the summer of 1886, Captain O'Shea broke with the Irish party and placed himself at the disposal of Parnell's opponents. Parnell appeared infrequently at the House of Commons and was virtually inaccessible to his lieutenants. He became the centre of public attention over the series 'Parnellism and Crime'* which appeared in *The Times* during 1887. The series was based on forged letters provided by a disreputable Dublin journalist, Richard Pigott.* While Parnell took no action against the newspaper his former supporter, Frank Hugh O'Donnell, did and lost. During the O'Donnell action, Parnell noted evidence which convinced him of the forgeries. He demanded a select committee of the House to investigate the charges so that he might clear his name. This was rejected but the House did establish a Special Parliamentary Commission which would examine not only *The Times'* letters but Parnell's whole career during and after the Land War.* Parnell's counsel during the sitting of the Special Commission (17 September 1888–22 November 1889) was Sir Charles Russell* who was assisted by H. H. Asquith.* Among those who gave evidence were O'Shea and a Fenian spy, Henri Le Caron.* Pigott gave evidence over two days (20–22 February) and, despite his shifty appearance in the witness box, emerged relatively unscathed until, in a moment of high drama, Russell elicited that Pigott wrote 'hesitancy' as 'hesitency' (as it appeared in the letters). When Parnell, who had not impressed while giving evidence on his own behalf, appeared in the House of Commons on 1 March, Gladstone led the Liberals in a standing ovation. The Report of the Special Commission appeared in February 1890, clearing Parnell

of all charges (although finding that he had supported boycotting).

On 24 December 1889 Captain O'Shea filed for divorce from Katharine, citing Parnell as co-respondent. The case did not come up for trial until 15 November 1890. In the meantime, Parnell assured his party that there was no need to fear the verdict as he would be completely exonerated. During January 1890 resolutions of confidence in his leadership were passed throughout the country. He did not contest the suit in November and Captain O'Shea's case was unopposed, apart from a watching brief for Mrs O'Shea held by Frank Lockwood. Parnell's two children by Mrs O'Shea, Claire (1883–1909) and Katharine (1884–1947), were placed in O'Shea's custody.

Despite the unfavourable verdict, resolutions of confidence in Parnell continued but a reaction had already set in. Michael Davitt* called for Parnell's resignation in *Labour World** (20 November). He was soon joined by members of the Liberal Party, the leaders of the Irish party and the Catholic hierarchy. However, Parnell was re-elected chairman of the party on 25 November when the members were unaware that Gladstone had informed Justin McCarthy* that so long as Parnell remained leader there could be no Liberal alliance. On the next day, Gladstone published his position in a letter to John Morley.* The storm broke when Parnell refused a request that he re-consider the chairmanship. On 28 November the Catholic hierarchy announced a meeting for 3 December. Parnell published a *Manifesto to the Irish People* in which he attacked Gladstone, the Liberals and a section of his own party (29 November). This alienated members of the party who were fund-raising in the USA (including Dillon and O'Brien). Before the party met for its fateful meeting on 1 December, the Archbishop of Dublin, William Walsh,* called on the members to 'act manfully'.

Seventy-three members were present at the meeting which continued until 6 December. On 3 December the standing committee of the hierarchy, at Maynooth, called on the Irish people to reject Parnell's leadership. Within Committee Room 15 of the House of Commons, attempts at compromise proved ineffectual as Parnell refused to make concessions. The party split on 6 December, when Justin McCarthy led 44 members out, leaving Parnell with 27 followers.

Parnell survived the split by less than a year. During that period he fought to maintain his political influence in some of the bitterest fighting in modern Irish political history. His political speeches broke with the cautious constitutionalism of the past, winning support from the Fenians, 'the hillside men'. His blatant appeal to the underground tradition shocked former adherents, who clashed physically with his supporters as he campaigned around the country. The by-election in North Kilkenny in December 1890 was a pointer to the future when his candidate was beaten by almost two to one. He supported the Balfour Land Act (*see* Land Acts) and attempted to woo working-class support in England. Another by-election, in North Sligo, was a less resounding defeat than Kilkenny. This time, the clergy were not united and his candidate lost by 2,493 votes to 3,261.

He married Katharine O'Shea on 25 June 1891 in Brighton where they took up residence. He returned to fight the third and last by-election in Carlow. By now the hierarchy, worried by the number of priests who had supported him in North Sligo, had issued a condemnation, (ironically, on the day of his wedding). In part, the hierarchy said that Parnell 'by his public misconduct, has utterly disqualified himself to be ... leader'. Only one bishop, Edward O'Dwyer* of Limerick, did not sign. Parnell failed in Carlow and also now lost the support of *The Freeman's Journal.* *

His health had deteriorated during the year. He travelled in September to Creggs on the Galway-Roscommon border and spoke in pouring rain. After resting in a local hotel he travelled to Dublin and from there to Brighton, where he died on 6 October in his wife's arms.

PARNELL, FRANCES ('FANNY') ISABEL (1849—82). Poet; b. Avondale, sister of Charles Stewart Parnell;* ed. privately. A Fenian sympathiser, while still a teenager she contributed patriotic verse to *The Irish People,* * the organ of the Irish Republican Brotherhood. While visiting the USA with her mother in 1874 her health failed and she remained there. She organised famine relief for Ireland in 1879 and became a close friend of Michael Davitt* at whose suggestion she founded the Ladies' Land League* in America. It was established in Ireland by her sister, Anna Catherine Parnell.* Many of her poems urging support for the Land League appeared in *United Ireland* and *The Nation.* Her most famous poem was 'Hold the Harvest'. She published a pamphlet, *Novels of Ireland,* in 1880. As her health deteriorated her themes became increasingly morbid. Her brother was deeply affected by her death.

PARNELL, HENRY BROOKE, 1st BARON CONGLETON (1776—1842). Politician (Whig); b. Queen's County (Laois); ed. Eton and Trinity College, Cambridge where he did not take a degree. MP for Maryborough (Portlaoise) in the Irish House of Commons, he opposed the Union,* after which he was MP, Queen's County (1802; 1806—32) and Portarlington (July—December 1802). Escheator of Munster (1802—06) and Commissioner of the Treasury in Ireland (February 1806—March 1807), he unsuccessfully demanded an inquiry into Tithes* (1809—11), and supported the demand for a general inquiry into the state of the country. Throughout his career he supported Catholic Emancipation.* He resigned as Secretary of War (1831–32) and Privy Councillor over the division on the Russo-Dutch War (1832). Four years later he became the first Paymaster General after the consolidation of the offices of Treasurer of the Navy and Paymaster of the Forces. As Baron Congleton, he entered the House of Lords in 1841. A depressive, he committed suicide. He was the grand-uncle of Charles Stewart Parnell* and the author of *History of the Penal Laws* (1808) and *Financial Reform* (1830).

PARNELL, JOHN HOWARD (1843–1923). Landowner; b. Avondale, elder brother of Charles Stewart Parnell;* ed. Paris, Chipping Norton and School of Mining where he was awarded a certificate in geology. He emigrated to the USA in 1866 and settled in Alabama. Following a visit from Charles, he was persuaded to return in 1872 and farmed his inheritance at Collure, Co. Armagh. He inherited the Avondale estate after his brother's death in 1891, but, unable to make a financial success of it, sold it in 1899 (five years later, at the suggestion of Sir Horance Plunkett,* it was purchased by the State). He was City Marshall of Dublin in 1898. He published *C. S. Parnell: A Memoir* in 1916.

PARNELL-HAYES WILLIAM (1777–1821). Landowner, politician and author; b. Avondale, Co. Wicklow; ed. Cambridge. His father, Sir John Parnell, inherited the Avondale estate from a cousin, Samuel Hayes, in 1795, and Sir William took the additional surname Hayes which was dropped by his successor, John Henry Parnell, the father of Charles Stewart Parnell.* He was the deputy lieutenant of Co. Wicklow (1817, 1819–20). Generally regarded as a good landlord, he published *An Enquiry into the cause of popular discontent in Ireland* by 'An Irish Country Gentleman' (1805), in which he was critical of landlords' agents and their treatment of the tenantry; *An Historical Apology for Irish Catholics* (1807),

Sermons (1816), *Maurice and Bergettam or, the Priest of Rothery* (a novel, 1818) and *Notes on need for government grants for educating Catholic poor* (1820).

'PARNELLISM AND CRIME'. Series of articles published by *The Times* of London, 1887–88, accusing Charles Stewart Parnell* and members of the Irish Parliamentary Party of having supported criminal conspiracy and murder during the Land War* of 1879–82. The first article appeared on 7 March 1887. A later article, published on 18 April, reproduced the following letter:

Dear Sir,
I am not surprised at your friend's anger but he and you should have known that to denounce the murders was the only course open to us. To do that promptly was plainly our best policy.

But you can tell him and all others concerned that though I regret the accident of Lord F. Cavendish's death, I cannot refuse to admit that Burke got no more that his deserts.

You are at liberty to show him this, and others whom you can trust also, but let not my address be known. He can write to House of Commons.
Yours very truly,
Chas. S. Parnell.

This damning publication, intended to show Parnell's approval of the Phoenix Park Murders,* was clearly designed to destroy him and wreck the alliance between the Irish party and the Liberals.

As a result of the series Frank Hugh O'Donnell* sued *The Times* for libel. Parnell sought a select committee of the House of Commons which established a Special Parliamentary Commission (the Parnell Commission). The Commission investigated his career and his associates over the previous ten years. O'Donnell .lost his case but the Special Commission continued to investigate Parnell who was eventually cleared. However, having examined *The Times'* evidence, Parnell uncovered the letter and revealed it to be the work of Richard Pigott.* A second series of articles on the same theme was written by Robert Anderson,* based on material supplied by Henri Le Caron.* The series cost *The Times* around £200,000 in damages. It lost circulation, and severely damaged its much-vaunted reputation for infallibility.

PARSONSTOWN TELESCOPE. Erected in the grounds of Birr Castle, King's County (Co. Offaly) in 1845 by the 3rd Earl of Rosse,* following a series of experiments which began in 1827. His experiments towards improving the reflecting telescope continued until 1839 when he successfully cast a three-foot speculum using home-made tools and equipment. Dissatisfied with the telescope's penetration, Lord Rosse began construction of a larger model, enlisting the aid of the Dublin-based optical firm of Thomas Grubb* for the specialised areas. After several failures, two specula, each six feet in diameter, four tons in weight and of fifty-four-foot focus, were cast in 1843.

The tube of the telescope was fifty-eight feet long and seven feet in diameter. It was slung on chains between two piers of masonry fifty feet high, seventy feet long and twenty-three feet apart. The speculum was supported in its tube by an intricate system of cast-iron platforms, triangles and levers. The telescope had limited horizontal movement which was compensated for by a vertical range of 110 degrees. The first observations began in February 1845. The results, which included the discovery of binary and triple stars, were laid before the Royal Society, of which Lord Rosse was President, on 19 June 1850.

Lord Rosse was estimated to have spent over £20,000 on the construction of his telescope, which, for many years, was the largest in the world. It can be seen in the Science Museum, London, and the remains of the observatory may be seen in the grounds of Birr Castle, Co. Offaly, in which a museum has been erected.

PARTITION BILL. *See* Government of Ireland Act (1920).

'PASS'. A letter of recommendation given to a favourite pupil by a hedge-schoolmaster, sometimes in rhyme. It was intended to facilitate the pupil in securing a post elsewhere in the country when he became a 'wandering scholar'.

PATRICIAN BROTHERS (THE BROTHERS OF ST PATRICK). Educational organisation, founded under simple vows by the Bishop of Kildare and Leighin, Daniel Delany, at Tullow, Co. Carlow in 1808.

'PATRIOT'. Newspaper founded by William Corbet in 1810 with the encouragement of the Chief Secretary, William Wellesley-Pole,* to support the government and the (Protestant) Ascendancy.* A financial failure, its circulation rarely rose above 700 until the editorship of J. T. Haydn* (1812–22). It later supported Catholic Emancipation* and lost government support. The title was changed to *The Statesman and Patriot* in 1828 but it failed to recover readers and ceased publication one year later.

PATTERN. A corruption of the word 'patron', it was a communal visit to the holy well associated with the patron saint of a district. The local community prayed at the wellside or in the surrounding area. Offerings of medals, coins, pieces of cloth and flowers were left at the well as thanksgiving for favours received or expected. Many of the wells were believed to have curative powers and the waters were drunk or applied to affected areas of the body. At the end of the prayers the community joined in dancing, singing and storytelling. As it was a holy-day and no work was done, drink was provided for the occasion and it was not uncommon for the evening to end amid fighting (*see* Faction-fighting). As a result of increasing disorder at patterns they were condemned by the church and the authorities. Daniel O'Connell* used his influence against them. Not many patterns survived the Famine of 1845–49* but some are still extant.

PATTERSON, ANNIE W. (1869–1934). Musician and author; b. Lurgan, Co. Armagh; ed. Alexandra College and the Royal Irish Academy of Music. She was Examiner in Music to the RIA (1892–95), to the Irish Intermediate Board of Education (1900–01, 1919–22), to the Cork Municipal School of Music (1914–19) and the Leinster School of Music (1919–26). An organist at several Dublin churches (1887–97) and conductor of the Dublin Choral Union, she was a founder-member of the Feis Ceoil (1897). She was Corporation Lecturer in Irish Music at UCC from 1924. Apart from her original compositions, she was the author of *The Story of Oratorio, Schumann, Chats with Music Lovers, Native Music of Ireland* and *Six Original Gaelic Songs* which she contributed to the Ivernia Irish Music series.

PEACE MOVEMENT. Founded in Northern Ireland by Miss Mairead Corrigan and Mrs Betty Williams in 1976 to mobilise public opinion against violence, after a number of children had been killed as a result of fighting between the British Army and the Provisional Irish Republican Army.* The 'Peace People', as they became known, were joined in their work by Mr Ciaran McKeown. The movement, protesting against violence and drawing attention to injustice, spread throughout Ireland, to the United Kingdom and the continent. It received aid from abroad to further its aims. The founders were awarded a Peace Foundation Award in 1976 and the Nobel Prize for Peace for 1976 in October 1977 (£80,000), 'for acting out of a

sense of conviction that individuals can make a contribution to peace'.

PEACE PRESERVATION POLICE. *See* Police.

PEARSE, PATRICK HENRY (1879–1916). Republican and writer; b. Dublin; ed. CBS and Royal University.* He was called to the Bar but did not practise. At the age of eleven, he started to learn Irish and his later reading of Old Irish literature and Irish history convinced him that only through a revival of the language and culture could Irish nationalism be fired. After a study of bilingual systems abroad, he founded his own school, St Enda's,* where he attempted to put his ideals into practice, aided by his brother, William Pearse,* and friends Thomas MacDonagh* and Con Colbert.*

Pearse was prominent in the Gaelic League* from 1896 and edited its journal, *An Claideamh Soluis,* * from 1903 until 1909. He also supported Sinn Fein and contributed to *The United Irishman* edited by Arthur Griffith. In addition, he edited *Macaoimh* at St Enda's (1909–13), a short-lived newspaper, *An Barr Buadh* (1912), and founded an unsuccessful society, Cumann na Saoru (The Society for Freedom, 1912).

Although he spoke from a platform in favour of Home Rule, along with John Redmond and Joseph Devlin, on 31 May 1912, Pearse's outlook changed as he became convinced that Britain would not keep faith in the face of the strong opposition to Home Rule from the Unionists and the Conservatives. Impatiently, he looked towards the most advanced nationalist paper of the time, *Irish Freedom,* * edited by Bulmer Hobson and financed by the Irish Republican Brotherhood.* He began to contribute to it, attracting the attention of the IRB with 'From a Heritage' (June 1913–February 1914). After becoming a founder-member of the Irish Volunteers* in November 1913 he was inducted into the IRB in December. As the (third)

Home Rule Bill* slowly progressed through the Commons and Lords, he wrote, 'This generation of Irishmen will be called upon in the very near future to make a very passionate assertion of nationality. The form in which the assertion shall be made must depend upon many things, more especially upon the passage or non-passage of the present Home Rule Bill' (June 1913).

In order to raise money for his financially ailing school and for the Volunteers, he visited the USA in February 1914. He met John Devoy* and Joseph McGarrity,* both of whom, impressed by his fervour, helped him to raise enough money to keep the school operating. Later in the year, the Volunteers were armed through the Howth Gun-running* but the movement split in September when Redmond called for support for the British war effort. Pearse was a leader of the secessionist Volunteers, holding the post of Director of Military Organisation. He informed McGarrity, on 24 September 1914, 'If at any time we seem to be too quiet, it is because we are awaiting a favourable moment for decisive action as regards the Volunteers.'

On 1 August 1915, speaking over the grave of the Fenian, Jeremiah O'Donovan Rossa,* he gave notice of nationalist unrest: 'Life springs from death: and from the graves of patriot men and women spring living nations. The Defenders of this Realm have worked well in secret and in the open. They think that they have pacified Ireland. They think they have purchased half of us and intimidated the other half. They think they have forseen everything, think that they have provided against everything; but the fools, the fools, the fools! – they have left us our Fenian dead, and while Ireland holds these graves, Ireland unfree shall never be at peace.'

At the same time he committed the Gaelic League to action. His declaration that it was a political body led to the resignation of Dr Douglas Hyde.* Pearse saw the League as a revolutionary force:

'The vital work to be done in the new Ireland will not be done so much by the Gaelic League itself as by men and movements that have sprung from the Gaelic League or have received from the Gaelic League a new baptism and a new life and grace. We must accustom ourselves to the thought of arms, to the use of arms. We may make mistakes in the beginning and shoot the wrong people, but bloodshed is a cleansing and a sanctifying thing, and the nation which regards it as the final horror has lost its manhood. There are many things more horrible than bloodshed; and slavery is one of them.'

He became a member of the Military Council* which planned the Easter Rising of 1916.* Despite the loss of the arms shipment on the *Aud* * and the countermanding order issued to the Volunteers by Eoin MacNeill,* whom he had not kept informed, he determined to press ahead with the rising on Easter Monday. As Chairman of the Provisional Government of the Irish Republic he read the Proclamation of Independence from the GPO. On Saturday 29 April, at 3.30 p.m., he surrendered to Brigadier-General Lowe in Parnell Street. Following a court-martial he was executed on 3 May.

Pearse's works were collected and edited from 1917 to 1922 by his former pupil, Desmond Ryan.* His works included *Three Lectures on Gaelic Topics* (1898), *An tAithriseóir* (The Reciter; edited with Tadhg Ó Donnchadha, 2 vols, 1900, 1902), *Bodach an Chóta Lachtna* (ed, 1906), *Iosagán agus Sgéalta Eile* (Little Jesus and Other Stories, 1907), *Bruidhean Chaorthainn: Scéal Fionnaidhneachtna* (ed, 1908), *Iosagán* (play, 1910), *An Rí* (The King, a play, 1911), *The Murder Machine* (1912), *An Sgoill: A Direct Method Course in Irish* (1913), *How Does She Stand?* (1914), *Suantraidhe agus Coltraidhe* (Songs of Sleep and Sorrow, 1914), *Specimens from an Irish Anthology* (1914), *Songs of the Irish Rebels* (1914), *Eoin* (play, 1915), *Ghosts* (1915), *The Master* (play, 1915), *An Mháthair agus Sgéalta Eile* (The Mother and Other Stories, 1916), and pamphlets: 'The Separatist Idea' (1916), 'The Spiritual Nation' (1916) and 'The Sovereign People' (1916).

PEARSE, WILLIAM (1881–1916). Republican; b. Dublin, younger brother of Patrick H. Pearse,* by whom he was deeply influenced; ed. CBS. He worked for some time in his father's stonework business. A member of the executive committee of the Wolfe Tone and United Irishmen Memorial Committee (1898), he followed his brother in to the Irish Volunteers.* He worked under Patrick at St Enda's. He was not a party to the planning of the Easter Rising of 1916* but took part in it. At his court martial he deliberately adopted a line which led to his execution on 4 May.

PEEL, SIR ROBERT (1788–1850). Politician (Tory and liberal Conservative), Chief Secretary (1812–18); Prime Minister (1834–35, 1841–46); b. Lancashire; ed. privately, at Tamworth, Harrow and at Christ Church, Oxford. After his father purchased him the Cashel, Co. Tipperary seat, he entered the House as a Tory supporter in April 1809. After a period as Under Secretary for War and the Colonies, he was appointed Chief Secretary for Ireland where his six-year term was the longest of the century.

From the moment he took up office, Peel was attacked by Daniel O'Connell* who, seeing in him an opponent of Catholic Emancipation,* dubbed him 'Orange Peel', '. . . a raw youth, squeezed out of I know not what factory in England . . .' Peel suppressed the Catholic Board* and revised sections of the Insurrection Act of 1807. In 1814 he introduced a coercion bill under which he created a new police force, the Peace Preservation Police, which were popularly known as 'Peelers'. (*see* Police). In 1815 he established a state subsidy for primary education by mak-

ing a grant to the non-denominational Kildare Place Society.* In that year, also, he challenged O'Connell to a duel. The latter stated that he had been traduced in parliament by Peel and defied him to 'use a single expression derogatory to his (O'Connell's) integrity or honour where he (Peel) was liable to personal account'. Peel issued a challenge and following a series of postponements, went to Ostend to meet O'Connell who was, however, arrested in England *en route.*

One of Peel's most important acts before leaving Ireland in May 1818 was the provision of £250,000 for relief works during the Famine of 1817. His experiences during this period provided him with some practical knowledge for the Famine of 1845–49* when he was Prime Minister.

Having resigned in 1827 from the Home Office, Peel agreed to serve in the Administration formed by the Duke of Wellington,* himself a former Chief Secretary. As a member of the administration at the Home Office, it fell to him to introduce Catholic Emancipation* which had been urged upon the reluctant George IV* as the alternative to civil war. To test reaction, Peel took the Chiltern Hundreds and stood for his Oxford seat (which he had held since 1817) and lost. On 3 March, he returned to office when he gained a seat at Westbury and helped to carry the Emancipation Bill which he introduced in 1829. When the government resigned in November 1830 he was again out of office.

The Whig ministry of Earl Grey set about introducing reform. In this, it had the support of O'Connell and Irish Repealers. Peel opposed reform, and when asked to form a ministry on condition that it supported reform, he refused. Grey carried the Reform Act of 1832 which was less radical than anticipated. This won Peel's support and he voted with Grey in an even more moderate Reform Act for Ireland in 1833. In the years 1833–34 he supported the Whig administration in sixteen out of twenty divisions.

Peel was in Rome in 1834 when he was sent for by William IV to become First Lord of the Treasury and Chancellor of the Exchequer. He dissolved parliament and returned with 100 extra supporters. However, when his government suffered defeat on the Irish and English Tithes Bills and on five other occasions, he resigned and was succeeded by Lord Melbourne.*

As a liberal Conservative Peel set about building a new party, winning support from prominent Whigs: E. G. Stanley (*see* Derby, 14th Earl), a former Chief Secretary, and James Graham. His new policy was to maintain the established constitution of the church and state. Peel's attempt to form an additional administration in 1839 was defeated on the 'bedchamber question' (his recommendation of certain changes in the Queen's household) and Melbourne returned to office until 1841. Peel's Irish policy (1841–46) was characterised by firmness and concession. He resolutely opposed the Repeal movement and defeated O'Connell's Repeal campaign in 1843. By the end of 1845 the potato blight had appeared, and Repeal was no longer a major issue. In 1845 also, Peel granted an annual endowment of £26,000 to Maynooth College* in the face of widespread opposition. He made a determined bid to end the vexed question of university education for Catholics when he introduced the Provincial Colleges Bill which established the Queen's Colleges.* The Colleges were welcomed by Young Ireland* but were roundly condemned as 'godless colleges' by members of the Catholic hierarchy and Daniel O'Connell. He also introduced the Charitable Donations and Bequests Act which was vehemently opposed by the Archbishop of Tuam, John MacHale,* but supported by the Archbishop of Dublin, Daniel Murray.*

For some time Peel had been considering the need for the repeal of the Corn Laws. The famine in Ireland now presented him with an opportunity to introduce the necessary legislation. However, he was defeated by the vested interests of the landowning community in the Commons, and resigned (9 December 1845). The Whig leader, Lord John Russell,* failed to form a government, and in January, Peel returned and immediately set about the repeal of the Corn Laws. Famine conditions in Ireland had inevitably produced discontent and he proposed a new coercion act. Coercion provided his opponents with an opportunity to launch a massive attack on him and on the very night his Repeal Bill was carried in the Lords, he was forced out of office by his defeat on coercion (29 June 1846). Before he left office he had set in train relief measures for Ireland. He had arranged for £100,000 worth of Indian meal (which became known as 'Peel's Brimstone') to be brought from the US and stored in Ireland. The political risks inherent in this act were considerable, as he lacked Cabinet approval. Peel intended that the corn should be used only as a stabilising agent in the market. His successor, Lord John Russell, had little visible effect on efforts to relieve famine-ravaged Ireland.

His son, Sir Robert Peel, 3rd Baronet (1822–95) a Liberal, was Chief Secretary (1861–65). A popular incumbent who travelled throughout Ireland, he proved unable to cope with the rise of the Irish Republican Brotherhood.* Later, disillusioned with the leadership of W. E. Gladstone,* he became a Conservative but lost his seat in 1889, having supported Home Rule.*

PEELERS. See Police.

'PEEL'S BRIMSTONE'. *See* Famine of 1845–49.

PEEP O'DAY BOYS. Secret agrarian society, confined to Protestants, operating in Ulster during the 1780s and 1790s. Following the battle of the Diamond in 1795 when the Peep O' Day Boys defeated a Catholic society, the Defenders, they formed a new society which they called the Orange Order.* *See also* Secret Societies.

PEOPLE'S DEMOCRACY. Socialist movement founded in Queen's University, Belfast, on 9 October 1968. The organisation was founded as a reaction to events in Derry City on 5 October when the Northern Ireland Civil Rights Association* was involved in a violent confrontation with the Royal Ulster Constabulary.* PD, whose founders included Michael Farrell, Bernadette Devlin (now Mrs Bernadette McAliskey) and Eamonn McCann, was open to non-university students and was non-sectarian. Like NICRA it sought equality of civil rights throughout Northern Ireland* and an end to discrimination against the Catholic minority population. It produced a newspaper, *The Free Citizen,* through which it demanded 'one-man, one-vote' and an end to repressive legislation, in particular the Civil Authorities (Northern Ireland) Special Powers Act.*

Against the advice of various other bodies PD organised a march from Belfast to Derry to begin on 1 January 1969. From the outset, the march, over a distance of seventy-five miles, was harried by militant loyalists led by Major Ronald Bunting. Major Bunting boasted that he had secured the help of 'the Loyal Citizens of Ulster . . . to hinder and harry it [the march]. . .' The marchers, whose intentions were to have a non-violent demonstration, were hindered and harried by a mob armed with bottles and studded batons. The RUC and the Special Constabulary* were accused by PD of making no attempt to protect the marchers from their assailants.

The worst encounter came a few miles outside Derry at Burntollet Bridge, on 4 January, when the unarmed marchers were subjected to indiscriminate violence while the police took almost no action to protect them. Further violence was triggered off by the arrival of the marchers in Derry and it spread to other Catholic areas in the North.

PD was denounced by the Prime Minister, Captain Terence O'Neill,* in a statement issued on 5 January when he called the supporters of the march 'mere hooligans' and praised the police 'who handled this most difficult situation as fairly and as firmly as they could'. However, the Report issued by the Cameron Commission* stated, '. . . our investigations had led us to the unhesitating conclusion that on the night of 4th/5th January a number of policemen were guilty of misconduct which involved assault and battery, malicious damage to property in streets in the predominantly Catholic Bogside area. . . . For such conduct among members of a disciplined and well-led force there can be no acceptable justification or excuse'. A few months afterwards, Bernadette Devlin was returned to Westminster as M.P. for Mid-Ulster, having defeated the widow of the former member (April 1969).

Although PD was never numerically significant it was considered dangerous enough by the government for its leaders to be interned in August 1971. However, as the situation deteriorated into a battle between the Provisional Irish Republican Army,* the British Army and the Protestant para-military groups, PD became a less significant organisation.

PEOPLE'S RIGHTS ASSOCIATION. Founded by Timothy M. Healy* in 1897 after he had broken with the Irish National Federation,* as a rival constituency organisation during the split in the Irish Parliamentary Party.* Healy joined the IPP when it was reunited under John Redmond* in 1900 through the efforts of the United Irish League.* However, when he refused to disband the PRA he was expelled from the parliamentary party and sat as an independent. At that stage the PRA was numerically small: a liberal estimate put the number of branches at around twenty, while the constabulary estimated that it only had a total of 228 members, most of whom were concentrated in Belfast.

PERCEVAL, ROBERT (1756–1839). Physician and reformer; b. Dublin; ed. TCD and Edinburgh; he was the first Professor of Chemistry at TCD (1783–1805), and a member of the Royal Irish Academy* (1785). Inspector of Apothecaries (1786), he was responsible for the foundation of the Dublin General Dispensary. Perceval was known as 'The Irish Howard' because of his efforts to secure prison reform. He was president of Sir Patrick Dun's Hospital (1799) and Physician to the Forces in Ireland (1819). Besides some religious works and several scientific papers in the *Transactions* of the RIA, he published *An Account of the Bequest of Sir Patrick Dun* (1804).

PERPETUAL COERCION BILL (July 1887). Powers granted to the Irish government to fight the Plan of Campaign.* The Lord Lieutenant was given wide powers to proclaim any Irish association illegal and to forbid the press to publish reports of meetings of any association so proclaimed. The provisions of the Bill were variously interpreted and some of the prosecutions were ridiculous in the extreme: a young lad was charged in open court with looking at a policeman 'with a humbugging sort of a smile'; an Italian organ-grinder who had taught his monkey to draw a toy pistol and fire it in the air had himself and the monkey arrested and the pistol confiscated, and a boy of ten was summoned for whistling a popular tune 'Harvey Duff', in the street 'with such a threatening air as to intimidate a magistrate'.

PERSICO, MONSIGNOR IGNAZIO (1823–95). Italian Capuchin priest. He served in the Vatican Diplomatic Service on whose behalf he came to Ireland along with the Under Secretary of Propaganda Fidei, Enrico Gualdi, to investigate the Plan of Campaign.* The Vatican was concerned about complaints from Ireland implicating priests in illegal activities. Monsignor Persico arrived on 7 July 1887 and began his mission by visiting the Archbishop of Armagh, Michael Logue,* and then moving south where he met the foremost hierarchical supporter of the Plan, the Archbishop of Cashel, Thomas William Croke,* on 29 August in Thurles. Persico personally sympathised with the Irish demand for Home Rule,* and was also sympathetic to the cause of the Irish tenants in their fight against the landlords during the Plan. However, like the Vatican, he was worried about clerical involvement in a movement which advocated boycotting etc. He enjoined the priests to avoid activities which might make them victims of the coercion act introduced during July 1887 by the Chief Secretary, A. J. Balfour (*see* Perpetual Coercion Bill).

Persico reported to Rome from Ireland until January 1888, and showed sympathy for the tenants' grievances but not for the form which their action was taking. While he was in Ireland British government representatives were seeking condemnation of the Plan from the Vatican. Persico was taken aback by the Papal Rescript of 20 April 1888 which denounced the Plan and condemned the boycotting. He was especially surprised at not having been given advance notice. The Rescript caused a strong anti-Vatican reaction among Irish nationalists, and the Pope, in correspondence with the Irish hierarchy in June 1888, cushioned the impact of the Rescript. Most Irish bishops blamed Persico for the Rescript and he was hurt by the condemnation he received in Ireland. He was later an Archbishop, a Cardinal and the Secretary of Propaganda Fidei.

PETRIE, GEORGE (1789–1866). Artist, antiquarian and music collector; b. Dublin; ed. Samuel Whyte's School, Dublin. Although he was intended for a medical career, he showed early artistic promise and was awarded the silver medal of the Royal Dublin Society's School in 1805. His career as an antiquarian began three years later when he travelled throughout Dublin and Wicklow collecting music and sketching ancient ecclesiastical architecture. During a visit to Wales (1810) and England (1813) he painted several landscapes; upon his return he painted extensively and illustrated many historical and travel books on Ireland. He was a constant exhibitor at the Royal Hibernian Academy* (1826-58) of which he became a member in 1828; he was the first water-colourist to be accepted and was never asked to fulfil his undertaking to submit works also in oils. His best-known painting was 'Gougane Barra'. Elected a member of the advisory council of the Royal Irish Academy* in 1830 he worked in the Topographical Section of the Ordnance Survey of Ireland* with John O'Donovan. The first number of his *Dublin Penny Journal* appeared on 30 June 1832.

Dr Petrie, who was awarded a Civil List Pension in 1849, made an immense contribution to the preservation of Irish music. He supplied Edward Bunting* with materials for his collections and furnished Thomas Moore* with a number of airs including 'Luggelaw'. His first collection, *Ancient Music of Ireland* (1853), contained 'Péarla an Bhrollaigh Bháin' ('The Snowy-Breasted Pearl') and the air later known as 'The Londonderry Air' ('Danny Boy'). The second collection, *Music of Ireland*, appeared in 1882. Apart from contributions on art and antiquities to learned and popular journals, he published *Essay on the Round Towers of Ireland* (1833) and *On the History and Antiquities of Tara Hill* (1839), for which he received gold medals from the RIA.

'PERVERTS'. Contemptuous epithet used by the Irish peasants to denote those who changed from the Catholic to the Protestant religion, especially during the Famine of 1845-49.* *See also* 'Jumper' and 'Souperism'.

'AN PHOBLACHT.' *An Phoblacht* first appeared on 20 June 1925, published by the Irish Republican Army.* Its editor was Peadar O'Donnell* and contributors included Frank Gallagher* and Frank Ryan.* Ryan also served as editor. The paper maintained a constant criticism of the W. T. Cosgrave administration. It was closely associated with Saor Eire* and was banned in 1931. Under O'Donnell's leadership, it supported Fianna Fail* in the call for the withholding of Land Annuities.* The paper was active in opposition to the Blueshirts* (1933-34). It ceased publication in 1937. Another newspaper called *An Phoblacht*, published by the Provisional IRA, appeared in May 1970.

PHOENIX NATIONAL AND LITERARY SOCIETIES. Republican societies founded in Skibbereen, Co. Cork, by Jeremiah O'Donovan Rossa* in 1856. Ostensibly literary-debating societies but, with 'Ireland for the Irish' as a motto, they were patently revolutionary. James Stephens,* during his tour of Ireland preparatory to establishing the Irish Republican Brotherhood,* was so impressed by their zeal that he recruited them in 1858. The Phoenix Clubs were raided in December 1858 and the leaders arrested but they were soon released for lack of evidence. By 1859, almost fully integrated into the IRB, the Phoenix societies were dissolved.

PHOENIX PARK MURDERS (6 May 1882). On 6 May 1882, four days after the resignation of the Chief Secretary, W. E. Forster, and the release of Charles Stewart Parnell under the terms of the Kilmainham 'Treaty',* the new Chief Secretary, Lord Frederick Cavendish,* and the Under Secretary, Thomas Henry Burke,* were assassinated outside the Vice-Regal Lodge in the Phoenix Park. The killings were the work of a Fenian splinter-group, the Invincibles.* The murders, performed with surgical knives smuggled from London, shocked public opinion in Ireland and Great Britain. Parnell, who believed that his work would be undone by the killings, offered his resignation to W. E. Gladstone. Gladstone, whose wife was related to Cavendish, persuaded him to remain as leader of the Irish Parliamentary Party.

James Carey,* a member of the Invincibles, informed on his companions and turned state's evidence. His revelations led to the execution of five of the principals involved, Brady, Kelly, Caffrey, Fagan and Curley, at Kilmainham between 14 May and 9 June 1883. Eight others were sentenced to long terms of imprisonment. Carey was later shot dead by an Invincible, Patrick O'Donnell, in Cape Town.

PIGOT, JOHN EDWARD (1822—71). Young Irelander and poet; b. Kilworth, Co. Cork; ed. locally and TCD, where he graduated B.A. in 1843. He was called to the Bar in 1844. Under the pen-name 'Fermoy' he contributed articles and poems to *The Nation** and was a member of the editorial board. A member of Young Ireland,* his work appeared also in *The Spirit of the Nation.** Pigot was a member of the Repeal Association.* Active in the Irish Confederation,* he was a member of the defence team during the state trials of John Mitchel* and William Smith O'Brien* in 1848. Closely associated with several cultural bodies, Pigot was joint honorary secretary of the Society for the Preservation and Publication of the Melodies of Ireland (1851). In this capacity he travelled throughout the country collecting old Irish airs and tunes which were used by George Petrie* and Patrick W. Joyce* in their published collections. Pigot's manuscripts in the Royal Irish Academy* include some 2,000 tunes. After emigrating to India in 1865 he established a thriving legal practice. He died while on holiday in Dublin.

PIGOTT, RICHARD (1828—89). Journalist and forger; b. Co. Meath; ed. locally. A supporter of nationalist causes for a period, he was imprisoned for sedition. Pigott had a poor reputation, and was at various times a pornographer and a blackmailer. He appeared to support the Home Rule League* and was the owner of the three ailing newspapers, *The Irishman, The Flag of Ireland* and *The Shamrock,* which he sold for £3,000 to the Irish Parliamentary Party* in 1881; they formed the basis for the nationalist *United Ireland** controlled by Charles Stewart Parnell.* During the transaction Pigott received documents bearing the signature of Parnell and used them for his subsequent forgeries.

In 1885 he was again in financial difficulties and he contacted Lord Richard Grosvenor, the Liberal Chief Whip, with a scheme to publicise material which would damage Parnell and the Irish party. Through Grosvenor he met a former London *Times* reporter, Edward Caulfield Houston, then secretary to the Irish Loyal and Patriotic Union,* who retained him to seek information implicating the Parnellites in crime. Pigott failed to find such information in his travels to Paris, Switzerland and the USA and, in despair of losing his income from Houston, forged letters in Paris. Houston was persuaded that the letters were genuine and sold them to *The Times* which did not check their authenticity, using them as the basis for a series of articles on 'Parnellism and Crime' from March 1887.

The letters led to a court action when Frank Hugh O'Donnell* sued *The Times,* claiming that he had been libelled by the articles in question. Although O'Donnell lost his case, a special Commission was established by the House of Commons which called Pigott as a witness. His forgery was revealed when Parnell's counsel, Sir Charles Russell,* asked him to write a number of words, including 'hesitancy'; Pigott spelled it 'hesitency', as it appeared in some of the letters. Further cross-examination revealed numerous contradictions in his testimony. In particular he denied that he had prior knowledge of the nature of *The Times'* series, whereas, letters which he had written to the Catholic Archbishop of Dublin, William Walsh,* made it clear that he did. He failed to make his appearance in court on 26 February and, having signed a confession which he almost immediately retracted, fled to Paris. From Paris he travelled to Madrid where he registered as 'Ronald Ponsonby' at the Hotel Embajadores on 28 February. When he was confronted by British policemen who wished to question him, he shot himself on the next day.

PIKE THEATRE. Fringe theatre founded in Dublin in 1953 by Alan Simpson and Carolyn Swift for the production of international drama. A very small theatre, seating around fifty, it mounted the first Irish productions of works by Samuel Beckett* and Brendan Behan.*

During the Dublin Drama Festival of 1957 the Pike became the centre of a controversy over the staging of Tennessee Williams' *The Rose Tatoo*. Following a complaint from a member of the public, the police demanded that Simpson take the production off as it contained 'objectionable passages'. Two days later, on 3 July, having refused to take off the production, he was arrested on a charge of producing an 'indecent and profane play for gain'. After spending the night in a cell Simpson posted bail and sought support for his stand. Support came from Behan, Frank O'Connor* and Donagh MacDonagh* but neither the Dublin Drama Festival nor the Gate Theatre,* where he had entered into a contract with Lord Longford,* would give support. During the hearing in the Dublin district court (4 July) a policeman giving evidence refused to disclose the source of the original complaint or to say what the 'objectionable passages' were. Simpson successfully appealed to the High Court and the charges were dropped.

Harold Hobson of *The Sunday Times* later claimed that his enthusiastic review of the production, during which he implied that a contraceptive had been dropped on stage, was responsible for the police action.

'PILOT.' Newspaper founded and edited by Richard Barrett in 1828 to provide support for Daniel O'Connell,* the Catholic Association* and the fight for Catholic Emancipation.* It later supported the Repeal Association.* The paper appeared three times per week and was viewed with hostility by the Irish executive. Barrett was several times prosecuted and imprisoned. Circulation was not large — between 700 and 1,000 — and material consisted almost exclusively of O'Connell's speeches and public letters. It was often involved in controversy with anti-O'Connellite newspapers. In 1834 the Castle withdrew its stamp and the paper appeared under the banner of *The Morning Register*. This persecution prompted its defence by the London *Times* and led to questions in the House of Commons so that it shortly re-appeared under its own banner. It ceased publication in 1849, two years after O'Connell's death.

PIRRIE, WILLIAM JAMES, 1st VISCOUNT (1847–1924). Shipbuilder; b. Quebec of Ulster parents and reared in Co. Down. Having entered Harland and Wolff's shipyard as an apprentice-draughtsman (1862), he proved so adept that he was co-opted to the Board of Directors in 1874. As chairman, from 1904, he was in sole control of the company. Under his direction, the shipyard built the biggest ships of the time, including the *Teutonic* (1889; 10,000 tons), *Oceanic* (1899; 17,000 tons) and *Titanic* (1911; 76,500 tons). Pirrie, who conceived the liners as 'floating hotels', recognised that oil was the fuel of the future and concluded a deal in 1912 by which he became a manufacturer of diesel engines in Glasgow. A director of the White Star and other shipping lines, he was reputed to have become a millionaire (he paid £250,000 for Witley Court, Surrey, in 1909). He had a chequered political career, becoming in turn Unionist, Liberal Unionist and Liberal. Lord Mayor of Belfast (1896–97) and the first Freeman of Belfast City, he failed to secure a parliamentary seat chiefly because his politics were too liberal for the Unionist, Orange and Conservative establishments. He supported the Independent Orange Order.* A Privy Councillor since 1897, he was raised to the peerage in 1906.

His wife, Margaret Pirrie (1857–1935), *née* Carlisle, was a noted philanthropist and was active in many charitable organisations. She was the first woman JP and the first woman to receive the Freedom of Belfast.

PISHOGUE (PISEÓG). Irish peasant belief that a charm or spell could be visited upon one by a form of sympathetic magic and defined by Mrs S. C. Hall* as a 'wise saw, a rural incantation, a charm, a sign, a cabalistic word'. Pishogues were generally directed towards obtaining cures of man and beast and increasing milk and butter yields, etc. They were of four principal kinds:
(1) Protective (from witchcraft, for example); fire was not allowed to leave a house in which butter was being churned nor was a person allowed to 'redden' his pipe in the house.
(2) Seeking an increase in yield; an instance of this sort of pishogue was the placing of a cow's after-birth under the milk-keelers to produce cream.
(3) Love charms; the object of these pishogues was to gain the affection of a loved one or to determine the identity of a future spouse or lover. Mrs S. C. Hall, quoting from an encounter with a woman known as 'Poll the Pishogue' at Newbridge, Co. Kildare, relates that 'Herbs used in love potions had to be gathered fasting in the bames of a full moon'. To ascertain the identity of a future

spouse or lover one had to visit the local abbey churchyard on May eve, put the right garter round the left knee and vice versa. The thumbs should be tied in the form of a cross with a peeled bark of rowan. The third snail found under the ivy was brought home between two plates and left with the twist of rowan until the morning. The following morning when the plates were opened the snail's trail on the rowan would contain the name of the future spouse.
(4a) Warding off and curing disease; for example, a reduction in the milk yield was prevented by placing a live cinder under the churn or iron nails were driven in a circle about it; or
(4b) Inflicting injury upon others; it was believed that by hiding eggs or raw meat in a neighbour's field his harvest would be adversely affected, or that if a cloth was dragged across a field wet by dew on May-eve the butter and milk produce on that farm would be destroyed.

Belief in pishogues still persists in some of the more isolated areas of the country.

PITT, WILLIAM (1759–1806). Politician (Tory); Prime Minister (1783–1801; 1804–06); b. Hayes, Bromley, in Kent; ed. privately and Pembroke Hall, Cambridge. After reading law at Lincoln's Inn he was called to the Bar in 1780 and entered politics as MP for Appleby one year later. His maiden speech in favour of economic reform was an outstanding success (26 February 1781). After serving briefly as Chancellor of the Exchequer in 1782 he was invited by George III* to form a government (1783–1801).

He failed in his attempt to establish Free Trade between Ireland and England (1784–85) but he succeeded in forcing the Irish Parliament to grant Catholic Relief in 1793. A supporter of Catholic Emancipation,* he intended that it should follow the Union* which became his prime objective following upon the rising of the United Irishmen* in 1798. The promise of Emancipation won support for the Union from the Catholic hierarchy led by John Thomas Troy.* Pitt met with strong opposition from Lord Clare* in Ireland and from George III. When the Union was secure and he became the first Prime Minister of the Imperial Parliament of Great Britain and Ireland (22 January 1801), he pressed for Emancipation. He met the King's resistance by announcing his resignation on 3 February but postponed it when the King became deranged. Upon the King's recovery, Pitt resigned on 14 March and was out of office until 1804.

During his period out of office he was dunned by creditors to whom he owed some £45,000; he declined offers of gifts from both the King and the London merchants. He also suffered from poor health, aggravated by excessive drinking. He was severely critical of the Addington administration's handling of the war with France which was renewed in 1803. Approached by the King to form another government, Pitt laid down two conditions: one was that Charles James Fox should be a member of the new administration, and the other was Emancipation. The King refused to include Fox in the government and extracted from Pitt a promise that he would not raise the question of Emancipation. Fearful for the King's sanity, Pitt conceded and formed a new government (1804–06). His final years as Prime Minister witnessed the rapid deterioration of his health.

PLAN KATHLEEN. Code name for a German invasion of Ireland proposed by the Irish Republican Army* during World War II (*see* Emergency). The plan, known to the Abwehr as the 'Artus Plan', proposed that German invading forces would aid the IRA in the overthrow of the government of Northern Ireland and the re-unification of Ireland as a thirty-two-county republic. A German agent, Hermann Goertz,* arrived in Ireland but his mission was a failure and the plan came to nothing.

PLAN OF CAMPAIGN. Stratagem employed by tenants against landlords between 1886 and 1891, prompted by the depression in the prices of dairy produce and cattle in the mid 1880s which left many tenants in arrears with rent. The Plan, conceived by Timothy M. Healy,* was organised by Tim Harrington,* William O'Brien* and John Dillon.* It was outlined in an article headed 'A Plan of Campaign' by Harrington which was published in *United Ireland** on 23 October 1886. The purpose of the Plan was to secure a reduction of rent: if the landlord refused to accept a reduced rent, the tenants were to pay no rent at all. The rents were then collected by campaigners who banked them in the name of a committee of trustees and were used to assist evicted tenants.

The Plan originated on the O'Grady estate in Co. Limerick in November 1886 and was then implemented by Dillon and O'Brien on the estate of the Marquess of Clanricarde* at Portumna, Co. Galway (19 November 1886). It spread to other estates, including the Lansdowne estate (Luggacurran, Co. Kerry), the Vandeleur' estate (Kilrush, Co. Clare), the Ponsonby estate (Youghal, Co. Cork), the Smith-Barry estate (Co. Tipperary), the de Freyne estate (Co. Roscommon), the O'Callaghan estate (Bodyke, Co. Clare), the Dillon estate (Co. Mayo), the Kingston estate (Mitchelstown, Co. Cork), and the Massareene estate, (Co. Louth). On all the estates the Plan was led by a member of the Irish Parliamentary Party or its constituency organisation, the National League. Some 20,000 tenants were involved.

The Plan was not supported by Charles Stewart Parnell,* leader of the Irish party, but he was unable to prevent it. In December 1886 when the government declared it to be 'an unlawful and criminal conspiracy', he persuaded O'Brien to confine it to the 116 estates upon which it was operating at that stage. However, the campaigners had support from the Catholic Archbishop of Dublin, William Walsh,* and from the Archbishop of Cashel, Thomas William Croke.* Many other bishops supported it, while opposition was led by the Bishop of Limerick, Edward O'Dwyer.*

The renewal of the Land War,* in the form of the Campaign, was a matter of grave concern to Lord Salisbury's Conservative government and, determined to crush it, he appointed his nephew, Arthur J. Balfour,* fresh from his attack on the Scottish Land League, to the Chief Secretaryship. Balfour secured a Perpetual Coercion Act* (1887) which was condemned by the Catholic hierarchy. Dillon and O'Brien were arrested, and, when their supporters started a public defence fund, Croke issued a 'No Tax Manifesto'* which prompted Balfour to consider imprisoning him also. Two priests, Fr Matt Ryan* and Fr Daniel Keller, both within Croke's archdiocese, were imprisoned. When Balfour defended Divisional Magistrate Thomas Plunkett's injunction to the police, 'Do not hesitate to shoot', in the House of Commons, O'Brien dubbed him 'Bloody' Balfour. Later in the year, nationalists were horrified at the Mitchelstown 'Massacre'.* Boycotting became widespread and the rising crime rate (*see* Agrarian Crime) and general unrest forced the government to seek Vatican assistance to suppress the clergymen involved in the Plan.

The Vatican despatched Monsignor Ignazio Persico* to Ireland in answer to British representations. Persico travelled throughout the country from July 1887 until January 1888, consulting prominent members of the hierarchy. The Vatican issued a Papal Rescript (20 April 1888) condemning the Plan, boycotting and clerical involvement, which Dr Croke and nationalists promptly ignored. A general resentment of the Vatican's intrusion into Irish affairs helped to win some support for the Plan which was by now

in financial difficulties. The organisers looked unavailingly to Parnell for help. In the course of a speech delivered to the Liberal Eighty Club, Parnell, fearing it would harm his alliance with the Liberals, virtually renounced his association with the Plan. The organisers were forced to seek financial assistance and Dillon embarked on a fund-raising drive in Australia and New Zealand (May 1889–April 1890) which raised some £33,000, but this was insufficient for their needs.

Balfour encouraged the landlords in 1889 to form an anti-tenant combination under the direction of the Tipperary landlord, A. H. Smith-Barry.* As the landlords' agent, Smith-Barry was authorised to buy up estates which were threatened by the Plan. This brought him into conflict with his own tenants in Tipperary town. When evicted they moved outside the town boundaries and built 'New' Tipperary* under the direction of Fr David Humphries* and O'Brien, just released from prison. The Tipperary project proved too costly for the Plan's leaders and this led to its defeat. By this time Parnell had been induced to give some support which helped in the formation of a Tenants' Defence Association* in Tipperary and this, along with Dillon's money, enabled the Plan to continue. The organisers had £84,000 in 1890 but this had shrunk to £48,000 within a year, by which time almost 1,500 tenants were receiving grants from Plan funds. In October Dillon and O'Brien jumped bail and escaped to France and from there to America where they were empowered by Parnell to raise more money (which he intended for the Irish party). In November, following the verdict in the *O'Shea v O'Shea and Parnell* divorce case the party split and the Campaign petered out. By 1893 the Campaign was over. It had resulted in settlements on eighty-four estates; on fifteen estates the tenants had gone back on the landlords' terms and no settlement had been reached on eighteen others.

PLUNKET, THOMAS, 2nd BARON PLUNKET (1792–1866). Evangelical Bishop of Tuam, Killala and Achonry (C.I.) (1839–66); b. Dublin, son of William Conyngham Plunket, 1st Baron Plunket;* ed. TCD. He was Dean of Down prior to his appointment to the bishopric of Tuam. Within a few years of taking up the Tuam diocese he became one of the best-known evangelicals in the country. His support for the Irish Church Missions to the Roman Catholics* and Rev. Edward Nangle* led to a religious war in Connaught between himself and the Catholic Archbishop of Tuam, John MacHale.* A highlight of the struggle was the so-called 'War in Partry' which led to questions in the House of Commons and attracted international attention (*see* Second Reformation). Plunket was denounced in November 1860 by *The Times* (London) for evicting Catholic tenants off his estate at Tourmakeady where his sister, Catherine Plunket, ran an evangelical school. By the time he died the evangelical movement in the West of Ireland was virtually dormant. He was the author of *Convert Confirmations: A Discourse Delivered to the Converts from Romanism in West Galway* (1851).

PLUNKET, WILLIAM CONYGHAM, 1st BARON PLUNKET (1764–1854). Lawyer and politician (Conservative); b. Enniskillen, Co. Fermanagh; ed. TCD where he received his B.A. in 1784. He was called to the Bar in 1787 and defended United Irishmen* (1797–98). Returned as MP for Charlemont (1798), he strongly opposed the Union* but later accepted office as Solicitor-General (1803). He was chief prosecutor at the trial of Robert Emmet.* As MP for Midhurst (1807–12) he supported Catholic Emancipation,* leading the fight after the death of Henry Grattan.* He was MP for Dublin University (TCD) from 1812. His Bill to secure Catholic Relief was successfully opposed by the Duke of York in the House of Lords in 1821.

Attorney-General in 1822, Plunket supported the Catholic Relief Bill introduced by Sir Francis Burdett* in 1825 (also blocked in the Lords). Raised to the peerage, he was appointed Chief Justice of the Court of Common Pleas in Ireland (1827) and was Lord Chancellor from 1830 until his resignation in 1841. Three of his children, none of whom supported his stand on Catholic Relief, were prominent members of the Church of Ireland, as Bishop of Tuam, Killala and Achonry (Thomas Plunket*), and Dean of Tuam and Vicar of Bray.

PLUNKET, WILLIAM CONYNGHAM, 4th BARON PLUNKET (1828–97). Archbishop of Dublin (C.I.) (1884–97); b. Dublin, grandson of William Conyngham Plunket, 1st Baron Plunket* and of Charles Kendal Bushe;* ed. Cheltenham and TCD. Following his ordination in 1857 he became chaplain and private secretary to his uncle, the evangelical Bishop of Tuam, Killala and Achonry, Thomas Plunket.* He gave active support in the West of Ireland to the Irish Church Missions to Roman Catholics (*see* Second Reformation). After his marriage to Anne, daughter of Benjamin Lee Guinness,* he was appointed to St Patrick's Cathedral, then being restored by his father-in-law. He was Bishop of Meath from 1876 to 1884 when he was translated to Dublin. As Archbishop he sought to achieve the unification of the Protestant Churches, and re-organised the Kildare Place Society* to establish the Church of Ireland Training College. He supported the Protestant movement in Spain and was president of the Italian Reform Society (1886). His writings include *Book for Tourists in Ireland* (1863), *Short Visit to the Connemara Missions* (1863), *All Things Are Ready: A sermon* (1865), *Church and the Census in Ireland* (1865) and *The Missionary Character and Responsibility of Our Church in This Land* (1865).

PLUNKETT, GEORGE NOBLE, COUNT (1851–1948). Antiquarian

and politician (Sinn Fein); b. Dublin; ed. Nice, Clongowes Wood College and TCD. President of the Society for the Preservation of the Irish language, he was vice-president of the Irish National Literary Society,* and active in a number of Irish cultural societies. He was founder and editor of *Hibernia* (1882–83). His title was a papal award. Count Plunkett was Director of the National Museum (1907–16), vice-president of the Royal Irish Academy (1908–09; 1911–14), which he represented on the Nobel Committee for Literature, and president of the Royal Society of Antiquaries of Ireland (RSAI). He contributed to *The Irish Monthly, The Nation, The Irishman, The Flag of Ireland, The Boston Pilot* and *North and South.*

His son, Joseph Mary Plunkett,* was one of the organisers of the Easter Rising of 1916. In the aftermath of the rising Count Plunkett became a political figure and was imprisoned. Aided by Sinn Fein* he was returned for North Roscommon in 1917 as an abstentionist independent. He held the seat in subsequent elections and was a member of the first Dail Eireann, holding the position of Minister for Foreign Affairs (January 1919–August 1921). He attended the Paris Peace Conference (1919) and accompanied Eamon de Valera* to London for the discussions with David Lloyd George* in July 1921. Minister for the Fine Arts but without a seat in the Cabinet (9 August 1921–January 1922), he opposed the Treaty. He did not take his seat in the Dail when returned for Co. Roscommon from 1922 to 1927 and continued to support Sinn Fein after de Valera broke with it to form Fianna Fail.* He was co-editor of *The Jacobite War in Ireland* (1894) and edited Stokes' *Early Christian Art in Ireland* (1911–15). His original works included *Sandro Botticelli* (1900), *Pinelli* (1904), *The Architecture of Dublin* (1908), *Arrows* (poems, 1921), *Echoes* (poems, 1928) and *Introduction to Church Symbolism* (1932).

PLUNKETT, SIR HORACE CURZON (1854–1932). Agriculturist and politician (Unionist); b. Gloucestershire; ed. Eton and Oxford. To improve his health he spent some ten years in Wyoming as a rancher. Upon his return to Ireland (1888) to manage the family estate in Co. Meath he was dismayed at the uneconomic and inefficient nature of Irish farming. He became one of a small number which included the 4th Lord Dunraven* and Fr Thomas Finlay* who began the Co-Operative Movement.* His membership of the Congested Districts Board* brought him into close contact with the primitive methods employed along the western seaboard. Plunkett believed that co-operation and self-help were the solutions for small and medium-sized farms and he sought to eliminate the middle-man. The first branch of the Co-Operative Movement was founded in Drumcollogher, Co. Limerick in 1890 and the movement spread, mainly in the dairying districts of the south and east. A co-ordinating body, the Irish Agricultural Organisation Society,* was formed in 1894. He interested his friend George Russell* in the movement and Russell became a travelling organiser and then full-time editor of the movement's newspaper, *The Irish Homestead.* * Plunkett, who had been returned as a Unionist MP for Dublin in 1892, organised the Recess Committee* which succeeded in securing a government department to aid agriculture, the Department of Agriculture and Technical Instruction,* of which he was vice-president until his resignation in 1907. His protégé, Thomas Patrick Gill,* who had also been a member of the Recess Committee, was appointed Secretary of the Department. After 1908 Plunkett lent his support to the campaign for Home Rule.*

He was a man of tremendous energy but possessed little tact. His work in agriculture and as a politician exposed him to attacks from virtually all sections of Irish public opinion. His Unionism had incurred the wrath of nationalists, his Protestantism made him suspect to Catholics, his desire to eliminate the middle-man from agriculture made him the bogey of rural shopkeepers.

At the height of the debate on the (third) Home Rule Bill,* he issued a pamphlet, *An Appeal to Ulster not to desert Ireland* (1914). He was chosen to act as Chairman of the Irish Convention*, 1917–18. The Convention was a failure and he was bitterly disappointed. In 1919 he founded the Irish Dominion League* but it was doomed – Dail Eireann* had already met and the War of Independence* had started.

He became a member of the Senate established in 1922 but one year later left Ireland permanently after his home, Kilteragh, was burned by republicans during the Civil War. Plunkett was the author of *Ireland in the New Century* (1904) which provoked a reply from Rev. M. O'Riordan under the title *Catholicity and Progress in Ireland* (1905). His autobiographical *Noblesse Oblige* appeared in 1908.

PLUNKETT, JOSEPH MARY (1887–1916). Poet and republican; b. Dublin, son of George Noble, Count Plunkett;* ed. privately and at Stonyhurst. Ill-health led to his spending much of his youth abroad (Sicily, Malta and Algeria). Widely read in the writings of Catholic mystics, he published his first volume of verse, *Circle and Sword,* in 1911, and became editor of *The Irish Review* founded by Padraic Colum;* his articles led to its suppression in November 1914. A member of the Irish Republican Brotherhood,* he joined the Irish Volunteers,* in which he became Director of Operations. He was an early member of the Military Council* which drew up the plans for the Easter Rising of 1916.*

He went to Germany in April 1915 to assist Sir Roger Casement* in securing aid for the rising from Germany. Casement, who felt that Plunkett's presence was an embarrassment, introduced him to mem-

bers of the German General Staff who were unimpressed by his personality and rejected his request for guns. Some aid, however, was sent on the *Aud** in April 1916. Plunkett was deeply interested in military tactics and in his position as Director of Operations, he displayed considerable ability, having drawn up plans for street-fighting in Dublin as early as 1914. He was co-author, with Sean MacDiarmada,* of the 'Castle Document'* which was intended to prompt moderates into supporting the rising. Despite the attempt by Eoin MacNeill* to prevent the insurrection, Plunkett strongly believed that it should go ahead, no matter how ill-starred. Shortly before the rising he underwent throat surgery and was dying when he left the convalescent home to take his place in the GPO where his ADC was Michael Collins.* He was a member of the Provisional Government formed by Patrick Pearse* and a signatory to the Proclamation of Independence. Following the collapse of the rising he was court-martialled and sentenced to death. On the eve of his execution he married his fiancée, Grace Gifford, who continued to support the republican struggle throughout the War of Independence and the Civil War. The *Poems of Joseph Mary Plunkett* appeared porthumously in 1916.

'POBLACHT NA hÉIREANN' ('THE IRISH REPUBLIC'). Republican news-sheet founded by Liam Mellows,* Frank Gallagher* and Robert Erskine Childers,* the first issue appeared on 3 January 1922. The editorial committee included Cathal Brugha* and Mary MacSwiney.* It was issued at a time when no major publication was opposing the Treaty.* *Poblacht na hÉireann* reflected the ideals of Eamon de Valera* and the republican leadership which was shortly in arms against the Provisional Government. After February, it was edited by Childers who was executed the following November. It ceased publication after the Civil War.

'POINT'. *See* 'Praties and Point'.

POINT ST CHARLES. Site near Montreal in Canada chosen for the establishment of immigrant landing-stations. The new stations helped to reduce typhus deaths from sixty to twenty per day. The Victoria Bridge and railway sidings now occupy the site of the sheds. At the entrance to the bridge there is a large stone with the following inscription:

'To preserve from desecration the remains of 6,000 immigrants who died from ship fever A.D. 1847−48 this stone is erected by the workmen of Messrs Peto, Brassey and Betts employed in the construction of the Victoria Bridge. A.D. 1859'.

POLICE. The first attempt to provide a police force for Ireland was by Act of George III in 1787 when the barony police were established. Known as 'Barnies', they were inadequate for the suppression of disturbances. It was a constant source of dissatisfaction to the authorities that the military forces in Ireland were generally required to act the role of police, further alienating the civilian population. Another attempt to establish an efficient force was made in 1814 with the creation of the Peace Preservation Force by Sir Robert Peel. This force, whose members became popularly known as 'Peelers', was at the disposal of the Lord Lieutenant for use in any district which had been 'proclaimed' as a disturbed area. During a period of intense agitation as a result of hunger and general discontent this force also proved inadequate, and in 1822 the County Constabulary was established. From 1822 there were two police forces in Ireland: the Peace Preservation Force worked independently in proclaimed districts and the County Constabulary preserved law and order throughout the country. To supervise the County Constabulary four provincial inspectors were appointed, each with complete responsibility for law and order with-in his area; sixteen constables were appointed to each barony. In all, there were 313 chief constables and 5,008 constables. The constables were frequently used in an attempt to suppress faction-fighting.*

Under the reforming Irish executive of 1835−41 the Under Secretary, Thomas Drummond,* remodelled the system under an Act of 1836. He absorbed all the existing police forces into a new body called the Irish Constabulary under an Inspector-General in Dublin.

He removed from magistrates the power to appoint constables (who were now to be appointed by the Lord Lieutenant) and a new code of discipline was introduced. By 1840 there were 8,500 constables stationed throughout the country. In 1867, as a reward for their role in suppressing the rising of the Irish Republican Brotherhood,* the force was awarded the prefix Royal. By this time there were 11,000 constables and officers stationed in 1,600 barracks. *See also* Royal Irish Constabulary, Dublin Metropolitan Police *and* Garda Siochana.

POOR LAW. A Commission of Inquiry into Poor Law in Ireland was established in 1833. The members included Richard Whately,* Church of Ireland Archbishop of Dublin; Daniel Murray,* Catholic Archbishop of Dublin; Richard More O'Ferrall,* William Nassau Senior,* A. R. Blake and J. E. Richeno; the secretary to the Commission was John Revans. In their Report the Commissioners found that there were 2,385,000 persons in want or distressed during thirty weeks of the year. The Commission also noted that agricultural wages varied from 6d (2½p) to 1s (5p) per day and were only available for a small part of the year. The poor depended on private charity which was estimated to amount to some £2,000,000 annually.

The Commissioners did not recommend the simple extension of the English Poor Law system. Instead, they produced a scheme of 'enactments calculated to promote the improvement of the country, and to extend the demand for free and profitable labour'. Their principal recommendations included subsidised and organised emigration, a Board of Improvement to supervise reclamation of land, the drainage and fencing of waste lands, the establishment of agricultural Model Schools and a scheme of public works to be administered by the Board of Works and the county boards.

When George Nicholls came to Ireland to investigate conditions in 1836 he had instructions which implied that he could ignore the Irish Commission's recommendations and set about establishing a system on the English model. In his first report to the government, he said, 'Ireland is now suffering under a circle of evils, producing and reproducing one another. Want of capital produces want of employment; want of employment, turbulence and misery; turbulence and misery, insecurity; insecurity prevents the introduction and accumulation of capital, and so on. Until this circle is broken, the evils must continue and probably increase'. After a month in Ireland he recommended to the Irish executive that the English Poor Law system should be extended to Ireland. Over the protests of Whately and the Commissioners the Chief Secretary, Viscount Morpeth,* accepted his recommendation.

The Bill introduced in 1837 to establish the Irish Poor Law system was opposed by Daniel O'Connell,* but was welcomed generally by the Catholic clergy. It received the Royal Assent on 31 July 1838. Under the Act, Ireland was divided into 130 Unions, each of which was centred on a market town where a workhouse, or union house, was built for the relief of the distressed. Indoor relief only was to be administered (no relief was to be granted to anyone who remained outside the workhouse). Work proceeded swiftly: twenty-two Unions were declared by the end of March 1839 and 104 one year later. The first workhouse was built in 1840 and the last in 1846. They were built to provide relief for between 80,000 and 100,000 persons.

Each workhouse was to be administered by a Board of Guardians consisting of representative ratepayers of the Union. Each Union was rated for the number of poor which it sent to the workhouse; half was to be paid by the tenants and half by the landlords. When the burden of paying the rate became too heavy for the tenants, an Amendment exempted those rated at £4 or less (*see* Poor Law Valuation). The Treasury advanced the money for building the workhouses. The Irish Poor Law was administered from Whitehall until 1847.

By the time the last workhouse was built, Ireland was in the throes of the Famine of 1845–49.* Indoor relief was hopelessly inadequate but outdoor relief was granted only on condition that the recipient did not have a quarter-acre or more or land (*see* Quarter-Acre Clause). The workhouses tottered under the weight thrust upon them and it became impossible to collect the Poor Rate with which to finance relief. In 1847 the Poor Law Extension Act separated the Irish Poor Law from the British and increased the number of Unions from 130 to 162. It also introduced the Quarter-Acre Clause and established a paid inspectorate. Inefficient Boards of Guardians were abolished and replaced by paid Guardians.

A total of 610,463 people received indoor relief in 1848 and 1,433,042 were granted outdoor relief. One year later the figures were 932,284 and 1,210,182. As the collection of rates became impossible, workhouses went bankrupt and the Treasury ordered that a Poor Rate of 5s (25p) in the pound should be collected. Despite widespread protest from those involved in Irish relief, the Treasury order remained in force. The old, sick and young were turned out of the workhouses to make room for the able-bodied who could be put to work.

After the Famine, the Poor Law and the workhouses remained detested symbols. Upon the establishment of the Free State they were abolished and the county unit replaced the Union for the purpose of administration of relief. *See also* Local Government.

POOR LAW UNION. The Poor Law was extended to Ireland in 1838 and the country divided into 130 Unions. Each Union was further divided into electoral divisions of which in 1847 there were 2,049. Each workhouse in the Union was supervised by a Board of Guardians who were representative of the electoral divisions. Relief was financed by a rate collected under the Poor Law Valuation.* In 1847, 82 Unions consisted of between 100,000 and 200,000 acres and 25 were over 200,000; 10 had a population of between 100,000 and 200,000 and none had a population of over 200,000. The 33 Unions in Leinster had an average population of 58,602; 35 in Munster had an average of 69,581; the 19 in Connaught had an average of 75,943, and the 43 in Ulster had an average of 54,933. The average population of each Union in the country was 62,879. *See also* Poor Law.

POOR LAW VALUATION (PLV). Valuation of property for the purpose of assessing the rates which financed the Unions for the administration of the Poor Law* introduced in 1838. Each electoral division within the Poor Law Union district was charged with a proportion of the total cost in respect of the number of persons from that division who had received relief in the workhouse. As some of the original valuations were made by tenant-farmers and others by surveyors, there was a wide variation in findings. The competence of the valuation was called into question and a more scientific survey was undertaken by Richard Griffith* between 1848 and 1865. This, officially known as the Primary Valuation,* became the recognised system of assessing the rates for official purposes.

POPE JOHN PAUL II IN IRELAND. Pope John Paul II paid a pastoral visit to Ireland from Saturday, 29 September to Monday, 1 October 1979. He was greeted at Dublin Airport by the President, Dr Patrick Hillery,* the Taoiseach, Jack Lynch,* and the Archbishop of Armagh and Primate of All Ireland, Dr Tomas O'Fiaich. The Pope then went by helicopter to the Phoenix Park where he concelebrated Mass before a crowd estimated to have been in excess of 1,250,000. He was assisted by eight cardinals, thirteen foreign archbishops and sixty-one foreign bishops, three Irish archbishops and twenty-five bishops. Two thousand five hundred priests distributed communion to over 750,000 people.

The Pope travelled to Killineer, near Drogheda, Co. Louth where, addressing a crowd of over 250,000, he appealed for peace in Northern Ireland: 'Now I wish to speak to all men and women engaged in violence. I appeal to you in language of passionate pleading. On my knees, I beg you to turn away from the paths of violence and to return to the ways of peace.' Upon his return to Dublin, Pope John Paul gave audiences to international journalists, the diplomatic corps and was received at Arus an Uachtarain by the President. The Pope was presented with a silver bowl made in Dublin in 1715. He presented the President with a box of gold, silver and bronze pontifical medals and planted a tree in the grounds of the presidential residence.

The papal party travelled on Sunday, 30 September to Ballybrit Racecourse, Galway, to concelebrate a Mass for Youth. *En route* he visited the monastic site at Clonmacnoise, Co. Offaly where he briefly addressed 20,000 people. In Galway the Youth Mass was attended by over 200,000 young people, representative of every parish in Ireland. From Galway the

Pope was flown to Knock, Co. Mayo,* scene of a reported apparition by the Virgin Mary in 1879. He spoke to a crowd of 400,000.

On the next day the Pope addressed seminarians at Maynooth College* and then travelled to Greenpark Racecourse, Limerick. He delivered a homily on the theme of the family to 400,000 people. The papal party then travelled to the USA from Shannon Airport.

POPE-MAGUIRE DISCUSSION. Celebrated discussion which took place in the lecture rooms of the Dublin Institution for six days (19–25 April 1827) between a noted evangelical preacher, Rev. Richard T. P. Pope, and Fr Tom Maguire. The discussion arose from the activities of Pope's 'Biblicals' or 'New Reformers'* in Co. Leitrim where 'Fr Tom', as he was popularly known, was the parish priest at Ballinamore. Fr Maguire had said, when speaking on National Education* at Carrick-on-Shannon, 'Were I to meet the arch-crusader himself (Mr Pope) . . . I would confine him to a few solid objections, such as that respecting the Socinian, which, if he would satisfactorily solve for me, I would myself consent to become a Biblical'.

By mutual agreement the discussion was chaired by a Protestant, Admiral Oliver, and a Catholic, Daniel O'Connell.* It was limited to three points by each party: Mr Pope chose infallibility, purgatory and transubstantiation. Fr Maguire chose the divine right of private judgement to pronounce upon the authenticity, integrity, and canonicity of scripture, and to determine its meaning in articles of faith; the justification of the Reformation and the Protestant Churches not possessing that unity which forms the distinctive mark of the true Church of Christ.

The discussion aroused a great deal of public interest among all denominations. Fr Maguire was adjudged the victor but in fact much of his argument had been provided by his publishers, Messrs Coyne, Tims and Curry, who published the *Discussion* later in the year.

POPE'S BRASS BAND. Facetious title for the Irish Brigade* at Westminster.

POPULATION. The following are the figures for the population of the thirty-two counties of Ireland until 1926. From 1926 the figures refer only to the population of the twenty-six counties of the Free State. Figures for the remaining six counties may be found in the entry on Northern Ireland.

1831	7,767,401	1926	2,971,992
1841	8,175,124	1936	2,968,420
1851	6,552,385	1946	2,955,107
1861	5,798,564	1951	2,960,593
1871	5,412,377	1956	2,898,264
1881	5,174,836	1961	2,818,341
1891	4,704,750	1966	2,884,002
1901	4,458,775	1971	2,978,248
1911	4,390,219	1979	3,364,881

POST OFFICE. The Irish Post Office came into existence in 1631 when King Charles I ordered his Post Master of England and Foreign Ports to open a regular communication by running posts between the metropolis and Edinburgh, West Chester, Holyhead and Ireland. The Penny Post in Ireland was introduced to Dublin on 10 October 1773. The first Secretary of the Irish Post Office was John Lees, who was appointed in 1784. He achieved a certain amount of legislative independence for the Irish administration. The Duke of Richmond became the first Postmaster-General of the united services when the British and Irish post offices were amalgamated in 1831.

The first Irish-America Telegraph Ocean Cable was laid in August 1858 but it failed. It was not successful until eight years later when the cable was completed between Newfoundland and Valentia Island, Co. Kerry. The first telephone exchange was opened by the United Telephone Company on the top floor of the Commercial Buildings in Dame Street,

Dublin, in 1880. A boy was employed on the switchboard but he was dismissed for playing marbles during working hours. Ireland's first telephone connection to Great Britain, from Donaghadee, Co. Down, to Port Patrick, Wigtown, Scotland, was laid in 1893 at a cost of £20,000. In 1913 the first telephone cable between the South of Ireland and Great Britain was laid from the Martello Tower in Howth, Co. Dublin, to Nevin in Wales.

The General Post Office in O'Connell Street (then Sackville Street) was the headquarters of the Provisional Government during the Easter Rising of 1916. In the course of the fighting during the week the building was largely destroyed. It was reconstructed under the supervision of Robert Cochrane and re-opened in 1929. The air mail service was inaugurated at 7.15 a.m. on 26 August 1929 at Oranmore Airport when Colonel Charles Russell flew via Dublin and Chester to Croydon where he arrived at 11.36 a.m. Air mail was first transported officially to the continent on 22 October 1932 when the second leg of a mail-carrying flight, Galway-Berlin, was flown by Colonel Russell.

In October 1979 two Interim Boards, Postal and Telecommunications, were appointed as a preliminary to the Post Office becoming a semi-state body. The Postal Board members were: Mr Fergal Quinn (chairman), Mrs Claire Browne, Mr Patrick Cardiff, Mr Daniel Grace, Mr Tony Halpin, Mr Brendan Murray, Mr Terry Quinlan, Mr J. H. D. Ryan and Mr J. T. Sheehan. The Telecommunications Board members were: Mr Michael W. J. Smurfit (chairman), Mr Denis Brosnan, Mr W. J. Chamberlaine, Mr S. De Paor, Mr Mark Hely-Hutchinson, Mrs Elizabeth Holden, Mr Harold O'Sullivan, Professor John O'Scanlon, Mr D. Edmund Williams.

POTEEN. Illicit, home-made whiskey, 'that has never seen the face of a gauger' (excise man), referred to sometimes as 'mountain dew'. Poteen became a familiar drink among the Irish peasantry because of the tax on 'parliament whiskey'. The duty rose from 4d (1½p) per gallon in 1661 when excise duties were reintroduced until it was 6s 1½d (30p) per gallon in 1815 when whiskey was selling at 10s (50p) per gallon. Making poteen was not considered a crime by the Irish peasants who took great delight in outwitting authority. Early in the nineteenth century it was made from malt but as this was inconvenient and increased the risk of detection it was soon replaced by raw grain; however, as grain growing declined in 'poteen districts' other materials were pressed into service, including sugar, porter, potatoes, apples and rhubarb. As the price of copper rose, tin vessels were most commonly used. Owing to the difficulties of transporting grain from remote areas, the spirit was distilled on the spot, usually where there was a plentiful supply of turf.

Poteen was most commonly made west of a line from Clare to Derry, but Cavan, Monaghan and Tyrone in southern Ulster were also areas of widespread illicit distillation. It was sold in the areas where it was made, and also transported to market towns and cities; in country districts it was often sold in 'shebeens'* where it was coloured with legal 'parliament' or 'government' whiskey. The price of the spirit varied according to the price of grain and the proliferation of poteen-making; in 1815 it was between 7s (35p) and 8s (40p) per gallon but this had fallen by 1823 to 2s 6d. (12½p); by 1850 the price varied between 3s 6d (17½p) and 7s (35p). In Connaught at the turn of the century it was sold for between 10s (50p) and 12s (60p). The price soared during World War I when it cost around 8s (40p) per pint. During the next two decades, it fell again until it was around 5s (25p) per pint. Currently it sells for between £2 and £3 per bottle (10 glasses). It is still made in Cavan, Connaught and North Munster. A commercially made 'poteen' is now available but has been unable to titillate the expert palate.

POUND. Enclosure in which cattle were kept when they were seized by the bailiff for non-payment of church rates, 'parish cess', etc. The cattle were returned to their owners when the sums due were paid up. Pounds were used in the eighteenth century and in the first half of the nineteenth. 'Hibernicus', writing in 1800, noted: 'There is no public establishment so much used in Ireland as the Pound; and the fees paid to the bailiffs in charge of these for indulgences, or dues arbitrarily imposed, are comparatively considerable. In consequence of ill-treatment in those places of confinement, it happens not only generally, but almost universally, that the cattle are much injured, often depreciated a third or more in value, whereby the poor peasant is made a serious sufferer.'

POWER, JOHN O'CONNOR (1848–1919). Fenian and politician (Nationalist); b. Ballinasloe, Co. Galway; ed. locally. After emigrating to Rochdale in 1861 he worked as a painter and formed a small business. A member of the Irish Republican Brotherhood,* he was involved in the raid on Chester Castle in 1867. Later in the year he was in Manchester during the rescue of Colonel Thomas J. Kelly* and Captain Timothy Deasy.* He was arrested in Dublin in 1868 and held for six months without trial. Following his release he entered St Jarlath's College, Tuam, where he studied for the priesthood and was an assistant teacher.

When he joined the Home Rule League* in 1873 his lead was followed by other Fenians who agreed to give Isaac Butt* and the constitutional approach a trial for four years. Returned as MP for Co. Mayo, he became a prominent obstructionist. He accompanied Charles Stewart Parnell,* whom he described as 'a mediocrity', to the USA in 1876 to present a congratulatory address to President Grant on the occasion of the centennial celebrations of American independence. (Grant refused them an audience.) Power remained in New York after Parnell returned to Ireland. He did not enjoy the confidence of John Devoy* or Clan na Gael* because of his parliamentary career.

His decision to continue in parliament after the IRB ordered the experiment to end led to his expulsion from the Supreme Council* in 1877. Although his Fenian background earned him suspicion within the Irish party, he was considered a possible candidate for the leadership in succession to Butt. In a newspaper letter on 6 December 1878 he accused Butt of being 'a traitor to the cause'. He claimed to have anticipated the New Departure* by some ten years, saying that it failed because of the death of George Henry Moore.* Power became the first MP to offer public support to the tenant-farmers' meeting at Irishtown, Co. Mayo,* 20 April 1879 and was shortly afterwards the first to join the Land League of Mayo.*

His ambition to lead the Irish party was shattered when Parnell was chosen in May 1880. He would not support Parnell in his attempt to remain neutral and was regarded with general suspicion. Following the Kilmainham 'Treaty'* he moved closer to the Liberal Party. Standing as a Liberal in the general election of 1885 (when Parnell called on the Irish voters in Britain to support the Conservatives) he lost his seat and retired from politics.

POWER, REV. PATRICK (1862–1951). Clergyman (R.C.) and archaeologist; b. Callaghane, near Waterford; ed. Catholic University School and St John's College, Waterford. After ordination in 1885 he ministered in Liverpool and in Australia. He was later attached to the Cathedral in Waterford where he was Diocesan Inspector of Schools. Lecturer in Archaeology at Maynooth (1910–31) and Professor of Archaeology at UCC (1931–34), his publications include *Place Names of Decies* (1907), *Parochial History of Waterford and Lismore* (1912), *Lives of Declan and Mochuda* (for the Irish Texts Society, 1915), *Place Names and Antiquities of South East Cork* (1917), *Ardmore-Deacglaim* (1919), *Prehistoric Ireland* (1922), *Early Christian Ireland (1925)*, *The Ancient Topography of Fermoy* (1931), *A Bishop of the Penal Times* (1932), *A Short History of Co. Waterford* (1933), *Waterford and Lismore* (1937), *The Cathedral and Priory of the Holy Trinity, Waterford* (1942), and *Lismore-Mochuda* (1946). He edited nineteen volumes of the *Journal* of the Waterford and South-East Ireland Archaeological Society.

POWIS COMMISSION. The Royal Commission of Inquiry into Primary Education in Ireland met from February 1868 to May 1870 under the chairmanship of Lord Powis. The Commission consisted of fourteen members: seven Catholic, five Church of Ireland and two Presbyterian representatives. Together with ten assistant commissioners, they examined the system of National Education* in Ireland, and produced eight volumes of evidence and conclusions. Their Report consisted of 129 conclusions and resolutions. Their recommendations included payment by results and compulsory attendance. They also recommended local contributions towards primary schooling and that varying textbooks should be allowed. An important recommendation was that where average daily attendance was less than twenty-five pupils the schools should be allowed to become denominational in effect. This enabled convent and brothers' schools to become part of the national education system. The Commission also criticised the Model Schools* and the system of training, recommending the virtual abolition of the Models. Nearly all the recommendations of the Commission were gradually implemented. Payment by results was introduced but it was unlike the system in England in that only a portion of the teachers' salaries was dependant upon results.

PRAEGER, ROBERT LLOYD (1865–1953). Naturalist; b. Holywood, Co. Down; ed. Royal Academical Institute, Belfast and Queen's College, Belfast from which he graduated in 1896. He was engaged on harbour and water engineering works, 1886–92, and became Assistant Librarian of TCD in 1893. In 1903 Praeger was appointed Librarian of the RIA and he became Librarian at the National Library (1920–24). He was President of the National Trust of Ireland (from 1928) and was President of the RIA (1931–34). Dr Praeger was active in founding *The Irish Naturalist*, of which he became editor, and was instrumental in setting up the Fauna and Flora Committee of the RIA. He travelled widely, including the Canaries and Balkans, in connection with his botanical writings and was the recipient of many honours from Irish universities. His works include *Irish Topographical Botany* (1901), *Tourist's Flora of the West of Ireland* (1934), *The Way That I Went* (1937), *Some Irish Naturalists* (1950), and *Natural History of Ireland* (1951). He contributed numerous papers on Irish botany and geology to the *Irish Naturalist, Journal of Botany, Proceedings* of the RIA, Journal of the Royal Horticultural Society and *Proceedings* of the Belfast Naturalist's Club.

'PRATIES AND POINT'. A familiar 'dish' among the Irish peasantry of the eighteenth and nineteenth centuries. When only a small portion of salt remained, the potato, instead of being dipped into it was 'as a sort of indulgence to the fancy', pointed at it instead. A variation on this pointing was to keep a portion of meat either on or hanging above the table; the potato was then rubbed against the meat in order to give it a flavour.

One writer described it as an 'imaginative dish'.

PRECURSOR SOCIETY. Founded in 1838 by Daniel O'Connell* to seek reforming legislation for Ireland with the implied threat that if not granted, a full demand would be made for Repeal. At this stage, O'Connell and the Repeal Party had been in an alliance with the Whigs for three years (*see* Lichfield House Compact) and the weakness of the Whig government led by Lord Melbourne* made it politic for O'Connell to make his demands. He believed that reforms would 'precede' Repeal. Many of his followers were under the misapprehension that the title meant that the Society would engage itself in cursing the government. *See also* Repeal Association.

PRESENTATION SISTERS. Order of nuns founded in 1776 by Nano Nagle. Primarily a teaching order, it was instructed by its foundress to devote itself to the education and care of the poor. The Order spread from Ireland and is now world-wide.

PRESIDENTS.
President of Dail Eireann (1919–22).
The President of Dail Eireann was the title given to Eamon de Valera* by the first Dail Eireann in April 1919. The office gave him the authority of Prime Minister. During his visit to the US (1919–20) he was called President of the Irish Republic, an office to which his followers elected him after they had rejected the Treaty in January 1922. De Valera resigned the Presidency of Dail Eireann on 9 January 1921 and lost the election on the same day to Arthur Griffith* by two votes (60–58). Griffith held the office until his death in August 1922. He was succeeded by William T. Cosgrave* who was also Chairman of the Provisional Government. When the Free State officially came into existence in December 1922, the head of the government became known as President of the Executive Council (cabinet).

President of the Executive Council (1922–37).
The Executive Council was the cabinet of the Free State and the President occupied the role of Prime Minister; the office lasted from 6 December 1922 until 29 December 1937. Cosgrave held the post from December 1922 until March 1932 when he was succeeded by de Valera who led Fianna Fail* to power for the first time in the general election of that year. De Valera set about dismantling the Treaty and substituted the Constitution of 1937 for the Constitution of 1922. Under the new Constitution the Executive Council and the title of President were abolished; the new head of the government would be known as Taoiseach and a new office, President of Eire, was substituted for the old office of Governor-General of the Free State.
President of Eire (1937–49) and of the *Republic of Ireland* (1949–   ).
The title of President has designated the head of the twenty-six county state from 1937; until 1949 the office was that of President of Eire but under the Republic of Ireland Act it became that of President of the Republic. The President is a member of the Oireachtas,* acting on the advice and authority of the government. He appoints the Taoiseach and on his advice appoints the members of the government; also, on the Taoiseach's advice, he accepts or terminates the appointment of members of the government. The President summons or dissolves Dail Eireann on the Taoiseach's advice. He may hold consultations with the Council of State.*

The President is the guardian of the Constitution and holds the following powers in addition to those mentioned above: he may send any bills (with two exceptions) to the Supreme Court; the exceptions are money bills or bills proposing to amend the Constitution. He may call a referendum on a bill at the request of a majority of the Senate and not less than one-third of the Dail if they instruct him not to approve a bill on the grounds that it 'contains a proposal of such national importance that the will of the people thereon ought to be ascertained'. He has 'absolute discretion' to refuse dissolution of the Dail to a Taoiseach who has lost his majority or who chooses to interpret a defeat as a loss of confidence. The powers of the President have been used sparingly and his primary function is to sign bills into law and perform the symbolic duties of a head of state. He is Commander-in-Chief of the national army and officers in the army hold their commissions from him. The Presidents have been: Dr Douglas Hyde (1938–45), Sean T. O'Kelly (1945–59), Eamon de Valera (1959–73), Erskine Hamilton Childers (1973–74), Cearbhall O'Dalaigh (1974–76), and Patrick Hillery (1976   ). Mr de Valera was the only person to hold all the offices of President (of Dail Eireann, of the Republic, of the Executive Council and of Ireland).

PRIMARY VALUATION. Known also as 'Griffith's Valuation', the Primary Valuation was carried out under the Valuation (Ireland) Act, 1852, directed by Richard Griffith* between 1852 and 1865. This valuation, which placed the assessment of rates for the administration of the Poor Law* on a uniform basis for the whole country, replaced the unsatisfactory Poor Law Valuation.* Rates payable under the Primary Valuation are a major source of revenue for local government.

For the Primary Valuation a distinction was drawn between tenements which consisted of land only and those upon which houses or other buildings had been erected, and land and buildings were valued separately. The net annual valuation of a tenement was defined under the Act as 'the rent for which one year with another, the same might in its actual state be reasonably expected to let from year to year with cost of repairs, insurance, maintenance, rates, taxes and all other public charges

except the tithe rent being paid by the tenement'. Land values were calculated on the basis of current prices, taking into account the fertility of the soil (and not according to the prices of 1850). Pasture land was to be valued at the price per acre proportionate to the number of cattle and sheep it may be capable of grazing during a year, according to the price per head prevailing in the neighbourhood for grazing. In addition, the quality of the 'herbage' and 'permanent' improvements (roads, drainage and fences) were taken into account. Other considerations were also taken into account, such as 'peculiar local circumstances' such as climate, elevation and shelter favourable to agriculture which would lead to an increase in valuation; where the 'peculiar local circumstances' were unfavourable there was to be a reduction. The Valuation (Ireland) Act 1852 is still the basic legislation for valuation. Comprehensive revaluations have been undertaken by only two local authorities: Dublin (1908–15) and Waterford (1924–26) cities. Private dwellings are no longer liable for rates since 1 January 1978 when that source of finance became a charge on central funds. *See also* Local Government.

PRIOMH-AIRE. 'First Minister' (Prime Minister); Irish title given to Eamon de Valera by the first Dail Eireann. In English he was known as 'President of Dail Eireann'. Following the creation of the Free State (December 1922), the head of the government was the President of the Executive Council.

'PRISON BARS'. Newspaper published by the Women's Prisoners' Defence League, 1937–38. It attempted to attract support for the release of the republicans imprisoned by the de Valera administration during 1936 and subsequently.

PROGRAMMES FOR ECONOMIC EXPANSION (1958–72). The three Programmes for Economic Expansion were an attempt to modernise the Irish economy. The first Programme (1958–63) was based on the White Paper 'Economic Development' drawn up by T. K. Whitaker* with the support of Sean Lemass* and adopted by the government in November 1958. The object of the Programme was to 'accelerate progress by strengthening public confidence after the stagnation of the 1950s, indicating the opportunities for development and encouraging a progressive and expansionist outlook'. The Whitaker Report indicated that in order to achieve these aims 'we must be prepared to take risks under all headings – social, commercial and financial – if we are to succeed in the drive for expansion'.

The Programme was adopted at an opportune moment to make maximum use of renewed world economic activity. During the period of the first Programme national income rose by 2 per cent compared with 0.5 per cent between 1952 and 1958. Real incomes rose by 4 per cent. This new-found prosperity was due to a rise in net agricultural output which increased by 9 per cent during the 1960s, and to manufacturing industry where value of output rose by 82 per cent (1959–68). The value of exports in 1960 was the highest for thirty years.

The second Programme (1963–68), drawn up by Whitaker and Lemass, capitalised on the economic growth achieved during the period of the first Programme. It set out to 'achieve the maximum sustainable rate of growth' in order to provide the rising standards made possible by the first Programme. One significant accompaniment of the second Programme was the re-organisation of the educational system by the Minister for Education, Donogh O'Malley,* in an attempt to bring education at all levels into line with the needs of the economy.

The third Programme was introduced by Lemass's successor, John ('Jack') Lynch.* Designed to cover the period from 1969 to 1972, it

was entitled 'Economic and Social Development'. It sought to take account of the social changes which had accompanied the revitalisation of the economy and was drawn up against the background of the National Industrial Economic Council's 'Report on Full Employment' which sought a growth rate of 17 per cent for the three-year period. The Programme projected an increase of 16,000 in employment and a reduction of emigration to an annual level of 12,000–13,000. A population of more than 3,000,000 was projected for 1972 (in 1971 the Census revealed a population of 2,978,248).

The third Programme collapsed in the face of an international recession. In 1973 the Fianna Fail government lost office to the National Coalition which did not attempt any new programmes for expansion in the light of adverse economic conditions.

PROGRESSIVE UNIONIST PARTY. Political party founded in Northern Ireland by W. J. Stewart to fight the general election of 1938. It was non-sectarian and, offering a radical housing programme and a demand for an end to the high rate of unemployment, hoped to attract the Catholic-Nationalist vote. It lost in the twelve constituencies which it contested, as it was unable to break the hold of the Ulster Unionist Party.

PROPERTY DEFENCE ASSOCIATION. Founded in 1880 to assist landlords against their tenants who were members of the Land League* during the Land War. Led by Lords Dunraven, Castletown, Rossmore, Colonel Nugent-Everard and A. H. Smith-Barry, the association served writs on tenants, provided caretakers on cleared holdings, combated boycotting and employed a reserve force to aid in evictions. The association was no longer necessary after 1882 but it was revived as a landlords' combination to fight the Plan of Campaign* under Smith-Barry.

PROPORTIONAL REPRESENTATION (PR). System of election used in Ireland. The first experiment with the system was made in Sligo in 1919. It was used for the first time officially in the local government elections of January 1920. Its first usage in a general election was in Northern Ireland for elections to the parliament of the new state held on 19 May 1921. However, it was abandoned in 1929 and the constituencies re-organised under the straight-vote system.

As used for general elections, Senate elections and local government elections in the Republic, the proportional representation system operates by means of the single-transferable vote in multi-member constituencies. Voters indicate their choices by placing numbers in order of preference against names on the ballot paper. Any paper which does not contain the number 1 against a candidate's name is invalid. Having voted No. 1, the voter may then vote for as many more candidates in order of choice as he wishes. A quota for election is set according to the Droop Quota which is represented by the formula:

$$Q = \frac{\text{No. of valid votes} + 1}{\text{No. of seats} + 1}$$

If no one is elected on the first count, votes are transferred according to the preferences expressed until all the seats are filled. Surplus or excess votes over the quota when reached by a candidate are distributed proportionally to the second or next available choices expressed by his supporters. When there are no surpluses to be distributed, and seats still remain to be filled, the candidate with the lowest number of votes is eliminated and his votes redistributed in accordance with the preferences indicated by his supporters. The process continues until all the seats are filled. It is possible, therefore, for a candidate to be elected without having reached the quota.

PR was the system chosen because the representatives of Dail Eireann, in particular the leader of the delegation, Arthur Griffith, and the representatives of the British government, favoured the system during the negotiations which led to the Treaty of December 1921. The argument in favour was that PR was the method of election best suited to providing representation of minorities (in this case, Unionists).

Attempts to abolish PR have been unsuccessful. Fianna Fail governments have twice held referendums to secure abolition of the system and its replacement by the single non-transferable vote in single-member constituencies. In the referendum of 1959, held on the same day as the presidential election which was won by the leader of Fianna Fail, Eamon de Valera, the result was 453,322 (48.2% of the valid poll) in favour of change and 486,989 (51.8%) against. In the second referendum, held in 1968, the result was 423,496 (39.2% of the valid poll) in favour of change and 657,898 (60.8%) against.

PROTECTION OF PERSON AND PROPERTY (IRELAND) ACT 1881. Coercion Bill introduced by the Chief Secretary, William Edward Forster,* to deal with the rising crime rate attributed to the Land League, (*see* Agrarian Crime). From its introduction on 24 January 1881, the Bill was opposed strenuously by Charles Stewart Parnell and the Irish Parliamentary Party, as it proposed to suspend the law in selected districts which were to be 'proclaimed'. The Irish members obstructed the Bill on its first reading and forced the House of Commons into a twenty-two-hour sitting on 25 January. On 31 January, they forced the House into a marathon forty-one-hour sitting, the second longest on record, and the longest of any legislature at that time. The Liberal government fought back against the obstruction and on 2 February, in order to end the forty-one-hour sitting, the Speaker introduced a motion of closure and guillotined the debate. Within a few days the first reading was passed and the Irish members had used the classical version of obstruction for the last time. The Bill became law in March.

PROTESTANT COLONISATION SOCIETY. Formed in 1830 when emigration was threatening the (Protestant) Ascendancy* in Ulster. The object of the Society was to ensure that lands vacated through emigration or other causes would continue to be owned by Protestants. The rules of the Society were distinctly sectarian:

'4th: Every tenant distinctly understands and agrees, that no Roman Catholic, under any pretence whatever, shall be allowed to reside or be employed in any Colony of the Society.

5th: Every colonist who shall marry a Roman Catholic shall, after due notice, retire from the colony, he being permitted to dispose of or carry away his private property'.

The Society, which numbered landed proprietors, parsons, military men and Fellows of Trinity College among its members, began its work on the lands of Sir Edmund Hayes in Co. Donegal. Seven Scottish settler-families were invited and had slated dwellings erected for them. The foundations of a Protestant Church were laid out and arrangements were made to increase the number of settlers.

The scheme was not a success and was abandoned after a few years. The original families returned to Scotland impoverished. The principle behind its foundation, however, lived on and several similar organisations were founded within the next decade, most notably the Protestant Tenantry Society in 1841.

PROTESTANT HOME RULE ASSOCIATION. Founded by Charles Hubert Oldham* and Edward Perceval Wright* in 1886 to bring together Protestant supporters of the (first) Home Rule Bill* introduced by W. E. Gladstone. The Protestant population was generally hostile to the idea of Home Rule and the Association soon disappeared.

PROTESTANT NATIONALIST PARTY. Political party founded in Ulster to fight the general election of 1892. The party secured nine seats (in Fermanagh, North Tyrone, North Antrim and North Derry) at the expense of the Irish Parliamentary Party.* Led by Rev. McAuley Brown, the party attracted Protestant liberals who were anti-Tory and anti-landlord. It looked for the 'expropriation of the landlords' who should be forced to sell out to the tenantry. It was not successful in securing a sizeable Catholic vote and was unable to combat Unionist-Conservative influence in the northern province. It disappeared at the turn of the century.

'PROTESTANT TELEGRAPH'. Propagandist newspaper founded by Noel Doherty and Rev. Ian Paisley* on 13 February 1966. It attacked the Church of Ireland, Catholicism, Captain Terence O'Neill* and the governments of Northern Ireland.

PROVINCIAL COLLEGES ACT. *See* Queen's Colleges.

PROVISIONAL GOVERNMENT (16 January–6 December 1922). The Provisional Government was established under Article 17 of the Treaty* for the administration of the 'southern' twenty-six Counties of Ireland until the establishment of the Free State.* It was granted 'the powers and machinery requisite for the discharge of its duties provided that every member of such provisional government shall have signified in writing his or her acceptance of this instrument (the Treaty). But this arrangement shall not continue in force beyond the expiration of twelve months from the date hereof (6 December 1921)'.

The government which was formed on 14 January 1922 under the chairmanship of Michael Collins* formally received its authority from Viscount FitzAlan of Derwent* on 16 January; it held full power from 1 April. Membership of the Provisional Government overlapped with membership of the government of Dail Eireann which was not recognised by Britain. The Dail government was answerable to the Dail while the Provisional Government was not, and for this reason, and because every member of the Provisional Government had undertaken to uphold the Treaty, its authority was not recognised by republicans led by Eamon de Valera.* This led to some confusion, as the republicans only addressed their queries to ministers in their capacity as ministers in the Dail government and not in their capacity as ministers of the Provisional Government.

The first Provisional Government was as follows (with the office held in the Dail government in parentheses): Michael Collins, Chairman and Finance (Finance); Eamon Duggan, Home Affairs (Home Affairs); W. T. Cosgrave, Local Government (Local Government); Joseph McGrath, Industries (Industries); Kevin O'Higgins, Economic Affairs (Economic Affairs); Fionan Lynch, Education; Patrick Hogan, Agriculture (Agriculture); J. J. Walsh, Postmaster-General, from April 1922; Eoin MacNeill, Minister without Portfolio; Hugh Kennedy, Law Officer.

The activities of the Provisional Government were financed by two loans. The first was a loan from the Bank of Ireland of £1,000,000 and the second a loan from the British government of £500,000, given with an injunction not to spend the money all at once. In addition to its financial problems the Provisional Government had to finance the new National Army in the Civil War* which broke out in June 1922.

Before the outbreak of Civil War the Provisional Government had responsibility for drafting the Constitution of 1922* and for arranging the general election of that year. It was agreed in January that, in order to give the people an opportunity to hear arguments for and against the Treaty, an election would not be held for three months. The date finally agreed on was 16 June. In May an agreement or pact was reached between Collins and de Valera for which reason the June election became known as the Pact Election.* However, the Constitution was not published until the day of the election, two days after Collins had repudiated the pact. The election was a victory for the Provisional Government.

Following the deaths of Arthur Griffith* on 12 August and of Collins ten days later, William T. Cosgrave assumed office as President of Dail Eireann and Chairman of the Provisional Government, as well as Minister for Finance. His government, which took office in September, also became the government of the third Dail. It was: Kevin O'Higgins (Home Affairs); Desmond Fitzgerald (Foreign Affairs); Richard Mulcahy (National Defence); Ernest Blythe (Local Government); Joseph McGrath (Labour, Industry and Commerce, Economic Affairs); Eoin MacNeill (Education); Patrick Hogan (Agriculture); J. J. Walsh (Postmaster-General); Hugh Kennedy (Law Officer). When the Free State came into existence on 6 December 1922 the Provisional Government became its first government, known as the Executive Council.* *See also* Governments.

PROVISIONAL IRA. *See* Irish Republican Army.

PROVISIONAL SINN FEIN. *See* Sinn Fein.

PUBLIC HEALTH (IRELAND) ACT, 1878. *See* Local Government.

PUBLIC RECORD OFFICE (PROI). The Public Record Office of Ireland, housed at the Four Courts, Dublin, was established in 1867 by the historian John Thomas Gilbert.* It houses seven miles of records relating to life in Ireland since 1210. The material is available in a variety of forms, ranging from parchment rolls to microfilm. The records have been gathered from central and local government offices and to a lesser extent, from private sources.

PUBLIC SAFETY ACTS. A series of Public Safety Acts were introduced by the Cumann na nGaedheal government from 1923 until 1927 in response to the unsettled conditions in the country as a result of activity directed against the state by the Irish Republican Army.* The Acts of 1923, 1924 and 1926 were introduced by Kevin O'Higgins,* Minister for Justice (known as Home Affairs until 1924). The 1927 Act was introduced by the government following his assassination.

Although the Irregulars (the anti-Treaty section of the IRA) had surrendered in May 1923, bringing the Civil War* to an end, O'Higgins considered it necessary to introduce a Public Safety (Emergency Powers) Act later in the year. The Act authorised the Minister for Justice to continue internment and also granted him powers to arrest and detain anyone considered a danger to public safety. *Habeas corpus* had been suspended during the Civil War but when the Appeal Court granted an application of *habeas corpus* the government did not consider that the state of the country warranted the full restoration of legal rights. Under the Act, which became law on 1 August, *habeas corpus* was again suspended and applications for the release of internees refused.

The general state of lawlessness, which had been a feature of Ireland during the War of Independence and Civil War, continued during 1924. Between August 1923 and February 1924, there had been 738 cases of arson and armed robbery. A new Public Safety Act in 1924 renewed the Minister's powers of detention and arrest. It renewed the penalty of flogging along with imprisonment for arson and armed robberies. O'Higgins was also concerned at the increase in other forms of law-breaking. Some 7,000 decrees for £170,000 worth of debts remained to be enforced as payment of rents, taxes and other debts had virtually ceased during the struggle for independence. The new Public Safety Act gave in-creased powers to sheriffs engaged in recovery of debts. By the end of the year it was felt that the Acts of 1923 and 1924 had led to an improvement in conditions. Towards the end of the year, some 12,000 republicans, men and women, had been released from internment.

Towards the end of 1925 there was an upsurge of republican activity in protest at the shelving· of the Boundary Commission.* Republicans had looked to the Commission to help bring about unification of the country. They were bitterly disappointed when a Financial Agreement between the Free State government and the British and Northern Ireland governments ensured that the border would become permanent. In 1926, twelve Garda barracks were attacked and two unarmed gardai killed. The government reacted with another Public Safety Act which again suspended *habeas corpus* and gave the Minister new powers of detention.

For a number of reasons, O'Higgins was unpopular with republicans. He was noted as a strong champion of law and order and was the most closely associated with the Public Safety Acts. He was also regarded as unsympathetic to the republican cause. On 10 July 1927 he was assassinated while walking to Mass. The government introduced a new Public Safety Act which outlawed any organisation dedicated to the overthrow of the state or the use of arms. Severe penalties for membership of such an organisation were laid down and the authorities were granted extensive powers of search and detention. A special court could inflict the death penalty or life imprisonment for unlawful possession of arms. The Act remained in force until December 1928.

PURSER, SARAH (1849–1943). Portraitist and stained-glass artist; b. Kingstown (Dun Laoghaire); ed. Switzerland and Dublin School of Art. After studying in France for six months at M. Julien's Art School (1878), she set up her own studio at

2 Leinster Street and exhibited at the Royal Hibernian Academy* in 1880. Through her friendship with the Gore-Booths of Sligo she received many portrait commissions until, as she said, she had 'gone through the aristocracy like measles'. She was a close friend of George W. Russell,* John Yeats,* and his sons Jack Butler Yeats* and William Butler Yeats,* and Sir Hugh Lane.* With the encouragement and help of Edward Martyn,* she opened a studio at 24 Pembroke Street and established *An Túr Gloine* (The Tower of Glass) which became the centre of the stained glass revival in Ireland. Founder of the Friends of the National Collections of Ireland to secure the fulfillment of the 'Lane Bequest', she played a leading role in the establishment of the Municipal Gallery of Modern Art (1934).

A woman of extraordinary vitality, she was noted for her sharpness of wit and epigram. Her indefatigable spirit was shown when, at the age of eighty-nine, she persuaded her friend Oliver St John Gogarty* to take her for her first aeroplane ride so that she could determine the faults in the roof of her house. Towards the end of her life, she estimated that she had earned £50,000 from her paintings.

Q

QUAKERS' CENTRAL RELIEF COMMITTEE. Founded in Dublin on 13 November 1846 by a Committee which included James Hack Tuke* and Marcus Goodbody. The Committee established soup-kitchens, built and equipped a fishing station, established a fish-curing establishment at Castletown Berehaven, and hired a trawler to augment the local fishing vessels.

Collections were organised throughout Britain and America, £505,000 was subscribed and numerous foodships were despatched from the US through the good offices of the Society. The Committee continued its efforts until June 1849 when it gave up relief work and in a letter to Lord John Russell,* the British Prime Minister, it stated, 'In the opinion of the Central Relief Committeee . . . the condition of our country has not improved in spite of the great exertions made by charitable bodies, and could not be improved until the land system of Ireland was reformed, which was a matter for legislation, not philanthropy'.

QUARANTOTTI RESCRIPT. *See* Veto.

QUARTER-ACRE CLAUSE. Section 10 of the Poor Law Extension Act of 1847 became known as the 'Quarter-Acre Clause'. The extension was prompted by the Famine of 1845–49* and allowed for outdoor as well as indoor relief. The Clause stated that 'occupiers of more than a quarter of an acre of land are not to be deemed destitute, nor to be relieved out of the poor-rates'. This caused much hardship in Ireland where many of the peasantry were in a state of starvation but were aware that if they gave up their holding in order to secure relief the landlord would pull down their cabin. The Clause thus had the effect of forwarding the movement in Irish agriculture from small holding to larger and more economical units. *See also* Poor Law.

QUEEN'S COLLEGES. University colleges established under the Provincial Colleges Act (1845) introduced by Sir Robert Peel* in an attempt to meet the demand for a Catholic system of higher education. The three colleges, in Belfast, Cork and Galway, were linked in 1850 to form the Queen's University in Ireland. A sum of £100,000 was provided for construction and they were granted an annual endowment of £30,000. The Queen's University was the first state-built university in British history.

The non-denominational colleges were not allowed Chairs of Theology funded by the state, but a private person could establish and endow a Chair of Theology for the religious instruction of each denomination within the college walls. There were denominational halls of residence and Deans of Residence. Each college was administered by a Senate and a Visitorial Board. No professor or lecturer could interfere with the religious beliefs of his students.

From the beginning the colleges were bedevilled by controversy. Their non-denominational nature earned them the title of the 'godless colleges' and was denounced by Daniel O'Connell* and the Catholic Archbishop of Tuam, John MacHale.* Young Ireland,* however, gave them a warm welcome. At first the colleges had a measure of support from the Catholic hierarchy led by Dr Crolly of Armagh and Dr Daniel Murray* of Dublin. The fundamental quarrel with the colleges was that the state retained the right to employ and dismiss personnel in secular subjects but refused to allow the right to the bishops. The campaign intensified when Dr MacHale went to Rome in 1847 and influenced the issue of papal rescripts condemning the colleges in 1847 and 1848.

They were condemned as a 'grave danger to the faith of Catholics' and 'dangerous to faith and morals'. It was suggested that the bishops should establish their own Catholic University. MacHale sought dual professorships (Catholic and Protestant) of anatomy, history, philosophy, etc. This idea was greeted without enthusiasm. The death of Dr Crolly, followed shortly afterwards by that of Dr Murray, both of whom had tentatively accepted the colleges, left the field to opponents of the system. Dr Paul Cullen,* who succeeded Crolly in 1848, was hostile. The Synod of Thurles* issued a condemnation in 1850 and this was followed a year later by another denunciation from Rome. Archbishop MacHale condemned them as an attempt to 'bribe Catholic youth into an abandonment of their religion', and the Bishop of Clonfert refused the sacraments to parents who allowed their children to enter the colleges.

In spite of this formidable opposition the colleges survived, although neither Cork nor Galway received more than a few hundred students. Belfast was the most successful of the three. Cardinal Cullen's attempt to establish a Catholic University was a failure and the demand for acceptable facilities for Catholic higher education continued until the establishment of the National University of Ireland.* This absorbed the Cork and Galway colleges, while the Queen's College in Belfast became the Queen's University of Belfast.

QUEEN'S COUNTY (LEIX OR LAOIS). Title for the territory of modern Co. Laois, so-named by English planters in honour of Queen Mary (reigned 1553–58) during the Plantation of Laois and Offaly. The official title of Queen's County was replaced by Laois upon the establishment of the Free State in 1922 when the administrative centre, Maryborough, was re-named Portloaise.

QUEEN'S UNIVERSITY IN IRELAND. *See* Queen's Colleges.

R

RADIO NA GAELTACHTA. A radio station established in 1972 to cater for the needs of the Irish-speaking communities within the gaeltachtai* in counties Donegal, Galway and Kerry. A service within Radio Telefis Eireann,* Radio na Gaeltachta first began transmission on 2 April 1972.

RADIO TELEFIS EIREANN (RTE). The national broadcasting service began transmission as Radio 2RN (the call-sign designated by London, phonetically reproducing the last words of the line 'Come back to Eireann'). The station was opened by Dr Douglas Hyde* at 7.45 p.m. on 1 January 1926. The first director was Seamus Clandillon* who held the post until 1935, when he was succeeded by Dr T. J. Kiernan; the first announcer was Seamus Hughes and the first musical director, Dr Vincent O'Brien. The name of the service was changed to Radio Eireann in 1932. The radio station moved to its studios at the General Post Office, Henry Street, Dublin, in 1928 and remained there until 1974 when it was moved to the new radio centre in Donnybrook, Dublin.

Five thousand radio licences were sold in 1926 but official estimates claimed that there were five times as many receivers. The figure rose to over 33,000 licences in 1933, 100,000 in 1937, and 500,000 in 1961. In 1978 the radio claimed 1,412,000 listeners (69 per cent). The Radio Eireann Players, a repertory company, was established by Riobeárd Ó Farachain in 1947. The Players gave their first stage performance as a company in October 1978.

The national television service was inaugurated on 1 January 1961 from studios at Montrose, Donnybrook. The title of the complete service was changed to Radio Telefis Eireann under the Broadcasting Authority (Amendment) Act, 1966. The second television channel, RTE 2, began transmission on 2 November 1978. Both the radio and television channels derive their support from licence fees and advertising revenue. A second radio channel opened in 1979.

RAFTERY, ANTHONY (c. 1784–1835). Poet; b. Kiltimagh, Co. Mayo. Blinded by smallpox as a child, he became a wandering bard, travelling throughout Mayo and Galway where he was known as 'The Kiltimagh Fiddler'. Although he was regarded as a poor musician, his songs, composed in the folk idiom, were popular among the peasantry and are still remembered in Irish-speaking parts of Connaught. His work was collected and published by Dr Douglas Hyde* as *Abhráin agus Dánta an Reachtabhraigh* (1933).

RAILWAYS IN IRELAND. The first railway to be authorised in Ireland was the Limerick and Waterford which obtained parliamentary approval in 1826. In 1834 the six-mile long Dublin and Kingstown was the first railway to be opened in Ireland. This was followed by the first sections of the Ulster Railway in 1839 and the Dublin and Drogheda in 1844. Intense railway speculation occured in 1835–36 and 1845–46 which paralleled the railway 'manias' in Britain. The speculation of the 1840s produced the principal trunk routes in the country. Dublin was linked with Cork in 1849, Galway in 1851 and Belfast in 1853.

By 1900 the main railway companies in the north of the country were the Great Northern Railway, the Belfast and Northern Counties and the Belfast and County Down. In the south of the country the main companies were the Great Southern and Western, the Midland Great Western and the Dublin and South Eastern. In 1922, when the Irish railway system had reached its greatest extent, there were 3,454 route miles of railway in the country, of which 2,896 miles were built to the Irish standard gauge of 5 feet 3 inches.

Following the establishment of the Free State* in 1922 the railways in the south were encouraged by the government to amalgamate. This resulted in the formation of the Great Southern Railway in 1925. The GNR, whose lines straddled the border between the Free State and Northern Ireland, continued its independent existence, as did the railway companies in Northern Ireland. In 1946 the railways in the south were nationalised and became part of Coras Iompar Eireann.* In the late 1940s parts of the BNCR and the B&CDR were taken over by the Belfast government to form part of the Ulster Transport Authority. By the early 1950s, the GNR was in severe financial difficulties and from 1952 to 1958 it was managed by a board with nominees from both governments. In 1958 this arrangement was ended and the company's assets were shared equally between the UTA and CIE.

Severe competition from road transport affected the traffic and profitability of Irish railways from the 1920s. Despite a revival during World War II, falling business resulted in widespread closures in the 1950s and 1960s. The 1970s, however, saw a revival of interest in railways and the authorities both north and south provided much-needed investment in rolling stock, track and facilities.

In addition to standard-gauge railways, Ireland once possessed an extensive network of narrow-gauge railways, mainly in rural areas. The principal narrow-gauge systems were in the counties of Donegal, Antrim, Cavan, Leitrim, Cork and Clare. The most celebrated narrow-gauge company was the West and South Clare. The West Clare was incorporated in 1884 and opened in 1887, running from Ennis to Miltown Malbay. The South Clare was incorporated in 1884 as an extension of the West Clare. It opened in 1892 and ran

from Miltown Malbay to Kilrush and Kilkee. Both lines operated as one system, with a total of fifty-three miles of track. It was the subject of a popular song, 'Are ye right there Michael' (1902) which led the company to take a libel action against the writer, Percy French.*

Most narrow-gauge lines were built to a gauge of three feet at the end of the nineteenth century and in the early twentieth century. Their construction was often encouraged by government financial assistance. The narrow-gauge lines were early victims of road competition and all had been closed by 1961.

RALAHINE AGRICULTURAL AND MANUFACTURING CO-OPERATIVE ASSOCIATION. Pioneering co-operative society founded in 1831 on the estate of John Scott Vandeleur at Ralahine, Co. Clare. Hoping to wean his tenantry away from the agrarian secret societies, the Lady Clares* and the Ribbonmen,* he brought Thomas Craig from England to advise on the establishment of the commune, which came into existence on 7 November 1831. The purpose of the commune was to acquire common capital and the mutual assurance of members 'against the evils of poverty, sickness, infirmity and old age, the attainments of a greater share of the comforts of life than the working class now possess, the mental and moral improvement of its adult members and the education of their children'.

The commune, consisting of twenty-one single adult men, seven married men and their wives, five single women, four orphan boys, three orphan girls and five infants under the age of nine (fifty-two persons in all), operated an estate of 618 acres. It was governed by a committee of nine, elected twice a year. Under an agreement between Vandeleur and the commune, the estate and property were to remain his at a rent of £700 per annum, until the co-operative could acquire the capital to purchase it. The commune was also paid £200 per annum for stock and equipment.

The Ralahine Co-Operative lasted only two years. It collapsed as a result of Vandeleur's reckless life; he was a noted gambler and fled the country after a losing streak. His creditors, refusing to recognise the commune, seized the estate. The experiment had attracted international attention. Craig's *History of Ralahine* was translated into several continental languages.

RATHCORMAC, CO. CORK. *See* Tithes.

RECESS COMMITTEE. Established in 1895 upon the proposal of Sir Horace Plunkett,* it was so called because its meetings were held during parliamentary recess. Its purpose was to consider the means by which Irish farmers could best be served and the manner in which suitable legislation could be achieved to assist them. The Committee's meetings during the session 1895–96 were attended by representatives of the Parnellite section of the Irish Parliamentary Party* under John Redmond,* by Unionists and by Liberal-Unionists. It was boycotted by the anti-Parnellites. The Committee's Report favoured assistance for Irish agriculture and recommended the creation of conditions which would allow farmers to help themselves once the administration and finance had been provided. Its recommendation also led to the establishment of the Department of Agriculture and Technical Instruction* in 1899.

REDINGTON, SIR THOMAS NICHOLAS (1815–62). Politician (Liberal); Under Secretary (1846–52); b. Oranmore, Co. Louth; ed. Oscott and Cambridge. He was MP for Dundalk (1837–46). The first Catholic to hold the post of Under Secretary, he incurred the hostility of both sides in his attempts to steer a neutral course between the Orange Order* and Catholic organisations. He held the post throughout the Famine of 1845–49* when the Irish administration was unable to cope with a disaster of such magnitude.

REDMOND, JOHN (1856–1918). Politician (Irish Parliamentary Party) b. Ballytrant, Co. Wexford; ed. Clongowes Wood College and TCD. Through the influence of his father, an MP, he was appointed to a clerkship in the House of Commons until returned as MP for New Ross (1881–85). An able speaker, he quickly established himself within the party and the National League* as a principal lieutenant of Charles Stewart Parnell.* During 1883–84, he toured Australia and the USA with his brother, William Redmond,* collecting £30,000. Having read law at Gray's Inn, he was called to the English Bar in 1885 and to the Irish Bar two years later, although he never practised. He sat as MP for North Wexford from 1885 until 1891.

Redmond was the leader of the minority which supported Parnell during the split of 1890. Sitting as MP for Waterford (1891–1918) he led the Parnellite remnant of the party, which had nine members in January 1892. He sat on the Recess Committee* and retained his contact with influential Irish-Americans, visiting the USA in 1895 and 1899.

When the rise of the United Irish League* led to the reunification of the Irish party in 1900 he was accepted as leader. His leadership of the party was not absolute and he was unable to retain the support of some of the old anti-Parnellites, notably William O'Brien* and T. M. Healy,* and their small band of followers. However, he continued to press for concessions for Ireland until the time came to raise the question of Home Rule. This opportunity came in 1910 when, after two general elections, H. H. Asquith* and the Liberals needed Irish support to secure the Parliament Act of 1911.* Redmond's support was won in return for the (third) Home Rule Bill,* introduced in 1912.

Opposition to Home Rule from the Ulster Unionist Party* led by Sir Edward Carson* constituted a serious threat. Redmond rejected partition as did the Unionists. Unionists were prepared finally to accept a measure of permanent exclusion from Home Rule but Redmond would concede nothing more than temporary exclusion.

By the summer of 1914, with Home Rule due to become law in September, Redmond was worried that hasty action by the Irish Volunteers might cause tension to increase. He confronted Volunteer leaders in June 1914 with a demand for half of the seats on the ruling committee. This was resisted by the Irish Republican Brotherhood but conceded by Eoin MacNeill, Bulmer Hobson and Colonel Maurice Moore.

Redmond and his chief lieutenant, John Dillon,* represented the Irish Party at the abortive Buckingham Palace Conference* in July. The Unionists were now prepared to settle for the exclusion of the six north-eastern counties from Home Rule. Redmond, however, wanted no partition, although early in 1914 he had reluctantly agreed to temporary exclusion. This situation was still unresolved when war broke out in August. In September, prior to its passage, Asquith incorporated two emergency provisos into the Act. The first was that Home Rule should not come into operation until parliament had an opportunity to make special provision for Ulster, and the second suspended the Act for the duration of the war. Redmond had secured Home Rule and was inundated with congratulatory messages from Ireland and abroad.

He offered the services of the Irish Volunteers for internal defence, but this was rejected by Asquith. In September, speaking at Woodenbridge, he called on the Volunteers to assist Britain by joining the British Army. Militant nationalists reacted angrily but the vast majority of the Volunteers answered his call. The minority, dominated by the IRB, retained the title Irish Volunteers and Redmond's followers became known as the National Volunteers.*

Redmond's description of the Easter Rising of 1916* as a 'German intrigue' was indicative of the extent to which he was out of touch with the nationalist Ireland of a new generation. His pleas, added to those of John Dillon, that the rebels should be treated leniently were ignored. Sinn Fein,* now his strongest opponents, re-organised during 1917 and became a mass movement under Eamon de Valera.* The new Prime Minister, David Lloyd George,* accepted Redmond's suggestion for an Irish Convention* to resolve the problem of Home Rule. Redmond died in March 1918, during the Convention at which he represented his party. Later that year, in the general election of December, his party was annihilated at the polls by Sinn Fein.

REDMOND, CAPTAIN WILLIAM ARCHER (1886–1932). Soldier and politician (Nationalist); b. Waterford, eldest son of John Redmond;* ed. Clongowes Wood and TCD. Called to the Bar (1910) he was MP for Tyrone (1910–18). During World War I, he served in the Irish Guards and was awarded the DSO (1917). He sat as MP for Waterford from 1918 until 1922 when he entered Dail Eireann as an independent, and founded the National League Party* in 1926. His party secured eight seats in the general election of June 1927 after which he committed the party's support to Fianna Fail* and Labour in the vote on the motion of no confidence in the Cosgrave administration. The motion was defeated due to the absence of Redmond's supporter, Alderman John Jinks (*see* Jinks Affair). His party was reduced to two after the general election of September 1927 and he joined Cumann na nGaedheal* in 1931.

REDMOND, WILLIAM HOEY KEARNEY (1861–1917). Politician (Irish Parliamentary Party); b. Wexford, younger brother of John Redmond;* ed. Clongowes Wood College. He was MP for Wexford (1883–85), Fermanagh (1885–92), and East Clare (1892–1917). Redmond and his brother John were involved in several fund-raising trips on behalf of the party, including a visit to Australia and the USA in 1883 when they raised £30,000. He accompanied Joseph Devlin* to the USA (February–June 1902) when they met President Theodore Roosevelt and established 200 branches of the United Irish League,* and was in Australia and the USA again in 1905. He supported his brother in accepting the leadership of Charles Stewart Parnell* after the split in the party. When he was refused a commission in the British Army in 1914 he enlisted as a private and rose to the rank of major before he was killed in action. A collection of articles which he contributed from the Western Front to the London *Chronicle* was published posthumously. He was also the author of *A Shooting Trip in the Australian Bush* (1898) and *The New Commonwealth*. His seat in East Clare was won by Eamon de Valera* in 1917.

REEVES, WILLIAM (1815–92). Bishop of Down, Connor and Dromore (C.I.); antiquarian; b. Charleville, Co. Cork; ed. TCD. Ordained in 1839, he became perpetual curate of Kilconriola, Co. Antrim before appointment to the bishopric. Apart from his articles of antiquarian interest which he contributed to a variety of learned journals, he was the author of *Ecclesiastical Antiquities of Down, Connor and Dromore* (1847), an edition of *Acts of Archbishop Colton* (1857) and *Life of St Columba* (1857).

REGIONAL TECHNICAL COLLEGES. *See* Commission on Higher Education.

REGISTRAR-GENERAL. The office of Registrar-General was created in 1845. The duties were extended by an act of 1863 to include:

1. The registration of births, deaths, marriages and successful vaccinations;

2. The compilation of emigration statistics, and the preparation of an annual report on the criminal and judicial statistics, and

3. The superintendence of the decennial census, for which a special commission was appointed of which the Registrar-General was chairman.

REGIUM DONUM. Sum payable to the Presbyterian Church in Ireland. It was introduced during the reign of Charles II in the amount of £600 per annum. After an increase in the amount by William III to £1,200 per annum, it was discontinued for a short time and then renewed in 1718 at the rate of £2,000 per annum. Under the terms of the Union it became a charge on the exchequer of the United Kingdom and in 1802 was paid directly to Presbyterian ministers at the rate of between £50 and £100 each per annum. Upon the Disestablishment of the Church of Ireland* it was abolished and the Presbyterian Church received a capital sum of £770,000 as compensation.

REILLY, THOMAS DEVIN (1824–54). Young Irelander and journalist; b. Monaghan; ed. TCD. Influenced by Charles Gavan Duffy,* he contributed to *The Nation** and was a prominent member of Young Ireland.* He supported the extremist policy of John Mitchel,* for whom he worked on *The United Irishman.** Following Mitchel's transportation he co-founded *The Irish Felon* with John Martin.* Reilly escaped while on bail in May 1848 and went to the USA where he worked as a journalist, editing *The Democratic Review*, and contributing to *The American Review, The People, The Whig Review* and the *Boston Protective Union*. His journalism reflected his aim of fomenting ill-will between America and Great Britain.

RELAPSING FEVER. Highly contagious disease endemic amongst the famine-stricken people during the Famine of 1845–49.* The crowded conditions of workhouses, public-works and soup-kitchens, and the severe winter of 1846–47, which caused people to huddle together for warmth, spread the disease-transmitting lice, exacting a high toll among a starving populace.

REMOVAL OF OATH ACT, 1933. The Constitution (Removal of Oath) Bill was introduced to the Dail by Eamon de Valera* on 20 April 1932. The purpose of the Bill was to amend the Constitution of 1922* through the removal of the Oath of Allegiance.* The Bill passed the Dail without amendment on 19 May but was rejected by the Senate where it met a particularly strong opposition from a leading lawyer, Senator Samuel Lombard Brown. The Senate sought to secure a clause to the effect that the Act would not come into force until an agreement was reached between the Free State and Britain providing that Article 4 of the Treaty should cease to have effect, and that this would be ratified by Dail Eireann. De Valera refused to consider this and the Bill waited to pass into law when the suspension period was up (18 November). In the interim de Valera called a general election and the Act came into force on 3 May 1933.

RENEHAN, REV. LAURENCE (1797–1857). Clergyman (R.C.) and scholar; b. Tipperary; ed. Kilkenny and Maynooth of which he was president (1845–57). He contributed many articles to literary and religious journals. His monument is a manuscript containing nearly 100 volumes on Irish ecclesiastical history. It was published in part as *Collection on Irish Church History* (1861) by Dr McCarthy, Bishop of Kerry.

REPEAL ASSOCIATION. The Association was founded by Daniel O'Connell* on 15 April 1840 to centralise his campaign in the bid for Repeal of the Union between Great Britain and Ireland and to establish a separate legislature in Dublin. Between 1835 and 1840 he had led the Repeal MPs in an alliance with the Whigs but achieved only moderate reform. By 1840, when it was obvious that the Whigs, then led by Lord Melbourne,* would shortly lose power, he withdrew from the House of Commons to carry the fight for Repeal to the country on the lines of the earlier Catholic Association* which had won Catholic Emancipation* through popular agitation in 1829.

The organisation of the Repeal Association was overseen by his son, John O'Connell,* the treasurer, Patrick Vincent Fitzpatrick,* and Thomas Steele.* A membership card was designed by the military historian, John Cornelius O'Callaghan.* Membership was divided into three classes: volunteers, who were life-members for a subscription of £10, ordinary members, who paid £1 per year and associates who paid one shilling (5p) per year. To finance Repeal he called for a Repeal Rent based on the highly successful Catholic Rent of the earlier agitation. Throughout Ireland 'Repeal Reading Rooms' were opened for free reading of books published by James Duffy* on Irish history, literature, art and music. The agitation was also supported by *The Pilot,* * Young Ireland and its organ, *The Nation.* *

Within two years Repeal was a popular cause. Its popularity was reflected by its revenues; by 1843 a total of £48,000 had been subscribed and in that year, the 'O'Connell Tribute' yielded £20,000. The staff at the Association headquarters, Conciliation Hall in Dublin, increased from seven clerks (1841) to forty-eight (1843). Throughout the country, thousands of voluntary workers, including many priests, worked for the cause. They organised the monster meetings, usually held on historic sites, where O'Connell addressed his followers.

However, the Repeal agitation differed from the earlier fight for Emancipation in two respects: Repeal did not have the backing of the Catholic hierarchy and priests who participated did not have official support; furthermore, Repeal did not have the support in England which Emancipation had had. Whigs, radicals and some conservatives, who had supported Emancipation on principle, did not support the breaking of the Union. In Ireland Emancipation had had support from Protestants but they would not support Repeal. As a consequence, support for Repeal was more homogenous and therefore easier for the government to handle.

Although Young Ireland* had thrown its support behind Repeal there were obvious tensions. O'Connell was now an old man, distrusted by the extremist elements of Young Ireland led by John Mitchel* and Thomas Francis Meagher.* They came to believe that if O'Connell's constitutionalism failed, then other methods should be used. However, the government's reaction, to remove from office anyone sympathetic to the movement, helped to secure temporary support for O'Connell from moderates led by William Smith O'Brien.*

O'Connell staked everything on 1843 being the Year of Repeal. The size of his audiences increased as his followers became convinced that Repeal was imminent. For his final meeting of the year he chose Clontarf for 8 October. The government proscribed the meeting and threatened to use gunboats if he proceeded with it. At the last moment, with hordes of people already making their way to Clontarf, he submitted and cancelled it. Shortly afterwards he was put on trial for conspiracy after he had called for delegates to attend the Council of Three Hundred* in Dublin. By the time he was released from prison, by order of the House of Lords in 1844, he was weakened both mentally and physically. Control of the Association fell completely to his son John, a man noted for his lack of intelligence and tact.

Divisions within the Association had arisen by 1845. A particularly strong dispute developed between O'Connell and Young Ireland over the Queen's Colleges.* At the same time the potato crop failed, and the tragedy of the Famine of 1845—49* struck. The breach between the Young Ireland radicals and the O'Connellites became complete in 1846 when John O'Connell, on his father's behalf, proposed a motion demanding a declaration that physical force could never be justified. Mitchel, Meagher and O'Brien broke with the Association.

O'Connell died in 1847. His son quickly alienated even some of the Association's staunchest supporters and it was soon dissolved. The legacy of Repeal remained, to be resurrected in the 1870s in the form of Home Rule.*

REPRESENTATIVE CHURCH BODY. Established after the Disestablishment of the Church of Ireland,* which came into effect in January 1871. Its purpose was to take over the churches and burial grounds in actual use and to oversee the distribution of the finances available to the Church of Ireland as a result of the disendowment which accompanied disestablishment.

REPUBLIC OF IRELAND ACT, 1948. Introduced by the first Inter-Party Government,* it repealed the External Relations Act* and declared that 'the description of the State shall be the Republic of Ireland'. The British government reacted by passing the Ireland Act.* The Republic of Ireland formally came into existence on Easter Monday, 1949.

REPUBLICAN CONGRESS. Socialist-republican movement founded in 1934 from Saor Eire,* following a split in the Irish Republican Army* in March. The Congress, led by Peadar O'Donnell,* George Gilmore* and

Frank Ryan,* sought the destruction of the 'ranch' farmers and the establishment of a workers' republic on the lines advocated by James Connolly,* whose daughter, Nora Connolly-O'Brien, was a member. In the 'Athlone Manifesto', issued on 8 April 1934, the Congress declared: 'We believe that a Republic or a united Ireland will never be achieved except through a struggle which uproots capitalism on its way. We cannot conceive of a free Ireland with a subject working class; we cannot conceive of a subject Ireland with a free working class'. The official newspaper, *Republican Congress,* was edited by the three leaders. The Congress was short lived, and faced bitter opposition from the orthodox IRA. When the Congress attempted to participate in the Wolfe Tone commemoration at Bodenstown on 17 June, there was a confrontation between the two groups. The Congress was itself divided between those who sought the immediate establishment of a workers' republic and those who wished to wait for a more opportune moment. The Congress split in October 1934 and was dissolved in 1935.

REPUBLICAN LABOUR PARTY. Founded by Harry Diamond in Belfast in 1953 as a splinter of the Labour Party.* Diamond was succeeded in the leadership in 1962 by Gerry Fitt.* Fitt led it until 1970 when he became a co-founder of the Social Democratic and Labour Party,* and was expelled from the RLP which fell apart shortly afterwards. It was always numerically weak and, apart from its opposition to partition, lacked any real policy. Its only electoral successes were in local government when members were returned to the Belfast Corporation, and in having Diamond and Paddy Kennedy returned to Stormont and Fitt returned to Westminster and Stormont.

REPUBLICANISM. *See* Irish Republican Brotherhood.

RESIDENT MAGISTRATES. The first resident magistrates were appointed under an Act of 1814. The position was open to barristers of at least six years' standing and each RM had at his disposal a Chief Constable and fifty sub-constables for deployment in any area proclaimed by the Lord Lieutenant as disturbed. Resident magistrates were also appointed after the reorganisation of the police system by Thomas Drummond* in 1836 (*see* Police). They replaced the Stipendiary Magistrates* and were appointed to each administrative district, generally on the basis of legal or administrative experience in the police or the army. The RM's reports formed a vital part of the intelligence network which kept Dublin Castle* in touch with the mood of the provinces. During periods of emergency, such as the Land War, 1879–82, 'Special' Resident Magistrates were appointed for the duration of the disturbance.

RESIGNED AND DISMISSED MEMBERS OF THE RIC AND DMP (1916–22). *See* Royal Irish Constabulary.

RESTORATION OF ORDER IN IRELAND ACT, 1920. Emergency legislation introduced during the War of Independence.* When it became law on 9 August 1920, it extended the terms of the Defence of the Realm Act (DORA)* and empowered the Commander-in-Chief, General Sir Nevil Macready,* to arrest and hold without trial anyone suspected of membership of Sinn Fein* or the Irish Republican Army.* Suspects could be tried by a secret court-martial and only a lawyer appointed by the Crown could be present for a charge involving the death penalty. Under the Act, coroner's inquests were suppressed (already in thirty-three cases coroners' inquests had indicted either the military or the police for murder). The Act led to increased activity by Auxiliaries* and Black and Tans.*

'RESURGENCE'. Newspaper published by a splinter group of the Irish Republican Army* in 1946. Suspicious of Clann na Poblachta* and the entry of republicans into orthodox politics, the newspaper first appeared in June but had ceased publication by December.

'RESURRECTION OF HUNGARY'. Series of twenty-seven articles by Arthur Griffith* which appeared in *The United Irishman* in 1904 and were published in book form later that year. Griffith first put forward the parallel between Ireland and Hungary at a convention of Cumann na nGaedheal* on 26 November 1902. He suggested that Irish MPs should withdraw from Westminster and together with representatives of the local authorities form a legislative assembly in Dublin, to be known as the Council of Three Hundred.* This was borrowed from Lajos Kossuth (1802–94) and the Hungarian nationalists who withdrew from the Austrian imperial parliament to form their own assembly in Budapest, an action which resulted in the Dual Monarchy of 1867 (the *Augsleich*). Griffith's concept of a 'Dual Monarchy' for Ireland and the rest of the United Kingdom had some support in Sinn Fein.*

REVOLUTIONARY WORKERS' GROUPS. Marxist groups founded in Dublin and Belfast during the economic depression (1929–30). They attempted to organise the unemployed. One of the leaders, James Larkin, Jnr,* edited their newspaper, *The Worker's Voice,* from August 1930. The groups were outlawed by the Cumann na nGaedheal government on 17 October 1931, along with other radical organisations, including Saor Eire.* Larkin was returned in the local elections, in the groups' interest, but failed to gain a seat in the general election of 1932. The Belfast branches of the RWG brought Catholic and Protestant workers together during 1932 under the leadership of Tommy Geehan.

Dublin members of the RWG were attacked by Catholic groups (*see* Great Strand Street, Siege of). They were also subjected to intimidation by Blueshirts.* At a convention in June 1932 the groups adopted a manifesto, 'Ireland's Path to Freedom'. A year later they helped to reestablish the Communist Party of Ireland.*

RIBBONMEN. Local groups which were part of an underground of agrarian secret societies known as the 'Ribbon Societies'. Members were known as 'Ribbonmen' in the nineteenth century as they had been known as 'Whiteboys' in the previous century. The first Ribbon Society appeared in 1826. Ribbonmen attempted to prevent exploitation of tenant-farmers and protested at payment of Tithes* and of high dues to the Catholic clergy. Their methods included intimidation by threatening violence, maiming cattle, burning crops and murder. Ribbonism was strongest in counties Roscommon, Queen's County (Laois), Kilkenny, Monaghan, Tipperary and Limerick, where farmers and agricultural labourers were at odds over conacre* and potato prices. As a rule the societies were most active during the winter. The following is a typical 'Ribbon Notice', dated 23 May 1851:

To Landlords, Agents, Bailiffs, Grippers, process-servers, and usurpers, or underminers who wish to step into the evicted tenants' property, and to all others concerned in Tyranny and Oppression of the Poor on the Bath Estate.
TAKE NOTICE
That you are hereby (under pain of a certain punishment which will inevitably occur), prohibited from evicting tenants, executing decrees, serving process, distraining for rent, or going into another's land, or to assist any tyrant, Landlord or Agent in his insatiable desire for depopulation. Recollect the fate of Mauleverer, on this his anniversary.

RICE, EDMUND IGNATIUS (1762–1844). Educationalist and philanthropist; founder of the Irish Christian Brothers;* b. Callan, Co. Kilkenny; ed. hedge-school, after which he spent two years at a Kilkenny boarding school. A businessman, he moved to Waterford following his wife's death shortly after the birth of their daughter, and joined his uncle's exporting business. He spent much of his personal fortune on the sick and the poor, and paying the debts of the imprisoned to secure their release. Distressed at the lack of educational facilities for the poor in Waterford, he established a school at Mount Sion (1802–03) in a converted stable. He befriended Charles Bianconi* to whom he taught English. He soon established other schools, in Clonmel (1806), Dungarvan (1806) and Cork (1811). Having taken religious vows along with eight others in 1808, he secured papal recognition for the Religious Brothers of Christian Schools in Ireland from Pius VII in 1820. Two years later he was elected superior-general of the new Order and occupied the position until his retirement in 1838. He continued to visit the Order's schools until old age prevented his leaving Mount Sion. The case for his beatification was opened in 1863.

RICHMOND COMMISSION. Appointed by Benjamin Disraeli* in August 1879, under the chairmanship of the Duke of Richmond, to investigate agricultural conditions in Great Britain and Ireland during the depression of the late 1870s. The preliminary report dealt mainly with Ireland. Like the Bessborough Commission* which issued its report a few weeks before Richmond (January 1881), the Richmond Report indicated that the Land Act of 1870 had been a failure (*see* Land Acts). The Commission also found that Irish tenants were in great misery and as a consequence there was widespread unrest throughout the country. The Richmond Commission isolated what it considered to be the cause of the Land War* of 1879–82. Some of the factors which it cited were the inclemency of the seasons and the consequent failure of the potato crop, foreign competition, and excessive competition for land which led to an arbitrary increase of rents, overcrowding in some areas and the subdivision of land. The commissioners recommended migration and emigration as a solution. A minority report, drafted by Lord Carlingford (*see* Fortescue-Parkinson, Chichester) recommended the legalisation of the Three Fs or Ulster Custom,* stating that there was no other solution to the problem.

ROANTREE, WILLIAM FRANCIS (1829–1918). Fenian; b. Leixlip, Co. Kildare. After emigrating to the USA he joined the navy and later served in the army in Nicaragua. Returning to Ireland in 1861, he became a principal organiser in the Irish Republican Brotherhood.* His centre around Leixlip became one of the biggest in Ireland (2,000 members). He replaced Patrick 'Pagan' O'Leary* as a Fenian recruiter, until his arrest in September 1865 when he was sentenced to ten years' imprisonment. As a result of agitation by the Amnesty Association* he was released along with John Devoy* and Jeremiah O'Donovan Rossa* whom he accompanied to the US where he settled as a commercial traveller in Philadelphia. He returned to Ireland in 1900 and worked for the Dublin Corporation.

ROBB, JOHN HANNA (1873–1956). Politician (Ulster Unionist); b. Clogher, Co. Tyrone; ed. Royal Belfast Academical Institute, Queen's College, Belfast, Gray's Inn and King's Inns. Called to the Bar in 1898, MP for Queen's University (1921–37), he was Parliamentary Secretary to the Minister for Education (1925–37), and Minister for Education and Leader of the Senate of Northern Ireland (1937–43). He was

Father of the Northern Ireland Bar (1939–43) and a County Court Judge in Armagh and Fermanagh (1943–54). He was the author of *The Law and Practice of Bankruptcy and arrangement in Ireland* (1907).

ROBINSON, ESMÉ STUART LENNOX (1886–1958). Dramatist; b. Cork; ed. Bandon Grammar School. A leading member of the so-called Cork 'School of Realists' – which included T. C. Murray* and challenge'd the peasant drama which had such a firm hold in Ireland during the 1920s – he was manager of the Abbey Theatre* (1910–23) where he also directed. His works include *The Clancy Name* (1908), *The Cross-Roads* (1909), *The Dreamers* (1915), *The Lost Leader* (1918), *The White Blackbird* (1925), and *The Far-Off Hills* (1928). Other works include *The Irish Theatre* (1939), *Curtain Up* (reminiscences, 1942) and *Ireland's Abbey Theatre 1899–1950* (1951). In addition, he edited *A Little Anthology of Modern Irish Verse* (1929), the *Journals* of Augusta, Lady Gregory (1946) and *The Oxford Book of Irish Verse* (with Donogh MacDonagh, 1956).

RODEN, 3rd EARL (1788–1880). Jocelyn, Robert; landowner and politician (Conservative). Jocelyn, who succeeded to the title in 1820, was the owner of an extensive estate at Tullymore Park, Castlewellan, Co. Down, and MP for Dundalk (1810–20). A prominent supporter of Protestant organisations, including the Hibernian Bible Society, the Sunday School Society, the Evangelical Alliance and the Protestant Orphans' Society, he was active in the Orange Order* of which he was Grand Master. The affray at Dolly's Brae* on 12 July 1849 occurred when Orangemen were returning from his home. Following censure by a Commission of Inquiry he was deprived of his office as a Commissioner of the Peace.

ROLLESTON, THOMAS WILLIAM (1857–1920). Scholar; b. Shinrone, King's County (Offaly); ed. St Columba's College and TCD. After living in Germany (1879–83), he returned to Ireland and edited the *Dublin University Review* (1885–86) and was a co-editor of the New Irish Library* (1893). He was honorary secretary of the Irish Literary Society* in London (1892–93), Taylorean Lecturer at Oxford (1892), and managing director and secretary of the Irish Industries Association (1894–97). After working as leader-writer on the Dublin *Daily Express* and the *Daily Chronicle* (1898–1900), he was organiser of lectures for the Department of Agriculture and Technical Instruction (1900–05), organiser of the Irish Historic Collection at the St Louis Exhibition (1904) and honorary secretary of the Irish Arts and Crafts Society (1898–1908). He settled in London in 1908. Apart from contributions to periodicals and journals and translations from the German, Greek and Irish, he was the author of *The Teaching of Epictetus* (1888), *Life of Lessing* (1889), *Treasury of Irish Poetry* (with his father-in-law, Stopford Brooke, 1900), *Imagination and Art in Gaelic Literature* (1900), *Parallel Paths: A Study in Biology, Ethics and Art* (1908), *Sea Spray* (poetry, 1909), *The High Deeds of Finn* (1910) and *Myths and Legends of the Celtic Race* (1911).

ROONEY, WILLIAM (1873–1901). Journalist and language revivalist; b. Dublin; ed. locally. He contributed to many Dublin periodicals during the 1890s and played an active role in the attempt to revive the Irish language (*see* Gaelic League). Despite his delicate health, he travelled throughout the country, often by night, sometimes to work with only a handful of students. Rooney deeply influenced the thinking of Arthur Griffith* with whom he founded *The United Irishman** and Cumann na nGaedheal.* He attacked Home

Rule* as not being sufficient to make Ireland 'a nation'.

ROS, AMANDA McKITTRICK (1860–1939). Author and eccentric; b. near Ballinahinch, Co. Down. After qualifying in Dublin as a teacher she married and then returned to Larne, in Co. Antrim. Her novels, written in a distinctive style, generally dealt with romantic themes. Described by one critic as the 'world's worst novelist', she possessed a vitriolic line in invective which she deployed against critics and lawyers. Her first novel was *Irene Iddesleigh* (1897); another, *Helen Huddleston,* contained such characters as Sir Christopher Currant, Sir Peter Plum, Madame Pear, Mrs Strawberry, Lilly Lentil and the Duke of Greengage.

ROSS, SIR JOHN (1854–1935). Lawyer and politician (Liberal); b. Co. Laois; ed. Derry City and TCD. After a call to the Bar in 1879 he became a QC in 1891. He was MP for Derry (1892–95). A judge in Chancery (1896–1921), he was Commissioner of Charitable Endowments and Bequests (1898) and a Privy Councillor (1919). He was the last Lord Chancellor of Ireland (1921–22). His publications included *The Years of My Pilgrimage* (1924), *Pilgrim Script* (1927) and *Essays and Addresses* (1930).

ROSSE, 3rd EARL (1800–67). Parsons, William; scientist and politician (Conservative); b. York; ed. Parsonstown (Birr), King's County (Offaly) where his family estate was situated, TCD and Magdalen College, Oxford. MP for King's County (1824–31), he was a member of the Royal Astronomical Society (1824) and of the Royal Society (1831). After retiring from politics he devoted himself to scientific research, with a particular emphasis on the improvement of the reflecting telescope. His work led to the construction of the Parsonstown Telescope.* He became President of the Royal Society (1849–54). Returned to the House of Lords as a Representative Irish Peer in 1845, he opposed the repeal of the Corn Laws and was an outspoken critic of secret societies.* During the Famine of 1845–49* he spent a considerable amount of his personal fortune on famine relief. His publications on Irish affairs included *Letters on the State of Ireland* (1847) and *A Few Words on the Relation of Landlord and Tenant* (1867).

ROYAL BLACK PRECEPTORY. Sometimes known as the Royal Black Institution, it is an Ulster Unionist Protestant organisation founded in Loughgall, Co. Armagh in 1796. Closely associated with the Orange Order,* which had been for long its rival, members of the Black Preceptory are dedicated to the 'maintenance of pure evangelical truth as contained in the written Word of God, as well as the dissemination of strict moral ethics'.

ROYAL DUBLIN SOCIETY (RDS). Established for 'improving husbandry, manufactures and other useful arts and sciences' on 25 June 1731. Incorporated by Royal Charter on 2 April 1750, the Society assumed the title 'Royal' in June 1820 when George IV* became its patron. The RDS has been responsible for many of Ireland's finest institutions, including the National Library,* National Museum,* National Gallery* and Botanic Gardens.* It was responsible for the first school of art (now the National College of Art) and many of Ireland's sculptors and artists studied in it. The RDS maintained a keen interest in scientific matters, making grants available for research, the acquisition of scientific collections and the purchase of scientific equipment. It published a series of *Statistical Surveys* of the Irish counties. The following is a list of those published (author and date in brackets): Antrim (Dubourdieu, 1812), Armagh (1804), Cavan (1802), Clare (Dutton, 1808), Cork (Townsend, 1810), Donegal (McParlan, 1802),

Down (Dubourdieu, 1802), Dublin (Archer, 1801), Galway (Dutton, 1824), Kildare (Rawson, 1807), Kilkenny (Tighe, 1802), King's County (Coote, 1801), Leitrim (Coote, 1802), Londonderry (1802), Mayo (McParlan, 1802), Monaghan (1801), Queen's County (Coote, 1801), Roscommon (Weld, 1832), Sligo (McParlan, 1802), Tyrone (McEvoy, 1802), Wexford (Fraser, 1807) and Wicklow (Fraser, 1801). The Survey of Tipperary, which was not published, is in the National Library.

The RDS possesses one of the most valuable libraries in Ireland, including complete sets of *Proceedings* and *Transactions* from learned societies in many parts of the world. It has published its own *Proceedings* since 1764. Part of the RDS collection formed the nucleus of the National Library (*see* Joly, Rev. Jasper). Its headquarters at Ballsbridge in Dublin is the centre for many exhibitions, displays and shows, including the famous Dublin Horse Show which was first held in 1868.

ROYAL HIBERNIAN ACADEMY. Incorporated by charter in 1823, the RHA's first president was William Ashford. Its purpose was to encourage Irish artists by offering them an annual opportunity of exhibiting their works. It was re-organised under a new charter in 1861.

ROYAL IRISH ACADEMY (RIA). Founded in 1785 by the 1st Earl of Charlemont, the RIA's purpose was to 'advance the studies of science, polite literature and antiquities'. The Academy was responsible, through patronage, for much of the historical and antiquarian research undertaken in Ireland during the nineteenth century. Its library contains 30,000 volumes, 2,500 rare manuscripts, 30,000 pamphlets and 1,700 sets of periodicals. Leading scholars associated with the Academy have included George Petrie* and Eoin MacNeill.* It receives a grant in aid from the government. Members, elected on the basis of scholarship,

number around 240. The RIA has published *Transactions* (1786–1907) and *Proceedings* has appeared since 1830.

ROYAL IRISH ACADEMY OF MUSIC. The RIAM, which evolved from the Antient Concert Society, was founded by Joseph Robinson in 1834. It was reorganised in 1856 as a state-subsidised charitable educational institution and received the title 'Royal' in 1872.

ROYAL IRISH CONSTABULARY (RIC). Armed police force formed as the Irish Constabulary by Thomas Drummond* in 1836 (*see* Police). The force was granted the title 'Royal' for its role in the suppression of the rising by the Irish Republican Brotherhood* in 1867. Members of the force, who were mainly Catholic, were recruited from among the tenant-farmer class and were removed to distant stations. Barracks were strategically centered in the most likely trouble spots.

The RIC was unpopular in many areas because it was used to assist at evictions and because, owing to the discontented state of the country throughout most of the nineteenth century and the early part of the twentieth, it filled a semi-military role. A highly efficient force, it supplied Dublin Castle* with most of its intelligence information.

Policemen were poorly paid and subject to a variety of officials, from sergeants upwards, most of whom were out of sympathy with the needs of those in the service. There were no recognised off-duty periods, days of rest or annual leave. A constable was confined to barracks at night. He could only marry after seven years' service and then his proposed bride had to meet with the approval of the authorities. Promotion was slow and opportunities for promotion were unequally distributed throughout the country. A constable could not vote in elections.

Officers were also subject to irksome regulations. Each officer had to keep a kit and horse, (a rule which was enforced long after the RIC had ceased to fill a military role). Officers also had to undergo military training, even when it was not relevant, and attend sessions of target practice.

Until 1919 there was no negotiating body within the RIC. In that year, T. J. McElligott* established a branch of the policemen's Representative Body and was dismissed from the force.

The strength of the force by 1870 was around 12,000. Until a re-organisation in 1881 it was commanded by inspectors. The country was then divided into five divisions outside of the Dublin Metropolitan Police areas (Co. Dublin and Co. Wicklow). Each division had a Divisional Magistrate (DM) with full powers over the entire force and complete responsibility for law and order. By 1885 the re-organisation was complete and the Divisional Magistrates were operating in the Western, South-Western, South-Eastern, Midland and Northern divisions.

Before the outbreak of World War I, recruitment into the RIC had fallen, due mainly to the unpopular nature of the job and the poor financial reward. There were also increasing resignations due to the belief that there would be no future within the service after Home Rule.* Morale was low, particularly when Assistant Commissioner David Harrell was dismissed following the Howth Gun-running.* Falling numbers presented the authorities with a problem during the war and the Police (Emergency Provisions) Act was introduced in 1915 to put an end to all resignations or retirement except for enlistment in the armed forces to serve at the front.

Following the Easter Rising of 1916* members of the force were regarded with even greater hostility by nationalists and members of the Irish Volunteers.* The RIC was the primary target of the Irish Republican Army* at the start of the War of Independence* as the police barracks were the most convenient symbol of

British imperialism in Ireland. The force was not equipped to fight a guerrilla war. Sinking morale in the face of hostility from their fellow-countrymen and the risk of death to their families proved too much for many policemen to take. In order to compensate for the shortfall in numbers as recruiting fell off and resignations increased, the government recruited an auxiliary force, the Auxiliaries,* and the Black and Tans.*

Whereas the RIC had for a long time been a police force doing a soldier's job, the new auxiliaries were ex-soldiers nominally expected to do a policeman's job and were given *carte blanche* to destroy the IRA. The brutality with which the Auxiliaries and the Black and Tans set about their task created unrest within the RIC, many of whose members refused to be associated with their actions. This led to an incident at Listowel RIC barracks in 1920 when Constable Jeremiah Mee* spoke for nationalist-minded policemen. Mee and others like him were dismissed. They were praised for their nationalism by republicans but were left without adequate means of support. Following the Treaty the RIC was disbanded and a new police force, the Civic Guards, was established (*see* Garda Siochana). In Northern Ireland members of the RIC were absorbed by the new Royal Ulster Constabulary.*

The Resigned and Dismissed Members of the RIC and DMP (1916−22) was founded by T. J. McElligott with the approval of Micheal Collins.* Its purpose was to protect the interests of members who had been dismissed on account of their nationalist sympathies. It mainly consisted of RIC men, as the DMP had not been in the firing-line to the same extent during the War of Independence. Dismissed and resigned members received little from the new order which was established after the Treaty. They were particularly dismayed by the financial agreement which ended the Economic War* in 1938 as it made no provision for them except that the British government took over liability for RIC pensions. Dismissed members had forfeited their pension rights in any case. *See also* Dublin Metropolitan Police.

ROYAL SOCIETY OF ANTIQUA-RIES OF IRELAND. Established from the Kilkenny Archaeological Society in 1849 by Rev. James Graves 'to preserve, examine and illustrate the ancient monuments of the history, language, arts, manners and customs of the past as connected with Ireland'. The RSAI, which was granted its charter in 1912, sponsors scholarly publications and a journal.

ROYAL ULSTER CONSTABU-LARY (RUC). Police force established in Northern Ireland on 1 June 1922 from among the Royal Irish Constabulary.* An armed force, the RUC was responsible not only for dealing with ordinary crime but also with the Irish Republican Army,* with the support of the Special Constabulary* and the Civil Authorities (Special Powers) Act 1922.* The RUC was partially disarmed in April 1970 in line with the recommendations of the Hunt Commission.*

ROYAL UNIVERSITY OF IRE-LAND. Examining body established by Benjamin Disraeli* under the University Education (Ireland) Act 1879. It was an attempt to solve the complex problems of higher education in Ireland. The Queen's Colleges* and Trinity College, Dublin were unacceptable to the Catholic hierarchy, while the Catholic University* had been restricted by lack of state support and by its lack of power to award degrees. Disraeli's solution was to establish the Royal University with power to award degrees. It was, in effect, a university with a staff but no student body. Students from all other institutions were free to sit for the examinations set by the Royal. It was an acceptable compromise and lasted until the National University of Ireland* and the

Queen's University of Belfast were established in 1908.

ROYAL ZOOLOGICAL SOCIETY OF IRELAND. Founded in 1830 as a non-profit making society. The gardens were opened to the public in September 1831. The Society is responsible for the zoological gardens in the Phoenix Park, Dublin and the study and display of natural history.

RUNDALE. System of landholding common in Ireland before the Famine of 1845–49.* It was mainly found in the western parts of the country during the nineteenth century. Land held in common was portioned out among tenant farmers, so that everyone received a share of both good and bad land. Allied to this system was 'changedale' which meant that there was a changeover of strips to ensure that tenants alternated between good and bad lands. In practice the system often meant that a tenant could have his individual strips scattered over many different fields, even to the number of thirty or forty, and as there were no fences in use there were frequent disputes over the precise location of land. In general, attempts were made to ensure a fair distribution of the good, middling and bad land, but according to Thomas Campbell Foster in his *Letters on the Condition of the People of Ireland,* 'Fights, tres‑ passes, confusion, disputes and assaults, were the natural and unavoidable consequence of this system'. The system was also sometimes known as 'Runrig'.

'RUNRIG'. *See* Rundale.

RURAL DISTRICT COUNCILS. *See* Local Government.

RUSSELL, CHARLES, 1st BARON RUSSELL OF KILLOWEN (1832–1900). Lawyer and politician (Liberal); b. Killane, Co. Down; ed. Castleknock College and TCD. He read law at King's Inns and was called to the Bar in 1859. MP (1880–94), he served as Attorney-General in 1886 and 1892 to 1894. Russell was retained by Charles Stewart Parnell* in 1888 as counsel during the Special Commission on *The Times'* series on 'Parnellism and Crime',* having earlier dissuaded him from suing *The Times* for libel. His cross-examination of Richard Pigott* revealed him as the forger of incriminating letters. He was later counsel for Mrs Katharine O'Shea* when her grand-aunt's will was contested. Recognised as the outstanding forensic orator of his time, Russell became Lord of Appeal in Ordinary (1894) and Lord Chief Justice of England. His biography was written by R. Barry O'Brien.*

RUSSELL, REV. CHARLES WILLIAM (1812—80). Clergyman (R.C.) author and President of Maynooth (1857—80); b. Killough, Co. Down; ed. Drogheda, Downpatrick and Maynooth where he was ordained in 1835. Fluent in seven languages, he was in the same year awarded the Chair of Humanities. He was the first Professor of Ecclesiastical History at Maynooth (1854—57), after which he became President of the college. Dr Russell was a close friend of Cardinal John Henry Newman* who acknowledged in his *Apologia Pro Vita Sua* (1864) that he had by his example 'perhaps more to do with my conversion than anyone else'. He contributed to leading periodicals including *The Dublin Review, The Edinburgh Review, The Irish Monthly* and Charles Dickens' *Household Words.* He wrote on Catholic doctrine and Irish historical and topographical matters for Chambers' *Encyclopaedia.*

RUSSELL, GEORGE WILLIAM ('AE') (1867—1935). Poet, journalist, mystic, economist and artist; b. Lurgan, Co. Armagh; ed. Rathmines School. He studied art at the Dublin Metropolitan School of Art, and worked as an assistant in Pim's Drapery, Dublin. He began to contribute to *The Irish Theosophist* in 1892, using the initials 'AE' by which he became well-known. Two years later he published his first volume of verse, *Homeward: Songs by the Way.* He joined the Irish Agricultural Organisation Society,* the central body of the Co-Operative Movement,* of which he became assistant secretary. As editor of the co-operative journal, *The Irish Homestead,* he attracted contributions from the leading writers of the day, including his close friend, William Butler Yeats.* Russell's writings on economic matters earned him an international reputation as an agronomist. *Co-Operation and Nationality* (1912) set out his ideas on the economics of the co-operative movement.

Russell was generous in his encouragement of literary talent and attendance at his soirées was regarded as a privilege. After he had been introduced to James Joyce* in 1902 he formed a very high opinion of his talent and introduced his name to a wide circle of influential literati.

As a polemicist he had a scathing style which was demonstrated in his attack on the Dublin employers, 'The Masters of Dublin' as he called them in his open letter, during the Lock-Out.* This experience of Dublin employer-worker relations prompted *The National Well-Being* (1916). He was invited to the USA by Franklin D. Roosevelt in 1935 to elaborate on the idea of employing young people on public works for two years. He undertook a heavy lecturing tour which undermined his health, and he died in England from cancer shortly after returning home.

His works include *Literary Ideals of Ireland* (1899), *Nuts of Knowledge* (privately printed, 1903), *The Divine Vision* (1904), *By Still Waters* (1906), *Deirdre* (1907), *The Hero in Man* (1909), *The Renewal of Youth* (1911), *Collected Poems* (1913), *Gods of War* (1915), *The Candle of Vision* (1919), *Vale and Other Poems* (1931), *Song and Its Foundations* (1932) and *The Aviators* (1933).

RUSSELL, LORD JOHN, 1st EARL
(1792–1878). Politician (Whig);
Prime Minister (1846–52; 1865–
66); b. Woburn Abbey, son of 6th
Duke of Bedford; ed. Westminster
School and privately at Woburn.
He visited Ireland for three months
in 1806 during his father's brief
Viceroyalty. After attending Edinburgh University (1809–12) he entered parliament in 1813. His Bills
for repeal of the Test Act and Corporations Act were carried in 1823,
enabling Catholics and dissenters to
become members of corporations. He
supported Daniel O'Connell* on
Catholic Emancipation.* He resigned
from Earl Grey's government when
the Reform Act of 1832 was rejected
by the Lords, but returned when Sir
Robert Peel* was unable to form a
new government; the Reform Act
became law on 7 June 1832. Russell
now visited Ireland and opposed the
demand by the Irish executive for
coercion. He advanced liberal views
on the tithes question and sought
an appropriations clause which would
convert the surplus to social ends.

Russell was not a party to the
Lichfield House Compact* between
Melbourne and O'Connell's Repealers.
He was Home Secretary and leader
of the Commons in Melbourne's
administration and presided over a
very liberal Irish executive, which
introduced important reforms (*see*
Police, Poor Law, Tithes *and* Munici-
pal Corporations Act). In Melbourne's
second administration (1837–41)
Russell served as Colonial Secretary.
Although leader of the opposition to
Peel's government (1841–46) he
supported Peel on the Maynooth
Grant and the repeal of the Corn
Laws. He succeeded Peel as Prime
Minister in 1846 when Peel carried
repeal but lost on the question of
coercion.

Russell came to government at a
period when the Famine of 1845–
49* was already spreading through
Ireland. He was handicapped in dealing with the crisis by the fact that he
was leading a minority government
and that, like his colleagues, he was
committed to free trade and *laissez
faire*. This governed decisions made
about Irish relief by himself and his
Chancellor of the Exchequer, Sir
Charles Wood.* In October 1846
Russell felt obliged to point out that,
although the potato crop had again
failed, 'It must be thoroughly understood that we cannot feed the
people'. Irish relief would have to
be provided from Irish resources.
Food was not to be sold below the
market price so as not to interfere
with normal trade.

He removed Lord Heytesbury*
from the Viceroyalty and replaced
him with the 4th Lord Bessborough.*
Russell allowed the distribution of
free soup but ordered that public
works should start closing down
(January 1847). He warned that no
food would be imported from abroad,
and against radical opposition, he
introduced coercion to deal with the
unrest produced by famine. He
continued to claim during 1847–48
that the financial crisis in England
made it impossible to provide aid
for Ireland.

The case for Irish relief suffered
in his eyes by the attempted rebellion of William Smith O'Brien* and
the Irish Confederation* in the
summer of 1848. To deal with the
impoverishment of Irish landlords
he introduced two Encumbered
Estates Acts* in 1848 and 1849, but
by then the worst of the Famine was
over.

He was the author of a number of
works, including *The Nun of Arrouca*
(1822), *Don Carlos* (1822) and
Memoirs of the Affairs of Europe
(1824).

RUSSELL, SEAN (1893–1940).
Republican; Chief of Staff, Irish
Republican Army,* 1938–39; b.
Dublin; ed. CBS, Fairview. A member of the Irish Volunteers,* he
fought in the Easter Rising of 1916*
and was interned. Upon release, he
was a member of Sinn Fein* and the
re-organised Volunteers. During the
War of Independence he was Director
of Munitions in the headquarters

514

staff of the IRA. Rejecting the Treaty,* Russell fought in the Civil War; following the republican surrender (May 1923) he remained active in the IRA. He visited Russia with Gerald Boland in 1926 in an attempt to secure arms for the republicans. Upon his return he broke with Eamon de Valera* and the constitutional republicans who founded Fianna Fail.*

Russell opposed the left-wing IRA which, led by Peadar O'Donnell and Frank Ryan, founded Saor Eire* in 1931. When approached by de Valera between 1932 and 1934, he refused to halt IRA drilling and parading in public unless Fianna Fail would guarantee a thirty-two-county republic within five years and thus the discussions ended. By 1936, when de Valera outlawed the IRA, Russell was its quartermaster-general and demanding an all-out war against Britain. This was opposed by Maurice ('Moss') Twomey* and Sean Mac-Bride* and he departed for the USA to win support from Joseph McGarrity and Clan na Gael. His tour of America led to court-martial and suspension from office in the IRA on his return to Ireland and he then returned to the US. However, at the IRA convention in April 1938 he secured a seat on the Army Council, and became Chief of Staff. He now pressed ahead with his plans for a war although the IRA was split. The 'war' started on 16 January 1939 with a series of explosions which culminated in the Coventry Explosion* (25 August 1939). Seeking additional American aid, he again visited the US. The European war prevented his return to Ireland but he managed to make his way to Italy and from there to Germany where he hoped to interest the Abwehr in arranging his repatriation. He met his old adversary, Frank Ryan,* and Admiral Canaris arranged for their transportation by U-boat to Ireland on 8 August. Russell died *en route* and was buried at sea 100 miles out of Galway Bay. Ryan was returned to Germany.

RUSSELL, THOMAS (1767–1803), United Irishman; b. Bessborough, Co. Cork. He served with the British Army in India (1782). Returning to Ireland, he held a commission in Belfast where he joined the United Irishmen* and became the first librarian of the Linenhall library. Arrested for his role as a United recruiting agent (1796), he was deported to Fort George in Scotland where he was held until 1802 without charge. While he was imprisoned the rebellion of 1798 was crushed. Russell had been leader-designate for Ulster where, according to Jemmy Hope,* his name alone was worth 50,000 men. Shortly after his release he was in Paris where he met Robert Emmet.* When Emmet was captured on 24 August 1803 after the failure of his rising, Russell came south to rescue him but was betrayed. Taken to Downpatrick and found guilty of high treason, he was hanged outside the jail gates. Known to his fellow United men as 'The Man from God Knows Where', he is the subject of a poem by Florence M. Wilson.

RUSSELL, THOMAS O'NEILL (1828–1908). Author and language revivalist; b. near Moate, Co. Westmeath, to a Quaker family. An enthusiastic language revivalist, he contributed to *The Irishman* in which he urged the preservation of Irish. He was suspected of sympathising with the Irish Republican Brotherhood* and emigrated to the USA after the rising of 1867. He spent thirty years in America, lecturing and writing on the language. After his return to Ireland in 1895 he continued his work through the Gaelic League.* His novels included *The Struggles of Dick Massey* (1860) under the pen-name 'Reginald Tierney'.

RUSSELL, THOMAS WALLACE, 1st EARL (1841–1920). Politician (Liberal); b. Cupar, Fife; ed. locally. After settling in Ireland in 1859 he worked as a draper's assistant in Donoughmore, Co. Tyrone. Active in the cause of temperance, he was secretary of the Dublin Temperance Association (1864) and played a prominent role in securing the Irish Sunday Closing Act (1878). Returned as MP for Preston in 1885, he opposed Home Rule, winning South Tyrone in 1886 when he defeated William O'Brien. He promoted the Land Acts Commission of 1894 and one year later became undersecretary of the Local Government Board. His support for Home Rule after 1900 lost him South Tyrone in 1910 but he won North Tyrone a year later. He founded the New Land Movement in Ulster, advocating compulsory purchase (which came in 1909). After serving as vice-president of the Department of Agriculture and Technical Instruction* (1907–18), he withdrew from public life. He published *England and the Empire* (1901), and *The Irish Land Question up to date* (1902).

RUSSIAN CROWN JEWELS. Part of the Russian Crown Jewels was accepted by the first Dail Eireann* as collateral for an interest-free loan of $25,000 to the Soviet Union authorised by the President of the Dail, Eamon de Valera,* while he was in the USA in 1920. This did not, however, prevent the Soviet government from rejecting a proposed trade agreement between the Irish Republic and the Soviet Union when Dr Patrick McCartan* visited the country.

The jewels were taken to Ireland by Harry Boland.* Following the Treaty which substituted the Free State for the Republic, Boland entrusted the jewels to his family with instructions that they should be given to de Valera when he came to power. De Valera formed the first Fianna Fail government in 1932 and the jewels lay in the office of a government department until they were discovered by P. J. McGilligan, Minister for Finance in the first Inter-Party Government* (1948–51). They were then returned to the USSR which repaid the $25,000.

'RUTHLESS WARFARE'. Article published anonymously but actually written by Ernest Blythe* in *An tÓglach,* the organ of the Irish Volunteers, in September 1918 during the anti-conscription campaign (*see* Conscription and Ireland). Blythe called on the Volunteers to regard any attempt to introduce conscription as an act of war which must be resisted by war: 'We must recognise that anyone, civilian or soldier, who assists directly or by connivance in this crime against Ireland merits no more consideration that a wild beast, and should be killed without mercy or hesitation as opportunity offers.'

RUTTLEDGE, PATRICK JOSEPH (1892–1952). Politician (Fianna Fail); b. Ballina, Co. Mayo; ed. locally and Dublin where he qualified as a solicitor. A member of the Irish Volunteers and Sinn Fein he fought in the War of Independence and was imprisoned. Returned as TD for Co. Mayo in May 1921 he opposed the Treaty and served in the Irregulars (anti-Treaty IRA) during the Civil War, as a member of the Army Council and of the Executive (April 1922). He was Minister for Justice in the republican cabinet formed by Eamon de Valera* in opposition to the Provisional Government,* and acted as President of the 'Republic' while de Valera was imprisoned (1923–24). Ruttledge supported de Valera in the break from Sinn Fein* (1926) and in the establishment of Fianna Fail, which first entered the Dail in 1927. He was Minister for Lands in the first Fianna Fail cabinet (March 1932–February 1933), Minister for Justice (February 1933–September 1939) and for Local Government and Public Health (September 1939–August 1941).

RYAN, DESMOND (1893–1964). Socialist republican and historian; b. London, son of William Patrick Ryan;* ed. London until the family moved to Dublin (1905) where he continued his education at Westland

Row CBS and St Enda's. While studying at UCD he lived in St Enda's* and was Patrick Pearse's secretary. A member of the Irish Volunteers,* he fought in the GPO during the Easter Rising of 1916,* after which he was interned. Following his release he worked on *The Freeman's Journal.* He supported the Treaty and, disillusioned by the Civil War, moved to London to work as a journalist. Later he returned to Ireland and established a poultry-farm near Swords, Co. Dublin.

A convinced socialist, having been influenced by the life and work of James Connolly,* he became an authority on the Irish Republican Brotherhood,* Pearse and other prominent nationalists. His writings include *The Man Called Pearse* (1919), *The Invisible Army* (1932), *Remembering Sion* (1934), *Unique Dictator* (a study of Eamon de Valera, 1936), *The Phoenix Flame: A Study of Fenianism and John Devoy* (1937), *The Sword of Light: From the Four Masters to Douglas Hyde* (1939), *The Rising: The Complete Story of Easter Week* (1948), and *The Fenian Chief* (1967). He edited the *Collected Works of Patrick Pearse* (1917–22), the *Collected Works of James Connolly* (1924) and was co-editor with William O'Brien* of *Devoy's Post Bag* (1948–53).

RYAN, FRANK (1902–44). Socialist republican; b. Elton, Co. Limerick; ed. St Colman's College, Fermoy and UCD. A member of Na Fianna Eireann,* he organised republican clubs at university where his studies were interrupted by membership of the Irish Republican Army* during the War of Independence.* Rejecting the Treaty,* he resumed his work in Celtic Studies at UCD where he edited *An Reult* to which he contributed under the pen-name 'Seachránuidhe'. Upon graduation (1925) he became a teacher while continuing his membership of the IRA. Closely associated with Peadar O'Donnell* and George Gilmore,* he was a founder-member of Comhairle na Poblachta* and Saor Eire.* He was also a co-editor of *An Phoblacht* (although he was quite deaf it was said that he could always hear an offer of money for the paper). He supported Eamon de Valera* and Fianna Fail* in the general election of 1932. A founder-member of the Republican Congress,* he edited the paper of that name.

Ryan was a leading opponent of the Irish quasi-fascist movement, the Blueshirts,* and organised IRA volunteers in support of the Spanish republican government during the Spanish Civil War* (1936–39). His eighty volunteers arrived in Albacete on 16 December 1936 to join the 15th International Brigade in which he held the rank of major. He was wounded in February 1937 at the battle of Jarama and returned home to recuperate. While in Dublin he unsuccessfully contested a seat in the 1937 general election. Returning to Spain, he was appointed to brigade staff as adjutant to General Miaja. Following capture at Calaceite during the Aragon offensive on 1 April 1938 he was held at Miranda del Ebro detention camp by the Francoists. At San Pedro de Cardenzas prison near Burgos he was court-martialled and sentenced to death. This was commuted to thirty years imprisonment following representations by de Valera and the Apostolic Delegate to Ireland. Further representations led to his release to Germany in August 1940.

Immediately upon his arrival in Berlin where he was known as 'Frank Richards' he was re-united with his former opponent in the IRA, Sean Russell,* who arranged for their transport to Ireland by U-boat. They sailed on 8 August. However, Russell died near the Orkneys and was buried at sea some 100 miles outside Galway (14 August) and Ryan returned to Germany. His health deteriorated and he failed to secure another chance to return to Ireland. He was buried in Loschwitz cemetery near Dresden. His remains were returned to Ireland for re-interment in Glasnevin cemetery, Dublin, in June 1979.

RYAN, DR JAMES (1891–1970). Politician (Sinn Fein and Fianna Fail); b. Tomcoole, Co. Wexford; ed. St Peter's· College, Ring and UCD where he qualified as a doctor (March 1917). A member of the Irish Volunteers while a medical student, he was in charge of the medical unit in the GPO during the Easter Rising of 1916 after which he was interned in Frongoch, Wales until August 1916. An active member of the re-organised Volunteers and Sinn Fein,* he was returned for Co. Wexford to the first Dail Eireann (December 1918). During the War of Independence he was imprisoned on Spike Island, Cork (1920–21). He was vice-chairman of the Wexford County Council (1919–22) and TD for the county (1921–65). After opposing the Treaty, he was a member of the Four Courts garrison (April – June 1922), after which he was imprisoned by the Provisional Government and went on hunger-strike.

An abstentionist member of the Dail, he was a founder-member of Fianna Fail* in 1926 and entered the Dail with his colleagues in September 1927. He was spokesman on agriculture until 1932, when, upon the formation of the first Fianna Fail* cabinet, he became Minister for Agriculture until 1947. He was Minister for Health and Social Welfare (1947–48) and for Finance (1951–54; 1957–65). As Minister for Finance he supported the Programmes for Economic Expansion.* Following his retirement from the Dail in 1965 he was a member of the Senate* for four years.

RYAN, DR MARK (1844–1940). Fenian; b. Kilconly, Tuam, Co. Galway; ed. at a hedge-school. Following eviction from their small-holding, the family moved to England. Ryan was sworn into the Irish Republican Brotherhood* by Michael Davitt* and then returned to Ireland to resume his education at St Jarlath's College, Tuam, where he was taught by Canon Ulick Bourke.* While studying medicine at Queen's College, Galway and in Dublin, he was an organiser for the IRB. After qualifying he moved to England where he remained and was a close associate of leading republicans, becoming a member of the Supreme Council.* He belonged to the extreme wing and after 1895 was leader of the Irish National Alliance.* A founder-member of the Gaelic League,* he also helped to found the Irish Literary Society.* His autobiography, *Fenian Memories,* was published in 1945.

RYAN, REV. MATTHEW, 'THE GENERAL' (1844–1937). Clergyman (R.C.) and land agitator who became popularly known as 'The General'; b. Kilduff, Pallasgreen, Co. Limerick; ed. locally, St Patrick's College, Thurles and Irish College, Paris where he was ordained (1871) and taught for a short time. Upon his return to the archdiocese of Cashel he was appointed to collect money for the cathedral in Thurles. As a curate in Lattin, Co. Tipperary (1876–86) he was active in the Land League,* which was also supported by his friend, the Archbishop of Cashel, Thomas William Croke.* In his next ministry, as curate in Hospital, Co. Limerick (1886–90), he played a leading role in the Plan of Campaign* on the Herbertstown estate. He held the monies for the tenants and was charged with bankruptcy in March 1887 by the state. At his trial in April, he refused to divulge details of the monies and was sentenced to two months' imprisonment for contempt of court. Upon appeal he was released on 24 May. Later in the year he was again imprisoned, in Limerick Jail (December 1887–January 1888) when he resisted all attempts to have him wear prison garb instead of clerical clothing. He was later curate in Solohead, Co. Tipperary (1890–97) and parish priest in Knockavella and Donaskeagh, Co. Tipperary (1897–

1937), where he was known affectionately as 'Father Matt'. A vice-president of the Gaelic League* for many years, he supported Sinn Fein after the Easter Rising of 1916 and rejected the Treaty.

RYAN, WILLIAM PATRICK (LIAM Ó RIÁIN) (1867–1942). Author; b. near Templemore, Co. Tipperary; ed. locally. After moving to England he worked as a journalist, on *The Catholic Times, The Sun, The Weekly Sun* (under T. P. O'Connor), *The Morning Leader* and *The Daily Chronicle*. Renowned for his socialist views, he was also closely connected with Irish societies, the Gaelic League,* the Southwark Literary Society* and the Irish Literary Society.*

He returned in 1905 to accept the editorship of *The Irish Peasant,* which, prior to its closure in December 1906, had become one of the most powerful organs of public opinion in Ireland. He criticised the Catholic Church for its opposition to nationalist movements and for its paternalism. His attitudes so concerned the hierarchy that it brought pressure on the McCann family which closed the paper. Ryan failed to make a success of *The Peasant* (1907) or *The Irish Nation* (1908–10), and returned to London where he continued his journalistic career, mostly on Labour newspapers. His son, Desmond Ryan,* was a distinguished journalist and historian.

His publications, sometimes under the pen-name 'Kelvin Kennedy', include *The Heart of Tipperary* (1893), *Starlight Through the Thatch* (1895), *Sidheóga ag Obair* (1904, winning an Oireachtas prize), *The Plough and the Cross* (1910, based on his struggle with the church over *The Irish Peasant*), *The Pope's Green Island* (1912), *Caomhin Ó Cearnaigh* (1913), *The Jug of Sorrow* (1914, produced at the Abbey Theatre), *The Irish Labour Movement* (1919) and *Gaelachas i gCéin* (1933).

S

SADLEIR, JOHN (1815–56). Businessman and politician (Nationalist); b. Shrone Hill, Co. Tipperary; ed. Clongowes Wood College. MP for Carlow (1847–53), he was a leading member of the Irish Brigade* and of the Catholic Defence Association.* He established the Irish Land Company to purchase estates under the Encumbered Estates Acts* and then founded the Tipperary Joint-Stock Bank to buy the Kingston estate in Mitchelstown, Co. Cork, on which the Land Company held a mortgage. This led to his becoming chairman of the London and County Joint Stock Company.

When the Irish Brigade, led by George Henry Moore,* co-operated with the Tenant League,* to form the Independent Irish Party,* Sadleir took the pledge not to accept government office. However, on 17 December 1852, he and William Keogh* broke their pledges and accepted office in Lord Aberdeen's ministry, earning notoriety and condemnation from nationalists. Sadleir became Lord of the Treasury and in 1853 was returned as MP for Sligo.

Sadleir speculated heavily in American railways, iron and sugar, and, as his investments failed, he embezzled from the Tipperary Joint-Stock Bank to the amount of £1,250,000. In January 1854 he lost a court action taken against him by one of his debtors for false imprisonment. His financial affairs in ruins and fearing discovery of his peculation, he committed suicide. His career provided Charles Dickens and Charles Lever* with material for their fiction.

ST ENDA'S. School founded in 1908 at Cullenswood House, Dublin, by Patrick Pearse,* for which he chose as a model Cuchulainn, under the motto, 'Courage in our hands, truth in our tongues and purity in our hearts'. Pearse, who attacked the prevailing educational system in a pamphlet, 'The Murder Machine', looked back to the ancient Irish custom of fosterage which would give him complete control of his pupils in an atmosphere steeped in the heroic tradition. The school was bilingual, Irish was taught by the direct method and it was advanced in its science teaching. St Ita's, a sister school for girls, and a mixed preparatory school were also attached.

During the first year the school had some twenty boarders and around fifty day-boys; in the next year there were thirty boarders and 100 day-boys, but subsequently the school ran into financial difficulties and as Pearse's nationalist reputation increased he received fewer pupils. The school was moved in 1910 to the Hermitage, a fifty-acre site near Dublin, which Pearse was never able to afford.

The teaching staff at St Enda's consisted of Pearse, his brother, William Pearse,* and their sister Margaret; Thomas MacDonagh,* his brother Joseph MacDonagh,* and Con Colbert* also assisted. Occasional lectures were delivered by W. B. Yeats,* Eoin MacNeill,* Mary Hayden,* Edward Martyn,* Alice Stopford Green* and Dr Douglas Hyde.* Among those who sent Pearse their children or relatives were Padraic Colum,* Stephen Gwynn,* William Bulfin,* D. P. Moran* and W. P. Ryan.* Ryan's son, Desmond Ryan,* lived at St Enda's while studying at UCD, acted as Pearse's secretary and took part in the Easter Rising of 1916.*

St Enda's was beset with financial problems. Between 1914 and 1916

it was kept open only through injections of money raised in the USA, from republican sources, in the main led by Joseph McGarrity* and Clan na Gael.* Preparations for the rising of 1916 took place in the basement where Desmond Ryan and Eamon Bulfin were occupied in making bombs. Following the rising, St Enda's was kept open by Pearse's mother and by Margaret. They were assisted by Joseph MacDonagh, who was headmaster for a time. The school was closed in 1935. The house and grounds were bequeathed by Mrs Pearse (d. 1932) to Margaret after whose death (1969) they were given to the state.

ST GERMANS, 3rd EARL (1798–1877). Eliot, Edward Granville; known as Lord Eliot until 1843; politician (Conservative); Chief Secretary (1841–45) and Lord Lieutenant (1852–55); ed. Westminster School and Christ Church, Oxford. Returned as MP for Liskeard in 1824, he was Lord Treasurer (1827–30) and Envoy to Spain (1835). Appointed to the Irish office by Sir Robert Peel,* he was faced with the Repeal agitation led by Daniel O'Connell.* He introduced an Arms Act in 1843 which restricted both the registration of arms and the importation of arms and ammunition. At the onset of the Famine of 1845–49,* he resigned office. His period as Lord Lieutenant was uneventful apart from the rise of the Tenant League* and the Independent Irish Party.*

SAINT JOHN AMBULANCE BRIGADE OF IRELAND. Founded in Ireland in the autumn of 1903 by Dr John Lumsden who formed the first brigade from among employees of Guinness' Brewery in Dublin where he was the Chief Medical Officer.

SAOR EIRE. Socialist-republican splinter group of the Irish Republican Army,* founded in September 1931 by Peadar O'Donnell,* Frank Ryan* and George Gilmore.* They sought the overthrow of 'British

Imperialism and its ally capitalism' in Ireland. Saor Eire, which appealed for support from workers and working farmers, had the support of *An Phoblacht,* * edited by Ryan and O'Donnell. The first national convention, organised by Sean Mac-Bride,* was held on 28 September when Sean Hayes was elected chairman. Resolutions favouring control of land and the public ownership of transport were passed and a national executive, including members of Cumann na mBan,* the IRA and left-wing members of the Labour Party,* was appointed.

The movement was regarded with suspicion by the Catholic hierarchy and the government. On 17 October 1931 the Cumann na nGaedheal government outlawed Saor Eire along with a number of other radical organisations. At the same time the hierarchy condemned it as communist in a joint pastoral published on 18 October, which stated that the two organisations, Saor Eire and the IRA, were 'sinful and irreligious' and that Catholics could not belong to them. The movement collapsed shortly afterwards. Many of the leaders were associated later with the Republican Congress.* Another organisation of the same name appeared in the 1960s.

SAOR ULADH. A splinter group of the Irish Republican Army* founded as the military wing of Fianna Uladh* in Co. Tyrone by Liam Kelly in 1954. It was largely confined to East Tyrone, but made occasional forays into Co. Fermanagh throughout the late 1950s. It was regarded with disapproval by the leaders of the IRA, the government of the Irish Republic and the government of Northern Ireland. During its short life, Saor Uladh attacked barracks of the Royal Ulster Constabulary* and destroyed a number of bridges, losing two members during the campaign which coincided with a renewal of the IRA campaign against Northern Ireland (1956–62).

SAUNDERSON, COLONEL EDWARD JAMES (1837–1906). Landowner and politician (Ulster Unionist Party); b. Ballinamallard, Co. Fermanagh. He spent his boyhood in Nice where he was educated. He returned to Ireland in 1858 to manage the estate upon which his considerable wealth was based. A commissioned officer in the Cavan Militia, 4th Battalion of the Royal Irish Fusiliers (1862), he was returned as Liberal MP for Cavan in 1865. Shortly afterwards he broke with W. E. Gladstone* over the Disestablishment of the Church of Ireland* and became a Conservative. Fearing for the future of the Protestant religion under Home Rule* as the Irish Parliamentary Party prospered under Charles Stewart Parnell, Saunderson joined the Orange Order* in 1882 and two years later became Deputy Grand Master for Ireland. He published *Two Irelands: or, Loyalty versus Treason* in 1884. Warning his co-religionists that they must be prepared to resist Home Rule and to use physical force if necessary, he was returned in the Conservative interest as MP for North Armagh in 1885. A popular speaker in the House of Commons, he was held in high regard for his wit and swashbuckling manner.

During 1885–86 he set about organising Ulster Unionists to resist Home Rule and brought Lord Randolph Churchill* to Belfast to assure them of Conservative support. By 1888 he was the recognised leader of the parliamentary Unionists. A leading member of the Ulster Loyalist Anti-Repeal Union* and later of the Irish Unionist Alliance,* he rejected an invitation to sit on the Recess Committee* in 1895 but was a member of the All-Ireland Committee in 1897. He refused to sit on the Land Conference* of 1902. Saunderson was succeeded as leader of the Ulster Unionists by Walter Long.*

SAURIN, WILLIAM (1757–1839). Lawyer and politician (Conservative);

b. Belfast, of Huguenot descent; ed. TCD. He was called to the Bar in 1780. As MP for Blessington, he opposed parliamentary reform and Catholic relief in the Irish House of Commons. A member of the Orange Order,* he prosecuted prominent United Irishmen* in 1798 and was a leader of the Irish Bar in opposition to the Act of Union, although he later accepted office as Solicitor-General (1807–22) where he was said to have enjoyed more power than the Lord Lieutenant. He led the prosecution during the trial of John Magee* for seditious libel on the Duke of Richmond in 1813 when Magee's counsel, Daniel O'Connell,* turned a four-hour speech for the defence into a savage attack on Saurin, the Irish executive and the bench itself. Mortified at his removal from office in 1822, Saurin rejected a peerage and the post of Lord Chief Justice to return to the practice of law. He continued to oppose O'Connell and Catholic Emancipation.*

SAVAGE, JOHN (1828–88). Young Irelander and Fenian; b. Dublin where he trained as an artist. A member of Young Ireland* and of the Irish Confederation,* he contributed to *The United Irishman** and *The Tribune.* He was a co-founder of *The Irish Felon.* His own paper, *The Patriot,* appeared in 1848 and was immediately suppressed by the government. Following the collapse of the Young Ireland rising at Ballingarry, Co. Tipperary* he made his escape and aided John O'Mahony* in the attempt to renew the rebellion. He then went to the USA where he continued his journalistic career. He was the leader-writer on *The Washington States' Journal* (1857) and contributed to *The Citizen,* published by John Mitchel.* A leading member of the Fenians, he joined the 69th Regiment, led by Thomas Francis Meagher,* during the American Civil War (1861–65). After the war he sought a rising in Ireland and when O'Mahony was deposed in 1867 Savage led the O'Mahony faction

although the movement was now seriously split. He published *'98 and '48* (1856) and *Fenian Heroes and Martyrs* (1868). His best-known poem was 'Shane's Head'.

SAYERS, PEIG (1873–1958). Known as the 'Queen of the Storytellers'; b. Dunquin, Co. Kerry. She spent the greater part of her life on the Great Blasket Island, where she was visited by many writers for her wealth of knowledge regarding local tradition. Her autobiography, *Peig* (1936), was edited by Máire Ní Chinnéide who also edited *Machtnamh Sean-Mná (Reflections of an Old Woman;* 1939). Peig was evacuated to the mainland along with her fellow-islanders in 1953 (*see* Blasket Islands). Her life story, *Beatha Peig Sayers,* was edited by her son, Mardhc Sayers.

SCALP. *See* Scalpeen.

SCALPEEN. Hole in the ground made *within* the walls of a peasant's cottage or hut from which the family had been evicted. It was roofed over with available materials – bracken, branches and sods of turf. Eventually, the people were driven from these by the landlord, who was aided by the police and military.

SCHOOL ATTENDANCE ACT (1926). Act which made it compulsory for children between the ages of six and fourteen to attend national schools (*see* National Education). The Act also gave the Minister for Education power to extend the school-leaving age to sixteen. Until this Act, attendance at school was governed by the Attendance Act of 1892 which left supervision to the discretion of the local authorities. Because this authority was not exercised to any significant degree attendance at school until the 1920s rarely rose above the level of 50 per cent.

SCOLLOPS. Rods of willow, hazel, briar or bog-fir used to pin down the thatch. The method used varied according to the area. The two methods in general use were: thrusting the rods in vertically at each end, or bent as huge hairpins to secure the tips of horizontal rods.

SCOUT ASSOCIATION OF IRELAND. Non-denominational scouting movement founded in 1908, following the principles laid down by Baden-Powell. It sought to develop the all-round personality of the scout. At the time of its foundation the Scout Association worried nationalists who felt that it might be anti-nationalist in tone, so Bulmer Hobson* and Countess Markievicz* organised Na Fianna Eireann.* In 1927 the Catholic Boy Scouts of Ireland* was founded by Fr Farrell in Dublin. The Scout Association now has 10,000 members. It is a member of the Federation of Irish Scout Associations and affiliated to the Boy Scout World Bureau.

SCRAWS OR SCRAGHS. Roofing sods for peasants' dwellings. The sods were some two to three feet wide and from two to three inches thick. They were rolled on to a stick and conveyed to the thatcher who laid them grass-side upwards on the roof-frame to serve as insulation and as a hold for the securing scollops.* A contemporary observer noted that they were used as bed-covering by the poverty-stricken cottiers* in the period before the Famine of 1845—49.*

SCULLY, DENIS (1773—1830). Lawyer; b. Kilfeakle, Co. Tipperary; ed. Cambridge. He built up a considerable reputation at the Bar, recognised as the leading Catholic advocate after Daniel O'Connell,* with whom he was associated in the struggle for Catholic Emancipation.* Scully was a leading member of the democratic faction within the movement for Emancipation (1812—29). He was the probable author of an article published by John Magee* which led to Magee's prosecution for

seditious libel on the Duke of Richmond. His *Statement of Penal Laws* (1812) led to the imprisonment of the publisher, Fitzpatrick.

SCURVY. Scurvy, previously unknown in Ireland, became general during the Famine of 1845—49* upon the substitution of Indian meal (which does not contain Vitamin C) for the potato.

SEANASCAL. *See* Ó Buachalla, Domhnall.

SEANCHAI. Storyteller. He inherited the function of the Old Irish bard (genealogist, local historian, guardian of the community's history). A seanchai was normally a member of a particular family which became the repository of stories, myths, legends and local and national history. He was generally supported by his community (although *see* Berry, James). The seanchai made a round of the community, telling his stories in a different house each night. Much of the seanchai's lore was unique and he guarded his vast store of tales jealously, handing them on to a chosen successor, but never writing them down. With the growth of the mass media in the early years of the twentieth century, he became obsolete as the younger generation turned to the wireless for their entertainment. The stories of several seanchais were recorded by the Irish Folklore Institute* and other bodies concerned with the preservation of native lore.

'SECOND REFORMATION'. Evangelical campaign organised by fundamentalists in the Church of Ireland and the Church of England in the 1820s, sometimes known as the 'New Reformation'.* Evangelical clergymen were known as 'Biblicals' or 'New Reformers'. The Second Reformation was most zealously prosecuted in Connaught where it had the encouragement of Thomas Plunket,* Bishop of Tuam. Among the most active evangelicals were Rev. Alexander R. C. Dallas,* founder of the Irish Church Missions to the Roman Catholics, Rev. Edward Nangle* and Rev. Hyacinth D'Arcy.* Opposition to the evangelicals in the west was led by the Archbishop of Tuam, John MacHale,* who particularly resented their proselytising campaign during the Famine of 1845–49.* He was assisted later by Rev. Patrick Lavelle.* The Second Reformation was opposed by moderates within the Church of Ireland and petered out during the 1860s, leaving a legacy of bitterness in its wake.

SECONDARY EDUCATION. Education for those between the stages of primary education and third-level studies was generally known as 'intermediate education' during the nineteenth century. There was no state provision for such education which was provided largely on a denominational basis. While Protestant grammar schools and endowed colleges provided such education from an early date, Catholic diocesan schools or colleges did not emerge until the last decade of the eighteenth century in the wake of the Catholic Relief Acts. Between 1783 and 1870 some forty-seven Catholic intermediate schools were opened. By 1871 there was a total of 587 intermediate schools of which 265 were for boys, 162 for girls and 160 mixed. Such schools offered instruction based on the humanities. Those which provided teaching in foreign languages were known as 'superior' schools.

Intermediate education was not organised until the passage of the Intermediate Education Act of 1878 which established an Intermediate Education Board for Ireland. The Board created three divisions, Junior, Middle and Senior, which obtained until 1924. The Board's duties included the organisation of a system of public examinations, the provision of certificates, prizes and exhibitions, and the allocation of finance to managers on the basis of results. This system of 'payment by results' was the main source of income for school managers. While the Board did not approve of the results system which was constantly criticised by its opponents, it was not completely abolished until 1924 and exerted a harmful influence through the encouragement of 'cramming'.

The numbers of students taking the Intermediate Board examinations showed a dramatic increase during the remainder of the century. When the examinations were first held in 1879 there were 3,954 candidates in the three grades. By 1880, the figure had risen to 5,561 and showed little increase until 1896 when there were 9,000 candidates. By 1907 there were 11,000 which did not change until 1924, when the system was reorganised.

Intermediate education was criticised for the lack of sound science teaching which led the Board to press for an inquiry, held in 1899. This inquiry recommended that more emphasis be placed on science and that 'payment by results' be abolished. This was followed by the Intermediate Education Act of 1900 which attempted to implement some of the recommendations although 'payment by results' continued. In the same year the newly-created Department of Agriculture and Technical Instruction* began to operate. The Technical Instructions Branch worked in close co-operation with the Intermediate Board.

There were now two separate 'secondary' systems in existence. The intermediate system catered for the middle and lower-middle classes, preparing pupils for a wide range of commercial and civil service posts and those who wished to undertake higher studies. The technical system catered for those in agriculture and allied fields, attempted to raise the standard of farming in Ireland and prepared pupils for the trades. Both systems operated separately until organised under the centralised control of the Department of Education in 1924.

From 1913 the Board paid fees to managers on the basis of inspections rather than solely in accordance with examination results. An Act of 1914 established a register of teachers and allocated their salaries by a grant of £40,000 to be distributed among qualified personnel. Four years later a Capitation Grant of £50,000 was made available for distribution on the basis of inspectors' reports.

A Commission of Inquiry was established in 1918 with a brief to enquire 'as to any improvement which may appear desirable to be made in the conditions of service and on the method of remuneration of teachers in Intermediate Schools in Ireland'. The Report, issued in March 1919, recommended pension schemes and the abolition of 'payment by results'; it also recommended that a capitation grant be paid for each pupil. The most important recommendation for the structure of intermediate education was that the division into Junior, Middle and Senior Grades be abolished, and replaced by an Intermediate and a Leaving Certificate. By this stage, the country was in the throes of the War of Independence,* and the government of Ireland collapsed in the face of growing allegiance to the first Dail Eireann.* By 1922 when the Free State was established, with its own Department of Education, the Report was ready for the new Free State department.

The new Department adopted the recommendations of the 1919 Report. The Intermediate Board was taken over by the Department in 1923 and a new programme for secondary schools was put into operation in August 1924. Secondary education was divided into two levels, Intermediate and Leaving. The Intermediate Certificate could be taken at around the age of sixteen by those who had followed a prescribed course for three or four years, and the Leaving Certificate could be taken by those aged around eighteen who had followed a prescribed course for two years. Irish and Mathematics were made essential subjects for the Intermediate Certificate and Irish was also essential for the Leaving Certificate. It was necessary to pass five subjects. A total of 1,841 pupils followed the first Intermediate Certificate course and 750 the Leaving Certificate.

In 1963–64 there were 557 secondary schools with an enrolment of 84,916; by the school year 1971–72, although the number of schools had increased by only two to 559, there was an enrolment of 149,629. In 1978 there were 537 secondary schools with an enrolment of 189,176 students, 246 vocational schools with an enrolment of 61,551, twenty community schools with 10,076 students and fourteen comprehensive schools with 7,750 students.

SECRET SOCIETIES. Agrarian secret societies were a common feature of Irish rural life in the eighteenth and nineteenth centuries. Many of them came into existence in response to landlord oppression, rising rents, the price of conacre* and labour duties etc.; others were in protest at the exactions of Protestant and Catholic clergy – tithes,* dues and offerings. The first widespread secret society was the Whiteboys,* founded in 1761, whose activities continued in one form or another into the nineteenth century. Secret societies had no political outlook but were founded for an immediate purpose and recruited in the main from the tenant class. The most active of them were the Blackfeet, the Carders,* the Defenders, the Hearts of Oak, (or Oakboys), the Hearts of Steel (or Steelboys), the Lady Clares,* the Peep O' Day Boys,* the Ribbonmen,* the Right Boys, the Terry Alts, the Thrashers and the Whitefeet. Elements of the secret societies were also found among the faction-fighters (*see* faction-fighting). The societies were led by anonymous individuals variously known as Captain Moonlight, Captain Rock, Captain Right, Captain Starlight, etc. Rough justice was meted out to anyone who betrayed the code of secrecy under which they operated. Their principal weapons were murder, assault, shooting into houses and other forms of intimidation, cattle-maiming and crop-burning.

In the second part of the nineteenth century a new kind of secret society appeared in the form of the Irish Republican Brotherhood.* It diverged from agrarian secret society traditions in that its membership was principally from towns and cities, that it had a long-term objective (to destroy British rule in Ireland), and that it had a rigid central organisation. The Land League* was not a secret society but it too aimed at the economic betterment of the tenant-farmers and the destruction of the landlord system, and many of its members resorted to violence.

In the twentieth century the Irish Republican Army,* because of its outlawed position, has taken on some of the characteristics and rhetoric of the old secret societies.

SENATE. The upper house of the Oireachtas;* upon the creation of the Free State* in December 1922 it was intended that the Senate should represent minority interests in the new state and include people with specialist knowledge or experience or a record of public service. Candidates for election had to be thirty-five years of age. The function and powers of the first Irish Senate were modelled on the British House of Lords. It could initiate legislation, amend it and also suspend it for 270 days. If legislation was presented to the Senate again at the end of the 270 days, and rejected again, it was deemed passed by Dail Eireann.* The Senate was granted twenty-one days in which to consider money bills which could not be suspended.

Among the first members of the Senate, which met on 11 December 1922, when the oath was administered by Eamon J. Duggan,* were W. B. Yeats,* Oliver St John Gogarty* and the Earls of Granard, Kerry, Mayo and Wicklow, all nominated by the President of the Executive Council, W. T. Cosgrave,* who nominated half the members; those elected by the Dail included Colonel Maurice Moore* and Mrs Alice Stopford Green.* Between 1922 and the abolition of the Senate in 1936 the Chairmen were Lord Glenavy (1922–28) and T. W. Westropp-Bennett (1928–36); vice-chairmen were James G. Douglas (1922–25), Westropp-Bennett (1925–28), Patrick W. Kenny (1928–31), M. F. O'Hanlon (1931–34) and Michael Comyn (1934–36). During that period the Senate initiated twenty-five bills, twelve of which were accepted by the Dail. It considered 489 bills (other than money bills) and proposed 1,831 amendments on 182 bills, most of which were accepted by the Dail. It exercised suspension on nine bills, two of which the Dail did not attempt to pass into law. Eamon de Valera* and Fianna Fail regarded the Senate with suspicion. He said, in February 1928, 'We think that the proper thing to do is to end the Senate and not attempt to mend it. It is costly, and we do not see any useful function that it really serves'. Sean Lemass* said, '. . . we think that this bulwark of imperialism should be abolished by the people's representatives on the first available opportunity we get'. A joint commission, of which de Valera and P. J. Ruttledge* were members, was established to examine the efficiency of the Senate. It recommended that the make-up of the body should be changed.

The Removal of Oath Act,* one of de Valera's first pieces of legislation, had a stormy passage through the Senate which held it up. De Valera accused the Senators of being hostile to his administration while having favoured that of his predecessor, Cosgrave. The Oath of Allegiance* was not in fact removed until 1933. During the general election of January 1933, de Valera promised to abolish the Senate 'as at present constituted'. Later, his Wearing of Uniform (Restriction) Bill, designed to embarrass the

Blueshirts,* was rejected in the Senate where he was accused of allowing the Irish Republican Army* to act as a police force and harass the Blueshirts. In 1934 he introduced a bill to abolish the Senate, which came into the House on 30 May 1934. The Chairman, Westropp-Bennett, rejected de Valera's accusation that the Senate had been partisan and accused him of attempting to establish a dictatorship. After the bill was rejected by 35 votes to 15, the period of suspension did not expire until 24 November 1935. The Senate next met on 28 May 1936 and adjourned *sine die*. The Dail passed a motion on 28 May to the effect that the Abolition Bill was deemed to have been passed by both Houses.

Under the Constitution of 1937* a Senate or Seanad was established. More firmly under the control of the government, it still had sixty members, forty-three elected on a vocational basis, three each for TCD and NUI and eleven nominated by the Taoiseach. The Senate now had ninety days' suspensory power (except for money bills which could only be suspended for twenty-one days). The new Senate which met for the first time in November 1938 became a second House for the political parties rather than a chamber of specialised knowledge. It became a haven for potential and defeated Dail deputies and for those who had retired from the Dail.

SENIOR, WILLIAM NASSAU (1790–1864). Economist; b. Berkshire; ed. Eton and Magdalen College, Oxford, where he received private tuition from Richard Whately.* After receiving his M.A. he read law and was called to the Bar (1819). Senior had a deep interest in Ireland of which he said, 'When Irish questions, or rather the Irish question (for there is but one) has been fixed for our attention, we have felt, like a dreamer in a nightmare, oppressed by the consciousness that great evil was rapidly advancing'. The first Professor of Political Economy at Oxford (where the Chair was founded by Thomas Drummond) from 1827 to 1832 and from 1847 to 1852, he supported Free Trade and sought parliamentary reform and the creation of a system of Poor Law.* He served as a member of the Commission on the Irish Poor Law (1833). Among his published works were *Letter to Lord Howick on a legal provision for the Irish Poor Law, Commutation of Tithes and a provision for the Irish Roman Catholic clergy* (1831) and *Journals, Conversations and Essays relating to Ireland* (2 vols, 1868).

'SEPARATIST'. Newspaper edited by P. S. O'Hegarty* from February to September 1922. While not formally an organ of the Irish Republican Brotherhood,* it was supported by the Supreme Council* which contributed £1,000 towards it. The paper accepted the Treaty* while looking for a complete break with Britain in the future.

SEXTON, THOMAS (1848–1932). Politician (Nationalist); b. Waterford; ed. locally, he joined the railway service at the age of thirteen. He entered politics as Home Rule MP for Sligo County (1880–85) and thereafter represented West Belfast (1886–92) and North Kerry (1892–96). High Sheriff of Dublin (1887), and Lord Mayor (1888–89), Sexton had played a prominent role in the Land League* and later in the Plan of Campaign.* When he became a member of the Irish Parliamentary Party,* he became the party's chief spokesman on finance. He was a brilliant public speaker and became known as 'silver-tongued Sexton' after W. E. Gladstone* commented during the debate on the Land Bill of 1881 (*see* Land Acts) that his (Sexton's) speech was the finest he had heard in the House of Commons. He was prosecuted for conspiracy but the charge failed (January 1881). Later that year, in October, Sexton was imprisoned along with Parnell. He was a signatory to the 'No Rent Manifesto',*

but was released from Kilmainham shortly afterwards when his health deteriorated. He played a leading role in the National League.* His loyalty to Parnell was demonstrated when he supported the appeal to the party's rebels to support Parnell's candidature of Captain W. H. O'Shea* during the Galway by-election (February 1886). In 1889 he represented Parnell at the inaugural meeting of the Tenants' Defence Association.* During the crisis over Parnell's leadership after the O'Shea divorce case, he proposed Parnell for the chairmanship of the party but then withdrew his support when it became clear that Parnell's continuation in the office could be at the expense of Home Rule. He retired from active politics in 1896 but continued in public life. He was chairman of *The Freeman's Journal,* 1892−1912, a member of the Royal Commission on Financial Committees (1894−96), and Viceregal Commissioner on Irish Railways (1906−10).

'SHAN VAN VOCHT, THE'. Separatist periodical founded in Belfast in 1896 by Alice Milligan* and Ethna Carbery* who jointly edited it. During its three years' existence, the periodical reflected nationalist thinking and published prose and poetry from leading nationalists of the era. The paper was taken over by Arthur Griffith* and *The United Irishman.*

SHANAVESTS. A fighting faction which started in Co. Tipperary and spread to Waterford, Limerick and Kerry (*see* faction-fighting). The Shanavest faction originated in Clonmel in 1805 after the hanging of Nicholas Hanly. A spectator who was asked by his friends to leave the scene of the execution said that he would not leave until 'I have seen the cravat put around Hanly's neck'. News of his statement reached Hanly's relations and friends who formed a rival faction known as the Caravats. In 1818 the Shanavests vowed to support each other for a period of four years and were thereafter known as the Four Year Olds while the Caravats took a vow for three years and became known as the Three Year Olds.

SHANNON FREE AIRPORT DEVELOPMENT CO. The Company was established in 1959 under the Shannon Free Airport Development Company Ltd Act, with particular responsibility for combatting unemployment in the Mid-Western Region of Ireland. Two years later the company oversaw the foundation of Shannon town − Ireland's first new town for over two centuries. Since its formation it has been a major contributor to the export market while devising flexible strategies to meet changing economic patterns. In 1977 under the Shannon Free Airport Development Bill, the company was further charged with the development of small indigenous industry. Its success in this field is apparent from 1978 figures: exports had increased by £6.9m. while imports were down by £4.5m. Eighty-one such projects were assisted by the company in 1978 giving an employment boost of six hundred and thirty-eight to the region. Through Investment Incentives, Training Grants, Duty-Free access to the EEC market, and Research and Development Grants, SFADCO in 1979 had over eighty-eight companies from Austria, Canada, Denmark, Germany, Japan, Luxembourg, Liechtenstein, Netherlands, South Africa, Switzerland, United Kingdom and the United States on their Shannon Industrial Estate employing some 5,400 workers and injecting a £115m. boost to the economy.

Since its establishment the company has responded to requests from United Nations agencies, other international bodies and foreign government agencies to share its experience and skills on development subjects. During 1978 it completed consultancy assignments, related to industrial development, in Bangladesh,

Colombia, Nicaragua and Sri Lanka.

The training element of the company's programme in 1978 comprised two courses on industrial free zones, funded by the Department of Foreign Affairs and UNIDO, and a new four-week course on Tourism Development. The latter course, funded by the Department of Foreign Affairs and the European Development Fund, was provided in conjunction with Bord Failte Eireann* and other tourism-related organisations.

A House Loan Scheme launched in 1976 was availed of by four hundred and thirty-nine tenants whose liabilities extended to £1.7m. at 31 December 1978. SFADCO works in close harmony with the Industrial Development Authority, Coras Trachtala,* Bord Failte and other related tourism and regional authorities. During 1978 it received £7,726 from the EEC in respect of a claim lodged in 1976. The total number of staff in the company (1978) was two hundred and ten, which represented an increase of fourteen on the previous year. The increase was due to the setting up of a new Business Services Division and to the staffing of field offices in Limerick, Ennis, Co. Clare and Nenagh, Co. Tipperary.

SHANNON SCHEME. The electrification of Ireland began with the Shannon Scheme, work on which commenced in August 1925 and was completed in 1929. The scheme was given state aid in excess of £10,000 under the Electricity (Supply) Act 1927 (*see* Electricity Supply Board). Prior to the commencement of work there was a protracted industrial dispute when the trade unions blacked the scheme in protest at the low wages being offered – thirty-two shillings (£1.60p) per week. Because of its geological advantages, Ardnacrusha, Co. Clare, was chosen for the location of the new scheme. The power station is at the end of a seven and a half mile head race which takes the water from a weir situated near O'Briensbridge on the Shannon;

a tail race of one and a half miles returns the water to the Shannon at the village of Parteen outside Limerick city. The head race is 300 feet wide at water level and some thirty-five feet deep.

SHAW, GEORGE BERNARD (1856–1950). Dramatist and critic; b. Dublin; ed. Wesley College. After moving to London in 1876 he worked briefly for the Edison Telephone Company and published a series of novels, all of them commercial failures. Turning to criticism, he became the leading music critic of his day, writing in T. P. O'Connor's *Star* and later in *The World* (under the pseudonym Corno di Bassetto). A socialist from 1882, he joined the Fabian Society two years later, of which, with Sidney and Beatrice Webb, he was a leader. In 1895 Shaw became drama critic of the *Saturday Review*.

He achieved economic independence through his marriage to Charlotte Payne-Townshend, a wealthy Fabian, in 1898 and concentrated on a literary career which spanned five decades. Although his first play, *Widowers' Houses,* was produced in 1892 he did not have any success until *John Bull's Other Island* was banned by the Lord Chamberlain in 1904. The ban did not apply to the Irish theatre and it was produced in Dublin.

Shaw's pacifism during World War I earned him notoriety and expulsion from the Dramatists' Club, and his penchant for controversy continued with the production of *O'Flaherty V.C.* in 1915 and his stand on the Easter Rising of 1916. He protested against the executions of the leaders, saying that 'an Irishman resorting to arms to achieve the independence of his country is doing only what Englishmen will do if it is their misfortune to be invaded and conquered by the Germans in the course of the present war'. The executions, he pointed out, were turning patriots into martyrs and handing the coun-

Shaw

try over to Sinn Fein. He then took up the defence of Sir Roger Casement.*

Shaw believed that Casement was a lost cause (he would not allow his wife to put money into the defence fund) but suggested that the line of defence should be an admission of guilt. He wished Casement to say, 'I am an Irishman, captured in a fair attempt to achieve the independence of my country'. While this accorded with Casement's own view, the defence put forward by Serjeant Sullivan was based on a legal technicality. Following the trial, Shaw continued to fight, presenting a petition to the Prime Minister, H. H. Asquith,* with the message that if Britain wanted to make a martyr out of Casement, it should hang him. His letter 'Shall Roger Casement Hang?'' was rejected by *The Times* but appeared in *The Manchester Guardian* (22 July 1916).

Shaw's reputation in Britain was restored with *St Joan* (1924) and a year later he won the Nobel Prize for Literature. He was a co-founder with W. B. Yeats* of the Irish Academy of Letters.* He declined British honours, turning down the Order of Merit and a peerage. He visited Russia in 1928 and at the age of seventy-five undertook a world tour, visiting four continents. His last years were spent at a cottage in Ayot St Lawrence in Hertfordshire (now a Shaw Museum). His death at the age of ninety-four resulted from complications following a fall while he was pruning his apple trees. He had been a life-long teetotaller and vegetarian. Shaw bequeathed part of his estate towards the introduction of a new alphabet, based on phonetics, a project which has not been realised although some of his own works have been published in this form. Royalties from *Pygmalion* (1912) accrue to the National Gallery.* Apart from his large body of plays, he was the author of tracts and pamphlets on socialism, including *Fabianism and the Empire* (1900) and *The Intelli-*

gent Woman's Guide to Socialism and Capitalism (1928).

SHAW, WILLIAM (1823–95). Businessman and politician (Whig); b. Cork; ed. Highbury. A minister to the Congregational Church in Cork (1846–50), he entered business in 1850 and met with some early success, becoming a director of the Munster Bank. MP for Bandon (1868–74) and for Co. Cork (1874–85), he was a member of the Home Rule Party under Isaac Butt,* whom he succeeded as chairman in 1879 (*see* Irish Parliamentary Party). In 1880 the principal contender for leadership of the party was Charles Stewart Parnell* and at the election in May, Shaw was not over-optimistic about his own chances – 'I have not the slightest intention of competing in popularity with Mr Parnell. Mr Parnell is a good-looking young man'. The result of the vote was twenty-three for Parnell against Shaw's eighteen. He did not support the party's radicals on the Land League,* and formally seceded from the party, followed by eleven other Whigs, in January 1881. He continued to support Gladstone and the Liberals on Home Rule. His bank failed in 1885, and thereafter he played no further part in public affairs.

SHAWE-TAYLOR, CAPTAIN JOHN. *See* Land Conference.

SHEBEEN. Illicit public-house. The word 'shebeen' was derived from the vessel of two to three quart capacity used to exact grain tolls. It was later used to measure drink to the peasantry who were the usual customers at these establishments. According to Maria Edgeworth* in *Castle Rackrent*, weak beer or 'taplash' was commonly available in shebeens, as was poteen (frequently coloured with legal whiskey).

SHEEHAN, REV. PATRICK AUGUSTUS, CANON (1852–1913). Clergyman (R.C.) and novelist; b. Mallow, Co. Cork; ed. National

530

School, Fermoy and at Maynooth where he was ordained in 1875. After ministering as a curate in Exeter (1875–77), Mallow (1877–81), Queenstown (Cobh) (1881–88) and Mallow again (1888–95), he became parish priest in Doneraile, Co. Cork (1895–1913). Most of his novels were written in the garden of his Doneraile home. A close friend of William O'Brien MP, the land agitator, Canon Sheehan's works display an acute observation of rural Ireland and the changes which were occurring. They were popular abroad. In Russia, Tolstoy called him '. . . the greatest living author', and he was highly admired in the USA. His works included *Geoffrey Austin, Student* (1895) and its sequel *The Triumph of Failure* (1899), *My New Curate* (1899), *Glenanaar* (1905), *The Blindness of Dr Gray* (1909), *Miriam Lucas* (1912) and *The Graves of Kilmorna* (1915). *Tristram Lloyd* (1928), his uncompleted last novel, was completed by Rev. Henry Gaffney.*

SHEEHY, DAVID (1843–1932). Politician (Irish Parliamentary Party) and land agitator; b. Broadford, Co. Limerick, brother of Fr Eugene Sheehy.* He established a milling business at Loughmore, near Templemore, Co. Tipperary, where he raised his family. A supporter of the Irish Republican Brotherhood* and of the Land League,* he was returned as MP for Galway (1885–1900) and South Meath (1903–08). He allied himself with John Dillon* and William O'Brien* during the Plan of Campaign,* for which he served eighteen months in prison. During the crisis over the leadership of Charles Stewart Parnell* (December 1890), he opposed Parnell's continuance, believing it would endanger the tenants' fight for fair rent. He was the father of Hanna Sheehy-Skeffington.*

SHEEHY, REV. EUGENE (1841–1917). Clergyman (R.C.) and land agitator; b. Broadford, Co. Limerick; ed. Mungret College and the Irish College, Paris, where he was ordained in 1868. While ministering as a curate in Kilmallock, Co. Limerick (1868–84) he was president of the local branch of the Land League.* His support of the land agitation earned him the popular title of 'The Land League Priest' and a period of imprisonment (May 1881). After moving to Bruree as Administrator (1884–86) he was Parish Priest from 1886 until he resigned through ill-health in 1909. During his early years there Eamon de Valera* was among his altar-boys. He organised a boycott of the local landlord family of Gubbins because of its policy of eviction.

Following his resignation he moved to Dublin where his three nieces, Hanna, married to Francis Sheehy-Skeffington,* Mary, married to Thomas Kettle,* and Mrs Cruise O'Brien, were active in nationalist organisations and the suffragette movement. His circle of friends in Dublin included Thomas J. Clarke* and Sean MacDiarmada,* leaders of the Irish Republican Brotherhood. He visited the USA on behalf of the Supreme Council in 1910. A founder-member of the Irish Volunteers,* he visited the GPO garrison to give spiritual aid during the Easter Rising of 1916, although in very poor health.

SHEEHY-SKEFFINGTON, FRANCIS (1878–1916). Socialist, journalist and pacifist; b. Francis Skeffington, Bailieborough, Co. Cavan; ed. locally and UCD where his friends included Thomas Kettle,* George Clancy* and James Joyce* who portrayed him as McCann in *A Portrait of the Artist as a Young Man.* He revived the Literary and Historical Society (1897), which had been dormant since 1891, and became its first auditor. An M.A. of the Royal University,* he was registrar of UCD from 1902 until 1904 when he resigned after a public dispute with the President (Fr William

Delany, S.J.) over the rights of women to academic status.

Upon his marriage to Hanna Sheehy in 1903 he adopted her name in addition to his own to show that marriage was no barrier to equality between the sexes. They worked together in a wide number of radical causes. He worked on *The Nationalist* (1906), *The National Democrat* (1908), and *The Irish Citizen.** During a lecture-tour of the USA in 1915 he was entertained by Clan na Gael* although he disapproved of republican violence. Sheehy-Skeffington supported the (third) Home Rule Bill* and disapproved of the Easter Rising of 1916.* While attempting to prevent looting during the rising he was arrested by Captain J. C. Bowen-Colthurst who had him executed after a drumhead court-martial. Bowen-Colthurst was subsequently adjudged guilty of murder but held to be insane.

Sheehy-Skeffington published 'Michael Davitt's Unfinished Campaign' in *Independent Review* (1906), and a *Life of Michael Davitt* (1908). His novel, *In Dark and Evil Days,* appeared in 1919.

SHEEHY-SKEFFINGTON, HANNA (1877–1946). Radical; b. Loughmore, Co. Tipperary; daughter of David Sheehy MP, and niece of Rev. Eugene Sheehy; a graduate of the Royal University. The founder of the Women Graduates' Association (1901) she was deeply involved in the suffragette movement, together with her husband, Francis Sheehy-Skeffington,* with whom she founded the Irish Women's Franchise League (1908). She was imprisoned in 1912 for breaking windows in protest at the exclusion of women from the franchise in the (third) Home Rule Bill.* During the Easter Rising of 1916* she carried messages to the GPO where her uncle, Fr Eugene Sheehy, gave spiritual aid to the rebels. She refused compensation of £10,000 from the British army for the death of her husband.

Mrs Sheehy-Skeffington under-took a lecture-tour of the USA in December 1916. During the next two years she called for support for Sinn Fein* and Irish independence, and succeeded, where other republicans failed, in meeting President Wilson (January 1918). Upon her return to Ireland she was arrested and imprisoned along with Mrs Kathleen Clarke,* Countess Markievicz* and Maud Gonne MacBride.* They were released after a hunger-strike. A member of the executive committee of Sinn Fein, she was a judge of the Dail Courts in South Dublin. Rejecting the Treaty, she supported the republicans during the Civil War, again visiting the USA. She later visited Russia (1929). Mrs Sheehy-Skeffington was arrested in Newry in 1933 and imprisoned in Northern Ireland for one month. She was a founder of the Women's Social and Progressive League. Her sisters, Mary and Kathleen, were respectively married to Thomas Kettle* and Cruise O'Brien.

SHEIL, RICHARD LALOR (1791–1851). Lawyer and politician (Repeal); b. Drumdowney, Co. Kilkenny; ed. Stonyhurst and TCD. While reading law at Lincoln's Inn (1811–17) he paid his way by writing plays: *Adelaide, or The Emigrant* (1814), *The Apostate* (1817), *Bellamira* (1818), *Evadne* (1819), *Mantoni* (1820) and *The Huguenot* (1822). His stilted style of writing was evident also in his public speaking. Sheil, who wished to secure Catholic Emancipation* with conditions, opposed Daniel O'Connell* during the controversy over the Veto (1813–15). After becoming a member of the Catholic Board* in 1813 he was closely associated with the fight for Emancipation. In 1821 he attacked O'Connell for subordinating Emancipation to the demand for parliamentary reform, but two years later he helped him to found the Catholic Association* and was active in the Clare by-election of 1828, when O'Connell won the seat.

Among the first Catholics to be

called to the Inner Bar in 1830, he became MP for Milborne Port after a defeat in Co. Louth which seat, however, he secured a year later. After winning the Tipperary seat (1833–41) he sat as a member of O'Connell's Repeal Party. Anxious to further relations between O'Connell's party and the Whigs, he assisted in bringing about the Lichfield House Compact.* During the next few years he enjoyed some sinecures: Commissioner of Greenwich Hospital (1838), Vice-President of the Board of Trade (1839) and Judge-Advocate (1841). He represented Dungarvan from 1841. Although he was not averse to enjoying his own positions, he made himself unpopular by bluntly refusing to seek patronage for his supporters. As Master of the Mint (1846–50) he was the cause of a celebrated controversy when he neglected to have the florin issue of 1849 stamped with the inscription 'Fidei Defensatrix Dei Gratia', causing the coin to become known as 'The Godless Florin'. He completed his career as ambassador to Florence. Sheil was popularly believed to have been the author of *Sketches of the Irish Bar* which appeared anonymously in the *New Monthly Magazine* from 1822. They had been written in collaboration with William H. Curran.

SHEPPARD, OLIVER (1865–1941). Sculptor; b. Dublin. After art-training he taught at the National College of Art, Dublin, where one of his pupils was William Pearse.* His best-known work is 'The Dying Cuchulainn', the memorial to the Easter Rising of 1916 in the GPO, O'Connell Street, Dublin; a professional Italian model posed for the body, the head was that of James Sleator, President of the Royal Hibernian Academy,* and the drape was the hide of a Russian mountain goat.

SIAMSA TÍRE. Folk theatre founded in Tralee, Co. Kerry by Fr Patrick Ahern in 1968. Known originally as Siamsóirí na Ríochta or 'players of the Kingdom' (of Kerry), the title derived from the Irish word *siamsa,* denoting the old Irish custom of neighbours visiting one another's houses to pass the time in the evenings. At first localised, the group of twenty-seven or so players formed Siamsa Tíre, the National Folk Theatre of Ireland, in 1972. Their entertainment, consisting of folk songs, dances, music and mime, has been performed internationally. Under the auspices of the siamsoirí the first Teach (house of) Siamsa was opened in 1974 in Finuge, North Kerry, to encourage the traditional modes of entertainment.

SIGERSON, DR GEORGE (1836–1925). Physician and scholar; b. Holyhill, near Strabane, Co. Tyrone, father of Dora Sigerson Shorter,* studied medicine and the arts, mainly in Paris. He translated and edited Charcot on diseases of the nervous system and his work on biology attracted the attention of Charles Darwin, among others. A fellow of the Royal University,* he was Professor of Biology at University College, Dublin, President of the National Library Society from 1893 and the author of an anthology, *Bards of the Gael and Gall* (1897). He was a member of the Senate of the Free State (1922–25).

SIGERSON SHORTER, DORA (1866–1918). Poet; b. Dublin, daughter of Dr George Sigerson; ed. privately. Following her marriage to Clement Shorter, editor of *The Illustrated London News,* in 1896, she lived in England. Her volumes included *Verses* (1893), *Ballads and Poems* (1899), *Collected Poems* (1909), *New Poems* (1912), *Love of Ireland* (1916), *The Sad Years and the Tricolour* (1918) and *Sixteen Dead Men and Other Poems of Easter Week* (1919).

'SILENCED PRIEST'. A Catholic clergyman who, for whatever reason, had been suspended by his superiors.

Many such priests were popularly believed to possess 'special powers' enabling them to cure sicknesses, or overcome the devil and 'evil spirits'. When all other resources failed the 'silenced' priest was often approached in time of trouble. George Bernard Shaw* has a portrait of one in *John Bull's Other Island. See also* 'Spoiled Priest'.

SIMMS, GEORGE OTTO 1919–). Archbishop of Armagh and Primate of All-Ireland (C.I.), 1969– 80. b. Dublin; ed. Donegal, Surrey, Cheltenham College and TCD; M.A. (1935), B.D. (1936) and Ph.D. (1950). After ministering in Dublin he taught at Lincoln Theological College (1938–39). He was Dean of Residence, TCD (1939–52), Dean of Cork (1952), Bishop of Cork, Cloyne and Ross (1952–56) and Archbishop of Dublin (1956–69). An authority on Irish illuminated manuscripts, he contributed to facsimile editions of *The Book of Kells* (1950–51) and *The Book of Durrow* (1960).

SINGER, DR PAUL (1911–). Philatelist; b. Bratislava; ed. Bratislava, Vienna, Lausanne (where he was awarded a doctorate in political science), Paris and the London School of Economics. He joined his father's finance company in 1931 in London, and was subsequently a director, until the company collapsed in October 1953 with liabilities of £45,000. Singer settled in Ireland with his wife and family early in 1954 and launched Shanahan's Stamp Auctions in February. Hundreds of small investors were attracted through newspaper advertising. When the company collapsed on 25 May 1959 with assets variously estimated at between £400,000 and £450,000, there were over 9,000 claims by investors and creditors, totalling just under £2,000,000. The collapse of the Singer stamp business resulted in one of the most intricate cases ever to come before Irish courts of law. He was twice tried by jury

for fraud and ultimately acquitted after a three-year battle which made Irish legal history.

SINN FEIN. Sinn Fein ('Ourselves') was a movement which developed between 1905 and 1908 under the direction of Arthur Griffith* and Bulmer Hobson,* absorbing the Dungannon Clubs,* the National Council* and Cumann na nGaedheal.* The title, frequently mistranslated as 'ourselves alone', was suggested to Griffith by Mary Lambert Butler (Máire de Buitléir). The first president was John Sweetman while Griffith and Hobson were vice-presidents. Other prominent members included W. T. Cosgrave,* Sean MacDiarmada,* Countess Markievicz* and Sean T. O'Kelly.

Sinn Fein's original concept of Irish independence was that of a dual monarchy as suggested by Griffith in his *Resurrection of Hungary** (1904). In essence, Griffith cited 'Grattan's Parliament' (1782–1800) as an example of Ireland's legislative independence. The movement spread to the US where the Sinn Fein League was founded in New York by Judge Daniel Cohalan* and John Devoy* in 1907 and the Sinn Fein League of America was founded in Buffalo one year later. The movement in Ireland also had a newspaper, *Sinn Fein,** edited by Griffith from 1906 until its suppression in 1914.

The Sinn Fein policy of 1908, influenced by the economic theories of Friedrich List, included the 'establishment of protection for Irish industries and commerce by combined action of the County Councils and Local Boards; development of . . . mineral resources; creation of a national civil service; national control and management of transport and of waste lands; reform of education; non-consumption as far as possible of articles requiring duty to the British exchequer; non-recognition of the British parliament'. In Griffith's words, 'Our declared object was to make England take one hand from Ireland's throat and the other out of Ireland's pocket'. The policy, however, had little initial impact as was demonstrated in the North Leitrim by-election of 1908 when C. J. Dolan, having resigned his membership of the Irish Parliamentary Party,* contested the seat as a Sinn Fein candidate and secured only one-third of the total poll.

Sinn Fein's anti-conscription stand during World War I (*see* Conscription and Ireland) helped to regain popular support for the movement. The Easter Rising of 1916* was described by the authorities as the 'Sinn Fein Rebellion' although in fact Sinn Fein had nothing to do with it. The executions and mass arrests in the wake of the rising alarmed many including George Bernard Shaw* who warned the Prime Minister, H. H. Asquith,* that government policy was handing Ireland over to Sinn Fein. Tim Healy put it more succinctly: '. . . The Sinn Feiners won in three years what we (the Irish Parliamentary Party) did not win in forty.'

Sinn Fein was reorganised in the spring of 1917 when Eamon de Valera* became president. Cathal Brugha* and Michael Collins* built the movement on a nation-wide basis on a platform of Irish independence and withdrawal from Westminster. A constitution was adopted at the Ard Fheis of 25 October 1917. While it incorporated the old ideals of the movement, it went much further. It read as follows:

I

1. The name of this organisation shall be Sinn Fein.
2. Sinn Fein aims at securing the international recognition of Ireland as an independent Irish Republic. Having achieved that status the Irish people may by referendum freely choose their own form of government.
3. This object shall be attained through the Sinn Fein organisation.
4. WHEREAS no law made without the authority and consent of the Irish people is, or ever can be, binding on their conscience.

Therefore, in accordance with the Resolution of Sinn Fein adopted in convention, 1905, a Constituent Assembly shall be convoked, comprising persons chosen by the Irish constituencies as the supreme national authority to speak and act in the name of the Irish people and to devise and formulate measures for the welfare of the whole people of Ireland,

Such as

(*a*) The Introduction of a Protective System for Irish industries and commerce by combined action of the Irish County Councils, Urban Councils, Rural Councils, Poor Law Boards, Harbour Boards and other bodies directly responsible to the Irish people.

(*b*) The establishment and maintenance under the direction of a National Assembly or other authority approved by the people of Ireland of an Irish Consular Service for the advancement of Irish commerce and Irish interests generally.

(*c*) The re-establishment of an Irish Mercantile Marine to facilitate direct trading between Ireland and the countries of continental Europe, America, Africa and the Far East.

(*d*) The industrial survey of Ireland and the development of its mineral resources under the auspices of a National Assembly or other national authoritiy approved by the people of Ireland.

(*e*) The establishment of a national stock exchange.

(*f*) The creation of a national civil service, embracing all the employees of the County Councils, Rural Councils, Poor Law Boards, Harbour Boards and other bodies responsible to the Irish people, by the institution of a common national qualifying examination (the latter at the discretion of local bodies).

(*g*) The establishment of Sinn Fein Courts of Arbitration for the speedy and satisfactory adjustment of disputes.

(*h*) The development of transit by rail, road and water, of waste lands for the national benefit by a national authority approved by the people of Ireland.

(*i*) The development of the Irish Sea Fisheries by National Assembly or other national authority approved by the people of Ireland.

(*j*) The reform of education, to render its basis national and industrial by the compulsory teaching of the Irish language, Irish history and Irish agricultural and manufacturing potentialities in the primary system, and, in addition, to elevate to a position of dominance in the university system Irish agriculture and economics.

(*k*) The abolition of the Poor Law system and substitution in its stead of adequate outdoor relief to the aged and infirm, and the employment of the able-bodied in the reclamation of waste lands, afforestation and other national and productive works.

II

A special meeting of the Executive may be summoned on three days' notice by the President on requisition presented to him, signed by six members of the Executive specifying the object for which the meeting is called.

In case of an urgent emergency, the President shall call all members of the Executive to an urgency [*sic*] meeting, and may take action in the name of the Executive in case he secures the approval of an absolute majority of the entire Executive. The action taken is to be reported for confirmation at the next ordinary meeting of the Executive.

III

That where Irish resources are being developed, or where industries exist, Sinn Feiners should make it their business to secure that workers are paid a living wage.

That the equality of men and women in this organisation be emphasised in all speeches and leaflets.

In an attempt to solve the Irish question, Redmond suggested the Irish Convention* to David Lloyd George.* The Convention, which sat during 1917–18, was boycotted by Sinn Fein. Later, in May 1918, over 100 leading Sinn Feiners were arrested during the 'German Plot' arrests. These included forty-seven Sinn Fein candidates in the general election of December 1918. Sinn Fein, which stood on an abstentionist platform, issued a *Manifesto to the Irish People* which said in part:

'Sinn Fein stands less for a political party then for the nation; it represents the old tradition of nationhood handed on from dead generations; it stands by the Proclamation of the Provisional Government of Easter 1916, re-asserting the inalienable right of the Irish nation to sovereign independence, reaffirming the determination of the Irish people to achieve it, and guaranteeing within the independent nation equal rights and equal opportunities to all its citizens.'

The election was a sweeping victory for Sinn Fein, which won seventy-three seats. The leader of the Irish Parliamentary Party, John Dillon, lost his seat in Mayo to de Valera. The Irish Party retained six seats and the Unionists won twenty-six.

The Sinn Fein MPs who were not imprisoned met in Dublin and formed the first Dail Eireann* on 19 January 1919. They issued a Declaration of Independence,* and adopted a constitution and Democratic Programme.* The Dail was to be the constituent assembly of the Irish Republic. Sinn Fein's leader, de Valera, who escaped from Lincoln Prison in February, went to America at the end of the year to secure support for the Dail. While the Dail regarded itself as the legitimate government of Ireland, the Irish Republican Army* waged the War of Independence* against the Crown forces.

The Treaty of December 1921 split Sinn Fein. Those who accepted the establishment of the Free State* formed Cumann na nGaedheal* under the leadership of W. T. Cosgrave.* Those who continued to call themselves Sinn Fein refused to recognise the legitimacy of the Free State and gave their allegiance to the survivors of the second Dail Eireann. When the Civil War* ended in 1923, some 12,000 men and women, members of the IRA and Sinn Fein, were interned until 1924. However, there were tensions within the movement and in 1925 the IRA separated from Sinn Fein.

De Valera, recognising the hopelessness of Sinn Fein's fundamentalist position, tabled a motion in 1926 to the effect that if the Oath of Allegiance* was removed it would be a question of policy and not of principle whether to enter the Dail. The motion was opposed by Fr Michael O'Flanagan* and his supporters and rejected by 223 votes to 218. De Valera left Sinn Fein to found Fianna Fail* which entered the Dail in 1927.

Throughout the 1930s and 1940s, Sinn Fein held to its platform of a British withdrawal from Northern Ireland and the reunification of the country. It refused to recognise Eire, which succeeded the Free State in 1937, or the Republic of Ireland which came into existence on Easter Monday 1949. While the IRA was outlawed in 1931 and 1936, Sinn Fein continued to operate freely as a political party. It had little success in general elections but did have occasional gains at local government level. Its biggest electoral success was in the general election of June 1927 when it won a seat in each of the East Cork, North Dublin, Kerry, North Mayo and Waterford constituencies, All five seats were lost in the following general election (September). The party gained some support from the IRA campaign which started in 1956 and took four seats in the 1957 general election, running as abstentionists. The four seats were lost in the 1961 election when the party's vote fell from 65,000 to 35,000 after it had run twenty candidates without success.

Sinn Fein changed direction during the 1960s. Under the leadership of Tomás MacGiolla, who took office in 1965, and influenced by Dr Roy Johnston and the Wolfe Tone Society,* the party moved to the left, a move supported by Cathal Goulding, leader of the IRA and editor of *The United Irishman.* *

Sinn Fein supporters were involved in the early marches organised by the Northern Ireland Civil Rights Association* for which the IRA sometimes acted as stewards. Events in Northern Ireland soon caused tensions within the Sinn Fein and IRA leadership. The republicanism of the northern part of the movement, whose Republican Clubs still carried the undiluted message of a united Ireland, had less appeal in Dublin where Sinn Fein had mingled socialism with traditional republican doctrine. This lack of empathy between the northern and southern parts of the movement needed little to precipitate another breach. The break occurred in January 1970 when the northern section, together with southern traditionalists, formed Provisional Sinn Fein, while the remainder called themselves Official Sinn Fein. A similar breach occurred within the IRA. Relations between the two groups deteriorated rapidly.

Provisional Sinn Fein. The Provisionals, fundamentalist in outlook, sought the Republic of 1916 and an All-Ireland parliament for a United Ireland. The President of Provisonal Sinn Fein was Ruadhri O'Bradaigh. It established headquarters at Kevin St, Dublin and published its own newspaper, *An Phoblacht.* * The Provisionals were numerically stronger than the Officials.

Official Sinn Fein. Sinn Fein, the Workers' Party (Official Sinn Fein), led by Mac Giolla, had its headquarters at Gardiner Place, Dublin, and published *The United Irishman.* It sought 'the complete overthrow of English rule in Ireland and the establishment of a democratic socialist republic, based on the proclamation of 1916.' The party, which offered an advanced radical programme, altered its name to Sinn Fein, the Workers' Party in January 1977.

'SINN FEIN'. Nationalist newspaper founded and edited by Arthur Griffith* as the organ of Sinn Fein (1906—14). It had small sales and was in financial trouble throughout its lifetime. Another paper of the same name was published by Sinn Fein in collaboration with the Irish Republican Army* from August 1923 until 1925 when it was replaced by *An Phoblacht.* *

SINN FEIN LEAGUE. Founded in April 1907 from a merger of the Dungannon Clubs* and Cumann na nGaedheal.* In September 1908, the Sinn Fein League merged with the National Council* to become Sinn Fein.*

'SIRIUS'. The *Sirius* was the first steamship to cross the Atlantic solely under steam. The ship was built for the St George Steam Packet Co. by Robert Menzies and Son of Leith, Scotland, at a cost of £27,000. The 412-ton vessel arrived in Cork on 9 August 1837 under the command of Lt Roger Langlands R.N., and was placed on the London-Cork route. At 10 a.m. on 3 April 1838 the vessel, now under the command of Lt Richard Roberts R.N., with a crew of thirty-eight, left Cork for New York. The *Sirius* had forty passengers who had paid fares varying from thirty-five guineas (saloon), twenty guineas (second-class cabin) to eight guineas for steerage. Its holds contained some 450 tons of coal, twenty tons of water and fifty-eight casks of resin. *Sirius* arrived in New York at 9 p.m. on 22 April having covered 2,897 miles in eighteen days at an average speed of 161 knots per day. Its highest speed during the voyage was 220 knots per day and its lowest eighty-five knots. On arrival at New York *Sirius*

had less than fifteen tons of coal in her hold.

SIRR, MAJOR HENRY CHARLES (1764—1841). Soldier and Dublin town major (head of police), 1798—1808; b. Dublin Castle. After serving in the British Army (1778—91) he became a wine merchant. As acting town-major in 1796 he played a leading part in the hunt for United Irishmen* who made three attempts to kill him. Most famous for the capture of Lord Edward Fitzgerald (1798), he later apprehended Robert Emmet* and Thomas Russell* in 1803. Having retired from the post of town-major he became a magistrate (1808—26) and was a founder-member of the Irish Society for Promoting Scriptural Education in the Irish Language. While Sirr was a notorious figure to subsequent generations of Irish nationalists (mainly because of his arrests of Fitzgerald and Emmet), he was very highly regarded by his superiors. A cultivated man, he built up a large collection of curiosities and antiquities which were later acquired by the Royal Irish Academy.*

SKIRMISHING FUND. A skirmishing fund was established by the Fenians* in the US at the suggestion of Jeremiah O'Donovan Rossa* in 1875. The purpose of the money was to finance activities directed at the harassment of British rule. John Devoy* and Dr William Carroll* managed to gain control of the fund for Clan na Gael* and used some of it to finance the New Departure* by providing money for Michael Davitt* and the Land League.* Some of the money was used in accordance with O'Donovan Rossa's aims when it helped to finance dynamiting (*see* Dynamiters).

SLEAN. A spade used by the Irish peasants, sometimes called a 'slane'. Used for cutting turf, it was narrower at the top than the bottom. Unlike the 'loy' it was fitted with two sides so as to be worked with either foot.

SLIDING COFFINS. Used during the Famine of 1845–49,* they were coffins with a sliding base so that when the bottom was drawn out the body would fall into the grave, leaving the coffin available for further use. A variation on the sliding coffin was the hinged coffin.

SLOAN, THOMAS HENRY (1870–1941). Trade unionist and politician (Independent); b. Belfast; ed. Belfast. He worked as a shipyard worker at Harland and Wolff's and was a prominent member of the Orange Order.* A leading member of the Belfast Protestant Association,* he criticised Colonel Edward J. Saunderson,* for which he was expelled from the Orange Order. Sloan then founded the Independent Orange Order* in 1902 with a strong working-class appeal. He was joined by Robert Lindsay Crawford,* and won the South Belfast seat vacated upon the death of William Johnston* in 1902. Sloan became part of the loose alliance between nationalist, labour and independent candidates in Belfast for the 1906 general election and held his seat until 1910.

SLUA MUIRI. Auxiliary of the Naval Service* established to replace the Maritime Inscription on 10 June 1947. The officers, formerly of the Maritime Inscription, were commissioned in the Reserve of Officers (An Slua Muiri). Two years later it was reorganised into five companies based in Army barracks in Dublin (2), Cork, Limerick and Waterford. The total strength at the end of 1979 was 392: 24 officers, 91 NCOs and 277 men.

SMIDDY, TIMOTHY A. (1875–1962). Economist and diplomat; b. Cork; ed. St Finbarr's, Queen's College, Cork, Paris and the Handelschochschule in Cologne. An M.A. of the Royal University, he was Professor of Economics at UCC (1909–24). He served in a wide variety of public posts: Economic Adviser to the Plenipotentiaries during the Treaty negotiations (October–December 1921), Envoy and Fiscal Agent of the Free State to the USA (1922–24), and Chairman of the Fiscal Committee of the Senate (1923). He was later Envoy Extraordinary and Minister Plenipotentiary in Washington (1924–29), High Commissioner in London (1929–30), and a delegate to the London Naval Conference (1930). Professor Smiddy was Chairman of the Free State Tariff Commission (1931–33), Chairman of the Free State Trade Loan Commission (from 1933), Chairman of the Summer Time Commission (1939–45), Director of the Central Bank of Ireland (1943–55) and Chairman of the Commission of Inquiry into Post-Emergency Agricultural Policy (1947).

SMITH, PATRICK (1901–). Politician (Sinn Fein and Fianna Fail); b. Tunnyduff, Co. Cavan; ed. National School. A member of the Irish Volunteers, during the War of Independence he was the youngest battalion commander in the Irish Republican Army. Following capture with his unit after a gun-fight in July 1921, he was sentenced to death. After the Treaty he was transferred to Mountjoy Jail and released in January 1922. He rejected the Treaty and supported the Irregulars – anti-Treaty IRA – during the Civil War when he was interned. While interned he was returned as abstentionist Sinn Fein candidate for Cavan.

A founder-member of Fianna Fail,* he was Parliamentary Secretary to Eamon de Valera* in 1938 and to the Minister for Finance (1943–46). Minister for Agriculture (January 1947–February 1948) and for Local Government (June 1951–June 1954, and March–November 1957) when he was also Minister for Social Welfare. He was again Minister for Agriculture from June 1959 until October 1964 when he resigned following a quarrel with Sean Lemass* over milk subsidies. Thereafter he remained a backbencher until June

1977 when he did not contest his seat. Having been first elected in 1923, he sat in Dail Eireann continuously from 1927 until 1977, the longest-serving TD of his time.

SMITH-BARRY, ARTHUR HUGH, 1st BARON BARRYMORE (1843–1925). Landowner and politician (Unionist); ed. Eton and Christ Church, Oxford. He was the owner of an estate in Co. Tipperary, worth £11,000 per annum, part of it embracing Tipperary town. Smith-Barry was Unionist MP for Co. Cork (1867–74) and for an English constituency from 1886 until 1900. He was prominent in opposition to Home Rule. He came to national prominence during the Plan of Campaign* when he became the agent for a landlords' syndicate established to resist the tenants' demand for rent reductions. This brought him into conflict with his Tipperary tenants in June 1889 and he was denounced by the Archbishop of Cashel, Thomas William Croke* for acting like 'an aggressive busybody'. When his tenants withheld their rents he evicted 152 of them in Tipperary town and this led to the foundation of a Tenants Defence League* and the establishment of 'New Tipperary'* to house the evicted tenants. He appealed in vain to Croke in an effort to get the tenants to pay their rents. The 'New Tipperary' project collapsed and he came to terms with his tenants in 1895. He was a member of the Irish Unionist Alliance* of which he was for a time chairman, and was later a member of the All-for-Ireland League.*

SMYLLIE, ROBERT M. (1894–1954). Journalist; b. Glasgow; reared in Sligo where he attended the Model and Grammar Schools before going to TCD. He was studying in Germany on the outbreak of World War I and was interned until 1918 when he escaped during the revolution in Berlin. Following his return to Ireland he was commissioned by *The Irish Times** to cover the Paris Peace Conference. This began his life-long association with the newspaper of which he was later editor, during the years when it became one of the country's most influential organs of public opinion. He once described its policy as 'to advocate the maintenance of a strong Commonwealth connection, while insisting, no less strongly, on Irish political independence . . .'

Smyllie was alleged to have been responsible, along with Major Bryan Cooper of Sligo, for ensuring the absence of Alderman John Jinks from the crucial vote of 'No Confidence' on the Cumann na nGaedheal government on 16 August 1927. (*see* Jinks Affair).

SMYTH, LT-COLONEL GERALD (1885–1920). Soldier; b. Dalhousie, India. He entered the British Army (1905) in the Royal Engineers. A captain (1914), he served in the British Expeditionary Force. He was wounded in action and awarded the DSO; as divisional commander of the Royal Irish Constabulary* in Munster (1920) on the recommendation of General Tudor,* he was responsible for the Auxiliaries* and Black and Tans* in his district. At Listowel RIC Barracks on 19 June 1920 he addressed the policemen, telling them that in dealing with the Irish Republican Army* and Sinn Fein,* 'The more you shoot the better I will like it, and I assure you no policeman will get into trouble for shooting any man'. This led to resignations from the RIC and an airing of general dissatisfaction within the police force. Representations on behalf of the constabulary were made by T. J. McElligott* and Jeremiah Mee.* Shortly afterwards Smyth was killed by the IRA in the Cork County Club.

SMYTH, PATRICK JAMES (1823–85). Young Irelander and politician (Home Rule); b. Dublin; ed. Clongowes Wood. He was a member of Young Ireland* and of the Irish Confederation.* Following the rising of 1848 he made his way to the USA. Smyth planned the escape from Tasmania of Young Ireland leaders, including that of John Mitchel* in 1854. He then rejected the idea of armed insurrection, returned to Ireland (1856) and was called to the Bar. For his services in organising an ambulance brigade during the Franco-Prussian War (1870–71) he was awarded the Legion of Honour by the French government. He entered politics as MP for Westmeath (1871), and was later considered a possible candidate for the leadership of the Home Rule Party. He won the Tipperary seat in the general election of 1880 after which Charles Stewart Parnell* became leader of the party. Smyth's opposition to the Land League* lost him popularity and in 1882 he resigned his seat, after which he lived in poverty for some time. He died within a few weeks of accepting the secretaryship of the Irish Loan Representative Fund for which he had been severely criticised in nationalist circles.

SOCIAL DEMOCRATIC AND LAB- OUR PARTY. Political party founded in Northern Ireland in August 1970 by members of the old Nationalist Party of Northern Ireland,* the Northern Ireland Labour Party,* the Republican Labour Party,* the National Democratic Party and civil rights activists (*see* Northern Ireland Civil Rights Association). The members of the executive were Gerry Fitt (chairman), John Hume (vice-chairman), Paddy Devlin, Austin Currie, Ivan Cooper, Patrick O'Hanlon and Senator Paddy Wilson. Clause two of the party's constitution stated that its aims included the following:

'To organise and maintain in Northern Ireland a socialist party. . . . To co-operate with the Irish Congress of Trade Unions in joint political or other action. . . . To promote the cause of Irish unity based on the consent of the majority of people in Northern Ireland. . . . To contest elections in Northern Ireland with a view to forming a government which will implement the following principles: (*a*) the abolition of all forms of religious, political, class or sex discrimination; the promotion of culture and the arts with a special responsibility to cherish and develop all aspects of our native culture; (*b*) the public ownership and democratic control of such essential industries and services as the common good requires; (*c*) the utilisation of its powers by the state, when and where necessary, to provide employment, by the establishment of publicly-owned industries.'

The SDLP led the parliamentary opposition at Stormont, pressing the Ulster Unionist Party,* which held a monopoly on government, for reform and concessions to the civil rights movement. Dissatisfaction with the Unionists culminated in the party's withdrawal from parliament in July 1971. A month later the Prime Minister, Brian Faulkner,* introduced internment in an attempt to destroy the Provisional Irish Republican Army.* This move further alienated the Catholic minority population and led to an escalation of violence. The situation in Northern Ireland continued to deteriorate and direct rule from Westminster was introduced in March 1972.

With Unionist government ended, the SDLP now called for a policy of co-operation with the Secretary of State for Northern Ireland, William Whitelaw, 'as a gesture of our confidence that meaningful political progress is now possible'. The party won nineteen seats in the election of 20 March 1973, which was held in order to form an Assembly of Northern Ireland with a power-sharing Executive. Talks were held with the Faulknerite Unionists and the Alliance Party* on 5 October, with a view to forming a coalition, and it was agreed that the SDLP would hold four posts in the Executive. The party was also represented at the talks which led to the Sunningdale Agreement* in December 1973. The four SDLP representatives on the Executive which took office on

1 January 1974 were Fitt (Deputy Chief Executive), Hume (Minister of Commerce), Devlin (Minister of Health and Social Security) and Currie (Minister of Local Government). In addition, two members of the party, Edward McGrady (Minister of Economic Planning) and Ivan Cooper (Minister of Community Relations), were non-voting members of the Executive. The Executive and the Assembly were brought down, however, by the United Ulster Unionist Council* and Northern Ireland reverted to direct rule (May 1974).

The SDLP lost two seats in the general election of 1 May 1975 for a Convention to draft a constitution for Northern Ireland. Its seventeen seats made it the second-largest single party in the Convention (the Official Unionists held nineteen). The Unionist coalition which made up the UUUC firmly rejected power-sharing, to which the SDLP remained committed. When each of the five main parties submitted a draft report the UUUC's had a majority but was rejected by Westminster which dissolved the Convention. The SDLP continued to represent moderate Catholic opinion in seeking power-sharing and the rejection of the IRA campaign.

The party had always been a coalition and now that its constitutional role in Northern Ireland had ended for the moment the strains began to show. In August 1977 Paddy Devlin and Ivan Cooper questioned the direction in which the party was moving. Devlin's criticisms led to his expulsion. It was also divided over Austin Currie's decision to oppose Frank Maguire in Fermanagh in the general election of 1979 when Currie was defeated. The party's decision not to attend a constitutional conference on Northern Ireland, originally called by Humphrey Atkins for December 1979, led to the resignation of Fitt from the leadership (November 1979). He was succeeded by John Hume. The party subsequently decided that it would attend the conference, which was held in January 1980.

SOCIALIST LABOUR PARTY. Founded in Dublin in November 1977 by ex-members of the Labour Party* and left-wing supporters. Its sole spokesman in the Dail was Dr Noel Browne* who had been returned as an Independent Labour TD in June 1977. The party's platform opposed coalition government, capitalism and imperialism. It also called for the withdrawal of the 'British presence in all its forms from the thirty-two counties of Ireland'.

SOCIALIST PARTY OF IRELAND. Formerly the Irish Socialist Republican Party* of James Connolly.* During his visit to America (1903–10) it became the SPI. Non-marxist and constitutional, it had a small membership. It was taken over in 1921 by Roderic Connolly,* son of James, and renamed the Communist Party of Ireland.*

SOCIETY FOR THE PROMOTION OF THE EDUCATION OF THE POOR IN IRELAND. *See* Kildare Place Society.

SOLEMN LEAGUE AND COVENANT. Ulster's Solemn League and Covenant was signed on 28 September 1912 throughout the province, as loyalists pledged themselves to resist Home Rule. The (third) Home Rule Bill* was certain to become law within two years, as the Parliament Act of 1911* had removed the absolute veto of the House of Lords. The leader in the signing ceremony was Sir Edward Carson.* Within a few days, 218,206 Ulstermen had signed the Covenant. Women were not invited to sign it but 228,991 women signed a declaration pledging support to their men in relation to Home Rule.

The text of the Covenant was:

Ulster's Solemn League and Covenant

Being convinced in our consciences that Home Rule would be

disastrous to the material well-being of Ulster as well as of the whole of Ireland, subversive of our civil and religious freedom, destructive of our citizenship and perilous to the unity of the Empire, we, whose names are underwritten, men of Ulster, loyal subjects of His Gracious Majesty King George V, humbly relying on the God whom our fathers in days of stress and trial confidently trusted, do hereby pledge ourselves in solemn Covenant throughout this our time of threatened calamity to stand by one another in defending for ourselves and our children our cherished position of equal citizenship in the United Kingdom and in using all means which may be found necesary to defeat the present conspiracy to set up a Home Rule Parliament in Ireland. And in the event of such a Parliament being forced upon us we further solemnly and mutually pledge ourselves to refuse to recognise its authority. In sure confidence that God will defend the right we hereto subscribe our names. And further, we individually declare that we have not already signed this Covenant.

The above was signed by me at

'Ulster Day', Saturday, 28th September, 1912.

God Save the King.

SOMERVILLE, EDITH ANNA OENONE (1858–1949). Novelist; b. Corfu where her father was serving in the British Army; ed. in West Carbery, Co. Cork. She studied art in Paris and later illustrated many of the books she wrote in association with her cousin, Violet Florence Martin.* A keen huntswoman, after settling in West Cork she became Master of Fox Hounds (1903), reestablished the pack in 1912 and led the hunt until 1919. She was a founder-member of the Irish Academy of Letters* (1932). Following the death of Violet Martin in 1915, Edith Somerville continued to publish books which, she claimed, had been written with her dead cousin through spiritual means. (The works which she wrote in collaboration are listed under Martin.)

After 1915 she published *Irish Memories* (1917), *An Enthusiast* (1921), *The Big House at Inver* (1925), *The States through Irish Eyes* (1931), *Notes of the Horn* (hunting verse, 1934), *The Sweet Cry of Hounds* (1936), *Records of the Somerville Family of Castlehaven and Drishane*, with Boyle Townshend Somerville (1940) and *Happy Days* (1946).

SOMERVILLE, VICE-ADMIRAL HENRY BOYLE (1864–1936). Naval officer; b. Castletownbere, Co. Cork, brother of the novelist, Edith O. Somerville.* After serving in the Royal Navy until 1919 he returned to his native village. He was a noted amateur archaeologist. Somerville was in the habit of providing local young men with references if they wished to join the British forces. This was interpreted by local republicans as recruiting for the armed forces. He was murdered on 24 March 1936 by members of the Irish Republican Army* who left a note: 'This agent sent fifty-two Irishmen to join the British Army in the last seven years'. His killers were never apprehended.

SOMERVILLE, SIR WILLIAM MEREDYTH, 1st BARON ATHLUMNEY (1802–73). Politician (Whig); Chief Secretary (1847–52); b. Co. Meath; ed. Christ Church, Oxford where he did not take a degree. He succeeded to the baronetcy in 1831. After serving in the diplomatic corps, he was Liberal MP for Drogheda (1837–52). In 1841 he sought the repeal of the Corn Laws and opposed coercion* in 1846. He was appointed to the Irish office by Lord John Russell,* entering it at a very difficult juncture during the Famine of 1845–49.* His office was handicapped by lack of finance for relief works, and he was extremely concerned by the Treasury's determination that Irish relief must come from Irish resources. His attempt to introduce a Land Bill to ease the lot of the tenantry by providing security of tenure was defeated by landlord interests in 1848. Somerville introduced a Bill to remove legal disabilities which debarred Catholics from becoming Lord Chancellors of Ireland, but withdrew it. Created Baron Athlumney of Somerville and Dollardstown in 1863, he supported the Disestablishment of the Church of Ireland* and the Land Act of 1870 (*see* Land Acts).

'SOUPERISM'. Highly emotive epithet for the practice among some Catholics of changing their religion in return for food and drink. In this way, some attempts were made to win converts to Protestantism from among the starving Catholic peasantry. Soupers were known sometimes colloquially as 'jumpers' or 'perverts'. The reason for the connotation was that most of those involved in the organisation of relief during the Famine of 1845–49* tended to belong to the Church of Ireland and many of them were clergymen of that Church, or of the Church of England. Their acts of charity were sometimes misinterpreted.

SOUTH, SEAN (1929–57). Republican; b. Limerick; ed. locally. A member of the Irish Republican Army,* he took part in a raid on Brookeborough RUC barracks on New Year's night, 1957, when he was killed as was his companion, an eighteen year-old youth from Monaghan, Fergal O'Hanlon. South and O'Hanlon became the most celebrated republican casualties of the campaign, which lasted until 1962. Both of them were the subjects of ballads, 'Sean Sabhat of Garryowen' and 'The Patriot Game'. South was also the subject of a poem by Criostóir Ó Floinn, 'Maraíodh Sean Sabhat Aréir', and a biography of the same title by Mainchin Seoighe (1964).

SOUTHERN IRELAND. Area of twenty-six counties designated in the Government of Ireland Act, 1920;* Northern Ireland consisted of the six north-eastern counties of Ulster. The Act was not recognised by Dail Eireann* which regarded itself as the legislative assembly for the Irish Republic declared on Easter Monday (*see* Easter Rising of 1916) and reaffirmed on 21 January 1919 upon the opening of the first Dail.

The Act provided that unless at least one-half of the members presented themselves to take an oath of allegiance the parliament of Southern Ireland should be dissolved and a crown colony government established. A general election was held on May 1921 which was treated by Sinn Fein* as an election to Dail Eireann.

The parliament of Southern Ireland was summoned to meet on 28 June 1921. Fifteen out of sixty-four Senators attended and four MPs out of 128 (the four were the Dublin University representatives). Following a fifteen-minute meeting, the parliament adjourned *sine die*. In July, a Truce led to the suspension of the War of Independence.* There was only one other meeting of the parliament when Arthur Griffith,* as President of Dail Eireann, summoned the assembly to meet on 14 January 1922 for the purpose of approving the Treaty,* and transferring power to the Provisional Government.* The meeting was attended by sixty TDs who favoured the Treaty and by the four members for Dublin University. It was boycotted by Eamon de Valera* and his anti-Treaty supporters. A motion of approval was passed on the Treaty and the Assembly elected a Provisional Government for the twenty-six counties designated under the Treaty (which were co-terminus with the area recognised in the Government of Ireland Act as Southern Ireland). Two days later, the Provisional Government met to prepare for the establishment of the Free State.

Soviets

SOUTHERN UNIONIST COMMITTEE.
The Committee, which was founded on 20 February 1918, represented southern Unionists who felt that they were not properly represented by the Irish Unionist Alliance.* They believed that their interests had not been upheld at the Irish Convention,* and that the Home Rule Act of 1914 (*see* third Home Rule Bill) could be set aside and a new settlement found. Led by William Jellett, MP for Dublin University (1919–21) and Henry de F. Montgomery,* they refused to accept that safeguards for their future under Irish self-government would be sufficient and were markedly hostile towards Sinn Fein.* The Committee was dissolved after the Treaty.*

SOUTHWARK LITERARY CLUB.
Founded on 4 January 1883 by Francis A. Fahy,* its objects were the cultivation and promotion of Irish history, art and literature and to provide a venue where Irish people with an interest in its objects might meet socially. The Club was supported by Sir Charles Gavan Duffy,* W. B. Yeats,* John O'Leary,* John Redmond,* T. D. Sullivan,* T. W. Rolleston,* R. Barry O'Brien,* D. P. Moran,* Justin McCarthy* and Dr Mark Ryan.* It sponsored lectures, amateur dramatics, concerts and dances, and had also a Junior Irish Club for young people. The Club, which was responsible for the publication of the poems of John Francis O'Donnell,* became the Irish Literary Society* in 1891. One year later, W. B. Yeats* and Dr Douglas Hyde* founded the Irish National Literary Society* in Dublin, inspired by the same ideas.

SOVIETS.
During the War of Independence* there were a number of forcible takeovers of businesses known as 'soviets' by the workers. The first such take-over occurred in Monaghan in January 1919 when Peadar O'Donnell* led a two-day takeover of a local business. The most famous soviet, however, was in Limerick, and began on 14 April 1919. A tense situation had developed in the city earlier that month when an imprisoned union organiser and republican, Bobby Byrne, was shot dead during a rescue attempt by local members of the Irish Volunteers.* His funeral was attended by some 15,000 people including the city fathers and became the occasion of a Sinn Fein demonstration. Under the Defence of the Realm Act,* martial law was invoked in areas of Limerick and, in protest, the workers called a general strike and established a 'soviet' which was organised by the Limerick United Trades and Labour Council. The Limerick Soviet received a wide press as international journalists were in the city to cover the stopover of Major Woods on his proposed air crossing of the Atlantic.

Limerick did not have the official support of the Irish labour movement and shortly ran into financial difficulties. The soviet commanded the allegiance of some 15,000 trade unionists. It issued a newspaper, *The Daily Bulletin*, to report its progress. On 24 April, the Catholic bishop and the Mayor of Limerick reached an agreement with the British military commander of the city and the strike was over. The Limerick Chamber of Commerce estimated that the employers had lost £250,000 in turnover and the workers some £45,000 in wages. There was a further development in Limerick in May 1920. The workers took over Cleeves' creamery at Knocklong when their wage demands were refused and they were locked out. Again, the trade union movement. with the sole exception of the Belfast Co-Operative Society, proved apathetic and the workers handed back control of the premises in less than a week.

Further takeovers, all of them destined to end in failure, occurred in 1921: in Co. Leitrim coal-miners established a soviet following the rejection of a wage-claim, in Cork workers took over the Harbour

Soyer

Board, in Drogheda a foundry was taken over; another takeover in Bruree, Co. Limerick again involved Cleeves, when workers there seized Cleeves' Mill and Bakery in August 1921, but handed back control within a few hours. A 'soviet' was established in Dublin where Liam O'Flaherty* seized the Rotunda on 18 January 1922. The small garrison, which included Peadar O'Donnell, was attacked by a hostile crowd and collapsed within two days. Three members of the Communist Party of Ireland,* Hedley, Dowling and McGrath, founded the Munster Council of Action in December 1921. They established two soviets, the last of which was at the Cork Flour Mills which were seized for a short time in February 1923.

SOYER, ALEXIS BENEIT (1809–58). French cook of the London Reform Club who arrived in Ireland in February 1847 at the invitation of the British government, to demonstrate his 'economical soup'—which he asserted 'had been tried and tested by numerous noblemen, Members of Parliament and several ladies . . . who have considered it very good and nourishing'. His 'Recipe No. 2' which enabled 100 gallons of soup to be made for less than £1 (including an allowance for fuel), was distributed, in a specially constructed kitchen, from 5 April 1847. Within two weeks of its opening, an estimated 8,750 people had passed through the doors daily. Soyer's 'Model Kitchen' was purchased by the government and handed over to the Relief Committee of the South Dublin Union, and Soyer returned to his London employment.

'SPALPEEN'. A wandering labourer who hired out his labour to farmers during the season of potato-picking. The word was derived from the Irish words 'sbeal' (scythe) and 'pingin' (penny). Carrying their scythes, spades or loys with them, the *spalpíní* hired themselves out upon agreed terms at a 'hiring-fair'.* The

spalpeen might hold a plot of land for himself on conacre* and the cash which he made from potato-picking would be vital to the family budget. Many of the *spailpíní* were landless wanderers also. They were a common feature of Irish rural life in the eighteenth century and into the first half of the nineteenth, but the Famine of 1845–49* ended their mode of existence. Many of the men who migrate from along the Western seaboard for the potato-picking season in England and Scotland are in the tradition of the *spailpíní.*

SPANISH CIVIL WAR (1936–39). When the civil war broke out in July 1936 Peadar O'Donnell,* a left-wing member of the Irish Republican Army,* urged the formation of the Connolly Column* to support the republican government. Led by Frank Ryan,* the column went to Spain as part of the Abraham Lincoln battalion of the International Brigade and was in action at Jarama where Irish casualties were high. The Catholic hierarchy and the right-wing Irish press supported General Franco and the rebels. General Eoin O'Duffy* led some 600 former Blueshirts* to Spain. They returned in the summer of 1937. The Fianna Fail* government of Eamon de Valera,* having initially supported a policy of neutrality, banning Irish involvement, followed the British and French lead by announcing recognition of General Franco's government on 28 February 1939.

SPECIAL CONSTABULARY. *See* Ulster Special Constabulary.

'SPECIAL MEN'. Category applied only to Irish political prisoners in English jails in the 1880s. The 'special men' received particularly harsh treatment and were nearly all imprisoned under the Treason-Felony Act of 1848. Their designation as 'special' seems to have made them targets for the hostility of the prison staffs. Among those who suffered in this

546

respect were Thomas J. Clarke,* John Daly,* Dr Thomas Gallagher* and Jeremiah O'Donovan Rossa.*

SPECIAL POWERS. *See* Civil Authority (Special Powers) Act, 1922.

SPENCER, JOHN POYNTZ, 5th EARL (1835–1910). Politician (Liberal); Lord Lieutenant (1869–74, 1882–85); b. Spencer House, London; ed. Harrow and Trinity College, Cambridge. MP for Northamptonshire South in 1857 until he became a peer and entered the House of Lords later in the year; he supported W. E. Gladstone* on the Disestablishment of the Church of Ireland* and became Lord Lieutenant. His plan to establish a firm but conciliatory style of government proved difficult in the prevailing political climate. He failed to win support from the Catholic Archbishop of Dublin, Paul Cullen,* who did not wish to become involved with Dublin Castle.* An outbreak of ribbonism (*see* Ribbonmen) in Westmeath led to increased coercion (the so-called 'Westmeath Act').

He was Lord President of the Council (1880–82) in Gladstone's second administration and supported the Land Act of 1881 (*see* Land Acts), and the Kilmainham 'Treaty'* with Charles Stewart Parnell.* The resignation of Lord Cowper* from the Viceroyalty over the 'Treaty' resulted in his return as Lord Lieutenant. When his Chief Secretary, Lord Frederick Cavendish,* was assassinated, new coercion measures were introduced in May 1882. Spencer's standing in Irish opinion declined over the next few years. He was attacked by Parnell and the Irish Parliamentary Party* over a miscarriage of justice in the Maamtrasna trials (1882). When he sought the renewal of sections of the Crimes Act in 1885 he was opposed by Joseph Chamberlain.* Gladstone's government fell in July 1885 over the budget introduced by Henry Culling Childers,* and the Conservatives formed a new government.

Spencer supported Gladstone on Home Rule* in 1886 when the Liberals returned and assisted in drafting the (first) Home Rule Bill* which was defeated in July. For the rest of his career he continued his support for Home Rule.

'SPIRIT OF THE NATION'. A collection of the best songs and ballads which appeared in *The Nation** in its first year. Published in 1843 by James Duffy,* it sold at the rate of 100 copies per day in July. *The New Spirit of the Nation* which was published in 1894 was equally successful.

'SPOILED PRIEST'. One who attended a seminary and studied for the priesthood but did not became an ordained priest in the Catholic Church was known as a 'spoiled priest'. Sometimes disowned by his family and rejected by his friends, he often became a wanderer, sometimes becoming a teacher away from his native countryside. It was considered a social disgrace to have a child who studied for the priesthood but who did not proceed to ordination. *See also* 'Silenced Priest'.

'SPONGINGHOUSE'. Slang for a debtor's prison. At one time prison staff were paid by fee and it became a regular practice for the sheriff to augment his income by preying upon the head jailer who in turn looked to his deputy and the latter to the inmates of the prison. This sytem continued until 1818, when, as the structure was modernised, the prison staff received a salary instead of a fee.

SPRING RICE, MARY ELLEN (1880–1924). Nationalist; b. Foynes, Co. Limerick, daughter of Lord Monteagle, owner of Mount Trenchard estate; ed. privately. A supporter of the Gaelic League* and a friend of Dr Douglas Hyde,* she arranged for the teaching of Irish in the national school in Foynes. In 1914 she accompanied Robert Erskine Childers* and wife on the *Asgard** and was a party to the Howth Gun-running.*

SQUAD, THE. Group of agents within the Special Intelligence Unit formed by Michael Collins* during the War of Independence.* Led by Patrick Daly, this small group, known colloquially as 'The Twelve Apostles', was the front line in Collins' battle with the G Division (Intelligence Unit) of Dublin Castle.* It also acted as a bodyguard for Collins. The Squad was responsible for the killing of British intelligence agents on 21 November 1921, provoking the reprisals which led to that day becoming known as Bloody Sunday.*

STACK, AUSTIN (1880–1929). Republican; politician (Sinn Fein); b. Tralee; ed. locally. Employed as an income-tax inspector for the Dingle region. He was a founder-member of the Irish Volunteers* in Kerry, and held the rank of Commandant for the Easter Rising of 1916.* Unaware that the *Aud** was arriving three days earlier than the scheduled date (23 April 1916), he failed to make contact with it. However, hearing that a stranger (Sir Roger Casement)* had been picked up on Banna Strand he went to Tralee police barracks to make enquiries and was himself arrested. During his period of imprisonment he was ostracised for a time by the Kerry Volunteers who held him responsible for not attempting to rescue Casement. He was released in June 1917, having led the fight for political prisoner status.

Elected an honorary secretary of Sinn Fein,* he was returned as Sinn Fein representative for West Kerry to the first Dail Eireann* (December 1918). He was Substitute Minister for Home Affairs (1920) and Minister for Home Affairs from August 1921 until January 1922. Close to Cathal Brugha,* Stack was suspicious of the publicity given to Michael Collins* who directed the Irish Republican Army.* He was among those who accompanied Eamon de Valera* to London for the talks with David Lloyd George* in July 1921 when he supported de Valera's rejection of the British terms. A leading opponent of the Treaty,* he supported the Irregulars (anti-Treaty IRA) during the Civil War* until he was captured in April 1923. While imprisoned in Kilmainham he led a hunger-strike which severely weakened his system. As an abstentionist republican he was returned for Sinn Fein for Co. Kerry and West Limerick in 1923.

STAINES, MICHAEL (1885–1955). Politician (Sinn Fein) and first Commissioner of the Civic Guards (1922); b. Newport, Co. Mayo; ed. National School. After moving to Dublin in 1902, he joined the Irish Republican Brotherhood* and became a member of the Supreme Council (1921–22). A member of the Irish Volunteers,* he took part in the Easter Rising of 1916 for which he was interned at Frongoch, Wales. He was prominent in the re-organised Volunteers and Sinn Fein. An alderman of the Dublin Corporation (1919–25), he was elected as Sinn Fein representative for St Michan's Division, Dublin, in December 1918. He was director of the Belfast Boycott* for the first Dail Eireann from 14 September 1920 and was closely associated with the Arbitration Courts.* Arrested shortly afterwards, he was interned until the Truce. Following his release, he accepted the Treaty and was reappointed director of the Boycott (19 January 1922). In February 1922 he became Commissioner of the new police force, the Civic Guards, which was known as the Garda Siochana* from August. He was succeeded in August by General Eoin O'Duffy* and was a member of the Senate from 1922 until 1936.

STANFORD, SIR CHARLES VIL-LIERS (1852–1924). Composer, organist and conductor; b. Dublin; ed. Cambridge where he graduated B.A. (1874). Following a study of Brahms' music in Germany he became Professor of Music at Cambridge and a teacher at the Royal College of Music. His pupils at Cambridge included Vaughan Williams, Bliss, Benjamin and Howells. Organist at Trinity College, Cambridge, conductor of the Bach Choir (1885–1902), he was also conductor of the Leeds Philharmonic Society and Leeds Music Festival. He edited *Music of Ireland* by George Petrie (1882). His compositions included five orchestral Irish *Rhapsodies,* several operas including *Shamus O'Brien, The Critic, The Travelling Companion,* seven symphonies, *The Revenge* and other cantatas. He also composed *Cushendall,* a song cycle, and church music. He was knighted in 1901.

STANLEY. EDWARD G., LORD. *See* Derby, 14th Earl.

'STATE OF THE COUNTRY'(1790–1831). Series of reports consisting of the reports of magistrates, army commanders and private individuals (often clergymen), dealing with the state of individual parts of the country in relation to law and order. They are kept in the State Paper Office and cover the period from the 1790 to 1831.

'STATION'. Custom peculiar to Ireland which probably dates from the time in the eighteenth century when it was not always possible for Catholics to have ready access to the sacraments. Stations were held twice yearly, usually during Lent, and in Autumn. The system worked in such a way as, for example, if there were ten houses in the townland, each one would be host to the station once every five years. The location of the station was announced in the church on the preceding Sunday, and all the people of the townland were expected to attend. The clergy heard Confession, offered Mass and distributed the Eucharist. The parish dues were then collected and the officiating priest or priests, altar-boys, and neighbours who attended were entertained to breakfast.

STAUNTON, MICHAEL (1788–1870). Journalist; b. Co. Clare. In his time he was described as 'the creator of the Irish press'. Editor of *The Freeman's Journal,** he founded the short-lived *Dublin Evening Herald* (1823–23) and *The Dublin Morning Register** (1824–43) with the encouragement of Daniel O'Connell.* Staunton, whose staff included Charles Gavan Duffy,* Thomas Davis* and John Blake Dillon,* did much to transform Irish newspapers from servile instruments of the government into independent organs of public opinion. Eventually, he fell into dispute with O'Connell who wanted a press which would make itself an uncritical instrument in the fight for Repeal. He denounced Young Ireland* and was Lord Mayor of Dublin in 1845. He was the author of *Hints for Harding* (1870).

STEELE, THOMAS (1788–1848). 'Head Pacificator' for Daniel O'Connell;* b. Derrymore, Co. Clare; ed. TCD and Cambridge. A prominent landlord in Clare, he bankrupted his estates providing aid for the patriot army in the Spanish War of 1823. After joining the Catholic Association* he became devoted to O'Connell and was a leading lieutenant in the Repeal Association.* His elaborate, grandiloquent mode of speech was incomprehensible to all but those closest to him. O'Connell, who dubbed him his 'Head Pacificator', encouraged him to adjudicate disputes among the Association's supporters. Steel was so overcome by O'Connell's death in 1847 that he attempted to kill himself by jumping off Waterloo Bridge in London. Although he was rescued, he died later as a result of the experience.

STEPHENS, JAMES (1824–1901). Republican; founder of the Irish Republican Brotherhood;* b. Kilkenny; ed. St Kieran's College, Kilkenny. After training as an engineer he worked on the Limerick-North Waterford railway line. A supporter of Young Ireland* and the Irish Confederation,* he served as ADC to William Smith O'Brien* in the 1848 rising at Ballingarry, Co. Tipperary* where he was wounded and reported killed. Reports of his death allayed the authorities' suspicions and he escaped to Paris where he met John O'Mahony* and Michael Doheny.* He was deeply influenced by French radicals and underground figures with whom he came into contact. After O'Mahony went to the USA in 1853, Stephens remained in Paris, earning a living by teaching English until he returned to Ireland in 1856 with the idea of establishing a new organisation.

A man of tremendous energy, over the next two years he travelled some 3,000 miles around the country, examining the feasibility of establishing a secret movement more durable than Young Ireland. This period earned him the title 'An Seabhac Siubhalach' ('The Wandering Hawk') which was anglicised to 'Shooks' or 'Mr Shooks'. He earned a living teaching French to the children of John Blake Dillon* who was now a constitutionalist. Much to Stephens' dismay, O'Mahony, settled in New York, was beginning to lose hope for a secret organisation in Ireland. However, in 1857 Stephens was contacted by an Emmet Monument Association emissary, Owen Considine, who gave instructions to set up a new movement. Stephens dispatched Joseph Denieffe* to New York to seek money for a new movement. Instead of the several thousand dollars which he expected to receive, he received 400 dollars and used it to establish a new organisation on 17 March 1858. At first called the Irish Revolutionary Brotherhood, it was later called the Irish Republican Brotherhood, a secret, oath-bound organisation. At the same time, O'Mahony founded an American auxiliary known as the Fenians,* the name by which the whole organisation became popularly known. Stephens recruited Jeremiah O'Donovan Rossa* into his new movement.

He spent much of 1859—60 in the US or France and then continued his work as Head Centre upon his return. In 1863 he established a newspaper, *The Irish People,* * with a staff including Thomas Clarke Luby,* O'Donovan Rossa, John O'Leary* and Charles J. Kickham.* He also brought together enthusiastic recruiting agents, including John Devoy,* William Roantree* and Patrick 'Pagan' O'Leary.* After the paper was suppressed and the leaders imprisoned in 1865 he evaded capture until November. Devoy then engineered his escape from Richmond Prison with the help of two sympathetic warders, Byrne and John Breslin.*

During 1864 his relations with O'Mahony and the American wing worsened considerably. The Americans, and many Irish members also, were annoyed by his dictatorial attitude. He constantly complained that the Americans were not supplying him with promised arms and money, and he exaggerated the numbers at his disposal. In addition, he made no secret of his poor opinion of the American Fenians. Finally, in 1865, the year in which O'Mahony believed the rising would occur, Thomas J. Kelly* arrived to examine the situation in Ireland. Stephens quoted figures of 85,000 members but Kelly found little evidence of such strength. After escaping from Richmond in December, Stephens persuaded Kelly to abandon plans for a rising for the moment. Early in 1866 he accompanied Kelly to New York where the Fenian movement was seriously divided. His attempts to bring the factions together were unsuccessful. By October he had failed either to heal the breach or raise badly-needed funds. The Americans now pressed for action but in December he again attempted to persuade them to postpone plans for a rising. This time they refused and he was deposed as Head Centre. Kelly, who succeeded him, was sent to Ireland in January 1867 with a group of Irish-Americans to plan the ill-fated rising of 1867.

Stephens left America for Paris where he lived until 1885, when the

French authorities, concerned over his possible involvement in the dynamiting activities of Clan na Gael (*see* Dyanamiters) expelled him. He moved to Switzerland and remained there until, through the intervention of Charles Stewart Parnell,* he was permitted to return to Ireland. He spent the remainder of his life in seclusion in Dublin with the exception of a brief appearance during the centenary celebrations for the United Irishmen in 1898, which had been organised by the Supreme Council of the IRB.

STEPHENS, JAMES (1882–1950). Poet and novelist; b. Dublin where his childhood was spent in the city's slums; ed. Meath Protestant Industrial School for boys. He worked as a clerk in a solicitor's office. His literary career began with the publication of some of his poems in *Sinn Fein*,* edited by Arthur Griffith.* His work met with encouragement from George W. Russell* who introduced him to W. B. Yeats* and George Moore.* Russell assisted in the publication of *Insurrections* (poetry, 1909). *The Charwoman's Daughter* appeared as a serial in *The Irish Review*, and appeared in book form in 1912 (under the title *Mary, Mary* in the US the same year). *The Crock of Gold* and *The Hill of Vision* also appeared in 1912. His appointment as registrar of the National Gallery* in 1915 gave him the security needed to continue writing, and further works included *The Insurrection in Dublin* (1916), *Reincarnations* (1918; translations from Irish poetry), *Irish Fairy Tales* (1920), *Deirdre* (1923) and *In the Land of Youth* (1924). Stephens moved to London in 1925 and quickly established himself as a broadcaster for the BBC. James Joyce* commented that the only writer with the imagination to complete *Finnegans Wake* would be Stephens.

STIPENDARY MAGISTRATE. Post officially created in 1814, initially confined to the metropolitan area of Dublin and extended to the rest of the country in 1822. One of the provisions of office was: 'No justice shall be assigned in any county if he have not land to the value of £20 by the year.' A further Act empowered the Lord Lieutenant 'to appoint by warrant under his hand and seal stipendary magistrates, and to dismiss them at his will and pleasure'. *See also* Resident Magistrate.

STOCKLEY, WILLIAM F. P. (1859–1943). Academic and politician (Sinn Fein); b. Templeogue, Co. Dublin; ed. Rathmines School and TCD. He taught English in Canada until 1905, and upon his return taught at UCC where he was later Professor of English. A member of Sinn Fein, he was an alderman of Cork Corporation (1920–25) and TD for the NUI constituency (1923–23). He supported Eamon de Valera after opposing the Treaty. His publications included critical works on Shakespeare and Newman.

STOKES, WHITLEY (1763–1845). Physician; b. Dublin; ed. TCD of which he became a Fellow (1788); M.D. (1793). A supporter of the United Irishmen* during the early years, he was suspended from his Fellowship in 1798. Regius Professor of Medicine at TCD (1830–43), in which he was succeeded by his son, William Stokes, he was noted for his scholarship and humanitarianism. He was highly praised for his exhaustive efforts during typhus epidemics in Dublin. His *English-Irish Dictionary* was published in 1814.

STOKES, WHITLEY (1830–1909). Lawyer and scholar; b. Dublin, son of Dr William Stokes;* ed. TCD. Called to the Bar in 1855, he served in India (1862–82). Stokes was a student of Old Irish and comparative languages (Breton and Cornish) and edited several translations from Irish. His extensive library was presented to University College, London. His works include *The Calendar of Oengus* (1880), *Saltair na Rann*

(1883), *Lives of the Saints from the Book of Lismore* (1889), *The Annals of Tigernach* (1897), *The Eulogy of Columba* (1899), *Da Derga's Hostel* (1901), and *The Martyrology of Oengus* (1905). He was associated with John Strachan* in publishing *Thesaurus Palaeohibernicus,* a two-volume collection of ancient glosses (1901–03).

STOKES, WILLIAM (1804–78). Physician; b. Dublin, son of Whitley Stokes (1763–1845). After studying medicine in Dublin and Edinburgh, he was awarded M.D. in 1825 and published one of the earliest treatises on the use of the stethoscope in the same year. Physician at the Meath Hospital, Stokes was founder of the Pathological Society (1838), Physician to the Queen in Ireland (1851) and President of the Royal Irish Academy* and of the Royal College of Physicians (1849–50). He succeeded his father as Professor of Medicine at TCD (1843). In addition to papers on a wide variety of medical topics, he published a *Life of George Petrie* (1878).

STONEY, GEORGE JOHNSTONE (1826–1911). Physicist; b. Oakley Park, King's County (Offaly); ed. TCD. Professor of Natural Philosophy at the Queen's College, Galway (*see* Queen's Colleges), secretary to the Queen's University in Ireland (1857–82) and to the Royal Dublin Society.* He published papers on physical optics, molecular physics and the kinetic theory of gases. He introduced the word 'electron' in 1891 to designate the elementary charge of electricity. Stoney assisted the Earl of Rosse* at the observatory in Parsonstown (*see* Parsonstown Telescope).

STORMONT. The home of the parliament of Northern Ireland, built in the grounds of Stormont Castle outside Belfast city. It was opened on 17 November 1932 by the Prince of Wales, later King Edward VIII (*see* Abdication Crisis). Until then parliament had met in the Council Chamber of Belfast City Hall and in the Assembly College, Belfast. The last sitting of the Northern Ireland parliament at Stormont was on 28 March 1972 when the House adjourned until 18 April. However, before that date the parliament was prorogued by the British government and direct rule was introduced in an attempt to find a solution to the conflict between the Catholic and Protestant communities. The Secretary of State for Northern Ireland, with offices in Stormont Castle, became responsible for the affairs of the province.

STRACHAN, JOHN (1862–1907). Scholar; b. Banffshire, Scotland. He assisted Kuno Meyer* in the foundation of the Summer School of Irish Learning in 1903, and published *Thesaurus Palaeohibernicus* (2 vols 1901–03) in association with Whitley Stokes.*

'STRADOGUE, SLEEPING IN'. Expression used for the custom among the Irish peasantry of sleeping naked. If a blanket was available it was used as a cover. In his *Sketches in Erris and Tyrawley* (1851), Caesar Otway* has a description of an Irish peasant cottage and its sleeping arrangements: '. . . stripping themselves entirely the whole family lie down at once and together, covering themselves with blankets if they have them, if not, with their day clothing, but they lie down decently and in order, the eldest daughter next the wall farthest from the door, then all the sisters according to their ages, next the mother, father and sons in succession, and then the strangers, whether the travelling pedlar; or tailor or beggar. Thus the strangers are kept aloof from the female part of the family and if there be an apparent community, there is great propriety of conduct.'

STRZELECKI, PAUL EDMUNDE, COUNT DE (1797–1873). Explorer and humanitarian; b. Poland. After leaving his native country in 1830 he travelled widely. He undertook a geological survey of Australia, during which he discovered the highest mountain in the country (7,316 feet), which he named Mount Kosciusko in honour of his country's statesman, Tadeusz Kosciusko. During the Famine of 1845—49,* he agreed to distribute relief in Connaught. Later, he told John Bright* that 'if the devil were to invent a scheme to destroy Ireland he could not have thought up anything more effectual than the principle and practice upon which landed property has been held and managed in Ireland'.

STUART, HENRY VILLIERS, 1st BARON (1803—74). Landowner and politician; ed. Eton. He had an estate at Dromana, Co. Waterford and was persuaded by Sir Thomas Wyse* to run as the Catholic Emancipation candidate in the Waterford by-election of 1826. With the support of Daniel O'Connell* and the Catholic Association,* he defeated the powerful Beresford family and won the seat. Lieutenant, Co. Waterford (1831—74), he was created Baron Stuart de Decies in 1839. His eldest son, Henry Windsor, failed to succeed to the title when a parliamentary committee ruled that there were doubts as to the validity of Stuart's marriage to Therese Pauline Ott of Vienna (alleged to have taken place in a Catholic church).

STUART, JAMES (1764—1840). His-torian and journalist; b. Armagh; ed. TCD. He was the first editor of *The Newry Telegraph* (1812) and *Newry Magazine* (1815—19). He edited *The Belfast News Letter* (1821—26) and founded *The Guardian* (1827). His publications included *Poems* (1811) and a *History of Armagh* (1819).

'STUDIES'. Irish journal which succeeded *New Ireland Review*★ in 1912. Sponsored by the Society of Jesus, it was edited from 1914 to 1950 by Fr Patrick J. Connolly (1875—1951). It attracts contributions from every aspect of cultural, academic, economic and literary life.

SUB-LETTING ACT, 1826. Act which attempted to prohibit the sub-letting of property by the tenant except with the consent of the proprietor. Sub-letting, with the consequent division of the land, was generally held to be responsible for the poor condition of the Irish peasantry. The Act also assisted landlords in their policy of consolidating landholdings at the expense of the tenantry who were in many cases evicted when their leases expired. Sub-division continued until it was brought to an end by the Famine of 1845—49.*

SUFFRAGETTES. *See* Irish Women's Suffrage Federation.

SULLIVAN, ALEXANDER (c. 1847—1913). Fenian and lawyer; b. either Canada or Maine of Cork parentage. He was reared in Amherst-burg, Ontario where his father served with the British Army. After living in Detroit, New Mexico and Washington, he moved to Chicago in 1872. Qualifying as a lawyer, Sullivan became active in republican politics and in Clan na Gael.* As a member of the Triangle* during the 1880s, he encouraged the Dynamiters.* He was National Chairman of the Clan (1881—85) and President of the Irish National League in America (1883—84). Sullivan was held responsible for the murder of Dr P. H. Cronin in 1889 (which discredited his leadership of the American Fenians) but remained an influential force in Irish-American politics for the rest of his life.

SULLIVAN, ALEXANDER MARTIN (1830—84). Journalist and politician (Nationalist); b. Bantry, Co. Cork, brother of Timothy Daniel Sullivan* and uncle of Timothy M. Healy.* A member of Young Ireland,* he worked as a journalist in Dublin and Liverpool (1853—55). He became proprietor and editor of *The Nation*★ in 1855. A constitutionalist, he opposed the Irish Republican Brotherhood,* which passed a death sentence on him in 1865. He owned *The Weekly News* for an article in which, eulogising the Manchester Martyrs,* he was imprisoned in 1868. A founder-member of the Home Rule League,* he entered politics as MP for Louth (1874–80). After a call to the Bar in 1876 he passed *The Nation* over to his brother, Timothy Daniel, in 1876. He was returned for Meath in 1880 but resigned following a heart-attack in 1881. Using £400 collected for him during his imprisonment in 1868 he erected a statue to Henry Grattan* in College Green, Dublin. His most popular works were *The Story of Ireland* (1867) and *New Ireland* (2 vols, 1878).

SULLIVAN, SIR EDWARD (1852–1928). Lawyer and politician (Liberal-Unionist); b. Dublin, son of Timothy Daniel Sullivan;* ed. Portora Royal, Enniskillen, and TCD. After studying law at King's Inns and the Middle Temple he was called to the Bar in 1888. MP for the Stephen's Green Division of Dublin (1888) and Chester-le-Street Division, Durham (1892), he was the author of *Dante's Comedy in English Prose – Part I: Hell* (1893), *Tales from Scott* (1894) *Buck Whaley's Memoirs* (1914) and *The Book of Kells* (1914).

SULLIVAN, TIMOTHY (1874–1949). Lawyer; b. Dublin, son of Timothy Daniel Sullivan;* ed. Belvedere College, Dublin. After studying law at King's Inns he was called to the Bar in 1895, and became KC in 1918. He married Maev, daughter of Timothy M. Healy.* Sullivan was first President of the Supreme Court and Chief Justice (1936–46).

SULLIVAN, TIMOTHY DANIEL (1827–1914). Journalist and politician (Irish Parliamentary Party); b. Bantry, Co. Cork, brother of Alexander Martin Sullivan* and uncle of T. M. Healy;* ed. locally. A supporter of Young Ireland,* he

contributed to *The Nation** which his brother purchased in 1855. He supported the Home Government Association* and the Home Rule League.* After taking over the editorship of *The Nation* in 1876 he employed Tim Healy as parliamentary correspondent.

A supporter of the Land League, and of Charles Stewart Parnell,* Sullivan entered politics as MP for Westmeath which he represented until 1885. He was Lord Mayor of Dublin (1886–87) and MP for Dublin (1885–92) and for West Donegal, (1892–1900). Soon recognised as the leader of the 'Bantry Band' (a group of Cork nationalists), he was prosecuted in November 1880 along with Parnell and the other Land League leaders (who were all acquitted in January 1881). Through his control of *The Nation* he was extremely influential both in Ireland and in the Irish party, and was a leader of the Plan of Campaign.* He was imprisoned under coercion in 1888 and wrote *Lays of Tullamore* while in prison.

Sullivan was a member of a fundraising delegation in the USA when the crisis arose over Parnell's involvement in the O'Shea divorce case. He was the only delegate to repudiate Parnell's leadership at that stage. Upon his return he was forced to sell *The Nation* which had been losing circulation to *The Freeman's Journal.**

He was the author of a number of popular ballads which included 'God Save Ireland', a song of the Manchester Martyrs* and the anthem of nationalists until 1916, and 'Song of the Canadian Woods' ('Ireland Boys Hurray'). His volumes included *Dunboy and Other Poems* (1861), *Speeches from the Dock* (co-edited with his brothers, 1867), *Green Leaves* (1885), *Poems* (1888), and *Recollections of Troubled Times in Ireland (1843–1904)* (1905).

SUNNINGDALE AGREEMENT. Agreement reached following tripartite talks at Sunningdale, Berkshire, 6–9

December 1973, between the British and Irish governments and the incoming Executive of Northern Ireland (*see* Assembly *in* Northern Ireland). Leaders in the talks were Edward Heath, British Prime Minister; Liam Cosgrave,* Irish Taoiseach; and Brian Faulkner,* leader of the Ulster Unionist Party* and Chief of the Executive to be installed on 1 January 1974. The Northern Ireland Social Democratic and Labour Party and the Alliance Party were also represented at the talks.

The talks, which had been initiated by Heath in an attempt to restore Northern Ireland to normality and clarify relations between Britain, Northern Ireland and the Republic, appeared to reach a wide measure of agreement. The British and Irish governments agreed that there should be no change in the status of Northern Ireland until a majority of the population had expressed support for such a change. It was also agreed to revive the idea of a Council of Ireland* and that there should be co-operation between Northern Ireland and the Republic on matters of law and order. The agreement was signed by the three leaders.

The Sunningdale Agreement was attacked by the Irish Republican Army,* loyalist leaders, Fianna Fail* and Unionist paramilitary groups. The government in the Republic was unable to grant recognition to Northern Ireland's constitutional position or to provide for the extradition of people wanted in Northern Ireland in connection with political crimes. The Ulster Unionist Council* rejected the Council of Ireland. In May, following a loyalist general strike, the power-sharing executive, over which Faulkner presided, was brought down. The Agreement had failed to stabilise the situation in Northern Ireland.

SUPREME COUNCIL (OF THE IRISH REPUBLICAN BROTHERHOOD). Directing body of the Irish Republican Brotherhood.* It consisted of eleven members, one from each of the four provinces of Ireland, one for Scotland, and one each for the North and South of England. Those seven were empowered to co-opt a further four members. As the IRB was an underground movement, meetings of the Supreme Council often took place outside of Ireland, usually in either London or Paris where many of the leaders had to seek refuge. The executive of the IRB consisted of the President, the Secretary and the Treasurer.

SWEAT-HOUSE. Normally a dry-stone corbelled structure in which sweating 'cures' were taken in summer and autumn. After a turf or bracken fire had been burning continuously for at least two days, the floor was swept and strewn with rushes. Five or six people were admitted at a time. The door was sealed with sods and smoke was allowed to escape through a hole in the roof. The occupants then sat naked, sweated profusely, and later cooled themselves in a stream or with buckets of water. A variation of the sweat-house was to have a huge fire burning for a few days, surrounded with cobbled stones. Buckets of water were thrown upon the stones, producing an effect not unlike a Turkish bath. Sweat-houses were frequented by kelp-gatherers, by people suffering from various complaints or by ladies attempting to improve their complexions.

SYNGE, JOHN MILLINGTON (1871–1909). Dramatist; b. Rathfarnham, Dublin; ed. TCD. Having spent much of his youth wandering in the Dublin mountains and the Wicklow hills, he studied music for a time at the Royal Irish Academy of Music and then went to Germany in 1893 to continue his studies. He travelled in Italy and France until, following the advice of William Butler Yeats* whom he met in Paris, he abandoned ideas of a career in music or painting and returned to Ireland. Yeats had advised him to seek his subject-matter in the Aran

Islands and to this end Synge spent his summers from 1899 to 1902 living with the islanders. Observation and the stories which he heard on Aran provided him with the material for *Riders to the Sea* and *The Playboy of the Western World.* It also provided him with the material for *The Aran Islands* which appeared in 1907 with illustrations by Yeats' brother, Jack Butler Yeats.* Synge's other travels in the West of Ireland led to the creation of a new idiom based, he claimed, totally on the speech of the peasantry among whom he had travelled.

He was closely associated with the foundation of the Abbey Theatre* of which he was appointed a director. *The Shadow of the Glen* (1904) aroused a storm of controversy. The story, of a young women who commits adultery, was denounced by nationalists as a slur on Irish womanhood. Arthur Griffith* in his *United Irishman* played a leading role in the attack on the play and its author. It was followed by *Riders to the Sea* (1904) which was accused by Patrick Pearse* of containing 'a sinister and unholy gospel . . .' (He was later, in 1913, to reverse his opinion of Synge and to describe him as '. . . one of the two or three men who have in our time made Ireland considerable in the eyes of the world . . .') Following *The Well of the Saints* (1905), which was again offensive to nationalists, his most controversial work, *The Playboy of the Western World,* was produced at the Abbey in 1907. The accompanying riots led to a bitter dispute between Yeats, its chief defender, and nationalists who claimed that it showed the Irish in a vicious and ridiculous light at a time when the nationalist aim was to project the image of a civilised people worthy of self-government.

Synge's most controversial play was to be internationally recognised as a masterpiece and as possibly the single most important play of the Irish literary revival. His realism, coupled with the poetry which springs so naturally from his peasant characters, broke with the sentimental stage-Irishry of nineteenth-century Irish drama which, written and produced by figures like Dion Boucicault, had been the accepted Irish fare outside of Ireland. In recognition of Synge's contribution to Irish drama Yeats, undaunted and to some extent thriving on the controversy, put on *The Tinker's Wedding* at the Abbey in 1908. By then Synge, dying from cancer, was unable to complete his last play, *Deirdre of the Sorrows,* written for his fiancée, the actress Maire O'Neill (Molly Allgood). His other works include *Poems and Translations* (1910) and *In Kerry, West Kerry, and Connemara* (1911).

SYNOD OF THURLES (22 August— 9 September 1850). Thurles, Co. Tipperary was the venue for the first national synod of the Catholic hierarchy to be held in Ireland since the middle ages. The synod was called by the newly-appointed Archbishop of Armagh, Paul Cullen,* acting under instructions from Rome, which was worried by the laxness of the administration of the church in Ireland. In the decree issued on 30 May 1850 Archbishop Cullen listed the purpose of the synod as the discovery of 'ways and means for preserving and strengthening the faith in Ireland and for warding off the dangers confronting Catholics; the fostering of divine worship and spread of devotion to the sacraments; definition of the duties and offices of the clergy; settlement of controversy and cultivation of the vineyard committed to the care of the bishops'.

The synod condemned the Queen's Colleges* and agreed to establish a Catholic University.* It called on pastors to increase the number of schools and to direct 'those pious associations for the diffusing of catechetical knowledge and the caring of the poor'. It accepted that each bishop would have discretion in relation to National Education* in his diocese. Secret societies* were condemned and the callous treatment of the peasantry during the Famine of 1845–49* was denounced.

Questions upon which the bishops could not agree were to be referred to Rome. Priests were forbidden to issue denunciations of people or movements from the altar or to say Mass after noon. It was decreed that the sacraments of baptism and marriage could be administered only in churches. Marriages between Catholics and non-Catholics were to be discouraged. A register of marriages and baptisms was to be kept in each church. Catholic clergy were not to engage in public disputation with members of other religions and the laity were forbidden to engage in discussions with non-Catholics. Priests were alerted to the dangers of proselytising (*see* Second Reformation), to combat which specially commissioned preachers were to be invited to give retreats. Sodalities were to be established for the laity and Catholic books were to be published to help strengthen the faith.

Decreta, Synodi Nationalis Totius Hiberniae was published in Dublin in 1851, but it took some time for the decrees to win acceptance. They were not popular with the clergy and three years after Thurles, Cullen, by then Archbishop of Dublin, complained that the decrees were not even observed in Thurles.

T

TAIBHDHEARC NA GAILLIMHE. Theatre for works in the Irish language founded with government support by Micheál MacLiammóir* in 1928 when the first production was his *Diarmuid agus Gráinne*. As well as directing, designing and acting in early productions during his four years with the theatre, he translated a number of plays into Irish. An Taibhdhearc is in receipt of a state subsidy.

TAISCE, AN (THE NATIONAL TRUST). Registered company limited by guarantee, founded 1948 and pledged to the conservation of the physical heritage and the natural and historical assets of Ireland.

TAKE. A 'take' was a portion of a farm which was given to tillage under the Irish land system in the early part of the nineteenth century. As described by Wakefield in *An Account of Ireland, Statistical and Political* (1812), the take was divided into between twenty and thirty lots. The lots were subdivided into fields, partitioned into smaller lots, each portion having one or two ridges which were held by their owners as long as the take was given over to tillage. Before the Famine of 1845–49,* the take system was disappearing. It had been conspicuous in Counties Kildare, Kilkenny and Tyrone.

TALBOT, MATT (1856–1925). Labourer; b. Dublin; ed. CBS, North Richmond Street. After many years of dissipation, he turned to a life of piety through reading St Augustine and *Lives of the Saints*. He modelled his penitential exercises on those of St Catherine of Siena and St Teresa of Avila. Talbot slept on a plank with a wooden block for a pillow and held vigils over a period of forty years. After his death in Jervis Street Hospital, it was discovered that he had worn chains around his body for so long that his stomach and back had been scarred with large grooves. There is a movement to have him beatified. *A Life of Matt Talbot* by Joseph Aloysius Glynn (1869–1951), which appeared in 1926, was translated into thirteen languages.

TALLY-WOMAN. An Irish girl or young woman who served as mistress to a member of the landlord class was known as a 'tally-woman'. It was customary in the eighteenth century for the landed gentry to select mistresses from among their tenantry. Such a woman lived in the 'big house' and enjoyed the life-style of her lover. If she became pregnant she was usually paid off in the form of cash or land and a marriage was arranged with one of the landlord's tenants. The custom died out during the Famine of 1845–49.*

TANAISTE. From the old Gaelic system of tanistry whereby the chief (or taoiseach) nominated his successor. In the Irish parliamentary system the Tanaiste is the deputy Taoiseach (or deputy Prime Minister).

TAOISEACH. Title for the leader or Prime Minister of the Irish government since December 1937. The word, chosen by Eamon de Valera,* and used in the Constitution of 1937, came from the Irish word for the chief of the tribe or family-group in the Gaelic system. From December 1922 until December 1937 the leader of the government was called the President of the Executive Council.

TECHNICAL EDUCATION. Under the Technical Instruction Act 1889 local authorities were empowered to raise a rate not in excess of one penny in the pound, to provide technical or manual instruction. Manual instruction was defined as instruction in the use of tools and processes of agriculture, modelling in clay, wood and other materials. Under the Local Government Act 1898 (*see* Local Government), technical education was placed under the County Councils. The Department of Agriculture and Technical Instruction* was established in 1899 and assumed responsibility for technical instruction. Technical instruction was also available in reformatory and industrial schools. In 1924 technical and all other education was placed under the Department of Education.

In 1926 the Minister for Education, J. M. O'Sullivan,* commissioned a report which led to the Vocational Education Act, 1930, which established thirty-eight vocational education committees (VECs) with responsibility for the provision of technical education. *See* Vocational Education.

TEMPORALITIES COMMISSION. Established after the Disestablishment of the Church of Ireland* in 1869, its purpose was to administer the revenues accruing to the property of the Church which was, from 1 January 1871, a voluntary body.

TENANT LEAGUE. Founded in August 1850 by Charles Gavan Duffy* and Frederick Lucas* in Dublin at a meeting attended by representatives of the Tenants' Protection Societies.* Initial support was forthcoming from the Ulster Tenant Right Association* led by William Sharman Crawford but this was lost, principally due to the involvement in the south of Catholic clergymen. Duffy, however, called his movement 'The League of North and South'. Among the clergy who supported the movement was Thomas William Croke (later Archbishop of Cashel), then a curate in Charleville, Co. Cork, who had proposed a 'tenant-right pledge' in a letter to *The Nation* (25 May 1850): 'We promise God, our country and each other, never to bid for any farm of land from which any industrious farmer in this district has been ejected.'

The aim of the League was to secure the three Fs of Fair Rent, Fixity of Tenure and Free Sale. To the larger tenant-farmer, in the wake of the Famine of 1845–49,* fixity of tenure was the main priority and the League never had the support of smaller tenants who were more concerned with fair rent. The founders wished to establish a parliamentary party of Irish MPs who would oppose any government not prepared to grant Tenant Right. This brought the League into alliance with the 'Irish Brigade'* led by George Henry Moore. Following the general election of July 1852 when fifty Tenant Righters, including Duffy and Lucas, had been returned a meeting was called for Dublin in September and the Independent Irish Party* was founded.

The cause of Tenant Right was seriously weakened when John Sadleir* and William Keogh* defected from the party in December. League supporters were also intimidated by hostile landlords. The most serious blow to the League's success however, was Lucas's decision to take his complaints about the Archbishop of Dublin, Paul Cullen,* to Rome. This move alienated clerical support. Lucas died in October 1855, shortly after the failure of his mission to Rome, and Duffy emigrated to Australia a month later. The League collapsed and the Independent Party disappeared by 1860. The demand for Tenant Right persisted and was taken up as a popular cause by the Land League* which secured it in the Land Act of 1881 (*see* Land Acts).

TENANT RIGHT. Free sale, one of the Three Fs,* also known as the Ulster Custom,* was the right of the tenant to sell occupancy of his holding to the highest bidder, subject to the approval by the landlord of the purchaser. This would allow the tenant to secure compensation for any improvements for which he was responsible on the land. Under tenant right, the tenant would be entitled to compensation for 'disturbance' (i.e., eviction), as a landlord who wished to evict would either have to allow the sale of tenant right or pay the outgoing tenant the market price. It was of importance to the larger tenant-farmers who organised the Tenant League* of the 1850s. Under the Land Act of 1870, tenant right was conceded wherever the custom could be shown to prevail, but this was a failure. It received legal recognition as one of the Three

Fs under the Land Act of 1881 (*see* Land Acts).

TENANTS' DEFENCE ASSOCIATION. Founded 15 October 1889 in Tipperary, the association was an inspiration of William O'Brien,* an organiser of the Plan of Campaign. The scheme had the support of Charles Stewart Parnell who was represented at the inaugural meeting by Thomas Sexton.* While Parnell disapproved of the Plan of Campaign, he supported the association under pressure from O'Brien who felt that it was necessary to retaliate against the landlords who were uniting to resist the Plan. The association was led by O'Brien and John Dillon,* but most of its finances were spent on New Tipperary.* The association broke up as a result of the split in the Irish Parliamentary Party (December 1890) over Parnell's involvement in the O'Shea divorce action.

TENANTS' PROTECTION SOCIETIES. Based on a suggestion by James Fintan Lalor,* the first tenants' protection society was founded in Callan, Co. Tipperary, by two Catholic curates, Frs O'Shea and Keeffe, in 1849. Their aim was to protect the tenants from the excessive demands of landlords, to secure a fair rent and prevent tenants from buying or renting land from which another had been evicted. During 1850 the Callan example spread to other areas as tenants, suffering from the effects of the Famine of 1845–49,* sought to secure improvements. The landlords retaliated: on the Earl of Derwent's estate in Callan, 442 tenants were evicted; over the country as a whole the figure was 100,000. In August 1850 Charles Gavan Duffy* invited the societies to send representatives to a meeting in Dublin where the Tenant League* was established to co-ordinate the fight.

THATCH. Traditional method of roofing once common throughout

Ireland. Isaac Weld, while engaged on the Royal Dublin Society's *Statistical Survey* in 1832, noted in Co. Roscommon that 'out of 517 houses, no less than 462 are thatched'. The materials used for roofing varied from area to area – dictated by financial consideration, availability and climatic conditions.

The following gives a general picture of the types of thatch used in different areas and conditions:

Barley Used in the most humble of dwellings only, and then on a limited scale.

Flax Occasionally used in Derry, Donegal and Fermanagh.

Heather Used in Donegal and other mountain districts; although this type of thatch was rough in appearance it presented a sturdy and durable roofing material.

Oat-straw Favoured in Kildare, Louth, Meath, Westmeath and Laois, this particular straw had a most beautiful golden sheen when new.

Reed Munster thatchers favoured the wild reed.

Rye This thatch was considered extremely durable if cut just before ripening. It was specially grown for thatching purposes in Donegal.

THOMPSON, WILLIAM (1785–1833). Political economist and social reformer; b. Rosscarbery, Co. Cork. The heir to a large fortune and estate, he became a radical democrat, socialist and supporter of female emancipation. He was influenced by the ideas of the French Revolution and during his travels on the continent and in England, came into contact with leading philosophers and economists of the era. His friends included Jeremy Bentham and David Ricardo.

Thompson started a co-operative farm on his estate at Rosscarbery where he granted long leases and taught his tenants modern methods of cultivation and scientific farming. He anticipated Karl Marx in the theory of surplus value, for which he received a footnote in *Das Kapital.* He published *An Inquiry into the principles of distribution of wealth*

most conducive to human happiness (1824), which while supporting the idea of a co-operative, rejected most of Robert Owen's theories; *Practical Considerations for the speedy and economic establishment of communities on the principle of co-operation* (1825) and *An Appeal of one half of the human race, women, against the pretensions of the other half, men, to retain them in political and thence in civil and domestic slavery* (1825).

After his death it was discovered that he had bequeathed his estate to the co-operative. His relatives challenged the will in an action which continued for twenty-five years to the benefit neither of themselves nor of the co-operative.

THOMPSON, WILLIAM (1805–52). Naturalist; b. Belfast; ed. locally. Having left the family linen business he devoted himself to nature studies and in 1832 commenced the systematic collection and arrangement of specimens of Irish fauna. After accompanying Forbes to the Levant in 1841, he contributed to the *Annals and Magazines of Natural History* and *Phycolagia Britannica.* President of the Natural History Society of Belfast (from 1843), he published *Report on the Fauna of Ireland – Division Vertabrate* (1840) and his major work, *The Natural History of Ireland* (4 vols, 1849–56).

'THOM'S DIRECTORY'. Compiled by Peter Wilson as the *Dublin Directory* in 1752, it was sold for threepence (1p). The *Directory* became the property of Alexander Thom in 1844 and henceforth bore his name.

THRASHERS. Agrarian secret society active in the 1820s and 1830s. *See* Secret Societies.

THREE Fs. Fixity of tenure, Fair rent and Free sale, known as the Three Fs, were demands of the Irish tenantry since the eighteenth century. The last of these, free sale, also known as Tenant Right,* generally obtained in Ulster and so was known as the Ulster Custom.* The Three Fs were conceded in the Land Act of 1881 (*see* Land Acts), under which Land Courts were empowered to arbitrate in disputes between landlords and tenants. While fixity of tenure and free sale were of value to the larger tenant-farmers, fair rent was of vital concern to the poorer tenants.

TINKERS. Tinkers, now officially known as 'itinerants', were descended from the dispossessed of the seventeenth and early eighteenth centuries who became tinsmiths from necessity. Prominent names among the 'travellers' are Cash, Coffey, Doherty, Maughan, McCarthy, MacDonagh, Reilly and Ward. The Irish tinkers developed a language of their own known as Shelta or Sheldry. As tinsmithing became an obsolete occupation with the arrival of synthetic containers, the tinkers attempted to find alternative work as traders. Their attempts to integrate in the settled community have been seriously hampered by prejudice.

TITHE APPLOTMENT. The Tithe Applotment books, dating from 1823–37, contain a record of the valuations assessed for each rural parish by the Parochial Commissioners, one of whom was appointed by the Church of Ireland bishop, and the other elected by the ratepayers. *See* Tithes.

TITHES. A tithe was 'the tenth part of the increase, yearly arising and renewing from the profits of lands, the stock upon lands, and the personal industry of the inhabitants' for the upkeep of the church. First introduced during the reign of Henry II, tithes were not paid outside of the area around Dublin until the reign of Elizabeth I when they were used for the upkeep of the Established Church of Ireland. As they were then payable by the Catholic population for the upkeep of a church to whose doctrines they did not subscribe, tithes became a chronic source of complaint and unrest into the nineteenth century.

There were three sources of tithes: *praedial*, from corn; *mixed*, from lambs, and *personal*, from money. They were divided into two major types: *great* or *rectoral*, on corn, hay and wood; and *small* or *vicarial*, on flax, garden produce and potatoes. The 'great' class made up two-thirds of the church's income from tithes. By an Irish Act of 1735 which forbade the tithe agistment payable upon pasturage and its produce, the main burden of paying tithes fell upon those who could least afford it. This Act was confirmed at the time of the Union. Payment was vigorously resisted by the Catholic and Presbyterian Churches and led to support for agrarian secret societies.*

Assessment of the tithes due was carried out by tithe-proctors who were often Catholic and held in contempt by their co-religionists. There were three methods of payment: in kind (tithe proctors were notorious for taking the best quality share of the produce); by fixed annual payment based upon acreage and by a variable tithe which depended on the output of the farm. In 1835 Church of Ireland revenues were calculated at £815,331, of which £531,782 came from tithes.

The 'tithe war', as it was known, was fought between 1830 and 1838. According to Lord Gort, speaking in the House of Lords in 1832, 242 homicides, 1,179 robberies, 401 burglaries, 568 burnings, 280 cases of cattle-maiming, 161 assaults, 203 riots and 723 attacks on houses were directly attributed to tithe-enforcement. The Chief Secretary, Lord Edward Stanley (*see* Derby, 14th Earl) fought against the evasion of tithe payment. The war started in Graiguenamanagh on the Carlow-Kilkenny border when the tithe proctor distrained the cattle of a Catholic priest, Fr Martin Doyle, who organised resistance with the approval of his bishop, James Doyle.* The resistance soon spread to the midlands.

In January 1831 when a magistrate

in Newtownbarry, Co. Wexford ordered out the yeomen at a sale of cattle which had been seized for non-payment of tithes, twelve people were killed. This was followed by incidents at Castlepollard, Co. Westmeath, Knocktopher, Co. Kilkenny and Wallstown, Co. Cork. The government issued 43,000 decrees against tithe evaders and spent £26,000 in order to collect £12,316. This was followed by concession when Lord Stanley introduced a Tithe Composition Bill which made the leaseholder above the tenant-at-will liable for payment but this made little impact. By 1833 arrears were estimated at over £1,000,000, and in June of that year the government advanced £1,000,000 to tithe-owners, subject to a 21 per cent reduction in the arrears for 1831–32.

Another attempt to solve the problem was made in 1834 by Edward John Littleton,* Stanley's successor, but the Bill was defeated in the Lords, after amendments had been secured by Daniel O'Connell.* In the same year there were two notorious incidents in the tithe war, at Doon, Co. Limerick and Rathcormac, Co. Cork.

There was a riot in Doon when the Church of Ireland rector, Rev. J. Coote, seized the cow of a Catholic priest in lieu of a tithe payment, and then offered the animal for sale at auction. Four thousand people attended and were confronted by sixty members of the 12th Lancers, five companies of the 92nd Highlanders and two artillery pieces. Doon became a rallying cry in the tithe war, which escalated when the Church of Ireland Archdeacon of Cloyne, Rev. William Ryder, who was also a Justice of the Peace, attempted to collect a forty-shilling tithe from a widow in Rathcormac, Mrs Ryan. Ryder, who was accompanied by police and troops of the 4th Royal Irish Dragoons and the 29th Regiment, entered the widow's cottage by a back window. While he was inside, there was a confrontation between the troops and local peasants. Nineteen people died in the fighting and thirty-five were wounded. Rev. Ryder, who had been popular in the neighbourhood before the incident, became a symbol of the tithe oppression.

Another attempt to deal with the problem was made in 1837 when a Bill was introduced by Viscount Morpeth.* It was unsuccessful but during the following year the Tithe Commutation Act removed a major grievance. Under the Act the tithe became a rent-charge at three-quarters of the old composition, payable twice yearly by the head landlord. He was allowed to add the charge to the rent of the immediate sub-tenants. By converting the tithe into a rent-charge, the Act removed the tithe-proctor and tithe-farmer and so removed the immediate source of discontent.

TODD, REV. JAMES HENTHORN (1805–69). Clergyman (C.I.) and scholar; b. Dublin; ed. TCD where he received his B.A. in 1825. He was elected to the Royal Irish Academy* in 1833, one year after his ordination, and became a Council member (1837), Secretary (1847–55) and President (1856–61). Founder of the Irish Archaeological Society (1841), he worked in close association with John O'Donovan* and Eugene O'Curry,* with whom he catalogued a large collection of Irish manuscripts while Librarian at TCD (from 1852). He quadrupled the library stock and procured transcripts of several Irish MSS in European libraries. He assisted O'Donovan in the preparation of O'Reilly's *Irish-English Dictionary* (1864). In addition to his own works, *Life of St Patrick* (1864) and *The Book of the Vaudois* (1865), he edited several works of antiquarian and religious interest, including *The Last Age of the Church* (1840), *An Apology for Lollard Doctrine* (1842), *The Irish Version of the Historia Britonum of Nennius* (1848), and *The Book of Hymns of the Ancient Church of Ireland* (1855).

TODHUNTER, JOHN (1839–1916). Doctor, poet and critic; b. Dublin; ed. York School, TCD, Paris and Vienna. After obtaining his M.D. in 1871 he practised medicine in Dublin. He taught English at Alexandra College, Dublin (1870–74) and later travelled on the continent and in Egypt before settling in London (1879), where he was active in the Irish Literary Society* and in the Gaelic League.* His works include *The Theory of the Beautiful* (1872), *Laurella and Other Poems* (1876), *The Banshee and Other Poems* (1888), *Life of Sarsfield* (1895), *Three Irish Bardic Tales* (1896), *Sound and Sweet Airs* (1905) and a translation of Heine's *Book of Songs* (1907).

TORRENS, WILLIAM TORRENS McCULLOUGH (1813–94). Politician (Independent Liberal) and reformer; b. Dublin; ed. TCD. After receiving his B.A. in 1833 he was called to the Irish Bar in 1836 and to the English Bar in 1855. He was an assistant commissioner on the Special Commission which enquired into the best system of Poor Law* to introduce into Ireland (1833–35), and a leading member of the Anti-Corn Law League. In 1842 he was co-founder with Sir Robert John Kane* of the Mechanics' Institute in Dublin, the first of its kind. Returned as an Independent Liberal MP for Dundalk, 1848–52. He stood unsuccessfully at Great Yarmouth in 1852 and did not sit again until 1857, when he won that seat, which he represented until 1865. He was then returned for the ancient borough of Finsbury, in London, which he represented until his retirement in 1885. An enlightened speaker on social topics, he supported the Reform Act of 1867 and carried an amendment which granted the franchise to lodgers. During the following year he introduced the Artisans' Dwelling Act ('Torrens Act') which allowed extensive clearance of slum districts. His Amendment to the Education Act of 1870 established the London School Board.

Torrens' publications include *Memoirs of the Right Hon. Richard Lalor Sheil* (2 vols, 1863), *The Life and Times of Sir James Graham* (2 vols, 1863), *Memoirs of Viscount Melbourne* (2 vols, 1878), *Life of Lord Wellesley* (2 vols, 1880), *Twenty Years in Parliament* (1893) and *History of Cabinets* (1894).

TÓSTAL, AN. From the Irish word for a 'pageant, array or muster', it was a National Festival organised with the support of the Fianna Fail government in 1953, during a severe economic depression. The idea was not a success and An Tóstal disappeared except in Drumshambo, Co. Leitrim where it has since been held. The Dublin Theatre Festival was a successful offshoot of An Tóstal.

TOWN COMMISSIONERS. *See* Local Government.

TOWNS IMPROVEMENT (IRELAND) ACT, 1854. *See* Local Government.

TOWNSEND, JOHN SEALY (1868–1957). Physicist; b. Galway; ed. TCD. The first scientist to determine the electrical charge on one ion of gas in 1897, he was the author of treatises on the *Theory of Ionisation of Gases by Collision* (1910) and *Electricity in Gases* (1915).

TRADE UNION ACT, 1941. Introduced by the Fianna Fail government in 1941, the Act met with strong resistance from the trade union movement. Under the Act a trade union would have to lodge a sum of money with the High Court in order to obtain from the government a licence which would enable it to take part in collective bargaining. It also stipulated that a tribunal should be established to determine that one union should be entitled to organise a particular category of workers if it could be demonstrated that the union had the support of the majority of workers in the particular category. It was also stipulated

563

that only an Irish-based union should receive sole negotiating rights from the tribunal (this was later held by the Supreme Court to be unconstitutional). The Act, which was supported by the Irish Transport and General Workers' Union,* the biggest union in the country, was opposed by the smaller unions with the support and leadership of James Larkin.*

TRAILL, DR ANTHONY (1838–1914). Physician and Provost of Trinity College, Dublin (1904–14); b. Co. Antrim; ed. TCD of which he became a Fellow in 1865. He was High Sheriff of Antrim, a representative of the landlords on the Fry Commission on the Land Acts (1897–98), a member of the Commissioners of National Education in Ireland (1901) and for many years chairman of the Portrush Electric Railway, one of the pioneering electric-railways. Traill published a variety of articles on the Church of Ireland, land and education. When he became Provost of Trinity, much to the chagrin of John Pentland Mahaffy,* he was the first medical man to hold the office.

TRAYNOR, OSCAR (1886–1963). Politician (Fianna Fail); b. Dublin; ed. CBS. A member of the Irish Volunteers, he fought in the Easter Rising of 1916 for which he was interned. Following his release he became active in the re-organised Sinn Fein* and was O/C of the Dublin Brigade of the Irish Republican Army during the War of Independence.* He organised one of the most successful IRA coups, when, on 25 May 1921, his Brigade burned the Custom House,* destroying important administrative documents. Traynor rejected the Treaty* and was active in the Civil War* when, as senior officer, he ordered the Four Courts* garrison to surrender in order to let him 'carry on the fight outside'. A founder-member of Fianna Fail,* he was Minster for Posts and Telegraphs (November 1936–September 1939), for Defence (September 1939–

February 1948; June 1951–June 1954) and for Justice (March 1957–October 1961).

TREACY, SEAN (1895–1920). Republican soldier; b. Solohead, Co. Tipperary; reared in Lackenacreena, Hollyford; ed. Hollyford National School and CBS, Tipperary. He joined the Gaelic League and the Irish Republican Brotherhood (1911) in which he became Centre of the Tipperary Circle. He was a close friend of Dan Breen* with whom he joined the Irish Volunteers* in 1913. After the Easter Rising of 1916 he played a major role in the reorganisation of the Volunteers and Sinn Fein.* He was imprisoned from August to November 1917 and from February until June 1918. In October 1918 he became Brigade vice-commandant of the Third Tipperary Brigade and was among those at the ambush at Soloheadbeg (21 January 1919) which started the War of Independence.* Treacy was wounded during the rescue of Sean Hogan at Knocklong (13 May 1919) and was subsequently on the run. He worked for a time in Dublin with Michael Collins and the Squad.* He took part in the attempt to assassinate Lord French at Ashtown (19 December 1919) and during 1920 was involved in the raids on Hollyford Barracks (10–11 May), Drangan Barracks (3 June) and Rear Cross Barracks (11 July). Having moved to Dublin in September, he was killed in a gun-battle in Talbot Street on 14 October 1920 when two of his assailants, Lieutenant Price and Sergeant Christian, were also killed.

TREASON ACT, 1939. Introduced on 30 May 1939 by the Fianna Fail government in response to the campaign conducted by the Irish Republican Army* against Northern Ireland and England. Under the Act treason was punishable by death. Shortly afterwards the government introduced the Offences Against the State Act.*

TREASON-FELONS. Nationalists found guilty under the Treason-Felony Act, 1848.* Sometimes known as 'Special Men',* they were treated with great harshness in British prisons.

TREASON-FELONY ACT, 1848. An Act rushed through parliament in order to give the Irish executive power to apprehend prominent members of Young Ireland.* Under the Act, the government could prosecute 'any person who, by open and advised speaking, compassed the intimidation of the crown or parliament'. The penalty for those found guilty under the Act was transportation for terms ranging from fourteen years to life. It received the royal assent on 22 April and in May, John Mitchel* became the first Young Irelander to be found guilty under it. *See also* 'Special Men'.

'TREASURY OF IRISH POETRY'. Edited by T. W. Rolleston* and Stopford Brooke, the collection appeared in 1900 at the height of the Irish literary revival and became the accepted anthology of Anglo-Irish poetry. Introductory notes were provided by William Butler Yeats,* Lionel Johnson, Dr Douglas Hyde* and George Sigerson.*

TREATY. The War of Independence,* which had broken out on 21 January 1919, on the same day as the Sinn Fein* representatives formed the first Dail Eireann* and reaffirmed the Irish Republic, ended with a Truce on 11 July 1921. Three days later, Eamon de Valera,* President of Dail Eireann, met with the British Prime Minister, David Lloyd George,* at 10 Downing Street. De Valera found Lloyd George's proposals unacceptable. His rejection was endorsed by the Dail and relayed to Lloyd George on 24 August.

As President of the Irish Republic (since August), de Valera accredited five members of his government to open negotiations with Britain in October on the basis of the 'Gairloch Formula'* proposed by Lloyd George:

In virtue of the authority vested in me by Dail Eireann, I hereby appoint Arthur Griffith, TD, Minister for Foreign Affairs; Michael Collins, TD, Minister for Finance; Robert C. Barton, TD, Minister for Economic Affairs; Edmund J. Duggan, TD, and George Gavan Duffy, TD, as Envoys Plenipotentiary of the Republic of Ireland to negotiate and conclude on behalf of Ireland, with the representatives of His Majesty George V, a treaty or treaties of settlement, association and accommodation between Ireland and the community of nations known as the British Commonwealth. In witness thereof I hereunder subscribe my name as President. Eamon de Valera.

Arthur Griffith,* Michael Collins* and Robert Barton,* Eamon Duggan* and George Gavan Duffy* were given the following written instructions:
1. The Plenipotentiaries have full powers as defined in their credentials.
2. It is understood, before decisions are finally reached on main questions, that a dispatch notifying the intention to make decisions will be sent to members of the cabinet in Dublin, and that a reply will be awaited by the Plenipotentiaries before the final decision is made.
3. It is also understood that a complete text of the draft Treaty about to be signed will be submitted to Dublin, and reply awaited.
4. In case of a break, the text of the final proposals from our side will be similarly submitted.
5. It is understood that the Cabinet in Dublin will be kept regularly informed of the progress of the negotiations.

Full negotiations with the British representatives began on 11 October in London. The British team was Lloyd George, Lord Birkenhead,* Winston S. Churchill,* Sir Hamar Greenwood,* Austen Chamberlain, L. Worthington Evans and Gordon Hewart.

During the negotiations de Valera

continued to press the Irish delegates to seek his formula of External Association* which had earlier been rejected by Lloyd George. The draft of the Treaty (or Articles of Agreement) which was discussed throughout October and November was presented to the Irish cabinet in Dublin and rejected on 3 December. There was dissatisfaction as to the status which Ireland would have (Dominion status), the form and degree of association with the Commonwealth, the Oath of Allegiance* and the question of the future of the six counties of Northern Ireland, (established since June 1921). It was understood by the delegates, as they returned to London, that the document would not be signed until it had once more been referred back to the Irish cabinet.

Negotiations with the British were resumed on 4 December and continued throughout the next day. On the evening of 5 December, Lloyd George confronted Griffith with an ultimatum: the Irish must sign the document or the war would be resumed within three days. Following further discussions between the Irish delegates the Treaty was signed at 2.20 a.m. on 6 December. Southern Ireland was to become a Free State with full Dominion status within the British Commonwealth of Nations.

At a cabinet meeting on 8 December the Treaty was accepted by four votes to three: for acceptance were Griffith, Collins, Barton and W. T. Cosgrave;* de Valera, Cathal Brugha* and Austin Stack* voted against. De Valera then published a repudiation of the document. The Dail debates on the Treaty continued throughout the Christmas period until 7 January 1922, when it was accepted by 64 votes to 57.

De Valera and his followers refused to recognise the Provisional Government* which was then established under the chairmanship of Collins. They did recognise the government of Dail Eireann, of which Griffith was elected President in place of de Valera. The British government recognised only the Provisional Government for the purpose of handing over authority in the Free State, which came into existence on 6 December 1922.

In the general election of 16 June 1922, the so-called Pact Election,* 620,283 votes were cast: 239,193 Pro-Treaty, 133,864 Anti-Treaty and 247,226 for others. Fifty-eight Pro-Treaty candidates were returned (later to form Cumann na nGaedheal), 35 Anti-Treaty and 17 for the Labour Party, seven Farmers, four Unionists and seven Independents. At the end of the month, when the Provisional Government attacked the republican garrison at the Four Courts, the Civil War* began.

The text of the Treaty, as the 'Articles of Agreement for a Treaty between Great Britain and Ireland, 6 December 1921' became more popularly known, was as follows:

1. Ireland shall have the same constitutional status in the community of Nations known as the British Empire as the Dominion of Canada, the Commonwealth of Australia, the Dominion of New Zealand, and the Union of South Africa, with a parliament having powers to make laws for the peace, order and good government of Ireland and an Executive responsible to that parliament, and shall be styled and known as the Irish Free State.

2. Subject to the provisions hereinafter set out, the position of the Irish Free State in relation to the Imperial parliament and government and otherwise shall be that of the Dominion of Canada, and the law, practice and constitutional usage governing the relationship of the Crown or the representative of the Crown and of the Imperial parliament to the Dominion of Canada shall govern their relationship to the Irish Free State.

3. The representative of the Crown in Ireland shall be appointed in like manner as the Governor-General of Canada, and in accordance with the practice observed in the making of such appointments.

4. The oath to be taken by members of the parliament of the Irish Free State shall be in the following form:
I . . . do solemnly swear true faith and allegiance to the Constitution of the Irish Free State as by law established and that I will be faithful to H.M. King George V, his heirs and successors by law, in virtue of the common citizenship of Ireland with Great Britain and her adherence to and membership of the group of nations forming the British Commonwealth of Nations.

5. The Irish Free State shall assume liability for the service of the Public Dept of the United Kingdom as existing at the date hereof and toward the payment of War Pensions as existing at that date in such proportion as may be fair and equitable, having regard to any just claims on the part of Ireland by way of set-off or counter-claim, the amount of such sums being determined in default of agreement by the arbitration of one or more independent persons being citizens of the British Empire.

6. Until an arrangement has been made between the British and Irish governments whereby the Irish Free State undertakes her own coastal defence, the defence by sea of Great Britain and Ireland shall be undertaken by His Majesty's Imperial Forces. But this shall not prevent the construction or maintenance by the government of the Irish Free State of such vessels as are necessary for the protection of the Revenue or the Fisheries. The foregoing provisions of this Article shall be reviewed at a conference of Representatives of the British and Irish governments, to be held at the expiration of five years from the date hereof with a view to the undertaking by Ireland of a share in her own coastal defence.

7. The government of the Irish Free State shall afford to His Majesty's Imperial Forces:
(*a*) In time of peace such harbour and other facilities as are indicated in the Annex hereto, or such other facilities as may from time to time be agreed between the British government and the government of the Irish Free State; and
(*b*) In time of war or of strained relations with a Foreign Power, such harbour and other facilities as the British government may require for the purposes of such defence as aforesaid.

8. With a view to securing the observance of the principle of international limitation of armaments, if the government of the Irish Free State establishes and maintains a military defence force, the establishments thereof shall not exceed in size such proportion of the military establishments maintained in Great Britain as that which the population of Ireland bears to the population of Great Britain.

9. The ports of Great Britain and the Irish Free State shall be freely open to the ships of the other country on payment of the customary port and other duties.

10. The government of the Irish Free State agrees to pay fair compensation on terms not less favourable than those accorded by the Act of 1920 to judges, officials, members of Police Forces, and other Public Servants who are discharged by it or who retire in consequence of the change of government effected in pursuance hereof. Provided that this agreement shall not apply to members of the Auxiliary Police Force or to persons recruited in Great Britain for the Royal Irish Constabulary during the two years next preceding the date hereof. The British government will assume responsibility for such compensation or pensions as may be payable to any of these excepted persons.

11. Until the expiration of one month from the passing of the Act of Parliament for the ratification of this instrument, the powers of the parliament and the government of the Irish Free State shall not be exercisable as respects Northern Ireland, and the provisions of the Government of Ireland Act, 1920, shall, so far as

they relate to Northern Ireland, remain in full force and effect, and no election shall be held for the return of members to serve in the parliament of the Irish Free State for constituencies in Northern Ireland, unless a resolution is passed by both houses of the parliament of Northern Ireland in favour of holding such election before the end of the said month.

12. If, before the expiration of the said month, an address is presented to His Majesty by both houses of parliament of Northern Ireland to that effect, the powers of the parliament and government of the Irish Free State shall no longer extend to Northern Ireland, and the provisions of the Government of Ireland Act, 1920 (including those relating to the Council of Ireland) shall, so far as they relate to Northern Ireland, continue to be of full force and effect, and this instrument shall have effect subject to the necessary modifications.

Provided that if such an address is so presented a Commission consisting of three persons, one to be appointed by the government of the Irish Free State, one to be appointed by the government of Northern Ireland and one who shall be Chairman to be appointed by the British government shall determine in accordance with the wishes of the inhabitants, so far as may be compatible with economic and geographic conditions, the boundaries between Northern Ireland and the rest of Ireland, and for purposes of the Government of Ireland Act, 1920, and of this instrument, the boundary of Northern Ireland shall be such as may be determined by such Commission.

13. For the purpose of the last foregoing article, the powers of the parliament of Southern Ireland under the Government of Ireland Act, 1920, to elect members of the Council of Ireland shall, after the parliament of the Irish Free State is constituted, be exercised by that parliament.

14. After the expiration of the said month, if no such address as is mentioned in Article 12 hereof is presented, the parliament and government of Northern Ireland shall continue to exercise as respects Northern Ireland the powers conferred on them by the Government of Ireland Act, 1920, but the parliament and government of the Irish Free State shall in Northern Ireland have in relation to matters in respect of which the parliament of Northern Ireland has not power to make laws under that Act (including matters which under the said Act are within the jurisdiction of the Council of Ireland) the same powers as in the rest of Ireland, subject to such other provisions as may be agreed in manner hereinafter appearing.

15. At any time after the date hereof the government of Northern Ireland and the Provisional Government of Southern Ireland hereinafter constituted may meet for the purpose of discussing the provisions subject to which the last foregoing article is to operate in the event of no such address as is therein mentioned being presented and those provisions may include:

(*a*) Safeguards with regard to patronage in Northern Ireland:

(*b*) Safeguards with regard to the collection of revenue in Northern Ireland:

(*c*) Safeguards with regard to import and export duties affecting the trade or industry of Northern Ireland:

(*d*) Safeguards for minorities in Northern Ireland:

(*e*) The settlement of the financial relations between Northern Ireland and the Irish Free State:

(*f*) The establishment and powers of a local militia in Northern Ireland and the relations of the Defence Forces of the Irish Free State and of Northern Ireland respectively:

and if at any such meeting provisions are agreed to, the same shall have effect as if they were included amongst the provisions subject to which the powers of the parliament and government of the Irish Free State are to be exercisable in Northern Ireland under Article 14 hereof.

16. Neither the parliament of the Irish Free State nor the parliament of Northern Ireland shall make any law so as either directly or indirectly to endow any religion or prohibit or restrict the free exercise thereof or give any preference or impose any disability on account of religious belief or religious status or affect prejudicially the right of any child to attend a school receiving public money without attending the religious instruction at the school or make any discrimination as respects State aid between schools under the management of different religious denominations or divert from any religious denomination or any educational institution any of its property except for public utility purposes and on payment of compensation.

17. By way of provisional arrangement for the administration of Southern Ireland during the interval which must elapse between the date hereof and the constitution of a parliament and government of the Irish Free State in accordance therewith, steps shall be taken forthwith for summoning a meeting of members of parliament elected for constituencies in Southern Ireland since the passing of the Government of Ireland Act, 1920, and for constituting a Provisional Government, and the British Government shall take the steps necessary to transfer to such Provisional Government the powers and machinery requisite for the discharge of its duties, provided that every member of such Provisional Government shall have signified in writing his or her acceptance of this instrument. But this arrangement shall not continue in force beyond the expiration of twelve months from the date hereof.

18. This instrument shall be submitted forthwith by His Majesty's Government for the approval of parliament and by the Irish signatories to a meeting summoned for the purpose of the members elected to sit in the House of Commons of Southern Ireland, and if approved shall be ratified by the necessary legislation.

On behalf of the Irish Delegation.

Signed
Art Ó Gríobhtha.
Micheál Ó Coileáin.
Riobárd Bartún.
Eudhmonn S. Ó Dúgáin.
Seórsa Ghabháin Uí Dhubhthaigh.

On behalf of the British Delegation.

Signed
D. Lloyd George.
Austen Chamberlain.
Birkenhead.
Winston S. Churchill.
L. Worthington-Evans.
Hamar Greenwood.
Gordon Hewart.
6th December 1921.

ANNEX

1. The following are the specific facilities required:

Dockyard port at Berehaven
(a) Admiralty property and rights to be retained as at the date hereof. Harbour defences to remain in charge of British care and maintenance parties.
Queenstown
(b) Harbour defences to remain in charge of British care and maintenance parties. Certain mooring buoys to be retained for use of His Majesty's ships.
Belfast Lough
(c) Harbour defences to remain in charge of British care and maintenance parties.
Lough Swilly
(d) Harbour defences to remain in charge of British care and maintenance parties.
Aviation
(e) Facilities in the neighbourhood of the above ports for coastal defence by air.
Oil Fuel Storage
(f) Haulbowline, Rathmullen – To be offered for sale to commercial companies under guarantee that purchasers shall maintain a certain minimum stock for Admiralty purposes.

2. A Convention shall be made between the British government and

the government of the Irish Free State to give effect to the following conditions:

(*a*) That submarine cables shall not be landed or wireless stations for communication with places outside Ireland be established except by agreement with the British government; that the existing cable landing rights and wireless concessions shall not be withdrawn except by agreement with the British government; and that the British government shall be entitled to land additional submarine cables or establish additional wireless stations for communication with places outside Ireland.

(*b*) That lighthouses, buoys, beacons, and any navigational marks or navigational aids shall be maintained by the government of the Irish Free State as at the date hereof and shall not be removed or added to except by agreement with the British government.

(*c*) That war signal stations shall be closed down and left in charge of care and maintenance parties, the government of the Irish Free State being offered the option of taking them over and working them for commercial purposes subject to Admiralty inspection, and guaranteeing the upkeep of existing telegraphic communication therewith.

3. A Convention shall be made between the same governments for the regulation of civil communication by air.

TREATY PORTS. Under an annex in the terms of the Treaty* Britain retained certain 'specific facilities' in Ireland, including four ports, three of which were in the Free State:* the dockyard at Berehaven, Queenstown (Cobh) and Lough Swilly. The Admiralty retained its properties and rights in those locations and undertook responsibility for harbour defences and maintenance parties. Under the agreement which ended the Economic War* in March 1938 and against the strong opposition of Winston Churchill, Britain conceded the Treaty Ports which were returned to what was then Eire.* British naval personnel withdrew from the Treaty Ports on 11 July 1938.

TRENCH, W. STEUART (1808–72). Land agent and author; b. Bellegrove, near Portarlington, Queen's County (Laois); ed. Royal School, Armagh and TCD. He won the gold medal of the Royal Agricultural Society for an essay on land reclamation in 1841. Trench served as land agent for the Shirley estate, Co. Monaghan (1843–45), the Lansdowne estate, Co. Kerry (from 1849), the estate of the Marquis of Bath in Co. Monaghan (from 1851) and Lord Digby's estate in the Midlands (from 1856). He recorded his experiences in *Realities of Irish Life* (1868) which went through five editions in its first year; his other works included *Ierne: A Tale* (1871) and *Sketches of Life and Character in Ireland* (1872).

TREVELYAN, SIR CHARLES EDWARD (1807–86). Civil servant; Assistant Secretary to the Treasury (1840–59); b. Taunton; ed. grammar school, Charterhouse and Haileybury. He joined the East India Co.'s Bengal service in 1826 and later became assistant commissioner in Delhi. After returning to England in 1838 he became assistant secretary to the Treasury in which capacity he virtually dictated Irish relief measures during the Famine of 1845–49.* Along with the Prime Minister, Lord John Russell,* and the Chancellor of the Exchequer, Sir Charles Wood,* Trevelyan was totally committed to free trade. In addition, he held the belief that the famine was the work of a benign Providence seeking to reduce an expanding population.

From March 1846 he controlled the public works through the disbursement of public funds. He defended the export of grain from Ireland on the grounds of free trade. When rioting broke out in protest at the exportation of corn, he deployed mobile columns of 2,000' troops provisioned with beef, pork and biscuits, 'to be directed on particular ports at short notice'. He was opposed to railway construction as a form of relief and successfully opposed Russell's scheme for the distribution of some £50,000 worth of seedlings to tenants. In 1848 he ceased Treasury grants to distressed Unions (Poor Law districts) in Ireland although by now there was an outbreak of cholera. Later in the year he was knighted for his services to Ireland.

Trevelyan made a major contribution to public service by his investigation into admission to the civil service. The Report which he issued with Sir Stafford Northcote, *The Organisation of the Permanent Civil Service* (1853), was responsible for a series of reforms which shaped the modern British civil service. He served again in India, as Governor of Madras (1859–60) and as finance minister (1862–65) when he instituted reforms in the public service. Upon his return to Britain he was involved in a variety of social questions. He was the author of *On the Education of the People of India* (1838) and *Christianity and Hinduism contrasted.* His son, George Otto Trevelyan,* was Chief Secretary (1882–84).

TREVELYAN, GEORGE OTTO (1838–1928). Politician (Liberal) and historian; Chief Secretary (1882–84); b. Tothley Temple, Leicestershire, son of Sir Charles Edward Trevelyan;* ed. Harrow and Trinity College, Cambridge. Having served as his father's secretary in India, he entered politics as MP for Tynemouth in 1865, and was Civil Lord of the Admiralty (1868) and Secretary of the Admiralty (1880). He succeeded the assassinated Lord Frederick Cavendish* at the Irish Office in May 1882. Trevelyan supported the extension of the household franchise in 1884. When W. E. Gladstone* led the Liberals back to power committed to Home Rule* in 1886, Trevelyan became Secretary for Scotland, but he resigned over the (first) Home Rule Bill* (April 1886). He was later reconciled to Home Rule and rejoined

Gladstone who again appointed him Secretary for Scotland (1892–94).

A nephew of Lord Macauley, Trevelyan was the author of *The Life and Letters of Lord Macauley* (2 vols, 1876), *The Early History of Charles James Fox* (1890), *The American Revolution* (6 vols, 1899–1914) and *George III and Charles Fox, 1778–1782* (2 vols, 1912–14).

TRIANGLE, THE. Code name for a triumvirate which dominated Clan na Gael* during the 1880s. It consisted of Alexander Sullivan,* Michael Boland and Denis Feeley who affixed a triangular mark instead of signatures to notices issued on their behalf. The Triangle encouraged terrorist activities in England and provided finance for the Dynamiters.* Principal opposition to their policy came from John Devoy.* Following the murder of Dr P. H. Cronin, of which Sullivan was accused, the Triangle was discredited in 1889.

TRICOLOUR – THE NATIONAL FLAG. Thomas Francis Meagher* returned from France in April 1848 with a gift of a tricolour from the citizens of France. When he presented it to a meeting of the Irish Confederation* in Dublin, John Mitchel* commented, 'I hope to see that flag one day waving as our national banner'. The flag was displayed during the Easter Rising of 1916* and captured national imagination as the banner of the new revolutionary Ireland. It was the official flag from 1922 until 1937 when its position as the national flag was enshrined in the Constitution of 1937: 'The national flag is the tricolour of green, white and orange' (Article 7). The colours are symbolic of union: the white of brotherhood joins the older Ireland (green) with the newer (orange) in a brotherhood of common nationality.

TRINITY COLLEGE, DUBLIN. Trinity College, Dublin University was founded in 1592, modelled on the residential colleges of Oxford and Cambridge. No part of the college erected during the reign of Elizabeth I now remains. Much of the splendid architecture of Trinity dates from the eighteenth century. As graduates were required to subscribe to the Oath of Supremacy, Trinity College became the centre of education for the (Protestant) Ascendancy.* Catholics were unable to take degrees until after 1793 but fellowships and scholarships were open only to members of the Established Church of Ireland.

An Act of Parliament of 1801 extended to Trinity the right to receive a copy of every book published in Great Britain and Ireland, provided that the library authorities claimed the copy within one year of publication. The library houses over 3,000 ancient manuscripts, including Egyptian papyri, the Palimsest Codex (Z) of St Matthew's Gospel which was uncovered by Professor John 'Jacky' Barrett (1753–1821), and also Greek, Latin and ancient Irish manuscripts. Other literary treasures include the Books of Kells, Durrow, Armagh, Leinster and the Yellow Book of Lecan. A harp, popularly known as Brian Boru's, is also on view in the Library.

TROY, JOHN THOMAS (1739–1823). Archbishop of Dublin (R.C.), 1784–1823; b. Porterstown, Co. Dublin; ed. Rome where he arrived at the age of fifteen to study for the priesthood and joined the Dominican Order (1756). Following his appointment as Bishop of Ossory (1776), Dr Troy was a strong supporter of the Dublin Castle authorities and several times condemned secret societies,* in particular the Whiteboys,* pronouncing excommunication upon those guilty of outrages. As Archbishop of Dublin he was identified with the Castle. He would not support the Catholic Committee* of the 1780s and 1790s, claiming that Catholic Emancipation* would be achieved through constitutional means and not through agitation. His concern that Irish clerical students should not go to France where they would be influenced by republican-democratic ideas, led to the foundation of Maynooth College* in 1795. In the same year, he attacked the Defenders* and the United Irishmen,* condemnations which he repeated during the rising of 1798.

Dr Troy presided over a meeting held in Maynooth in January 1799 when the hierarchy considered guarantees for the Church connected with the Union.* The four archbishops and six bishops signed a resolution accepting Emancipation together with the Veto.* However, the Union was not followed by Emancipation (*see* **George III** *and* **Pitt, William**) but the issue of the Veto continued through his term as Archbishop of Dublin until it was defeated by Daniel O'Connell* and the populists in 1815. One of his last major public appearances was to lay the foundation-stone of the Pro-Cathedral in Marlborough Street, Dublin (1815). He was succeeded by Daniel Murray.*

TRUCE. King George V* appealed for peace between Great Britain and Ireland on 22 June 1921 while opening the parliament of Northern Ireland and two days later Eamon de Valera,* President of Dail Eireann, received an invitation from the British Prime Minister, David Lloyd George,* to attend talks. As a preliminary to the talks a Truce was agreed between de Valera and General Sir Nevil Macready* on 9 July, to come into effect on 11 July. Although discussions between Lloyd George and de Valera broke down, the uneasy truce continued throughout August and September. The deadlock was broken on 30 September when Lloyd George's 'Gairloch Formula'* was accepted as the basis for new discussions which began on 11 October and concluded on 6 December when the Treaty* was signed.

'TRUCK'. Name for a system of payment by kind instead of wages to labourers. It was outlawed by Acts of 1715, 1729, 1745 and 1841 but persisted until the Famine of 1845–49.*

TUBERCULOSIS. A major cause of death in Ireland throughout the nineteenth and into the twentieth century, sometimes known as the 'Irish disease'. The largest number of fatalities were in the age group 20–34. The decadal death figures for the period 1871–1910 per 100,000 of population were:

1871–80	260
1881–90	267
1891–1900	277
1900–10	263

The TB Prevention (Ireland) Act of 1908 established hospitals to treat those suffering from the disease. County councils and borough corporations were authorised to provide clinics and sanatoria but little impact was made as they were inadequately staffed and financed. The death rate from the disease continued to increase as local authorities failed to meet their obligations.

The disease was finally tackled by Dr Noel Browne,* Minister for Health in the first Inter-Party Government (1948–51). Dr Browne, whose family had suffered from the disease, launched a major campaign to eradicate TB, establishing emergency sanatoria throughout the country. The death rate fell below 100 per 100,000 of population until by 1952 it had been reduced to forty (or 1,187 persons) and by 1957 to twenty-four (or 694 persons).

The death rate from the disease in Northern Ireland fell within the same period from thirty per 100,000 (or 410 persons) to thirteen (or 175 persons).

TUDOR, MAJOR-GENERAL SIR HUGH H. (1871–1965). Soldier; Chief of Police (1920–22); b. Exeter. After being commissioned, he served in the Boer War and in World War I, when he was wounded in both campaigns. As Chief of Police in Ireland he was responsible for the co-ordination of the Dublin Metropolitan Police* and the Royal Irish Constabulary* during the War of Independence.* He had to replace the secret service which had been rendered ineffective by Michael Collins* and the Irish Republican Army.* Tudor was criticised for the behaviour of the Auxiliaries* and the Black and Tans* and admitted that there was much drunkeness among the men under his command. He was subsequently Air Vice-Marshall and GOC in Palestine (1922).

TUKE, JAMES HACK (1819–96). Philanthropist; b. York of a Quaker family; ed. Friends' School, York. He entered the family tea and coffee business where he remained until 1852 when he became a banker. Tuke accompanied his fellow-Quaker, William Edward Forster,* to Ireland to distribute relief in the West of Ireland during the Famine of 1845–49.* His experiences were published as *A Visit to Connaught in 1847* (1847). In 1848 he contracted fever while aiding Irish refugees in York. He returned to Ireland during the famine in Connaught in 1880 at the request of Forster, who was then Chief Secretary. Tuke urged the introduction of the Three Fs* and family emigration to end agrarian unrest. He returned in 1881 and 1882 to administer a fund established with government support to assist Irish emigrants, 1,200 of whom were helped to the USA. A year later, 5,380 were assisted and 2,800 in 1884, many of them personally selected by Tuke. He distributed famine relief seed potatoes during 1885–86. His comments on the West of Ireland were answered in some measure by the creation of the Congested Districts' Board* in 1889–90. He was an advisor to the Board which oversaw another of his suggestions, the creation of a light railway system in Connaught.

He published 'Peasant Proprietors at Home' in *Nineteenth Century* (1880), *Achill and the West of Ireland: Report of the Distribution of the Seed Potato Fund* (1886) and *The Condition of Donegal* (1889).

TURBARY-RIGHT. Ancient right to cut turf in a bog, it was dependent upon land-holding. The land to which turbury-right was attached did not necessarily have to adjoin the bog.

TWOMEY, MAURICE 'MOSS' (1896–1978). Republican; Chief of Staff of the Irish Republican Army* (1927–36); b. Clondulane, Fermoy, Cork; ed. CBS. A member of the Irish Volunteers* from 1914, he was Staff Commandant of the 1st Southern Division of the IRA during the War of Independence* when he was a close associate of Liam Lynch.* Rejecting the Treaty,* he supported the Irregulars (anti-Treaty IRA) during the Civil War,*and, following his capture in Dublin, was imprisoned on 6 April 1923. After his release in 1924 he resumed his career in the IRA and broke with Sinn Fein*(1925) becoming Chief of Staff two years later. Twomey and the IRA leadership supported Fianna Fail* during

1932–33 and helped to combat the Blueshirts.* He opposed the socialist wing of the IRA, Republican Congress.* When the Fianna Fail government outlawed the IRA in 1936 he went on the run but was captured and imprisoned until 1938 and succeeded as Chief of Staff by Sean Mac-Bride.* He opposed Sean Russell* and the militants who declared war on Britain in 1939. Twomey established a grocery and newsagent's business in Dublin where he lived for the rest of his life.

TYNAN HINKSON, KATHARINE (1861–1931). Poet; b. Dublin; ed. Dominican Convent, Drogheda, to the age of fourteen. An early supporter of the Ladies' Land League,* she was influenced by John O'Leary* and was closely associated with W. B. Yeats* and other literary figures in the national literary revival of the 1890s. Her best-known poem was 'Sheep and Lambs' ('All in the April evening') and her many volumes of verse included *Shamrocks* (1887), *Irish Poems* (1913) and *Collected Poems* (1930).

U

ULSTER CONSTITUTION DEFENCE COMMITTEE. Founded by Noel Doherty and Rev. Ian Paisley* in 1966 in protest against republican commemorations of the Easter Rising of 1916. Rev. Paisley's committee, jocularly known as 'The Twelve Apostles', led the opposition to any form of *rapprochement* between Northern Ireland and the Republic of Ireland. The UCDC, which formed a subsidiary, the Ulster Protestant Volunteers,* stated that they were '. . . one united society of Protestant patriots pledged by all lawful methods to uphold and maintain the Con-

stitution of Northern Ireland as an integral part of the United Kingdom as long as the United Kingdom maintains a Protestant Monarchy and the terms of the Revolutionary Settlement'. Membership was open only to 'those who have been born Protestant'. The Committee warned that 'when the authorities act contrary to the Constitution the body (UCDC) will take whatever steps it thinks fit to expose such unconstitutional acts'. Reacting to the growth of the Northern Ireland Civil Rights Association,* the Committee and Rev. Paisley were associated with the short-lived Protestant Unionist Party and later with the Democratic Unionist Party.*

ULSTER CUSTOM. The Ulster Custom was the recognition of the tenant's saleable interest in his holdings and was one of the Three Fs.* The custom was found principally in Ulster, as a result of which there was less land agitation in that province than throughout the rest of the country. The demand for the custom, which was of importance to the bigger tenant-farmers, grew during the 1850s (*see* Tenant League), but it was not granted legal recognition until 1881 (*see* Land Acts).

ULSTER DEFENCE ASSOCIATION. Paramilitary organisation founded in Northern Ireland in August 1971 as an umbrella for local defence associations which had been formed around Belfast to combat the Irish Republican Army.* These local organisations were formed into the UDA by Charles Harding Smith, leader of the Woodvale Defence Association. The UDA, which adopted the motto *Cedenta Arma Togae* ('Law before Violence') stated that its aim was 'to see law restored everywhere, including the no-go areas' i.e., Catholic areas of Derry and Belfast.

The local defence associations within the UDA were not under central control and the organisation was rent by struggles as the stronger personalities struggled for leadership. The chairman, Harding Smith, was imprisoned in 1972 and his successor, James Anderson, holding the rank of major-general, reorganised the UDA with a thirteen-man inner council. The chief spokesman was Tommy Herron (later killed) under whom there were eleven colonels and lieutenant-colonels. The council stated that if the British Army, with which the UDA hitherto had good relations, did not break down the barricades and enter the 'no-go' areas, the UDA would do so itself. During May and June 1972, it built up Protestant 'no-go' areas. However, the British Army entered the Catholic 'no-go' areas and in September also raided UDA headquarters, where bombing equipment was uncovered. Anderson and Herron were arrested and the UDA co-operated closely with the Ulster Volunter Force* for an armed attack on a Catholic housing estate in Larne. It moved further away from the Protestant political movement, Vanguard,* and was shortly afterwards involved in a series of shoot-outs with the British Army. These ended after a truce was agreed. The UDA was involved in sporadic outbursts of violence over the next few years, sometimes using the cover-name Ulster Freedom Fighters. A demand from within the movement for 'more socialist-orientated policies' did not lead to anything.

ULSTER DEFENCE REGIMENT (UDR). Military force established in Northern Ireland in 1970, following the recommendations of the Hunt Commission* and the disbandment of the 'B' Specials (*see* Ulster Special Constabulary). Contrary to the intentions of the Commission, some members of the UDR were recruited from the 'B' Specials. The UDR, which was divided into full and part-time members, assisted the Royal Ulster Constabulary* and the British Army in the fight against the Irish Republican Army.*

ULSTER DEFENCE UNION. Founded by Colonel Edward J. Saunderson* in 1894 to collect funds and organise resistance to Home Rule.* In the event, the (second) Home Rule Bill,* introduced by W. E. Gladstone,* was defeated in the House of Lords. *See also* Union Defence League, Ulster Unionist Council *and* Ulster Unionist Party.

ULSTER GOVERNMENT. *See* Solemn League and Covenant.

ULSTER LIBERAL UNIONIST COMMITTEE. Following a meeting between Ulster Liberals and Conservatives in April 1886 the Ulster Liberal Unionist Committee was established on 4 June 1886, the month before the vote on the (first) Home Rule Bill.* The Committee's purpose was to organise opposition to Home Rule* by providing speakers for meetings in Britain. The Bill was defeated in the House of Commons one month later. The Liberal Unionists remained a strong force in Ulster politics and helped to organise the Unionist Convention of 1892. The Committee was entitled to twelve delegates to the Ulster Unionist Council* from 1905 to 1929.

ULSTER LITERARY THEATRE. The ULT had its origins in the Irish Literary Theatre,* and sought, by providing a native peasant drama, to accomplish for Belfast and Ulster what the Abbey Theatre* was doing in the south. Its first season opened on 7 December 1904 with a play by Bulmer Hobson,* *Brian of Banba*, and *The Reformers* by Lewis Purcell. The ULT never had the repertory of actors and writers upon which the Abbey relied for support and disappeared in the 1930s.

ULSTER LOYALIST ANTI-REPEAL UNION. Founded in Belfast on 8 January 1886 as the Ulster Loyalist Anti-Repeal Committee, a rival to the Irish Loyal and Patriotic Union,* dedicated to fighting the (first) Home Rule Bill* which was to be introduced by W. E. Gladstone in April. Supported by Ulster landowners, businessmen and Protestant clergymen, the ULAU was opposed to any form of self-government for Ireland. The committee, which met weekly and rotated the chair, had the support of the *Belfast News Letter*, the editor of which, Henderson, was treasurer. By March the Union had twenty local associations and during that month organised a series of anti-Home Rule meetings which brought it closer to the Orange Order.* Support was sought from Protestants in Scotland and England and members of the committee helped

to organise the visit to Belfast of Lord Randolph Churchill.* The Union was heavily involved in the sectarian rioting which broke out in Belfast during the summer of 1886. Following the defeat of the Home Rule Bill (July 1886) the leaders of the Union remained active in the Unionist interest and were prominent in the Ulster Unionist Party.* The Union was dissolved in 1911.

ULSTER PROTESTANT ACTION. Based on the Ulster Protestant League* of the 1930s, UPA was a Loyalist-Protestant movement in the 1950s. During a period of economic depression in Northern Ireland, the UPA encouraged the employment of Protestants only and discrimination against the minority Catholic population. In the late 1950s it was dominated by Rev. Ian Paisley.* Among its members who continued careers as militant Unionists were Noel Doherty, later active in the Ulster Protestant Volunteers* and Gusty Spence, founder of the revived Ulster Volunteer Force* in 1966.

ULSTER PROTESTANT LEAGUE. Founded in 1931, the UPL's purpose was discrimination against the minority Catholic population of Northern Ireland. The League called on Protestant employers not to employ Catholic workers and asked Protestants not to work or do business with Catholics. It was a response to the heavy unemployment in Northern Ireland as a result of the worldwide depression in the years after 1929. As economic conditions improved the League began to lose support. Ulster Protestant Action* was revived for the same purpose in the 1950s.

ULSTER PROTESTANT VOLUNTEERS. Founded in 1966 by Noel Doherty and Rev. Ian Paisley* as a subsidiary of Paisley's Ulster Constitution Defence Committee.* Described by Rev. Paisley as 'constitutional, democratic, open and legal', it was not open to Roman Catholics, and the constitution also debarred members of the Royal Ulster Constabulary.* A major figure in the organisation was Major Ronald Bunting, who also claimed leadership of a number of one-man and sometimes fictional organisations. In the beginning the Volunteers had an unofficial connection with the Ulster Volunteer Force* through Doherty. Members, who wore red, white and blue sashes while parading, saw themselves as guardians of the Union which they claimed was under attack from republicans and 'Lundyite' Unionist politicians led by the Prime Minister, Captain Terence O'Neill.* Bunting led the attack on the People's Democracy which took place at Burntollet Bridge in January 1969. The UPV collapsed during the early 1970s. *See also* Ulster Volunter Force.

ULSTER REFORM CLUB. Founded in 1880 by the Ulster Liberals to mark the election victory and the return of W. E. Gladstone* as Prime Minister, it remained the centre of the Ulster Liberal organisation. After the defeat of the (first) Home Rule Bill* in 1886 the club came under the control of the Liberal Unionists who were led by Frederick Crawford.* The club's members were dedicated to the preservation of the Union,* and included many industrial and commercial leaders who identified their prosperity with the Union. After 1905 the club was affiliated to the Ulster Unionist Council* on which it had a strong influence.

ULSTER SPECIAL CONSTABULARY. The Ulster Special Constabulary was established in Northern Ireland to supplement the official police force, the Royal Ulster Constabulary,* in 1921. The state of Northern Ireland came into existence at a time of acute unrest in Ireland; the War of Independence* was still being fought in the south and it was felt necessary to protect the new state from the Irish Republican Army* which had support within the Catholic community in the north. Recruitment into the Special Constabulary was mainly

from among the revived Ulster Volunteer Force.* There were three categories of Special Constabulary, the 'A', 'B' and 'C'.

The 'A' Special Constables were attached to the RUC. A full-time body based in barracks, members had to undergo a medical inspection, were armed and uniformed, and paid around £3 17s 6d (£3.87½p) per week. Members were given a six-month contract with the RUC.

The 'B' Specials were more numerous. They did not have to undergo a medical inspection (nor did Class 'C') and they selected their own officers. While on duty they were uniformed and armed but their arms were supposed to remain in local barracks when they were not on duty (these regulations were generally not enforced). The 'B' Specials had to perform a half night's duty per week or one full night per fortnight. They were paid 4s (20p) per half-night or double that per full night (this sum was to cover dress, meals and travelling expenses). They served in their home districts and each patrol consisted of three or four members with one RUC man. 'C' Specials were a general reserve, unpaid and only called out in an emergency.

The Special Constabulary was entirely Protestant and many members were also in the Orange Order.* The 'A' and 'C' Specials were not used after the 1920s. The 'B' Specials were particularly active in attempts to contain the Northern Ireland Civil Rights Association* and the People's Democracy.* Clashes between the RUC, the Specials, loyalists and the civil rights marchers led to violence during 1968–69. As a result of the recommendations of the Hunt Commission* the force was disbanded in April 1970 but many of the members were absorbed into the new Ulster Defence Regiment.*

ULSTER TENANT RIGHT ASSOCIATION. Founded in 1847 by William Sharman Crawford,* Dr Edward Maginn,* Bishop of Derry and James McKnight, following the defeat of Crawford's tenant right bill which had sought to legalise the Ulster Custom.* Representatives of the Ulster movement attended a conference called by Charles Gavan Duffy* in Dublin (August 1850) at which the Tenant League* was established. Although the new movement was sometimes called the 'League of North and South', the Northern tenants took little part.

ULSTER UNIONIST COUNCIL. Following the devolution proposal of August 1904, a Unionist Council was proposed on 2 December. The Ulster Unionist Council was formally constituted at a meeting in the Ulster Hall, Belfast, on 3 March 1905, with the aim of acting 'as a further connecting link between Ulster Unionists and their parliamentary representatives; to settle in consultation with them the parliamentary policy', and 'generally to advance and defend the interests of Ulster Unionists'. Its first president was the 2nd Duke of Abercorn* and the first chairman was Colonel E. J. Saunderson,* leader of the Ulster Unionist Party. It drew its original 200 members from local Unionist associations, the Orange Order,* MPs and peers. Saunderson was succeeded by Walter Long* in 1906 and a year later the Council organised the Joint Committee of Unionist Associations of Ireland.* Sir Edward Carson* became leader in 1910.

Membership of the UUC expanded to meet changing circumstances. As it prepared to fight the (third) Home Rule Bill* (1912–14), it was increased to 370 members in 1911. As part of the campaign to resist Home Rule, the Council organised the Solemn League and Covenant* in September 1912 and the Ulster Volunteer Force* in January 1913. It appointed a Provisional Government for Ulster in September 1913 and organised the Larne-Gun-running* in April 1914. The Council was represented at the Irish Convention* (1917–18) after which membership was expanded in 1918 to 432. It re-

luctantly accepted the Government of Ireland Act, 1920,* and played a leading role in the creation of the state of Northern Ireland, all of whose governments were subsequently formed by the Ulster Unionist Party. All the Unionist MPs for northern constituencies were members of the Council's standing committee.

The Council adopted a new constitution in 1946, which stated that its aim was 'To maintain Northern Ireland as an integral part of the United Kingdom and to uphold and defend the Constitution and Parliament of Northern Ireland'.

The Council, which has its headquarters at Glengall Street, Belfast, was, in 1905, the first such organisation in Ireland to have a full-time, professional staff. The Secretary from 1906 to 1921 was Richard Dawson Bates* whose successors, were Wilson Hungerford (1921–41), William (Billy) Douglas (1941–63) and James O'Bailie (1963–   ). Organisations affiliated to the Council have been the Ulster Unionist Labour Association,* the Ulster Women's Unionist Council* and the Ulster Young Unionist Council.*

ULSTER UNIONIST LABOUR ASSOCIATION. The Ulster Unionist Party* leadership was not representative of the working class and in an attempt to win trade unionists' support the UULA was founded in June 1918. Its purpose was to be the 'medium of expression of the ideas of trade unionists' and 'to expose the real aims and objects of socialism and other anti-British movements'. Sir Edward Carson,* who became president, and John Miller Andrews,* who became chairman, were the only two non-trade unionists on the committee. In the general election of December 1918 three Labour Unionists were returned for Shankill (North Belfast), St Andrews (South Belfast), and Victoria (East Belfast). They sat on the Conservative benches at Westminster and lost their seats to Northern Ireland Labour Party candidates in 1925. The Association, which opened two working men's clubs (in East Belfast, 1921, and North Belfast, 1924), lost members during the economic recession of the 1920s and 1930s. There was a small revival during the 1950s but the UULA did not lead to a noticeable increase in working class influence within the Unionist Party.

ULSTER UNIONIST PARTY. The Ulster Unionists were the strongest element in the general Unionist movement from 1886 (*see* Unionist Party). Led by Colonel E. J. Saunderson,* they formed the Ulster Unionist Council* in 1905 as a central body through which to fight Irish home rule. Following Saunderson's death in 1906 the Ulster Unionists were led by an Englishman, Walter Long, until 1910 and from then until 1921 by Sir Edward Carson.* Carson was succeeded by Sir James Craig (*see* Craigavon, 1st Viscount) who became the first Prime Minister of the state of Northern Ireland (1921). The Ulster Unionist Party provided all the governments of Northern Ireland until the introduction of direct rule from Westminster in March 1972 and had strong contacts with the Orange Order,* of which all Unionist leaders were prominent members.

The Unionist Party remained united until the late 1960s when, in the premiership of Capt. Terence O'Neill,* the rise of the Northern Ireland Civil Rights Association* and the demand by the minority Catholic population for full civil rights placed the party under considerable strain. In the early 1970s, other forms of Unionism appeared in the shape of the Democratic Unionist Party* and the Vanguard* movement. The United Ulster Unionist Council,* a coalition of traditionalists, was set up in 1974 in an attempt to restore Unionist unity. It included the Unionist Party as a constituent, but no longer dominant, element. It succeeded in bringing about the collapse of the power-sharing Executive set up under the Sunningdale Agreement,* but by 1977 had itself broken up. The UUP

seemed to suffer from this break-up more than the DUP, to which it appeared to be losing ground as the 1970s drew to a close.

The leaders of the party since Sir James Craig's death in 1940 have been:

John Miller Andrews (1940–43)
Sir Basil Brooke,
    Lord Brookeborough (1953–63)
Captain Terence O'Neill (1963–69)
James Chichester-Clark (1969–71)
Arthur Brian Deane Faulkner
    (1971–74)
Henry William (Harry) West
    (1974–79)
James Henry Molyneaux
    (1979–   )

The strength of the Ulster Unionist Party in Stormont general elections since 1921 has been:

1921	40	1949	37
1925	32	1953	38
1929	37	1958	37
1933	36	1962	34
1938	39	1965	36
1945	33	1969	36

In the 1969 election, in addition to the thirty-six officially sponsored Unionists elected, a further three Unofficial Unionists were returned. These were candidates who ran against official party nominees who had declared their opposition to the O'Neill reform package. Out of a total of thirty-nine Unionist MPs, official and unofficial, returned in this election, twenty-seven were pro-O'Neill, ten anti-O'Neill and two were unclear in their attitude to the Prime Minister.

For a list of the governments of Northern Ireland formed by the Ulster Unionist Party *see* Northern Ireland.

ULSTER   VOLUNTEER   FORCE (UVF). Founded in January 1913 by the Ulster Unionist Council* from among local corps in Ulster, its purpose was to resist the implementation of Home Rule* which was due to become law in 1914. Finance for the Volunteers was provided by Ulster businessmen and the landed gentry, who assumed the leadership of the new force. Aid also came from England: Rudyard Kipling provided £50,000 and a poem, 'Ulster 1913', and financial aid also came from the Duke of Bedford, Lord Iveagh (*see* Guinness, Edward Cecil) and Lord Rothschild. Volunteer leaders were James Craig (*see* Craigavon, Lord), Sir Edward Carson* and Frederick Crawford.* Sir George Richardson was appointed Commander in July 1913 after he was nominated for the post by Field-Marshall Lord Roberts, while Lord Milner selected British army officers to train the force. General Sir Henry Wilson,* attached to army headquarters in London, showed his support as did army officers stationed at the Curragh (*see* Curragh Incident). Numbers were limited to 100,000 who were between the ages of seventeen and sixty-five and signatories of the Solemn League and Covenant* of September 1912. In September 1913 the Volunteers became the Army of Ulster when the Ulster Unionist Council appointed the Provisional Government of Ulster.

The UVF was able to operate in the open because drilling was legal when authorised by two magistrates. As most magistrates were either members or sympathetic to their aims, public appearances were commonplace. However, it was clear that the aims of the UVF were illegal when Carson said, 'Drilling is illegal, the Volunteers are illegal and the government knows they are illegal, and the government does not interefere with them', and told his followers, 'Don't be afraid of illegalities'. Their example was followed in Dublin where Irish nationalists established the Irish Volunteers.* The UVF were armed after the Larne Gun-running* of April 1914 which secured them 25,000 guns and 3,000,000 rounds of ammunition. By that time the Curragh Incident had demonstrated to H. H. Asquith and the Liberal government that the army in Ireland could not be relied upon to act against Ulster.

Upon the outbreak of World War I in August 1914, the UVF answered Carson's call to join the defence of the Empire. The force was incorporated into the British Army as the 36th (Ulster) Division. One month later, Home Rule became law, allowing for temporary partition but with suspension of the Act for the duration of the war. In 1916 the UVF division was virtually wiped out at the Somme where the Ulstermen displayed conspicuous gallantry.

By the end of the war the Irish situation had changed as a result of the Easter Rising of 1916* and the rise of Sinn Fein.* The War of Independence* broke out in 1919 and in 1920 David Lloyd George* sought to solve the Irish question by the Government of Ireland Act* which divided the island into Northern Ireland and Southern Ireland. Carson requested that UVF men should have preference for recruitment into the new Ulster Special Constabulary* and this was arranged by Colonel Sir William Spender. The UVF was then disbanded.

The UVF's tradition of defending the Union against the Irish Republican Army* and republicanism was revived in 1966, when there were republican commemorations in Northern Ireland for the fiftieth anniversary of the Easter Rising of 1916. The UVF revival was organised by a noted loyalist, 'Gusty' Spence. Many Catholics, unconnected with the republican movement, were objects of attack and there were a number of murders. The serious nature of the new UVF was made public on 21 May when a statement signed by 'William Johnston, Chief-of-Staff of the UVF', appeared in Belfast newspapers. It stated, 'From this day we declare war against the IRA. . . . Known IRA men will be executed mercilessly and without hesitation. . . . We will not tolerate any interference from any source and we solemnly warn the authorities to make no more speeches of appeasement.' Members of the UVF were also supporting the loyalist spokesman, Rev. Ian Paisley.*

On 28 June 1966 the Prime

Minister, Captain Terence O'Neill* proscribed the UVF and on the same day, Spence and two others were charged with conspiring '. . . between 1 March and 27 June . . . to incite ill-will among different classes and creeds of the Queen's subjects, to create a public disturbance and disorder and murder persons who might be opposed to their opinions'. They were found guilty and sentenced to life imprisonment (14 October).

The rise of the Northern Ireland Civil Rights Association* gave a new lease of life to the UVF. There was a series of bombings, some of them attributed to the UVF, during 1969. Captain O'Neill, unable to satisfy the civil rights movement and contain the loyalist reaction, fell from power on 28 April. His successor, Major James Dawson Chichester-Clark,* failed to suppress the violence as the Catholic and Protestant populations moved towards civil war. British troops arrived in August.

A Protestant mob, led, it was alleged, by members of the UVF attacked a Catholic church on the Newtownards Road with petrol bombs in August and when the army – already overstretched in West Belfast – did not appear in answer to a call for aid, the IRA turned out to protect the church. The ensuing gun battle lasted six hours and resulted in the deaths of four men.

The UVF was disorganised during 1971 although violent acts were carried out in its name. A new paramilitary force, the Ulster Defence Association* (UDA) was founded in August 1971, and, fearing a loss of support, the UVF re-organised in an attempt to gain control of the new loyalist army. In its attempt to impress loyalists the UVF was a party to some very violent actions and outrages. The tone was set by a warning which appeared in the *Belfast News Letter* on 8 March 1972: for every member of the armed forces who was killed, the UVF would kill ten republicans.

Political initiatives failed as Union-ism fragmented (1972–74) and the paramilitaries on both sides filled the vacuum. The UVF was again proscribed in 1974 but the pattern of bombings, assassination, murder and reprisal, which had emerged, continued into the 1980s.

ULSTER WOMEN'S UNIONIST COUNCIL. Founded on 23 January 1911 for 'the maintenance of the legislative Union between Great Britain and Ireland on the unimpaired integrity of which we believe our civil and religious liberties depend'. Mainly upper and middle class, its first President was the Duchess of Abercorn and another leader was the Marchioness of Londonderry. The Council, which had a membership of between 40,000 and 50,000 members during its early years, stated its support for the Ulster Unionist Party* on 18 January 1912: 'We will stand by our husbands, our brothers, and our sons, in whatever steps they may be forced to take in defending our liberties against the tyranny of Home Rule.' The UWUC organised signatures for the Solemn League and Covenant,* supported the Ulster Volunteer Force* and addressed meetings in Britain during the passage of the (third) Home Rule Bill* in 1913–14.

The Council had twelve representatives on the Ulster Unionist Council* from 1918 to 1929. Since 1944 it has had six representatives and has been active in organising weekend seminars for the study of Unionism. It has also been active in fund-raising and maintaining an up-to-date electoral register.

ULSTER WORKERS' COUNCIL. Loyalist council formed in Northern Ireland in 1974. Opposed to direct rule, the power-sharing Executive of the Assembly of Northern Ireland, and the Sunningdale Agreement,* the Council called a general strike in May. The strike paralysed Northern Ireland, bringing down the Chief Executive, Brian Faulkner,* and the Assembly.

Rev. Ian Paisley's followers continued to have influence within the Council but attempts in 1977 to elicit support for a general strike, under the umbrella of the United Unionist Action Council, failed. This strike was supported by the Ulster Volunteer Force* and the Ulster Defence Association* but there was minimal disruption of the economy as the Council failed to involve the power-workers.

ULSTER YOUNG UNIONIST COUNCIL. Youth branch of the Ulster Unionist Party* established in Belfast in 1946. In its earlier days the Council organised weekend seminars to study economic, social and political questions. It was reorganised in May 1964 to play a more positive role within the party. By 1970 it had sixty-eight branches. Among those who emerged from the youth movement to full-time political careers were William Craig,* John Taylor and Mrs Anne Dickson.

ULTIMATE FINANCIAL AGREEMENT. Agreement between the government of the Free State and the British government signed in March 1926. Under the terms of the agreement the Free State ratified its undertaking to pay Land Annuities to the British Exchequer and also took responsibility for pensions payable to former members of the Royal Irish Constabulary. The agreement was signed on the Free State's behalf by W. T. Cosgrave* and his Minister for Finance, Ernest Blythe.* The financial commitments, to the total of £5,000,000 were never presented to the Dail for ratification and so became a matter of extreme political importance when attacked by Fianna Fail* during the depression, 1929–32.

ULTRAMONTANISM. Attitude which recognises the absolute authority of the Pope in matters of faith and morals, literally a recognition of the Papal authority 'beyond the mountains' (i.e., the Alps). Ultramontanism was introduced into the Irish Catholic Church by Dr Paul

Cullen,* who was appointed Archbishop of Armagh in 1849 and became Archbishop of Dublin three years later, with a brief from the Vatican to bring the Irish church into line with Roman practice.

UNBAPTISED CHILDREN. Children who died without baptism were not allowed burial in consecrated ground. Most parishes had special places known as 'killeens' or 'little graveyards' for their interment. The unbaptised were also sometimes buried on the north side of graveyards or on boundary lines.

UNDER SECRETARY. A permanent official in the Irish administration, answerable to the Chief Secretary.* He headed the Civil Service in Ireland.

UNION, ACT OF. Ireland had its own parliament from 1295 to 1800. Parliament's legislative authority was restricted until 1782 by 'Poynings Law' (1494) and the 'Sixth of George I' (1719). However, with the repeal of these Acts in 1782 the independent Irish parliament, also known as 'Grattan's parliament' after Henry Grattan,* came into existence. It lasted until 1800. The idea of a legislative union of Great Britain and Ireland had been considered in the seventeenth and several times during the eighteenth century. The grant of independence in 1782 gave the impression that the idea had been dropped permanently but the situation was changed by the war with France and the rising of the republican United Irishmen* in 1798. The possibility of Ireland's becoming a base for an attack on England was demonstrated when an expedition under General Humbert landed at Killala, Co. Mayo, on 22 August to aid the United men. The rising, which was put down with great savagery by government forces, secured support from influential members of the establishment for a union of the two parliaments.

In the Lord Lieutenant's speech

from the throne to the Irish parliament on 22 January 1799 there was no direct reference to a union but he did refer to the need to adopt measures which would strengthen the powers and resources of the Empire. This veiled reference led to an attempt by George Ponsonby (1755–1817) to secure an amendment. Ponsonby moved that the above reference be deleted from the address and that the House should maintain 'the undoubted birthright of the people of Ireland to have a free and independent legislature'. The motion was lost by one vote (106–105) but two days later it was carried by five votes (111–106). In an attempt to capitalise on this evidence of anti-Unionist support Ponsonby sought a pledge from the House that it would never again entertain the idea of union. However, the move failed.

William Pitt* believed that the union could only be meaningful if it was carried by a strong majority. To this end, he sought the support of the Catholic hierarchy which, under the Archbishop of Dublin, John Thomas Troy,* showed itself prepared to accept the union if it were followed by Catholic Emancipation.* In this concession, Pitt was supported by the Lord Lieutenant, Lord Cornwallis,* and the Chief Secretary, Lord Castlereagh.* Emancipation was strongly opposed by the influential Lord Chancellor, Lord Clare.* Cornwallis was authorised to assure the Catholic hierarchy that emancipation would follow the union. The leading opponents of the union, with Ponsonby, were the Chancellor of the Exchequer, Sir John Parnell (1744–1801) who lost his post, and the Speaker of the House of Commons, John Foster (1740–1829), later the most heavily compensated member of the parliament although he did not waver in his opposition to the measure.

Castlereagh and Clare were responsible for turning the government's earlier defeat into an ultimate victory. The Catholic hierarchy having been won over, Catholic property-owners were promised law and order and the middle classes prosperity. One failure was with the Catholic barristers, who, led by Daniel O'Connell,* feared that they would have much to lose if the judicial systems were united; (this did not happen). Members of the Protestant churches had been alarmed by the rising of 1798 and their support was gained by promises of guarantees of protection for the Established Church and the Presbyterian Church. Many, who controlled pocket and rotten boroughs (a feature which made the Irish parliament completely unrepresentative of the people) were promised generous compensation of money, patronage and titles. In all, £1,250,000 was spent buying out the boroughs at an average of £15,000 per seat, paid equally to those who supported and opposed.

By January 1800, when the parliament assembled, the government had its majority. After listening to a plea from Henry Grattan that the Union be rejected, the House voted 138–96 in its favour on 22 January. On 6 February, the proposals were carried by 158 to 115 votes. The motion was carried in both the British and Irish Houses on 28 March and 'An Act for the Union of Great Britain and Ireland' received the Royal Assent on 1 August 1800. It came into effect on 1 January 1801. The union was not immediately followed by emancipation as George III* refused to consider it and Pitt had to concede.

The Act, which contained eight articles, provided for Irish representation in the House of Lords of twenty-eight temporal and four spiritual lords. Representation in the House of Commons was 100: two for each county, two each for Dublin and Cork cities, one each for thirty-one boroughs and towns and one for Dublin University. The Established Churches of Ireland and England were united, and guaranteed to be 'an essential and fundamental part of the Union'. Under article six, equality in matters of commerce was granted, as was free trade, except for different rates of duties on certain home-produced goods and foreign imports. (There would, however, be a system of countervailing duties on goods passing from one country to the other.) Selected manufactures, including cotton and woollen goods, would attract customs' duties for twenty years. Ireland and England were to have separate exchequers and separate responsibilities for their respective national debts. Ireland was to contribute two-seventeenths to the expenditure of the United Kingdom, subject to periodic review. Under certain conditions the exchequers and national debts could be united (this was done in 1817). Under article 8 all laws in force at the time of the union, and the civil and ecclesiastical courts, were to remain as they were, unless they should be altered by the imperial parliament. Organised opposition to the union began during the 1830s when Daniel O'Connell led a group of Repeal MPs at Westminster. Failing to achieve a significant breakthrough, they established the Repeal Association* which sought repeal of the Act of Union and a reversion to the independent parliament of 1782–1800. Later, the union was attacked by Isaac Butt,* Charles Stewart Parnell* and John Redmond,* the leaders of the Irish Parliamentary Party* which sought a domestic parliament for Ireland within the United Kingdom. A more extreme position, complete separation of Ireland from England, was taken up by the Irish Republican Brotherhood.* Separatism became the demand of Sinn Fein* which, in January 1919, established the first Dail Eireann.* During the War of Independence* the British government introduced the Government of Ireland Act, 1920* which proposed separate parliaments for Northern Ireland* (the six north-eastern counties) and 'Southern Ireland'. This did not appease Sinn Fein which continued to fight until 1921 when the Treaty* was agreed. The union ended and government of Ireland was assumed

in January 1922 by the Provisional Government.*

UNION DEFENCE LEAGUE. Founded in 1907 by Walter Long,* its aim was to combat Home Rule* which the League assumed would be introduced soon by the Liberal government. However, H. H. Asquith* did not come to terms with the Irish Parliamentary Party* until the end of 1909 and the (third) Home Rule Bill* was not introduced until 1912. In anticipation of the Bill, the UDL entered into the Londonderry House Agreement* with the Joint Committee of Unionist Associations of Ireland* on 6 April 1911. Under the agreement the UDL was to collect money and organise anti-Home Rule propaganda in England, Scotland and Wales. Home Rule became law in September 1914 but was suspended for the duration of World War I.

UNION, POOR LAW. *See* Poor Law Union.

UNIONIST ANTI-PARTITION LEAGUE. Formed by influential southern Unionists* in 1919 after they had seceded from the Irish Unionist Alliance.* Led by Lord Midleton,* they sought a solution to the Irish demand for Home Rule which would leave them with a role in an independent Ireland. By this time Sinn Fein, to which they were opposed, had formed the first Dail Eireann and declared an Irish Republic. The War of Independence had started. Members of the League met with Eamon de Valera in July 1921 and later with Arthur Griffith. They were assured that they would have representation in an independent Ireland. The League opposed the Treaty but members were granted generous representation in the Senate of the Free State which was established in December 1922.

UNIONIST CLUBS. The Unionist Clubs were founded in 1893 to organise opposition to the (second) Home Rule Bill* introduced that year by W. E. Gladstone.* A Unionist Clubs' Council was founded in Belfast as a central body. The Bill was defeated in the House of Lords but the Unionist Clubs remained vigilant on behalf of Ulster Unionists.* The Clubs were represented on the Ulster Unionist Council,* founded in 1904.

UNIONIST PARTY. The organisation of the Unionist movement began in the south with the foundation of the Irish Loyal and Patriotic Union* in May 1885. From 1891 it was known as the Irish Unionist Alliance.* As a result of the general election of November 1885 which returned the Conservatives to power, there were eighteen Irish Unionists in the House of Commons, sixteen of them representing Ulster constituencies. With the support of the Irish Parliamentary Party* led by Charles Stewart Parnell* the Liberals replaced the Conservatives in January 1886. W. E. Gladstone* formed his new administration committed to the (first) Home Rule Bill.* The Ulster Loyalist Anti-Repeal Union* was founded on 8 January and later in the month the Irish Unionist Party was formed in the House of Commons to support the Conservatives in opposition to the Bill. The Bill was defeated in June and the Liberals lost the general election in July. The threat of Home Rule faded. Nineteen Unionists had been returned, seventeen in Ulster constituencies.

The general election of 1892 which returned the Liberals to power brought twenty-three Unionists into the Commons, nineteen representing Ulster constituencies. They prepared to organise resistance to Gladstone's (second) Home Rule Bill.* Unionist clubs, later an important feature of Unionist organisation, were formed in January 1893. Gladstone carried his Bill through the Commons but the Unionists had enough support to defeat it in the House of Lords. Lord Rosebery, who had no personal commitment to Home Rule, succeeded Gladstone as Liberal Prime

Minister in 1894. The Liberals lost the general election of July 1895 when twenty-one Unionists were returned, eighteen for Ulster constituencies. The Unionist figures were unchanged in the general election of 1900, by which time the party was led by Colonel E. J. Saunderson.*

The Devolution proposal put forward by the Irish Reform Association* in 1904 led to the foundation of the Ulster Unionist Council* as a central executive for Ulster opposition to Home Rule. The fall of the Conservative government in 1905 and the success of the Liberals in the 1906 general election led to the establishment of the Joint Committee of Unionist Associations* (1907). Colonel Saunderson, who died in 1906, was replaced as Unionist leader by Walter Long,* a British Conservative politician. Unionists produced a stream of anti-Home Rule propaganda and were superbly organised when H. H. Asquith,* having become dependent on the votes of John Redmond and the Irish Parliamentary Party for the struggle with the House of Lords, became pledged to Home Rule immediately before the general election of January 1910.

Twenty-one Unionists were returned, eighteen for Ulster constituencies, and a month later Sir Edward Carson* became their leader. Following a second general election (in December 1910), when the Unionists lost two seats (one of them in Ulster), Asquith introduced the Parliament Act, 1911,* which reduced the Lords' delaying power on Bills to a maximum of two years. This ensured the success of the (third) Home Rule Bill* which Asquith introduced in 1912.

Southern Unionists were now concerned to seek protection within a Home Rule framework while the Ulster Unionists were utterly determined to prevent Home Rule. At a demonstration at Craigavon, the home of Sir James Craig, on 23 September 1911, Unionists threatened open defiance of Asquith's policy and were publicly supported by

Andrew Bonar Law* of the Conservative Party. Two days later the Ulster Unionist Council, at Carson's urging, prepared the establishment of a provisional government of Ulster in the event of Home Rule. Demonstrations in Ulster and throughout Great Britain reiterated Unionist determination to resist.

The Ulster Unionists formed the Ulster Volunteer Force* in January 1913, recruiting from among those who had signed the Solemn League and Covenant* the previous September. Asquith discovered in March 1914 that the army in Ireland could not be depended upon to act against Ulster (*see* Curragh Incident). The Unionists were represented at the abortive Buckingham Palace Conference* in July when European considerations were occupying the government's attention. By agreement with Carson and Redmond, the Home Rule Act received the Royal Assent on 18 September 1914, accompanied by a suspensory act and a proviso that gave parliament a further opportunity to make separate provision for Ulster. The Ulster Unionists were determined to exclude the six north-eastern counties of Ulster from Home Rule.

By the time World War I ended in November 1918 the Easter Rising of 1916* in Dublin and its aftermath had hardened nationalist determination to secure full independence; Home Rule was no longer regarded as adequate. Sinn Fein,* under the leadership of Eamon de Valera,* had become a mass movement. The Irish Convention* (1917–18) which the new Prime Minister, David Lloyd George,* had hoped would provide a solution, was attended by the Unionists but was boycotted by Sinn Fein. The general election of December 1918 resulted in a sweeping victory for Sinn Fein (seventy-three seats) and a crushing defeat for the Irish Parliamentary Party (six seats). Twenty-six Unionists were returned, twenty-three of them in Ulster constituencies. The Sinn Fein representatives formed the first Dail Eireann on 21 January 1919 and issued a Declaration of Independence which proclaimed an all-Ireland republic. The Irish Unionist Alliance* split and Lord Midleton and his supporters formed the Unionist Anti-Partition League,* representative in the main of southern Unionists. The War of Independence,* waged by the Irish Republican Army* against the Royal Irish Constabulary* and military, also started in January 1919.

Lloyd George's new attempt to solve the Irish question was the Government of Ireland Act, 1920.* Two Irish states were to be established: a six-county state of Northern Ireland and a twenty-six county state of Southern Ireland. Sinn Fein, ignoring the new state of Northern Ireland, recognised only the all-Ireland assembly in Dublin which claimed to legislate for the Irish republic.

The southern Unionists held discussions through the Unionist Anti-Partition League with de Valera in Dublin between 2 and 8 July 1921. A Truce between the IRA and the Crown forces was reached three days later and in October negotiations began between the representatives of Dail Eireann and the British government. During these negotiations, which resulted in a Treaty* (6 December), the leader of the Irish delegation, Arthur Griffith,* met representatives of the southern Unionists, including Midleton and Archbishop Bernard of Dublin. They discussed safeguards for the Unionist population under Home Rule. Their discussions were reported to de Valera. The Unionists sought a Senate to guard their interests in an independent Ireland.

When the Treaty was signed on 6 December Lloyd George was assured that the southern Unionists would be protected in their property and religion and that' they would have a voice in the new Free State. The Anti-Partition League was dissolved and at the beginning of 1922 the Irish Unionist Alliance wound up its affairs. The southern Unionists were given generous representation in the Senate of the Free State (appointed in December 1922). The Civil War, however, revived Unionist fears and they were the subject of attacks on their persons and property by the Irregulars (anti-Treaty IRA). Many of them left the country. Those who remained were allowed to pursue their interests without hindrance in the Free State. For further information *see* Ulster Unionist Party.

UNIONIST PARTY OF NORTHERN IRELAND. Founded by Brian Faulkner* on 24 June 1974 following the collapse of the Assembly of Northern Ireland. The UPNI contained members of the Ulster Unionist Party* who continued to support Faulkner and represented a further step in the fragmentation of the Unionist movement. Following Faulkner's death (January 1977) the party was led by Anne L. Dickson. The UPNI held five seats in the Constitutional Convention of Northern Ireland (1975).

'UNITED IRELAND'. Newspaper founded by Charles Stewart Parnell* from *The Flag of Ireland* which was purchased from Richard Pigott.* The paper, which was edited by William O'Brien* until 1890, first appeared on 13 August 1881, and became the official organ of the Land League and the Irish Parliamentary Party. After O'Brien's imprisonment in October 1881 the paper was published by the Ladies' Land League. The paper again supported the land agitation in 1886 when Tim Harrington* wrote an article called 'A Plan of Campaign' which was published on 23 October 1886 (*see* Plan of Campaign). *United Ireland* provoked a bitter dispute with the Catholic hierarchy after defending John Dillon* from an attack by Edward O'Dwyer,* Bishop of Limerick, who condemned the boycotting tactics of the Plan (August 1890).

Parnell seized control of the paper when O'Brien's deputy, Matthew Bodkin, criticised his continuing

leadership of the party (6 December 1890). Bodkin brought out a substitute, *'Suppressed' United Ireland*, later *The Insuppressible*, which ceased publication on 24 January 1891. *United Ireland* ceased publication in 1898. Cumann na nGaedheal* published a newspaper called *United Ireland* in the early 1930s.

UNITED IRELAND PARTY. English name of the political party more popularly known as Fine Gael.*

UNITED IRISH LEAGUE (UIL). Agrarian organisation founded by William O'Brien, MP* on 23 January 1898 at Westport, Co. Mayo. A response to the depressed state of agriculture in the west, its name commemorated the United Irishmen* whose centenary was celebrated during that year. With Michael Davitt* as president, the League, under its slogan 'The Land for the People', called for the redistribution of large estates among the small farmers and attacked land-grabbers. It quickly gathered support and had fifty-three branches by October, mainly in Mayo. The League soon spread beyond Connaught and by April 1900 was claiming 462 branches with 60,000 to 80,000 members in twenty-five counties. It also had its own newspaper, *The Irish People,** edited by O'Brien (1899–1908).

The rapid growth of the UIL alarmed the various factions of the Irish Parliamentary Party,* which had been split since the crisis over the leadership of Charles Stewart Parnell* (December 1890). Fearing that the political initiative would fall to O'Brien, John Dillon* and John Redmond* re-united the party in 1900 and invited O'Brien to join them. Redmond then assumed the presidency of the League which became the new constituency organisation of the Irish party. By 1901 there were 100,000 members, and Redmond carried the League to the USA, despite the opposition of John Devoy* and Clan na Gael.*

The League lost support in 1914

when Redmond called on the Irish Volunteers* to aid Britain in the war effort and four years later was destroyed outside of Ulster when Sinn Fein* annihilated the Irish Party at the polls. It continued to operate in Ulster where it was the organ of Joseph Devlin* and his small band of nationalists until 1928.

'UNITED IRISHMAN'. Newspaper founded by John Mitchel* in 1847 after he broke with *The Nation.** It became the principal organ for advanced republican views and despite its price of 2s (10p) it sold 5,000 copies on its first day of issue. Mitchel, who was influenced by James Fintan Lalor* on the land issue, sought an armed insurrection and called on the tenantry, suffering from the Famine of 1845–49,* to withhold payment of rent and poor-rate, boycott those who did pay and to withhold the harvest. He published instructions on street warfare. The paper was suppressed in 1848 and Mitchel tried and transported for fourteen years.

Arthur Griffith,* who had been deeply influenced by Mitchel, revived the title *United Irishman* for his own weekly paper which appeared from 1899 to 1906. First issued on 4 March 1899, it became the organ of Cumann na nGaedheal* and advocated self-government for Ireland. Contributors included W. B. Yeats* and George Russell.* Griffith's series of articles on the 'Resurrection of Hungary'* appeared in *The United Irishman* during 1904. Two years later it was replaced by his new paper, *Sinn Fein.**

The United Irishman was the title for the official monthly organ of the Irish Republican Army* and Sinn Fein,* issued since 1948. By 1957 its circulation was around 120,000. Following the split in the republican movement (January 1970) it became the organ of the Official (Gardiner Place) wing of Sinn Fein.

UNITED IRISHMEN. The Society of United Irishmen, or the United Irish Society, was founded in Belfast in October 1791 and in Dublin, one month later. At the start the society drew its support from Presbyterians in Ulster, and from Protestants and liberals seeking parliamentary reform. There were others, like Theobald Wolfe Tone, who, inspired by the French Revolution, sought to establish a republic. Its aims were viewed with hostility by the political and religious establishment and the government moved to suppress it in May 1794. The United Irishmen then went underground and was reconstituted in 1795 as a secret, oath-bound society dedicated to the establishment of a republic. By 1798 it had around 250,000 members, on paper, and had taken root among the Catholic peasantry. The repressive measures undertaken by General Edward Lake drove the society into revolt in 1798. The rising was suppressed with great savagery and the movement destroyed. The government, alarmed by the rising, set about implementing the legislative union of the Irish and English parliaments (*see* Union, Act of). The unsuccessful attempt by Robert Emmet* to organise a rising in 1803 spelt the death of the movement.

The ideals of Wolfe Tone and the United Irishmen continued to be a potent force in Irish history. They influenced Thomas Davis,* John Mitchel,* the Irish Republican Brotherhood* and James Connolly.* The centenary celebrations to commemorate the rising of 1798 were organised by the IRB in 1898 and became a rallying-point for all shades of nationalist opinion.

UNITED IRISHWOMEN. The women's branch of the Co-Operative Movement,* founded in 1910, it later became the Irish Countrywomen's Association* (ICA).

UNITED NATIONS AND IRELAND. Although Ireland did participate in specialist agencies of the UN, the country did not become a member until 14 December 1955; until then Ireland's membership had been vetoed by the USSR (as early as 1946). Ireland became a member in 1955 as a result of a package deal which permitted the entry also of Albania, Austria, Bulgaria, Cambodia, Ceylon, Finland, Hungary, Italy, Jordan, Laos, Libya, Portugal, Rumania and Spain. Application for Ireland's membership had been handled by the Minister for External Affairs in the second Inter-Party Government, Liam Cosgrave.*

When the country took its seat at the UN during the session of 1956 the Irish delegation was led by Frederick H. Boland,* later president of the General Assembly. Irish policy in relation to the United Nations as laid down by Mr Cosgrave had three aspects: it pledged to abide by the UN Charter; it would maintain independence so as not to be 'associated with particular blocs or groups so far as possible'; but, at the same time, it was stated that the country would support those powers which were dedicated to preserving freedom from communism (in effect, Ireland was identifying herself with Canada, the US and Western Europe).

In 1957 when the Inter-Party Government fell from power, Frank Aiken* became the new Minister for External Affairs, an office which he held until 1969. He looked to the United Nations, without success, for an agreement on the non-proliferation of nuclear arms, sought controls to restrain imperialist ambitions and repeatedly sought discussions on the admission of the People's Republic of China. He had little success with the first two and when the admission of the People's Republic did come up finally in 1961, Ireland opposed it. In 1961 a member of the Irish delegation, Dr Conor Cruise O'Brien, was chosen to represent the secretary-general of the UN (Dag Hammar-skjold) in Katanga. Later that year, Dr O'Brien resigned and left the Irish Department of External Affairs. During the 1960s and 1970s Irish troops served on UN peace-keeping missions in the Middle East, Cyprus, Kashmir and the Lebanon. Sean Mac-Bride* was UN Commissioner in Namibia until 1977.

UNITED TRADES ASSOCIATION. Formed in 1863 by thirty Dublin trades unions, which sought to protect labour and encourage native manufactures and not, as they put it, 'to interfere with the legitimate progress of trade' but 'to push trade in every manner possible'. In 1864 it sought to form a federation of all the trades unions in the country but when the Trades Union Congress in Britain was formed in 1868 the United Trades Association found it easier to continue under the general umbrella of the TUC; in any case, many important Irish unions had their headquarters in England. An Irish Trades Union Congress* was founded in 1894.

UNITED ULSTER UNIONIST COUNCIL (UUUC). Also known as the Loyalist Coalition, it was founded in Northern Ireland in 1974 with the aim of bringing down the power-sharing Executive and Assembly of Northern Ireland (*see* Northern Ireland). The parties on the council were the Official Unionists led by Harry West, the Democratic Unionist Party* led by Rev. Ian Paisley* and the Vanguard Unionist Party led by William Craig* (*see* Ulster Unionists). The UUUC co-operated with the Ulster Workers' Council* in the organisation of a general strike which brought down the Assembly. The coalition had the support of loyalist paramilitary groups. The UUUC won 47 out of 78 seats in the election to the Convention to draft a constitution for Northern Ireland (1 May 1975). William Craig, hitherto one of the most hardline loyalists, suggested that loyalists could form an emergency coalition with the Social Democratic and Labour Party* if devolved government returned to Northern Ireland. This was rejected by Rev. Paisley and other partners by thirty-seven votes to one, and Craig was expelled from the coalition on 23 October.

The coalition submitted a report for the consideration of the Convention, in which it condemned the

SDLP and demanded majority rule through a Westminster-style parliament in Northern Ireland. This stand was rejected by other parties but the UUUC report was accepted in the Convention by forty-two votes to thirty-one. It was then rejected by the British government. The life of the Convention was then extended until 7 May 1976 but when no further progress had been made in the spring of 1976 it was dissolved. The coalition subsequently fell apart.

UNITY PROPOSALS (MAY 1922). Put forward by officers of the Irish Republican Army* in an attempt to bridge the gap between the pro- and anti-Treatyite factions (*see* Treaty). The proposals read:

We, the undersigned officers of the IRA, realising the gravity of the present situation in Ireland, and appreciating the fact that if the present drift is maintained a conflict of comrades is inevitable, declare that this would be the greatest calamity in Irish history, and would leave Ireland broken for generations.

To avert this catastrophe we believe that a closing of the ranks all round is necessary.

We suggest to all leaders, army and political, and all citizens and soldiers of Ireland the advisability of a unification of forces on the basis of acceptance and utilisation of our present national position in the best interests of Ireland; and we require that nothing shall be done which would prejudice our position or dissipate our strength. We feel that on this basis alone can the situation best be faced, viz:

(1) The acceptance of that fact – admitted by all sides – that the majority of the people of Ireland are willing to accept the Treaty.

(2) An agreed election with a view to

(3) Forming a government which will have the confidence of the whole country.

(4) Army unification on above basis.

Signed
Tom Hales, S. O'Hegarty, Sean Moylan, Eoin O'Duffy, Micheál O Coileáin, Dan Breen, H. Murphy, F. O'Donoghue, R. J. Mulcahy, Gearóid O'Sullivan.

UNIVERSITY EDUCATION. *See* Trinity College, Dublin; Maynooth College; Queen's Colleges; Catholic University; Royal University *and* National University of Ireland.

UNIVERSITY EDUCATION (IRELAND) ACT, 1879. *See* Royal University of Ireland.

URBAN DISTRICT COUNCILS. *See* Local Government.

V

VACCINATION. Introduced to Ireland in 1800 when John Milner Barry* used it in his native Cork.

VALUATION ACT (IRELAND) 1852. *See* Primary Valuation.

VANGUARD. Ulster Unionist organisation founded by William Craig* in February 1972 as a reaction to the attempts of the government of Northern Ireland, led by Brian Faulkner,* to introduce reforms under pressure from the British government. Vanguard demanded the maintenance of Northern Ireland under the Stormont government within the United Kingdom. It sought the restoration of internal security to the government and expressed total opposition to a united Ireland. Vanguard, which was seeking a return to the pre-1969 state in Northern Ireland, alarmed moderates when Craig began to attend demonstrations accompanied by motor-cycle escorts of beleathered young men, after which he made speeches which appeared to call for a pogrom of those suspected of disloyalty to Northern Ireland. The Ulster Defence Association* operated under the Vanguard umbrella for a time.

Upon the introduction of direct rule from Westminster in March 1972, there was a further fragmentation in the Ulster Unionist Party.* Craig broke with Faulkner and established the Vanguard Unionist Progressive Party. Vanguard candidates won seven seats to the Assembly of Nortern Ireland in June 1973, and, as part of the United Ulster Unionist Council,* worked to destroy the power-sharing Executive formed under Brian Faulkner* in January 1974. At one stage it advocated an independent Ulster rather than direct rule. However, when Craig expressed support for an emergency coalition between the Social Democratic and Labour Party* and the loyalists he was expelled from the Council and lost the leadership of Vanguard. With the fall of the Assembly and the failure of the Constitutional Convention (1975), Vanguard, like other small political parties in Northern Ireland, became for the moment largely irrelevant. It was subsequently reabsorbed into the Official Unionist Party and ceased to function as a separate movement.

VANGUARD UNIONIST PROGRESSIVE PARTY. *See* Vanguard.

VESEY-FITZGERALD, WILLIAM (1783–1843). Landowner and politician (Conservative); b. Ennis, Co. Clare; ed. Oxford. MP for Ennis (1808–12; 1813–18; 1831–32) and for Clare county (1818–28), he was Lord of the Irish Treasury and Privy Councillor (1810) and English Privy Councillor (1812). He was Envoy Extraordinary to Sweden (1820–23) and Paymaster-General of the

Forces (1826). When he was selected by the Duke of Wellington* to be President of the Board of Trade in 1828, he had to seek re-election. Although his sympathies were with Catholic Emancipation* and he was a popular landlord, the Catholic Association* opposed him and put Daniel O'Connell* forward for the Clare seat. O'Connell's victory in Clare marked the last stage of the fight for Emancipation which was granted one year later. The Government found Vesey-Fitzgerald another seat (Newport, Cornwall). He was re-elected for Ennis in 1831. Sir Robert Peel* created him Lord Fitzgerald of Desmond and Clan Gibbon in 1835. He was again President of the Board of Trade (1841–43).

VETO. The veto, mooted as an accompaniment to Catholic Emancipation,* would have granted the British government the right to veto the appointment of Catholic bishops and archbishops in Ireland to whom it had 'any proper objection'. In return for the veto the state would provide for the payment of Catholic clergymen. At a meeting in Maynooth* in January 1799, the acceptance of the veto was favoured by the four archbishops, including John Thomas Troy,* Archbishop of Dublin, and six bishops, who hoped that Union* would be accompanied by Emancipation. After the Union, however, George III* extracted from William Pitt* a promise that Emancipation would not be raised. The controversy over the veto continued for more than two decades.

The veto was raised in 1805 by Sir John Cox Hippisley and three years later it had the support of the Whigs, when Henry Grattan* introduced a Catholic Relief Bill which included the veto. It had clerical support in the early stages, but later in the year the bishops rejected it. While Emancipation accompanied by the veto had support from the aristocratic and propertied elements on the Catholic Committee* there was a strong opposition led by

Daniel O'Connell.* He had clerical and episcopal support which rejected the veto when it was again raised in 1810. Grattan introduced another Bill in 1813, this time without the veto. When Lord Castlereagh* attempted to amend it to include securities Grattan rejected it. The Bill, in any event, was lost.

The battle between the aristocratic leadership of the Catholic movement for Emancipation and the populists led by O'Connell reached crisis point in 1814 when the Vatican vice-prefect of the Congregation for the Propagation of the Faith, Monsignor Quarantotti, issued a rescript favouring the veto. He was speaking on behalf of Pope Pius VII, then the prisoner of Napoleon. The rescript was denounced by the bishops and O'Connell, and led to the rout of the aristocratic leadership of the emancipationists. The Pope, following his release, announced his acceptance of the veto in 1815 and in February 1816 pointed out to the Irish bishops that he was acting in accordance with established custom in not appointing to bishoprics people who were 'displeasing to the powers under whom the dioceses to be administered were situated'. The question of the veto lay dormant for some time after that. In 1825 a Relief Bill introduced by Sir Francis Burdett,* supported by O'Connell, included two 'wings' instead of the old veto: they were state payment of the clergy and the disenfranchisement of the forty-shilling freeholders.* The Bill was lost in the House of Lords. Emancipation was granted without the veto in 1829.

VICTORIA, QUEEN (1819–1901). Queen of the United Kingdom of Great Britain and Ireland (1837–1901) and Empress of India (1876–1901); b. Kensington Palace, London, where she was raised and educated. She married Prince Albert of Saxe-Coburg (1840) who acted as her private secretary afterwards. Her first Prime Minister, Lord Melbourne,* was her political mentor. Personally distressed by the agitation of Daniel O'Connell and the Repeal Association,* she encouraged Sir Robert Peel* on the Maynooth Grant (1845; *see* Maynooth), and treated with contempt the Protestant protests which followed. She also supported Peel on the repeal of the Corn Laws.

During the Famine of 1845–49, she contributed £2,000 to the British Relief Association,* but became known to generations of nationalists as 'The Famine Queen'. Shortly after one William Hamilton of Adare, Co. Limerick, fired a blank charge at her while she was driving in London on 19 May 1849, she paid her first visit to Ireland. Her party arrived at Cobh, Co. Cork, which was renamed Queenstown in her honour, in August. After travelling by yacht to Kingstown (Dun Laoghaire) she spent four days at the Vice-Regal Lodge in the Phoenix Park. The Queen was enthusiastically received during her visit and before moving to Belfast she created the Prince of Wales Earl of Dublin (10 September) and gave the name Patrick to her third son, Prince Arthur (22 June 1850).

The Queen was disturbed by the Protestant outcry at the Pope's decision to revive the Catholic bishoprics in England (*see* Ecclesiastical Titles Bill). When Lord John Russell* was succeeded as Prime Minister by the 14th Earl of Derby* in 1852, Derby's short-lived government included Benjamin Disraeli* as Chancellor of the Exchequer. She returned in August 1853 to open the Dublin Exhibition organised by William Dargan.* Upon her arrival at Kingstown (Dun Laoghaire), she was met by a reported one million people. On her third visit in August 1858 she visited the Prince of Wales at the Curragh and travelled to Co. Kerry. She stayed at Kenmare House and was hostess at a levée at Muckross House, Killarney, where her guests included O'Connell's brother, James.

W. E. Gladstone* disconcerted her. She criticised one of his first Acts, the Disestablishment of the Church of Ireland* and considered him a dangerous radical (she said of him that he addressed her as though she were a public meeting). The Queen rejected Gladstone's suggestion that the office of Lord Lieutenant of Ireland should be abolished and replaced by the Prince of Wales in permanent residence in Dublin.

She urged strong government for Ireland during the Land War,* encouraging W. E. Forster* to break the Land League. Forster and the Queen were in agreement on the Kilmainham 'Treaty'* of which she strongly disapproved. She held a poor opinion of Charles Stewart Parnell* and the Irish Parliamentary Party,* calling its members '. . . low, disreputable men, who were elected by order of Parnell'. When the Irish pressed for Home Rule she opposed it on the grounds that to break the Union would be repugnant to her Coronation Oath. The Queen again visited Ireland (4–25 April 1900) and stayed at the Vice-Regal Lodge. Despite nationalist protests organised by Maud Gonne* and James Connolly,* she was well received and was given an Address of Welcome by the Dublin Corporation.

VILLIERS-STUART, HENRY. *See* Stuart, Henry Villiers.

VOCATIONAL EDUCATION. The Vocational Education Act of 1930 reorganised technical instruction in the Free State and provided education at a low cost for pupils whose needs were not catered for in the existing secondary school system. This form of education had been the responsibility of the technical instruction section of the Department of Agriculture and Technical Instruction* since 1899. Vocational education was designed for 'trades, manufactures, commerce and other industrial pursuits'. Apprenticeship courses were offered, some leading to professional qualifications, and much of the teaching was through night classes. The system was geared to the needs of a rural community. Funds for the vocational schools

were provided from central funds and from local rates. Co-educational and non-denominational, the schools were administered by thirty-eight local Vocational Education Committees, to be selected by local authorities and to be representative of commercial, industrial, educational and cultural interests. Eight of the fourteen seats on each committee were to be filled by the local authority. Their purpose was to oversee the provision of continuing education, to 'supplement education provided in elementary schools' and to include 'general and practical training in preparation for employment'.

The distinction which obtained between secondary schools and vocational schools was broken down to a large extent when the latter began to offer Intermediate and Leaving Certificate courses after 1967. In 1978 there were 246 Vocational Schools offering general classes to 61,551 students. *See also* Secondary Education.

'VOICE OF LABOUR'. Newspaper, organ of the Labour Party* and trade union movement, which appeared from October 1922 until 1927, edited by Cathal O'Shannon.* It was succeeded by *The Irishman* (1927–30) and *The Watchword of Labour* (1930–32).

VOLUNTARY HEALTH INSURANCE BOARD. Founded in 1957 under the Voluntary Health Insurance Act as a statutory corporation to operate various voluntary health insurance schemes.

VOLUNTEER POLITICAL PARTY. Founded in April 1974 by Kenneth Gibson as an ultra-loyalist political branch of the Ulster Volunteer Force.* Gibson secured 6 per cent of the vote when he contested West Belfast in the Westminster general election of October 1974. In the same month, the UVF was again proscribed and the VPP disappeared.

W

WAGES' STANDSTILL ORDER (1941). Introduced during the Emergency* by the Fianna Fail government in an effort to protect the economy. The Order, steered through by Sean Lemass,* prevented trade unions from striking for higher wages by removing legal protection for strike action. It was strongly resisted by James Larkin* and was repealed in 1946.

WAKE. Custom of remaining with a corpse until its removal to the church. Normally the laying out of a body was done by some female neighbours. The corpse was first cleaned and clothed in a habit. A crucifix was placed on the breast and rosary beads were entwined in the fingers. In some areas it was customary to place a prayer-book or bible under the chin of the deceased. As soon as these formalities had been concluded, candles were lit near the corpse and the relatives brought formally into its presence. A lament known as a keen* was then performed. Chief mourners provided food, drink, snuff and pipes of tobacco for those in attendance. On entering a wake house, the visitor made his way to the side of the corpse and prayed silently for a few moments. He then expressed his sympathy to the relatives. A crowd collected at the wakehouse. Drink was freely taken and dancing and merrymaking, including the playing of special 'wake-games', occurred. Many of these games were of pre-Christian origin and had distinct sexual undertones. It was said that in rural Ireland 'many a wedding was made at a wake'. The Catholic Church condemned the custom of drinking at a wake on numerous occasions. By decree of the synod of Dublin (July 1831) priests were ordered to forbid their congregation to provide tobacco at wakes or to spend money on things which would lead people to commit sin. The Synod of Ardagh (October 1835), under the chairmanship of Dr William Higgins, condemned utterly the custom of making alcoholic drinks available at wakes and funerals. The Synod of Maynooth (1875) completely forbade the practice of giving out alcoholic drink at wakes as a 'disgrace to Christian communities'. Bishops were exhorted to penalise those found guilty of such misbehaviour. In the diocese of Ardagh and Clonmacnoise, on 17 February 1903, the bishop, Dr Hoare, issued a notice which was displayed in all churches of the dioceses, forbidding, under pain of mortal sin, the drinking of alcohol at wakes or funerals. Mass would not be offered in any house in which this regulation was not observed. Wakes in the West of Ireland were known to last for a week, which provoked Mary Little to comment that 'In some parts of Ireland the sleep which knows no waking is always followed by a wake which knows no sleeping'. The custom is still extant in some areas.

WALKER, WILLIAM (1870–1918). Trade unionist; b. Belfast. Employed at the Harland and Wolff shipyards, he helped to organise its semi-skilled labour force and became a delegate to Belfast Trades Council and to the first Irish Trades Union Congress* (1894) of which he was appointed Secretary. As a full-time official of the Textile Operatives Society of Ireland, Walker was recognised as the most important labour leader in Ireland. His bitter feud with James Connolly* stemmed from the latter's criticism of Walker's support for Ulster Unionists.* Although a prominent member of the British Labour Party, Walker failed in three attempts to gain a Belfast seat to Westminster. Following his appointment as a National Insurance Inspector, he lost much of his trade-union support and his influence gradually waned. His pamphlet, *The Irish Ques-*

tion (1908), stated his belief that Home Rule* would hamper Irish economic progress.

'WALKERITES'. Followers of the 'Church of God', a fundamentalist church founded by Rev. John Walker (1768–1833), who broke from the Church of Ireland in 1804.

WALSH, EDWARD (1805–50). Folklorist and Irish language enthusiast; b. Derry city; ed. chiefly in Cork. He worked as a tutor and schoolmaster before his appointment as sub-editor of *The Dublin Monitor* through the influence of his friend Charles Gavan Duffy.* While a schoolmaster at the convict settlement at Spike Island, Cork, in November 1848, Walsh met John Mitchel,* then in transit to Tasmania. Mitchel describes the meeting in *Jail Journal:* '. . . Poor Walsh! He has a family of young children; he seems broken in health and spirits; ruin has been on his tracks for years, and I think has him in the wind at last. There are more contented galley-slaves toiling at Spike than the schoolmaster . . .' Walsh spent his last days as a schoolteacher in the Cork workhouse. As a folklorist Walsh is considered second only to Thomas Crofton Croker,* while his ability as a lyricist earned him the unstinted admiration of W. B. Yeats.* Apart from his many translations, his works include *Reliques of Jacobite Poetry* (1844) and *Irish Popular Songs* (1847).

WALSH, JOHN EDWARD (1816–69). Lawyer and essayist; b. Dublin; ed. TCD where he had a brilliant academic career and was a prominent member of TCD Historical Society. Called to the Bar in 1839, and QC in 1857, he was Attorney-General in 1866, and Master of the Rolls (1866). He died in Paris. His essays and sketches of pre-Famine life in Ireland appeared in the *Dublin University Magazine** and were published as *Ireland Sixty Years Ago* in 1847.

WALSH, JOHN STEPHEN (1835–94). Land agitator; b. Milford, Co. Cork but moved as a child with his parents to Middlesborough, England. Walsh became an active member of the Irish Republican Brotherhood* and was an early supporter of the Land League.* As an IRB agent he was involved in the rescue of Fenian prisoners from Fremantle, Australia, on the *Catalpa.** He was strongly suspected by the authorities of involvement in the Phoenix Park Murders.* Walsh fled via France to the USA where he was active in Clan na Gael* among whom he was known as 'John Walsh of Middlesborough'. He died, impoverished, in New York.

WALSH, WILLIAM JOSEPH (1841–1921). Archbishop of Dublin (R.C.), 1885–1921; b. Dublin; ed. St Laurence O'Toole Seminary, Dublin, Catholic University* and St Patrick's College, Maynooth, where he had a brilliant academic career. He became Professor of Dogmatic and Moral Theology (1867–78), Vice-President, Maynooth (1878–80), and President from 1880 until his appointment to the See of Dublin in 1885. His appointment to the archdiocese was opposed by the British government, aware of his strong nationalist sympathies as indicated by his support for the Land League,* Charles Stewart Parnell* and the Irish Parliamentary Party.* Dr Walsh was a member of the Senate of the Royal University of Ireland (1883–84) and pressed for a Catholic system of national, intermediate and university education.

With Thomas William Croke,* Archbishop of Cashel, he lent his support to the Plan of Campaign.* When the crisis arose in the Irish party over Parnell's involvement in the O'Shea divorce case (November–December 1890), the Archbishop played a leading role in restraining Catholic clergy from becoming involved in the leadership crisis within the Irish party. He himself remained publicly aloof from the leadership struggle until 3 December, when he sent a telegram to the party calling on it to 'act manfully'. Later that day the Standing Committee recommended that the Irish people reject Parnell's continuing leadership and three days later the party split on the issue.

During the 1890s the Archbishop was closely connected with the controversy over bimetallism upon which he was an authority, advocating the use of silver currency. He published *Bimetallism and Monometallism* in 1893 which was translated into German the same year and into French in 1894.

An indefatigable nationalist, he supported Sinn Fein* and vehemently opposed the Government of Ireland Act, 1920* which partitioned the country. Dr Walsh served on many public bodies during his long public career including Commissioner of Intermediate Education (1892–1919), Commissioner of Charitable Donations and Bequests (1893), Commissioner of National Education (1895–1901), Consultative Commissioner of Education for the Department of Agriculture and Technical Instruction (1900–04), and on the Senate of the National University of Ireland of which in 1908 he became the first Chancellor.

He was a prolific writer and contributed articles of Catholic and national interest to *The Nation, Freeman's Journal,* *Irish Ecclesiastical Record, Contemporary Review, Fortnightly Review, Dublin Review* etc. His writings include *Louise Lateau* (1876), *Harmony of the Gospel* (1879), *Tractatus de Actibus Humanis* (1880), *The Queen's Colleges and the Royal University* (No. 1, 1883, No. 2, 1884), *Officium Defunctorum et Ordo Exsequiarum* (1884), *Grammar of Gregorian Music* (1885), *Addresses on Irish Education* (1890), *Statement of the Chief Grievances of Irish Catholics in the Matter of Education* (1890), *The Irish University Question* (1897), *Trinity College and the University of Dublin* (1902), *The Irish University Question: Trinity College and its Medical School* (1906),

The Motu Proprio Quantavis Diligentia and its Critics (1912), *O'Connell and Archbishop Murray, and the Board of Charitable Donations and Bequests* (1916). He was also the author of *A Plain Exposition of the Land Act of 1881* (1881).

WAR OF INDEPENDENCE (1919–21). The War of Independence began on 21 January 1919 when members of the Third Tipperary Brigade of the Irish Volunteers,* led by Sean Treacy* and Dan Breen,* ambushed and killed two members of the Royal Irish Constabulary* at Soloheadbeg, Co. Tipperary. As the year progressed, small bands of Volunteers made lightning raids against the RIC, banks, post offices and, eventually, tax offices. Squads of soldiers and police were ambushed by antagonists who then faded into the rural background where they were protected in 'safe' houses. Volunteer leaders became the new nationalist folk heroes: *see* Aiken, Frank; Barry, Tom; Lynch, Liam; MacEoin, Seán; O'Malley, Ernie. It was estimated that, in all, no more than 2,000 Volunteers were involved in the struggle against 50,000 soldiers and policemen by 1921.

On the same day as the Soloheadbeg ambush the Sinn Fein MPs who had been returned at the general election of December 1918 formed the first Dail Eireann* and issued a Declaration of Independence. During the following August the Volunteers, who had formed the army of the Republic proclaimed by Patrick Pearse,* at the start of the Easter Rising of 1916,* took an oath of allegiance to the Dail and became the Irish Republican Army.* While the Dail's Minister for Defence was Cathal Brugha,* it was his colleague, Michael Collins,* Minister for Finance and Director of Intelligence of the Volunteers, who enjoyed the confidence of the IRA and who acted as coordinator for the scattered bands. After the Easter Rising the British government made an unsuccessful attempt to solve the Irish question through the Irish Convention.* The next attempt was the Government of Ireland Act, 1920,* which was ignored in the south during the War but which led to the establishment of the six-county state of Northern Ireland in 1921. The Prime Minister, David Lloyd George,* refused to recognise the Dail, which was outlawed, or the status of the IRA as an army. He also refused to recognise the existence of a war between Ireland and Great Britain although increasingly embarrassed by the financial and military demands which the struggle was making on his resources. The policy of reprisals adopted by the RIC and their reinforcements, the Auxiliaries* and the Black and Tans,* after the summer of 1920, led to questions in the House of Commons and to calls upon the government by the British press to find a solution to the Irish question.

The Dail established 'Arbitration Courts' which adjudicated in frequent land disputes. As republican courts spread, the IRA acted as a police force and British law ceased to operate in parts of the country. On 3 and 4 April 1920, a further blow to British administration in Ireland was struck when the IRA raided and destroyed tax offices around the country. No further taxes were collected until the establishment of the Free State* in December 1922. The IRA strengthened its hold over the population as police and military counter-measures alienated the civilian population. Arthur Griffith* estimated that between 1 January 1919 and 31 July 1920 there had been 38,720 armed raids upon private houses, 4,982 arrests, 1,604 armed assaults, 102 sackings and shootings-up in towns and seventy-seven murders, including those of women and children; all this, he claimed, was the work of Crown forces.

During 1920 the IRA began to use the hunger-strike as a weapon to draw attention to the state of Ireland. Republicans in Mountjoy Jail went on hunger-strike on 5 April. A week later, the Irish Trades Union Congress* called a general strike; the hunger-strikers were released three days later. Later in the year the hunger-strike became a deadly weapon and highlighted the Irish demand for sovereign independence when Terence MacSwiney* died in Brixton Prison on 25 October, having survived for seventy-four days without food.

The war between the IRA and the police, who acted without any apparent controls, was pursued with a new fury. The police went on indiscriminate rampages through villages and towns. The IRA burned loyalist houses. The Catholic hierarchy condemned the violence. While individual bishops such as Michael Fogarty* of Killaloe (himself the victim of a police attempt upon his life) showed sympathy for Dail Eireann and the republican cause, the hierarchy as a body never granted formal recognition to the struggle for independence. Eighteen RIC men had died during 1919 but by the end of 1920 165 policemen had been killed and 251 wounded. Military casualties were on a smaller scale. There were attempts to secure a peace in the second half of 1920. The Assistant Under-Secretary for Ireland, Sir Alfred Cope,* played a leading role in putting out feelers to the IRA, with Lloyd George's consent. Other attempts were made by the Archbishop of Perth, Dr Clune, who came to Ireland to attend the funeral of his nephew, Conor Clune, murdered in prison on Bloody Sunday (21 November 1920).* With Lloyd George's consent he tested the Irish attitude towards peace negotiations. He failed to make any progress in his meetings with Griffith, Collins and Eoin MacNeill,* as the IRA would not consent to lay down arms as a preliminary to peace talks.

Eamon de Valera,* President of Dail Eireann, having returned from the USA in January 1921, secured permission from the Dail on 11 March 1921 to announce a formal 'state of war with England'. This belated proposal had the effect of demonstrating to Irishmen that the Dail was now assuming responsibility for the actions of the IRA while, at the same time, indicating to England Irish determination to press on with the struggle. Meanwhile, the British press intensified its attack on the government for its failure to find a solution.

A new initiative came on 22 June when George V* opened the parliament of Northern Ireland, and, in the course of his speech, which had been prepared by Lloyd George, pleaded for an end to the war. At the same time de Valera was invited by Lloyd George to attend a conference in London.

Details for a Truce were worked out between General Sir Nevil Macready* and the IRA. It came into force on 11 July 1921 and, though an uneasy peace, it held until the Dail sent a team of plenipotentiaries, headed by Griffith and Collins, to London in October. A Treaty* was signed on 6 December, accepting Dominion status as a Free State within the British Commonwealth of Nations.

The following incidents indicate the nature of the struggle which took place during the War of Independence:

13 May 1919

Knocklong, Co. Limerick: units of the 3rd Tipperary Brigade, led by Dan Breen and Sean Treacy, rescued their comrade, Sean Hogan, from the Dublin-Cork train. Two policemen were killed and Breen and Treacy seriously wounded.

17 November 1919

Bantry Bay, Co. Cork: units of the Cork No. 3 (West) Brigade, commanded by Maurice Donegan, raided a sloop and made away with arms and ammunition.

14 February 1920

Shantonagh, Ballytrain, Co. Monaghan: 120 members of the Monaghan Brigade, led by Ernie O'Malley and Eoin O'Duffy, destroyed the RIC barracks and accepted the surrender of seven policemen. This was the first RIC barracks in Ulster to be captured.

27 April 1920

Ballylanders, Co. Limerick: Thomas Malone, known then as 'Sean Forde', led the East Limerick Brigade in an attack on the RIC barracks. The five policemen surrendered and one IRA man was wounded.

5 June 1920

Midleton, Co. Cork: units of the Cork No. 1 Brigade ambushed a motor-cycle detachment of the Cameron Highlanders at Mile Bush. The troops were disarmed. Later that day troops shot up Midleton.

11 July 1920

Rear Cross, Co. Tipperary: units of the 3rd Tipperary, South Tipperary and East Limerick Brigades, led by Dan Breen, Ernie O'Malley and Sean Treacy, attacked the RIC barracks which was destroyed in the action, and a number of policemen killed. Breen, O'Malley and Treacy were wounded.

22 September 1920

Rineen Cross, near Miltown Malbay, Co. Clare: the 4th Battalion of the Mid-Clare Brigade, commanded by Ignatius O'Neill and Patrick Lehane, ambushed six policemen, killing all of them. The IRA made a successful retreat when attacked by 150 troops who arrived on the scene of the ambush. As a result of the action, troops burned Ennistymon, Lahinch and Miltown Malbay in reprisal. On the same day, houses in Tuam, Co. Galway and Galway city, and Drumshambo, Co. Leitrim were sacked.

28 September 1920

Mallow, Co. Cork: units of the Cork No. 2 (North) Brigade, led by Liam Lynch and Ernie O'Malley, captured the only military barracks to be taken by the IRA during the War. Having taken the barracks, the home of the 17th Lancers, they secured twenty-seven rifles, two machine-guns and boxes of ammunition before retreating to Lombardstown. The duty-sergeant was killed during the raid. British troops then sacked the town of Mallow, including Cleeve's creamery. Other towns shot up and partially wrecked that day included Liscarroll, Co. Cork; Dunkerrin, King's Co. (Offaly); Clonmore, Co. Carlow; Ballyshannon, Co. Donegal; Listowel, Co. Kerry and Drimoleague, Co. Cork. The policy of reprisals was condemned by the London *Times*.

30 September 1920

Trim, Co. Meath: the Trim Battalion of the Meath Brigade, acting on intelligence provided by T. J. McElligott, captured and destroyed the RIC barracks. In reprisals, the town was shot up and almost one-quarter of the houses destroyed on the next day.

28 October 1920

Thomastown, Co. Tipperary: the 4th Battalion of the Tipperary No. 3 (South) Brigade, led by Dinny Lacey ambushed a lorryload of troops. Later that day, there were police reprisals in the area.

2–9 November 1920

Ballinalee, Co. Longford: following a series of sackings in the area, Sean MacEoin of the Longford Brigade, IRA, shot down RIC men who were burning down a priest's house in Granard. Expecting reprisals, he organised the defence of Ballinalee, which was vacated on 3 November, and prevented its being sacked over the next few days. Following a pitched battle with the military forces on the night of 8–9 November his units withdrew from the town, which was burned.

13 November 1920

Lisnagall, Co. Tipperary: a column of the Tipperary (South) Brigade ambushed Black and Tans, lost five men and several were injured. Over the next three days, reprisals included the burning of business premises in Tipperary and surrounding towns, to the estimated amount of £36,000.

21 November 1920

Dublin, Bloody Sunday.*

28 November 1920

Kilmichael, Co. Cork; the Cork No. 3 (West) Brigade under Tom Barry ambushed sixteen Auxiliaries, all of whom were killed, including Lt-Col Crake, by the thirty-six IRA men. As a result the Auxiliary division at Macroom Castle ordered that 'All male inhabitants of Macroom and all males passing through Macroom shall not appear in public with their hands in their pockets', on pain of being shot on sight. Martial law was declared in Cork county and city, Tipperary and Limerick county and city.

11 December 1920

Cork city: following an IRA ambush of Auxiliaries at Dillon's Cross, Auxiliaries and Black and Tans went on a rampage of burning and looting. Between 10 p.m., and 3 a.m., they inflicted damage to the amount of between £2,000,000 and £3,000,000, the major part of it in Patrick Street. Several thousand workers were rendered unemployed as a result. The British Labour Party Commission (at that time investigating atrocities in Ireland) took evidence which identified those responsible as members of the Crown forces, although their involvement was denied by the authorities. A military inquiry under the command of Major-General Strickland, from which lawyers and the press were excluded, produced a report which was suppressed by the Cabinet.

18 December 1920

Monreal, Co. Clare: Units of the Mid-Clare Brigade, commanded by Ignatius O'Neill, ambushed three lorries of military and police, near Ennistymon, killing sixteen and wounding fourteen.

20 January 1921

Thirty-six men of units of the East Clare Brigade, commanded by Michael Brennan, ambushed police at Glenwood House, near Castlelake, in Co. Clare. All except two of the ten policemen were killed or mortally wounded. That evening and during the next day the police and military fired buildings in Kilkishen, O'Brien's Bridge, Broadford, Clonecurry, Lissane, Ballykelly, Aclare, Belvoir, Knockatureen and Sixmilebridge.

28 January 1921

Tureengariffe, two miles west of Ballydesmond, Co. Kerry: the Newmarket Battalion of the Cork No. 2 (North) Brigade and East Kerry Volunteers under Sean Moylan ambushed Major-General Philip Armstrong Holmes, Divisional Commander of Police for Cork and Kerry, and his escort. The police surrendered, after one had been killed and the remainder wounded after they ran out of ammunition. There were police reprisals on Knocknagree and Ballydesmond during the next few days.

3 February 1921

Dromkeen, Co. Limerick: units of the East and Mid-Limerick Brigades, commanded by D. O'Hannigan, ambushed a detachment of thirteen police (three Regulars and ten Black and Tans), three miles from Pallas. Two policemen survived the action.

11 February 1921

Drishanebeg, Co. Cork: the Millstreet column of the Cork No. 2 (North) Brigade halted the Tralee-Mallow train two miles from Millstreet and engaged troops of the First Royal Fusiliers, who finally surrendered when seven had been seriously wounded.

5 March 1921

Clonbanin, Co. Cork: in a raid planned by Liam Lynch, nearly 100 members of the Cork No. 2 (North) Brigade and the Kerry No. 2 Brigade, commanded by Sean Moylan, ambushed Brigadier-General Cummins and his escort. Thirteen troops were killed and fifteen wounded; the IRA had no casualties.

19 March 1921

Crossbarry, Co. Cork: in one of the biggest engagements of the War, 100 men of the Cork No. 3 (West) Brigade under Tom Barry, engaged some 1,000 troops of the Essex and Hampshire Regiments. Three IRA men were killed and four wounded while British casualties were placed at thirty-nine killed and forty-seven wounded.

21 March 1921

Headford, Co. Kerry: a column of the Kerry No. 2 Brigade, commanded by Dan Allman and Thomas McEllistrim, attacked troops of the First Royal Fusiliers on the Kenmare train at Headford junction. The IRA failed to gain badly needed arms from the troops and Allman was killed, as was one volunteer.

23 March 1921

Scramogue, Co. Roscommon: units of the North and South Roscommon Brigades, commanded by Sean Leavy and Martin Fallon, ambushed the 9th Lancers two miles from Strokestown. The Lancers, under Captain Sir Alfred Peek (who was killed), were escorting two Black and Tans who had been accused of smashing the windows of Elphin Church. The prisoners survived the ambush and were later killed by the IRA.

3 May 1921

Tourmakeady, Co. Mayo: units of the South Mayo Brigade, under Tom Maguire (who was wounded six times during the action), ambushed RIC constables in the early hours of the morning and then retreated to the Partry Mountains where they were attacked by some 600 troops. Following intensive fighting until nightfall, the British troops withdrew. The RIC barracks at Derrypark, Kinniry and Cuilmore were vacated within a short time.

1 June 1921

Castlemaine, Co. Kerry: the 6th Battalion of the Kerry No. 1 Brigade, commanded by Tom O'Connor, ambushed a detachment of Black and Tans, two of whom escaped.

16 June 1921

Rathcoole, Co. Cork: One hundred and thirty-eight men of units of the Cork No. 2 (North) Brigade, using land-mines, ambushed Auxiliaries, killing about half of them. There were no IRA casualties in the action but there were police reprisals against the local population.

'WATCHWORD OF LABOUR'. See *Voice of Labour.*

WEBB, ALFRED JOHN (1834–1908). Writer and politician (Irish Parliamentary Party); b. Dublin where he worked as a printer in his father's business. Webb was an early member of the Home Rule League. He was also a member of Dublin Corporation, Dublin Port and Docks Board and was elected to the RSAI in 1884. He travelled widely on the continent, India and the USA. Webb was elected MP for West Waterford in 1890 and held the seat until 1895. His best-known work, *A Compendium of Irish Biography,* appeared in 1878.

WELLESLEY, RICHARD COLLEY, 2nd EARL OF MORNINGTON AND MARQUESS (1760–1842). Lord Lieutenant (1821–28; 1833–34); b. Dangan Castle, Co. Meath, eldest brother of Arthur Wellesley, later Duke of Wellington;* ed. Eton and Oxford. Having succeeded as Lord Mornington in 1781, he became an Irish peer as a Marquess in 1799. He was Governor of Madras (1797) and Governor-General of India where Arthur was serving in the army. He pressed the second Mahratta War (1803–05), after which he was dismissed from the post and returned to England. Wellesley was Ambassador to Spain (1808) while his younger brother was commanding in Portugal, but was recalled to become Foreign Secretary in the administrations of the Duke of Portland and Spencer Perceval. Claiming support for Catholic Emancipation,* he refused to serve in the government formed by Lord Liverpool in 1812, an example followed by his younger brother, William Wellesley-Pole,* then Irish Chief Secretary.

In spite of his earlier refusal, Wellesley accepted the Irish office from Liverpool in 1821, where his support for Emancipation made him a popular choice for the Lord Lieutenancy. Wellesley's attempts to steer a neutral course between Irish nationalists and the Orange Order* earned him the suspicion of the (Protestant) Ascendancy.* After he ordered the Lord Mayor of Dublin to proclaim an Orange demonstration to decorate King William's statue in College Green on the King's birthday (4 December 1822), a bottle was thrown at him in the Theatre Royal (14 December).

Wellesley suspended *habeas corpus* during Whiteboy agitation over tithes* and conacre.* He re-organised the police and reformed the magistracy, by removing the more bigoted from office. During the famine of the 1820s, he organised famine relief for Ireland at home and in England. The Duke of Wellington, who became Prime Minister in January 1828, did not intend to concede Emancipation and recalled Wellesley from office, replacing him with the 1st Marquess of Anglesey* (who also had to be recalled because he favoured it). Wellesley returned as Viceroy in 1833 but was recalled when Lord Grey's ministry fell. After failing to secure the post from Lord Melbourne,* he retired from public service. A notorious womaniser and spendthrift, Wellesley was a constant source of embarrassment to his family and made himself an object of ridicule on many occasions.

WELLESLEY-POLE, WILLIAM, 3rd EARL OF MORNINGTON (1763–1845). Politician (Conservative); Chief Secretary (1809–12); b. Dangan Castle, Co. Meath, elder brother of Arthur Wellesley, later Duke of Wellington;* ed. Eton. He assumed the additional surname Pole upon inheriting the Queen's Co. (Laois) estate of his uncle, William Pole. MP for Trim in the Irish House of Commons (1783–90) and for East Lowe (1790–94) and Queen's Co. (1801–21) in the imperial parliament, he chose the title 'Welling-

601

ton' for his brother when the latter was created Duke. He was Clerk of the Ordnance in 1802 and Secretary to the Admiralty from 1807 until he succeeded Arthur as Chief Secretary in 1809. At first opposed to Catholic Emancipation,* Wellesley-Pole made himself unpopular in Ireland for his use of the Convention Act. Under the influence of his brother, Richard Colley Wellesley,* he turned to support Emancipation. Having resigned when he refused to serve in Lord Liverpool's administration, he was succeeded in the Irish office by Sir Robert Peel,* but two years later accepted office as Master of the Mint. First raised to the peerage as Baron Maryborough (1821), and having served as Postmaster-General (1834—35), he succeeded to the title of Lord Mornington upon Richard's death (1842).

WELLINGTON, DUKE OF (1769—1852). Wellesley, Arthur; soldier known as 'The Iron Duke'; Chief Secretary (1807—09); Prime Minister (1828—30); b. Dublin; ed. Eton, Brighton and the School of Equitation, Angers, France. An ensign in the 73rd Highland Regiment (1787), he became a lieutenant in the 76th (December 1787) and ADC to the Lord Lieutenant of Ireland (1788—94). MP for Trim in the Irish House of Commons (1790—95), he became a major in the 33rd Foot (April 1793), lieutenant-colonel (September) and colonel (1796).

He commanded the 33rd Foot in India (1797) where he remained until 1805 while his eldest brother, Richard Colley Wellesley,* was Governor-General. He was Governor of Mysore in 1799 and became a major-general in 1802, after which he fought in the second Mahratta War (1803—05). After returning to England in 1805 he succeeded Lord Cornwallis* in January 1806 as Colonel of the 33rd. He became MP for Rye in 1806 and in April married Kitty Pakenham.

Upon his appointment by the Duke of Portland to the Irish Chief Secretaryship, Wellesley sought to ad-

minister Ireland — then demanding Catholic Emancipation,* to which he was opposed — with mildness. He criticised absentee landlords and forbade triumphalist processions on the anniversary of the defeat of the United Irishmen.* He reluctantly fulfilled one of the main functions of the Chief Secretary, dispensation of patronage. Alarmed by the Treaty of Tilsit between Napoleon and the Tsar of Russia, he devoted his attention to the defence of Ireland, because of the possibility of a French invasion. During the summer of 1807, when he heard rumours of a British expedition to the continent, he demanded to be relieved of the Irish Office which he officially vacated in April 1809, to be succeeded by his brother, William Wellesley-Pole.* He served in Denmark where he defeated the Danish militia (July—September 1807).

Wellesley commanded in the Iberian Peninsula from July 1808 until the abdication of Napoleon in 1814. As a reward for his services, he was created the first Duke of Wellington (3 May 1814) and returned to England for victory celebrations in June. He was appointed Ambassador to the French court in August and attended the Congress of Vienna. On 25 March 1815, five days after Napoleon re-entered Paris, Wellington was appointed Commander-in-Chief of the British and Dutch-Belgian forces and began to assemble the allied army which met and defeated Napoleon at Waterloo (18 June).

Wellington became Prime Minister in January 1828 at the height of the Irish agitation for Emancipation which was led by Daniel O'Connell.* Supported by his Home Secretary, Sir Robert Peel,* he agreed to the conditions laid down by George IV,* that Emancipation should not become a cabinet issue. However, the appointment of William Vesey-Fitzgerald* to the Board of Trade led to the Clare by-election and a victory for Daniel O'Connell. Wellington realised that the right of Catholic MPs to take their seats without subscribing to the Oath of Supremacy could no longer be denied without the risk of civil war in Ireland. He and Peel won the King's approval, but only after threatening their resignations, and Emancipation became law in April 1829. Following his defeat in 1830 when a new government was formed by Earl Grey, Wellington became the elder statesman of the Tory party. He had a snappy, taciturn style of communication and was celebrated for his dryness and use of irony. With reference to his Irish birth, he was reputed to have remarked that being born in a stable did not make one a horse.

WESTMINSTER, STATUTE OF (1930). The Statute of Westminster implemented a resolution taken in 1930 at the Imperial Conference of that year when the Free State was represented by P. J. McGilligan.* The Statute provide that no law made by the parliament of a Dominion should be void and inoperative on the grounds that it was repugnant to the law of England. The parliament of a Dominion should have the power to repeal or amend any existing or future act of parliament of the United Kingdom insofar as the same was part of the law of a Dominion. The parliament of a Dominion was granted the full power to make laws having extra-territorial operation. It was also provided that no future act of the United Kingdom parliament should extend to a Dominion unless it was expressly declared in that Act that the Dominion had requested and consented to its enactment. This last was opposed by Winston Churchill* who pointed out that this would enable Dail Eireann* to repudiate the Treaty,* and by the Secretary of State for Dominion Affairs, L. S. Amery, who said that the Free State* must be treated as other Dominions. The Statute received the royal assent on 11 December 1931.

WHATELY, RICHARD (1787–1863). Theologian and Archbishop of Dublin (C.I.), 1831–63; b. London; ed. privately and at Oriel College, Oxford where he took B.A. (1808) and M.A. (1812). While at Oxford he tutored William Nassau Senior* whom he later succeeded as Drummond Professor of Political Economics (1829–31).

Although not happy with his translation to Dublin in 1831, the new Archbishop quickly involved himself in the social, cultural and political life of the country. A supporter of Catholic Emancipation,* he sought Poor Law and National Education reforms. In this latter association he enjoyed a good relationship with Daniel Murray,* his Catholic counterpart. Further evidence of his liberal views was his support for the Maynooth Grant and his plea for the state endowment of Catholic clergy. He suggested the abolition of the viceroyalty and its replacement with an increased number of royal visits. He also advocated a radical programme of prison reform. Whately was an outspoken critic of evangelicalism and disapproved of the widespread agitation aroused by the tithes.*

He was connected with most of the leading scientific associations of the period and shortly after his election to the RIA he became its vice-president (1848), a founder-member of the Statistical Society of Dublin (1847), the Society for Promoting Scientific Inquiries into Social Questions (1850), the Statistical Department of the British Association in Belfast (1852) and in Dublin (1857). The Archbishop sought the abolition of the Parliamentary Oath and was the founder of the Society for Protecting the Rights of Conscience (1851).

Mildly eccentric, Whately was patently ill at ease during social visits. His discomfiture was manifested by a rather disquieting habit of raising his right leg and doubling it back over the thigh of the left one, whilst grasping his instep with both hands. Such behaviour wreaked havoc with his hosts' chairs and the Lord

Lieutenant, Lord Anglesey,* lost six of his finest in this manner. On another celebrated occasion Chief Justice John Doherty* reached into his pocket for his handkerchief only to find the Archbishop's black-shod foot reposing therein.

A prolific writer, Whateley's first major literary work, *Historic Doubts Relative to Napoleon Bonaparte* (1819), satirised scepticism by reducing to absurdity the application of logic to the scriptures. *Logic* appeared in 1826 and was followed by *Rhetoric* in 1828. In all he produced over twenty major religious works. His educational manuals included *Introductory Lectures in Political Economics* (1831), *Easy Lessons on Money Matters* (1837), *Introductory Lessons on the British Constitution* (1854), and *Introductory Lessons on Mind* (1859). He edited *Remarks on the Character of Shakespeare* (1839), by his uncle Thomas Whately, *Bacon's Essays* (1856), *Paley's Moral Philosophy* (1859), and *View of Christian Evidences* (1859).

WHIDDY ISLAND DISASTER (8 January 1979). A French oil-tanker, the 150,000 ton *Betelgeuse*, built in 1968, exploded at the Gulf Oil terminal on Whiddy Island, in Bantry Bay, Co. Cork, following a fire on board. Fifty people were killed, including forty-three members of the crew and seven local Gulf Oil workers. Eighty thousand tons of oil, or two-thirds of the cargo, had been unloaded onto the Gulf Oil terminal when the explosion occurred.

An inquiry into the disaster began in Bantry in May and following an adjournment sat at the headquarters of the Incorporated Law Society, Blackhall Place, Dublin, from October. Judge Declan Costello was sole tribunal judge and was assisted by specially appointed Irish government assessors: Dr Hugh Kenneth Black, a former British Home Office explosives expert (Dr Black however resigned after the first four weeks of the inquiry claiming dissatisfaction with its progress and stating that he felt his reputation was at stake); Captain Donald Hindle, who had command experience with two of the world's largest oil tankers; Mr Gerard Van Zon, a Dutch shipping expert; and Mr Jens Wilse, a Norwegian naval architect.

The Inquiry ended on 20 December 1979 having sat for some seventy days and heard evidence from over one hundred witnesses. Having cost slightly in excess of £3m. it was the costliest inquiry since the foundation of the state. Its report, published in July 1980, laid the blame for the disaster on the two oil companies involved, Total, the owners of the *Betelguese*, and Gulf.

WHITAKER, THOMAS KENNETH (1916–   ). Civil servant and economist; b. Rostrevor, Co. Down; ed. CBS, Drogheda. He entered the civil service in 1934 and was attached to the Department of Finance four years later. After becoming Secretary of the Department in 1956 he advocated long-term planning to assist the development of the Irish economy. His *Economic Development*, backed by Sean Lemass* and Dr James Ryan,* was adopted by the government as a White Paper (May 1958) and formed the basis for the First Programme for Economic Expansion adopted in November 1958 (*see* Programmes for Economic Expansion).

Whitaker, who was awarded M.Sc. (Econ.) by the University of London and D. Econ.Sc. by the National University of Ireland, was a director of the Central Bank of Ireland from 1958 to 1969 and Governor from 1969 until his retirement in 1976. He was President of the Economic and Social Research Institute, on the governing body of the School of Celtic Studies and a member of the council of the Statistical and Social Inquiry Society of Ireland. After retiring from the Central Bank he became Chancellor of the National

University and Chairman of Bord na Gaeilge.

WHITE, CAPTAIN JAMES ROBERT ('JACK') (1879–1946). Soldier; b. Whitehall, Broughshane, near Bally-mena, Co. Antrim, son of Field-Marshal Sir George White (one of the most decorated soldiers of his time); ed. Winchester and Sandhurst Military Academy. Commissioned in the Gordon Highlanders (1897), he served in South Africa during the Boer War when he received the DSO. He served as ADC to his father, Governor of Gibraltar until 1905, and later served in India. Upon returning to Europe he spent a short time as adjutant of the Territorial Battalion of the Gordon Highlanders (in Aberdeen) before going to Bohemia to teach, after which he spent some time in Canada.

Upon his return to Ireland, White supported Home Rule.* On 24 October 1913, he spoke alongside Sir Roger Casement,* with whom he later quarrelled, at a meeting organised by Rev. J. B. Armour,* at Bally-money, Co. Antrim. Soon completely involved in the nationalist cause, he was horrified by the conditions in the Dublin slums and in 1913 supported James Larkin* during the Lock-Out.* With Larkin's encouragement he organised the Irish Citizen Army,* with the aims of boosting the workers' morale and protecting them from employer and police intimidation. He was arrested during a workers' march to the Mansion House in 1914. Later, dissatisfied with the Citizen Army, he left it (May 1914) and became an organiser in Derry and Tyrone for the Irish Volunteers,* but was dismissed when he called on Britain to recognise them as an Irish defence force. He served in France with an ambulance corps until 1916. Following the Easter Rising of 1916* he organised a Welsh miners' strike to save James Connolly and was imprisoned at Pentonville Prison (where he arrived the day before Casement, with whom he was reconciled, was hanged). He later settled in Northern Ireland and

published his autobiography, *Misfit,* in 1930.

WHITE CROSS. Sinn Fein organisation founded 1 February 1921 to assist in the distribution of the American-based White Cross Fund. The purpose of the fund was to assist republicans and their families who were suffering hardship through involvement in the War of Independence. The funds were also applied to aid expelled Catholic workers from Northern Ireland and to others not otherwise entitled to compensation. Active in its organisation were Arthur Griffith* and Maud Gonne* and its patrons included Cardinal Logue.* The accounts of the White Cross published on 31 August 1921 reveal that it had collected £1,374,795. The major contributions came from private American sources (£1,250,000), John, Count Mc-Cormack* (£35,000), American Red Cross Fund (£12,500), private English sources (£9,517), Canadian sources (£8,659), Pope Benedict XV (£5,000), and Scottish sources (£3,814).

WHITE QUAKERS. *See* Jacob, Joshua.

WHITEBOYS. Agrarian secret society, founded in Tipperary in 1761, so-called from their wearing white shirts to better identify each other at night. Originally called 'Levellers', Whiteboy leaders called themselves Captain Lightfoot, Slasher, Cropper, Echo, Fear-not and Burnstack, etc. The names in many instances were quite apposite. Their principal grievances were landlord exactions, tithes,* insecurity of land tenure, wages, hearth-money, tolls, and unemployment. The Whiteboy movement, which spread throughout Munster, was strongest in the counties of Cork, Kilkenny, Waterford and Limerick. Its association with atrocities earned the condemnation of the Catholic church and the secular authorities during the 1770s. Other organisations such as the Ribbonmen* modelled themselves on the Whiteboys in their oaths of allegiance and methods. *See also* Secret Societies *and* Doneraile Conspiracy.

WHITESIDE, JAMES (1806–76). Lawyer; b. Delgany, Co. Wicklow; ed. TCD and London. He was called to the Irish Bar in 1830 and was appointed QC in 1842. He defended Daniel O'Connell,* Charles Gavan Duffy* and their colleagues in 1843, and William Smith O'Brien* in 1848. A brilliant advocate, Whiteside's appearance in a case brought crowds to the courtroom. Following his election as MP for Enniskillen in 1852 he became a leading Conservative spokesman. Appointments which he held included Solicitor-General (1852), Attorney-General for Ireland (1858, 1866) and Lord Chief Justice (from 1866). He contributed to the leading periodicals and journals of the day and published works on his extensive Italian travels. An edition of his collected essays and lectures was published as *Life and Death of the Irish Parliament* in 1869.

WILDE, JANE FRANCESCA, LADY (1826–96). Poetess and folklorist; b. Co. Wexford *née* Elgee; mother of Oscar Wilde.* Her interest in Irish nationalism was aroused through the poetry of Richard D'Alton Williams* in *The Nation** to which she became a regular contributor under the pen-name 'Speranza'. She married Sir William Wilde* in 1851 and, following his death in 1876, moved to London. Her later years were spent in poor circumstances despite the international success of her son, Oscar. Her works include *Poems* (1864), *Driftwood from Scandanavia* (folklore, 1884), *Ancient Legends of Ireland* (1887), *Ancient Cures* (1891), *Men Women and Books* (1891). Her best-known poem is 'The Famine Year'.

WILDE, OSCAR FINGAL O'FLAHERTIE WILLS (1854–1900). Poet and playwright; b. Dublin; the son of Sir William

Wilde* and Jane, Lady Wilde* ('Speranza'); ed. TCD where he was influenced by John Pentland Mahaffy* and at Magdalen College, Oxford, where he won the Newdigate Prize for poetry. He became the centre of an aesthetic cult with a reputation for brilliant epigrams, wit and scholarship, and was burlesqued as 'Bunthorne' in Gilbert and Sullivan's *Patience* (1881). Wilde lectured in the US on aesthetic philosophy in 1882 when he gained notoriety by his aesthetic eccentricities. Tried on charges of sodomy, convicted and imprisoned (1895–97). He moved via Italy to Paris where, under the name 'Sebastian Melmoth', he lived frugally, and was received into the Roman Catholic Church on his deathbed. His writings include *The Happy Prince* (1888), *Lord Arthur Saville's Crime* (1891), *The Picture of Dorian Gray* (1891), *Lady Windermere's Fan* (1892), *A Woman of No Importance* (1893), *An Ideal Husband* (1895), and *The Importance of Being Earnest* (1895). His *Salome* (1893) written in French, was staged in Paris with Sarah Bernhardt in the title role (1894) and was later made the libretto of an opera by Richard Strauss. Wilde's *Ballad of Reading Gaol*, reflecting his prison experiences, appeared anonymously in 1898.

WILDE, SIR WILLIAM ROBERT WILLS (1815–76). Surgeon and writer; b. Co. Roscommon; husband of Jane Francesca Elgee ('Speranza'; *see* Wilde, Jane Francesca, Lady) whom he married in 1851, and father of Oscar Wilde;* ed. London, Berlin and Vienna. He was knighted in 1864 for his services as Medical Commissioner to the Irish Census of 1841 and 1851. The inventor of an ophthalmoscope, Wilde introduced a new form of treatment for mastoiditis which is still in general use. A man of wide generosity, he freely gave to the poor and contributed the first £1,000 he earned to the founding of St Mark's Ophthalmic Hospital, Dublin. He travelled extensively and in

1840 published *Narrative of a Voyage to Madeira and Tenerife* (2 vols). He fathered three children before his marriage and in 1859 was involved in a libel case with a patient, a Miss Travers, which entailed heavy legal costs. In the last decade of his life, his practice fell into decline and when he died his widow was left financially insecure. His other works include *Beauties of the Boyne and Blackwater* (1849), *The Closing Years of the Life of Dean Swift* (1849), *The Epidemics of Ireland* (1851), *Catalogue of the contents of the Museum of the RIA* (3 vols, 1858) and *Lough Corrib and Lough Mask* (1867).

WILLIAMS, RICHARD D'ALTON (1822–62). Young Ireland poet; b. Dublin, he spent his childhood at Grenanstown, Co. Tipperary; ed. by the Jesuit Fathers at Tullabeg, Queen's County (Laois), and St Patrick's College, Carlow. He studied medicine in Dublin (from 1843) and in that year also, the first of his many contributions to *The Nation*, 'The Munster War Song' (under the nom-de-plume 'Shamrock') appeared. As a student attached to St Vincent's Hospital, Dublin, he wrote some of his most popular poetry, 'The Dying Girl', 'The Sister of Charity' and the humorous series, 'Misadventures of a Medical Student'. A founder-member of the Dublin Society of St Vincent de Paul, Williams was active in the treatment of cholera victims in the city during the Famine of 1845–49.* He was a member of Young Ireland and was a council member of the Irish Confederation.* He assisted his friend Kevin Izod O'Doherty* with the founding of the *Irish Tribune* to which he also contributed verse. Williams was arrested on charges of treason in the wake of the 1848 rising, but was acquitted. He emigrated to the US in 1851 and settled in Mobile, Alabama, where he became Professor of Belles Lettres at the Jesuit University. He died of tuberculosis shortly after writing his last work, 'Song of the Irish-American Regiments'.

Shortly after his death, a group of Irish-American soldiers passing through the town visited the cemetery and were touched at his humble grave. A collection was arranged among the ranks and a slab of Carrara marble inset with an oak-wreath enclosing a sprig of shamrock was erected over his grave. Part of the inscription reads '. . . as a slight testimonial of their esteem for his unsullied patriotism and his exalted devotion to the Cause of Irish Freedom . . .'

WILLS, REV. JAMES (1790–1868). Clergyman (C.I.), poet and biographer; b. Co. Roscommon; ed. TCD. He went to the Middle Temple to study law but instead entered religion. After returning to Ireland he held various livings including those of Suirville and Kilmacow, Co. Waterford. He resided for some time in Dublin and contributed to *Blackwood's Magazine*, *The Dublin Penny Journal* and *Dublin University Magazine** of which he was editor (1822–38). With Rev. Caeser Otway* he founded the *Irish Quarterly Review*. Dr Wills was appointed Donnellan lecturer TCD in 1855. His chief work, *Lives of Illustrious Irishmen* (6 vols, 1839–45), earned him a wide reputation and he received £1,000 in royalties on its publication. An enlarged work, *The Irish Nation, its History and Biography*, was posthumously re-issued (8 vols, 1875), completed by F. Willis.

WILSON, GENERAL SIR HENRY (1864–1922). Soldier and politician (Conservative); b. Currygrane, Co. Longford; ed. Marlborough School. Having failed to gain entrance to Woolwich or Sandhurst Military Colleges, Wilson was commissioned in the 6th Batt., Rifle Brigade of the Longford Militia. He served in the 18th Royal Irish Brigade in 1884 and subsequently saw action in the Boer War. Attached to headquarters staff in 1901, he became brigadier general in 1907 and was transferred to the War Office in 1910. He was Assistant Chief of General Staff of the British Expeditionary Force to France in 1914. While at army headquarters, Wilson supported British army officers in the Curragh Incident.* Highly regarded by the Prime Minister, David Lloyd George,* Wilson was a staunch supporter of the Orange Order* and Unionist tradition and in particular their unremitting opposition to Home Rule.* During the War of Independence,* he suggested that one solution to the 'troubles' would be to execute the Sinn Fein leaders. He became adviser on security to the government of the new state of Northern Ireland. Wilson opposed British participation in the League of Nations and disagreed with Lloyd George on the terms of the Versailles settlement. His major difference with the Prime Minister concerned the manner in which the war in Ireland was being conducted (Wilson felt that the British forces were being too lenient). Returned as MP for Co. Down (1921), he was adviser on security matters to Sir James Craig (*see* Craigavon, Lord). On 22 June Wilson was assassinated on the steps of 36 Eaton Place by two republicans, Dunne and O'Sullivan.

WIMBORNE, 1st VISCOUNT (1873–1939). Churchill-Guest, Ivor; politician (Conservative); Lord Lieutenant (1915–18); grandson of the 7th Duke of Marlborough; ed. Eton and Trinity College, Cambridge. Having fought in the Boer War, Wimborne was elected MP for Plymouth (1900–06) and for Cardiff District (1906–10). Paymaster-General (1910–12), Wimborne's next major appointment was as Lord Lieutenant. Upon arrival in Ireland in 1915 he was briefed by the Chief Secretary, Augustine Birrell,* and Under-Secretary, Mathew Nathan,* on the political climate of the country. Lulled into a sense of complacency occasioned by the split in the Irish Volunteers* caused by thousands of Volunteers responding to the appeal of John Redmond* to enlist in the British army, the authorities were apparently unaware of a strong republican undercurrent. The Easter Rising of 1916* took them by surprise and harsh measures, including the execution of its leaders, were taken to suppress it. Wimborne commented '... sternest measures are being taken and will be taken for the prompt suppression of the existing disturbances and the restoration of order'. Public reaction to the methods used by General Maxwell* to restore order caused widespread support for the re-constituted Sinn Fein movement. During 1917 the government was under strong pressure to extend conscription to Ireland (*see* Conscription and Ireland). It was felt that such a measure would require a stronger personality than Wimborne, and he was replaced by Lord French* of Ypres.

'WISE PERSON'. Usually an old person of either sex held to have special powers and knowledge including the gift of prophecy. The 'wise' person was held in great awe by the community and was consulted in times of sickness, trouble or doubt. They were commonly believed to have knowledge of the faeries and to know how to circumvent and placate them. Many such people were denounced by the clergy who were apprehensive of the wise person's influence and standing in the community. The most famous of the wise people was the Co. Clare-born Biddy Early.*

WOLFE TONE SOCIETY. Founded in 1963 by Dr Roy Johnston 'to work out a synthesis between traditional republican populism and socialism'. Under the influence of Dr Johnston the Irish Republican Army* and Sinn Fein* moved to the left during the 1960s until the upsurge of violence in Northern Ireland in 1969–70.

WOOD, SIR CHARLES, 1st VISCOUNT HALIFAX (1800–85). Politician (Liberal); Chancellor of the Exchequer (1846—52); b. England; ed. Eton and Oriel College, Oxford, where he graduated B.A. in 1821. He was MP for Grimsby (1826), Wareham (1831), and Halifax (1832—65). Wood held the post of Joint Secretary of the Treasury until becoming Secretary of the Admiralty (1835—39). He took office as Chancellor of the Exchequer in the administration formed by Lord John Russell* in 1846. A supporter of *laissez faire* as was the Prime Minister and the overlord at the Treasury, Charles Edward Trevelyan,* Wood was resolutely opposed to new expenditure and to raising additional taxes. His solution to the crisis provoked by the Famine of 1845—49* was to encourage Irish self-sufficiency. As a Malthusian, he held that the Famine would be beneficial in reducing the population to manageable proportions. Wood was deeply influenced by Trevelyan with whom he agreed that should the potato crop again fail in 1846, there would be no importation of food and that market forces must be allowed to operate without interference. As famine conditions worsened, Wood announced on 8 July that £4,500,000 (half of the money advanced to Ireland from the Treasury), would be forgiven but that there would be no further aid. In September he insisted that the Poor Law rates (*see* Poor Law) should be collected regardless of hardship and that force should be used, if necessary. The Lord Lieutenant, Lord Clarendon,* intervened, however, and the rate was reduced from five to three shillings.

By the time Wood vacated the Chancellory in 1851, he was a despised figure in Ireland (where it wasn't generally known that he had subscribed £200 from his own pocket for famine relief). From 1853 to 1859 he held various offices under Aberdeen and Palmerston, and was raised to the peerage as Lord Halifax in 1866, having retired from politics following a serious accident.

WORKERS' DEFENCE CORPS. Founded in June 1929, the WDC drew its support principally from among Dublin trade unionists and left-wing elements of the Irish Republican Army.* Following its first convention on 7 July which was attended by prominent left-wing members of the IRA, including Frank Ryan,* Michael Price and Geoffrey Coulter, the WDC was renamed the Irish Labour Defence League. On 17 October 1931, it was outlawed by the government, along with Saor Eire,* the Workers' Revolutionary Party,* The Irish Working Farmers' Committee* and several other radical and communist organisations.

WORKERS' PARTY OF IRELAND. Founded by Roderic Connolly,* Captain James Robert ('Jack') White* and members of the defunct Communist Party of Ireland* in May 1926. They failed to secure affiliation to the Comintern and were advised by Moscow to join the Irish Workers' League of James Larkin.* Their aim was to establish a workers' state. The WPI published a weekly newspaper, *The Irish Hammer and Plough* (22 May—16 October 1926). Members of the WPI, which was no longer active after 1927, founded the James Connolly Workers' Education Club in 1928. The Club founded the Irish National Unemployed Movement which lasted into the 1930s. They were later active in the Revolutionary Workers' Group* and the Communist Party of Ireland.

'WORKERS' REPUBLIC'. Socialist weekly newspaper founded by James Connolly* as the organ of the Irish Socialist Republican Party* in August 1898. The paper, which made an uncompromising stand for the rights of labour, failed after eleven issues and ceased publication temporarily in October. It appeared irregularly, depending on Connolly's financial circumstances, and a second series ran from May 1899 until the presses were smashed by the Dublin Metropolitan

Police* in December, after Connolly organised a pro-Boer rally. He revived it again in May 1900 but it collapsed shortly afterwards. Another series ran from October 1900 until January 1902 and yet another from March to June 1903. Following the collapse of *The Irish Worker** Connolly revived *The Workers' Republic* again (May 1915–16). His son, Roderic Connolly, published a paper of the same name during 1921–22.

WORKERS' REVOLUTIONARY PARTY. Socialist organisation founded by Peadar O'Donnell* on 13 March 1930; he edited its newspaper, *The Workers' Voice.* Many prominent members were also members of the Irish Republican Army. The WRP was part of an upsurge of radical activity which, during the economic depression of the late 1920s, alarmed the Cumann na nGaedheal government. On 17 October 1931 the government banned a number of organisations including the WRP.

WORKERS' UNION OF IRELAND. Syndicalist trade union founded in June 1924 by Peter and James Larkin.* Following his return from the US James Larkin failed to wrest control of his old union, the Irish Transport and General Workers' Union,* from William O'Brien.* The WUI succeeded in attracting some 60,000 Dublin members from the ITGWU, but made little impact outside the capital. Through O'Brien's influence, the WUI was excluded from the Irish Trade Union Congress* until 1945 when it became affiliated and the ITGWU disaffiliated and formed the Congress of Irish Unions.* In 1947, the WUI expanded and accepted members from the Electricity Supply Board,* Aer Lingus,* Guinness and other large employments. It was affiliated to the new Irish Congress of Trade Unions* in 1959 when the breach in the labour movement was healed. By 1977 the WUI had some 35,000 members. Its general secretaries have been James Larkin (1924–47), James Larkin Jnr* (1947–

69), Denis Larkin* (1969–77) and Paddy Cardiff (1977–   ).

WOULFE, STEPHEN (1787–1840). Lawyer and politician (Liberal); b. Ennis, Co. Clare; ed. TCD where he was one of the first Catholics to be admitted. Woulfe, who was called to the Bar in 1814, opposed Daniel O'Connell* on the Veto* and was prominent in the demand for Catholic Emancipation.* MP for Cashel (1835), he was Attorney-General (1837) and one year later became the first Catholic to hold the office of Chief Baron of the Irish Exchequer.

WRIGHT, EDWARD PERCEVAL (1834–1910). Naturalist; b. Dublin; ed. TCD where, following his ordination, he became Professor of Botany (1869–1904). He travelled widely studying the botany of Portugal, the Seychelles and Sicily. An authority on the geology and botany of Ireland, he founded *Natural History Review* of which he was editor for some years. A member of the RIA, of which he was later Secretary, he was President of the RSAI. A supporter of Isaac Butt* and the Home Rule League, Wright founded the Protestant Home Rule Association.* His brother, Rev. Charles Henry Hamilton Wright (1836–1909), linguist and scholar, published a *Grammar of Modern Irish* in 1855.

'WRIT OF PROHIBITION'. The Writ was applied for on 17 June 1920 by Michael Comyn, senior counsel to the Irish Republican Army, to test the legality of the military courts by whom all applications for *habeas corpus* had been refused. The writ was refused in Ireland on the grounds that a state of war existed (although the British Prime Minister, David Lloyd George* was at pains to deny this), and was heard by the House of Lords. The decision on 28 July 1920 was in favour of the appellant and the military courts and executions ordered by them were deemed illegal. At the time of the issue of the writ, forty-two members of the Irish

Volunteers* were under sentence of death by military courts and all were subsequently released.

WYNDHAM ACT, 1903. *See* Land Acts.

WYNDHAM, GEORGE (1863–1913). Politician (Conservative); Chief Secretary (1900–05); his mother was a grand-daughter of Lord Edward Fitzgerald and Wyndham was also related to the 4th Earl of Dunraven.* He saw service with the Coldstream Guards from 1883 and in 1887 was appointed private secretary to Arthur J. Balfour.* While Chief Secretary, Wyndham supported the policy of constructive legislation inaugurated by Balfour with which the Conservatives intended to 'kill Home Rule with kindness'. His approach, however, incurred the hostility of the Ulster Unionists* particularly when Wyndham encouraged Lord Dunraven and the Land Conference of 1902.* Wyndham's Land Act of 1903 (*see* Land Acts) extended the policy of land purchase and incorporated many of the recommendations of the Land Conference. He was widely criticised by Unionists for his attempts to find a permanent solution to the land problem which would serve the mutual interests of landlord and tenant. Wyndham failed in his effort to solve the university question (*see* National University of Ireland). Unionist pressure finally forced his resignation in 1905 and he left the Irish office with his health impaired. A regular contributor to the *Natural Observer* and the *New Review*, he published North's *Plutarch* (1895–96), *Shakespeare's Classics* (1898) and *Ronsard and La Pleiade* (1906).

WYNNE, THOMAS (1838–1900). Photographer; b. USA. He returned to Ireland as a child and settled in Castlebar, Co. Mayo, where he was educated. After starting a career as a photographer he travelled throughout the West of Ireland. His work

from 1860 to his death forms a remarkable study of contemporary Irish life, including the Land War and famine in the West, and is preserved in the National Library. He established branches of his business in Loughrea, Co. Galway; Portarlington, King's Co. (Offaly) and Tipperary.

WYSE, SIR THOMAS (1791–1862). Politician (Liberal) and reformer; b. St John's Manor, Co. Waterford; ed. Stonyhurst and TCD where he was among the first Catholic students. While reading law at Lincoln's Inn (1813) he travelled on the continent. He married Letitia Bonaparte in Rome in 1821 but they separated after seven years. An early supporter of the Catholic Association,* after settling in Waterford in 1825 Wyse played a leading role in the campaign for Catholic Emancipation.* A talented organiser, he led the campaign against the powerful Beresford faction in the Waterford by-election of 1826 and secured the return of the pro-Emancipationist, Villiers Stuart.* On the eve of Emancipation in 1829 he published *A Letter to My Fellow Countrymen,* calling for the dissolution of the Catholic Association. In the same year, he published an *Historical Sketch of the late Catholic Association* (2 vols). After his return as MP for Tipperary (1830) he supported the Reform Bill of 1832.

Passionately interested in education, Wyse proposed a progressive plan for National Education to Lord Edward Stanley (*see* Derby, 14th Earl), some of which was incorporated into the scheme introduced in 1831, though without acknowledgement to Wyse. Retiring from his Tipperary seat in 1832, he unsuccessfully contested Waterford but was returned for the constituency in 1835, although in dispute with Daniel O'Connell,* for whom he had a personal dislike. Chairman of the Commission of Inquiry into National Education, his Report anticipated Intermediate Education (*see*

Secondary Education), provincial colleges (*see* Queen's Colleges) and a second university (*see* University Education). He published *Educational Reform* (1837) and was co-founder of the Central Society for Education. From 1839 to 1841, he was Lord of the Treasury in the government formed by Lord Melbourne.* After

the state trials he sought the release of O'Connell in 1844. Wyse was Secretary to the Board of Control for India in 1846 and a year later lost his Waterford seat. He became Ambassador to Athens in 1849 and won high regard for his efforts to strengthen relations between England and Greece.

Y

YEATS, JOHN BUTLER (1839–1922). Artist; b. Tullylish, Co. Down; ed. Douglas, Isle of Man and TCD. He studied art at Heatherleys Art School (1867), the Royal Academy and the Slade School of Art. He settled in Dublin (1902) and, while following a legal career, devoted much of his leisure time to painting, producing a succession of portraits including those of his sons, Jack Butler Yeats* and W. B. Yeats* (now in the National Gallery). He moved to New York in 1907 and remained there for the rest of his life. His *Essays, Irish and American*, appeared in 1918. *Extracts from the Letters of John Butler Yeats* was edited by Ezra Pound and *Further Letters of John Butler Yeats* was edited by Lennox Robinson (1920).

YEATS, JOHN (JACK) BUTLER (1871–1957). Artist and writer; b. London, son of John Butler Yeats* and younger brother of William Butler Yeats;* ed. principally in Sligo (1878–86) and from 1888 at art school in London. On his return to Ireland in 1900 he began a career as a painter in watercolours and also worked as an illustrator for the family business, Cuala Press. His first commercial work appeared in *The Vegetarian* in 1888 and he subsequently worked for the *Daily Graphic* and the *Manchester Guardian*. Yeats exhibited throughout America and Europe. He took up oil painting in

1915 and was celebrated for his romantic landscapes and in particular his depiction of life in the West of Ireland. His best-known paintings include 'The Tinker', 'The Circus Clown', 'The Rake', 'Man from Aranmore', 'Empty Creels' and 'Face in the Shadow'. A skilful illustrator, he published a monthly *Broadsheet* (1902–03, 1908–15). He was also author of *Life in the West of Ireland* (1912), *Sligo* (1930), *Sailing and Sailing Swiftly* (1933), *The Amaranthen* (1933), *The Charmed Life* (1938), *Ah Well!* (1942), *And To You Also* (1944) and *The Careless Flower* (1947). His plays include *Apparitions* (1933), *Harlequin's Positions* (1939), *La La Noo* (1943) and *In Sand* (1949).

YEATS, WILLIAM BUTLER (1865–1939). Poet; b. Dublin, son of John Butler Yeats* and brother of Jack Butler Yeats;* ed. London and High School, Dublin. He studied art at the Dublin Metropolitan School of Art (1883–86). Yeats published his first lyrics in *The Dublin University Review* in 1885, and two years later, joined the Blavatsky Lodge of the Theosophical Society. He worked for some time as literary correspondent for the American newspapers, *Providence Study Journal* and *The Boston Pilot*. His interest in Irish myth was stimulated by living in the West of Ireland and through contact with John O'Leary* to whom he dedicated

Poems and Ballads of Young Ireland (1888, co-edited with Douglas Hyde). Yeats' first volume of poetry, *The Wanderings of Oisin*, was published along with *Crossways* (1889). In the same year he began collaboration with Edwin Ellis on a three-volume edition of Blake's works which appeared in 1893. He first met Maud Gonne* in 1889 and thereafter she symbolised for him the spirit of tragic beauty and Irish nationalism. He was a founder-member of the Irish Literary Society* and the Irish National Literary Society* in 1892. His friendship with Augusta, Lady Gregory* began in 1896. Yeats encouraged John Millington Synge* to spend some time in the Aran Islands to mature his developing talents. A founder-member of the Irish Literary Theatre,* Yeats' *Cathleen ni Houlihan* (1902) with Maud Gonne in the lead, was written expressly for the ILT, which, two years later, became the Abbey Theatre,* of which he was a director. His ambitious forty-lecture tour of the US in 1903 was a complete success. Upon his return he learned of Maud Gonne's marriage to Major John MacBride.*

The pre-1916 period found Yeats disillusioned by the materialistic concern of the Irish bourgeouisie and the spirit of narrow-minded nationalism which he viewed with distaste. He met Ezra Pound (who later became his secretary) in 1908 and had a strong influence on the American poet. Upon his return from another successful American lecture tour in 1912 Yeats shared a cottage with Pound in England. Yeats refused the offer of a knighthood in 1915 and a year later proposed to Maud Gonne, whose husband had been executed for his part in the Easter Rising of 1916. Maud Gonne refused his offer and in 1917 he married Georgie Hyde-Lees. He lived in Thoor Ballylee, near Lady Gregory's Coole Park estate, from 1922.

The Civil War horrified Yeats and upon the creation of the Irish Free State he became a member of the Senate. During 1922–28 he proved a constant source of irritation and annoyance to the highly conservative political and church establishments, proposing a number of liberal measures including divorce legislation. In 1923 Yeats became the first Irishman to receive the Nobel Prize for Literature. From 1924, he spent a considerable time abroad, particularly in France. His health suffered in his last years and he underwent a Steinach rejuvenation operation. One of his last major literary undertakings was his editorship of the controversial *Oxford Book of Poetry* in 1936. He moved to France in 1938 and died at Cap Martin. His body was returned to Ireland in 1948 and re-interred in Drumcliffe Churchyard, Co. Sligo, under a self-composed epitaph:

> *Cast a cold eye*
> *On life, on death.*
> *Horseman, pass by!*

Apart from the works already mentioned, he was the author of *John Sherman* (a novel, 1891), *The Countess Cathleen and Various Legends and Lyrics* (1892), *The Celtic Twilight* (tales which he took down from an old Sligo-man, Paddy Flynn; 1893), *Poems of William Blake* (1893), *A Book of Irish Verse* (1895), *Poems* (1895), *The Secret Rose* (1897), *The Wind Among the Reeds* (1899), *The Shadowy Waters* (1900), *Ideas of Good and Evil* (1903), *The Old Age of Queen Maeve* (1903), *Baile an Ailinn* (1903), *Hour Glass and Other Plays* (1904), *The King's Threshold* (1904), *The Shadowy Waters* (1906), *Deirdre* (1907), *Collected Poems* (6 vols, 1908), *The Green Helmet and Other Poems* (1910), *John Synge and the Ireland of His Time* (1911), *Plays for an Irish Theatre* (1912), *The Two Kings* and *Responsibilities* (1914), *Reveries* (1916), *Per Amica Silentia Lunae* (1918), *The Cutting of an Agate* (1919), *The Wild Swans at Coole* (1919), *Michael Robartes and the Dancer* (1921), *Seven Poems and a Fragment* (1922), *The Trembling of the Veil* (privately; 1922), *Later Poems* (1923), *Plays in Prose and*

Verse (1923), *Plays and Controversies* (1923), *The Gift of Harun-al-Rashid* (1923), *Essays* (1924), *Early Poems and Stories* (1925), *Autobiographies* (1926), *The Tower* (1928), *Selected Poems, Lyrical and Narrative* (1929), *The Winding Stair* (1929), *Words for Music, Perhaps* (1932), *Collected Poems* (1933), *Wheels and Butterflies* (1934), *Collected Plays* (1934), *A Full Moon in March* (1935), *Dramatis Personae* (1936) and *The Essays of W. B. Yeats, 1931–36* (1938). *Last Poems* was published posthumously in 1940.

YOUNG, REV. HENRY (1786–1869). Clergyman (R.C.); b. Dublin; ed. Rome where he was ordained in 1810. On his return to Ireland he became curate at St Michan's and Harold's Cross, Dublin (1819–27). Noted for his charity and piety, he travelled throughout Leinster preaching at fairs, missions and retreats. He was an outspoken opponent of intemperance and of faction fighting.* A friend and supporter of Daniel O'Connell,* he spoke and celebrated mass at many of his meetings. Despite a self-imposed life of austerity during which he frequently partook of only one meal a day and slept in barns and out-houses, Fr Young lived to be the oldest priest in Ireland. He made several translations of religious works and was joint-author of a *Breviary* in 1822.

YOUNG IRELAND. Nationalist movement led by Thomas Davis,* Charles Gavan Duffy* and John Blake Dillon* and inspired by their newspaper *The Nation*,* which began publication in October 1842. Young Ireland attracted young members of the middle class, many of whom supported Daniel O'Connell* and the Repeal Association* but whose aspirations went further than simple Repeal. Young Ireland aimed at a nationalism which would 'establish internal union and external independence'. The lead came from Davis and the movement's success stemmed largely from the popularity of *The Nation*. Relations between O'Connell's 'Old Ireland' and the younger movement were uneasy. Young Ireland disapproved of his alliance with the Whigs (1835–40). In 1844, when O'Connell gave acceptance to a proposal for a federal solution to the demand for Repeal, Young Ireland attacked him bitterly and continued to remain suspicious of him after he had long abandoned the idea. O'Connell also had a poor relationship with William Smith O'Brien,* the parliamentary spokesman for Young Ireland, while the Liberator's son, John O'Connell,* displayed an open contempt for the movement.

The establishment of the Queen's Colleges* by Sir Robert Peel in 1845 was welcomed by Young Ireland, but the Colleges were condemned by O'Connell and by the influential Archbishop of Tuam, John MacHale.* This dispute further widened the breach and, following the death of Davis in that year, relations between O'Connell and Young Ireland quickly deteriorated.

The outbreak of the Famine of 1845–49* gave the impetus for a radical solution to the Irish question. Young Ireland now attracted a number of less moderate adherents including John Mitchel,* who replaced Davis on *The Nation*, Thomas Devin Reilly,* Thomas Francis Meagher,* Thomas Darcy McGee,* John Martin* and Michael Doheny.* Mitchel's writings indicated that Young Ireland would ultimately consider the use of physical force, a solution which was anathema to O'Connell who in 1845 sought a further alliance with the Whigs. The break occurred in 1846 when O'Connell demanded that members of the Repeal Association should pledge that under no circumstances could physical force be justified. O'Brien and Mitchel led Young Ireland out of the Repeal Association and the breach with O'Connell was complete.

The potato failure of 1845 had been repeated in 1846 and the position of the tenant-farmers became desperate. Peel's administration had been replaced by a government led by Lord John Russell* which proved insensitive to the Irish crisis. Young Ireland split in 1847 and Duffy and O'Brien organised the Irish Confederation* through Confederate Clubs. Mitchel openly preached sedition in his new paper, *The United Irishman,* which was suppressed and Mitchel transported for fourteen years to Tasmania.

The Confederation, impressed by the revolution in France in February 1848, now sought an armed uprising in Ireland. In July 1848 Smith O'Brien led a badly armed and disorganised insurrection at Ballingarry, Co. Tipperary.* Its collapse was followed by the arrest or flight of the Young Ireland leaders and the movement quickly disintegrated.

YOUNG IRELAND ASSOCIATION. Title assumed by the National Guard or Blueshirts* after they were banned by the Fianna Fail government in 1933. A youth organisation, on the lines of contemporary right-wing movements, the YIA was closely associated with Fine Gael.* It faded within a short period.

YOUNG ULSTER. Founded in 1892 by Frederick Crawford,* it was a secret movement dedicated to the maintenance of the Union and opposition to Home Rule.* Members had to possess either a revolver, a Mortini Henry rifle or a cavalry Winchester carbine, in addition to 100 rounds of ammunition. YU was absorbed by much larger Unionist organisations when the (second) Home Rule Bill* introduced by W. E. Gladstone* was defeated in the House of Lords in 1893. *See* Unionist Party *and* Ulster Unionist Party.

Z

'ZOZIMUS' (MICHAEL MORAN) (1794—1846). Street singer and ballad writer; b. Faddle Alley in the Dublin Liberties. Blind from infancy, he was the last of the Dublin gleemen. Possessed of an extraordinary memory and a powerful voice, Zozimus 'performed' principally at Essex Bridge, Wood Quay, Church Street, Dame Street, Capel Street, Sackville (now O'Connell) Street, Grafton Street, Henry Street, and Conciliation Hall. His most popular ballads were 'St Patrick was a Gentleman', 'The Life of St Mary of Egypt', 'Maguire's Triumph' and 'The Finding of Moses'.

When arriving at his chosen pitch, Zozimus began each performance with:

> Ye sons and daughters of Erin, attend,
> Gather round poor Zozimus, yer friend;
> Listen boys, until yez hear,
> My charming song so dear.

For many years after Moran's death an enterprising contemporary, McGee, made 'a pretty penny' by having himself led through the streets of Dublin labelled as 'The Real, Identical, Irish Zozimus'.

A DICTIONARY OF IRISH HISTORY 1800-1980

D.J. Hickey   J.E. Doherty

Hickey and Doherty's DICTIONARY OF IRISH HISTORY first appeared in hardback in 1980 and immediately became an invaluable reference work for everyone with even a passing interest in Irish history. For serious students, it is simply indispensable.

Now re-issued in paperback, it will resume its place alongside other standard works of reference in Irish life. It offers a unique and wide-ranging account — in readily accessible form — of the political, social and military events, economic and demographic developments, and artistic movements, and individual personalities which have determined the course of modern Irish history.

'This is a valuable addition to the Gill and Macmillan series of dictionaries on Irish affairs and its two thousand references will prove useful to a great variety of people.' — *The Irish Times*

'This pioneering effort will remain an invaluable work of reference.'
— *British Book News*

'The authors of this dictionary decided to include as many entries as possible on social affairs, the arts, folk customs, economics and the like. This decision has raised their dictionary from the merely useful to the delightful.' — *The Economist*

'This is a hardy book, one which should be found on every proverbial library shelf.' — *Irish Literary Supplement*

THE AUTHORS

Denis J. Hickey was born in Limerick in 1937. He lived in London for over twenty years, working first as a _____ later in telecommunications. He now works as a telecomm_____ ord Telecom in Limerick. He is married with t___

James Doherty was born in Co. Sligo in 1946. He _____ cated in Ballina, Co. Mayo and in University College, Galway. He is a history teacher in Limerick, where he lives with his wife and two children.

0 7171 1567 4

ISBN 0-7171-1567-4

9 780717 115679

GREENES BOOKSHOP
£17.99